Y0-BZG-806

Favorite Brand Name™

Cookies

Publications International, Ltd.
Favorite Brand Name Recipes at www.fbnr.com

Copyright © 2000 Publications International, Ltd.
All rights reserved. This publication may not be reproduced or quoted in whole or in part by any means whatsoever without written permission from:

Louis Weber, CEO
Publications International, Ltd.
7373 North Cicero Avenue
Lincolnwood, Illinois 60712

Permission is never granted for commercial purposes.

Favorite Brand Name is a trademark of Publications International, Ltd.

All recipes and photographs that contain specific brand names are copyrighted by those companies and/or associations, unless otherwise specified. All photographs *except* those on pages 23, 57, 63, 109, 131, 133, 141, 261, 265, 277, 285, 295, 309 and 321 copyright © Publications International, Ltd.

DOLE® is a registered trademark of Dole Food Company, Inc.

Carnation, Libby's, Nestlé and Toll House are registered trademarks of Nestlé.

Some of the products listed in this publication may be in limited distribution.

Front cover photography by Proffitt Photography Ltd., Chicago.

Pictured on the front cover *(clockwise from top left):* Linzer Sandwich Cookies *(page 300),* Moons and Stars *(page 348),* Chocolate Chip Shortbread *(page 82),* Three Great Tastes Blond Brownies *(page 200),* Danish Raspberry Ribbons *(page 280)* and Oatmeal Candied Chipper *(page 82).*
Pictured on the jacket flaps: Almond Crescents *(page 146)* and Hershey's White Chip Brownies *(page 192).*
Pictured on the contents page: Peanut Butter Chocolate Chippers *(page 88).*
Pictured on the back cover *(clockwise from top):* Hershey's "Perfectly Chocolate" Chocolate Chip Cookies *(page 72),* Sandwich Cookies *(page 208),* Tiny Mini Kisses™ Peanut Blossoms *(page 60)* and Strawberry Oat Bars *(page 240).*

ISBN-13: 978-1-4127-2282-7
ISBN-10: 1-4127-2282-9

Library of Congress Catalog Card Number: 2005925711

Manufactured in China.

8 7 6 5 4 3 2 1

Microwave Cooking: Microwave ovens vary in wattage. Use the cooking times as guidelines and check for doneness before adding more time.

Preparation/Cooking Times: Preparation times are based on the approximate amount of time required to assemble the recipe before cooking, baking, chilling or serving. These times include preparation steps such as measuring, chopping and mixing. The fact that some preparations and cooking can be done simultaneously is taken into account. Preparation of optional ingredients and serving suggestions are not included.

Contents

Cookie Basics

Baking cookies is a much-loved, time-honored American tradition. What other food could welcome children home from school, star at community bake sales, and help celebrate countless holidays and special occasions? Cookies are everywhere! Whether you're whipping up a quick snack for your family or putting together a beautiful gift basket, the more cookie recipes you have, the better. You'll find all the great cookie recipes you could ever want right here in this book, along with helpful information on preparing, baking and storing your cookies.

General Guidelines

Take the guesswork out of cookie baking by practicing the following techniques:

- Read the entire recipe before beginning to make sure you have all the necessary ingredients and baking utensils.
- Remove butter, margarine and cream cheese from the refrigerator to soften, if necessary.
- Toast and chop nuts, peel and slice fruit, and melt chocolate before preparing the cookie dough.
- Measure all the ingredients accurately and assemble them in the order they are called for in the recipe.
- When making bar cookies or brownies, use the pan specified in the recipe. Prepare the pans according to the recipe directions. Adjust oven racks and preheat the oven. Check oven temperature for accuracy with an oven thermometer.
- Follow recipe directions and baking times exactly. Check for doneness using the test given in the recipe.

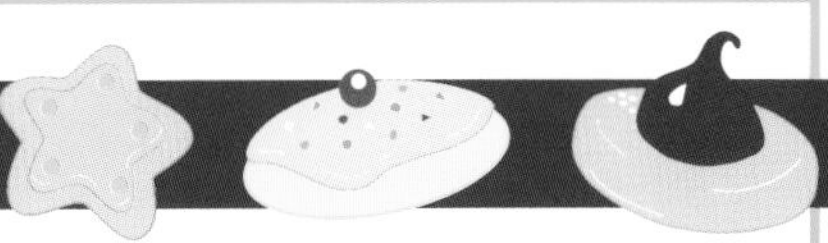

Melting Chocolate

Make sure the utensils you use for melting chocolate are completely dry. Moisture makes the chocolate become stiff and grainy. If this happens, add ½ teaspoon shortening (not butter) for each ounce of chocolate and stir until smooth. Chocolate scorches easily, and once scorched cannot be used. Follow one of these three methods for successful melting.

Double Boiler: This is the safest method because it prevents scorching. Place the chocolate in the top of a double boiler or in a bowl over hot, not boiling, water; stir until smooth. (Make sure the water remains just below a simmer and is one inch below the top pan.) Be careful that no steam or water gets into the chocolate.

Direct Heat: Place the chocolate in a heavy saucepan and melt over very low heat, stirring constantly. Remove the chocolate from the heat as soon as it is melted. Be sure to watch the chocolate carefully since it is easily scorched with this method.

Microwave Oven: Place an unwrapped 1-ounce square or 1 cup of chips in a small microwavable bowl. Microwave on High (100%) 1 to 1½ minutes, stirring after 1 minute. Stir the chocolate at 30-second intervals until smooth. Be sure to stir microwaved chocolate since it retains its original shape, even when melted.

Preparation

The seemingly endless variety of cookies can actually be divided into five basic types: bar, drop, refrigerator, rolled and shaped. These types are determined by the consistency of the dough and how it is formed into cookies.

Bar Cookies: Bar cookies and brownies are some of the easiest cookies to make—simply mix the batter, spread it in the pan and bake. These cookies are also quick to prepare since they bake all at once rather than in batches on a cookie sheet.

Always use the pan size called for in the recipe. Substituting a different pan will affect the cookies' texture: a smaller pan will make the bars more cakey, while a larger pan will produce flatter bars with a drier texture.

Most bar cookies should cool in the pan on a wire rack until barely warm before they are cut into squares. Try cutting bar cookies into triangles or diamonds for a festive new shape. To make serving easy, remove a corner piece first, then remove the rest.

Drop Cookies: These cookies are named for the way they are formed on the cookie sheet. The soft dough mounds when dropped from a spoon and then flattens slightly during baking. Space the mounds of dough about 2 inches apart on the cookie sheets to allow for spreading unless the recipe directs otherwise.

Cookies that are uniform in size and shape will finish baking at the same time. To easily shape drop cookies into a uniform size, use an ice cream scoop with a release bar.

Refrigerator Cookies: Refrigerator doughs are perfect for preparing in advance. Tightly wrapped rolls of dough can be stored in the refrigerator for up to one week or frozen for up to six weeks. These rich doughs are ready to be sliced and baked at a moment's notice.

Always shape the dough into rolls before chilling. Shaping is easier if you first place the dough on a piece of waxed paper or plastic wrap. If desired, you can gently press chopped nuts, flaked coconut or colored sugar into the roll. Before chilling, wrap the rolls securely in plastic wrap so that air cannot penetrate the dough and cause it to dry out.

Use gentle pressure and a back-and-forth sawing motion when slicing the rolls so the cookies will keep their nice round shape. Rotating the roll while slicing also prevents one side from flattening.

Rolled Cookies: Rolled or cutout cookies are made from stiff doughs that are rolled out and cut into fancy shapes with floured cookie cutters, a knife or a pastry wheel.

Chill the cookie dough before rolling for easier handling. Remove only enough dough from the refrigerator to work with at one time. Save any trimmings and reroll them all at once to prevent the dough from becoming tough.

Shaped Cookies: These cookies can be simply hand-shaped into balls or crescents, forced through a cookie press into more complex shapes or baked in cookie molds.

By using different plates in a cookie press, spritz cookies can be formed into many shapes. If your first efforts are not successful, just transfer the dough back to the cookie press and try again.

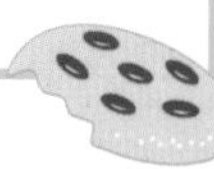

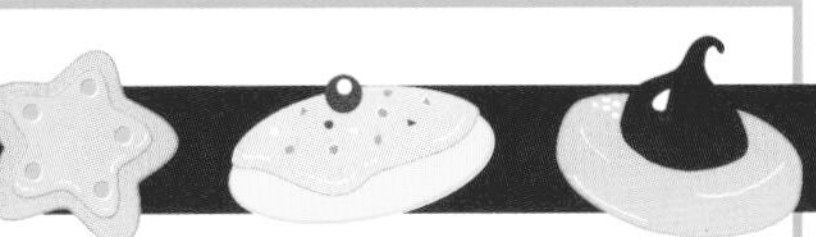

Baking

The best cookie sheets to use are those with little or no sides. They allow the heat to circulate evenly during baking and promote even browning. Another way to promote even baking and browning is to place only one cookie sheet at a time in the center of the oven. If you do use more than one sheet at a time, rotate the cookie sheets from top to bottom and front to back halfway through the baking time.

When a recipe calls for greasing the cookie sheets, use shortening or a nonstick cooking spray for the best results. Lining the cookie sheets with parchment paper is an alternative to greasing. It eliminates cleanup, bakes the cookies more evenly and allows them to cool right on the paper instead of on wire racks. Allow cookie sheets to cool between batches; the dough will spread if placed on a hot cookie sheet.

Most cookies should be removed from cookie sheets immediately after baking and placed in a single layer on wire racks to cool. Fragile cookies may need to cool slightly on the cookie sheet before being moved. Always cool cookies completely before stacking and storing. Bar cookies and brownies may be cooled and stored in the baking pan.

Storing

Unbaked cookie dough can be refrigerated for up to one week or frozen for up to six weeks. Rolls of dough should be sealed tightly in plastic wrap; other doughs should be stored in airtight containers. Label dough with baking information for convenience.

Store soft and crisp cookies separately at room temperature to prevent changes in texture and flavor. Keep soft cookies in airtight containers. If the cookies begin to dry out, add a piece of apple or bread to the container to help them retain moisture. Store crisp cookies in containers with loose-fitting lids to prevent moisture build-up. If they become soggy, heat undecorated cookies in a 300°F oven for 3 to 5 minutes to restore crispness. Store cookies with sticky glazes, fragile decorations and icings in single layers between sheets of waxed paper. Bar cookies and brownies may be stored in their own baking pans, covered with aluminum foil or plastic wrap when cool.

Cookie Jar Classics

Double Chocolate Walnut Drops

- **¾ cup (1½ sticks) butter or margarine, softened**
- **¾ cup granulated sugar**
- **¾ cup firmly packed light brown sugar**
- **1 large egg**
- **1 teaspoon vanilla extract**
- **2¼ cups all-purpose flour**
- **⅓ cup unsweetened cocoa powder**
- **1 teaspoon baking soda**
- **½ teaspoon salt**
- **1¾ cups "M&M's"® Chocolate Mini Baking Bits**
- **1 cup coarsely chopped English or black walnuts**

Preheat oven to 350°F. Lightly grease cookie sheets; set aside. In large bowl cream butter and sugars until light and fluffy; beat in egg and vanilla. In medium bowl combine flour, cocoa powder, baking soda and salt; add to creamed mixture. Stir in "M&M's"® Chocolate Mini Baking Bits and nuts. Drop by heaping tablespoonfuls about 2 inches apart onto prepared cookie sheets. Bake 12 to 14 minutes for chewy cookies or 14 to 16 minutes for crispy cookies. Cool completely on wire racks. Store in tightly covered container.

Makes about 4 dozen cookies

Variation: *Shape dough into 2-inch-thick roll. Cover with plastic wrap; refrigerate. When ready to bake, slice dough into ¼-inch-thick slices and bake as directed.*

Double Chocolate Walnut Drops

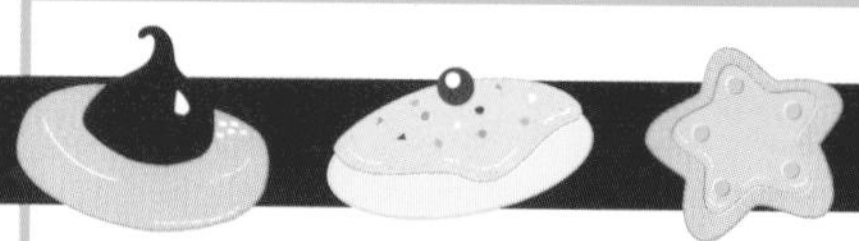

Peanut Gems

- 2½ cups all-purpose flour
- 1 teaspoon baking powder
- ⅛ teaspoon salt
- 1 cup butter, softened
- 1 cup packed light brown sugar
- 2 eggs
- 2 teaspoons vanilla
- 1½ cups cocktail peanuts, finely chopped
- Powdered sugar (optional)

Preheat oven to 350°F. Combine flour, baking powder and salt in small bowl.

Beat butter in large bowl with electric mixer at medium speed until smooth. Gradually beat in brown sugar; increase speed to medium-high and beat until light and fluffy. Beat in eggs, one at a time, until fluffy. Beat in vanilla. Gradually stir in flour mixture until blended. Stir in peanuts.

Drop heaping tablespoonfuls of dough about 1 inch apart onto ungreased cookie sheets; flatten slightly with hands.

Bake 12 minutes or until set. Let cookies stand on cookie sheets 5 minutes; transfer to wire racks to cool completely. Dust cookies with powdered sugar, if desired. Store in airtight container.

Makes 30 cookies

Chocolate-Dipped Oat Cookies

- 2 cups uncooked rolled oats
- ¾ cup firmly packed brown sugar
- ½ cup vegetable oil
- ½ cup finely chopped walnuts
- 1 egg
- 2 teaspoons grated orange peel
- ¼ teaspoon salt
- 1 package (12 ounces) milk chocolate chips

Combine oats, sugar, oil, walnuts, egg, orange peel and salt in large bowl until blended. Cover; refrigerate overnight.

Preheat oven to 350°F. Lightly grease cookie sheets or line with parchment paper. Melt chocolate chips in top of double boiler over hot, not boiling, water; keep warm. Shape oat mixture into large marble-sized balls. Place 2 inches apart on prepared cookie sheets.

Bake 10 to 12 minutes or until golden and crisp. Cool 10 minutes on wire racks. Dip tops of cookies, one at a time, into melted chocolate. Place on waxed paper; cool until chocolate is set.

Makes about 6 dozen cookies

Peanut Gems

Baker's® Coconut Chocolate Jumbles

½ cup (1 stick) butter *or* margarine
½ cup granulated sugar
¼ cup firmly packed brown sugar
1 egg
½ teaspoon vanilla
1 cup flour
1 teaspoon baking soda
¼ teaspoon salt
6 squares BAKER'S® Semi-Sweet Baking Chocolate Squares *or* BAKER'S® Premium White Baking Chocolate Squares, chopped
1 package (7 ounces) BAKER'S® ANGEL FLAKE® Coconut (2⅔ cups)
1 cup *each* chopped, toasted walnuts and raisins

HEAT oven to 350°F.

BEAT butter and sugars in large bowl with electric mixer on medium speed until light and fluffy. Beat in egg and vanilla. Mix in flour, baking soda and salt. Stir in chocolate, coconut, walnuts and raisins.

DROP by rounded tablespoonfuls, 1½ inches apart, onto ungreased cookie sheets.

BAKE 10 to 12 minutes or until golden brown. Cool 2 to 3 minutes; remove from cookie sheets. Cool completely on wire racks. Store in tightly covered container.

Makes about 3 dozen cookies

Prep Time: 15 minutes
Baking Time: 12 minutes

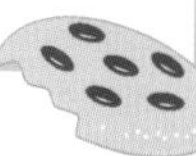

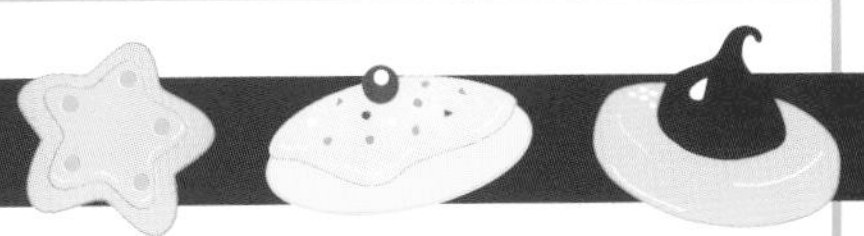

Hermits

MAZOLA NO STICK® Cooking Spray
3 cups flour
2 teaspoons pumpkin pie spice
¾ teaspoon baking powder
¾ teaspoon baking soda
¼ teaspoon salt
½ cup (1 stick) MAZOLA® Margarine, softened
1 cup packed brown sugar
2 eggs
½ cup KARO® Dark Corn Syrup
1 cup raisins
1 cup coarsely chopped walnuts
2 tablespoons finely chopped crystallized ginger (optional)

1. Preheat oven to 350°F. Spray cookie sheets with cooking spray. In medium bowl combine flour, pumpkin pie spice, baking powder, baking soda and salt.

2. In large bowl with mixer at medium speed, beat margarine and brown sugar until fluffy. Beat in eggs and corn syrup. Reduce speed; beat in flour mixture until blended. Stir in raisins, walnuts and ginger.

3. Drop by heaping teaspoonfuls 1½ inches apart on prepared cookie sheets.

4. Bake 12 minutes until golden and lightly browned at edges. Cool several minutes before removing from pan. Remove; cool completely on wire rack.

Makes about 4 dozen cookies

Note: *Soft or chewy cookies such as Hermits should always be stored in an airtight container to keep them fresh. If tightly wrapped in moisture-proof packaging, these cookies will keep well in the freezer up to 6 months.*

Prep Time: 25 minutes
Bake Time: 12 minutes, plus cooling

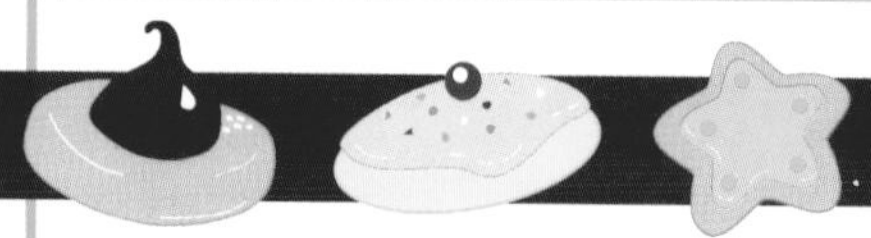

Classic Refrigerator Sugar Cookies

1 cup butter, softened
1 cup sugar
1 egg
1 teaspoon vanilla
2 cups all-purpose flour
2 teaspoons baking powder
Dash nutmeg
¼ cup milk
Colored sprinkles or melted semisweet chocolate* (optional)

**To dip 24 cookies, melt 1 cup chocolate chips in small saucepan over very low heat until smooth.*

Beat butter in large bowl with electric mixer at medium speed until smooth. Add sugar; beat until well blended. Add egg and vanilla; beat until well blended.

Combine flour, baking powder and nutmeg in medium bowl. Add flour mixture and milk alternately to butter mixture, beating at low speed after each addition until well blended.

Shape dough into 2 logs, each about 2 inches in diameter and 6 inches long. Roll logs in colored sprinkles, if desired, coating evenly (about ¼ cup sprinkles per roll). Or, leave rolls plain and decorate with melted chocolate after baking. Wrap each roll in plastic wrap. Refrigerate 2 to 3 hours or overnight.

Preheat oven to 350°F. Grease cookie sheets. Cut logs into ¼-inch-thick slices; place 1 inch apart on prepared cookie sheets. (Keep unbaked logs and sliced cookies chilled until ready to bake.)

Bake 8 to 10 minutes or until edges are golden brown. Transfer to wire racks to cool.

Dip plain cookies in melted chocolate or drizzle chocolate over cookies with fork or spoon, if desired. Set cookies on wire racks until chocolate is set. Store in airtight container.

Makes about 48 cookies

Classic Refrigerator Sugar Cookies

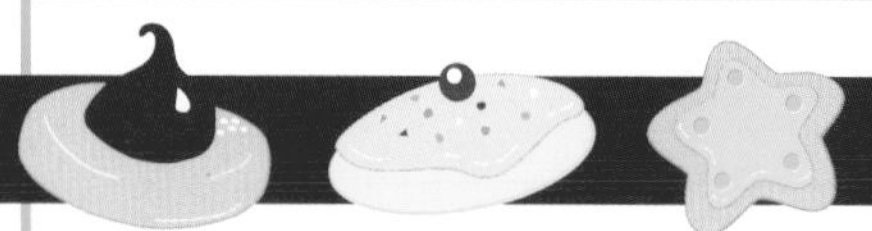

Peanut Butter and Chocolate Spirals

1 package (20 ounces) refrigerated sugar cookie dough
1 package (20 ounces) refrigerated peanut butter cookie dough
¼ cup unsweetened cocoa powder
⅓ cup peanut butter-flavored chips, chopped
¼ cup all-purpose flour
⅓ cup miniature chocolate chips

1. Remove each dough from wrapper according to package directions.

2. Place sugar cookie dough and cocoa in large bowl; mix with fork to blend. Stir in peanut butter chips.

3. Place peanut butter cookie dough and flour in another large bowl; mix with fork to blend. Stir in chocolate chips. Divide each dough in half; refrigerate 1 hour.

4. Roll each dough on floured surface to 12×6-inch rectangle. Layer each half of peanut butter dough onto each half of chocolate dough. Roll up dough, starting at long end to form 2 (12-inch) rolls. Refrigerate 1 hour.

5. Preheat oven to 375°F. Cut dough into ½-inch-thick slices. Place cookies 2 inches apart on ungreased cookie sheets.

6. Bake 10 to 12 minutes or until lightly browned. Remove to wire racks; cool completely. *Makes 4 dozen cookies*

Peanut Butter and Chocolate Spirals

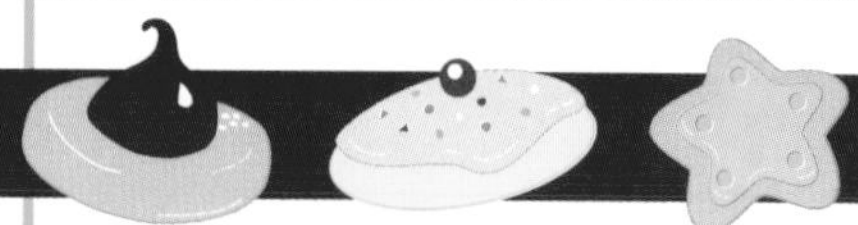

Reese's® Chewy Chocolate Cookies

1¼ cups butter or margarine, softened
2 cups sugar
2 eggs
2 teaspoons vanilla extract
2 cups all-purpose flour
¾ cup HERSHEY'S® Cocoa
1 teaspoon baking soda
½ teaspoon salt
1⅔ cups (10-ounce package) REESE'S® Peanut Butter Chips
½ cup finely chopped nuts (optional)

1. Heat oven to 350°F. Beat butter and sugar in large bowl until light and fluffy. Add eggs and vanilla; beat well. In medium bowl, combine flour, cocoa, baking soda and salt; gradually blend into butter mixture. Stir in peanut butter chips and nuts, if desired. Drop by rounded teaspoonfuls onto ungreased cookie sheets.

2. Bake 8 to 9 minutes. (Do not overbake; cookies will be soft. They will puff while baking and flatten while cooling). Cool slightly; remove from cookie sheets to wire racks. Cool completely. *Makes about 4½ dozen cookies*

Reese's® Chewy Chocolate Pan Cookies: Spread dough into greased 15½×10½×1-inch jelly-roll pan. Bake at 350°F for 20 minutes or until set. Cool completely in pan on wire rack; cut into bars. Makes about 4 dozen bars.

Reese's® Chewy Chocolate Cookie Ice Cream Sandwiches: Prepare Reese's® Chewy Chocolate Cookies as directed; cool. Place small scoop of slightly softened vanilla ice cream between flat sides of two cookies. Gently press together. Serve immediately or wrap and freeze.

High Altitude Directions: Decrease sugar to 1⅔ cups. Increase flour to 2 cups plus 2 tablespoons. Decrease baking soda to ¾ teaspoon. Add 2 teaspoons water with flour mixture. Bake at 350°F 7 to 8 minutes. Makes about 6 dozen cookies.

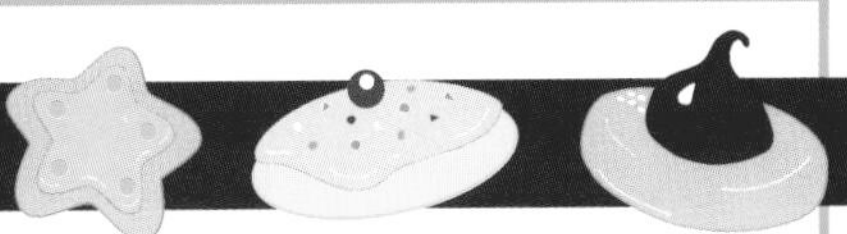

Granola Apple Cookies

- 1 cup packed brown sugar
- 3/4 cup margarine or butter, softened
- 1 egg
- 3/4 cup MOTT'S® Natural Apple Sauce
- 1 teaspoon vanilla
- 3 cups granola with dates and raisins
- 1 1/2 cups all-purpose flour
- 1 teaspoon baking powder
- 1/2 teaspoon baking soda
- 1 teaspoon ground cinnamon
- 1/2 teaspoon allspice
- 1/2 teaspoon salt
- 1 cup flaked coconut
- 1 cup unsalted sunflower nuts

In large bowl, combine brown sugar, margarine, egg, apple sauce and vanilla; beat well. Stir in remaining ingredients; mix well. Refrigerate 1 to 2 hours or until firm enough to handle.

Preheat oven to 375°F. Grease cookie sheets. Drop dough by teaspoonfuls 2 inches apart onto prepared cookie sheets. Bake 11 to 13 minutes or until edges are light golden brown. Immediately remove from cookie sheets. Cool on wire racks. Store cookies in airtight container to retain their soft, chewy texture.

Makes about 5 dozen cookies

Note: *For larger cookies, press 1/4 cup dough for each cookie 3 inches apart onto greased cookie sheets. Bake at 375°F for 13 to 15 minutes.*

Tip

Don't grease your cookie sheets too heavily; it can cause cookies to spread and overbrown on the bottom.

Lip-Smacking Lemon Cookies

½ cup butter, softened
1 cup sugar
1 egg
2 tablespoons lemon juice
2 teaspoons grated lemon peel
2 cups all-purpose flour
1 teaspoon baking powder
⅛ teaspoon salt
Dash ground nutmeg

Tip

One medium lemon will yield about 3 tablespoons juice and 2 to 3 teaspoons grated peel.

Beat butter in large bowl with electric mixer at medium speed until smooth. Add sugar; beat until well blended. Add egg, lemon juice and peel; beat until well blended.

Combine flour, baking powder, salt and nutmeg in large bowl. Gradually add flour mixture to butter mixture at low speed, blending well after each addition.

Shape dough into 2 logs, each about 1½ inches in diameter and 6½ inches long. Wrap each log in plastic wrap. Refrigerate 2 to 3 hours or up to 3 days.

Preheat oven to 350°F. Grease cookie sheets. Cut logs into ¼-inch-thick slices; place 1 inch apart on cookie sheets.

Bake about 15 minutes or until edges are light brown. Transfer to wire rack to cool. Store in airtight container.

Makes about 48 cookies

Lip-Smacking Lemon Cookies

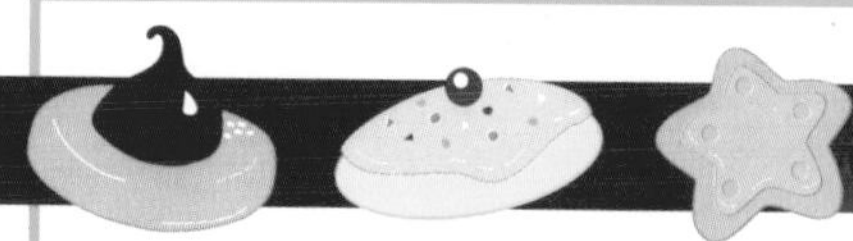

Peanut Butter Chewies

1 Butter Flavor* CRISCO® Stick or 1 cup Butter Flavor* CRISCO® all-vegetable shortening
1½ cups creamy peanut butter
1½ cups firmly packed brown sugar
2 eggs
1 can (14 ounces) sweetened condensed milk
2 teaspoons vanilla
2 cups all-purpose flour
1 teaspoon baking soda
1 teaspoon salt
1½ cups chopped pecans

**Butter Flavor Crisco® is artificially flavored.*

1. Heat oven to 350°F. Place sheets of foil on countertop for cooling cookies.

2. Combine 1 cup shortening, peanut butter and sugar in large bowl. Beat at medium speed of electric mixer until well blended. Beat in eggs, sweetened condensed milk and vanilla.

3. Combine flour, baking soda and salt. Mix into shortening mixture at low speed until just blended. Stir in pecans.

4. Drop rounded tablespoonfuls of dough 2 inches apart onto ungreased baking sheets.

5. Bake one baking sheet at a time at 350°F for 10 to 11 minutes or until lightly browned on bottom. *Do not overbake.* Cool 2 minutes on baking sheets. Remove cookies to foil to cool completely.

Makes about 4 dozen cookies

Peanut Butter Chewies

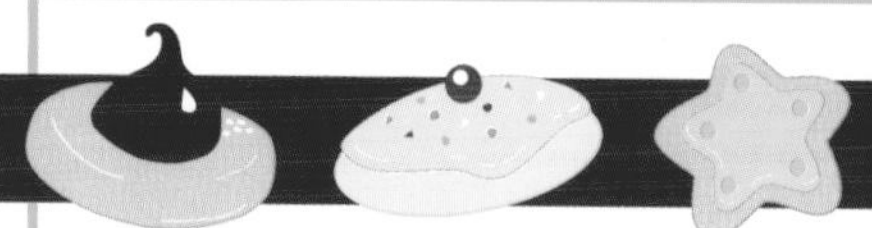

Oatmeal Butterscotch Cookies

- **¾ cup (1½ sticks) butter or margarine, softened**
- **¾ cup granulated sugar**
- **¾ cup packed light brown sugar**
- **2 eggs**
- **1 teaspoon vanilla extract**
- **1¼ cups all-purpose flour**
- **1 teaspoon baking soda**
- **½ teaspoon ground cinnamon**
- **½ teaspoon salt**
- **3 cups quick-cooking or regular rolled oats**
- **1⅔ cups (10-ounce package) HERSHEY®S Butterscotch Chips**

1. Heat oven to 375°F.

2. Beat butter, granulated sugar and brown sugar in large bowl until well blended. Add eggs and vanilla; blend thoroughly. Stir together flour, baking soda, cinnamon and salt; gradually add to butter mixture, beating until well blended. Stir in oats and butterscotch chips; mix well. Drop by teaspoons onto ungreased cookie sheet.

3. Bake 8 to 10 minutes or until golden brown. Cool slightly; remove from cookie sheet to wire rack. Cool completely.

Makes about 4 dozen cookies

Tip

To soften cold butter, cut a stick into ½-inch slices and place on a microwavable plate. Heat at MEDIUM-LOW (30% power) about 30 seconds.

Oatmeal Butterscotch Cookies

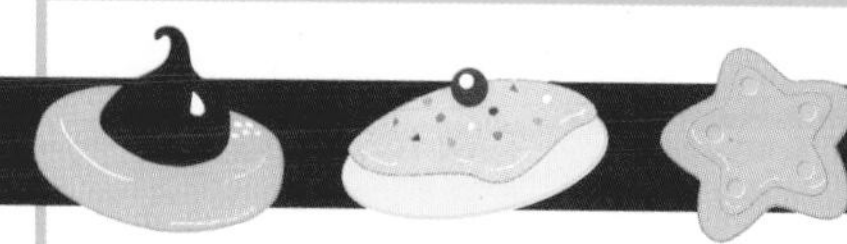

Mexican Wedding Cookies

1 cup pecan pieces or halves
1 cup butter, softened
2 cups powdered sugar, divided
2 cups all-purpose flour, divided
2 teaspoons vanilla
⅛ teaspoon salt

Place pecans in food processor. Process using on/off pulsing action until pecans are ground, but not pasty.

Beat butter and ½ cup powdered sugar in large bowl with electric mixer at medium speed until light and fluffy. Gradually add 1 cup flour, vanilla and salt. Beat at low speed until well blended. Stir in remaining 1 cup flour and ground nuts with spoon.

Shape dough into a ball; wrap in plastic wrap and refrigerate 1 hour or until firm.

Preheat oven to 350°F. Shape tablespoons of dough into 1-inch balls. Place 1 inch apart on ungreased cookie sheets.

Bake 12 to 15 minutes or until pale golden brown. Let cookies stand on cookie sheets 2 minutes.

Meanwhile, place 1 cup powdered sugar in 13×9-inch glass dish. Transfer hot cookies to powdered sugar. Roll cookies in powdered sugar, coating well. Let cookies cool in sugar.

Sift remaining ½ cup powdered sugar over sugar-coated cookies before serving. Store tightly covered at room temperature or freeze up to 1 month.

Makes about 48 cookies

Mexican Wedding Cookies

Smucker's® Grandmother's Jelly Cookies

- 1½ cups sugar
- 1 cup butter or margarine, softened
- 1 egg
- 1½ teaspoons vanilla extract
- 3½ cups all-purpose flour
- 1 teaspoon salt
- ¾ cup SMUCKER'S® Red Raspberry, Strawberry or Peach Preserves

In large bowl, cream together sugar and butter until light and fluffy. Add egg and vanilla; beat well. Stir in flour and salt; mix well. Stir to make smooth dough. (If batter gets too hard to handle, mix with hands.) Cover and refrigerate about 2 hours.

Preheat oven to 375°F. Lightly grease baking sheets. On lightly floured board, roll out half of dough to about ⅛-inch thickness. Cut out cookies with 2½-inch round cookie cutter. Roll out remaining dough; cut with 2½-inch cutter with hole in center. Place on baking sheets. Bake 8 to 10 minutes or until lightly browned. Cool about 30 minutes.

To serve, spread preserves on plain cookies; top with cookies with holes.

Makes approximately 3 dozen cookies

Classic Peanut Butter Cookies

- 1 cup unsalted butter, softened
- 1 cup crunchy peanut butter
- 1 cup granulated sugar
- 1 cup light brown sugar, firmly packed
- 2 eggs
- 2½ cups all-purpose flour
- 1 teaspoon baking powder
- 1½ teaspoons baking soda
- ½ teaspoon salt

Beat butter, peanut butter and sugars until creamy. Beat in eggs. In separate bowl, sift flour, baking powder, baking soda and salt. Stir into batter until blended. Refrigerate 1 hour. Roll dough into 1-inch balls and place on baking sheets. Flatten each ball with fork, making criss-cross pattern. Bake in preheated 375°F oven about 10 minutes or until cookies begin to brown. Do not overbake.

Makes 4 dozen cookies

Favorite recipe from Peanut Advisory Board

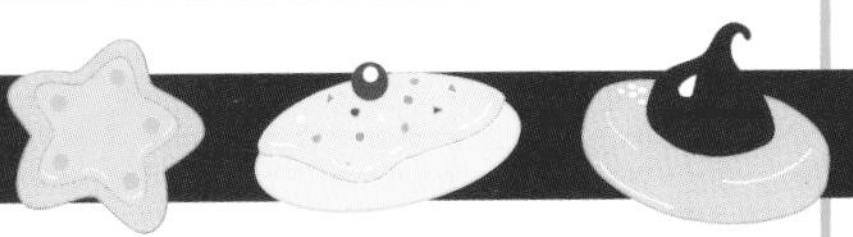

Baker's® One Bowl® Coconut Macaroons

1 package (14 ounces) BAKER'S® ANGEL FLAKE® Coconut (5⅓ cups)
⅔ cup sugar
6 tablespoons flour
¼ teaspoon salt
4 egg whites
1 teaspoon almond extract

HEAT oven to 325°F.

MIX coconut, sugar, flour and salt in large bowl. Stir in egg whites and almond extract until well blended.

DROP by teaspoonfuls onto greased and floured cookie sheets. Press 1 whole candied cherry or whole natural almond into center of each cookie, if desired.

BAKE 20 minutes or until edges of cookies are golden brown. Immediately remove from cookie sheets. Cool on wire racks. *Makes about 3 dozen cookies*

Chocolate Dipped Macaroons: Prepare Coconut Macaroons as directed. Cool. Melt 1 package (8 squares) Baker's® Semi-Sweet Baking Chocolate as directed on package. Dip cookies halfway into chocolate or drizzle tops of cookies with chocolate; let excess chocolate drip off. Let stand at room temperature or refrigerate on wax paper-lined tray 30 minutes or until chocolate is firm.

White Chocolate Coconut Macaroons: Prepare Coconut Macaroons as directed, adding 3 squares Baker's® Premium White Baking Chocolate, chopped, to coconut mixture.

Chocolate Macaroons: Prepare Coconut Macaroons as directed, adding 2 squares Baker's® Semi-Sweet Baking Chocolate, melted, to coconut mixture.

Prep Time: 15 minutes
Bake Time: 20 minutes

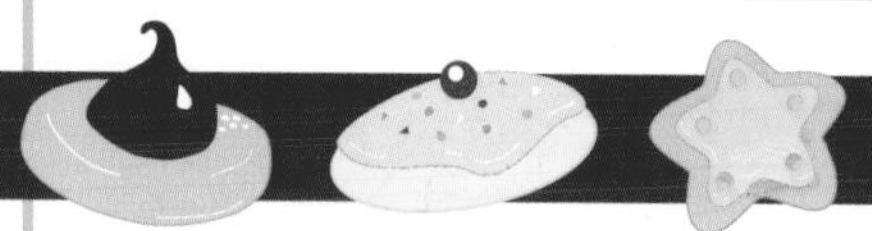

Chocolate Crackletops

- 2 cups all-purpose flour
- 2 teaspoons baking powder
- 2 cups granulated sugar
- ½ cup (1 stick) butter or margarine
- 4 squares (1 ounce each) unsweetened baking chocolate, chopped
- 4 large eggs, lightly beaten
- 2 teaspoons vanilla extract
- 1¾ cups "M&M's"® Chocolate Mini Baking Bits
- Additional granulated sugar

Combine flour and baking powder; set aside. In 2-quart saucepan over medium heat combine 2 cups sugar, butter and chocolate, stirring until butter and chocolate are melted; remove from heat. Gradually stir in eggs and vanilla. Stir in flour mixture until well blended. Chill mixture 1 hour. Stir in "M&M's"® Chocolate Mini Baking Bits; chill mixture an additional 1 hour.

Preheat oven to 350°F. Line cookie sheets with foil. With sugar-dusted hands, roll dough into 1-inch balls; roll balls in additional granulated sugar. Place about 2 inches apart onto prepared cookie sheets. Bake 10 to 12 minutes. Do not overbake. Cool completely on wire racks. Store in tightly covered container. *Makes about 5 dozen cookies*

Oatmeal Pecan Scotchies

- ½ cup margarine or butter, softened
- ½ cup packed light brown sugar
- 1 egg
- 1¼ cups all-purpose flour
- 1 cup old-fashioned rolled oats
- 1 teaspoon DAVIS® Baking Powder
- ¼ cup milk
- ½ cup PLANTERS® Pecan Pieces
- ½ cup butterscotch chips

1. Beat margarine or butter and sugar in large bowl with mixer at medium speed until creamy. Blend in egg.

2. Mix flour, oats and baking powder in small bowl. Alternately stir flour mixture and milk into egg mixture. Stir in pecans and butterscotch chips.

3. Drop batter by rounded teaspoonfuls onto ungreased baking sheets. Bake at 350°F for 12 to 15 minutes or until lightly golden. Remove from pan; cool on wire rack. Store in airtight container. *Makes 4 dozen cookies*

Chocolate Crackletops

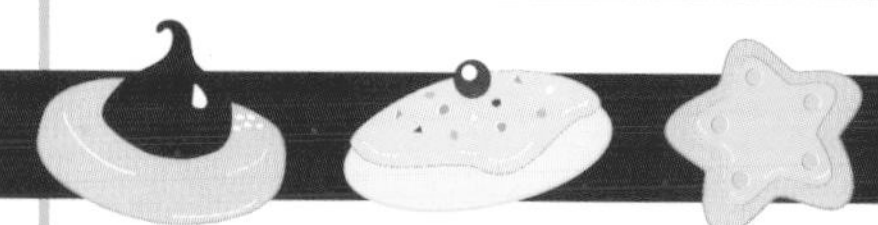

Spicy Oatmeal Raisin Cookies

- **1 package DUNCAN HINES® Moist Deluxe Spice Cake Mix**
- **4 egg whites**
- **1 cup uncooked quick-cooking oats (not instant or old-fashioned)**
- **½ cup vegetable oil**
- **½ cup raisins**

Preheat oven to 350°F. Grease cookie sheets.

Combine cake mix, egg whites, oats and oil in large mixing bowl. Beat at low speed with electric mixer until blended. Stir in raisins. Drop by rounded teaspoons onto prepared cookie sheets.

Bake 7 to 9 minutes or until lightly browned. Cool 1 minute on cookie sheets. Remove to cooling racks; cool completely.

Makes about 4 dozen cookies

Chocolate & Peanut-Butter Tweed Cookies

- **1 cup butter, softened**
- **½ cup packed light brown sugar**
- **¼ cup granulated sugar**
- **1 egg**
- **¼ teaspoon baking soda**
- **2½ cups all-purpose flour**
- **½ cup each semisweet chocolate chips and peanut butter chips, chopped***

**Chips can be chopped in a food processor.*

Beat butter and sugars in large bowl with electric mixer until smooth. Add egg and baking soda; beat until light and fluffy. Stir in flour until dough is smooth. Blend in chopped chips. Divide dough into 4 parts. Shape each part into a roll, about 1½ inches in diameter. Wrap in plastic wrap; refrigerate until firm, at least 1 hour or up to 2 weeks. (For longer storage, freeze up to 6 weeks.)

Preheat oven to 375°F. Lightly grease cookie sheets or line with parchment paper. Cut rolls into ⅛-inch-thick slices; place 2 inches apart on prepared cookie sheets. Bake 10 to 12 minutes or until lightly browned. Remove to wire racks to cool.

Makes about 6 dozen cookies

Spicy Oatmeal Raisin Cookies

Peanut Butter Brickle Cookies

- 1½ cups all-purpose flour
- 1 cup granulated sugar
- 1 cup butter or margarine, softened
- ½ cup peanut butter
- 1 egg
- 2 tablespoons packed light brown sugar
- ½ teaspoon baking soda
- 1 teaspoon vanilla
- 1 package (6 ounces) almond brickle bits

Preheat oven to 350°F. Grease cookie sheets. Combine flour, granulated sugar, butter, peanut butter, egg, brown sugar, baking soda and vanilla in large bowl. Beat at medium speed of electric mixer 2 to 3 minutes until well blended, scraping bowl often. Stir in almond brickle bits.

Shape rounded teaspoonfuls of dough into 1-inch balls. Place 2 inches apart on prepared cookie sheets. Flatten cookies to ⅛-inch thickness with bottom of glass covered with waxed paper. Bake 7 to 9 minutes or until edges are very lightly browned.

Makes about 4 dozen cookies

Hershey®s Classic Milk Chocolate Chip Cookies

- 1 cup (2 sticks) butter, softened
- ¾ cup granulated sugar
- ¾ cup packed light brown sugar
- 1 teaspoon vanilla extract
- 2 eggs
- 2¼ cups all-purpose flour
- 1 teaspoon baking soda
- ½ teaspoon salt
- 2 cups (11.5-ounce package) HERSHEY®S Milk Chocolate Chips
- 1 cup chopped nuts (optional)

1. Heat oven to 375°F.

2. Beat butter, granulated sugar, brown sugar and vanilla in large bowl. Add eggs; beat well. Stir together flour, baking soda and salt; gradually add to butter mixture, beating until well blended. Stir in chocolate chips and nuts, if desired. Drop by teaspoons onto ungreased cookie sheet.

3. Bake 8 to 10 minutes or until lightly browned. Cool slightly; remove from cookie sheet to wire rack. Cool completely.

Makes about 5 dozen cookies

Pan Recipe: *Spread batter into greased 15½×10½×1-inch jelly-roll pan. Bake at 375°F 20 minutes or until lightly browned. Cool completely. Cut into bars. Makes about 48 bars.*

Peanut Butter Brickle Cookies

Jammy Pinwheels

1¼ cups granulated sugar
1 Butter Flavor* CRISCO® Stick or 1 cup Butter Flavor* CRISCO® all-vegetable shortening plus additional for greasing
2 eggs
¼ cup light corn syrup or regular pancake syrup
1 tablespoon vanilla
3 cups all-purpose flour (plus 2 tablespoons), divided
¾ teaspoon baking powder
½ teaspoon baking soda
½ teaspoon salt
1 cup apricot, strawberry or seedless raspberry jam

**Butter Flavor Crisco® is artificially flavored.*

1. Place sugar and 1 cup shortening in large bowl. Beat at medium speed of electric mixer until well blended. Add eggs, syrup and vanilla; beat until well blended and fluffy.

2. Combine 3 cups flour, baking powder, baking soda and salt. Add gradually to shortening mixture, beating at low speed until well blended.

3. Divide dough in half. Pat each half into thick rectangle. Sprinkle about 1 tablespoon flour on large sheet of waxed paper. Place rectangle of dough on floured paper. Turn dough over; cover with another large sheet of waxed paper. Roll dough into 12×8-inch rectangle about ⅛ inch thick. Trim edges. Slide dough and waxed paper onto ungreased baking sheets. Refrigerate 20 minutes or until firm. Repeat with remaining dough.

4. Heat oven to 375°F. Grease baking sheets. Place sheets of foil on counter for cooling cookies.

5. Place chilled dough rectangle on work surface. Remove top sheet of waxed paper. Cut dough into 2-inch squares. Place squares 2 inches apart on prepared baking sheets. Make a 1-inch diagonal cut from each corner of square almost to center. Place 1 teaspoon jam in center. Lift every other corner and bring together in center of cookie. Repeat with remaining dough.

6. Bake at 375°F for 7 to 10 minutes or until edges of cookies are golden brown. *Do not overbake.* Cool 2 minutes on baking sheet. Remove cookies to foil to cool completely.

Makes about 4 dozen cookies

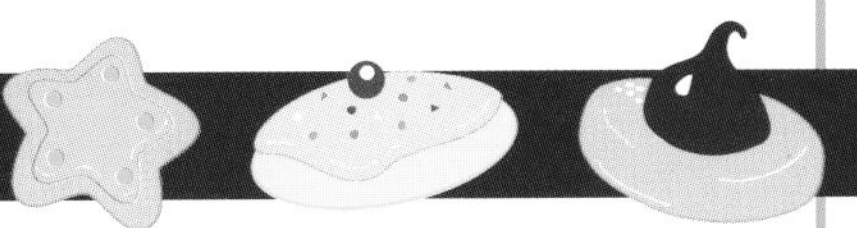

Soft Spicy Molasses Cookies

2 cups all-purpose flour
1 cup sugar
¾ cup butter, softened
⅓ cup light molasses
3 tablespoons milk
1 egg
½ teaspoon baking soda
½ teaspoon ground ginger
½ teaspoon ground cinnamon
½ teaspoon ground cloves
⅛ teaspoon salt
Sugar for rolling

Combine flour, 1 cup sugar, butter, molasses, milk, egg, baking soda, ginger, cinnamon, cloves and salt in large bowl. Beat at low speed of electric mixer 2 to 3 minutes until well blended. Cover; refrigerate until firm enough to handle, at least 4 hours or overnight.

Preheat oven to 350°F. Shape rounded teaspoonfuls of dough into 1-inch balls. Roll in sugar. Place 2 inches apart on ungreased cookie sheets. Bake 10 to 12 minutes or until slightly firm to the touch. Remove immediately.

Makes about 4 dozen cookies

Pecan Drops

¾ cup sugar
½ cup margarine or butter, softened
¼ cup egg substitute
1 teaspoon vanilla extract
2 cups all-purpose flour
⅔ cup PLANTERS® Pecans, finely chopped
3 tablespoons jam, jelly or preserves, any flavor

In small bowl, with electric mixer at medium speed, cream sugar and margarine. Add egg substitute and vanilla; beat 1 minute. Stir in flour until blended. Refrigerate dough 1 hour.

Form dough into 36 (1¼-inch) balls; roll in pecans, pressing into dough. Place 2 inches apart on greased cookie sheets. Indent center of each ball with thumb or back of wooden spoon. Bake at 350°F for 10 minutes; remove from oven. Spoon ¼ teaspoon jam into each cookie indentation. Bake 2 to 5 more minutes or until lightly browned. Remove from sheets; cool on wire racks.

Makes about 3 dozen cookies

Crispy Oat Drops

1 cup (2 sticks) butter or margarine, softened
½ cup granulated sugar
½ cup firmly packed light brown sugar
1 large egg
2 cups all-purpose flour
½ cup quick-cooking or old-fashioned oats, uncooked
1 teaspoon cream of tartar
½ teaspoon baking soda
¼ teaspoon salt
1¾ cups "M&M's"® Semi-Sweet Chocolate Mini Baking Bits
1 cup toasted rice cereal
½ cup shredded coconut
½ cup coarsely chopped pecans

Preheat oven to 350°F. In large bowl cream butter and sugars until light and fluffy; beat in egg. In medium bowl combine flour, oats, cream of tartar, baking soda and salt; blend flour mixture into creamed mixture. Stir in "M&M's"® Semi-Sweet Chocolate Mini Baking Bits, cereal, coconut and pecans. Drop by heaping tablespoonfuls about 2 inches apart onto ungreased cookie sheets. Bake 10 to 13 minutes or until lightly browned. Cool completely on wire racks. Store in tightly covered container. *Makes about 4 dozen cookies*

Tip 

Quick-cooking rolled oats and old-fashioned rolled oats are essentially the same; the quick-cooking oats simply cook faster because they have been rolled into thinner flakes.

Crispy Oat Drops

Hershey®s Soft & Chewy Cookies

- 1 cup (2 sticks) butter (no substitutes)
- ¾ cup packed light brown sugar
- ½ cup granulated sugar
- ¼ cup light corn syrup
- 1 egg
- 2 teaspoons vanilla extract
- 2½ cups all-purpose flour
- 1 teaspoon baking soda
- ¼ teaspoon salt
- 1 package (10 to 12 ounces) HERSHEY®S Bake Shoppe pieces (any flavor)

1. Heat oven to 350°F.

2. Beat butter, brown sugar and granulated sugar in large bowl until light and fluffy. Add corn syrup, egg and vanilla; beat well. Stir together flour, baking soda and salt; gradually add to butter mixture, beating until well blended. Stir in any flavor Bake Shoppe pieces. Drop by rounded teaspoons onto ungreased cookie sheet.

3. Bake 8 to 10 minutes or until lightly browned and almost set. Cool slightly; remove from cookie sheet to wire rack. Cool completely. Cookies will be softer the second day.

Makes about 3½ dozen cookies

Chocolate Chocolate Cookies: *Decrease flour to 2¼ cups and add ¼ cup HERSHEY®S Cocoa or HERSHEY®S European Style Cocoa.*

Hershey's® Soft & Chewy Cookies

Ranger Cookies

- **1 cup (2 sticks) margarine or butter, softened**
- **1 cup granulated sugar**
- **1 cup firmly packed brown sugar**
- **2 eggs**
- **1 teaspoon vanilla**
- **2 cups all-purpose flour**
- **1 teaspoon baking soda**
- **½ teaspoon baking powder**
- **½ teaspoon salt (optional)**
- **2 cups QUAKER® Oats (quick or old fashioned, uncooked)**
- **2 cups corn flakes cereal**
- **½ cup flaked or shredded coconut**
- **½ cup chopped nuts**

Heat oven to 350°F. Beat margarine and sugars until creamy. Add eggs and vanilla; beat well. Add combined flour, baking soda, baking powder and salt; mix well. Stir in oats, corn flakes, coconut and nuts; mix well. Drop dough by heaping tablespoonfuls onto ungreased cookie sheet. Bake 10 to 12 minutes or until light golden brown. Cool 1 minute on cookie sheet; remove to wire rack. Cool completely. Store tightly covered.

Makes 2 dozen large cookies

Tip

Hardened brown sugar can be softened quickly in the microwave. Place one cup sugar in a covered microwavable dish; heat at HIGH 30 to 60 seconds. Repeat if necessary.

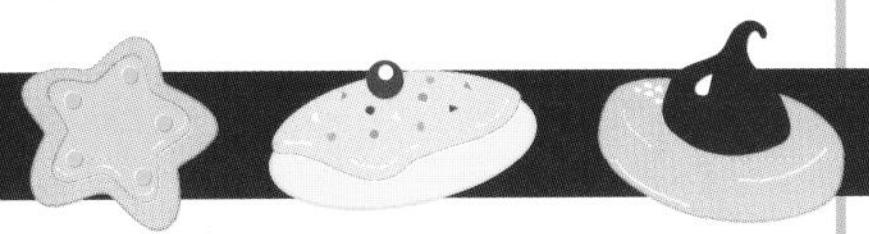

Baker's® One Bowl® Super Chunk Cookies

1 package (8 squares) BAKER'S® Semi-Sweet Baking Chocolate
½ cup (1 stick) butter *or* margarine
½ cup *each* granulated sugar and firmly packed brown sugar
1 egg
1 teaspoon vanilla
1 cup flour
1 cup quick-cooking rolled oats
½ teaspoon baking soda
½ cup chopped nuts (optional)

HEAT oven to 375°F. Break chocolate squares in half; cut each half into 3 chunks.

BEAT butter, sugars, egg and vanilla in large bowl with electric mixer on medium speed 1 minute or until well blended. Beat in flour, oats and baking soda on low speed until combined. Stir in chocolate and nuts.

DROP by rounded tablespoonfuls onto ungreased cookie sheet.

BAKE 10 minutes or until lightly browned. Cool on cookie sheet 2 minutes. Cool completely on wire racks.

Makes about 2 dozen cookies

Variation: Prepare as directed, substituting 1 cup lightly toasted Baker's® Angel Flake® Coconut for the nuts.

Prep Time: 10 minutes
Bake Time: 10 minutes

Chocolate Clouds

- **3 egg whites, at room temperature**
- **1/8 teaspoon cream of tartar**
- **3/4 cup sugar**
- **1 teaspoon vanilla extract**
- **2 tablespoons HERSHEY®S Cocoa**
- **2 cups (12-ounce package) HERSHEY®S Semi-Sweet Chocolate Chips**

Heat oven to 300°F. Cover cookie sheet with parchment paper or foil.

Beat egg whites and cream of tartar in large bowl at high speed of electric mixer until soft peaks form. Gradually add sugar and vanilla, beating well after each addition until stiff peaks hold, sugar is dissolved and mixture is glossy. Sift cocoa onto egg white mixture; gently fold just until combined. Fold in chocolate chips. Drop by heaping tablespoons onto prepared cookie sheet.

Bake 35 to 45 minutes or just until dry. Cool slightly; peel paper from cookies. Store, covered, at room temperature.

Makes 30 cookies

Peanutty Crisscrosses

- **3/4 cup (1 1/2 sticks) margarine or butter, softened**
- **1 cup peanut butter**
- **1 1/2 cups firmly packed brown sugar**
- **1/3 cup water**
- **1 egg**
- **1 teaspoon vanilla**
- **3 cups QUAKER® Oats (quick or old fashioned, uncooked)**
- **1 1/2 cups all-purpose flour**
- **1/2 teaspoon baking soda**
- **Granulated sugar**

Beat together margarine, peanut butter and sugar until creamy. Add water, egg and vanilla; beat well. Add combined oats, flour and baking soda. Cover; chill about 1 hour.

Heat oven to 350°F. Shape dough into 1-inch balls. Place on ungreased cookie sheet; flatten with tines of fork, dipped in granulated sugar, to form crisscross pattern. Bake 9 to 10 minutes or until edges are golden brown. Cool 2 minutes on cookie sheet; remove to wire rack. Cool completely. Store in tightly covered container.

Makes about 7 dozen cookies

Chocolate Clouds

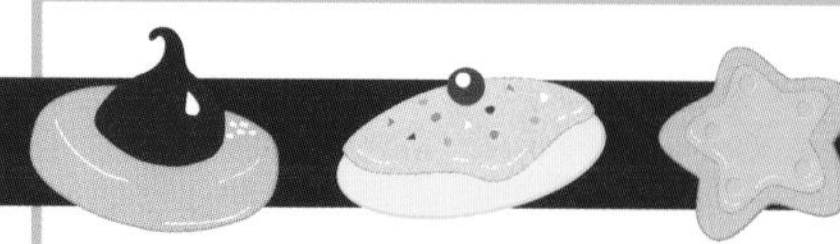

Molasses Spice Cookies

1 cup granulated sugar
¾ cup shortening
¼ cup molasses
1 large egg, beaten
2 cups all-purpose flour
2 teaspoons baking soda
1 teaspoon ground cinnamon
1 teaspoon ground cloves
1 teaspoon ground ginger
¼ teaspoon dry mustard
¼ teaspoon salt
½ cup granulated brown sugar

1. Preheat oven to 375°F. Grease cookie sheets; set aside.

2. Beat granulated sugar and shortening about 5 minutes in large bowl until light and fluffy. Add molasses and egg; beat until fluffy.

3. Combine flour, baking soda, cinnamon, cloves, ginger, mustard and salt in medium bowl. Add to shortening mixture; mix until just combined.

4. Place brown sugar in shallow dish. Roll tablespoonfuls of dough into 1-inch balls; roll in sugar to coat. Place 2 inches apart on prepared cookie sheets. Bake 15 minutes or until lightly browned. Let cookies stand on cookie sheets 2 minutes. Remove cookies to wire racks; cool completely.

Makes about 6 dozen cookies

Chunky Chocolate Cookies

1 cup butter, softened
¾ cup granulated sugar
¾ cup packed light brown sugar
2 eggs
1½ teaspoons vanilla
2¼ cups all-purpose flour
1 teaspoon baking soda
½ teaspoon salt
1 cup chopped walnuts
1 (8-ounce) milk chocolate candy bar, cut into ½-inch pieces

Preheat oven to 375°F. Combine butter, granulated sugar, brown sugar, eggs and vanilla in large bowl. Beat at medium speed of electric mixer, scraping bowl often, until well blended, 1 to 2 minutes. Add flour, baking soda and salt. Continue beating until well mixed, 1 to 2 minutes. Stir in walnuts and chocolate. Drop rounded tablespoonfuls of dough 2 inches apart onto ungreased cookie sheets.

Bake 9 to 11 minutes or until lightly browned. Cool 1 minute on cookie sheets; remove immediately to wire racks.

Makes about 3 dozen cookies

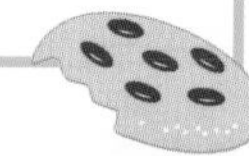

Molasses Spice Cookies

Golden Gingersnaps

- **1 package DUNCAN HINES® Golden Sugar Cookie Mix**
- **1 egg**
- **1 tablespoon water**
- **1 tablespoon light molasses**
- **1½ teaspoons ground ginger**
- **1 teaspoon ground cinnamon**
- **½ teaspoon baking soda**
- **¼ cup granulated sugar**
- **1 tablespoon milk**
- **⅓ cup finely chopped pecans**

Preheat oven to 375°F. Grease cookie sheets.

Combine cookie mix, egg, water, molasses, ginger, cinnamon and baking soda in large bowl. Stir until thoroughly blended. Drop by level tablespoonfuls into sugar. Roll to completely cover. Place 2 inches apart onto prepared cookie sheets. Flatten slightly with bottom of drinking glass. Brush tops lightly with milk. Sprinkle with pecans. Bake 9 minutes for chewy cookies or 10 minutes for crisp cookies. Cool 2 minutes on cookie sheets. Remove to cooling racks. Cool completely. Store in airtight container. *Makes 3 dozen cookies*

Loaded Oatmeal Cookies

- **¾ cup butter, softened**
- **1 cup packed brown sugar**
- **1 egg**
- **1 tablespoon milk**
- **1 teaspoon vanilla extract**
- **1½ cups uncooked quick oats**
- **1 cup all-purpose flour**
- **½ teaspoon baking soda**
- **½ teaspoon salt**
- **½ teaspoon ground cinnamon**
- **1 cup (6 ounces) semisweet chocolate chips**
- **1 cup (6 ounces) butterscotch chips**
- **¾ cup raisins**
- **½ cup chopped walnuts**

Preheat oven to 350°F. Beat butter and brown sugar in large bowl until creamy. Beat in egg, milk and vanilla until light and fluffy. Mix in oats, flour, baking soda, salt and cinnamon until well blended. Stir in chips, raisins and walnuts. Drop rounded tablespoonfuls of dough 2 inches apart onto ungreased cookie sheets.

Bake 12 to 15 minutes or until lightly browned around edges. Cool 2 minutes on cookie sheets. Remove to wire racks; cool completely. Store in airtight container.

Makes about 3 dozen cookies

Golden Gingersnaps

Baker's® Chocolate Sugar Cookies

- **2 cups all-purpose flour**
- **1 teaspoon baking soda**
- **¼ teaspoon salt**
- **3 squares BAKER'S® Unsweetened Baking Chocolate**
- **1 cup (2 sticks) butter *or* margarine**
- **1 cup sugar**
- **1 egg**
- **1 teaspoon vanilla**
- **Additional sugar**

HEAT oven to 375°F. Mix flour, baking soda and salt in medium bowl.

MICROWAVE chocolate and butter in large microwavable bowl on HIGH 2 minutes or until butter is melted. Stir until chocolate is completely melted.

STIR 1 cup sugar into melted chocolate mixture until well blended. Mix in egg and vanilla until completely blended. Stir in flour mixture until well blended. Refrigerate dough about 15 minutes or until easy to handle.

SHAPE dough into 1-inch balls; roll in additional sugar. Place on ungreased cookie sheets.

BAKE 8 to 10 minutes or until set. (If flatter, crisper cookies are desired, flatten with bottom of glass before baking.) Remove from cookie sheets. Cool on wire racks. Store in tightly covered container. *Makes about 3½ dozen cookies*

Melting Chocolate on Top of Stove: Melt chocolate and butter in 3-quart heavy saucepan on low heat; stir constantly until chocolate is just melted. Remove from heat. Continue as directed.

Jam-Filled Chocolate Sugar Cookies: Prepare Baker's® Chocolate Sugar Cookie dough as directed. Roll in finely chopped nuts in place of sugar. Make indentation in each ball; fill center with your favorite jam. Bake as directed.

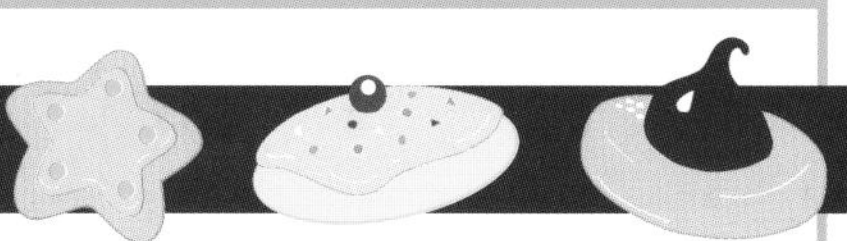

Chocolate-Caramel Sugar Cookies: *Prepare Baker's® Chocolate Sugar Cookie dough as directed. Roll in finely chopped nuts in place of sugar. Make indentation in each ball; bake as directed. Microwave 1 package (14 ounces) KRAFT® Caramels with 2 tablespoons milk in microwavable bowl on HIGH 3 minutes or until melted, stirring after 2 minutes. Fill centers of cookies with caramel mixture. Drizzle with melted Baker's® Semi-Sweet Baking Chocolate.*

Prep Time: 20 minutes plus refrigerating
Bake Time: 10 minutes

Simpler Than Sin Peanut Chocolate Cookies

- **1 cup PETER PAN® Extra Crunchy Peanut Butter**
- **1 cup sugar**
- **1 egg, room temperature and beaten**
- **2 teaspoons vanilla**
- **1 (6-ounce) dark or milk chocolate candy bar, broken into squares**

Preheat oven to 350°F. In medium bowl, combine Peter Pan® Peanut Butter, sugar, egg and vanilla; mix well. Roll dough into 1-inch balls. Place on ungreased cookie sheet 2 inches apart. Bake 12 minutes. Remove from oven and place chocolate squares in center of each cookie. Bake an additional 5 to 7 minutes or until cookies are lightly golden around edges. Cool 5 minutes. Remove to wire rack. Cool.

Makes about 24 cookies

Prep Time: 10 minutes
Bake Time: 19 minutes

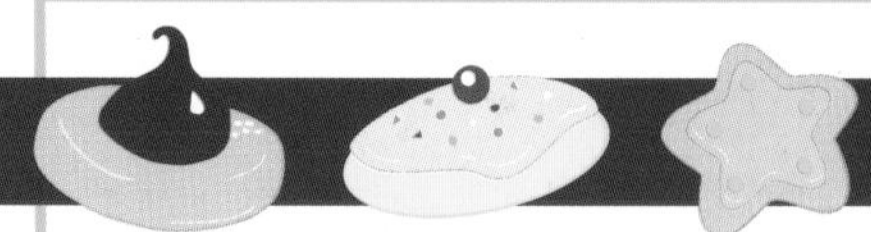

Date-Nut Macaroons

- **1 (8-ounce) package pitted dates, chopped**
- **1½ cups flaked coconut**
- **1 cup PLANTERS® Pecan Halves, chopped**
- **¾ cup sweetened condensed milk (not evaporated milk)**
- **½ teaspoon vanilla extract**

Preheat oven to 350°F.

In medium bowl, combine dates, coconut and nuts; blend in sweetened condensed milk and vanilla. Drop by rounded tablespoonfuls onto greased and floured cookie sheets. Bake 10 to 12 minutes or until light golden brown. Carefully remove from cookie sheets; cool completely on wire racks. Store in airtight container.

Makes about 2 dozen cookies

Double Chocolate Cookies

- **2¼ cups all-purpose flour**
- **1 teaspoon baking soda**
- **1 teaspoon salt**
- **1 cup (2 sticks) butter or margarine, softened**
- **¾ cup granulated sugar**
- **¾ cup firmly packed brown sugar**
- **1 teaspoon vanilla extract**
- **2 eggs**
- **2 (2-ounce) envelopes NESTLÉ® Choco-Bake® Unsweetened Chocolate Flavor**
- **2 cups (12-ounce package) NESTLÉ® TOLL HOUSE® Semi-Sweet Chocolate Morsels**
- **1 cup chopped walnuts**

COMBINE flour, baking soda and salt in small bowl. Beat butter, granulated sugar, brown sugar and vanilla in large mixer bowl. Beat in eggs and Choco-Bake. Gradually beat in flour mixture. Stir in morsels and nuts. Drop by rounded tablespoons onto ungreased baking sheets.

BAKE in preheated 375°F. oven for 8 to 10 minutes or until edges are set but centers are still slightly soft. Let stand for 2 minutes; remove to wire racks to cool completely.

Makes about 6 dozen 2½-inch cookies

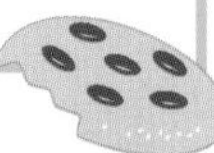

Date-Nut Macaroons

Chocolate Malted Cookies

½ cup butter, softened
½ cup shortening
1¾ cups powdered sugar, divided
1 teaspoon vanilla
2 cups all-purpose flour
1 cup malted milk powder, divided
¼ cup unsweetened cocoa powder

1. Beat butter, shortening, ¾ cup powdered sugar and vanilla in large bowl with electric mixer at high speed.

2. Add flour, ½ cup malted milk powder and cocoa; beat at low speed until well blended. Refrigerate several hours or overnight.

3. Preheat oven to 350°F. Shape slightly mounded teaspoonfuls of dough into balls.

4. Place dough balls about 2 inches apart on ungreased cookie sheets.

5. Bake 14 to 16 minutes or until lightly browned.

6. Meanwhile, combine remaining 1 cup powdered sugar and ½ cup malted milk powder in medium bowl.

7. Remove cookies to wire racks; cool 5 minutes. Roll cookies in powdered sugar mixture.

Makes about 4 dozen cookies

Tip: *Substitute 6 ounces melted semisweet chocolate for the 1 cup powdered sugar and ½ cup malted milk powder used to roll the cookies. Instead, dip cookies in melted chocolate and let dry on wire racks until coating is set.*

Chocolate Malted Cookies

Original Nestlé® Toll House® Chocolate Chip Cookies

2¼ cups all-purpose flour
1 teaspoon baking soda
1 teaspoon salt
1 cup (2 sticks) butter, softened
¾ cup granulated sugar
¾ cup packed brown sugar
1 teaspoon vanilla extract
2 eggs
2 cups (12-ounce package) NESTLÉ® TOLL HOUSE® Semi-Sweet Chocolate Morsels
1 cup chopped nuts

COMBINE flour, baking soda and salt in small bowl. Beat butter, granulated sugar, brown sugar and vanilla in large mixer bowl. Add eggs, one at a time, beating well after each addition. Gradually beat in flour mixture. Stir in morsels and nuts. Drop by rounded tablespoons onto ungreased baking sheets.

BAKE in preheated 375°F. oven for 9 to 11 minutes or until golden brown. Cool on baking sheets for 2 minutes; remove to wire racks to cool completely.

Makes about 5 dozen cookies

Pan Cookie Variation: PREPARE dough as directed. Spread into greased 15½×10½-inch jelly-roll pan. Bake in preheated 375°F. oven for 20 to 25 minutes or until golden brown. Cool in pan on wire rack. Makes 4 dozen bars.

Slice and Bake Cookie Variation: PREPARE dough as directed. Divide in half; wrap in wax paper. Chill for 1 hour or until firm. Shape each half into 15-inch log; wrap in wax paper. Chill for 30 minutes. Cut into ½-inch-thick slices; place on ungreased baking sheets. Bake in preheated 375°F. oven for 8 to 10 minutes or until golden brown. Cool on baking sheets for 2 minutes; remove to wire racks to cool completely. Makes about 5 dozen cookies.*

**May be stored in refrigerator for up to 1 week or in freezer for up to 8 weeks.*

Original Nestlé® Toll House® Chocolate Chip Cookies

Lemon Pecan Cookies

- 1⅔ cups (10-ounce package) HERSHEY®S Premier White Chips, divided
- 2¼ cups all-purpose flour
- ¾ cup sugar
- 2 eggs
- ¾ teaspoon baking soda
- ½ teaspoon freshly grated lemon peel
- ¼ teaspoon lemon extract
- ½ cup (1 stick) butter or margarine
- ¾ cup chopped pecans
- Lemon Drizzle (recipe follows)

1. Heat oven to 350°F. Reserve 2 tablespoons white chips for drizzle.

2. Combine flour, sugar, eggs, baking soda, lemon peel and lemon extract in large bowl. Place remaining white chips and butter in medium microwave-safe bowl. Microwave at HIGH (100%) 1 minute; stir. If necessary, microwave at HIGH an additional 15 seconds at a time, stirring after each heating, just until chips and butter are melted when stirred. Add chip mixture to flour mixture; beat until blended. Stir in pecans. Drop dough by rounded teaspoons onto ungreased cookie sheet.

3. Bake 9 to 11 minutes or until very slightly golden around edges. Remove from cookie sheet to wire rack. Cool completely. Prepare Lemon Drizzle; lightly drizzle over cookies.

Makes about 3½ dozen cookies

Lemon Drizzle: *Place reserved 2 tablespoons white chips and ½ teaspoon shortening (do not use butter, margarine, spread or oil) in microwave-safe bowl. Microwave at HIGH (100%) 30 seconds; stir. If necessary, microwave at HIGH an additional 15 seconds at a time, stirring after each heating, just until chips are melted when smooth. Stir in a few drops food color and a few drops lemon extract, if desired.*

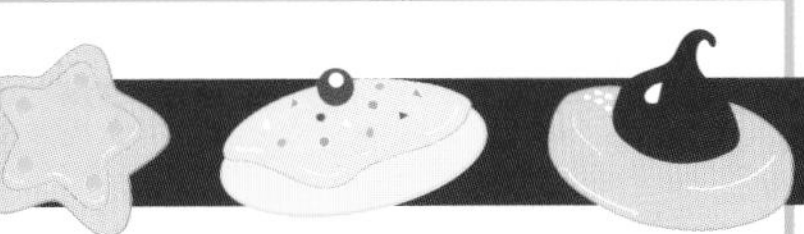

Fudge Cookies

- 1 cup (6 ounces) semisweet chocolate chips
- ½ cup butter or margarine, softened
- 1 cup granulated sugar
- 2 eggs
- 1½ cups all-purpose flour
- Dash salt
- 1½ cups coarsely chopped pecans or walnuts
- Fudge Frosting (recipe follows)

Preheat oven to 375°F. Lightly grease cookie sheets or line with parchment paper. Melt chocolate chips in top of double boiler over hot, not boiling, water. Remove from heat; cool. Beat butter, granulated sugar and eggs in large bowl until smooth. Beat in melted chocolate. Gradually add flour and salt, mixing until smooth. Stir in nuts. Drop dough by rounded teaspoonfuls 2 inches apart onto prepared cookie sheets. Bake 10 to 12 minutes or until slightly firm. Cool 5 minutes on cookie sheet, then remove to wire racks. While cookies bake, prepare Fudge Frosting. Frost cookies while still warm. Cool until frosting is set. *Makes about 5 dozen cookies*

Fudge Frosting

- 1 square (1 ounce) semisweet chocolate
- 3 tablespoons heavy cream
- 1 cup powdered sugar
- 1 teaspoon vanilla

Melt chocolate with cream in small heavy saucepan over medium heat, stirring until chocolate melts completely. Remove from heat; beat in powdered sugar and vanilla. Spread over cookies while frosting is still warm.

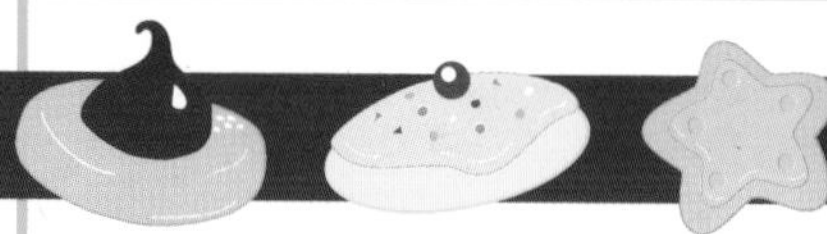

Tiny Mini Kisses™ Peanut Blossoms

¾ cup REESE'S® Creamy Peanut Butter
½ cup shortening
⅓ cup granulated sugar
⅓ cup packed light brown sugar
1 egg
3 tablespoons milk
1 teaspoon vanilla extract
1½ cups all-purpose flour
½ teaspoon baking soda
½ teaspoon salt
Granulated sugar
HERSHEY'S® MINI KISSES™ Semi-Sweet *or* Milk Chocolate Baking Pieces

1. Heat oven to 350°F.

2. Beat peanut butter and shortening in large bowl with electric mixer until well mixed. Add ⅓ cup granulated sugar and brown sugar; beat well. Add egg, milk and vanilla; beat until fluffy. Stir together flour, baking soda and salt; gradually add to peanut butter mixture, beating until blended. Shape into ½-inch balls. Roll in granulated sugar; place on ungreased cookie sheet.

3. Bake 5 to 6 minutes or until set. Immediately press MINI KISS™ into center of each cookie. Remove from cookie sheet to wire rack.

Makes about 14 dozen cookies

Variation: For larger cookies, shape dough into 1-inch balls. Roll in granulated sugar. Place on ungreased cookie sheet. Bake 10 minutes or until set. Immediately place 3 MINI KISSES™ in center of each cookie, pressing down slightly. Remove from cookie sheet to wire rack. Cool completely.

Tiny Mini Kisses™ Peanut Blossoms

Chockful of Chips

Oatmeal Scotch Chippers

- 1¼ Butter Flavor* CRISCO® Sticks or 1¼ cups Butter Flavor* CRISCO® all-vegetable shortening
- 1½ cups firmly packed brown sugar
- 1 cup granulated sugar
- 3 eggs
- 1¼ cups crunchy peanut butter
- 4½ cups rolled oats
- 2 teaspoons baking soda
- 1 cup semisweet chocolate chips
- 1 cup butterscotch-flavored chips
- 1 cup chopped walnuts

**Butter Flavor Crisco is artificially flavored.*

1. Heat oven to 350°F. Place sheets of foil on countertop for cooling cookies.

2. Combine 1¼ cups shortening, brown sugar and granulated sugar in large bowl. Beat at medium speed of electric mixer until well blended. Beat in eggs. Add peanut butter. Beat until blended.

3. Combine oats and baking soda. Stir into shortening mixture with spoon. Stir in chocolate chips, butterscotch chips and nuts until blended.

4. Drop by rounded teaspoonfuls 2 inches apart onto ungreased baking sheets.

5. Bake one baking sheet at a time at 350°F for 10 to 11 minutes or until lightly browned. *Do not overbake.* Cool 2 minutes on baking sheet. Remove cookies to foil to cool completely.

Makes about 6 dozen cookies

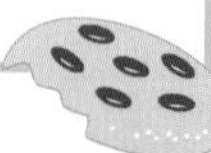

Oatmeal Scotch Chippers

Three-in-One Chocolate Chip Cookies

6 tablespoons butter or margarine, softened
½ cup packed light brown sugar
¼ cup granulated sugar
1 egg
1 teaspoon vanilla extract
1½ cups all-purpose flour
½ teaspoon baking soda
¼ teaspoon salt
2 cups (12-ounce package) HERSHEY'S Semi-Sweet Chocolate Chips

Beat butter, brown sugar and granulated sugar in large bowl until light and fluffy. Add egg and vanilla; beat well. Stir together flour, baking soda and salt; gradually blend into butter mixture. Stir in chocolate chips. Shape and bake cookies into one of the three versions below.

Giant Cookies: Prepare dough. Heat oven to 350°F. Line 12×⅝-inch round pizza pan with foil. Pat dough evenly into prepared pan to within ¾ inch of edge. Bake 15 to 18 minutes or until lightly browned. Cool completely; cut into wedges. Decorate or garnish as desired. Makes about 8 servings (one 12-inch cookie).

Medium-Size Refrigerator Cookies: Prepare dough. On wax paper, shape into 2 rolls, 1½ inches in diameter. Wrap in wax paper; cover with plastic wrap. Refrigerate several hours, or until firm enough to slice. Heat oven to 350°F. Remove rolls from refrigerator; remove wrapping. With sharp knife, cut into ¼-inch-wide slices. Place on ungreased cookie sheet, about 3 inches apart. Bake 8 to 10 minutes or until lightly browned. Cool slightly; remove from cookie sheet to wire rack. Cool completely. Makes about 2½ dozen (2½-inch) cookies.

Miniature Cookies: Prepare dough. Heat oven to 350°F. Drop dough by ¼ teaspoons onto ungreased cookie sheet, about 1½ inches apart. (Or, spoon dough into disposable plastic frosting bag; cut about ¼ inch off tip. Squeeze batter by ¼ teaspoons onto ungreased cookie sheet.) Bake 5 to 7 minutes or just until set. Cool slightly; remove from cookie sheet to wire rack. Cool completely. Makes about 18½ dozen (¾-inch) cookies.

Three-in-One Chocolate Chip Cookies

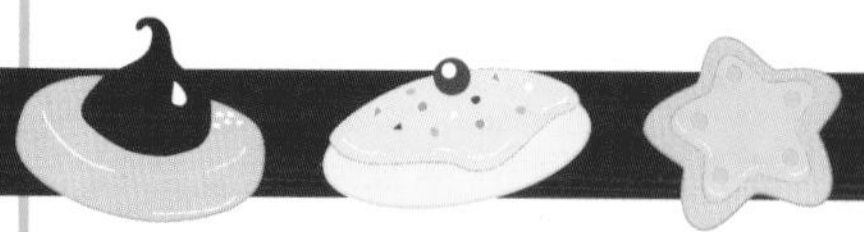

Banana Chocolate Chip Softies

- **1¼ cups all-purpose flour**
- **1 teaspoon baking powder**
- **½ teaspoon salt**
- **⅓ cup butter or margarine, softened**
- **⅓ cup granulated sugar**
- **⅓ cup firmly packed light brown sugar**
- **1 ripe, medium banana, mashed**
- **1 large egg**
- **1 teaspoon vanilla**
- **1 cup milk chocolate chips**
- **½ cup coarsely chopped walnuts (optional)**

Preheat oven to 375°F. Lightly grease cookie sheets.

Place flour, baking powder and salt in small bowl; stir to combine.

Beat butter, granulated sugar and brown sugar in large bowl with electric mixer at medium speed until light and fluffy. Beat in banana, egg and vanilla. Add flour mixture. Beat at low speed until well blended. Stir in chips and walnuts with mixing spoon. (Dough will be soft.)

Drop rounded teaspoonfuls of dough 2 inches apart onto prepared cookie sheets.

Bake 9 to 11 minutes or until edges are golden brown. Let cookies stand on cookie sheets 2 minutes. Remove cookies with spatula to wire racks; cool completely. Store tightly covered at room temperature. These cookies do not freeze well.

Makes about 3 dozen cookies

Banana Chocolate Chip Softies

Mrs. J's Chip Cookies

4 cups crispy rice cereal
1 milk chocolate crunch bar (5 ounces), broken into squares
2 cups all-purpose flour
1 teaspoon baking powder
1 teaspoon baking soda
¼ teaspoon salt
1 cup butter or margarine, softened
1 cup granulated sugar
1 cup packed light brown sugar
2 eggs
1 teaspoon vanilla
1 package (12 ounces) semisweet chocolate chips
1½ cups chopped walnuts

Preheat oven to 375°F. Line cookie sheets with parchment paper or leave ungreased. Process cereal in blender or food processor until pulverized. Add chocolate bar; continue processing until both chocolate and cereal are completely ground. Add flour, baking powder, baking soda and salt; process until blended. Beat butter and sugars in large bowl until well blended. Add eggs; beat until light. Blend in vanilla. Add flour mixture; blend until smooth. Stir in chocolate chips and walnuts until blended. Shape dough into walnut-sized balls. Place 2 inches apart on cookie sheets. Bake 10 to 12 minutes or until firm in center. *Do not overbake*. Remove to wire racks to cool.

Makes about 8 dozen cookies

Crunchy Chocolate Chip Cookies

2¼ cups unsifted all-purpose flour
1 teaspoon ARM & HAMMER® Baking Soda
1 teaspoon salt
1 cup softened margarine or butter
¾ cup granulated sugar
¾ cup packed brown sugar
1 teaspoon vanilla extract
2 eggs
2 cups (12 ounces) semisweet chocolate chips
1 cup chopped nuts (peanuts, walnuts or pecans)

Preheat oven to 375°F. Sift together flour, Baking Soda and salt in small bowl. Beat margarine, sugars and vanilla in large bowl with electric mixer until creamy. Beat in eggs. Gradually add flour mixture; mix well. Stir in chocolate chips and nuts. Drop by rounded teaspoons onto ungreased cookie sheets. Bake 8 minutes or until lightly browned.

Makes about 8 dozen (2-inch) cookies

Tip

Don't store crisp and soft cookies in the same container--it will cause the crisp cookies to soften quickly.

Chocolate Chip Almond Biscotti

2¾ cups all-purpose flour
1½ teaspoons baking powder
¼ teaspoon salt
½ cup butter, softened
1 cup sugar
3 eggs
3 tablespoons almond-flavored liqueur
1 tablespoon water
1 cup mini semisweet chocolate chips
1 cup sliced almonds, toasted and chopped

1. Place flour, baking powder and salt in medium bowl; stir to combine.

2. Beat butter and sugar in large bowl with electric mixer at medium speed until light and fluffy. Beat in eggs, 1 at a time. Beat in liqueur and water. Gradually add flour mixture. Beat at low speed just until blended. Stir in chips and almonds.

3. Divide dough into fourths. Spread each quarter evenly down center of waxed paper. Using waxed paper to hold dough, roll it back and forth to form a 15-inch log. Wrap in plastic wrap. Refrigerate until firm, about 2 hours.

4. Preheat oven to 375°F. Lightly grease cookie sheet. Unwrap and place each log on prepared cookie sheet. With floured hands, shape each log 2 inches wide and ½ inch thick.

5. Bake 15 minutes. Remove cookie sheet from oven. Cut each log with serrated knife into 1-inch-thick diagonal slices. Place slices, cut side up, on cookie sheet; bake 7 minutes. Turn cookies over; bake 7 minutes or until cut surfaces are golden brown and cookies are dry. Remove cookies with spatula to wire racks; cool completely. Store tightly covered at room temperature or freeze up to 3 months.

Makes about 4 dozen cookies

Chocolate Chip Almond Biscotti

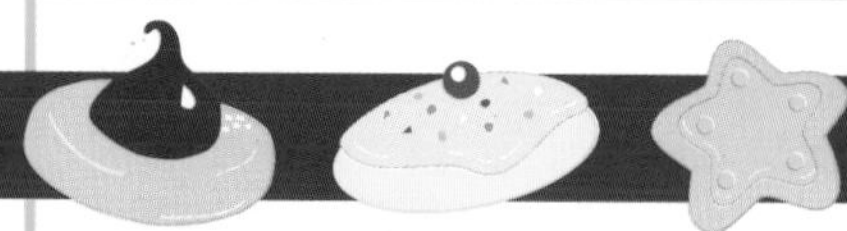

Hershey®s "Perfectly Chocolate" Chocolate Chip Cookies

2¼ cups all-purpose flour
⅓ cup HERSHEY®S Cocoa
1 teaspoon baking soda
½ teaspoon salt
1 cup (2 sticks) butter or margarine, softened
¾ cup granulated sugar
¾ cup packed light brown sugar
1 teaspoon vanilla extract
2 eggs
2 cups (12-ounce package) HERSHEY®S Semi-Sweet Chocolate Chips
1 cup chopped nuts (optional)

1. Heat oven to 375°F.

2. Stir together flour, cocoa, baking soda and salt. Beat butter, granulated sugar, brown sugar and vanilla in large bowl on medium speed of electric mixer until creamy. Add eggs; beat well. Gradually add flour mixture, beating until well blended. Stir in chocolate chips and nuts, if desired. Drop by rounded teaspoons onto ungreased cookie sheet.

3. Bake 8 to 10 minutes or until set. Cool slightly; remove from cookie sheet to wire rack.

Makes about 5 dozen cookies

Tip

Use shiny cookie sheets for the best cookie baking results. Dark cookie sheets can cause the bottoms of the cookies to be dark.

Hershey®s "Perfectly Chocolate" Chocolate Chip Cookies

Chocolate-Pecan Angels

- **1 cup mini semisweet chocolate chips**
- **1 cup chopped pecans, toasted**
- **1 cup sifted powdered sugar**
- **1 egg white**

Preheat oven to 350°F. Grease cookie sheets. Combine chips, pecans and powdered sugar in medium bowl. Add egg white; mix well. Drop batter by teaspoonfuls 2 inches apart onto prepared cookie sheets.

Bake 11 to 12 minutes until edges are light golden brown. Let cookies stand on cookie sheets 1 minute. Remove cookies to wire racks; cool completely.

Makes about 3 dozen cookies

Mini Chip Snowball Cookies

- **1½ cups (3 sticks) butter, softened**
- **¾ cup powdered sugar**
- **1 tablespoon vanilla extract**
- **½ teaspoon salt**
- **3 cups all-purpose flour**
- **2 cups (12-ounce package) NESTLÉ® TOLL HOUSE® Semi-Sweet Chocolate Mini Morsels**
- **½ cup finely chopped nuts**
- **Powdered sugar**

BEAT butter, sugar, vanilla and salt in large mixer bowl until creamy. Gradually beat in flour; stir in morsels and nuts. Shape level tablespoonfuls of dough into 1¼-inch balls. Place on ungreased baking sheets.

BAKE in preheated 375°F. oven for 10 to 12 minutes or until cookies are set and lightly browned. Remove from oven. Sift powdered sugar over hot cookies on baking sheet. Let stand for 10 minutes; remove to wire racks to cool completely. Sprinkle with additional powdered sugar if desired. Store in airtight containers.

Makes 5 dozen cookies

Chocolate-Pecan Angels

Double Chocolate Banana Cookies

3 to 4 extra-ripe, medium DOLE® Bananas, peeled
2 cups rolled oats
2 cups sugar
1¾ cups all-purpose flour
½ cup unsweetened cocoa powder
1 teaspoon baking soda
½ teaspoon salt
2 eggs, slightly beaten
1¼ cups margarine, melted
1 cup DOLE® Chopped Natural Almonds, toasted
2 cups semisweet chocolate chips

• Purée bananas in blender; measure 2 cups for recipe.

• Combine oats, sugar, flour, cocoa, baking soda and salt until well mixed. Stir in bananas, eggs and margarine until blended. Stir in almonds and chocolate chips.

• Refrigerate batter 1 hour or until mixture becomes partially firm (batter runs during baking if too soft).

• Measure ¼ cup batter for each cookie; drop onto greased cookie sheet. Flatten slightly with spatula.

• Bake in 350°F oven 15 to 17 minutes until cookies are golden brown. Remove to wire rack to cool.

Makes about 2½ dozen (3-inch) cookies

Prep Time: 15 minutes
Chill Time: 1 hour
Bake Time: 17 minutes/batch

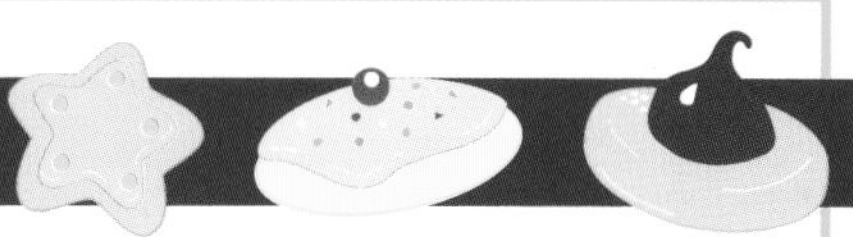

Giant Raisin-Chip Frisbees

- 1 cup butter or margarine, softened
- 1 cup packed brown sugar
- ½ cup granulated sugar
- 2 eggs
- 1 teaspoon vanilla
- 1½ cups all-purpose flour
- ¼ cup unsweetened cocoa powder
- 1 teaspoon baking soda
- 1 cup (6 ounces) semisweet chocolate chips
- ¾ cup raisins
- ¾ cup chopped walnuts

Preheat oven to 350°F. Line cookie sheets with parchment paper or lightly grease and dust with flour.

Beat butter with both sugars in large bowl. Add eggs and vanilla; beat until light. Combine flour, cocoa and baking soda in small bowl. Add to butter mixture with chocolate chips, raisins and walnuts; stir until well blended.

Scoop out about ½ cupful of dough for each cookie. Place on prepared cookie sheets, spacing about 5 inches apart. Using knife dipped in water, smooth balls of dough out to about 3½ inches in diameter. Bake 10 to 12 minutes or until golden. Remove to wire racks to cool.

Makes about 16 cookies

Forgotten Chips Cookies

- 2 egg whites
- ⅛ teaspoon cream of tartar
- ⅛ teaspoon salt
- ⅔ cup sugar
- 1 teaspoon vanilla extract
- 1 cup HERSHEY'S® Semi-Sweet Chocolate Chips or Milk Chocolate Chips

1. Heat oven to 375°F. Lightly grease cookie sheets.

2. Beat egg whites with cream of tartar and salt in small bowl until soft peaks form. Gradually add sugar, beating until stiff peaks form. Carefully fold in vanilla extract and chocolate chips. Drop by teaspoonfuls onto prepared cookie sheets.

3. Place cookie sheets in heated oven; immediately turn off oven and allow cookies to remain in oven six hours or overnight without opening door. Remove cookies from cookie sheets. Store in airtight container in cool, dry place.

Makes about 2½ dozen cookies

Almond Milk Chocolate Chippers

½ cup slivered almonds
1¼ cups all-purpose flour
½ teaspoon baking soda
½ teaspoon salt
½ cup butter, softened
½ cup firmly packed light brown sugar
⅓ cup granulated sugar
1 large egg
2 tablespoons almond-flavored liqueur
1 cup milk chocolate chips

1. Preheat oven to 350°F. To toast almonds, spread on baking sheet. Bake 8 to 10 minutes or until golden brown, stirring frequently. Remove almonds from pan and cool; set aside.

2. *Increase oven temperature to 375°F.* Combine flour, baking soda and salt in small bowl.

3. Beat butter, brown sugar and granulated sugar in large bowl until light and fluffy. Beat in egg until well blended. Beat in liqueur. Gradually add flour mixture. Beat until well blended. Stir in chips and almonds.

4. Drop dough by rounded teaspoonfuls 2 inches apart onto ungreased cookie sheets.

5. Bake 9 to 10 minutes or until edges are golden brown. Let cookies stand on cookie sheets 2 minutes. Remove cookies to wire racks; cool completely. Store tightly covered at room temperature or freeze up to 3 months.

Makes about 3 dozen cookies

Almond Milk Chocolate Chippers

Chocolate Chip Shortbread

- ½ cup butter, softened
- ½ cup sugar
- 1 teaspoon vanilla
- 1 cup all-purpose flour
- ¼ teaspoon salt
- ½ cup mini semisweet chocolate chips

Preheat oven to 375°F.

Beat butter and sugar in large bowl with electric mixer at medium speed until light and fluffy. Beat in vanilla. Add flour and salt; beat at low speed. Stir in chips.

Divide dough in half. Press each half into ungreased 8-inch round cake pan.

Bake 12 minutes or until edges are golden brown. Score shortbread with sharp knife, taking care not to cut completely through shortbread. Make 8 wedges per pan.

Let pans stand on wire racks 10 minutes. Invert shortbread onto wire racks; cool completely. Break into triangles.

Makes 16 cookies

Hershey®s White Chip Chocolate Cookies

- 1 cup (2 sticks) butter or margarine, softened
- 2 cups sugar
- 2 eggs
- 2 teaspoons vanilla extract
- 2 cups all-purpose flour
- ¾ cup HERSHEY®S Cocoa
- 1 teaspoon baking soda
- ½ teaspoon salt
- 1⅔ cups (10-ounce package) HERSHEY®S Premier White Chips

1. Heat oven to 350°F.

2. Beat butter and sugar in large bowl until creamy. Add eggs and vanilla extract; beat until light and fluffy. Stir together flour, cocoa, baking soda and salt; gradually blend into butter mixture. Stir in white chips. Drop by rounded teaspoons onto ungreased cookie sheet.

3. Bake 8 to 9 minutes. (Do not overbake; cookies will be soft. They will puff while baking and flatten upon cooling.) Cool slightly; remove from cookie sheet to wire racks. Cool completely.

Makes about 4½ dozen cookies

Chocolate Chip Shortbread

Oatmeal Candied Chippers

- ¾ cup butter, softened
- ¾ cup granulated sugar
- ¾ cup packed light brown sugar
- 3 tablespoons milk
- 1 egg
- 2 teaspoons vanilla
- ¾ cup all-purpose flour
- ¾ teaspoon salt
- ½ teaspoon baking soda
- 3 cups uncooked rolled oats
- 1⅓ cups (10-ounce package) candy-coated semisweet chocolate chips or candy-coated chocolate pieces

Preheat oven to 375°F. Grease cookie sheets; set aside. Beat butter, granulated sugar and brown sugar in large bowl until light and fluffy. Add milk, egg and vanilla; beat well. Add flour, salt and baking soda. Beat until well combined. Stir in oats and chocolate chips.

Drop by rounded tablespoonfuls 2 inches apart on prepared cookie sheets. Bake 10 to 12 minutes until edges are golden brown. Let cookies stand 2 minutes on cookie sheets. Remove cookies to wire racks; cool completely.

Makes about 4 dozen cookies

Tip

For a delicious change of pace, substitute your favorite candy bars, chopped, for the candy-coated chips.

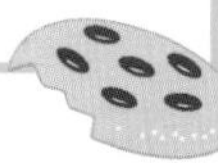

Oatmeal Candied Chippers

Hershey®'s Great American Chocolate Chip Cookies

1 cup (2 sticks) butter, softened
¾ cup granulated sugar
¾ cup packed light brown sugar
1 teaspoon vanilla extract
2 eggs
2¼ cups all-purpose flour
1 teaspoon baking soda
½ teaspoon salt
2 cups (12-ounce package) HERSHEY®'S Semi-Sweet Chocolate Chips
1 cup chopped nuts (optional)

1. Heat oven to 375°F.

2. Beat butter, granulated sugar, brown sugar and vanilla in large mixer bowl until creamy. Add eggs; beat well. Stir together flour, baking soda and salt; gradually add to butter mixture, beating well. Stir in chocolate chips and nuts, if desired. Drop dough by rounded teaspoons onto ungreased cookie sheet.

3. Bake 8 to 10 minutes or until lightly browned. Cool slightly; remove from cookie sheet to wire rack. Cool completely.

Makes about 6 dozen cookies

Hershey®'s Great American Chocolate Chip Pan Cookies: Spread dough into greased 15½×10½×1-inch jelly-roll pan. Bake at 375°F for 20 minutes or until lightly browned. Cool completely in pan on wire rack. Cut into bars. Makes about 48 bars.

Skor® & Chocolate Chip Cookies: Omit 1 cup HERSHEY®'S Semi-Sweet Chocolate Chips and nuts; replace with 1 cup finely chopped SKOR® bars. Drop onto cookie sheets and bake as directed.

Great American Ice Cream Sandwiches: Prepare cookies as directed. Place one small scoop slightly softened vanilla ice cream between flat sides of two cookies. Gently press together. Wrap and freeze.

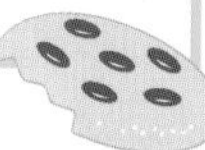

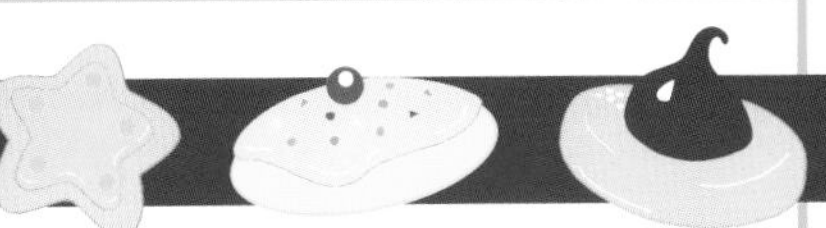

Peanutty Double Chip Cookies

- ½ cup butter or margarine, softened
- ¾ cup packed light brown sugar
- ¾ cup granulated sugar
- 2 eggs
- 1 teaspoon baking soda
- 1 teaspoon vanilla
- 2 cups all-purpose flour
- 1 cup chunky peanut butter
- 1 cup (6 ounces) semisweet or milk chocolate chips
- 1 cup (6 ounces) peanut butter chips

Preheat oven to 350°F. Lightly grease cookie sheets or line with parchment paper. Beat butter and sugars in large bowl until blended. Add eggs, baking soda and vanilla; beat until light. Blend in flour and peanut butter until dough is stiff and smooth. Stir in chocolate and peanut butter chips. Drop dough by teaspoonfuls 2 inches apart onto prepared cookie sheets. Press cookies down with tines of fork to flatten slightly. Bake 12 minutes or until just barely done. *Do not overbake.* Remove to wire racks to cool.

Makes about 5 dozen cookies

Chocolate Chip Macaroons

- 2½ cups flaked coconut
- ⅔ cup mini semisweet chocolate chips
- ⅔ cup sweetened condensed milk
- 1 teaspoon vanilla

Preheat oven to 350°F. Grease cookie sheets. Combine coconut, chocolate chips, milk and vanilla in medium bowl; mix until well blended. Drop dough by rounded teaspoonfuls 2 inches apart onto greased cookie sheets. Press dough gently with back of spoon to flatten slightly. Bake 10 to 12 minutes or until light golden brown. Let cookies stand on cookie sheets 1 minute. Remove cookies to wire racks; cool completely.

Makes about 3½ dozen cookies

Oatmeal Chocolate Chip Cookies

- 1 can (20 ounces) DOLE® Crushed Pineapple
- 1½ cups brown sugar, packed
- 1 cup margarine, softened
- 1 egg
- ¼ teaspoon almond extract
- 4 cups rolled oats, uncooked
- 2 cups flour
- 1 teaspoon baking powder
- 1 teaspoon salt
- 1 teaspoon ground cinnamon
- ½ teaspoon ground nutmeg
- 1 package (12 ounces) semisweet chocolate chips
- ¾ cup DOLE® Slivered Almonds, toasted
- 2 cups flaked coconut

• Preheat oven to 350°F. Grease cookie sheets. Drain pineapple well, reserving ½ cup syrup.

• In large bowl, beat brown sugar and margarine until light and fluffy. Beat in egg. Beat in pineapple, reserved ½ cup liquid and almond extract.

• In small bowl, combine oats, flour, baking powder, salt, cinnamon and nutmeg. Add to margarine mixture; beat until blended. Stir in chocolate chips, almonds and coconut.

• Drop by heaping tablespoonfuls onto prepared cookie sheets. Flatten cookies slightly with back of spoon. Bake 20 to 25 minutes or until golden. Cool on wire racks.

Makes about 5 dozen cookies

Chocolate Chip Macaroons

Peanut Butter Chocolate Chippers

1 cup creamy or chunky peanut butter
1 cup firmly packed light brown sugar
1 large egg
¾ cup milk chocolate chips
Granulated sugar

1. Preheat oven to 350°F.

2. Combine peanut butter, brown sugar and egg in medium bowl; mix until well blended. Add chips; mix well.

3. Roll heaping tablespoonfuls of dough into 1½-inch balls. Place balls 2 inches apart on ungreased cookie sheets.

4. Dip table fork into granulated sugar; press criss-cross fashion onto each ball, flattening to ½-inch thickness.

5. Bake 12 minutes or until set. Let cookies stand on cookie sheets 2 minutes. Remove cookies to wire racks; cool completely. *Makes about 2 dozen cookies*

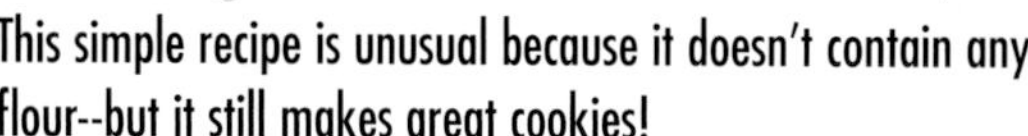

This simple recipe is unusual because it doesn't contain any flour--but it still makes great cookies!

Peanut Butter Chocolate Chippers

Chocolate Macadamia Chewies

- **¾ cup (1½ sticks) butter or margarine, softened**
- **⅔ cup firmly packed light brown sugar**
- **1 large egg**
- **1 teaspoon vanilla extract**
- **1¾ cups all-purpose flour**
- **¾ teaspoon baking soda**
- **¼ teaspoon salt**
- **¾ cup (3½ ounces) coarsely chopped macadamia nuts**
- **½ cup shredded coconut**
- **1¾ cups "M&M's"® Chocolate Mini Baking Bits**

Preheat oven to 350°F. In large bowl cream butter and sugar until light and fluffy; beat in egg and vanilla. In medium bowl combine flour, baking soda and salt; blend into creamed mixture. Blend in nuts and coconut. Stir in "M&M's"® Chocolate Mini Baking Bits. Drop by heaping teaspoonfuls about 2 inches apart onto ungreased cookie sheets; flatten slightly with back of spoon. Bake 8 to 10 minutes or until set. Do not overbake. Cool 1 minute on cookie sheets; cool completely on wire racks. Store in tightly covered container.

Makes about 4 dozen cookies

Chocolate Macadamia Chewies

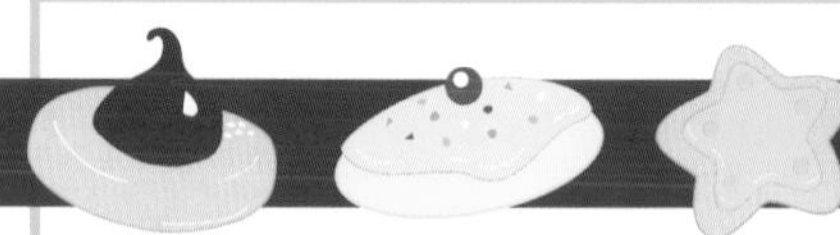

Double Chocolate Oat Drops

MAZOLA NO STICK® Cooking Spray
2 cups (12 ounces) semisweet chocolate chips, divided
¼ cup (½ stick) MAZOLA® Margarine
⅔ cup KARO® Light or Dark Corn Syrup
2 eggs
¼ teaspoon salt
4 cups uncooked quick oats
⅔ cup packed brown sugar
1 cup coarsely chopped walnuts
1 cup flaked coconut

1. Preheat oven to 350°F. Spray cookie sheets with cooking spray.

2. In medium heavy saucepan over low heat, combine 1 cup chocolate chips and margarine; stir just until melted. Remove from heat. Stir in corn syrup, eggs and salt.

3. In large bowl combine oats, brown sugar, walnuts and coconut. Add chocolate mixture; mix well. Stir in remaining 1 cup chocolate chips.

4. Drop by tablespoonfuls onto prepared cookie sheets. Bake 15 minutes (cookies will not change much in appearance during baking). Cool 5 minutes on cookie sheet or until firm. Remove; cool completely on wire rack.

Makes about 3 dozen cookies

Chocolate-Dipped Oat Drops: *In medium heavy saucepan over low heat, stir 1½ cups (9 ounces) semisweet chocolate chips until melted and smooth. Dip half of each cookie in melted chocolate. Place on waxed paper to cool.*

Tip: *Use your microwave oven to eliminate the risks of melting chocolate on top of the stove. To melt 1 (1-ounce) square, microwave on HIGH (100%) 1 to 2 minutes. For 2 squares, 1½ to 2½ minutes is sufficient. For chocolate chips, allow 1½ to 2½ minutes for 1 cup (6 ounces). Remember that the chocolate will not lose its shape in the microwave oven, so stir often to avoid overheating.*

Prep Time: 20 minutes
Bake Time: 15 minutes, plus cooling

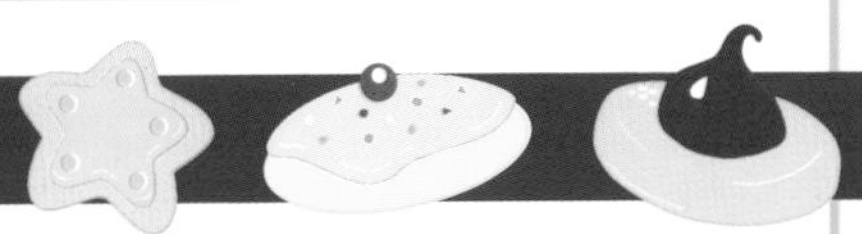

Baker's® Double Chocolate Chunk Cookies

- **1 package (8 squares) BAKER'S® Semi-Sweet Baking Chocolate, divided**
- **½ cup (1 stick) butter *or* margarine**
- **½ cup granulated sugar**
- **¼ cup firmly packed brown sugar**
- **1 egg**
- **1 teaspoon vanilla**
- **1 cup flour**
- **½ teaspoon CALUMET® Baking Powder**
- **¼ teaspoon salt**
- **¾ cup chopped walnuts (optional)**

HEAT oven to 375°F.

MICROWAVE 1 square chocolate in microwavable bowl on HIGH 1 to 2 minutes until almost melted, stirring halfway through heating time. Stir until chocolate is completely melted.

CUT 3 squares chocolate into large (½-inch) chunks; set aside.

BEAT butter until light and fluffy. Gradually beat in sugars. Mix in egg and vanilla. Stir in melted chocolate. Mix in flour, baking powder and salt. Stir in chocolate chunks and walnuts. Refrigerate dough 30 minutes.

DROP dough by rounded tablespoonfuls, about 2 inches apart, onto greased cookie sheets.

BAKE for 8 to 10 minutes or until lightly browned. Cool 2 minutes; remove from cookie sheets.

MICROWAVE remaining 4 squares chocolate in microwavable bowl on HIGH 1½ to 2 minutes until almost melted, stirring halfway through heating time. Stir until completely melted.

DIP ½ of each cookie into melted chocolate. Let stand until chocolate is firm. *Makes about 2 dozen (3-inch) cookies*

Melting Chocolate on Top of Stove: Heat chocolate in heavy saucepan on very low heat, stirring constantly, until just melted. Remove from heat. Continue as directed.

Tip: Do not overbake cookies. They will be soft when done and firm up upon cooling.

Prep Time: 20 minutes plus refrigerating
Bake Time: 10 minutes

Tracy's Pizza-Pan Cookies

1 cup butter or margarine, softened
¾ cup granulated sugar
¾ cup packed brown sugar
1 package (8 ounces) cream cheese, softened
1 teaspoon vanilla
2 eggs
2¼ cups all-purpose flour
1 teaspoon baking soda
¼ teaspoon salt
1 package (12 ounces) semisweet chocolate chips
1 cup chopped walnuts or pecans

Preheat oven to 375°F. Lightly grease two 12-inch pizza pans.

Beat butter, sugars, cream cheese and vanilla in large bowl. Add eggs; beat until well blended. Combine flour, baking soda and salt in small bowl. Add to creamed mixture; blend well. Stir in chocolate chips and nuts. Divide dough in half; press each half evenly into prepared pans.

Bake 20 to 25 minutes or until lightly browned around edges. Cool completely in pans on wire racks. To serve, cut into slim wedges or break into pieces. *Makes two (12-inch) cookies*

Tip

To soften cream cheese for recipes, remove from the wrapper and place in a microwavable bowl. Microwave at MEDIUM (50%) 1½ to 2 minutes or until slightly softened, turning the bowl after 1 minute.

Tracy's Pizza-Pan Cookie

Chocolate Chip 'n Oatmeal Cookies

1 package (18.25 or 18.5 ounces) yellow cake mix
1 cup quick-cooking rolled oats, uncooked
¾ cup butter or margarine, softened
2 eggs
1 cup HERSHEY®S Semi-Sweet Chocolate Chips

1. Heat oven to 350°F.

2. Combine cake mix, oats, butter and eggs in large bowl; mix well. Stir in chocolate chips. Drop by rounded teaspoons onto ungreased cookie sheets.

3. Bake 10 to 12 minutes or until very lightly browned. Cool slightly; remove from cookie sheets to wire racks. Cool completely. *Makes about 4 dozen cookies*

San Francisco Cookies

2 extra-ripe, medium DOLE® Bananas, cut into chunks
2 cups granola
1½ cups all-purpose flour
1 cup packed brown sugar
1 teaspoon baking powder
1 teaspoon ground cinnamon
2 eggs
½ cup margarine, melted
¼ cup vegetable oil
1 cup chocolate chips

- Preheat oven to 350°F. Lightly grease cookie sheets. In food processor or blender, process bananas until puréed (1 cup).

- Combine granola, flour, sugar, baking powder and cinnamon in large bowl. Beat in puréed bananas, eggs, margarine and oil. Stir in chocolate chips.

- Drop by ¼ cupfuls onto prepared cookie sheets. Spread dough into 2½- to 3-inch circles. Bake about 16 minutes or until golden. Remove to wire racks to cool.

Makes about 16 cookies

Chocolate Chip 'n Oatmeal Cookies

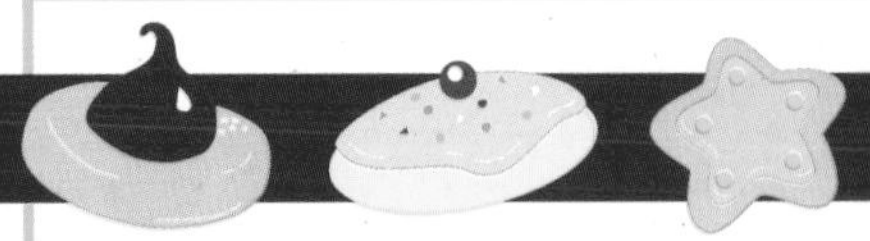

Orange-Walnut Chippers

- 1 cup packed light brown sugar
- ½ cup butter or margarine, softened
- 1 large egg
- 1 tablespoon grated orange peel
- ½ cup all-purpose flour
- ¼ teaspoon baking soda
- ¼ teaspoon salt
- 1½ cups uncooked rolled oats
- 1 cup semisweet chocolate chips
- ½ cup coarsely chopped walnuts

Preheat oven to 375°F. Lightly grease cookie sheets; set aside.

Beat sugar and butter in large bowl until light and fluffy. Beat in egg and orange peel. Add flour, baking soda and salt to butter mixture. Beat until well blended. Stir in oats, chips and nuts. Drop by rounded teaspoonfuls 2 inches apart onto prepared cookie sheets.

Bake 10 to 12 minutes or until golden brown. Let cookies stand on cookie sheets 2 minutes. Remove cookies to wire racks; cool completely. *Makes about 3 dozen cookies*

Tip

One medium orange yields 1 to 2 tablespoons grated peel, which can be frozen for up to six months.

Orange-Walnut Chippers

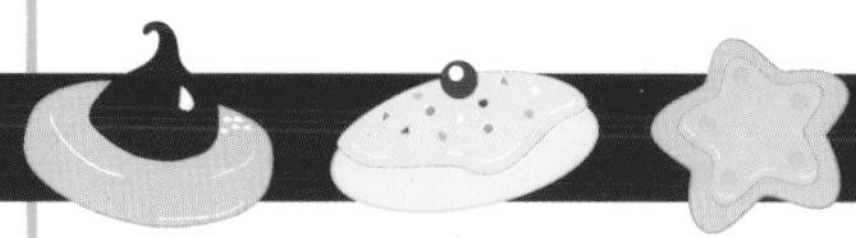

Peanut Butter Chip Oatmeal Cookies

- **1 cup (2 sticks) butter or margarine, softened**
- **¼ cup shortening**
- **2 cups packed light brown sugar**
- **1 tablespoon milk**
- **2 teaspoons vanilla extract**
- **1 egg**
- **2 cups all-purpose flour**
- **1⅔ cups (10-ounce package) REESE'S® Peanut Butter Chips**
- **1½ cups quick-cooking or regular rolled oats**
- **½ cup chopped walnuts**
- **½ teaspoon baking soda**
- **½ teaspoon salt**

1. Heat oven to 375°F.

2. Beat butter, shortening, brown sugar, milk, vanilla and egg in large mixer bowl until light and fluffy. Add remaining ingredients; mix until well blended. Drop dough by rounded teaspoonfuls about 2 inches apart onto ungreased cookie sheet.

3. Bake until light brown, 10 to 12 minutes for soft cookies or 12 to 14 minutes for crisp cookies. Remove from cookie sheet to wire rack. Cool completely.

Makes about 6 dozen cookies

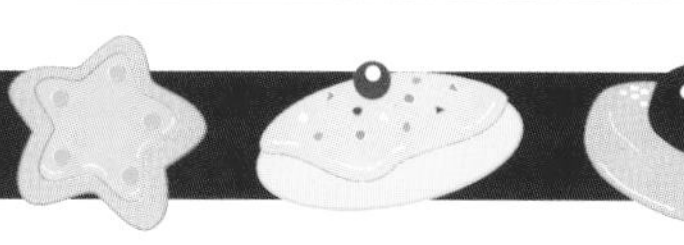

Oatmeal Treasures

COOKIES

- **¾ Butter Flavor* CRISCO® Stick or ¾ cup Butter Flavor* CRISCO® all-vegetable shortening plus additional for greasing**
- **1¼ cups firmly packed light brown sugar**
- **1 egg**
- **⅓ cup milk**
- **1½ teaspoons vanilla**
- **3 cups quick oats, uncooked**
- **1 cup all-purpose flour**
- **½ teaspoon baking soda**
- **½ teaspoon salt**
- **1 cup milk chocolate chips**
- **½ cup flake coconut**

DRIZZLE

- **⅓ cup white chocolate baking pieces**
- **1 tablespoon plus 2 teaspoons Butter Flavor* CRISCO® Stick or 1 tablespoon plus 2 teaspoons Butter Flavor* CRISCO®, divided**
- **⅓ cup semi-sweet chocolate chips**

**Butter Flavor Crisco® is artificially flavored.*

1. Heat oven to 375°F. Grease baking sheets with shortening. Place sheets of foil on countertop for cooling cookies.

2. For cookies, combine ¾ cup shortening, brown sugar, egg, milk and vanilla in large bowl. Beat at medium speed of electric mixer until well blended.

3. Combine oats, flour, baking soda and salt. Mix into creamed mixture at low speed just until blended. Stir in milk chocolate chips and coconut.

4. Drop rounded tablespoonfuls of dough 2 inches apart onto ungreased baking sheet.

5. Bake one baking sheet at a time at 375°F for 10 to 12 minutes or until lightly browned. *Do not overbake.* Cool 2 minutes on baking sheet. Remove cookies to foil to cool completely.

6. For drizzle, place white chocolate pieces and 1 tablespoon shortening in heavy resealable plastic bag or microwave-safe bowl. Microwave at 50% (MEDIUM) for 1 minute. Knead or stir and repeat, if necessary, until completely smooth. Cut tiny tip off corner of bag. Drizzle over top of each cookie. Melt semi-sweet chocolate chips and remaining 2 teaspoons shortening as directed for white chocolate. Drizzle again over top of each cookie. *Makes about 2½ dozen cookies*

Cowboy Cookies

- ½ cup butter or margarine, softened
- ½ cup packed light brown sugar
- ¼ cup granulated sugar
- 1 egg
- 1 teaspoon vanilla
- 1 cup all-purpose flour
- 2 tablespoons unsweetened cocoa powder
- ½ teaspoon baking powder
- ¼ teaspoon baking soda
- 1 cup uncooked rolled oats
- 1 cup (6 ounces) semisweet chocolate chips
- ½ cup raisins
- ½ cup chopped nuts

Preheat oven to 375°F. Lightly grease cookie sheets or line with parchment paper.

Beat butter with sugars in large bowl until blended. Add egg and vanilla; beat until fluffy. Combine flour, cocoa, baking powder and baking soda in small bowl; stir into butter mixture. Add oats, chocolate chips, raisins and nuts. Drop by rounded teaspoonfuls 2 inches apart onto prepared cookie sheets.

Bake 10 to 12 minutes or until lightly browned around edges. Remove to wire racks to cool.

Makes about 4 dozen cookies

Tip

Using parchment paper on your cookie sheets makes kitchen cleanup a breeze. It is available at gourmet kitchenware stores and at many supermarkets.

Cowboy Cookies

Out of the Ordinary

Chocolate Macadamia Cookies

1 package DUNCAN HINES® Chocolate Chip Cookie Mix
¼ cup unsweetened cocoa powder
⅓ cup vegetable oil
1 egg
3 tablespoons water
⅔ cup coarsely chopped macadamia nuts

Preheat oven to 375°F.

Combine cookie mix and cocoa in large bowl. Add oil, egg and water. Stir until thoroughly blended. Stir in macadamia nuts. Drop by rounded teaspoonfuls 2 inches apart onto *ungreased* cookie sheets.

Bake 8 to 10 minutes or until set. Cool 1 minute on cookie sheets. Remove to cooling racks. Cool completely.

Makes 3 dozen cookies

Chocolate Macadamia Cookies

Peanut Butter Chip Orange Cookies

½ cup (1 stick) butter or margarine, softened
½ cup shortening
¾ cup granulated sugar
¾ cup packed light brown sugar
2 eggs
1 tablespoon freshly grated orange peel
1 teaspoon vanilla extract
2¼ cups all-purpose flour
1 teaspoon baking soda
1 teaspoon salt
¼ cup orange juice
1⅔ cups (10-ounce package) REESE'S® Peanut Butter Chips

1. Heat oven to 350°F.

2. Beat butter, shortening, granulated sugar and brown sugar in large bowl until light and fluffy. Add eggs, orange peel and vanilla; beat until blended. Stir together flour, baking soda and salt; add alternately with orange juice to butter mixture, beating until well blended. Stir in peanut butter chips. Drop by teaspoons onto ungreased cookie sheet.

3. Bake 8 to 10 minutes or until lightly browned. Cool slightly; remove from cookie sheet to wire rack. Cool completely.

Makes about 6 dozen cookies

Tip: Cool cookie sheets completely before putting more cookie dough on them. Dropping cookie dough on warm cookie sheets causes excess spread.

Peanut Butter Chip Orange Cookies

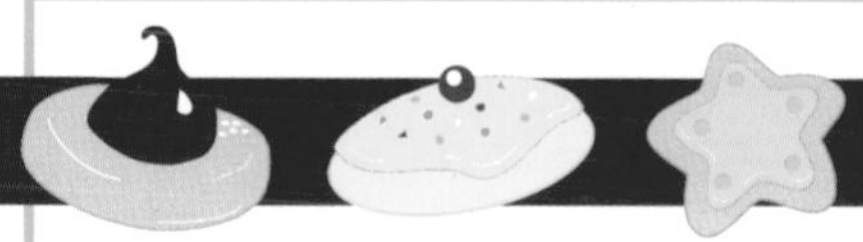

Jam-Up Oatmeal Cookies

1 Butter Flavor* CRISCO® Stick or 1 cup Butter Flavor* CRISCO® all-vegetable shortening plus additional for greasing
1½ cups firmly packed brown sugar
2 eggs
2 teaspoons almond extract
2 cups all-purpose flour
1 teaspoon baking powder
1 teaspoon salt
½ teaspoon baking soda
2½ cups quick oats (not instant or old fashioned), uncooked
1 cup finely chopped pecans
1 jar (12 ounces) strawberry jam
Sugar for sprinkling

**Butter Flavor Crisco® is artificially flavored.*

1. Combine 1 cup shortening and brown sugar in large bowl. Beat at medium speed of electric mixer until well blended. Beat in eggs and almond extract.

2. Combine flour, baking powder, salt and baking soda. Mix into shortening mixture at low speed until just blended. Stir in oats and chopped nuts with spoon. Cover and refrigerate at least 1 hour.

3. Heat oven to 350°F. Grease baking sheets with shortening. Place sheets of foil on countertop for cooling cookies.

4. Roll out dough, half at a time, to about ¼-inch thickness on floured surface. Cut out with 2½-inch round cookie cutter. Place 1 teaspoonful of jam in center of half of the rounds. Top with remaining rounds. Press edges to seal. Prick centers; sprinkle with sugar. Place 1 inch apart on baking sheets.

5. Bake one baking sheet at a time at 350°F for 12 to 15 minutes or until lightly browned. *Do not overbake.* Cool 2 minutes on baking sheets. Remove cookies to foil to cool completely. *Makes about 2 dozen cookies*

Jam-Up Oatmeal Cookies

Chocolate Edged Lace Cookies

⅔ cup ground almonds
½ cup butter
½ cup sugar
2 tablespoons milk
1 tablespoon flour
4 ounces dark sweet or bittersweet chocolate candy bar, broken into pieces

Preheat oven to 325°F. Grease cookie sheets very lightly. Combine almonds, butter, sugar, milk and flour in large skillet. Cook and stir over low heat until well blended. Keep mixture warm over very low heat while forming and baking cookies.

Drop tablespoonfuls of batter 2 inches apart on prepared cookie sheets. Bake 6 minutes or until cookies are golden brown. Let cookies stand on cookie sheets 30 seconds to 1 minute before loosening with thin spatula. (If cookies become too brittle to remove, warm them briefly in oven.) Remove cookies to wire rack;* cool.

Melt chocolate in small, heavy saucepan over low heat, stirring constantly. Tilt saucepan to pool chocolate at one end; dip edge of each cookie in chocolate, turning cookie slowly so entire edge is tinged with chocolate. Let cookies stand on waxed paper until chocolate is set.

Makes about 2 dozen cookies

**For tuile-shaped cookies, balance a wooden spoon over two cans of the same height. Working quickly while cookies are still hot, drape the cookies (bottom side down) over the handle of the spoon so that both sides hang down and form a taco shape. When firm, transfer to wire rack to cool completely. Dip both edges of cooled cookies into chocolate.*

Chocolate Edged Lace Cookies

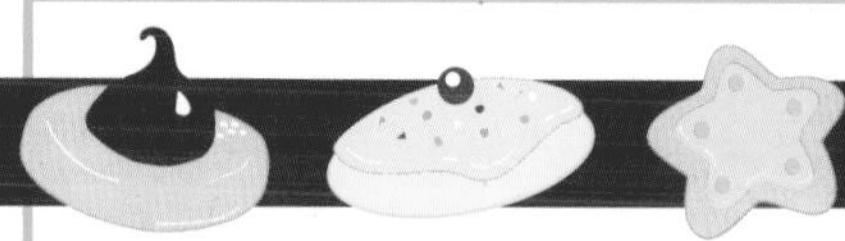

Peanut Butter Knockouts

- **1 package DUNCAN HINES® Peanut Butter Cookie Mix**
- **1 whole egg**
- **1 (3-ounce) package cream cheese, softened**
- **¼ cup creamy peanut butter**
- **1 egg yolk**
- **2½ tablespoons granulated sugar**
- **Dash salt (optional)**
- **½ cup semisweet mini chocolate chips (optional)**
- **½ cup semisweet chocolate chips**
- **2 teaspoons shortening**

Preheat oven to 375°F.

Combine cookie mix, contents of peanut butter packet from mix and whole egg in large bowl. Stir until thoroughly blended. Shape dough into 36 (about 1-inch) balls. Place 2 inches apart onto *ungreased* cookie sheets. Press thumb gently in center of each cookie.

Combine cream cheese, peanut butter, egg yolk, sugar and salt in medium bowl. Beat at medium speed with electric mixer until blended. Stir in mini chocolate chips, if desired. Fill center of each cookie with rounded teaspoonful of filling. Bake 8 to 10 minutes or until light golden brown. Cool 2 minutes on cookie sheets. Remove to cooling racks. Cool completely.

Place chocolate chips and shortening in small resealable plastic bag; seal. Place bag in bowl of hot water for several minutes. Dry bag with towel. Knead bag until contents are blended and chocolate is smooth. Snip tiny hole in corner of bag. Drizzle contents over cookies. Allow drizzle to set before storing cookies between layers of waxed paper in airtight container.

Makes 3 dozen cookies

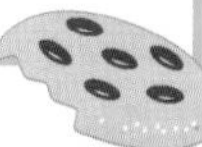

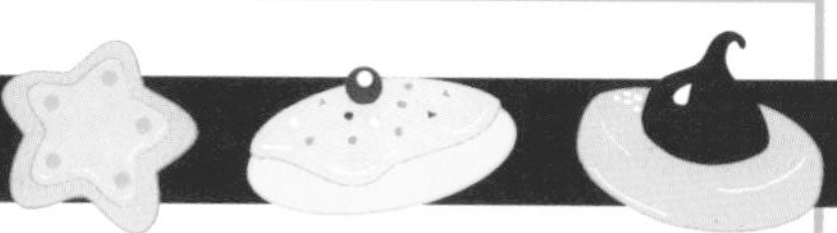

Snow Caps

- 3 egg whites, room temperature
- ¼ teaspoon cream of tartar
- ¾ cup sugar
- ½ teaspoon vanilla extract
- 1 cup (6 ounces) semisweet chocolate chips
- 4 ounces white chocolate, grated

Preheat oven to 200°F. Line baking sheets with plain ungreased brown paper such as heavy brown paper bags (not recycled). Combine egg whites and cream of tartar in large bowl of electric mixer. Beat at highest speed until mixture is just frothy. Add sugar, 1 tablespoon at a time, beating well after each addition. Beat until stiff peaks form. Add vanilla; beat 1 minute. Fold in chocolate chips. Drop mixture by teaspoonfuls onto prepared baking sheets. Bake 2 hours or until meringues are thoroughly dry to touch but not browned, rotating baking sheets halfway through baking. Turn off heat and leave in closed oven 3 to 4 hours or until completely dry. Remove from oven and cool completely. Carefully remove meringues from paper.

Bring water in bottom of double boiler to a boil; turn off heat. Place white chocolate in top of double boiler; place over hot water. Stir constantly until chocolate melts. Dip top of each meringue into melted chocolate. Place on waxed paper to dry. Store at room temperature in a tightly covered container.

Makes about 6 dozen cookies

Apple Pie Wedges

1 cup butter, softened
⅔ cup sugar
1 egg yolk
⅓ cup apple butter
2⅓ cups all-purpose flour
1 teaspoon ground cinnamon
½ teaspoon apple pie spice
½ teaspoon vanilla

1. Beat butter and sugar in medium bowl at medium speed of electric mixer until fluffy.

2. Add egg yolk and apple butter; mix well. Add flour, cinnamon, apple pie spice and vanilla; beat at low speed until well blended.

3. Divide dough in half. Shape each half into 6-inch disc and wrap in plastic wrap. Refrigerate 30 minutes.

4. Preheat oven to 325°F. Invert 1 disc of dough into ungreased 9-inch round pie plate.

5. Press dough into plate with lightly floured hand, covering plate completely.

6. Flute edge using handle of wooden spoon. Deeply score into 8 wedges.

7. Prick surface using tines of fork. Repeat steps with remaining disc of dough and another pie plate.

8. Bake 35 minutes or until golden brown. Remove to wire rack; cool completely. Cut into wedges.

Makes 16 wedges

Tip: Serve these tasty cookies warm with a big scoop of vanilla or cinnamon-flavored ice cream.

Apple Pie Wedges

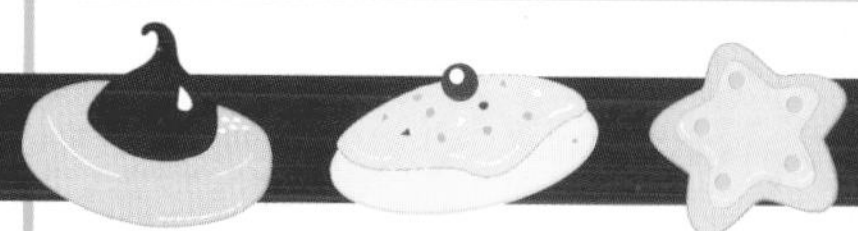

Cocoa Crinkle Sandwiches

1¾ cups all-purpose flour
½ cup unsweetened cocoa
1 teaspoon baking soda
¼ teaspoon salt
½ cup butter
1¾ cups sugar, divided
2 eggs
2 teaspoons vanilla
1 can (16 ounces) chocolate or favorite flavor frosting
½ cup crushed candy canes* (optional)

**To crush candy canes, place candy in sealed heavy-duty plastic food storage bag. Break into pieces with heavy object (such as meat mallet or can of vegetables); crush pieces with rolling pin.*

Combine flour, cocoa, baking soda and salt in medium bowl.

Melt butter in large saucepan over medium heat; cool slightly. Add 1¼ cups sugar; whisk until smooth. Whisk in eggs, 1 at a time, until blended. Stir in vanilla until smooth. Stir in flour mixture just until combined. Wrap dough in plastic wrap; refrigerate 2 hours.

Preheat oven to 350°F. Grease cookie sheets. Shape dough into 1-inch balls. Place remaining ½ cup sugar in shallow bowl; roll balls in sugar. Place 1½ inches apart on cookie sheets.

Bake12 minutes or until cookies feel set to the touch. Let cookies stand on cookie sheets 5 minutes; transfer to wire racks to cool completely.

Stir frosting until soft and smooth. Place crushed candy canes on piece of waxed paper. Spread about 2 teaspoons frosting over flat side of one cookie. Place second cookie, flat side down, over frosting, pressing down to allow frosting to squeeze out slightly between cookies. Press exposed frosting into crushed candy canes. Repeat with remaining cookies. Store in airtight container.

Makes about 20 sandwich cookies (about 40 unfilled cookies)

Cocoa Crinkle Sandwiches

Spicy Lemon Crescents

1 cup (2 sticks) butter or margarine, softened
1½ cups powdered sugar, divided
½ teaspoon lemon extract
½ teaspoon grated lemon zest
2 cups cake flour
½ cup finely chopped almonds, walnuts or pecans
1 teaspoon ground cinnamon
½ teaspoon ground cardamom
½ teaspoon ground nutmeg
1¾ cups "M&M's"® Chocolate Mini Baking Bits

Preheat oven to 375°F. Lightly grease cookie sheets; set aside. In large bowl cream butter and ½ cup sugar; add lemon extract and zest until well blended. In medium bowl combine flour, nuts, cinnamon, cardamom and nutmeg; add to creamed mixture until well blended. Stir in "M&M's"® Chocolate Mini Baking Bits. Using 1 tablespoon of dough at a time, form into crescent shapes; place about 2 inches apart onto prepared cookie sheets. Bake 12 to 14 minutes or until edges are golden. Cool 2 minutes on cookie sheets. Gently roll warm crescents in remaining 1 cup sugar. Cool completely on wire racks. Store in tightly covered container.

Makes about 2 dozen cookies

Spicy Lemon Crescents

Mocha Cookies

- 2 tablespoons plus 1½ teaspoons instant coffee granules
- 1½ tablespoons skim milk
- ⅓ cup packed light brown sugar
- ¼ cup granulated sugar
- ¼ cup margarine
- 1 egg
- ½ teaspoon almond extract
- 2 cups all-purpose flour, sifted
- ¼ cup wheat flakes
- ½ teaspoon ground cinnamon
- ¼ teaspoon baking powder

Preheat oven to 350°F. Spray cookie sheets with nonstick cooking spray. Dissolve coffee granules in milk. In large bowl, beat brown sugar, granulated sugar and margarine until smooth and creamy. Beat in egg, almond extract and coffee mixture. Combine flour, wheat flakes, cinnamon and baking powder; gradually beat flour mixture into sugar mixture. Drop by teaspoonfuls onto prepared cookie sheets; flatten with back of fork. Bake 8 to 10 minutes.

Makes about 40 cookies

Favorite recipe from The Sugar Association, Inc.

Tip

Let your cookie sheets cool to room temperature before adding more dough and baking another batch of cookies. Hot cookie sheets will cause the dough to melt and spread, affecting the cookies' final texture.

Mocha Cookies

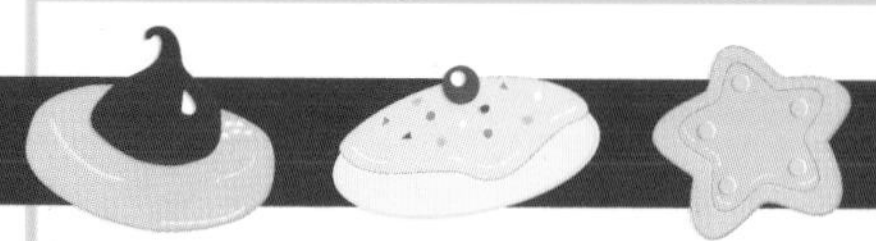

Date Pinwheel Cookies

- 1¼ cups dates, pitted and finely chopped
- ¾ cup orange juice
- ½ cup granulated sugar
- 1 tablespoon butter
- 3 cups plus 1 tablespoon all-purpose flour, divided
- 2 teaspoons vanilla, divided
- 4 ounces cream cheese
- ¼ cup vegetable shortening
- 1 cup packed brown sugar
- 2 eggs
- 1 teaspoon baking soda
- ½ teaspoon salt

1. Heat dates, orange juice, granulated sugar, butter and 1 tablespoon flour in medium saucepan over medium heat. Cook 10 minutes or until thick, stirring frequently; remove from heat. Stir in 1 teaspoon vanilla; set aside to cool.

2. Beat cream cheese, shortening and brown sugar about 3 minutes in large bowl until light and fluffy. Add eggs and remaining 1 teaspoon vanilla; beat 2 minutes longer.

3. Combine 3 cups flour, baking soda and salt in medium bowl. Add to shortening mixture; stir just until blended. Divide dough in half. Roll one half of dough on lightly floured work surface into 12×9-inch rectangle. Spread half of date mixture over dough. Spread evenly, leaving ¼-inch border on top short edge. Starting at short side, tightly roll up dough jelly-roll style. Wrap in plastic wrap; freeze for at least 1 hour. Repeat with remaining dough.

4. Preheat oven to 350°F. Grease cookie sheets. Unwrap dough. Using heavy thread or dental floss, cut dough into ¼-inch slices. Place slices 1 inch apart on prepared cookie sheets.

5. Bake 12 minutes or until lightly browned. Let cookies stand on cookie sheets 2 minutes. Remove cookies to wire rack; cool completely.

Makes 6 dozen cookies

Date Pinwheel Cookies

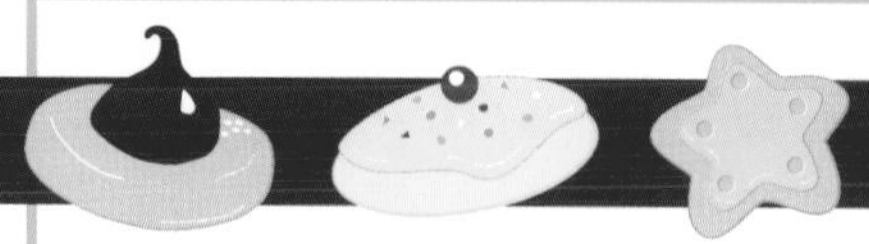

Heavenly Oatmeal Hearts

COOKIES

- **¾ Butter Flavor* CRISCO® Stick or ¾ cup Butter Flavor* CRISCO® all-vegetable shortening plus additional for greasing**
- **1¼ cups packed brown sugar**
- **1 egg**
- **⅓ cup milk**
- **1½ teaspoons vanilla**
- **3 cups quick oats, uncooked**
- **1 cup all-purpose flour**
- **1½ teaspoons cinnamon**
- **½ teaspoon baking soda**
- **½ teaspoon salt**
- **1 cup milk chocolate chips**
- **1 cup white chocolate baking pieces**
- **1 cup honey-roasted peanuts, chopped**

DRIZZLE

- **½ cup milk chocolate chips**
- **½ cup white chocolate baking pieces**
- **1 teaspoon Butter Flavor* CRISCO® Stick or 1 teaspoon Butter Flavor* CRISCO® all-vegetable shortening**

**Butter Flavor Crisco® is artificially flavored.*

1. Heat oven to 375°F. Grease baking sheets. Place sheets of foil on countertop for cooling cookies.

2. For cookies, combine ¾ cup shortening, brown sugar, egg, milk and vanilla in large bowl. Beat at medium speed of electric mixer until well blended.

3. Combine oats, flour, cinnamon, baking soda and salt. Mix into creamed mixture at low speed just until blended. Stir in chips, baking pieces and nuts.

4. Place 3-inch heart-shaped cookie cutter on prepared baking sheet. Place ⅓ cup dough inside cutter. Press to edges and level. Remove cutter. Repeat to form remaining cookies, spacing 2½ inches apart.

5. Bake one baking sheet at a time at 375°F for 10 to 12 minutes or until lightly browned. *Do not overbake.* Cool 2 minutes on baking sheet. Remove cookies to foil to cool completely.

6. For drizzle, place both chips in separate heavy resealable sandwich bags. Add ½ teaspoon shortening to each bag. Seal. Microwave 1 bag at 50% power (MEDIUM). Knead bag after 1 minute. Repeat until mixture is smooth. Repeat with remaining bag. Cut tiny piece off corner of each bag. Squeeze out and drizzle both mixtures over cookies. To serve, cut cookies in half, if desired.

Makes 2½ dozen heart cookies

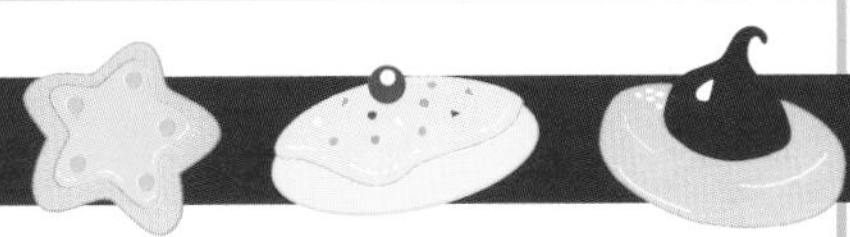

Peppersass Cookies

2¼ cups all-purpose flour
½ teaspoon baking soda
½ teaspoon salt
1½ cups sugar, divided
⅔ cup butter or margarine, at room temperature
1 egg
2 teaspoons TABASCO® brand Pepper Sauce
1 teaspoon vanilla extract

Combine flour, baking soda and salt in small bowl. Beat 1 cup sugar and butter in large bowl with electric mixer at low speed until well blended. Add egg, TABASCO® Sauce, vanilla and flour mixture; beat until smooth.

Divide dough in half; place halves on plastic wrap. Shape each half into log about 1½ inches in diameter. Cover and refrigerate until firm, 2 to 3 hours or overnight.

Preheat oven to 350°F. Place remaining ½ cup sugar in shallow dish. Cut dough logs into ¼-inch-thick slices; dip each slice in sugar. Place slices 1 inch apart on ungreased cookie sheets. Bake 10 to 12 minutes or until cookies are golden around the edges. Cool on wire racks.

Makes about 5 dozen cookies

Milk Chocolate Florentine Cookies

⅔ cup butter
2 cups quick oats, uncooked
1 cup granulated sugar
⅔ cup all-purpose flour
¼ cup light or dark corn syrup
¼ cup milk
1 teaspoon vanilla extract
¼ teaspoon salt
2 cups (11.5-ounce package) NESTLÉ® TOLL HOUSE® Milk Chocolate Morsels

MELT butter in medium saucepan; remove from heat. Stir in oats, sugar, flour, corn syrup, milk, vanilla and salt; mix well. Drop by level teaspoonfuls, about 3 inches apart, onto foil-lined baking sheets. Spread thinly with rubber spatula.

BAKE in preheated 375°F. oven for 6 to 8 minutes, until golden brown; cool on baking sheets on wire racks. Peel foil from cookies.

MICROWAVE morsels in medium microwave-safe bowl on MEDIUM-HIGH (70%) power for 1 minute; stir. Microwave at additional 10- to 20-second intervals, stirring until smooth. Spread thin layer of melted chocolate on flat side of *half* the cookies. Top with remaining cookies.

Makes about 3½ dozen sandwich cookies

Cashew-Lemon Shortbread Cookies

- **½ cup roasted cashews**
- **1 cup butter, softened**
- **½ cup sugar**
- **2 teaspoons lemon extract**
- **1 teaspoon vanilla**
- **2 cups all-purpose flour**
- **Additional sugar**

1. Preheat oven to 325°F. Place cashews in food processor; process until finely ground. Add butter, sugar, lemon extract and vanilla; process until well blended. Add flour; process using on/off pulsing action until dough is well blended and begins to form a ball.

2. Shape dough into 1½-inch balls; roll in additional sugar. Place about 2 inches apart onto ungreased baking sheets; flatten with bottom of glass.

3. Bake cookies 17 to 19 minutes or just until set and edges are lightly browned. Remove cookies from baking sheets to wire rack to cool. *Makes 2 to 2½ dozen cookies*

Chocolate Sugar Drops

- **½ cup butter or margarine, softened**
- **½ cup vegetable oil**
- **½ cup powdered sugar**
- **½ cup granulated sugar**
- **1 egg**
- **2 cups all-purpose flour**
- **¼ cup unsweetened cocoa**
- **½ teaspoon baking soda**
- **½ teaspoon cream of tartar**
- **¼ teaspoon salt**
- **1 teaspoon vanilla**
- **Additional granulated sugar**

Beat butter, oil, powdered sugar, ½ cup granulated sugar and egg in large bowl until light and fluffy. Combine flour, cocoa, baking soda, cream of tartar and salt in small bowl. Add to butter mixture with vanilla, stirring until dough is smooth. Cover; refrigerate 30 minutes or overnight, if desired.

Preheat oven to 350°F. Lightly grease cookie sheets or line with parchment paper. Shape dough into marble-sized balls. Place 2 inches apart on prepared cookie sheets. Flatten each cookie to about ⅓-inch thickness with bottom of greased glass dipped in additional granulated sugar.

Bake 10 minutes or until firm. *Do not overbake.* Remove to wire racks to cool. *Makes about 5 dozen cookies*

Cashew-Lemon Shortbread Cookies

Marbled Biscotti

- **½ cup (1 stick) butter or margarine, softened**
- **1 cup granulated sugar**
- **2 large eggs**
- **1 teaspoon vanilla extract**
- **2½ cups all-purpose flour**
- **1 teaspoon baking powder**
- **1 teaspoon baking soda**
- **1¾ cups "M&M's"® Chocolate Mini Baking Bits, divided**
- **1 cup slivered almonds, toasted***
- **¼ cup unsweetened cocoa powder**
- **2 tablespoons instant coffee granules**

**To toast almonds, spread in single layer on baking sheet. Bake at 350°F for 7 to 10 minutes until light golden, stirring occasionally. Remove almonds from pan and cool completely before using.*

Preheat oven to 350°F. Lightly grease cookie sheets; set aside. In large bowl cream butter and sugar until light and fluffy; beat in eggs and vanilla. In medium bowl combine flour, baking powder and baking soda; blend into creamed mixture. Dough will be stiff. Stir in 1¼ cups "M&M's"® Chocolate Mini Baking Bits and nuts. Divide dough in half. Add cocoa powder and coffee granules to half of the dough, mixing to blend. On well-floured surface, gently knead doughs together just enough to marble. Divide dough in half and gently roll each half into 12×2-inch log; place on prepared cookie sheets at least 4 inches apart. Press remaining ½ cup "M&M's"® Chocolate Mini Baking Bits onto outside of both logs. Bake 25 minutes. Dough will spread. Cool logs 15 to 20 minutes. Slice each log into 12 slices; arrange on cookie sheet cut-side down. Bake an additional 10 minutes. (For softer biscotti, omit second baking.) Cool completely. Store in tightly covered container.

Makes 24 pieces

Marbled Biscotti

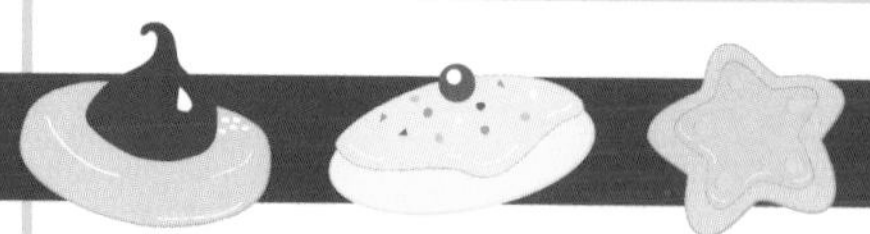

Chocolate Peanut Butter Cup Cookies

COOKIES

- **1 cup semi-sweet chocolate chips**
- **2 squares (1 ounce each) unsweetened baking chocolate**
- **1 cup sugar**
- **½ Butter Flavor* CRISCO® Stick or ½ cup Butter Flavor* CRISCO® all-vegetable shortening**
- **2 eggs**
- **1 teaspoon salt**
- **1 teaspoon vanilla**
- **1½ cups plus 2 tablespoons all-purpose flour**
- **½ teaspoon baking soda**
- **¾ cup finely chopped peanuts**
- **36 miniature peanut butter cups, unwrapped**

DRIZZLE

- **1 cup peanut butter chips**

**Butter Flavor Crisco® is artificially flavored.*

1. Heat oven to 350°F. Place sheets of foil on countertop for cooling cookies.

2. For cookies, combine chocolate chips and chocolate squares in microwave-safe measuring cup or bowl. Microwave at 50% (MEDIUM). Stir after 2 minutes. Repeat until smooth (or melt on rangetop in small saucepan on very low heat). Cool slightly.

3. Combine sugar and ½ cup shortening in large bowl. Beat at medium speed of electric mixer until blended and crumbly. Beat in eggs, one at a time, then salt and vanilla. Reduce speed to low. Add chocolate slowly. Mix until well blended. Stir in flour and baking soda with spoon until well blended. Shape dough into 1¼-inch balls. Roll in nuts. Place 2 inches apart on ungreased baking sheet.

4. Bake at 350°F for 8 to 10 minutes or until set. *Do not overbake.* Press peanut butter cup into center of each cookie immediately. Press cookie against cup. Cool 2 minutes on baking sheet before removing to cooling rack. Cool completely.

5. For drizzle, place peanut butter chips in heavy resealable sandwich bag. Seal. Microwave at 50% (MEDIUM). Knead bag after 1 minute. Repeat until smooth (or melt by placing bag in hot water). Cut tiny tip off corner of bag. Squeeze out and drizzle over cookies.

Makes 3 dozen cookies

Chocolate Peanut Butter Cup Cookies

Raspberry Almond Sandwich Cookies

1 package DUNCAN HINES® Golden Sugar Cookie Mix
1 egg
¼ cup vegetable oil
1 tablespoon water
¾ teaspoon almond extract
1⅓ cups sliced natural almonds, broken
Seedless red raspberry jam

Tip

Sandwich cookies should be stored in layers separated by waxed paper to prevent them from sticking together.

Preheat oven to 375°F.

Combine cookie mix, egg, oil, water and almond extract in large bowl. Stir until thoroughly blended. Drop half of dough by level teaspoonfuls 2 inches apart onto *ungreased* cookie sheets. (Dough will spread during baking to 1½ to 1¾ inches.)

Place almonds on waxed paper. Drop remaining half of dough by level teaspoonfuls onto nuts. Place almond side up 2 inches apart onto *ungreased* cookie sheets.

Bake both plain and almond cookies 6 minutes or until set but not browned. Cool 1 minute on cookie sheets. Remove to cooling racks. Cool completely.

Spread bottoms of plain cookies with jam; top with almond cookies. Press together to make sandwiches. Store in airtight container.

Makes 6 dozen sandwich cookies

Raspberry Almond Sandwich Cookies

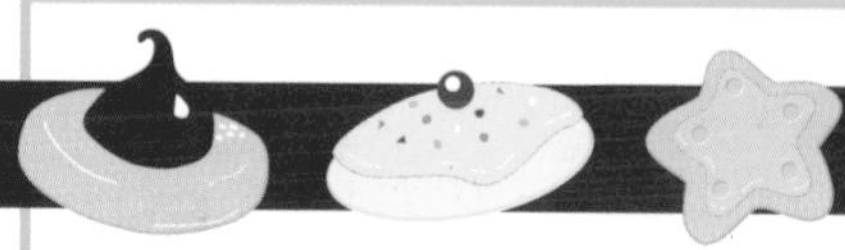

Macaroon Kiss Cookies

- ⅓ cup butter or margarine, softened
- 1 package (3 ounces) cream cheese, softened
- ¾ cup sugar
- 1 egg yolk
- 2 teaspoons almond extract
- 2 teaspoons orange juice
- 1¼ cups all-purpose flour
- 2 teaspoons baking powder
- ¼ teaspoon salt
- 5 cups MOUNDS® Sweetened Coconut Flakes, divided
- 1 bag (8 ounces) HERSHEY®S KISSES® Milk Chocolates

1. Beat together butter, cream cheese and sugar in large bowl. Add egg yolk, almond extract and orange juice; beat well. Stir together flour, baking powder and salt; gradually add to butter mixture. Stir in 3 cups coconut. Cover; refrigerate 1 hour or until firm enough to handle.

2. Heat oven to 350°F. Shape dough into 1-inch balls; roll in remaining 2 cups coconut. Place on ungreased cookie sheets.

3. Bake 10 to 12 minutes or until lightly browned. Meanwhile, remove wrappers from chocolate pieces. Remove cookies from oven; immediately press chocolate piece in center of each cookie. Cool 1 minute. Carefully remove from cookie sheets to wire racks. Cool completely.

Makes about 4½ dozen cookies

Snow-Covered Almond Crescents

- 1 cup (2 sticks) margarine or butter, softened
- ¾ cup powdered sugar
- ½ teaspoon almond extract or 2 teaspoons vanilla extract
- 2 cups all-purpose flour
- ¼ teaspoon salt (optional)
- 1 cup QUAKER® Oats (quick or old fashioned, uncooked)
- ½ cup finely chopped almonds
- Additional powdered sugar

Preheat oven to 325°F. Beat margarine, ¾ cup powdered sugar and almond extract until fluffy. Add flour and salt; mix until well blended. Stir in oats and almonds. Shape level measuring tablespoonfuls of dough into crescents. Place on ungreased cookie sheet about 2 inches apart.

Bake 14 to 17 minutes or until bottoms are light golden brown. Remove to wire rack. Sift additional powdered sugar generously over warm cookies. Cool completely. Store tightly covered.

Makes about 4 dozen cookies

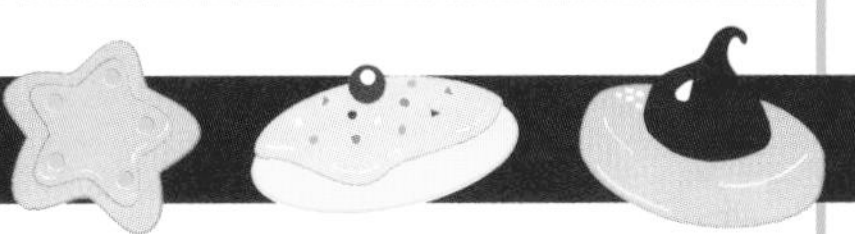

Slice 'n' Bake Ginger Wafers

½ cup butter or margarine, softened
1 cup packed brown sugar
¼ cup light molasses
1 egg
2 teaspoons ground ginger
1 teaspoon grated orange peel
¼ teaspoon salt
¼ teaspoon ground cinnamon
¼ teaspoon ground cloves
2 cups all-purpose flour

1. Beat butter, sugar and molasses in large bowl until light and fluffy. Add egg, ginger, orange peel, salt, cinnamon and cloves; beat until well blended. Stir in flour until well blended. (Dough will be very stiff.)

2. Divide dough in half. Roll each half into 8×1½-inch log. Wrap logs in waxed paper or plastic wrap; refrigerate at least 5 hours or up to 3 days.

3. Preheat oven to 350°F. Cut dough into ¼-inch-thick slices. Place about 2 inches apart onto ungreased baking sheets. Bake 12 to 14 minutes or until set. Remove from baking sheet to wire rack to cool. *Makes about 4½ dozen cookies*

Serving Suggestion: Dip half of each cookie in melted white chocolate or drizzle cookies with a glaze of 1¼ cups powdered sugar and 2 tablespoons orange juice. Or, cut cookie dough into ⅛-inch-thick slices; bake and sandwich melted caramel candy or peanut butter between cookies.

Banana Crescents

½ cup DOLE® Chopped Almonds, toasted
6 tablespoons sugar, divided
½ cup margarine, cut into pieces
1½ cups plus 2 tablespoons all-purpose flour
⅛ teaspoon salt
1 extra-ripe, medium DOLE® Banana, peeled
2 to 3 ounces semisweet chocolate chips

- Pulverize almonds with 2 tablespoons sugar.
- Beat margarine, almonds, remaining 4 tablespoons sugar, flour and salt.
- Purée banana; add to almond mixture and mix until well blended.
- Roll tablespoonfuls of dough into logs, then shape into crescents. Place on ungreased cookie sheet. Bake in 375°F oven 25 minutes or until golden. Cool on wire rack.
- Melt chocolate in microwavable dish at MEDIUM (50% power) 1½ to 2 minutes, stirring once. Dip ends of cookies in chocolate. Refrigerate until chocolate is set.

Makes 2 dozen cookies

Triple Chocolate Cookies

1 package DUNCAN HINES® Moist Deluxe® Swiss Chocolate Cake Mix
½ cup butter or margarine, melted
1 egg
½ cup semisweet chocolate chips
½ cup milk chocolate chips
½ cup coarsely chopped white chocolate
½ cup chopped pecans

1. Preheat oven to 375°F.
2. Combine cake mix, melted butter and egg in large bowl. Beat at low speed with electric mixer until blended. Stir in all 3 chocolates and pecans.
3. Drop by rounded tablespoonfuls onto ungreased baking sheets. Bake at 375°F 9 to 11 minutes. Cool 1 minute on baking sheet. Remove to cooling racks.

Makes 3½ to 4 dozen cookies

Tip: Cookies may be stored in an airtight container in freezer for up to 6 months.

Banana Crescents

Fudge Meringues

- 1/3 cup unsweetened cocoa powder
- 2 tablespoons all-purpose flour
- 1 square (1 ounce) semisweet chocolate, finely chopped
- 3 egg whites
- 1/4 teaspoon cream of tartar
- 1/4 teaspoon salt
- 2 cups powdered sugar

1. Preheat oven to 300°F. Combine cocoa, flour and chocolate in small bowl; set aside. Beat egg whites in medium bowl with electric mixer at high speed until foamy. Add cream of tartar and salt; beat until soft peaks form. Gradually beat in powdered sugar; beat until stiff peaks form. Fold in chocolate mixture.

2. Drop mixture by rounded tablespoonfuls onto cookie sheets lined with parchment paper. Bake 20 minutes or until cookies are crisp when lightly touched with fingertip (cookies will crack). Slide parchment paper onto wire racks; cool completely. Carefully remove cookies from parchment paper. Cookies are best when eaten the day they are baked but can be stored in an airtight container for up to 2 days. Cookies will become crispier when stored.

Makes 2 dozen cookies

Honey Carrot Cookies

- 1 cup sugar
- 1/2 cup butter, softened
- 2 eggs
- 3 tablespoons honey
- 1 teaspoon vanilla
- 2 1/4 cups all-purpose flour
- 2 teaspoons baking soda
- 1/2 teaspoon nutmeg
- 1/4 teaspoon salt
- 1/2 cup shredded carrot

Preheat oven to 325°F. Combine sugar and butter in large bowl. Beat well. Add eggs, honey and vanilla; beat until well mixed. Combine flour, baking soda, nutmeg and salt in medium bowl. Stir dry ingredients into butter mixture; mix well. Stir in carrot. Using well-floured hands, shape rounded teaspoonfuls of dough into 1-inch balls. Place 2 inches apart on ungreased cookie sheets.

Bake 13 to 18 minutes or until edges are lightly browned. Remove immediately to wire racks to cool.

Makes about 3 dozen cookies

Fudge Meringues

Oatmeal Apple Cookies

1¼ cups firmly packed brown sugar
¾ Butter Flavor* CRISCO® Stick *or* ¾ cup Butter Flavor* CRISCO® all-vegetable shortening plus additional for greasing
¼ cup milk
1 egg
1½ teaspoons vanilla
1 cup all-purpose flour
1¼ teaspoons ground cinnamon
½ teaspoon salt
¼ teaspoon baking soda
¼ teaspoon ground nutmeg
3 cups quick-cooking oats (not instant or old-fashioned), uncooked
1 cup diced, peeled apples
¾ cup raisins (optional)
¾ cup coarsely chopped walnuts (optional)

**Butter Flavor Crisco® is artificially flavored.*

1. Heat oven to 375°F. Grease baking sheet. Place sheets of foil on countertop for cooling cookies.

2. Combine brown sugar, ¾ cup shortening, milk, egg and vanilla in large bowl. Beat at medium speed of electric mixer until well blended and creamy.

3. Combine flour, cinnamon, salt, baking soda and nutmeg. Add gradually to creamed mixture at low speed. Mix just until blended. Stir in, one at a time, oats, apples, raisins and nuts with spoon. Drop by rounded tablespoonfuls 2 inches apart onto prepared baking sheet.

4. Bake at 375°F for 13 minutes or until set. *Do not overbake.* Cool 2 minutes on baking sheet. Remove cookies to foil to cool completely.

Makes about 2½ dozen cookies

Oatmeal Apple Cookies

Drizzled Raspberry Crinkles

1⅔ cups (10-ounce package) HERSHEY'S® Raspberry Chips, divided
1 cup (2 sticks) butter or margarine, softened
1 cup packed light brown sugar
¾ cup granulated sugar
2 eggs
1 teaspoon vanilla extract
2½ cups all-purpose flour
⅓ cup HERSHEY'S® Cocoa
1 teaspoon baking powder
1 teaspoon baking soda
1½ teaspoons shortening (do not use butter, margarine, spread or oil)

1. Heat oven to 350°F.

2. Set aside ½ cup raspberry chips. In small microwave-safe bowl, place remaining chips. Microwave at HIGH (100%) 1 minute or until melted when stirred.

3. Beat butter, brown sugar and granulated sugar in large bowl until well blended. Add melted chips; beat until well blended. Beat in eggs and vanilla. Stir together flour, cocoa, baking powder and baking soda. Gradually beat into chocolate mixture. Drop by rounded teaspoons onto ungreased cookie sheet.

4. Bake 8 to 9 minutes for chewy cookies or 10 to 11 minutes for crisp cookies. Cool slightly. Remove from cookie sheet to wire rack. Cool completely.

5. Place reserved chips and shortening in small microwave-safe bowl. Microwave at HIGH 30 seconds or until chips are melted when stirred. Drizzle over cookies.

Makes about 5 dozen cookies

Drizzled Raspberry Crinkles

Chocolate-Flecked Pirouettes

- **½ cup butter or margarine, softened**
- **½ cup sugar**
- **2 egg whites**
- **1 teaspoon vanilla**
- **½ cup all-purpose flour**
- **⅓ cup coarsely grated bittersweet or dark sweet chocolate bar (about 2 ounces)**

1. Preheat oven to 400°F. Grease cookie sheets well; set aside.

2. Beat butter and sugar in small bowl with electric mixer at medium speed until light and fluffy. Beat in egg whites, 1 at a time. Beat in vanilla. Add flour; beat at low speed just until blended. Gently fold in grated chocolate with rubber spatula.

3. Drop teaspoonfuls of batter 4 inches apart onto prepared cookie sheets. Spread dough into 2-inch rounds with small spatula. Make only 3 or 4 rounds per sheet.

4. Bake 1 sheet at a time 4 to 5 minutes until edges are barely golden. *Do not overbake.*

5. Remove from oven and quickly loosen edge of 1 cookie from baking sheet with thin spatula. Quickly roll cookie around clean handle of wooden spoon overlapping edges to form cigar shape. Repeat with remaining cookies. (If cookies become too firm to shape, return to oven for a few seconds to soften.) Slide cookie off handle to wire rack; cool completely.

6. Store tightly covered at room temperature or freeze up to 3 months.

Makes about 3 dozen cookies

Chocolate-Flecked Pirouettes

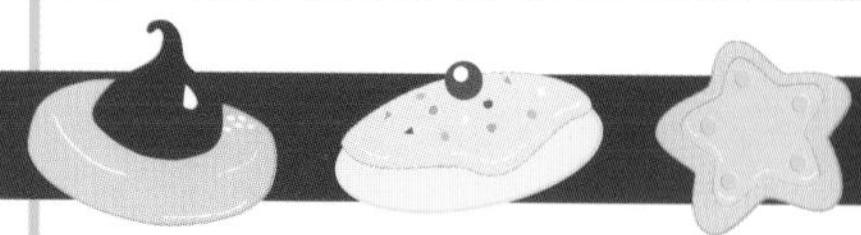

Almond Crescents

1 cup butter, softened
⅓ cup granulated sugar
1¾ cups all-purpose flour
¼ cup cornstarch
1 teaspoon vanilla extract
1½ cups ground toasted almonds*
Chocolate Glaze (recipe follows) or powdered sugar

**To toast almonds, spread on cookie sheet. Bake at 325°F for 4 minutes or until fragrant and golden.*

Preheat oven to 325°F. Beat butter and granulated sugar in large bowl until creamy. Mix in flour, cornstarch and vanilla. Stir in almonds. Shape tablespoonfuls of dough into crescents. Place 2 inches apart on ungreased cookie sheets. Bake 22 to 25 minutes or until light brown. Cool 1 minute. Remove to wire racks; cool completely. Prepare Chocolate Glaze; drizzle over cookies. Allow chocolate to set, then store in airtight container. Or, before serving, sprinkle with powdered sugar.

Makes about 3 dozen cookies

Chocolate Glaze: *Place ½ cup semisweet chocolate chips and 1 tablespoon butter or margarine in small resealable plastic bag. Place bag in bowl of hot water for 2 to 3 minutes or until chocolate is softened. Dry with paper towel. Knead until chocolate mixture is smooth. Cut off very tiny corner of bag. Drizzle chocolate mixture over cookies.*

Almond Crescents

Chocolate-Raspberry Kolachy

2 squares (1 ounce each) semisweet chocolate, coarsely chopped
1½ cups all-purpose flour
¼ teaspoon baking soda
¼ teaspoon salt
½ cup butter or margarine, softened
3 ounces cream cheese or light cream cheese, softened
⅓ cup granulated sugar
1 teaspoon vanilla
Seedless raspberry jam
Powdered sugar

Place chocolate in 1-cup glass measure. Microwave at HIGH (100% power) 1 to 2 minutes or until chocolate is melted, stirring after 1 minute.

Combine flour, baking soda and salt in small bowl; stir well. Beat butter and cream cheese in large bowl with electric mixer at medium speed until well blended. Beat in granulated sugar until light and fluffy. Beat in vanilla and chocolate. Gradually add flour mixture. Beat at low speed just until blended. Divide dough in half; flatten each half into a disc. Wrap separately in plastic wrap. Refrigerate 1 to 2 hours or until firm.

Preheat oven to 375°F. Lightly grease cookie sheets. Roll each dough disc of dough on well-floured surface to ¼- to ⅛-inch thickness. Cut out with 3-inch round cookie cutter. Place 2 inches apart on prepared cookie sheets. Place rounded ½ teaspoon jam in center of each circle. Bring three edges of dough circles up over jam; pinch edges together to seal, leaving center of triangle slightly open.

Bake 10 minutes or until set. Let cookies stand on cookie sheets 2 minutes. Remove cookies with spatula to wire racks; cool completely. Just before serving, sprinkle with powdered sugar. Store tightly covered in refrigerator; let stand for 30 minutes at room temperature before serving.

Makes about 1½ dozen cookies

Note: *These cookies do not freeze well.*

Chocolate-Raspberry Kolachy Cups: *Fit dough circles into greased mini-muffin cups; fill with heaping teaspoon of jam. Bake 10 minutes or until set. Let pans stand on wire racks; cool completely. Dust with powdered sugar before serving.*

Chocolate-Raspberry Kolachy

Peanut Butter and Chocolate Cookie Sandwich Cookies

½ cup REESE'S® Peanut Butter Chips
3 tablespoons plus ½ cup (1 stick) butter or margarine, softened and divided
1¼ cups sugar, divided
¼ cup light corn syrup
1 egg
1 teaspoon vanilla extract
2 cups plus 2 tablespoons all-purpose flour, divided
2 teaspoons baking soda
¼ teaspoon salt
½ cup HERSHEY'S® Cocoa
5 tablespoons butter or margarine, melted
Additional sugar
About 2 dozen large marshmallows

1. Heat oven to 350°F. Melt peanut butter chips and 3 tablespoons softened butter in small saucepan over very low heat. Remove from heat; cool slightly.

2. Beat remaining ½ cup softened butter and 1 cup sugar in large bowl until light and fluffy. Add corn syrup, egg and vanilla; blend thoroughly. Stir together 2 cups flour, baking soda and salt; add to butter mixture, blending well. Remove 1¼ cups batter and place in small bowl; with wooden spoon stir in the remaining 2 tablespoons flour and peanut butter chip mixture.

3. Blend cocoa, remaining ¼ cup sugar and 5 tablespoons melted butter into remaining batter. Refrigerate both batters 5 to 10 minutes or until firm enough to handle. Roll each dough into 1-inch balls; roll in sugar. Place on ungreased cookie sheets.

4. Bake 10 to 11 minutes or until set. Cool slightly; remove from cookie sheets to wire racks. Cool completely. Place 1 marshmallow on flat side of 1 chocolate cookie. Microwave at MEDIUM (50%) 10 seconds or until marshmallow is softened; place a peanut butter cookie over marshmallow, pressing down slightly. Repeat for remaining cookies. Serve immediately. *Makes about 2 dozen cookie sandwiches*

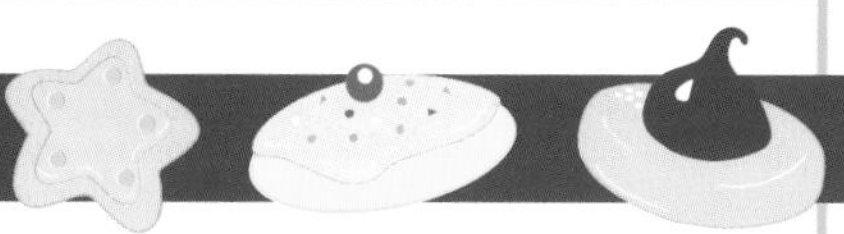

Pineapple Raisin Jumbles

2 cans (8 ounces each) DOLE® Crushed Pineapple
½ cup margarine, softened
½ cup sugar
1 teaspoon vanilla extract
1 cup all-purpose flour
4 teaspoons grated orange peel
1 cup DOLE® Blanched Slivered Almonds, toasted
1 cup DOLE® Seedless Raisins

• Preheat oven to 350°F. Drain pineapple well, pressing out excess liquid with back of spoon.

• In large bowl, beat margarine and sugar until light and fluffy. Stir in pineapple and vanilla. Beat in flour and orange peel. Stir in almonds and raisins.

• Drop heaping tablespoons of dough 2 inches apart onto greased cookie sheets.

• Bake 20 to 22 minutes or until firm. Cool on wire racks.

Makes 2 to 2½ dozen cookies

Walnut Crescents

3¾ cups flour
½ teaspoon cinnamon
1½ cups (3 sticks) MAZOLA® Margarine or butter
¾ cup KARO® Light or Dark Corn Syrup
1 tablespoon vanilla
2¼ cups ground walnuts
1½ cups confectioners sugar

1. In medium bowl combine flour and cinnamon; set aside.

2. In large bowl with mixer at medium speed, beat margarine until creamy. Gradually beat in corn syrup and vanilla until well blended. Stir in flour mixture and walnuts.

3. Cover; refrigerate several hours or until easy to handle.

4. Preheat oven to 350°F. Shape rounded teaspoonfuls of dough into 2-inch-long rolls. Place 2 inches apart on ungreased cookie sheets, curving to form crescents.

5. Bake 15 to 18 minutes or until bottoms are lightly browned. Remove from cookie sheets; cool completely on wire racks. Roll in confectioners sugar.

Makes about 8 dozen cookies

Chocolate-Dipped Cinnamon Thins

1¼ cups all-purpose flour
1½ teaspoons ground cinnamon
¼ teaspoon salt
1 cup unsalted butter, softened
1 cup powdered sugar
1 large egg
1 teaspoon vanilla
4 ounces broken bittersweet chocolate candy bar, melted

1. Place flour, cinnamon, and salt in small bowl; stir to combine.

2. Beat butter in large bowl with electric mixer at medium speed until light and fluffy. Add sugar; beat well. Add egg and vanilla. Gradually add flour mixture. Beat at low speed just until blended.

3. Place dough on sheet of waxed paper. Using waxed paper to hold dough, roll it back and forth to form a log about 12 inches long and 2½ inches wide.

4. Securely wrap log in plastic wrap. Refrigerate at least 2 hours or until firm. (Log may be frozen up to 3 months; thaw in refrigerator before baking.)

5. Preheat oven to 350°F. Cut dough with long, sharp knife into ¼-inch-thick slices. Place 2 inches apart on ungreased cookie sheets.

6. Bake 10 minutes or until set. Let cookies stand on cookie sheets 2 minutes. Remove cookies with spatula to wire racks; cool completely.

7. Dip each cookie into chocolate, coating 1 inch up sides. Transfer to wire racks or waxed paper; let stand at cool room temperature about 40 minutes until chocolate is set.

8. Store cookies between sheets of waxed paper at cool room temperature or in refrigerator. These cookies do not freeze well. *Makes about 2 dozen cookies*

Chocolate-Dipped Cinnamon Thins

Choco-Caramel Delights

½ cup (1 stick) butter or margarine, softened
⅔ cup sugar
1 egg, separated
2 tablespoons milk
1 teaspoon vanilla extract
1 cup all-purpose flour
⅓ cup HERSHEY'S® Cocoa
¼ teaspoon salt
1 cup finely chopped pecans
Caramel Filling (recipe follows)
½ cup HERSHEY'S® Semi-Sweet Chocolate Chips
1 teaspoon shortening (do not use butter, margarine, spread or oil)

1. Beat butter, sugar, egg yolk, milk and vanilla in medium bowl until blended. Stir together flour, cocoa and salt; blend into butter mixture. Refrigerate dough at least 1 hour or until firm enough to handle.

2. Heat oven to 350°F. Lightly grease cookie sheet.

3. Beat egg white slightly. Shape dough into 1-inch balls. Dip each ball into egg white; roll in pecans to coat. Place on prepared cookie sheet. Press thumb gently in center of each ball. Bake 10 to 12 minutes or until set.

4. Meanwhile, prepare Caramel Filling. Remove cookies from oven; press center of each cookie again with thumb to make indentation. Immediately spoon about ½ teaspoon Caramel Filling in center of each cookie. Carefully remove from cookie sheets; cool on wire racks.

5. Place chocolate chips and shortening in small microwave-safe bowl. Microwave at HIGH (100%) 1 minute or until softened; stir. Allow to stand several minutes to finish melting; stir until smooth. Place wax paper under wire rack with cookies. Drizzle chocolate mixture over top of cookies.

Makes about 2 dozen cookies

Caramel Filling: In small saucepan, combine 14 unwrapped light caramels and 3 tablespoons whipping cream. Cook over low heat, stirring frequently, until caramels are melted and mixture is smooth.

Choco-Caramel Delights

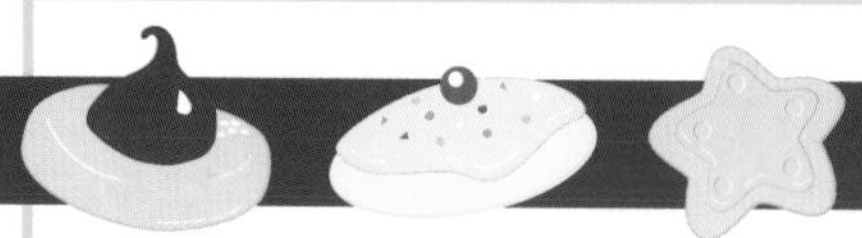

Chocolate Biscotti Nuggets

¾ cup old-fashioned or quick oats
2¼ cups all-purpose flour
1½ teaspoons baking powder
½ teaspoon salt
¾ cup chopped dates
½ cup coarsely chopped toasted pecans
½ cup honey
2 large eggs
1 teaspoon vanilla
½ cup (1 stick) butter, melted
Grated peel of 2 oranges

CHOCOLATE COATING
1¾ cups semisweet dark chocolate or white chocolate chips
4 teaspoons shortening

1. Grease baking sheet; set aside. Preheat oven to 350°F.

2. Place oats in food processor; process until oats resemble coarse flour. Combine oats, flour, baking powder and salt in large bowl. Stir in dates and pecans.

3. Whisk together honey, eggs and vanilla in medium bowl. Add melted butter and orange peel. Stir egg mixture into oat mixture just until blended. Turn out dough onto lightly floured surface; flatten slightly. Knead until dough holds together, adding flour if necessary to prevent sticking. Divide dough into 3 equal pieces; roll each into 9×½-inch log. Carefully transfer logs to prepared baking sheet, spacing about 2 inches apart. If dough cracks, pat back into shape.

4. Bake logs 25 to 30 minutes or until lightly golden but still soft. Remove from oven. Reduce oven temperature to 275°F. Let logs cool on baking sheet 10 minutes. Trim ends using serrated knife. Slice logs on slight diagonal about ¾ inch thick. Arrange biscotti on their sides on baking sheet. Return to oven and bake 15 to 20 minutes or until lightly golden. Turn biscotti over and bake 10 to 15 minutes longer. Remove biscotti to wire rack to cool completely.

5. Brush individual biscotti with dry pastry brush to remove any loose crumbs. Heat chocolate chips and shortening in small heavy saucepan over very low heat until melted and smooth. Dip half of each biscotti slice into melted chocolate, letting any excess run off. Place on prepared baking sheet. Let stand until set. Store in waxed paper-lined tin at room temperature. *Makes about 36 biscotti slices*

Chocolate Biscotti Nuggets

Mexican Chocolate Macaroons

1 package (8 ounces) semisweet baking chocolate, divided
1¾ cups plus ⅓ cup whole almonds, divided
¾ cup sugar
1 teaspoon ground cinnamon
1 teaspoon vanilla
2 egg whites

Tip

To handle sticky doughs more easily, flour your hands before shaping the cookies. Or, wet your hands with water and keep them wet as long as you are working with the dough.

1. Preheat oven to 400°F. Grease baking sheets; set aside.

2. Place 5 squares of chocolate in food processor; process until coarsely chopped. Add 1¾ cups almonds and sugar; process using on/off pulsing action until mixture is finely ground. Add cinnamon, vanilla and egg whites; process just until mixture forms moist dough.

3. Form dough into 1-inch balls (dough will be sticky). Place about 2 inches apart onto prepared baking sheets. Press 1 almond on top of each cookie.

4. Bake 8 to 10 minutes or just until set. Cool 2 minutes on baking sheets. Remove cookies from baking sheets to wire rack to cool.

5. Heat remaining 3 squares chocolate in small saucepan over very low heat until melted. Spoon chocolate into small resealable plastic food storage bag. Cut small corner off bottom of bag with scissors. Drizzle chocolate over cookies.

Makes 3 dozen cookies

Tip: For longer storage, allow cookies to stand until chocolate drizzle is set. Store in airtight containers.

Mexican Chocolate Macaroons

Cappuccino Cookies

1 cup butter, softened
2 cups firmly packed brown sugar
2 tablespoons milk
2 tablespoons instant coffee granules
2 eggs
1 teaspoon rum extract
½ teaspoon vanilla
4 cups all-purpose flour
1 teaspoon baking powder
½ teaspoon ground nutmeg
¼ teaspoon salt
Chocolate sprinkles or melted semisweet and/or white chocolate chips (optional)

Beat butter in large bowl with electric mixer at medium speed until smooth. Add brown sugar; beat until well blended.

Heat milk in small saucepan over low heat; add coffee granules, stirring to dissolve. Add milk mixture, eggs, rum extract and vanilla to butter mixture. Beat at medium speed until well blended.

Combine flour, baking powder, nutmeg and salt in large bowl. Gradually add flour mixture to butter mixture, beating at low speed after each addition until blended.

Shape dough into 2 logs, about 2 inches in diameter and 8 inches long. (Dough will be soft; sprinkle lightly with flour if too sticky to handle.)

Roll logs in chocolate sprinkles, if desired, coating evenly (⅓ cup sprinkles per roll). Or, leave rolls plain and dip in melted chocolate after baking. Wrap each log in plastic wrap; refrigerate overnight.

Preheat oven to 350°F. Grease cookie sheets. Cut rolls into ¼-inch-thick slices; place 1 inch apart on cookie sheets. (Keep unbaked rolls and sliced cookies chilled until ready to bake.)

Bake 10 to 12 minutes or until golden brown. Transfer to wire racks to cool. Dip plain cookies in melted semisweet or white chocolate, if desired. Store in airtight container.

Makes about 60 cookies

Cappuccino Cookies

Southern Belle White Chocolate Cookies

- ½ cup PETER PAN® Creamy Peanut Butter
- ¼ cup WESSON® Vegetable Oil
- ¼ cup (½ stick) butter
- ½ cup granulated sugar
- ½ cup firmly packed brown sugar
- 1 egg, at room temperature, slightly beaten
- 2 teaspoons vanilla
- ½ teaspoon baking soda
- ½ teaspoon baking powder
- 1¼ cups all-purpose flour
- 2 (4-ounce) bars white confection candy bar for baking and eating, broken into small chunks
- 1⅓ cups coarsely chopped macadamia nuts

Preheat oven to 350°F. In a large mixing bowl, using an electric mixer, beat Peter Pan® Peanut Butter, Wesson® Oil and butter together until creamy. Add *next 6* ingredients, ending with baking powder; beat on medium speed until well blended. Add flour and continue mixing until well blended. Fold candy chunks and nuts into cookie dough. Place heaping tablespoons of dough onto an ungreased cookie sheet 1½ inches apart, pressing dough down slightly with the back of spoon. Bake 10 to 12 minutes or until lightly brown around edges. Remove from cookie sheet; cool on wire rack.

Makes 1½ dozen cookies

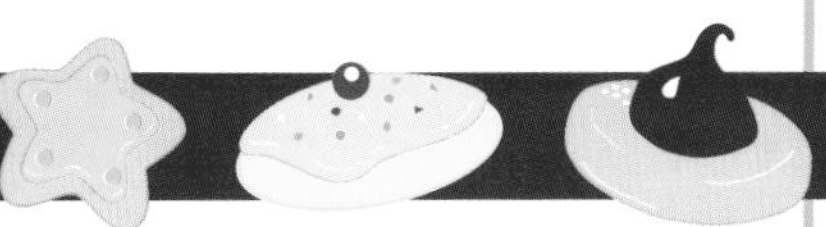

Peanut Butter Spritz Sandwiches

1 package DUNCAN HINES® Peanut Butter Cookie Mix
¼ cup vegetable oil
1 egg
4 bars (1.55 ounces each) milk chocolate

Tip

If you're baking more than one sheet of cookies at a time, rotate them from front to back and top to bottom halfway through the baking time to prevent overbrowning.

1. Preheat oven to 375°F.

2. Combine cookie mix, peanut butter packet from mix, oil and egg in large bowl. Stir until thoroughly blended. Fill cookie press with dough. Press desired shapes 2 inches apart onto ungreased baking sheet. Bake at 375°F for 7 to 9 minutes or until set but not browned. Cool 1 minute on baking sheet.

3. Cut each milk chocolate bar into 12 sections by following division marks on bars.

4. To assemble, carefully remove one cookie from cookie sheet. Place one milk chocolate section on bottom of warm cookie; top with second cookie. Press together to make sandwich. Repeat with remaining cookies. Place sandwich cookies on wire rack until chocolate is set. Store in airtight container. *Makes 3½ to 4 dozen sandwich cookies*

Tip: For best appearance, use cookie press plates that give solid shapes.

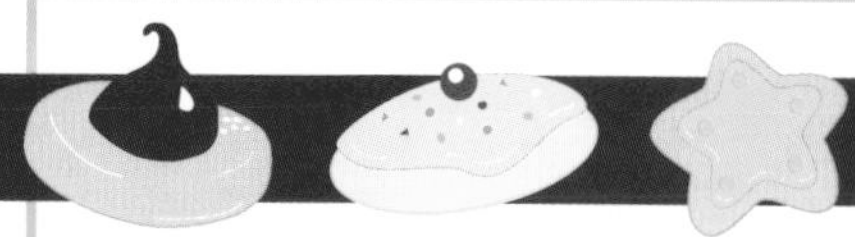

Chocolate Almond Biscotti

3 cups all-purpose flour
½ cup unsweetened cocoa
2 teaspoons baking powder
½ teaspoon salt
1 cup granulated sugar
⅔ cup FLEISCHMANN'S® Original Margarine, softened
¾ cup EGG BEATERS® Healthy Real Egg Product
1 teaspoon almond extract
½ cup whole blanched almonds, toasted and coarsely chopped
Powdered Sugar Glaze (recipe follows)

In medium bowl, combine flour, cocoa, baking powder and salt; set aside.

In large bowl, with electric mixer at medium speed, beat granulated sugar and margarine for 2 minutes or until creamy. Add Egg Beaters® and almond extract; beat well. With electric mixer at low speed, gradually add flour mixture, beating just until blended; stir in almonds.

On lightly greased baking sheet, form dough into two (12×2½-inch) logs. Bake at 350°F for 25 to 30 minutes or until toothpick inserted in centers comes out clean. Remove from sheet; cool on wire racks 15 minutes.

Using serrated knife, slice each log diagonally into 12 (1-inch-thick) slices; place, cut-sides up, on same baking sheet. Bake at 350°F for 12 to 15 minutes on each side or until cookies are crisp and edges are browned. Remove from sheet; cool completely on wire rack. Drizzle tops with Powdered Sugar Glaze. *Makes 2 dozen cookies*

Powdered Sugar Glaze: In small bowl, combine 1 cup powdered sugar and 5 to 6 teaspoons water until smooth.

Prep Time: 25 minutes
Cook Time: 45 minutes

Chocolate Almond Biscotti

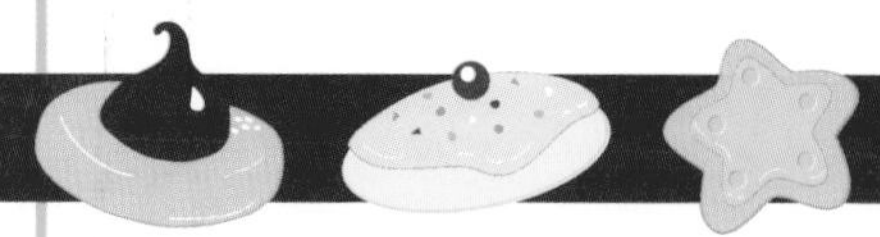

Greeting Card Cookies

½ cup (1 stick) butter or margarine, softened
¾ cup sugar
1 egg
1 teaspoon vanilla extract
1½ cups all-purpose flour
⅓ cup HERSHEY'S® Cocoa
½ teaspoon baking powder
½ teaspoon baking soda
¼ teaspoon salt
Decorative Frosting (recipe follows)

1. Beat butter, sugar, egg and vanilla in large bowl until light and fluffy. Stir together flour, cocoa, baking powder, baking soda and salt; add to butter mixture, blending well. Refrigerate about 1 hour or until firm enough to roll. Cut cardboard rectangle for pattern, 2½×4 inches; wrap in plastic wrap.

2. Heat oven to 350°F. Lightly grease cookie sheet. On lightly floured board or between two pieces of waxed paper, roll out half of dough to ¼-inch thickness. For each cookie, place pattern on dough; cut through dough around pattern with sharp paring knife. (Save dough trimmings and reroll for remaining cookies.) Carefully place cutouts on prepared cookie sheet.

3. Bake 8 to 10 minutes or until set. Cool 1 minute on cookie sheet. (If cookies have lost their shape, trim irregular edges while cookies are still hot.) Carefully transfer to wire rack. Repeat procedure with remaining dough.

4. Prepare Decorative Frosting; spoon into pastry bag fitted with decorating tip. Pipe names or greetings onto cookies; decorate as desired. *Makes about 12 cookies*

Decorative Frosting

3 cups powdered sugar
⅓ cup shortening
2 to 3 tablespoons milk
Food color (optional)

Beat sugar and shortening in small bowl; gradually add milk, beating until smooth and slightly thickened. Cover until ready to use. If desired, divide frosting into two bowls; tint with food color.

Greeting Card Cookies

Brownie Bonanza

Derby Brownies

1 package DUNCAN HINES® Walnut Brownie Mix
½ cup (1 stick) butter or margarine, softened
1 pound confectioners' sugar (about 3½ to 4 cups)
2 tablespoons bourbon or milk
1 container DUNCAN HINES® Dark Chocolate Frosting

Preheat oven to 350°F. Grease bottom only of 13×9-inch pan.

Prepare brownie mix as directed on package for cake-like brownies. Pour into prepared pan. Bake 24 to 27 minutes or until set. Cool completely in pan. Beat butter until smooth in large mixing bowl; stir in sugar and bourbon. Beat until smooth and of spreading consistency. Spread over brownies; chill. Top with frosting. Chill 2 to 4 hours. Cut into bars and serve at room temperature. *Makes 24 brownies*

Derby Brownies

Fabulous Blonde Brownies

1¾ cups all-purpose flour
1 teaspoon baking powder
¼ teaspoon salt
1 cup (6 ounces) white chocolate chips
1 cup (4 ounces) blanched whole almonds, coarsely chopped
1 cup English toffee bits
⅔ cup margarine or butter, softened
1½ cups packed light brown sugar
2 eggs
2 teaspoons vanilla

Preheat oven to 350°F. Lightly grease 13×9-inch baking pan.

Combine flour, baking powder and salt in small bowl; mix well. Combine white chocolate, almonds and toffee in medium bowl; mix well.

Beat margarine and brown sugar in large bowl with electric mixer at medium speed until light and fluffy. Beat in eggs and vanilla. Add flour mixture; beat at low speed until well blended. Stir in ¾ cup of white chocolate mixture. Spread evenly into prepared pan.

Bake 20 minutes. Immediately after removing brownies from oven, sprinkle remaining white chocolate mixture evenly over brownies. Press down lightly. Bake 15 to 20 minutes or until wooden pick inserted into center comes out clean. Cool brownies completely in pan on wire rack. Cut into 2×1½-inch bars. *Makes 3 dozen brownies*

Fabulous Blonde Brownies

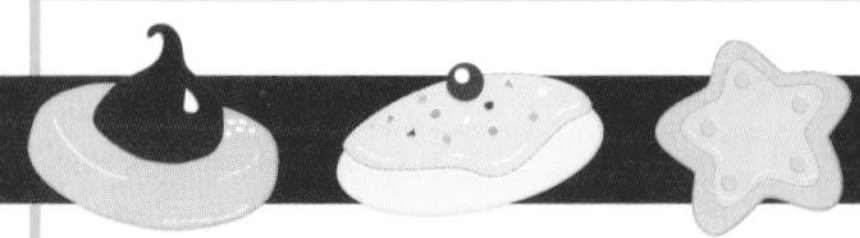

Brownie Turtle Cookies

2 squares (1 ounce each) unsweetened baking chocolate
⅓ cup solid vegetable shortening
1 cup granulated sugar
½ teaspoon vanilla extract
2 large eggs
1¼ cups all-purpose flour
½ teaspoon baking powder
½ teaspoon salt
1 cup "M&M's"® Milk Chocolate Mini Baking Bits, divided
1 cup pecan halves
⅓ cup caramel ice cream topping
⅓ cup shredded coconut
⅓ cup finely chopped pecans

Preheat oven to 350°F. Lightly grease cookie sheets; set aside. Heat chocolate and shortening in 2-quart saucepan over low heat, stirring constantly until melted; remove from heat. Mix in sugar, vanilla and eggs. Blend in flour, baking powder and salt. Stir in ⅔ cup "M&M's"® Milk Chocolate Mini Baking Bits. For each cookie, arrange 3 pecan halves, with ends almost touching at center, on prepared cookie sheets. Drop dough by rounded teaspoonfuls onto center of each group of pecans; mound the dough slightly. Bake 8 to 10 minutes just until set. Do not overbake. Cool completely on wire racks. In small bowl combine ice cream topping, coconut and chopped nuts; top each cookie with about 1½ teaspoons mixture. Press remaining ⅓ cup "M&M's"® Milk Chocolate Mini Baking Bits into topping.

Makes about 2½ dozen cookies

Brownie Turtle Cookies

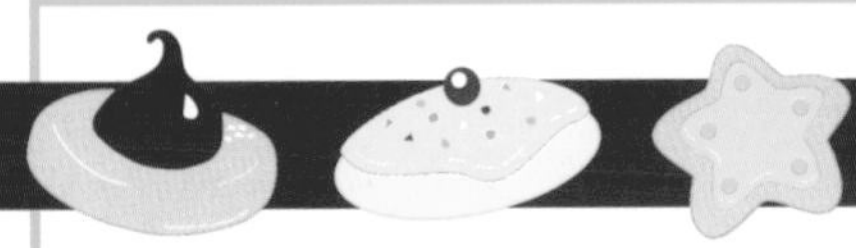

Orange Cappuccino Brownies

- ¾ cup butter
- 2 squares (1 ounce each) semisweet chocolate, coarsely chopped
- 2 squares (1 ounce each) unsweetened chocolate, coarsely chopped
- 1¾ cups granulated sugar
- 1 tablespoon instant espresso powder or instant coffee granules
- 3 eggs
- ¼ cup orange-flavored liqueur
- 2 teaspoons grated orange peel
- 1 cup all-purpose flour
- 1 package (12 ounces) semisweet chocolate chips
- 2 tablespoons shortening

Preheat oven to 350°F. Grease 13×9-inch baking pan.

Melt butter and chopped chocolates in large, heavy saucepan over low heat, stirring constantly. Stir in granulated sugar and espresso powder. Remove from heat. Cool slightly. Beat in eggs, 1 at a time. Whisk in liqueur and orange peel. Beat flour into chocolate mixture just until blended. Spread batter evenly in prepared pan.

Bake 25 to 30 minutes or until center is just set. Remove pan to wire rack. Meanwhile, melt chocolate chips and shortening in small, heavy saucepan over low heat, stirring constantly. Immediately, spread hot chocolate mixture over warm brownies. Cool completely in pan on wire rack. Cut into 2-inch squares. *Makes about 2 dozen brownies*

Tip

One medium orange yields 1 to 2 tablespoons grated peel, which can be frozen for up to six months.

Orange Cappuccino Brownies

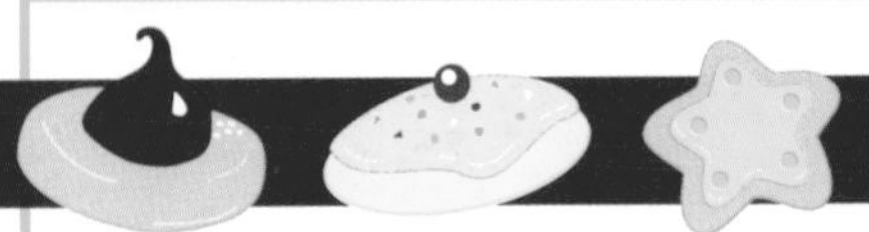

Sensational Peppermint Pattie Brownies

24 small (1½-inch) YORK® Peppermint Patties
1½ cups (3 sticks) butter or margarine, melted
3 cups sugar
1 tablespoon vanilla extract
5 eggs
2 cups all-purpose flour
1 cup HERSHEY'®S Cocoa
1 teaspoon baking powder
1 teaspoon salt

1. Heat oven to 350°F. Remove wrappers from peppermint patties. Grease 13×9×2-inch baking pan.

2. Stir together butter, sugar and vanilla in large bowl. Add eggs; beat until well blended. Stir together flour, cocoa, baking powder and salt; gradually add to butter mixture, blending well. Reserve 2 cups batter. Spread remaining batter into prepared pan. Arrange peppermint patties about ½ inch apart in single layer over batter. Spread reserved batter over patties.

3. Bake 50 to 55 minutes or until brownies pull away from sides of pan. Cool completely in pan on wire rack.

Makes about 36 brownies

Peanut Butter Chip Brownies

½ cup butter or margarine
4 squares (1 ounce each) semisweet chocolate
½ cup sugar
2 eggs
1 teaspoon vanilla
½ cup all-purpose flour
1 package (12 ounces) peanut butter chips
1 cup (6 ounces) milk chocolate chips

Preheat oven to 350°F. Grease 8-inch square baking pan. Melt butter and semisweet chocolate in small, heavy saucepan over low heat, stirring just until chocolate melts completely. Remove from heat; cool. Beat sugar and eggs in large bowl until light and fluffy. Blend in vanilla and chocolate mixture. Stir in flour until blended; fold in peanut butter chips. Spread batter evenly in prepared pan.

Bake 25 to 30 minutes or just until firm and dry in center. Remove from oven; sprinkle milk chocolate chips over top. Place pan on wire rack. When chocolate chips have melted, spread over brownies. Refrigerate until chocolate topping is set. Cut into 2-inch squares.

Makes 16 brownies

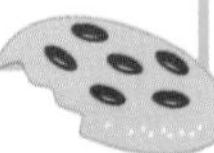

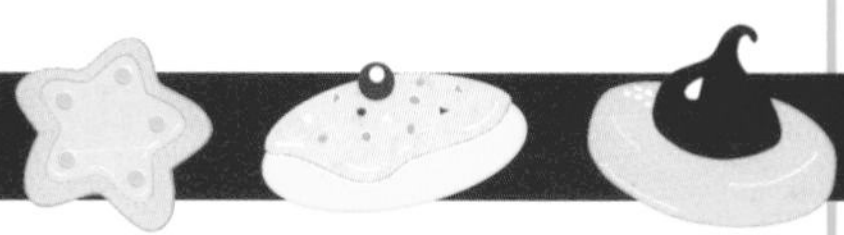

Devil's Fudge Brownies

- ½ cup (1 stick) butter or margarine, softened
- 1 cup granulated sugar
- 2 large eggs
- 2 tablespoons FRANK'S® REDHOT® Sauce
- 1 teaspoon vanilla extract
- ⅔ cup all-purpose flour
- ½ cup unsweetened cocoa
- ¼ teaspoon baking soda
- 1 cup chopped pecans
- ½ cup mini chocolate chips
- Pecan halves
- Confectioners' sugar
- Ice cream (optional)
- Fudge sauce (optional)

Beat butter, granulated sugar, eggs, REDHOT sauce and vanilla in large bowl of electric mixer on medium speed until light and fluffy. Blend in flour, cocoa and baking soda. Beat until smooth. Stir in chopped nuts and mini chips. Spread into greased deep-dish 9-inch microwave-safe pie plate. Arrange pecan halves on top.

Place pie plate on top of inverted custard cup in microwave oven. Microwave, uncovered, on HIGH 6 minutes or until toothpick inserted in center comes out clean, turning once. (Brownie may appear moist on surface. Do not overcook.) Cool completely on wire rack.

Dust top with confectioners' sugar. Cut into wedges. Serve with ice cream and fudge sauce, if desired.

Makes 8 servings

Prep Time: 20 minutes
Cook Time: 6 minutes

Butterscotch Brownies

- **1 cup butterscotch-flavored chips**
- **½ cup packed light brown sugar**
- **¼ cup butter, softened**
- **2 eggs**
- **½ teaspoon vanilla**
- **1 cup all-purpose flour**
- **½ teaspoon baking powder**
- **¼ teaspoon salt**
- **1 cup semisweet chocolate chips**

Preheat oven to 350°F. Grease 9-inch square baking pan. Melt butterscotch chips in small saucepan over low heat, stirring constantly; set aside.

Beat sugar and butter in large bowl until light and fluffy. Beat in eggs, one at a time, scraping down side of bowl after each addition. Beat in vanilla and melted butterscotch chips. Combine flour, baking powder and salt in small bowl; add to butter mixture. Beat until well blended. Spread batter evenly in prepared pan.

Bake 20 to 25 minutes or until golden brown and center is set. Remove pan from oven and immediately sprinkle with chocolate chips. Let stand about 4 minutes or until chocolate is melted. Spread chocolate evenly over top. Place pan on wire rack; cool completely. Cut into 2¼-inch squares.

Makes about 16 brownies

Nuggets o' Gold Brownies

- **3 ounces unsweetened baking chocolate**
- **¼ cup WESSON® Vegetable Oil**
- **2 eggs**
- **1 cup sugar**
- **¼ teaspoon salt**
- **1 teaspoon vanilla extract**
- **½ cup all-purpose flour**
- **1 (3.8-ounce) BUTTERFINGER® Candy Bar, coarsely chopped**

In microwave-safe measuring cup, heat chocolate 2 minutes on HIGH in microwave oven. Stir and continue heating in 30 second intervals until chocolate is completely melted. Stir in oil and set aside to cool. In mixing bowl, beat eggs until foamy. Whisk in sugar, then add salt and vanilla. Stir in chocolate mixture then mix in flour until all ingredients are moistened. Gently fold in candy. Pour batter into a 9-inch greased baking pan and bake at 350°F for 25 to 30 minutes or until edges begin to leave sides of pan. Cool before cutting.

Makes 20 brownies

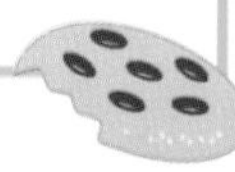

Butterscotch Brownies

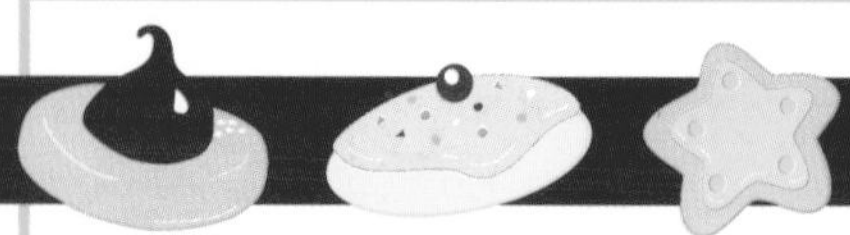

Irish Brownies

- **4 squares (1 ounce each) semisweet baking chocolate, coarsely chopped**
- **½ cup butter or margarine**
- **½ cup sugar**
- **2 eggs**
- **¼ cup Irish cream liqueur**
- **1 cup all-purpose flour**
- **½ teaspoon baking powder**
- **¼ teaspoon salt**
- **Irish Cream Frosting (recipe follows)**

Preheat oven to 350°F. Grease 8-inch square baking pan. Melt chocolate and butter in medium, heavy saucepan over low heat, stirring constantly. Remove from heat. Stir in sugar. Beat in eggs, 1 at a time, with wire whisk. Whisk in Irish cream. Combine flour, baking powder and salt in small bowl; stir into chocolate mixture until just blended. Spread batter evenly in prepared pan.

Bake 22 to 25 minutes or until center is set. Remove pan to wire rack; cool completely before frosting. Spread Irish Cream Frosting over cooled brownies. Chill at least 1 hour or until frosting is set. Cut into 2-inch squares.

Makes about 16 brownies

Irish Cream Frosting

- **2 ounces cream cheese (¼ cup), softened**
- **2 tablespoons butter or margarine, softened**
- **2 tablespoons Irish cream liqueur**
- **1½ cups powdered sugar**

Beat cream cheese and butter in small bowl with electric mixer at medium speed until smooth. Beat in Irish cream. Gradually beat in powdered sugar until smooth.

Makes about ⅔ cup frosting

Irish Brownies

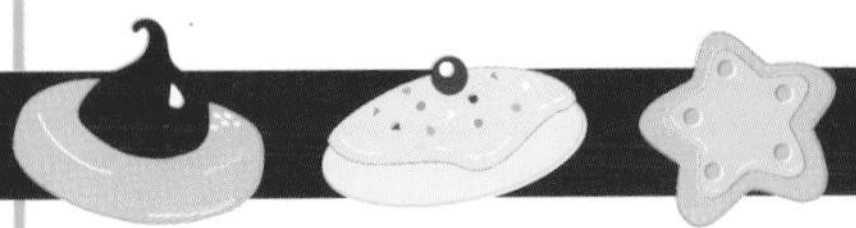

Quick & Easy Fudgey Brownies

4 bars (1 ounce each) HERSHEY®S Unsweetened Baking Chocolate, broken into pieces
¾ cup (1½ sticks) butter or margarine
2 cups sugar
3 eggs
1½ teaspoons vanilla extract
1 cup all-purpose flour
1 cup chopped nuts (optional)
Creamy Quick Chocolate Frosting (recipe follows, optional)

Heat oven to 350°F. Grease 13×9×2-inch baking pan.

Place chocolate and butter in large microwave-safe bowl. Microwave at HIGH 1½ to 2 minutes or until chocolate is melted and mixture is smooth when stirred. Add sugar; stir with spoon until well blended. Add eggs and vanilla; mix well. Add flour and nuts, if desired; stir until well blended. Spread into prepared pan.

Bake 30 to 35 minutes or until wooden pick inserted in center comes out almost clean. Cool in pan on wire rack.

Frost with Quick & Easy Chocolate Frosting, if desired. Cut into squares. *Makes about 24 brownies*

Creamy Quick Chocolate Frosting

3 tablespoons butter or margarine
3 bars (1 ounce each) HERSHEY®S Unsweetened Baking Chocolate, broken into pieces
3 cups powdered sugar
½ cup milk
1 teaspoon vanilla extract
⅛ teaspoon salt

Melt butter and chocolate in saucepan over very low heat. Cook, stirring constantly, until chocolate is melted and mixture is smooth. Pour into large bowl; add powdered sugar, milk, vanilla and salt. Beat on medium speed of electric mixer until well blended. If necessary, refrigerate 10 minutes or until of spreading consistency. *Makes about 2 cups frosting*

Quick & Easy Fudgey Brownies

Heavenly Hash Brownies

1 cup butter
¼ cup unsweetened cocoa powder
4 eggs
1¼ cups granulated sugar
2 cups chopped walnuts or pecans
1½ cups all-purpose flour
2 teaspoons vanilla
Creamy Cocoa Icing (recipe follows)
1 package (10 ounces) miniature marshmallows*

**For best results, use fresh marshmallows.*

Preheat oven to 350°F. Grease 13×9-inch baking pan. Melt butter in 2-quart saucepan; stir in cocoa. Remove from heat; beat in eggs and granulated sugar. Blend in nuts, flour and vanilla. Spread batter evenly in prepared pan.

Bake 20 to 25 minutes or until wooden pick inserted in center comes out clean. Do not overbake. Meanwhile, prepare Creamy Cocoa Icing. Remove brownies from oven. Immediately sprinkle marshmallows over hot brownies. Pour hot icing evenly over marshmallows. Cool in pan on wire rack. Cut into 2-inch squares.

Makes about 2 dozen brownies

Creamy Cocoa Icing

6 tablespoons butter or margarine
¾ cup undiluted evaporated milk
6 cups powdered sugar
¾ cup unsweetened cocoa powder

Melt butter in 2-quart saucepan. Add milk, powdered sugar and cocoa. Stir over low heat until smooth and creamy.

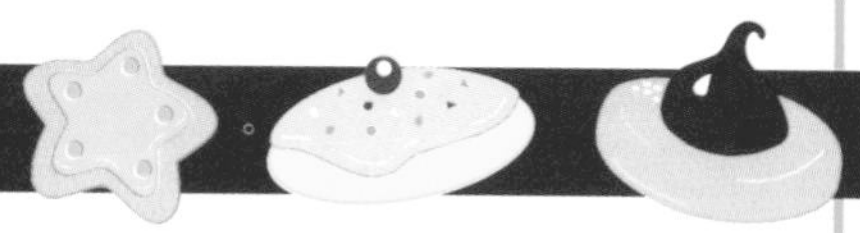

Baker's® Raspberry Truffle Brownies

BROWNIE LAYER:

- **4 squares BAKER'S® Unsweetened Baking Chocolate**
- **¾ cup (1½ sticks) butter *or* margarine**
- **2 cups sugar**
- **3 eggs**
- **1 teaspoon vanilla**
- **1 cup flour**
- **1 cup coarsely chopped macadamia nuts *or* toasted almonds**
- **¼ cup seedless raspberry jam**

GLAZE:

- **1 cup whipping (heavy) cream**
- **6 squares BAKER'S® Semi-Sweet Baking Chocolate, finely chopped**
- **2 squares BAKER'S® Unsweetened Baking Chocolate, finely chopped**
- **3 tablespoons seedless raspberry jam**

BROWNIE LAYER

HEAT oven to 350°F (325°F for glass baking dish). Line 13×9-inch baking pan with foil. Grease foil.

MICROWAVE chocolate and butter in large microwavable bowl on HIGH 2 minutes or until butter is melted. Stir until chocolate is completely melted.

STIR sugar into chocolate mixture until well blended. Mix in eggs and vanilla. Stir in flour and nuts until well blended. Spread in prepared pan.

BAKE 30 to 35 minutes or until toothpick inserted in center comes out with fudgy crumbs. DO NOT OVERBAKE. Cool in pan. Spread jam over brownies.

GLAZE

MICROWAVE cream in medium microwavable bowl on HIGH 45 seconds or until simmering. Stir in chopped chocolates and jam until chocolates are melted and mixture is smooth. Spread glaze over jam layer on brownies.

REFRIGERATE 1 hour or until glaze is set. Lift out of pan onto cutting board. Cut into diamond-shaped bars. Garnish with fresh raspberries, if desired.

Makes about 3 dozen brownies

Prep Time: 20 minutes plus refrigerating
Bake Time: 35 minutes

German Chocolate Brownies

- 1 package DUNCAN HINES® Milk Chocolate Chunk Brownie Mix
- 2 eggs
- 1/3 cup water
- 1/3 cup vegetable oil
- 1/2 cup packed brown sugar
- 2 tablespoons butter or margarine, softened
- 1 tablespoon all-purpose flour
- 1/2 cup chopped pecans
- 1/2 cup flaked coconut

Preheat oven to 350°F. Grease bottom only of 13×9-inch pan.

Combine brownie mix, eggs, water and oil in large bowl. Stir with spoon until well blended, about 50 strokes. Spread into prepared pan.

Combine sugar, butter and flour in small bowl. Mix until well blended. Stir in pecans and coconut. Sprinkle mixture over batter. Bake 25 to 30 minutes or until topping is browned. Cool completely in pan. Cut into bars.

Makes 24 brownies

Tip: *Always mix brownies by hand. Never use an electric mixer.*

Deep Dish Brownies

- 3/4 cup (1 1/2 sticks) butter or margarine, melted
- 1 1/2 cups sugar
- 1 1/2 teaspoons vanilla extract
- 3 eggs
- 3/4 cup all-purpose flour
- 1/2 cup HERSHEY®S Cocoa
- 1/2 teaspoon baking powder
- 1/2 teaspoon salt

1. Heat oven to 350°F. Grease 8-inch square baking pan.

2. Blend butter, sugar and vanilla in medium bowl. Add eggs; using spoon, beat well. Combine flour, cocoa, baking powder and salt; gradually add to egg mixture, beating until well blended. Spread batter into prepared pan.

3. Bake 40 to 45 minutes or until brownies begin to pull away from sides of pan. Cool completely in pan on wire rack. Cut into squares.

Makes about 16 brownies

Variation: *Stir 1 cup REESE'S® Peanut Butter Chips or HERSHEY®S Semi-Sweet Chocolate Chips into batter before spreading into pan. Proceed as directed.*

German Chocolate Brownies

Minted Chocolate Chip Brownies

- **¾ cup granulated sugar**
- **½ cup butter**
- **2 tablespoons water**
- **1 cup semisweet chocolate chips or mini semisweet chocolate chips**
- **1½ teaspoons vanilla**
- **2 eggs**
- **1¼ cups all-purpose flour**
- **½ teaspoon baking soda**
- **½ teaspoon salt**
- **1 cup mint chocolate chips**
- **Powdered sugar for garnish**

Preheat oven to 350°F. Grease 9-inch square baking pan. Combine sugar, butter and water in medium microwavable bowl. Microwave on HIGH 2½ to 3 minutes or until butter is melted. Stir in semisweet chips; stir gently until chips are melted and mixture is well blended. Stir in vanilla; let stand 5 minutes to cool.

Beat eggs into chocolate mixture, 1 at a time. Combine flour, baking soda and salt in small bowl; add to chocolate mixture. Stir in mint chocolate chips. Spread into prepared pan.

Bake 25 minutes for fudgy brownies or 30 minutes for cakelike brownies.

Remove pan to wire rack; cool completely. Cut into 2¼-inch squares. Sprinkle with powdered sugar, if desired.

Makes about 16 brownies

Philadelphia® Marble Brownies

- **1 package (21½ ounces) brownie mix**
- **1 package (8 ounces) PHILADELPHIA® Cream Cheese, softened**
- **⅓ cup sugar**
- **½ teaspoon vanilla**
- **1 egg**
- **1 cup BAKER'S® Semi-Sweet Real Chocolate Chips**

PREPARE brownie mix as directed on package. Spread in greased 13×9-inch baking pan.

MIX cream cheese, sugar and vanilla with electric mixer on medium speed until well blended. Add egg; mix well. Pour over brownie mixture; cut through batter with knife several times for marble effect. Sprinkle with chips.

BAKE at 350°F for 35 to 40 minutes or until cream cheese mixture is lightly browned. Cool in pan on wire rack. Cut into squares.

Makes 24 brownies

Prep Time: 20 minutes plus cooling
Bake Time: 40 minutes

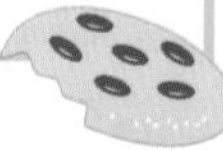

Minted Chocolate Chip Brownies

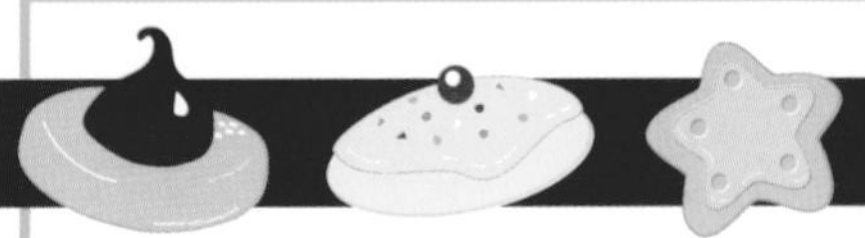

Peanut Butter Marbled Brownies

- **4 ounces cream cheese, softened**
- **½ cup peanut butter**
- **2 tablespoons sugar**
- **1 egg**
- **1 package (20 to 22 ounces) brownie mix plus ingredients to prepare mix**
- **¾ cup lightly salted cocktail peanuts**

Preheat oven to 350°F. Lightly grease 13×9-inch baking pan. Beat cream cheese, peanut butter, sugar and egg in medium bowl with electric mixer at medium speed until blended.

Prepare brownie mix according to package directions. Spread brownie mixture evenly in prepared pan. Spoon peanut butter mixture in dollops over brownie mixture. Swirl peanut butter mixture into brownie mixture with tip of knife. Sprinkle peanuts on top; lightly press peanuts down.

Bake 30 to 35 minutes or until wooden pick inserted into center comes out almost clean. (Do not overbake.) Cool brownies completely in pan on wire rack. Cut into 2-inch squares.

Makes 2 dozen brownies

Chewy Chocolate Brownies

- **¾ cup granulated sugar**
- **½ cup (1 stick) butter or margarine**
- **2 tablespoons water**
- **4 bars (2 ounces *each*) NESTLÉ® TOLL HOUSE® Semi-Sweet Baking Chocolate, broken into pieces**
- **2 eggs**
- **2 teaspoons vanilla extract**
- **1 cup all-purpose flour**
- **¼ teaspoon baking soda**
- **¼ teaspoon salt**
- **½ cup chopped nuts (optional)**

MICROWAVE sugar, butter and water in large, microwave-safe bowl on HIGH (100%) power for 3 minutes until mixture boils, stirring once. Add baking bars; stir until melted.

STIR in eggs one at a time until well blended. Stir in vanilla. Add flour, baking soda and salt; stir well. Stir in nuts. Pour into greased 13×9-inch baking pan.

BAKE in preheated 350°F. oven for 16 to 20 minutes until wooden pick inserted in center comes out still slightly sticky. Cool in pan on wire rack.

Makes about 2 dozen brownies

Saucepan Method: BRING sugar, butter and water in medium saucepan just to a boil, stirring constantly. Remove from heat. Proceed as directed.

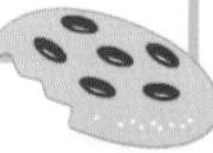

Peanut Butter Marbled Brownies

Hershey's® White Chip Brownies

- 4 eggs
- 1¼ cups sugar
- ½ cup (1 stick) butter or margarine, melted
- 2 teaspoons vanilla extract
- 1⅓ cups all-purpose flour
- ⅔ cup HERSHEY'®S Cocoa
- 1 teaspoon baking powder
- ½ teaspoon salt
- 1⅔ cups (10-ounce package) HERSHEY'®S Premier White Chips

1. Heat oven to 350°F. Grease 13×9×2-inch baking pan.

2. Beat eggs in large bowl until foamy; gradually beat in sugar. Add butter and vanilla; beat until blended. Stir together flour, cocoa, baking powder and salt; add to egg mixture, beating until blended. Stir in white chips. Spread batter into prepared pan.

3. Bake 25 to 30 minutes or until brownies begin to pull away from sides of pan. Cool completely in pan on wire rack. Cut into squares. *Makes about 36 brownies*

Tip: Brownies and bar cookies cut into different shapes can add interest to a plate of simple square cookies. Cut cookies into different size rectangles or make triangles by cutting them into 2- to 2½-inch squares; then cut each square in half diagonally. To make diamond shapes, cut straight lines 1 or 1½ inches apart the length of the baking pan, then cut straight lines 1½ inches apart diagonally across the pan.

Prep Time: 15 minutes
Bake Time: 25 minutes
Cool Time: 2 hours

Hershey®s White Chip Brownies

Double-Decker Confetti Brownies

- 3/4 cup (1 1/2 sticks) butter or margarine, softened
- 1 cup granulated sugar
- 1 cup firmly packed light brown sugar
- 3 large eggs
- 1 teaspoon vanilla extract
- 2 1/2 cups all-purpose flour, divided
- 2 1/2 teaspoons baking powder
- 1/2 teaspoon salt
- 1/3 cup unsweetened cocoa powder
- 1 tablespoon butter or margarine, melted
- 1 cup "M&M's"® Semi-Sweet Chocolate Mini Baking Bits, divided

Preheat oven to 350°F. Lightly grease 13×9×2-inch baking pan; set aside. In large bowl cream butter and sugars until light and fluffy; beat in eggs and vanilla. In medium bowl combine 2 1/4 cups flour, baking powder and salt; blend into creamed mixture. Divide batter in half. Blend together cocoa powder and melted butter; stir into one half of the dough. Spread cocoa dough evenly into prepared baking pan. Stir remaining 1/4 cup flour and 1/2 cup "M&M's"® Semi-Sweet Chocolate Mini Baking Bits into remaining dough; spread evenly over cocoa dough in pan. Sprinkle with remaining 1/2 cup "M&M's"® Semi-Sweet Chocolate Mini Baking Bits. Bake 25 to 30 minutes or until edges start to pull away from sides of pan. Cool completely. Cut into bars. Store in tightly covered container.

Makes 24 brownies

Double-Decker Confetti Brownies

Rich Chocolate Caramel Brownies

1 package (18.25 to 18.5 ounces) devil's food or chocolate cake mix
1 cup chopped nuts
½ cup (1 stick) butter or margarine, melted
1 cup undiluted CARNATION® Evaporated Milk, divided
35 (10 ounces) light caramels, unwrapped
1 cup (6 ounces) NESTLÉ® TOLL HOUSE® Semi-Sweet Chocolate Morsels

COMBINE cake mix and nuts in large bowl; stir in butter. Stir in ⅔ *cup* evaporated milk (batter will be thick). Spread *half* of batter into greased 13×9-inch baking pan. Bake in preheated 350°F. oven for 15 minutes.

COMBINE caramels and *remaining* evaporated milk in small saucepan. Cook over low heat, stirring constantly, for about 10 minutes or until caramels are melted. Sprinkle chocolate morsels over baked layer; drizzle caramel mixture over top. Drop *remaining* batter by heaping teaspoon over caramel mixture. Bake for additional 20 to 25 minutes (top layer will be soft). Cool completely on wire rack.

Makes about 48 brownies

Variation: For Rich Chocolate Butterscotch Brownies, pour 12.25-ounce jar of butterscotch-flavored topping over Nestlé® Toll House® Semi-Sweet Chocolate Morsels, instead of melting caramels with ⅓ cup evaporated milk.

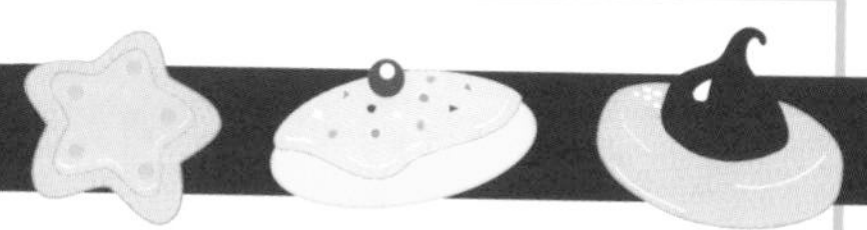

Double Fudge Brownie Bars

- 1 package DUNCAN HINES® Double Fudge Brownie Mix
- 2 eggs
- ⅓ cup water
- ¼ cup vegetable oil
- 1 (6-ounce) package semisweet chocolate chips
- 1 cup peanut butter chips
- ½ cup chopped pecans
- 1 cup flaked coconut
- 1 (14-ounce) can sweetened condensed milk

Preheat oven to 350°F. Grease bottom only of 13×9-inch pan.

Combine brownie mix, contents of fudge packet from mix, eggs, water and oil in large bowl. Stir with spoon until well blended, about 50 strokes. Spread in prepared pan. Bake 18 minutes. Remove from oven. Sprinkle chocolate chips over brownie base, then sprinkle with peanut butter chips, pecans and coconut. Pour milk over top. Bake 22 to 25 minutes or until light golden brown. Cool completely in pan. Cut into bars.

Makes 20 to 24 bars

Tip: For a delicious flavor variation, substitute butterscotch-flavored chips for the peanut butter chips.

Tip

Sweetened condensed milk is a mixture of whole milk and sugar that is heated until about 60 percent of the water evaporates, resulting in a sticky, sweet mixture frequently used in baked goods. Unopened sweetened condensed milk should be stored at room temperature for up to six months. Once opened, store unused milk in an airtight container in the refrigerator for up to five days.

Chocolate Espresso Brownies

- **4 squares (1 ounce each) unsweetened chocolate**
- **1 cup sugar**
- **¼ cup Prune Purée (recipe follows) or prepared prune butter**
- **3 egg whites**
- **1 to 2 tablespoons instant espresso coffee powder**
- **1 teaspoon baking powder**
- **1 teaspoon salt**
- **1 teaspoon vanilla**
- **½ cup all-purpose flour**
- **Powdered sugar (optional)**

Preheat oven to 350°F. Coat 8-inch square baking pan with vegetable cooking spray. In small heavy saucepan, melt chocolate over very low heat, stirring until melted and smooth. Remove from heat; cool. In mixer bowl, beat chocolate and remaining ingredients except flour and powdered sugar at medium speed until well blended; mix in flour. Spread batter evenly in prepared pan. Bake in center of oven about 30 minutes until pick inserted into center comes out clean. Cool completely in pan on wire rack. Dust with powdered sugar. Cut into 1⅓-inch squares. *Makes 36 brownies*

Prune Purée: *Combine 1⅓ cups (8 ounces) pitted prunes and 6 tablespoons hot water in container of food processor or blender. Pulse on and off until prunes are finely chopped and smooth. Store leftovers in a covered container in the refrigerator for up to two months. Makes 1 cup.*

Favorite recipe from California Prune Board

Chocolate Espresso Brownies

Three Great Tastes Blond Brownies

2 cups packed light brown sugar
1 cup (2 sticks) butter or margarine, melted
2 eggs
2 teaspoons vanilla extract
2 cups all-purpose flour
1 teaspoon salt
⅔ cup (of each) HERSHEY'S® Semi-Sweet Chocolate Chips, REESE'S® Peanut Butter Chips, and HERSHEY'S® Premier White Chips
Chocolate Chip Drizzle (recipe follows)

1. Heat oven to 350°F. Grease 15½×10½×1-inch jelly-roll pan.

2. Stir together brown sugar and butter in large bowl; beat in eggs and vanilla until smooth. Add flour and salt, beating just until blended; stir in chocolate, peanut butter and white chips. Spread batter into prepared pan.

3. Bake 25 to 30 minutes or until wooden pick inserted in center comes out clean. Cool completely in pan on wire rack. Cut into bars. With tines of fork, drizzle Chocolate Chip Drizzle randomly over bars. *Makes about 72 bars*

Chocolate Chip Drizzle: In small microwave-safe bowl, place ¼ cup HERSHEY'S® Semi-Sweet Chocolate Chips and ¼ teaspoon shortening (do not use butter, margarine, spread or oil). Microwave at HIGH (100%) 30 seconds to 1 minute; stir until chips are melted and mixture is smooth.

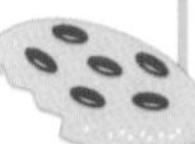

Three Great Tastes Blond Brownies

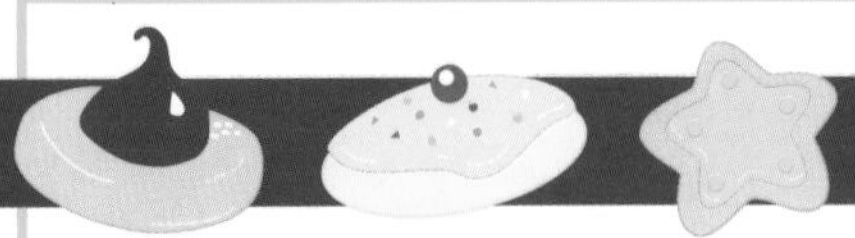

Triple Chocolate Brownies

- **3 squares (1 ounce each) unsweetened chocolate, coarsely chopped**
- **2 squares (1 ounce each) semisweet chocolate, coarsely chopped**
- **½ cup butter**
- **1 cup all-purpose flour**
- **½ teaspoon salt**
- **¼ teaspoon baking powder**
- **1½ cups sugar**
- **3 large eggs**
- **1 teaspoon vanilla**
- **¼ cup sour cream**
- **½ cup milk chocolate chips**
- **Powdered sugar (optional)**

Preheat oven to 350°F. Lightly grease 13×9-inch baking pan.

Place unsweetened chocolate, semisweet chocolate and butter in medium microwavable bowl. Microwave at HIGH 2 minutes or until butter is melted; stir until chocolate is completely melted. Cool to room temperature.

Place flour, salt and baking powder in small bowl; stir to combine.

Beat sugar, eggs and vanilla in large bowl with electric mixer at medium speed until slightly thickened. Beat in chocolate mixture until well combined. Add flour mixture; beat at low speed until blended. Add sour cream; beat at low speed until combined. Stir in milk chocolate chips. Spread mixture evenly into prepared pan.

Bake 20 to 25 minutes or until toothpick inserted into center comes out almost clean. (Do not overbake.) Cool brownies completely in pan on wire rack. Cut into 2-inch squares. Place powdered sugar in fine-mesh strainer; sprinkle over brownies, if desired.

Store tightly covered at room temperature or freeze up to 3 months.

Makes 2 dozen brownies

Triple Chocolate Brownies

A Bevy of Bars

Rich Chocolate Chip Toffee Bars

2⅓ cups all-purpose flour
⅔ cup packed light brown sugar
¾ cup (1½ sticks) butter or margarine
1 egg, slightly beaten
2 cups (12-ounce package) HERSHEY'S® Semi-Sweet Chocolate Chips, divided
1 cup coarsely chopped nuts
1 can (14 ounces) sweetened condensed milk (not evaporated milk)
1¾ cups (10-ounce package) SKOR® English Toffee Bits, divided

1. Heat oven to 350°F. Grease 13×9×2-inch baking pan.

2. Stir together flour and brown sugar in large bowl. Cut in butter with pastry blender until mixture resembles coarse crumbs. Add egg; mix well. Stir in 1½ cups chocolate chips and nuts. Reserve 1½ cups mixture. Press remaining crumb mixture onto bottom of prepared pan.

3. Bake 10 minutes. Pour sweetened condensed milk evenly over hot crust. Top with 1½ cups toffee bits. Sprinkle reserved crumb mixture and remaining ½ cup chips over top.

4. Bake 25 to 30 minutes or until golden brown. Sprinkle with remaining ¼ cup toffee bits. Cool completely in pan on wire rack. Cut into bars. *Makes about 36 bars*

Rich Chocolate Chip Toffee Bars

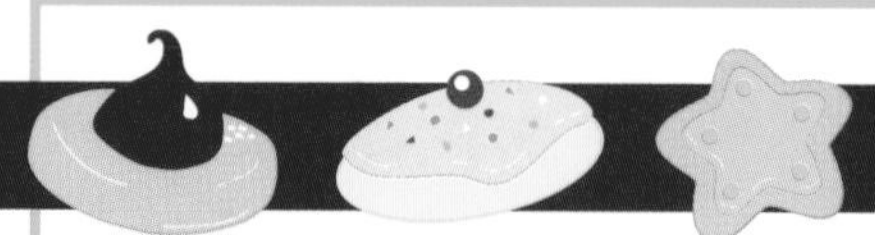

Choco Cheesecake Squares

- **1/3 cup butter, softened**
- **1/3 cup packed light brown sugar**
- **1 cup plus 1 tablespoon all-purpose flour, divided**
- **1/2 cup chopped pecans (optional)**
- **1 cup semisweet chocolate chips**
- **1 package (8 ounces) cream cheese, softened**
- **1/4 cup granulated sugar**
- **1 large egg**
- **1 teaspoon vanilla**

Preheat oven to 350°F. Grease 8-inch square baking pan; set aside. Beat butter and brown sugar in large bowl until light and fluffy. Add 1 cup flour. Beat until well combined. Stir in nuts, if desired. (Mixture will be crumbly.) Press evenly into prepared pan. Bake 15 minutes.

Place chocolate chips in glass measuring cup. Melt in microwave oven at HIGH 2½ to 3 minutes, stirring after 2 minutes. Beat cream cheese and granulated sugar in medium bowl until light and fluffy. Add remaining 1 tablespoon flour, egg and vanilla; beat until smooth. Gradually stir in melted chocolate, mixing well. Pour cream cheese mixture over partially baked crust. Return to oven; bake 15 minutes or until set. Remove pan to wire rack; cool completely. Cut into 2-inch squares. *Makes about 16 squares*

Buttery Lemon Bars

CRUST

- **1¼ cups all-purpose flour**
- **½ cup butter, softened**
- **¼ cup powdered sugar**
- **½ teaspoon vanilla**

FILLING

- **1 cup granulated sugar**
- **2 eggs**
- **⅓ cup fresh lemon juice**
- **2 tablespoons all-purpose flour**
- **Grated peel of 1 lemon**
- **Powdered sugar**

1. Preheat oven to 350°F.

2. Combine all crust ingredients in small bowl. Beat at low speed 2 to 3 minutes until mixture is crumbly. Press onto bottom of 8-inch square baking pan. Bake 15 to 20 minutes or until edges are lightly browned.

3. Combine all filling ingredients except powdered sugar in small bowl. Beat at low speed until well mixed.

4. Pour filling over hot crust. Continue baking 15 to 18 minutes or until filling is set. Sprinkle with powdered sugar; cool completely. Cut into bars; sprinkle again with powdered sugar. *Makes about 16 bars*

Choco Cheesecake Squares

Mini Kisses™ Coconut Macaroon Bars

- **3¾ cups (10-ounce package) MOUNDS® Sweetened Coconut Flakes**
- **¾ cup sugar**
- **¼ cup all-purpose flour**
- **¼ teaspoon salt**
- **3 egg whites**
- **1 whole egg, slightly beaten**
- **1 teaspoon almond extract**
- **1 cup HERSHEY®S MINI KISSES™ Milk Chocolate Baking Pieces**

1. Heat oven to 350°F. Lightly grease 9-inch square baking pan.

2. Stir together coconut, sugar, flour and salt in large bowl. Add egg whites, whole egg and almond extract; stir until well blended. Stir in MINI KISSES. Spread mixture into prepared pan, covering all chocolate pieces with coconut mixture.

3. Bake 35 minutes or until lightly browned. Cool completely in pan on wire rack. Cover with foil; allow to stand at room temperature about 8 hours or overnight. Cut into bars.

Makes about 24 bars

Variation: Omit MINI KISSES in batter. Immediately after removing pan from oven, place desired number of chocolate pieces on top, pressing down lightly. Cool completely. Cut into bars.

Prep Time: 15 minutes
Bake Time: 35 minutes
Cool Time: 9 hours

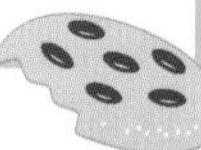

Mini Kisses™ Coconut Macaroon Bars

Chocolate Cheesecake Bars

CRUST

1 cup graham cracker crumbs
¼ cup firmly packed brown sugar
⅓ Butter Flavor* CRISCO® Stick *or* ⅓ cup Butter Flavor* CRISCO® all-vegetable shortening, melted

FILLING

1 package (8 ounces) cream cheese, softened
½ cup granulated sugar
3 tablespoons cocoa
2 eggs
1 tablespoon all-purpose flour
½ teaspoon vanilla

TOPPING

2 tablespoons Butter Flavor* CRISCO® Stick *or* 2 tablespoons Butter Flavor* CRISCO® all-vegetable shortening
1 package (3 ounces) cream cheese, softened
1 cup powdered sugar
½ teaspoon vanilla

**Butter Flavor Crisco® is artificially flavored.*

1. Heat oven to 350°F. Place cooling rack on countertop.

2. For crust, combine graham cracker crumbs and brown sugar. Stir in melted shortening. Press into ungreased 8-inch square baking pan.

3. Bake at 350°F for 10 minutes. *Do not overbake.*

4. For filling, beat 8-ounce package cream cheese in small bowl at medium speed of electric mixer until smooth. Add, one at a time, granulated sugar, cocoa, eggs, flour and vanilla. Mix well after each addition. Pour over baked crust.

5. Bake for 30 minutes. *Do not overbake.* Cool to room temperature on cooling rack.

6. For topping, combine 2 tablespoons shortening and 3-ounce package cream cheese in small bowl. Beat at medium speed until well blended. Add powdered sugar and vanilla. Beat until smooth. Spread over filling. Cut into bars about 2×1½ inches. Refrigerate. *Makes 20 bars*

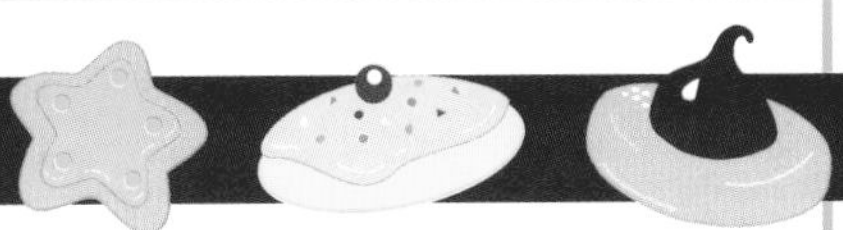

Mott's® Chewy Oatmeal Raisin Squares

1 cup raisins
1 cup rolled oats
¾ cup boiling water
1 cup granulated sugar
½ cup MOTT'S® Natural Apple Sauce
¼ cup MOTT'S® Grandma's® Molasses
1 whole egg
2 egg whites, lightly beaten
2 tablespoons vegetable oil
1 teaspoon vanilla extract
2 cups all-purpose flour
1½ teaspoons baking powder
½ teaspoon baking soda
1 teaspoon cinnamon
½ teaspoon ground cloves
½ teaspoon salt

1. Preheat oven to 400°F. Spray 13×9-inch baking pan with nonstick cooking spray.

2. In medium bowl, combine raisins and rolled oats. Pour boiling water over ingredients; mix until moistened. Set aside.

3. In large bowl, combine sugar, apple sauce, molasses, whole egg, egg whites, oil and vanilla.

4. In separate medium bowl, combine flour, baking powder, baking soda, spices and salt.

5. Add flour mixture to apple sauce mixture; mix until ingredients are combined. Stir in raisin-oatmeal mixture.

6. Spread batter evenly into prepared pan. Bake 12 to 15 minutes. Place pan on cooling rack to cool.

7. Let cool 15 minutes before cutting into squares.

Makes 16 servings

Coconut Pecan Bars

1¼ cups granulated sugar, divided
½ cup plus 3 tablespoons all-purpose flour, divided
1½ cups finely chopped pecans, divided
¾ cup (1½ sticks) butter or margarine, softened, divided
2 large eggs
1 tablespoon vanilla extract
1¾ cups "M&M's"® Chocolate Mini Baking Bits, divided
1 cup shredded coconut

Preheat oven to 350°F. Lightly grease 13×9×2-inch baking pan; set aside. In large bowl combine ¾ cup sugar, ½ cup flour and ½ cup nuts; add ¼ cup melted butter and mix well. Press mixture onto bottom of prepared pan. Bake 10 minutes or until set; cool slightly. In large bowl cream remaining ½ cup butter and ½ cup sugar; beat in eggs and vanilla. Combine 1 cup "M&M's"® Chocolate Mini Baking Bits and remaining 3 tablespoons flour; stir into creamed mixture. Spread mixture over cooled crust. Combine coconut and remaining 1 cup nuts; sprinkle over batter. Sprinkle remaining ¾ cup "M&M's"® Chocolate Mini Baking Bits over coconut and nuts; pat down lightly. Bake 25 to 30 minutes or until set. Cool completely. Cut into bars. Store in tightly covered container.

Makes 24 bars

Tip 

Cut brownies and bar cookies into triangles or diamonds for a festive new look. To make serving easy, remove a corner piece first; then remove the rest.

Coconut Pecan Bars

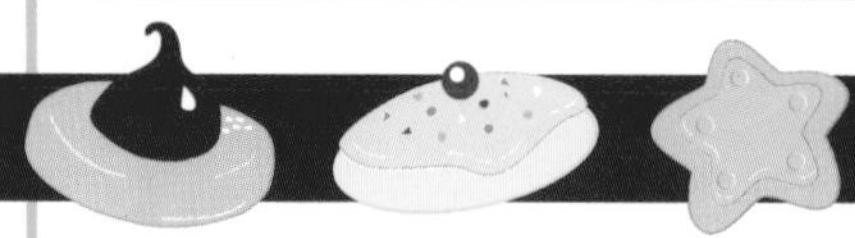

Butterscotch Blondies

- **¾ cup (1½ sticks) butter or margarine, softened**
- **¾ cup packed light brown sugar**
- **½ cup granulated sugar**
- **2 eggs**
- **2 cups all-purpose flour**
- **1 teaspoon baking soda**
- **½ teaspoon salt**
- **1⅔ cups (10-ounce package) HERSHEY®S Butterscotch Chips**
- **1 cup chopped nuts (optional)**

1. Heat oven to 350°F. Grease 13×9×2-inch baking pan.

2. Beat butter, brown sugar and granulated sugar in large bowl until creamy. Add eggs; beat well. Stir together flour, baking soda and salt; gradually add to butter mixture, blending well. Stir in butterscotch chips and nuts, if desired. Spread into prepared pan.

3. Bake 30 to 35 minutes or until top is golden brown and center is set. Cool completely in pan on wire rack. Cut into bars. *Makes about 36 bars*

Orange Chess Bars

CRUST

- **1 package DUNCAN HINES® Moist Deluxe Orange Supreme Cake Mix**
- **½ cup vegetable oil**
- **⅓ cup chopped pecans**

TOPPING

- **1 pound confectioners sugar (3½ to 4 cups)**
- **1 (8-ounce) package cream cheese, softened**
- **2 eggs**
- **2 teaspoons grated orange peel**

1. Preheat oven to 350°F. Grease 13×9-inch baking pan.

2. For crust, combine cake mix, oil and pecans in large bowl. Stir until blended (mixture will be crumbly). Press in bottom of prepared pan.

3. For topping, combine confectioners sugar and cream cheese in large bowl. Beat at low speed with electric mixer until blended. Add eggs and orange peel. Beat at low speed until blended. Pour over crust. Bake 30 to 35 minutes or until topping is set. Cool. Refrigerate until ready to serve. Cut into bars. *Makes about 24 bars*

Butterscotch Blondies

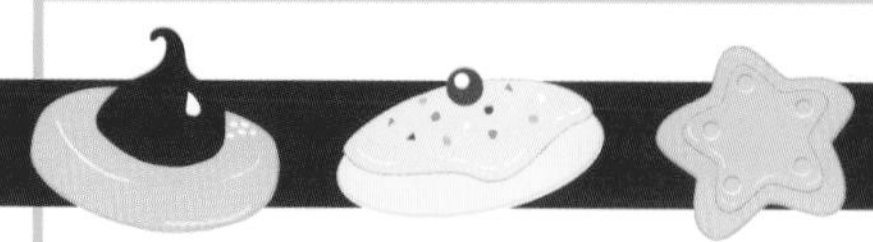

Fruit and Oat Squares

- 1 cup all-purpose flour
- 1 cup uncooked quick oats
- ¾ cup packed light brown sugar
- ½ teaspoon baking soda
- ¼ teaspoon salt
- ¼ teaspoon ground cinnamon
- ⅓ cup margarine or butter, melted
- ¾ cup apricot, cherry or other fruit flavor preserves

1. Preheat oven to 350°F. Spray 9-inch square baking pan with nonstick cooking spray; set aside.

2. Combine flour, oats, brown sugar, baking soda, salt and cinnamon in medium bowl; mix well. Add margarine; stir with fork until mixture is crumbly. Reserve ¾ cup crumb mixture for topping. Press remaining crumb mixture evenly onto bottom of prepared pan. Bake 5 to 7 minutes or until lightly browned. Spread preserves onto crust; sprinkle with reserved crumb mixture.

3. Bake 20 to 25 minutes or until golden brown. Cool completely in pan on wire rack. Cut into 16 squares.

Makes 16 servings

"Everything but the Kitchen Sink" Bar Cookies

- 1 package (18 ounces) refrigerated chocolate chip cookie dough
- 1 jar (7 ounces) marshmallow creme
- ½ cup creamy peanut butter
- 1½ cups toasted corn cereal
- ½ cup miniature candy-coated chocolate pieces

1. Preheat oven to 350°F. Grease 13×9-inch baking pan. Remove dough from wrapper according to package directions.

2. Press dough into prepared baking pan. Bake 13 minutes.

3. Remove baking pan from oven. Drop teaspoonfuls of marshmallow creme and peanut butter over hot cookie base.

4. Bake 1 minute. Carefully spread marshmallow creme and peanut butter over cookie base.

5. Sprinkle cereal and chocolate pieces over melted marshmallow and peanut butter mixture.

6. Bake 7 minutes. Cool completely on wire rack. Cut into 2-inch bars.

Makes 3 dozen bar cookies

Fruit and Oat Squares

Chocolate Peppermint Bars

CRUST

1¾ cups all-purpose flour
1½ cups confectioners sugar
½ cup unsweetened cocoa powder
1 Butter Flavor* CRISCO® Stick or 1 cup Butter Flavor* CRISCO® all-vegetable shortening
2 tablespoons milk

TOPPING

1 package (8 ounces) cream cheese, softened
1 can (14 ounces) sweetened condensed milk
1 egg
1 teaspoon peppermint extract
Red food color
½ cup coarsely crushed hard peppermint candies (about 20 to 24)

**Butter Flavor Crisco® is artificially flavored.*

1. Heat oven to 350°F. Place cooling rack on counter for cooling bars.

2. For crust, combine flour, confectioners sugar and cocoa powder in large bowl. Beat in 1 cup shortening and milk on low speed of electric mixer until mixture is crumbly. Reserve 1¾ cups of mixture for topping. Press remainder into ungreased 13×9-inch baking pan.

3. Bake at 350°F for 15 minutes.

4. For topping, beat cream cheese in medium bowl at medium speed. Beat in condensed milk gradually. Beat until mixture is smooth. Beat in egg and peppermint extract. Add food color until desired shade of red is achieved. Mix well. Stir in chopped candies.

5. Pour mixture over baked crust. Sprinkle reserved crumb topping evenly over cream cheese filling.

6. Bake at 350°F for 25 to 30 minutes or until filling is set. *Do not overbake.* Cool in pan. Loosen from sides of pan with knife or spatula. Refrigerate until ready to serve. Cut into bars approximately 2×1½-inches. *Makes 3 dozen bars*

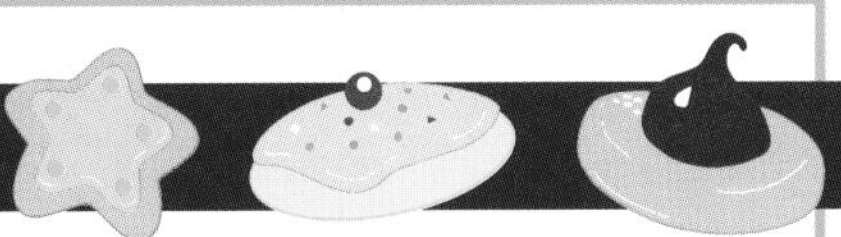

Brownie Caramel Pecan Bars

½ cup sugar
2 tablespoons butter or margarine
2 tablespoons water
2 cups (12-ounce package) HERSHEY'S® Semi-Sweet Chocolate Chips, divided
2 eggs
1 teaspoon vanilla extract
⅔ cup all-purpose flour
¼ teaspoon baking soda
¼ teaspoon salt
Caramel Topping (recipe follows)
1 cup pecan pieces

1. Heat oven to 350°F. Line 9-inch square baking pan with foil, extending foil over edges of pan. Grease and flour foil.

2. In medium saucepan, combine sugar, butter and water; cook over low heat, stirring constantly, until mixture boils. Remove from heat. Immediately add 1 cup chocolate chips; stir until melted. Beat in eggs and vanilla until well blended. Stir together flour, baking soda and salt; stir into chocolate mixture. Spread batter into prepared pan.

3. Bake 15 to 20 minutes or until brownies begin to pull away from sides of pan. Meanwhile, prepare Caramel Topping. Remove brownies from oven; immediately and carefully spread with prepared topping. Sprinkle remaining 1 cup chips and pecans over topping. Cool completely in pan on wire rack, being careful not to disturb chips while soft. Lift out of pan. Cut into bars. *Makes about 16 bars*

Caramel Topping: Remove wrappers from 25 caramels. In medium microwave-safe bowl, place ¼ cup (½ stick) butter or margarine, caramels and 2 tablespoons milk. Microwave at HIGH (100%) 1 minute; stir. Microwave an additional 1 to 2 minutes, stirring every 30 seconds, or until caramels are melted and mixture is smooth when stirred. Use immediately.

Oatmeal Toffee Bars

- **1 cup (2 sticks) butter or margarine, softened**
- **½ cup packed light brown sugar**
- **½ cup granulated sugar**
- **2 eggs**
- **1 teaspoon vanilla extract**
- **1½ cups all-purpose flour**
- **1 teaspoon baking soda**
- **½ teaspoon ground cinnamon**
- **½ teaspoon salt**
- **3 cups quick-cooking or regular rolled oats**
- **1¾ cups (10-ounce package) SKOR® English Toffee Bits or 1¾ cups HEATH® Bits 'O Brickle, divided**

1. Heat oven to 350°F. Grease 13×9×2-inch baking pan.

2. Beat butter, brown sugar and granulated sugar in large bowl until well blended. Add eggs and vanilla; beat well. Stir together flour, baking soda, cinnamon and salt; gradually add to butter mixture, beating until well blended. Stir in oats and 1⅓ cups toffee bits (mixture will be stiff). Spread mixture into prepared pan.

3. Bake 25 minutes or until wooden pick inserted in center comes out clean. Immediately sprinkle remaining toffee bits over surface. Cool completely in pan on wire rack. Cut into bars. *Makes about 36 bars*

Tip: Bar cookies can be cut into different shapes for variety. To cut into triangles, cut cookie bars into 2- to 3-inch squares, then diagonally cut each square in half. To make diamond shapes, cut parallel lines 2 inches apart across the length of the pan, then cut diagonal lines 2 inches apart.

Oatmeal Toffee Bars

Spiced Chocolate Pecan Squares

COOKIE BASE

- **1 cup all-purpose flour**
- **½ cup packed light brown sugar**
- **½ teaspoon baking soda**
- **¼ cup (½ stick) butter or margarine, softened**

TOPPING

- **1 package (8 ounces) semi-sweet chocolate baking squares**
- **2 large eggs**
- **¼ cup packed light brown sugar**
- **¼ cup light corn syrup**
- **2 tablespoons FRENCH'S® Worcestershire Sauce**
- **1 tablespoon vanilla extract**
- **1½ cups chopped pecans or walnuts, divided**

Preheat oven to 375°F. To prepare cookie base, place flour, ½ cup sugar and baking soda in food processor or bowl of electric mixer. Process or mix 10 seconds. Add butter. Process or beat 30 seconds or until mixture resembles fine crumbs. Press evenly into bottom of greased 9-inch baking pan. Bake 15 minutes.

Meanwhile, to prepare topping, place chocolate in microwave-safe bowl. Microwave, uncovered, on HIGH 2 minutes or until chocolate is melted, stirring until chocolate is smooth; set aside.

Place eggs, ¼ cup sugar, corn syrup, Worcestershire and vanilla in food processor or bowl of electric mixer. Process or beat until well blended. Add melted chocolate. Process or beat until smooth. Stir in 1 cup nuts. Pour chocolate mixture over cookie base. Sprinkle with remaining ½ cup nuts. Bake 40 minutes or until toothpick inserted into center comes out with slightly fudgy crumbs. (Cookie will be slightly puffed along edges.) Cool completely on wire rack. To serve, cut into squares. *Makes 16 servings*

Prep Time: 20 minutes
Cook Time: 55 minutes

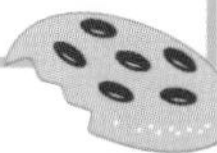

Spiced Chocolate Pecan Squares

Raspberry Coconut Layer Bars

1⅔ cups graham cracker crumbs
½ cup butter or margarine, melted
2⅔ cups (7-ounce package) flaked coconut
1¼ cups (14-ounce can) CARNATION® Sweetened Condensed Milk
1 cup red raspberry jam or preserves
⅓ cup finely chopped walnuts, toasted
½ cup NESTLÉ® TOLL HOUSE® Semi-Sweet Chocolate Morsels, melted
¼ cup (1½ ounces) chopped NESTLÉ® Premier White Baking Bar, melted

COMBINE graham cracker crumbs and butter in medium bowl. Spread evenly over bottom of 13×9-inch baking pan, pressing to make compact crust. Sprinkle with coconut; pour sweetened condensed milk evenly over coconut.

BAKE in preheated 350°F. oven 20 to 25 minutes or until lightly browned; cool.

SPREAD jam over coconut layer; chill for 3 to 4 hours. Sprinkle with walnuts. Drizzle semi-sweet chocolate then white chocolate over top layer to make lacy effect; chill. Cut into 3×1½-inch bars. *Makes 24 bar cookies*

Tip

Crush graham crackers quickly and easily by placing them in a sealed plastic food storage bag, then running a rolling pin over the bag several times to pulverize them.

Raspberry Coconut Layer Bars

Caramel Apple Bars

CRUST

- **¾ Butter Flavor* CRISCO® Stick or ¾ cup Butter Flavor* CRISCO® all-vegetable shortening plus additional for greasing**
- **1 cup firmly packed light brown sugar**
- **1 egg**
- **1½ cups all-purpose flour**
- **½ teaspoon salt**
- **½ teaspoon baking soda**
- **1¾ cups quick oats, uncooked**

FILLING

- **3 to 4 Granny Smith or Golden Delicious apples, peeled and cut into ½-inch dice (about 4 cups)**
- **2 tablespoons all-purpose flour**
- **1 teaspoon lemon juice**
- **1 bag (14 ounces) caramel candy, unwrapped**

**Butter Flavor Crisco® is artificially flavored.*

1. Heat oven to 350°F. Grease 13×9×2-inch baking pan with shortening.

2. For crust, combine shortening and brown sugar in large bowl. Beat at medium speed of electric mixer. Add egg to creamed mixture. Beat until well blended.

3. Combine 1½ cups flour, salt and baking soda. Add to creamed mixture gradually. Add in oats. Mix until blended. Reserve 1¼ cups of mixture for topping. Press remaining mixture into prepared pan.

4. Bake at 350°F for 10 minutes.

5. For filling, toss apples with 2 tablespoons flour and lemon juice. Distribute apple mixture evenly over partially baked crust. Press in lightly.

6. Place caramels in microwave-safe bowl. Microwave at HIGH (100%) for 1 minute. Stir. Repeat until caramels are melted. Drizzle melted caramel evenly over apples. Crumble reserved topping evenly over caramel.

7. Bake at 350°F for 30 to 40 minutes, or until apples are tender and top is golden brown. Loosen caramel from sides of pan with knife. Cool completely. *Do not overbake.* Cut into 1½-inch bars. Cover tightly with plastic wrap to store.

Makes about 4 dozen bars

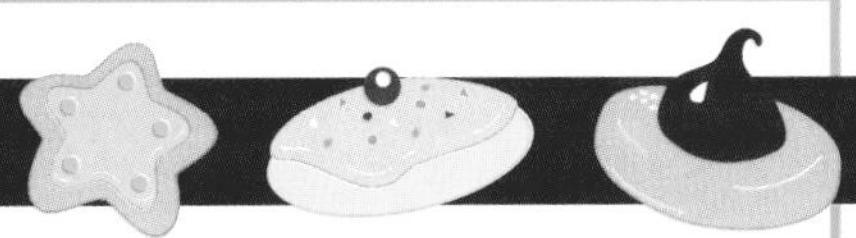

Baker's® Mississippi Mud Bars

- **½ cup (1 stick) butter or margarine**
- **¾ cup firmly packed brown sugar**
- **1 egg**
- **1 teaspoon vanilla**
- **1 cup flour**
- **½ teaspoon baking soda**
- **¼ teaspoon salt**
- **1 package (8 squares) BAKER'S® Semi-Sweet Baking Chocolate, chopped, divided**
- **1 package (6 squares) BAKER'S® Premium White Baking Chocolate, chopped, divided**
- **1 cup chopped walnuts, divided**

HEAT oven to 350°F. Line 9-inch square baking pan with foil. Grease foil.

BEAT butter, sugar, egg and vanilla in large bowl with electric mixer on medium speed until light and fluffy. Mix in flour, baking soda and salt. Stir in ½ each of the semi-sweet and white chocolates and ½ cup of the walnuts. Spread in prepared pan.

BAKE 25 minutes or until toothpick inserted in center comes out almost clean. DO NOT OVERBAKE. Remove from oven. Sprinkle with remaining semi-sweet and white chocolates. Cover with foil. Let stand 5 minutes or until chocolates are melted. Swirl with knife to marbleize. Sprinkle with remaining ½ cup walnuts. Cool in pan on wire rack until chocolate is firm. Cut into 2×1-inch bars. Store in tightly covered container.

Makes 3 dozen bars

Prep Time: 20 minutes
Bake Time: 25 minutes

No-Bake Pineapple Marmalade Squares

- 1 cup graham cracker crumbs
- ½ cup plus 2 tablespoons sugar, divided
- ¼ cup light margarine, melted
- 1 cup fat free or light sour cream
- 4 ounces light cream cheese, softened
- ¼ cup orange marmalade or apricot fruit spread, divided
- 1 can (20 ounces) DOLE® Crushed Pineapple
- 1 envelope unflavored gelatin

• Combine graham cracker crumbs, 2 tablespoons sugar and margarine in 8-inch square glass baking dish; pat mixture firmly and evenly onto bottom of dish. Freeze 10 minutes.

• Beat sour cream, cream cheese, remaining ½ cup sugar and 1 tablespoon marmalade in medium bowl until smooth and blended; set aside.

• Drain pineapple; reserve ¼ cup juice.

• Sprinkle gelatin over reserved juice in small saucepan; let stand 1 minute. Cook and stir over low heat until gelatin dissolves.

• Beat gelatin mixture into sour cream mixture until well blended. Spoon mixture evenly over crust.

• Stir together pineapple and remaining 3 tablespoons marmalade in small bowl until blended. Evenly spoon over sour cream filling. Cover and refrigerate 2 hours or until firm.

Makes 16 servings

Oat-Y Nut Bars

- ½ cup butter
- ½ cup honey
- ¼ cup corn syrup
- ¼ cup packed brown sugar
- 2¾ cups uncooked quick oats
- ⅔ cup raisins
- ½ cup salted peanuts

Preheat oven to 300°F. Grease 9-inch square baking pan. Melt butter with honey, corn syrup and brown sugar in medium saucepan over medium heat, stirring constantly. Bring to a boil; boil 8 minutes until mixture thickens slightly. Stir in oats, raisins and peanuts until well blended. Press evenly into prepared pan.

Bake 45 to 50 minutes or until golden brown. Place pan on wire rack; score top into 2-inch squares. Cool completely. Cut into bars.

Makes 16 bars

No-Bake Pineapple Marmalade Squares

Fruit and Nut Bars

- **1 cup unsifted all-purpose flour**
- **1 cup quick oats**
- **⅔ cup brown sugar**
- **2 teaspoons baking soda**
- **½ teaspoon salt**
- **½ teaspoon cinnamon**
- **⅔ cup buttermilk**
- **3 tablespoons vegetable oil**
- **2 egg whites, lightly beaten**
- **1 Washington Golden Delicious apple, cored and chopped**
- **½ cup dried cranberries or raisins, chopped**
- **¼ cup chopped nuts**
- **2 tablespoons flaked coconut (optional)**

1. Heat oven to 375°F. Lightly grease 9-inch square baking pan. In large mixing bowl, combine flour, oats, brown sugar, baking soda, salt and cinnamon; stir to blend.

2. Add buttermilk, oil and egg whites; beat with electric mixer just until mixed. Stir in apple, dried fruit and nuts; spread evenly in pan and top with coconut, if desired. Bake 20 to 25 minutes or until cake tester inserted in center comes out clean. Cool and cut into 10 bars. *Makes 10 bars*

Favorite recipe from Washington Apple Commission

Tip 

Always use the pan size called for in the recipe. Substituting a different pan will affect the cookies' texture—a smaller pan will give the bars a more cakelike texture and a larger pan will produce a flatter bar with a drier texture.

Fruit and Nut Bars

Chippy Chewy Bars

- ½ cup (1 stick) butter or margarine
- 1½ cups graham cracker crumbs
- 1⅔ cups (10-ounce package) REESE'S® Peanut Butter Chips, divided
- 1½ cups MOUNDS® Sweetened Coconut Flakes
- 1 can (14 ounces) sweetened condensed milk (not evaporated milk)
- 1 cup HERSHEY'S Semi-Sweet Chocolate Chips or HERSHEY'S MINI CHIPS™ Semi-Sweet Chocolate
- 1½ teaspoons shortening (do not use butter, margarine, spread or oil)

1. Heat oven to 350°F.

2. Place butter in 13×9×2-inch baking pan. Heat in oven until melted. Remove pan from oven. Sprinkle graham cracker crumbs evenly over butter; press down with fork. Layer 1 cup peanut butter chips over crumbs; sprinkle coconut over peanut butter chips. Layer remaining ⅔ cup peanut butter chips over coconut; drizzle sweetened condensed milk evenly over top. Press down firmly.

3. Bake 20 minutes or until lightly browned.

4. Place chocolate chips and shortening in small microwave-safe bowl. Microwave at HIGH (100%) 1 minute; stir. If necessary, microwave at HIGH an additional 15 seconds at a time, stirring after each heating, just until chips are melted when stirred. Drizzle evenly over top of baked mixture. Cool completely in pan on wire rack. Cut into bars.

Makes about 48 bars

Note: *For lighter drizzle, use ½ cup chocolate chips and ¾ teaspoon shortening. Microwave at HIGH 30 seconds to 1 minute; stir. If necessary, microwave at HIGH an additional 15 seconds at a time, stirring after each heating, just until chips are melted when stirred.*

Chippy Chewy Bars

Oatmeal Praline Cheese Bars

COOKIE BASE

- **1¼ cups firmly packed light brown sugar**
- **¾ Butter Flavor* CRISCO® Stick or ¾ cup Butter Flavor* CRISCO® all-vegetable shortening plus additional for greasing**
- **1 egg**
- **⅓ cup milk**
- **1½ teaspoons vanilla**
- **1½ cups quick oats, uncooked**
- **1 cup all-purpose flour**
- **1 cup finely chopped pecans**
- **¼ cup toasted wheat germ**
- **½ teaspoon baking soda**
- **½ teaspoon salt**
- **½ teaspoon cinnamon**

TOPPING

- **1 package (8 ounces) cream cheese, softened**
- **⅓ cup firmly packed light brown sugar**
- **2 eggs**
- **½ teaspoon vanilla**
- **½ teaspoon salt**
- **½ cup almond brickle chips**
- **½ cup finely chopped pecans**

**Butter Flavor Crisco® is artificially flavored.*

1. Heat oven to 350°F. Grease 13×9-inch baking pan. Place cooling rack on countertop.

2. For cookie base, place brown sugar, ¾ cup shortening, egg, milk and vanilla in large bowl. Beat at medium speed of electric mixer until well blended.

3. Combine oats, flour, pecans, wheat germ, baking soda, salt and cinnamon. Add to shortening mixture; beat at low speed just until blended.

4. Spread dough onto bottom of prepared pan.

5. Bake at 350°F for 15 to 17 minutes or until surface is light golden brown and edges pull away from sides of pan. *Do not overbake.*

6. For topping, place cream cheese, brown sugar, eggs, vanilla and salt in medium bowl. Beat at medium speed of electric mixer until smooth. Pour mixture over cookie base. Sprinkle with almond brickle chips and pecans.

7. Bake 15 to 17 minutes longer or until topping is set. *Do not overbake.* Cool completely on cooling rack. Cut into 2×1½-inch bars. Refrigerate.

Makes about 3 dozen bars

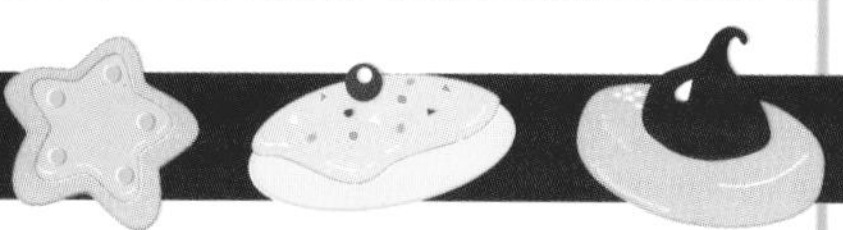

Baker's® Chocolate Pecan Pie Bars

- **2 cups flour**
- **2 cups sugar, divided**
- **1 cup (2 sticks) butter or margarine, softened**
- **¼ teaspoon salt**
- **1½ cups corn syrup**
- **6 squares BAKER'S® Semi-Sweet Baking Chocolate**
- **4 eggs, slightly beaten**
- **1½ teaspoons vanilla**
- **2½ cups chopped pecans**

HEAT oven to 350°F. Lightly grease sides of 15×10×1-inch baking pan.

BEAT flour, ½ cup of the sugar, butter and salt in large bowl with electric mixer on medium speed until mixture resembles coarse crumbs. Press firmly and evenly into prepared baking pan. Bake 20 minutes or until lightly browned.

MICROWAVE corn syrup and chocolate in large microwavable bowl on HIGH 2½ minutes or until chocolate is almost melted, stirring halfway through heating time. Stir until chocolate is completely melted. Mix in remaining 1½ cups sugar, eggs and vanilla until blended. Stir in pecans. Pour filling over hot crust; spread evenly.

BAKE 35 minutes or until filling is firm around edges and slightly soft in center. Cool completely in pan on wire rack.

Makes 48 bars

Melting Chocolate on Top of Stove: Heat corn syrup and chocolate in heavy 3-quart saucepan on very low heat, stirring constantly until chocolate is just melted. Remove from heat. Continue as directed above.

Prep Time: 20 minutes
Bake Time: 55 minutes

No-Bake Chocolate Oat Bars

1 cup butter
½ cup firmly packed brown sugar
1 teaspoon vanilla
3 cups uncooked quick-cooking oats
1 cup semisweet chocolate chips
½ cup crunchy or creamy peanut butter

Grease 9-inch square baking pan. Melt butter in large saucepan over medium heat. Add brown sugar and vanilla; mix well.

Stir in oats. Cook over low heat 2 to 3 minutes or until ingredients are well blended. Press half of mixture into prepared pan. Use back of large spoon to spread mixture evenly.

Meanwhile, melt chocolate chips in small heavy saucepan over low heat, stirring occasionally. Stir in peanut butter. Pour chocolate mixture over oat mixture in pan; spread evenly with knife or back of spoon. Crumble remaining oat mixture over chocolate layer, pressing in gently. Cover and refrigerate 2 to 3 hours or overnight.

Bring to room temperature before cutting into bars. (Bars can be frozen; let thaw about 10 minutes or more before serving.)

Makes 32 bars

Tip

Cookies, brownies and bars always make great gifts. Place them in a paper-lined tin or on a decorative plate covered with plastic wrap and tied with colorful ribbon. For a special touch, include the recipe.

No-Bake Chocolate Oat Bars

Chocolate Chip Cookie Bars

- **1¼ cups firmly packed light brown sugar**
- **¾ Butter Flavor* CRISCO® Stick or ¾ cup Butter Flavor* CRISCO® all-vegetable shortening plus additional for greasing**
- **2 tablespoons milk**
- **1 tablespoon vanilla**
- **1 egg**
- **1¾ cups all-purpose flour**
- **1 teaspoon salt**
- **¾ teaspoon baking soda**
- **1 cup (6 ounces) semisweet chocolate chips**
- **1 cup coarsely chopped pecans** (optional)**

**Butter Flavor Crisco® is artificially flavored.*

***If pecans are omitted, add an additional ½ cup semisweet chocolate chips.*

1. Heat oven to 350°F. Grease 13×9-inch baking pan. Place cooling rack on countertop.

2. Place brown sugar, shortening, milk and vanilla in large bowl. Beat at medium speed of electric mixer until well blended. Add egg; beat well.

3. Combine flour, salt and baking soda. Add to shortening mixture; beat at low speed just until blended. Stir in chocolate chips and pecans, if desired.

4. Press dough evenly onto bottom of prepared pan.

5. Bake at 350°F for 20 to 25 minutes or until lightly browned and firm in the center. *Do not overbake.* Cool completely on cooling rack. Cut into 2×1½-inch bars.

Makes about 3 dozen bars

Chocolate Chip Cookie Bars

Strawberry Oat Bars

- 1 cup butter, softened
- 1 cup firmly packed light brown sugar
- 2 cups uncooked quick oats
- 1 cup all-purpose flour
- 2 teaspoons baking soda
- ½ teaspoon ground cinnamon
- ¼ teaspoon salt
- 1 can (21 ounces) strawberry pie filling
- ¾ teaspoon almond extract

Preheat oven to 375°F. Beat butter in large bowl with electric mixer at medium speed until smooth. Add brown sugar; beat until well blended.

Combine oats, flour, baking soda, cinnamon and salt in large bowl; mix well. Add flour mixture to butter mixture, beating on low speed until well blended and crumbly.

Spread ⅔ of crumb mixture in bottom of ungreased 13×9-inch baking pan, pressing down to form firm layer. Bake 15 minutes; let cool 5 minutes on wire rack

Meanwhile, place strawberry filling in food processor or blender; process until smooth. Stir in almond extract.

Pour strawberry mixture over partially baked crust. Sprinkle remaining crumb mixture evenly over strawberry layer.

Return pan to oven; bake 20 to 25 minutes or until topping is golden brown and filling is slightly bubbly. Let cool completely on wire rack before cutting into bars.

Makes about 4 dozen bars

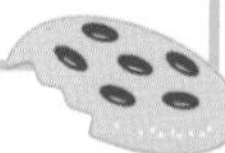

Strawberry Oat Bars

Chocolate Caramel Bars

CRUST

MAZOLA NO STICK® Cooking Spray
2 cups flour
¾ cup (1½ sticks) MAZOLA® Margarine or butter, slightly softened
½ cup packed brown sugar
¼ teaspoon salt
1 cup (6 ounces) semisweet or milk chocolate chips

CARAMEL

¾ cup (1½ sticks) MAZOLA® Margarine or butter
1 cup packed brown sugar
⅓ cup KARO® Light or Dark Corn Syrup
1 teaspoon vanilla
½ cup chopped walnuts

FOR CRUST:

1. Preheat oven to 350°F. Spray 13×9×2-inch baking pan with cooking spray.

2. In large bowl with mixer at medium speed, beat flour, margarine, brown sugar and salt until mixture resembles coarse crumbs; press firmly into prepared pan.

3. Bake 15 minutes or until golden brown. Sprinkle chocolate chips over hot crust; let stand 5 minutes or until shiny and soft. Spread chocolate evenly; set aside.

FOR CARAMEL:

4. In heavy 2-quart saucepan combine margarine, brown sugar, corn syrup and vanilla. Stirring frequently, bring to a boil over medium heat. Without stirring, boil 4 minutes.

5. Pour over chocolate; spread evenly. Sprinkle with walnuts.

6. Cool completely. Refrigerate 1 hour to set chocolate; let stand at room temperature until softened.

7. Cut into 48 (1-inch) bars. Store in tightly covered container at room temperature. *Makes about 4 dozen bars*

Prep Time: 30 minutes
Bake Time: 15 minutes, plus cooling and chilling

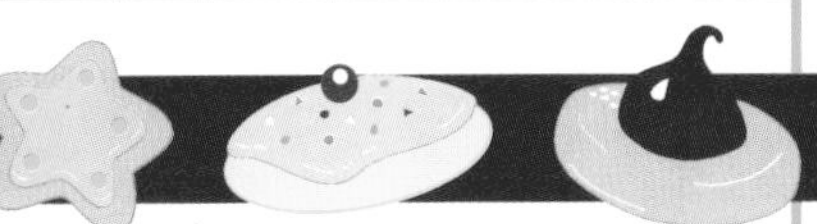

Double Chocolate Crispy Bars

- **6 cups crispy rice cereal**
- **½ cup peanut butter**
- **⅓ cup butter or margarine**
- **2 squares (1 ounce each) unsweetened chocolate**
- **1 package (8 ounces) marshmallows**
- **1 cup (6 ounces) semisweet chocolate chips or 6 ounces bittersweet chocolate, chopped**
- **6 ounces white chocolate, chopped**
- **2 teaspoons shortening, divided**

Preheat oven to 350°F. Line 13×9-inch pan with waxed paper. Spread cereal on cookie sheet; toast in oven 10 minutes or until crispy; place in large bowl. Meanwhile, combine peanut butter, butter and unsweetened chocolate in large heavy saucepan. Stir over low heat until chocolate is melted. Add marshmallows; stir until melted and smooth. Pour chocolate mixture over cereal; mix until evenly coated. Press firmly into prepared pan. Place semisweet and white chocolates into separate bowls. Add 1 teaspoon shortening to each bowl. Place bowls over very warm water; stir until chocolates are melted. Spread top of bars with melted semisweet chocolate; cool until chocolate is set. Turn bars out of pan onto a sheet of waxed paper, chocolate side down. Remove waxed paper from bottom of bars; spread white chocolate over surface. Cool until chocolate is set. Cut into 2×1½-inch bars using sharp, thin knife.

Makes about 3 dozen bars

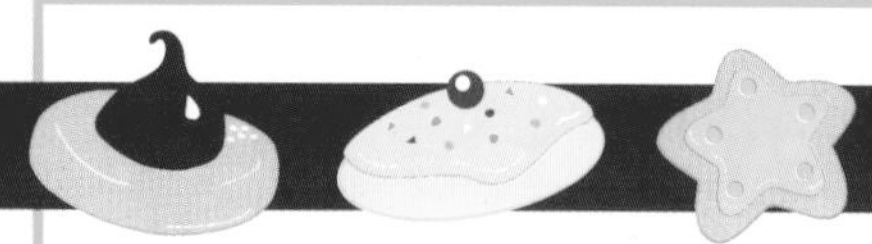

Cinnamony Apple Streusel Bars

- 1¼ cups graham cracker crumbs
- 1¼ cups all-purpose flour
- ¾ cup packed brown sugar, divided
- ¼ cup granulated sugar
- 1 teaspoon ground cinnamon
- ¾ cup butter or margarine, melted
- 2 cups chopped apples (2 medium apples, cored and peeled)
- Glaze (recipe follows)

Preheat oven to 350°F. Grease 13×9-inch baking pan. Combine graham cracker crumbs, flour, ½ cup brown sugar, granulated sugar, cinnamon and melted butter in large bowl until well blended; reserve 1 cup. Press remaining crumb mixture into bottom of prepared pan.

Bake 8 minutes. Remove from oven; set aside. Toss apples with remaining ¼ cup brown sugar in medium bowl until brown sugar is dissolved; arrange apples over baked crust. Sprinkle reserved 1 cup crumb mixture over filling. Bake 30 to 35 minutes more or until apples are tender. Remove pan to wire rack; cool completely. Drizzle with Glaze. Cut into bars.

Makes 3 dozen bars

Glaze: *Combine ½ cup powdered sugar and 1 tablespoon milk in small bowl until well blended.*

Peachy Oatmeal Bars

CRUMB MIXTURE

- 1½ cups all-purpose flour
- 1 cup uncooked rolled oats
- ½ cup sugar
- ¾ cup butter, melted
- ½ teaspoon baking soda
- ¼ teaspoon salt
- 2 teaspoons almond extract

FILLING

- ¾ cup peach preserves
- ⅓ cup flaked coconut

Preheat oven to 350°F. Grease 9-inch square baking pan.

Combine flour, oats, sugar, butter, baking soda, salt and almond extract in large bowl. Beat with electric mixer at low speed 1 to 2 minutes until mixture is crumbly. Reserve ¾ cup crumb mixture; press remaining crumb mixture onto bottom of prepared baking pan.

Spread peach preserves to within ½ inch of edge of crumb mixture; sprinkle reserved crumb mixture and coconut over top. Bake 22 to 27 minutes or until edges are lightly browned. Cool completely. Cut into bars.

Makes 24 to 30 bars

Cinnamony Apple Streusel Bars

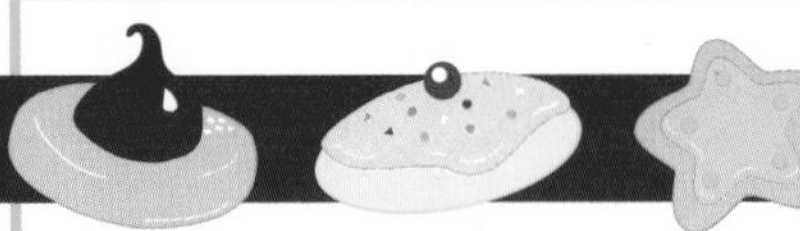

Oatmeal Chocolate Cherry Bars

½ cup (1 stick) butter or margarine, softened
¼ cup solid vegetable shortening
1 cup firmly packed light brown sugar
1 large egg
1 teaspoon vanilla extract
2½ cups quick-cooking or old-fashioned oats, uncooked
1 cup all-purpose flour
1 teaspoon baking soda
1¾ cups "M&M's"® Chocolate Mini Baking Bits, divided
1 cup dried cherries, plumped*

**To plump cherries, pour 1½ cups boiling water over cherries and let stand 10 minutes. Drain well and use as directed.*

Preheat oven to 350°F. Lightly grease 13×9×2-inch baking pan; set aside. In large bowl cream butter and shortening until light and fluffy; beat in sugar, egg and vanilla. In medium bowl combine oats, flour and baking soda; blend into creamed mixture. Stir in 1¼ cups "M&M's"® Chocolate Mini Baking Bits and cherries. Spread batter evenly in prepared pan; top with remaining ½ cup "M&M's"® Chocolate Mini Baking Bits. Bake 25 to 30 minutes or until toothpick inserted in center comes out clean. Cool completely. Cut into squares. Store in tightly covered container. *Makes 24 bars*

Variation: *To make cookies, drop dough by rounded tablespoonfuls about 2 inches apart onto lightly greased cookie sheets; place 4 to 5 pieces of remaining ½ cup "M&M's"® Chocolate Mini Baking Bits on top of each cookie. Bake 13 to 15 minutes. Cool 2 to 3 minutes on cookie sheets; remove to wire racks to cool completely. Store in tightly covered container. Makes about 4 dozen cookies.*

Oatmeal Chocolate Cherry Bars

Peanut Butter Chocolate No-Bake Bars

BARS
- **1 cup peanut butter**
- **½ cup light corn syrup**
- **½ cup powdered sugar**
- **2 tablespoons margarine or butter**
- **2 cups QUAKER® Oats (quick or old fashioned, uncooked)**

TOPPING
- **1 cup (6 ounces) semisweet chocolate pieces**
- **2 tablespoons peanut butter**
- **¼ cup chopped peanuts (optional)**

1. For bars, in medium saucepan, heat peanut butter, corn syrup, powdered sugar and margarine over medium-low heat until margarine is melted, stirring frequently. Remove from heat. Stir in oats, mixing well.

2. Spread onto bottom of *ungreased* 8- or 9-inch square pan; set aside.

3. For topping, place chocolate pieces in medium-size microwavable bowl. Microwave on HIGH 1 to 2 minutes, stirring every 30 seconds until smooth.

4. Stir in peanut butter until well blended.

5. Spread evenly over oats layer. Sprinkle with chopped nuts, if desired. Refrigerate 30 minutes or until chocolate is set.

6. Cut into bars with sharp knife. If bars are difficult to cut, let stand about 10 minutes. Store tightly covered at room temperature.

Makes 24 bars

Festive Fruited White Chip Blondies

- **½ cup (1 stick) butter or margarine**
- **1⅔ cups (10-ounce package) HERSHEY®S Premier White Chips, divided**
- **2 eggs**
- **¼ cup granulated sugar**
- **1¼ cups all-purpose flour**
- **⅓ cup orange juice**
- **¾ cup cranberries, chopped**
- **¼ cup chopped dried apricots**
- **½ cup coarsely chopped nuts**
- **¼ cup packed light brown sugar**

1. Heat oven to 325°F. Grease and flour 9-inch square baking pan.

2. Melt butter in medium saucepan; stir in 1 cup white chips. In large bowl, beat eggs until foamy. Add granulated sugar; beat until thick and pale yellow in color. Add flour, orange juice and white chip mixture; beat just until combined. Spread one-half of batter, about 1¼ cups, into prepared pan.

3. Bake 15 minutes until edges are lightly browned; remove from oven.

4. Stir cranberries, apricots and remaining ⅔ cup white chips into remaining one-half of batter; spread over top of hot baked mixture. Stir together nuts and brown sugar; sprinkle over top.

5. Bake 25 to 30 minutes or until edges are lightly browned. Cool completely in pan on wire rack. Cut into bars.

Makes about 16 bars

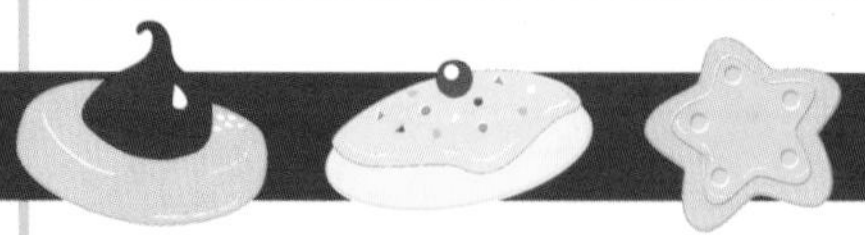

Praline Bars

- **¾ cup butter or margarine, softened**
- **1 cup sugar, divided**
- **1 teaspoon vanilla, divided**
- **1½ cups flour**
- **2 packages (8 ounces each) PHILADELPHIA® Cream Cheese, softened**
- **2 eggs**
- **½ cup almond brickle chips**
- **3 tablespoons caramel ice cream topping**

MIX butter, ½ cup of the sugar and ½ teaspoon of the vanilla with electric mixer on medium speed until light and fluffy. Gradually add flour, mixing on low speed until blended. Press onto bottom of 13×9-inch pan. Bake at 350°F for 20 to 23 minutes or until lightly browned.

MIX cream cheese, remaining ½ cup sugar and ½ teaspoon vanilla with electric mixer on medium speed until well blended. Add eggs; mix well. Blend in chips. Pour over crust. Dot top of cream cheese mixture with topping. Cut through batter with knife several times for marble effect.

BAKE at 350°F for 30 minutes. Cool in pan on wire rack. Cut into bars.

Makes 2 dozen

Prep Time: 30 minutes
Bake Time: 30 minutes

Microwave Double Peanut Bars

- **½ cup light brown sugar**
- **½ cup light corn syrup or honey**
- **½ cup creamy peanut butter**
- **6 shredded wheat biscuits, coarsely crushed**
- **¾ cup raisins**
- **½ cup chopped peanuts**

In 2-quart microwavable bowl, blend sugar, corn syrup and peanut butter. Microwave on HIGH (100% power) 1 to 1½ minutes until bubbly. Stir until smooth. Quickly stir in cereal, raisins and peanuts. Press evenly into greased 8- or 9-inch square baking pan. Cool. Cut into bars.

Makes 2 dozen bars

Favorite recipe from Peanut Advisory Board

Praline Bars

Oatmeal Carmelita Bars

¾ Butter Flavor* CRISCO® stick or ¾ cup Butter Flavor* CRISCO® all-vegetable shortening, melted, plus additional for greasing
1½ cups quick oats (not instant or old fashioned), uncooked
¾ cup firmly packed brown sugar
½ cup plus 3 tablespoons all-purpose flour, divided
½ cup whole wheat flour
½ teaspoon baking soda
¼ teaspoon cinnamon
1⅓ cups milk chocolate chips
½ cup chopped walnuts
1 jar (12.5 ounces) or ¾ cup caramel ice cream topping

**Butter Flavor Crisco is artificially flavored.*

1. Heat oven to 350°F. Grease bottom and sides of 9-inch square baking pan with shortening. Place wire rack on countertop to cool bars.

2. Combine ¾ cup shortening, oats, sugar, ½ cup all-purpose flour, whole wheat flour, baking soda and cinnamon in large bowl. Mix at low speed of electric mixer until crumbs form. Reserve ½ cup for topping. Press remaining crumbs into prepared pan.

3. Bake at 350°F for 10 minutes. Sprinkle chocolate chips and nuts over crust.

4. Combine caramel topping and remaining 3 tablespoons all-purpose flour. Stir until well blended. Drizzle over chocolate chips and nuts. Sprinkle reserved ½ cup crumbs over caramel topping.

5. Return to oven. Bake for 20 to 25 minutes or until golden brown. *Do not overbake.* Run spatula around edge of pan before cooling. Cool completely in pan on wire rack. Cut into 1½×1½-inch squares. *Makes 3 dozen squares*

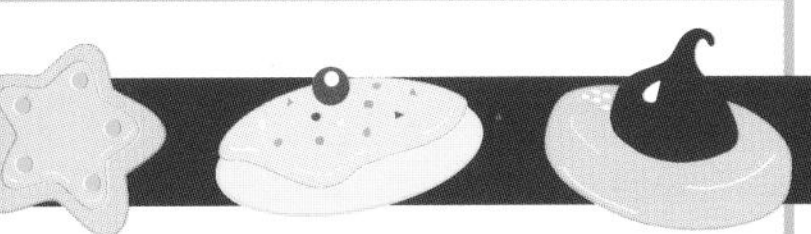

Double-Decker Cereal Treats

1⅔ cups (10-ounce package) REESE'S® Peanut Butter Chips
2 tablespoons vegetable oil
2 teaspoons vanilla extract, divided
2 cups (12-ounce package) HERSHEY'S Semi-Sweet Chocolate Chips
2 cups light corn syrup
1⅓ cups packed light brown sugar
12 cups crisp rice cereal, divided

1. Line 15½×10½×1-inch jelly-roll pan with foil, extending foil over edges of pan.

2. Place peanut butter chips, oil and 1 teaspoon vanilla in large bowl. Place chocolate chips and remaining 1 teaspoon vanilla in second large bowl. Stir together corn syrup and brown sugar in large saucepan; cook over medium heat, stirring constantly, until mixture comes to full rolling boil. Remove from heat. Immediately pour half of hot mixture into each reserved bowl; stir each mixture until chips are melted and mixture is smooth. Immediately stir 6 cups rice cereal into each of the two mixtures. Spread peanut butter mixture into prepared pan; spread chocolate mixture over top of peanut butter layer.

3. Cool completely. Use foil to lift treats out of pan; peel off foil. Cut treats into bars. Store in tightly covered container in cool, dry place. *Makes about 6 dozen pieces*

Marvelous Cookie Bars

½ cup (1 stick) butter or margarine, softened
1 cup firmly packed light brown sugar
2 large eggs
1⅓ cups all-purpose flour
1 cup quick-cooking or old-fashioned oats, uncooked
⅓ cup unsweetened cocoa powder
1 teaspoon baking powder
½ teaspoon salt
¼ teaspoon baking soda
½ cup chopped walnuts, divided
1 cup "M&M's"® Semi-Sweet Chocolate Mini Baking Bits, divided
½ cup cherry preserves
¼ cup shredded coconut

Preheat oven to 350°F. Lightly grease 9×9×2-inch baking pan; set aside. In large bowl cream butter and sugar until light and fluffy; beat in eggs. In medium bowl combine flour, oats, cocoa powder, baking powder, salt and baking soda; blend into creamed mixture. Stir in ¼ cup nuts and ¾ cup "M&M's"® Semi-Sweet Chocolate Mini Baking Bits. Reserve 1 cup dough; spread remaining dough into prepared pan. Combine preserves, coconut and remaining ¼ cup nuts; spread evenly over dough to within ½ inch of edge. Drop reserved dough by rounded teaspoonfuls over preserves mixture; sprinkle with remaining ¼ cup "M&M's"® Semi-Sweet Chocolate Mini Baking Bits. Bake 25 to 30 minutes or until slightly firm near edges. Cool completely. Cut into bars. Store in tightly covered container. *Makes 16 bars*

Marvelous Cookie Bars

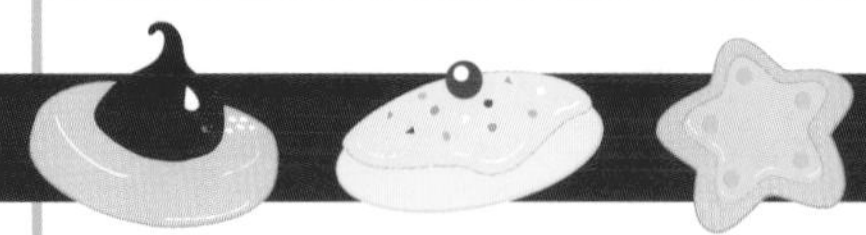

Chocolate Chips and Raspberry Bars

1½ cups all-purpose flour
½ cup sugar
½ teaspoon baking powder
½ teaspoon salt
½ cup (1 stick) butter or margarine, softened
1 egg, beaten
¼ cup milk
¼ teaspoon vanilla extract
¾ cup raspberry preserves
1 cup HERSHEY'®S Semi-Sweet Chocolate Chips

1. Heat oven to 400°F. Grease 13×9×2-inch baking pan.

2. Stir together flour, sugar, baking powder and salt in large bowl. Cut in butter with pastry blender until mixture resembles coarse crumbs. Add egg, milk and vanilla; beat on medium speed of electric mixer until well blended.

3. Reserve ½ cup mixture for topping. Spread remaining mixture onto bottom of prepared pan (this will be a very thin layer). Spread preserves evenly over dough; sprinkle chocolate chips over top. Drop reserved dough by ½ teaspoons over chips.

4. Bake 25 minutes or until golden. Cool completely in pan on wire rack. Cut into bars. *Makes about 32 bars*

Tip: Rich, buttery bar cookies and brownies freeze extremely well. Freeze in airtight containers or freezer bags for up to three months. Thaw at room temperature.

Chocolate Chips and Raspberry Bars

Holiday Treats

Christmas Tree Platter

1 recipe Christmas Ornament Cookie dough (page 306)
2 cups sifted powdered sugar
2 tablespoons milk or lemon juice
Assorted food colors, colored sugars and assorted small decors

1. Preheat oven to 350°F. Prepare dough; divide dough in half. Reserve 1 half; refrigerate remaining dough. Roll reserved half of dough to ⅛-inch thickness.

2. Cut out tree shapes with cookie cutters. Place on ungreased cookie sheets.

3. Bake 10 to 12 minutes or until edges are lightly browned. Remove to wire racks; cool completely.

4. Repeat with remaining half of dough. Reroll scraps; cut into small circles for ornaments, squares and rectangles for gift boxes and tree trunks.

5. Bake 8 to 12 minutes, depending on size of cookies.

6. Mix sugar and milk for icing. Tint most of icing green and a smaller amount red or other colors for ornaments and boxes. Spread green icing on trees. Sprinkle ornaments and boxes with colored sugars or decorate as desired. Arrange cookies on flat platter to resemble tree as shown in photo.

Makes about 1 dozen cookies

Christmas Tree Platter

Pinwheels

1 package DUNCAN HINES® Golden Sugar Cookie Mix
1 egg
¼ cup vegetable oil
1½ tablespoons water
1 egg white, lightly beaten
Coarse decorating sugar
18 candied maraschino cherries, halved

1. Preheat oven to 375°F.

2. Combine cookie mix, egg, oil and water in large bowl. Stir until thoroughly blended. Roll dough to ⅛-inch thickness on lightly floured surface. Cut into 2½-inch squares. Place each square 1 inch apart on ungreased baking sheet. Cut 1-inch slits diagonally from each corner towards center. Fold every other corner tip towards center. Brush tops with egg white. Sprinkle with sugar. Place cherry half on center of each pinwheel. Bake at 375°F for 8 to 9 minutes or until edges are lightly golden brown. Remove to cooling racks. Cool completely. Store between layers of waxed paper in airtight containers. *Makes 3 dozen cookies*

Tip: You may substitute granulated sugar for coarse decorating sugar, if desired.

Pinwheels

Yuletide Linzer Bars

- 1⅓ cups butter or margarine, softened
- ¾ cup sugar
- 1 egg
- 1 teaspoon grated lemon peel
- 2½ cups all-purpose flour
- 1½ cups whole almonds, ground
- 1 teaspoon ground cinnamon
- ¾ cup raspberry preserves
- Powdered sugar

Preheat oven to 350°F. Grease 13×9-inch baking pan.

Beat butter and sugar in large bowl with electric mixer until creamy. Beat in egg and lemon peel until blended. Mix in flour, almonds and cinnamon until well blended.

Press 2 cups dough into bottom of prepared pan. Spread preserves over crust. Press remaining dough, a small amount at a time, evenly over preserves.

Bake 35 to 40 minutes until golden brown. Cool in pan on wire rack. Sprinkle with powdered sugar; cut into bars.

Makes 36 bars

Santa's Chocolate Cookies

- 1 cup margarine or butter
- ⅔ cup semisweet chocolate chips
- ¾ cup sugar
- 1 egg
- ½ teaspoon vanilla
- 2 cups all-purpose flour
- Apricot jam, melted semisweet chocolate, chopped almonds, frosting, coconut or colored sprinkles (optional)

Preheat oven to 350°F. Melt margarine and chocolate together in small saucepan over low heat or microwave for 2 minutes at HIGH until completely melted. Combine chocolate mixture and sugar in large bowl. Add egg and vanilla; stir well. Add flour; stir well. Refrigerate 30 minutes or until firm.

Shape dough into 1-inch balls. Place 1 inch apart on ungreased cookie sheets. If desired, flatten balls with bottom of drinking glass, shape into logs or make a depression in center and fill with apricot jam.

Bake 8 to 10 minutes or until set. Remove to wire racks to cool completely. Decorate as desired with melted chocolate, almonds, frosting, coconut or colored sprinkles.

Makes about 3 dozen cookies

Yuletide Linzer Bars

Gingerbread Kids

2 ripe, small DOLE® Bananas
4 cups all-purpose flour
1½ teaspoons ground ginger
1 teaspoon baking soda
1 teaspoon ground cinnamon
½ cup butter, softened
½ cup packed brown sugar
½ cup dark molasses
Prepared icing and candies

Tip

Before measuring molasses, lightly coat a measuring cup with nonstick cooking spray so the molasses will slide out easily instead of clinging to the cup.

• Purée bananas in blender. Combine flour, ginger, baking soda and cinnamon. Cream butter and sugar until light and fluffy. Beat in molasses and bananas until blended. Stir in flour mixture with wooden spoon until completely blended. (Dough will be stiff.) Cover; refrigerate 1 hour.

• Preheat oven to 375°F. Divide dough into 4 parts. Roll out each part to ⅛-inch thickness on lightly floured surface. Cut out cookies using small gingerbread people cutters. Use favorite cookie cutters for any smaller amounts of remaining dough.

• Bake on greased cookie sheets 10 to 15 minutes or until just brown around edges. Cool completely on wire racks. Decorate as desired with favorite icing and candies.

Makes 30 to 35 cookies

Gingerbread Kids

Pumpkin White Chocolate Drops

2 cups butter or margarine, softened
2 cups granulated sugar
1 can (16 ounces) solid pack pumpkin
2 eggs
4 cups all-purpose flour
2 teaspoons pumpkin pie spice
1 teaspoon baking powder
½ teaspoon baking soda
1 bag (12 ounces) vanilla baking chips
1 container (16 ounces) ready-to-spread cream cheese frosting
¼ cup packed brown sugar

1. Preheat oven to 375°F. Grease cookie sheets.

2. Beat butter and sugar in large bowl until light and fluffy. Add pumpkin and eggs; beat until smooth. Add flour, pumpkin pie spice, baking powder and baking soda; beat just until well blended. Stir in chips.

3. Drop dough by teaspoonfuls about 2 inches apart onto cookie sheets. Bake about 16 minutes or until set and bottoms are brown. Cool 1 minute on cookie sheets. Remove from cookie sheets to wire rack to cool.

4. Combine frosting and brown sugar in small bowl. Spread on warm cookies. *Makes about 6 dozen cookies*

Pumpkin White Chocolate Drops

Kringle's Cutouts

1¼ cups granulated sugar
1 Butter Flavor* CRISCO® Stick or 1 cup Butter Flavor* CRISCO® all-vegetable shortening
2 eggs
¼ cup light corn syrup or regular pancake syrup
1 teaspoon vanilla
3 cups plus 4 tablespoons all-purpose flour, divided
¾ teaspoon baking powder
½ teaspoon baking soda
½ teaspoon salt
Colored sugar, decors and prepared frosting (optional)

**Butter Flavor Crisco® is artificially flavored.*

1. Combine sugar and 1 cup shortening in large bowl. Beat at medium speed of electric mixer until well blended. Add eggs, syrup and vanilla. Beat until well blended and fluffy.

2. Combine 3 cups flour, baking powder, baking soda and salt. Add gradually to creamed mixture at low speed. Mix until well blended.

3. Divide dough into 4 quarters. Cover and refrigerate at least two hours or overnight.

4. Heat oven to 375°F. Place sheets of foil on countertop for cooling cookies.

5. Spread 1 tablespoon flour on large sheet of waxed paper. Place one quarter of dough on floured paper. Flatten slightly with hands. Turn dough over. Cover with another large sheet of waxed paper. Roll dough to ¼-inch thickness. Remove top layer of waxed paper. Cut out with seasonal cookie cutters. Place cutouts 2 inches apart on ungreased baking sheets. Roll and cut out remaining dough. Sprinkle with colored sugar and decors or leave plain to frost when cool.

6. Bake at 375°F for 5 to 9 minutes, depending on size of cookies. (Bake small, thin cookies about 5 minutes; larger cookies about 9 minutes.) *Do not overbake.* Cool 2 minutes on baking sheet. Remove cookies to foil to cool completely.

Makes 3 to 4 dozen cookies (depending on size and shape)

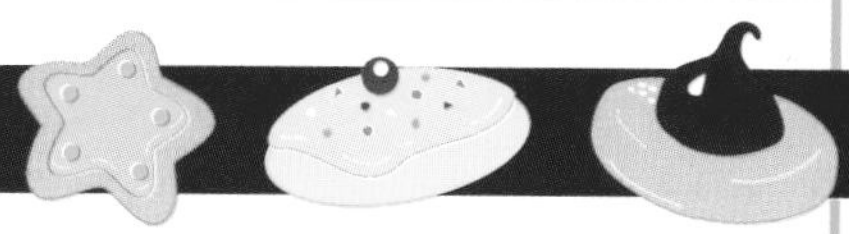

Honey Nut Rugelach

- 1 cup butter or margarine, softened
- 3 ounces cream cheese, softened
- ½ cup honey, divided
- 2 cups flour
- 1 teaspoon lemon juice
- 1 teaspoon ground cinnamon, divided
- 1 cup finely chopped walnuts
- ½ cup dried cherries or cranberries

Cream butter and cream cheese until fluffy. Add 3 tablespoons honey and mix well. Mix in flour until dough holds together. Form into a ball, wrap and refrigerate 2 hours or longer. Divide dough into 4 equal portions. On floured surface, roll one portion of dough into 9-inch circle. Combine 2 tablespoons honey and lemon juice; mix well. Brush dough with ¼ of honey mixture; sprinkle with ¼ teaspoon cinnamon. Combine walnuts and cherries in small bowl; drizzle with remaining 3 tablespoons honey and mix well. Spread ¼ of walnut mixture onto circle of dough, stopping ½ inch from outer edge. Cut circle into 8 triangular pieces. Roll up dough staring at wide outer edge and rolling toward tip. Gently bend both ends to form a crescent. Place on oiled parchment paper-lined baking sheet and refrigerate 20 minutes or longer. Repeat with remaining dough and filling. Bake at 350°F 20 to 25 minutes or until golden brown. Cool on wire racks.

Makes 32 cookies

Freezing Tip: *Unbaked cookies can be placed in freezer-safe containers or bags and frozen until ready to bake.*

Favorite recipe from National Honey Board

Cranberry Cheese Bars

- **2 cups all-purpose flour**
- **1½ cups quick-cooking or old-fashioned oats, uncooked**
- **¾ cup plus 1 tablespoon firmly packed light brown sugar, divided**
- **1 cup (2 sticks) butter or margarine, softened**
- **1¾ cups "M&M's"® Chocolate Mini Baking Bits, divided**
- **1 (8-ounce) package cream cheese**
- **1 (14-ounce) can sweetened condensed milk**
- **¼ cup lemon juice**
- **1 teaspoon vanilla extract**
- **2 tablespoons cornstarch**
- **1 (16-ounce) can whole berry cranberry sauce**

Preheat oven to 350°F. Lightly grease 13×9×2-inch baking pan; set aside. In large bowl combine flour, oats, ¾ cup sugar and butter; mix until crumbly. Reserve 1½ cups crumb mixture for topping. Stir ½ cup "M&M's"® Chocolate Mini Baking Bits into remaining crumb mixture; press into prepared pan. Bake 15 minutes. Cool completely. In large bowl beat cream cheese until light and fluffy; gradually mix in condensed milk, lemon juice and vanilla until smooth. Pour evenly over crust. In small bowl combine remaining 1 tablespoon sugar, cornstarch and cranberry sauce. Spoon over cream cheese mixture. Stir remaining 1¼ cups "M&M's"® Chocolate Mini Baking Bits into reserved crumb mixture. Sprinkle over cranberry mixture. Bake 40 minutes. Cool at room temperature; refrigerate before cutting. Store in refrigerator in tightly covered container. *Makes 32 bars*

Cranberry Cheese Bars

Maple Walnut Meringues

- ⅓ cup powdered sugar
- ½ cup plus ⅓ cup ground walnuts, divided
- ¾ cup packed light brown sugar
- 3 egg whites, at room temperature
- Pinch salt
- ⅛ teaspoon cream of tartar
- 1 teaspoon maple extract

Place 1 oven rack in the top third of oven and 1 oven rack in the bottom third of oven; preheat oven to 300°F. Line 2 large cookie sheets with aluminum foil, shiny side up.

Stir powdered sugar and ½ cup walnuts with fork in medium bowl; set aside. Crumble brown sugar into small bowl; set aside.

Beat egg whites and salt in large bowl with electric mixer at high speed until foamy. Add cream of tartar; beat 30 seconds or until mixture forms soft peaks. Sprinkle brown sugar, 1 tablespoon at a time, over egg white mixture; beat at high speed until each addition is completely absorbed. Beat 2 to 3 minutes or until mixture forms stiff peaks. Beat in maple extract at low speed. Fold in walnut mixture with large rubber spatula.

Drop level tablespoonfuls of dough to form mounds about 1 inch apart on prepared cookie sheets. Sprinkle cookies with remaining ⅓ cup ground walnuts. Bake 25 minutes or until cookies feel dry on surface but remain soft inside. (Rotate cookie sheets from top to bottom halfway through baking time.)

Slide foil with cookies onto wire racks; cool completely. Carefully remove cookies from foil. Store in airtight container with waxed paper between layers of cookies. Cookies are best the day they are baked. *Makes about 36 cookies*

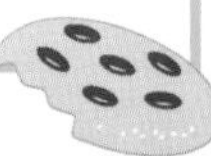

Maple Walnut Meringues

Molded Scotch Shortbread

1½ cups all-purpose flour
¼ teaspoon salt
¾ cup butter, softened
⅓ cup sugar
1 egg

Tip

To measure flour accurately, spoon it into a dry measure until the measure is overflowing. Then, with a straight-edged metal spatula, sweep across the top of the measure. Don't scoop the flour with the measure or tap the measure on the counter, because this will compact the flour and result in an inaccurate measure.

1. Preheat oven to temperature recommended by shortbread mold manufacturer. Combine flour and salt in medium bowl.

2. Beat butter and sugar in large bowl with electric mixer at medium speed until light and fluffy. Beat in egg. Gradually add flour mixture. Beat at low speed until well blended.

3. Spray 10-inch ceramic shortbread mold with nonstick cooking spray.* Press dough firmly into mold. Bake, cool and remove from mold according to manufacturer's directions.

Makes 1 shortbread mold or 24 cookies

**If mold is not available, preheat oven to 350°F. Shape tablespoonfuls of dough into 1-inch balls. Place 2 inches apart on ungreased cookie sheets; press with fork to flatten. Bake 18 to 20 minutes or until edges are lightly browned. Let cookies stand on cookie sheets 2 minutes; transfer to wire racks to cool completely. Store tightly covered at room temperature or freeze up to 3 months.*

Molded Scotch Shortbread

Spritz Christmas Trees

- 1/3 cup (3 1/2 ounces) almond paste
- 1 egg
- 1 package DUNCAN HINES® Golden Sugar Cookie Mix
- 8 drops green food coloring
- 1 container DUNCAN HINES® Vanilla Frosting
- Cinnamon candies, for garnish

1. Preheat oven to 375°F.

2. Combine almond paste and egg in large bowl. Beat at low speed with electric mixer until blended. Add contents of buttery flavor packet from Mix and green food coloring. Beat until smooth and evenly tinted. Add cookie mix. Beat at low speed until thoroughly blended.

3. Fit cookie press with Christmas tree plate; fill with dough. Force dough through press, 2 inches apart, onto ungreased cookie sheets. Bake at 375°F for 6 to 7 minutes or until set but not browned. Cool 1 minute on cookie sheets. Remove to cooling racks. Cool completely.

4. To decorate, fill resealable plastic bag half full with vanilla frosting. Do not seal bag. Cut pinpoint hole in bottom corner of bag. Pipe small dot of frosting onto tip of one cookie tree and top with cinnamon candy. Repeat with remaining cookies. Pipe remaining frosting to form garland on cookie trees. Allow frosting to set before storing between layers of waxed paper in airtight container. *Makes about 5 dozen cookies*

Spritz Christmas Trees

Christmas Stained Glass Cookies

- Colored hard candy
- ¾ cup butter or margarine, softened
- ¾ cup granulated sugar
- 2 eggs
- 1 teaspoon vanilla extract
- 3 cups all-purpose flour
- 1 teaspoon baking powder
- Frosting (optional)
- Small decorative candies (optional)

Separate colors of hard candy into resealable plastic freezer bags. Crush with mallet or hammer to equal about ⅓ cup crushed candy; set aside. In mixing bowl, cream butter and sugar. Beat in eggs and vanilla. In another bowl sift together flour and baking powder. Gradually stir flour mixture into butter mixture until dough is very stiff. Wrap in plastic wrap and chill about 3 hours.

Preheat oven to 375°F. Roll out dough to ⅛-inch thickness on lightly floured surface. Additional flour may be added to dough if necessary. Cut out cookies using large Christmas cookie cutters. Transfer cookies to foil-lined baking sheet. Using small Christmas cookie cutter of the same shape as large one, cut out and remove dough from center of each cookie.* Fill cut out sections with crushed candy. If using cookies as hanging ornaments, make holes at tops of cookies for string with drinking straw or chopstick. Bake 7 to 9 minutes or until cookies are lightly browned and candy is melted. Slide foil off baking sheets. When cool, carefully loosen cookies from foil. Use frosting and candy for additional decorations, if desired.

Makes about 2½ dozen medium-sized cookies

**For different designs, other cookie cutter shapes can be used to cut out center of cookies (i.e., small circle and star-shaped cutters can be used to cut out ornament designs on large Christmas tree cookies).*

Favorite recipe from The Sugar Association, Inc.

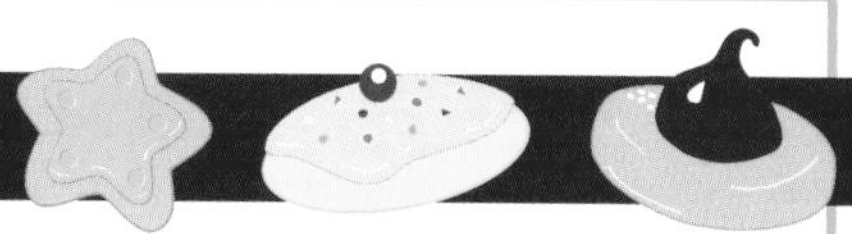

Chocolate Chip Cranberry Cheese Bars

1 cup (2 sticks) butter or margarine, softened
1 cup packed brown sugar
2 cups all-purpose flour
1½ cups quick or old-fashioned oats
2 teaspoons grated orange peel
2 cups (12-ounce package) NESTLÉ® TOLL HOUSE® Semi-Sweet Chocolate Morsels
1 cup (4 ounces) dried cranberries
1 package (8 ounces) cream cheese, softened
1¼ cups (14-ounce can) CARNATION® Sweetened Condensed Milk

BEAT butter and brown sugar in large mixer bowl until creamy. Gradually beat in flour, oats and orange peel until crumbly. Stir in morsels and cranberries; reserve 2 cups mixture. Press remaining mixture onto bottom of greased 13×9-inch baking pan.

BAKE in preheated 350°F. oven for 15 minutes. Beat cream cheese in small mixer bowl until smooth. Gradually beat in sweetened condensed milk. Pour over hot crust; sprinkle with reserved flour mixture. Bake for additional 25 to 30 minutes or until center is set. Cool in pan on wire rack.

Makes about 3 dozen bars

Tip

Cookies, brownies and bars make great gifts. Place them in a paper-lined tin or on a decorative plate covered with plastic wrap and tied with colorful ribbon. For a special touch, include the recipe.

Danish Raspberry Ribbons

1 cup butter, softened
½ cup granulated sugar
1 large egg
2 tablespoons milk
2 tablespoons vanilla
¼ teaspoon almond extract
2⅔ cups all-purpose flour, divided
6 tablespoons seedless raspberry jam
Glaze (recipe follows)

1. Beat butter and sugar in large bowl with electric mixer at medium speed until light and fluffy. Beat in egg, milk, vanilla and almond extract until well blended.

2. Gradually add 1½ cups flour. Beat at low speed until well blended. Stir in enough remaining flour with spoon to form stiff dough. Form dough into disc; wrap in plastic wrap and refrigerate until firm, at least 30 minutes or overnight.

3. Preheat oven to 375°F. Cut dough into 6 equal pieces. Rewrap 3 dough pieces and return to refrigerator. With floured hands, shape each piece of dough into 12-inch-long, ¾-inch-thick rope.

4. Place ropes 2 inches apart on ungreased cookie sheets. Make lengthwise ¼-inch-deep groove down center of each rope with handle of wooden spoon or finger. (Ropes will flatten to ½-inch-thick strips.)

5. Bake 12 minutes. Remove from oven; spoon 1 tablespoon jam into each groove. Return to oven; bake 5 to 7 minutes longer or until strips are light golden brown. Cool strips 15 minutes on cookie sheet.

6. Prepare Glaze. Drizzle strips with Glaze; let stand 5 minutes to dry. Cut cookie strips at 45° angle into 1-inch slices. Place cookies on wire racks; cool completely. Repeat with remaining dough. Store tightly covered between sheets of waxed paper at room temperature.

Makes about 5½ dozen cookies

Glaze: *Blend ½ cup powdered sugar, 1 tablespoon milk and 1 teaspoon vanilla until smooth.*

Danish Raspberry Ribbons

Snowmen

1 package (20 ounces) refrigerated chocolate chip cookie dough
1½ cups sifted powdered sugar
2 tablespoons milk
Candy corn, gum drops, chocolate chips, licorice and other assorted small candies

1. Preheat oven to 375°F.

2. Cut dough into 12 equal sections. Divide each section into 3 balls: large, medium and small for each snowman.

3. For each snowman, place 3 balls in row, ¼ inch apart, on ungreased cookie sheet. Repeat with remaining dough.

4. Bake 10 to 12 minutes or until edges are very lightly browned. Cool 4 minutes on cookie sheets. Remove to wire racks; cool completely.

5. Mix powdered sugar and milk in medium bowl until smooth. Pour over cookies. Let cookies stand 20 minutes or until set.

6. Decorate to create faces, hats and arms with assorted candies. *Makes 1 dozen cookies*

Snowmen

Sugar Cookie Wreaths

1 package DUNCAN HINES® Golden Sugar Cookie Mix
1 egg
¼ cup vegetable oil
1 tablespoon water
Green food coloring
Candied or maraschino cherry pieces

Tip

When reusing cookie sheets for several batches of cookies, cool the sheets completely before placing dough on them. The dough will soften and begin to spread on a hot baking sheet.

1. Preheat oven to 375°F.

2. Combine cookie mix, egg, oil and water in large bowl. Stir until thoroughly blended.

3. Tint dough with green food coloring. Stir until desired color. Form into balls the size of miniature marshmallows. For each wreath, arrange 9 or 10 balls, with sides touching, into a ring. Place wreaths 2 inches apart on ungreased baking sheets. Flatten slightly with fingers. Place small piece of candied cherry on each ball.

4. Bake at 375°F for 5 to 7 minutes or until set but not browned. Cool 1 minute on baking sheets. Remove to cooling racks. Cool completely. Store in airtight container.

Makes 4 dozen cookies

Tip: Instead of tinting dough green, coat balls with green sugar crystals.

Sugar Cookie Wreaths

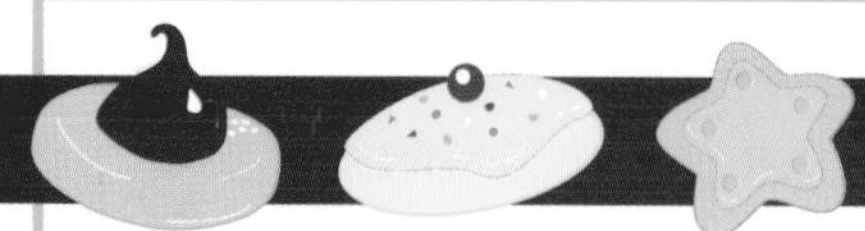

Apple-Cranberry Crescent Cookies

1¼ cups chopped apples
½ cup dried cranberries
½ cup reduced-fat sour cream
¼ cup cholesterol-free egg substitute
¼ cup margarine or butter, melted
3 tablespoons sugar, divided
1 package quick-rise yeast
1 teaspoon vanilla
2 cups all-purpose flour
1 teaspoon ground cinnamon
1 tablespoon reduced-fat (2%) milk

1. Preheat oven to 350°F. Lightly coat cookie sheet with nonstick cooking spray.

2. Place apples and cranberries in food processor or blender; pulse to finely chop. Set aside.

3. Combine sour cream, egg substitute, margarine and 2 tablespoons sugar in medium bowl. Add yeast and vanilla. Add flour; stir to form ball. Turn dough out onto lightly floured work surface. Knead 1 minute. Cover with plastic wrap; allow to stand 10 minutes.

4. Divide dough into thirds. Roll one portion into 12-inch circle. Spread with ⅓ apple mixture (about ¼ cup). Cut dough to make 8 wedges. Roll up each wedge beginning at outside edge. Place on prepared cookie sheet; turn ends of cookies to form crescents. Repeat with remaining dough and apple mixture.

5. Combine remaining 1 tablespoon sugar and cinnamon in small bowl. Lightly brush cookies with milk; sprinkle with sugar-cinnamon mixture. Bake cookies 18 to 20 minutes or until lightly browned. *Makes 24 cookies*

Apple-Cranberry Crescent Cookies

Apricot-Filled Pastries

Apricot Filling (recipe follows)
2¼ cups flour
⅔ cup sugar
1 cup (2 sticks) cold MAZOLA® Margarine or butter
2 egg yolks, lightly beaten
½ cup sour cream
Confectioners sugar

1. Prepare Apricot Filling; set aside.

2. In large bowl combine flour and sugar. With pastry blender or 2 knives, cut in margarine until mixture resembles coarse crumbs. Stir in egg yolks and sour cream until mixed.

3. Turn onto floured surface; knead just until smooth. Divide dough into quarters. Cover; refrigerate 20 minutes.

4. Preheat oven to 375°F. On floured pastry cloth with stockinette-covered rolling pin, roll one piece of dough at a time into 10-inch square. (Keep remaining dough refrigerated.)

5. Cut dough into 2-inch squares. Place ½ teaspoon Apricot Filling diagonally across each square. Moisten 2 opposite corners with water; fold over filling, overlapping slightly. Place on ungreased cookie sheets.

6. Bake 10 to 12 minutes or until edges are lightly browned. Cool on wire racks.

7. Just before serving, sprinkle with confectioners sugar. Store in tightly covered container up to 3 weeks.

Makes about 8 dozen pastries

Apricot Filling: In 1-quart saucepan bring 1 cup dried apricots and 1 cup water to boil over medium-high heat. Reduce heat; cover and simmer 5 minutes. Drain. Place apricots and ½ cup KARO® Light Corn Syrup in blender container or food processor. Cover and blend on high speed 2 minutes or until smooth. Cool completely.

Prep Time: 90 minutes, plus chilling
Bake Time: 10 minutes, plus cooling

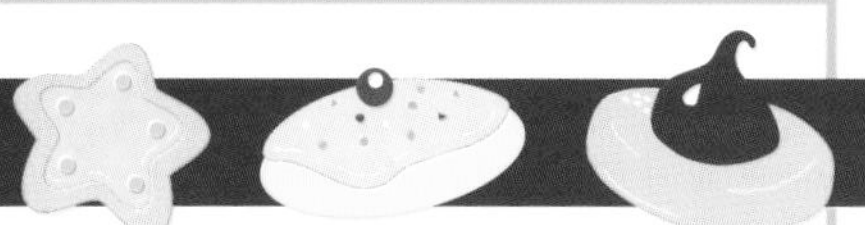

Chocolate Raspberry Thumbprints

- ½ cup (1 stick) butter or margarine, softened
- ½ cup granulated sugar
- ½ cup firmly packed light brown sugar
- 1 large egg
- 1 teaspoon vanilla extract
- 2 cups all-purpose flour
- ½ teaspoon baking powder
- 1¾ cups "M&M's"® Chocolate Mini Baking Bits, divided
- Powdered sugar
- ½ cup raspberry jam

In large microwave-safe bowl melt butter in microwave; add sugars and mix well. Stir in egg and vanilla. In medium bowl combine flour and baking powder; blend into butter mixture. Stir in 1¼ cups "M&M's"® Chocolate Mini Baking Bits; refrigerate dough 1 hour. Preheat oven to 350°F. Lightly grease cookie sheets. Roll dough into 1-inch balls and place about 2 inches apart onto prepared cookie sheets. Make an indentation in center of each ball with thumb. Bake 8 to 10 minutes. Remove from oven and reindent, if necessary; transfer to wire racks. Lightly dust warm cookies with powdered sugar; fill each indentation with ½ teaspoon raspberry jam. Sprinkle with remaining ½ cup "M&M's"® Chocolate Mini Baking Bits. Cool completely. Dust with additional powdered sugar, if desired. Store in tightly covered container.

Makes about 4 dozen cookies

Jolly Peanut Butter Gingerbread Cookies

1⅔ cups (10-ounce package) REESE'S® Peanut Butter Chips
¾ cup (1½ sticks) butter or margarine, softened
1 cup packed light brown sugar
1 cup dark corn syrup
2 eggs
5 cups all-purpose flour
1 teaspoon baking soda
½ teaspoon ground cinnamon
¼ teaspoon ground ginger
¼ teaspoon salt

1. Place peanut butter chips in small microwave-safe bowl. Microwave at HIGH (100%) 1 to 2 minutes or until chips are melted when stirred. In large bowl, beat melted peanut butter chips and butter until well blended. Add brown sugar, corn syrup and eggs; beat until light and fluffy. Stir together flour, baking soda, cinnamon, ginger and salt. Add half of flour mixture to butter mixture; beat on low speed of electric mixer until smooth. With wooden spoon, stir in remaining flour mixture until well blended. Divide into thirds; wrap each in plastic wrap. Refrigerate at least 1 hour or until dough is firm enough to roll.

2. Heat oven to 325°F.

3. Roll 1 dough portion at a time to ⅛-inch thickness on lightly floured surface; with floured cookie cutters, cut into holiday shapes. Place on ungreased cookie sheet.

4. Bake 10 to 12 minutes or until set and lightly browned. Cool slightly; remove from cookie sheet to wire rack. Cool completely. Frost and decorate as desired.

Makes about 6 dozen cookies

Jolly Peanut Butter Gingerbread Cookies

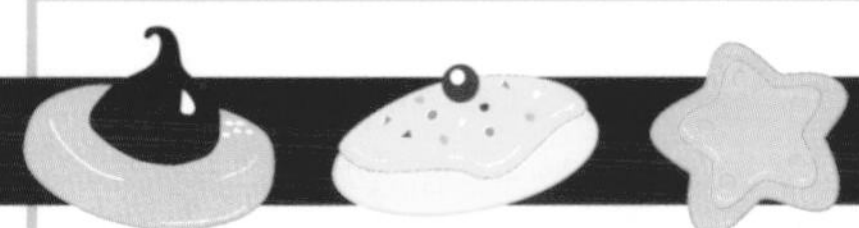

Pfeffernusse

3½ cups all-purpose flour
2 teaspoons baking powder
1½ teaspoons ground cinnamon
1 teaspoon ground ginger
½ teaspoon baking soda
½ teaspoon salt
½ teaspoon ground cloves
½ teaspoon ground cardamom
¼ teaspoon black pepper
1 cup butter, softened
1 cup granulated sugar
¼ cup dark molasses
1 egg
Powdered sugar

Combine flour, baking powder, cinnamon, ginger, baking soda, salt, cloves, cardamom and pepper in large bowl.

Beat butter and sugar in large bowl with electric mixer at medium speed until light and fluffy. Beat in molasses and egg. Gradually add flour mixture. Beat at low speed until dough forms. Shape dough into disk; wrap in plastic wrap and refrigerate until firm, 30 minutes or up to 3 days.

Preheat oven to 350°F. Grease cookie sheets. Roll dough into 1-inch balls. Place 2 inches apart on prepared cookie sheets.

Bake 12 to 14 minutes or until golden brown. Transfer cookies to wire racks; dust with sifted powdered sugar. Cool completely. Store tightly covered at room temperature or freeze up to 3 months. *Makes about 60 cookies*

Pfeffernusse

Pumpkin Jingle Bars

- ¾ cup MIRACLE WHIP® Salad Dressing
- 1 package (2-layer size) spice cake mix
- 1 can (16 ounces) can pumpkin
- 3 eggs
- Sifted powdered sugar
- Vanilla frosting
- Red and green gum drops, sliced

• Mix first 4 ingredients in large bowl at medium speed of electric mixer until well blended. Pour into greased 15½×10½×1-inch baking pan.

• Bake at 350°F 18 to 20 minutes or until edges pull away from sides of pan. Cool.

• Sprinkle with sugar. Cut into bars. Decorate with frosting and gum drops. *Makes about 3 dozen bars*

Prep Time: 5 minutes
Cook Time: 20 minutes

Gingersnaps

- 2½ cups all-purpose flour
- 1½ teaspoons ground ginger
- 1 teaspoon baking soda
- 1 teaspoon ground allspice
- ½ teaspoon salt
- 1½ cups sugar
- 2 tablespoons margarine, softened
- ½ cup MOTT'S® Apple Sauce
- ¼ cup GRANDMA'S® Molasses

1. Preheat oven to 375°F. Spray cookie sheet with nonstick cooking spray.

2. In medium bowl, sift together flour, ginger, baking soda, allspice and salt.

3. In large bowl, beat sugar and margarine with electric mixer at medium speed until blended. Whisk in apple sauce and molasses.

4. Add flour mixture to apple sauce mixture; stir until well blended.

5. Drop rounded tablespoonfuls of dough 1 inch apart onto prepared cookie sheet. Flatten each slightly with moistened fingertips.

6. Bake 12 to 15 minutes or until firm. Cool completely on wire rack. *Makes 3 dozen cookies*

Pumpkin Jingle Bars

Date-Nut Cookies

- **1 cup chopped dates**
- **½ cup water**
- **1¾ cups all-purpose flour**
- **½ teaspoon baking powder**
- **⅛ teaspoon salt**
- **½ cup butter, softened**
- **½ cup packed dark brown sugar**
- **1 egg**
- **2 teaspoons rum extract**
- **½ cup walnut pieces, chopped**

Soak dates in water in small bowl at least 30 minutes or up to 2 hours.

Preheat oven to 350°F. Grease cookie sheets. Combine flour, baking powder and salt in medium bowl.

Beat butter in large bowl at medium speed until smooth. Gradually beat in brown sugar; increase speed to high and beat until light and fluffy. Beat in egg and rum extract until fluffy. Gradually stir in flour mixture alternately with date mixture, mixing just until combined after each addition. Stir in walnuts until blended.

Drop level tablespoonfuls of dough about 1½ inches apart onto prepared cookie sheets. Bake 14 minutes or until just set. Transfer to wire racks to cool completely. Store in airtight container.

Makes 24 cookies

Date-Nut Cookies

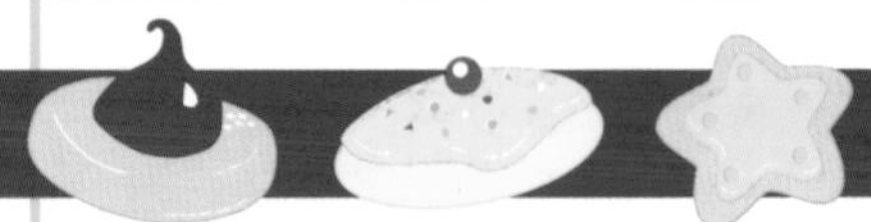

Pumpkin Cheesecake Bars

BASE AND TOPPING
- **2 cups all-purpose flour**
- **⅔ cup packed light brown sugar**
- **½ cup (1 stick) butter or margarine**
- **1 cup finely chopped pecans**

PUMPKIN CREAM CHEESE FILLING
- **11 ounces (one 8-ounce package and one 3-ounce package) cream cheese, softened**
- **1¼ cups granulated sugar**
- **1½ teaspoons vanilla extract**
- **1½ teaspoons ground cinnamon**
- **½ teaspoon ground allspice**
- **¾ cup LIBBY'S® Solid Pack Pumpkin**
- **3 eggs**
- **Glazed Pecans (recipe follows)**

FOR BASE AND TOPPING

COMBINE flour and brown sugar in medium bowl. Cut in butter with pastry blender or two knives until mixture resembles coarse crumbs; stir in nuts. Reserve 1½ cups mixture for topping; press remaining mixture onto bottom of ungreased 13×9-inch baking pan. Bake in preheated 350°F. oven for 15 minutes.

FOR PUMPKIN CREAM CHEESE FILLING

BEAT cream cheese, granulated sugar, vanilla, cinnamon and allspice in large mixer bowl. Beat in pumpkin and eggs. Spread over crust; sprinkle with reserved topping. Bake in 350°F. oven for 25 to 30 minutes or until center is set. Cool in pan on wire rack; chill for several hours or until firm. Cut into bars; place Glazed Pecan half on each bar.

Makes 32 bars or 64 triangles

Glazed Pecans: PLACE waxed paper under greased wire rack. Bring ¼ cup dark corn syrup to a boil in medium saucepan; boil, stirring constantly, for 1 minute. Remove from heat; stir in 30 pecan halves. Remove pecan halves to wire rack. Turn right side up; separate. Cool.

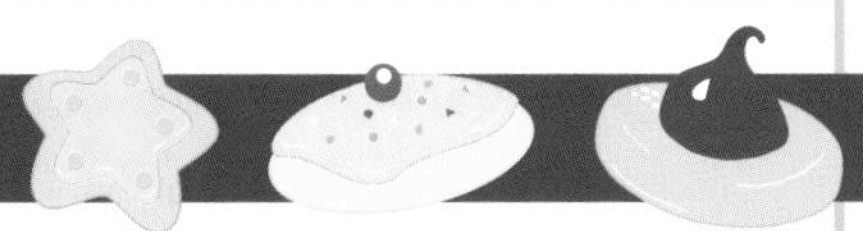

Peanut Butter Cut-Outs

- ½ cup SKIPPY® Creamy Peanut Butter
- 6 tablespoons MAZOLA® Margarine or butter, softened
- ½ cup packed brown sugar
- ⅓ cup KARO® Light or Dark Corn Syrup
- 1 egg
- 2 cups flour, divided
- 1½ teaspoons baking powder
- 1 teaspoon cinnamon (optional)
- ⅛ teaspoon salt

1. In large bowl with mixer at medium speed, beat peanut butter, margarine, brown sugar, corn syrup and egg until smooth. Reduce speed; beat in 1 cup flour, baking powder, cinnamon and salt. With spoon stir in remaining 1 cup flour.

2. Divide dough in half. Between two sheets of waxed paper on large cookie sheets, roll each half of dough ¼ inch thick. Refrigerate until firm, about 1 hour.

3. Preheat oven to 350°F. Remove top piece of waxed paper. With floured cookie cutters, cut dough into shapes. Place on ungreased cookie sheets.

4. Bake 10 minutes or until lightly browned. Do not overbake. Let stand on cookie sheets 2 minutes. Remove from cookie sheets; cool completely on wire racks. Reroll dough trimmings and cut additional cookies. Decorate as desired.

Makes about 5 dozen cookies

Note: *Use scraps of dough to create details on cookies.*

Prep Time: 20 minutes, plus chilling and decorating
Bake Time: 10 minutes, plus cooling

Linzer Sandwich Cookies

1⅓ cups all-purpose flour
¼ teaspoon baking powder
¼ teaspoon salt
¾ cup granulated sugar
½ cup butter, softened
1 large egg
1 teaspoon vanilla
Powdered sugar (optional)
Seedless raspberry jam

Place flour, baking powder and salt in small bowl; stir to combine. Beat granulated sugar and butter in medium bowl with electric mixer at medium speed until light and fluffy. Beat in egg and vanilla. Gradually add flour mixture. Beat at low speed until dough forms. Divide dough in half; cover and refrigerate 2 hours or until firm.

Preheat oven to 375°F. Working with 1 portion at a time, roll out dough on lightly floured surface to 3/16-inch thickness. Cut dough into desired shapes with floured cookie cutters. Cut out equal numbers of each shape. (If dough becomes too soft, refrigerate several minutes before continuing.) Cut 1-inch centers out of half the cookies of each shape. Reroll trimmings and cut out more cookies. Place cookies 1½ to 2 inches apart on ungreased cookie sheets. Bake 7 to 9 minutes or until edges are lightly brown. Let cookies stand on cookie sheets 1 to 2 minutes. Remove cookies to wire racks; cool completely.

Sprinkle cookies with holes with powdered sugar, if desired. Spread 1 teaspoon jam on flat side of whole cookies, spreading almost to edges. Place cookies with holes, flat side down, over jam. Store tightly covered at room temperature or freeze up to 3 months. *Makes about 2 dozen cookies*

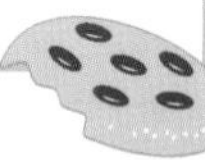

Linzer Sandwich Cookies

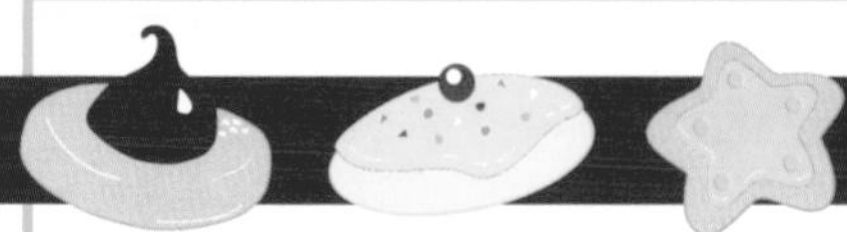

Chocolate Sugar Spritz

2 squares (1 ounce each) unsweetened chocolate, coarsely chopped
2¼ cups all-purpose flour
¼ teaspoon salt
1 cup butter or margarine, softened
¾ cup granulated sugar
1 large egg
1 teaspoon almond extract
½ cup powdered sugar
1 teaspoon ground cinnamon

1. Preheat oven to 400°F.

2. Melt chocolate in small, heavy saucepan over low heat, stirring constantly.

3. Combine flour and salt in small bowl; stir to combine.

4. Beat butter and granulated sugar in large bowl with electric mixer at medium speed until light and fluffy. Beat in egg and almond extract. Beat in chocolate. Gradually add flour mixture with mixing spoon. (Dough will be stiff.)

5. Fit cookie press with desired plate (or change plates for different shapes after first batch). Fill press with dough; press dough 1 inch apart onto ungreased cookie sheets.

6. Bake 7 minutes or until just set.

7. Combine powdered sugar and cinnamon in small bowl. Transfer to fine-mesh strainer and sprinkle over hot cookies while they are still on cookie sheets. Remove cookies to wire racks; cool completely.

8. Store tightly covered at room temperature. These cookies do not freeze well.

Makes 4 to 5 dozen cookies

Chocolate Sugar Spritz

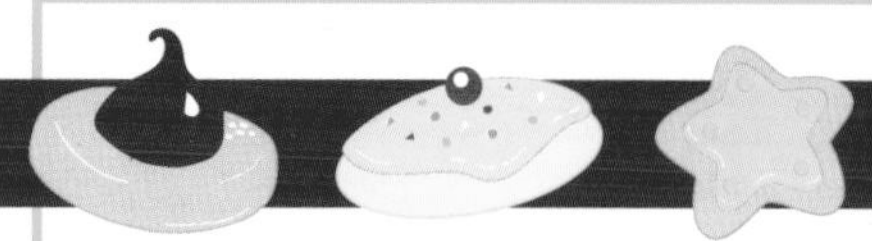

Rum Fruitcake Cookies

1 cup sugar
¾ cup vegetable shortening
3 large eggs
⅓ cup orange juice
1 tablespoon rum extract
3 cups all-purpose flour
2 teaspoons baking powder
1 teaspoon baking soda
1 teaspoon salt
2 cups (8 ounces) candied fruit
1 cup raisins
1 cup nuts, coarsely chopped

1. Preheat oven to 375°F. Lightly grease cookie sheets; set aside. Beat sugar and shortening in large bowl until fluffy. Add eggs, orange juice and rum extract; beat 2 minutes longer.

2. Combine flour, baking powder, baking soda and salt in small bowl. Add fruit, raisins and nuts. Stir into creamed mixture. Drop dough by rounded teaspoonfuls 2 inches apart onto prepared cookie sheets. Bake 10 to 12 minutes or until golden. Let cookies stand on cookie sheets 2 minutes. Remove to wire rack; cool completely.

Makes about 6 dozen cookies

Linzer Tarts

1 cup margarine or butter, softened
1 cup granulated sugar
2 cups all-purpose flour
1 cup PLANTERS® Slivered Almonds, chopped
1 teaspoon grated lemon peel
¼ teaspoon ground cinnamon
⅓ cup raspberry preserves
Powdered sugar

In large bowl with electric mixer at high speed, beat margarine and sugar until light and fluffy. Stir in flour, almonds, lemon peel and cinnamon until blended. Cover; refrigerate 2 hours.

Divide dough in half. On floured surface, roll out half of dough to ⅛-inch thickness. Using 2½-inch round cookie cutter, cut circles from dough. Reroll scraps to make additional rounds. Cut out ½-inch circles from centers of half the rounds. Repeat with remaining dough. Place on ungreased cookie sheets.

Bake at 325°F for 12 to 15 minutes or until lightly browned. Remove from cookie sheets; cool on wire racks. Spread preserves on flat side of whole cookies. Top with cut-out cookies to make sandwiches. Dust with powdered sugar.

Makes about 2 dozen cookies

Rum Fruitcake Cookies

Christmas Ornament Cookies

2¼ cups all-purpose flour
¼ teaspoon salt
1 cup sugar
¾ cup butter, softened
1 large egg
1 teaspoon vanilla
1 teaspoon almond extract
Icing (recipe follows)
Assorted candies or decors

Place flour and salt in medium bowl; stir to combine. Beat sugar and butter in large bowl with electric mixer at medium speed until light and fluffy. Beat in egg, vanilla and almond extract. Gradually add flour mixture. Beat at low speed until well blended. Divide dough in half; cover and refrigerate 30 minutes or until firm.

Preheat oven to 350°F. Working with 1 portion at a time, roll out dough on lightly floured surface to ¼-inch thickness. Cut dough into desired shapes with assorted floured cookie cutters. Reroll trimmings and cut out more cookies. Place cutouts on ungreased baking sheets. Using drinking straw or tip of sharp knife, cut hole near top of each cookie to allow for piece of ribbon or string to be inserted for hanger. Bake 10 to 12 minutes or until edges are golden brown. Let cookies stand on baking sheets 1 minute. Remove cookies to wire racks; cool completely.

Prepare Icing. Spoon Icing into small resealable plastic food storage bag. Cut off very tiny corner of bag; pipe Icing decoratively over cookies. Decorate with candies as desired. Let stand at room temperature 40 minutes or until set. Thread ribbon through each cookie hole to hang as Christmas tree ornaments. *Makes about 2 dozen cookies*

Icing: *Blend 2 cups powdered sugar and 2 tablespoons milk or lemon juice; stir until smooth. Tint with food color, if desired.*

Holiday Truffles

3 tablespoons heavy cream
1 tablespoon instant coffee granules
2 cups semisweet or milk chocolate chips
½ cup FLEISCHMANN'S® Original Margarine
1 teaspoon vanilla extract
Crushed cookie crumbs, chopped nuts, toasted coconut, melted white chocolate, colored sprinkles

1. Blend heavy cream and coffee in small bowl; let stand 5 minutes to dissolve.

2. Melt chocolate chips in medium saucepan over low heat until smooth. Remove from heat. With wire whisk, beat in margarine, heavy cream mixture and vanilla until smooth. Place in bowl; refrigerate until firm, about 3 hours.

3. Shape teaspoonfuls of mixture into balls and coat with cookie crumbs, chopped nuts, coconut, melted white chocolate or colored sprinkles until well coated. Store in airtight container in refrigerator. *Makes 2½ dozen cookies*

Prep Time: 30 minutes
Cook Time: 5 minutes
Chill Time: 3 hours
Total Time: 3 hours and 35 minutes

Peanut Butter Bears

- **1 cup SKIPPY® Creamy Peanut Butter**
- **1 cup (2 sticks) MAZOLA® Margarine or butter, softened**
- **1 cup packed brown sugar**
- **⅔ cup KARO® Light or Dark Corn Syrup**
- **2 eggs**
- **4 cups flour, divided**
- **1 tablespoon baking powder**
- **1 teaspoon cinnamon (optional)**
- **¼ teaspoon salt**

1. In large bowl with mixer at medium speed, beat peanut butter, margarine, brown sugar, corn syrup and eggs until smooth. Reduce speed; beat in 2 cups flour, baking powder, cinnamon and salt. With spoon, stir in remaining 2 cups flour. Wrap dough in plastic wrap; refrigerate 2 hours.

2. Preheat oven to 325°F. Divide dough in half; set aside half.

3. On floured surface roll out half the dough to ⅛-inch thickness. Cut with floured bear cookie cutter. Repeat with remaining dough.

4. Use scraps of dough to make bear faces. Make one small ball of dough for muzzle. Form 3 smaller balls of dough and press gently to create eyes and nose.

5. Bake bears on ungreased cookie sheets 10 minutes or until lightly browned. Remove from cookie sheets; cool completely on wire rack. Decorate as desired using frosting to create paws, ears and bow ties. *Makes about 3 dozen bears*

Prep Time: 35 minutes plus chilling
Bake Time: 10 minutes plus cooling

Peanut Butter Bears

Almost Homemade

Quick Chocolate Softies

- 1 package (18.25 ounces) devil's food cake mix
- ⅓ cup water
- ¼ cup butter, softened
- 1 egg
- 1 cup white chocolate baking chips
- ½ cup coarsely chopped walnuts

Preheat oven to 350°F. Grease cookie sheets. Combine cake mix, water, butter and egg in large bowl. Beat with electric mixer at low speed until moistened. Increase speed to medium; beat 1 minute. (Dough will be thick.) Stir in chips and nuts; mix until well blended. Drop dough by heaping teaspoonfuls 2 inches apart onto prepared cookie sheets.

Bake 10 to 12 minutes or until set. Let cookies stand on cookie sheets 1 minute. Remove cookies to wire racks; cool completely. *Makes about 4 dozen cookies*

Quick Chocolate Softies

Lemon Bars

- 1 package DUNCAN HINES® Moist Deluxe Lemon Supreme Cake Mix
- 3 eggs, divided
- ⅓ cup butter-flavor shortening
- ½ cup granulated sugar
- ¼ cup lemon juice
- 2 teaspoons grated lemon peel
- ½ teaspoon baking powder
- ¼ teaspoon salt
- Confectioners' sugar

Preheat oven to 350°F.

Combine cake mix, 1 egg and shortening in large mixing bowl. Beat at low speed with electric mixer until crumbs form. Reserve 1 cup. Pat remaining mixture lightly into *ungreased* 13×9-inch pan. Bake 15 minutes or until lightly browned.

Combine remaining 2 eggs, granulated sugar, lemon juice, lemon peel, baking powder and salt in medium mixing bowl. Beat at medium speed with electric mixer until light and foamy. Pour over hot crust. Sprinkle with reserved crumb mixture.

Bake 15 minutes or until lightly browned. Sprinkle with confectioners' sugar. Cool in pan. Cut into bars.

Makes 30 to 32 bars

Tip: These bars are also delicious using DUNCAN HINES® Moist Deluxe Yellow Cake Mix.

Lemon Bars

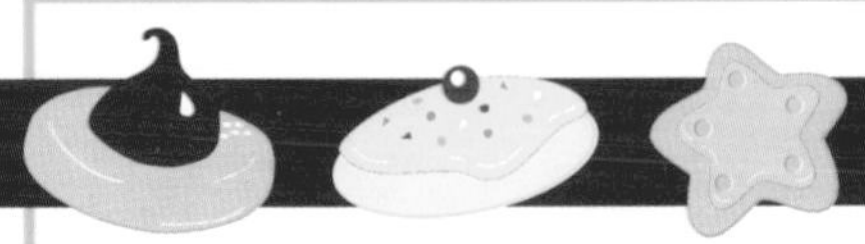

Chocolate Mint Ravioli Cookies

1 package (15 ounces) refrigerated pie crusts
1 bar (7 ounces) cookies 'n' mint chocolate candy
1 egg
1 tablespoon water
Powdered sugar

Tip

Don't like mint? Just use your favorite candy bar for the filling instead of the cookies 'n' mint bar.

1. Preheat oven to 400°F. Unfold 1 pie crust on lightly floured surface. Roll into 13-inch circle. Using 2½-inch cutters, cut pastry into 24 (2½-inch) circles with cookie cutters, rerolling scraps if necessary. Repeat with remaining pie crust.

2. Separate candy bar into pieces marked in chocolate. Cut each chocolate piece in half. Beat egg and water together in small bowl with fork. Brush half of pastry circles lightly with egg mixture. Place 1 piece of chocolate in center of each circle (there will be some candy bar left over). Top with remaining pastry circles. Seal edges with tines of fork.

3. Place on ungreased baking sheets. Brush with egg mixture.

4. Bake 8 to 10 minutes or until golden brown. Remove from cookie sheets; cool completely on wire rack. Dust with powdered sugar. *Makes 2 dozen cookies*

Prep and Cook Time: 30 minutes

Chocolate Mint Ravioli Cookies

Sugar Doodles

- **1 package (22.3 ounces) golden sugar cookie mix**
- **2 eggs**
- **⅓ cup oil**
- **1 teaspoon water**
- **½ cup (of each) HERSHEY'S® Butterscotch Chips, HERSHEY'S® Semi-Sweet Chocolate Chips and REESE'S® Peanut Butter Chips**
- **5 tablespoons colored sugar**
- **1 tablespoon granulated sugar**

1. Heat oven to 375°F.

2. Empty cookie mix into large bowl. Break up any lumps. Add eggs, oil and water to mix; stir with spoon or fork until well blended. Stir in butterscotch chips, chocolate chips and peanut butter chips. Cover; refrigerate dough about 1 hour.

3. Shape dough into 1½-inch balls. Place colored sugar and granulated sugar in large reclosable plastic bag; shake well to blend. Place 2 balls into bag; reclose bag and shake well. Place balls 2 inches apart on ungreased cookie sheet. Repeat until all balls are coated with sugar mixture.

4. Bake 8 to 10 minutes or until set. Cool slightly; remove from cookie sheet to wire rack. Cool completely.

Makes about 2½ dozen cookies

Cocoa Sugar Doodles: Substitute 5 tablespoons granulated sugar and ¾ teaspoon HERSHEY'S® Cocoa or HERSHEY'S® European Style Cocoa for amounts of colored and granulated sugars above.

Rainbow Sugar Doodles: Substitute about 1¾ teaspoons each of blue, pink and yellow colored sugar for the 5 tablespoons colored sugar called for above.

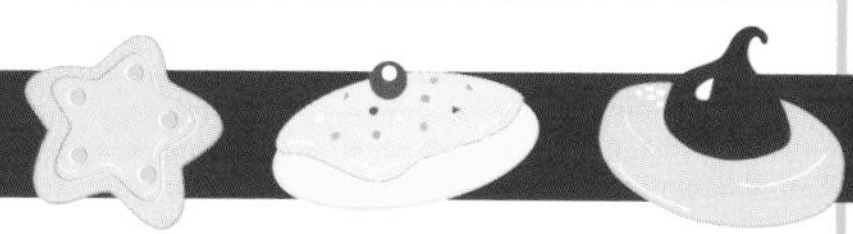

Elephant Ears

- 1 package (17¼ ounces) frozen puff pastry, thawed according to package directions
- 1 egg, beaten
- ¼ cup sugar, divided
- 2 squares (1 ounce each) semisweet chocolate

Preheat oven to 375°F. Grease cookie sheets; sprinkle lightly with water. Roll one sheet of pastry to 12×10-inch rectangle. Brush with egg; sprinkle with 1 tablespoon sugar. Tightly roll up 10-inch sides, meeting in center. Brush center with egg and seal rolls tightly together; turn over. Cut into ⅜-inch-thick slices. Place slices on prepared cookie sheets. Sprinkle with 1 tablespoon sugar. Repeat with remaining pastry, egg and sugar. Bake 16 to 18 minutes until golden brown. Remove to wire racks; cool completely.

Melt chocolate in small saucepan over low heat, stirring constantly. Remove from heat. Spread bottoms of cookies with chocolate. Place on wire rack, chocolate side up. Let stand until chocolate is set. Store between layers of waxed paper in airtight containers.

Makes about 4 dozen cookies

Peanutty Picnic Brownies

- 1 package DUNCAN HINES® Double Fudge Brownie Mix
- 1 cup quick-cooking oats (not instant or old-fashioned)
- 1 egg
- ⅓ cup water
- ⅓ cup vegetable oil plus additional for greasing
- ¾ cup peanut butter chips
- ⅓ cup chopped peanuts

1. Preheat oven to 350°F. Grease bottom of 13×9-inch pan.

2. Combine brownie mix, oats, egg, water and oil in large bowl. Stir with spoon until well blended, about 50 strokes. Stir in peanut butter chips. Spread in prepared pan. Sprinkle with peanuts. Bake at 350°F for 25 to 28 minutes or until set. *Do not overbake.* Cool completely. Cut into bars.

Makes about 24 brownies

Crispy Thumbprint Cookies

1 package (18.25 ounces) yellow cake mix
½ cup vegetable oil
1 egg
3 cups crisp rice cereal, crushed
½ cup chopped walnuts
Raspberry or strawberry preserves or thin chocolate mint candies, cut in half

1. Preheat oven to 375°F.

2. Combine cake mix, oil, egg and ¼ cup water. Beat at medium speed of electric mixer until well blended. Add cereal and walnuts; mix until well blended.

3. Drop by heaping teaspoonfuls about 2 inches apart onto ungreased baking sheets. Use thumb to make indentation in each cookie. Spoon about ½ teaspoon preserves into center of each cookie. (Or, place ½ of mint candy in center of each cookie).

4. Bake 9 to 11 minutes or until golden brown. Cool cookies 1 minute on baking sheet; remove from baking sheet to wire rack to cool completely. *Makes 3 dozen cookies*

Prep and Cook Time: 30 minutes

Chewy Chocolate Cookies

1 package (2-layer size) chocolate cake mix
2 eggs
1 cup MIRACLE WHIP® or MIRACLE WHIP® LIGHT Dressing
1 cup BAKER'S® Semi-Sweet Real Chocolate Chips
½ cup chopped walnuts

• Mix cake mix, eggs and dressing in large bowl with electric mixer on medium speed until blended. Stir in remaining ingredients. Drop by rounded teaspoonfuls onto greased cookie sheets.

• Bake at 350°F for 10 to 12 minutes or until edges are lightly browned. *Makes 4 dozen cookies*

Prep Time: 10 minutes
Bake Time: 12 minutes

Crispy Thumbprint Cookies

Orange Pecan Gems

- **1 package DUNCAN HINES® Moist Deluxe Orange Supreme Cake Mix**
- **1 container (8 ounces) vanilla low fat yogurt**
- **1 egg**
- **2 tablespoons butter or margarine, softened**
- **1 cup finely chopped pecans**
- **1 cup pecan halves**

1. Preheat oven to 350°F. Grease cookie sheets.

2. Combine cake mix, yogurt, egg, butter and chopped pecans in large bowl. Beat at low speed with electric mixer until blended. Drop by rounded teaspoonfuls 2 inches apart onto prepared cookie sheets. Press pecan half onto center of each cookie. Bake at 350°F for 11 to 13 minutes or until golden brown. Cool 1 minute on cookie sheets. Remove to cooling racks. Cool completely. Store in airtight container.

Makes about 4½ to 5 dozen cookies

Creamy Cappuccino Brownies

- **1 package (21 to 24 ounces) brownie mix**
- **1 tablespoon coffee crystals *or* 1 teaspoon espresso powder**
- **2 tablespoons warm water**
- **1 cup (8 ounces) Wisconsin Mascarpone cheese**
- **3 tablespoons sugar**
- **1 egg**
- **Powdered sugar**

Grease bottom of 13×9-inch baking pan. Prepare brownie mix according to package directions. Pour half of batter into prepared pan. Dissolve coffee crystals in water; add Mascarpone, sugar and egg. Blend until smooth. Drop by spoonfuls over brownie batter; top with remaining brownie batter. With knife, swirl cheese mixture through brownies creating a marbled effect. Bake at 375°F 30 to 35 minutes or until toothpick inserted in center comes out clean. Sprinkle with powdered sugar. *Makes 2 dozen brownies*

Favorite recipe from Wisconsin Milk Marketing Board

Orange Pecan Gems

Pumpkin Snack Bars

CAKE

1 package (2-layer size) spice cake mix
1 can (16 ounces) pumpkin
¾ cup MIRACLE WHIP® or MIRACLE WHIP® LIGHT Dressing
3 eggs

FROSTING

3½ cups powdered sugar
½ cup (1 stick) butter or margarine, softened
2 tablespoons milk
1 teaspoon vanilla

CAKE

- Heat oven to 350°F.
- Blend cake mix, pumpkin, dressing and eggs with electric mixer on medium speed until well blended. Pour into greased 15×10×1-inch baking pan.
- Bake 18 to 20 minutes or until toothpick inserted in center comes out clean. Cool completely on wire rack.

FROSTING

- Blend all ingredients with electric mixer on low speed until moistened. Beat on high speed until light and fluffy. Spread over cake. Cut into bars. *Makes about 3 dozen bars*

Prep Time: 20 minutes
Cook Time: 20 minutes

Tip

A 1-pound bag of powdered sugar contains 4 cups unsifted powdered sugar (4½ cups sifted).

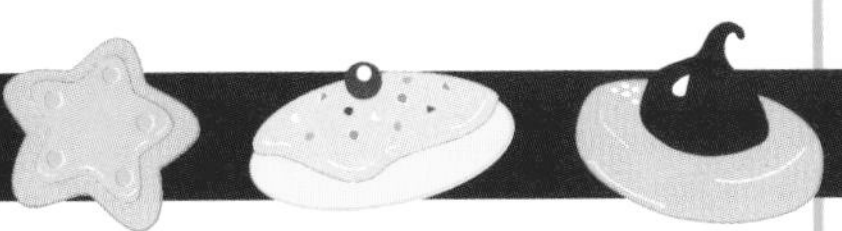

Fudgy Walnut Cookie Wedges

- 1 package (20 ounces) refrigerated cookie dough, any flavor
- 2 cups (12-ounce package) HERSHEY'S® Semi-Sweet Chocolate Chips
- 2 tablespoons butter or margarine
- 1 can (14 ounces) sweetened condensed milk (not evaporated milk)
- 1 teaspoon vanilla extract
- ½ cup chopped walnuts

1. Heat oven to 350°F.

2. Divide cookie dough into thirds. With floured hands, press on bottom of 3 aluminum foil-lined 9-inch round cake pans or press into 9-inch circles on ungreased cookie sheets.

3. Bake 10 to 20 minutes or until golden. Cool. Melt chips and butter with sweetened condensed milk in heavy saucepan over medium heat. Cook and stir until thickened, about 5 minutes. Remove from heat; add vanilla.

4. Spread over cookie circles. Top with walnuts. Chill. Cut into wedges. Store loosely covered at room temperature.

Makes about 36 wedges

Strawberry Streusel Squares

1 package (about 18 ounces) yellow cake mix, divided
3 tablespoons uncooked old-fashioned oats
1 tablespoon margarine
1½ cups sliced strawberries
¾ cup plus 2 tablespoons water, divided
¾ cup diced strawberries
3 egg whites
⅓ cup unsweetened applesauce
½ teaspoon cinnamon
⅛ teaspoon nutmeg

1. Preheat oven to 350°F. Spray 13×9-inch baking pan with nonstick cooking spray; lightly coat with flour.

2. Combine ½ cup cake mix and oats in small bowl. Cut in margarine until mixture resembles coarse crumbs; set aside.

3. Place 1½ cups sliced strawberries and 2 tablespoons water in blender or food processor. Process until smooth. Transfer to small bowl and stir in ¾ cup diced strawberries. Set aside.

4. Place remaining cake mix in large bowl. Add ¾ cup water, egg whites, applesauce, cinnamon and nutmeg. Blend 30 seconds at low speed or just until moistened. Beat at medium speed 2 minutes. Pour batter into prepared pan.

5. Spoon strawberry mixture evenly over batter, spreading lightly. Sprinkle evenly with oat mixture. Bake 31 to 34 minutes or until wooden toothpick inserted into center comes out clean. Cool completely in pan on wire rack.

Makes 12 servings

Strawberry Streusel Squares

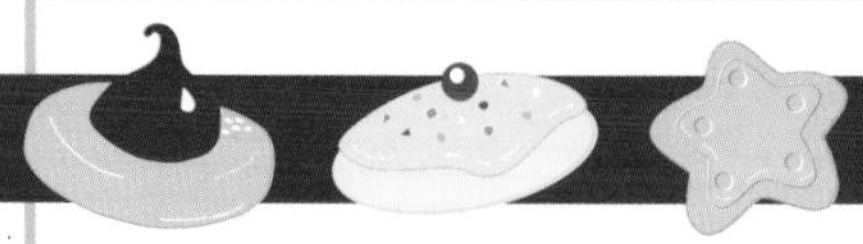

Cookie Pizza

1 package (20 ounces) refrigerated sugar or peanut butter cookie dough
All-purpose flour (optional)
6 ounces (1 cup) semisweet chocolate chips
1 tablespoon plus 2 teaspoons shortening, divided
¼ cup white chocolate chips
Gummy fruit, chocolate-covered peanuts, assorted roasted nuts, raisins, jelly beans and other assorted candies

1. Preheat oven to 350°F. Generously grease 12-inch pizza pan. Remove dough from wrapper according to package directions.

2. Sprinkle dough with flour to minimize sticking, if necessary. Press dough into bottom of prepared pan, leaving about ¼-inch space between edge of dough and pan.

3. Bake 14 to 23 minutes or until golden brown and set in center. Cool completely in pan on wire rack, running spatula between cookie crust and pan after 10 to 15 minutes to loosen.

4. Melt semisweet chocolate chips and 1 tablespoon shortening in microwavable bowl on HIGH (100%) 1 minute; stir. Repeat process at 10- to 20-second intervals until smooth.

5. Melt white chocolate chips and remaining 2 teaspoons shortening in another microwavable bowl on MEDIUM-HIGH (70%) 1 minute; stir. Repeat process at 10- to 20-second intervals until smooth.

6. Spread melted semisweet chocolate mixture over crust to within 1 inch of edge. Decorate with desired toppings.

7. Drizzle melted white chocolate over toppings to resemble melted mozzarella cheese. Cut and serve.

Makes 10 to 12 pizza slices

Cookie Pizza

Vanilla Butter Crescents

- **1 package DUNCAN HINES® Moist Deluxe French Vanilla Flavor Cake Mix**
- **¾ cup butter, softened**
- **1 vanilla bean, very finely chopped (see Tip)**
- **1 cup finely chopped pecans or walnuts**
- **Confectioners' sugar**

1. Preheat oven to 350°F.

2. Place cake mix and butter in large bowl. Cut in butter with pastry blender or 2 knives. Stir in vanilla bean and pecans. Since mixture is crumbly, it may be helpful to work dough with hands to blend until mixture holds together. Shape dough into balls. Roll 1 ball between palms until 4 inches long. Shape into crescent. Repeat with remaining balls. Place 2 inches apart on ungreased baking sheets. Bake at 350°F for 10 to 12 minutes or until light golden brown around edges. Cool 2 minutes on baking sheets. Remove to cooling racks. Dust with confectioners' sugar. Cool completely. Dust with additional confectioners' sugar, if desired. Store in airtight container. *Makes 4 dozen cookies*

Tip: *To quickly chop vanilla bean, place in work bowl of food processor fitted with knife blade. Process until finely chopped.*

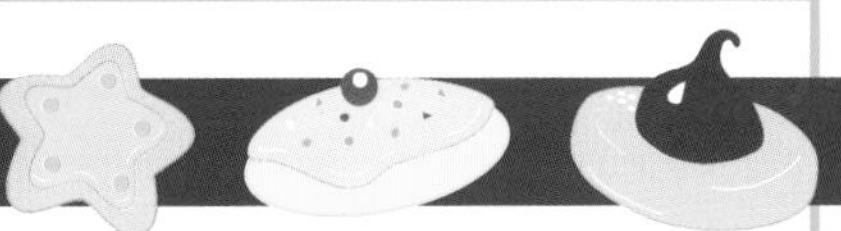

Rocky Road Squares

- **1 package (21.5 ounces) fudge brownie mix calling for ½ cup water**
- **Vegetable oil, per package directions**
- **Egg(s), per package directions**
- **½ cup CARNATION® Evaporated Milk**
- **2 cups miniature marshmallows**
- **1½ cups coarsely chopped DIAMOND® Walnuts**
- **1 cup (6 ounces) NESTLÉ® TOLL HOUSE® Semi-Sweet Chocolate Morsels**

PREPARE brownie mix according to package directions, using oil and egg(s); substitute evaporated milk for water. Spread into greased 13×9-inch baking pan. Bake according to package directions; do not overbake. Remove from oven. Top with marshmallows, walnuts and morsels.

BAKE for 3 to 5 minutes or just until topping is warm and begins to melt together. Cool for 20 to 30 minutes before cutting into squares. *Makes 24 brownies*

Tip

You can prevent marshmallows from drying out by storing them in a tightly sealed plastic bag in the freezer.

Chocolate Caramel Nut Bars

- **1 package (18¼ ounces) devil's food cake mix**
- **¾ cup butter or margarine, melted**
- **½ cup milk, divided**
- **60 vanilla caramels**
- **1 cup cashews**
- **1 cup semisweet chocolate chips**

Preheat oven to 350°F. Grease 13×9-inch baking pan. Combine cake mix, butter and ¼ cup milk in medium bowl; mix well. Press half of batter into bottom of prepared pan.

Bake 7 to 8 minutes or until batter just begins to form crust. Remove from oven.

Meanwhile, combine caramels and remaining ¼ cup milk in heavy medium saucepan. Cook over low heat, stirring often, about 5 minutes or until caramels are melted and mixture is smooth.

Pour melted caramel mixture over partially baked crust. Combine cashews and chocolate chips in small bowl; sprinkle over caramel mixture.

Drop spoonfuls of remaining batter evenly over nut mixture. Return pan to oven; bake 18 to 20 minutes more or until top cake layer springs back when lightly touched. (Caramel center will be soft.) Let cool on wire rack before cutting into squares or bars. (Bars can be frozen; let thaw 20 to 25 minutes before serving.)

Makes about 48 bars

Chocolate Caramel Nut Bars

Surprise Cookies

1 package (about 18 ounces) refrigerated sugar cookie dough
All-purpose flour (optional)
Any combination of walnut halves, whole almonds, chocolate-covered raisins or caramel candy squares
Assorted colored sugars

1. Grease cookie sheets. Remove dough from wrapper according to package directions.

2. Divide dough into 4 equal sections. Reserve 1 section; cover and refrigerate remaining 3 sections.

3. Roll reserved dough to ¼-inch thickness. Sprinkle with flour to minimize sticking, if necessary.

4. Cut out 3-inch square cookie with sharp knife. Transfer cookie to prepared cookie sheet.

5. Place desired "surprise" filling in center of cookie. (If using caramel candy square, place so that caramel forms diamond shape within square.)

6. Bring up 4 corners of dough towards center; pinch gently to seal. Repeat steps with remaining dough and fillings, placing cookies about 2 inches apart on prepared cookie sheets. Sprinkle with colored sugar, if desired.

7. Freeze cookies 20 minutes. Preheat oven to 350°F.

8. Bake 9 to 11 minutes or until edges are lightly browned. Remove to wire racks; cool completely.

Makes about 14 cookies

Tip: Make extra batches of these simple cookies and store in freezer in heavy-duty freezer bags. Take out a few at a time for kids' after-school treats.

Surprise Cookies

Banana Berry Brownie Pizza

⅓ cup cold water
1 package (15 ounces) brownie mix
¼ cup oil
1 egg
1 package (8 ounces) PHILADELPHIA® Cream Cheese, softened
¼ cup sugar
1 egg
1 teaspoon vanilla
Strawberry slices
Banana slices
2 squares (1 ounce each) BAKER'S® Semi-Sweet Chocolate, melted

PREHEAT oven to 350°F. Bring water to boil.

MIX together brownie mix, boiled water, oil and egg in large bowl until well blended.

POUR into greased and floured 12-inch pizza pan.

BAKE 25 minutes.

BEAT cream cheese, sugar, egg and vanilla in small mixing bowl at medium speed with electric mixer until well blended. Pour over crust.

BAKE 15 minutes. Cool. Top with fruit; drizzle with chocolate. Garnish with mint leaves, if desired.

Makes 10 to 12 servings

Microwave Tip: To melt chocolate, place unwrapped chocolate squares in small bowl. Microwave on HIGH 1 to 2 minutes or until almost melted. Stir until smooth.

Prep Time: 35 minutes
Cook Time: 40 minutes

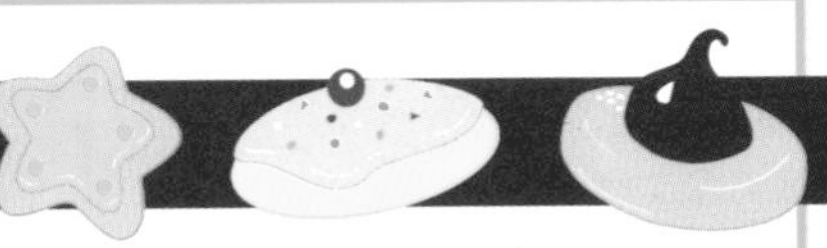

Sweet Walnut Maple Bars

CRUST

1 package DUNCAN HINES® Moist Deluxe Yellow Cake Mix, divided
⅓ cup butter or margarine, melted
1 egg

TOPPING

1⅓ cups MRS. BUTTERWORTH'S® Maple Syrup
3 eggs
⅓ cup firmly packed light brown sugar
½ teaspoon maple flavoring or vanilla extract
1 cup chopped walnuts

1. Preheat oven to 350°F. Grease 13×9×2-inch pan.

2. **For crust,** reserve ⅔ cup cake mix; set aside. Combine remaining cake mix, melted butter and egg in large bowl. Stir until thoroughly blended. (Mixture will be crumbly.) Press into pan. Bake at 350°F for 15 to 20 minutes or until light golden brown.

3. **For topping,** combine reserved cake mix, maple syrup, eggs, brown sugar and maple flavoring in large bowl. Beat at low speed with electric mixer for 3 minutes. Pour over crust. Sprinkle with walnuts. Bake at 350°F for 30 to 35 minutes or until filling is set. Cool completely. Cut into bars. Store leftover cookie bars in refrigerator. *Makes 24 bars*

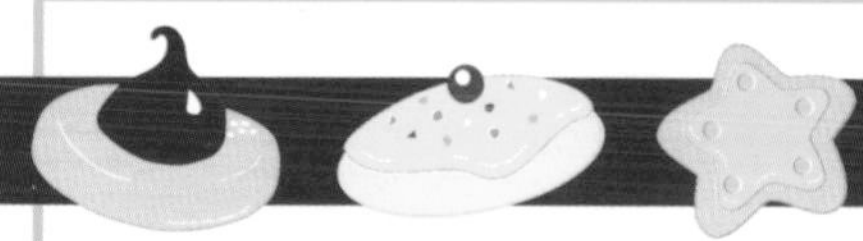

Ultimate Brownies

½ cup MIRACLE WHIP® Salad Dressing
2 eggs, beaten
¼ cup cold water
1 package (21.5 ounces) fudge brownie mix
3 milk chocolate bars (7 ounces each), divided
Walnut halves (optional)

• Preheat oven to 350°F.

• Mix together salad dressing, eggs and water until well blended. Stir in brownie mix, mixing just until moistened.

• Coarsely chop 2 chocolate bars; stir into brownie mixture. Pour into greased 13×9-inch baking pan.

• Bake 30 to 35 minutes or until edges begin to pull away from sides of pan. Immediately top with remaining chocolate bar, chopped. Let stand about 5 minutes or until melted; spread evenly over brownies. Garnish with walnut halves, if desired. Cool. Cut into squares.

Makes about 24 brownies

Easy Peanutty Snickerdoodles

3 tablespoons sugar
3 teaspoons ground cinnamon
1 package (22.3 ounces) golden sugar cookie mix
2 eggs
⅓ cup vegetable oil
1 teaspoon water
1 cup REESE'S® Peanut Butter Chips

1. Heat oven to 375°F. Stir together sugar and cinnamon in small bowl; set aside.

2. Empty cookie mix into large bowl. Break up any lumps. Add eggs, oil and water; stir with spoon or fork until well blended. Stir in peanut butter chips. Shape dough into 1-inch balls. (If dough is too soft, cover and refrigerate about 1 hour.) Roll balls in cinnamon-sugar; place on ungreased cookie sheet.

3. Bake 9 to 11 minutes or until set. Cool slightly; remove from cookie sheet to wire rack. Cool completely.

Makes about 3½ dozen cookies

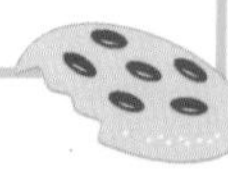

Ultimate Brownies

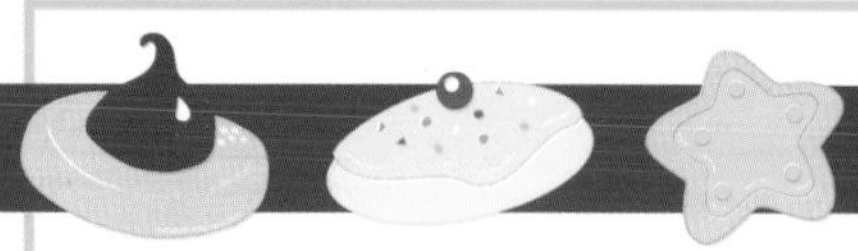

Oatmeal Brownie Gems

2¾ cups quick-cooking or old-fashioned oats, uncooked
1 cup all-purpose flour
1 cup firmly packed light brown sugar
1 cup coarsely chopped walnuts
1 teaspoon baking soda
1 cup butter or margarine, melted
1¾ cups "M&M's"® Semi-Sweet Chocolate Mini Baking Bits
1 (19- to 21-ounce) package fudge brownie mix, prepared according to package directions for fudge-like brownies

Preheat oven to 350°F. In large bowl combine oats, flour, sugar, nuts and baking soda; add butter until mixture forms coarse crumbs. Toss in "M&M's"® Semi-Sweet Chocolate Mini Baking Bits until evenly distributed. Reserve 3 cups mixture. Pat remaining mixture onto bottom of 15×10×1-inch pan to form crust. Pour prepared brownie mix over crust, carefully spreading into thin layer. Sprinkle reserved crumb mixture over top of brownie mixture; pat down lightly. Bake 25 to 30 minutes or until toothpick inserted in center comes out with moist crumbs. Cool completely. Cut into bars. Store in tightly covered container.

Makes 48 bars

Tip

To melt butter in the microwave, place 1 cup (2 sticks) of butter in a microwavable dish. Cover with plastic wrap and heat at HIGH 1½ to 2 minutes.

Oatmeal Brownie Gems

Chocolate Caramel Brownies

1 package (18¼ to 18½ ounces) devil's food or chocolate cake mix
1 cup chopped nuts
½ cup (1 stick) butter or margarine, melted
1 cup *undiluted* CARNATION® Evaporated Milk, divided
35 light caramels (10 ounces)
1 cup (6-ounce package) NESTLÉ® TOLL HOUSE® Semi-Sweet Chocolate Morsels

COMBINE cake mix and nuts in large bowl; stir in butter. Stir in ½ cup evaporated milk (batter will be thick). Spread half of batter in greased 13×9-inch baking pan.

BAKE in preheated 350°F. oven for 15 minutes.

COMBINE caramels and remaining evaporated milk in small saucepan; cook over low heat, stirring occasionally, until caramels are melted. Sprinkle morsels over baked layer. Drizzle melted caramels over chocolate morsels, carefully spreading to cover chocolate layer. Drop remaining half of batter in heaping teaspoons over caramel mixture.

RETURN to oven; bake 20 to 25 minutes longer (top layer will be soft). Cool completely before cutting.

Makes 48 brownies

Banana Chocolate Chip Cookies

2 extra-ripe, medium DOLE® Bananas, peeled
1 package (17.5 ounces) chocolate chip cookie mix
½ teaspoon ground cinnamon
1 egg, lightly beaten
1 teaspoon vanilla extract
1 cup toasted wheat germ

- Mash bananas with fork. Measure 1 cup.
- Combine cookie mix and cinnamon. Stir in contents of enclosed flavoring packet, mashed bananas, egg and vanilla until well blended. Stir in wheat germ.
- Drop batter by heaping tablespoonfuls 2 inches apart onto cookie sheets coated with cooking spray. Shape cookies with back of spoon. Bake in 375°F oven 10 to 12 minutes until lightly browned. Cool on wire racks. *Makes 18 cookies*

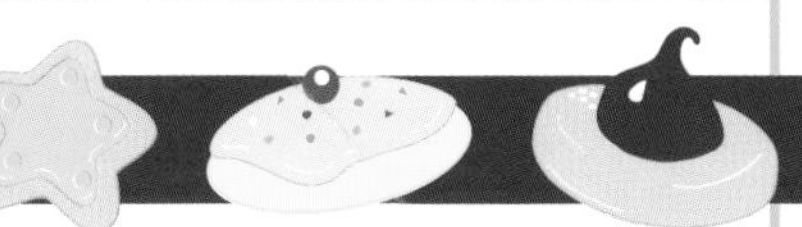

Peanut Maple Triangles

1¼ cups powdered sugar, divided
½ cup creamy peanut butter
¼ cup plus 3 tablespoons maple-flavored syrup, divided
1 package (17½ ounces) frozen puff pastry dough, thawed

1. Preheat oven to 400°F. Combine ¼ cup powdered sugar, peanut butter and ¼ cup maple syrup in small bowl until well blended; set aside.

2. Cut pastry dough into 3-inch-wide strips. Place rounded teaspoon peanut butter mixture about 1 inch from 1 end of each strip.

3. Starting at end of each strip with filling, fold corner of pastry dough over filling so it lines up with other side of strip, forming a triangle. Continue folding like a flag in triangular shape, using entire strip. Repeat process with remaining pastry dough and filling.

4. Place triangles about 2 inches apart onto ungreased baking sheets, seam-side down; spray with cooking spray. Bake 6 to 8 minutes or until golden brown. Remove from baking sheets to wire rack to cool.

5. Combine remaining 1 cup powdered sugar, 3 tablespoons syrup and 1 to 2 tablespoons water in small bowl. Glaze cookies just before serving. *Makes 28 cookies*

Note: *For longer storage, do not glaze cookies and store loosely covered so pastry dough remains crisp. Glaze before serving.*

Prep and Bake Time: 30 minutes

Festive Fudge Blossoms

¼ cup butter or margarine, softened
1 box (18.25 ounces) chocolate fudge cake mix
1 egg, slightly beaten
2 tablespoons water
¾ to 1 cup finely chopped walnuts
48 chocolate star candies

1. Preheat oven to 350°F. Cut butter into cake mix in large bowl until mixture resembles coarse crumbs. Stir in egg and water until well blended.

2. Shape dough into ½-inch balls; roll in walnuts, pressing nuts gently into dough. Place about 2 inches apart on ungreased baking sheets.

3. Bake cookies 12 minutes or until puffed and nearly set. Place chocolate star in center of each cookie; bake 1 minute more. Cool 2 minutes on baking sheet. Remove cookies from baking sheets to wire rack to cool completely.

Makes 4 dozen cookies

Spicy Sour Cream Cookies

1 package DUNCAN HINES® Moist Deluxe Spice Cake Mix
1 cup sour cream
1 cup chopped pecans or walnuts
¼ cup butter or margarine, softened
1 egg

1. Preheat oven to 350°F. Grease cookie sheets.

2. Combine cake mix, sour cream, pecans, butter and egg in large bowl. Mix at low speed with electric mixer until blended.

3. Drop dough by rounded teaspoonfuls onto prepared cookie sheets. Bake 9 to 11 minutes or until lightly browned. Cool 2 minutes on cookie sheets. Remove to cooling racks; cool completely.

Makes about 4½ dozen cookies

Festive Fudge Blossoms

Especially for Kids

Crayon Cookies

1 cup butter, softened
2 teaspoons vanilla
½ cup powdered sugar
2¼ cups all-purpose flour
¼ teaspoon salt
Assorted paste food colorings
1½ cups chocolate chips
1½ teaspoons shortening

1. Preheat oven to 350°F. Grease cookie sheets. Beat butter and vanilla in large bowl at high speed of electric mixer until fluffy. Add sugar; beat at medium speed until blended. Combine flour and salt in small bowl. Gradually add to butter mixture.

2. Divide dough into 10 equal sections. Reserve 1 section; cover and refrigerate remaining 9 sections. Combine reserved section and desired food coloring in small bowl; blend well.

3. Cut dough into 2 equal sections. Roll each section into 5-inch log. Pinch one end to resemble crayon tip. Place cookies 2 inches apart on prepared cookie sheets. Repeat with remaining 9 sections of dough and desired food colorings.

4. Bake 15 to 18 minutes or until edges are lightly browned. Cool completely on cookie sheets.

5. Combine chocolate chips and shortening in small microwavable bowl. Microwave at HIGH 1 to 1½ minutes or until smooth. Decorate with chocolate mixture as shown in photo.

Makes 20 cookies

Crayon Cookies

Happy Cookie Pops

1½ cups granulated sugar
1 cup butter-flavored solid vegetable shortening
2 large eggs
1 teaspoon vanilla extract
2¾ cups all-purpose flour
1 teaspoon baking powder
½ teaspoon baking soda
1¾ cups "M&M's"® Chocolate Mini Baking Bits, divided
Additional granulated sugar
2½ dozen flat wooden ice cream sticks
Prepared frostings
Tubes of decorator's icing

In large bowl cream 1½ cups sugar and shortening until light and fluffy; beat in eggs and vanilla. In medium bowl combine flour, baking powder and baking soda; blend into creamed mixture. Stir in 1¼ cups "M&M's"® Chocolate Mini Baking Bits. Wrap and refrigerate dough 1 hour.

Preheat oven to 375°F. Roll 1½ tablespoons dough into ball and roll in granulated sugar. Insert ice cream stick into each ball. Place about 2 inches apart onto ungreased cookie sheets; gently flatten, using bottom of small plate. On half the cookies, make a smiling face by placing some of the remaining "M&M's"® Chocolate Mini Baking Bits on the surface; leave other cookies for decorating after baking. Bake all cookies 10 to 12 minutes or until golden. Cool 2 minutes on cookie sheets; cool completely on wire racks. Decorate cookies as desired using frostings, decorator's icing and remaining "M&M's"® Chocolate Mini Baking Bits. Store in single layer in tightly covered container.

Makes 2½ dozen cookies

Variation: *For chocolate cookies, combine ⅓ cup unsweetened cocoa powder with flour, baking powder and baking soda; continue as directed.*

Happy Cookie Pops

Moons and Stars

- 1 cup butter, softened
- 1 cup sugar
- 1 egg
- 2 teaspoons lemon peel
- ½ teaspoon almond extract
- 3 cups all-purpose flour
- ½ cup ground almonds
- All-purpose flour (optional)
- Assorted colored icings, hard candies and colored sprinkles

1. Preheat oven to 350°F. Grease cookie sheets.

2. Beat butter, sugar, egg, lemon peel and almond extract in large bowl at medium speed of electric mixer until light and fluffy.

3. Combine flour and almonds in medium bowl. Add flour mixture to butter mixture; stir just until combined.

4. Roll dough on lightly floured surface to ⅛- to ¼-inch thickness. Cut out cookies using moon and star cookie cutters. Place cookies 2 inches apart on prepared cookie sheets.

5. Bake 7 to 9 minutes or until set but not browned. Cool on cookie sheets 2 minutes. Remove to wire rack; cool completely.

6. Decorate cookies with icings, sugars and sprinkles as shown in photo. *Makes about 4 dozen cookies*

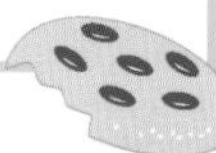

Moons and Stars

Chocolate Surprise Cookies

- **2¾ cups all-purpose flour**
- **¾ cup unsweetened cocoa powder**
- **½ teaspoon baking powder**
- **½ teaspoon baking soda**
- **1 cup (2 sticks) butter or margarine, softened**
- **1½ cups packed light brown sugar**
- **½ cup plus 1 tablespoon granulated sugar, divided**
- **2 eggs**
- **1 teaspoon vanilla**
- **1 cup chopped pecans, divided**
- **1 package (9 ounces) caramels coated in milk chocolate**
- **3 squares (1 ounce each) white chocolate, coarsely chopped**

Preheat oven to 375°F. Combine flour, cocoa, baking powder and baking soda in medium bowl; set aside.

Beat butter, brown sugar and ½ cup granulated sugar with electric mixer at medium speed until light and fluffy; beat in eggs and vanilla. Gradually add flour mixture and ½ cup pecans; beat well. Cover dough; refrigerate 15 minutes or until firm enough to roll into balls.

Place remaining ½ cup pecans and 1 tablespoon sugar in shallow dish. Roll tablespoonful of dough around 1 caramel candy, covering completely; press one side into nut mixture. Place, nut side up, on ungreased cookie sheet. Repeat with additional dough and candies, placing 3 inches apart.

Bake 10 to 12 minutes or until set and slightly cracked. Let stand on cookie sheet 2 minutes. Transfer cookies to wire rack; cool completely.

Place white chocolate pieces in small resealable plastic freezer bag; seal bag. Microwave at MEDIUM (50% power) 2 minutes. Turn bag over; microwave 2 to 3 minutes or until melted. Knead bag until chocolate is smooth. Cut off tiny corner of bag; drizzle chocolate onto cookies. Let stand about 30 minutes or until chocolate is set.

Makes about 3½ dozen cookies

Chocolate Surprise Cookies

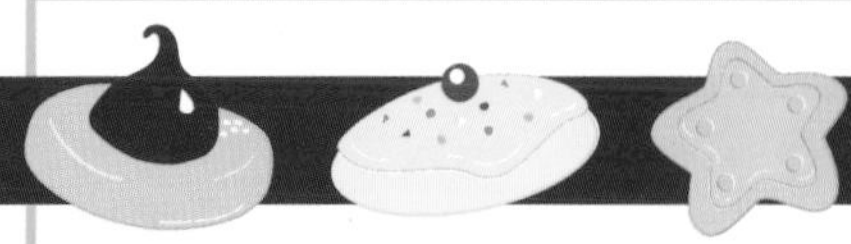

Sugar Cookie Pizza

- **1 package DUNCAN HINES® Golden Sugar Cookie Mix**
- **½ cup semisweet mini chocolate coated candy pieces**
- **1 container DUNCAN HINES® Vanilla or Chocolate Frosting (optional)**

Preheat oven to 350°F.

Prepare cookie mix as directed on package. Spread onto lightly greased 12-inch pizza pan. Sprinkle candy pieces evenly over cookie dough; press down gently. Bake 15 to 20 minutes or until golden brown. Cool 3 to 4 minutes in pan. Remove from pan; cool completely. Decorate with frosting, if desired. *Makes 12 servings*

Flourless Peanut Butter Cookies

- **1 cup peanut butter**
- **1 cup packed light brown sugar**
- **1 egg**
- **24 milk chocolate candy stars or other solid milk chocolate candy**

Preheat oven to 350°F. Combine peanut butter, sugar and egg in medium bowl until blended and smooth.

Shape dough into 24 balls about 1½ inches in diameter. Place 2 inches apart on ungreased cookie sheets. Press one chocolate star on top of each cookie. Bake 10 to 12 minutes or until set. Transfer to wire racks to cool completely.

Makes about 2 dozen cookies

Sugar Cookie Pizza

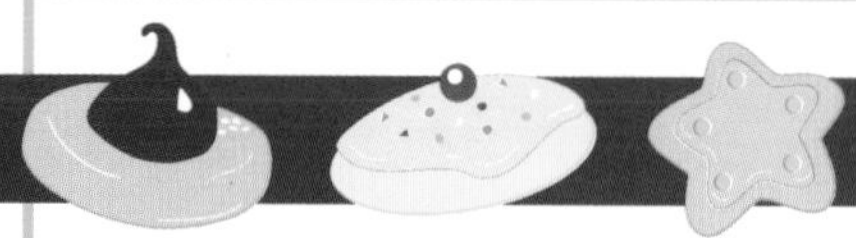

Peanut Butter and Jelly Sandwich Cookies

1 package (about 18 ounces) refrigerated sugar cookie dough
1 tablespoon unsweetened cocoa powder
All-purpose flour (optional)
1¾ cups creamy peanut butter
½ cup grape jam or jelly

1. Remove dough from wrapper according to package directions. Reserve ¼ section of dough; cover and refrigerate remaining ¾ section of dough. Combine reserved dough and cocoa in small bowl; refrigerate.

2. Shape remaining ¾ section dough into 5½-inch log. Sprinkle with flour to minimize sticking, if necessary. Remove chocolate dough from refrigerator; roll on sheet of waxed paper to 9½×6½-inch rectangle. Place dough log in center of rectangle.

3. Bring waxed paper edges and chocolate dough up and together over log. Press gently on top and sides of dough so entire log is wrapped in chocolate dough. Flatten log slightly to form square. Wrap in waxed paper. Freeze 10 minutes.

4. Preheat oven to 350°F. Remove waxed paper from dough. Cut dough into ¼-inch slices. Place slices 2 inches apart on ungreased cookie sheets. Reshape dough edges into square, if necessary. Press dough slightly to form indentation so dough resembles slice of bread.

5. Bake 8 to 11 minutes or until lightly browned. Remove from oven and straighten cookie edges with spatula. Cool 2 minutes on cookie sheets. Remove to wire racks; cool.

6. To make sandwich, spread about 1 tablespoon peanut butter on underside of 1 cookie. Spread about ½ tablespoon jam over peanut butter; top with second cookie, pressing gently. Repeat with remaining cookies.

Makes 11 sandwich cookies

Tip: Cut each sandwich diagonally in half for a smaller cookie and fun look.

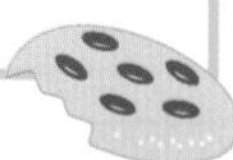

Peanut Butter and Jelly Sandwich Cookies

Cookie Pops

1 package (20 ounces) refrigerated sugar cookie dough
All-purpose flour (optional)
20 (4-inch) lollipop sticks
Assorted colored sugars, frostings, glazes and gels

1. Preheat oven to 350°F. Grease cookie sheets.

2. Remove dough from wrapper according to package directions. Sprinkle with flour to minimize sticking, if necessary.

3. Cut dough in half. Reserve 1 half; refrigerate remaining dough. Roll reserved dough to ⅛-inch thickness. Cut out cookies using 3½-inch cookie cutters.

4. Place lollipop sticks on cookies so that tips of sticks are imbedded in cookies. Carefully turn cookies so sticks are in back; place on prepared cookie sheets. Repeat with remaining dough.

5. Bake 7 to 11 minutes or until edges are lightly browned. Cool cookies on cookie sheets 2 minutes. Remove cookies to wire racks; cool completely.

6. Decorate with colored sugars, frostings, glazes and gels as desired. *Makes 20 cookies*

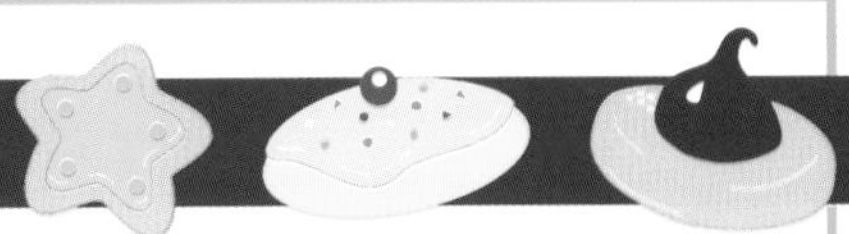

Caramel Marshmallow Bars

CRUMB MIXTURE
- **1¼ cups all-purpose flour**
- **½ cup sugar**
- **½ cup butter or margarine, softened**
- **¼ cup graham cracker crumbs**
- **¼ teaspoon salt**
- **½ cup chopped salted peanuts**

FILLING
- **¾ cup caramel ice cream topping**
- **½ cup salted peanuts**
- **½ cups miniature marshmallows**
- **½ cup milk chocolate chips**

Preheat oven to 350°F. Grease and flour 9-inch square baking pan. For crumb mixture, combine flour, sugar, butter, graham cracker crumbs and salt in small mixer bowl. Beat with electric mixer at low speed 1 to 2 minutes until mixture is crumbly. Stir in nuts. Reserve ¾ cup crumb mixture. Press remaining crumb mixture onto bottom of prepared pan. Bake 10 to 12 minutes or until lightly browned.

For filling, spread caramel topping evenly over hot crust. Sprinkle with nuts, marshmallows and chocolate chips. Crumble ¾ cup reserved crumb mixture over chocolate chips. Continue baking 10 to 12 minutes or until marshmallows just start to brown. Cool on wire rack about 30 minutes. Cover; refrigerate 1 to 2 hours or until firm. Cut into bars.

Makes about 30 bars

Tip: For an extra special treat, serve these kid-pleasing bars with a scoop of ice cream.

Peanuts

½ cup butter or margarine, softened
¼ cup shortening
¼ cup creamy peanut butter
1 cup powdered sugar, sifted
1 egg yolk
1 teaspoon vanilla
1¾ cups all-purpose flour
1 cup finely ground honey-roasted peanuts, divided
Peanut Buttery Frosting (recipe follows)

1. Beat butter, shortening and peanut butter in large bowl at medium speed of electric mixer. Gradually add sugar, beating until smooth. Add egg yolk and vanilla; beat well. Add flour; mix well. Stir in ⅓ cup ground peanuts. Cover dough; refrigerate 1 hour.

2. Prepare Peanut Buttery Frosting. Preheat oven to 350°F. Grease cookie sheets. Shape dough into 1-inch balls. Place 2 balls, side by side and slightly touching, on prepared cookie sheet. Gently flatten balls with fingertips and form into "peanut" shape. Repeat steps with remaining dough.

3. Bake 16 to 18 minutes or until edges are lightly browned. Cool on cookie sheets 5 minutes. Remove cookies to wire racks; cool completely.

4. Place remaining ⅔ cup ground peanuts in shallow dish. Spread about 2 teaspoons Peanut Buttery Frosting evenly over top of each cookie. Coat with ground peanuts.

Makes about 2 dozen cookies

Peanut Buttery Frosting

½ cup butter or margarine, softened
½ cup creamy peanut butter
2 cups powdered sugar, sifted
½ teaspoon vanilla
3 to 6 tablespoons milk

Beat butter and peanut butter in medium bowl at medium speed of electric mixer until smooth. Gradually add sugar and vanilla until blended but crumbly. Add milk, 1 tablespoon at a time, until smooth. Refrigerate until ready to use.

Makes 1⅓ cups frosting

Peanuts

Handprints

1 package (20 ounces) refrigerated cookie dough, any flavor
All-purpose flour (optional)
Cookie glazes, frostings, nondairy whipped topping, peanut butter and assorted candies

1. Grease cookie sheets. Remove dough from wrapper according to package directions.

2. Cut dough into 4 equal sections. Reserve 1 section; refrigerate remaining 3 sections. Sprinkle reserved dough with flour to minimize sticking, if necessary.

3. Roll dough on prepared cookie sheet to 5×7-inch rectangle.

4. Place hand, palm-side down, on dough. Carefully cut around outline of hand with knife. Remove scraps. Separate fingers as much as possible using small spatula. Pat fingers outward to lengthen slightly. Repeat steps with remaining dough.

5. Freeze dough 15 minutes. Preheat oven to 350°F.

6. Bake 7 to 13 minutes or until cookies are set and edges are golden brown. Cool completely on cookie sheets.

7. Decorate as desired. *Makes 4 adult handprint cookies*

Tip: To get the kids involved, let them use their hands to make the handprints. Be sure that an adult is available to cut around the outline with a knife. The kids will enjoy seeing how their handprints bake into big cookies.

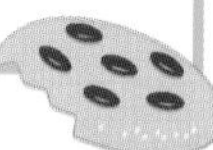

Handprints

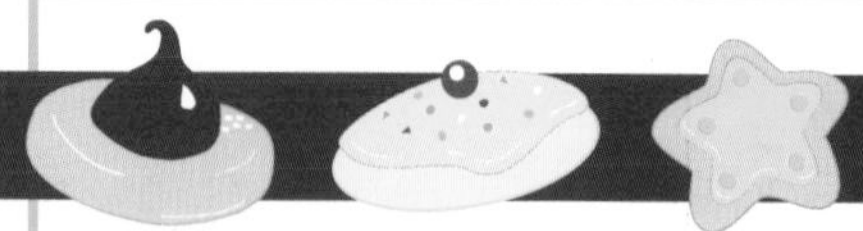

Sandwich Cookies

1 package (20 ounces) refrigerated cookie dough, any flavor
All-purpose flour (optional)
Any combination of colored frostings, peanut butter or assorted ice creams
Colored sprinkles, chocolate-covered raisins, miniature candy-coated chocolate pieces and other assorted small candies

1. Preheat oven to 350°F. Grease cookie sheets.

2. Remove dough from wrapper according to package directions.

3. Cut dough into 4 equal sections. Reserve 1 section; refrigerate remaining 3 sections.

4. Roll reserved dough to ¼-inch thickness. Sprinkle with flour to minimize sticking, if necessary.

5. Cut out cookies using ¾-inch round cookie cutter. Transfer cookies to prepared cookie sheets, placing about 2 inches apart. Repeat steps with remaining dough.

6. Bake 8 to 11 minutes or until edges are lightly browned. Remove to wire racks; cool completely.

7. To make sandwich, spread about 1 tablespoon desired filling on bottom of 1 cookie. Top with second cookie, pressing gently.

8. Roll side of sandwich in desired decorations. Repeat with remaining cookies.

Makes about 20 to 24 sandwich cookies

Tip: Be creative—make sandwich cookies using 2 or more flavors of refrigerated cookie dough. Mix and match to see how many flavor combinations you can come up with.

Sandwich Cookies

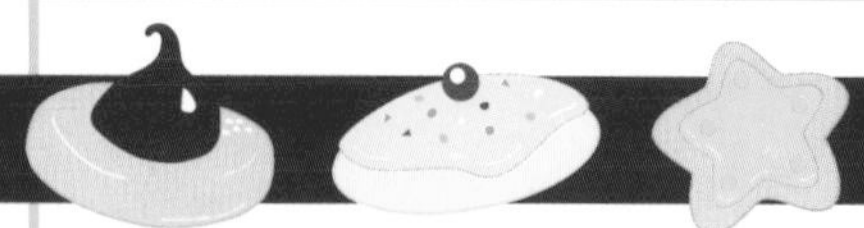

Mini Pizza Cookies

1 20-ounce tube of refrigerated sugar cookie dough
2 cups (16 ounces) prepared pink frosting
"M&M's"® Chocolate Mini Baking Bits
Variety of additional toppings such as shredded coconut, granola, raisins, nuts, small pretzels, snack mixes, sunflower seeds, popped corn and mini marshmallows

Preheat oven to 350°F. Lightly grease cookie sheets; set aside. Divide dough into 8 equal portions. On lightly floured surface, roll each portion of dough into ¼-inch-thick circle; place about 2 inches apart onto prepared cookie sheets. Bake 10 to 13 minutes or until golden brown on edges. Cool completely on wire racks. Spread top of each pizza with frosting; sprinkle with "M&M's"® Chocolate Mini Baking Bits and 2 or 3 suggested toppings. *Makes 8 cookies*

Tip

These cookies are a great activity for a kids' party, or even for a special after-school treat—kids will love creating and eating their own masterpieces!

Mini Pizza Cookies

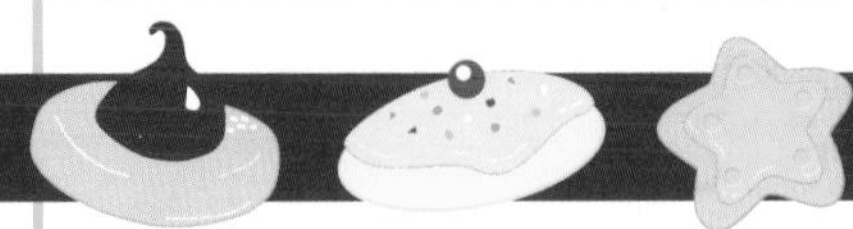

Peanut Butter Pizza Cookies

1¼ cups firmly packed light brown sugar
¾ cup creamy peanut butter
½ CRISCO® Stick or ½ cup CRISCO® all-vegetable shortening
3 tablespoons milk
1 tablespoon vanilla
1 egg
1¾ cups all-purpose flour
¾ teaspoon salt
¾ teaspoon baking soda
8 ounces white baking chocolate, chopped
Decorative candies

1. Heat oven to 375°F. Place sheets of foil on countertop for cooling cookies.

2. Combine brown sugar, peanut butter, shortening, milk and vanilla in large bowl. Beat at medium speed of electric mixer until well blended. Add egg. Beat just until blended.

3. Combine flour, salt and baking soda. Add to creamed mixture at low speed. Mix just until blended.

4. Divide dough in half. Form each half into a ball. Place 1 ball of dough onto center of ungreased pizza pan or baking sheet. Spread dough with fingers to form a 12-inch circle. Repeat with other ball of dough.

5. Bake one baking sheet at a time at 375°F for 10 to 12 minutes, or until lightly browned. *Do not overbake.* Cool 2 minutes on baking sheet. Remove with large spatula to foil to cool completely.

6. Place white chocolate in a shallow microwave-safe bowl. Microwave on 100% (HIGH) for 30 seconds. Stir. Repeat at 30 second intervals until white chocolate is melted.

7. Spread melted white chocolate on center of cooled cookies to within ½ inch of edge. Decorate with candies. Set completely. Cut into wedges. *Makes 2 pizzas*

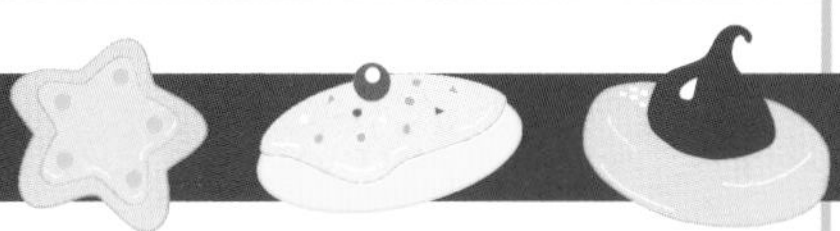

PB & J Cookie Sandwiches

- ½ cup butter or margarine, softened
- ½ cup creamy peanut butter
- ¼ cup solid vegetable shortening
- 1 cup firmly packed light brown sugar
- 1 large egg
- 1 teaspoon vanilla extract
- 1⅔ cups all-purpose flour
- 1 teaspoon baking soda
- ½ teaspoon baking powder
- 1 cup "M&M's"® Milk Chocolate Mini Baking Bits
- ½ cup finely chopped peanuts
- ½ cup grape or strawberry jam

Preheat oven to 350°F. In large bowl cream butter, peanut butter, shortening and sugar until light and fluffy; beat in egg and vanilla. In medium bowl combine flour, baking soda and baking powder; blend into creamed mixture. Stir in "M&M's"® Milk Chocolate Mini Baking Bits and nuts. Drop by rounded teaspoonfuls onto ungreased cookie sheets. Bake 8 to 10 minutes or until light golden. Let cool 2 minutes on cookie sheets; remove to wire racks to cool completely. Just before serving, spread ½ teaspoon jam on bottom of one cookie; top with second cookie. Store in tightly covered container.

Makes about 2 dozen sandwich cookies

Fruity Cookie Rings and Twists

1 package (20 ounces) refrigerated sugar cookie dough
3 cups fruit-flavored cereal, crushed and divided

Tip

Be creative! Try making the cookies in a variety of shapes in addition to rings and twists: form the ropes of dough into pretzels, snails, hearts or alphabet letters.

1. Remove dough from wrapper according to package directions.

2. Combine dough and ½ cup cereal in large bowl. Divide dough into 32 balls. Refrigerate 1 hour.

3. Preheat oven to 375°F. Roll dough balls into 6- to 8-inch-long ropes. Roll ropes in remaining cereal to coat; shape into rings or fold in half and twist.

4. Place cookies 2 inches apart on ungreased cookie sheets.

5. Bake 10 to 11 minutes or until lightly browned. Remove to wire racks; cool completely. *Makes 32 cookies*

Tip: These cookie rings can be transformed into Christmas tree ornaments by poking a hole in each unbaked ring using a drinking straw. Bake cookies and decorate with colored gels and small candies to resemble wreaths. Loop thin ribbon through holes and tie together.

Fruity Cookie Rings and Twists

Critters-in-Holes

48 chewy caramel candies coated in milk chocolate
48 pieces candy corn
Miniature candy-coated chocolate pieces
1 container frosting, any flavor
1 package (20 ounces) refrigerated peanut butter cookie dough

1. Cut slit into side of 1 caramel candy using sharp knife.

2. Carefully insert 1 piece candy corn into slit. Repeat with remaining caramel candies and candy corn.

3. Attach miniature chocolate pieces to caramel candies to resemble "eyes," using frosting as glue. Decorate as desired.

4. Preheat oven to 350°F. Grease 12 (1¾-inch) muffin cups.

5. Remove dough from wrapper according to package directions. Cut dough into 12 (1-inch) slices. Cut each slice into 4 equal sections. Place 1 section of dough into each muffin cup.

6. Bake 9 minutes. Remove from oven and immediately press 1 decorated caramel candy into center of each cookie. Repeat with remaining ingredients. Remove to wire racks; cool completely. *Makes 4 dozen cookies*

Critters-in-Holes

Kids' Favorite Jumbo Chippers

- **1 cup butter, softened**
- **¾ cup granulated sugar**
- **¾ cup packed brown sugar**
- **2 eggs**
- **1 teaspoon vanilla**
- **2¼ cups all-purpose flour**
- **1 teaspoon baking soda**
- **¾ teaspoon salt**
- **1 package (9 ounces) candy-coated chocolate pieces**
- **1 cup peanut butter flavored chips**

Preheat oven to 375°F. Beat butter, granulated sugar and brown sugar in large bowl until light and fluffy. Beat in eggs and vanilla. Add flour, baking soda and salt. Beat until well blended. Stir in chocolate pieces and peanut butter chips. Drop by rounded tablespoonfuls 3 inches apart onto ungreased cookie sheets. Bake 10 to 12 minutes or until edges are golden brown. Let cookies stand on cookie sheets 2 minutes. Remove cookies to wire racks; cool completely.

Makes 3 dozen cookies

Note: *For a change of pace, substitute white chocolate chips, chocolate chips, chocolate-covered raisins, toffee bits or any of your kids' favorite candy pieces for the candy-coated chocolate pieces.*

Crispy Cocoa Bars

- **¼ cup (½ stick) margarine**
- **¼ cup HERSHEY'®S Cocoa**
- **5 cups miniature marshmallows**
- **5 cups crisp rice cereal**

Spray 13×9×2-inch pan with vegetable cooking spray.

Melt margarine in large saucepan over low heat; stir in cocoa and marshmallows. Cook over low heat, stirring constantly, until marshmallows are melted and mixture is smooth and well blended. Continue cooking 1 minute, stirring constantly. Remove from heat.

Add cereal; stir until coated. Lightly spray spatula with vegetable cooking spray; press mixture into prepared pan. Cool completely. Cut into bars.

Makes 24 bars

Kids' Favorite Jumbo Chippers

Acknowledgments

The publisher would like to thank the companies and organizations listed below for the use of their recipes and photographs in this publication.

Arm & Hammer Division, Church & Dwight Co., Inc.
Bestfoods
California Prune Board
ConAgra Grocery Products Company
Dole Food Company, Inc.
Duncan Hines® and Moist Deluxe® are registered trademarks of Aurora Foods Inc.
Egg Beaters®
Fleischmann's® Original Spread
Hershey Foods Corporation
Kraft Foods, Inc.
M&M/MARS
McIlhenny Company (TABASCO® brand Pepper Sauce)
MOTT'S® Inc., a division of Cadbury Beverages Inc.
National Honey Board
Nestlé USA, Inc.
Peanut Advisory Board
PLANTERS® Baking Nuts
The Procter & Gamble Company
The Quaker® Oatmeal Kitchens
Reckitt Benckiser
The J.M. Smucker Company
The Sugar Association, Inc.
Washington Apple Commission
Wisconsin Milk Marketing Board

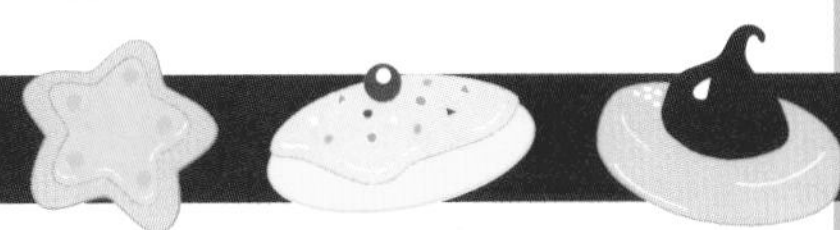

Index

Index

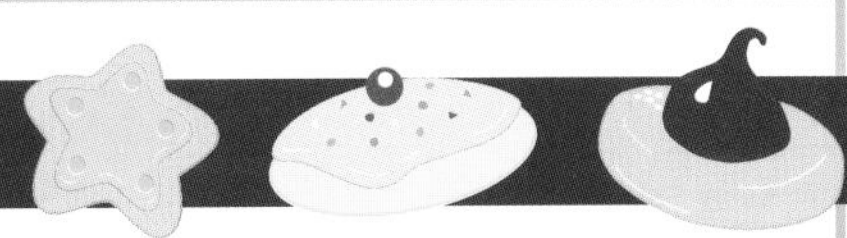

Index

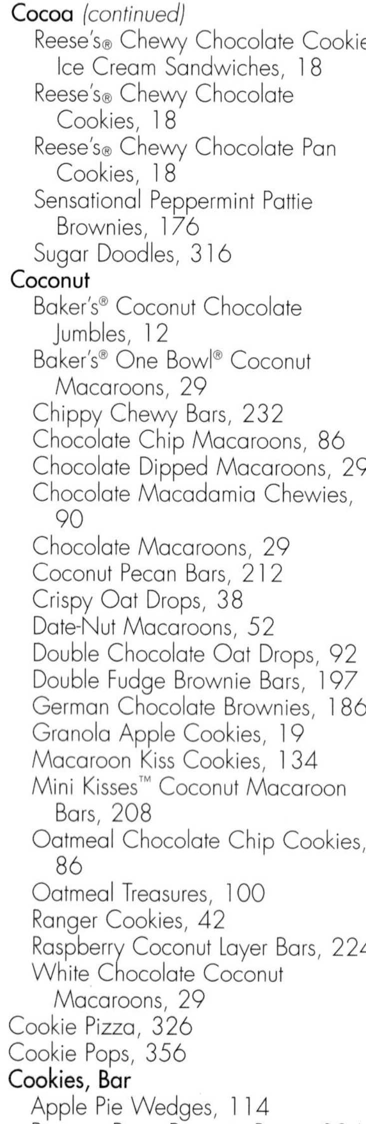

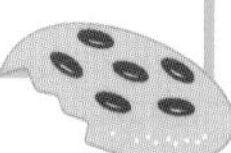

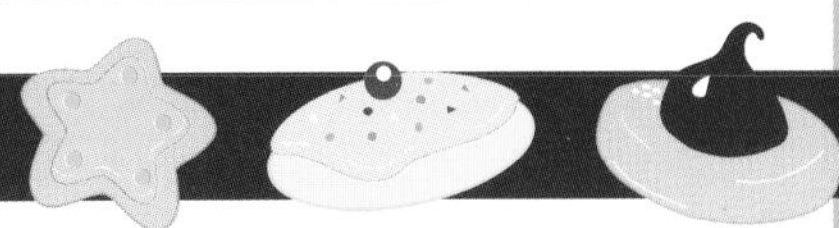

Index

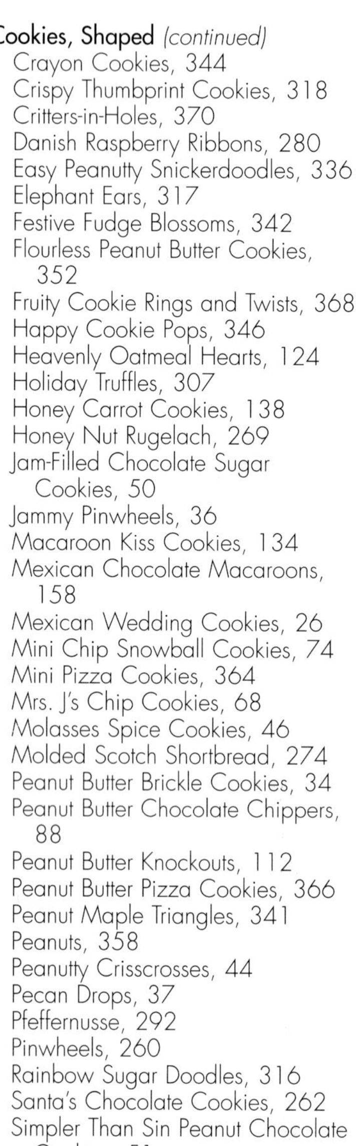

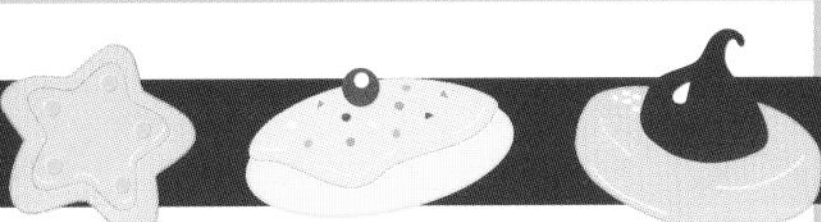

Index

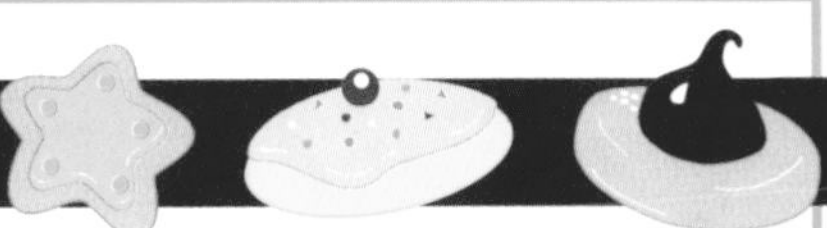

METRIC CONVERSION CHART

VOLUME MEASUREMENTS (dry)

1/8 teaspoon = 0.5 mL
1/4 teaspoon = 1 mL
1/2 teaspoon = 2 mL
3/4 teaspoon = 4 mL
1 teaspoon = 5 mL
1 tablespoon = 15 mL
2 tablespoons = 30 mL
1/4 cup = 60 mL
1/3 cup = 75 mL
1/2 cup = 125 mL
2/3 cup = 150 mL
3/4 cup = 175 mL
1 cup = 250 mL
2 cups = 1 pint = 500 mL
3 cups = 750 mL
4 cups = 1 quart = 1 L

VOLUME MEASUREMENTS (fluid)

1 fluid ounce (2 tablespoons) = 30 mL
4 fluid ounces (1/2 cup) = 125 mL
8 fluid ounces (1 cup) = 250 mL
12 fluid ounces (1 1/2 cups) = 375 mL
16 fluid ounces (2 cups) = 500 mL

WEIGHTS (mass)

1/2 ounce = 15 g
1 ounce = 30 g
3 ounces = 90 g
4 ounces = 120 g
8 ounces = 225 g
10 ounces = 285 g
12 ounces = 360 g
16 ounces = 1 pound = 450 g

DIMENSIONS

1/16 inch = 2 mm
1/8 inch = 3 mm
1/4 inch = 6 mm
1/2 inch = 1.5 cm
3/4 inch = 2 cm
1 inch = 2.5 cm

OVEN TEMPERATURES

250°F = 120°C
275°F = 140°C
300°F = 150°C
325°F = 160°C
350°F = 180°C
375°F = 190°C
400°F = 200°C
425°F = 220°C
450°F = 230°C

BAKING PAN SIZES

Utensil	Size in Inches/Quarts	Metric Volume	Size in Centimeters
Baking or Cake Pan (square or rectangular)	8×8×2	2 L	20×20×5
	9×9×2	2.5 L	23×23×5
	12×8×2	3 L	30×20×5
	13×9×2	3.5 L	33×23×5
Loaf Pan	8×4×3	1.5 L	20×10×7
	9×5×3	2 L	23×13×7
Round Layer Cake Pan	8×1½	1.2 L	20×4
	9×1½	1.5 L	23×4
Pie Plate	8×1¼	750 mL	20×3
	9×1¼	1 L	23×3
Baking Dish or Casserole	1 quart	1 L	—
	1½ quart	1.5 L	—
	2 quart	2 L	—

Y0-BRM-580

A DICTIONARY OF BATTLES

A DICTIONARY OF BATTLES

DAVID EGGENBERGER

THOMAS Y. CROWELL COMPANY

New York, Established 1834

To the infantry soldier of every age

who held the MOS (Military Occupation Specialty) of rifleman,

or its equivalent.

25141
MAR 4 1976

Maps by Donald T. Pitcher

Copyright © 1967 by David Eggenberger

All rights reserved. Except for use in a review, the reproduction or utilization of this work in any form or by any electronic, mechanical, or other means, now known or hereafter invented, including photocopying and recording, and in any information storage and retrieval system is forbidden without the written permission of the publisher.
Published in Canada by Fitzhenry & Whiteside Limited, Toronto.

Manufactured in the United States of America
by Vail-Ballou Press, Inc., Binghamton, N.Y.

ISBN 0-690-23744-8

4 5 6 7 8 9 10

Ref.
D
25
A2.E35

PREFACE

This book attempts to provide the essential details of all the major battles in recorded history. It covers more than 1,560 separate and distinct military engagements, from the first battle of Megiddo in 1479 B.C. to the fighting in Vietnam during the 1960's. The battles are listed alphabetically and identified by war, revolution, political movement, and so on. As far as possible, the entry for each battle presents the strategic situation, date of combat, military commanders, number of troops involved, tactics employed, casualties, and consequences of the action. With few exceptions each battle takes the name of its geographic location, whether it be a world-famous site such as Rome or a once-obscure hamlet in South Vietnam. This is true even for battles that may be equally well known by another name. What is called in Great Britain the Glorious First of June (June 1, 1794) is treated in this book under the title Ushant II, Lose-coat Field under Empingham, and two battles identified as Spurs under Guinegate and Courtrai. The only exceptions to this placement are the English-Scots battle at Cowton Moor, which is listed under the better-known name of (The) Standard; the American-British naval battle called Chesapeake vs. Shannon; the 1942 American carrier-based bombing of Japan, which President F. D. Roosevelt reported as originating in Shangri-La; and three World War II naval engagements listed under the names of the principal ships involved —*Graf Spee, Bismarck,* and *Prince of Wales–Repulse.*

Battle names are derived from the place names in use at the time of the engagement. Thus the 1302 conflict in Belgium is called the battle of Courtrai rather than the modern name of Kortrijk. In all such cases, however, the modern name is also given in the text. (In like manner military commanders are called by their rank at the time of the battle, without regard to the several grades of general and admiral). Roman numerals are used to show the occurrence of more than one battle at a particular site. Thus the battles of 1778 and 1794 at Ushant are entitled Ushant I and Ushant II, respectively.

In addition to entries for major battles there are about 150 brief entries that identify parts of larger battles and cross-refer to them. Examples are: Kasserine Pass (to Tunisia), Jackson (to Vicksburg), and Freeman's Farm (to Saratoga). Well-known variant names of battles are listed in the text as cross-reference entries. Also included within the alphabetical arrangement are more than eighty entries for the major wars of the world, from the Persian-Greek wars to the Vietnam conflict. These entries contain cross references, in chronological order, to the names of battles in each conflict. In addition there are dozens of entries for countries and geographical areas, with chronological cross references to the war entries and to entries for battles that are not associated with a broad-scale conflict.

The cross references found at the end of almost every entry list the relevant battles that immediately preceded and followed. Those battles that are a part of a named war or a series of related conflicts also carry a cross reference to the appropriate parent entry.

A battle is usually defined as a general fight or encounter between hostile military forces. Some of the elements of the definition include length of time of the encounter, scale (intensity) of fighting, size of the forces involved, influence on a particular campaign, and decisiveness of the action. A battle may be further defined by distinguishing it from a skirmish, a raid, or a siege. This book, however, uses the term battle in the broadest sense—that is, as a confrontation between opposing armed forces that resulted in casualties or in a change in the military situation. Under this definition many prolonged holding operations (such as those at Vicksburg and Plevna) are treated as battles even though a major feature may have been one of siege. Similarly, Dieppe is called a battle in this book although the action was planned and executed as a raid on an enemy-held town. The need to broaden the definition of a battle has been highlighted by warfare in the twentieth century in which entire countries became a single battlefield and the military action was sustained over a period of weeks or even months. This trend began in World War I with such battles as Serbia and Rumania, continued into the 1930's with Ethiopia and Albania, and culminated in World War II with such battles as Poland, Norway, and Britain. The clearest example of a nation becoming a theater of action was the fighting in Russia resulting from the German invasion of 1941. The struggle for the Soviet Union, a contest spread over thousands of miles and lasting three years, has been rightly called history's greatest continuous land battle.

It might be argued that some of the engagements in South Vietnam reported in this book fail to meet even the modern definition of a battle. Yet, in terms of national effort, international attention, and sheer intensity of fighting, each of these encounters seems to merit a place in history equal to (or perhaps even exceeding) that accorded such battles as those fought by Xenophon's Ten Thousand at Cunaxa, the Crusaders at Jerusalem, or General J. E. B. Stuart's cavalry at Bristoe Station.

As stated earlier, the battle descriptions in this book are listed under the geographic locations. This arrangement indicates that Jerusalem, the site of nine separate battles, has been the most fought-over place in the world. Next in line for this unenviable distinction are Adrianople (Edirne), Constantinople (Istanbul), and Rome, each the site of seven battles; Warsaw, with six; Pavia, five; and Alexandria, Baghdad, Paris, Prague, and Ravenna, four. The present-day importance of most of these cities testifies to man's inherent capability to endure and build anew.

DAVID EGGENBERGER

CONTENTS

BATTLE MAPS

Battle Maps

A DICTIONARY OF BATTLES

A

Aachen (World War II). This first German city to fall to the Allies was captured in bitter fighting between October 13 and 20, 1944. *See* Siegfried Line.

Abensberg (Napoleonic Empire Wars), 1809. When the armies of Napoleon I bogged down in Spain, Austria declared war on France for the fourth time since 1792. With 200,000 reorganized troops, Archduke Charles Louis, brother of Emperor Francis I, began crossing the Inn River on April 10, 1809. Marching into Bavaria south of the Danube River, Charles hoped to trap the III French Corps of Marshal Louis Davout at Regensberg (Ratisbon). Realizing his danger, Davout fought his way 18 miles southwest on April 19 to link up with Marshal François Lefebvre's VII Corps at Abensberg. Meanwhile, Napoleon hurried forward from Paris to take direct command. On April 20 he sent a provisional corps (25,000 men), commanded by Marshal Jean Lannes, south of Abensberg against the thinly stretched Austrian center. A hard-hitting French attack thrust between the wings of Charles's army. The archduke's right wing pulled back to Eggmühl (Eckmühl), south of Regensberg, while Gen. Baron Johann Hiller's left wing retreated south toward Landshut, on the Isar River. French casualties were few; the Austrians lost 2,700 killed and wounded and 4,000 prisoners. *See* Oporto; Sacile; Landshut; Napoleonic Empire Wars.

Abukir (Wars of the French Revolution), 1799. While Napoleon Bonaparte was withdrawing to Egypt from his repulse at Acre in May 1799, a Turkish expeditionary force of 18,000 men under Mustafa IV landed at Abukir, east of Alexandria, on July 15. Napoleon hurriedly regrouped his Egyptian forces and moved against the Turkish positions on the Abukir peninsula with 7,700 men. On July 25 a fierce French assault cracked the first Turkish defense line in an hour, shattering the force of 8,000 enemy troops. Continuing their artillery-supported attack against the second line, the French rolled up this position as well, killing or scattering another 6,000 of Mustafa's men. Pressing on up the peninsula, Napoleon destroyed the entire army, except for a few thousand that held out in Fort Abukir until August 2. In all, Turkish losses were 2,000 killed, 10–11,000 drowned trying to escape, and 3,000 captured. French casualties numbered 150 killed and 750 wounded.

Learning that the armies of the French Directory had been suffering serious defeats in Italy and Germany, Napoleon embarked for France on August 22. He left Gen. Jean Kléber to command the army in Egypt. *See* Acre III; Trebbia River II; Stokach I; Montebello; Alexandria III; French Revolution Wars.

Abu Klea (War for the Sudan), 1885. Seven months after Gen. George "Chinese" Gordon was trapped in Khartoum by the Sudanese Mahdists, a relief expedition left Cairo. Commanded by Gen. Sir Garnet Wolseley, the column pressed up the Nile toward Khartoum, 800 miles away. In northern Sudan Wolseley sent an 1,800-man camel corps under Gen. Sir Herbert Stewart directly across country, where the Nile makes a great bend to the east. At Abu Klea, a caravan stop 63 miles southwest of Ed Damer, Stewart's troops encountered almost 10,000 Mahdist followers of Mohammed Ahmed. In a desperate hand-to-hand battle on January 17, the Sudanese were repulsed with more than a thousand killed. Anglo-Egyptian casualties were 168.

Stewart's corps fought its way to the Nile two days later, but their commander was mortally wounded. On January 24 the force, now under Lord Charles Beresford, began moving upriver to Khartoum, where they arrived four days later—and 48 hours too late to save Gordon. *See* Khartoum; Atbara; Sudan, War for the.

Aclea (Danish Invasions of Britain), 851. The increasingly deep thrusts of the Danish Vikings into Britain brought on the major battle of Aclea (Oakley), south of the Thames. King Ethelwulf, son of Egbert and father of Alfred, deployed his Wessex army to meet the invaders. In a fierce struggle his men repelled the Danes. The successful defense helped establish Wessex as the premier state among the heptarchial kingdoms of Britain. But it was the only major victory of the West Saxons over the Danes during Ethelwulf's lifetime. *See* Hingston Down; York; Danish Invasions of Britain.

Acragas (Carthaginian Invasion of Sicily),

406 B.C. The Carthaginian scourge of Sicily, which began in 409, made Acragas (Agrigentum), on the southwest coast, the target three years later. Employing the same tactics he had used successfully at Selinus and Himera, Hannibal (not to be confused with the famed general of the Punic Wars) laid siege to the city, which was commanded by Dexippus, a Spartan. Although an epidemic swept through the Carthaginian camp, killing Hannibal and many others, Himilco, a cousin, succeeded to the command and continued the siege.

As in the earlier battles, a force of Syracusans, this time 35,000 men commanded by Daphnaeus, marched to the relief of the city. Under the walls of Acragas a pitched battle took place, in which the Carthaginians were partially defeated. However, dissension broke out among the Sicilians, and many mercenaries deserted. Finally, after eight months, the entire garrison abandoned the city, which was then occupied by the victorious Himilco. *See* Selinus-Himera; Syracuse II.

Acre I (Third Crusade), 1189–1191. The crushing Christian defeat at Tiberias and subsequent loss of Jerusalem in 1187 left the Turkish general Saladin master of the Near East except for the Frankish hold on Tyre. By luck, Conrad of Montferrat (in Italy) arrived at Tyre with a shipload of French knights in the summer of 1187, just in time to help repulse Saladin's attack on the city. For the next year Conrad built up his strength by recruiting armed pilgrims to his standard. Then, in July 1188, Saladin paroled Guy of Lusignan, the defeated king of Jerusalem. The two Christian leaders immediately quarreled over supreme command. Finally, in August 1189, King Guy marched out to attack the Moslem garrison at Acre, 20 miles to the south. Conrad followed in September.

Acre, a powerful fortress built on a peninsula, defied capture. The two rival Christian leaders, with about 30,000 men in all, prepared siege lines a mile to the east on the Hill of Turon. A mile still farther east Saladin built countersiege lines. A deadlock developed, in which both sides suffered more from disease and hunger than from combat, throughout 1190.

Meanwhile the three greatest kings of Europe were moving eastward in the Third Crusade. First to start was the red-bearded Frederick I, Barbarossa, Holy Roman emperor. Frederick led a strong contingent of Germans through the Balkans and Asia Minor but drowned in the Calycadnus (Göksu) River in Cicilia on June 10, 1190. His large army soon melted away and his son Frederick V of Swabia arrived in front of Acre in October with only 1,000 men-at-arms. The other two kings—colorless Philip II, Augustus, of France and flamboyant Richard I, Coeur de Lion, of England—set off in the summer of 1190, somewhat reluctant allies. They wintered in Sicily. Philip then sailed directly to Acre, arriving there on April 20, 1191. Richard stopped over at Cyprus to wrest that island from the Byzantine Empire and did not land on the beach at Acre until June 8.

The Christian host that had assembled at Acre quarreled too much among themselves to launch a unified assault on the fortress. But their piecemeal attacks, coupled with the tight blockade instituted by their ships in the harbor, forced the Moslem garrison to capitulate on July 12, ending the two-year siege. The victory brought new quarreling among the crusade commanders. Leopold, duke of Austria (who led the German contingent after the death of Frederick of Swabia in the last year of the siege), and King Philip sailed for Europe; Conrad sulked in Tyre; Richard, allied with King Guy, became sole leader of the crusade. When Saladin refused to honor the surrender terms of the Acre garrison, Richard executed all 2,700 Moslem captives. He then took the coast road south toward Jerusalem. *See* Jerusalem VIII; Arsouf; Crusades.

Acre II (Crusader-Turkish Wars), 1291. By 1290 the Christian kingdom of Jerusalem had been reduced to a few fortresses on the coast, ruled by the absent King Henry II (III of Cyprus). That year street rioting between Christians and Moslems in Acre, the strongest of the remaining Frankish forts, prompted the Egyptian sultan Al-Ashraf to organize an offensive against Acre. On April 6, 1291, the Mamelukes, with 60,000 horsemen and 100,000 foot soldiers, laid siege to the city. Amalric, brother of King Henry, commanded the Christian garrison, which consisted of 1,000 mounted men and 15,000 infantry.

Despite heavy bombardment from Egyptian siege engines, Acre resisted stoutly. On May 4 King Henry arrived from Cyprus with reinforcements—100 knights and 2,000 infantry—but they were not enough to counterbalance the steady attrition brought on by Moslem attacks. The outer wall fell on May 15, and in a general assault three days later the Mamelukes stormed the inner gates and burst into the city. The king and his brother escaped with a few nobles to Cyprus, while other Christians fought hopelessly in the streets. By the end of the day the Mameluke victory was complete. Most of the defenders died fighting; the others fell into captivity and were sold off as slaves. Acre was thoroughly sacked and its fortifications demolished.

On the following day, May 19, the garrison at Tyre abandoned that city in the face of a threatened attack. Sidon and Beirut fell in July, the Mount Carmel monasteries in August. By the end of the summer the last of the Frankish warriors had been erased from the Asian mainland. Syria and Palestine lay under Moslem dominion as complete as that in 1097 when the First Crusade began. *See* Tripoli, in Lebanon; Crusades.

Acre III (Wars of the French Revolution), 1799. During the summer of 1798 Napoleon Bonaparte had conquered Egypt only to be cut off from Europe by the defeat of his fleet at the Nile by the British navy. He then turned eastward, on February 6, 1799, to carry the war against Turkey into Syria. With 13,000 men and 52 cannon Napoleon brushed past weak Turkish resistance to reach Jaffa on March 7. Here more than 1,000 Turkish soldiers who had broken parole to defend the city were recaptured and shot. On March 18 the French arrived at Acre, which was defended by a Turkish force under Ahmed Pasha, called Djezzar (the Butcher). Aiding Turkish resistance was a British task force of two vessels under Sidney Smith, which protected all the city except the landward side from attack. Napoleon settled down to besiege Acre.

A month later a Turkish column approached the city from the southeast. Napoleon detached Gen. Jean Kléber's division to hold off this advance. On April 16 Kléber, with the aid of a second French force, routed the Turks at Mount Tabor. Acre, however, continued to hold out against all French efforts to break into the city. Finally, when plague struck Napoleon's troops, he raised the siege on the night of May 20 and withdrew toward Egypt. In all, he had lost 2,200 dead, including 1,000 from disease. *See* Pyramids; Abukir; French Revolution Wars.

Acre IV (Egyptian Revolt against Turkey), 1840. The growing power of Mehemet (Mohammed) Ali of Egypt in the Near East alarmed the major nations of Europe. In the summer of 1839 Egyptian forces had destroyed a strong Turkish army at Nizib and captured the sultan's fleet at Alexandria. Mahmud II had died and had been succeeded by his 16-year-old son, Abdul-Medjid I, who was powerless to oust the Egyptians from Syria. Great Britain, Austria, Prussia, and Russia (with France opposing) then intervened. The English admiral Robert Stopford took an allied fleet into the eastern Mediterranean. On November 3 Stopford's ships bombarded Acre, in modern Israel, reduced the defenses, and stormed the town. The Egyptian forces of Gen. Ibrahim Pasha, son of Mehemet Ali, evacuated Acre and soon all of Syria. The following year Mehemet Ali agreed to return the Turkish fleet and abandon claims to Syria in exchange for the hereditary rule of Egypt. *See* Nizib; Oltenita; Egyptian Revolt against Turkey.

Acroïnum (Moslem-Byzantine Wars), 739. Twenty years after they had been driven away from Constantinople, the Arabs surged back into Asia Minor. The Byzantine emperor Leo III, the Isaurian, met the new invasion at Acroïnum (Akroinon), in ancient Phrygia, in 739. In a great battle the Moslems of the Hisham caliphate were defeated and turned back toward Damascus. This check in Asia Minor followed the blunting of Moslem thrusts on the two extremes of their empire—France and China—and was the last aggression of the Ommiad dynasty. *See* Constantinople IV; Tours; Kashgar; Moslem Conquests.

Actium (Wars of the Second Triumvirate), 31 B.C. Mark Antony's commitment of Roman resources to Egypt and Cleopatra VII ensured a showdown with his rival triumvir Octavian. While Antony's fortunes in Rome were in decline, the 32-year-old Octavian had been steadily winning popular favor by substituting moderation and mercy for earlier cruelties. In May 32 B.C. Antony formally divorced Octavian's sister Octavia. Octavian then publicized Antony's will, which deeded various Roman possessions to the children of his affair with Cleopatra. Roman sentiment became so outraged that Octavian was directed to make war on Egypt.

Early in 31 B.C. Octavian landed an army of 40,000 men in Epirus, on the west coast of Greece. Just to the south, in the Ambracian Gulf, stood Antony's Roman-Egyptian fleet. On the promontory of Actium, on the south side of the gulf, stood Antony's army, numbering also about 40,000 men. For months the two antagonists eyed each other without giving battle. During this time, however, Octavian's ships cut Antony's supply line from the Peloponnesus back to Egypt. Finally, at dawn on September 2, 31 B.C., Antony risked everything on a naval battle. With a superiority in numbers

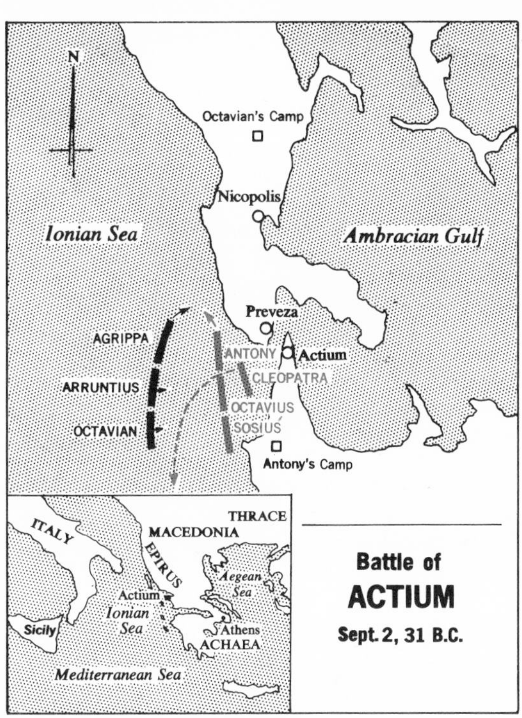

Battle of ACTIUM Sept. 2, 31 B.C.

(480 against slightly more than 400) and in the size of its warships, the Roman-Egyptian navy sailed into the Ionian Sea, seeking an early advantage over the lighter Liburnian (two banks of oars) vessels of Octavian. Antony himself commanded the right squadron, Marcus Octavius the center, C. Sosius the left. Cleopatra's squadron stood in the rear, to the right of center. Opposing this formation were the three enemy squadrons commanded by, from left to right, Marcus Vipsanius Agrippa, Arruntius, and Octavian.

Each side tried to turn the opponent's northern flank. In the afternoon Antony's center and left began giving way. Cleopatra then sailed her 60 Egyptian ships between the two struggling armadas and left the scene of battle. Antony transferred to a quinquereme (five banks of oars) and followed, boarding the Egyptian flagship *Antonia* farther out in the Ionian Sea. The leaderless Antonian navy was now hopelessly beaten. Octavian's swifter Liburnians, dodging the rams and missiles of the heavier vessels, methodically set fire to the opposing warships. At the end of ten hours of fighting, the few survivors of Antony's burning fleet surrendered. Five thousand of his men were dead.

On land the flight of Antony caused equal consternation among the troops. They became even more frustrated when their leader, P. Crassus Canidius, fled to Egypt also. Octavian refused to attack them. Each day desertions increased. By September 9 the entire army had melted away.

In Rome popular clamor forced Octavian to launch an invasion of Egypt the following year. He arrived at Alexandria on August 1, 30 B.C. The still powerful army (11 legions) Antony had stationed to defend Egypt promptly deserted to the enemy. Antony and, then, Cleopatra committed suicide. Octavian looted the Ptolemaic treasures, exacted a tribute, and returned to Rome as sole master of the Western world. Three years later the senate conferred upon him the title "Augustus" (exalted). As such he became the first ruler of the Roman Empire that was to endure for the next 500 years. The battle of Actium had determined that Europe's cultural axis would not be turned toward the East. *See* Phraaspa; Naulochus; Lippe River; Second Triumvirate, Wars of the.

Adana (Byzantine-Moslem Wars), 964. The continuation of the century-old Byzantine counteroffensive against the Moslems in Asia Minor fell to coregents in 963: the widow Theophano and the able general Nicephorus II Phocas. Nicephorus, the conqueror of Crete, took an army over the Taurus Mountains to swoop down on Adana, near the eastern Mediterranean coast. The strong Moslem garrison was subdued. A year later the aggressive Byzantine general rode 23 miles to the west to take Tarsus, the chief city of Cilicia and birthplace of Saint Paul. Nicephorus, who married his attractive coregent, now stood ready to attack the disintegrating Moslem empire in Syria. *See* Samosata; Candia I; Aleppo-Antioch; Moslem Conquests.

Admiralty Islands (World War II). Particularly Los Negros and Manus, seized from the Japanese by U.S. troops between February 29 and March 18, 1944. *See* Rabaul.

Adrianople I (Civil Wars of the Roman Empire), 323. After nine years of uneasy peace, the inevitable conflict broke out between the two Roman emperors—Constantine I, ruler of the West, and Licinianus Licinius, sovereign of the East. One of the basic points of difference between the two rulers was the Christian religion, which Constantine tolerated but Licinius persecuted. The immediate cause of the civil war was a dispute over the prime responsibility for repelling Gothic invasions of the Balkans. Constantine marched into Thrace with an army of more than 50,000 men. At Adrianople (Hadrianopolis, or modern Edirne), 130 miles northwest of Byzantium (later Constantinople), he encountered an army of similar size under Licinius. On July 3 Constantine skillfully maneuvered the eastern army out of its entrenched position. In the open, his disciplined veterans overpowered Licinius' inexperienced troops. More than 20,000 died in a fierce battle that found Licinius retreating into Byzantium. *See* Cibalae; Byzantium II; Roman Empire.

Adrianople II (Gothic Invasions of the Roman Empire), 378. Pushed from the north by the savage Huns, the Visigoths received permission from Valens, Roman emperor of the East, to settle south of the Danube in 376. But conflict with the Romans in the area soon led to open fighting, in which much of Thrace was devastated, the following year. Valens marched a Roman army against

the semicivilized Goths, who were commanded by a chieftain named Fritigern. Ten miles from Adrianople (Edirne), the Romans came up against the massed enemy. Valens, without waiting for reinforcements that were on the way from Italy, launched an attack on August 9, 378, while the Gothic cavalry was off on a foraging expedition. Deploying his own cavalry on both wings, Valens drove the Goths back on their wagon barricade. But at that moment the barbarian horsemen returned unexpectedly and quickly routed the Roman cavalry. The Gothic cavalry then rode down the helpless legionaries, methodically cutting their formations to pieces. Some 20,000 of the 30,000 Roman infantry were killed, including Valens. (It was a slaughter reminiscent of Cannae, almost 600 years earlier, and one that would not be repeated until 1382 at Roosebeke.) The Goths moved on Adrianople itself but could not penetrate the city's walls.

This battle of Adrianople is one of the most decisive in history. It established the supremacy of cavalry over infantry for the next thousand years. And it demonstrated that barbarians could overwhelm a Roman army inside the empire's frontiers. Adrianople was the greatest loss suffered by a Roman army since the German victory at Teutoburger Wald in A.D. 9. Theodosius I (the Great), who became emperor of the Eastern Empire the following year, patched together an uneasy peace with the Goths, but the eventual destruction of Rome was now certain. *See* Châlons-sur-Marne I; Aquileia II; Roman Empire.

Adrianople III (Wars of the Byzantine Empire), 972. A new threat appeared on the European borders of the Byzantine Empire in the middle of the tenth century. Under Sviatoslav, the duke of Kiev, the Russians crossed the Balkan Mountains and seized Philippopolis (Plovdiv) in 969. They pressed on south along the valley of the Maritsa toward Constantinople. From the Byzantine capital the energetic general John I Zimisces, guardian of youthful Emperor Basil II, marched out to meet the invading infantry. Near Adrianople (Edirne) a combined force of 30,000 Imperial infantry and cavalry blocked the advance of the 60,000 Russians. The veteran Byzantine foot archers riddled the enemy ranks with arrows; the cavalry then routed them with a hard charge. With the aid of Byzantine ships on the Danube, John I drove the Russians completely out of Bulgaria. But this victory proved to be a mixed blessing. It enabled another Balkan opponent of the Byzantines, the Bulgars, to increase their strength. Meanwhile Sviatoslav and his survivors, on their way back to Kiev, were attacked by Patzinaks (Pechenegs); the duke was killed. *See* Aleppo-Antioch; Novgorod; Sofia.

Adrianople IV (Fourth Crusade), 1205. After conquering and sacking Constantinople in 1204, the Latin crusaders under Baldwin I (IX of Flanders) and the Venetian doge Enrico Dandolo marched northwest toward Bulgaria. Here Kaloyan (Yoannitsa), third Asen ruler of the Bulgarian Empire, had refused to acknowledge the supremacy of Baldwin. To meet the mounted army from Constantinople, Kaloyan supplemented his Bulgars with local Greeks and Turkish Cumans. The rival armies met at Adrianople (Edirne) on April 15. When the Bulgar cavalry feigned a withdrawal, the Latin knights (mostly Franks) rode in hot pursuit. The Bulgars suddenly wheeled about and assaulted their disorganized foe. The Count of Blois and many other Latins fell in the ensuing rout. Pressing their advantage, the Bulgars swept the field, capturing Baldwin, who later died (or was murdered) in captivity. Kaloyan went on to ravage much of Thrace and Macedonia. *See* Stara Zagora; Constantinople V; Philippopolis II; Crusades.

Adrianople V (Byzantine-Bulgarian Wars), 1254. During the half-century that Latin emperors ruled at Constantinople (1204–61), incessant warfare gripped the states of the Near East. Bulgaria, under the youthful ruler Michael Asen, lost southern Thrace and part of Macedonia to the Nicaean emperor John III Ducas (Vatatzes). When the aggressive John died in 1254, Michael sought to regain his lost territories. He marched to Adrianople (Edirne) the same year. Here he encountered the army of John's successor, Theodore II Lascaris. The Bulgarians were thoroughly beaten. Four years later the Asen line of rulers died out, and in the next century Turkey absorbed the Second Bulgarian Empire. *See* Klokotnitsa; Constantinople VI.

Adrianople VI (Capture by Ottoman Turks), 1365. The great Serbian leader Stephen Dushan, the self-proclaimed emperor of the Serbs, Greeks, Bulgars, and Albanians, took Adrianople (Edirne) from the Byzantine Empire on his thrust toward Constantinople in 1355. But he died on December 20 of that year, ending his hope of consolidating the Balkans against the growing power of the Ottoman Turks. Dushan's concern was well taken. The Turks, who had established themselves in Europe at Gallipoli in 1354, began overrunning Thrace. In 1365, under Murad I, they attacked and seized the historic crossroads town of Adrianople, 130 miles northwest of Constantinople. The city became the capital of the Ottomans, replacing Bursa, in 1366. *See* Bursa; Maritsa River.

Adrianople VII (First Balkan War), 1913. Although Bulgaria agreed to an armistice with Turkey on December 3, 1912, Czar Ferdinand I kept his troops near Constantinople and Adrianople (Edirne), 130 miles to the northwest. During the negotiations the Turkish government agreed to give up Adrianople. Thereupon a *coup d'état* in Constantinople overthrew the ministry of Mohammed V. Nationalists led by Enver Bey determined to hold on to the city. On February 3, 1913, the war resumed, with the Bulgarians investing Adrianople. The city was forced to capitulate on March 26. This battle ended the war, except for the continuing siege of Shkodër (Scutari) by Montenegro. A peace treaty was signed at London on May 30. (During the Second Balkan War, Turkey took advantage of the quarreling among its enemies to reoccupy and hold Adrianople.) *See* Ioannina; Shkodër II; Balkan Wars.

Aduwa (Italian-Ethiopian War I), 1896. The Italian protectorate over Ethiopia (Abyssinia), secured by treaty in 1889, was overthrown by King of Kings Menelik II six years later. From the Italian colony of Eritrea, along the Red Sea, the government of King Humbert I sent troops into northern Ethiopia in March 1895. The invasion force, commanded by Gen. Oreste Baratieri, suffered two minor setbacks at the hands of the Ethiopian forces. To redeem his nation's prestige, Premier Francesco Crispi ordered the Italian general to fight and win a major victory. At Aduwa, about 80 miles south of Asmara, Eritrea, Baratieri encountered some 80,000 Ethiopians led by Menelik himself. On March 1, 1896, the 20,000-man Italian army was virtually wiped out by the massed attacks of the Ethiopians. It was one of the worst defeats ever suffered by a European power in colonial warfare. The disaster forced Baratieri to retire from the army and brought the downfall of Crispi's cabinet. Italy sued for peace, signing the Treaty of Addis Ababa on October 26, which recognized the independence of Ethiopia. It was in part to revenge Aduwa that Benito Mussolini invaded Ethiopia in 1935. *See* Ethiopia.

Adwalton Moor (English Civil War), 1643. During the second year of the bitter Civil War, the Cavalier forces of Charles I won local successes over the Roundheads in the west and around Oxford. In Yorkshire the Royalists drew their chief support from William Cavendish, earl of Newcastle. When a Roundhead army, led by Lord Ferdinando Fairfax and his son Sir Thomas, laid siege to York early in 1643, Newcastle relieved the city. The two hostile forces maneuvered for position and then met head on at Adwalton (Atherton) Moor near Bradford. On June 30 the Cavaliers overwhelmed the Fairfaxes, leaving Charles's supporters in control of all Yorkshire except the city of Hull. *See* Stratton; Chalgrove Field; Selby; English Civil War.

Aegates Islands (First Punic War), 241 B.C. The 23-year-old First Punic War, which had settled down to a Roman-Carthaginian contest for Sicily, reached a climax in a naval battle off the west coast of the island. After its disastrous defeat at Drepanum, Rome had rebuilt and retrained its fleet. Now 200 quinqueremes under G. Lutatius Catulus encountered the Carthaginian navy in the Aegates (Egadi) Islands. In a heavy storm on March 10, 241 B.C., the Roman galleys annihilated the heretofore strong naval force of the Punic republic. Fifty of the Carthaginian ships were sunk and 70 captured.

With his navy wiped out, Hamilcar Barca (father of Hannibal) accepted peace terms for Carthage. He agreed to the payment of 3,200 talents and the surrender of Carthage's claim to Sicily, which had stood for almost 250 years. Rome made Sicily, except for the allied city of Syracuse, its first province. (It later seized both Sardinia and Corsica.)

One of the evacuees from the Carthaginian stronghold at Mount Eryx (Monte San Giuliano) was the six-year-old Hannibal. With his father, the young man swore never to be a friend of the Romans, an oath the Italian city would have reason to recall many times during the Second Punic War. *See* Drepanum; Saguntum; Punic Wars.

Aegina (First Peloponnesian War), 458–457 B.C. In the developing rupture between Sparta and Athens, the island state of Aegina (in the Saronic Gulf) allied itself with the Peloponnesians. However, the Athenian fleet sailed into Aegina's home waters to defeat the Aeginetan navy and invade the island. In a siege of a little less than two years, the Athenians under Leosthenes conquered Aegina and forced it to accept membership in the Athens-dominated Delian League in 457 B.C. Sparta then entered the war and sent an army across the Corinthian Isthmus into Boeotia. *See* Tanagra-Oenophyta; Peloponnesian Wars.

Aegospotami (Great Peloponnesian War), 405 B.C. After the Athenian victory in the Arginusae Islands, Conon took his fleet to Aegospotami on the Dardanelles (the Hellespont). Across the strait lay the reorganized navy of Sparta, under the resourceful Lysander who was now restored to command. In August Conon sailed the Athenian fleet across the strait four days in a row, vainly trying to bring on a major engagement. On the fifth day the Athenian ships made another challenge, turned about, and carelessly returned to their anchorage. At this moment Lysander's 180 ships suddenly dashed across the strait and fell upon the surprised and disorganized Athenians. The Spartans seized all but 20 of Conon's 170 galleys and killed the captured seamen.

The battle shattered the naval power of Athens. In November Lysander sailed up to the Piraeus and laid siege to Athens itself. None of its remaining allies came to the aid of the once-powerful city-state. Inside the city, Cleophon, who had succeeded Cleon as head of the Athenian war party, was deposed and executed. Theramenes surrendered the starvation-stricken city to Lysander in April 404. The Spartan general ordered the destruction of the long walls connecting Athens with the Piraeus, the impressment of Athenian shipping, and the forced alliance of Athens to the Spartan league. The long and bitter Peloponnesian Wars were over. But civil war among the Greek city-states would continue for another 66 years, until it was ended by Macedonian dictatorship. *See* Arginusae Islands; Cunaxa; Haliartus; Peloponnesian Wars.

Afghan-British Wars I and II (1839–1842, 1878–1880). Both wars between the British in India and the Afghans were in large part provoked by Russian efforts to dominate Afghanistan. Although the British managed to pacify Afghanistan in the two conflicts, the price was high.

First Afghan War

Kabul II	1842

Second Afghan War

Peiwar Pass	1878
Maiwand	1880
Kandahar	1880

Agendicum (Gallic Wars), 52 B.C. When Julius Caesar moved south from Avaricum (Bourges) with six Roman legions, he sent Titus Labienus north to the Seine Valley with four legions. Labienus had just crossed to the north side of the Seine when word came of Caesar's defeat at Gergovia. Sensing victory, a large force of Gauls under Camulogenus took up a position south of the river, cutting off the Romans from their base at Agendicum (Sens). Another Gallic tribe began assembling north of Labienus. Labienus now gave up all thought of taking Paris. Instead, he recrossed the Seine in the face of Camulogenus' army and delivered a vigorous attack against the far more numerous foe. The veteran, tightly disciplined legionaries cut their way through the Gauls, inflicting heavy losses. (Camulogenus was killed.) Safely back at their base, Labienus' legions were joined by Caesar's force from the south. The reunited Roman army now moved toward the Gallic stronghold at Alesia. *See* Gergovia; Alesia; Gallic Wars.

Agincourt (Hundred Years' War), 1415. The renewed English invasion of 1415 found France ruled by a mad king, Charles VI. From his conquest of Harfleur on September 22, Henry V marched northward toward Calais with his English army of about 1,000 knights and men-at-arms and some 5,000 archers. Unable to cross the lower Somme because of flooding and French defenses, the English had to swing inland to cross above Amiens. This detour enabled a French army of 20,000 men under the constable Charles d'Albret and the marshal Jean Bouciquaut II to interpose itself between the invaders and Calais. Henry had no choice but to fight. At the village of Agincourt, 33 miles northwest of Arras, he chose a position between two patches of woods that narrowed the front to 1,200 yards. Sending his horses to the rear, he deployed his men-at-arms in three divisions abreast, each supported by a group of archers on either flank. To his front lay ploughed fields, heavy with mud after a week of rain.

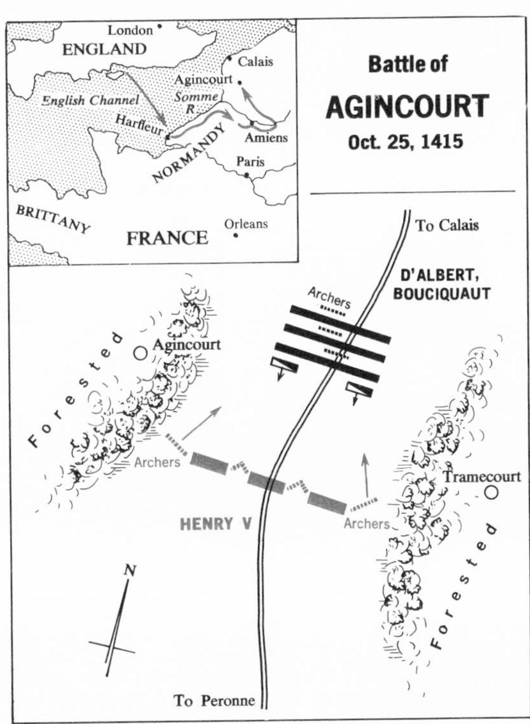

The French, with most of their numerical superiority lost on the cramped front, also dismounted and deployed in three lines in depth. Little use was made of their crossbowmen or heavy cannon. At eleven o'clock on October 25 the English opened the battle by advancing their archers to bring the longbows within killing range (about 250 yards). The first French line, led by a cavalry spearhead, plodded forward through the mud. Although suffering terrible casualties from English arrows, they reached Henry's front ranks, only to be repulsed when the archers exchanged their bows for axes and swords. Then the second line, under the Duc d'Alençon, pressed forward to continue the deadly hand-to-hand struggle. It, too, was finally beaten back, leaving the duke dead on the field, and many wounded, as well as able-bodied, prisoners in the hands of the English. At this moment the French camp followers broke into Henry's camp, seeking plunder. Believing himself attacked in the rear while the third line of the enemy stood intact on his front, the king ordered the massacre of all prisoners. Thus perished much of the remaining warrior arm of the French nobility.

After extinguishing the threat to their rear, the English braced to meet a new assault. But the French tnird line, shaken by the heaps of corpses to their front, recoiled without making an effective charge. The battle had ended in less than three hours with 7,000 French casualties. D'Albret was dead and Bouciquaut a prisoner. English losses were reported no higher than 1,600. At odds larger than 3 to 1, England had won one of the great victories of military history.

With the way now open Henry marched on to the English base at Calais, reaching there on November 16. Buoyed by the dramatic victory at Agincourt, he returned two years later to launch a systematic conquest of all Normandy. *See* Harfleur; Rouen II; Hundred Years' War.

Agnadello (French Wars in Italy), 1509. Although forced out of southern Italy by the Spanish, Louis XII of France held on to Milan and in 1507 sent his Swiss pikemen mercenaries to storm and take Genoa. Then, in an abrupt diplomatic switch, Louis joined Ferdinand (V of Castile, II of Aragon, III of Naples), Holy Roman Emperor Maximilian I, and Pope Julius II in the League of Cambrai on December 10, 1508. This alliance was aimed at reducing the city-state of Venice. On May 14 of the following year the army of Louis, 30,000 strong, fought the Venetian army of similar size at Agnadello in Cremona province of northern Italy. The French overpowered the Italian army, inflicting several thousand casualties and capturing the Venetian artillery. As a consequence the satellite cities of Venice were divided among Louis, Maximilian, Ferdinand, and the pope.

But when Venice refused to surrender, the unsteady League broke up. In 1510 Pope Julius changed sides. Then Ferdinand did likewise. The stage was now set for a resumption of French-Spanish fighting. *See* Garigliano River; Ravenna IV.

Ahvenanmaa (Great Northern War), 1714. After his crushing defeat at the hands of the Russians near Poltava in 1709, the Swedish king Charles XII remained with the Turks for five years fruitlessly trying to foment a Moslem attack on Czar Peter I, the Great. Meanwhile, at home Sweden was beset by a reinvigorated coalition of enemies —Denmark (Frederick IV), Poland (Augustus II), Prussia (Frederick William I), and, of course, Russia. In the summer of 1714 a Russian expedition of 30 warships and 180 galleys sailed out of the Gulf of Finland to attack the Swedish island of Ahvenanmaa (Aland), at the mouth of the Gulf of Bothnia. The formidable force under Adm. Fëdor Apraksin (Apraxin) reached the island on July 14. The defending Swedish navy, although outnumbered 3 to 1, fought valiantly for three hours before succumbing to the Russian assault. When Peter's ground troops occupied Ahvenanmaa (part of present-day Finland), it marked the first major Russian naval triumph in history. *See* Poltava; Stralsund II; Great Northern War.

Ain Jalut (Mongol Conquest of Western Asia), 1260. The Mongol army of Hulagu, grandson of Genghis Khan, pressed westward into Syria and Palestine after its crushing victory over the Moslems of Baghdad. On learning of the death of Mangu Khan, the Mongol leader in the east and older brother of Hulagu, the invaders turned back. However, a Mameluke army of Egypt, which had been preparing to resist the Mongol advance, now swung over to the offensive. The Mamelukes, commanded by Baybars I (Bibars), caught up with the withdrawing Mongol rear guard at Ain Jalut near the Sea of Galilee in September 1260. The invaders' rear guard was cut to pieces by Mameluke cavalry. When the main body wheeled about to help out, it was attacked and put to flight. The battle of Ain Jalut, the first Mongol defeat in the West, ended Hulagu's invasion. Meanwhile, the former slave Baybars, who had built the Mameluke rule of Egypt into a major Moslem military power, captured Damascus and took over the sultanate of Syria as well. *See* Baghdad I; Antioch III; Mongol Wars.

Aisne-Marne rivers (World War I). The second half of the battle of Marne River II, during July 18–August 6, 1918, in which an Allied offensive eliminated the German salient northeast of Paris. *See* Marne River II.

Aisne River I (World War I), 1914. After their defeat in the first battle of the Marne River, the German armies pulled back to the high ground just north of the Aisne River, a westward flowing tributary of the Oise. They were in a strong position, under the new German commander Erich von Falkenhayn (who replaced Field Marshal Helmuth von Moltke), when the French forces of Field Marshal Joseph Joffre attacked across the Aisne River. The German armies, aligned from west to east, were the First (Alexander von Kluck); Seventh (Josias von Heeringen), which had been moved westward from Alsace; Second (Karl von Bülow); and then the Third, Fourth, Fifth, and Sixth stretching eastward to the Swiss frontier.

For his attack, Joffre pushed forward the Allied left-wing (west) armies—Sixth (Michel Joseph Maunoury), British Expeditionary Force (Sir John French), and Fifth (Louis Franchet d'Esperey). Farther to the east stood the Ninth, Fourth, Third, Second, and First armies. Despite a fierce attack beginning on September 14, the Allies could make only small gains against a well-prepared position protected by artillery that had previously registered its fire. On September 18 Joffre called off the offensive. This first battle of the Aisne marked the transition from the open combat of the initial campaigns to the stabilized trench warfare which would characterize the Western Front for the remainder of the war.

During the last two days of the Aisne offensive, Joffre had begun shifting troops to the northwest in an effort to strike the exposed German flank at Noyon. Falkenhayn quickly shifted reserves to this region and in turn tried to outflank the Allies. Both sides continued this strategy of attempting to envelop the opponent's northern flank until the Allies reached the sea at Nieuwpoort, Belgium, in the first week in October. This ended the so-called Race to the Sea. *See* Marne River I; Ypres I; World War I.

Aisne River II (World War I), 1917. Following by a week the British attack at Arras, Gen. Robert Nivelle, new French commander on the Western Front, launched his long-awaited offensive on the Aisne River between Soissons and Reims. The attack, on a 50-mile front, began on April 16, two armies abreast—the Sixth of Gen. Charles Mangin in the Soissons sector to the left, the Fifth of Gen. Olivier Mazel on the right. Both forces served under army group commander Gen. Joseph Alfred Micheler. Following a prolonged artillery bombardment, French troops rushed forward courageously but were soon checked by heavy machine-gun fire from Gen. Max Boehn's Seventh Army in the Chemin des Dames area and from Gen. Fritz von Below's First Army to the east. Three-fourths of France's 200 tanks were knocked out or broke down before rendering any effective aid.

Doggedly Nivelle pushed the attack. The Germans abandoned Fort Malmaison and later most of the Chemin des Dames area. On April 20 Gen. Denis Duchêne's Tenth Army moved to the front between the Sixth and Fifth armies. But German awareness of Nivelle's plans had allowed commanders Field Marshal Paul von Hindenburg and Gen. Erich Ludendorff to concentrate huge reserves behind the front lines. French assaults became increasingly costly. ·Finally the offensive petered out on May 9. Six days later Gen. Henri Pétain, who had become chief of staff on April 29, succeeded Nivelle. Meanwhile, the demoralized French troops had broken out in open mutiny. Pétain eventually re-established control. Although 23,385 mutineers were convicted, only 55 were shot. The number of French casualties in Nivelle's unfortunate attack is officially listed at 96,000, but some critics claim the number to be almost twice as large. German losses were 163,000. *See* Arras II; Messines; World War I.

Aisne River III (World War I), 1918. The third German offensive of 1918 to be launched by Gen. Erich Ludendorff struck the French in the Chemin des Dames area in front of the Aisne River. This naturally strong sector was lightly held by the French Sixth Army of Gen. Denis Duchêne. For the attack Ludendorff quietly reinforced his First (Fritz von Below) and Seventh (Max von Boehn) armies to a total of 41 divisions. Soon after midnight on May 27 the German artillery began blasting the entire sector with 4,600 guns. It was one of the heaviest bombardments of the war. Before dawn 17 German divisions in the first wave stormed the Chemin des Dames on a nine-mile front. The attack swept away Duchêne's lines and captured intact bridges over the Aisne. By nightfall the Germans had carved out a 13-mile bulge in the French front between Soissons and Reims, the greatest one-day advance since the Western Front was stabilized almost four years before.

Ludendorff had planned the offensive as a diversion before again striking the British in Flanders. But now he threw in all available reserves to exploit the sudden breakthrough south of the Aisne. Soissons, near the right (northwestern) flank of the German offensive, fell on May 28. Two days later the Germans stood on the Marne River at Château-Thierry, only 37 miles from Paris. With the three French armies of Gen. Henri Pétain being steadily forced back, the Allied commander in chief, Gen. Ferdinand Foch, rushed rear area units to the front. The American general John Pershing's 3rd Division (Joseph Dickman) reached Château-Thierry on June 1 and for three days fought fiercely to hold the Marne crossings. To the west, the American 2nd Division (Omar Bundy) counterattacked the nose of the advance to regain Belleau Wood. Finally, on June 6, the German offensive, which had gained 35 miles, ended, with Ludendorff holding a large salient pointed at Paris. Meanwhile the first American victory of the war had been won at Cantigny. *See* Lys River; Cantigny; Noyon-Montdidier; World War I.

Ajnadain (Moslem Conquest of Syria), 634. Under the caliphate of, first, Abu-Bakr and then Omar I, large forces of Moslem cavalry burst out of Arabia to invade both Syria and Persia. The attack toward Syria was checked at Ajnadain (Jannabatain), southwest of Jerusalem, by a Byzantine army under Theodorus, brother of the Byzantine emperor Heraclius. However, the Moslem general Khālid ibn-al-Walīd made a dramatic forced march from Hira across the Syrian desert with reinforcements. The combined Arabian force of some 45,000 troops routed the more numerous Byzantine army on July 30, 634. Khālid pressed on northward toward Damascus. *See* Hira; Pella; Moslem Conquests.

Alamance Creek (Colonial Wars of the United States), 1771. In the colony of North Carolina the people of the upper (western) section, chiefly Scotch-Irish, stood apart from the inhabitants of the east and south, who controlled the machinery of government. Calling themselves Regulators, the former complained of discrimination and refused to let courts sit in their area. The royal governor, William Tryon, organized a force of 1,018 militia and 30 light cavalry. Marching westward, Tryon began putting down the rebellion by destroying homes and farms. At Alamance Creek, 20 miles west of Hillsboro, the royal forces encountered about 2,000 unorganized and half-armed Regulators on May 16, 1771. In a two-hour pitched battle, 20 Regulators were killed, many wounded, and 12 captured (6 of whom were later hanged). The attackers lost 9 killed and 61 wounded. This battle ended the fighting, but it had important repercussions in the Revolutionary War, which began four years later. When most of the people of the low country turned patriot, the Regulators opposed them by remaining loyal to England. *See* Moore's Creek Bridge.

Alam Halfa (World War II), 1942. A month after having his long drive across Cyrenaica and western Egypt stopped at El Alamein, Field Marshal Erwin Rommel drove his *Panzerarmee Afrika* at the key east-west ridge of Alam Halfa, deep in the right center of the British Alamein position. This was Rommel's last attempt to break through to the Nile Valley and also the first battle in which Gen. Bernard Montgomery commanded the British Eighth Army. On August 31 three veteran German armored divisions turned the British southern flank but then were stopped cold by a model British defense, aided by heavy artillery and air bombardment, at Alam Halfa. On the fourth day Rommel pulled back his armored salient to a defensive north-south line. His casualties were heavier than the British losses of 1,750. The Eighth Army resumed its build-up for the second battle of El Alamein, now less than two months away. *See* El Alamein I; El Alamein II; World War II.

Alamo (Texan War of Independence), 1836. Several years of strife between the government of Mexico and its constituent state of Texas led to increasing demands for independence by the American settlers north of the Rio Grande. To put down the revolt, the Mexican general Antonio de Santa Anna marched into Texas at the head of some 6,000 troops. At San Antonio 188 American troops took refuge in the Alamo, a Spanish Franciscan mission that had been converted into a fort. Santa Anna laid siege to the fort on February 23, 1836, with 3,000 men. For 12 days the sharpshooting American riflemen held off the assaults of the Mexicans, inflicting hundreds of casualties. The defenders included such famous American frontier heroes as William B. Travis, the commandant; Davy Crockett; James Bowie; and James Bonham. Finally, on March 6, a massive Mexican attack stormed into the Alamo. In a no-quarter fight every defender (except for 30 women and children) was slain. This massacre gave rise to the war cry "Remember the Alamo!" About 1,600 Mexicans died in the siege and final assault. It was the first of eight battles that Santa Anna would fight against American troops. He marched eastward, destroying American settlements in his path, to reach Galveston Bay five weeks later.

Meanwhile, in a convention at Washington, Texas, on March 2, had proclaimed its independence from Mexico. Sam Houston was named commander of the army. *See* San Jacinto River; Texan War of Independence.

Alarcos (Spanish-Moslem Wars), 1195. In the century after the Spanish counteroffensive in the south had been checked at Zallaka (1086), the Christian-Moslem conflict fell under the larger shadow of a dynastic struggle among the Moors. The Almoravids, who had defeated Alfonso VI of Castile and León, were steadily displaced by another Berber sect from North Africa, the Almohads. Beginning in 1147, the new Islamic force took over control of southern Spain. Its greatest general, al-Mansur, encountered the Christian army of Alfonso VIII of Castile in 1195 at Alarcos in south-central Spain. On July 18 the Moors won an overwhelming victory, inflicting thousands of casualties. The few Spanish survivors, including Alfonso, fled northeast through Ciudad Real to the fortress at Calatrava. But this stronghold also fell to Moorish attack two years later. Alfonso had to accept a humiliating peace. *See* Saragossa I; Las Navas de Tolosa.

Albania (Conquest by Italy), 1939. Benito Mussolini, dictator of Italy, had long interfered in the affairs of Albania. When King Zog I continued to resist such demands as the allowance of a Fascist party in Albania, Italian naval and army forces moved across the Adriatic Sea. On April 7, 1939, Italian ships bombarded Albanian coastal towns while landing troops on the beaches. Albania could offer little resistance to the conquest. Zog and his queen fled into exile. The crown of Albania passed to Victor Emmanuel III of Italy. *See* Ethiopia.

Alcácer do Sal (Portuguese-Moslem Wars), 1217. Portugal's third king, Alfonso II, the Fat, continued the campaign of pushing back the Moors that was launched by his father, Sancho I, and grandfather, Alfonso I. In 1217 the Portuguese army attacked the Moorish stronghold at Alcácer do Sal in the Estremadura of the southwest. The troops of Alfonso routed the enemy, driving the Moslems farther south. *See* Santarém I; Aljubarrota.

Alcántara (Spanish Conquest of Portugal), 1580. Portugal, which had been steadily declining during the sixteenth century, received a crippling blow when King Cardinal Henry died in 1580 leaving no clear heir in the house of Aviz. The most popular claimant to the throne was Dom Antonio, the prior of Crato. But the high clergy and some of the nobility threw their support to King Philip II of Spain. Philip sent an army under the veteran Duke of Alva westward to enforce his claim. At Alcántara, on the Tagus River near the present Spanish-Portuguese border, the duke met Antonio's army of peasants and townspeople on August 25, 1580. The Portuguese were routed, Antonio fleeing into exile at Paris. Lisbon yielded to the new conqueror, and Portugal became a realm of the Spanish throne until 1640. *See* Alcázarquivir; Montijo.

Alcazarquivir (Portuguese Invasion of Morocco),

1578. The Portuguese king Sebastian took personal charge of an invasion of Morocco in 1578. Aided by a Moorish pretender to the throne of Fes (Fez), the Portuguese army attacked Alcazarquivir (El Qsar el Kbir), 60 miles south of Tangier, on August 4. In a fierce encounter the invaders were defeated and Sebastian was killed. Also slain were the Moorish pretender and the king of Fes, thus giving the name Battle of Three Kings. The victory of the Moors ended the Portuguese attempt at Moroccan conquest. *See* Alcántara.

Alcolea (Deposition of Isabella II), 1868. The tempestuous and authoritarian reign of Queen Isabella II of Spain finally brought an open revolution in 1868. Rebel forces under Francisco Serrano met the royal army at Alcolea on the Guadalquivir River just east of Cordova on September 28. The rebels won a decisive victory. Isabella fled to France the following day. A provisional government ruled Spain until King Amadeo I came to the throne in 1871. Meanwhile, the search for a royal ruler helped lead to the Franco-Prussian War. *See* Wissembourg.

Aleppo (Moslem Conquest of Syria), 638. After organizing their conquest of Damascus and breaking into Jerusalem, the Arabs stood ready to ride on into northern Syria. In 638 Khālid ibn-al-Walīd led his Moslem cavalry into Emesa (Homs), Antioch, and Aleppo. Only in the latter city did he meet stubborn resistance. Although Aleppo itself surrendered readily, the Byzantine garrison took refuge in the citadel where they defied capture for five months. At last the besieged commander, named Youkinna, surrendered the fort and became a convert to Mohammedanism. This battle ended the last resistance in Syria to Moslem domination. Only the Taurus Mountains prevented the Arabian flood from sweeping on into Asia Minor. *See* Yarmuk River; Jerusalem VI; Moslem Conquests.

Aleppo-Antioch (Byzantine-Moslem Wars), 969. The Byzantine counteroffensive against the Moslems had rewon most of Asia Minor by 965. The able general Nicephorus II Phocas then took his veteran army into northern Syria. Here the cities of Aleppo and Antioch had lain under Arab rule for 330 years. But now the Moslem empire was seriously weakened by a long series of internal squabblings. Nicephorus stormed and recaptured both Aleppo and Antioch (60 miles to the west) in 969. Before the year was out, however, the general was murdered by his nephew John I Zimisces (who promptly married Nicephorus' attractive widow, Theophano). The Moslems later regained Aleppo, but only for a short while. *See* Adana; Damascus II; Moslem Conquests.

Alesia (Gallic Wars), 52 B.C. Julius Caesar, who had failed to quell the Gallic uprising early in 52 B.C. by splitting his Roman legions into two forces, reunited his army at Agendicum (Sens). He then marched southeastward toward the Mandubian fortress of Alesia (just north of Dijon). En route, the Roman army was attacked by a large cavalry force under Vercingetorix, commander in chief of the Gauls. But the well-disciplined legions formed a hollow square, beat off the enemy horsemen, and forced Vercingetorix back to Alesia. Reaching the heavily fortified town, Caesar began extensive siege works that stretched nine and a half miles around Alesia. Inside the town Vercingetorix drove out the Mandubii, with their wives and children, to conserve food supplies for his 50,000 warriors.

Knowing that the battle for Alesia would prove to be decisive, Vercingetorix called for a force of 100,000 Gallic infantry and 8,000 cavalry to assemble a mile west of the Roman circumvallation. This huge force attacked Caesar's lines all one afternoon. They were finally driven off with terrible losses by the 40,000 legionaries (including some hired German cavalry), who made good use of their strong defensive works and skillful deployment. The besieged then attempted a large-scale breakout in a night attack, but again the Roman lines held. A third attempt to raise the siege was directed by Vercassivellaunus, son-in-law of Vercingetorix. From the heights of Mont Rea, to the north, the Gauls struck savagely at the two legions holding that part of the line. Caesar prevented a breakthrough by personally leading a reserve of five cohorts (battalions) to the hard-hit sector. With Caesar's scarlet cloak providing instant recognition for both friend and foe, his men counterattacked vigorously. The relieving force was shattered; Vercassivellaunus became a prisoner.

The garrison, anxiously watching the fight outside their walls, now lost all hope. Vercingetorix surrendered Alesia, even though the month's supply of food had not been exhausted. (He was taken to Rome in chains and beheaded.) When the news of the victory reached Italy, public thanksgiving was celebrated for 20 days. The last of the rebellious Gauls were rounded up the following year. Caesar's conquest was now complete. *See* Agendicum; Carrhae I; Rubicon River; Gallic Wars.

Aleutian Islands (World War II), 1943. At the high tide of Japan's conquests in the Pacific, a powerful Japanese naval task force struck at Midway early in June 1942. To divert U.S. attention from this principal target, a smaller force under Adm. Moshiro Hosogaya steamed across the northern Pacific toward the Aleutian Islands. On June 3 and 4, during the Midway battle in the Central Pacific, Japanese carrier-based bombers blasted the U.S. naval and air base at Dutch Harbor on the Aleutian island of Unalaska. Three days later Japanese troops landed on the island of Kiska and on Attu, 150 miles farther west.

At the end of a long supply line, Japan made no further effort to advance eastward along the

Aleutian chain. This gave Gen. Simon Buckner, commander of the Alaska-Aleutian area, time to establish new U.S. bases on Adak and Amchitka islands. General William Butler's 11th Air Force and Adm. Thomas Kinkaid's naval force brought the two Japanese-held islands under increasingly heavy attacks. Then on May 11, 1943, the U.S. 7th Infantry Division invaded Attu at three places—Holtz Bay and Chichagof Harbor in the north and Massacre Bay in the south. General A. E. Brown's troops drove the Japanese defenders into the mountainous interior. Fighting in severe cold and heavy fog, the U.S. troops' two-pronged attack slowly squeezed the Japanese into an untenable position. On May 29 the hard-pressed defenders launched a desperate counterattack. When this was beaten back, enemy resistance collapsed the following day. In all, 2,350 Japanese were killed (or committed suicide) and 28 captured. United States losses were 552 killed and 1,140 wounded.

The United States then stepped up its air and naval bombardment of Kiska and on August 15 began landing a force of 29,000 Americans and 5,300 Canadians. The landing party found the island deserted. Under cover of a heavy fog, Japan had secretly evacuated its entire Kiska garrison some days earlier. The reconquest of the Aleutians secured the U.S. northern flank in the Pacific and freed American fighting strength for the continuation of the offensive in the Central and Southwest Pacific. *See* Midway; Solomon Islands; Tarawa-Makin; World War II.

Alexandria I (Wars of the First Triumvirate), 48–47 B.C. Learning that Pompey the Great had fled to Egypt after the battle of Pharsalus, Julius Caesar promptly sailed to Alexandria. Here he found the Egyptian throne contested between Ptolemy XII and his sister (also his wife) Cleopatra VII. (Pompey had already been murdered.) Caesar ordered both claimants to report to him on October 7, 48 B.C., for a decision as to the rightful ruler. Cleopatra complied, but the 13-year-old Ptolemy declined. Instead, he ordered his general Achillas to move on Alexandria and arrest the impudent Roman.

With only 3,200 men at his disposal, Caesar turned the royal palace into a fortress. Here his staunch legionaries fought off Achillas' 20,000 troops for five months. To avoid a fatal siege, Caesar sent a detachment into the harbor to occupy the island of Pharos. This action held the harbor open for a relief force, which finally arrived late in March 47 B.C. The combined Roman force routed Achillas' army. Ptolemy drowned in the Nile attempting to escape. With Caesar's support, Cleopatra and her 11-year-old brother, Ptolemy XIII, became joint rulers of Egypt. Three months later, in June, Caesar left Egypt for Syria. *See* Pharsalus; Zela; First Triumvirate, Wars of the.

Alexandria II (Moslem Conquest of Egypt), 642. The Arabian victory at al-Fustât (Old Cairo) opened the way for an attack on Alexandria, Egypt's greatest city and the naval base of the Byzantine Empire. Alexandria was defended by 50,000 troops, but the garrison was demoralized and uncertain in the face of half their number of Moslem invaders commanded by the able general Amr ibn-al-As. For 11 months of alternate siege and truce, the city held out against the Moslems, who had only cavalry to attack the fortifications. Finally the patriarch of Alexandria, Cyrus, who was himself hostile to Constantinople, surrendered the city. Under the arranged terms the inhabitants were to pay tribute in return for security of person, property, and religious exercise. The Moslems now stood masters of all Egypt.

Three years later, in 645, the appearance of a Byzantine fleet outside Alexandria prompted the residents to rebel against their Arabian conquerors. But Amr crushed the revolt as effectively as he had taken the city originally. *See* al-Fustât; Tripoli I.

Alexandria III (Wars of the French Revolution), 1801. When Napoleon Bonaparte embarked for France on August 22, 1799, he left Gen. Jean Kléber in command of the French forces in Egypt. Kléber negotiated with the Turks in an effort to evacuate his army, but in June of the following year he was assassinated. His replacement, Gen. Baron Jacques de Menou, proved to be incapable. Great Britain, taking advantage of the growing French weaknesses, landed an expeditionary force of 14,000 men at Abukir Bay on March 8, 1801. Led by Gen. Sir Ralph Abercromby, the British moved down the peninsula toward Alexandria, to the west. Menou marched out from the city to attack the invaders on March 21. In a four-hour fight the French were thrown back with a loss of 3,000 men. British casualties totaled 1,400, including the fatally wounded Abercromby. This defeat was decisive for the French. Cairo surrendered in June and Alexandria in August to the new British commander, Gen. Sir John Hely-Hutchinson (later Lord Hutchinson). The remnants of Menou's force were returned to France, and Egypt was restored to the rule of the Turkish sultan Selim III. Meanwhile, however, France had knocked all of Great Britain's allies out of the war in Europe. *See* Abukir; Hohenlinden; Copenhagen I; French Revolution Wars.

Alexandria IV (Egyptian Revolt), 1882. Great Britain joined France in control of the Suez Canal (opened 1869) when Benjamin Disraeli bought the shares of the Egyptian khedive Ismail in 1875. Six years later Col. Arabi Pasha led a revolution against the two European powers, which were administering Egyptian finances. To guard the western entrance to the Nile River, Arabi began constructing forts at Alexandria. The British government ordered the Egyptians to cease this work. When Arabi refused, Adm. Frederick Beauchamp Seymour took a squadron of eight warships and five gunboats into the harbor. On July 11, 1882, the British ships opened fire on Alexandria's forts. By the evening of the second day the fortifications had been demolished. A landing party then occupied Alexandria. The Suez Canal remained secure. *See* Tell el-Kebir.

Alexandria, La. (American Civil War). A rearguard action, between May 1 and 8, 1864, during the Federal general Nathaniel Banks's withdrawal from his Red River offensive. *See* Sabine Crossroads–Pleasant Hill.

Alford (English Civil War), 1645. At the same time that Charles I's Cavaliers were losing the Civil War in England, their Royalist counterparts in Scotland were defeating all opposition. To check the victorious campaigns of the king's Scottish lieutenant, the Marquis of Montrose (James Graham), the Covenanters organized a new army under Gen. William Baillie. This force marched upon Montrose and, it appeared to Baillie, drove him beyond the Don River in Aberdeen County. But when Baillie carried his pursuit across the river, he found that Montrose had led him into a trap at Alford. On July 2, 1645, the Covenanters resumed their advance, only to be repulsed with heavy losses. Both sides then maneuvered to the southwest, each seeking an advantageous position for a showdown battle. *See* Naseby; Auldearn; Kilsyth; English Civil War.

al-Fustât (Moslem Conquest of Egypt), 641. The aggressive Moslem caliph Omar I remained unsatisfied with the swift Arabian conquests of Syria (including Palestine) and Persia. In 639 he sent an Arabian army under the general Amr ibn-al-As westward toward Egypt, then held by the Byzantine Empire. With 4,000 horsemen, Amr rode along the ancient road of conquest, seizing Pelusium and then Heliopolis, at the edge of the Nile delta, in 640. The Byzantine army prepared to defend Egypt at the old Roman settlement of Babylon on the Nile. The capable Amr encamped at al-Fustât (later to become Old Cairo) and laid siege to Babylon. The Moslem army, steadily augmented by fresh recruits, prosecuted the siege vigorously. On April 9, 641, the Byzantine garrison surrendered. Amr promptly moved down the Nile to Alexandria, Egypt's greatest city. *See* Aleppo; Nihawand; Alexandria II; Moslem Conquests.

Algeciras (Spanish-Moslem Wars), 1344. The decisive victory of Alfonso XI over the Spanish and African Moslems at Río Salado in 1340 enabled him to move on the Atlantic seaport of Algeciras. His army of Castile (and León) laid siege to the city. With the Moorish reserve strength dissipated during the long Christian counteroffensive, Algeciras could expect no relief. It capitulated in 1344. The city was virtually destroyed. To the east only the independent kingdom of Granada remained of the Moorish power in Spain. But the attempts to reduce this stronghold were long delayed by preoccupation with the Hundred Years' War and by dynastic quarrels. *See* Río Salado; Nájera.

Alghero (Aragonese Conquest of Sardinia), 1353. The island of Sardinia came under the control of the Doria family of Genoa early in the twelfth century. In 1353, however, Pedro IV of Aragon landed an expeditionary force at Alghero on the northwest corner of the island. The Genoese were chased off Sardinia, which remained under the rule of the crown of Aragon for almost 400 years. *See* Messina II.

Alhama de Granada (Spanish-Moslem Wars), 1482. The union of Castile and Aragon (through the marriage of Isabella I and Ferdinand II) in 1479 provided the military strength to war on the last Moslem enclave in Spain—the kingdom of Granada in the south. The Christian offensive began on February 28, 1482, with an attack on Alhama de Granada, a key defensive point 24 miles southwest of the Moorish capital of Granada. Surprising the garrison, a Spanish army under the Marquis of Cadiz stormed into the fortress and seized it. Abul Hassan, the Moslem king of Granada, took the fortress under siege five days later. But the Spaniards held on firmly. When King Ferdinand (who took the number V of Castile) sent out a large relieving force, the Moors withdrew. The hard campaign to reconquer Granada had opened successfully. *See* Toro; Loja.

Aligarh (Maratha-British War II), 1803. The Second Maratha War fought by the British in India broke out during the administration of Gov.-Gen. Lord Richard Wellesley. In the north Gen. Gerard Lake, the victor of Vinegar Hill during the Irish Rebellion, led a British and allied Indian army against Aligarh, the key Maratha fortress, 43 miles north of Agra. On August 28, 1803, Lake's troops stormed into the fortress and captured it at a cost of 200 casualties. The victorious army moved on to take Delhi on September 11 and Agra on October 4. *See* Laswari; Assaye; Maratha-British Wars.

Aliwal (Sikh-British War I), 1846. The third battle of the war found an Anglo-Indian army pushing the Sikhs back to the Sutlej River. At Aliwal in East Punjab, 90 miles southeast of Lahore, Sir Harry Smith with 10,000 men attacked a Sikh force twice as large on January 28. The third charge by Smith's cavalry routed the stubborn enemy, who fled across the river, where many drowned. One more battle remained to be fought in this war, about 45 miles downstream. *See* Ferozeshah; Sobraon; Sikh-British Wars.

Aljubarrota (Spanish-Portuguese Wars), 1385. A

dynastic quarrel with Castile endangered the independence of Portugal when its king, Ferdinand I, died in 1383. Ferdinand's illegitimate half brother, John, grand master of the Aviz order of knights, assumed the regency. But the Portuguese crown was claimed by John I of Castile, husband of Ferdinand's daughter Beatrice. The Castilian John marched into Portugal at the head of an 18,000-man army to enforce his claim. The Portuguese John assembled a force of some 7,000 men, which included hundreds of English and Gascon veterans of the Hundred Years' War. The two armies clashed in a showdown battle at Aljubarrota, about 50 miles north of Lisbon, on August 14, 1385. Imitating successful English tactics in the use of archers and men-at-arms, the Portuguese decisively defeated the Castilian force (which included some French). John of Castile was forced to abandon his claim to the Portuguese throne, while the victorious John had himself crowned as John I, the first of the Aviz dynasty that would rule Portugal the next 200 years. *See* Montiel; Ceuta.

Alkmaar I (Netherlands War of Independence), 1573. After capturing Haarlem, the Spanish troops of the Duke of Alva moved to take Alkmaar, 20 miles to the northwest of Amsterdam. Alva's natural son Don Frederic of Toledo again commanded the attack. With 16,000 men the Spaniard struck the city on August 21, 1573. He was beaten off by a stubborn defense carried out by only 2,000 soldiers and armed townspeople. Don Frederic then laid siege to the city. The Alkmaarites retaliated by opening the dikes and flooding the land. An inland Spanish fleet under the Comte Bossu (Jean de Henin-Lietard) sought to come up to help the besiegers. It was met in the Zuider Zee by a Dutch naval force under Adm. Dirkzoon. The Dutch "Sea Beggars" destroyed the Spanish ships, capturing Bossu. On October 8 the Spanish had to abandon the siege. Alkmaar thus became the first city in the Netherlands to resist successfully the iron hand of Philip II. It was also Alva's last battle again the Dutch; he was succeeded by Don Luis de Requeséns. *See* Haarlem; Walcheren; Leyden; Netherlands War of Independence.

Alkmaar II (Wars of the French Revolution), 1799. Of all the offensives launched by the Second Coalition powers against the armies of the French Directory in 1799, only the one in Holland failed to make any headway. Here Frederick Augustus, duke of York and Albany, second son of Great Britain's George III, commanded a combined British-Russian force. Driven out of the southern Netherlands in September, the 30,000 allied troops moved northward to challenge the French army of comparable size at Alkmaar. In an indecisive battle on October 2 the allies seized the town but then were promptly bottled up by the French commander, Gen. Guillaume Brune. Sixteen days later the English duke signed the Convention of Alkmaar, in which he released all French prisoners in exchange for a safe evacuation of the British and Russian armies from the Netherlands. Angered at the lack of support from Great Britain and Austria, Czar Paul I took Russia out of the Coalition on October 22. *See* Bergen op Zoom II; Zurich II; Stockach II; French Revolution Wars.

Allia (Gallic Invasion of Rome), 390 B.C. Six years after their victory at Veii, the Romans faced a new threat from the north. A horde of Gauls under the semilegendary Brennus swept out of the Po Valley and overran Etruria. At the Allia River, about 11 miles north of Rome, some 40,000 Romans under Quintus Sulpicius tried to halt the invaders. The barbarians of Brennus broke through the defenders' line on July 18 and in the pursuit that followed inflicted heavy losses on the Romans. Entering Rome, the Gauls methodically sacked and burned the city, except for the Capitol, which resisted capture. After a siege of several months, Brennus withdrew his army upon payment of a reported 1,000 pounds of gold.

The Gauls continued to raid the outlying parts of Rome for the next 50 years but never succeeded in retaking the city. Peace terms were finally agreed on about 334 B.C. *See* Veii; Roman Republic.

Almansa (War of the Spanish Succession), 1707. The English-led allied naval attacks on Spain, which had taken Gibraltar (1704) and Barcelona (1705), switched to a land offensive in 1706. From Lisbon, the Earl of Galway, a Huguenot named Henri de Massue, marquis de Ruvigny, led an English-Dutch-Portuguese army of 15,000 men eastward to Madrid. He entered the city in June, proclaiming Archduke Charles of Austria (future Holy Roman Emperor Charles VI) Charles III of Spain. But finding no support among the Castilian people (who preferred the Bourbon king Philip V), Galway withdrew eastward to the Valencian coast. The following spring Galway was maneuvered into combat by Louis XIV's general, the Duke of Berwick (James Fitz-james, the natural son of King James II of England and the Duke of Marlborough's sister Arabella). At Almansa, 60 miles southwest of Valencia, Berwick with a superior Franco-Spanish force fell on Galway's army on April 25. In a bloody battle the capable Berwick routed the allies so thoroughly that the attempt to unseat Philip V ended in dismal failure. *See* Barcelona I; Stollhofen; Spanish Succession, War of the.

Alma River (Crimean War), 1854. When Great Britain and France joined Turkey in the war against Russia, the scene of battle shifted to the Crimean peninsula (except for two abortive allied expeditions in the Baltic Sea). On September 14 an English-French army of 26,000 men landed at the northwest base of the peninsula and began marching on the Sevastopol naval base. General Lord Raglan (Fitzroy Somerset) of Britain and Marshal Armand Saint-Arnaud of France shared the allied command. At the Alma River the allies found their route blocked by Russian troops under Prince Aleksandr Menshikov. They attacked nevertheless, on September 20. In a sharp struggle in which the British carried the weight of the assault, the Russians were driven off the heights south of the river. Menshikov lost 1,200 killed and more than 4,000 captured, many of them wounded by British bayonets. Raglan suffered about 3,000 casualties; Saint-Arnaud, 1,000. The latter died of cholera after the battle and was succeeded by Gen. François Canrobert. The thrust toward Sevastopol continued. *See* Silistra; Bomarsund; Sevastopol I; Crimean War.

Alnwick I (English-Scottish Wars), 1093. The forceful rule of William II, Rufus, brought the northwestern counties of Cumberland and Westmorland under English rule in the spring of 1093. This aggression provoked Malcolm III, Canmore, of Scotland to invade Northumberland. The Scots' army penetrated to the Aln River, laying siege to Alnwick Castle on the north side of the town. William sent an army north to relieve the garrison. On November 13 the English ambushed the besieging Scots, killing Malcolm and his eldest son, Edward. The invasion collapsed. *See* Rochester I; Tinchebray.

Alnwick II (English-Scottish Wars), 1174. As had his grandfather David I before him, William I, the Lion, of Scotland invaded Northumberland during the reign of Henry II. Allied with young Henry, eldest son of the English ruler, the Scots reached the Aln River and laid siege to Alnwick Castle. Henry II sent a relieving army of knights to the north, which surprised and routed the besiegers on June 13, 1174. William was captured and sent to prison in Normandy. He was able to secure his release only by recognizing English hegemony over Scotland. Under Henry's successor, however, Scotland regained its independence by paying 10,000 marks toward the Third Crusade expenses of Richard I. *See* Wallingford; Berwick upon Tweed.

Alte Veste. *See* Fürth.

Amberg (Wars of the French Revolution), 1796. While Napoleon Bonaparte campaigned in northern Italy, the French Revolutionary government launched a twin offensive beyond the Rhine against the German states of the Holy Roman Empire (Francis II). In 1795 Gen. Jean Jourdan led the Army of the Sambre-and-Meuse across the lower Rhine into Franconia, while Gen. Charles Pichegru took the Army of the Rhine-and-Moselle over the upper Rhine into Swabia and Bavaria. By the summer of 1796 most of south Germany had fallen to the French drives. But then Archduke Charles Louis, brother of the emperor, mounted a counterattack with an Austrian army of 48,000. On August 24 Charles attacked and defeated Jourdan's 45,000-man force at Amberg, 35 miles east of Nürnberg. The French fell back to the northwest, while the Austrians pressed forward, widening the gap between the two invading armies. *See* Castiglione delle Stiviere; Würzburg; French Revolution Wars.

American Civil War (1861–1865). The issue of slavery, particularly in the new states being formed from western territories, drove an ever larger wedge between the free states of the North and the slaveholding states in the South. When the Republican candidate for President of the United States, Abraham Lincoln, won election on November 6, 1860, the situation reached a crisis. South Carolina seceded from the Union on December 20, declaring that its sovereignty now stood in jeopardy. Six other states followed suit from January 9 to February 1, 1861: Mississippi, Florida, Alabama, Georgia, Louisiana, and Texas. On February 4 delegates from the seceding states formed the Confederate States of America, with Jefferson Davis elected President. Federal forts and arsenals were seized throughout the South. Confederate shore batteries forced the surrender of Fort Sumter outside Charleston, S.C., on April 13. President Lincoln then called for 75,000 volunteers to put down the "insurrection" against the United States. From April 17 to May 20, four more states left the Union: Virginia, Arkansas, Tennessee, and North Carolina. The Confederate government established its capital at Richmond, Va., and mobilized for war. Its chief aim was to force the North to recognize its independence. The 23 states of the North and West, under the leadership of Lincoln, sought originally only to restore the Union. However, after the President's Emancipation Proclamation of January 1, 1863, freeing the slaves became an almost equally important objective.

For four years the United States was torn by bitter civil war. The major theater of operations was east of the Appalachians, especially in northern Virginia between the two hostile capitals of Washington, D.C., and Richmond. From the Appalachians westward to the Mississippi River an important secondary theater developed. The last two Confederate armies in the field surrendered on April 9 and 18, 1865. In the costliest war in United States history (in the proportion of casualties to participants), the Confederate government was decisively defeated, the Union preserved, and slavery abolished. In all, the North mobilized 1,557,000 men, the South 1,082,000. Federal losses were 359,528 dead (of these 110,070 were killed or mortally wounded in battle), 275,175 wounded. Confederate casualties were 258,000 dead (including 94,000 battle deaths) and more than 100,000 reported wounded.

Fort Sumter	1861
Philippi, W. Va.	1861
Big Bethel	1861
Rich Mountain	1861
Bull Run I	1861
Wilson's Creek	1861
Cheat Mountain	1861
Ball's Bluff	1861
Belmont	1861
Mill Springs	1862
Fort Henry	1862
Roanoke Island	1862
Fort Donelson	1862
Pea Ridge	1862
Hampton Roads	1862
Kernstown I	1862
Island No. 10	1862
New Madrid	1862
Shiloh	1862
New Orleans II	1862
Yorktown II	1862
Williamsburg	1862
McDowell	1862
Front Royal	1862
Winchester I	1862
Fair Oaks	1862
Cross Keys–Fort Republic	1862
Seven Days	1862
Mechanicsville	1862
Gaines's Mill	1862
Savage's Station	1862
Frayser's Farm	1862
Malvern Hill	1862
Cedar Mountain	1862
Bull Run II	1862
Groveton	1862
Chantilly	1862
Richmond, Ky.	1862
Harpers Ferry	1862
Antietam Creek	1862
South Mountain	1862
Crampton's Gap	1862
Iuka	1862
Corinth, Miss.	1862
Perryville	1862
Prairie Grove	1862
Fredericksburg	1862
Chickasaw Bluffs	1862
Stones River	1862–1863
Arkansas Post	1863
Charleston III	1863
Fort Wagner	1863
Chancellorsville	1863
Salem Church	1863
Port Hudson	1863
Brandy Station	1863
Winchester II	1863
Gettysburg	1863
Vicksburg	1863
Port Gibson	1863
Jackson	1863
Champion's Hill	1863
Big Black River	1863
Chickamauga	1863
Bristoe Station	1863
Chattanooga	1863
Orchard Knob–Indian Hill	1863
Lookout Mountain	1863
Missionary Ridge	1863
Knoxville	1863
Olustee	1864
Sabine Crossroads–Pleasant Hill	1864
Alexandria, La.	1864
Fort Pillow	1864
Wilderness	1864
Spotsylvania	1864
Yellow Tavern	1864
Drewry's Bluff	1864
Resaca	1864
New Market	1864
North Anna River	1864
Cold Harbor	1864
Piedmont	1864
Brices Cross Roads	1864
Trevilian Station	1864
Petersburg	1864–1865
Crater	1864
Fort Stedman	1865
Lynchburg	1864
Kenesaw Mountain	1864
New Hope Church	1864
Monocacy River	1864
Tupelo	1864
Atlanta	1864
Peach Tree Creek	1864
Kernstown II	1864
Mobile Bay	1864
Winchester III	1864
Fisher's Hill	1864
Cedar Creek	1864
Franklin	1864
Spring Hill	1864
Nashville	1864
Savannah III	1864
Fort Fisher	1865
Bentonville	1865
Five Forks	1865
Appomattox River	1865
Sayler's Creek	1865

American Revolution, War of the (1775–1783). A strong American resentment against British rule developed after the successful conclusion of the French and Indian War. Widening the gap between the 13 colonies and the mother country were the

Stamp Act (1765), the Boston Massacre (1770), the Boston Tea Party (1773), and the Intolerable Acts (1774). The first pitched battles between colonial militia and British regulars took place at Lexington and Concord, both in Massachusetts, on April 19, 1775. On July 4, 1776, American patriots announced their Declaration of Independence. This historic act, together with the decisive U.S. victory at Saratoga in 1777, gained the allegiance of France. Although largely successful in the field, Britain steadily dissipated its strength against the stubborn resistance of Gen. George Washington's Continental troops. The largest English army in America was finally cornered at Yorktown, Va. The surrender there in 1781 ended the fighting only for Great Britain's erstwhile colonies (and their allied French ground troops). Meanwhile Great Britain had become engaged in a fierce maritime conflict with France (1778), Spain (1779), and the Netherlands (1780). The 1783 Treaty of Versailles ended the war. The independence of the United States was acknowledged, conquests in India were mutually restored, and Florida and Minorca ceded to Spain.

Lexington and Concord 1775
Fort Ticonderoga II 1775
Bunker Hill 1775
  Boston 1775–1776
Great Bridge 1775
Quebec III 1775
  Saint Johns 1775
Moores Creek Bridge 1776
Charleston I 1776
  Fort Moultrie 1776
Long Island 1776
Valcour Island 1776
White Plains 1776
  Harlem Heights 1776
Fort Washington 1776
Trenton 1776
Princeton 1777
Danbury 1777
Fort Ticonderoga III 1777
  Hubbardton 1777
Fort Stanwix 1777
  Oriskany 1777
Bennington 1777
Cooch's Bridge 1777
Brandywine Creek 1777
Paoli 1777
Germantown 1777
Saratoga 1777
  Freeman's Farm 1777
  Bemis Heights 1777
  Fort Clinton and Fort Montgomery 1777
Fort Mercer and Fort Mifflin 1777
Carrickfergus 1778
Monmouth 1778
Ushant I 1778
Newport 1778
Savannah I 1778
Port Royal Island 1779
Kettle Creek 1779
Vincennes 1779
Briar Creek 1779
Stono Ferry 1779
Grenada 1779
Stony Point 1779
Paulus Hook 1779
Newtown 1779
Savannah II 1779
Flamborough Head 1779
Gibraltar II 1779–1783
Saint Vincent Cape I 1780
Charleston II 1780
Waxhaw Creek 1780
Camden 1780
  Fishing Creek 1780
Kings Mountain 1780
Cowpens 1781
Guilford Courthouse 1781
Praia 1781
Hobkirk's Hill 1781
Ninety Six 1781
Dogger Bank I 1781
Chesapeake Capes 1781
Eutaw Springs 1781
Yorktown I 1781
Minorca II 1782
Madras III 1782
Trincomalee I 1782
Saintes, Les 1782
Cuddalore I 1782
Trincomalee II 1782
Cuddalore II 1783

Amida I (Roman-Persian Wars), 359. The second war between Constantius II and the Sassanian Persian Empire found Shapur (Sapor) II again invading Roman territory in Mesopotamia. This time his objective was Amida (Diyarbekir), on the right bank of the Tigris River. For 73 days the Roman garrison held out against the aggressive Persian siege. Finally Shapur's army stormed the fortress and massacred the defenders. Although the Persians were victorious, the long, bitter battle had cost them 30,000 casualties. Shapur now felt too weak to continue the campaign and withdrew to his capital of Ctesiphon. But the respite in the prolonged Roman-Persian conflict was short-lived. Four years later the struggle was renewed by the Roman emperor Julian. *See* Singara; Argentoratum; Tigris River; Roman Empire.

Amida II (Byzantine-Persian Wars), 502. At the beginning of the sixth century the Byzantine emperor Anastasius I reneged on his share of the expenses incurred by Persia in defending the

Derbent Gateway (a pass through the Caucasus Mountains near the Caspian Sea) against northern nomads. The Sassanid ruler of Persia, Kavadh I, then reopened the historic war against Rome-Constantinople. As 156 years earlier, the chief Persian attack was against the Roman fortress of Amida (Diyarbekir), on the right bank of the Tigris. The garrison resisted stubbornly for three months, taking a toll of thousands of Persian besiegers. But finally a night attack led by Kavadh himself breached the walls and conquered the fortress. A reported 80,000 (probably much exaggerated) soldiers and civilians fell to the invaders' swords. The following year, however, Persia made peace with Anastasius on terms of the *status quo ante bellum. See* Tigris River; Dara.

Amiens (World War I), 1918. Two days after the German salient on the Marne River had been eliminated, the Allied commander in chief, Marshal Ferdinand Foch, launched his second offensive of 1918. This attack, under the British field marshal Sir Douglas Haig, was scheduled to reduce the enemy salient jutting toward Amiens, thus clearing the Amiens–Paris railway from hostile artillery fire. The chief striking force was the British Fourth Army of Gen. Sir Henry Rawlinson, whose 17 divisions included one American division, the four divisions of the Canadian Corps, and the five divisions of the Australian Corps. Supported by 400 tanks, Rawlinson attacked eastward from Amiens on August 8 against the 20 worn German divisions of the Second (Georg von der Marwitz) and Eighteenth (Oskar von Hutier) armies. Behind tanks and a rolling artillery barrage, the British advanced on a ten-mile front. They took 16,000 prisoners in two hours and by nightfall had penetrated nine miles into the enemy lines. The German commander in chief, Gen. Erich Ludendorff, called it the "black day" of his army—for the first time entire units collapsed. On the right (south) of Rawlinson, the French First Army of Gen. Marie Eugène Debeney had also made some progress.

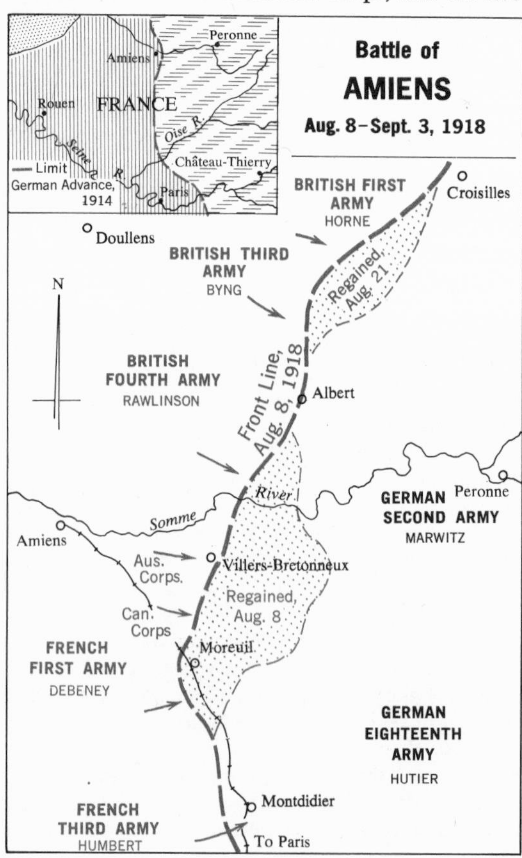

Although the British advance slowed down after the first day, it continued to grind forward. On August 10 the French Third Army of Georges Humbert struck the southern face of the salient, driving the Germans out of Montdidier. After a pause the British Third Army (Sir Julian Byng), to the north of Rawlinson, joined the attack on August 21, followed by the British First Army (Sir Henry Horne), still farther north. Ludendorff then ordered a general withdrawal to the east along a 30-mile front. When the Allies pursued closely, he was forced to fall back to the Hindenburg Line on September 3. This eliminated the Amiens salient that had been carved out by the Germans five months earlier. Ludendorff's losses during the battle of Amiens totaled 75,000, including almost 30,000 captured. The French lost 24,000 men, the British 22,000. Amiens marked the turning point on the Western Front. *See* Marne River II; Saint-Mihiel; World War I.

Amorium (Moslem-Byzantine Wars), 838. The periodic struggle for Asia Minor erupted again during the reign of the Byzantine emperor Theophilus. At the frontier post of Amorium, in ancient Phrygia, the Byzantines fought a pitched battle against the Moslems of Caliph al-Mutasim, son of the great Harun al-Rashid. The Byzantine cavalry was driven from the field. Al-Mutasim then surrounded the fort. After a bloody siege of almost two months, the Moslems broke in and massacred the garrison. The fighting then died down again. *See* Heraclea Pontica; Samosata; Moslem Conquests.

Amphipolis (Great Peloponnesian War), 422 B.C. Sparta carried the Great Peloponnesian War to the Athenian colonies of northeastern Greece in 424. An expedition under the able general Brasidas captured the city of Amphipolis in eastern Macedonia and began stirring up rebellion in the cities of Thrace. When the offshore Athenian fleet under Thucydides failed to take effective action, Cleon exiled the commander, who later won great fame as an historian of the war.

In 422 Cleon personally led an attack against Amphipolis. But Brasidas welcomed the opportunity to fight and sortied from the city to meet the Athenians. At the first clash of the two forces, Cleon's left collapsed. The weakened center and the right flank offered some resistance, but they too soon broke and fled, taking heavy losses. In the close fighting of the pursuit, both Cleon and Brasidas were killed.

The death of the two leading belligerents induced Sparta and Athens to accept peace the following year. Called the Peace of Nicias, the truce was scheduled for 50 years. But the terms of the treaty applied only to the two principal city-states, and the allies of both sides continued the quarrel. During this semiwar, Athens resolved to attack in Sicily. *See* Delium; Syracuse I; Peloponnesian Wars.

Angaur (World War II). During the U.S. marines' assault on Peleliu Island, the 81st Infantry Division overran Angaur Island, to the south, during September 17–19, 1944. *See* Peleliu-Angaur.

Angora (Tamerlane's Invasion of Turkey), 1402. Following his decisive victory at Nicopolis in 1396, the Ottoman sultan Bajazet I (Bayazid) resumed his siege of Constantinople. But the Turkish attack had to be suspended again when a Tatar army under Tamerlane (Timur Lenk, or Timur the Lame) swept through Aleppo and Damascus into Asia Minor. Bajazet hurried eastward to meet the new threat. With his army augmented by Christian levies, the sultan reached Angora (Ankara) in west-central Asia Minor. Here stood the Mongol host of Tamerlane, which had seized Baghdad in 1393 and caved in the eastern part of the Ottoman Empire. On July 20, 1402, the two armies, both strong in cavalry, clashed head on. During the desperate fighting most of the Turkish vassals deserted, giving Tamerlane complete mastery of the field. Bajazet was taken prisoner and died in captivity the next year. Although Tamerlane, the Prince of Destruction, died two years later, before he could launch a new conquest, it took the Ottoman Empire more than a decade to regain its former vitality. *See* Baghdad II; Nicopolis; Salonika I; Mongol Wars.

An Lao Valley (Vietnam War), 1966. Since their establishment in 1954, the Viet Cong had held the South China Sea coast from Qui Nhon northward along Route 1 almost to Chu Lai. An American and allied offensive to clear these Binh Dinh plains led to the heaviest fighting of the war up to that time. The center of the battle was An Lao Valley, about 280 miles northeast of Saigon. On January 25, 12,000 men of the U.S. 1st Air Cavalry, South Vietnamese airborne, and South Korean marines struck northward toward An Lao in the first division-size attack of the war (called Operation White Wing). Three days later 5,000 U.S. marines, supported by 2,000 South Vietnamese troops, attacked south and west toward An Lao (Operation Double Eagle) in a large-scale pincers movement. In a three-week battle the coordinated attack killed about 1,800 enemy soldiers. But the great bulk of the Communist force in the area—estimated at two to four regiments—escaped into the hills to the west. Casualties for the U.S. and South Vietnamese troops totaled several hundred. *See* South Vietnam; Chu Pong–Ia Drang River; A Shau; Vietnam War.

Antietam Creek (American Civil War), 1862. After his victory at Bull Run II, the Confederate general Robert E. Lee turned north, crossing the Potomac River during September 4–6 to invade Maryland. He then divided his army of 65,000 men by sending Gen. Thomas (Stonewall) Jackson westward to attack Harpers Ferry. The capture of this Potomac crossing would open up a protected Confederate supply line down the Shenandoah Valley. The remainder of the Southern army moved from Frederick to Hagerstown, Md.

In Washington, D.C., Gen. John Pope's battered Army of Virginia was absorbed into the major Federal striking force, the Army of the Potomac. Gen. George McClellan, restored to top command, began moving slowly northwest toward Frederick with some 84,000 troops. On September 13 McClellan reached Frederick. Here he learned that Lee's army, to his front, was widely scattered. Still, McClellan moved with extreme caution. At daylight on September 14 he sent Gen. Ambrose Burnside, commander of his right wing, with two corps to Turner's Gap in South Mountain. The Federals arrived at noon to find the pass held by Gen. Daniel Hill's division, later supported by Gen. James Longstreet's division. The ensuing battle of South Mountain lasted into the night. Finally the Confederates were beaten back, outflanked on the right (north) by Gen. Joseph Hooker's I Corps and on the left by Gen. Jesse Reno's IX Corps. Although the action was a Federal victory, the Confederate defense had given Lee an extra day to reassemble his army. Among the 1,813 Federal casualties was the mortally wounded Reno. Hill and Longstreet lost 2,685 men.

As Burnside was forcing his way through Turner's Gap, McClellan's left wing under Gen. William Franklin (VI Corps) attacked westward through Crampton's Gap, four miles to the south. West of this height, the Confederate general Lafayette McLaws, who also commanded Gen. Richard Anderson's division, was supporting General Jackson's determined offensive against Harpers Ferry. McLaws turned to confront Franklin. Driven out of the pass, the Confederates fell back southward down Pleasant Valley. Here McLaws bluffed the Federal commander into hesitating. While Franklin (who had lost only 533 men) delayed, Harpers Ferry fell early the following morning (September 15). Federal indecision had given the Confederates another tactical advantage.

After losing both mountain passes, Lee planned to withdraw to the south side of the Potomac. But when he learned that Jackson had taken

Antietam Creek

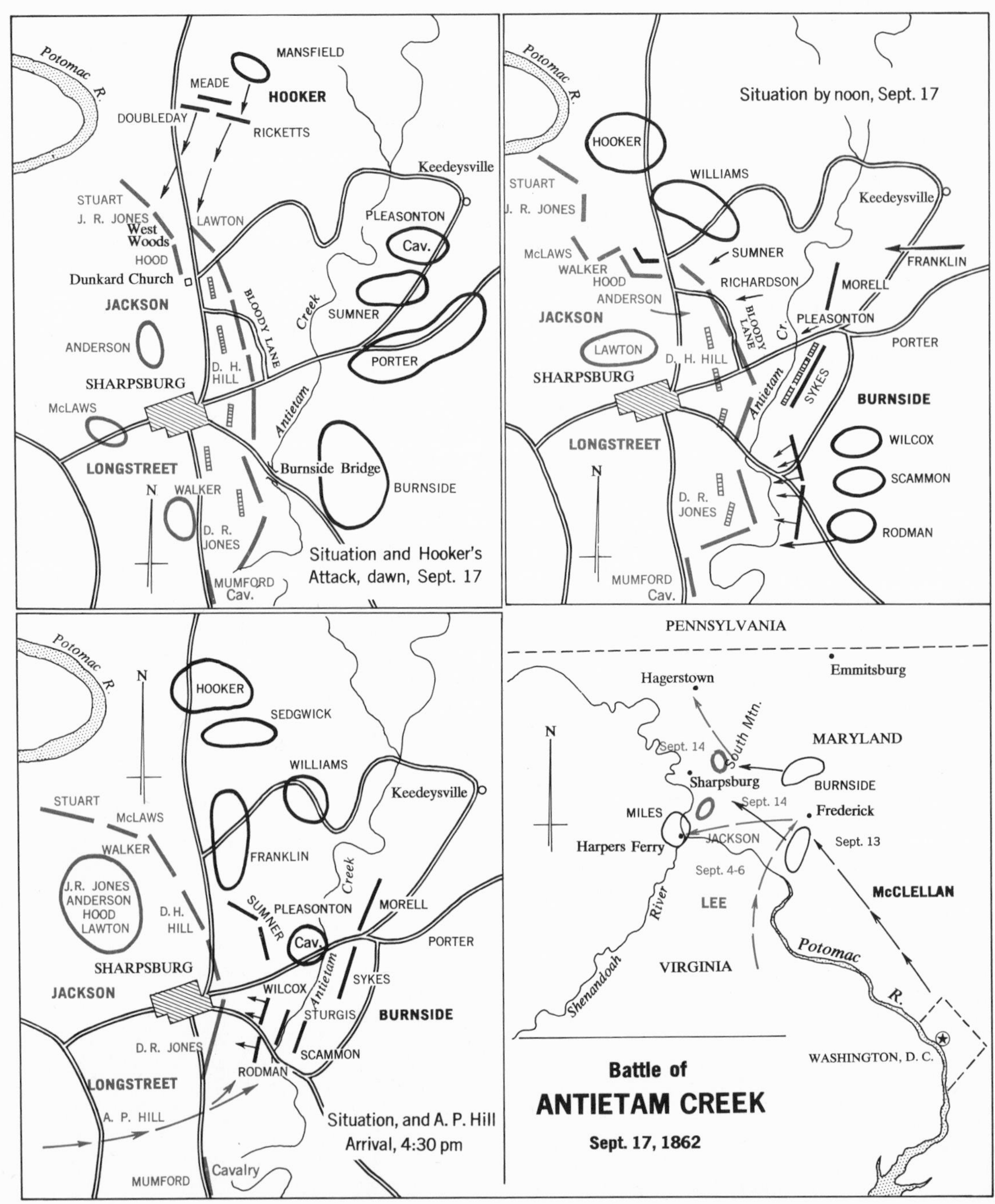

Harpers Ferry and was marching northward to join him at Sharpsburg, Lee took up a defensive position behind Antietam Creek, awaiting McClellan's attack. It was a risky decision. The Confederate army numbered only 20,000 at this time, while the oncoming Federal Army of the Potomac consisted of 75,000 troops. However, McClellan moved up slowly and spent all of September 16 organizing his attack for the following day. Meanwhile Jackson arrived from his victory at Harpers Ferry with 11,000 men, and another 10,000 were on the way.

The Federal attack began at dawn on September 17 on the north end of the line and spread across the front to the center and finally to the extreme southern flank by late afternoon. This piecemeal assault nullified McClellan's marked numerical superiority. On the northern flank, Gen. Joseph Hooker's I Corps drove the Confederate left past

Dunkard Church and West Woods, until it was finally checked by the hard-fighting troops of Gens. John Hood and J. E. B. Stuart. Hooker was wounded and Gen. Joseph Mansfield, commander of the supporting XIII Corps, killed.

In the center Gen. Edwin Sumner committed his II Corps precipitously only to have Gen. John Sedgwick's division thrown back with 2,200 casualties. However, the divisions of Gen. William French and Gen. Israel Richardson fought their way forward, driving the Confederates of Gen. Daniel Hill out of a sunken road now called Bloody Lane. By noon Lee's center in front of Sharpsburg and his left flank to the north stood in grave danger. Only Federal lethargy prevented a total rout.

At the southern end of the front Gen. Ambrose Burnside launched his attack against the Confederate right flank about noon. During the next four hours the Federals swarmed across Antietam Creek, driving back Gen. James Longstreet's men to the southern edge of Sharpsburg. At this decisive moment the tide of battle abruptly changed. General Ambrose P. Hill's division arrived from Harpers Ferry to strike Burnside's IX Corps in the flank and send it reeling back to Antietam Creek. This check to the Federal advance saved the Confederate army and ended the battle. Antietam is often called the "bloodiest single day of the war." Lee lost 13,724 men (including 2,700 killed), McClellan 12,140 (including 2,108 killed).

Lee remained in position during the day of September 18, then began withdrawing across the Potomac that night. Federal pursuit was negligible. Despite the failure to win a larger victory, President Abraham Lincoln used the occasion to announce the Emancipation Proclamation effective January 1, 1863. The character of the conflict now changed from a war to preserve the Union to a crusade to free the slaves. *See* Bull Run II; Harpers Ferry; Fredericksburg; American Civil War.

Antioch I (First Crusade), 1097–1098. After a difficult four-month march through hostile territory, the crusaders reached the plain of Antioch on October 20, 1097. The strongly defended city stood on the southern bank of the Orontes River below Mount Silpius. In command was the Turkish chieftain Yaghi-Siyan. The crusaders stormed across the Iron Bridge east of Antioch, then turned downstream to encamp north of the city. A long siege set in. The command of the European army was still vested in a council of war, of which the two chief figures were Bohemond of Taranto and his rival for supreme leadership, Raymond IV of Toulouse.

The siege was as difficult for the Crusaders to endure as for the Turks. Hunger and disease weakened both sides. On December 29 the garrison made a determined sally to raise the siege but was beaten back by the Christian knights. Two days later a Turkish relief force from Damascus was repulsed. A more serious threat to the crusaders came on February 9, 1098, when a large Turkish relief army from Aleppo advanced near to Antioch. Bohemond broke the attack with a slashing charge by 700 mounted knights. In March 1098 the garrison made its last futile sally. They then settled back to await the arrival of the greatest Turkish lord of the region, Kerboga of Mosul, who was moving on Antioch with a seemingly invincible force. Fortunately for the crusaders, Kerboga delayed his arrival by three weeks in a fruitless siege of Edessa (Urfa), which was held by Baldwin of Boulogne.

In the meantime, Bohemond persuaded a traitor in the garrison to help open the Bridge Gate to the Christians the night of June 2–3. The crusaders poured into the city. In an orgy of killing, all of Antioch except the citadel was taken by the following evening. Yaghi-Siyan was slain. Four days later Kerboga's Turkish army arrived and took over the citadel from the original garrison troops. He launched a strong assault from the citadel downhill into the town but was beaten back in a fierce fight.

Sensing a quick collapse by the Europeans, who were short of food, Kerboga prepared to besiege the city. The Turkish leader was right about the inability of the crusaders to undergo a long siege, but he underestimated their fighting qualities. On June 28 Bohemond marched his entire force, now mostly on foot, across the Orontes River. Maneuvering smartly in the face of the enemy, the crusaders advanced on the Turkish army, which bolted almost immediately. Thousands of the fleeing soldiers were overtaken and killed along the river bank. Kerboga returned to Mosul with only a few survivors from his once powerful army. Following this decisive victory, the Turks in the citadel promptly surrendered. After resting and reorganizing for six months, the crusaders stood ready to move on their ultimate objective, Jerusalem. *See* Dorylaeum I; Tarsus; Jerusalem VII; Crusades.

Antioch II (Crusader-Turkish Wars), 1119. The failure of the First Crusade to take the Moslem stronghold at Aleppo kept the Christian states of Antioch and Edessa (Urfa) in constant danger. In the spring of 1119 the Turkish lord of Aleppo, Ilghazi, suddenly marched on Antioch, which was commanded by Roger of Salerno as regent for young King Bohemond II. Roger requested help from Tripoli, in Lebanon, and from Jerusalem and then rode out hoping to contain the Turkish invasion of his principality. On the night of June 28 the Norman knights camped near Ilghazi's troops. They awoke in the morning to find themselves surrounded by mounted enemy bowmen. All but a few knights, together with the infantry and the usual camp followers, were either killed or captured. The French gave the battle site the name Ager Sanguinis, or Field of Blood. Roger was among the dead. Both Antioch and Edessa now lay open to Turkish capture. But instead of pressing on, Ilghazi returned to Aleppo, where he amused the populace by torturing to death his Christian prisoners. Baldwin II of Jerusalem took over the regency of Antioch for young Bohemond II. *See* Ramleh I; Dyrrachium III; Edessa II; Crusades.

Antioch III (Crusader-Turkish Wars), 1268. After consolidating his position as sultan of Egypt and Syria, the Mameluke Baybars I (Bibars) launched an offensive against the remaining Frankish holdings in the Near East. In 1265 he captured Caesarea and Arsouf. Three years later he took Jaffa and, after feinting at Tripoli, seized the port of Saint Simeon. He then besieged the great fortress of Antioch, which had been held by Christians since 1098. On May 18, 1268, he assaulted the walls of the city with a Moslem army far superior to the Frankish defenders. Antioch fell. After killing or removing all the people of the city, Baybars razed the walls and other fortifications. The once great fortress never flourished again. *See* El Mansûra; Ain Jalut; Tunis II; Tripoli in Lebanon; Crusades.

Antwerp I (Netherlands War of Independence), 1584–1585. The largest city in the Spanish Netherlands, Antwerp suffered two attacks by the troops of Philip II during the Dutch War for Independence. On November 4, 1576, the Spanish garrison mutinied against its officers and sacked the city for two days and nights, a violence (named the Spanish Fury) in which some 8,000 people were killed. Eight years later, with the townspeople again in control of the city, Antwerp was attacked by the troops of the Duke of Parma (Alessandro Farnese), the fourth commander sent out from Madrid to crush the Dutch revolt. The city cut nearby dikes to limit the assault to a narrow front, which was successfully defended. Meanwhile, however, Parma built a fortified bridge over the Schelde, which cut off Antwerp from all supplies by sea. Finally, after 14 months of hardship, the city capitulated in 1585. *See* Maastricht I; Zutphen; Netherlands War of Independence.

Antwerp II (World War I), 1914. When the German invasion smashed through Liège and Namur in August, the main Belgian army of 150,000 men fell back to a second line based on Antwerp. To protect the German rear, Gen. Erich von Falkenhayn turned on the Belgian port after the battle of Aisne River I had begun stabilizing the Western Front. On October 1 heavy German siege guns under Gen. Hans von Beseler began knocking out Antwerp's forts one by one. Finally, on October 6, King Albert I of Belgium moved his army out of the city southwestward along the Flemish coast. During the retreat the king met a British force under Gen. Henry Rawlinson, which was marching forward from Oostende in a belated effort to help Belgium hold the city. The combined army continued to fall back, with the Belgian army taking a position on the extreme left of the Allied line between the North Sea and Diksmuide. Antwerp surrendered on October 9. *See* Namur II; Aisne River I; Ypres I; World War I.

Anual (Riffian War in Morocco), 1921. The Berber tribes of the Er Rif, a hilly coastal area in northern Morocco, revolted in 1921 against Spanish rule. Under the leadership of Abd-el-Krim, the Moorish Riffians surrounded a Spanish force of 20,000 at Anual on July 21. Some 12,000 Spanish troops were killed; their commander, Fernández Silvestre, committed suicide. After this disaster, Abd-el-Krim forced the Spanish out of the interior by the end of 1924. The chief then began attacking French forces to the west. Finally a combined French and Spanish army under Marshal Henri Pétain subdued the Riffians, capturing Abd-el-Krim on May 26, 1926, and sending him into exile.

Anzio (World War II), 1944. Late in 1943 the Allied advance on Rome became blocked at the Gustav-Cassino Line. General Sir Harold Alexander, commander of the ground forces in Italy, then launched an amphibious attack (Operation Shingle) 70 miles behind the German lines at Anzio, 30 miles south of Rome. Early in the morning of January 22 the VI Corps, under Gen. John Lucas, landed on the beach at Anzio, the British 1st Infantry Division on the left (north), the U.S. 3rd Infantry Division on the right. Despite little opposition, the invaders moved inland slowly. Before VI Corps could cut Highway 7 between Rome and Cassino, Field Marshal Albert Kesselring rushed up the German Fourteenth Army (Gen. Mackensen) to seal off the perimeter, on February 3. The Allies then dug in their beachhead (15 miles long and 7 miles deep) to defend against the expected counterattack and sent in the 5th and 56th British and U.S. 1st Armored and 45th Infantry divisions as reinforcements. During this period VI Corps lost 6,923 men in killed, wounded, and missing.

The Nazis counterattacked on February 16 with four divisions supported by 450 guns, which shelled the crowded lodgment mercilessly (almost 18,000 vehicles had been landed at Anzio during the first two weeks of the invasion). With their backs to the sea, the Allied soldiers fought doggedly and at the end of two days had blunted the German thrust. A second German counterattack late in February was also beaten back, and by March 1 the beachhead stood secure.

Although the Anzio landings failed to achieve a quick conquest of Rome, the fortified perimeter served as a springboard from which VI Corps troops could later join the rest of the Fifth Army in a joint attack toward Rome. Meanwhile, Lucas was relieved by Gen. Lucian Truscott and the corps re-formed to include seven divisions (British 5th and 1st, U.S. 45th, 36th, 34th, 3rd, and 1st Armored). On May 23 VI Corps lunged out of its beachhead and crossed Highway 7 the following day. The next day it linked up with the II Corps of Fifth Army, which was fighting its way northward after breaking through the Gustav-Cassino Line earlier in the month. Both corps then drove on Rome. *See* Gustav-Cassino Line; Gothic Line; World War II.

Appomattox River (American Civil War), 1865. After the defeat of his right flank at Five Forks, Va., on April 1, the Confederate commander, Gen. Robert E. Lee, decided to evacuate both Petersburg and Richmond. On the night of April 2–3 the exhausted, near-starving Army of Northern Virginia began retreating westward below the Appomattox River. Lee hoped to take his 30,000 men around the Federal left flank to join up with Gen. Joseph Johnston's army, which was falling back in North Carolina before the advance of Gen. William Sherman. However, the Federal commander in chief, Gen. U. S. Grant, who had 125,000 men available, drove his subordinates hard to block Lee's escape. General Philip Sheridan's cavalry corps cut the railroad to the south on April 5, forcing Lee farther westward. The next day the Federal II Corps of Gen. Andrew Humphreys overwhelmed Lee's rear guard at Sayler's Creek, taking about 7,000 prisoners, including Richard Ewell and five other generals. Federal losses were 1,180, including 166 killed.

The tightening pursuit forced Lee to cross to the north side of the Appomattox at Farmville on April 7. He continued the westward retreat the following day, pursued by Humphreys and the VI Corps of Gen. Horatio Wright. But now Sheridan, with Gen. Charles Griffin's V Corps and Gen. Edward Ord's Army of the James, had raced past Lee's southern flank to take a blocking position at Appomattox Station. Early on April 9 the Confederate division of Gen. John Gordon (1,600 infantry) tried to break through to open the route to Lynchburg. The last attack of the Army of Northern Virginia was beaten back. At 4 P.M. that day the encircled Lee surrendered his sword and his army to the victorious Grant at Appomattox Court House, a few miles to the northwest. Grant's vigorous pursuit stands as one of the most successful operations of its kind in history. In North Carolina, Gen. Joseph Johnston surrendered the last major Confederate army in the field on April 18, West of the Mississippi River, Gen. Edmund Kirby-Smith surrendered at Shreveport on May 26. The four-year war was over at last. *See* Five Forks; Petersburg; Bentonville; American Civil War.

Apulia (Moslem Wars with Byzantine Empire), 875–880. The resurgent military strength of the Byzantine Empire under Basil I first struck the Moslems in Asia Minor. Then turning to the west, Basil sent an expedition from Constantinople to Italy, where the Arabs had earlier won control of the lower peninsula. In 875 the Byzantines landed at Bari on the southeast coast and drove out the Moslem garrison. Five years later the operation was successfully repeated at the southern port of Tarentum (Taranto). When the Byzantines extended their control to Calabria in 885, Constantinople created two new themes, or provinces. Ironically, these themes were the refuge of Christians from Sicily, which was being overrun by the Moslems at the same time. *See* Samosata; Taormina; Erzurum; Moslem Conquests.

Aquae Sextiae (Gauls' Attack on Rome), 102 B.C. The overwhelming Gallic victory at Arausio in 105 prompted Rome to recall Gaius Marius and his army from Numidia. Marius marched into northern Italy to defend the Po Valley against a Gallic invasion. Fortunately for Rome the invaders had imprudently divided their forces after their triumph in France. The Cimbri swung to the east to enter Italy through the Brenner Pass; the Teutones advanced over Little Saint Bernard Pass in the western Alps.

Marius attacked the Teutones first. His well-trained legions drove the Gauls back through the mountains. Pursuing vigorously, the Romans overtook the enemy at Aquae Sextiae (Aix-en-Provence), on the lower Rhone. The Teutones were virtually annihilated. Marius then turned back to help Quintus Lutatius Catulus, who had been harassing the Cimbri with a second Roman army. *See* Arausio; Vercellae; Roman Republic.

Aquidaban River (Paraguayan War), 1870. When Francisco López became president of Paraguay in 1862, he used his dictatorial powers to build up the strongest army in South America. Aiming at the establishment of a Greater Paraguay, López intervened in Uruguay, supporting the Blancos party. This led to war with the Uruguayan Colorado party (Venancio Flores), with Argentina, and with Brazil in 1865. López took the offensive. In a short war his well-trained army might have been victorious. But with a population of only a million to draw upon, his armed forces were steadily whittled down by the guerrilla activities of his more populous neighbors. On December 31, 1868, the Allies pushed into Asunción. Finally, in 1870, López was driven back to the Aquidaban River in north-central Paraguay. On May 1 his surviving troops were overwhelmed by a larger allied (chiefly Brazilian) army under Gen. Camera. López was killed. The five-year war had reduced the population of Paraguay to less than 250,000, of whom only 28,000 were males over the age of 15. The country never recovered the power achieved under López. *See* Montevideo.

Aquileia I (Germanic Invasion of Italy), 166–167. In the middle of 166 three Germanic tribes swarmed across the Alps into northeastern Italy:

the Marcomanni of Bohemia, the Qûadi of Moravia, and the Iazyges of Hungary. The barbarians attacked Aquileia, at the head of the Adriatic. Repulsed at the walls of the town, they left it under siege and swept on to Opitergium (Oderzo). They ravaged and burned this town before moving on to the Piave River. Here the Roman emperor Marcus Aurelius met the threat with a hastily assembled force of legionaries—the main Roman army was still in the East, and the entire empire was scourged by the bubonic plague.

Marcus Aurelius managed to throw back the invaders and the following year raised the siege of Aquileia. This defensive victory was achieved largely because the barbarians lacked a single, capable commander. When the enemy threat along the northeast frontier persisted, Rome finally accepted a compromise peace. The original border was re-established. But in return Marcus allowed barbarians to settle within the Roman Empire—a precedent destined to have serious consequences later on. *See* Philippopolis I; Roman Empire.

Aquileia II (Civil Wars of the Roman Empire), 394. Theodosius I, the Great, ruler of the Eastern Roman Empire, had beheaded Magnus Maximus, a pretender to the Western Roman throne, at Aquileia in 388. Valentinian II, placed back on the Western throne, was again unseated and this time killed in 392. The new pretender, the pagan Eugenius of Gaul, drew his support from a Frankish general named Arbogast. For the second time Theodosius marched out from his capital of Constantinople to put down an insurrection in Italy. Forcing his way through the Julian Alps, Theodosius encountered the enemy at the head of the Adriatic, east of Aquileia, on September 5, 394. Despite a day-long attack, the imperial troops made little headway against the rebels. On the second day, however, Theodosius' army crushed the enemy force. Eugenius was beheaded and Arbogast committed suicide. Pagan worship again became forbidden.

The battle of Aquileia reunited the Roman Empire once more, but it was to be the last time. Theodosius died the following year and the empire was divided between his two sons, Arcadius, ruler in the East, and Honorius, emperor of the West. Although not planned so, this division proved to be permanent. *See* Adrianople II; Pollentia; Roman Empire.

Aquileia III (Wars of the Western Roman Empire), 452. After being defeated at Châlons-sur-Marne in his invasion of Gaul, Attila led his Huns eastward across the Rhine in 451. From their central European stronghold, the Huns swarmed through the Alps the following year and descended upon northern Italy. Aquileia, at the head of the Adriatic, was stormed and then sacked and burned. (Refugees from the city sought safety in the lagoons along the coast and thereby founded the city of Venice.) Just when Rome and all the peninsula seemed doomed, Pope Leo I persuaded Attila (probably with the promise of a large tribute) to abandon his raid. The Huns withdrew across the Alps, where Attila died the following year. His death ended the Hun menace but not the incursion of other barbarians into the heart of the empire. *See* Châlons-sur-Marne II; Rome II; Roman Empire.

Arausio (Gauls' Attack on Rome), 105 B.C. The extension of Roman influence into southern France brought the aggressive Italian republic into conflict with the Gauls across the Alps. (The Cisalpine Gauls had been subdued by 222 B.C.) In 106 B.C. Quintus Servilius Caepio's legionaries raised the Gallic siege of Toulouse. But the following year Caepio's Roman army was surrounded at Arausio (Orange) on the Rhone River by a combined force of Cimbri and Teutones. The Romans were soundly beaten with losses estimated in the thousands. The Gauls then moved eastward to the Alpine passes leading into Italy. *See* Muthul River; Aquae Sextiae; Roman Republic.

Arbedo (Swiss-Milanese Wars), 1422. A dispute over possession of the city of Bellinzona led to war between the Swiss cantons and the duchy of Milan in 1422. The Swiss deployed their solid phalanx of 4,000 halberds and pikes at Arbedo, in present-day Ticino canton, on June 30. Opposing them stood the mounted *condottiere* cavalry commanded by Francesco Bussone, known as Carmagnola. When the sturdy mountaineers repulsed his cavalry charge, the Milanese general dismounted his 6,000 men. He then sent them against the Swiss in a massed column. In a savage encounter, the lances and swords of the more numerous Milanese gradually prevailed. A total Swiss defeat was in the making when Carmagnola ordered a brief halt to the advance in order to guard against an exaggerated threat to his rear. This respite enabled the Swiss to withdraw from the field. But their percentage of losses was high for the number of men engaged. And Arbedo is sometimes called the worst defeat suffered by the mountaineer infantry in the fourteenth and fifteenth centuries. *See* Näfels; Saint Jacob-en-Birs; Giornico.

Arbela-Gaugamela (Macedonian Conquests), 331 B.C. Retracing his route from Egypt early in 331 B.C., Alexander III, the Great, marched through Syria and crossed both the Euphrates and Tigris rivers. East of the latter river, King Darius III determined to make an all-out attempt to destroy the Macedonian invader and thus preserve his Persian Empire. He established a headquarters at Arbela and then moved 20 miles northeast to a plains region at Gaugamela (Erbil in modern Iraq), near the ancient ruins of Nineveh. Here he ordered the terrain smoothed down as level as a parade ground to increase the speed and effectiveness of his 200 scythe-bearing chariots. With great care Darius posted his chariots in the front line, supported by formations of archers and cavalry. Behind these forces stood a great mass of infantry with some 40,000 light horsemen guarding the flanks. The total strength of the Persian horde has been estimated at 250,000 men, plus 15 war elephants.

Alexander, aware that a large force stood astride his route, marched his battle-wise troops—40,000 infantry, 7,000 cavalry—to within sight of the Persian army. He then encamped for four days of rest and preparation. On October 1, 331 B.C., the outnumbered but better-trained Macedonians organized for an attack. Because the long Persian line extended beyond both his flanks, Alexander for the first time held back reserve forces on the wings. The Macedonian commander opened the battle with an attack from his right (west), where he had posted the archers, javelin men, and most of his cavalry. In the fierce fighting that followed, Alexander's phalanx had a difficult time pressing forward, while his center, and especially the left (under Parmenio), stood in grave danger of engulfment by the more numerous Persian forces.

A break in the battle occurred when so much of the Persian cavalry (Scythians and Bactrians) became embroiled in the combat on the west flank that they left their infantry in the center uncovered. Alexander himself led a hard charge of his personal cavalry (the Companions) into the gap, penetrated the Persian line, and then wheeled to assail the enemy's flank and rear. This sudden stroke relieved the pressure on Alexander's own center and left and turned the tide of battle. Darius took flight and panic soon spread through the Asiatic ranks. Although they still greatly outnumbered their European foe, the Persians fled for their lives and in so doing became easy targets for the closely pursuing Macedonians. A fearful slaughter took place for some 50 miles of the chase, which was finally called off at midnight. Casualty estimates vary from 40,000 to 90,000 for the Persians, 100 to 500 for the Macedonians. Darius III escaped to Bactria (in modern Afghanistan), only to be assassinated there by Bessus, one of his satraps, the following year.

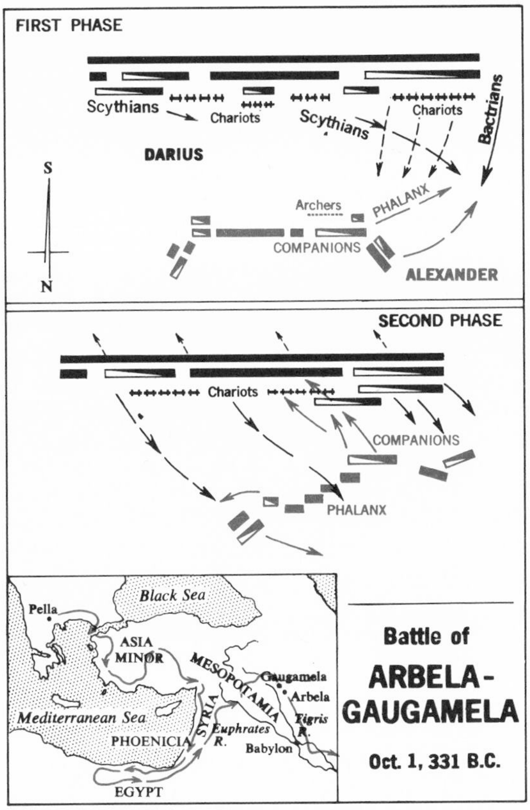

The Macedonian victory at Arbela-Gaugamela was one of the decisive battles of history. It sent the mighty Persian Empire, founded by Cyrus the Elder, into a decline from which it never recovered. Alexander the Great, for a time threatened with a defeat which would have erased his entire force, now stood master of Asia. And the way lay open for additional conquests farther east. *See* Gaza I; Megalopolis; Hydaspes River; Macedonian Conquests.

Arcis-sur-Aube (Napoleonic Empire Wars), 1814. Believing that his subordinates could hold the line of the Aisne River against allied thrusts from the north, Napoleon I marched southward to strike the 90,000-man army of Prince Karl von Schwarzenberg. The Austrian army, concentrated between the Aube and Seine rivers, had a more than 3-to-1 superiority. Yet when the French struck his northern flank at Arcis-sur-Aube on March 20, Schwarzenberg barely held his ground. He lost 2,500 men. Napoleon, with 1,700 casualties, could not afford to resume the attack. Instead he marched quickly northeast, planning to destroy the allied communications in Lorraine. He called for Marshals Auguste Marmont and Édouard Mortier to join him. But their 17,000 troops bumped into Schwarzenberg at Fere-Champenoise on March 25 and were driven back toward Paris, 75 miles to the west. With Napoleon now hopelessly cut off to the east, the emboldened allies marched on Paris. *See* Reims; Paris I; Napoleonic Empire Wars.

Arcole (Wars of the French Revolution), 1796. Despite his setback at Caldiero on November 12, Napoleon Bonaparte resolved to attack the Austrians again before they could unite against the outnumbered French army. East of his base at Verona stood the main Austrian body of 24,000 troops under Gen. Josef Alvinczy (Baron von

Battle of ARBELA-GAUGAMELA Oct. 1, 331 B.C.

Borberek). On the night of November 14 Napoleon with 19,000 men swung wide to his right (south) to cross the Adige River and threaten the rear of Alvinczy's force. On the following day the French were stopped at Arcole by a strongly held bridge over the small Alpone River. Swampy terrain made maneuver impossible. The bridge had to be taken. But successive French charges were beaten back all that day. Napoleon resumed the attack the next day (November 16), and though he obtained no breakthrough, the pressure of the French assaults forced Alvinczy to move back from Verona to defend the Austrian left rear. On the third day of the French offensive Gen. Pierre Augureau's division crossed the Alpone below Arcole. The widened French front finally squeezed the Austrians out of Arcole. Alvinczy fell back northeast. He had lost the initiative and more than 6,000 men. Napoleon's casualties in the three-day battle totaled 4,600.

Meanwhile the second Austrian column, advancing down the Adige Valley under Gen. Baron Paul Davidovich, moved too slowly to aid Alvinczy or to push through to relieve the siege of Mantua. Both sides now encamped to rest and reorganize. *See* Caldiero I; Mantua; Rivoli Veronese; French Revolution Wars.

Arcot (Carnatic War in India), 1751. During a native civil war in the Indian peninsula, French forces under Marquis Joseph Dupleix took sides and besieged Trichinopoly, 200 miles southwest of Madras. Here Mahomet Ali, the British candidate for the viceroyalty of the Deccan, was trapped. To relieve the pressure on Trichinopoly, Ensign Robert Clive (later Lord Clive) took command of 200 Europeans and 600 Indians and marched on Arcot, 65 miles west of Madras. He seized this capital of the French-aligned Indian potentate on September 20, 1751. The hostile Indians and the French rushed back from Trichinopoly to attack Clive. For 50 days the young English commander repulsed the attacks of a force 20 times larger than his own. Finally, with food and ammunition nearly exhausted, Arcot was relieved by a friendly Maratha chieftain. The power of Dupleix and the French in India was checked, and Mahomet Ali ascended the throne the following year. The Carnatic was secure for Great Britain. *See* Madras I; Calcutta.

Ardennes I (World War I). The east-central part of the massive battle fought along the French frontier during August 20–24, 1914, in which the first French and German offensives of the war met head on. *See* Frontiers of France.

Ardennes II (World War II), 1944–1945. Popularly called the Battle of the Bulge. In the fall of 1944 the stubborn Nazi defense of the Siegfried Line allowed the German armies some time to reorganize. Hitler then ordered Field Marshal Karl von Rundstedt to launch a major counteroffensive, aimed at recapturing Liége and Antwerp and thus cutting in two Gen. Dwight Eisenhower's Allied forces stretched from the North Sea to Switzerland. The second German objective was the destruction of the four Allied armies north of the line Bastogne–Brussels–Antwerp: the Canadian First, British Second, U.S. Ninth, and most of the U.S. First. Hitler chose the Ardennes (site of his spectacular 1940 breakthrough) as the point of attack. Here Gen. Troy Middleton's U.S. VIII Corps was thinly spread across a 75-mile front from Monschau south to Echternach.

Hidden by dense fog, the Nazi attack (Operation Watch on the Rhine) began early on December 16. Schutzstaffel (SS) Gen. Sepp Dietrich's Sixth Panzer Army was charged with the main thrust, supported on the left by the Fifth Panzer (Hasso von Manteuffel) and the Seventh (Ernst Brandenberger) armies. The massive assault by 20 divisions caught the Americans by surprise and sent the 28th and 106th Infantry and 9th Armored divisions reeling back in disarray. A special Nazi unit (under Col. Otto Skorzeny) disguised as Americans penetrated the rear, disrupting communications and transportation. Adding to the Allied confusion was a parachute drop of 1,000 men under Col. Friedrich von der Heydte near Malmédy. This unit attempted to block off Allied reinforcements coming into the Ardennes from the north.

The sudden German thrust drove a bulge in the First Army (Courtney Hodges) line. But on the north shoulder Gen. Leonard Gerow's V Corps quickly organized a stout defense that deflected the main axis of the Sixth Panzer Army's attack southward. Here again, the Nazis were held up from December 17 to 23 by a sturdy roadblock thrown up by the U.S. 7th Armored Division at Saint-Vith. (On this northern shoulder of the attack 125 American prisoners were massacred by SS troops near Malmédy on December 23.)

Slowed down in the north, Field Marshal Walter Model, in direct command of the offensive, then switched the major German effort to the Fifth Panzer Army. Racing westward, Manteuffel's armor reached Bastogne on December 20. To hold this vital road junction, the U.S. 101st Airborne had been hurried forward from reserve to join part of the 10th Armored and other command fragments. Under Gen. Anthony McAuliffe, a tough Allied defensive perimeter threw back the Nazi attacks. Unable to break into Bastogne, German infantry surrounded the town while Panzer units drove around it and continued toward the Meuse. Farther south, the German Seventh Army made but little progress. On December 20 Eisenhower placed all American forces in the northern half of the bulge under the temporary

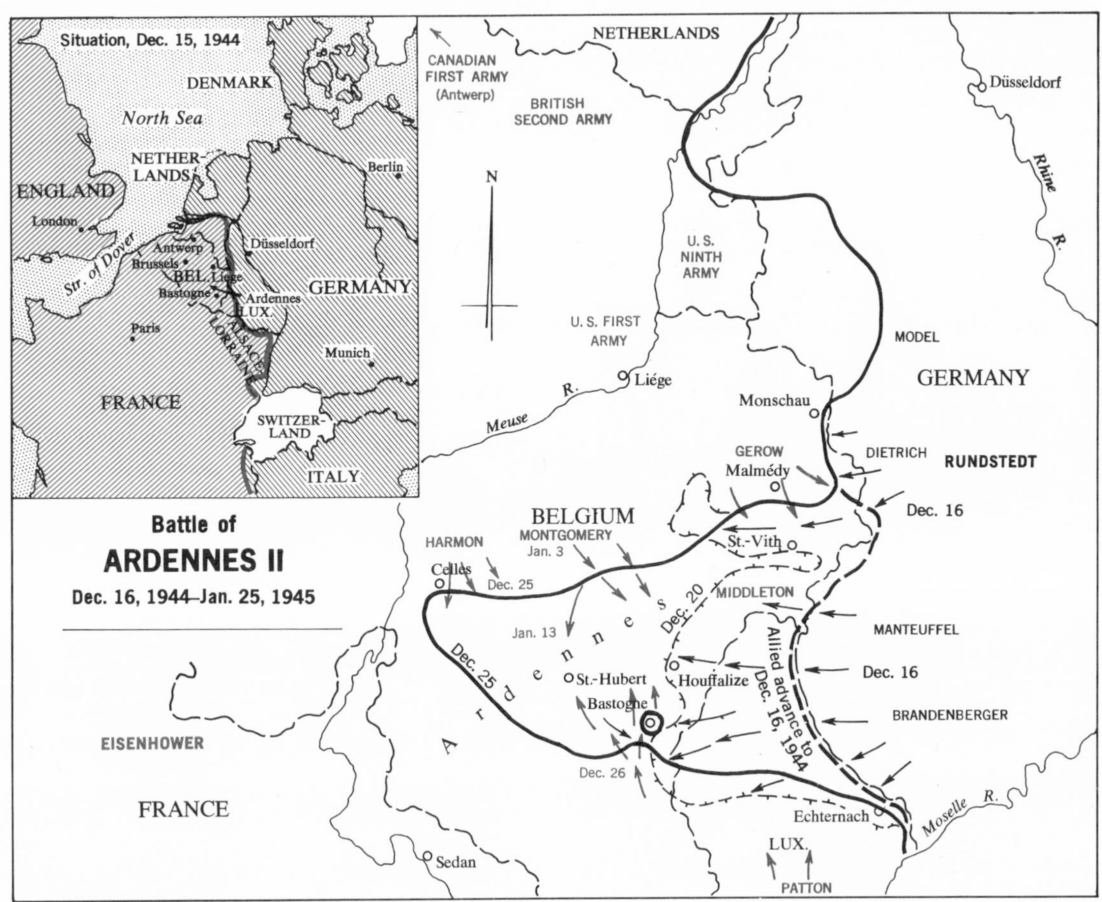

command of the British field marshal Sir Bernard Montgomery. At the same time Gen. George Patton's Third Army was ordered to turn north to attack the southern flank of the German wedge.

During the first week of the battle, Allied air power had been immobilized by bad weather. On December 23, however, clearer skies brought British and U.S. planes into the fray, attacking German columns and supplying encircled Bastogne by air. Two days later, near Celles, the U.S. 2nd Armored Division (Ernest Harmon) struck the 2nd Panzer at the western tip of the Ardennes bulge. A decisive two-day battle bent back the Nazi spearhead, 60 miles from the starting line. Thirty-five miles to the southeast, Patton's 4th Armored Division punched a narrow corridor into beleaguered Bastogne (December 26), where McAuliffe had ridiculed an earlier German surrender proposal by replying "Nuts." The whirlwind Nazi offensive had now been stopped, but the long, costly elimination of the bulge into the Allied line still lay ahead.

On the southern flank of the Ardennes three Third Army corps fought off fierce German attempts to cut the corridor into Bastogne and slowly pressed northward. On the northwest and northern faces of the bulge, Montgomery stabilized his front and then attacked on January 3 with the British XXX Corps (Bryan Horrocks) and the U.S. VII (Lawton Collins). On January 8 Model began a skillful, fighting retreat that successfully pulled back every major German unit. British and American patrols made contact near Saint-Hubert on January 13, and three days later a solid front was re-established when the U.S. 2nd (from the north) and 11th (from the south) Armored divisions linked up at Houffalize. The First Army, but not the Ninth, then came again under control of Gen. Omar Bradley's Twelfth Army Group. By January 25 the original front had been restored.

Meanwhile, to the south in Alsace-Lorraine, the German First Army (Gen. Obstfelder) had launched an attack on January 1 toward the Laverne Gap. Here Gen. Jacob Devers' Sixth Army Group had been forced to cover the hole left by the shift of Third Army troops to the Ardennes. Although the Nazi attack gained ground initially, Gen. Alexander Patch's U.S. Seventh Army retained its organization and held firm behind the Moder River on January 20. Still farther south,

Gen. Jean de Lattre de Tassigny's First French Army, reinforced by four U.S. divisions, pinched off the Colmar Pocket west of the Rhine between January 20 and February 9.

With the end of this secondary fighting along the upper Rhine, the battle of the Ardennes came to a close. Hitler's daring gamble cost the Germans almost 200,000 casualties, 600 tanks and assault guns, and more than 1,500 aircraft. The Allies lost about 60,000 men in killed, wounded, and missing. The Ardennes battle delayed the Allied offensive toward the Rhine by six weeks. But the destruction of virtually all Nazi reserve strength helped ensure the final defeat of Germany. *See* Siegfried Line; Rhineland; World War II.

Argaon (Maratha-British War II), 1803. Following the bloody British victory against the Marathas at Assaye in September 1803, Gen. Arthur Wellesley (later Duke of Wellington) marched against the enemy at Argaon (Argaum) in Berar. Wellesley, younger brother of Gov. Gen. Lord Richard Wellesley, attacked the stronghold on November 29. The initial assault by the British and allied native troops was repulsed. But Wellesley rallied his men to make a second effort, which carried Argaon. The Marathas were totally routed. This victory ended the Maratha War in central India. In the north, however, Gen. Gerard Lake fought on against another sect. *See* Assaye; Farrukhabad; Maratha-British Wars.

Argentan (World War II). The southern prong of the Falaise-Argentan pincers that closed on a large body of German troops on August 19, 1944. *See* Falaise-Argentan Pocket.

Argentina. *See* Latin America.

Argentoratum (Germanic Invasion of the Roman Empire), 357. To deal with the western barbarians, Emperor Constantius II appointed his cousin Julian as caesar (governor) for Britain, Spain, and Gaul in 355. The choice was a happy one. Julian's aggressive leadership and tactical skill drove most of the Alamanni, Franks, and other Germanic tribes out of the middle Rhine Valley in little more than a year. In the summer of 357, however, the Roman army of 13,000 men encountered a Germanic army three times as large at Argentoratum (Strasbourg). Launching a violent attack against the superior force, Julian routed the barbarians, inflicting some 6,000 casualties. Chnodomar, the Alamanni chief, was taken prisoner. Roman losses totaled only 250.

When the Persian War flared up again in 359, Constantius ordered Julian and his army to the East. Instead, the Gallic troops revolted and proclaimed Julian emperor. Before a new civil war could begin, Constantius died suddenly of a fever. Julian then became undisputed ruler of the empire and marched against Persia on his own. *See* Mursa; Amida I; Roman Empire.

Arginusae Islands (Great Peloponnesian War), 406 B.C. After the Spartan naval victory over Athens off Notium in 407, both fleets received new commanders. Conon took charge of the Athenian vessels, while Callicratidas replaced Lysander as commander of the Peloponnesian navy. The two new leaders fought a naval action off the island of Lesbos the following year. The Athenian fleet suffered the loss of 30 ships. The remaining 40 fled into the harbor at Mytilene where they were promptly blockaded.

Athens then sent its last navy reserves, about 150 triremes, to the eastern Aegean. In a fierce encounter among the Arginusae Islands, the Athenian navy regained the upper hand by destroying 70 of the 120 Peloponnesian ships. Callicratidas was killed. But the battle proved to be the last Athenian victory in the war. During the fighting, 25 of Conon's ships had been wrecked. When the shipwrecked sailors drowned in a storm, eight leading Athenian officers were charged with neglect of duty. Six were sentenced to death; the other two fled into exile. The loss of these key commanders markedly weakened the effectiveness of the Athenian fleet in a decisive battle the following year. *See* Cyzicus I; Aegospotami; Peloponnesian Wars.

Argonne Forest (World War I). A wooded plateau between the Aisne and Meuse rivers that was cleared of Germans by the American First Army between September 26 and October 31, 1918. *See* Meuse River–Argonne Forest.

Arkansas Post (American Civil War), 1863. While Gen. William Sherman was leading his fruitless Federal expedition against Vicksburg by way of Chickasaw Bluffs, Gen. John McClernand received approval from Washington, D.C., to lead a second attack on the Mississippi river port. On January 2 McClernand arrived at Miliken's Bend to take over Sherman's command. But instead of attacking Vicksburg, he moved the 29,000-man Federal army 50 miles up the Arkansas River against Arkansas Post. Here the Confederate general Thomas Churchill had some 4,500 troops to defend Fort Hindman.

McClernand took his army up the river in transports, landing three miles below Arkansas Post on the night of January 9. The next day the Federals, supported by 13 gunboats under Adm. David Porter, marched along the east bank toward the fort. It was not until January 11, however, that McClernand could launch a coordinated attack by his land and naval forces. By 3 P.M. Porter's gunboats had silenced the Confederate artillery. Fort Hindman then surrendered, as did the Southern troops manning the outlying defenses. The attack cost 1,061 Federal casualties. When Gen. U. S. Grant, commander in the West, learned of McClernand's operation, he ordered an immediate withdrawal so that the troops could be employed against the far more important objective of Vicksburg. *See* Chickasaw Bluffs; Vicksburg; American Civil War.

Arnhem (World War II). An Allied airdrop of three divisions, on September 17, 1944, in an effort to secure bridges over the lower Rhine behind German lines; the attempt was crushed by German counterattacks on September 25. *See* Siegfried Line.

Arques (French Religious Wars), 1589. The murder of King Henry III on July 31, 1589, left France without a Valois male heir to the throne. Henry of Navarre (later Henry IV), the Huguenot leader, claimed the crown, but his claim was disputed by the Catholic party (Holy League) and its champion, the Duc de Mayenne (Charles de Lorraine of the Guise family). Henry, with an army of some 9,000 men, took up a strong position in the marshes of Arques, south of Dieppe, near the Normandy coast. Here he was attacked by a markedly superior Catholic force under De Mayenne on September 21, 1589. Because of the unfavorable terrain the latter could commit only a few thousand of his men at a time. This enabled Henry to beat back each attack in piecemeal fashion. Finally De Mayenne was forced to withdraw, leaving more dead on the field than the total number in Henry's army. But the decisive battle for the throne of France had yet to be fought. *See* Coutras; Ivry-la-Bataille; French Religious Wars.

Arrah (Indian Mutiny), 1857. Near the eastern limits of the Great Mutiny in India, three native regiments attacked a house in Arrah, 35 miles west of Patna. From July 25 until August 3, 16 Englishmen and 60 Sikh police held off every assault by the mutineers. Relief came from a small British column commanded by Maj. Vincent Eyre, ending one of the most courageous defenses in the savage revolt in the Ganges Valley. *See* Lucknow; Cawnpore II; Indian Mutiny.

Arras I (Spanish-French Wars), 1654. The long war between Spain and France was in its 18th year in 1652 when Louis II, the Great Condé, deserted the country of Louis XIV to become a general in the Spanish army of Philip IV. In this role Condé found himself opposed by his old antagonist in the civil disturbances of the Fronde, the French marshal the Vicomte de Turenne. Both commanders were wily, skillful generals, adept at maneuver as well as at battle. The duel that followed (called the Spanish Fronde) took place chiefly in the Spanish Netherlands and northern France. Throughout the campaign of 1653 neither side gained an advantage. Then, in the summer of the following year, the Great Condé laid siege to the French-held town of Arras, in the present Pas-de-Calais department. But on the night of August 24–25, Turenne suddenly attacked the Spanish lines of circumvallation. The besiegers were routed with a loss of 3,000 men. Only with great difficulty did Condé regroup his force and fall back eastward to Cambrai. *See* Lens; Faubourg St. Antoine; Valenciennes; Thirty Years' War.

Arras II (World War I), 1917. The main Allied offensive of 1917, as planned by the new French commander on the Western Front, Gen. Robert Nivelle, was aimed at the Aisne River sector. To draw German reserves northward, the British Expeditionary Force of Field Marshal Sir Douglas Haig planned an attack a week earlier at Arras. Meanwhile, from February 23 to April 5, the German armies had made a voluntary eastward withdrawal to the strongly defended Hindenburg Line, named for Field Marshal Paul von Hindenburg. On April 9 Haig launched his offensive after five days of preparatory bombardment (including gas) by 2,800 guns. On the left (north of Arras) the Canadian Corps of Gen. Henry Horne's First Army stormed up to the crest of Vimy Ridge on the first day. To the south the Third Army of Gen. Sir Edmund Allenby punched forward three and a half miles. The exuberant British prepared to exploit their openings but were rudely disappointed. The German Sixth Army commander on this front, Baron Ludwig von Falkenhausen, had ample reserves standing 15 miles farther east. These troops now moved up quickly to check the British advance. On the far right (south) Haig committed the Fifth Army of Gen. Hubert Gough to the attack, but here the German first line held fast. The British continued to press their thoroughly checked offensive until May 3 to divert attention from the French attack in the south and, later, Haig's preparation for a new assault at Ypres (Ieper). Along the 20-mile front the British had inflicted about 75,000 casualties on the Germans at a cost to themselves of 84,000 men. *See* Somme River I; Aisne River II; Ypres III; World War I.

Arsanias River (Parthian Wars of the Roman Empire), A.D. 62. The successful campaign of Gnaeus Domitius Corbulo in 58 and 59 restored Armenia to Roman control. But to the southeast, Vologesus I of Parthia remained hostile and in 61 launched a two-pronged attack on Armenia and Syria. Corbulo withdrew his main body of troops to guard against the invasion of Syria, calling on Rome to send a second army into Armenia. Dissatisfied with this prudent action, Emperor Nero sent a new general, Caesennius Paetus, to direct the Roman offensive.

Paetus launched a bold attack in 62. He soon found himself outmaneuvered and surrounded by Parthians on the Arsanias (Murat Suyu) River, a tributary of the Euphrates. Corbulo rushed to the rescue but could not arrive in time to prevent the surrender of Paetus. Despite this setback, Corbulo negotiated a satisfactory peace the following year.

Vologesus' brother Tiridates was allowed to resume his rule over Armenia, but as a vassal of Rome. (He traveled to Italy to receive the crown from Nero in 66.) *See* Tigranocerta II; Ctesiphon I; Roman Empire.

Arsouf (Third Crusade), 1191. Following his capture of Acre in July, Richard the Lion-Hearted took the army of the Third Crusade southward along the Mediterranean coast. Saladin's Turkish army marched parallel to the Christian column, keeping itself always between Richard and his ultimate objective, Jerusalem. The Christians passed through Haifa and Caesarea without incident, but on September 7 at Arsouf (Arsuf) the Moslems suddenly attacked. In the first onslaught, Sudanese spearmen drove in Richard's flank guard of infantry. Then the Mameluke horsebowmen charged the rear column of mounted knights, the Hospitallers. Planning to force a decisive engagement, Richard ordered his men to fight a strictly defensive battle until the enemy became too committed to retreat successfully. But the undisciplined knights countercharged prematurely, and although they routed the Mamelukes, most of the latter escaped into woods.

From Arsouf, the English king marched ten miles farther south to Jaffa, which he refortified. Saladin hurried forward to demolish Ashkelon so that the Christians could not use it as a base from which to turn inland to Jerusalem. For months the two armies marched and countermarched. Richard took Darum, the last coastal strongpoint before Sinai, and repulsed Saladin's attack on Jaffa. But he could find no way to liberate Jerusalem or to hold it, even if he could drive out the Turks. Finally, on September 2, 1192, a five-year truce was arranged—the Christians would keep the coastal towns (except Ashkelon), giving access to Moslem traders; Saladin would hold the holy places but allow visits by unarmed pilgrims. Henry of Champagne, nephew to Richard, became king of Jerusalem (consisting of a narrow strip of coastline), marrying Isabella, the widow of Conrad of Montferrat, who had been assassinated. Guy of Lusignan bought Cyprus from Richard and set up an independent Christian kingdom there, which would last until conquered by the Ottoman Turks in 1571. Richard the Lion-Hearted sailed for home in October, and the Third crusade came to a close with the Holy City still in Moslem hands. *See* Acre I; Constantinople V; Crusades.

Artaxata (Parthian Wars of the Roman Empire), A.D. 58. During the reign of Nero, Vologesus I of Parthia challenged Roman rule by placing his brother Tiridates I on the throne of Armenia. Nero sent Gnaeus Domitius Corbulo, veteran of fighting against the Germans, to the East. In the spring of 58 Corbulo launched a campaign to reconquer Armenia. Despite Tiridates' implacable guerrilla warfare, the Roman army managed to seize the ancient capital of Artaxata by the end of the year. The city was destroyed. *See* Tigranocerta II; Roman Empire.

Artois I (World War I). One of the series of flanking maneuvers by both Germany and the French-British Allies, during September 27–October 10, 1914, in the misnamed Race to the Sea—from Noyon northward to the Belgian coast. *See* Aisne River I; Ypres I.

Artois II (World War I), 1915. During the battle of Ypres (Ieper) II, the French field marshal Joseph Joffre continued his build-up of forces in Artois. Finally on May 9, preceded by a massive artillery bombardment, the French launched an offensive on a six-mile front north of Arras. In the first days of the attack the German lines, commanded by Gen. Erich von Falkenhayn, were pushed back three miles. French troops secured a foothold on key Vimy Ridge but were subsequently thrown back by furious German counterattacks. The battle then became one of attrition until it ended on June 18. Joffre lost 100,000 men; the Germans suffered 75,000 casualties. *See* Ypres II; Champagne II; World War I.

Artois-Loos (World War I), 1915. Field Marshal Joseph Joffre's major French offensive in Champagne was accompanied by a coordinated attack by French and British armies in Artois. North of Arras, Gen. Victor d'Urbal led the French Tenth Army in an attack against German positions in the Vimy Ridge area on September 25. At the same time the British First Army under Gen. Sir Douglas Haig, using poison gas for the first time, drove against the village of Loos, still farther north. Both Allied attacks won some ground initially but were soon checked by German counterattacks directed by Gen. Erich von Falkenhayn. The British assault petered out on October 8, the French halted a week later in what is sometimes called the third battle of Artois. French losses were 190,000, British casualties 60,000. The defending Germans lost 178,000 men. Two months later Haig replaced Sir John French as British commander in France. Artois-Loos ended the fighting in northern France in 1915. *See* Champagne II; Verdun; World War I.

Asculum I (Rise of Rome), 279 B.C. Following his victory at Heraclea, King Pyrrhus marched north into Apulia with a combined force of 40,000 Epirot and Italiote troops. At Asculum (Ascoli Satriano) he encountered an equal force of Romans, under Sulpicius Saverrio, who were trying to raise a siege laid against the city. As in the battle the previous year, both sides fought furiously. But again Epirot cavalry proved the decisive element, and the Romans were finally forced to fall back.

The battle cost the Roman legions 6,000 men; the Epirots lost 3,500. Realizing that Rome could supply replacements much more easily than the Greeks, Pyrrhus exclaimed, "Another such victory and we are lost" (thus the term "Pyrrhic victory").

Pyrrhus then moved to Sicily to aid the Greek city-states there against Carthage, which had concluded a peace treaty with Rome. But after only indifferent success, he returned to Italy. *See* Heraclea; Beneventum; Roman Republic.

Asculum II (Roman Social War), 90–89 B.C. Discontented with the rights granted by Rome, some allied tribes revolted. Led by the Marsi in the north and the Samnites in the south, a new republic of Italia was set up with the capital at Corfinium in Samnium. The cause of the allies (socii) became hopeless when the Etrurians, Latins, and some of the southern cities refused to join the revolt. The chief fighting was at Asculum on the eastern side of the peninsula. Here Roman citizens were massacred in 90 B.C., but the city was recaptured by legionaries the following year. But Rome did not need a decisive military victory. An offer of citizenship to all Italians who applied for it within 60 days ended the so-called Social War. *See* Roman Republic.

A Shau (Vietnam War), 1966. Increased U.S. military strength in South Vietnam, which began in the summer of 1965, seemed to have checked the Communist take-over of that country. Then on March 9, 1966, a force of some 3,000 North Vietnamese regular troops suddenly struck the isolated Special Forces camp at A Shau, 55 miles west of Da Nang and 360 miles north of Saigon. The camp, a triangular log fortress (480 feet on each side) that stood only three miles from the Laotian border, was held by 17 U.S. Special Forces men (the "Green Berets") and 360 Montagnard and Nung tribesmen. Weakened by Viet Cong infiltration and denied effective air support by foul weather, the camp fell after 39 hours of sustained attack. Helicopters rescued 200 defenders during and after the Communist assault, including 12 Special Forces men. A few others were believed to have escaped into the jungle. Six U.S. aircraft—three planes and three helicopters—were lost in the battle. At least 500 North Vietnamese were killed. It was the first loss of a Special Forces camp since the Viet Cong stormed Dak Sut in the central highlands, 290 miles north of Saigon, on August 19, 1965. *See* South Vietnam; An Lao Valley; Vietnam War.

Ashdown (Danish Invasions of Britain), 871. The Danish conquerors steadily overran all the Saxon kingdoms of eastern Britain, occupying London and fortifying a camp at Reading, 40 miles to the west. Only the kingdom of Wessex stood in the way of complete subjugation. When the Danes penetrated the Berkshire hills, the Wessex king Ethelred I and his brother Alfred deployed the West Saxon army to meet them. As the invaders approached on January 8, Ethelred tarried at his prayers, so Alfred took command. Leading an uphill charge "like a wild boar," as one witness described it, Alfred checked the Danish advance. For hours the combatants battled for the hilltop until the Vikings finally gave way. The Saxons pursued hotly, strewing the Berkshire hills with the bodies of the Danes fleeing back to Reading.

The battle of Ashdown gave the Saxons their first real hope of beating back the invaders. A Danish victory here would probably have led to the stamping out of Christianity in Britain. The Vikings were only temporarily halted, however. More battles would have to be fought before the year was out. *See* Hoxne; Reading; Danish Invasions of Britain.

Ash Hollow (Sioux Wars), 1855. One of the early battles with the Indians west of the Mississippi River grew out of Sioux and Cheyenne attacks on emigrants along the California Trail. The situation became acute when Lt. J. L. Grattan and 18 men were killed near Fort Laramie, Wyo., on August 19, 1854. On August 5 of the following year Gen. W. S. Harney left Fort Leavenworth, Kans., with 1,200 troops. The punitive expedition caught up with Little Thunder's band of Brûlé Sioux at Ash Hollow, west of Fort Kearny (near Grand Island), Nebr. Here on September 3 Harney's men virtually destroyed the Indian force, killing 136 warriors. *See* Killdeer Mountain; Indian Wars in the United States.

Ashingdon (Rise of England), 1016. After a year-long contest for the throne of England, Edmund II (Ironside) of Wessex and Canute of the Danes fought a decisive battle at Ashingdon (Assandun) in Essex. Edmund, who had gained a slight advantage in earlier struggles, seemed again on the way to victory with his Saxon army when his brother-in-law Edric deserted to the Danes with some men of Hereford. This action tipped the scales against the English. Canute's men charged forward to rout Edmund's army and inflict a severe defeat on the Saxons on October 18, 1016.

Soon after the battle the two leaders made peace. Canute received all of England except Wessex, which remained under Edmund. When Edmund died the next month, Wessex also accepted Danish rule. Canute proved to be an able king. His descendants were weak, however, and after five years of turmoil, Godwin, earl of Wessex, succeeded in re-establishing the Saxon line by crowning Edward the Confessor king of the English in 1042. *See* Pen; Fulford; Danish Invasions of Britain.

Ashkelon I (First Crusade), 1099. The crusaders had no sooner taken Jerusalem when a great army of Moslems marched up from Egypt and encamped at Ashkelon on the Palestinian coast west of the Holy City. Despite being heavily outnumbered, the Christian leaders took the offensive. Commanded by Godfrey of Bouillon, Tancred of Taranto, and Robert of Normandy, the armored crusaders rode out of Jerusalem toward the enemy. At dawn on August 12 the knights surprised the Moslems with a sudden charge into the center of their camp. In the melee that followed, the entire Egyptian army was shattered. Some of the survivors found refuge in the fortress of Ashkelon. Here the garrison refused surrender, and the victorious crusaders returned to Jerusalem, satisfied that they had eliminated the threat to their rule. (The fortress remained a threat to crusader communications until taken by Baldwin III of Jerusalem in 1153.)

This battle ended the offensive phase of the First Crusade. Five little Christian states were now set up in Outremer, as the Franks called the region from Cilicia south to Sinai: Antioch, under Bohemond of Taranto; Edessa (Urfa), under Baldwin of Boulogne; Tripoli, in Lebanon, under Raymond IV of Toulouse; Jerusalem, under Godfrey of Bouillon; and Galilee, under Tancred, nephew of Bohemond. *See* Jerusalem VII; Melitene III; Crusades.

Ashkelon II (Crusader-Turkish Wars), 1153. For more than 50 years the Egyptian fortress of Ashkelon had posed a threat to the Christian kingdom of Jerusalem. From Ashkelon, Moslem bands frequently cut the 35-mile highway between Jerusalem and its Mediterranean port of Jaffa. Finally, in 1153, King Baldwin III, aided by a strong force of Knights Templars, marched on Ashkelon. More than 40 Templars were killed when they rashly tried to capture the fortress singlehandedly for their order. The garrison finally surrendered to the Christian army. Baldwin then gave the city—the gateway to Egypt—to his brother Amalric, the Count of Jaffa and later (1162) King Amalric I of Jerusalem. The capture of Ashkelon was to be the first step in the conquest of strife-torn Egypt. But the Franks could never muster enough strength to take the Nile kingdom. In 1169 it became too late, for the able Syrian warrior Saladin took over control of Egypt that year. *See* Damascus III; Ramleh II; Crusades.

Asiago (World War I), 1916. After beating back the first five Italian assaults along the Isonzo River front, the Austrian commander in chief, Field Marshal Count Conrad von Hötzendorf, resolved to take the offensive in the Trentino. From other fronts he shifted 15 divisions and much heavy artillery to a line south of Trent, aiming to drive into the northern Italian plain. Here the capture of Padua, 22 miles west of Venice, would cut off the Italian forces in the Carnic Alps and along the Isonzo. Organized as the Eleventh Army (archduke Eugene), 15 Austrian divisions attacked southward from the Trentino bulge on May 15. The Italian First Army of Gen. Roberto Brusati was caught unprepared despite ample warnings of the enemy offensive. Asiago, the gateway through the foot of the Dolomite Alps, fell to the Austrians, as did Arsiero to the southwest, both on May 31.

The Italian supreme commander, Gen. Count Cadorna, hurriedly brought troops westward by rail from the Isonzo. But the Austrian offensive soon halted, handicapped by difficult terrain, a lack of reserves, and the need to shift some troops back to the Russian front. By June 17 the invaders had pulled back almost to their starting point. Eight days later Cadorna counterattacked with his Fifth Army but found the Austrians too entrenched to dislodge. This ended the battle, with casualties on each side of about 100,000. The Italians now resumed their futile attacks on the Isonzo. *See* Isonzo River; Caporetto; World War I.

Aspern-Essling (Napoleonic Empire Wars), 1809. To the surprise of Napoleon I, the Austrian government of Francis I did not sue for peace when the French army stormed into Vienna on May 10, 1809. Instead Archduke Charles Louis, brother of the beleaguered emperor, built up the Austrian army to some 95,000 men and took up a position across the Danube, northeast of the city. Four miles below Vienna Napoleon constructed a bridge to Löbau Island, near the far bank, on May 20 and began sending troops across later that day. By the following noon 23,000 French troops had crossed the river and seized the small stone-house villages of Aspern and Essling. Marshal André Masséna's IV Corps held Aspern on the left (northwest) and Marshal Jean Lannes's II Corps stood in Essling. That afternoon Charles's Austrians counterattacked in strength. Despite their inferiority in infantry, cavalry, and artillery, the French grimly held on to their cramped bridgehead until nightfall ended the fighting.

During the night of May 21–22 the troops of Marshal Jean Bessières moved across the Danube to bring the French strength up to 48,000 infantry, 7,000 cavalry, and 144 guns. In the morning Lannes assaulted the Austrian center, but stout resistance checked his advance. Bitter fighting took place all around the rim of the perimeter. The Austrians could not drive the French into the river, and Napoleon's troops could not break out. (The Danube bridge had been smashed, blocking French reinforcements and limiting the supply of ammunition.) Finally calling off his attack, Charles contented himself with pounding the bridgehead with most of his 264 guns. Although the French held on, the Austrian artillery took a cruel toll, including the capable Lannes, who had served Napoleon for 13 years. (Masséna was later created Prince d'Essling for his part in the battle.) At nightfall the French pulled back to Löbau Island. They had lost almost 20,000 men in the most severe check Napoleon had yet received. Austrian casualties totaled more than 23,000. For six weeks Napoleon crouched on Löbau Island, building up his strength for a new attack across the river. *See* Eggmühl; Raab; Wagram; Napoleonic Empire Wars.

Aspromonte (Italian Wars of Independence), 1862. When the kingdom of Italy under Victor Emmanuel II was proclaimed on March 17, 1861, Rome was excluded. Here French troops stood in support of Pope Pius IX, who refused annexation by the new nation. When negotiations dragged, Giuseppe Garibaldi, one of the leading patriots in the unification of Italy, came out of retirement to arouse popular sentiment against the papacy. Early in 1862 Garibaldi organized a force in Sicily to liberate Rome. On August 24 he crossed to the mainland and in defiance of the Italian government prepared to march on Rome. Fearful of French intervention, Victor Emmanuel II sent an army under the marchese Georgio Guido (Pallavicino-Trivulzio) to halt the rebels. At Aspromonte in the southern Apennines the royal troops met and defeated Garibaldi's men on August 29. Garibaldi was wounded and captured along with hundreds of others. The Italian government granted amnesties five weeks later. *See* Gaeta; Custoza II; Italian Wars of Independence.

Assaye (Maratha-British War II), 1803. During the Second Maratha War, British Gov.-Gen. Lord Richard Wellesley directed the operations of two armies in India—that of Gen. Gerard Lake in the north and that of Gen. Arthur Wellesley (Lord Wellesley's younger brother and later Duke of Wellington) in the south-central part of the peninsula. General Wellesley took the field against the Marathas in the fall of 1803 with 4,500 British and allied native troops. At Assaye, in Hyderabad, this force met a Maratha army some six times larger on September 23. The Marathas were thoroughly routed, but Wellesley suffered casualties to more than a third of his force. For the numbers engaged, this was one of the bloodiest battles in the long career of the British general. *See* Aligarh; Argaon; Maratha-British Wars.

Astrakhan I (Conquest by Ivan IV), 1554–1556. After capturing Kazan on the upper Volga in 1552, Ivan IV, the Terrible, marched southward down the river. In 1554 he reached Astrakhan, a Tatar stronghold at the head of the Volga delta. The Mongolian defenders resisted fiercely, forcing Ivan to conduct a siege of the city. Astrakhan finally fell in 1556, giving Russia control of the entire course of the Volga and opening the way to the east and southeast. *See* Kazan; Polotsk.

Astrakhan II (Turkish Invasion of Russia), 1569. Three years after becoming sultan of the Ottoman Turks, Selim II sought to implement his dream of digging a canal between the Don and Volga rivers. Such a waterway would make it possible for the Turkish fleet to sail from the Black Sea into the Caspian Sea. A Moslem army, sent into southern Russia in 1569, laid siege to Astrakhan, at the head of the Volga delta. The city, which Ivan IV, the Terrible, had taken from the Mongols only 13 years before, resisted bravely. A relieving army, sent out by Ivan, arrived in time to attack the besiegers' lines and drive them off. The brilliant but heavy-drinking Selim then abandoned his Russian project. *See* Szigetvár.

Atbara (War for the Sudan), 1898. After the Anglo-Egyptian defeat and the death of Gen. George Gordon at Khartoum in 1885, the Mahdi ruled most of Sudan. The increased activity of France, Belgium, and Italy in Africa finally prompted the British government to launch a campaign of reconquest from Egypt. Under Gen. Horatio Herbert (later Lord) Kitchener, a force of 15,000 British and Egyptian troops invaded Sudan in March 1896. Proceeding southward cautiously and building a railroad as he advanced, Kitchener took Dongola on September 21 and Abu Hamed on August 7, 1897. The following spring the expedition reached Atbara, where the Nile receives its last tributary, the Atbara River. Here a large force of Mahdists had taken up a strong position behind a stockade (zareba). Despite being markedly outnumbered, Kitchener's troops attacked and routed the Sudanese on April 8. Some 6,000 Sudanese were killed or captured, a third of the enemy army. Anglo-Egyptian casualties totaled 570. Kitchener then pushed on up the Nile. *See* Khartoum; Omdurman; Sudan, War for the.

Athens-Piraeus (First Mithridatic War), 86 B.C. One of the native kingdoms that arose during the wars of the Hellenistic monarchies in the third century B.C. was Pontus on the southern shore of the Black Sea. Under the able King Mithridates VI Eupator, Pontus began conquering its weaker neighbors and soon came into conflict with Rome. In 88 B.C. Mithridates, who had assumed the role of liberator of the Greeks, sent an army to occupy Athens. He also ordered the killing of all Italians in Asia Minor.

In Rome, the choice of a general to campaign against Mithridates provoked civil war between Gaius Marius and his former lieutenant L. Cornelius Sulla. Sulla drove Marius from Rome, seized control of the government, and then took his army into Greece. Here Archelaus, a Pontic general sent out by Mithridates, held Athens and its port of Piraeus. In 86 B.C. Sulla stormed into both Athens and Piraeus. The Pontic army, although greatly superior in numbers, fell back northwest into Boeotia. *See* Chaeronea II; Mithridatic Wars.

Atlanta (American Civil War), 1864. Reverting

to his campaign of maneuver after the Federal repulse at Kenesaw Mountain, Gen. William Sherman began crossing the Chattahoochee River above the Confederate position of Gen. Joseph Johnston on July 9. Johnston, who had only about half the 100,000 troops available to Sherman, fell back once more. Confederate President Jefferson Davis replaced Johnston with the more aggressive Gen. John Hood on July 17. Sherman pressed on southward toward Atlanta, the South's most important transportation, manufacturing, supply and medical center. On the right, Gen. George Thomas' Army of the Cumberland began crossing Peach Tree Creek, north of the city, while Gen. John Schofield (Army of the Ohio) and Gen. James McPherson (Army of the Tennessee) closed in from the northeast and east.

Hood, seeing an opportunity to strike Thomas' force while it was isolated, sent forward the corps of Gens. Alexander Stewart and William Hardee, from left (west) to right. The Confederate attack along Peach Tree Creek began about 3 P.M. on July 20. It was fiercely conducted but futile. Three hours later the attack ended with 2,500 killed or wounded, chiefly in Stewart's corps. Federal losses were 1,600. Hood withdrew into the defenses of Atlanta the following day.

Believing Hood was evacuating the city, Sherman sent McPherson on a wide pursuing movement to the southeast. Instead of withdrawing, Hood sent Hardee's corps on an overnight 15-mile march to strike the exposed southern flank of the Federals, on July 22. In one of the most desperate struggles of the war the Confederate attack, later supported by Gen. Benjamin Cheatham's corps (Hood's former corps), was stopped with a loss of 8,000 men. Federal casualties were 3,700, including the slain McPherson. General Oliver Howard took over the Army of the Tennessee.

Sherman now shifted Howard's corps from the far left (east) to the extreme right. Here the Federals were moving past Ezra Church, southwest of Atlanta, when they were attacked by Gen. Stephen Lee's corps (formerly commanded by Cheatham) on July 28. Hood sent part of Stewart's corps to help, but the Federals held their ground for the third time in nine days. On August 5 and 6 Sherman resumed his efforts to turn Hood's left (southwest) flank and to cut the railroads leading into Atlanta from the south. The Confederates held off the attack of Schofield and part of Thomas' army at Utoy Creek. But their situation was hopeless.

On August 26 Sherman began moving his entire force in a deep envelopment of Atlanta from the west, with the armies of Schofield, Thomas, and Howard, from north to south. The Montgomery railroad was cut on August 27, the Macon line four days later. Hardee, the only Confederate corps commander in this area, fell back to Lovejoy's Station, 25 miles to the south. Here he fought, on August 31 and September 1, against the growing Federal concentration at nearby Jonesboro. At 5 P.M. on September 1 Hood abandoned Atlanta to link up with Hardee. The capture of the city, culminating a 140-mile advance from Chattanooga, had cost Sherman 21,656 casualties. Confederate losses totaled 27,565.

On September 11 Hood began moving west and north for an offensive against Sherman's supply and communication lines in Tennessee. Sherman sent Thomas northward to watch Hood and on November 15 cut loose from Atlanta to "march to the sea" at Savannah, where he could be supplied by the Federal navy. Much of Atlanta was set afire. *See* Kenesaw Mountain; Franklin; Savannah III; American Civil War.

Atlantic Ocean I (World War I), 1915–1917. Both Great Britain and Germany entered the war with formidable surface fleets. But except for the 1916 battle of Jutland and four smaller actions, the two hostile navies served chiefly as blockading forces, while watching each other warily. This left the Atlantic Ocean open to a three-year struggle between German submarines and Allied merchant ships. Under the command of High Adm. Alfred von Tirpitz, German underseas craft instituted a blockade of Great Britain on February 18, 1915. Allied ships were torpedoed without warning. The sinking of the British liner *Lusitania* on May 7, 1915, took 1,198 lives, including 139 Americans. The United States and Germany moved to the brink of war that summer. But on September 1, 1915, the German government promised to give warning and to provide for the safety of noncombatants if the liners offered no resistance and did not attempt to escape. There was no relief for merchant vessels, however. The toll steadily mounted.

On March 1, 1916, German submarines, now under Adm. Eduard von Capelle, broadened their campaign against all ships in the Atlantic. But again American pressure forced a reduction in unrestricted U-boat attacks, beginning on May 10. Meanwhile light cruisers slipped through the British blockade to add to the growing total of Allied shipping losses. During the last months of 1916, more than a hundred submarines were sinking 300,000 tons of shipping a month. These losses reached a peak in April 1917 when 875,000 tons were destroyed, more than half of the total being British. This was far more shipping than could be constructed each month. The British Isles stood in grave danger of being completely cut off. Then, largely on the insistence of Prime Minister David Lloyd George, the Allies began moving ships in convoys. With the employment of the first convoy on May 10, shipping losses dropped dramatically. American ships helped turn the tide, as did the increased use of destroyers and submarine chasers and the development of the depth bomb.

By October 1 Germany had destroyed about eight million tons of shipping. But 50 submarines had been lost and the 134 still in operation were becoming less and less effective against the convoy system. At year's end the Allies were constructing more shipping than was being destroyed. The lifeline to Great Britain stood secure, giving the Allies the victory in the battle of the Atlantic. *See* Dogger Bank II; Jutland; World War I.

Atlantic Ocean II (World War II), 1940–1944. German efforts to strangle Great Britain by air and sea blockade turned the entire Atlantic Ocean into a battlefield. Nazi weapons were mines sown in British harbors and shipping lanes, long-range bombers operating from the coastline of western Europe, marauding surface raiders commanded by the German naval chieftan Adm. Erich Raeder, and the deadly submarines of Adm. Karl Doenitz' U-boat fleet.

With the fall of France, Germany intensified its Atlantic attack. From June 1, 1940, to July 1, 1941, Britain lost 899 ships totaling 4 million gross tons (plus an additional 471 Allied and neutral vessels of 1.8 million tons). For 1941 Allied and neutral losses were 1,141 ships, amounting to 350,000 tons a month. This loss was three times the combined productive capacity of British and American shipyards. And sinkings were not the only naval casualties. By March 1941 more than 2.6 million tons of damaged shipping had accumulated in British ports. The high toll of Allied and neutral shipping was sharply reflected in the import of cargo into Great Britain. From more than 1.2 million tons (exclusive of oil) a week in June 1940, imports fell to a weekly average of little more than .8 million by the end of the year.

The greatest peril to Allied shipping came from the U-boats. These vessels often traveled in underwater wolf packs, guided to targets by scouting aircraft from advanced land bases. Torpedoes from submarines accounted for about one-half of all ships sunk. In 1941 German production of submarines reached 15 to 18 a month, and the total fleet had grown to 250, of which 100 were always operational.

Second only to the submarine as a destroyer of ships was the airplane, particularly the Focke-Wulf. German superiority in the air enabled bombers to destroy one-fourth of all Allied and neutral shipping lost at sea.

For attack on the surface, Germany had powerful capital ships that roamed the Atlantic as solitary killers, a threat to merchantmen, troop ships, and the smaller-gunned vessels of the Allied navies. During February and March 1941 the battle cruisers *Scharnhorst* and *Gneisenau* sank or captured 22 ships amounting to 115,000 tons. In a five-month raid against Atlantic shipping ending in April 1941, the cruiser *Scheer* accounted for 16 ships totaling 93,000 tons. In all, German surface raiders sank about 700,000 tons of shipping during 1940–41.

To escort merchant ships across the Atlantic, Great Britain in July 1941 instituted the convoy system, first employed in World War I. For protection, the convoys had a variable (but maximum available) component of Allied capital ships, destroyers, corvettes, and aircraft from small (baby) carriers and from nearby bases in Greenland, Iceland, and the British Isles. In September 1941 the first true escort carrier, H.M.S. *Audacity,* operating six aircraft from its flying deck, came into service.

In this life-or-death struggle on the water Britain's Royal Navy fought unflinchingly. The pocket battleship *Admiral Graf Spee,* raiding in the South Atlantic, had been damaged and forced to scuttle in December 1939. Then in May 1941 the battleship *Bismarck* was located in the North Atlantic and sunk.

In 1942 the combined German air and sea attacks almost choked off Allied shipping in the Atlantic. Early in the year 12 to 15 of Doenitz' U-boats began striking off the coast of North America, concentrating on tankers. In January, 31 ships, totaling almost 200,000 tons, were sunk in the western Atlantic and Caribbean Sea. During the months that followed, the number of sinkings in this sector grew alarmingly—May, 91 vessels totaling 452,000 tons; June, 80 ships, 416,000 tons. During the first six months of 1942, the Allies (and neutrals) lost a total of 900 ships totaling more than 4 million tons.

Thereafter the losses dropped sharply as a result of improved Allied tactics and equipment. There was closer cooperation between air and sea forces. Vessels were being equipped with seagoing radar, while some merchantmen were fitted to catapult fighter planes into the air to challenge the deadly Focke-Wulfs. Convoys became stronger and more experienced, and the United States instituted coastal convoys on April 1, 1942. During the first six months of the year 14 submarines were destroyed, but in July alone another 14 were sunk and in October the number destroyed reached 16. Yet despite these losses, the number of U-boats in operation doubled in 1942 to almost 200.

A vital extension of the battle of the Atlantic was the sending of Arctic convoys, loaded with basic supplies for Russia, to Murmansk and Archangel. During 1941 and 1942, 102 British ships and 117 U.S. vessels arrived safely at the northern Russian ports with vehicles, tanks, aircraft, ammunition, and fuel. But 22 British and 42

U.S. merchantmen were lost to German air and sea attacks. Hardest hit among the convoys was P.Q. 17, which lost 23 of 34 cargo ships in June and July 1942. (In all, 40 convoys carried 3,700,000 tons of cargo to Russia with a loss of 91 merchantmen and 300,000 tons of supplies.)

Total losses for Allied (and neutral) shipping in 1942 were 1,570 ships with 7.7 million tons (plus hundreds of ships that had to be laid up for repair). Despite this heavy toll Adolf Hitler berated the German navy and on January 30, 1943, forced Raeder to resign. Doenitz became navy supreme commander, leading to emphasis on renewed submarine attacks.

The battle of the Atlantic reached a climax in the spring of 1943. Germany put into action the greatest number of U-boats in history, 235. Ship sinkings in the Atlantic alone rose to more than 500,000 tons a month. But at the same time the Allied sea and air forces were destroying more Nazi submarines than ever before—12 in March, 15 in April, 40 in May. The U-boat attacks began to waver under these heavy losses. In April Atlantic shipping losses dropped to 253,000 tons, in May to 206,000 tons. Doenitz then recalled most of his submarine fleet to rest, refit, and go out again in less hazardous waters. The battle with the U-boats was won. In June the total Atlantic losses fell to 28,000 tons, the lowest monthly total since 1940. In the last three months of 1943 there came two more clear signs of the Allied victory. For the first time the number of submarines destroyed exceeded the number of merchant ships sunk, 53 to 47. And new construction outstripped losses for the first time in the war. By the end of the year the Allies could show a net gain of almost 11,000,000 tons from the 14,600,000 tons of shipping built that year.

The blunting of the U-boat menace was accompanied by other successes in the air and on the surface. The ever growing Allied air strength, particularly in longer-range fighter planes, sharply reduced shipping losses from Nazi bomber attack. Then, on December 26, 1943, came a notable surface victory. The German battle cruiser *Scharnhorst,* in an attack on an Arctic convoy off Spitsbergen, was engaged and sunk by a British force led by the 35,000-ton battleship *Duke of York* under command of Adm. Sir Bruce Fraser, leader of the British Home Fleet. Only 36 of the 1,970 German seamen survived. (The Nazi sister ship, the *Gneisenau,* never recovered from damage inflicted by a mine on a run from Brest to Kiel on February 11, 1942.) The last remaining German heavy ship threat, the 42,000-ton *Tirpitz,* had already been immobilized by air attacks at various western European ports. Finally it was cornered at Tromsö Fiord, Norway, where on November 12, 1944, 29 British Lancasters zoomed in for a deadly attack. The battleship was destroyed and more than half of its 1,900-man crew killed, at a cost of one bomber. With this victory the long, grueling battle of the Atlantic at last drew to a close.

In all, British and American shipyards built 45,600,000 gross tons of merchant shipping in World War II. Allied and neutral losses totaled 23,500,000 tons, of which 14,000,000 were destroyed by submarines. The Axis lost 781 U-boats, more than half of which (415) were accounted for by air attack. *See* "Graf Spee"; "Bismarck"; World War II.

Attu (World War II). The Aleutian island held in greatest strength by the Japanese, Attu was invaded and liberated by U.S. troops between May 11 and 30, 1943. *See* Aleutian Islands.

Auerstedt (Napoleonic Empire Wars). An overwhelming French victory, directed by Marshal Louis Davout, over a superior Prussian army on October 14, 1806, while Napoleon I was winning a second triumph the same day at Jena. *See* Jena-Auerstedt.

Aughrim (Resistance to the Glorious Revolution), 1691. After winning the crucial battle of the Boyne River against the Catholic army of deposed James II, William III returned to England. He left the Dutch-born general Godert de Ginkel (future Earl of Athlone) in charge of subduing the Jacobite rebellion in Ireland. In 1691 Ginkel completed the conquest of Athlone, on the upper Shannon River, then marched westward. At Aughrim, 30 miles east of Galway, he encountered the rebels in an open field. Led by Patrick Sarsfield, earl of Lucan, and the French general the Marquis de Saint Ruth, the Catholic army fought fiercely against the royalist troops on July 12, 1691. But Ginkel turned the Irish flank and killed Saint Ruth in storming the Irish entrenchments. The rebels then bolted, losing several thousand men in the flight. Lucan took refuge in Limerick, which earlier had successfully resisted siege by William III. *See* Boyne River; Limerick; Jacobite Insurrections.

Augsburg League, War of the. *See* Grand Alliance, War of the.

Augusta (Second, or Dutch, War of Louis XIV), 1676. Three months after an indecisive naval battle off Stromboli, the French and Dutch-Spanish fleets clashed again off Augusta (Agosta), on the southeast coast of Sicily. The French had 29 ships of the line under the Marquis Duquesne to oppose 17 Dutch and 10 Spanish warships commanded by the 69-year-old Adm. Michel de Ruyter of the Netherlands. On April 22 the allied navies fought a hopeless battle against Duquesne's superior force—a situation worsened by inept seamanship on the part of the Spanish. Although no decisive verdict was reached, De Ruyter received a mortal wound, ending one of the glorious naval careers of the seventeenth century. A month later the French fleet surprised the Dutch and Spanish ships at anchor in Palermo and routed them. This ended the fighting in the Mediterranean. Two years later Sicily was restored to Spanish control by the Treaties of Nijmegen. *See* Stromboli; Mons I; Louis XIV, Wars of.

Auldearn (English Civil War), 1645. While England was convulsed by civil war, Scotland became a secondary theater of operations. Under the leadership of the Marquis of Montrose (James Graham), the supporters of King Charles I steadily beat down Covenanter opposition from one end of Scotland to the other. Early in 1645 new opposition to Montrose appeared in the person of Gen. Sir John Urry (or Hurry), a professional soldier who had already changed sides twice in the war. Urry, intent on harrying the lands of the Gordons in Nairn County, was intercepted at Auldearn, east of Nairn, on May 9 by Montrose's army. Despite the fact that the 2,200 Royalists were again heavily outnumbered, they routed Urry's force, to continue their string of victories. *See* Inverlochy; Alford; English Civil War.

Auray (Hundred Years' War), 1364. Only four years after the Treaty of Bretigny, hostilities between England and France broke out again, this time over possession of the duchy of Brittany. John de Montfort, who claimed the peninsula for England, sent a force under John Chandos to besiege Auray. Charles de Blois and the able general Bertrand du Guesclin marched a French army to the relief of the town. In an assault on the siege lines on September 29, 1364, the French were repulsed and then routed by a flank attack. Charles de Blois was killed and Du Guesclin captured (although later ransomed). The town then surrendered to the English. De Montfort's claim won recognition from France's Charles V the following year, but the new ruler of Brittany steered a neutral course between the two great warring powers. *See* Poitiers; Nájera; Châteauneuf-de-Randon; Hundred Years' War.

Austerlitz (Napoleonic Empire Wars), 1805. The relentless French advance northward from Vienna reached Brünn (Brno) in Moravia, 70 miles away, on November 19, 1805. Here Napoleon I halted to rest his 70,000 troops, hoping to bring on a major battle from his Russian (Alexander I) and Austrian (Holy Roman Emperor Francis II) opponents. From Olmütz the allied emperors did indeed plan a counteroffensive. Late in November 85,000 Russian and Austrian troops began shifting southwestward, planning to hit Napoleon's right wing and cut him off from Vienna. Napoleon, in turn, baited a trap by withdrawing from the Pratzen Plateau, just west of the village of Austerlitz.

The allies quickly occupied the Pratzen Plateau and at daybreak on December 2 launched their main assault against the French right (south). Here the Russian general Count Friedrich von Buxhöwden with 40,000 men began pressing against the 10,500 French in Marshal Louis Davout's III Corps. While Davout resisted stubbornly behind Goldbach Brook, Napoleon threw his main punch at the Allied center. (About this time, 8 A.M., the sun broke through heavy mists; Napoleon accepted as a good omen this "sun of Austerlitz.") Marshal Nicolas Soult led 20,000 French infantry in an attack that drove the Russians and Austrians off the Pratzen Plateau. Grand Duke Konstantin Pavlovich, brother of the Russian czar, threw in the allied reserve, but the French swept forward to pierce the enemy's center by 10 A.M.

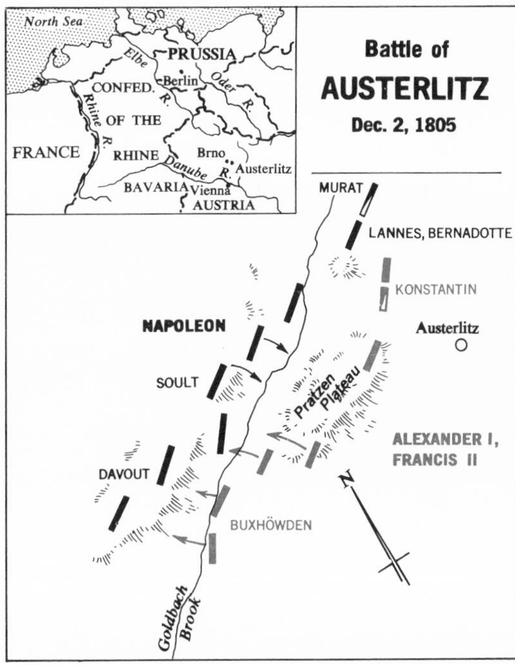

Meanwhile, on the north, the corps of Marshals Jean Lannes and Jean Bernadotte (later King Charles XIV John of Sweden and Norway), supported by Marshal Joachim Murat's cavalry, began striking the enemy right wing. Despite the efforts of the allied field commander, Mikhail Kutuzov, to effect a rally, his forces began to give way and soon were streaming back through Austerlitz. When Davout counterattacked across the Goldbach, the entire allied line collapsed in complete disorder. The French were too exhausted to pursue vigorously. Napoleon lost 2,000 killed and 7,000 wounded. The Russians and Austrians suffered 15,000 killed and wounded and 11,000 prisoners.

The overwhelming French triumph at Austerlitz, often called the Battle of the Three Emperors, wrecked the Third Coalition. Alexander I took his armies back into Russia. Francis II signed the Treaty of Pressburg on December 26, ceding great blocks of territory. The following year the ancient Holy Roman Empire was formally abolished, with the emperor assuming the title Francis I of "Austria." Prussia, which had been on the point of joining the coalition before Austerlitz, signed a treaty of peace with Napoleon. *See* Oberhollabrunn; Cape Town; Saalfeld; Napoleonic Empire Wars.

Austria. For the list of early battles fought by Austria *see* German States of the Holy Roman Empire; Napoleonic Empire Wars. Austria was an independent kingdom from 1806 until 1867, when it became the senior partner in a dual monarchy with Hungary. It became a republic in 1918. In 1945 it was the site of a nationwide battle (*see* following entry).

See Napoleon's Hundred Days	
See Italian Wars of Independence	
See Hungarian Revolt	
Dybböl	1864
See Seven Weeks' War	
See World War I	
See World War II	

Austria (World War II), 1945. The Russian sweep through the Balkans in late 1944 and capture of Budapest on February 18, 1945, doomed Austria. In March the Second Ukrainian Army of Gen. Radion Malinovski drove into Austria from the southeast in two great thrusts. On the right, one force marched up the Danube, captured Vienna in fighting during April 8–13, and then moved west toward the American Seventh Army near Linz. The Americans, under Gen. Alexander Patch, had invaded Austria from Bavaria late in April. Meanwhile, the left wing thrust westward into upper Austria and then turned south, seeking a link-up with the British Eighth Army advancing through the Alps from Italy. Before firm contacts could be made between the Russians and the two Allied armies, Germany surrendered unconditionally on May 8. *See* Balkans; Hungary (World War II); Germany, East; World War II.

Austrian Succession, War of the (1740–1748). When Maria Theresa succeeded her father, Charles VI, as Holy Roman Emperor, her right to reign was challenged by three candidates—Charles Albert, elector of Bavaria; Philip V, king of Spain; and Augustus III, king of Poland and elector of Saxony. At the same time Frederick II, the Great, of Prussia claimed the province of Silesia, then under the rule of Maria Theresa. The Prussians seized the disputed province during 1740–41, in the so-called First Silesian War. This conflict then merged into the larger War of the Austrian Succession. France, Spain, and Bavaria allied themselves with Prussia, while Great Britain, the Netherlands, and Sardinia (Savoy) supported Maria Theresa and Austria. Frederick took Prussia out of the war in 1742. But two years later he started the Second Silesian War against Austria (and Saxony), which was concluded in 1745. Bavaria withdrew from the war the same year; Russia entered on the side of Austria in 1746 but played a minor role. The fighting spread to North America (where it was called King George's War), Italy, the high seas, and India. Finally in 1748 the Peace of Aachen ended the war. Most of the conquered territory was restored, except for Silesia, which passed to Prussia. Maria Theresa's rule (the Pragmatic Sanction) was guaranteed, and her husband won recognition as Holy Roman Emperor Francis I. *See also* King George's War.

Mollwitz	1741
Chotusitz	1742
Dettingen	1743
Toulon II	1744
Velletri	1744
Prague III	1744
Cuneo	1744
Fontenoy	1745
Hohenfriedeberg	1745
Louisbourg I	1745
Soor	1745
Hennersdorf	1745
Kesselsdorf	1745
Madras I	1746
Rocourt	1746
Finisterre Cape I	1747
Lauffeld	1747
Bergen op Zoom I	1747
Finisterre Cape II	1747
Maastricht III	1748

Avaricum (Gallic Wars), 52 B.C. During a relentless six-year campaign (with fighting generally limited to the summer months), Julius Caesar's Roman legions seemed to have conquered most of Gaul. But many fierce tribal leaders remained unsubdued. In the winter of 53–52 B.C. the Carnutes swooped down on Orleans (Cenabum) and massacred the Roman inhabitants. A renewed spirit of revolt flashed through the country, sparked by the leadership of a young Arvernian, Vercingetorix. Caesar hurried back from Italy.

Marching swiftly up the Rhone-Saône Valley at the head of two legions, Caesar turned left (west) and in a sudden stroke liberated Orleans. Crossing the Loire, to the south side, he moved toward Avaricum (Bourges), the largest of the Biturigan towns. Although Vercingetorix had imposed a scorched-earth policy on the Gauls in order to deprive the Romans of supplies, he allowed the Bituriges to defend Avaricum. This was to prove a tragic mistake for the inhabitants. The legionaries brushed aside Gallic resistance and laid siege to the town. After beating off all efforts to raise the siege,

Caesar's troops stormed into Avaricum. Sparing neither women nor children, the Romans killed all but 800 out of a population of about 40,000.

Caesar now divided his force, sending Titus Labienus with four legions north to the Seine, while he took six legions south up the Allier Valley. *See* Tongres; Gergovia; Agendicum; Gallic Wars.

Axholme (Second Baron's War of England), 1265. Some of the survivors of the decisive defeat of the barons' forces at Evesham took refuge at the so-called Isle of Axholme in the fens of northern Lincolnshire. Here they were joined by young Simon de Montfort, who had escaped the royalist siege of Kenilworth Castle. (The elder Montfort, earl of Leicester, had died at Evesham.) King Henry III was too old and frail to disturb the Axholme rebels, but his energetic son Prince Edward (later Edward I) closed in on the Montfortians. In December of 1265 Edward forced the surrender of the refugee barons on the promise of sparing their lives. Young Montfort fled overseas the following year, but some of the rebels broke their parole to enlist with another rebel force holding out at Ely. *See* Evesham; Chesterfield; Ely II; Barons' Wars.

Ayacucho (Peruvian War of Independence), 1824. After the patriot victory over the Spaniards at Junín on August 24, Antonio de Sucre pressed farther into the highlands in pursuit. At Ayacucho, 200 miles southeast of Lima, Sucre's 5,800-man army caught up with the 9,300 royalists of Viceroy José de La Serna and Gen. José Canterac. The patriots attacked on December 9, winning a decisive victory at a cost of less than 1,000 casualties. More than 2,000 royalists were killed and wounded and more than 3,500 captured. Among the prisoners was La Serna, who signed a capitulation agreeing to withdraw all royal troops from Peru. This victory ensured the independence of Peru.

Pushing into Upper Peru, Sucre convened a congress at Chuquisaca, which proclaimed the independence of a new state. It was called Bolivia, in honor of Simón Bolívar, who helped to organize the republic. *See* Junín.

Azov (Russian-Turkish Wars), 1696 .The Turkish-held fortress of Azov, which commanded the Sea of Azov and the entrance to the Black Sea, had long been an objective of Peter I, the Great, of Russia. In 1695 the Russian czar led a land attack against Azov, which the Turks repulsed. The following year, however, Peter tried again, this time launching an assault both by land and sea. The fortress fell on July 28. Fifteen years later Peter found himself surrounded on the Pruth River by a vastly superior Turkish force. Forced to buy his way out, Peter surrendered title to Azov, among other concessions. (Azov was finally conquered for Russia under Czarina Anna in 1739.) *See* Slankamen; Senta.

B

Babylon (Conquest by Persia), 539 B.C. The mighty Persian Empire of Cyrus the Great came into conflict with Babylonia when the then reigning Chaldean dynasty was on the decline under Nabonidus. In 539 B.C. Cyrus moved on the city of Babylon with 40,000 men. The Babylonian army under Nabonidus' son Belshazzar fell back behind the formidable walls of the capital on the Euphrates River. Marching downstream (southward), Cyrus halted long enough to divert the waters of the Euphrates and then entered the surprised city on the dry stream bed. The fall of Babylon ended the Chaldean dynasty. Nabonidus became a prisoner; Belshazzar was killed. Cyrus released the Jews from their Babylonian captivity. Persia now ruled from the Indus to the Mediterranean. *See* Sardis; Pelusium.

Badajoz (Napoleonic Empire Wars), 1812. After reducing the French-held fortress at Ciudad Rodrigo in January 1812, Gen. Lord Wellington (Arthur Wellesley) turned southward to attack Badajoz, the second stronghold barring his way into western Spain. Strongly held by a garrison of French, Germans, and loyal Spanish, Badajoz defied quick capture. But Wellington, at the head of a British, Portuguese, and rebel Spanish force, began a vigorous investment of the fortress in March. By April 5 the besiegers had breached the defenses enough to warrant an assault. In a savage attack Wellington stormed into the town and captured it. The victors, who had suffered 3,500 casualties in the battle, took their revenge on the town and its defeated garrison for two days. The route into Spain now lay open to Wellington, who had driven a wedge between the French armies of Marshal Auguste Marmont in the north and Marshal Nicolas Soult in the south. *See* Ciudad Rodrigo; Salamanca; Napoleonic Empire Wars.

Bad Axe (Black Hawk War), 1832. Forced west of the Mississippi River in 1831, the Sauk and Fox Indians recrossed to the east side the following April. Led by Black Hawk, after whom the summer war was named, several hundred Indians terrorized western Illinois and Wisconsin without doing any real damage. Finally a force of 400 regulars and 900 militia penned the Indians against the Mississippi River at the mouth of the Bad Axe in southwestern Wisconsin. Here on August 2, Gen. Henry Atkinson's command dealt the Indians a crushing blow, ending the war. The Sauk and Fox were resettled in western Iowa. *See* Indian Wars in the United States.

Badonicus, Mons. *See* Mons Badonicus.

Badr (Mohammed's Conquest of Arabia), 624. A year and a half after Mohammed made the 210-mile flight northward from Mecca to Medina (the hegira), he launched his first military operation. With 300 loyal followers, he set out to intercept a caravan on its return from Syria to Mecca. The caravan was defended by a thousand Meccans, led by Abu Sufyan of the Koreish (Mohammed's tribe). At Badr in the Hejaz of western Arabia Mohammed's men routed the larger enemy force and captured the caravan. It was the first of a long series of battles won by the hard-riding desert cavalry of the Arabian Moslems. *See* Ohod; Moslem Conquests.

Baghdad I (Mongol Conquest of Western Asia), 1258. While Mangu Khan, grandson of Genghis Khan and third ruler of the Mongol Empire, was conquering China, he sent his brother Hulagu westward to attack the cities of Islam. In 1256 Hulagu's Mongol army swarmed through the Near East, annihilating the Assassin sect, which had spread terror through the region for more than 150 years. Two years later Hulagu attacked Baghdad, the center of Moslem strength in Asia. The Mongols stormed into the city on February 15, 1258, and sacked it ruthlessly. Mustasim, last of the original line of Abbassid caliphs, which had ruled since 750, fell into Mongol hands. He was trampled to death by horses, leaving Mameluke Egypt the last stronghold of Moslem culture. Hulagu pressed on westward into Syria. *See* Mohi; Ain Jalut; Baghdad II; Mongol Wars.

Baghdad II (Conquests of Tamerlane), 1401. During his first foray into Persia from Samarkand, the Mongol conqueror Tamerlane (Timur Lenk, or Timur the Lame) captured Baghdad in 1393. But when the invading host moved on, the city revolted, threw out the Mongol governor, and reestablished its own rule. Eight years later, after conquests as far apart as Russia and India, Tamerlane again swept into Persia. On July 23, 1401, his fierce-fighting troops stormed into Baghdad. The city fell, and the Mongol victors methodically took their revenge for the earlier uprising. Tens of thousands of citizens were massacred and Baghdad was laid waste. Tamerlane then plunged westward into Syria. *See* Delhi I; Angora; Mongol Wars.

Baghdad III (Turkish-Persian Wars), 1534. While Suleiman I, the Magnificent, was fighting the West on land and sea, trouble erupted in Persia. Revitalized by Shah Thamasp after their crushing defeat at Chaldiran in 1514, the Persians recaptured Tabriz in 1526. The shah increased his threat to the Turks by opening negotiations with Charles V, Holy Roman Emperor. Suleiman then turned his back on Europe and marched a large army into Persia. Tabriz again fell to the Turks. Pushing onward, the invaders stormed and captured Baghdad in 1534. This victory stamped out the Persian revolt, although Baghdad was not formally incorporated into the Ottoman Empire until 1638. *See* Vienna I; Tunis III.

Baghdad IV (World War I), 1917. The new British commander in Mesopotamia, Gen. Sir Frederick Maude, built up his manpower and supplies until he was ready to launch a fresh Anglo-Indian offensive up the Tigris River to Baghdad. On December 13, 1916, Maude moved out from Basra with almost 50,000 men. Advancing methodically toward the Turkish fortress of Kut-al-Imara, Maude spent two months eliminating the Turkish detachments south of the river. On February 17 he began a series of well-planned strikes against the fortress, held by some 12,000 Turks under Gen. Kara Bekr Bey. These maneuvers forced the evacuation of Kut-al-Imara eight days later.

Methodically fighting his way upriver, Maude reached the Turkish defenses on the Diyala River, ten miles below Baghdad, on March 4. His skillful deployment forced the 11,000 Turks to abandon their lines without a major fight. The outmaneuvered Turkish army of Gen. Halil Pasha then withdrew to the north of Baghdad. Maude marched into the city on March 11, taking 9,000 prisoners. *See* Kut-al-Imara II; Ramadi; World War I.

Bagradas River (Wars of the First Triumvirate), 49 B.C. The conquest of North Africa started well for the forces loyal to Julius Caesar. After routing the Pompeian army at Utica, G. Scribonius Curio marched his two Caesarian legions inland to the Bagradas (Medjerda) River. But here he was attacked by a strong force of Numidian cavalry under their king, Juba I, an ally of Pompey. The skillful African horsemen (who had contributed so much to Hannibal's campaign in Italy 150 years earlier) dispersed the Roman cavalry and then surrounded the infantry. Unable to defend themselves against the swift, hard-hitting Numidians, the legionaries were cut down one by one. Among the slain was Curio. The Pompeian adherents now held Africa, but this was a secondary theater. The decisive battle had yet to be fought, in Greece as well as in Africa. *See* Utica II; Pharsalus; Ruspina; First Triumvirate, Wars of the.

Bailén (Napoleonic Empire Wars), 1808. When Napoleon I installed his older brother, Joseph Bonaparte, as king of Spain in place of Charles IV, most of the nation erupted in revolt against the French. The ensuing struggle took the name Peninsular War. Faced with a hostile countryside, a French army of 20,000 men under Gen. Comte Pierre Dupont de l'Etang began withdrawing from southern Spain toward Madrid in the summer of 1808. The column was severely harassed by some 30,000 hastily assembled Spanish troops commanded by Francisco de Castaños (later Duque de Bailén). Finally, on July 19 at Bailén, 20 miles north of Jaen, the French were forced to fight for water. Unable to break loose, and after suffering 2,000 casualties, Dupont de l'Étang surrendered his entire force. The capitulation of a Napoleonic army rocked all of Europe. The French government evacuated Madrid, withdrawing northeast behind the Ebro River. This retreat isolated the French army of Marshal Andoche Junot in Portugal. *See* Saragossa II; Vimeiro; Napoleonic Empire Wars.

Balaclava (Crimean War), 1854. During the British-French siege of Sevastopol, allied supplies came in through the port of Balaclava, eight miles southeast of the besieged fortress. On October 25 the Russians under Prince Aleksandr Menshikov made a sudden attack on the allied base. Caught by surprise, the British commander, Gen. Lord Raglan (Fitzroy Somerset), threw out a "thin red line"—the 93rd Highlanders under Gen. Sir Colin Campbell—to stop the enemy advance. Raglan then ordered the cavalry division of Gen. Lord Lucan (George Bingham) to counterattack. The Heavy Brigade (Sir James Scarlett) drove back 3,000 Russian horsemen. But Lucan failed to follow up his advantage, giving the Russians time to re-form. Then, instead of having the Light Brigade clear the causeway leading to Balaclava as he intended, Lucan, through a staff officer's error, sent his force up a heavily defended valley to the north.

The brigade of 673 horsemen, led by Gen. Lord Cardigan (James Brudenell), made one of the famous charges in history. Supported by the French Chasseurs d'Afrique, it swept through the guns at the head of the valley. But Cardigan had to turn back, altogether losing 113 killed and 134 wounded in a senseless operation. A French general, Pierre Bosquet, who witnessed the assault, is reported to have remarked, "It is magnificent but it is not war." This attack ended the battle with Balaclava still in the hands of the allies. *See* Sevastopol I; Crimean War.

Balathista (Byzantine-Bulgarian Wars), 1014. The growing power of the Bulgarian Empire of Tsar Samuel forced the Byzantine emperor Basil II to undertake one of the most brutal campaigns in history. Beginning in 996, the Byzantine and Bulgar armies see-sawed in indecisive combat from Adrianople (Edirne) westward into Macedonia and Greece proper. Finally, in 1014, Basil managed to trap a large Bulgar force at Balathista in the valley of the Struma River, which flows into the Aegean Sea. The Byzantine army overwhelmed its opponents, taking some 15,000 prisoners. Basil ordered their eyes put out. A few men were each spared one eye to serve as guides for the return of the blinded captives to Samuel. The shock of seeing his mutilated warriors was too much for the Bulgar emperor. He died on the spot. Four years later Samuel's successors made peace with Basil II (now called Bulgaroktonos, or "slayer of the Bulgarians") and the Bulgars were incorporated into the Byzantine Empire. *See* Sofia; Stara Zagora.

Balkans (World War II), 1944–1945. In March 1944 two Russian army groups had plunged westward out of the Ukraine, collapsing the German defenses in front of them. On the north, Gen. Georgi Zhukov crossed the upper Prut to drive a wedge along the northern border of Rumania. On his left, Gen. Ivan Konev drove through Moldavia to cross the Prut at Jassy (Iasi). At that point the Russian offensive halted for five months to reorganize and resupply.

On August 20, 1944, the Red armies renewed their assault upon Rumania. This time the main thrust was against the German salient still held between the Dniester and Prut rivers. Generals Rodion Malinovski and Fedor Tolbukhin attacked southwest, crossed the lower Prut, and pressed on toward the lower Danube. The Rumanian government of King Michael capitulated on August 23. Many Rumanian troops then changed sides and turned their guns on the German army. The sudden collapse in this sector led to the destruction of 16 German divisions in Gen. Friessner's Army Group South Ukraine. Galati, at the mouth of the Danube, fell on August 27. Three days later Russian forces occupied Bucharest and the valuable Ploesti oil fields.

On September 8 the Russians under Tolbukhin crossed the Danube boundary into Bulgaria, which immediately changed sides and joined the Russians. Sofia was occupied on September 19. The German troops in Bulgaria were disarmed and imprisoned.

Meanwhile, a wide sweep by the Russian left wing drove up the Danube Valley to reach the Yugoslav frontier at Turnu Severin on September 6. Aided by strong partisan forces, Tolbukhin's army drove back Field Marshal Maximilian von Weich's Southeast Army Group ("F") and captured Belgrade on October 20. Inside this sweep Malinovski's army pushed into Hungary from the south. *See* Ukraine; Hungary (World War II); World War II.

Balkan Wars (1885; 1912–1913). For more than a quarter of a century the weakening control of the Turkish Empire, the rising influence of Russia, and the strong nationalistic feelings among the inhabitants made the Balkan Peninsula an international trouble spot. Serbia and Montenegro won their independence from Turkey in 1878. Seven years later Serbia went to war with Bulgaria, then an autonomous principality, over the latter's annexation of Eastern Rumelia. Other European powers intervened to re-establish the *status quo.*

Slivnica	1885
Pirot	1885

Mutual hostility toward Turkey drew Bulgaria and Serbia into a joint alliance on March 13, 1912. Greece (independent since 1829) and Montenegro also associated themselves with this anti-Ottoman league. Then, on October 8, Montenegro declared war on Turkey, followed by Greece on October 18. A day earlier Sultan Mohammed V had declared war on Serbia and Bulgaria. Fighting was officially ended by the Treaty of London, signed on May 30, 1913. Turkey ceded Macedonia, abandoned claims to Crete, and recognized the independence of Albania.

Kirk-Kilissa	1912
Kumanovo	1912
Monastir	1912
Lüleburgaz	1912
Çatalca	1912
Shkodër II	1913
Ioannina	1913
Adrianople VII	1912–1913

The Second Balkan War, which started on June 29, 1913, found the former anti-Turkish allies, plus Rumania (independent since 1878) and later Turkey, aligned against Bulgaria. It was a war without a major battle. Bulgarian troops commanded by Gen. Mikhail Savov attacked westward against Serbia and Greece without a declaration of war. The double offensive gained ground initially but soon petered out, whereupon both Serbia and Greece launched counteroffensives. Rumania joined in the attack toward Sofia, while Turkey seized Adrianople (Edirne). By July 31 the Bulgarian government of Czar Ferdinand I was suing for peace. On August 10 the Treaty of Bucharest forced Bulgaria to cede various territories to its enemies. In a second treaty signed at Constantinople on September 29, Bulgaria surrendered to Turkey the city of Adrianople and pulled back its boundaries to the line of the Maritsa River. Crete passed to Greece.

Ball's Bluff (American Civil War), 1861. Following the Federal defeat at the first battle of Bull Run, President Abraham Lincoln appointed Gen. George McClellan to organize the future Army of the Potomac. McClellan moved too slowly to satisfy public opinion in the North. To carry the war to the South, Col. Edward Baker received permission to attack the Confederate position at Ball's Bluff on the Potomac River, 33 miles northwest of Washington, D.C. On October 21 Baker sent out a column that was promptly ambushed by the Confederate general Nathan Evans, veteran of first Bull Run. Baker and 48 others were killed, 158 suffered wounds, and 714 were captured or missing. Evans lost 33 killed, 115 wounded, and one missing. Although of no military importance, the battle aroused much criticism in the North about the ineptness of Union leadership. *See* Bull Run I; American Civil War.

Bamian (Mongol Conquest of Central Asia), 1221. By the autumn of 1221 Genghis Khan's Mongol horde had overrun virtually all of the former Khwarizm Empire of central Asia. One of the Mongol columns was pushing westward into modern Iran, while another was raiding west of the Caspian Sea. The Great Khan himself with 40,000 men now turned southeast in search of the late Shah Mohammed's son Jalal-ad-Din, who had raised a new Khwarizm army to oppose the Mongol conquerors. Genghis rode into Afghanistan, where he found his route blocked by the defiant city of Bamian in the pass between the Hindu Kush on the left (east) and the Koh-i-Baba on the right (southwest). The Mongols laid siege to the city. During this operation a youthful grandson (son of Ogadai) of the Khan was killed below the city's walls. With cold fury the Mongol chief ordered a relentless assault on Bamian. Despite heavy Mongol casualties, the city was taken. All human life was extinguished and the buildings were burned to the ground. Even the Mongols called Bamian the City of Sorrow. Genghis Khan resumed his pursuit of the Moslem army of Jalal-ad-Din. *See* Merv; Indus River; Mongol Wars.

Banbury (Wars of the Roses), 1469. After only eight years of rule the Yorkist (white rose) party of Edward IV began to break apart. The king's marriage to Elizabeth Woodville and his honoring of the Woodville family, plus his alliance with Burgundy on the Continent, alienated the powerful Neville family, headed by Richard, Earl of Warwick, nicknamed the Kingmaker. Warwick, who wanted an alliance with France, received support from George, the Duke of Clarence, younger brother of the king.

In the spring of 1469 discontented elements provoked an uprising in Yorkshire. Edward left London for the north, ordering the Earls of Pembroke and Devon to join him in putting down the rebellion. With levies from Wales and the western counties, the loyal nobles marched into Oxfordshire. But on July 26 at Edgcott, six miles northeast of Banbury, they were intercepted and routed by a rebel force under a so-called Robin of Redesdale, a friend of Warwick. Almost 200 royalist nobles, including Pembroke and Devon, were either killed in the battle or beheaded afterward. Meanwhile, Warwick himself and the Duke of Clarence crossed over from Calais to enforce their will upon the defenseless Edward IV. *See* Hexham; Losecoat Field; Roses, Wars of the.

Bannockburn (English-Scottish Wars), 1314. After the English repulse at Loudon Hill and the death of Edward I in 1307, the ineffectual Edward II abandoned the war against Scotland. During the next seven years, Robert I, the Bruce, united Scotland under his rule and forced the English out of all castles north of the Tweed except Berwick and Stirling. When the latter fortresses came under siege, Edward II marched north with a strong army of 15,000 men, including 2,000 armored knights. To meet the English attack, Robert deployed some 8,000 spearmen on a small rise overlooking Bannock Burn (brook), a tributary of the Forth. He anchored his left flank in a patch of dense woods, his right on a bend in the stream. For a reserve Robert held back a force of 500 mounted knights.

On the morning of June 24 the large English army was still splashing across the Bannock, preparing to charge up the slope against the Scottish lines. The Bruce seized the opportunity to attack on a 2,000-yard front, with four schiltrons (circles of spearmen) echeloned to the left. The two sides became locked together in a deadly struggle. Edward sent his archers around the Scottish left flank, but Bruce's cavalry, under the marshal Sir Robert Keith, drove them back into the great mass of English troops. The spears of the tough Scots created havoc among the cramped men and horses of the invaders. Finally the English front broke and began to fall back. The Scots pressed their advantage, turning the retreat into a rout. Edward barely managed to escape capture. But the vast majority of his men, exhausted by their attack and bogged down in the marshy ground along the Bannock, fell victim to Scottish spears or drowned trying to escape. It was the greatest loss ever suffered by English knighthood in a single day. Some 4,000 Scots were killed.

The battle of Bannockburn ended English hopes of conquering Scotland by force. Stirling Castle immediately fell to Bruce. (Berwick surrendered four years later.) Meanwhile, Edward returned to his court, where new troubles awaited him from his barons at home and from an Irish uprising abroad. *See* Loudon Hill; Dundalk; Boroughbridge.

Bantry Bay (War of the Grand Alliance), 1689. The first sea battle of the war between France and

England grew out of Louis XIV's efforts to support the counterrevolution of deposed James II against England's William III and Mary. James had landed in Ireland on March 14, 1689, to organize a Catholic army as an instrument of regaining his throne. Two months later a French fleet under the Marquis de Châteaurenault entered Bantry Bay, off Ireland's southwest coast, carrying reinforcements to James. Here the French were attacked by an English naval force under Adm. Arthur Herbert (later Earl of Torrington) on May 11. The English attack was beaten off and the reinforcements were landed. But French aid was not strong enough to turn the tide in favor of James. On the Continent, however, French troops were soon to prove superior to the armies of the Grand Alliance (also called the League of Augsburg). In America, the conflict was called King William's War. *See* Londonderry; Port Royal I; Fleurus II; Beachy Head; Grand Alliance, War of the.

Bapaume (Franco-Prussian War), 1871. One of the civilian armies that took the field in defense of France after the Sedan disaster was commanded by Gen. Louis Faidherbe. On New Year's Day this force marched toward Péronne, in northern France, then under siege by the Prussian First Army of Gen. August von Goeben. The Prussians met the French at Bapaume, on January 2 and 3. Although Faidherbe's troops scored a few small gains, they were unable to dislodge the better-trained enemy. The French had to pull back, and Péronne fell on January 9. Another crushing blow struck the new Third Republic three days later at Le Mans. *See* Coulmiers; Le Mans; Paris II; Franco-Prussian War.

Barcelona I (War of the Spanish Succession), 1705. The English and Dutch, who had taken and defended Gibraltar in 1704, pressed their attack against Spain the following year. A fleet under Adm. Sir Cloudesley Shovell carried the Earl of Peterborough (Charles Mordaunt) and 6,000 English troops to Barcelona in August. Landing north of the city, Peterborough besieged Barcelona, held for Philip V by a French-Catalan garrison. By a bold night march, the English surprised and captured the fortified hill of Montjuich, south of the city. One of those killed in the fighting was Prince George of Hesse-Darmstadt, a hero in the Gibraltar assault the year before. The fall of this key strong point led to the surrender of Barcelona on October 9. Archduke Charles (and future Charles VI) of the Holy Roman Empire, son of Leopold I, was installed as Charles III of Spain. The following year the allies would strike from Portugal into central Spain. *See* Málaga II; Blenheim; Almansa; Spanish Succession, War of the.

Barcelona II (Spanish Civil War), 1938–1939. With Republican Spain cut in two, Generalissimo Francisco Franco prepared a massive offensive against the Catalonia pocket in the east. Six Nationalist armies took positions from the Pyrenees southward to the mouth of the Ebro River. On December 23 the broad-front attack got under way. The Republican defenders under Gen. Hernández Sarabia, bled white by the battle of the Ebro in the fall, were soon driven back all along the line. The Segre River, a northern tributary of the Ebro, was crossed by the four Italian divisions of Gen. Gastone Gambara and the Army of Navarre commanded by Gen. José Solchaga. The Republicans reeled back toward Barcelona. To the south Borjas Blancas fell on January 4. With Nationalist armor smashing steadily forward, the Republican withdrawal soon became a rout. On January 14 Gen. Juan de Yagüe's Moroccans lunged across the lower Ebro to seize Tarragona.

The shattered Republican forces fled back into Barcelona, which was blasted continuously by Nationalist air raids. By January 24 Yagüe, Solchaga, and Gambara, from south to north, had reached the Llobregat River, three miles from the Catalan capital. Juan Negrín and the government hurriedly escaped northeast to Gerona. On January 26 Nationalist troops poured into a virtually deserted Barcelona. Almost half a million people had headed for the French border. Between February 5 and 10, 230,000 civilians, 10,000 wounded, and 250,000 Republican troops crossed the Pyrenees into France. Hard on their heels, the Nationalists occupied Gerona on February 5 and closed up to the border five days later. Negrín and other Republican leaders assembled in Toulouse and then returned by air to the Madrid-Valencia pocket, the last part of Spain still held by the government. *See* Ebro River; Madrid; Spanish Civil War.

Bardia (World War II), 1941. In Great Britain's first offensive of the North African campaign, the British XIII Corps, formerly called the Western Desert Force, crossed the Egyptian frontier into Libya, following its victory at Sidi Barrâni. At the small Mediterranean port of Bardia, Gen. Sir Richard O'Connor's army surrounded 45,000 troops of the Italian Tenth Army, under the overall command of Marshal Rodolpho Graziani, on January 3, 1941. Under heavy fire the 6th Australian Division bridged a deep antitank ditch, which enabled the 7th Armoured Division to penetrate the defenses. In two days of fighting the Italians suffered 40,000 casualties, the great majority of which were captured. British casualties were light.

Leaving mop-up operations to the infantry, the 7th Armoured raced west along the coast road (Via Balbia) to the fortress of Tobruk. *See* Sidi Barrâni; Tobruk I; World War II.

Barletta (French-Spanish Wars in Italy), 1502. Ferdinand (V of Castile, II of Aragon) had joined the Holy League to expel the French of Charles

VIII from Italy in 1495. Five years later, however, he joined with Charles's successor, Louis XII, in the Treaty of Granada, which divided the kingdom of Naples between Spain and France. The new allies raced into southern Italy and subdued it in little more than a year. By July 1502, however, fighting broke out between the two victorious armies. The French heavy cavalry and efficient artillery train, supported by Scottish bowmen and Swiss pikemen, proved superior. But in 1502 outside the walls of Barletta, on Italy's Adriatic Coast, the veteran Spanish captain Gonzalo de Córdoba revived the tactics of the ancient Roman legions. Relying on well-trained infantry armed only with a buckler and short thrusting sword, the Spanish fought at such close quarters that the long-handled pikes of the Swiss became useless. It was Spain's first victory over the French. From this battle the Spanish infantry continued to improve until it became the best in Europe and remained so for more than a century. *See* Fornovo; Cerignola.

Barnet (Wars of the Roses), 1471. The sudden thrust of Edward IV to London and his resumption of the English throne revitalized the Yorkists (white rose) once again. Prompted by the king's successful coup, his younger brother, the Duke of Clarence, deserted the Lancastrian (red rose) cause and joined Edward. Despite this loss, the Earl of Warwick, called the Kingmaker, now at the head of the Lancastrian army, forced a battle with the royalist forces at Barnet, 12 miles north of London. The two forces clashed head on in a thick fog on April 14, 1471. Warwick's right wing overlapped Edward's left, but in the limited visibility became confused and failed to exploit its advantage. Meanwhile Edward's right had crushed in the enemy's left and, wheeling about, struck the center of the Lancastrian forces. This attack broke Warwick's ranks. In attempting to flee, the Kingmaker was overtaken and slain. So died one of the great English soldiers of the Middle Ages. A combined total of almost a thousand knights lay dead on the misty field. But Edward's crown remained in jeopardy. On the day of the battle Queen Margaret, wife of the imprisoned Henry VI, landed at Weymouth with a second Lancastrian army to which the western counties began to rally. *See* Ravenspur II; Tewkesbury; Roses, Wars of the.

Barons' Wars of England I and **II** (1215–1217, 1264–1267). Opposition to King John of England by many nobles brought on civil war, called the First Barons' War. Despite the signing of the Magna Carta, the barons wanted Prince Louis, son of Philip II of France, to take over the English throne. After John's death, he was succeeded by his son, Henry III. In the Treaty of Kingston-on-Thames, signed in 1217, Louis relinquished his claim to the English crown. There were two more battles however before the fighting ended.

Rochester II	1215
Dover I	1216–1217
Lincoln II	1217
Sandwich I	1217
Bytham	1220
Bedford	1224

Henry III, who had established his claim to the English throne in the First Barons' War, was faced with a second civil war in 1264. The revolt in this Second Barons' War was spearheaded by the king's brother-in-law, Simon de Montfort (earl of Leicester). After Montfort was killed in 1265, the king crushed the rebellion in three more battles.

Northampton I	1264
Rochester III	1264
Lewes	1264
Kenilworth	1265–1266
Evesham	1265
Axholme	1265
Chesterfield	1266
Ely II	1266–1267

Bar-sur-Aube (Napoleonic Empire Wars), 1814. Following his victory at Montereau on February 18, 1814, Napoleon I continued to push back the allied army of Prince Karl von Schwarzenberg. The Austrian commander abandoned Troyes on February 23, continuing his eastward retreat beyond the Aube River. Leaving Marshal Nicolas Oudinot to conduct the pursuit, Napoleon marched northward to where the Prussian field marshal general Gebhard von Blücher was again threatening Paris by moving down the Marne Valley. With the pressure against him relaxed, Schwarzenberg prepared a counterattack toward Bar-sur-Aube. On February 27 the Russian corps of the Prince of Sayn-Wittgenstein-Ludwigsburg and the Bavarian corps under Gen. (later prince and field marshal) Karl Wrede struck Oudinot, who held a poor position astride the Aube. Outnumbered and outfought, the French marshal suffered a sharp defeat and fell back to Troyes. *See* Montereau; Craonne; Napoleonic Empire Wars.

Basra (Moslem Civil Wars), 656. Islam suffered its first civil war during the rule of its fourth caliph, Ali. The leaders of the revolt were old associates of Mohammed—Zobair, his cousin; Talha, a companion; and Aisha, daughter of abu-Bakr and one of the wives of the Prophet. The rebels seized Basra (Bassorah in the *Arabian Nights*), near the head of the Persian Gulf, in 656. Ali rode to the port with some 29,000 loyal troops. On December 9 he fought a pitched battle for possession of Basra. Although the rebels had a superiority in numbers, they were decisively beaten. Zobair and Talha were killed and Aisha was captured. This struggle is often called the Battle of the Camel; each of the reported 70 men who held the bridle of Aisha's camel was killed in turn in the fight which raged around the Prophet's widow.

But the battle of Basra did not end the revolt. The governor of Syria, Muawiyah, also sought the caliphate. *See* Lycia; Siffin; Moslem Conquests.

Bassano (Wars of the French Revolution), 1796. After driving one Austrian column out of Trent on September 5, 1796, Napoleon Bonaparte turned southeast down the valley of the Brenta in pursuit of the main enemy army under Field Marshal Count Dagobert von Wurmser. The Austrian commander, who had launched a hesitating offensive toward Mantua, now hurriedly tried to concentrate his forces at Bassano. But the swiftly marching French army brushed past a Croatian rear guard posted at Primolano on September 7, to strike Bassano the following day. General Pierre Augereau attacked down the left (east) bank of the Brenta, Gen. André Masséna down the right bank. The Austrian defense collapsed in wild disorder. A group of 3,000 escaped eastward toward Trieste, while Wurmser led 12,000 survivors southward to refuge in Mantua five days later. The French victory netted 3,000 prisoners, 35 cannon, and more than 200 wagons. *See* Caliano; Mantua; Caldiero I; French Revolution Wars.

Bastogne (World War II). A successful American defense of a key road junction, between December 20 and 26, 1944, that helped thwart the German advance in the Ardennes. *See* Ardennes II.

Bataan-Corregidor (World War II), 1942. When strong Japanese landings on both northern and southern Luzon closed in on Manila in late December 1941, Gen. Douglas MacArthur withdrew his American-Filipino command to the rugged peninsula of Bataan on the west coast. By New Year's Day 15,000 Americans and 65,000 (only 10,000 of whom were well-trained) Filipinos had successfully assembled in Bataan. MacArthur established a 15-mile-wide defensive line across the neck of the peninsula, from Subic Bay on the South China Sea on the left eastward to Manila Bay on the right. General Jonathan Wainwright commanded the western half of the line (I Corps), Gen. George Parker the eastern half (II Corps). Just off the southern coast of the 30-mile-long peninsula, MacArthur and President Manuel Quezon set up headquarters on the fortified island rock of Corregidor in the mouth of Manila Bay.

It was hoped that the Bataan position could be held until the arrival of U.S. naval, air, and ground reinforcements. But the continuing Japanese push into the Central and Southwest Pacific increased the isolation of the Philippines. MacArthur had only a few remaining fighter planes to dispute enemy air supremacy and no navy except small craft. The troops received only half-rations from the beginning. Medical supplies, ammunition, and weapons were severely limited.

General Masaharu Homma's Fourteenth Army launched the Japanese offensive the night of January 10 with an attack against the eastern half of the line (the Abucay position). Parker's men repulsed the thrust. During the fighting, Lt. Alexander Nininger, Jr., became the first Medal of Honor winner (posthumously) in World War II. Relentless Japanese pressure on both ends of the line forced MacArthur to order a general retreat on January 22 to the east-west Pilar–Bagac road, across the middle of Bataan. Four days later the command was forced back on the east to Orion. Here the defenders dug in for an all-out stand. But now food and medical supplies were so scarce that a thousand men a day were entering the two hospitals at the southern tip of Bataan. Almost three-fourths of the front-line troops suffered from malaria.

On the order of President F. D. Roosevelt, MacArthur and his personal staff were evacuated by PT (Patrol Torpedo) boat on the night of March 11–12 to Mindanao. From there a B-17 bomber flew MacArthur to Australia, where he became supreme commander of Allied forces in the Southwest Pacific. Wainwright took charge of all forces in the Philippines, with Gen. Albert Jones replacing Wainwright as commander of I Corps and Gen. Edward King assuming command of the Bataan troops.

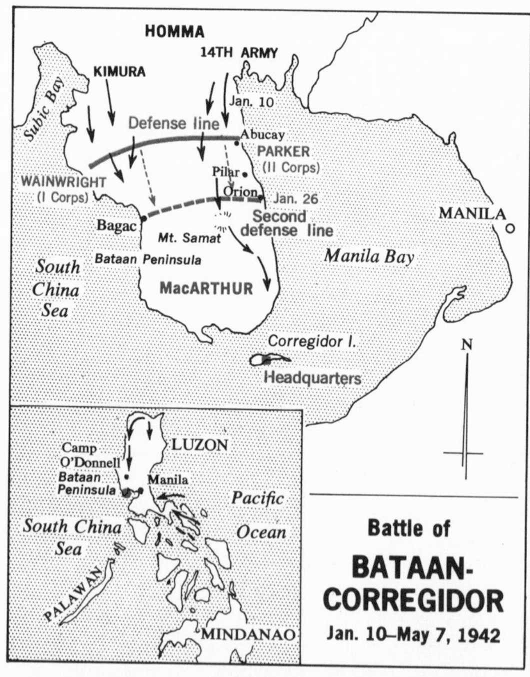

Battle of
BATAAN-CORREGIDOR
Jan. 10–May 7, 1942

On April 3 Homma launched a devastating barrage against the Fil-American position, with incendiaries burning many of the defenders out of their foxholes. Japanese troops punched a wide hole in the eastern half of the line on April 5, capturing Mount Samat, which gave them a commanding view of the now crumbling defenses. During the next two days relentless Japanese attacks annihilated the II Corps front. By April 8 the starved and disease-ridden defenders were thoroughly beaten. That night 2,000 nurses and others escaped from the smoldering peninsula to Corregidor in small boats. On the morning of April 9 King surrendered some 76,000 men, including 12,000 Americans. It was the worst capitulation in U.S. history. The Japanese captors then started the prisoners on a brutal march of 55 miles up the Bataan Peninsula to San Fernando, where freight cars took the suffering survivors farther north to Camp O'Donnell, beyond Clark Field. Deprived of food, water, and rest, beaten and murdered all along the route, an estimated 7,000 to 10,000 men (including 2,330 Americans) died during the Death March to prison. (After the war Homma and Gen. Tomoyuki Yamashita, the conqueror of Singapore who had assumed supreme command in the Philippines late in the campaign, were tried and executed as war criminals for their responsibility in the march.)

On Corregidor Wainwright and 13,000 others were suffering through a devastating artillery bombardment that seemed to grow heavier each day. On May 4 alone, Homma's siege guns on Bataan churned the island with 16,000 shells. The almost continuous drumfire caused more than a thousand casualties among the 4,000 troops defending the beaches. (The others huddled together inside the large Malinta Tunnel.) On the night of May 5 two battalions of Japanese infantry landed on the northeast shore of Corregidor. Under cover of artillery and mortar fire, the invaders methodically pressed toward the eastern mouth of Malinta Tunnel. By midmorning Japanese tanks had joined the attack. Wainwright then signaled that he was surrendering the island. But holding the 11,000 Corregidor prisoners as helpless hostages, Homma refused to accept the surrender until the American general ordered a cease-fire for all troops still resisting in the Philippines. Wainwright finally capitulated at midnight of May 6–7. The long, always one-sided battle was over. But the stout Filipino-American defense had slowed the Japanese onslaught. Moreover, it was to be the last major defeat suffered by the Allies in the Pacific. *See* Philippine Islands; Coral Sea; Leyte; World War II.

Batoche (Canadian Rebellion), 1885. Fearful of losing land titles in the incorporation of Northwest Territories into the Dominion of Canada, Louis Riel led an uprising of métis (French halfbreeds). His rebels captured Fort Garry (Winnipeg) but disbanded upon the approach of a force under Col. Garnet Wolseley (later Lord Wolseley) in September 1870. Fifteen years later Riel led a second revolt in Manitoba and Saskatchewan. Driven westward, the rebels made a stand at Batoche, in south-central Saskatchewan, against a government army led by Gen. Middleton. On May 12 Batoche fell with a loss of 220 rebels, as against 54 casualties suffered by Middleton. Riel surrendered three days later, was convicted of treason, and was hanged. *See* Toronto.

Bautzen (Napoleonic Empire Wars), 1813. After their defeat at Lützen on May 2, 1813, the Russian and Prussian armies of the Prince of Sayn-Wittgenstein-Ludwigsburg and Gen. Gebhard von Blücher fell back eastward between the Elbe and Oder rivers. Napoleon I pursued slowly, occupying Dresden and converting it into his principal advance base. Thirty miles to the northeast the allied monarchs, Alexander I of Russia and Frederick William III of Prussia, ordered a stand at Bautzen, on the Spree River. Pressing forward with 115,000 troops, Napoleon forced a crossing of the Spree at Bautzen on May 20. Meanwhile Marshal Michel Ney's newly constituted army of 84,000 men bridged the river farther downstream. On the following day Napoleon resumed his frontal attack, while Ney struck the allied right from the north. Unfortunately for the French, Ney's attack lacked vigor, enabling Wittgenstein to withdraw his 96,000-man army in good order. Each side suffered about 20,000 casualties in the indecisive two-day battle. The allies fell back into Silesia, where a truce, during June 4–August 10, took effect. Two days after the armistice ended, Austria (Francis I, father-in-law of Napoleon) declared war on France for the fifth time since 1792. Meanwhile a defeat at Vitoria forced the French to abandon Spain. *See* Lützen II; Vitoria; Grossbeeren; Napoleonic Empire Wars.

Baza (Spanish-Moslem Wars), 1489. After driving in the Moorish defenses west of Granada, capital of the Moslem kingdom in Spain, Ferdinand (V of Castile, II of Aragon) launched an offensive east of the city. Here stood two enemy strong points: Baza, 50 miles northeast of Granada inland, and Almería, 50 miles to the southeast on the coast. In June a large Spanish army took Baza under siege. Despite a fierce Moorish defense, the well-fortified city had to surrender on December 4. Meanwhile, Almería, offering little resistance, had fallen, depriving the Moslem kingdom of its last outlet to the sea. Granada itself, now effectively isolated, became the next Spanish objective. *See* Málaga I; Granada.

Beachy Head (War of the Grand Alliance), 1690. The second battle of the war at sea found the French fleet (70 ships) under Adm. the Comte de Tourville dominating the waters off England. Arthur Herbert, newly created earl of Torrington and first lord of the admiralty, had to divide his English fleet between Ireland (to cover King William III's operations) and the English Channel. However, when Tourville arrived off Cornwall on June 30, 1690, Torrington had to fight, even though his Channel force consisted of only 56 English and Dutch ships. The two hostile fleets maneuvered eastward until they reached Beachy Head in East Sussex. On July 10 Torrington, having the wind advantage, attacked the French. But his disposition was faulty and the Dutch in the van suffered severely. The allies lost 12 ships; the French none.

Torrington withdrew up the Thames, where he became the first to proclaim the strategic concept of maintaining a "fleet in being," thus safeguarding England against invasion. Torrington was court-martialed for lack of aggressiveness but acquitted. Meanwhile, Tourville threw away his opportunity for an even greater victory by failing to pursue vigorously. Two years later he would pay a heavy price for his sluggish actions at Beachy Head. *See* Bantry Bay; Fleurus II; La Hogue; Grand Alliance, War of the.

Bear Paw Mountains (Nez Percé War), 1877. When the United States attempted to move the southern Nez Percé Indians from their reservation in northeastern Oregon, Chief Joseph took the entire tribe into the mountains of northern Idaho. General Oliver Howard sent troops to round up the Indians. Although a total of 2,000 troops became actually engaged against him, Joseph, with 300 warriors, fought one of the longest and most skillful delaying actions in history. On June 17, 1877, he repulsed an attack in White Bird Canyon, inflicting 40 casualties on a 100-man force commanded by Capt. David Perry. Again on July 11 and 12 he beat back an attack by Howard on the Clearwater River. Joseph then crossed the Bitter Root Mountains eastward into Montana. At Big Hole River on August 9 he was surprised by a column under Col. John Gibbon. Joseph lost 89 killed (including women and children) but escaped a third time. Gibbon suffered 31 killed and 38 wounded.

Swinging southward into Wyoming, Joseph suddenly doubled back into Montana, heading for the Canadian border. At Canyon Creek he turned, on September 13, to repulse an attack directed by Col. Samuel Sturgis. But now a new force entered the field. From Fort Keogh, Wyo., Gen. Nelson Miles marched 267 miles northward in 12 days to intercept the fleeing Indians. On September 30 Miles closed in on Joseph in the Bear Paw Mountains of Montana, only 30 miles from the border. The doughty chief held out for five more days before finally surrendering to Howard himself. During the rugged 2,000-mile retreat of the entire tribe, Joseph lost a total of 239 men, women, and children. He inflicted 266 casualties on the pursuing troops. The Nez Percé war was over. Only one major Indian battle remained to be fought in the American West. *See* Wolf Mountain; Wounded Knee Creek; Indian Wars in the United States.

Beaugé (Hundred Years' War), 1421. Ignoring the 1420 Treaty of Troyes, a combined Orleanist French and Scottish force began raiding English holdings in southern Normandy and Maine. The brother of Henry V, Thomas, duke of Clarence, set off in pursuit with an English army. Outdistancing his infantry, Clarence's cavalry caught up with the raiders. But the latter, commanded by the Earl of Buchan (John Stewart, later constable of France), turned and gave battle on March 21, 1421. The English cavalry was surrounded at Beaugé in Anjou and cut to pieces. Clarence lay among the slain. Although the infantry arrived later to drive the French from the field, the battle of Beaugé stands as one of the few defeats handed the English in the Hundred Years' War. *See* Rouen II; Cravant; Hundred Years' War.

Beauséjour (French and Indian War), 1755. The British and their American colonists launched three widely separated operations against the French and their Indian allies in 1755. The first striking column to go into action was a force of 2,000 New Englanders and a few British regulars, under the command of Lt. Col. Robert Monckton, assisted by Lt. Col. John Winslow. Carried in English ships to New Brunswick, the army seized Saint John at the mouth of the Saint John River and then attacked the French fort of Beauséjour on the southeastern coast. After only a few days resistance the garrison surrendered on June 19. By the end of the month all the Bay of Fundy area lay under British control. However the New York column failed to take its objective, and in Pennsylvania the British offensive met disaster. *See* Fort Necessity; Monongahela River; George, Lake; French and Indian War.

Beda Fomm (World War II), 1941. After taking Tobruk, Gen. Sir Richard O'Connor continued the first British offensive in Libya. The goal of the British XIII Corps was Benghazi, 240 miles to the west. While the 6th Australian Infantry moved west along the Mediterranean coast road, the 7th Armoured raced southwest through the inland desert. On February 5 the armor reached the coast at Beda Fomm, well beyond Benghazi, blocking the retreat into Tripoli of Marshal Rodolpho Graziani's Italian Tenth Army. After two days of futile effort to break through the British defenses, the entire Italian army of 20,000 men surrendered. British casualties were 9 killed and 15 wounded. The important port of Benghazi had fallen at equally small cost to the British, who now halted at El Agheila.

O'Connor's victory at Beda Fomm concluded the first British offensive in North Africa, a ten-week, 500-mile drive that annihilated the Italian Tenth Army of 130,000 men, 400 tanks, and 1,290 guns. Total British casualties were 1,744 killed, wounded, and missing. At this point the tide of war changed drastically in Africa. The British XIII

Corps was stripped to send aid to Greece, and the German general Erwin Rommel was sent to Tripoli at the head of the newly formed Afrika Korps. O'Connor himself was captured by Rommel's troops two months later in an Axis offensive that retook all of Cyrenaica except Tobruk with comparative ease. *See* Tobruk I; Salûm–Halfaya Pass; Tobruk II; World War II.

Bedford (First Barons' War of England), 1224. The last battle of the First Barons' War came seven years after the peace treaty had been signed at Kingston-on-Thames. One of the strongest captains who had fought on the royalist side, Fawkes de Bréauté, refused to yield to government control and order. In 1224 he was outlawed. His brother William retaliated by imprisoning a royal justice in Bedford Castle, 48 miles northwest of London. Young Henry III's stern justiciar, Hubert de Burgh (later earl of Kent), marched against Bedford and took it under siege. After two months Bedford surrendered, on August 14, when the castle was successfully mined. William and 23 surviving knights were hanged in front of the castle walls on the following day. Fawkes was permitted to go into exile. *See* Sandwich I; Bytham; Saintes; Barons' Wars.

Bedriacum (Civil Wars of the Roman Empire), A.D. 69. Nero's highhanded reign finally brought his downfall as emperor of Rome in June A.D. 68. The new ruler, Servius Sulpicius Galba, won the throne through the strength of his Spanish legions. But the German legions had another candidate for emperor, and early in January 69 they proclaimed Aulus Vitellius the legitimate successor to Nero. This action was enough to overthrow Galba. He was murdered on January 15 and replaced by Marcus Salvius Otho. While Otho hesitated, hoping for a peaceful solution, Vitellius sent two armies through the Alpine passes into northwest Italy, under Alienus Caecina and Fabius Valens. These two forces, composed largely of German and Gallic auxiliaries, debouched into the upper valley of the Po.

Otho hurried northward. Whereas once he had delayed too long, now he launched an attack before all his troops were assembled. At Bedriacum, outside Cremona, his advance column encountered the Vitellians on April 19. The emperor's legions were checked and fell back. Although this defeat was far from decisive, Otho committed suicide. The leaderless imperial forces then swore fidelity to Vitellius, and the Roman senate hastily proclaimed him emperor. But the new ruler had no better luck than his two predecessors in that strife-torn year of 69. The legions of the East—Judea, Syria, Egypt—had their own candidate for emperor, Titus Flavius Vespasian. *See* Jotapata; Cremona I; Roman Empire.

Beecher Island (Cheyenne and Arapahoe War), 1868. In September 1868 during the savage Indian warfare of the 1860's in the Great Plains, Col. George Forsyth marched into Colorado from Fort Wallace, Kans., at the head of a picked force of 50 men. On the night of September 16 the group camped along the Arickaree fork of the Republican River. At dawn, Forsyth's force was attacked by some 750 Cheyennes, Arapahoes, and Sioux. The frontiersmen retreated to a small island in the dry bed of the river, while the Indians opened a steady fire and attacked in waves. In the afternoon the Cheyenne chief, Roman Nose, arrived to lead a new charge. But this too was beaten back by the deadly sharpshooting of the repeating rifles in the hands of the frontiersmen. By nightfall Roman Nose was slain. Forsyth had suffered 7 killed and 17 wounded. One of the dead was his second-in-command, Lt. Frederick Beecher, for whom the island was later named.

The Indians then settled down to a siege. Forsyth sent two men back to Fort Wallace for help. Two troops of the 10th Cavalry raised the siege on the ninth day. The survivors were nearly dead from starvation and exhaustion. *See* Fort Phil Kearny; Washita River; Indian Wars in the United States.

Belgrade I (Invasion by Ottoman Turks), 1456. After his capture of Constantinople in 1453, Mohammed II, the Conqueror, marched his Ottoman Turks into the Balkans. Southern Serbia fell under his control. On the Danube, Belgrade was taken under siege in 1456. The city seemed doomed, but János Hunyadi, veteran of many battles against the Turks, led a Hungarian army to the relief of Belgrade. In a battle outside the city's walls, Hunyadi routed the Turkish invaders, who were then forced to raise the siege. It was the Hungarian's greatest victory. Hunyadi died soon afterward, and the stout defense of Belgrade proved to be only a temporary check to the Turkish conquest of southeastern Europe. *See* Constantinople VII; Negroponte.

Belgrade II (Turkish Conquests of Balkans), 1521. When Suleiman I, the Magnificent (or the Lawgiver, in Turkey), replaced his father, Selim I, as sultan of the Ottoman Turks in 1520, Europe found itself in new trouble. The Ottomans' northwestward route of aggression, blocked by János Hunyadi at Belgrade in 1456, was resumed. With a disciplined army of Janizaries and powerful artillery, Suleiman again marched on Belgrade, key Christian bastion in the Balkans at the junction of the Danube and Save rivers. Now there was no Hunyadi to rally the Hungarians of Louis II and other Westerners. After blasting gaps in the fortifications with mines, the Turks stormed into the undermanned city in 1521. The fall of Belgrade opened Hungary, Austria, and even Germany to Turkish raiding parties. But Suleiman would spend the next five years concentrating on building up his sea power. *See* Rhodes; Mohács.

Belleau Wood (World War I), 1918. Early in June the third German offensive of 1918 bogged down northeast of Paris, ending the battle of Aisne River III. At their deepest penetration the troops of Gen. Erich Ludendorff held Vaux on the vital Metz–Paris road and Belleau Wood, just to the northwest. To drive the Germans out of Belleau Wood, the American commander, Gen. John Pershing, sent the 2nd Division (Omar Bundy) forward in a counterattack on June 6. The major burden of the attack fell to the marine brigade of Gen. James Harbord, assisted by the 3rd Infantry Brigade of Gen. Edward Lewis. Day after day the Americans slugged their way through Belleau Wood against four German divisions. The mile-square, forested area was not cleared until July 1; Vaux was recaptured the same day. The first large-scale battle fought by American soldiers in the war cost the 2nd Division 9,777 casualties, including 1,811 killed. More than 1,600 Germans were taken prisoner. *See* Aisne River III; Noyon-Montdidier; World War I.

Belmont (American Civil War), 1861. The narrow Confederate victory at Wilson's Creek in August left much of Missouri under Southern domination. Across the Mississippi River in western Kentucky, Gen. Leonidas Polk held Columbus for the South. From Cairo, Ill., at the mouth of the Ohio River, the Federal general U. S. Grant made small spoiling attacks down both banks of the Mississippi early in November. Grant himself took 3,114 men in transports 12 miles down the river. On November 7 he landed three miles above Belmont, Mo., and marched on the Confederate camp, held by elements of Gen. Sterling Price's command. Fighting through thick woods, the Federals drove the Southerners to the river's edge where the latter came under the protection of the Confederate guns across the Mississippi. Polk now sent 10,000 troops to the west bank, hoping to cut the Federals off from their transports. But Grant fought free and successfully re-embarked for Cairo. He had suffered 607 casualties. It was the first battle in Grant's climb to commander in chief of the Union armies. Of the 4,000 Confederates actually engaged, 642 were lost. *See* Wilson's Creek; Fort Henry; American Civil War.

Bemis Heights (War of the American Revolution). The second battle of Saratoga, on October 7, 1777; an American victory which led directly to the surrender of Gen. John Burgoyne ten days later. *See* Saratoga.

Benevento (French Invasion of Italy), 1266. During the civil turmoil in Italy in the thirteenth century, Manfred, the illegitimate son of Holy Roman Emperor Frederich II, made himself king of the Two Sicilies. The papacy asked for help from the French. Charles I of Anjou, brother of Saint Louis IX, went to southern Italy at the head of a French army. At Benevento on February 26, 1266, he defeated the forces of Manfred, who was killed in the battle. Charles then proclaimed himself king of Naples and Sicily. *See* Cortenuova; Tagliacozzo.

Beneventum (Rise of Rome), 275 B.C. After an indifferent four-year campaign in Sicily, King Pyrrhus of Epirus returned to Italy to aid Tarentum in its struggle against Rome. Remembering his two notable victories in 280 and 279, thousands of Samnites, Bruttians, Lucanians, Sabines, and Italiotes joined his Epirot ranks. At the Samnium town of Beneventum, 130 miles southeast of Rome, the Roman commander, Manius Curius Dentatus, took up a strong position and awaited the coalition's attack.

Pyrrhus opened the battle with a night attack against the Roman camp. But the well-trained legionaries sprang to arms quickly and drove off the attackers with considerable losses, including eight elephants. Encouraged by this success, Dentatus resolved to strike at Pyrrhus' position on a nearby plain. The first legion attack crumpled in the face of stubborn Epirot resistance, aided in

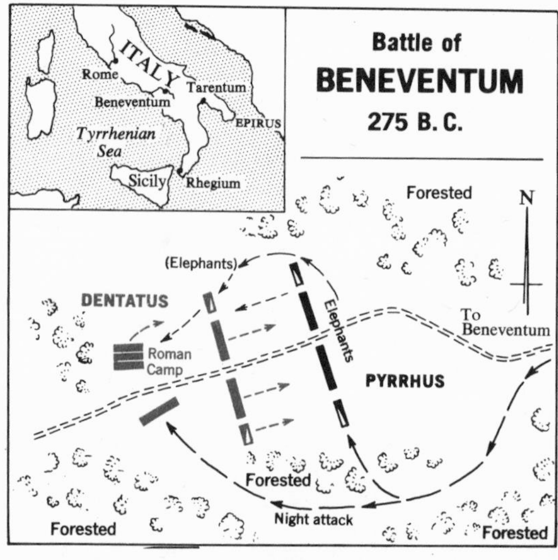

part by elephants. In a second effort, however, the Romans managed to stampede the elephants back through the lines of the enemy. A follow-up attack against the disordered Greek phalanx put a sudden end to the battle, with the invaders fleeing the field.

The Roman victory at Beneventum ended Pyrrhus' invasion of Italy. He soon returned to Greece (where he was killed three years later), leaving the Italiotes without a strong leader to oppose Rome. In 272 Roman troops seized Tarentum and destroyed its defenses. Two years later the subjugation of southern Italy was completed with the capture of Rhegium, on the toe of the peninsula. The republic of Rome now stood master of all Italy from the Rubicon (Fiumicino) River at Rimini to the Strait of Messina, across from Sicily. *See* Asculum I; Messina I; Roman Republic.

Bennington (War of the American Revolution), 1777. While the British expedition of Gen. John Burgoyne pushed laboriously southward from Canada through the wilderness to the upper Hudson, the other two prongs of the planned multiple offensive against Albany failed to come to his aid. (Colonel Barry St. Leger was unsuccessfully besieging Fort Stanwix in western New York State; Gen. Sir William Howe had left New York City, but instead of moving northward, he sailed against Philadelphia.) Burgoyne plowed doggedly forward during the summer of 1777 but often moved no more than one mile a day. Supplies grew short. Finally, on August 11, Lt. Col. Friedrich Baum was sent southeast with 800 men, chiefly Germans, to raid the American supply depot at Bennington, Vt. Here the militia general John Stark had collected a volunteer force of 2,000 New England riflemen. Stark moved west of the town to meet the invaders. On August 16 the militiamen encircled Baum's position on a hill overlooking the Walloomsac River. In a sharp fight Baum was mortally wounded and his army shattered.

A second German column of 642 men, sent out by Burgoyne, arrived at the moment of the American victory. Led by Lt. Col. Heinrich Breymann, the newcomers seriously threatened the disorganized militia. But just before sunset 330 American reinforcements, under the command of Lt. Col. Seth Warner, marched up to check and then drive back the mercenaries. Breymann, with a loss of a third of his force, withdrew to the main British position along the Hudson. In the long day's fighting 207 Germans were killed and 700 captured (plus four brass fieldpieces). American losses were 30 killed and 40 wounded. With this defeat Burgoyne's position became even more desperate. *See* Ticonderoga III; Fort Stanwix; Saratoga; American Revolution.

Bentonville (American Civil War), 1865. The Federal march to the sea and subsequent occupation of Savannah, Ga., on December 21, 1864, had again split the Confederacy in two. After refitting his 60,000-man army, Gen. William Sherman began moving northward through the Carolinas on February 1, 1865. As on the march from Atlanta, the army was divided into two wings: Gen. Oliver Howard commanded the right (Army of the Tennessee), Gen. Henry Slocum the left (Army of Georgia). On February 16 Sherman reached Columbia, S.C., which was more than half burned the following day (probably by accident). As the Federals moved into North Carolina, Gen. Joseph Johnston at Raleigh collected all available Confederate forces to check Sherman. When Slocum's left wing reached Bentonville, Johnston blocked his route with about 17,000 men on March 19. In a day of inconclusive fighting both sides held their ground. Two days later Sherman began moving up his other wing, plus the forces of Gens. John Schofield and Alfred Terry, which had marched inland from the coast to Goldsboro. Faced with overwhelming numbers, Johnston withdrew. He had lost 2,600 men. Federal casualties numbered 1,646.

Sherman then paused to organize his forces for a march into Virginia to link up with the Federal commander in chief, Gen. U. S. Grant. But when Johnston heard of the surrender of Gen. Robert E. Lee's Confederate army at Appomattox, he too capitulated, on April 18. Except for minor actions in Alabama and west of the Mississippi River, the bitter four-year war was over. *See* Savannah III; Appomattox River; American Civil War.

Beresteczko (Polish-Cossack War), 1651. Under the leadership of Cossack hetman Bogdan Chmielnicki, the Ukraine had won a semi-independent status by the mid-seventeenth century. In 1651, however, the Polish king, John II Casimir, assembled a large army to deal with the Cossacks. On July 1 the Poles met an equally large force under Chmielnicki at Beresteczko, about 30 miles south of Lutsk, in northwestern Ukrainia. In a savage battle the Poles swept the field. The shattered Cossacks then allied themselves with Czar Alexis of Russia, ending Ukrainian hopes for independence. After long years of intermittent fighting, Poland ceded the eastern Ukraine and Smolensk to Russia in 1667.

Berezina River (Napoleonic Empire Wars), 1812. The retreat of the French army from Moscow, begun on October 19, 1812, soon became a nightmare of hardship and terror for the troops of Napoleon I. Desperately short of supplies and hounded by Russian hit-and-run attacks on both flanks and in the rear, the Grande Armée suffered cruelly. Forced by Russian resistance to take the northern route, the French ran into the first snow on November 4 and bitter cold weather thereafter. On November 9 the retreating column straggled into Smolensk. Ten days later Napoleon reached Orsha, 70 miles to the west, with only 25,000 effectives. Eighty miles farther west he found the Russians holding the bridge over the Berezina River at Borisov. On November 26 the II Corps of Marshal Nicolas Oudinot forced a crossing at Studenka, eight miles to the north. Deceiving the Russians west of the river until the last minute and then fighting off sporadic attacks, Napoleon moved most of his army across at Studenka on November 27 and 28. Claude Victor's IX Corps held the temporary bridges open during the third night, throwing back a last attack by the Prince of Sayn-Wittgenstein-Ludwigsburg, who came up too late to block the crossing. Although the great bulk of Napoleon's effectives crossed the Berezina, some 10,000 stragglers had to be abandoned on the east bank when the bridges were burned early on November 29.

Ploughing doggedly forward, the French army reached Vilna on December 9 (Napoleon had left for Paris four days before) and the Niemen River on December 13. Here the crossing was made over the solidly frozen stream, with Marshal Michel Ney reportedly the last French soldier to leave Russian soil. Field Marshal Mikhail Kutuzov, the Russian commander, whose troops suffered as much from the sub-zero weather as did his quarry, abandoned the pursuit here. In all, he had lost 250,000 men, plus an unknown number of Cossack irregulars. French losses during the most disastrous retreat in history exceeded 400,000 men, 1,000 cannon, and 175,000 horses.

During the French agony Napoleon had received scant help from the allies on his flanks—the Prussians on the north under Gen. Count Hans Yorck (York) von Wartenburg and the Austrians on the south commanded by Prince Karl von Schwarzenberg. This double defection foretold more trouble for France the following year. *See* Maloyaroslavets; Lützen II; Napoleonic Empire Wars.

Bergen (Seven Years' War), 1759. Bouncing back from their 1758 defeat at Crefeld, the French recrossed the Rhine the following spring. Under Victor François, duc de Broglie, the army of Louis XV moved up the Main Valley to occupy Bergen, 10 miles northeast of Frankfurt. To block this latest advance against Prussia, the field marshal Ferdinand, duke of Brunswick, the victor of Crefeld and the western commander of Frederick II, the Great, moved up with a force of almost 40,000 Germans. On April 13 Ferdinand attacked the French garrison in Bergen. He received a sharp repulse. Forced to fall back, the Prussian general retreated northward to the Weser River. The French followed on a broad front. *See* Crefeld; Minden II; Seven Years' War.

Bergen op Zoom I (War of the Austrian Succession), 1747. Before the British-Dutch-Austrian allies could recover from their defeat at Lauffeld, they found the French besieging the port of Bergen op Zoom on the Schelde estuary at the other (western) end of the Netherlands. A French column, which Marshal Comte Maurice de Saxe had sent out from Lauffeld under Count Ulrich von Löwendal, reached the city on July 15. The English-Dutch garrison resisted stubbornly, inflicting heavy casualties by making vigorous sorties. However, on September 18 the French made a sudden assault that gained a lodgment inside the walls, and the city surrendered. Löwendal now marched back eastward to rejoin Saxe. *See* Lauffeld; Maastricht III; Austrian Succession, War of the.

Bergen op Zoom II (Wars of the French Revolution), 1799. The multiple offensive launched by the Second Coalition in 1799 drove back the armies of the French Directory in Germany, Switzerland, and Italy. To keep up the pressure against France, another front was opened in the Netherlands by Great Britain (George III) and Russia (Paul I). Here, Frederick Augustus, duke of York and Albany, second son of George III, commanded a British army, which in alliance with a Russian force gave the allies some 35,000 men. A French army of comparable size under Gen. Dominique Vandamme moved to repel the invading force in the southern Netherlands. Near Bergen op Zoom on September 19 Vandamme launched a fierce attack that broke the Russian army posted on one allied flank. Although the British held their ground, the collapse of the Russians forced the Duke of York and Albany to retreat to the north. French casualties totaled 3,000. The British lost only 500, but the Russians lost 3,500, plus most of their artillery. *See* Stokach I; Zurich II; Novi Ligure; Alkmaar II; French Revolution Wars.

Berlin (World War II), 1945. By the spring of 1945 three great Russian army groups had closed to the Oder-Neisse river line, less than 50 miles from Berlin. The greatest threat to the German capital stood at Küstrin (Kostrzyn), where Marshal Georgi Zhukov had ordered the First White Russian Army Group (Vassili Sokolovski) to seize a bridgehead west of the Oder. On April 16, preceded by a devastating air and artillery bombardment, Russian tanks roared out of the bridgehead and headed for Berlin. Simultaneous Russian attacks to the north and south protected Zhukov's flanks and shattered German defenses along the central Oder, commanded by Gen. Gotthard Heinrici.

On April 20 armored spearheads plunged into the eastern suburbs of Berlin. While one of Sokolovski's tank columns swept around north of the city, an armored thrust from the south came from Marshal Ivan Konev's First Ukrainian Army Group. These two arms closed a pincers west of Berlin on April 25. (Meanwhile, north of Zhukov's thrust, the third army group—the Second White Russian of Konstantin Rokossovski—plunged westward to the lower Elbe River.)

Zhukov's forces now hammered their way into the city, leaving a vast sea of rubble in their wake. Russian troops took Tempelhof airfield on April 26 and advanced methodically into the heart of the city—Unter den Linden and the Tiergarten. Some German units fought fanatically street-by-street and building-by-building. But their defenses proved futile and only added to the fiery destruction of the city. On May 1 the Russians captured the Reichstag building. The previous day, Adolf Hitler had taken his own life in his Berlin headquarters bunker. Finally, on May 2, the ranking German officer left in the city, Gen. Kurt Weidling, surrendered the 135,000 remaining Nazi defenders of Berlin. The Russians had captured their biggest prize of the war. *See* Germany, East; Germany, West; World War II.

Berwick upon Tweed (English-Scottish Wars), 1296. When Edward I arbitrated the dispute over the Scottish crown in favor of John de Baliol in 1292, many Scots nobles resented the English intrusion in their affairs. Three years later the nobles took Scotland into an alliance with France, then at war with England. The English king judged this to be a hostile action that called for retaliation. He marched an army northward toward Berwick on the Tweed River at the border between the two nations. The Scots hurriedly threw up defensive works, but Edward's army stormed into the city on March 28. Employing calculated terror as an instrument of national policy, the English slaughtered thousands. Berwick was thoroughly sacked, reducing it from an important commercial center to a minor seaport within a few hours. The city was then fortified and made into an English military base. *See* Radnor; Dunbar I.

Bezetha (Jewish Wars of the Roman Empire), A.D. 66. During the last years of Emperor Nero's reign, mismanagement by Roman officials, coupled with the terrorist activities of the Zealots, brought bloody anarchy to Judea. In September 66 the Roman garrison of Jerusalem was overpowered and butchered. Cestius Gallus, governor of Syria, led an army into Jerusalem but could not take the Temple, which was held by a rebel force. Unable to obtain supplies in the hostile city, Gallus began a withdrawal. In the northern suburb of Bezetha (Bezatha) his column was attacked by a strong force of Jewish revolutionaries. The Romans lost 6,000 men, all their baggage, and their siege train. This defeat forced Gallus to fall back into Syria. Nero then ordered Titus Flavius Vespasian, an obscure senator, to put down the Jewish uprising. *See* Jotapata; Roman Empire.

Biak Island (World War II). Part of the battle of New Guinea; the island was taken from the Japanese by Allied troops during May 27–June 20, 1944. *See* New Guinea.

Bibracte (Gallic Wars), 58 B.C. In 60 B.C. Rome came under the firm control of the First Triumvirate—Julius Caesar, Marcus Licinius Crassus, Pompey the Great. Caesar then marched an army across the Alps into modern France (his assigned sphere of action), where a conquest of the Gauls would bring personal riches and an enviable military reputation. At Bibracte (Autun, in east-central France) he encountered a large force of Helvetii who were trying to migrate westward from Switzerland. Caesar posted his six legions on high ground, where they fought off the Helvetii for several hours. Superior discipline and heavier armament enabled the legionaries to rout their more numerous opponents by nightfall. Pressing forward, Caesar's troops captured the enemy's transport (carts) and their camp. The Helvetii surrendered to Roman domination, while Caesar moved northward. *See* Vesontio; Gallic Wars.

Big Bethel (American Civil War), 1861. At the outbreak of the Civil War, Federal troops under Gen. Benjamin Butler held Fort Monroe at the entrance to Hampton Roads in southeastern Virginia. On June 10 Butler sent 4,400 men to attack the Confederate outpost at Big Bethel, ten miles to the northwest. Anticipating the Federal advance, Col. John Magruder, Confederate commander on the peninsula (between the York and James rivers), ordered Col. Daniel Hill to counterattack with 1,400 Southern troops. In a poorly managed battle Hill's men forced the Federals to fall back to Fort Monroe with 76 casualties. Confederate losses were 11. This action would soon be overshadowed by a major battle in northern Virginia. *See* Philippi, W. Va.; Bull Run I; American Civil War.

Big Black River (American Civil War). The last attempt by Gen. John Pemberton to prevent his Confederate army from being bottled up in Vicksburg by Gen. U. S. Grant's Federal army, on May 17, 1863. *See* Vicksburg.

Bilbao (Spanish Civil War), 1937. Checked in his drive to capture Madrid, Nationalist generalissimo Francisco Franco ordered an attack in the north against the Basque stronghold of Bilbao. On March 31 Gen. Emilio Mola launched an offensive northwest toward Bilbao with 50,000 Nationalist troops. The Basque commander, Gen. Francisco Llano de la Encomienda, who had some 40,000 poorly armed men, was forced to give ground steadily. He yielded Durango and Guernica on April 28 after both towns had suffered terribly from Nationalist air attacks. During the 11-week offensive Mola died in an airplane crash, on June 3, and was succeeded by Gen. Fidel Dávila, who continued to press the attack. By June 11 the Nationalists had reached the so-called Ring of Iron defenses guarding Bilbao. Under cover of a heavy artillery bombardment, the Nationalists penetrated the Basque lines the following day. The Ring of Iron now crumbled. Civilians were evacuated to the west on the night of June 13–14. Five nights later the survivors of the Basque army, now led by Gen. Mariano Gamir Ulíbarri, abandoned their capital. Nationalist troops entered the city on June 19. The Basque independence movement, which had been aligned with the Republicans, collapsed. *See* Madrid; Santander; Spanish Civil War.

"Bismarck" (World War II), 1941. At the height of the battle of the Atlantic the 45,000-ton German battleship *Bismarck,* commanded by Adm. Lutjens, slipped into the North Atlantic to prey on Allied shipping. The most powerful ship in commission, it was the first to have radar-controlled guns for use in night firing. Located by British scout planes off the coast of Greenland, the pride of the German fleet was attacked early on May 24 by a Royal Navy squadron with four capital ships. Within minutes the eight 15-inch guns of the *Bismarck* sank the battle cruiser *Hood* (only 3 of 1,500 seamen survived) and severely damaged the battleship *Prince of Wales.* But the Royal Navy kept the German dreadnought under surveillance during a 2,500-mile chase to the southeast.

Meanwhile, Adm. Sir John Tovey, commander of the British Home Fleet, was converging all naval strength possible in the North Atlantic. On the fourth day, the *Bismarck* was cornered and attacked 400 miles from Brest by the battleships *King George V* and *Rodney,* the cruisers *Norfolk* and *Dorsetshire,* and torpedo-bombers from the carrier *Ark Royal.* A torpedo attack by the *Rodney* was the first example in history of one battleship torpedoing another. The crashing rain of shells and torpedoes gradually silenced the German guns. On May 27 at 10:40 A.M., torpedoes from the *Dorsetshire* made the kill. Almost 2,000 German seamen, including Lutjens, perished with their ship. *See* Atlantic Ocean II; World War II.

Bismarck Sea (World War II), 1943. After the Allied victory in Papua in eastern New Guinea, Japan tried to reinforce its garrison at Lae and Salamaua on the Huon Gulf. A 16-ship convoy steaming west from Rabaul, New Britain, was located in the Bismarck Sea by the U.S. Fifth Air Force (George Kenney) and the Royal Australian Air Force. In a four-day aerial onslaught on March 2–5 Allied planes sank four destroyers and all eight transports. American PT boats joined in the attack on the surface. Less than 1,000 of the 7,000-man Japanese force reached New Guinea. Thereafter Japan limited traffic in the Bismarck Sea to small, nighttime operations. *See* New Guinea; Rabaul; World War II.

Bladensburg (War of 1812), 1814. The centermost of the three British offensives against the United States in 1814 was an expeditionary force sent against the East Coast. Planned as a diversion in support of the thrust into New York from Canada, this force also had the mission of retaliating for the American burning of York (Toronto) in the previous April. A British fleet under Adm. (later Sir) George Cockburn sailed up Chesapeake Bay to the mouth of the Patuxent River in Maryland on August 19. (The American commodore Joshua Barney quickly blew up his flotilla of gunboats on the river to prevent their seizure by the British.) At Benedict the fleet landed 4,000 troops, many of them veterans of the Peninsular Campaign in the Napoleonic wars, under Gen. Robert Ross. Finding no opposition, Ross marched northward to Washington, D.C. Here the incompetent Gen. William H. Winder (who had been captured earlier at Stoney Creek and then exchanged) hastily organized a mixed force of about 6,000 men, all militia except for a few hundred regulars and Barney's 400 seamen. On August 24 he marched seven miles northeast to block the British route to Washington at Bladensburg. At the first British attack the American army fled. Only Barney's sailors and marines fought well in a futile rear-guard action. Total American casualties were 26 killed, 51 wounded. The British suffered 64 killed and 185 wounded.

With the city's only defenders hopelessly scattered, President James Madison and other government officials fled across the Potomac River into Virginia. Detachments from the British army entered Washington and set fire to the Capitol, White House, and other public buildings (except the Patent Office) and some private buildings. On the following day the invaders returned to their transports on the Patuxent and sailed toward Baltimore. *See* Champlain, Lake; Fort McHenry; New Orleans I; War of 1812.

Blenheim (War of the Spanish Succession), 1704. The Duke of Marlborough's invasion of Bavaria had interposed the allied army between Vienna and the French along the upper Danube. After winning the battle of Donauwörth on July 2, the duke (John Churchill) passed over to the right bank to threaten Augsburg, but when he found the French concentrating north of the river he recrossed to that side. Here he was joined by the Holy Roman Empire army of Prince Eugene of Savoy. Marlborough, determined to fight a decisive battle, sent the reluctant Louis William I, margrave of Baden-Baden, eastward to besiege Ingolstadt. He then deployed his 52,000 men along the small Nebel River, which flows southward into the Danube. Marlborough himself commanded the center, Gen. Lord John Cutts the left (nearest the river), and Prince Eugene, with cavalry and Prussian infantry, the right. Opposing the allies were two French armies totaling almost 60,000 men—Marshal Comte Ferdinand de Marsin, with Maximilian II Emanuel, elector of Bavaria, held the left, while Marshal Comte Camille de Tallard commanded the right, which was anchored in the village of Blenheim, three miles downriver from Höchstädt (scene of a battle the year before).

Marlborough opened the battle early on August 13 by sending Cutts against Tallard's Blenheim position. Two fierce assaults were thrown back by the French. Meanwhile Eugene was heavily engaged on the right wing. The British-Austrian allies seemed stopped all along the line, but the French center had been weakened by the sending of support to both flanks. Here, late in the after-

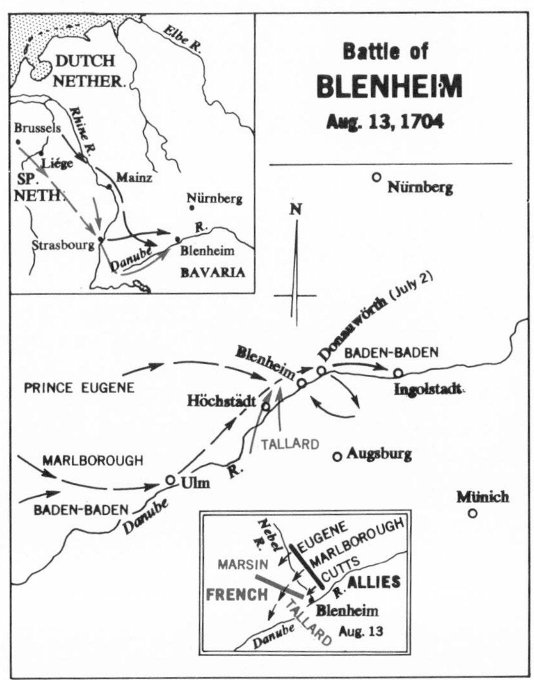

noon, Marlborough concentrated a powerful 8,000-man cavalry force. Storming across the Nebel, the allied cavalry struck and routed the French horsemen in the center. Then, wheeling left, the duke drove thousands of enemy horse and infantry to their death in the Danube. This maneuver split the French in two and trapped the great mass of enemy infantry in Blenheim. At the same time Eugene, on the right, swept forward, scattering the French to his front. The allied victory was complete. Some 13,000 Franco-Bavarians, including the bulk of the French infantry in Blenheim, surrendered. Tallard himself became a prisoner of war. Another 15,000 of the vanquished were killed, wounded, or drowned. Marlborough's losses were 12,000.

The battle of Blenheim saved Vienna, knocked Bavaria out of the war, and drove the French survivors back to the Rhine. It ranks as one of the decisive battles of history. *See* Donauwörth; Cassano d'Adda I; Ramillies; Spanish Succession, War of the.

Bloemfontein (South African War II), 1900. The British victory at Paardeberg on February 27 opened the way for an all-out offensive against the Boers in the Orange Free State. General Lord Frederick Roberts, now heavily reinforced, marched on Bloemfontein, capital of the hostile state, from the west. On March 31 Roberts' troops stormed into the city. Driving the remaining Boer forces in front of them, the British turned north. They arrived at Kroonstad on May 12. Twelve days later the Orange Free State, resistance crushed, was annexed by Great Britain. *See* Paardeberg; Johannesburg; South African Wars.

Blood River (Boer-Zulu War), 1838. Frustrated by British rule in the Cape Colony, about 10,000 Boer (Dutch) farmers and cattlemen made the Great Trek to the north and east of the Orange River during 1835–37. In Natal the immigrants came into conflict with the Zulus, led by Dingaan. On February 6, 1838, Zulu tribesmen massacred the Boer leader Piet Retief and 60 followers in Natal and pushed on eastward to destroy the coastal city of Durban. On December 16, 500 Boers under Andries Pretorius made a stand along the Blood River, repulsing attacks by 10,000 Zulus under Dingaan. Some 3,000 Zulus were killed. (This victory is commemorated in the national holiday of Dingaan's Day, or the Day of the Covenant, December 16, in South Africa.) The Boers founded the Natal Republic around the town of Pietermaritzburg the following year. In 1840 Dingaan was overthrown by his brother Umpanda, with Boer help. *See* Boomplaats.

Bloody Week. *See* Paris III.

Blore Heath (Wars of the Roses), 1459. The rebel Yorkist victory at Saint Albans led to four years of uneasy peace between King Henry VI's house of Lancaster (red rose) and the forces of Richard of York (white rose). But fighting broke out again in 1459 in western England at Blore Heath, Staffordshire. A group of Yorkist knights under the Earl of Salisbury fought a pitched battle with royalist men-at-arms. The rebels inflicted a stinging defeat on Henry's troops on September 22. Salisbury then marched on south to join up with Richard's main body. *See* Saint Albans I; Ludford; Roses, Wars of the.

Blue Licks (Indian Wars in the United States), 1782. A mixed force of 240 hostile Indians and Canadians raided southward across the Ohio River to attack Bryan's Station, a small fort near present-day Lexington, Ky., on August 15, 1782. Failing to take the fort, the raiders, who were commanded by Simon Girty, withdrew on August 18. Hoping to entice the militia into following, the Indians left a well-marked route of retreat. A force of 182 hastily assembled militia set off in pursuit. On the morning of August 19 the pioneers overtook the Indians at Blue Licks, on the right bank of the Licking River, 40 miles northeast of Lexington. Their commander, Col. Daniel Boone, wanted to wait for reinforcements. But Maj. Hugh McGary and other leaders led a charge straight into an ambush. About 70 of the militia were killed; another 20 were captured or seriously wounded. Although Girty's force suffered only 7 killed and 10 wounded, it withdrew across the Ohio River. This was the last Indian battle within the borders of the present state of Kentucky. *See* Point Pleasant; Indian Wars in the United States.

Boer Wars. Two conflicts (1880–1881, 1899–1902) between the British in South Africa and the descendants of Dutch settlers, called Boers. *See* South African Wars I and II.

Boer-Zulu War. *See* Blood River.

Bolivia. *See* Latin America.

Bomarsund (Crimean War), 1854. As their first action upon entering the Crimean War, Great Britain and France sent a joint expedition into the Baltic Sea. On August 16 the allied fleet under Adm. Sir Charles Napier bombarded the Russian-held fort of Bomarsund on Ahvenanmaa Island in the Gulf of Bothnia. A landing force of chiefly French soldiers seized the fort the same day. Here the offensive bogged down, however, as did a second expedition sent to the Baltic the following year. Thereafter, allied efforts were concentrated against Sevastopol in the Crimea. *See* Silistra; Alma River; Crimean War.

Boomplaats (Orange Free State War), 1848. The British Cape Colony, which had annexed Natal in 1844, claimed the territory to the west, between the Orange and Vaal rivers, four years later. Led by Andries Pretorius, the Boers in the area revolted. On August 29 Pretorius and 1,000 rebels were defeated at Boomplaats by a British force of similar size under Gen. Sir Harry Smith. Total casualties were less than 100. Great Britain set up the Orange River Sovereignty. But in 1854 the British withdrew south of the Orange River, allowing the Boers to establish the Orange Free State. *See* Blood River; Laing's Nek.

Borneo (World War II). As part of the Allied campaign to liberate the Philippine Islands, an Australian force began the invasion of Japanese-held Borneo on June 10, 1945. *See* Southern Philippines–Borneo.

Bornhöved (Wars of Scandinavia), 1227. The conquests of the Danish king Waldemar II, the Victorious, made him the most powerful ruler in northern Europe early in the thirteenth century. In 1227, however, the German province of Dithmarschen, in Schleswig-Holstein, rebelled. The royal army was severely beaten at Bornhöved, ending Danish control of the province. Waldemar's loss here marked the turning point in his conquests. His last 14 years of rule were devoted to domestic reform. Meanwhile, to the south, the German princes became involved in the machinations of the Holy Roman Empire. *See* Reval.

Borodino (Napoleonic Empire Wars), 1812. Following the French capture of Smolensk on August 18, 1812, Napoleon I sent his columns deeper into Russia. Czar Alexander I put Field Marshal Mikhail Kutuzov in charge of the Russian armies, but the retreat continued. On September 5 Marshal Joachim Murat's French cavalry, probing 160 miles northeast of Smolensk, found Kutuzov hastily fortifying a line behind the little town of Borodino. Napoleon spent the next day deploying 86,000 infantry, 28,000 cavalry, and 587 guns against the Russian's 72,000 infantry, 18,000 cavalry and 640 guns (plus 17,000 Cossacks and militia).

Early on September 7 Marshal Louis Davout led the assault of the French right wing. On the left Eugène de Beauharnais, Napoleon's stepson, initiated an attack against Borodino. Throughout the morning the fighting see-sawed back and forth. But by noon the French artillery dominated the battlefield, inflicting thousands of casualties, including the mortally wounded Prince Pëtr Bagration, commander of the Second Russian Army. Kutuzov pulled his troops back to the next ridge. The French, however, were too battered to pursue. In the bloodiest battle of the century Russia suffered 45,000 casualties, Napoleon between 28,000 and 30,000.

Kutuzov retreated 70 miles northeast to Moscow but then abandoned the city to prevent its destruction. French advance elements entered the Russian capital on September 14. On the following night a terrible fire broke out, which in three days destroyed most of the city. After five weeks of uncertainty, Napoleon left Moscow on October 19, planning to retreat toward the southwest. *See* Smolensk I; Maloyaroslavets; Napoleonic Empire Wars.

Boroughbridge (Barons' Revolt in England), 1322. The weak rule of Edward II encouraged power grabs by many of the barons, particularly Thomas, earl of Lancaster, nephew of the king, and the Marcher lords of Wales. In 1321 Edward resolved to defend the position of his court favorite Hugh le Despenser (later Earl of Winchester) and his son, also named Hugh. He marched an army northward. The Lancastrian force, seeking to escape across the border to link up with Scottish allies, found its route blocked at the Ure River in Yorkshire. On March 16 they attacked Edward's royalists at Boroughbridge but suffered a severe defeat. The battle was an early example of a successful defense by dismounted men-at-arms and archers against cavalry. A second royalist army moved up behind the blocked Lancastrians the following day, forcing the rebels to surrender. The earl was taken prisoner and beheaded at Pontefract.

The Despensers seemed firmly in control of the English government. But final tragedy stood just a few years away. In 1326 Edward II was deposed by a clique made up of his wife, Isabella; Roger Mortimer, her paramour and one of the rebellious Marcher lords; and other dissident barons. Both Despensers were hanged, and Edward himself was brutally murdered the following year. His eldest son, Edward III, assumed the English crown. *See* Myton; Byland.

Boston (War of the American Revolution). A loose siege conducted by Gen. George Washington's colonial troops from April 20, 1775, until the British evacuation on March 17, 1776; the turning point was the emplacement of Gen. Henry Knox's artillery on Dorchester Heights, south of the city. *See* Bunker Hill.

Bosworth Field (Wars of the Roses), 1485. Although Edward IV had seemingly ended the civil war with his Yorkist (white rose) triumph at Tewkesbury, new strife developed upon his death 12 years later, in 1483. He was succeeded by his 13-year-old son, Edward V. But the Duke of Gloucester, paternal uncle of the young king, seized power as Richard III and threw the boy and his younger brother, the Duke of York, into the Tower of London. Both princes were murdered before the end of the year. The double murder aroused widespread indignation against the usurper Richard. Taking advantage of the king's unpopularity, Henry Tudor, Earl of Richmond, invaded southwest Wales at Milford Haven, on August 7, 1485. Henry, who was descended from both the Yorkist (white rose) and Lancastrian (red rose) houses, marched northeastward through Shrewsbury and Stafford. Recruits flocked to his standard, augmenting his original 2,000-man force to an army of 5,000.

Meanwhile, Richard III, supported by the Duke of Norfolk and the Earl of Northumberland, moved westward to Leicester with a royal army of 10,000 men. On August 22 the king encountered the rebel force two miles south of the village of Market Bosworth. The royalists had a 2-to-1 advantage in numbers, plus an additional 6,000 men under Thomas Lord Stanley and his brother Sir William, who stood off on the two flanks. Cannon fire and archery opened the battle, before the two lines became locked in deadly combat. At this point Northumberland held himself aloof from the fray, while the Stanley brothers turned their coats and threw their support to Henry. This action brought a quick decision. The Yorkists were overwhelmed. A valiant warrior, Richard died fighting (as did the Duke of Norfolk). The royal crown, which Richard had worn into battle, was picked out of a bush and placed on Henry's head. The 30-year Wars of the Roses were over. As Henry VII the victor inaugurated the rule of the house of Tudor over England, which would last until 1603. *See* Tewkesbury; East Stoke; Roses, Wars of the.

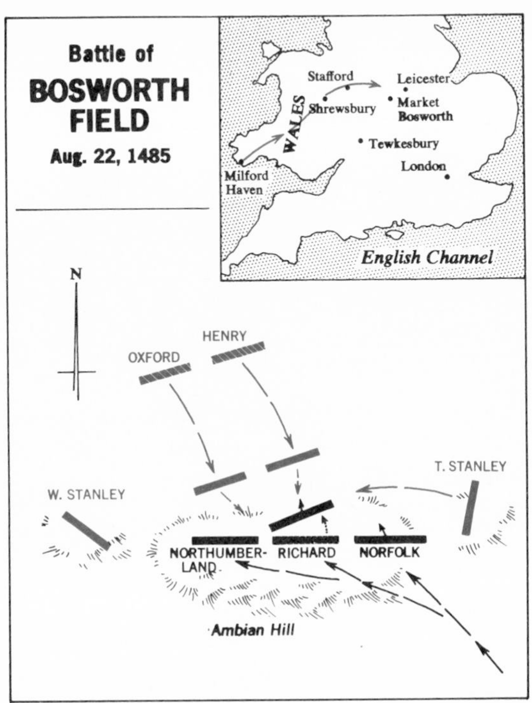

Bothwell Bridge (Scottish Covenanters' Revolt), 1679. The revolt of the Covenanters against the harsh measures of Charles II's secretary of state for Scottish affairs, the Duke of Lauderdale (John Maitland), had resulted in an English royalist defeat at Drumclog on June 11, 1679. However, the beaten troops of the Viscount Dundee (John Graham of Claverhouse) were almost immediately reinforced by fresh troops commanded by the Duke of Monmouth (James Scott), natural son of Charles II. On July 2 the entire royalist force fell on the Covenanters at Bothwell Bridge over the Clyde in Lanark County. The rebels were crushed with heavy losses. After the battle, however, Monmouth showed a clemency that won him great personal popularity. *See* Drumclog; Sedgemoor.

Bougainville (World War II). A Japanese-held island in the northern Solomons, invaded by U.S. marines at Empress Augusta Bay on November 1, 1943. *See* Solomon Islands.

Boulogne (English-French Wars), 1544. To check the growing power of France under Francis I, England's Henry VIII made an alliance with Holy Roman Emperor Charles V, a Spanish Hapsburg. A joint invasion of France was planned. Henry, with an army, crossed the Channel to his English base at Calais in 1544 and marched southward to lay siege to the seaport of Boulogne. For two months the city resisted, until finally forced to surrender on September 14. The garrison was allowed to evacuate Boulogne in peace. But the joint invasion progressed no farther. Charles made a separate peace with France five days later. The English continued to hold Boulogne until 1550, when it was sold back to France. Meanwhile, Henry had also tried to reduce Scotland, France's ally on his northern border. After burning Edinburgh, however, the English expedition was turned back at Ancrum Moor in 1545. *See* Guinegate; Solway Moss; Saint-Quentin I.

Bouvines (English-French Wars), 1214. Following the English naval victory at Damme, King John I organized a two-pronged invasion of the

France of Philip II Augustus. The English king personally led an expedition against Poitou in west-central France in 1214. The attack soon collapsed, failing even to draw Philip to the south. The main English effort took place in the north. Here John had forged a coalition consisting of an English force under the Earl of Salisbury, Holy Roman Empire troops led by Emperor Otto IV (nephew of John), and units from the Low Countries commanded by the Count of Flanders and other princes. Undaunted by this seemingly formidable array, Philip's army of 10,000 men, supported only by Frederick I of Sicily (future Holy Roman Emperor Frederick II), rode out to meet the 15,000 invaders at Bouvines in northeastern France on July 27, 1214. In a single day the French won a decisive victory, slaying 170 English and Flemish knights and capturing for ransom another 128 men-at-arms. Uncounted thousands of infantry lay dead on the field.

The victory, which produced a strong nationalistic spirit in France, shattered the coalition. The Count of Flanders was taken prisoner; Otto withdrew to Brunswick. The defeat ended all hope of England's recovery of territory north of the Loire and so weakened John's position at home that he had to sign the Magna Carta the following year. *See* Damme; Rochester II.

Bovianum (Second Samnite War), 305 B.C. Except for Apulia and Lucania, most of the central Italian states sided with Samnium against Rome in the Second Samnite War. However, the growing power of the legion formation enabled the Romans to subdue their foes one by one. Two other factors contributed to Rome's increasing military might. A war fleet was developed, and in 312 Appius Claudius began construction of the great Via Appia, linking the city to its conquests in the south.

In 308 the Roman army began methodically to ravage the Samnite cities and soon laid siege to Bovianum, the capital. When Statius Gellius brought up a force of Samnites to relieve the city in 305, he suffered a crushing defeat at the hands of Titus Minucius, although the Roman general was killed in the fray. This battle destroyed the power of Samnium, which sued for peace the following year. Rome now held undisputed hegemony over Campania. *See* Caudine Forks; Camerinum; Samnite Wars.

Boxer Rebellion (1900–1901). An uprising against European settlements in eastern China. It was largely put down by the capture of Peking by an allied force on August 14, 1900. *See* Peking III.

Boyacá (Colombian War of Independence), 1819. In eight years of intermittent guerrilla warfare, patriot Simón Bolívar had failed to throw off Spanish rule in New Granada in northwestern South America. Then in 1819, with a newly organized army that included many British volunteers, Bolívar made a new attempt. With an army of 3,200, he moved up the Orinoco River and crossed the Andes Mountains in a rugged 700-mile march. He arrived in modern Colombia with only a third of his original force. But reinforced by local patriots, he occupied Boyacá, interposing his army between 2,500 Spanish troops and their base at Bogotá. On August 7 the royalists attacked. Despite their superior numbers, the Spanish were decisively repulsed, their commander and some 1,600 men being captured. Bolívar, who had lost only 66 men, marched into Bogotá three days later. Colombia was at last free. *See* Carabobo.

Boyne River (Resistance to the Glorious Revolution), 1690. The growing strength of the deposed James II in Ireland forced his successor, William III, to take the field in person in 1690. Landing in the northeast at Carrickfergus, William marched southward with some 35,000 English troops to the line of the Boyne held by James, who was supported by the Irish Jacobite the Earl of Lucan (Patrick Sarsfield). On July 1 William sent out Duke Friedrich von Schomberg to force a passage of the Boyne three miles west of Drogheda. Another detachment crossed the river farther upstream to take the Catholic army in flank. The coordinated attack routed James's forces with a loss of more than a thousand men. The English losses were only half as great but included Schomberg, the veteran soldier of fortune. James fled to France, where he was welcomed and supported by Louis XIV. Dublin and Waterford capitulated quickly, but Limerick resisted William's advance. By the end of the year the Duke of Marlborough (John Churchill) had subdued all of southern Ireland. *See* Londonderry; Aughrim; Jacobite Insurrections.

Bramham Moor (Percy Revolt against Henry IV), 1408. Two years after the death of his son Sir Henry (Hotspur) at Shrewsbury in 1403, Henry Percy, earl of Northumberland, revolted a second time against Henry IV. When royalist forces under Ralph Neville, earl of Westmorland, marched northward, Percy fled across the border into Scotland. His confederates—Archbishop Scrope of York and Thomas Mowbray, earl of Nottingham—were captured and beheaded. Early in 1408, however, the tough 66-year-old Percy, aided by Thomas Bardolph and some Scots, recrossed the border to stir up the north country against the crown. He met little success and at Bramham Moor in Yorkshire was trapped by a royalist force under Thomas Rokeby, sheriff of the county, on February 19. The rebels suffered a striking defeat, both Percy and Bardolph falling in the battle. This ended the Percy family revolt. *See* Shrewsbury.

Brandy Station (American Civil War), 1863.

When the front along the Rappahannock River appeared deadlocked after the battle of Chancellorsville, Gen. Robert E. Lee began shifting his Confederate Army of Northern Virginia westward. To watch Lee, the Federal commander of the Army of the Potomac, Gen. Joseph Hooker, sent out his cavalry corps under Gen. Alfred Pleasonton. With 11,000 men, including two infantry brigades, Pleasonton crossed the upper Rappahannock early on June 9 and headed for Culpeper. Four miles beyond the river the Federal horsemen surprised the Confederate cavalry corps of Gen. J. E. B. Stuart at Brandy Station. Stuart's 10,000 men reacted quickly, however, to fight back in what quickly became the biggest cavalry battle in American history. For hours both sides charged and countercharged in a wild saber-swinging melee. In midafternoon Gen. Robert Rodes's infantry division began arriving in support of Stuart. Pleasonton then withdrew. He had suffered 936 casualties (including 486 captured). Stuart lost fewer men—523—but drew much criticism for being caught unprepared by the sudden Federal thrust, which confirmed the fact of Lee's westward movement. *See* Chancellorsville; Winchester II; American Civil War.

Brandywine Creek (War of the American Revolution), 1777. In the summer of the third year of the war the British under Gen. John Burgoyne launched a major advance from Canada toward Albany, N.Y. But instead of aiding this offensive, Gen. Sir William Howe, British commander in New York City, embarked 15,000 troops on July 23 and sailed up the Chesapeake Bay, aiming at the U.S. capital at Philadelphia. Howe landed at the Head of Elk on the upper bay on August 25. As Howe marched northeast toward Philadelphia, Gen. George Washington with some 10,500 men crossed the Delaware from New Jersey to take up a defensive position behind Brandywine Creek.

On September 11 Howe attacked. He sent a 5,000-man force under Gen. Baron von Knyphausen to make a feint against the American center at Chad's Ford, held by Gen. Nathanael Greene. Meanwhile, the British general Lord Cornwallis with 10,000 men circled wide to the northwest, crossed the upper Brandywine, and struck the exposed American right flank. The commander on this wing, Gen. John Sullivan, attempted to change his front to meet the unexpected attack but was overwhelmed. At this moment Knyphausen opened his frontal assault across Chad's Ford. The American army bolted to the rear with 1,000 killed, wounded, and captured. British losses were less than 600, including 90 killed. Only valiant action by Greene kept the retreat from becoming a disorderly rout. Washington's troops halted at Chester and re-formed, still between Howe and Philadelphia. The British encamped on the battlefield, meanwhile taking possession of Wilmington, Del. *See* Princeton; Cooch's Bridge; Paoli; American Revolution.

Brazil. *See* Latin America.

Breda (Netherlands War of Independence), 1625. The long Dutch War for Independence against Spain merged with the Thirty Years' War in 1622. Three years later Spanish troops under Ambrogio di Spinola attacked the fortress city of Breda in the southern Netherlands. When the city resisted, Spinola besieged it in a grip of iron. Frederick Henry, who had succeeded his half brother Maurice of Nassau earlier in the year as stadholder of the Dutch Republic, marched an army to Breda. But Spinola drove off the relief force. Near starvation after more than six months of siege, the garrison surrendered on June 5, 1625. The Spanish victory was soon swallowed up by the larger events of the Thirty Years' War, and in 1637 Frederick Henry liberated the city from the Spanish. *See* Oostende; Fleurus I; Netherlands War of Independence.

Breisach (Thirty Years' War), 1638. After their victory at Rheinfelden in March 1638, the suddenly revitalized Franco-German army of Bernhard, duke of Saxe-Weimar, moved on Breisach. This strong Baden fortress on the right bank of the Rhine, ten miles west of Freiburg, had long been held by the Holy Roman Empire (Ferdinand III). As Saxe-Weimar approached Breisach, a Bavarian force rushed to intercept him but was beaten back on July 30. By mid-August a siege had been instituted, with the aid of French troops under the Vicomte de Turenne. A second Imperial attempt to relieve this gateway to Germany was made by Charles IV of Lorraine in October. Again Saxe-Weimar's lines held fast. By now the Imperial garrison had been starved into cannibalism. Finally, on December 17, Breisach surrendered, and the anti-Hapsburg forces of the French cardinal the Duc de Richelieu stood supreme along the upper Rhine.

Saxe-Weimar died the following year, at the age of 35. His army, variously called Weimarians or Bernardines, then passed under the direct control of Richelieu. *See* Rheinfelden; Breitenfeld II; Thirty Years' War.

Breitenfeld I (Thirty Years' War), 1631. Eleven days after marching into Saxony, Field Marshal the Count of Tilly's army of the Holy Roman Empire (Ferdinand II) seized Leipzig, on September 15, 1631. The Catholic invasion of Saxony had prompted John George I, elector of Saxony, to join forces with the Swedish army of Gustavus II. The combined Protestant army (26,000 Swedes, 16,000 Saxons) hurried southward across the Elbe to intercept Tilly. On September 18 this force reached the village of Breitenfeld, six miles north of Leipzig. Tilly, outnumbered by several thousand men, hoped to withstand the enemy behind the barricades of the city. But his second-in-command, Gen. Count Gottfried zu Pappenheim, committed the Catholic army to a major battle just north of Leipzig (and east of Breitenfeld) that same day.

At nine o'clock on a hot, windy morning Tilly advanced on Breitenfeld, his infantry in the center, cavalry on both wings. On his left, Pappenheim's cavalry struck the Protestant right flank (commanded by Gen. Johan Banér) but was stopped by a skillful Swedish deployment of alternate squares of horsemen and infantry. On the Catholic right, however, the Imperial horsemen under Count Fürstenberg charged and routed the Saxons opposite them. John George's raw troops fled in panic, abandoning their guns. The Elector himself rode 15 miles eastward to Eilenburg. Gustavus, however, turned his Swedish infantry to seal off the breach in his left flank (which was under Field Marshal Gustaf Horn). Meanwhile, his well-drilled musketeers continued to pour volleys into the

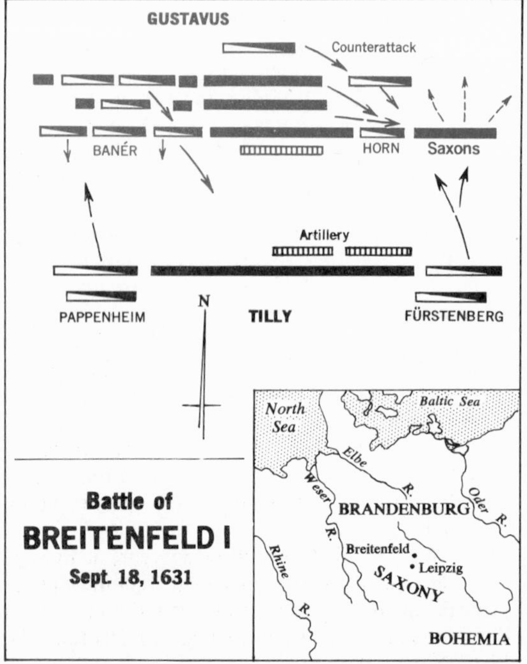

Battle of
BREITENFELD I
Sept. 18, 1631

Imperials at three times the rate and effectiveness of Tilly's return fire. This heavy volume broke up every charge of the Catholic cavalry for seven hours. Then, late in the afternoon, the Swedish king brought up his reserve of a thousand horsemen to lead a furious counterattack. The assault on the now-weary Imperial army shattered their lines. Tilly himself was wounded in the neck, chest, and right arm. His army bolted, losing heavily in a vigorous pursuit by the Swedes. Only a hard-fighting rear-guard action by Pappenheim prevented the rout from being worse than it was. Twelve thousand Imperials fell at Breitenfeld and on the bloody road back to Leipzig. Another 7,000 were lost through capture, plus all 20 pieces of artillery. Protestant losses were less than 3,000, and less than a third of these were Swedes. Leipzig was now untenable for the Catholic army. On the following morning Tilly began a retreat northwestward to Halle.

The battle of Breitenfeld marked a turning point in the Thirty Year's War. It was the first major Protestant victory and, as such, strengthened resistance to Catholic Hapsburg rule all across Europe. It also established Gustavus as the supreme military commander of his time. The Swedish king, called Gustavus Adolphus, now divided his forces. John George I collected his skittish Saxon force and sent them into Bohemia under Baron Hans Georg von Arnim. Prague was occupied on November 15. Meanwhile Gustavus himself marched southwest through Erfurt and Wurzburg into The Palatinate. *See* Werben; Rain; Thirty Years' War.

Breitenfeld II (Thirty Years' War), 1642. During the last decade of the long, terrible war, peace feelers filled the air. Largely because of the confusing rumors that resulted, fighting became uncoordinated and spasmodic. In eastern Germany the Swedish commander, Field Marshal Johan Banér, had died in 1641. His successor, Field Marshal Lennart Torstenson, sought to knock Saxony out of the war the following year. Torstenson was besieging Leipzig with somewhat less than 20,000 men when an army of the Holy Roman Empire marched to the relief of the city on November 2, 1642. The Swedish field marshal, finding himself outnumbered, withdrew six miles northwestward to Breitenfeld, site of a major battle 11 years earlier. The Imperials under Archduke Leopold William, brother of Emperor Ferdinand III, and Gen. Octavio Piccolomini (duke of Amalfi) pursued hotly. When the Swedes turned to fight, Leopold William prepared to charge under cover of a heavy artillery bombardment. But before the Imperial cavalry on the left could deploy, they were themselves struck hard by the Swedish horsemen on that flank. Torstenson's sudden assault routed the Austrian cavalry. The Swedish field marshal then wheeled to the left to drive back the Imperial infantry who were attacking in the center. This success enabled the entire Protestant army to converge on the enemy's isolated right wing. Those who did not flee surrendered wholesale. The battle ended almost as suddenly as it had begun.

Leopold William, having lost 5,000 in killed or wounded and an equal number of captured, fell back into Bohemia. Soon thereafter he resigned his command. Baron Franz von Mercy, a Bavarian field marshal, then took charge of the Imperial forces. He would remain relatively inactive for more than a year. Meanwhile, the Spanish branch of the Hapsburg house suffered a crushing defeat in what is now northeast France. *See* Breisach; Rocroi; Tuttlingen; Thirty Years' War.

Brémule (English-French Wars), 1119. The victory of Henry I at Tinchebray overcame almost all resistance to English control over Normandy. Louis VI of France, however, refused to recognize Henry's rule in northwestern France. He built an alliance with dissident Normans, the Count of Anjou, and the Count of Flanders to support the claim of William Clito, nephew of Henry, to the dukedom. On August 20, 1119, knights representing this alliance encountered a small Anglo-Norman force at Brémule. Henry's armored horsemen won the field. Although less than a thousand knights were engaged, the battle marked a turning point in the struggle for Normandy. Henry's claim became established beyond dispute. *See* Tinchebray; Standard.

Brentford (English Civil War), 1642. After the drawn battle of Edgehill late in October 1642, Charles I resumed his march on London with the Cavalier army. Meanwhile the Roundhead army under Robert Devereux, 3rd earl of Essex, fell back, seeking to join forces with the Londoners, who were hostile to the English king. At Brentford, ten miles up the Thames from the capital, Prince Rupert of Germany, nephew of Charles, led a Cavalier cavalry charge that inflicted a sharp defeat on the Roundheads on November 12. But the Royalist victory did not prevent Essex from linking up with the London troops. As a result, when the Cavaliers came upon the united enemy at Turnham Green a few days later, Charles had to give up his advance on London. He then withdrew to his capital at Oxford. *See* Edgehill; Grantham; Stratton; English Civil War.

Breslau (Seven Years' War), 1757. While Frederick II, the Great, was stopping the French advance in the west at Rossbach, a simultaneous attack endangered Prussia from the south. Here an Austrian army of the Holy Roman Empire pushed into Silesia. Under the command of Prince Charles of Lorraine (Karl Alexander), brother-in-law of Empress Maria Theresa, the Austrians masked the fortress of Schweidnitz (Swidnica) and marched northeast toward Breslau (Wroclaw) on the Oder River. The Prussian commander in this sector, August Wilhelm, duke of Brunswick-Bevern, threw up a roadblock with some 20,000 men outside the city's walls. But the Imperial army, enjoying a 3-to-1 superiority, overpowered the defenders on November 22, 1757. The Prussians lost almost a third of their army. Brunswick-Bevern was captured. The survivors withdrew into Breslau, then abandoned the city to fall back beyond the Oder. Both Schweidnitz and Breslau surrendered in a few days. Meanwhile Frederick was hurrying back from Saxony to meet this newest threat to his country. *See* Rossbach; Leuthen; Seven Years' War.

Briar Creek (War of the American Revolution), 1779. Encouraged by small American victories at Port Royal Island and Kettle Creek in February 1779, Gen. Benjamin Lincoln, commander in the South, resolved to recover Georgia. From Purysburg, S.C., he sent out a force under Gen. John Ashe to liberate Augusta. The British troops in Augusta began withdrawing southeast toward Savannah. The Americans (1,400 North Carolina militia, 100 Georgia Continentals) crossed the Savannah River and started in pursuit. But the British commander in Georgia, Gen. Augustine Prevost, devised a trap. When Ashe reached the north bank of Briar Creek, he found only a small enemy force across the stream. The Americans encamped carelessly, unaware that Prevost had sent 900 men across the creek above Ashe. On March 3 Prevost's force suddenly struck the rear of Ashe's camp. Most of the militia fled without firing a shot, leaving the Continentals to be overwhelmed. More than 350 Americans were killed, drowned in flight, or captured. Hundreds of others melted away to their homes. Prevost lost only 5 killed and 11 wounded. *See* Kettle Creek; Stono Ferry; American Revolution.

Brices Cross Roads (American Civil War), 1864. During the Federal drive on Atlanta, a force was sent out from Memphis on June 2 to destroy the Confederate cavalry of Gen. Nathan Forrest, who had been raiding Federal communication lines in Tennessee. Under the command of Gen. Samuel Sturgis, 4,800 infantry, 3,000 cavalry, and 18 guns moved to Brices Cross Roads, in northeastern Mississippi, on June 10. Learning of the Federal advance, Forrest with 3,500 cavalry rode quickly to the road junction to attack the enemy horsemen before the Federal infantry could deploy. The Confederates launched their assault about 1 P.M. They drove back the Federal cavalry and continued to press forward against the infantry coming into position. By 5 P.M. Sturgis' force had collapsed and was retreating to Stubb's plantation, ten miles to the north. Federal losses were 223 killed, 394 wounded, and 1,623 captured, plus 16 of their 18 guns and 250 wagons. Forrest, who defeated an army more than twice the size of his own, suffered 492 casualties. Sturgis was not condemned by an investigative board but never received another command. *See* Resaca; Tupelo; American Civil War.

Brielle (Netherlands War of Independence), 1572. When the Netherlands revolted against Spanish rule in 1567, King Philip II sent the Duke of Alva with 20,000 troops to suppress the rebels. Alva ruthlessly stamped out resistance within a year; the Dutch leader, William I (the Silent) of Orange, fled into Germany. In 1572, however, the

Dutch fleet of privateers, called the Sea Beggars, landed on Voorne Island, 14 miles west of Rotterdam. Under the command of William de la Marck and William of Blois (Lord of Teslong), the Dutch sailors took the fortress of Brielle (Brill) on April 1. It was the first patriot victory of the rebellion, which nine years later would result in independence for the seven northern provinces (modern Netherlands). *See* Haarlem; Netherlands War of Independence.

Brienne (Napoleonic Empire Wars), 1814. When Napoleon I withdrew into France in the autumn of 1813, he hurriedly organized a defensive line to the northeast with some 117,000 troops. The allies pressed forward. Prince Karl von Schwarzenberg marched his Austrian army of 50,000 across the Swiss frontier on December 21; Field Marshal Gen. Gebhard von Blücher bridged the Rhine on January 1. Taking advantage of Blücher's scattered forces, Napoleon suddenly struck eastward to Brienne, 23 miles northeast of Troyes, on January 29. His eager French conscripts routed the Prussian veterans, inflicting 4,000 casualties at a loss of 3,000 to themselves. The French pushed on to occupy La Rothière, while Blücher and Schwarzenberg halted to plan a joint offensive. *See* Hanau; La Rothière; Napoleonic Empire Wars.

Brihuega (War of the Spanish Succession), 1710. Although the English-dominated allies were successful against France in northern Italy and only a little less so on the western front, Spain itself proved to be a different story. Here the mass of the people (except the Catalonians) supported the Bourbon Philip V, grandson of France's Louis XIV. After setbacks at Almansa and Toulon in 1707, the allies remained quietly in Barcelona for three years. In 1710, however, James, Earl of Stanhope, led another abortive expedition toward Madrid in an effort to replace Philip with Archduke Charles of Austria (future Holy Roman Emperor Charles VI). Repulsed at the Spanish capital, Stanhope began falling back toward Barcelona. Fifty miles northeast of Madrid the allied army was attacked at Brihuega by a Franco-Spanish force under Marshal Louis Joseph, Duc de Vendôme. Although the allied army fought valiantly, it was surrounded and forced to surrender on December 9. Thereafter the allies held only Barcelona, until the 1713 Treaty of Utrecht, when that city too was given up, although it did not come into actual Spanish possession until September 11, 1714. *See* Turin; Toulon I; Malplaquet; Denain; Spanish Succession, War of the.

Bristoe Station (American Civil War), 1863. The three months after Gettysburg were a period of complex maneuvering for the Federal Army of the Potomac (Gen. George Meade) and the opposing Confederate Army of Northern Virginia (Gen. Robert E. Lee). On October 9 Lee moved northward against the west flank of Meade, who withdrew cautiously 40 miles to Centreville. During this well-ordered retreat, Gen. Ambrose Hill's III Corps overtook the Federal rear guard near Bristoe Station. Seeing a chance to crush the Federal III Corps of Gen. William French, Hill attacked briskly on October 14. The Confederate advance, however, blundered straight into the overlooked Federal II Corps of Gen. Gouverneur Warren. This force, well entrenched behind a railroad embankment, opened up with a devastating infantry and artillery fire. Two brigades of Gen. Henry Heth's division charged the strong enemy position and lost 700 and 602 men, respectively. In all, Hill's corps suffered 1,900 casualties against a Federal loss of 548.

Unable to gain an advantage over his more numerous foe (47,000 to 77,000), Lee returned to his position south of the Rapidan River. In a rearguard action along the Rappahannock on November 7, Lee lost another 2,023 men, from Gen. Richard Ewell's II Corps. Except for Meade's abortive offensive toward Mine Run during November 26–December 1, both armies retired into winter quarters. *See* Gettysburg; Wilderness; American Civil War.

Britain (World War II), 1940–1941. Following the fall of France, only Great Britain held out against the all-victorious German war machine. With his ground forces stopped at the English Channel, Adolf Hitler attempted conquest by aerial bombardment or, failing in that, planned to destroy British naval and air defenses and thus open the way to Nazi invasion of the island (Operation Sea Lion). For this air assault Gen. Hermann Goering's German *Luftwaffe,* based chiefly on French and Belgian airfields, had about 2,670 planes—1,015 bombers (Junkers, Dorniers, Heinkels), 350 dive bombers (Stukas), 930 fighters, and 375 heavy fighters (Focke-Wulfs, Messerschmitts). Opposed were about 600 Royal Air Force (RAF) fighters—Hurricanes and Spitfires—commanded by Air Chief Marshal Sir Hugh Dowding. The battle—the first in history to be fought exclusively in the air—took place in three successive but overlapping phases.

The first heavy air attack on Britain, on July 10, 1940, opened the phase of the German air offensive aimed at neutralizing the southern ports from Dover west to Plymouth. This was prime invasion territory, and waves of bombers escorted by fighters roared almost daily across the Channel to blast shipping and harbor installations. The climax of this phase occurred on August 15, when some 940 German aircraft attacked both southern and northern England. About 76 were shot down at a loss of 34 RAF fighters (plus 21 bombers destroyed on the ground).

Meanwhile, the *Luftwaffe* had launched the second phase of its offensive by stepping up attacks on airfields, aircraft factories, and radar stations in an effort to strangle the RAF. During the critical two weeks of this phase (August 24–September 6), relentless Nazi attacks destroyed or badly damaged 466 Hurricanes and Spitfires with a loss of 103 pilots killed and 128 seriously wounded. (This was one-fourth of the total pilot strength in the 50 operational RAF fighter squadrons.) German losses, however, were twice as great in aircraft and even greater in pilots. On September 7 the Germans began switching their attack to the air defenses of London, with about 300 planes making the first massive daylight raid on the city. Eight days later the largest attack on London found more than 400 planes blasting the capital; 56 were shot down by RAF fighters and antiaircraft fire.

The costly September 15 raid convinced Goering that daylight attacks were futile. He then concentrated on the third (and last) phase of the battle of Britain—a nighttime blitz of the capital. This attack, which had started on September 7, was to continue unceasingly for 57 nights. During this time an average of 200 planes a night smashed at the city with high-explosive and incendiary bombs. October 15 was an especially brutal night—480 German planes dropped 386 tons of high explosive and 70,000 incendiary bombs. British defenses consisted of six squadrons of night fighters and about 2,000 antiaircraft guns.

The repetitive, heavy raids killed more than 43,000 British and wounded five times that number, caused tremendous property damage, and curtailed war and food production. But the change to night attack made it clear that British fighter pilots in "their finest hour" had broken the back of the *Luftwaffe* bomber offensive and unequivocally ended Nazi invasion plans. Although the air battle raged on for another two months (to November 3), the issue had been settled in September. During the four crucial months of the battle of Britain, the RAF lost 915 fighter aircraft, 481 men in killed, prisoners, or missing, and 422 wounded. German aircraft losses were 1,733 (although the British claimed 2,698 kills).

Beginning on November 4, German night attacks shifted to Britain's key industrial centers. Coventry was blasted by 600 tons of high explosives from 500 aircraft on the night of November 14. Birmingham was heavily raided between November 19 and 22. London was again struck savagely on December 29, with almost 1,500 different fires started. Throughout the winter of 1940–41 German bombing attacks continued, with heavy emphasis on port cities as part of the battle of the Atlantic aimed at cutting Great Britain's lifeline. During this time British air defenses destroyed an average of 15 to 20 planes a month. In the first ten days of May alone, 70 *Luftwaffe* planes were shot down by ever improving defensive weapons—more antiaircraft guns (almost 500 in London alone), better radar, and the addition of rocket batteries. The last incendiary attack on London, on May 10, was the most destructive of the entire blitz. Bombers started more than 2,000 fires and killed or injured over 3,000 people, at a cost of 16 planes (the most planes destroyed in a night attack throughout the blitz). But this was the *Luftwaffe*'s last major strike in the battle of Britain—the first defeat for Adolf Hitler's Germany. Five weeks later virtually all Nazi military resources were thrown into the attack on Soviet Russia. *See* France (World War II); Soviet Union (World War II); Atlantic Ocean II; German Vengeance-Weapon Bombardment; World War II.

Brunanburh (Rise of England), 937. The West Saxon ruler Athelstan walked in the king-sized footsteps of his father and grandfather, Edward the Elder and Alfred the Great. He brought under his control the Norse kingdom of York and the Britons of Strathclyde. However, when he marched into Scotland, the entire north erupted against him—Picts and Scots of Constantine III, Britons, vikings of King Olaf Godfreyson of Dublin, and some other Irish. The northerners fought against Athelstan's army in a great two-day battle at Brunanburh, near the English-Scottish border. The Saxons of Wessex and Mercia (including some Danes) won an overwhelming victory that was celebrated in an Icelandic saga and an Old English poem. Athelstan stood supreme in the greater part of what is now England, a position later held by his brothers Edmund I and then Edred. *See* Tempsford; Stainmore.

Brunete (Spanish Civil War). A counterattack by Republican forces during July 6–25, 1937, against the Nationalist army besieging Madrid; it gained little ground at a high cost in casualties. *See* Madrid.

Brunkeberg (Danish-Swedish Wars), 1471. The ambitious Christian I of Denmark and Norway sought to enforce the Union of Kalmar by bringing Sweden firmly under his single monarchy. But a Swedish noble, Sten Sture (the Elder), led a patriot force to meet Christian's army at Brunkeberg (now part of Stockholm) on October 10, 1471. The Swedes won a sweeping victory, ending the Danish campaign of conquest. Sweden continued under the rule of a regency. (The Union of Kalmar—Denmark, Norway, Sweden—finally broke up in 1523, when Sweden became independent under Gustavus I.)

Brusilov Offensive. *See* Kovel-Stanislav.

Buena Vista (U.S.-Mexican War), 1847. Early in 1847 the United States government withdrew 9,000 troops from Gen. Zachary Taylor's command in northern Mexico to launch an amphibious expedition against Veracruz. Taylor was ordered to remain on the defensive along the Monterrey-Saltillo line. Instead, the frustrated general took the offensive, marching southwest beyond Saltillo during February 5–14. Meanwhile the Mexican general Antonio de Santa Anna collected about 20,000 troops at San Luis Potosí and began moving northward toward the Americans. Taylor, with only 4,800 men, largely inexperienced volunteers, withdrew to a defile along the road near Buena Vista.

Santa Anna, pushing forward rapidly, reached the American position with more than 14,000 troops. When Taylor refused a demand to surrender, the Mexicans attacked on February 22. The long march had so exhausted Santa Anna's command that his ill-trained army could not take advantage of their 3-to-1 superiority in numbers. In a two-day fight the Mexican army was beaten off with at least 1,500 casualties, including 500 killed. American losses were 267 killed, 456 wounded, and 23 missing. Santa Anna retreated toward Mexico City, where he took office as president on March 21.

The battle of Buena Vista ended the war in northern Mexico. Taylor remained in command until relieved at his own request in November. Meanwhile the theater of operations shifted to the eastern coast of Mexico. *See* Monterrey; Veracruz; U.S.-Mexican War.

Buenos Aires (Napoleonic Empire Wars), 1806–1807. In the long struggle against the French Empire of Napoleon I, Great Britain struck at the overseas possessions of France and its allies wherever possible. On June 27, 1806, a British expedition of 1,500 men under Col. William Carr Beresford (later Lord Beresford) landed on the coast of Argentina aiming to seize Buenos Aires, then held by Spain. Before Beresford could be reinforced, however, he was counterattacked by an Argentine force led by Santiago de Liniers, a French naval officer in the service of Charles IV. The British were overwhelmed and forced to surrender.

A second British force, 10,000 men under Gen. John Whitelocke, which had occupied Montevideo in 1806, moved against Buenos Aires the following year. But again Liniers rallied the Argentines and forced Whitelocke to withdraw from the Río de la Plata area. This double defense aroused national feeling, and direct Spanish rule was never restored. *See* Finisterre Cape III; Cape Town; Napoleonic Empire Wars.

Bukhara (Mongol Conquest of Central Asia), 1220. When the Mongol horde of Genghis Khan swept out of the northeast, the Khwarizm Empire of Persia was a rich land embracing modern Iran, Afghanistan, Turkistan, and parts of northern India. Mohammed, the reigning shah, threw out a defensive line along the Jaxartes River (Syr Darya). But in February 1220 some 100,000 mounted Mongols penetrated this thin line in four columns, commanded by the Great Khan himself, two of his sons—Juji (Juchi) and Jagatai (Chagatai)—and a general named Chépé. While the three columns of his subordinates converged to crumple the shah's right (southern) flank near Samarkand, the Great Khan with 40,000 horsemen executed a giant turning movement in the north to threaten Bukhara (Bokhara) from the rear (west). For extent and precision Genghis Khan's invasion of Khwarizm has not been surpassed in military history.

Caught between swiftly closing pincers, Shah Mohammed concentrated against Juji's column but was repulsed with heavy loss. Bukhara was abandoned by Mohammed, and after a brief siege it fell to the invaders. As a lesson to his enemies, Genghis Khan ordered a merciless slaughter of the inhabitants, after which the city was sacked and burned. The Mongols moved to close the pincers against Samarkand. *See* Khojend; Samarkand; Mongol Wars.

Bulawayo (British conquest of the Matabeles), 1893. The discovery of gold in Mashonaland of Southern Rhodesia brought in many white settlers. Lobengula, chief of the Matabeles, granted safe transit to the South Africa Company of Cecil Rhodes. But in 1893 he led an uprising against both the Mashonas and the British. Near the Matabele capital of Bulawayo, 380 miles north of Pretoria, the rebels were mowed down by British machine-gun fire on October 23. Pressing forward, the British occupied Bulawayo on November 4. The revolt ended with the death of Lobengula two months later. *See* Majuba Hill; Doornkop.

Bulgaria. The first organized Slavic power in the Balkans, Bulgaria enjoyed a brief period of independence from the Byzantine Empire in the Middle Ages. It then came under the rule of the Ottoman Turks for 500 years. *See* Turkey. Bulgaria achieved partial autonomy in 1879, complete independence in 1908.

Stara Zagora	1189
Adrianople IV	1205
Philippopolis II	1208
Trnovo	1218
Klokotnitsa	1230
Adrianople V	1254
Nicopolis	1396

See Balkan Wars
See World War I
See World War II

"Bulge, Battle of the." *See* Ardennes II

Bull Run I (American Civil War), 1861. The popular view in the North that the Confederate forces could be easily crushed led to a premature offensive in northern Virginia. From Alexandria, Gen. Irvin McDowell marched southwest to Centreville, reaching there on July 18 with almost 35,000 Federal troops. Alert to the Union advance,

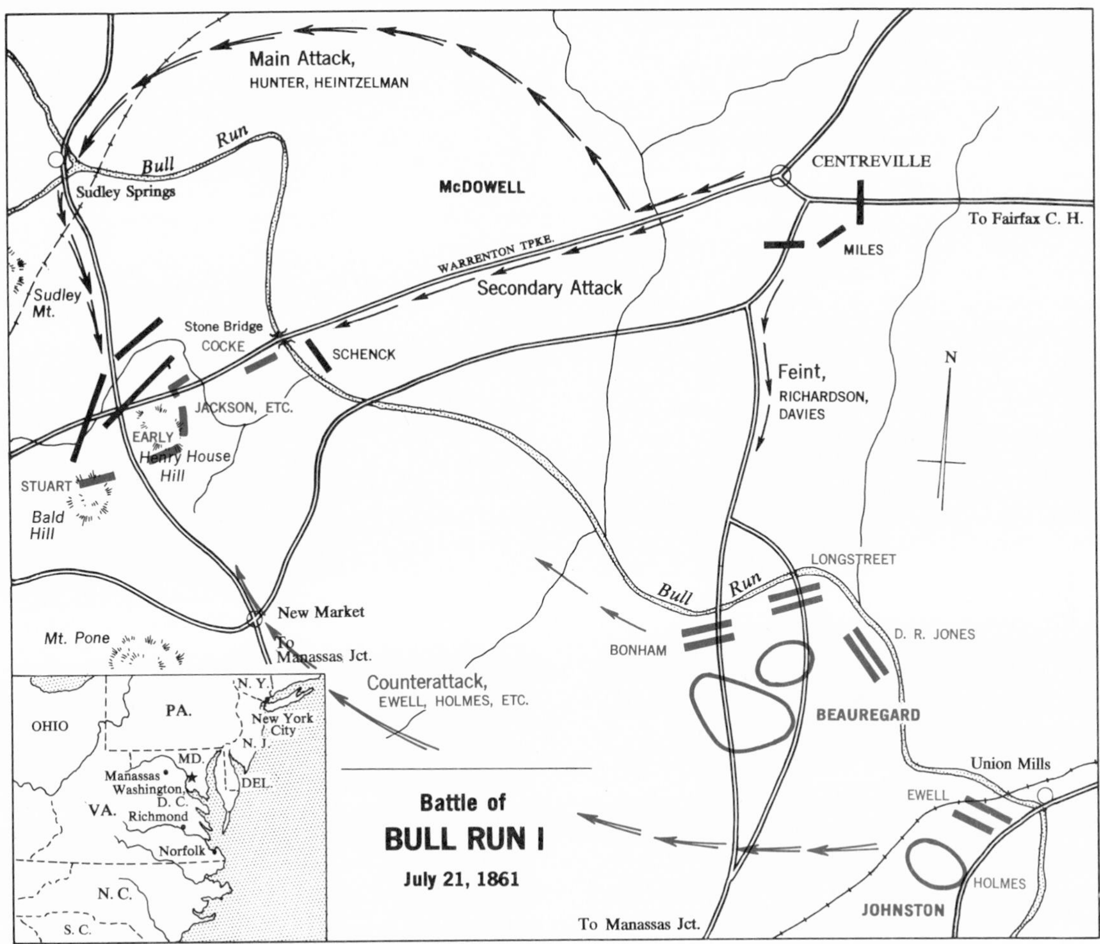

Battle of
BULL RUN I
July 21, 1861

Gen. Pierre Beauregard concentrated 20,000 Confederate soldiers at Manassas, a key railroad junction. Here he was joined by Gen. Joseph Johnston, who had eluded the Federal commander, Gen. Robert Patterson, in present-day West Virigina and brought in 9,000 Confederates by railroad. It was the first strategic use of railroad transportation in military history.

McDowell, whose troops were largely poorly trained militia, spent two precious days closing up to the stream called Bull Run. Then, on the morning of July 21, the Federal commander attacked in a turning movement aimed at the enemy left (west). Three divisions crossed Bull Run upstream at Sudley Springs, driving the Confederate flank back to Henry House Hill. Here the brigade of Col. Thomas Jackson (and other Southern troops) held firm. This led Gen. Barnard Bee to encourage his own men with the shout: "Look at Jackson's brigade; it stands like a stone wall!" Thus both the commander and his brigade earned the name "Stonewall" for the duration of the war.

While the rest of the 14-mile front remained relatively quiet, both sides hurriedly shifted reserves to the west. By 4 P.M. the Confederates had not only checked the Federal advance but had begun their own counterattack. McDowell ordered his exposed right to withdraw across Bull Run, back to Centreville. The retreat soon became a disorganized flight, with the entire army scurrying all the way back to Washington, D.C. Fortunately for the Union, the victorious Confederates could mount only a hesitant and confused pursuit that was soon called off. In this first major battle of the war the Federals lost 2,896 men killed, wounded, or captured. Total Confederate casualties were 1,982. To rebuild the Federal forces into what would become the Army of the Potomac, President Abraham Lincoln called in Gen. George McClellan from West Virginia; McDowell would revert to a division commander. *See* Philippi, W. Va.; Rich Mountain; Ball's Bluff; American Civil War.

Bull Run II (American Civil War), 1862. The Confederate commander, Gen. Robert E. Lee, determined to strike Gen. John Pope's Army of Virginia before it could be reinforced by Gen. George McClellan's much larger Federal force, which was moving up the Potomac River. To do this, Lee divided his army on August 24. From the south side of the Rappahannock River, he sent Gen. Thomas (Stonewall) Jackson upriver to circle behind Pope's 75,000 troops deployed along the Orange and Alexandria Railroad, south of Manassas. Two nights later the fast-marching Jackson stood at Manassas, across Pope's lines of communication. Meanwhile the Confederate general James Longstreet moved his command to a position at Orleans, 30 miles to the west. On August 27 Jackson seized what Federal stores he could use, destroyed the rest, and beat back a small, foolhardy attack by Gen. George Taylor, who was assigned to guard the Union Mills railroad bridge over Bull Run. After destroying the bridge, Jackson moved up Bull Run to assume a defensive position at Stony Ridge near Sudley Springs. Pope, meanwhile, marched hurriedly northward to attack Jackson before Longstreet could interfere. But confused by the movements of Jackson and his division commanders—Gens. Ambrose Hill, Richard Ewell, and William Taliaferro—Pope scattered his units over too wide an area to control.

Moving eastward on the Warrenton Turnpike, Gen. Rufus King's division of Pope's command unknowingly crossed the front of Jackson's corps in the late afternoon of August 28. The Confederate divisions of Ewell and Taliaferro fell on King's men at Groveton. In one of the fiercest small actions of the war both sides suffered heavy casualties before the Federals withdrew at midnight. Both Ewell (who lost a leg) and Taliaferro were wounded.

On August 29 Pope hurled three corps at Jackson on Stony Ridge—from south to north, I (Franz Sigel), IX (Jesse Reno), and III (Samuel Heintzelman). But the poorly coordinated frontal attacks were repulsed. During this fight Pope paid the penalty of not blocking out Longstreet at Bull Run Mountain. The four-division Confederate corps arrived on Jackson's right (south) at noon, in a position to drive between Pope's main force and Gen. Fitz-John Porter's V Corps two miles to the south. But Longstreet missed the opportunity to score a decisive triumph for Lee. (Porter, confused by Pope's ambiguous orders, was later court-martialed and dismissed from the army; he was cleared 20 years later.)

Still misinterpreting the situation, Pope launched an attack on Jackson again the following day (August 30). The Confederate army held and then counterattacked. On the south Longstreet's corps, driving eastward, caved in Pope's left flank. Only a stubborn defense of Henry House Hill prevented a major Federal defeat. That night the Union Army withdrew northward across Bull Run to Centreville. Lee did not pursue. Instead, he sent Jackson northward to circle behind Centreville to Fairfax Court House. On September 1 Pope sent two divisions under Gens. Isaac Stevens and Philip Kearny to intercept Jackson. The two hostile forces met at Chantilly. In a hard fight Jackson's tired troops failed to break through, despite their superior numbers. Both Stevens and Kearny were killed, among the 1,300 Federal casualties. Confederate losses were 800. When Longstreet came up that night, Pope retired to Fairfax and the following day withdrew into the fortifications of Washington, D.C. Thus Bull Run II ended with the Southern armies on the offensive and the Federal forces beaten and demoralized by poor leadership. The five-day battle cost Lee 9,197 casualties (19 percent of his strength), while Federal losses totaled 16,054 (21 percent of their strength). *See* Cedar Mountain; Harpers Ferry; American Civil War.

Bunker Hill (War of the American Revolution), 1775. After the sharp repulse of his raiding party at Lexington and Concord in April, Gen. Thomas Gage concentrated the British occupation troops in the city of Boston. The American militia then closed in to conduct a loose siege under the direction of Gen. Artemas Ward. On the night of June 16, 1,600 colonists under Col. William Prescott moved out on the Charlestown Peninsula, a half-mile north of Boston across the Charles River. By mistake they fortified Breed's Hill, forward of the intended objective of Bunker Hill. While the Americans continued to erect earthworks the following day, Gage ordered a frontal assault on the new position. That afternoon Gen. Sir William Howe landed on the tip of the peninsula with 2,100 British troops. Advancing up the hill in tight formation, the redcoats met a murderous musket and cannon fire that drove them back. A second attack was also repulsed. Then, strengthened by 400 fresh troops under Gen. Sir Henry Clinton, Howe launched a third assault with bayonets fixed. The Americans, now running short of powder, were driven off Breed's Hill. Bunker Hill, held by Gen. Israel Putnam, also was abandoned. Howe had the opportunity to turn the retreat into a disastrous rout. But he halted the British pursuit at the base of the peninsula. In the first pitched battle of the American Revolution, the British suffered 1,054 casualties, a high proportion of them officers, including 226 killed. American losses were 140 dead, 271 wounded, and 30 captured, out of some 1,500 troops actually engaged.

Two weeks after the battle of Bunker Hill, Gen. George Washington arrived at Cambridge to take command of the American army. The siege of Boston was resumed. Finally, on March 17, 1776, after the colonials had fortified Dorchester Heights, to the south, the British evacuated the city and sailed to Halifax, in Canada. *See* Lexington and Concord; Fort Ticonderoga II; Long Island; American Revolution.

Burkersdorf (Seven Years' War), 1762. After the Pyrrhic victory of Frederick II, the Great, over the Austrians at Torgau late in 1760, the emphasis in the Seven Years' War turned to military and diplomatic maneuvering. The death of George II in Great Britain led to decreased aid to Frederick's Prussia. But this loss was balanced by the withdrawal of Russia from the Austrian-French alliance after the death of Empress Elizabeth early in 1762. Meanwhile, however, the Holy Roman Empire's (Maria Theresa) army of Field Marshal Count Leopold von Daun stayed in the field to oppose Frederick. It was more than a year and a half after the battle of Torgau before the two veteran opponents faced each other again in open battle. The encounter took place at Burkersdorf (Burkatów) in Silesia, on July 21, 1762. Frederick's Prussians drove the Austrians from the field, but casualties were few and no advantage was gained. The war-weary armies would meet only one more time before the long conflict ended. *See* Torgau; Havana; Freiberg; Seven Years' War.

Burma I (World War II), 1942. The seizure of Thailand in December 1941 gave the Japanese advanced bases in Southeast Asia to support their thrust down the Malay Peninsula to the south and to threaten Burma from the east. While Gen. Tomoyuki Yamashita was smashing through Singapore, the Japanese Fifteenth Army invaded Burma on January 16. Within two weeks the invaders overran southeast Burma, including Moulmein, up to the lower Salween River. By February 20 Japanese pressure forced the British-Indian 17th Division to give up this line and fall back across the Sittang River. Heavily attacked during the withdrawal, only 3,300 men escaped over the river to aid in the defense of Rangoon, which was now threatened. Some 250 miles to the north the 1st Burma Division, after being relieved in the South Shan states by the Chinese Sixth Army, moved to Toungoo to guard the chief northward route to Mandalay.

General Sir Harold Alexander arrived on March 5 to take over the defense of Burma from Gen. T. J. Hutton. Encircled Rangoon had to be evacuated four days later. Lower Burma was lost and upper Burma, to which the British retreated, was in jeopardy. Here the U.S. general Joseph Stilwell commanded the Fifth and Sixth (understrength) Chinese armies.

On March 24 the Japanese began pressing northward up the Sittang, Irrawaddy, and Chindwin rivers. Toungoo fell on March 31. Mandalay was taken on May 1, but a more serious loss occurred two days earlier, when a Japanese advance from the east captured Lashio, the southern terminus of the Burma Road. The cutting of the vital supply line to Kunming severed the last overland route to China. With the battle of Burma lost, India-based aircraft evacuated 8,600 wounded and others. The remainder of Alexander's and Stilwell's commands labored 250 miles through jungles and over mountains to reach Assam Province, inside the border of India, on May 17. Stilwell reported the Allied defeat "a hell of a beating." Japan now owned a major foothold on the Bay of Bengal in the Indian Ocean. *See* China II; Ceylon; Malaya; Burma II; World War II.

Burma II (World War II), 1943–1945. To open an overland supply route to China, the Allies launched an offensive from India against Japanese-held Burma in December 1943. From Ledo, the U.S. general Joseph Stilwell led two American-trained Chinese divisions southeast into the Burmese jungles toward Myitkyina. Behind Stilwell's advance, U.S. engineers under Gen. Lewis Pick constructed the Ledo (later called the Stilwell) Road, designed to link up with the Burma Road more than 300 miles away.

On January 19 the battle to regain Burma spread to the south, where the British XV Corps attacked down the Arakan coast toward Akyab. But fierce resistance by the Japanese Twenty-eighth Army checked this advance. To the north, the British general Orde Wingate's Chindits conducted guerrilla warfare behind the Japanese lines in the Indaw area of central Burma. The effectiveness of the Chindits became severly curtailed, however, when Wingate was killed in an air crash on March 24.

Meanwhile, on March 8, the Japanese Fifteenth Army (Renya Mutaguchi) launched a major assault against the British Fourteenth Army (William Slim) at Imphal. By the end of the month the Japanese attack had isolated 60,000 British and Indian troops. Although supplies had to be flown in by air, Slim's troops held fast and thus prevented an enemy penetration into India. It was not until June 22, however, that Adm. Lord Louis Mountbatten, commander in chief for Southeast Asia, could break the Japanese grip on Imphal. The futile attack cost the Japanese 13,000 killed and four times that many deaths from wounds, disease, and starvation.

In the north, 200 miles away, Stilwell's two Chinese divisions, now aided by the U.S. general Frank Merrill's Marauders, drove doggedly forward. Air support came from Gen. Clayton Bissell's India-based U.S. 10th Air Force. Then, in a quick blow, the airfield at Myitkyina was captured on May 17. Stilwell now stood halfway across Burma. But the Japanese Thirty-third Army clung to the town until August 3, and monsoon rains prohibited further Allied advances.

Despite his successful offensive, Stilwell, who also served as chief of staff to Generalissimo Chiang Kai-shek, was relieved on October 19. His command was divided between the U.S. generals

Albert Wedemeyer (China) and Daniel Sultan (India-Burma). After the monsoon season the Allies, under the British general Sir Oliver Leese, ground commander, resumed their advance—Sultan from the north, Slim from the northwest and west. On December 16 these two forces linked up and pushed south toward Mandalay against the Japanese who were now commanded by Gen. Hyotaro Kimura. Meanwhile Marshal Wei Lihuang's Chinese Expeditionary Force was fighting its way down the Burma Road and on March 7 recaptured Lashio. This advance reopened the overland supply route to Kunming by way of the new Stilwell Road from Ledo. In the difficult drive to the south the British assumed the major burden. Mandalay fell on March 20 to Slim's Fourteenth Army, which drove relentlessly forward to capture Prome, on the lower Irrawaddy, on May 2 and Pegu, on the Mandalay–Rangoon railroad, on the same day. Rangoon fell to a British XV Corps amphibious assault on May 3. The Japanese hold on Burma was broken completely just as another monsoon season began. *See* Burma I; China II; World War II.

Burmese-British Wars (1824–1885). In three minor conflicts, Great Britain steadily extended its control over Burma. Operating from India, the modern British armies easily overpowered the native forces. The victorious commanders were Gen. Sir Archibald Campbell, 1824–26, Gen. Henry Godwin, 1852–53, and Gen. Sir Harry Prendergast, 1885.

Bursa (Rise of Ottoman Turks), 1317–1326. The first Turkish empire, that of the Seljuks, ruled much of Asia Minor during the time of the Crusades. In the mid-thirteenth century, however, Mongol invasions from the east broke up the Seljuk Empire into a series of local tribal dynasties. One of these tribes, led by Osman I (or Othman, and hence Ottoman Turks), gradually gained ascendancy over its rivals. In 1317 Osman's army, strong in mounted bowmen, laid siege to Bursa (Brusa), a Byzantine outpost 13 miles southeast of the Sea of Marmara. The embattled garrison, under the absentee command of Emperor Andronicus II, held out for nine years. It was finally starved into submission by Osman's son and heir, Orkhan I, in 1326. Bursa became the capital of the embryonic Ottoman Empire (until replaced by Adrianople in 1366). Orkhan continued to overrun Byzantine territory in Asia Minor, and in 1354, taking advantage of civil strife in Constantinople, made a permanent lodgment in Europe at Gallipoli. *See* Erzincan; Adrianople VI.

Bushy Run (Pontiac's Rebellion), 1763. As a result of the French and Indian War, Great Britain won possession of North America north of the Ohio River in 1763. Friction with the Indians led to an uprising the same year. The Indian leader was Pontiac, an Ottawa chief. From May 16 to June 20 Pontiac's followers destroyed every British post west of Niagara except Detroit and Fort Pitt, both of which were under siege. In southwestern Pennsylvania Col. Henry Bouquet, a Swiss soldier of fortune in the service of King George III, marched to the relief of Fort Pitt. At Bushy Run, 30 miles southeast of the fort, Bouquet encountered a large force of hostile Indians. In a two-day battle, on August 5–6, the British regulars routed the Indians despite heavy casualties to themselves. Bouquet relieved Fort Pitt four days later. Outside Detroit, Pontiac raised the siege in November. After more than two more years of raids the chief agreed to a peace treaty on July 24, 1766. *See* Indian Wars in the United States.

Bussaco (Napoleonic Empire Wars), 1810. With Austria again knocked out of the war in 1809, Napoleon I was free to concentrate on the Iberian Peninsula. Here he hoped to subdue the Spanish (ensuring his brother Joseph's hold on the throne) and to drive the British out of Portugal. To protect the British position at Lisbon, Gen. Lord Wellington (Arthur Wellesley) constructed a series of fortified lines on the heights of the Torres Vedras during the winter of 1809–10. In the following summer Marshal André Masséna, at the head of 80,000 French troops, overwhelmed Spanish opposition to march into Portugal. Wellington pulled back to the heights of Bussaco, 125 miles northeast of Lisbon, where he attempted to block the French with 25,000 British and 25,000 Portuguese.

On September 27 Masséna attacked with his main army of 60,000 men. In a stiff fight Wellington checked Masséna's advance but then continued his retreat to behind the Torres Vedras. He had lost 1,200 allied troops; Masséna's casualties totaled 4,600. The French marshal pursued but, finding the British position too formidable to assault, went into winter quarters. Throughout the cold-weather months Wellington hounded his enemy by hit-and-run attacks and by shutting off the French flow of supplies. Finally, in the spring, Masséna withdrew into Spain, leaving more than 20,000 men captured, killed, or dead of disease and starvation. Portugal stood free, while Wellington organized an offensive for the following year. *See* Wagram; Talavera de la Reina; Fuentes de Oñoro; Napoleonic Empire Wars.

Buxar (British Conquest of Bengal), 1764. The nawab of Bengal, Mir Kasim, led an uprising against the British in India in 1763. His troops seized Patna on the Ganges River and massacred about 125 European prisoners. To put down the rebellion, an army of several thousand British and allied native soldiers under Maj. Hector Munro took the field against Mir Kasim. Munro's army met the rebels on October 23, 1764, at Buxar

(Baxar), 77 miles west of Patna. Although greatly outnumbered, the British routed their opponents, inflicting heavy losses. Mir Kasim fled to Oudh, and the British domination of Bengal was re-established. *See* Panipat III;

Byland (English-Scottish Wars), 1322. The battle of Myton in 1319 brought a three-year peace to the English-Scottish border warfare. As soon as the truce ended, Robert I, the Bruce, again invaded England. Edward II, fresh from his victory over the rebellious English barons at Boroughbridge, retaliated by marching into southeastern Scotland. But he was almost immediately forced back, closely pursued by Robert's Scots. Edward continued to retreat, reaching Byland, 20 miles north of York, on October 14. Here his army was attacked and routed. The English king narrowly avoided capture. This defeat compelled Edward to formally acknowledge Scottish independence, which became official with the signing of the Treaty of Northampton in 1328, the year after Edward's murder. *See* Myton; Boroughbridge; Dupplin Moor.

Bytham (First Barons' War of England), 1220. Despite the official end of the Barons' War in 1217, many lords and mercenary captains refused to yield the castles they had held for John and later for his son Henry III. With the death of the regent, William Marshal (1st earl of Pembroke and Strigul), in 1219 the government's recovery of these strong points fell to Hubert de Burgh (later earl of Kent), acting for the young king. In 1220 opposition to the royal program flared into open defiance, when the Earl of Aumâle refused to give up two royal castles and the private castle of Bytham in Lincolnshire. De Burgh took Bytham under siege. After overcoming a short resistance, he captured the castle, compelling the earl's obedience. This battle ended armed opposition, although similar trouble broke out four years later at Bedford. *See* Sandwich I; Bedford; Barons' Wars.

Byzantine Empire (395–1453). The Eastern Roman Empire came into existence in 395 with the death of Flavius Theodosius I, who had reunited the Roman Empire under his rule the previous year. He was succeeded by his two sons—Honorius, emperor of the Western Roman Empire, and Arcadius, ruler in the East of what was to be called the Byzantine Empire. In 474 Zeno the Isaurian became the first ruler to take the name Byzantine (for Byzantium, the original name of Constantinople) emperor. For almost a thousand years the Byzantine Empire, with its center at Constantinople, ruled much of southern and southeastern Europe and western Asia. When Constantinople fell to the forces of the Fourth Crusade, the empire went into eclipse until it was restored in 1261 under Michael VIII. Finally in 1453 the aggressive Ottoman Turks, who had overrun all the Imperial lands but the capital, swept into Constantinople and ended the Byzantine Empire. For later battles and wars of the major heir to the empire *see* Turkey.

Amida II	502
Dara	528
Callinicum	531
Constantinople I	532
Carthage II	533–534
Tricameron	534
Rome III	536–538
Rome IV	546–547
Taginae	552
Casilinum	554
Constantinople II	559
Melitene I	578
Viminacium	601
Jerusalem V	615
Nineveh II	627
Ajnadain	634
Pella	635
Damascus I	635
Yarmuk River	636
Aleppo	638
al-Fustât	641
Alexandria II	642
Tripoli I	643
Lycia	655
Constantinople III	673–678
Carthage III	698
Constantinople IV	717–718
Ravenna II	729
Acroinum	739
Heraclea Pontica	806
Amorium	838
Samosata	873
Apulia	875–880
Taormina	902
Erzurum	928
Melitene II	934
Candia I	960–961
Adana	964
Aleppo-Antioch	969
Adrianople III	972
Damascus II	976
Sofia	981
Crotone	982
Balathista	1014
Manzikert	1071
Dyrrachium II	1081
Dyrrachium III	1108
Philomelion	1116
Myriocephalon	1176
Stara Zagora	1189
Constantinople V	1204
Klokotnitsa	1230
Adrianople V	1254
Constantinople VI	1261
Bursa	1317–1326
Constantinople VII	1453

Byzantium I (Civil Wars of the Roman Empire), 194–196. When Emperor Publius Helvius Pertinax was assassinated in 193, a rich senator, Didius Julianus, claimed the throne. But the real struggle for rule came from three military commanders—Clodius Albinus of Britain, Septimius Severus of Pannonia, and Pescennius Niger of Egypt. Severus, nearest to Rome, marched on the capital and assumed the title of emperor. Julianus was killed.

Severus turned to the East to attack the legions of Niger. He blockaded a large enemy force in Byzantium (later Constantinople) in 194. The remainder of Niger's troops were attacked and driven out of Cyzicus, Nicaea, and Issus in Asia Minor. Niger himself was captured south of Issus at the Cilician Gates and beheaded. Severus then concentrated on the siege of Byzantium. In the spring of 196 his forces stormed into the city and thoroughly sacked it. With the East under firm control, Severus hurried back to Rome to challenge Albinus, who had been building a rival force in Gaul. *See* Lugdunum; Roman Empire.

Byzantium II (Civil Wars of the Roman Empire), 323–324. Following up his victory at Adrianople on July 3, 323, Constantine I, western ruler of the Roman Empire, pursued the defeated Licinianus Licinius to Byzantium. Here the latter, head of the Eastern Empire, deployed his army to resist Constantine's siege. Licinius himself crossed the Bosporus into Asia to raise an army to relieve Byzantium.

Meanwhile, at sea the Dardanelles (Hellespont), water gateway to the Sea of Marmara, was held by Licinius' fleet of 350 vessels, commanded by Amandus. To bottle up Byzantium on the water side, Constantine ordered his armada of 200 galleys into action under the direction of his son Crispus. In two days of fighting, the lighter, faster vessels of Crispus forced the Dardanelles passage and routed the enemy navy with a loss of 150 ships and 5,000 men. Constantine was free to send a large part of his army across the Bosporus to attack Licinius at Chrysopolis (Üsküdar). After winning a decisive battle there on September 18, 324, he returned to prosecute the siege of Byzantium. The city soon surrendered. The Roman Empire was at last reunited under one ruler, Constantine I, the Great. Six years later the emperor ordered the rebuilt Byzantium to be named Constantinople, which would become the capital of the Eastern Roman, or Byzantine, Empire. *See* Adrianople I; Chrysopolis; Roman Empire.

C

Cadiz (English-Spanish Wars), 1587. During the long, brutal war between Spain and the Netherlands provinces, Elizabeth I of England aided the Low Countries. Particularly effective against the ships of the Spanish king, Philip II, was the English navy of Sir Francis Drake, Sir John Hawkins, and Lord Charles Howard of Effingham. On April 29, 1587, Drake boldly sailed a task force of 30 to 40 ships into Cadiz, Spain's most important Atlantic port. Defying the shore batteries of the Duke of Medina-Sidonia (Alonso de Guzmán), the English fleet sank or captured about 30 Spanish ships of all sizes, without the loss of a ship or a man. For a total of three days Drake raided along the southwestern coasts of Spain and Portugal before returning to England. The attack on Cadiz (called by Drake "singeing the king of Spain's beard") is believed to have delayed the sailing of the Invincible Armada by at least a year. *See* Zutphen; Spanish Armada.

Caesarea (Jewish Wars of the Roman Empire), 135. During the reign of Hadrian, Judea again revolted against Roman rule and institutions. The immediate cause was Emperor Hadrian's order to rebuild Jerusalem as a Graeco-Roman city. Led by Simon Bar Cocheba (Bar Kokhba), the Jews began a systematic expulsion of all Roman forces from Judea in 132. The tide turned, however, when the veteran Roman general Sextus Julius Severus arrived to take charge of the legionaries. In a hard-fought campaign he ruthlessly crushed the revolt by destroying 50 Jewish strong points and hundreds of villages. The Roman reconquest was completed in 135 when Severus captured the seaport of Caesarea (Qisarya), 55 miles northwest of Jerusalem. Bar Cocheba was killed. Tens of thousands of Jewish combatants perished during the savage three-year struggle. *See* Jerusalem IV; Roman Empire.

Cairo (Turkish Invasion of Egypt), 1517. After crushing the Mameluke army and slaying the Egyptian sultan at Marj-Dabik in 1516, Selim I, the Grim, took his Ottoman Turk force of Janizaries into Egypt itself. On January 22, 1517, making good use of his artillery, Selim blasted his way into Cairo. His troops promptly sacked the city. The new sultan, Tuman Bey, was executed and the caliph sent to Constantinople. The Turks, now in control of the Mohammedan holy places in Arabia, left Egypt under the rule of a governor-general. *See* Marj-Dabik; Rhodes.

Cajamarca (Spanish Conquest of Peru), 1532. The Spanish conquistador Francisco Pizarro marched into the interior of Peru with 62 horsemen and 102 infantry in 1532. Later in the year he reached Cajamarca on a plateau on the east slope of the Andes. Here on November 16 he met a large army of Incas commanded by Atahualpa. By a ruse Pizarro seized the Inca chief, which paralyzed the Indians' ability to fight. Despite receiving a huge ransom of gold and silver, the Spaniards killed Atahualpa the following year. With the death of their sovereign, the Incas became an easy conquest for Pizarro. *See* Tenochtitlán.

Calais I (Hundred Years' War), 1346–1347. Following his decisive victory over the French army of Philip VI at Crécy, England's Edward III marched northwest to Calais. Nine days later, on September 4, 1346, the English took the city under siege. The townspeople, led by Jean de Vienne, resisted stubbornly, holding the invaders at bay despite what was probably the first use of artillery (called bombards) in a military operation. During the course of the long siege, six burghers reportedly surrendered to the English, offering their lives as ransom for their fellow citizens; they were spared on the intervention of Edward's wife, Queen Philippa. At the beginning of August 1347 a French relief army appeared but, finding the English siege lines too strong to attack, moved off. The long-suffering garrison then capitulated on August 4. Edward evacuated the French population and turned Calais into an advanced military base for operations on the Continent. The city remained in English hands until early in 1558. *See* Crécy; Winchelsea; Hundred Years' War.

Calais II (English-French Wars), 1558. The marriage of the English queen Mary I to Philip II of Spain forced England to take the side of the Hapsburgs in their long struggle with Valois kings of France. English support aided the Spanish victory at Saint-Quentin in 1557. But later that year a French army under the Duc de Guise (François de Lorraine) marched on Calais, which had been England's toehold on the Continent since 1357. Mary refused to aid the garrison with either reinforcements or money. After a siege of five days, Calais surrendered on January 6, 1558. By a treaty signed the following year, France's Henry II promised to return the city in eight years. But Calais remained lost to England, and Mary is reported to have said in sorrow that the word "Calais" would be engraved on her heart. *See* Boulogne; Saint-Quentin I; Gravelines.

Calatafimi (Italian Wars of Independence), 1860. The Italian War of Independence against Austria received a severe setback in 1859 when France (Louis Napoleon III) suddenly withdrew as an ally. But the unrest in the several states of Italy continued. On May 11, 1860, Giuseppe Garibaldi landed in western Sicily with a thousand Redshirts to aid an uprising against the Austrian-dominated kingdom of Naples (Francis II). Augmented by a thousand or more Sicilian recruits, Garibaldi attacked the Neapolitan army at Calatafimi in the northwest on May 15. The rebels defeated several thousand troops of Francis II and went on to seize Palermo 12 days later. *See* Solferino; Milazzo; Italian Wars of Independence.

Calcutta (Seven Years' War), 1756. A new Moslem ruler of Bengal, Siraj-ud-daula (Surajah Dowlah), came to power in 1756. Fearing entrapment in the new English-French war, he struck first. At the head of a large Indian army, he attacked the British at Calcutta, on the Hooghly River, on June 16, 1756. Most of the Europeans fled to nearby ships, leaving only 190 men to defend Fort William. After undergoing a three-day assault, the fort surrendered on June 20. According to one report, 146 of the captured were pushed into an 18-by-15-foot prison cell for the night; by morning all except 23 had died in the Black Hole of Calcutta.

In January of the following year Lt. Col. Robert Clive, with 900 European and 1,500 Indian soldiers, recaptured Calcutta. Clive then repulsed a counterattack by some 40,000 of Siraj-ud-daula's men. In March he went on to take Chandernagor, a French post 21 miles up the Hooghly River, before falling back to Madras. But now a crucial battle loomed for the control of all Bengal. *See* Arcot; Minorca I; Plassey; Seven Years' War.

Calderón Bridge (Mexican War of Independence), 1811. The Spanish rule of modern Mexico received its first threat from a revolt of the masses led by a Creole priest, Miguel Hidalgo y Costilla. On September 16, 1810, Hidalgo organized a revolt in the northwestern province of Guanajuato. Marching on Mexico City, the rebels built up to a force of 80,000 men. Near the capital the poorly organized horde was turned back by 6,000 Spaniards under Gen. Felix Calleja del Rey on November 6. The rebels fled, pursued by the royalists. On January 17, 1811, Calleja's troops caught up with their quarry at the Bridge of Calderón, near Guadalajara, 280 miles northwest of the capital. The revolutionists suffered a crushing defeat. Hidalgo and his two lieutenants, Ignacio Allende and Juan Aldama, tried to escape, were captured, and were executed. Calleja earned the nickname "the Butcher" for his treatment of prisoners. The leadership of the revolt now passed to José Morelos, who in turn was captured and executed on December 22, 1815. *See* Calpulalpam.

Caldiero I (Wars of the French Revolution), 1796. Early in November 1796 Austria made a third large-scale attempt to crush Napoleon Bonaparte's 40,000 troops in northern Italy. From the north Gen. Baron Paul Davidovich with 18,000 troops drove into Trent and then pressed the French back down the Adige Valley to Rivoli. At this point he halted to await developments. Meanwhile, Gen. Josef Alvinczy (Baron von Borberek) marched his 29,000 men westward to Vicenza, routing the French outposts in his path. From November 2 to 6 Napoleon lost 5,000 men to the twin Austrian offensives. But the temporary encampment of Davidovich gave the French the opportunity to concentrate against Alvinczy. From Verona, Napoleon sent the divisions of Gen. André Masséna (on the left) and Gen. Pierre Augereau (on the right) eastward to attack Alvinczy's advance guard of 8,000 men. Slowed up by a fierce sleet storm in their faces, the 12,000 French were unable to reach Caldiero, five miles eastward. On November 12, while the Austrian lead elements held their ground, Alvinczy moved up his main body to hurl back the attackers. In this first defeat for Napoleon the French lost 2,000 men; 5 general officers were wounded. Napoleon withdrew to Verona, but instead of waiting there for the Austrian columns to converge against him, he renewed the offensive. *See* Bassano; Arcole; French Revolution Wars.

Caldiero II (Napoleonic Empire Wars), 1805. One of the main objectives of the French thrust to the Danube below Ulm was to force a general withdrawal of the three Austrian armies of Holy Roman Emperor Francis II. Each of the three was commanded by a brother of the emperor—Archduke Ferdinand at Ulm, Archduke John in the Tyrol, Archduke Charles Louis in northern Italy. While Napoleon I himself directed the drive southeast through Germany, he sent Marshal Michel Ney with 7,500 French troops and a Bavarian force to press southward against the 40,000 troops of John. At the same time Marshal André Masséna with an army of 37,000 men was to attack eastward and push the 50,000 troops of Charles out of Italy.

The able Charles, foreseeing the squeeze against his position, made a spoiling attack on October 30, 1805, against the French at Caldiero, five miles east of Verona. Masséna's troops beat back the assault, but the battle gave the Austrians time to send their baggage train eastward. From Caldiero Masséna relentlessly pressed eastward, while Charles fought only rear-guard actions. When the archduke reached the Tagliamento River, near the head of the Adriatic, he halted long enough to cover John's withdrawal from the Tyrol. Both Austrian armies then continued their retreat into what is now Hungary. Meanwhile the emperor's forces along the Danube were falling back to Vienna and beyond. *See* Ulm; Oberhollabrunn; Napoleonic Empire Wars.

Caliano (Wars of the French Revolution), 1796. When the Austrian field marshal Count Dagobert von Wurmser fell back north and east of northern Italy's Lake Garda in August 1796, Napoleon Bonaparte followed cautiously. But the French commander struck quickly upon learning that his opponent had divided his army. While keeping an eye on Wurmser, who had moved southeast of Trent, Napoleon sent Gen. André Masséna northward up the Adige Valley. Here an Austrian army of 20,000 men under Gen. Baron Paul Davidovich held the road leading into Trent. On September 4 the French army pressed forward to drive Davidovich's advance guard out of Marco. On the following day Napoleon himself directed a ten-mile advance to Caliano. A furious charge following an artillery barrage swept the Austrians out of the town. With a two-day loss of 6,000 men and 20 cannon, Davidovich abandoned Trent, 15 miles to the north, and retreated into the Alps. Napoleon then wheeled his army to the right (east) to take up the pursuit of Wurmser's main body. *See* Castiglione delle Stiviere; Bassano; French Revolution Wars.

Callinicum (Byzantine-Persian Wars), 531. The victory of the Byzantine army, under Belisarius, at Dara in 528 checked the Persian advance into northern Mesopotomia. Three years later, however, the Sassanid ruler of Persia, Kavadh I, resumed the offensive. He struck at Callinicum on the east bank of the Euphrates River, routing the Byzantine army. Belisarius saved most of his troops by taking refuge on the islands in the river. With this indecisive action, the war ended. Belisarius returned to Constantinople where Emperor Justinian I was planning a restoration of the Roman Empire in the West. *See* Dara; Constantinople I.

Calpulalpam (Mexican War of Reform), 1860. A series of religious and political reforms by a liberal government beginning in 1855 led to civil war two years later. The Liberals, under Benito Juárez, established their capital at Vera Cruz in opposition to the Conservatives, who held Mexico City. (The United States recognized the government of the Liberals on April 6, 1859.) After three years of conflict, the two hostile armies met in a showdown battle on December 22, 1860, at Calpulalpam, 40 miles northeast of Mexico City. The forces of Juárez, led by Jesús Gonzáles Ortega, won decisively and marched into the capital. The defeated leader, Miguel Miramón, fled into exile. This battle ended the War of the Reform, with Juárez installed as president. *See* Puebla II.

Calven (Swiss-Swabian War), 1499. The second major battle of the frontier war between the confederated Swiss cantons and the troops of Holy Roman Emperor Maximilian I took place a month after the first clash. As at Frastenz, Maximilian's Imperial army, chiefly from the duchy of Swabia, occupied a strong position, at Calven in present-day Italian Venezia Tridentina. On May 22, 1499, the outnumbered Swiss infantry charged head on into their opponents, wielding their deadly pikes and halberds. The Swabians fled the field, enabling the Swiss of Graubünden (Grisons) to secure their independence. A third, and final, battle would end the war. *See* Frastenz; Dornach.

Cambrai (World War I), 1917. The impending Russian-German armistice threatened to free large elements of the German army for use on the Western Front. Before these troops could come into line against the Allies, the British field marshal Sir Douglas Haig resolved to launch one more offensive in northern France. On November 20 he sent the Third Army of Gen. Sir Julian Byng against the German position southwest of Cambrai. To catch the enemy by surprise, Haig conducted no preliminary bombardment. Instead, the attack was spearheaded by 324 tanks. The first massed tank assault in history carved a six-mile-wide hole in the lines held by Gen. Georg von der Marwitz' Second German Army. British infantry poured through the gap for three miles. By nightfall, however, German resistance and mechanical failures among the tanks had stalled the attack along the Saint-Quentin Canal. Despite furious fighting, especially around Bourlon Wood, the British could make no farther penetration of the Hindenburg Line. Meanwhile, the German operational commander on the Western Front, Gen. Erich Ludendorff, massed reinforcements on both flanks of the British penetration. On November 30 a strong counterattack began driving forward south of the salient. On the night of December 4 Haig ordered a withdrawal, ending the battle with no overall gain in territory.

The battle of Cambrai cost the British 43,000 casualties, of whom 6,000 were prisoners taken on the first day of the German counteroffensive, and 158 guns. German losses were 41,000, including 11,000 captured, and 138 guns. *See* Ypres III; Somme River II; World War I.

Cambrai–Saint-Quentin (World War I), 1918. A day after the American-French attack in the south, the Allied commander in chief, Marshal Ferdinand Foch, launched the western half of his gigantic pincers offensive on the Western Front. From Cambrai south to Saint-Quentin, four allied armies under the immediate direction of the British field marshal Sir Douglas Haig stood poised to attack: the British First (Sir Henry Horne), Third (Sir Julian Byng), and Fourth (Sir Henry Rawlinson), and the French First (Marie Debeney). On September 27 the two northern armies attacked, followed two days later by Rawlinson and Debeney. The German armies of Gen. Max von Boehn, suffering under heavy Allied artillery fire, yielded the line of the Saint-Quentin Canal. Even the famed Hindenburg Line collapsed under relentless Allied pressure. Cambrai was enveloped on September 30, Saint-Quentin evacuated on October 1. Four days later the British held the entire defensive position. General Erich Ludendorff, chief German operations officer in the west, withdrew his forces to the line of the Selle River, a tributary of the Schelde.

The Allied drive continued on October 17. The Selle line was forced in the south on October 19 and in the north the following day. A week later Ludendorff resigned and was replaced by Gen. Wilhelm Groener. By the end of October the Germans had been forced back behind the Schelde. As Haig's armies closed up to the river, they were joined on their left (north) by three armies under King Albert I of Belgium—Belgian, French Sixth, British Second—which had pushed eastward through Flanders. To the south the French Fifth and Tenth armies maintained constant pressure on the German lines to prevent reserves from moving either northward against Haig or southward against the American offensive of Gen. John Pershing.

On November 1 Haig resumed his offensive on a 30-mile front. The Schelde line was turned. By the time of the armistice on November 11, one of his Canadian divisions had reached Mons, while King Albert's troops to the north held Ghent. Meanwhile the southern arm of the pincers had been making equal progress. Foch's two offensives never converged, but the steady thrust of both arms thoroughly defeated the German armies on the Western Front. *See* Amiens; Meuse River–Argonne Forest; World War I.

Camden (War of the American Revolution), 1780. With the surrender of Charleston, S.C., on May 12, 1780, American resistance in the South collapsed, except for guerrilla operations conducted by Andrew Pickens, Francis Marion, and Thomas Sumter. In the summer, however, the U.S. Congress commissioned Gen. Horatio Gates to organize a new army around a core of 900 Continental troops detached by Gen. George Washington from his New York base. Gates took command on July 25 in North Carolina. With 3,000 men he began a slow march southward toward the British base at Camden, S.C.

On August 15 Gates began a night march to Sanders Creek, seven miles north of Camden. In the darkness the Americans bumped into the British army of Gen. Lord Charles Cornwallis, who had moved northward to meet Gates. Although the British had a smaller force (2,239 men), they attacked at dawn. The formal advance of the redcoats with their bayonets at the ready was too much for the inexperienced American troops. The North Carolina militia of Gen. Richard Caswell in the center bolted to the rear. On the left Gen. Edward Stevens' Virginia militia also panicked and fled to the north. On the right the Delaware and Maryland Continentals, under Gen. Baron de Kalb, held their ground for almost an hour before being outflanked and crushed between converging British columns. De Kalb fell with eleven wounds. Among the Continentals, 650 were killed or captured, many of the latter wounded. Militia losses were 100 killed or wounded and 300 captured. British casualties totaled only 324.

As the routed American army hurried northward, Col. Banastre Tarleton's British cavalry pursued. At Fishing Creek, in South Carolina, Tarleton overtook a retreating detachment of 700 men under Sumter. A sudden attack on August 18 killed another 150 Americans, while 300 more were taken prisoner. This setback opened the way for Cornwallis to invade North Carolina. It also completed the ruin of Gates, who had led the 200-mile flight to Hillsboro, N.C. The victor at Saratoga lost his command after suffering one of the greatest disasters in American military history at Camden. *See* Waxhaw Creek; Kings Mountain; American Revolution.

"Camel, Battle of the." *See* Basra

Camerinum (Third Samnite War), 298 B.C. Six years after conceding defeat in the Second Samnite War, Samnium made a last effort to arrest the growing power of Rome. The Lucanians, Etruscans, and Gauls joined the Samnites to form a hostile ring around Rome and its new possession of Campania.

The war started auspiciously for the anti-Rome coalition. Two Roman legions commanded by Lucius Scipio were sent to Camerinum, 90 miles northeast of Rome, to hold a pass in the Apennines through which the Gauls were expected to advance. Here in 298 B.C. Scipio was attacked by a combined force of Gauls and Samnites under Gellius Equatius. The Roman army was badly defeated, one of its legions (about 4,200 men) being cut to pieces. *See* Bovianum; Sentinum; Samnite Wars.

Campaldino (Wars of Italy), 1289. In the tumultuous Guelph-Ghibelline struggle Florence served as a center of Guelph strength against the Imperial power of the Holy Roman Empire. To the southeast, Arezzo held a Ghibelline force. On June 11, 1289, armies from the two hostile cities clashed at Campaldino on the upper Arno River. The Florentine army routed its opponents. One of the members of the victorious force was Dante. *See* Messina II; Curzola.

Camperdown (Irish Rebellion), 1797. During the Irish revolt against Great Britain (George III), the insurgents appealed for aid to the Netherlands, then under the domination of the French Directory. A Dutch fleet of 16 ships under Adm. Jan Willem de Winter put out from Texel in the fall of 1797. However, it was intercepted in the North Sea off Camperdown in the northern Netherlands by a British fleet commanded by Adm. Adam Duncan (later Lord Duncan). On October 11 the two forces fought a savage naval battle in which nine Dutch ships were captured without the loss of a British vessel. Each side suffered more than a thousand killed and wounded, while the Dutch also lost 5,000 captured. The defeat of this expedition blocked all important aid from abroad to the Irish rebels. The battle of Camperdown may also be considered as part of the Wars of the French Revolution. *See* Saint Vincent Cape II; Vinegar Hill; French Revolution Wars.

Canada. As a British colony Canada was the site of battles in six wars involving the mother country, the United States, or both. Two local rebellions were quelled, one prior to and one following the establishment of dominion status in 1867. In both World Wars Canada sent troops to fight alongside British and other allied armies in western Europe.

Port Royal I (King William's War) 1690
Port Royal II (Queen Anne's War) 1710
Louisbourg I (King George's War) 1745
See French and Indian War
See American Revolution
See War of 1812
Toronto 1837
Batoche 1885
See World War I
See World War II

Candia I (Byzantine Reconquest of Crete), 960–961. Continuing the offensive against the crumbling Moslem domain, the Byzantine Empire sent an expedition to Crete. Under the experienced general Nicephorus Phocas, the Constantinopolitan fleet of 3,000 vessels opened the invasion with an assault on Candia (Heraklion), on the north shore of the island late in 960. For six months the Byzantines pressed home their attack. Crete finally fell in March 961. The Moslems were killed, expelled, or converted to Christianity. The recapture of Crete enabled the Byzantine navy to win back Cyprus, Rhodes, and the other islands of the eastern Mediterranean. *See* Melitene II; Adana; Moslem Conquests.

Candia II (Venetian-Turkish Wars), 1646–1669. Despite the declining strength of the Ottomans after the 1571 battle of Lepanto, the Turks still hungered to possess Crete. This island had been controlled by Venice since the time of the Fourth Crusade. In 1648 Sultan Ibrahim I seized the city of Canea, on the northwest coast of Crete, after a two-month siege. But Candia (Heraklion), 60 miles to the east, resisted capture, whereupon the Turks launched a new siege against this city. The small garrison of Venetians and Greeks under Francesco Morosini resisted stubbornly and received periodic reinforcements and supplies from the strong Venetian fleet. Ibrahim fell in 1648 and was replaced by Mohammed IV, but the fight for Candia went on. In 1656 the Venetian navy temporarily closed the Dardanelles, which caused great suffering in Constantinople as well as among the Ottomans on Crete; but the Turks still clung to their siege lines. Finally, even with some aid from France, the defenders of Candia could hold out no longer. On September 27, 1669, the city surrendered to Mohammed's grand vizier, Fazil Ahmed Kuprili. Venice agreed to surrender all claims to Crete except for three fortified posts on the island. *See* Khotin I; Szentgotthárd.

Cannae (Second Punic War), 216 B.C. While Quintus Fabius Maximus Verrucosus harassed Hannibal in southern Italy, Rome built a new army of 85,000 men. This huge force, double the size of the Carthaginian army, crossed the Apennines and prepared to corner Hannibal at the village of Cannae (modern Barletta), near the Adriatic coast. In charge of the eight Roman legions were the consuls Gaius Terentius Varro and Lucius Aemilius Paulus.

On August 3 the Roman army attacked the Carthaginian lines which were drawn up on the plains outside the deserted village on the Aufidus (Ofanto) River. Moving westward from the sea, the legionaries slowly forced back Hannibal's center. But the Carthaginian withdrawal was planned. The flanks held fast, and soon the Romans became wedged into a large salient, the foot soldiers massed ever tighter by the push of men from the back. Meanwhile Hanno, son of Bomilcar, led a charge of heavy cavalry past the right flank of the Roman lines, then turned and routed the enemy horsemen on both wings. Just as Hannibal's center seemed about to collapse, Hanno's cavalry struck the rear of the Roman army, completing its encirclement. Assailed on all sides, the legionaries were cut to pieces where they stood. More than 50,000 Romans died at Cannae; 4,500 were captured. Among the dead were Consul Paulus, 29 of 33 military tribunes,

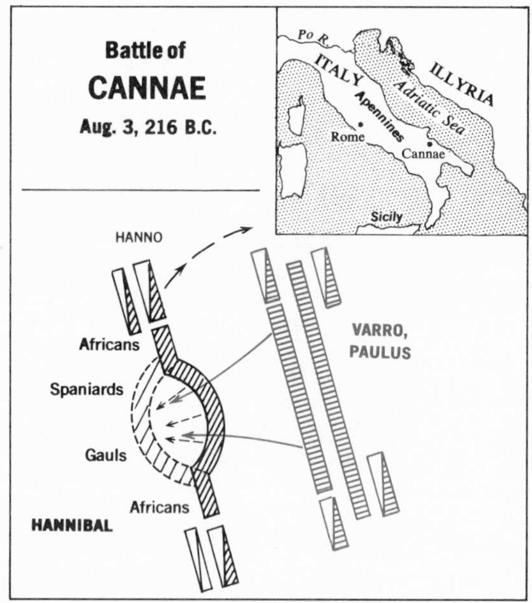

and 80 senators. It was Rome's greatest defeat and one of the classic envelopments in history. The Carthaginians suffered 5,700 casualties.

Hannibal had now destroyed all of Rome's fighting forces except the defensive troops inside the capital. But he still could not attack the city itself. His strongest arm, the African and Spanish cavalry, would be useless in an assault on the walls of Rome. And he lacked the heavy equipment necessary to besiege the city. The Carthaginian marched across the mountains to Capua, the second largest city of Italy, where he established his headquarters. Capua, and almost all the southern part of the peninsula, welcomed him as an ally. Across the Strait of Messina, Syracuse also threw off Roman rule. *See* Trasimeno Lake; Nola; Punic Wars.

Cantigny (World War I), 1918. As the first American troops began coming into the Allied line on the Western Front, Gen. John Pershing insisted that they be committed as units under his direct command. This was agreed to by the Allied commander in chief, Gen. Ferdinand Foch. In the Somme River sector the American 1st Division (Robert Bullard) took over a part of the front occupied by the French First Army of Gen. Marie Debeney. To the east stood the village of Cantigny, held by the German Eighteenth Army (Oskar von Hutier). On May 28, the second day of the huge German offensive on the Aisne River to the south, the Americans attacked and captured Cantigny, taking 200 prisoners. The new troops held the village despite fierce counterattacks. Although the tactical significance of the battle was small, the first American division-size offensive provided a psychological lift to the Allies. The battle cost the victors 1,607 casualties, including 199 killed. Four days later the 2nd and 3rd divisions went into action on the Marne River. *See* Aisne River III; Belleau Wood; World War I.

Cape. For battle sites beginning with this word, see name of cape. For **Cape Saint Vincent,** for example, see **Saint Vincent Cape.**

Cape Town (Napoleonic Empire Wars), 1806. The Dutch settlement at Cape Town, South Africa, became a pawn in the Revolutionary Wars of France when the Netherlands fell under the control of Paris. Cape Town was occupied by Great Britain in 1795 but restored to Dutch rule by the 1803 Treaty of Amiens. Upon the renewal of the war against France by the Third Coalition in 1805, Great Britain sent an expeditionary force against Cape Town. Led by Gen. Sir David Baird, some 6,000 British landed at Saldanha Bay on the southwest coast on January 8, 1806. Repulsing a combined Dutch and French counterattack, Baird secured the beachhead and went on to seize Cape Town, which remained in British hands even after the end of the war in 1815. *See* Finisterre Cape III; Buenos Aires; Napoleonic Empire Wars.

Caporetto (World War I), 1917. The eleven Italian assaults on the Isonzo River line had failed to break the stalemate on the Austrian front in the northeast, by the autumn of 1917. The Italian supreme commander, Gen. Count Cadorna, then ordered his Second and Third armies in this sector to go over to the defensive. Meanwhile, Germany had decided to help Austria deliver a knockout blow to Italy. Seven German divisions were united with eight Austrian divisions to form a new Fourteenth Army, under the German general Otto von Below, veteran of the Western Front. Below moved his force toward Caporetto on the northern flank of the Isonzo lines, opposite the Italian Second Army of Gen. Luigi Capello. On Below's left and right flanks the Austrian Fifth and Tenth armies prepared to make secondary attacks against the Italian Third and Fourth armies, respectively.

The German-Austrian offensive opened before dawn on October 24 with a massive six-hour artillery bombardment. The primed infantry then rushed forward to Caporetto. Capello had neglected the defenses on his front, giving his troops little protection. The infantry assault carried ten miles the first day and tore the Second Army to pieces. As the German-led Fourteenth Army thrust farther westward, the Austrian units on its flanks forced the withdrawal of the Italian Fourth and Third armies.

Cadorna planned to make a stand on the Tagliamento River. But on the night of November 2–3, Below's advance guards forced a crossing upstream near Cornino. The Italian retreat then continued to the Piave River, 70 miles behind the starting line. Here the German-Austrian advance finally halted on November 12, having outrun its supplies. The defeat at Caporetto, sometimes called the Twelfth Battle of the Isonzo, cost the Italians 275,000 prisoners, plus another 45,000 in killed and wounded. Along the Piave a defensive line was organized by Gen. Armando Diaz, who had replaced Cadorna. Six French and five British divisions arrived from the Western Front to bolster the sagging Italian armies. *See* Isonzo River; Asiago; Piave River; World War I.

Capua (Second Punic War), 212–211 B.C. When Hannibal established his Carthaginian headquarters at Capua in southwestern Italy, he made that city a focal point of Roman attention. A Roman army was organized to lay siege to Capua. Hannibal relieved the immediate pressure on the city by suddenly marching south and seizing Tarentum (Taranto), on the southern coast, in 212 B.C. (But a Roman garrison holding out in a citadel at the harbor's mouth prevented the Carthaginian fleet from using the port.) Returning to Capua, Hannibal tried to lure the enemy away by marching to within a mile of Rome. But the Roman legions refused to abandon the siege, and Hannibal had to turn away.

By now Quintus Fulvius Flaccus had circumvallated Capua with a double wall held by 60,000 Romans. The city's position was hopeless and it was forced to surrender. Fifty-three of Capua's senators faced execution; other officials were sold into slavery. *See* Nola; Metaurus River; Punic Wars.

Carabobo (Venezuelan War of Independence), 1821. The liberation of Colombia in 1819 furnished Simón Bolívar with men and supplies to resume the rebellion in Venezuela. Bolívar, now the president of Colombia, moved into Venezuela in 1821, uniting his army with that of José Páez. On June 24 the combined patriot force of 6,500 men attacked a smaller army of royalists at Carabobo, about 100 miles west of Caracas. The Spaniards, commanded by Gen. Miguel de La Torre, suffered a crushing defeat, in large part due to the valor of a British battalion fighting on the side of the patriots. Five days later Bolívar entered Caracas in triumph. The freedom of Venezuela stood secure. *See* Boyacá; Pichincha.

Carberry Hill (Scottish Rebellion against Mary), 1567. The third marriage of Mary, Queen of Scots, to the Earl of Bothwell (James Hepburn) on May 15, 1567, provoked an uprising among the nobles of the country. A rebel force challenged the royal army at Carberry Hill, east of Edinburgh, the following month. Early in the battle, on June 15, Mary's troops deserted her cause. The queen was taken captive and forced to dismiss Bothwell. Imprisoned at Lochleven Castle in east-central Scotland she agreed to abdicate in favor of her son, the future James VI (son of her second husband, Lord Darnley). Mary escaped, however, to try to regain the throne. *See* Pinkie; Langside.

Carbiesdale (English Civil War), 1650. When his Scottish Cavalier army fell apart at Philiphaugh in 1645, the brilliant general the 1st Marquis of Montrose (James Graham) fled to the Continent. Here he supported the claims of the pretender Charles II to the English throne. Five years later Montrose returned to Scotland to rally Royalists against the Commonwealth of Oliver Cromwell. He landed in Caithness with 1,500 men, a third of whom were Swedish mercenaries. But few Scots supported the rebel movement, and on April 27, 1650, Montrose was caught by a surprise Commonwealth attack at Carbiesdale in northern Scotland's Ross County. The attacking cavalry routed the rebel force. Montrose was betrayed into capture and hanged at Edinburgh on May 21. His body was dismembered for distribution at the scenes of his 1645 triumphs. Ironically, at the same time the victorious Duke of Argyll and other Covenanters were preparing to make war on England in behalf of Charles II. *See* Philiphaugh; Dunbar II; English Civil War.

Carchemish (Babylonian-Egyptian War), 605 B.C. The Egyptian army of Necho II, which crushed Judah in 609, stayed on in western Asia to war with Babylon's Chaldean dynasty. After three years of indifferent fighting, Nabopolassar turned over his Chaldean army to his son Nebuchadnezzar II (Nabuchodonosor). At Carchemish on the Euphrates River (at the Syrian border), Nebuchadnezzar launched his brilliant military career with a crushing defeat of the Egyptians. This battle cost Egypt its Asiatic possessions. *See* Megiddo II; Jerusalem I.

Carham (Rise of Scotland), 1016. After repelling the Danish invaders at Mortlack, Malcolm II of Scotland turned to consolidating his rule. In the south the Scots' expansion brought them into conflict with the Northumbrians. Malcolm's army, assisted by Strathclyde Britons under Oswain the Bald, clashed with a Northumbrian force led by the earl, Uhtred, on the Tweed River. Malcolm won a clear victory. This battle confirmed the Scots' possession of the Central Lowlands—the valleys of the Tay, Forth, and Clyde. *See* Mortlack; Dunsinane.

Carlist Wars (1834–1839, 1873–1876). During the reign of Isabella II of Spain, Don Carlos, son of Charles IV, claimed the throne and gained the support of the Church and much of the northern provinces. Great Britain, France, and Portugal supported Isabella. The English general George de Lacy Evans led a brigade against the guerrilla forces of the pretender, who called himself Charles V. The Carlists could make no headway and ended their revolt on August 31, 1839. Don Carlos took refuge abroad.

The Second Carlist War took place during the formation of the first Spanish republic in 1873, the rebels uniting behind Don Carlos VII, grandson of the first pretender. Only guerrilla fighting ensued. Two years later a separate revolution restored the monarchy in the person of Don Carlos' cousin Alfonso XII, son of Isabella. In February 1876 the thwarted rebels again yielded. Don Carlos fled into exile.

Carrhae I (Wars of the First Triumvirate), 53 B.C. When Rome's First Triumvirate assigned themselves spheres of action, Marcus Licinius Crassus took Syria (Julius Caesar received Gaul and Pompey the Great, Spain). Crassus hurried east to intervene in a dynastic quarrel among the Parthians. At Carrhae (Haran) in northern Mesopotamia, Crassus' army encountered a Parthian force commanded by Orodes I, the anti-Roman claimant to the throne. The Parthians fought their cavalry skillfully, harassing the Romans with hit-and-run attacks. When the more heavily armed legionaries charged the elusive horsemen, their ranks became scattered. The Parthians then turned upon Crassus and cut down his detachments in detail. Of the 6,000 Romans actually engaged, 5,500 were killed. The others were captured, including Crassus, who was promptly executed.

With the death of Crassus, and with Caesar busy fighting the Gauls across the Alps, Pompey the Great became virtual dictator of Rome. *See* Alesia; Rubicon River; First Triumvirate, Wars of the.

Carrhae II (Persian Wars of the Roman Empire), 296. Another of the numerous wars between the Roman Empire and Sassanian Persia broke out during the reign of Diocletian. Diocletian sent his son-in-law (and future emperor) Galerius to the East with an imperial army. The Roman legions encountered the Persian army under Narses at Carrhae (Haran), in northern Mesopotamia, scene of the defeat and death of the triumvir Crassus in 53 B.C. History repeated itself, as the legionaries suffered a second severe defeat at this ancient communication center.

Galerius, however, received reinforcements during the winter and the following year pursued the victorious Persian host into Armenia. Catching Narses by surprise in a night attack, the Romans reversed the decision at Carrhae by almost annihilating the Asiatics. With this battle, the two opponents made peace. Rome regained Mesopotamia and was allowed to continue its hegemony over Armenia. *See* Edessa I; Verona; Singara; Roman Empire.

Carrickfergus (War of the American Revolution), 1778. To carry the naval war into British home waters, Capt. John Paul Jones sailed from Portsmouth, N.H., in the American warship the *Ranger* in November 1777. After raiding the northwest coast of England, Jones put in at Carrickfergus in Northern Ireland on April 24, 1778. Here he found the British warship *Drake,* equipped with 20 guns. Jones opened fire and within 30 minutes the 18 guns of the *Ranger* had killed the *Drake*'s captain and 40 of its crew. Jones lost 6 men. It was the first defeat of a British warship by an American naval vessel. Jones later sailed for France to try to organize a fleet for a heavier attack on England. *See* Flamborough Head; American Revolution.

Carrizal (U.S. Expedition against Villa), 1916. The raid on Columbus, N.M., by the Mexican guerrilla force of Francisco (Pancho) Villa aroused the United States. General John J. Pershing was sent southward across the border with a provisional cavalry division to bring Villa to justice. Many Mexicans regarded Pershing's force as an invasion army, rather than as a punitive expedition against a bandit leader who was also sought by the government of Venustiano Carranza. Despite the local hostility, Pershing pressed deep into Mexico. At Carrizal, 85 miles south of Ciudad Juárez, a body of Mexican regulars barred the way. Pershing routed them in a short skirmish on June 21. He then continued his 400-mile advance into Mexico. Although Villa escaped, the expedition broke up the bandit army into small, disorganized bands. At the continued insistence of President Carranza, Pershing's force was ordered withdrawn on February 5, 1917. *See* Columbus, N.M.

Carthage. The ancient city and state in North Africa (in modern Tunisia) became a military power in the western Mediterranean in large part at the expense of Greek cities in Sicily. Its growth brought Carthage into conflict with Rome, however, resulting in the three Punic Wars. In the third conflict Carthage was destroyed by a Roman army under the younger Scipio.

Himera	480 B.C.
Selinus-Himera	409 B.C.
Acragas	406 B.C.
Syracuse II	387 B.C.
Crimisus River	341 B.C.
Himera River	311 B.C.

See Punic Wars

Carthage I (Third Punic War), 149–146 B.C. At the end of the Second Punic War Carthage had been stripped of most of its wealth and of all its Mediterranean possessions. But during the next 50 years it rebuilt its economy to the point where it again rivaled Rome as a commercial power. Many Romans regretted that the African city had been allowed to revive. Marcus Porcius Cato, in particular, ended each of his speeches in the Roman senate with the words "Carthage must be destroyed."

The pretext for a new attack on the city came when Carthage quarreled with Numidia, its western neighbor and an ally of Rome. The senate sent an army to Utica, 20 miles away, in 150 B.C. Carthage offered to submit and even sent 300 children from its leading families to Sicily as hostages. But when Rome demanded that the city be vacated, the Carthaginians refused. The legions then attacked. For three years the citizens of Carthage courageously held off the better-trained and heavier-armed Roman army. In the third year of the war Publius Cornelius Scipio Aemilianus took charge of the legions and pressed the attack vigorously, as his grandfather Scipio Africanus had done in the Second Punic conflict. But even after the Romans had breached the triple walls of the city, the Carthaginians fought in the streets until they were completely overcome. Of the 50,000 survivors, some escaped into the interior; the rest were sold into slavery. The city was burned to the ground, never to rise again. Carthage had been wiped off the map. *See* Zama; Numantia; Punic Wars.

Carthage II (Wars of the Byzantine Empire), 533–534. Under the rule of Justinian I, the Great, the Byzantine (or Eastern Roman) Empire launched a long campaign to recover the territories of the Western Roman Empire that had been inundated by barbarians. The first blow was directed at Carthage, the chief city of North Africa, where the Vandals had been established for more than a hundred years. In the summer of 533 Belisarius sailed from Constantinople to the Tunisian coast with a force of 5,000 cavalry and 10,000 infantry. Landing below Carthage, Belisarius marched on the city from the east. Ten miles from his objective he surprised a large body of dismounted Vandal horsemen, under Gelimer. In a sudden charge the Imperials routed the enemy on September 14 and entered the city the following day. While Belisarius rested and reorganized his troops in Carthage, Gelimer camped with his Vandal force 18 miles to the southwest at Tricameron for the remainder of the year.

Early in 534 Belisarius suddenly rode out of the city and struck hard at the Vandals, who were positioned behind a stream. When Gelimer fled on horseback, his men followed in great disarray. The Imperials had won an easy victory, losing only 50 men compared to the enemy's loss of 800. Later, Gelimer was captured and sent to Constantinople as a prisoner. The Vandal kingdom had ceased to exist. Belisarius was recalled briefly to the Byzantine capital where Justinian was planning the reconquest of Italy. *See* Constantinople I; Rome III.

Carthage III (Moslem Conquest of North Africa), 698. The Moslem conquest of North Africa, which had engulfed Tripoli in 655, thrust on westward under Okba (Oqba). In 670 he founded Kairouan, later to become a holy city of Islam, and then, bypassing northern Tunisia, raided as far west as Tangier. Okba, the nephew of the conqueror of Egypt Amr ibn-al-As, was killed on the return march in 683 (and raised to sainthood by the Arabs). His successor, Hasan ibn No'man, consolidated the conquest by attacking the Tunisian cities of Utica and Carthage, the last outposts of the Byzantine Empire in Africa. Hasan's hard-riding cavalrymen burst into Utica, destroyed it, and then moved 15 miles southeast to Carthage. Here the Byzantine garrison again crumbled in the face of a fierce Arab onslaught. The ancient city was reduced to the status of an obscure village.

The Berber tribesmen, who had resisted the Arabs more effectively than the Byzantines, accepted peace a few years later. All North Africa now passed under Moslem rule. *See* Tripoli I; Río Barbate; Moslem Conquests.

Casilinum (Wars of the Byzantine Empire), 554. The Byzantine general Narses had no sooner reconquered Italy for the empire of Justinian I than the Franks poured across the Alps. The outnumbered Imperial troops barricaded themselves in the towns while the flood swept down the peninsula. Finally at Casilinum (Capua), 20 miles north of Naples, Narses deployed 18,000 Byzantine troops to challenge the main body of Franks, 30,000 strong, under Buccelin. As was their custom, the Frankish infantry charged head on, wielding their deadly, short-handled axes (the francisca). Narses stopped the head of the Frankish column with Roman infantry and the dismounted heavy cavalry of his Herule auxiliaries. At the same time he sent his mounted archers against both flanks of the invaders. The entire body of Franks was trapped and cut to pieces. Buccelin was killed. In an age in which cavalry was becoming predominant, even the fierce Frankish infantry could not compete against well-mounted troops.

This battle ended the Frankish invasion. The remnants pulled back beyond the Alps. From that time until his recall in 567, the aged eunuch Narses ably ruled the whole of Italy for his emperor in Constantinople. *See* Taginae; Constantinople II.

Cassano d'Adda I (War of the Spanish Succession), 1705. The war in northern Italy, which had been relatively quiet after the 1702 battle of Luzzara, flared up again with the return of Prince Eugene of Savoy in 1705. Eugene, supported by Victor Amadeus II, duke of Savoy, organized an attack on the French line at Cassano, on the Adda River, 16 miles east of Milan. On August 16 the Imperial army struck the French, who were commanded by Philippe de Vendôme (Grand Prior), brother of Marshal Louis Joseph, duc de Vendôme, the chief general of Louis XIV in Italy. Despite a disadvantage in numbers, the Imperials penetrated the French positions. However, the Duc de Vendôme arrived in time to reorganize the French and eventually drive the Imperials back. Each side lost several thousand men, and Philippe fell into disgrace for his faulty leadership. The Italian theater then became inactive again until the following year. *See* Luzzara; Blenheim; Turin; Spanish Succession, War of the.

Cassano d'Adda II (Wars of the French Revolution), 1799. The new Austrian offensive against the French in northern Italy picked up momentum in the spring of 1799 with the arrival of an allied Russian army under Field Marshal Count Aleksandr Suvorov. Driven westward after the defeat at Magnano, the French general Jean Moreau dug in to defend the Adda River line. Here, at Cassano, 16 miles east of Milan, Suvorov's Russians and an Austrian army commanded by Gen. Baron Michael von Melas stormed against the French position on April 27. Despite a loss of 6,000 men, the allies routed the outnumbered French, taking 7,000 prisoners. Suvorov entered Milan in triumph and then pressed on to occupy Turin on May 27. Meanwhile, the French continued to fall back toward Genoa. *See* Magnano; Trebbia River II; French Revolution Wars.

Cassel (French-Flemish Wars), 1328. Two bloody battles with France early in the fourteenth century had secured independence for Flanders but had engendered strong hostility between the two states. Soon after Philip VI of Valois ascended the throne of France in 1328, a new war broke out. The mounted knights of France met the foot soldiers of Flanders at Cassel, northeast of Saint-Omer, later that year (August). As at Mons-en-Pévèle 24 years before, the Flemish pikemen could not hold their ground against the hard-charging French cavalry. The Flemings, including their leader, Nicolas Zannequin, were ridden down and killed by the thousands. This crushing victory secured French domination over the Flemings for another 50 years. Philip reinstated the Count of Flanders as his authority over the erstwhile rebels. *See* Mons-en-Pévèle; Roosebeke.

Cassino (World War II). An Italian hill town occupying a key position in the German Gustav Line south of Rome; it was attacked four times by Allied troops from early February until May 17, 1944, when it finally fell to Polish troops. *See* Gustav-Cassino Line.

Castelfidardo (Italian Wars of Independence), 1860. After the Redshirts of Giuseppe Garibaldi occupied Naples on September 7, they prepared to march on Rome. This alarmed Conte Camillo di Cavour of Piedmont, who feared the intervention of France (Louis Napoleon III). With the consent of King Victor Emmanuel II, he sent a Piedmontese army southward to the Papal State. Negotiations with Giacomo Cardinal Antonelli, representative of Pope Pius IX, fell through. The Piedmontese, commanded by Col. Enrico Cialdini (later Duca di Gaeta), then marched into papal territory. At Castelfidardo, near the Adriatic coast south of Ancona, Cialdini met the papal army, under Gen. Louis de Lamoricière, on September 18. The Piedmontese won an overwhelming victory. Marching on to the south, the victors linked up with Garibaldi. The combined Italian force then turned southwestward against the Neapolitan army of King Francis II of the Two Sicilies, now at Gaeta. Meanwhile both Naples and Sicily voted by plebiscite to unite with Piedmont. *See* Milazzo; Gaeta; Italian Wars of Independence.

Castelnaudary (French Civil Wars), 1632. After erasing the military power of the Huguenots, Louis XIII and his minister Cardinal Richelieu were troubled by a revolt among the French nobility. The uprising was led by Duc Henri II de Montmorency, marshal of France, and by Gaston, duc d'Orleans, brother of the king and sworn enemy of the cardinal. The royal army met the rebel force at Castelnaudary in southern France on September 1, 1632. Richelieu's troops won a decisive victory. Montmorency was captured and later beheaded. This battle ended the conspiracy. *See* La Rochelle II.

Castiglione delle Stiviere (Wars of the French Revolution), 1796. While Napoleon Bonaparte's main army was routing an Austrian column at Lonato, west of Lake Garda, on August 3, a French division under Gen. Pierre Augereau held off the chief Austrian army south of the lake at Castiglione delle Stiviere. Two days later Napoleon massed most of the French troops (30,000 men) against the 24,000 Austrians under Field Marshal Count Dagobert von Wurmser. In a pitched battle east of the town, the Austrian left (south) was turned and Wurmser driven across the Mincio River. The Austrians lost 2,000 men and all their artillery. (Augereau was later made Duc de Castiglione by Louis XVIII.) When Napoleon began crossing the Mincio on the following day, Wurmser fell back through Verona. Except for the 15,000 troops still holding Mantua, the Austrian summer offensive had collapsed completely. But in Germany the French armies were suffering a similar fate. *See* Lonato; Mantua; Caliano; Amberg; French Revolution Wars.

Castillon (Hundred Years' War), 1453. The French offensive of Charles VII in 1450–51 drove the English out of France (except Calais). When Aquitaine revolted against the new French rule, however, England's Henry VI sent a fresh army to Bordeaux under John Talbot, earl of Shrewsbury, in 1452. Shrewsbury pressed eastward to Castillon, 26 miles up the Dordogne River. Here the French were besieging the hostile town. When the English made a rash attack on the French siege lines, on July 17, 1453, they were cut down by artillery fire and then routed by a counterattack. Shrewsbury was killed and most of his 6,000-man army destroyed.

The battle of Castillon ended the Hundred

Years' War. Bordeaux opened its gates to the French on October 19, with the remaining English under Edmund Beaufort, 2nd duke of Somerset, permitted to sail for home from La Rochelle. Despite the stirring English victories of Crécy, Poitiers, Agincourt, and Verneuil, France had driven the enemy from the Continent (except for the small bridgehead of Calais, which was yielded in 1588). *See* Formigny; Guinegate; Hundred Years' War.

Çatalca (First Balkan War). A heavily fortified line from the Black Sea to the Sea of Marmara that protected the Turkish city of Constantinople against Bulgarian attack on November 17 and 18, 1912. *See* Lüleburgaz.

Caucasus (World War II), 1942–1943. During the winter of 1941–42 the German armies held more than 1,500 miles of front deep in Russia, with only minor withdrawals to the west. By spring, however, the bitter cold and, to a lesser degree, Russian counterattacks had taken so many casualties that there was not sufficient German strength to resume an advance along the entire front, as had been carried out the previous year. Hitler then chose to concentrate on the southern sector and strike for Stalingrad and for the Caucasus oil fields. Here the German armies stood along the upper Donetz and the Mius rivers. The Mius line was the most advanced position in Russia and only 50 miles from Rostov, the gateway to the Caucasus. The attack into the Caucasus was assigned to a specially created Army Group "A" directed by Field Marshal Siegmund von List (soon to be relieved). Farther north the new Army Group "B" became the left flank guard under Field Marshal Maximilian von Weichs (who replaced the original commander, Fedor von Bock, on July 13).

Before the German drive could begin, Marshal Semën Timoshenko launched an attack against Kharkov on May 12. Progress was slow, and five days later the German Seventeenth Army counterattacked viciously, regained all lost ground, and took 80,000 prisoners by May 31. The premature Russian commitment helped open the way for the last great German offensive in the East. It began on June 22 with the left wing advancing from Kursk toward Voronezh on the Don River. Farther south the spearheading Fourth Panzer Army of Gen. Hermann Hoth reached the Don at the great bend a hundred miles from the starting line early in July and then turned southeast. Hoth's *Panzers* continued to slant down the corridor between the Don and the Donetz. They were followed by Gen. Friedrich von Paulus' Sixth Army, which was headed for Stalingrad.

With his left screened by the Fourth Panzer to the north, Gen. Paul von Kleist now launched the principal thrust. Starting near Kharkov, the First Panzer Army (15 divisions) raced southeast to cross the lower Don above Rostov on July 22. At the same time the German Seventeenth Army, south and west of the Donetz, pressed eastward to close on Kleist's right and back up his advance. Rostov fell on July 27.

East of the Don, the German armor crossed the flooded Manych River where the Russians had blown up a dam. Then Kleist's *Panzers* broke out to the south in three columns between the Black and Caspian seas. The right (west) column reached the more westerly oil fields at Maikop, 200 miles beyond Rostov, on August 9, while the center and left approached the Caucasus foothills 150 miles farther southeast. Just across the mountains lay the main oil fields, and a little beyond, an opening to the whole Middle East. But then the drive slowed. Fuel for the tanks became increasingly difficult to supply. The fighting at Stalingrad began to siphon off Kleist's strength—some motorized troops, his flak corps, and most of his air force. There was also an exposed left flank between Stalingrad and the Caspian to protect. And Russian resistance, directed by General Ivan Iyulenev, tightened—800 bombers began to strike at the *Panzer* divisions.

Checked at the Terek River, Kleist forced a passage downstream (to the east) at Mozdok early in September. But the *Panzers* had run their course. By November 18 the front was stabilized. Meanwhile, on the west, Novorossisk was taken on September 11, but the seacoast drive of the Seventeenth Army bogged down at Tuapse, 90 miles deeper into the Caucasus.

Army Group "A," which came officially under Kleist's command on November 22, remained in its exposed Caucasus position through December. In January, however, a Russian counterthrust down the Don River from the Stalingrad sector threatened to cut off retreat. The Germans began pulling out of the Caucasus. When the Russians were only 42 miles from the Rostov gateway, Kleist's forces were still 390 miles to the southeast and pressed hard by pursuing Russians under Gen. Ivan Maslennikov. Nevertheless, by helping Gen. Erich von Manstein's newly formed Army Group Don (later Army Group South) hold open Rostov, Kleist was able to withdraw across the lower Don just before the gate was slammed shut on February 14. Kleist was promoted to field marshal for this feat. The only German force left in the Caucasus held a small bridgehead at Novorossisk.

But even west of the Don, Kleist's and Manstein's army groups were imperiled by Russian advances made in early 1943 under the direction of Marshal Georgi Zhukov. Continuing a southward drive from the Stalingrad pincer, Gen. Nikolai Vatutin's armies had crossed the Donetz at Izyum on February 5. At the same time from the upper Don, Gen. Filip Golikov had struck westward to Kursk on February 7. Kharkov fell to this joint offensive on February 16. Now, however, an early thaw slowed the Russian momentum. This gave Manstein time to regroup 9 *Panzer* and 12 infantry divisions in the Stalino sector and launch a counterattack. Aided by Field Marshal Gunther von Kluge's Army Group Central, Manstein's armies fought their way north to the Donetz and retook Kharkov on March 15. But here the German drive collapsed on the thawing steppes. The entire southern front then quieted down until midsummer 1943. *See* Soviet Union (World War II); Crimea; Stalingrad; Ukraine; World War II.

Caudine Forks (Second Samnite War), 321 B.C. The First Samnite War (343–341 B.C.) left unsettled the intense competition between the hill people of Samnium and the Romans for possession of the rich plains of Campania, along the Tyrrhenian Sea. In 327 B.C. a Roman force moved halfway across Campania to occupy Naples. The Samnites retaliated the following year by blocking the Latin Way route from Rome south to Fregellae. The Romans then sought to outflank the Samnites by making an alliance with Lucera in Apulia province on the eastern side of the peninsula. In 321 B.C. a large Roman army under Consuls Sp. Postumius and T. Veturius, moving eastward toward Lucera, was trapped by the Samnite Pontius in the narrow Apennine Mountain pass called Caudine Forks. Failing to fight their way out of the ambush, the Romans surrendered to Pontius and were marched out under the yoke, a humiliation Rome always remembered.

The defeat at Caudine Forks hastened the evolution of the Roman military organization. Finding the phalanx too stiff and heavy for rough terrain, the Romans designed the famed legion. In the beginning this unit consisted of 30 maniples (each of 120 men) plus 5 maniples in reserve. The legion was deployed in three lines arranged in checkerboard fashion to provide maximum power and maneuverability.

After the disaster suffered at Caudine Forks, the Roman army gradually regained its strength. In 318 B.C. it seized most of the Campanian plains, and five years later it raised the siege of Fregellae. *See* Trifanum; Bovianum; Samnite Wars.

Cawnpore I (Indian Mutiny), 1857. When the Great Mutiny broke out at Meerut in May, Nana Sahib (Dandhu Panth), a disgruntled Maratha, took charge of 3,000 Sepoy rebels at Cawnpore, 245 miles southeast of Delhi. On June 6 he laid siege to the city. For 20 days the garrison of 900 British and loyal Indians, half of whom were women and children, held out. Then, on a promise of safe conduct by Nana Sahib, the besieged began filing out of Cawnpore for boats on the Ganges River on June 26. The mutineers opened fire, killing all the men and herding the surviving women and children into prison. A relief column under Gen. Sir Henry Havelock had pushed to within 20 miles of the city on July 15, when Nana Sahib ordered five assassins to kill all remaining prisoners and to throw their bodies down a well. Havelock's force reached the stricken city two days later. *See* Delhi II; Indian Mutiny.

Cawnpore II (Indian Mutiny), 1857. After the midsummer massacres at Cawnpore, the Sepoy mutineers, under Tantia Topi, lieutenant of chief rebel Nana Sahib, held the upper hand in the Cawnpore area. In November the British commander in chief, Sir Colin Campbell, relieved Lucknow and then turned southwest to Cawnpore. Campbell encountered a much larger force of 25,000 rebels outside the city on December 6. In a slashing assault Campbell routed the mutineers, who suffered heavy losses at the hands of pursuing British cavalry. Campbell lost only 99 men. Tantia Topi fled to Jhansi. *See* Lucknow; Jhansi; Indian Mutiny.

Cedar Creek (American Civil War), 1864. Believing the Confederates to be thoroughly defeated in the Shenandoah Valley, Gen. Philip Sheridan withdrew northward and prepared to send Federal reinforcements to Gen. U. S. Grant's main army in front of Petersburg. On October 18 Sheridan was on his way back from a conference in Washington, D.C. His army of 31,000 men, under the temporary command of Gen. Horatio Wright of the VI Corps, stood along Cedar Creek near Middletown, Va. That night the Confederate general Jubal Early, who had cautiously followed the Federals down the valley, moved into position for an attack the following day.

At dawn Early's II Corps (18,400 men) suddenly struck the forward Federal position held by Gen. George Crook's XIX Corps. The surprised bluecoats fell back in confusion, as did the VI Corps when the Confederate attack drove deeper into the Federal lines. Wright rallied his command briefly, west of Middletown, then withdrew to a new position north of the village. The Confederates, who had taken 1,300 prisoners and 18 guns, halted to loot the enemy camp. Early did not press his advantage, expecting the Federals to retreat farther. But Sheridan, riding hard to the sound of battle from Winchester, 14 miles away, had arrived and was reorganizing his army for a counterattack. Late in the afternoon the Federals swept forward against the unprepared Confederates. In a few minutes the battle had turned around. Early's corps was driven from the field, losing most of its artillery, supplies, and baggage wagons. In all, the Confederates lost 2,000 in killed and wounded (including the slain division commander Stephen Ramseur) and 1,000 missing. The day's fighting cost the Federals 5,665 men, of whom 1,591 were missing.

The battle of Cedar Creek virtually ended the

war in the Shenandoah Valley. Early's corps disintegrated until he had little more than 1,000 men. This force was wiped out by Gen. George Custer's cavalry at Waynesboro, Va., on March 2 of the following year. Meanwhile Sheridan, with most of his troops, rejoined Grant at Petersburg. *See* Fisher's Hill; Petersburg; American Civil War.

Cedar Mountain (American Civil War), 1862. To correct the Federal failures in the Shenandoah Valley campaign, President Abraham Lincoln created the Army of Virginia, with Gen. John Pope in command, on June 26. (On that same day Confederate Gen. Robert E. Lee initiated the Seven Days battle that would repulse Gen. George McClellan's drive on Richmond by way of the peninsula.) Pope sent Gen. Nathaniel Banks's II Corps toward the key Confederate railroad junction of Gordonsville. But Lee ordered Gen. Thomas (Stonewall) Jackson, who was northeast of Richmond, to get there first. Jackson did. Lee, becoming convinced of McClellan's continued inactivity east of Richmond, then reinforced Jackson to 24,000 troops by giving him Gen. Ambrose Hill's division on July 27. Jackson promptly marched north, meeting Banks at Cedar Mountain on August 9. The Federal commander struck first, caving in Jackson's left flank and killing Gen. Charles Winder who was leading the old Stonewall Division. However, the timely arrival of Hill permitted a counterattack, which checked and then drove back the now outnumbered Federals. The battle cost Banks 2,353 casualties, Jackson 1,338.

When Lee learned that McClellan was evacuating the peninsula, he hurried his entire army northward to strike Pope before the latter could be reinforced. The Federal general fell back north of the Rappahannock River. *See* Cross Keys; Port Republic; Seven Days; Bull Run II; American Civil War.

Celles (World War II). The deepest point of penetration in the Ardennes by German armor, which was blocked by the U.S. 2nd Armored Division on December 24 and 25, 1944. *See* Ardennes II.

Cerignola (French-Spanish Wars in Italy), 1503. The struggle between the French of Louis XII and the Spanish of Ferdinand (V of Castile, II of Aragon) for the possession of southern Italy began in July 1502. Early French superiority became nullified with the indecisive battle of Barletta, on the Adriatic coast, later that year. The two armies clashed again on April 28, 1503, at Cerignola, 20 miles to the west. To the deadly short sword and buckler of his Spanish infantry, Gonzalo de Córdoba had added a corps of arquebusiers. When the French infantry, including hired Swiss pikemen, charged the Spanish position in a vineyard, the musketeers took a deadly toll of their assailants. A Spanish counterattack then routed the French, capturing the enemy's artillery train before it could be put into action.

Louis XII hurried reinforcements to Italy to augment the survivors of Cerignola, who began falling back westward across the peninsula. Naples was abandoned to the Spanish on May 13, the French retreating across the Garigliano River. *See* Barletta; Garigliano River.

Cerro Gordo (U.S.-Mexican War), 1847. After consolidating his hold on Veracruz, Gen. Winfield Scott with some 8,500 American troops began marching westward toward Mexico City on April 8. At the mountain pass at Cerro Gordo, 55 miles inland, Scott's advance was blocked by about 12,000 Mexicans under Gen. Antonio de Santa Anna. The column halted while Capts. Robert E. Lee, George B. McClellan, and other engineer officers made a reconnaissance of the Mexican position. A premature American attack by Gen. David Twiggs on Santa Anna's left, on April 17, opened the battle before Scott had completely deployed his troops for an enveloping operation against both enemy flanks. The main assault took place the following day. In fierce fighting that included much hand-to-hand combat, the Americans swept through the pass. Santa Anna fell back. He lost 204 officers and 2,837 men by capture alone, plus 43 guns and 4,000 small arms. U.S. casualties were 63 killed, 337 wounded.

Scott pressed forward almost 20 miles to occupy Jalapa on April 19. On May 15 he reached Puebla, 65 miles short of Mexico City. With his ranks depleted by disease and the expiration of short-term enlistments, Scott held up here. On August 6 Gen. Franklin Pierce arrived with 3,000 fresh troops, bringing the American strength up to more than 10,000 effectives. Scott resumed his march the following day. *See* Veracruz; Contreras-Churubusco; U.S.-Mexican War.

Český-Brod (Hussite Wars), 1434. After terrorizing eastern Europe for 14 years, the Hussites resumed their internal struggle between the extreme Taborites and the moderate Utraquists. The decisive battle came on May 30, 1434, at Český-Brod (Böhmisch-Brod; also called Lipan), 19 miles east of Prague. Andrew Procop the Great (there was also a Procop the Little), the heir of Jan Zizka, led the Taborites against an army backed by the nobles and conservatives. The murderous clash left 18,000 dead on the field, including both Procops. The Taborites suffered the greater losses, but the flower of Bohemian manhood perished at Český-Brod. Thus the Hussites themselves accomplished what no foreign army had been able to do—they shattered the precocious military might of Bohemia. Two years later the exhausted nation bowed to Sigismund, who also ruled Hungary and the Holy Roman Empire, as the king of Bohemia, and also acknowledged (but not permanently) the dictates of the Roman Catholic Church. *See* Ústí nad Laben; Hussite Wars.

Çeşme (Turkish-Russian Wars), 1770. When Catherine II, the Great, of Russia joined Austria and Prussia in a combined squeeze against Poland, Turkey declared war on Russia. The empress sent the Russian fleet of 50 sail under Count Aleksei Orlov into the eastern Mediterranean. On July 5, 1770, Orlov met the larger Turkish fleet of Sultan Mustafa III at Çeşme, west of Smyrna. In a one-sided battle the entire force of Turkish ships was destroyed. Much of the Russian victory came from the attack of a division of ships under Sir Samuel Greig, a Scottish naval officer in the service of Catherine. After four more years of setbacks in land fighting, Mustafa's successor, Abdul-Hamid I, signed the Treaty of Kuchuk Kainarji with Russia on July 21, 1774, yielding important territorial claims in southeastern Europe. (Meanwhile, Poland had suffered its first partition in 1772.) *See* Focsani.

Ceuta (Portuguese Invasion of Africa), 1415. John I, who had established the Aviz dynasty in Portugal in 1385, consolidated his rule and then looked to expansion overseas. In 1415 he led an expedition against the Moslem trading center of Ceuta on the African side of the Strait of Gibraltar. His Portuguese force stormed into the town and seized it on August 24. The capture of Ceuta launched the first of a series of battles in which the Portuguese sought to build an empire in Africa.

One of John's aides at Ceuta was his third son, who later gained greater fame as Prince Henry the Navigator by sparking the Portuguese voyages of discovery. *See* Aljubarrota; Tangier.

Ceylon (World War II), 1942. Japanese naval victories in the South China Sea and the Java Sea forced the British to rebuild their Eastern fleet hurriedly. On March 24 Adm. Sir James Somerville, former commander of Force H at Gibraltar, arrived at Colombo, Ceylon, to direct defensive operations in the Indian Ocean. A strong Japanese force, including five carriers and four battleships, entered the Bay of Bengal and struck at Colombo with about 80 dive bombers on April 5. This attack, commanded by Adm. Chuichi Nagumo, who had led the Japanese attack on Pearl Harbor, damaged the port and sank a destroyer and an armed merchant cruiser in the harbor. The Japanese lost 21 planes; 19 British fighters and 6 naval aircraft were shot down. Later that day waves of Japanese dive bombers attacked the British cruisers *Dorsetshire* and *Cornwall* south of Ceylon. Both ships were sunk in 15 minutes, with a loss of 29 officers and 395 seamen. Fortunately for the British, Somerville's other ships were at sea between Ceylon and Port T at Addu Atoll, 600 miles to the southwest.

Japanese carrier bombers raided Ceylon again on April 6, striking at Trincomalee's dock and airfield. A small carrier and a destroyer were sunk offshore with a loss of over 300 British seamen. The Japanese lost 15 of 54 planes to Ceylon-based fighters; 11 British planes were shot down. During the next few days 93,000 tons of Allied merchant shipping were destroyed in the Bay of Bengal, demonstrating Japanese control of the eastern Indian Ocean.

Britain's Eastern fleet then pulled back to Bombay on the west coast of India and to Kilindini on the east coast of Africa. But the Japanese also withdrew from the Indian Ocean at that time, shifting their offensive southward toward Australia and eastward toward Midway. *See* Burma I; Madagascar; Java Sea; Coral Sea; World War II.

Chacabuco (Chilean War of Independence), 1817. The first Chilean independence movement, led by José de Carrera and Bernardo O'Higgins, was crushed by the royal Spanish government in 1814. Three years later José de San Martín, from his revolutionary base at Mendoza in western Argentina, began a march across the Andes Mountains with some 5,200 men. Three weeks later San Martín, with O'Higgins, arrived at Chacabuco, just north of Santiago in central Chile. Here the rebels met and defeated the Spanish army on February 12 in a single, well-organized assault. The rebels moved on to occupy Santiago where O'Higgins became "supreme director." A year later the independence of Chile was proclaimed. *See* Rancagua; Maipo River.

Chaeronea I (Macedonian Conquests), 338 B.C. In the twenty years after the mutually disastrous battle of Mantinea, the leaderless Greek city-states further exhausted themselves in continued and confused civil warfare. The so-called Social War (357–55), or "War of the Allies" of Athens, only weakened the Athenian fleet. Then, in 355, controversy over possession of the shrine at Delphi, a source of conflict for more than 200 years, led to the Third Sacred War, which lasted until 346. Meanwhile, in northeast Greece a mortal threat to the democratic city-states was rapidly developing.

In 359 a strong leader, Philip II, took the throne of the somewhat backward country of Macedonia. The new king quickly formed the world's first standing army, organized a hard-hitting cavalry arm, and strengthened the phalanx by increasing its depth from 8 to 16 ranks. He also increased the length of the infantry spear by a third, to 21 feet, and reinstituted the ancient 7-foot javelin, or casting spear. During the first two years of his reign, Philip's new army secured the northern and eastern frontiers of Macedonia against barbarian raids. He then launched a well-planned campaign to conquer all of Greece. In 352 the Macedonian army won a foothold in central Greece by capturing the Thessalian seaport of Volos on the

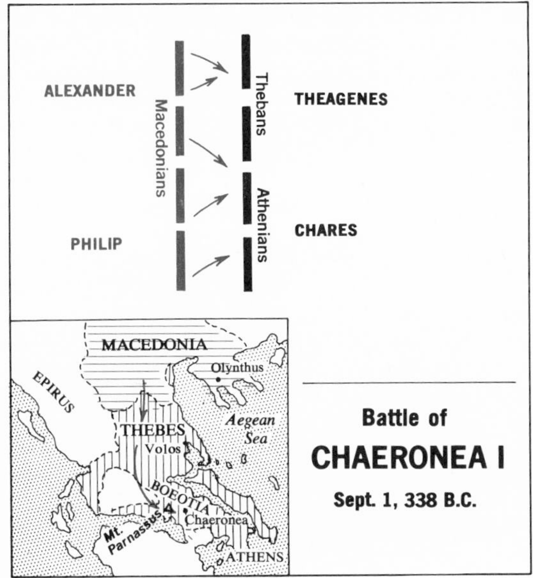

Battle of
CHAERONEA I
Sept. 1, 338 B.C.

Pagasaean (Volos) Gulf. Four years later Philip defied Athens by seizing its colonial city of Olynthus, on the Macedonian coast.

The great Athenian Demosthenes, in a series of impassioned orations, sought to awaken Greece to its growing peril. But the city-states paid no heed and in 339 became embroiled in yet another conflict, the Fourth Sacred War. Philip promptly intervened. Athens and Thebes made a hasty alliance, which was later joined by other Greek states. But the Macedonian army, marching southward, routed the allies' advance guard at Amphissa, west of Mount Parnassus, and pushed deeper into Boeotia. At Chaeronea on September 1, 338 B.C., Philip's 40,000 veterans encountered an equal force of Athenians (on the left) and Thebans (on the right), commanded by Chares and Theagenes, respectively. The desperate fighting of the allies kept the issue in doubt for hours. Finally a cavalry charge led by Philip's 18-year-old son Alexander broke the Theban line on the right; the Sacred Band cavalry, founded by Epaminondas, died to the last man. This action exposed the Athenian flank and rear. The battle became a rout. Some 6,000 Athenians were killed and another 2,000 captured. Few of the Thebans survived. The Macedonians' overwhelming victory over the citizen-soldiers is one of the decisive battles of history. It ended the long years of freedom for the city-states. From this time forward Greece would be troubled by periods of strong authoritarian control. *See* Mantinea; Thebes; Macedonian Conquests.

Chaeronea II (First Mithridatic War), 86 B.C. The Pontic army that Mithridates VI Eupator sent from Asia Minor into Greece greatly outnumbered the relieving force of 30,000 Romans commanded by L. Cornelius Sulla. Nevertheless, the better-trained Roman legions routed the Pontines from Athens and Piraeus. Archelaus, the Asiatic general, then withdrew northwest into Boeotia. Following closely, Sulla attacked at Chaeronea. The Romans routed the larger enemy force, driving them toward Orchomenus, six miles farther north. *See* Athens-Piraeus; Orchomenus; Mithridatic Wars.

Chalchuapa (Central American War), 1885. After their liberation from Spain in 1823, the states of Central America sought periodically to establish themselves in a union. An attempt to organize such a union by force was made in 1885 by Justo Rufino Barrios, president of Guatemala. He won the support of Honduras, but Costa Rica, Nicaragua, and El Salvador opposed him. Disregarding all protests, Barrios placed himself at the head of an army of unification and invaded El Salvador. At Chalchuapa on April 2, the aggressors were defeated by an army of Salvadorians. Barrios was killed, and another effort to form an isthmian federation collapsed.

Chaldiran (Turkish Invasion of Persia), 1514. When Selim I, the Grim, became sultan of the Ottoman Turks, the West received a reprieve. An ardent Mohammedan, Selim concentrated on stamping out heretic sects. After executing thousands of Shiittes at home, he marched a 50,000-man army into Persia. On August 23, 1514, the Turks overwhelmed the Persian cavalry host of Shah Ismail I at Chaldiran, east of the Euphrates, in Armenia. The decisive element was the Ottoman handguns and artillery, which riddled the superior force of Persian cavalry. Selim went on to occupy Azerbaijan and Kurdistan. Only the refusal of the Janizaries to advance farther prevented greater Turkish conquests. *See* Lepanto I; Marj-Dabik.

Chalgrove Field (English Civil War), 1643. While Cavalier forces won local successes in the west and north against the Roundheads during the second year of the Civil War, Charles I maintained his headquarters at Oxford. Here his cavalry, commanded by his nephew Prince Rupert of Germany, carried out raids against the Parliamentarian forces in the southeast. While returning from a raid on June 18, Rupert's horsemen were intercepted by a Roundhead force at Chalgrove, a few miles from Oxford. The able prince led a sudden charge that routed the enemy cavalry. The Roundhead commander, Col. John Hampden, long a prominent foe of the crown, fell mortally wounded. Although the battle was a minor one, it persuaded the supreme Roundhead commander, Robert Devereux (3rd earl of Essex), to give up plans to besiege Oxford. *See* Stratton; Adwalton Moor; English Civil War.

Châlons-sur-Marne I (Germanic Invasions of the Roman Empire), 366. Nine years after the Alamanni had been turned back at Argentoratum

(Strasbourg), the fierce Germanic tribe invaded Gaul again. This time they reached Châlons-sur-Marne, 95 miles east of Paris, before being checked by a Roman army under Emperor Valentinian I. In an all-day battle, the legionaries crushed the invaders, killing 6,000 and taking 4,000 prisoners. Roman losses were 1,200.

Valentinian, probably the last of the able emperors in the West, carried the war across the Rhine the following year. He subdued the Alamanni so thoroughly that, except for a brief flare-up in 378, they remained quiet for 25 years. *See* Argentoratum; Tigris River; Adrianople II; Roman Empire.

Châlons-sur-Marne II (Wars of the Western Roman Empire), 451. During the first half of the fifth century, the Asiatic Huns had established their supremacy over the other barbarbian tribes of central Europe. Led by Attila, "the Scourge of God," the Huns overran most of the Balkans during 447–50, exacting a large tribute from Theodosius II, ruler of the Eastern Roman Empire. In 450 Attila suddenly turned to the west and sent his 40,000 Hun warriors into Gaul on a broad front stretching from Belgium to Metz. Paris was by-passed, but Orleans came under siege.

Flavius Aëtius, military commander of the Western Roman Empire (under Emperor Valentinian III), allied himself with the Visigoth king, Theodoric I, son of Alaric. The combined armies marched to the relief of Orleans on June 14 and drove the Huns back (northward) to the Catalaunian Plains south of Méry-sur-Seine. The Roman

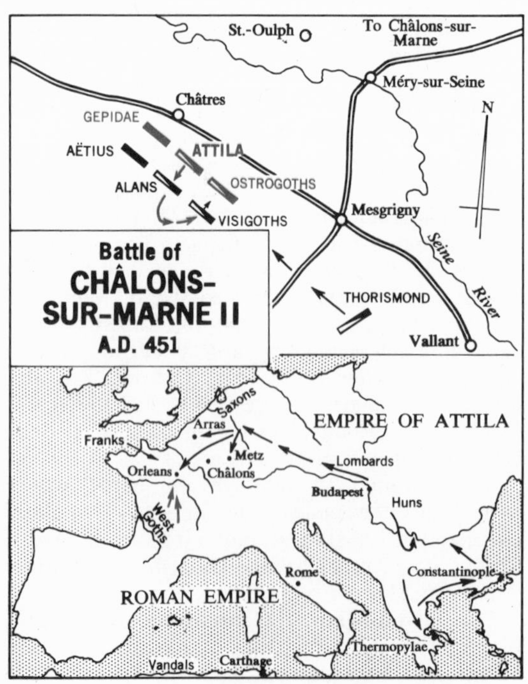

and Visigoth army followed. About June 20 the allies and the Huns fought a pitched cavalry battle on these open plains. The imperial forces held firm on one wing (under Aëtius). The Alans in the center gave way, endangering the right flank. Here, however, the Visigoth heavy mounted troops rode down the Hun horsemen opposite them. Theodoric, who fell in this counterattack, was succeeded by his son Thorismond. Attila, having suffered heavy losses, withdrew to his camp between the Seine and the Marne rivers. And even though Aëtius failed to renew the attack the following day, the Huns retreated back across the Rhine.

Châlons-sur-Marne (more accurately called Méry-sur-Seine) is sometimes called one of the decisive battles of history. It did check the Hun invasion of Gaul. But by allowing Attila to escape with most of his army, Aëtius left the door open for another Hun raid on the Western Empire, to come the following year. *See* Rome I; Hippo Regius; Aquileia III; Roman Empire.

Champagne I (World War I), 1914–1915. Despite heavy losses on both sides and the increasing evidence that the Western Front had become deadlocked, the Germans and Allies continued to slug away at each other through the winter of 1914–15. The French commander in chief, Field Marshal Joseph Joffre, concentrated most of his effort in Champagne, beginning on December 20. But the German defenses of Gen. Erich von Falkenhayn proved to be unyielding. The French attacks were finally called off on March 17. German entrenchments, defended by machine guns, had again demonstrated superiority over courage and bayonets. *See* Ypres I; Champagne II; World War I.

Champagne II (World War I), 1915. The quietness that had prevailed through most of the summer on the Western Front was shattered by a major French offensive in Champagne, beginning on September 25. Planned by the French field marshal Joseph Joffre, it was carried out by the French Second Army of Gen. Henri Pétain and the Fourth Army of Gen. Fernand Langle de Cary. Attacking from Reims westward to the Argonne Forest, the French gained several miles before they were thrown back by German counterattacks ordered by Gen. Erich von Falkenhayn. The battle drew to a bloody close on November 6, with both sides holding their original positions. Joffre's troops had captured 25,000 Germans and 150 field guns but only at a cost of 145,000 casualties. A complementary Allied attack in Artois was equally unsuccessful. *See* Artois II; Artois-Loos; World War I.

Champagne–Marne River (World War I). The German offensive during July 15–17, 1918, which carried southward across the Marne River to open the second battle of the Marne. *See* Marne River II.

Champaubert-Montmirail (Napoleonic Empire Wars), 1814. As the several columns of the Prussian field marshal general Gebhard von Blücher pressed toward Paris from the east, they became too separated to be mutually supporting. Napoleon I seized this opportunity to launch an offensive. With 30,000 troops and 120 guns, the French emperor marched secretly northeast from Nogent-sur-Seine. Despite muddy roads, the French moved quickly. On February 10, 1814, they struck an isolated allied corps at Champaubert and destroyed it. Turning westward, Napoleon interposed his army between two other Blücher corps near Montmirail the following day. In a hard fight the French defeated one enemy force west of Montmirail and drove the second northward toward Château-Thierry. Napoleon turned right (north) on February 12 and continued his attack. The defeated invaders, under Gen. Count Hans Yorck (York) von Wartenburg, finally escaped pursuit across the Marne River. In the two-day combat they lost 7,000 men and 20 guns. French casualties totaled 2,500.

Blücher, learning of Napoleon's offensive, hurried westward with the rest of his army, hoping to strike the French rear. Marshal Auguste Marmont fought a skillful delaying action back to Vauchamps, four miles east of Montmirail. This gave Napoleon time to countermarch to Marmont's assistance. On February 14 the French struck and turned back Blücher's advance guard. The Prussian commander immediately began to retreat through Champaubert. East of this village his route of withdrawal was blocked by a French corps under Gen. Emmanuel de Grouchy. Blücher finally fought free. Heading for Châlons-sur-Marne, he dropped off a Russian division at Étoges. This force was virtually destroyed by Marmont's pursuit late that night. It was a disastrous day for Blücher, who lost 7,000 men, 16 guns, and most of his supply trains. However, to the south the advance of his colleague Prince Karl von Schwarzenberg across the Seine forced Napoleon to move to that sector. The five-day offensive of the French emperor, which shattered the allied army advancing down the Marne Valley, ranks as one of the great achievements in military history. *See* La Rothière; Montereau; Napoleonic Empire Wars.

Champion's Hill (American Civil War). Having routed one Confederate army at Jackson, Miss., Gen. U. S. Grant turned westward to drive Gen. John Pemberton's force back toward Vicksburg, on May 16, 1863. *See* Vicksburg.

Champlain, Lake (War of 1812), 1814. The northernmost of the three British offensives against the United States in 1814 was a joint land and water thrust from Canada down Lake Champlain in New York State. Under the command of Gen. Sir George Prevost, an army of 11,000 men, many of them veterans of the successful Peninsular Campaign of the Napoleonic Wars, left the Saint Lawrence frontier on August 31 to march down the west side of the lake. The American army at Plattsburg consisted of only 3,300 regulars and militia under Gen. Alexander Macomb. Rather than risk a battle against such overwhelming odds, Macomb fell back south of the Saranac River below Plattsburg. Prevost occupied the village on September 6 and then waited for his naval support to arrive. This was a fleet of 4 ships and 12 gunboats, mounting a total of 92 guns and carrying 800 men, commanded by Capt. George Downie.

The American naval commander on Lake Champlain, Capt. Thomas Macdonough, had long sensed that the key to the defense of upper New York lay in the control of the waterway. He had therefore built up a fleet of four ships and ten gunboats that mounted a total of 86 guns and

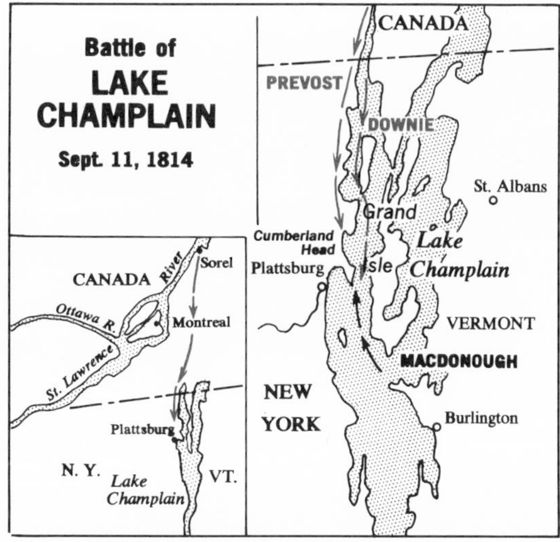

carried 850 men. When Downie's ships entered the lake, Macdonough deployed his vessels in a narrow channel across the bay from Plattsburg and ordered anchors to be dropped. Here he hoped to neutralize the British long-range guns with his own short-range pieces. On September 11 the British ships rounded Cumberland Head to open the battle at a range of 500 yards. For two hours a gun duel raged with no marked advantage to either side. Then Macdonough in the *Saratoga* moved out to attack the enemy flagship, *Confiance,* and forced Downie to strike his flag. Within 30 minutes the battle was over, with the four British warships seized or destroyed, 57 of their crewmen killed, and 72 wounded. American casualties were only slightly less—52 killed, 58 wounded—but no ships were lost. It was one of the few times in history that ships at anchor won a naval battle.

During the battle Prevost's shore batteries had unaccountably remained silent. Now, with the loss of his naval arm, the British commander was forced to retreat back to Canada. Prevost was relieved, but to no avail—Lake Champlain proved to be the last battle of the war in the North. *See* Bladensburg; Fort McHenry; New Orleans I; War of 1812.

Chancellorsville (American Civil War), 1863. When Gen. Joseph Hooker took command of the Army of the Potomac after the disastrous Federal defeat at Fredericksburg, his forces held the north bank of the Rappahannock. Across the river Gen. Robert E. Lee's Army of Northern Virginia guarded every possible crossing against Federal attack. On April 27 Hooker began a movement to turn Lee's left (west) flank by sending Gen. Henry Slocum upstream with three corps (V, XI, XII). Crossing the Rappahannock at Kelly's Ford and the Rapidan at Germania Ford, Slocum reached Chancellorsville with 42,000 men on April 29, in the rear of Lee's 53,000 troops, who were facing northeast toward Fredericksburg. Gen. Darius Crouch then crossed the river with 12,000 men to take up a position behind Slocum. On that same day Gen. John Sedgwick sent part of the I and VI Corps (total of 40,000 men) across the Rappahannock below Fredericksburg.

The Federal offensive seemed to pin Lee between two strong enemy armies. But on April 30 the Confederate commander left Gen. Jubal Early's reinforced division to hold off Sedgwick on the east, while moving the rest of his army against Hooker's main force to the west. Here the Federals did not begin to advance until almost noon of May 1. In a region of tangled underbrush and second-growth timber, appropriately called "the Wilderness," the two armies clashed indecisively. Hooker then unexpectedly called off the attack in favor of fortifying a position around Chancellorsville.

Lee reacted quickly. Early on the following morning he sent Gen. Thomas (Stonewall) Jackson with 26,000 men of the II Corps on a 14-mile circuit of the Federal position to strike from the west. (The exposed Federal right flank had been detected by Gen. J. E. B. Stuart's cavalry.) By 6 P.M. Jackson was in position and attacking the right wing XI Corps of Gen. Oliver Howard. The Confederates had gained some advantage by nightfall. But in the dusk Jackson was mortally wounded accidentally by his own men (he died May 10). As the second-in-command, Gen. Ambrose P. Hill, had been wounded, Stuart took over the corps. Hooker continued to surrender the initiative by contracting his perimeter defense, enabling the separated wings of Lee's army on this front to reestablish communications. At daybreak on May 3 Stuart renewed the assault from the west against the III Corps of Gen. Daniel Sickles and the XII of Henry Slocum. By noon Hooker, who had been slightly wounded, pulled his army northward into a prepared position that looked southward from the junction of the Rapidan and Rappahannock rivers.

Also on the morning of May 3, Sedgwick, 12 miles to the east, began to move toward the Chancellorsville battle. Four times he assaulted Marye's Heights—the scene of heavy fighting during the battle of Fredericksburg, before he finally drove off Early's division. Perceiving this new danger, Lee left Stuart with 25,000 men to try to contain Hooker's force of 75,000 and marched Gen. Lafayette McLaws eastward with 20,000 troops. McLaws reached Salem Church at 3 P.M. and checked Sedgwick's advance. On the following day (May 4) Early returned to the fight and occupied Marye's Heights, in the Federal rear. Sedgwick's 19,000 men were now surrounded on three sides by 21,000 Confederates, who, however, attacked unsuccessfully. Under cover of darkness Sedgwick withdrew to the north side of the Rappahannock.

Lee now turned back westward to attack Hooker, who had been strangely inactive during the action of Salem Church. But the Federal commander had lost all his combativeness. On the night of May 5–6 he began withdrawing his entire force across the Rappahannock. Hooker's only battle as commander of the Army of the Potomac had cost 17,278 in killed, wounded, and missing. Lee's casualties were 12,821, but they included the irreplaceable Stonewall Jackson. The Army of Northern Virginia would never again display the military ingenuity it had shown at Chancellorsville. *See* Fredericksburg; Brandy Station; American Civil War.

Chantilly (American Civil War). The third and last action of Bull Run II, on September 1, 1862, in which the Confederate general Robert E. Lee drove the Federal armies back into the defenses of Washington, D.C. *See* Bull Run II.

Chapultepec (U.S.-Mexican War), 1847. For his final assault on Mexico City the American general Winfield Scott deployed 7,200 men southwest of the capital. Here rose the rocky, 200-foot-high hill of Chapultepec, where the Mexican president, Gen. Antonio de Santa Anna, had posted 1,000 troops. Another 4,000 Mexicans manned secondary fortifications in the area, while some 10,000 stood behind the walls of the city itself. Early on September 13 Scott's artillery opened a bombardment of Chapultepec. Then at 8 A.M. the divisions of Gen. John Quitman (4th) and Gen. Gideon Pillow (3rd) began ascending the hill. Despite heavy enemy fire, Pillow's Americans steadily climbed the slope, aided by ladders and pickaxes. By 9:30 A.M. they had reached and cleared the summit despite the stiff resistance of Los Niños, about 100 boy cadets who defended the Mexican Military

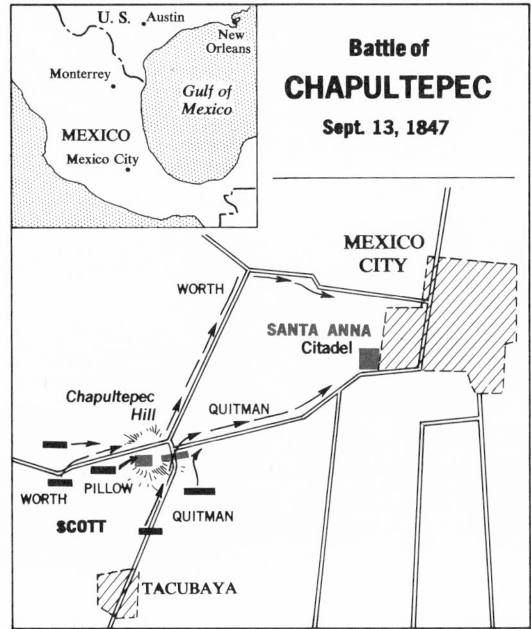

Academy. The fall of Chapultepec opened the causeways to the western *garitas* (stone police-customs stations) of the city. By evening the divisions of Gen. William Worth (1st) and Quitman had stormed and taken two of these *garitas*. The attack cost Scott 130 killed, 703 wounded, and 29 missing.

That night the American army hacked its way through the city's walls with picks and crowbars. Pouring into the capital, U.S. troops raised their flag over the National Palace, marines standing guard over the "halls of Montezuma." After a few days of disorder, Scott established firm control over Mexico City, from which Santa Anna had earlier fled to Puebla. One more battle would conclude the war. *See* Contreras-Churubusco; Molino del Rey; Puebla I; U.S.-Mexican War.

Charlemagne, Conquests of (773–796). Charlemagne, or Charles I, became king of all the Franks in 768. His campaigns to Christianize western Europe took him into Italy, Spain, Germany, and the upper Balkans. In 800 he was rewarded in Rome by being crowned Emperor of the West, a title that later came to be called Holy Roman Emperor.

Pavia IV	773–774
Roncesvalles	778
Süntelberg	782
Tisza River	795–796

Charleroi (World War I). The west-central part of the massive battle fought along the French frontier during August 20–24, 1914, in which the first French and German offensives of the war met head on. *See* Frontiers of France.

Charleston I (War of the American Revolution), 1776. After being forced to abandon his plan to strike North Carolina, the British commander, Gen. Sir Henry Clinton, resolved to capture Charleston, S.C. Here the American general Charles Lee was hastily organizing a defense of the city. The chief American strong point was a palmetto-log fort on Sullivan's Island at the northern entrance to the harbor. It was manned by a South Carolina regiment of 413 infantry and 22 artillerymen, all commanded by Col. William Moultrie.

The British expeditionary force arrived off Charleston on June 4, 1776. Five days later the British troop commander, Gen. Lord Charles Cornwallis, began landing men on nearby Long Island to the north. From here, however, the British soldiers could not force a crossing to Sullivan's Island and took no part in the subsequent battle. Finally, on June 28, Adm. Sir Peter Parker with nine British warships closed in to bombard the fort at the harbor's mouth. The 21 artillery pieces of the colonials replied. It was a hot duel. British guns fired at more than seven times the American rate. But American gunnery was more accurate. In the day-long battle two British warships were crippled (*Bristol* and *Experiment*) and a third, the *Actaeon*, ran aground. In the invading fleet 64 men were killed and 131 wounded. American casualties totaled 17 dead and 20 wounded. Clinton ordered the ships withdrawn that night. The repulse ended active British operations in the South for more than two years. Meanwhile the sturdy palmetto fort was named Moultrie in honor of the gallant commander who had saved Charleston from almost certain capture. *See* Moores Creek Bridge; Savannah I; American Revolution.

Charleston II (War of the American Revolution), 1780. In the sixth year of the war the British commander in the United States, Gen. Sir Henry Clinton, stepped up the offensive in the South. Embarking 8,500 troops at New York City, Clinton sailed to South Carolina, where he landed on February 11 on Johns Island, 30 miles south of Charleston. While the fleet blockaded the harbor, Clinton and his second-in-command, Gen. Lord Charles Cornwallis, pushed slowly northward, crossing the Ashley River on March 29. Meanwhile the American commander in the South, Gen. Benjamin Lincoln, had been drawing all available troops into the city. He now had 2,650 Continentals and 2,500 militia to hold three miles of fortified lines. Outside the defenses the British attackers, built up to 10,000 men, plus 5,000 seamen, worked their way toward the city by parallels.

Northeast of Charleston, across the Cooper River, Lincoln had posted Gen. Isaac Huger with 500 men to protect the American line of communications to the north. On April 14 this force became the object of a sudden British thrust. Colonel Banastre Tarleton's British Legion, composed of both cavalry and infantry, struck Huger's camp at 3 A.M. and swept it away. Tarleton pressed on down the left bank of the Cooper, cutting off Lincoln's last avenue of retreat. By May 8 the British investment was complete and a final assault readied. At this point Lincoln asked for a truce in order to consider surrender terms. Four days later the American army marched out of Charleston and laid down its arms. The number of prisoners—Continentals, militia, and armed citizens—came to 5,466 (89 Continentals had been killed and 189 wounded during the siege). In addition, a huge quantity of military stores fell into the hands of the victors. At a cost of only 265 casualties, Great Britain had won its greatest victory of the war over the former colonies. Three weeks later Clinton sailed back to New York, leaving Cornwallis to complete the subjugation of the American South. *See* Savannah II; Waxhaw Creek; Camden; American Revolution.

Charleston III (American Civil War), 1863. The first of a long series of Federal attempts to capture Charleston, S.C., was launched by Adm. Samuel Du Pont. On April 7 he sent nine warships against Fort Sumter in the mouth of the harbor but was repulsed with one ship sunk and several crippled. A joint army-navy expedition, commanded by Gen. Quincy Gillmore and Adm. John Dahlgren, attacked Fort Wagner on Morris Island at the south entrance to Charleston harbor, on July 11. Gillmore sent a brigade commanded by Gen. George Strong against the fort, defended by 1,200 Confederates under Gen. William Taliaferro. The assault was repulsed with 339 Federal casualties as opposed to the 12 men lost by the Southerners.

The Federals then brought up siege artillery, and under cover of this fire Gen. Truman Seymour led two brigades in a new assault on July 18. The attackers gained a foothold in Fort Wagner before being hurled back. Seymour was wounded and both his brigade commanders, Strong and H. S. Putnam, were killed. In all, 1,515 Federals were killed, wounded, or missing out of the 5,264-man force. Taliaferro, who commanded 1,785 men at that time, suffered 174 casualties. When Gillmore pressed his formal siege operations, the Confederates abandoned Morris Island, on the night of September 6–7.

It was an insignificant conquest, however. Fort Sumter continued to hold out, and on September 8 its defenders inflicted 125 casualties on a landing party of 400 Federals who attempted a surprise attack. Thereafter Charleston, under the overall command of Gen. Pierre Beauregard, remained secure from attack for a year and a half, although Federal naval forces continued to blockade the harbor. On February 17, 1865, the city was evacuated to escape the northward march of the Federal army of Gen. William Sherman. *See* Fort Sumter; American Civil War.

Château Gaillard (English-French Wars), 1203–1204. During the long war between England and France for possession of Normandy, Richard I, Coeur de Lion, built a commanding fortress at Les Andelys on the Seine. Called Château Gaillard, the military castle defended the English hold on Rouen through the end of Richard's reign in 1199. However, his successor, John, proved to be no match for the French king, Philip II Augustus. In September 1203 Philip's knights drove back the English army and laid siege to Château Gaillard, defended by Roger de Lacy. In March of the following year the fortress, weakened by mines, fell, opening the French road to Rouen and endangering the entire English hold on Normandy. *See* Gisors; Rouen I.

Chateaugay River (War of 1812), 1813. The second American attempt in two years to take Montreal got under way in the fall of 1813. While Gen. James Wilkinson descended the Saint Lawrence, Gen. Wade Hampton led a coordinated thrust northward from Plattsburg, N.Y. With about 4,000 troops Hampton crossed the Canadian border on September 19 and then moved west to the Chateaugay River. He marched downstream to within 15 miles from the river's mouth, which is 14 miles above Montreal, and then sat down to await the arrival of Wilkinson's force. On October 26 Hampton fought an inconclusive battle against a much smaller force of Canadian militia. Failing to win the enemy position, the lethargic American commander fell back on Plattsburg without notifying Wilkinson of his withdrawal. Hampton was allowed to resign from the army the following March. *See* Queenston Heights; Chrysler's Farm; War of 1812.

Châteauneuf-de-Randon (Hundred Years' War), 1380. After the crushing loss at Poitiers in 1356, France was too enfeebled and demoralized to field a major army against the English invaders. Almost all French resistance centered on Bertrand du Guesclin, who was called "the Eagle of Brittany." This able commander rallied his countrymen by a long, desperate guerrilla warfare. Twice captured and ransomed, he harassed the English armies from Spain northward to Normandy. In 1380 Du Guesclin's irregular force besieged and eventually won the surrender of the English garrison in the fortress of Châteauneuf-de-Randon in south-central France. But the work and privations of the prolonged campaign took the life of the 60-year-old patriot. *See* Poitiers; Auray; Montiel; Margate; Hundred Years' War.

Château-Thierry (World War I). A village on the Marne River, site of an early clash between German and American troops on June 1, 1918, in the battle of Aisne River III; it was liberated by an Allied counteroffensive on July 21. *See* Aisne River III; Marne River II.

Chatham (Second English-Dutch War), 1667.

While England, France, and Holland wrangled over peace terms to end the second English-Dutch naval war, Charles II allowed his fleet to fall into disrepair. Taking advantage of this weakness, Adm. Michel de Ruyter sailed the Dutch navy into English waters. On June 14, 1667, some 60 Netherlands warships bombarded Sheerness on the Isle of Sheppey in the Thames estuary. They then forced their way up the Thames as far as Gravesend, 22 miles from London, and up the Medway to Chatham. At this naval base the Dutch burned four vessels and towed away the *Royal Charles* (of Lowestoft fame). This disaster marked the low point of England's naval power—the fires could be seen in London. Charles II consented to the Treaties of Breda the following month. Little was decided, except for the possession of New Amsterdam (New York), which passed to England. *See* Lowestoft; North Foreland II; Pentland Hills; Southwold Bay; English-Dutch Wars.

Chattanooga (American Civil War), 1863. Following the Federal defeat at Chickamauga, Ga., Gen. William Rosecrans withdrew supinely into Chattanooga. Confederate commander Braxton Bragg likewise disdained to take the initiative and settled down to a siege of the city. The tortuous Federal supply line from Bridgeport, Ala., downriver, threatened Rosecrans' army with starvation. In Washington, an exasperated President Abraham Lincoln made Gen. U. S. Grant supreme commander of the Federal armies between the Alleghenies and the Mississippi River. General George Thomas took over command of the Army of the Cumberland at Chattanooga, where Grant arrived on October 23. General William Sherman's Army of the Tennessee was moved from Corinth, Miss., to Thomas' left, upriver from Chattanooga. A third force, three Federal divisions under Gen. Joseph Hooker, occupied Bridgeport.

The first Federal offensive, during October 26–28, opened a short supply line south of the Tennessee River from Bridgeport into Chattanooga. Hooker, whose troops stood guard over this vital artery, repulsed a night attack at Wauhatchie on October 28–29. With the Federal supply line ensured, Grant organized a limited attack. On November 23 Thomas moved eastward to seize Orchard Knob and Indian Hill, the chief outposts of Bragg's main position on Missionary Ridge. The Confederate corps of Gen. John Breckinridge fell back to the main defensive position. The following day Sherman crossed the river to take up a position against Bragg's right flank, north of Missionary Ridge. That same day Hooker attacked eastward between the Tennessee River and Lookout Mountain. Finding this defile only weakly guarded, the Federals turned to ascend the 1,100-foot height. Again resistance was surprisingly weak. Hooker's men swept the Confederates off

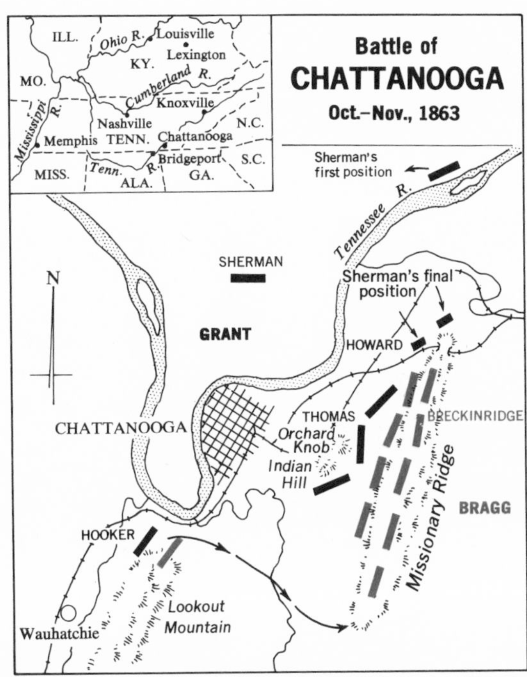

Lookout Mountain in an action later called the "Battle above the Clouds."

On November 25 Grant ordered a double envelopment of Bragg's Missionary Ridge position—Sherman to assault the north flank, Hooker the south. By midafternoon neither attack had made any progress. Grant then sent Thomas' army forward in a frontal attack in an attempt to secure the lowest of the three Confederate defensive lines on Missionary Ridge. The charge carried the entrenchments, but when the Federals found themselves exposed to fire from the upper lines, they continued to ascend the ridge. In a clear case of soldiers taking the initiative away from their commanders, Thomas' army drove the startled defenders off the height. Within an hour and a half Bragg's army was routed with a loss of 2,000 prisoners. The discredited Confederate commander fell back to Dalton, Ga. His defeat at Chattanooga cut a vital line of lateral communications in the South and opened the way for a Federal drive on Atlanta. Bragg, who had 64,000 men in his command, lost a total of 361 killed, 2,160 wounded, and 4,146 missing at Chattanooga. Grant's casualties among the 56,000 Federal troops employed were 753 killed, 4,722 wounded, 349 missing. *See* Chickamauga; Knoxville; Resaca; American Civil War.

Cheat Mountain (American Civil War), 1861. During the summer of 1861, Gen. George McClellan had conquered much of present-day West Virginia for the Union. To recover this territory, the Confederate general Robert E. Lee led six brigades against the Federal positions on Cheat Mountain and at the village of Elkwater, seven miles to the west. Lee launched a two-pronged attack on September 10. But hampered by rough terrain and weak leadership among his brigade commanders, the future Confederate hero made no progress on either front. On February 15 he withdrew, reporting few casualties. However, the Federal commander, Gen. Joseph Reynolds, claimed 20 prisoners and estimated 100 Confederate dead and wounded. This battle is chiefly notable as Lee's first combat action in the four-year Civil War. *See* Rich Mountain; American Civil War.

Cherbourg (World War II). The first large port captured by the Allies from the Germans on June 27, 1944, after the invasion of Normandy. *See* Normandy.

Cheriton (English Civil War), 1644. In the third year of the Civil War, Gen. Lord Ralph Hopton, who led Charles I's forces in the west, continued to be one of the most agressive Cavalier commanders. In March 1644 Hopton launched a drive into the Roundhead stronghold of southeastern England. In Kent, however, he was challenged at Cheriton by his old antagonist, Gen. Sir William Waller. Here, near the coast west of Dover on March 29, Hopton's Cavaliers were defeated and forced to pull back to Cornwall. (Two years later Hopton was encircled at Truro, surrendered, and fled England with Prince Charles.) Waller promptly marched northwest into Oxfordshire to engage the central forces of the king. But meanwhile a more dangerous threat to the crown came from the north, where a strong Scottish army had crossed the Tweed and moved into Yorkshire. *See* Newbury I; Selby; Cropredy Bridge; English Civil War.

Chernaya River (Crimean War), 1855. During the almost year-long siege of Russian-held Sevastopol, a new ally joined Great Britain, France and Turkey. To increase Italian prestige in the struggle for independence, Count Camillo di Cavour persuaded Victor Emmanuel II of Sardinia to send a Piedmontese division to the Crimea. These troops, commanded by the Marchese di La Marmora (Alfonso Ferrero), were in the allied line east of Sevastopol when the Russians made a large-scale sortie on August 16. Three Russian divisions led by Prince Mikhail Gorchakov swarmed against the allied position. They were repulsed, however, by the Piedmontese, the British (under Sir James Simpson) and the French (directed by Aimable Pélissier). Russian losses totaled almost 5,000. Allied casualties were about 1,200. This was the last attempt of the besieged to break out of the city. The initiative now passed to the allies. *See* Sevastopol I; Crimean War.

Chesapeake Capes (War of the American Revolution), 1781. When Gen. Lord Charles Cornwallis moved his British army northward into Virginia in the spring of 1781, the American and French commanders seized the opportunity to deliver a decisive blow. General George Washington, assisted by the French general the Comte de Rochambeau, began marching southward from New York in August. Meanwhile, in perfect coordination, the French admiral the Comte de Grasse sailed from the West Indies with 24 ships of the line led by his flagship, *Ville de Paris*. De Grasse entered Chesapeake Bay and anchored just inside the capes on August 30. This movement shut off all possibility of Cornwallis' escape by sea and prevented any naval reinforcements from reaching the English commander, who was now bottled up at Yorktown, Va., on the peninsula between the York and James rivers.

An English fleet of 19 warships under Adm. Thomas Graves had sailed from New York for the Chesapeake in August. Graves arrived off capes Charles and Henry on September 5. De Grasse promptly left the bay to engage the enemy fleet. In a two-hour battle late in the afternoon, the English suffered the heavier casualties. Graves,

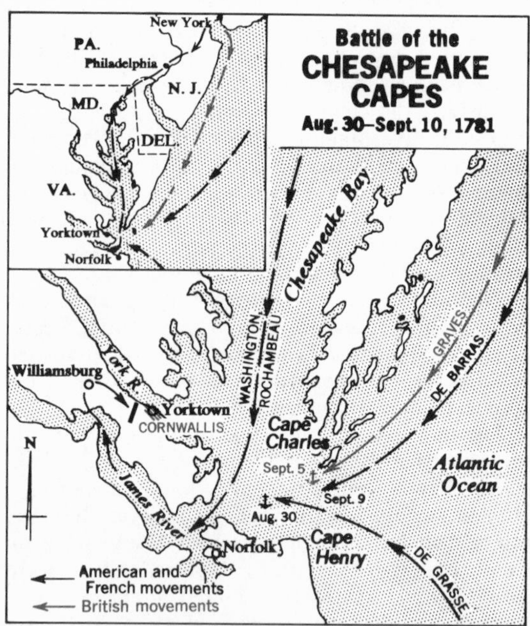

from his flagship, the *London,* worsened his numerical inferiority by such a faulty disposition that the seven ships of Adm. Lord Samuel Hood failed to get into the action. For the next three days both fleets maneuvered outside the capes without coming to grips. On September 9 a second French fleet of eight warships under the Comte de Barras, which had sailed from Newport, R.I., carrying the siege train for Washington's army, slipped into Chesapeake Bay. Graves was now hopelessly outnumbered. He set sail for New York the following day. English casualties were 336, French losses 221.

Although the battle of the Chesapeake Capes was one of maneuver more than of combat, it was nevertheless of crucial importance. The establishment of the French navy at the mouth of Chesapeake Bay ensured the doom of Cornwallis in Virginia. De Grasse had been able to land 3,000 French troops, under the Marquis de Saint-Simon, to support the allied ground campaign. And the arrival of the French siege train aboard De Barras' ships contributed much to the allied victory at Yorktown six weeks later. *See* Guilford Courthouse; Yorktown I; American Revolution.

"Chesapeake" vs. "Shannon" (War of 1812), 1813. The 38-gun frigate U.S.S. *Chesapeake* under Capt. James Lawrence sailed out of Boston harbor on June 1, 1813. Thirty miles out to sea the American warship encountered the British *Shannon,* also of 38 guns, commanded by Capt. (later Sir) Philip Broke. In a 15-minute action the more experienced British gunners disabled the *Chesapeake,* which was then captured by a boarding party and brought into Halifax, Nova Scotia. British casualties numbered 83 out of a crew of 330. Among the 146 Americans killed or wounded (out of a crew of 379) was Lawrence, whose last words were reported to have been, "Don't give up the ship!" This order became the rallying cry of the U.S. Navy for the remainder of the war. *See* Stoney Creek; Erie, Lake; War of 1812.

Chester (Teutonic Conquest of Britain), c. 616. The aggressive Anglo-Saxon kingdom of Northumbria pressed westward under the leadership of King Ethelfrith. Sometime about 616 Ethelfrith's army reached the Dee River at Chester. Here the Northumbrians encountered a force of Britons under Solomon of the Welsh kingdom of Powys. A group of monks from a monastery at Bangor came forward to pray for the success of their fellow Britons. They were promptly massacred. The Northumbrians then attacked and routed Solomon's army. By pushing on to the Irish Sea, the conquerors drove a wedge between the Britons of modern Wales and those of Strathclyde, to the north. This action, coupled with the earlier Teutonic victory at Dyrham to the south, completely isolated the Welsh peninsula from the rest of Britain. *See* Dyrham; Degsastan; Heathfield.

Chesterfield (Second Barons' War of England), 1266. Despite the defeat and death of their leader, Simon de Montfort (earl of Leicester), at Evesham in 1265, the dissident barons made one more attempt to impose their power on Henry III and his son Prince Edward (later Edward I). The Earl of Derby rallied an army of knights to the barons' cause in north-central England. At Chesterfield in Derbyshire this force met a royalist army commanded by Henry of Almaine, nephew of the king, on May 15. In the last pitched battle of the war the barons were soundly defeated. Derby was captured, but some survivors escaped to join other fugitives at Ely. *See* Evesham; Ely II; Barons' Wars.

Chiari (War of the Spanish Succession), 1701. Three years after the 1697 Treaty of Ryswick had ended the War of the Grand Alliance against Louis XIV's France and Charles II's Spain, the Spanish king died, leaving no Hapsburg successor. Louis claimed the Spanish throne for his grandson Philip of Anjou (Philip V), while Holy Roman Emperor Leopold I made the identical claim for his son Charles (future Emperor Charles VI). France was supported by Bavaria, but the other members of the Grand Alliance (chiefly England and Holland) sided with the Empire. The ensuing War of the Spanish Succession opened the following summer, when Prince Eugene of Savoy led an Imperial (Austrian) army from the Tirol into northern Italy. Crossing neutral Venetian territory, the able Eugene outmaneuvered the French marshal Nicolas de Catinat at Carpi, in Emilia. Catinat was replaced by Marshal the Duc de Villeroi. When Eugene moved northwest into Lombardy, Villeroi attacked him at Chiari on September 1, 1701. The prince occupied a strong position, and after two hours of bloody fighting the French were repulsed, losing 3,000 men, to only 150 Austrian losses. Eugene turned back to besiege Mantua, while Villeroi also marched southward, to Cremona on the Po River. *See* Namur I; Cremona II; Spanish Succession, War of the.

Chickamauga (American Civil War), 1863. For six months after the hard-fought battle of Stones River, both hostile armies in eastern Tennessee remained inactive. Then in June the Federal general William Rosecrans maneuvered from Murfreesboro toward Tullahoma so skillfully that the Confederate commander, Gen. Braxton Bragg, withdrew south of the Tennessee River to Chattanooga on July 4. (At this time the Confederates were suffering decisive defeats on two other fronts —at Gettysburg, Pa., and Vicksburg, Miss.) Rosecrans delayed again and then crossed the Tennessee southwest of Chattanooga early in September. He marched eastward to get behind Chattanooga, three corps abreast but widely separated on a 40-mile front: Gen. Thomas Crittenden (XXI) on the north, Gen. George Thomas (XIV) in the center, and Gen. Alexander McCook (XX) to the south.

Bragg quickly evacuated Chattanooga, on September 8, and began moving his army 22 miles southward to Lafayette, Ga., opposite the Federal center. For ten days both sides maneuvered for advantage over poor roads in wooded, mountainous terrain. During this time Crittenden occupied Chattanooga and then marched southward to join Rosecrans' main body. Finally Bragg concentrated three corps west of Chickamauga Creek in position to attack Crittenden, thereby turning the Federals left and cutting them off from their new lines of communication back through Chattanooga. On September 19 the Confederate corps of Gens. William H. Walker, John Hood (leading James Longstreet's two divisions), and Simon Buckner, from north to south, made a frontal attack against the Federals. They had expected to strike the enemy's extreme left flank but instead ran into the corps of Thomas, who had moved up to the left rear of Crittenden. It was a day of confused, indecisive fighting.

On September 20 Bragg renewed the attack, first from his right center where Gen. Leonidas Polk had taken command, and then extending across the front to the south wing, now directed by Longstreet. The assault by Longstreet accidentally found a gap in the Federal line. Rosecrans' right was rolled up and forced back on his left. Believing the battle lost, the Federal commander, followed by the corps of Crittenden and McCook, withdrew to the northwest. Although now pressed from the south (by Longstreet) as well as from the east (by Polk), Thomas grimly held his corps in place. Early in the afternoon he was reinforced from the north by the alert commander of the reserve corps, Gen. Gordon Granger. Thomas' firm stand, which earned him the nickname "Rock of Chickamauga," limited the Federal defeat. He withdrew to Rossville Gap that night. Rosecrans pulled his entire army into Chattanooga. Bragg, whose failure to pursue vigorously cost the Confederates a major triumph, closed up to the city and besieged it.

Of the 58,000 Federal troops at Chickamauga, 1,657 were killed, 9,756 wounded, and 4,757 missing. Confederate casualties among their 66,000 effectives were 2,312 killed, 14,677 wounded, 1,468 missing. In addition to Thomas, who replaced Rosecrans on October 19, Granger too gained in reputation as a result of his performance in the battle. McCook and Crittenden, the other corps commanders, were relieved. The reputation of several of the victorious generals also suffered—Polk, Daniel Hill, and Thomas Hindman were all relieved. Longstreet received praise for his aggressiveness. *See* Stones River; Gettysburg; Vicksburg; Chattanooga; American Civil War.

Chickasaw Bluffs (American Civil War), 1862. From his positions in western Tennessee and northern Mississippi, the Federal general U. S. Grant began an overland march on the key Confederate river port of Vicksburg on the Mississippi. By December 20 he had penetrated 15 miles south of Oxford when a cavalry raid by Gen. Earl Van Dorn destroyed his advance base at Holly Springs, Miss. This loss, plus repeated attacks on Federal communications by the cavalry of Gen. Nathan Forrest, forced Grant to withdraw. He next sent Gen. William Sherman with 32,000 men down the Mississippi River from Memphis. Sherman landed on the banks of the Yazoo River, just above Vicksburg, on December 26. Advancing slowly through difficult, swampy terrain, the Federal expedition stood in position to assault Chickasaw Bluffs, overlooking the Mississippi, three days later. By now, however, the Vicksburg garrison had grown from 6,000 Confederates to more than 12,000 (and more reinforcements arrived daily), under the supreme command of Gen. John Pemberton.

On December 29 Sherman's troops attacked, only to be checked by murderous fire from the bluffs. Deprived of effective artillery support by the virtually impassable bayous, the Federals had no way of neutralizing the strong Confederate defenses. Sherman waited two days and then took his troops across the Mississippi to Louisiana, opposite Vicksburg. He had suffered 1,776 casualties in contrast to Pemberton's loss of 207 men. The Confederate stronghold would resist successfully for another six months. *See* Corinth, Miss.; Vicksburg; American Civil War.

Chihuahua (U.S.-Mexican War), 1847. While pausing in Sante Fe, N.M., en route to California, Col. Stephen W. Kearny, head of the U.S. "Army of the West," determined to send an expedition farther south into Mexico. On September 23, 1846, Col. Alexander Doniphan left Santa Fe with the 1st Regiment of Missouri Mounted Volunteers. Brushing past feeble Mexican opposition, Doniphan reached El Paso on December 27, suffering only seven wounded. On February 8 the American expedition crossed the Rio Grande and rode on southward. Again resistance was negligible. Doniphan entered Chihuahua on March 1 with only one man killed and eleven wounded. From here he moved southeast to Saltillo and eventually back to transports on the Rio Grande. On their 3,500-mile march across deserts and mountains the Americans inflicted more than 600 casualties (half of them killed) on the enemy. Meanwhile, more than 400 miles to the southeast of Chihuahua, Gen. Zachary Taylor's army fought a major battle. *See* San Pasqual; Buena Vista; U.S.-Mexican War.

Chile. *See* Latin America.

Chilianwala (Sikh-British War II), 1849. When his frontal assault against the Sikhs failed at Ramnagar Gen. Sir Hugh Gough took his Anglo-Indian army up the Chenab River. Here he crossed against weak opposition, turning the Sikh left flank. Pressing forward in West Punjab, Gough reached Chilianwala, five miles from the Jhelum River. At this village almost 40,000 Sikhs entrenched themselves to ward off Gough's attack by a much smaller force. On January 14 the Anglo-Indians assaulted the enemy position. In a fierce fight the defenders were driven back, but Gough's casualties were so heavy he could not pursue until he received reinforcements. Three of his regiments had lost their colors. *See* Ramnagar; Gujrat; Sikh-British Wars.

China. The major battles and wars fought by what are now the two nations of China are listed below. For earlier history *see* Mongol Wars.

Nanking I	1356
Peking II	1644
Fort Zealandia	1661–1662
Taku	1860
See Chinese-Japanese War I	
Peking III	1900
Tsingtao	1914
Yenan	1934–1935
See Chinese-Japanese War II	
See World War II	
See Chinese Civil War	

China I (Chinese-Japanese War II), 1937–1941. Some Japanese leaders began hungering for an empire on the continent of Asia early in the twentieth century. As China strained for increased unification and nationalism, Japan's timetable for conquest quickened. Under the guise of helping to establish order, many Japanese troops took up stations in China. On September 18, 1931, Japanese soldiers in the northeastern city of Mukden attacked Chinese police in Manchuria. With this fighting as a pretext, Japan occupied the province and in February 1932 set up the puppet state of Manchukuo. Japan's hostile intent became overt on July 7, 1937, when Japanese and Chinese troops clashed at the Marco Polo bridge in Lukouchiao on the outskirts of the ancient Chinese capital of Peking (Peiping). Seizing upon this "incident," Japan launched an open attack aimed at subduing all of China. There was no declaration of war.

Japanese strategy called for a quick conquest of the coast to shut off all foreign aid, followed by a destruction of Chinese armies in the field. Generalissimo Chiang Kai-shek, who commanded the Chinese, planned to trade space for time, avoid a decisive engagement, and eventually wear down the invaders. Although the Chinese often fought stubbornly for key cities, they could not stand for long against superior discipline, better weapons, and complete control of the air.

From bases in Manchukuo (Manchuria), Japanese troops poured into northern China, occupying Peking on July 28 and Tientsin the following day. In central China, Shanghai, the chief port and largest city, was attacked on August 13, 1937, by land, sea, and air. The Chinese resisted for three months until they were finally driven back by 200,000 Japanese troops on November 8. Nearby Soochow fell on November 20, and Hangchow, to the south, surrendered on December 24. Meanwhile, the Japanese had marched up the Yangtze River to attack the capital of Nanking. Chiang then moved his headquarters 600 miles up the river to Hankow (one of the triple cities of Han (Wuhan); the capital was established another 600 miles farther upriver at Chungking. The fall of Nanking on December 13 triggered a wave of atrocities within the prostrate city. Japanese troops wantonly slaughtered some 40,000 civilians and ravaged thousands of women. This "rape of Nanking," coupled with the merciless bombing of undefended cities, outraged world opinion. Earlier, anti-Japanese feeling had been provoked by the attack and sinking of the United States river gunboat *Panay* on the Yangtze on December 12. By the end of 1937 Japan held most of North China (although Tsingtao held out until January 10), part of Inner Mongolia, and the important central Chinese cities around the mouth of the Yangtze River.

In 1938 the Japanese extended their conquests in three directions. From the north they advanced southward to the Yellow (Hwang Ho) River, taking Kaifeng on June 6. The only important Chinese victory came in this sector when two Japanese divisions were routed at Taierhchwang in southern Shantung province, between March 31 and April 9, by troops under the command of Gen. Li Tsung-jên. The second Japanese drive took place along the southern coast, where the invaders captured Amoy on May 10 and Canton on October 21. In central China Japan scored its third series of victories by moving upriver on both banks of the Yangtze to overrun Hankow on October 25. Twelve Japanese divisions aided in the capture of this key railroad junction.

Beginning in 1939, the character of the "incident" changed. Japan had found that it could not win a quick, decisive battle. Chinese troops melted into the interior only to reappear as guerrilla forces harassing the Japanese flanks, rear, and lines of communication. Even in conquered areas Japanese control was often restricted to important cities and railroad lines. Japan then set up a puppet Chinese government at Nanking in March 1940 and began exploiting resources under its military grip. But all Japanese peace overtures were firmly rejected by Chiang, who at this time enjoyed the support of Mao Tse-tung's Chinese Communists.

In two endeavors, however, Japan was highly successful—control of the air and the coastal blockade. Chunking and other strategic points were subjected to savage aerial assault. And the blockade shut off supplies so effectively that China could mount no major counteroffensive. On July 18, 1940, Great Britain closed the Burma Road, the chief source of overland supply. Three months later, however, this 1,500-mile highway from Lashio, Burma, to Kunming, in Yunan Province, was reopened. The Japanese seizure of Indochinese air bases had demonstrated that appeasement only encouraged further aggression.

Japan then halted military operations, content to harvest the Chinese territory then under its control. At Chungking, Chiang also remained immobile, confident that World War II would soon spread to the Far East and bring him strong allies against the invader. Japanese headquarters reported that the fighting had cost 800,000 Chinese lives, 50,000 Japanese. During 1940 and 1941 many of the Japanese economic gains were offset by the necessity of maintaining a 1,000,000-man army in occupation of China. When Japan sought to enlarge its new order in the East by attacking the United States on December 7, 1941, the four-year China "incident" merged into World War II. *See* Yenan; China II; Chinese-Japanese War II.

China II (World War II), 1941–1945. The day after Japanese attacks in the Pacific brought that theater into World War II, China declared war on Japan (as well as on Germany and Italy). This step enlarged the Sino-Japanese fighting of the four-year China "incident" into a full-scale war. Generalissimo Chiang Kai-shek became supreme commander of the Allies on the China front. He sent three of his best armies (5th, 6th, and 66th) to the Burma border where they came under the command of the U.S. general Joseph Stilwell. But the suddenness and ferocity of the Japanese offensive gave the Allies no time to prepare adequate defenses. Japan took the surrender of Thailand on December 9 and three days later marched across that nation to the Burmese border. Burma came under attack on January 16. Despite sometimes fierce resistance, Japanese ground and air forces pushed relentlessly forward. Lashio, the southern terminus of the vital Burma Road to Kunming, fell on April 29. One Japanese force then wheeled northward to attack western Yunnan Province, the back door to China, while the main advance continued in Burma. By May 15 Burma had been overrun and the Chinese expeditionary force sadly decimated. Of the latter, one part retreated westward with Stilwell to Ledo on the Indian border; the remainder withdrew to Chinese soil to help in the defense of Yunnan.

The most effective Allied aid came in the air. After the Japanese cut the Burma Road, the U.S. Air Transport Command flew supplies from India over the 500-mile hump of the Himalayas to Kunming. Earlier, in August 1941, a small group of U.S. pilots, the American Volunteer Group, or Flying Tigers, had organized at Kunming under Claire Chennault. With only 50 planes, this group shot down 284 Japanese planes and destroyed another 100 on the ground. On July 4, 1942, the Flying Tigers became a part of the U.S. military establishment, under Gen. Chennault. The following year the enlarged group, which by then had won local air superiority in southwestern China, became the U.S. 14th Air Force.

On the ground, Japan launched a series of offensives designed to extend its area of control, wipe out the growing number of Chinese-American air bases, and carve out a south-north corridor (Canton–Hankow–Peking) through China. The first major attack came late in 1941 against Changsha, in south-central Hunan Province. This was repulsed with heavy losses on January 15, 1942, by the apparently improving Chinese army. During the summer the Japanese attacked in east-central China along the Chekiang-Kiangsi border to neutralize the Chuhsien airfield. In the north the Japanese pressed westward to the upper Yellow (Hwang Ho) River, but they made no real effort to bridge that waterway. This line was defended by Mao Tse-tung's Chinese Communists, headquartered at Yenan. Ostensibly allied with Chiang's forces, Mao's troops often proved to be faithless friends, and the Japanese feared that a major offensive in this sector might heal China's internal strife.

In 1943 Japanese troops launched a drive westward in Hupeh Province that for a time seemed to threaten the wartime capital of Chungking. But by May 31 Chinese resistance had forced back the attackers. A second drive, this time to the south in Hunan Province, began on November 2 with 100,000 Japanese attacking the rice-bowl center of Changteh. In savage fighting with heavy losses on both sides, the Chinese threw back the enemy by late December. This victory resulted in large part from the assistance provided by 280 China-based U.S. bombers. It was the first time that strong air forces had supported Chinese ground troops.

The battle of China increased in tempo in 1944. In April Japan stepped up its attacks (called Operation Ichi-Go) against air bases, particularly in south-central China. Bitter fighting took place in Kiangsi and Kwangsi. In these provinces the Japanese managed to capture seven airfields, which had taken tens of thousands of laborers months to build by hand. In their long-time efforts to win control of the vital Peking–Canton railroad, the Japanese were equally successful. An attack in April forced the Chinese out of the strategic point of Chengchow in Honan, on the Peking–Hankow (Wuhan) line, and by June 17 the Japanese had cleared the entire line north of the Yangtze. South of the river, ten Japanese divisions drove into Changsha on June 19 and pushed down the Hankow–Canton railroad to Hengyang in southern Hunan. Here the Chinese Tenth Army under Gen. Hsueh-Yueh fought almost to the last man before succumbing on August 8. The remainder of the line running south into Canton fell to the Japanese six months later. But even after this vital trans-China artery was completely in Japanese hands, it was so thoroughly wrecked that the Japanese were never able to use it to serve the entire Canton–Peking route.

Despite the many Japanese successes in the east, 1944 proved to be the turning point for the Allies in southwestern China. In January Allied forces (including American-trained Chinese divisions and the first U.S. troops to fight in Asia) began to attack from India across northern Burma. This offensive, led by Stilwell (under the Southeast Asia commander, the British admiral Lord Louis Mountbatten), drove steadily toward China's Yunnan Province. At the same time Marshal Wei Lihuang launched a drive down the Burma Road from Kunming with 12 Chinese divisions. These advances were designed to connect the Burma Road with the Stilwell Road being built eastward behind Stilwell's offensive from Ledo, 300 miles away. (In October 1944, the U.S. general Albert Wedemeyer replaced Stilwell in China, while the U.S. general Daniel Sultan took over the India-Burma forces.)

On January 28, 1945, troops from the Burma and Yunnan fronts linked up 75 miles north of Lashio. On March 7 Lashio itself was taken, opening the Ledo–Burma road for truck convoys to Kunming. Meanwhile, U.S. B-29 Superfortress bombers, operating from hand-built bases deep in the interior of China, were hammering at far-flung Japanese targets.

In 1945 the retrained and re-equipped Chinese army seized the initiative on several fronts. In western Hunan a Japanese attack on the Chihkiang airfield resulted in a decisive Chinese victory. In Kwangsi Chinese troops liberated Nanning and regained the key air bases of Liuchow (in June) and Kweilin (in July) that had been lost in the 1944 Japanese offensive. To the east the Chinese won a base on the coast in May by capturing Kowloon, opposite Hong Kong. Guerrilla activity became intense. But the victories in China were only a small part of the increasingly heavy Allied blows against Japan—at sea, in the air, and on islands in the Pacific.

Finally, on August 14, 1945, Japan accepted the Allied terms of unconditional surrender. General Yasutsugu Okamura, commander of the Japanese expeditionary army in China, surrendered to Generalissimo Chiang, ending more than eight years of Sino-Japanese hostilities that had begun with the "incident" at Marco Polo Bridge. (The Japanese Kwantung army in Manchuria yielded to the Soviet Union.) Total Chinese casualties amounted to more than 3,200,000 officers and men, including some 1,319,000 killed. Civilian casualties were probably higher. *See* Pearl Harbor; China I; Burma I; Burma II; World War II.

Chinese Civil War (1946–1949). During both the China "incident" of 1937–41 and World War II, which followed, the Chinese Communists of Mao Tse-tung and the Kuomintang Nationalists of Generalissimo Chiang Kai-shek had in large part cooperated against the invading Japanese. But with the defeat of Japan in 1945 the rivalry between the two Chinese forces flared into open warfare. During the Japanese war Communist military strength had increased, while the Kuomintang armies had deteriorated due to corruption and incompetence. Even with heavy U.S. military aid, which continued through most of the civil war, Chiang was unable to re-establish control over Chinese territory. It was not until March 15, seven months after Japan's surrender, that Chiang occupied Mukden, the key city in southern Manchuria.

Meanwhile, Communist troops in North China geared up to fight for control of all Manchuria. The fighting broke out in this area and spread through most of central and eastern China during the next three and a half years. During this time the Communist armies overwhelmed the Nationalist forces in every theater. Late in 1949 Chiang fled with the remnants of his government to Formosa. China had become a Communist power destined to throw an ever-lengthening shadow over world affairs. In the meantime, Chiang's so-called Republic of China continued to hold only Formosa, even though it was the only "China" represented in the United Nations.

Szepingkai	1946
Sungari River	1947
Mukden II	1947–1948
Kaifeng	1948
Tsinan	1948
Hwai-Hai	1948–1949
Nanking III	1949

Chinese-Japanese War I (1894–1895). Ten years of vying for possession of Korea flared into open hostilities on July 27, 1894, when the Japanese regent in Korea declared war on China. Four days later Japan and China officially went to war against each other. The unorganized troops of Chinese emperor Kuang Hsü were no match for the modern Japanese armies. On April 17, 1895, China accepted the Treaty of Shimonoseki, which recognized the independence of Korea and ceded Formosa, the Pescadores Islands, and the Liaotung Peninsula to Japan. In addition China agreed to pay a large indemnity.

Pyongyang	1894
Yalu River I	1894
Port Arthur I	1894
Weihaiwei	1895

Chinese-Japanese War II (1937–1945). The second war between China and Japan in less than half a century began with an "incident" at Marco Polo Bridge, near Peking, on July 7, 1937. Four years later the undeclared war merged with World War II. The Allied victory over Japan in this conflict enabled China to free its soil of Japanese occupation troops. *See* World War II.

China I	1937–1941
Shanghai	1937
Nanking	1937
Taierhchwang	1938
China II	1941–1945

Chioggia (Venetian-Genoese Wars), 1379. Following the Genoese naval victory at Pulj (Pola), Pietro Doria captured the Venetian port of Chioggia in northeastern Italy. He then besieged Venice itself, 15 miles to the north. However, Vittorio Pisano, commander of the Venetian fleet, in turn blockaded the Genoese galleys in the channel. In attempting to fight their way out into the Adriatic on December 23, 1379, the Genoese suffered a crushing defeat, losing most of their ships and several thousand seamen. This battle, the final struggle in what is often called the War of Chioggia, destroyed the sea power of Genoa. *See* Pulj.

Chippenham (Danish Invasions of Britain), 878. The five-year truce King Alfred the Great of Wessex had secured in 871 was shattered by the aggressive new Danish leader Guthrum. Throughout 877 the Danes raided Dorset, Somerset, and Devon counties, while Alfred sought to check the invaders from his headquarters at Chippenham in Wiltshire. Early in January 878 the Saxon soldiers were busy celebrating Twelfth Night when the Danes suddenly swept down on them. The surprise attack destroyed the Wessex army. Many were killed; some fled over the Channel to France; and others melted away into the forests. Alfred himself became a fugitive at Athelney in Somersetshire. All Britain south of the Thames lay at the mercy of the Danes.

While in hiding, Alfred kept in communication with his tormented people. Cheered by news of a successful guerrilla action at Exmoor, the king ordered a general mobilization for the end of May. A decisive counteroffensive was in the making. *See* Wilton; Edington; Danish Invasions of Britain.

Chippewa River (War of 1812), 1814. In the spring of 1814 both Great Britain and the United States prepared new offensives. The Americans leaped off first. On July 3 Gen. Jacob Brown with 3,500 U.S. troops crossed the Niagara River into Canada and seized Fort Erie, at the junction of the river and Lake Erie. The British army under Gen. Phineas Riall fell back to the Chippewa River, 16 miles to the north. Here Riall, who was serving under the British commander Gen. (later Sir) Gordon Drummond, deployed some 1,500 men on a plain near the river. Brown ordered an attack by the brigade (1,300 men) of Gen. Winfield Scott. In a half-hour battle on July 5, Scott's brigade broke the British line, killing 137 and wounding 375. The Americans lost 48 killed and 227 wounded.

The battle of Chippewa was the first action of the war in which American regular army troops faced British regulars, some of them veterans of the Napoleonic Wars in Spain. When the British fell back to the north, Brown pursued. *See* Chrysler's Farm; Lundy's Lane; War of 1812.

Chotusitz (War of the Austrian Succession), 1742. Following the Prussian victory of Frederick II, the Great, over the Austrians at Mollwitz in April 1741, the War of the Austrian Succession became a series of large-scale maneuvers. Finally, in the spring of 1742, Prince Charles (Karl Alexander) of Lorraine, brother-in-law of Holy Roman Empress Maria Theresa, tried to throw back the Prussian invasion of Bohemia. His Austrian army encountered that of Frederick at Chotusitz, 50 miles southeast of Prague, on May 17. In a bitter struggle the steady-firing Prussian infantry gradually wore down the Austrians, who were then driven from the field by Frederick's cavalry (which he had reorganized after their poor performance at Mollwitz). The defeated Austrians lost all their artillery and several thousand men. A month later Maria Theresa, to free the empire for action against other enemies, made a separate peace with Prussia. Frederick withdrew (temporarily) from the war. This ended the First Silesian conflict. *See* Mollwitz; Dettingen; Austrian Succession, War of the.

Chrysler's Farm (War of 1812), 1813. For the second thrust at Montreal in two years, the United States assigned Gen. James Wilkinson to replace Gen. Henry Dearborn. Wilkinson was to descend the Saint Lawrence River in an attack coordinated with a march northward through upper New York State by Gen. Wade Hampton. Leaving Sackets Harbor, N.Y., with 8,000 troops on October 17, 1813, Wilkinson began moving down the Saint Lawrence two weeks later. On November 10 the flotilla halted at Chrysler's Farm, on the north bank, 90 miles above Montreal. Here the American commander dispatched 2,000 men under Gen. John Boyd to check an enemy force in his rear. On the following day Boyd's army was severely defeated by some 800 British commanded by Col. J. W. Morrison. American losses were 102 killed, 237 wounded, and more than 100 captured. British casualties came to only 22 killed, 48 wounded, and 12 missing. This setback, coupled with the news that Hampton had abandoned his attack, led Wilkinson to go into winter quarters.

The failure of the twin American offensive prompted the British to seize the initiative. General John Vincent, who had been forced in May to evacuate Fort George at the southwestern end of Lake Ontario, returned to occupy the fort on December 10. Eight days later the British captured nearby Fort Niagara and then burned Black Rock and Buffalo before the end of the year. Thus, after two years of war the American forces in New York State had been checkmated at every point. Both Wilkinson and Hampton were relieved the following spring. *See* Chateaugay River; Chippewa River; War of 1812.

Chrysopolis (Civil Wars of the Roman Empire), 324. Under the aggressive leadership of Constantine I, the army of the Western Roman Empire had defeated Licinianus Licinius' Eastern Empire forces at Adrianople and laid siege to the enemy stronghold at Byzantium (later Constantinople). To raise the siege, Licinius crossed the Bosporus into Asia to assemble a new army. But before this force could be transported to Europe, Licinius' fleet was smashed in the Dardanelles by Constantine's navy, commanded by his son Crispus. This naval battle altered the entire strategy of the campaign. With his newly acquired control of the water passageway, Constantine crossed the Bosporus with an experienced force drawn from the siege lines around Byzantium. At Chrysopolis (Scutari, later Üsküdar), on the northeast shore of the Sea of Marmara, he attacked the large army of recruits gathered by Licinius. In a deadly assault on September 18, Constantine's regulars killed almost 20,000 of the 50,000 men opposing them. Licinius was captured and the following year was executed. Constantine returned to Byzantium to prosecute the siege of that city. *See* Adrianople I; Byzantium II; Roman Empire.

Chu Pong–Ia Drang River (Vietnam War), 1965. To seek out and destroy Communist forces, a battalion of the U.S. 1st Cavalry Division (Airmobile) landed by helicopter at the foot of Chu Pong Mountain, near the Cambodian border, on November 14. Here the Americans found the 66th North Vietnamese Regiment. For four days the battalion fought off the regular enemy troops. Tactical aircraft flew 260 sorties over the battleground, and even B-52 bombers from Guam supported the American perimeter set up around the helicopter landing zone, called X-Ray. By November 17 the landing force had secured its position. Outside the perimeter lay 890 Communist dead, with probably more killed farther away by artillery and aircraft.

Pushing northward, some 500 air cavalrymen crossed the Ia Drang River only to run into another large force of North Vietnamese soldiers. In the savage fight that followed, the United States suffered more casualties than ever before in the Vietnam War. Some 350 Communist regulars were killed in the Ia Drang Valley. South Vietnamese paratroopers moved in two days later to relieve the battered cavalry troopers. The weeklong twin battle took the lives of 240 Americans, wounded 470 others. More than 2,200 Communist dead were counted. *See* South Vietnam; Plei Me; An Lao Valley; Vietnam War.

Churubusco (U.S.-Mexican War). A Mexican strongpoint south of Mexico City, the second objective to fall to Gen. Winfield Scott's offensive of August 7–20, 1847. *See* Contreras-Churubusco.

Cibalae (Civil Wars of the Roman Empire), 314. Eight years of conflict during the early reign of Emperor Constantine I had left only two contenders for the throne of the Roman Empire—Constantine himself in the West and Licinianus Licinius in the East. Constantine took an army of 20,000 men into Pannonia, where he encountered a force of 35,000 Illyrian troops under Licinius. The two armies clashed at Cibalae on the Sava River on October 8. Constantine repulsed his rival's first attack but, in launching a counterthrust, took heavy losses before finally breaking Licinius' lines. The defeated Illyrians retreated southward into Thrace.

Constantine pursued and on the plains of Mardiensis (Jarbiensis) dealt Licinius a second defeat. The latter now withdrew into the mountains of Macedonia. Realizing that to win a decisive victory would mean a long and bloody continuation of the struggle, Constantine came to terms with his rival. The Roman Empire was peacefully redivided between the two men. This agreement brought nine years of peace. *See* Heraclea Propontis; Adrianople I; Roman Empire.

Ciudad Rodrigo (Napoleonic Empire Wars), 1812. After spending seven months reorganizing his British, Portuguese, and Spanish army, Gen. Lord Wellington (Arthur Wellesley) renewed his offensive against French-held Spain early in 1812. Barring his northern route through León to Madrid stood the fortress of Ciudad Rodrigo, inside the Spanish frontier 53 miles southwest of Salamanca. Here the French marshal Auguste Marmont had posted a garrison of 2,000 men with 150 guns. Marching through winter snows, Wellington reached the fortress on January 8. He spent ten days investing Ciudad Rodrigo. Then, on January 19, in a bloody assault British troops stormed into the fortress and took the surrender of the 1,500 survivors. The successful siege cost Wellington 1,300 men, more than half of them lost during the final attack. The English general then turned southward 120 miles to Badajoz, which blocked the route into Andalusia. *See* La Albuera; Badajoz; Napoleonic Empire Wars.

Clastidium (Conquest of Cisalpine Gaul), 222 B.C. After stopping the invasion of Etruria by the Italian Celts, called the Cisalpine Gauls, Rome sent its legions northward to the Po Valley, homeland of the Gauls. Roman troops under Gaius Flaminius crossed the Po River in 223 and methodically reduced the Gallic settlements around modern Milan. The next year the Gauls rallied to fight a major battle with the Romans south of the river at Clastidium. The legionaries won decisively. In this battle the Roman general Marcus Claudius Marcellus killed the Gallic chief, Britomartus, in single combat. The defeat took the steam out of the Gauls' revolt, and they agreed to accept Roman rule. However, with the arrival of Hannibal four years later, many Gauls again took up arms against Rome. *See* Telamon; Trebbia River I; Roman Republic.

Clermont (*Jacquerie* Uprising in France), 1358. The chaos that gripped France during the Hundred Years' War with England deepened when King John II became a prisoner of war in 1356. Two years later a peasant uprising, called the *Jacquerie,* swept north-central France. The immediate cause of the outbreak was an order from the Estates General in Paris that the castles and country houses of the nobility should be repaired and strengthened (against the ravages of the roving "free companies" of former soldiers). In protest against this forced labor, the peasants revolted in an orgy of murder and pillage. Finally a great mass of peasants, led by Guillaume Cale, was attacked near Clermont, 41 miles north of Paris, by an armed force assembled by the local authorities. In the ensuing battle some 800 peasants were massacred. Cale himself was captured and beheaded after being tortured. Similar reprisals conducted by Charles II, the Bad, of Navarre, the future captain general of Paris, smashed the *Jacquerie* within a few weeks of the climactic battle of Clermont. Thousands of peasants were butchered during this time. *See* Poitiers.

Clontarf (Danish Invasion of Ireland), 1014. The fierce Danish raids that Sweyn I, Forkbeard, directed against Britain early in the eleventh century struck Ireland in the spring of 1014. A large group of invaders landed near Dublin. On April 23 King Brian Boru (Boramha) led an Irish army against them at Clontarf. The Danes were beaten and driven back to their ships with a loss estimated at 6,000 men. Brian, who had ruled for 12 years, and his son were both killed. Sweyn also died that year. The Danish attacks now shifted back to England. *See* Mortlack; Carham; Pen.

Cnidus (Greek City-States' Wars), 394 B.C. The only naval battle of the Corinthian War found Persia supplying Athens and its allies with money, men, and ships. In 394 the combined Athenian-Persian fleet encountered 120 Spartan ships off Cnidus, on the southwest coast of Asia Minor. Commanded by the Athenian Conon and the Persian Pharnabazus, the allied galleys won a decisive victory over the Spartan navy under Pisander. Pisander was killed. This defeat dealt a severe blow to Sparta's bid for maritime supremacy in the Aegean. *See* Coronea II; Naxos; Greek City-States' Wars.

Coblenz (Gallic Wars), 55 B.C. Just when Julius Caesar seemed to have subdued Gaul, after a three-year campaign, new trouble arose in the north. Two Germanic tribes, the Usipetes and Tencteri, crossed the lower Rhine and stirred several Gallic bands to new revolt. Caesar marched north to meet the invaders. When the Germanic leaders approached the Roman camp for a parley, they were promptly arrested. The legionaries then attacked and drove the enemy into the triangle made by the confluence of the Moselle with the Rhine. The entire force was either killed or drowned trying to escape across the water.

Caesar then determined to overawe the local tribes. In a remarkable engineering feat, his soldiers built a bridge over the Rhine in ten days. The Romans crossed over and spent the next 18 days east of the Rhine. After this demonstration of force, Caesar returned to the left bank and destroyed the bridge behind him. *See* Morbihan Gulf; Verulamium I; Tongres; Gallic Wars.

Cold Harbor (American Civil War), 1864. From the North Anna River the Federal commander, Gen. U. S. Grant, again moved the Army of the Potomac by its left flank. Its next objective was the road junction of Old Cold Harbor, ten miles northeast of Richmond. For the fourth time Gen. Robert E. Lee shifted his Army of Northern Virginia to keep it between Grant and the Confederate capital. Aggressive as always, Lee hurried the I Corps of Gen. Richard Anderson forward to seize Cold Harbor. Early on June 1 the Confederates attacked toward the crossroads, occupied only by the two slim cavalry divisions of Gen. Philip Sheridan. In a sharp fight the Federals barely held their ground until Gen. Horatio Wright's VI Corps came up at 9 A.M. to repulse the assault. Both armies then moved into position, facing each other on a seven-mile front that stretched roughly north–south between Totopotomoy Creek and the Chickahominy River. About 6 P.M. Wright and Gen. William Smith (XVIII Corps) counterattacked Anderson but failed to break the Confederate line. The loss of 2,200 Federals in this attack demonstrated the new-found effectiveness of defensive troops fighting behind entrenchments.

Grant now resolved to take advantage of his great numerical superiority—108,000 men against the 59,000 available to Lee. At 4:30 A.M. on June 3 he ordered three of his corps to effect a massive penetration of the Confederate center and right (south), held by Anderson and Gen. Ambrose Hill (III Corps), respectively. The attacking Federal corps were (from north to south) Smith, Wright, and Gen. Winfield Hancock (II Corps). The blue-coated troops charged bravely but ran into a murderous frontal and enfilade fire. Within an hour the assault had been stopped all along the line with 7,000 Federals dead or wounded. Lee's losses were probably less than 1,500. General George Meade, in immediate command of the Army of the Potomac, then called off the attack. The bleeding Federals dug in where they halted.

For the next eight days the two armies fought from their respective trenches within a hundred yards of each other.

The costly repulse at Cold Harbor caused Grant to change his tactics. In the month-long drive on Richmond that started in the Wilderness he had suffered more than 50,000 casualties, in contrast to Lee's losses of 30,000. On the night of June 12–13 he began a southward march to cross the James River, circling east of Richmond to attack Petersburg, 23 miles south of the Confederate capital. *See* North Anna River; Trevilian Station; Petersburg; American Civil War.

Colenso (South African War II), 1899. To take the offensive against the Boers of commander in chief Petrus Joubert, Gen. Sir Redvers Buller deployed the British army on three fronts. Two of these columns had already met defeat when Buller himself marched to the relief of Ladysmith in the second week in December. At Colenso, 14 miles south of Ladysmith, he found the Boers holding the far bank of the Tugela River. Buller attacked on December 15. Despite the gallantry of the British frontal assault, the Boers, under Gen. Louis Botha, held their ground and returned a deadly fire. Buller finally called off the attack after suffering more than 1,000 casualties. It was the third defeat endured by British troops during "Black Week."

At this point Gen. Lord Frederick Roberts was put in command of the British forces in South Africa, with Gen. Lord Kitchener as his chief of staff. Buller retained command on the Natal front. *See* Ladysmith; Stormberg; Magersfontein; Spion Kop; South African Wars.

Colline Gate (Marius-Sulla Civil War), 82 B.C. While Rome was torn by civil war between the popular party and the aristocrats of Lucius Cornelius Sulla, the Samnites took the opportunity to rebel. In November 82 B.C. Pontius led an attack of Samnites and anti-Sulla Romans against the capital city. At the Colline Gate, in the inner wall of Rome (northeast corner), Sulla's legions fought an all-night battle against the invaders. Finally gaining the upper hand, the defenders put Pontius to rout, capturing 4,000 of his men. Meanwhile, to the northeast, Sulla's lieutenant Quintus Caecilius Metellus (Pius) defeated a second rebel army at Faventia (Faenza). The victory of Sulla's aristocratic party was now complete. Sulla reformed the government of Rome and then voluntarily retired in 79 B.C. *See* Mount Tifata; Mount Vesuvius; Roman Republic.

Colombey (Franco-Prussian War), 1870. After three defeats in three days along the northeast borders of France, the troops of Napoleon III began to fall back to Metz, under the command of Marshal Achille Bazaine. The shaken French forces were followed by three Prussian armies under the direction of Gen. (later Count) Helmuth von Moltke. At Colombey, four miles east of Metz, the Prussian First Army of Gen. Karl von Steinmetz overtook the retreating French on August 14. A sharp fight took place here and at the nearby towns of Borny and Courcelles. Each side suffered several thousand casualties, the French taking the heavier losses. The retreat continued. *See* Wörth; Spicheren; Mars-la-Tour; Franco-Prussian War.

Colombia. *See* Latin America.

Columbus, N.M. (Raid by Villa), 1916. In the anarchy that gripped Mexico after 1914, several leaders set up their own revolutionary governments. The local dictator in the north was Francisco (Pancho) Villa. On the night of March 8–9, 1916, Villa, with more than 500 mounted men, crossed the border to raid Columbus, N.M. The invaders burnt part of the town before they were driven off by 350 officers and men of the 13th U.S. Cavalry on the following day. About 190 Mexicans were killed or wounded. American losses were 7 soldiers and 8 civilians killed, 5 soldiers and 2 civilians wounded. The American government sent a punitive expedition after Villa. *See* Carrizal.

Concord (War of the American Revolution). The second part of the opening battle of American colonists against the British, on April 19, 1775. *See* Lexington and Concord.

Constantine (Conquest by French), 1837. France, which had occupied Algiers and appointed Comte Bertrand Clausel governor in 1830, could make no headway against Constantine, 200 miles to the east. An attack by Clausel himself was repulsed by the Berbers with many casualties in the autumn of 1836. The next year, however, 10,000 French-Algerian troops laid siege to the city on October 6. The Constantine garrison finally yielded one week later. France stood secure along most of the Algerian coast. *See* Isly River.

Constantinople I (Nika Revolt), 532. During the fifth year of the Byzantine emperor Justinian I's reign, Constantinople was torn by strife between two factions that developed out of the chariot racing teams in the city's circus, its chief entertainment. Long at odds, the so-called Blues and Greens fell to open street rioting in January 532. The outbreak took its name from the rebels' circus cry, "Nika" (Victory). After a week of wanton murder and the burning of city buildings, Justinian prepared to abandon his throne. He was persuaded to stay on only through the firmness of his wife, Theodora. Realizing that strong military action was the only alternative to flight, Justinian, on January 18, ordered the hero of the Persian war, Belisarius, to put down the street fighting. At the head of 2,500 barbarian mercenaries, Belisarius forced his way into the circus arena, the Hippodrome, where 30,000 rioters had gathered to proclaim their own emperor. In a ruthless assault with swords, the small Imperial force slaughtered virtually all the helplessly trapped rebels.

The suppression of the Nika Revolt solidified Justinian's position as emperor. It enabled him to carry out three projects important to history: the reconquest of the Western Roman Empire from the barbarians, the building of Saint Sophia Church in Constantinople, and the publication of the *Corpus Juris Civilis,* the foundation of the law practiced in most of continental Europe today. *See* Callinicum; Carthage II.

Constantinople II (Wars of the Byzantine Empire), 559. During the winter of 558–559, a fierce horde of Huns and Slavs crossed the frozen Danube and plundered southward toward Constantinople. Led by their khan, Zabergan, the invaders easily penetrated the long walls providing the city's first line of defense. Sergius, commander of the Byzantine militia, was taken prisoner. In this grave emergency the retired military hero Belisarius collected a small force of his demobilized veterans and rode out once more to defend the empire of Justinian I. At the village of Chettus, Belisarius' 300 veteran cavalrymen and an ill-trained citizen-soldiery bluffed a charge so convincingly that the 7,000 barbarians turned and fled. Continuing to give the impression that he commanded a much larger force than he actually had, Belisarius pursued. The worried invaders abandoned their camp at Melantiadum and pulled back to the Danube. In his last battle Belisarius saved Constantinople and again demonstrated his surpassing tactical skill. *See* Rome IV.

Constantinople III (Moslem-Byzantine Wars), 673–678. The militant Moslems who had burst out of Arabia in 634 to overrun all of western Asia reached the walls of Constantinople in April 673. For five months the Arab army and fleet of Caliph Muawiyah I besieged the Byzantine capital, pressing to gain an entry into the city. The armed forces of Constantine IV fought back stubbornly. On land they were aided by the strength of the city's walls; at sea the discharge of liquid "Greek fire" (believed to be a combination of quicklime, naphtha, sulfur, and sea water, it remained a Byzantine state secret and a potent weapon both on sea and land for centuries) created havoc among the Moslem ships that had forced the Dardanelles. In September the Arabs retired to winter quarters.

Although they had failed to take Constantinople in their initial surge, the Moslems continued to blockade the city and launched new attacks every year for five years. Finally, in 677, the Byzantine navy destroyed the Arab fleet at Syllaeum and secured a favorable 30-year peace the following year. The five-year siege cost the attackers more than 30,000 men. Constantinople had proved itself to be the sturdy bastion of eastern Europe against the hitherto all-engulfing Moslem tide. *See* Lycia; Constantinople IV; Moslem Conquests.

Constantinople IV (Moslem-Byzantine Wars), 717–718. The second great Arab attack on Constantinople was led by Maslama, brother of the Ommiad caliph Suleiman. With a fleet of almost 2,000 ships, Maslama attacked with the largest armada assembled in the early Middle Ages. His ships forced their way into the Sea of Marmara but found the passage into the Golden Horn blocked by a huge chain. On land, the army of Emperor Leo III, the Isaurian, from behind the great walls of the city, fought off 50,000 invaders, beginning on August 15, 717. After a year-long siege, in which his reinforced army suffered heavy casualties and his navy lost many ships to the Byzantines' "Greek fire," (believed to be a combination of quicklime, naphtha, sulfur, and sea water, it was a Byzantine state secret and a potent weapon both on sea and land for centuries), Maslama abandoned the attack. During the withdrawal most of the Arabian fleet was destroyed in a storm. The long retreat across Asia Minor proved equally disastrous to the Moslem cavalry. The expedition against Constantinople cost Islam an estimated 40,000 deaths. Although ground forces from Damascus would overrun Asia Minor 20 years later, Constantinople never again stood in such danger of Arab conquest. *See* Constantinople III; Covadonga; Constantinople V; Moslem Conquests.

Constantinople V (Fourth Crusade), 1204. When Pope Innocent III preached the Fourth Crusade, he called for an attack on Egypt. However, the French baronage, who made up most of the military force, made an alliance with Venice and switched the objective to Constantinople, capital of the Byzantine Empire. Carried across the Adriatic in Venetian galleys, the 15,000 crusaders seized the Christian city of Zara (Zadar) on the Dalmatian coast in November 1202 and sacked it. A furious Pope Innocent excommunicated the crusaders, who were led by the blind Venetian doge Enrico Dandolo and Boniface III of Montferrat (in Italy). Undaunted, the marauding force sailed to Constantinople in June of the following year. They unseated the Byzantine emperor Alexius III Angelus and restored the deposed (and blinded) Isaac II Angelus and his son Alexius IV Angelus to the throne. When the crusaders demanded heavy tribute, the residents revolted, on January 25, 1204, and proclaimed Alexius V, emperor. Alexius IV was killed; his father, Isaac, died a few days later.

The new Byzantine emperor demanded that the crusaders leave the vicinity of the city. But the

Europeans stormed the capital on April 12, and for the first time in its almost 900-year history, Constantinople fell to an invader. A fearful sack followed. Alexius V fled but was captured and executed. A new Latin Empire of the East was proclaimed with Baldwin I (IX of Flanders) the first ruler. The ravishing of Constantinople discredited the crusading movement (although the excommunication was later lifted) and eased the westward advance of the Turks.

The once-powerful Byzantine Empire crumbled into several separate states. A younger Comnenus, Alexius, and his brother David set up the empire of Trebizond on the Black Sea (which would endure until conquered by the Ottoman Turks in 1461). Theodore I, Lascaris, organized the empire of Nicaea. Michael Angelus Comnenus became ruler of Epirus. Boniface of Montferrat took over Thessalonica. Other states were set up in Athens, Achaia, Rhodes, and the Meander Valley of Asia Minor. Meanwhile Venice grabbed most of the valuable commercial posts of the fallen empire. *See* Arsouf; Adrianople IV; Crusades.

Constantinople VI (Reconquest by Byzantines), 1261. The Latin Empire of the East had come into being with the capture of Constantinople by the Fourth Crusade in 1204. Never a strong military power, it relied chiefly on the Venetian fleet for protection against its numerous enemies. Its most formidable opponent was the state of Nicaea, in Asia Minor, which stood as the heir of the Byzantine Empire. When Michael VIII, Palaeologus, assumed power in Nicaea in 1259, he immediately laid plans to reconquer Constantinople. He made an alliance with Genoa, the major naval rival of Venice, promising trade privileges in a reconstituted Byzantine Empire. On July 25, 1261, with the Venetian fleet absent, Michael sent an army across the Bosporus under Alexius Strategopulos. The invaders, numbering only about a thousand armored horsemen, stormed into Constantinople and captured it. Baldwin II, the fifth Latin emperor, fled for his life. Michael reestablished the Byzantine Empire. The Palaeologus line continued to rule at Constantinople until the city, and empire, fell to the Ottoman Turks in 1453. *See* Constantinople V; Bursa.

Constantinople VII (Conquest by Turks), 1453. The great city of Constantinople, eastern bastion of Christendom and capital of the Byzantine Empire, had for centuries defied attack from all enemies. Beginning in 1396, the Ottoman Turks had three times laid siege to the city, only to abandon each in favor of more pressing military requirements elsewhere in their Islamic empire. In April 1453, however, the Turkish sultan Mohammed II, soon to be called the Conqueror, launched a new attack on Constantinople, after making extensive preparations. With 80,000 picked troops and an artillery train of 70 pieces, Mohammed took the city under siege.

The Turks had picked a good time to attack. The once great Byzantine Empire had crumbled into decay, and Constantine XI Palaeologus ruled over little but the capital itself. He could call on only some 7,000 troops to garrison the 13 miles of triple walls that surrounded the city. The walls had always been Constantinople's strongest defense, but now they were subjected to the most destructive artillery barrage known up to that time. Moslem cannon pounded breaches in the walls, through which their infantry attacked on April 18, and May 7, 12, and 21. But each time the garrison, led by John (Giovanni) Giustiniani, threw back the assaults and partially repaired the openings.

Constantine could expect no relief from the outside. His navy had disintegrated. A heavy iron chain across the Golden Horn shut out the Turkish

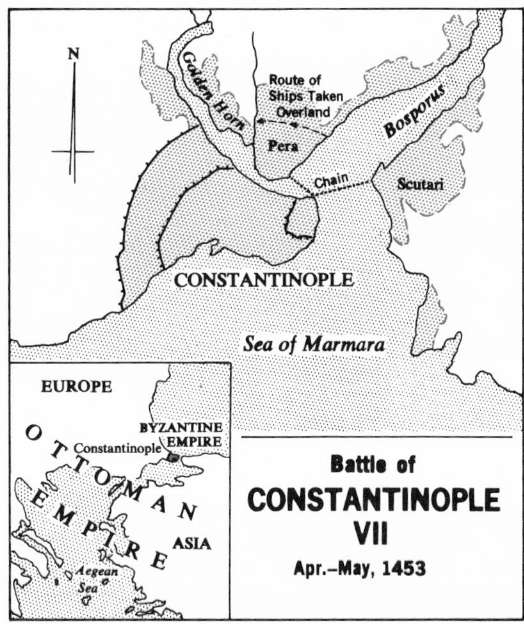

Battle of
CONSTANTINOPLE VII
Apr.–May, 1453

fleet from the harbor. But during the siege the Turks had dragged some 70 light ships across a mile of land to enter the upper end of the Golden Horn, completely blockading the city.

On May 29, after 50 days of relentless artillery bombardment, the Ottomans launched a major assault featuring 12,000 Janizary infantrymen. Pouring through the broken walls in several places, the Turks swarmed into the city. Constantine, Giustiniani, and most of the native troops, mercenaries, and Venetian and Genoese sailors died in a futile effort to stem the Mohammedan tide. Thousands of civilians were massacred while other thousands were enslaved. For three days the city suffered a thorough pillage at the hands of the victorious troops. On the following Friday, prayers to Allah were offered in the historic Christian church of Saint Sophia.

The fall of Constantinople ended the thousand-year Byzantine, or Eastern, Empire. When the Peloponnesus surrendered in 1460, and Trebizond on the Black Sea capitulated the following year, the last of the Greek states had been erased by the Ottoman Turks. In less than a century Constantinople (renamed Istanbul in 1930) would become the religious and political capital of the Mohammedan world. The siege and capture of Constantinople ranks as one of the decisive battles of history. And the key role of artillery in this struggle would cast a major shadow over all subsequent battles. *See* Kossovo II; Belgrade I.

Contreras-Churubusco (U.S.-Mexican War), 1847. With his American army built up to some 10,000 effectives, Gen. Winfield Scott left Puebla on August 7 for Mexico City, 65 miles to the west. He pushed into the Valley of Mexico four days later. Here Gen. Antonio de Santa Anna, now the president of Mexico, had concentrated about 20,000 troops, chiefly at Contreras and Churubusco. These points guarded the approaches to the Mexican capital from the south. On August 19 an American detachment of 3,300 men under Gen. Gideon Pillow attacked Contreras, held by Gen. Gabriel Valencia. The attackers were repulsed, but on the second day the 5,000 Mexican defenders were routed with 700 killed and 800 captured. The Americans, who were led chiefly by Gen. Persifor Smith, suffered 60 killed and wounded.

Pushing forward toward the capital, Scott launched an assault against Santa Anna's new position at Churubusco later that day. Here the Mexicans had converted a church and convent into a strong fortress. Scott's troops captured the improvised position only after a hard fight that cost 133 killed and over 900 wounded. These losses, plus those at Contreras and a total of 40 missing from the dual battle, amounted to about 7 percent of the entire American army. The twin defeat had been even more costly for Santa Anna, however. In all, he had lost more than a third of his army. With the Americans now only five miles from Mexico City, Santa Anna withdrew into the capital and requested an armistice in order to consider peace proposals. Fighting was suspended on August 24. When negotiations collapsed on September 7, Scott resumed the offensive. *See* Cerro Gordo; Molino del Rey; Chapultepec; U.S.-Mexican War.

Cooch's Bridge (War of the American Revolution), 1777. When Gen. Sir William Howe landed on the upper Chesapeake Bay on August 25, 1777, he marched his British army of 15,000 men toward Philadelphia in two columns. The right-hand (eastward) column, under Gen. Lord Cornwallis, marched into Delaware. Here on the Christina River, the American commander in chief, Gen. George Washington, had posted Gen. William Maxwell with 720 men to delay the British advance. When Cornwallis' van reached the vicinity of Cooch's Bridge on September 3, a brisk fight ensued. Maxwell's men inflicted some 30 casualties before the weight of enemy numbers forced them to abandon their position and fall back on the main American army, with a loss of 30 men killed. *See* Princeton; Brandywine Creek; American Revolution.

Copenhagen I (Wars of the French Revolution), 1801. Although a British offensive was successfully liberating Egypt from French control early in 1801, elsewhere the government of George III stood on the defensive. The victories of Napoleon Bonaparte in Europe had wrecked the Second Coalition and left England the only power still at war with France. To add to British troubles, the now neutral nations of Russia, Prussia, Sweden, and Denmark formed the Northern Convention to resist the claimed rights of the belligerents (really England) in the Baltic.

On April 2 Adm. Sir Hyde Parker took a fleet of 20 British warships into Copenhagen harbor to deliver an ultimatum to Crown Prince Frederick, regent for the insane Christian VII, king of Denmark and Norway. The Danes opened fire with shore batteries. Parker ordered his ships to withdraw, but his second-in-command, Adm. Lord Nelson, ignored the signal. Under Nelson's direction, the British naval guns silenced the shore batteries and then attacked and disabled the anchored Danish fleet of ten vessels. Denmark accepted a truce on the following day. This British victory, plus the assassination of the Russian czar, Paul I, dissolved the Northern Convention. (The new Russian ruler, Alexander I, was friendly toward Great Britain.)

After a year of inaction, Great Britain and France signed the Treaty of Amiens on March 27, 1802, terminating the war. But peace lasted only 14 months before these two belligerents clashed again. *See* Alexandria III; Hohenlinden; Finisterre Cape III; French Revolution Wars.

Copenhagen II (Napoleonic Empire Wars), 1807. The British government of King George III learned that a secret clause in the French-Russian Treaty of Tilsit (July 7, 1807) provided for Napoleon I to seize the Danish navy and thus gain control of the entrance to the Baltic Sea. Admiral James Gambier (later Lord Gambier) was promptly sent into Köge (Kjöge) Bight south of Copenhagen with a fleet of 20 British warships. Gambier landed an expeditionary force of 18,000 British and Hannoverian troops during August 16–18, commanded by Gen. Lord Cathcart (William Schaw). The invaders began to invest the Danish capital. On August 29 a relieving force of Danes was beaten off by Gen. Sir Arthur Wellesley (later Duke of Wellington). The British fleet then moved in closer and joined in the land bombardment of the city during September 2–5. Two days later Danish Crown Prince Frederick, regent for the insane Christian VII of Denmark and Norway, surrendered the Danish fleet of 18 ships. The British then withdrew. *See* Friedland; Napoleonic Empire Wars.

Coral Sea (World War II), 1942. At the end of April 1942 the Japanese resumed their thus far all-victorious advance in the Pacific. Darkening the threat to Australia, a Japanese invasion force under Adm. Shigeyoshi Inouye left Rabaul, New Britain, for Port Moresby on the south side of New Guinea on May 4. At the same time, a strong striking force headed by the carriers *Shokaku* and *Zuikaku* moved into the Coral Sea, northeast of Australia. Meanwhile, the United States hurriedly assembled a naval task force, also in the Coral Sea, commanded by Adm. Frank Fletcher.

On May 7 Fletcher's planes from the carriers *Yorktown* and *Lexington* struck at the Japanese invasion fleet north of the Louisiade Archipelago. The enemy carrier *Shoho* was sunk and the transports, stripped of their air cover, turned back. The next day the two main naval forces, of equal size and striking power, located each other in the Coral Sea. There followed the first sea battle in history in which surface ships did not exchange a shot. The battle was fought at long range with carrier planes. United States planes damaged the carrier *Shokaku* at a cost of 33 of 82 attacking aircraft. The Japanese sank the *Lexington,* a destroyer, and a tanker, but lost 43 of 69 planes. American casualties were 543. Despite the heavier losses, the United States had checked the enemy advance for the first time in the war. Port Moresby was saved and the Japanese were driven back from the Coral Sea. Within a month the United States won a more decisive battle in the mid-Pacific. *See* Java Sea; New Guinea; Midway; World War II.

Cordova (Spanish-Moslem Wars), 1236. Despite the decisive Christian victory at Las Navas de Tolosa in 1212, the reconquest of southern Spain from the Moors moved slowly, chiefly because of frequent civil strife among the Christian states. In 1227 Alfonso IX of León took Badajoz, in the southwest. Three years later the war against the Moors speeded up when the kingdoms of León and Castile became permanently united under Alfonso's son Ferdinand III, the Saint. A strong ruler, Ferdinand marched his army against Cordova on the Guadalquivir River. This flourishing city had served as the capital of Moorish Spain since the eighth century. Ferdinand's troops stormed into Cordova and captured it in 1236. Other successes quickly followed. Seville, to the southwest, fell two years later; Jaén, to the east, capitulated in 1246. Ferdinand's son and successor, Alfonso X, seized Cadiz in 1262.

Meanwhile, James I, the Conqueror, of Aragon, pushed his kingdom to the Mediterranean by taking Valencia in 1238 and Mercia in 1266. Now only the southern tip of Andalusia and Granada remained as Moorish strongholds in Spain. The successors of Alfonso X continued the counteroffensive toward Gibraltar, but to the east the Moslem commander of Granada, having agreed to serve as Ferdinand's vassal, obtained security for his city until 1482. *See* Las Navas de Tolosa; Río Salado.

Corinth (Roman Conquest of Greece), 146 B.C. After the fall of Macedonia the Achaean League became the last independent power in Greece. In 151 B.C. Rome returned the 1,000 hostages taken from the Achaean cities to Italy 16 years earlier. But rivalry with Sparta, which had been a satellite of Rome since early in the second century B.C., provoked new hostilities between the Achaean League and the aggressive republic across the Adriatic. When the League attacked Sparta, a strong Roman force intervened and began a systematic conquest of the upper Peloponnesus, which the outnumbered Achaeans were helpless to prevent. Finally the Roman general Lucius Mummius (Achaicus) captured the key Achaean city of Corinth. The Greek inhabitants were massacred and the city was sacked. This erased the Achaean League. The Roman conquest of Greece was now complete. *See* Pydna; Roman Republic.

Corinth, Miss. (American Civil War), 1862. The defeat of Gen. Sterling Price's Confederate army at Iuka prompted the senior Confederate general, Earl Van Dorn, to unite all his forces at Ripley, Miss. With a combined total of 22,000 men Van Dorn then marched northward. His objective was Corinth, 28 miles to the northeast, which was held by Gen. William Rosecrans with 23,000 Federal troops. Underestimating the size of the defending force, Van Dorn attacked Corinth on October 3. The first Confederate assault drove in the exterior Federal lines. But thereafter, Rosecrans' army fought back fiercely. Van Dorn realized he was outmatched and tried to retreat westward the following day. He was forced to fight a strong rear-guard action all the way back to Ripley, before Rosecrans, who had been reinforced by troops sent forward by Gen. U. S. Grant, abandoned the pursuit. The Confederates suffered 2,470 in killed or wounded and another 1,763 missing (of whom at least 300 were captured). Federal losses were 2,520. *See* Iuka; Chickasaw Bluffs; American Civil War.

Corinthian War. *See* Haliartus; Coronea II; Cnidus.

Coronea I (First Peloponnesian War), 447 B.C. Although Pericles provided great diplomatic skill, Athenian hegemony did not bring peace to the cities of central Greece. Much of the unrest stemmed from the knowledge that only 150 miles away stood the Laconian city of Sparta, ever ready to intervene against its natural rival. In 447 Boeotia revolted and at its western city of Coronea defeated an Athenian force under Tolmides, who had been sent to quell the uprising. In a trade for the freedom of many Athenian prisoners, Boeotia was allowed to re-establish its pro-Spartan league under the hegemony of Thebes.

The following year Pericles had to put down a revolt on the island of Euboea. Then Megara, taking up the cue, withdrew from the Athenian confederacy. Rather than hazard further hostilities, Athens signed a 30-year peace treaty with Sparta late in 446. Each city agreed to recognize its rival's existing theater of influence. But the treaty lasted for only half of its intended span; by 431 Athens and Sparta were again in conflict, in the Great Peloponnesian War. *See* Tanagra-Oenophyta; Plataea II; Peloponnesian Wars.

Coronea II (Greek City-States' Wars), 394 B.C. The surprising Spartan defeat at Haliartus forced Agesilaus II to call off his expedition in Asia Minor in order to prosecute the Corinthian War at home. Returning to Greece through the Gulf of Corinth, Agesilaus pushed his way inland and defeated a larger force of anti-Spartan allies at Coronea, in Boeotia. The victory, however, proved inconclusive against the coalition, which continued to resist Spartan hegemony. Sparta laid siege to Corinth, but in 390 the Athenian general Iphicrates relieved the city. This action ended the Corinthian War, but it by no means brought peace to the belligerent city-states of Greece. *See* Haliartus; Cnidus; Naxos; Greek City-States' Wars.

Coronel (World War I), 1914. At the outbreak of war eight German cruisers were on the high seas or foreign station. From the Orient the admiral Count Maximilian von Spee sailed for South America. Arriving off Coronel, Chile, on November 1 with five cruisers, Spee encountered an inferior British squadron commanded by Adm. Sir Christopher Cradock. In a short fight the Germans sank Cradock's only two armored cruisers, the *Good Hope* and *Monmouth*. The light cruiser *Glasgow* escaped, along with an armed merchant cruiser. Cradock went down with the *Good Hope*. British naval reinforcements were immediately sent into the South Atlantic from the Grand Fleet. *See* Heligoland Bight; Falkland Islands; World War I.

Corregidor (World War II). An island in the mouth of Manila Bay captured by the Japanese on May 6–7, 1942; it was retaken by American troops on February 16, 1945. *See* Bataan-Corregidor; Luzon.

Cortenuova (German Invasion of Italy), 1237. The long struggle between the German emperors of the Holy Roman Empire and the Italian cities dominated much of the later Middle Ages. Generally the German Welfs (Italian Guelphs) wanted local autonomy; the German Waiblings (Italian Ghibellines), chiefly the Hohenstaufen dynasty, sought to impose a strong Imperial rule over the Italian cities. In 1237 Frederick II of the Holy Roman Empire attacked the Guelph forces of the revived Lombard League at Cortenuova. The Imperial army routed the Italians on November 27. Frederick then moved on to smash Milan, which had played a leading role in the cities' resistance to Imperial power. *See* Legnano; Benevento.

Corunna Road (Spanish Civil War). A month-long battle, during December 13, 1936–January 15, 1937, in which the rebel Nationalists cut the road leading northward from Republican-held Madrid. *See* Madrid.

Corupedion (Wars of the Hellenistic Monarchies), 281 B.C. Twenty years after the battle of Ipsus had divided up the spoils of Alexander the Great's empire, two of the Diadochi (successors) fought each other for possession of Asia Minor. At Corupedion in ancient Lydia the Macedonian troops, then under the command of Lysimachus, lined up against the Syrians under Seleucus I. Both armies watched while the two octogenarian generals fought in hand-to-hand combat. Seleucus killed his opponent, and his army then routed the Macedonians to make the Syrian victory complete.

Seleucus had become undisputed master of Asia Minor. But when he tried to take over Macedonia the following year, he was assassinated. His son Antiochus I (called Soter) succeeded to the Seleucid throne. The new ruler concentrated on Asian affairs, leaving the troubled rule of Macedonia to Antigonus II (Gonatas). The third Hellenistic monarchy to emerge from Alexander's conquests, Egypt, continued to be ruled by the Ptolemaic dynasty. *See* Ipsus; Pergamum; Hellenistic Monarchies, Wars of the.

Costa Rica. *See* Chalchuapa.

Coulmiers (Franco-Prussian War), 1870. The crushing defeat at Sedan, the fall of Metz, and the siege of Paris destroyed all the regular armed forces of France. But under the leadership of the new Third Republic and the inspiration of Léon Gambetta, the people in the provinces flew to arms against the Prussian army of occupation. A force organized at Tours under Gen. Louis d'Aurelle de Paladines marched on Coulmiers, west of Orleans, on November 9. Here the civilian-soldiers encountered a Bavarian corps, which they defeated after a hard fight. Unfortunately for France, it was the only clear victory for the provincial armies. *See* Sedan; Paris II; Bapaume; Franco-Prussian War.

Courtrai (French-Flemish Wars), 1302. The harsh French rule of Philip IV, the Fair, provoked a Flemish revolt on May 18, 1302, called the Matins of Bruges. To put down the uprising, the Comte d'Artois marched to Courtrai (Kortrijk) in West Flanders with an army of knights from France and the Flemish nobility, supported by hired Genoese crossbowmen and German cavalry. Opposing this impressive array stood a force of Flemish weavers and other workingmen, armed chiefly with heavy pikes. Under the command of Count Guy de Dampierre, the Flemish army deployed skillfully among the waterways of the region.

On July 11 the feudal army charged without waiting for the crossbowmen to soften up the Flemings. Lacking discipline and unable to maneuver, the attackers soon became disorganized. The pikemen fought fiercely, inflicting heavy casualties on both horses and men who became mired in the soft ground. Thousands of French were killed, including Artois and 63 other nobles. When the last of the French had fled the field, the victors picked up 700 gilt spurs from dead knights, thus giving rise to the name "battle of the Spurs." (For another engagement called the battle of the Spurs *see* Guinegate.) France later reasserted its dominion over Flanders, but the battle stands as one of the great victories of infantry over armored cavalry in the Middle Ages. *See* Mons-en-Pévèle.

Coutras (French Religious Wars), 1587. The seven civil and religious uprisings which had torn France for a quarter of a century after 1562 had settled no issue between the Huguenots and the Catholic Valois kings of France. A new outbreak in 1585 was complicated by the intervention of King Philip II of Spain and the Catholic Holy League and by an internal French struggle to succeed King Henry III. In this struggle, which was called the War of the Three Henrys, the chief participants were the Valois king himself, Henry I de Lorraine (Duc de Guise), an ardent Catholic; and Henry of Navarre (later Henry IV), Protestant brother-in-law of the king. After many months of maneuvering, the hostile religious forces met at Coutras, in southwest France, for a showdown battle, on October 20, 1587. Henry of Navarre, a capable commander, skillfully deployed his 6,300 men on a narrow front between wooded heights, placing musketeers between squadrons of cavalry. The Catholic army of 10,000 men under the Duc de Joyeuse charged the Huguenot line, only to be riddled by gunfire and then routed by a mounted counterattack. Joyeuse and 3,500 of his men were killed, while Navarre suffered only 200 casualties.

Aroused by the defeat at Coutras, Henry of Guise marched into Paris to depose the incompetent Henry III and to take over the Holy League crusade. The king fled on May 12, 1588, but ordered the assassination of De Guise later that year. The Catholic party now revolted and King Henry fled once more, this time to the Huguenot camp of Henry of Navarre. Here he was murdered in 1589, ending the Valois line of kings but not the French religious wars. *See* Moncontour; Arques; French Religious Wars.

Covadonga (Moslem Conquest of Spain), 718. Beginning with the invasion of 711, the hard-riding Moslem cavalry met only weak resistance in overrunning all of Spain but the northwest corner. In 718, however, Pelayo, the Gothic chieftain in the mountains of Asturias, rallied a Christian army to challenge the invaders. At Covadonga, five miles from Cangas de Ónis, Pelayo threw back the invaders so thoroughly that this part of Spain remained free of Moslem control. The battle marked the end of the conquest of Spain but not the last of the Moslem attacks in western Europe. Southern France was under almost constant attack, and 14 years later a powerful Islamic force crossed the Pyrenees into central France. *See* Río Barbate; Toulouse I; Moslem Conquests.

Cowpens (War of the American Revolution), 1781. Despite the patriot victory at Kings Mountain in October 1781, American strength in the South was at a low ebb when Gen. Nathanael Greene assumed command on December 3 at Charlotte, N.C. The capable Greene promptly began reorganizing his forces. He then moved to Cheraw, S.C., while sending Gen. Daniel Morgan to make a sweep west of the British base at Winnsboro. The British commander in the South, Gen. Lord Charles Cornwallis, ordered Col. Banastre Tarleton to pursue Morgan. At the head of 1,100 well-trained men, Tarleton caught up with Morgan at Cowpens, a broad plain in the Piedmont region of South Carolina. Morgan made a stand with his back and left flank against the Broad River.

Although Morgan had as many men as Tarleton, the great majority of the American force consisted of raw militia. Morgan compensated for the inexperience of his troops by skillful deployment. In front of his position he posted 150 expert riflemen from Georgia and North Carolina. Some 150 yards to the rear of this line he organized 300 North and South Carolina militia under Gen. Andrew Pickens. Another 150 yards to the rear stood the main American line of 450 men, Continentals flanked by two Virginia militia detachments. Colonel William Washington's 125 mounted men constituted the only reserve.

On January 17 Tarleton's Legion charged the American position. As instructed by Morgan, the sharpshooters fired and then fell back to the second line, which fired two volleys before it too fell back. The British pressed on to the main line of resistance despite severe casualties. After a deadly half-hour battle, this American line also withdrew. The attackers rushed forward anticipating a complete victory. But Morgan had organized his successive and orderly withdrawals to build up the pressure of a coiled spring. His entire force suddenly wheeled about and counterattacked the disorganized British. At the same time Washington's cavalry struck their flank and rear. The British army wavered and then bolted in disorder, leaving 100 dead and 229 wounded on the field. Another 600 were taken prisoner. American losses were 12 killed, 60 wounded.

After the battle, Morgan promptly retreated to the northeast before he could be trapped by Cornwallis' main army, which now began to move against him. Hurrying across four unbridged rivers, Morgan linked up with Greene at Guilford Courthouse, N.C., on February 9. Six days later the reunited American army crossed the Dan River into Virginia. Cornwallis, hard on their heels, was stymied on the south bank for lack of boats. (Unfortunately for the American cause, ill health prevented the able Morgan from taking the field again.) *See* Kings Mountain; Guilford Courthouse; American Revolution.

Cracow (Mongol Invasion of Europe), 1241. After conquering most of Russia during 1237–40 the Mongol horde of Subotai and Batu Khan (grandson of Genghis Khan) swept westward to the Lvov (Lemberg)-Przemyśl area. From here the main body rode south across the Carpathians to the plains of Hungary, while a single column under Kaidu, another of Genghis' grandsons, plunged westward across the Vistula River. Near Cracow (Kraków) the Polish king Boleslav V had assembled an army of mounted knights to oppose the invaders. At the first Mongol attack, on the village of Szylow on March 3, 1241, the Polish king cravenly fled the field. The now leaderless Poles crumbled under the Mongol arrows, which preceded the usual sword-slashing cavalry attack. Using the same missile-and-shock tactics, the invaders swept on to take Cracow and then Breslau (Wroclaw). Meanwhile, a second European army was hastily forming farther west near Liegnitz (Legnica). *See* Kiev I; Liegnitz I; Mohi; Mongol Wars.

Crampton's Gap (American Civil War). The capture of this pass through South Mountain by Gen. George McClellan's Federal troops on September 14, 1862, preceded the larger battles of Harpers Ferry and Antietam Creek. *See* Harpers Ferry; Antietam Creek.

Crannon (Macedonian Conquests), 322 B.C. The news of the death of Alexander III, the Great, sparked a revolt against Macedonia in Athens. Urged on by the great orator Demosthenes, Leosthenes led a force of Greek rebels into Thessaly to attack the Macedonian governor, Antipater, at Lamia in 323 B.C. Meanwhile, at sea Athens tried to cut communications between the Macedonians in Asia and those in Greece. But the new Athenian fleet was destroyed in a naval engagement in the Cyclades Islands. This action opened the way for Macedonian reinforcements to reach Antipater in Thessaly. At Crannon in 322 B.C. the Greek rebels were defeated and the revolt collapsed. Athens was occupied and its leaders were taken prisoner, ending the so-called Lamian War. Demosthenes took poison to escape capture. *See* Hydaspes River; Ipsus; Macedonian Conquests.

Craonne (Napoleonic Empire Wars), 1814. While Napoleon I was driving the main allied army away from Paris up the Seine and Aube valleys, the Prussian field marshal Gebhard von Blücher launched a new attack on the capital down the Marne. Struck repeatedly on his left (south) flank, Blücher sidled northward, finally retreating across the Aisne during March 4–5. Napoleon took up the pursuit. Blücher determined to make a stand on the Craonne Plateau, 15 miles southeast of Laon, while enveloping the French right rear with a Russian corps under Field Marshal Baron Ferdinand von Wintzingerode. But before the allied offensive could be launched, Napoleon assaulted Craonne on March 7 with 37,000 troops, aiming to encircle the town. Although the French failed to trap Blücher's troops, their attack forced the much larger allied army back on Laon. The battle, which cost Napoleon 5,400 casualties to the enemy's 5,000, would be the French emperor's next-to-last victory of the campaign. *See* Bar-sur-Aube; Laon; Napoleonic Empire Wars.

Crater (American Civil War). A huge Federal mine was exploded on July 30, 1864, under the Confederate lines east of Petersburg in a futile effort to break through to the city; the ensuing struggle in the blasted area is sometimes called the battle of the Crater. *See* Petersburg.

Cravant (Hundred Years' War), 1423. With the death of Henry V in 1422, the Duke of Bedford (John of Lancaster), regent for his youthful nephew Henry VI, took over the direction of the English campaign in France. He began to reduce methodically all Orleanist French resistance north of the Loire. At Cravant, southeast of Laon, Bedford's army encountered a combined French and Scottish force under the earls of Buchan (John Stewart) and Douglas (Archibald, 4th earl of Douglas), respectively, fighting in the interest of the dauphin Charles (future Charles VII). On August 1, 1423, the Orleanist allies fought bravely, but they were slaughtered by the deadly longbows of the English, who were supported by their French friends, the Burgundians. The English conquest of northern France rolled on. *See* Beaugé; Verneuil; Hundred Years' War.

Crécy (Hundred Years' War), 1346. Capitalizing

on the English mastery of the Channel won at the battle of Sluys (Sluis), Edward III landed an invasion force in Normandy on July 12, 1346. The English army of about 10,000 men marched northward, plundering the countryside. King Philip VI, at the head of the French army of 12,000 men—8,000 mailed horsemen, 4,000 hired Genoese crossbowman—pursued the invaders across the Somme River. At Crécy, 12 miles north of Abbeville, Edward halted. His men-at-arms dismounted and took up strong defensive positions, each of the three corps protected by wings of archers wielding the deadly longbow.

After reconnoitering the English position late in the afternoon of August 26, Philip ordered his attack deferred until the following day. But the French vanguard continued to press forward until the whole army was inadvertently committed. The Genoese crossbowmen opened the battle but soon found themselves being cut to pieces by the English longbowmen who were able to fire six times more rapidly. When the outfought mercenaries bolted to the rear, Philip's cavalry charged through them toward the English archers, only to pile up in a bloody heap of horses and men before the continued shower of arrows. Pressed from the rear, the French attacked again and again until nightfall brought a merciful end to the uneven struggle. More than a third of the French army lay dead on the field, the great majority victims of English arrows. Among the dead was the blind Bohemian king, John of Luxemburg. English losses were less than 100.

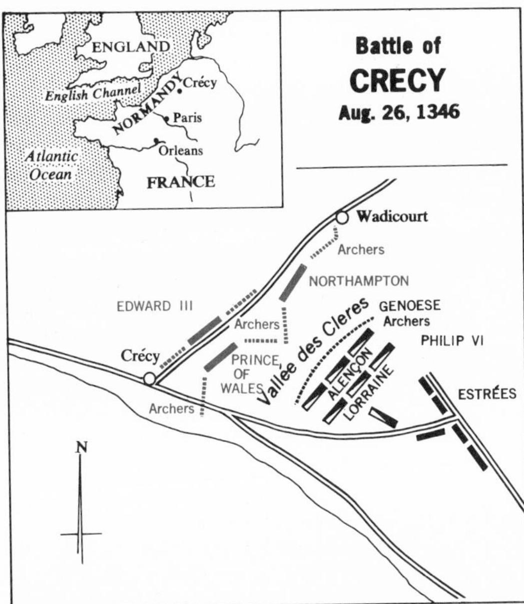

The introduction of the longbow with a killing range up to 250 yards, the corresponding decline of the mounted knight, and the rise of England to an international military power all combine to make Crécy one of history's most decisive battles. With the shattered French army no longer a threat, Edward turned northwest to Calais. *See* Sluys; Calais I; Hundred Years' War.

Crefeld (Seven Years' War), 1758. While Frederick II, the Great, was campaigning against Austria in 1758, a second Prussian army took the field against the French. The able field marshal Ferdinand, duke of Brunswick, at the head of an army of 30,000 men from Brunswick, Hesse, and Hannover, marched westward. The main body of French, which had been severely mauled at Rossbach the previous year, fell back under the Comte de Clermont. Pressing forward in the Ruhr Valley, Ferdinand drove the retreating enemy over the Rhine. Here Clermont made a stand at Crefeld (Krefeld). The aggressive, well-disciplined Prussian army attacked on June 23 and utterly routed the numerically superior French army. Ferdinand then turned back to campaign in Hannover, the fief of Prussia's ally King George II of Great Britain. Meanwhile, another ponderous Russian army was invading East Prussia. *See* Olmütz; Zorndorf; Seven Years' War.

Cremona I (Civil Wars of the Roman Empire), A.D. 69. The civil war in Italy that catapulted Aulus Vitellius to ruler of the Roman Empire provoked an equally violent reaction in the East. In Egypt, Syria, and Judea the legions united in support of Titus Flavius Vespasian for emperor. Joining this coalition were the 40,000 troops in the province of Pannonia, west of the Danube. Without waiting for additional support, Antonius Primus marched this force around the head of the Adriatic and invaded Italy.

Vitellius sent out an imperial army under Caecina to repel this threat. But Caecina, despite the fact that he had superior numbers, continued to fall back, to the Adige River and then to the Po. Then he abandoned his army altogether and fled. The aggressive Primus pursued the leaderless imperials westward and caught up with them before they could take refuge within the walls of Cremona. Here the frustrated Vitellians turned and fought back savagely. For a day and a night the battle raged. Finally Primus' troops scattered their opponents and entered the town. Cremona was sacked and burned.

Primus now marched on Rome, which was also the objective of another force of Vespasians under Mucianus, the governor of Syria, who had landed in Italy with legionaries from the East. Vitellius tried to abdicate, but his friends resisted the double invasion of the capital. Much of Rome was destroyed and Vitellius killed before the resistance was crushed on December 21. Vespasian, although he had not yet arrived from Jerusalem, stood victorious. Rome had its fourth emperor of the year. *See* Bedriacum; Jerusalem IV; Roman Empire.

Cremona II (War of the Spanish Succession), 1702. Five months after repulsing a French attack at Chiari in Lombardy, Italy, Prince Eugene of Savoy took the offensive again. He struck westward with his Austrian army of the Holy Roman Empire (Leopold I) to Cremona, on the Po River. On February 1, 1702, Eugene made a night attack that caught the French garrison, under Marshal the Duc de Villeroi, completely by surprise. Storming into the city, the Austrians captured the French marshal and several other high-ranking officers; another 1,000 French were killed. However, the citadel held out, and when a relieving French army approached Cremona, Eugene had to withdraw. *See* Chiari; Luzzara; Spanish Succession, War of the.

Crete (World War II), 1941. When the German Twelfth Army overran Greece in a crushing three-week attack in April, 26,000 British and Imperial troops were evacuated to Crete. There they joined another 1,500 British troops, plus a force of 14,000 Greeks. Because of their hasty evacuation and continued German dominance in the air, the Allied force on Crete (largely Australians and New Zealanders) was short of supplies, weapons, and communications. Germany quickly organized an airborne assault on Crete under the command of Gen. Kurt Student. On May 20, preceded by heavy bombings, the Germans began landing parachutists and glider troops at the two airfields of Maleme and Rethymnon and at the harbor of Heraklion (Candia)—all on the north side of the island. About 7,000 German troops landed the first day, 22,000 by the end of the week. It was the first entirely airborne assault in history.

The Crete defenders, commanded by the New Zealand general Bernard Freyberg, fought back hard against the assault from the sky and took a heavy toll of the XI Air Corps invaders. But they suffered relentless attack from German aircraft and were gradually overwhelmed.

By May 27 the battle was lost, and on that and the following night 16,500 of the British force were evacuated, chiefly to Egypt. Most of the 13,000 Allied casualties on the island were prisoners, the last surrendering on May 31. British naval losses totaled more than 2,000 men, with three cruisers and six destroyers sunk. German personnel casualties included more than 5,600 killed in action, a heavy percentage of them parachutists. Another 5,000 Germans were killed when their Crete-bound convoys were routed by the British Eastern Mediterranean fleet under Adm. Sir Andrew Cunningham. The battle of Crete ended Germany's campaign in southeastern Europe. The next Nazi attack would come against an erstwhile ally, the Soviet Union. *See* Greece (World War II); Soviet Union (World War II); World War II.

Crimea (World War II), 1941–1944. In the 1941 German invasion of the Soviet Union, Field Marshal Karl von Rundstedt's southern army group swept through the Ukraine beyond the Crimean Peninsula. In October the back-up Eleventh Army of Gen. Erich von Manstein began to attack the peninsula itself. Mainstein broke through the fortified Perekop Isthmus on November 8 and quickly overran all the Crimea except the Black Sea port of Sevastopol, which resisted savagely. To the east, the Kerch Peninsula was taken but lost again in a Russian counteroffensive in December.

Manstein held both Sevastopol and the Kerch under siege until the following spring. Then, on May 7, 1942, with 15 divisions (including 2 *Panzer* and 5 Rumanian), he smashed at the Kerch defenses and overcame them in six days. Part of the three Russian divisions escaped across the Kerch Strait to the Taman Peninsula in the Caucasus; the rest were captured as part of the 150,000 Russian casualties. Turning back to the western Crimea, Manstein attacked Sevastopol on June 3. After a savage month-long assault, the battered city surrendered on July 1, ending a 245-day siege. Some 90,000 prisoners were taken. (Manstein and five of his divisions were then transferred to the Leningrad front to repeat the Crimean assault tactics, but in that city the besieged Russians held fast.) Thus the Soviet Union lost its chief Black Sea base just as the 1942 German offensive in the Caucasus threatened to sweep down the entire eastern shore.

In November 1943 Gen. Fedor Tolbukhin's drive along the northern shores of the Sea of Azov and the Black Sea bottled up the German forces still in the Crimea. In the following spring Gen. Ivan Petrov's Caucasus army drove the German forces in the Taman Peninsula across the strait to Kerch. The Russians crossed the Kerch Strait in pursuit, timing their attack with Tolbukhin's thrust at the Perekop Isthmus defenses in the north on April 8. Tolbukhin broke into the Crimea after three days of fighting. The German Seventeenth Army, now holding the Crimea, had to fall back to Sevastopol. Here the German garrison held out 24 days, finally surrendering on May 9. The last Germans in the Crimea capitulated three days later. The entire Fourth (southern) Ukranian front was now clear. *See* Soviet Union (World War II); Leningrad; Caucasus; Ukraine; World War II.

Crimean War (1853–1856). The long-standing rivalry between Russia and Turkey broke out in war again in 1853. Chief causes were the claims of Russia (Nicholas I) to the protection of the Holy Places in the Near East and to the Orthodox Christians throughout the empire of Turkey (Abdul Medjid I). When Russia occupied the Danubian principalities of Wallachia and Moldavia, the Ottoman sultan declared war, on October 4. England and France entered on Turkey's side in 1854 and Sardinia a year later. The final peace treaty, signed at Paris on March 30, 1856, settled none of the issues but did check growing Russian designs upon the weakening Turkish Empire.

Oltenita	1853
Sinope	1853
Silistra	1854
Bomarsund	1854
Alma River	1854
Sevastopol I	1854–1855
Balaclava	1854
Inkerman	1854
Chernaya River	1855
Melakhov	1855
Redan	1855
Kars I	1855

Crimisus River (Carthaginian Invasion of Sicily), 341 B.C. The repetitive conflict between Syracuse and Carthage for control of Sicily broke out again in 341 B.C. In that year a large force of Carthaginians, including 2,500 members of the Sacred Band (so grouped because of their high birth), moved inland from the west coast to the Crimisus River. Timoleon, the Sicilian commander, found himself greatly outnumbered. But by attacking the Carthaginians as they were crossing the river, he was able to strike and disperse the Sacred Band while it was separated from the main body. Partly hidden by a heavy rainstorm, Timoleon pressed his attack vigorously until the enemy fled the field, leaving 10,000 dead and 15,000 prisoner. Thousands of others drowned trying to recross the river.

Despite the overwhelming Syracusan victory, Carthage maintained a hold on Sicily until the Roman wars in the next century. *See* Syracuse II; Himera River; Punic Wars.

Cropredy Bridge (English Civil War), 1644. In the summer of the third year of the English Civil War, Charles I, from his Oxford headquarters, faced a Roundhead advance in Yorkshire and another from the southeast. The more immediate danger came from Gen. Sir William Waller, who had marched up from Kent to attack Oxford from the rear. Charles sent out a Cavalier force that encountered Waller's Roundheads at Cropredy Bridge over the Cherwell, three miles north of Banbury. On June 29, 1644, the Royalists attacked and routed Waller's force, inflicting severe casualties. With this threat eliminated, Charles ordered his cavalry commander (and nephew), Prince Rupert of Germany, northward to relieve the hard-pressed city of York. *See* Selby; Cheriton; Marston Moor; English Civil War.

Cross Keys–Port Republic (American Civil War), 1862. After escaping the Federal trap at Strasburg in June, Gen. Thomas (Stonewall) Jackson continued to withdraw up the Shenandoah Valley. Federal Gen. John Frémont with 12,000 troops pursued up the North Fork; Gen. James Shields with 5,000 men, up the South Fork (Luray Valley). At Port Republic Jackson turned, on June 7, to face the advancing Union columns which, because of Massanutten Mountain, could unite against his 15,000 men only at this place. The Confederate general Richard Ewell was sent four miles northwest to Cross Keys to hold off Frémont, whose column launched a halfhearted attack against Ewell's 6,500 men on June 8. The Confederates on this flank checked the assault and then drove it back. Leaving a brigade at Cross Keys to hold Frémont, Ewell marched to Port Republic to rejoin Jackson.

The following day (June 9) Jackson launched an attack down the right bank of the South Fork against Shields. His three assault brigades fought without gain for four hours. Then the arrival of Ewell's force swept the Federals out of their positions. Shields fell back northward. During the two-day battle at Cross Keys, Frémont lost 114 killed, 443 wounded, and 127 missing, while Ewell suffered 41 killed, 232 wounded, and 15 missing. At Port Republic Federal casualties were 1,018, including 450 prisoners; Confederate losses, about 800. The double check to the Federal advance ended the 1862 campaign in the valley. The Confederate objective of tying down large Union forces west of the Blue Ridge had succeeded. Jackson remained at Brown's Gap, an exit eastward across the Blue Ridge, until ordered to the Richmond area on June 17. Here a major battle had already been fought in Gen. George McClellan's attack on the Confederate capital. *See* Winchester I; Fair Oaks; Seven Days; American Civil War.

Crotone (German Invasion of Italy), 982. The Holy Roman Emperor Otto II marched from Germany to Rome in 981. He drove out Crescentius I, the Roman duke, and restored Pope Benedict VII. Otto then launched a rash campaign to expel the Moslems from southern Italy and Sicily. On July 13, 982, he attacked Crotone, on the Gulf of Taranto, by both land and sea. The Germans, however, found themselves faced with an alliance between the Byzantine Empire and the Moslems under the caliph of Egypt. Otto's ships were sunk and his army of knights, although fighting bravely, overcome. The expedition collapsed with the death of Otto the following year. Southern Italy remained closed to the Holy Roman Empire for another two centuries. *See* Lechfield; Sant' Angelo; Moslem Conquests.

Crusades (1096–1291). The Byzantine emperor Alexius I Comnenus' appeal for help against the Seljuk Turks prompted Pope Urban II to convene the Synod of Clermont in 1095. The Pope called for a crusade to free the Holy Land from the Seljuks. Eight distinct crusades followed, interspersed with local battles between Christians and the Moslem Turks. At the end of 200 years of fighting the crusades died out, with Palestine and Syria still under Turkish rule.

First Crusade

Nicaea	1097
Dorylaeum I	1097
Tarsus	1097
Antioch I	1097–1098
Jerusalem VII	1099
Ashkelon I	1099
Melitene III	1100
Mersivan	1101
Ereğli I	1101
Ereğli II	1101
Ramleh I	1102
Crusader-Turkish Wars	
Antioch II	1119
Edessa II	1144
Second Crusade	
Dorylaeum II	1147
Damascus III	1148
Crusader-Turkish Wars	
Ashkelon II	1153
Ramleh II	1177
Tiberias	1187
Jerusalem VIII	1187
Third Crusade	
Acre I	1189–1191
Arsouf	1191
Fourth Crusade	
Constantinople V	1204
Adrianople IV	1205
Philippopolis II	1208
Fifth Crusade	
Damietta	1218–1221
Sixth Crusade	
La Forbie	1244
Seventh Crusade	
El Mansûra	1250
Crusader-Turkish Wars	
Antioch III	1268
Eighth Crusade	
Tunis II	1270
Crusader-Turkish Wars	
Tripoli, in Lebanon	1289
Acre II	1291

Ctesiphon I (Parthian Wars of the Roman Empire), 165. The eastern kingdom of Parthia, one of the oldest and strongest enemies of the Roman Empire, provoked another war during the reign of Marcus Aurelius, in 162. Under Vologesus III, Parthian troops conquered Armenia and threatened Syria. To re-establish Roman rule, Lucius Verus and Avidius Cassius took two armies into the East. Cassius marched into modern Iraq and in 165 captured and burned the Parthian capital of Ctesiphon on the east bank of the Tigris. When Verus invaded Media, to the north, Vologesus sued for peace and ceded upper Mesopotamia. It was Rome's greatest victory in the East since the days of Pompey the Great. *See* Arsanias River; Ctesiphon II; Roman Empire.

Ctesiphon II (Parthian Wars of the Roman Empire), 197–198. While Septimius Severus was fighting his way to rule over the Roman Empire, the Eastern kingdom of Parthia made still another attempt to throw Rome out of Asia. Under Vologesus IV, a Parthian army overran Mesopotamia as far west as Nisibis (Nusaybin), on the modern Turkish-Syrian border. Severus organized a large force of legionaries and marched to the east. He relieved the siege of Nisibis in 197 and, driving Vologesus' army before him, reached the Parthian capital of Ctesiphon, on the east bank of the Tigris. The Romans stormed into the city, taking tens of thousands of soldiers and citizens prisoner. Ctesiphon was thoroughly plundered. The decisive Roman triumph induced Vologesus to accept peace the following year. *See* Ctesiphon I; Lugdunum; Roman Empire.

Ctesiphon III (World War I), 1915. Less than two months after his capture of Kut-al-Imara, the British general Sir Charles Townshend was on the march again with his Anglo-Indian army. His objective was Baghdad, 100 miles up the Tigris River. At Ctesiphon, on the east bank of the river 20 miles from Baghdad, Townshend encountered a well-entrenched Turkish force under Gen. Nur-ud-din. Recklessly, he ordered an attack on November 22, although his 14,000 men were markedly outnumbered. The British army advanced hesitantly. They were repulsed sharply, suffering 4,500 casualties. Townshend evacuated his sick and wounded back to Kut-al-Imara and then fell back himself on December 3. *See* Kut-al-Imara I and II; World War I.

Cuba. *See* Latin America.

Cuddalore I (War of the American Revolution), 1782. The third naval battle of 1782 between the British and the French in the Bay of Bengal took place south of Cuddalore, on the east coast of India. Again it was the French commander, Adm. Pierre André de Suffren, who seized the initiative. On July 6 with 11 ships of the line (one of the original 12 had been crippled in a storm the previous day), he attacked the British fleet of 11 warships captained by Adm. Sir Edward Hughes. In a running fight of several hours the French inflicted the greater ship damage but suffered more casualties. The battle was not resumed the following day. Hughes retired to Madras, while Suffren sailed south to Ceylon. *See* Trincomalee I; Trincomalee II; American Revolution.

Cuddalore II (War of the American Revolution), 1783. In the British-French struggle for control in India, the success of land fighting depended heavily upon local domination of the seacoast. When the

French admiral Pierre André de Suffren routed the British fleet off Madras in February 1782, he was able to land troops that helped capture Cuddalore, on April 4. A year later the British command in India launched an attack to regain the seaport. By June 13 Cuddalore lay under siege. Suffren hurriedly sailed north from Ceylon with 15 ships of the line. At his approach, the British fleet commander, Adm. Sir Edward Hughes, moved his 18 warships out to sea and waited for an opportunity to attack. Meanwhile, the aggressive Suffren sailed right up to the town, anchored on June 17, and embarked 1,200 men from the garrison to fill vacancies in his gun crews. On June 20, while Hughes still waited for a favorable wind, Suffren attacked late in the afternoon. This fifth engagement between the two commanders was as indecisive as all the others—not a ship was lost. Hughes pulled back to Madras the following day, leaving the besiegers isolated and short of supplies. But before either side could make a decisive move, news of the preliminary peace treaty reached Cuddalore on June 29. This, then, was the last battle of the eight-year War of the American Revolution. *See* Trincomalee II; Yorktown I; American Revolution.

Culloden Moor ("the Forty-five"), 1746. After successfully mauling their English pursuers at Falkirk, the Scottish Jacobite followers of the Young Pretender, Prince Charles Edward, marched northward to occupy Inverness. The reorganized English army, under King George II's son the Duke of Cumberland (William Augustus), followed. Northeast of Inverness, Cumberland forced the rebels to fight a showdown battle at Culloden Moor on April 16, 1746. Skillfully placing his artillery, Cumberland, with some 10,000 men, beat off every charge of the outnumbered Highlanders. Then the royal cavalry counterattacked and swept the field. The regular English horsemen cut down the fleeing Scots, including the wounded. Cumberland's "no-quarter" generalship and ruthless slaughter of the Jacobite rebels at Culloden gave him the title "Butcher." Royalist losses were only about 300. Prince Charles barely escaped with his life, and the last chance of a Stuart restoration vanished forever. James Edward, the Old Pretender, died in 1766, and Prince Charles 22 years later, without issue. *See* Falkirk II; Jacobite Insurrections.

Cumae (Wars of Sicily), 474 B.C. Six years after Syracuse had established supremacy in Sicily at the battle of Himera, the island was threatened by the southward expansion of Etruria on the mainland of Italy. In 474 B.C. Hiero (Hieron) I, brother of Gelon, took the Syracusan fleet up the west coast of Italy. At Cumae, Hiero encountered the Etruscan navy and in a fierce sea battle turned back the enemy galleys. The victory enabled Syracuse to retain its dominance of the central Mediterranean, while Etruscan power began to decline. *See* Himera; Syracuse I.

Cunaxa (Persian-Greek Wars), 401 B.C. After its victory in the Great Peloponnesian War, Sparta attempted to win control of Asia Minor. In 401 B.C. Sparta made an alliance with the Persian prince Cyrus the Younger, who was in revolt against his older brother the king of Persia, Artaxerxes II (called Mnemon). Clearchus with 13,000 Greek mercenaries joined Cyrus' army of Asiatics at Sardis in Asia Minor, and marched into Babylonia. At the town of Cunaxa the rebels encountered a superior force led by Artaxerxes. Although the Greek phalanx gave a good account of itself, the allied force suffered a crushing defeat. Cyrus was killed. Clearchus and the other Greek leaders were captured and executed.

Xenophon of Athens took command of the Greeks and in a torturous two-year retreat led the "Ten Thousand" back to the Black Sea where they sailed for home. Only half the band survived the 4,000-mile retreat to cry "The sea! The sea!" at the sight of open water. The hardships of the journey were later described by Xenophon in his history the *Anabasis*, or "going up." *See* Eurymedon River; Aegospotami; Haliartus; Persian-Greek Wars.

Cuneo (War of the Austrian Succession), 1744. The second major battle of the desultory war in Italy grew out of a siege that France (Louis XV) and Spain (Philip V) were conducting against Cuneo (Coni), 70 miles west of Genoa. The allied besiegers were led by Prince Louis de Conti of France and by Philip, son of the Spanish king and brother of the Neapolitan monarch Charles IV. To relieve the city, the king of Sardinia (Savoy), Charles Emmanuel I, marched on Cuneo in concert with an Austrian army of the Holy Roman Empire (Maria Theresa) commanded by Gen. Johann Lobkowitz. On September 30, 1744, the Sardinian king attacked the Franco-Spanish force at Madonna del Olmo. In a sharp struggle he was driven back. Conti, however, failed to take the Cuneo fortress and on October 22 retreated eastward into Dauphiné for winter quarters. Thus the year ended with the Austro-Sardinian army still standing between the divided enemy forces in Italy. *See* Velletri; Fontenoy; Austrian Succession, War of the.

Curzola (Venetian-Genoese Wars), 1299. The growing maritime power of Venice found a strong rival in the sea strength of Genoa, across the Italian peninsula. Venetian vessels dominated the eastern Mediterranean through most of the thirteenth century. But new opposition arose when Venice made a treaty with the Turks in Asia Minor in 1289. Ten years later its navy was challenged by Genoese ships at the island of Curzola (Korčula), off the Dalmatian coast. The Genoese won a decisive victory. One of the several thousand Venetians taken prisoner was Marco Polo. The peace negotiated later that year brought no important change in the relative strengths of the two sea powers. *See* Campaldino; Pulj.

"Custer's Last Stand." *See* Little Bighorn River.

Custoza I (Italian Wars of Independence), 1848. For 33 years after the Napoleonic Wars ended in 1815, Italy remained divided into nine separate states, all more or less dominated by the Austrian Empire. Dissatisfaction with Austrian rule came to a head in Milan, the chief city of Lombardy, during March 18–22, 1848. In the "Five Days of Milan" a fierce uprising expelled the Austrian army of Field Marshal Joseph Radetzky. Allying himself with the Milanese rebels, Charles Albert, king of Sardinia (Piedmont), declared war on Austria (Ferdinand I). Piedmontese troops, joined by other Italian rebels, met Radetzky's army at Custoza, 11 miles southwest of Verona, on July 24. The Austrians won overwhelmingly, driving Charles Albert's army out of Lombardy. On August 9 an armistice, displeasing to both sides, took effect. *See* Tolentino; Rieti; Novara II; Italian Wars of Independence.

Custoza II (Italian Wars of Independence), 1866. After successful negotiations to have Louis Napoleon III evacuate his French troops from Rome by 1867, the new kingdom of Italy under Victor Emmanuel II turned its attention to Austria. The government of Franz Josef I still held Venice and surrounding territory. On June 20 Italy declared war on Austria and sent an army under Gen. the Marchese di La Marmora (Alfonso Ferrero) eastward across the Mincio River. Four days later the Italians met the Austrian army of Archduke Albert at Custoza, 11 miles southwest of Verona. The better organized Austrians drove back the Italians in great confusion. Franz Josef, however, was more concerned with his war against Prussia and on July 3 agreed to cede Venice to Italy, via France. But this did not end the Italian war. *See* Aspromonte; Vis; Italian Wars of Independence.

Cynoscephalae I (Greek City-States' Wars), 364 B.C. After its victory at Leuctra, Thebes discovered that the maintenance of hegemony over Greece brought numerous military problems. The chief threat in the north was Alexander of Pherae, who ruled much of Thessaly. In 364 the able Theban commander Pelopidas, one of the leaders at Leuctra, marched against the despotic Alexander. Both armies, intent on seizing the heights of Cynoscephalae in southwest Thessaly, reached there simultaneously. A bitter battle developed. The Theban cavalry won the opening round by driving back the enemy horse, but at a cost of time, which allowed Alexander's infantry to gain the heights. Only after a prolonged attack were the Thebans able to dislodge the enemy and put them to flight. During the fighting, however, Pelopidas was killed, depriving Thebes of a commander second only to Epaminondas. *See* Leuctra; Mantinea; Greek City-States' Wars.

Cynoscephalae II (Second Macedonian War), 197 B.C. In the confused and almost continual warfare that ravaged Greece in the third century B.C., Philip V of Macedonia emerged as the dominant leader. From 215 to 205 Philip's aggressions carried him into conflict with Rome in the First Macedonian War. But after indecisive fighting, both sides agreed to peace terms. Then in 200 Rhodes and Pergamum appealed to Rome to curb Philip's obvious designs on such territories as the Dardanelles (Hellespont) and Egypt. Most of the Greek cities joined the anti-Macedonian alliance.

Rome sent Titus Quinctius Flamininus into Greece at the head of 20,000 legionaries. At the heights of Cynoscephalae, in southeast Thessaly, the Roman legion met the Macedonian phalanx for the first time. After a hard fight Philip and his Macedonians received a thorough beating, almost half of their 20,000-man force being killed or wounded. Roman losses were much smaller.

As a consequence of the defeat, Philip was forced to turn over his fleet, pay a large indemnity, and withdraw from Greece. Flamininus proclaimed the "independence" of Greece at the Isthmian Games in Corinth the following year, ending the Second Macedonian War. But independence only brought a new enemy on the scene, Antiochus III of Syria and, in less than 30 years, new strife in Greece. *See* Sellasia; Panion; Thermopylae II; Pydna; Macedonian Wars.

Cynossema (Great Peloponnesian War), 411 B.C. Four years after the crushing defeat at Syracuse, Athens had partly rebuilt its fleet and resumed the naval war with Sparta. (The 50-year Peace of Nicias had been formally broken in 414, after lasting only seven years.) Alcibiades, recalled to power in Athens, sent a force of 76 triremes into the eastern Aegean Sea under Gens. Thrasybulus and Theramenes. In 411 this fleet defeated the Peloponnesian navy, commanded by Mindarus, in a battle off Cynossema in eastern Thrace. *See* Syracuse I; Cyzicus I; Peloponnesian Wars.

Cyprus (Conquest by Turks), 1570–1571. During the sultanate of Selim II, the Ottoman Turks demanded the control of Cyprus, the last Venetian outpost in the eastern Mediterranean. The island, which had been conquered by the crusading Richard I (the Lion-Hearted) of England in 1191, had been Venice's most valuable base in the East since 1489. When the Venetians refused to give up Cyprus, a Turkish force of 50,000 men attacked the island in July 1570. Philip II of Spain offered to help, as did Pope Pius V. But no relieving fleet reached Cyprus. Meanwhile, the Ottomans overran all of the island except the port of Famagusta on the east coast. Here a garrison of 7,000 Venetians and Cypriots held out until August 3, 1571, when it too surrendered. In violation of the surrender terms, the Venetian governor, Marco Antonio Bragadino, and several of his lieutenants were executed. This massacre aroused the new Holy League that had been forming in Europe against the Turks. *See* Astrakhan II; Malta I; Lepanto II.

Cyzicus I (Great Peloponnesian War), 410 B.C. Despite his naval defeat at Cynossema in 411, the Spartan admiral Mindarus took the offensive by blockading the Athenian colony at Cyzicus in Asia Minor. To relieve the colony, Alcibiades sent out a fleet of Athenian triremes. The Athenians caught the Spartan fleet by surprise in 410. Mindarus was killed and the Peloponnesian navy virtually annihilated. Athens again stood supreme at sea. *See* Cynossema; Notium; Peloponnesian Wars.

Cyzicus II (Third Mithridatic War), 73 B.C. A year after the end of the First Mithridatic War, a Roman army under L. Licinius Murena attempted an invasion of Pontus. When Mithridates VI Eupator refused to give ground (83–82 B.C.), the Second Mithridatic War ended, with no change in the established peace terms. The Pontic king stayed alert, however, and, when he saw Rome beset by domestic strife, launched a new campaign of conquest in 74 B.C. A Roman army under L. Licinius Lucullus marched to the relief of Cyzicus on the southern coast of Propontus (Sea of Marmara). Because Mithridates had a far larger force, Lucullus avoided a pitched battle and concentrated on hit-and-run attacks against the Asiatics' flanks and rear. These tactics not only raised the siege of Cyzicus but gradually eroded the Pontic army. Mithridates finally fled to the court of his son-in-law Tigranes the Great of Armenia. *See* Orchomenus; Tigranocerta I; Mithridatic Wars.

Czechoslovakia (World War II), 1945. The massive Russian offensive to the west during the winter of 1944–45 clamped a three-pronged pincers on German-held Czechoslovakia. Marshal Ivan Konev's First Ukrainian Army struck southward from Saxony. General Andrei Yeremenko's Fourth Ukranian Army entered from the east, while in the south the Third Ukrainian Army of Marshal Fedor Tolbukhin marched into central Czechoslovakia. While Czech patriots revolted in Prague, the American Third Army of Gen. George Patton plunged across the western border from Germany to Pilsen in April. Before these four converging forces could link up at Prague, Germany surrendered unconditionally on May 8. *See* Balkans; Poland–East Prussia; Austria (World War II); Germany, East; World War II.

D

Dakar (World War II), 1940. Three months after the fall of France, a British naval force under Adm. John Cunningham and Free French troops under Gen. Charles de Gaulle attempted to seize the strategic port and air base of Dakar, in French West Africa (this area is now Senegal). The attack was repulsed at sea by forces loyal to the Vichy government of France, commanded by the local governor, Pierre F. Boisson, on September 23–25.

Following the Anglo-American invasion of French North Africa on November 8, 1942, Dakar came under Allied control without a struggle. *See* France (World War II); Oran II; Northwest Africa; World War II.

Damascus I (Moslem Conquest of Syria), 635. From his victory at Pella, in northern Palestine, Khālid ibn-al-Walīd took his Arabian horsemen into Syria. As the Moslems approached Damascus, the Byzantine garrison threw up a strong defense. When the Arabs began to besiege Damascus, Emperor Heraclius ordered one of his generals, named Werdan, to relieve the city. There followed a swift series of maneuvers that established Khālid as one of the best generals of his era. He began pulling away from Damascus to meet Werdan, but as he did so the garrison sallied out to attack his rear. Khālid wheeled quickly and smashed this assault with heavy losses to the Byzantines. Then he turned back to confront and drive off the Werdan relieving force. The energetic Moslem turned again to lock Damascus in a siege that forced the city to surrender on September 4, 635. An Arabian column rode 85 miles to the north to take Emesa (Homs) as well.

Emperor Heraclius had not given up, however. From Constantinople he ordered two armies to march into Syria, from the north and the southwest. Khālid prudently withdrew from both Emesa and Damascus to more favorable ground near the Jordan River. A major battle now loomed. *See* Pella; Yarmuk River; Moslem Conquests.

Damascus II (Byzantine-Moslem Wars), 976. Acting for the youthful Byzantine emperor Basil II, the able general John I Zimisces continued the counteroffensive against the Moslem empire in Syria. In 974 he completed Nicephorus II Phocas' conquest of the northern part of the province and then pushed into central and southern Syria. The veteran Byzantine cavalry routed the defenders of the crumbling Moslem caliphate at every point. In 976 John seized Damascus against only weak resistance. He advanced south toward Jerusalem but had to withdraw when faced by a large enemy army in southern Palestine.

Twenty years later Basil II himself routed the last of the Arabians from Syria, incorporating the area into the Byzantine Empire. *See* Aleppo-Antioch; Sofia; Moslem Conquests.

Damascus III (Second Crusade), 1148. Only the two princely leaders, Louis VII of France and Conrad III of the Holy Roman Empire, plus a handful of knights reached Syria-Palestine from the disasters suffered by the Second Crusade in Asia Minor. Nevertheless, the survivors joined forces with Baldwin III of Jerusalem for an attack on the Turks in the summer of 1148. The great Moslem leader Nureddin of Mosul and Aleppo was by far the chief threat to the Christian Frankish states. But instead of attacking him, the crusaders chose to assault Damascus, which was under the rule of a somewhat friendly emir. The crusaders' objective was to occupy this stronghold and thus cut the road between the two Moslem capitals of Baghdad and Cairo.

The largest Christian army heretofore seen in the Holy Land assembled at Acre and marched on Damascus. The crusading knights drove through the outer defenses to the walls of the city by July 25. But they had no sooner begun their siege when they learned that Nureddin was marching to the relief of Damascus with a strong army of Turks. On July 28 the crusaders broke the siege and began falling back to Galilee. The hit-and-run tactics of Nureddin's mounted bowmen inflicted heavy casualties on the way. By autumn the large Christian force had dispersed. Conrad immediately departed for Europe, and Louis left the following year. Thus the Second Crusade ended with nothing accomplished. Damascus fell to Nureddin six years later, in 1154. *See* Dorylaeum II; Ashkelon II; Crusades.

Damietta (Fifth Crusade), 1218–1221. After

overthrowing the Byzantine Empire of Constantinople on the Fourth Crusade, Christian Europe again turned its hostility on the Turks. Believing that Egypt was the weak spot in the Moslem Empire, forces from Acre and Sicily converged in May 1218 on Damietta, the Egyptian port on the eastern Nile Delta. The new crusade included John of Brienne (France), who was titular king of Jerusalem, the Duke of Austria, a French contingent, the military orders of Hospitallers and Templars, and in September a second force of French and English led by the Count of Nevers and Cardinal Pelagius, who was the papal legate of Honorius III. Damietta became a long siege operation, partly because the Crusaders would not unite behind a single commander and partly because the powerful Frederick II, king of Germany and Holy Roman Emperor, was expected to arrive and take personal charge of the expedition at any time. Meanwhile the sultan of Egypt, Malik al-Kamil, kept his army of Mamelukes upriver between the crusaders and his capital of Cairo.

In November 1219, after 16 months of siege interspersed with frequent truce negotiations, the Christian army captured Damietta by storm. But the victory was minimal and only accentuated the disputes among the leaders of the crusade. Finally, in July 1221, after almost two more years of deadlock in which Frederick II still dallied in Europe, Cardinal Pelagius took command and began marching southward up the Damietta branch of the Nile toward Cairo. The strong force of 5,000 men-at-arms and 40,000 foot soldiers soon floundered amid the flooding waters of the lower Nile. The hastily constructed Moslem fortress at El Mansûra blocked their advance. And when the Egyptian fleet slipped past the crusaders downstream, Cardinal Pelagius wisely asked for peace. The sultan of Egypt agreed to let the crusaders withdraw unmolested if they would evacuate Damietta and leave the country. Pelagius accepted the terms, and in September the Christian army sailed for Europe, ending another crusade that failed. *See* Constantinople V: La Forbie; Crusades.

Damme (English-French Wars), 1213. After chasing the English army of King John out of France north of the Loire, Philip II Augustus considered invading Britain itself. First, however, he attacked Flanders by both land and sea. The Count of Flanders asked England for aid, and King John sent out the fleet that had been stationed at Portsmouth guarding against invasion. Led by the Earl of Salisbury, some 500 English ships crossed the Channel. They caught the French fleet by surprise off Damme in the Zwyn estuary in late March 1213. In a one-sided battle virtually all of Philip's ships were burned or captured. The initiative now passed to John, who began forming a coalition against the French. Meanwhile, the barons of northern France took part in the Albigensian Crusade. *See* Rouen I; Muret; Bouvines.

Danbury (War of the American Revolution), 1777. During the winter of 1776–77, American forces in New England established a large magazine of supplies at Danbury, Conn. In the spring the British commander in New York City, Gen. Sir William Howe, sent out an expedition to destroy the rebel base. William Tryon, royal governor of New York and a general in the British army, landed near Fairfield, Conn., on the evening of April 25 with about 2,000 men. Unopposed by the Americans, Tryon marched into Danbury the following day and burned down the storehouses. The British began their return march to the coast on April 27.

At the time of the raid Gen. Benedict Arnold was in New Haven, threatening to resign his commission. But when he learned of the destruction of Danbury, Arnold collected 700 militiamen and hurried to interpose this force between Tryon and his ships. At Ridgefield the British broke through the improvised American position. Although Arnold's men continued to harass the enemy column, Tryon managed to re-embark his troops near Norwalk on April 28. In all, the raiders lost almost 200 men. American casualties were 200 killed and 40 wounded. Arnold's heroism won him the recognition he sought and led to his later valuable service at Fort Stanwix and Saratoga. *See* American Revolution.

Danish Invasions of Britain (837–1016). Beginning in 837, Danish Vikings invaded the island of Britain periodically for almost 200 years. After 865 the Danes maintained a large army in Britain. Most of the island's defense fell to the West Saxon kingdom of Wessex. Finally, in 1016, peace was established when a Danish state under Canute the Great was recognized by the Wessex king Edmund II (Ironside). The Danish dynasty died out in 1042.

Hingston Down	837
Aclea	851
York	867
Hoxne	870
Ashdown	871
Reading	871
Wilton	871
Chippenham	878
Edington	878
Tettenhall	910
Tempsford	918
Maldon	991
Nairn	1009
Mortlack	1010
Pen	1016
Ashingdon	1016

Dan no Ura (Rise of Japanese Feudalism), 1185.

The beginning of feudal rule in Japan grew out of a civil war between the Taira and Minamoto clans. In 1185 at Dan no Ura (the east end of Shimonoseki), on the southwestern end of Honshu, the two clans clashed in a naval battle at the Inland Sea's western outlet. The Minamoto force, led by Yoshitsune, totally defeated the Taira. Antoku, the child-emperor supported by the Taira, was killed in the battle. Yoshitsune's older brother, Yoritomo, became the virtual ruler of Japan. His descendants remained in power until replaced by the Hojo family in 1219. *See* Hakata Bay.

Danzig I (War of the Polish Succession), 1733–1734. On the death of Augustus II, the Strong, king of Poland (and elector of Saxony), the majority of Polish nobles wanted the new monarch to be Stanislas Leszczyński, father-in-law of France's Louis XV. France, Spain, and Sardinia (Savoy) took up arms for Leszczyński. A rival candidate, Augustus III, son of the late king, won the support of Russia (Anna) and Austria (Charles VI of the Holy Roman Empire). In October 1733 a large Russian army under Field Marshal Count Burkhard von Münnich laid siege to the Polish city of Danzig, at the mouth of the Vistula River. The garrison served under Leszczyński himself. Despite French efforts in the Baltic to relieve the city, Danzig capitulated on June 2, 1734. It was the only major Austrian-Russian victory of the war. Leszczyński fled to Prussia. The main theater of fighting then shifted to Italy and, to a lesser degree, to the Rhine. *See* Parma; Phillipsburg; Polish Succession, War of the.

Danzig II (Napoleonic Empire Wars), 1807. When Napoleon I crushed the main Prussian armies in 1806 and moved eastward against Russia, he was content to bypass Danzig, near the mouth of the Vistula River. In March of the following year he sent Marshal François Lefebvre with an army of 18,000 men to reduce the city, which now jeopardized his left rear. Lefebvre cleared the area of enemy troops and began an investment of Danzig on April 1. Inside the city the garrison of 15,000 Prussians and Russians was commanded by the Count von Kalckreuth.

To relieve the city, the Russian commander, Gen. Levin Bennigsen, sent a two-pronged amphibious expedition westward along the Baltic coast. But the Russian prong was repulsed on May 15, and the Prussian attack collapsed completely a day later. Lefebvre stood ready for a final assault on May 21, when Kalckreuth asked for a truce. The garrison, now reduced to 7,000 effectives, surrendered five days later. (Lefebvre later became Duc de Dantzig.) Napoleon had now cleared the way for a spring offensive against the main Russian army south of Königsberg (Kaliningrad). *See* Eylau; Heilsberg; Friedland; Napoleonic Empire Wars.

Dara (Byzantine-Persian Wars), 528. To strengthen its frontier against Persia the Byzantine Empire built a new fort at Dara in northern Mesopotomia. This action provoked the Sassanid ruler of Persia, Kavadh I, into a new war against Constantinople in 526. The Persian army pushed steadily westward. But as it approached Dara, the garrison commander Belisarius sallied out to meet the invaders in the open. When Belisarius supplemented his frontal assault with a flank attack by a force of hard-riding Huns, the Persian army bolted, leaving 8,000 dead on the field. The victory so pleased Emperor Justinian I that he made Belisarius chief commander in the East. *See* Amida II; Callinicum.

Dardanelles (World War I), 1915. With the Western Front completely deadlocked, British First Lord of the Admiralty Winston Churchill persuaded the Allies to open a new front, against Turkey. The plan was to force passage of the Dardanelles in order to attack Constantinople. A clearance of the Dardanelles and later the Bosporus would also establish a supply route to Russia on the Black Sea. The British admiral, Sir Sackville Carden, with 12 aged French and British warships, began the battle on February 19. During the next four weeks Carden's naval gunfire reduced the forts at Cape Helles and Kum Kale at the entrance to the Dardanelles. Minesweepers, working at night, sought to clear the 11 belts of mines that guarded the inner waterway called The Narrows, leading to the Sea of Marmara (and to Constantinople).

Carden's health then broke, and he was replaced by Adm. Sir John de Robeck. Robeck decided to make an all-out, daylight assault on March 18 with minesweepers preceding the warships. Unknown to the Allies, however, German advisor Gen. Otto Liman von Sanders had meanwhile greatly strengthened Turkish defenses on both sides of the waterway. Robeck's attack got under way at 10 A.M. In four hours his warships had closed to The Narrows, but Turkish field guns were taking a heavy toll of the minesweepers. A French battleship, the *Bouvet,* had been destroyed by an unswept mine. Now another battleship and a cruiser were lost, and a second cruiser damaged by mines. Two other ships were crippled by gunfire. At this point Robeck lost his nerve and withdrew. Never again in the war would the Allies come so close to Constantinople. A purely naval attack was discarded in favor of a land operation against Gallipoli. This too was promoted by Churchill, and when it fizzled, he was removed from the British cabinet. *See* Gallipoli; World War I.

Darwin (World War II), 1942. During December 1941 and the early months of 1942, Japanese sea, air, and land forces swept aside all opposition in the 4,000-mile arc of islands stretching from the Malay Peninsula to Australia. One of the ultimate targets of this surge was Australia itself. On February 19 Adm. Chuichi Nagumo, who had led the Japanese attack on Pearl Harbor, sent 80 carrier-based planes, supplemented by land-based bombers from Celebes, in a savage raid on the northern Australian port of Darwin. The attack destroyed docks, warehouses, and the airport and sank or damaged all of the 17 ships in the harbor, including the U.S. destroyer *Peary*. Five Japanese planes were shot down at a cost of 22 Allied aircraft. *See* East Indies; Coral Sea; World War II.

Dego (Wars of the French Revolution), 1796. The victory of Napoleon Bonaparte at Montenotte in northwestern Italy, on April 12, 1796, had driven a French wedge between the Austrian army of Gen. Baron Jean de Beaulieu on the right (east) and the Sardinian (Piedmontese) troops of King Victor Amadeus II on the left (west). Realizing that the combined allied force outnumbered his 40,000 French by at least 25 percent, Napoleon hurried to drive the wedge deeper. On April 14 he pushed northwest to attack the 4,000 Sardinians and Austrians at Dego. The garrison surrendered. But when Gen. André Masséna left the town weakly guarded, an Austrian column recaptured it the following morning. Napoleon counterattacked later that day and drove the enemy out of Dego to the north. The Sardinian army fell back to the west to protect the capital at Turin, while on the other flank Beaulieu remained strangely inactive. *See* Montenotte; Mondovì; French Revolution Wars.

Degsastan (Teutonic Conquest of Britain), 603. The Scots and Picts of Dalriada under King Aedan left their home in northern Scotland to invade the Angle kingdom of Northumbria in 603. In the battle of Degsastan (site uncertain) the Northumbrians of King Ethelfrith defeated the invaders and turned them back. It was more than 400 years before the Scots could gain possession of the lowlands south of the Firth of Forth. *See* Dyrham; Chester; Carham.

Delhi I (Conquests of Tamerlane), 1398. With Persia and the Golden Horde of Russia subdued, the Mongol conqueror Tamerlane (Timur Lenk, or Timur the Lame) turned to India. His pretext for invasion was that the sultans of Delhi were too tolerant of Hinduism among their subjects. Tamerlane, a ferocious Mohammedan, marched southeast from his capital at Samarkand, crossing the Indus in September 1398. On December 17 he met the Indian army of Mahmud Tughlak at Panipat, 53 miles north of Delhi. Tamerlane's cavalry host destroyed the enemy force. Plundering into Delhi, the Mongol invaders razed the city to the ground. Tamerlane then turned northeast to attack Meerut. *See* Kandurcha; Meerut; Mongol Wars.

Delhi II (Indian Mutiny), 1857. When the Great Mutiny spread to Delhi, the Indian rebels seized the city, killing all Europeans they could find. Perceiving that this city held the key to the revolt, Gen. Sir Henry Barnard assembled 3,000 troops, chiefly British, and on June 8 occupied a nearby ridge. However, his force was too small to attack the 30,000 mutineers inside Delhi frontally or even to institute a tight siege. Nevertheless, the British held on grimly until reinforced early in August by Gen. John Nicholson, who had marched almost 30 miles a day for three weeks from the Punjab. On September 14 the combined force attacked and in six days of violent street fighting captured the city. Nicholson was killed, but the victory at Delhi proved to be the first step in containing the mutiny. *See* Cawnpore I; Lucknow; Indian Mutiny.

Delium (Great Peloponnesian War), 424 B.C. While Athens had been victorious in several battles at sea, the Peloponnesian army remained the dominant land power. In 424 the Athenian leader Cleon launched an offensive against Boeotia from two directions. Demosthenes was to invade the Spartan ally from the west, the general Hippocrates from the east. Demosthenes' advance was checked by a Theban force, however, leaving Hippocrates to carry on the attack alone. On a plain near the Boeotian seaport of Delium, the Athenians, about 17,000 strong, met an equal force of Boeotians and Thebans, commanded by Pagondas. After a fierce struggle the Athenian phalanx was broken. Hippocrates was killed and his army put to rout. The Peloponnesian ground forces remained supreme. *See* Pylos-Sphacteria; Amphipolis; Peloponnesian Wars.

Denain (War of the Spanish Succession), 1712. Unable to find mutually acceptable peace terms, the allies and Louis XIV of France fought on, even though both sides wanted a settlement after the terrible slaughter in 1709 at Malplaquet. In 1711 the incomparable allied commander, the Duke of Marlborough (John Churchill), was dismissed by the English government. That same year Holy Roman Emperor Joseph I died and was succeeded by his brother Charles VI, who was also the allied candidate for the throne of Spain as Charles III. The uniting of Spain and the Empire under a Hapsburg monarch was as much to be feared as the original cause of the war—the uniting of Spain and France under the house of Bourbon. England withdrew from the war in 1712. But the Dutch, Prussians, and Austrians remained in the field under the Imperial general Prince Eugene of Savoy.

In the summer of 1712 Eugene launched an offensive against the French line of forts in the Spanish Netherlands. But Marshal Duc Claude de Villars, the able commander of Louis XIV's army, made a quick march and cut the allied supply line at Denain on the Schelde, 26 miles southeast of Lille. Here Eugene had placed a large part of his force under the Dutch general the Earl of Albemarle (Arnold van Keppel). On July 24 Villars fell on this allied army and drove it into the Schelde. Eugene could not come up in time to prevent a loss of 8,000 men, at a cost to the French of only 500.

The battle of Denain was the last serious battle of the War of the Spanish Succession. Except for the Empire, the shattered coalition against Louis XIV agreed to the Treaty of Utrecht the following spring. Philip V of the house of Bourbon won recognition as the ruler of Spain, which ceded Sicily to Savoy and Gibraltar and Minorca to Great Britain. Charles VI and the Holy Roman Empire fought on for another indecisive year before signing the treaties of Rastatt and Baden in 1714. In all, the chief loser was Spain, which surrendered modern Belgium to the Empire as the then named Austrian Netherlands. *See* Malplaquet; Brihuega; Spanish Succession, War of the.

Denmark. *See* Danish Invasions of Britain, Scandinavia.

Dennewitz (Napoleonic Empire Wars), 1813. The defeat of his pursuing force at Kulm-Priesten on August 30, 1813, prohibited Napoleon I from winning a major victory over the allied Russian-Prussian-Austrian army south of Dresden. The French emperor then switched to the defensive, while sending Marshal Michel Ney northward to attack Berlin. At Wittenberg Ney took over the command of Marshal Nicolas Oudinot, who had been defeated by Swedish Crown Prince Jean Bernadotte (former French marshal) in August. On September 6, while marching through Dennewitz, 42 miles southwest of Berlin, Ney blundered into an allied trap set by Bernadotte. A Prussian army under Gen. Baron Friedrich von Bülow struck the unwary French column in flank. Ney turned his troops to hold off the attack. But despite a stubborn resistance, he was driven back all the way to Torgau on the Elbe, suffering a loss of 10,000 men. Allied casualties totaled 7,000. Napoleon now decided to retire behind the Elbe, with Leipzig to be his central position. *See* Kulm-Priesten; Grossbeeren; Leipzig; Napoleonic Empire Wars.

Dessau Bridge (Thirty Years' War), 1626. The entrance of King Christian IV of Denmark and Norway into the Thirty Years' War in 1625 gave new hope to the Protestant (anti-Hapsburg) forces. A coordinated attack was planned on the Catholic armies of Field Marshal the Count of Tilly and Gen. Albrecht von Wallenstein in the spring of the following year. Christian was to advance up the Weser to assault Tilly, while Gen. Count Ernst von Mansfeld marched into the bishopric of Magdeburg to challenge Wallenstein. Mansfeld, at the head of a mercenary army of 12,000 men, was off the mark first. But Wallenstein learned of his opponent's movement and hurried some 20,000 men from his Holy Roman Empire (Ferdinand II) army to Dessau on the Elbe River. Here he established a strong bridgehead east of the river, blocking Mansfeld's passage. On April 25 the veteran Protestant general attacked the Imperial force of Wallenstein, who was fighting his first major battle. With his infantry and artillery skillfully concealed to mask their strength, Wallenstein turned the Dessau Bridge into a deathtrap for the Protestant forces. Mansfeld, relying on the massed weight of his charge, was bloodily repulsed, leaving a third of his men dead on the field.

It was the last battle for the veteran German general who had helped launch the war eight years earlier in Bohemia. Turning back, he moved up the Oder into Silesia. From there he struck for the Dalmatian coast but died en route. His army immediately disintegrated. Meanwhile Wallenstein, who had started in pursuit of Mansfeld, halted and detached 8,000 men to reinforce Tilly near Brunswick. *See* Stadtlohn; Lutter am Barenberge; Thirty Years' War.

Detroit (War of 1812), 1812. A three-pronged invasion of Canada became the first objective of the United States in the war. The first offensive to get under way was in the West, where Gen. William Hull was to invade Canada from Detroit. With 2,200 men, Hull crossed the Detroit River on July 12. He penetrated only to Windsor, Ontario, and then pulled back to Detroit on August 8. When a Canadian force of 2,000 under Gen. Isaac Brock appeared outside Detroit, Hull inexplicably surrendered, on August 16. (On the previous day the garrison at Fort Dearborn, now Chicago, was wiped out after evacuating the post upon Hull's garbled instructions.) With the British now in firm control of western Lake Erie and the Michigan country, Brock moved to the eastern end of the lake. Hull was later court-martialed and sentenced to death for cowardice and neglect of duty, but the sentence was remitted. *See* Fort Dearborn; Queenston Heights; War of 1812.

Dettingen (War of the Austrian Succession), 1743. When Frederick II, the Great, took Prussia out of the war in 1742, the French position in Bohemia became untenable. To escape Austria's counteroffensive the French retreated westward into Germany, suffering terrible losses during the winter of 1742–43. At the same time their Bavarian allies were being pushed up the Danube Valley toward the Rhine. The Austrian armies of disputed Holy Roman Empress Maria Theresa were everywhere victorious. Now Austria's ally Great Britain began marching an army from the lower Rhine toward the Main Valley, planning to drive a wedge between the French and the Bavarians. Instead the French marshal Duc Adrien Noailles trapped the 37,000 English, Hannoverians, and Hessians in a narrow defile between Aschaffenburg and Hanau along the Main. Posting 28,000 men at the river end of the valley, Noailles prepared to fall on the enemy's rear at the other end. However, King George II, who personally commanded the allied army, received a good break when the French cavalry to his front attacked prematurely, on June 27, at the village of Dettingen. Leading his infantry in a fierce countercharge, the king routed the 28,000-man French force before Noailles could come to their rescue. Some 5,000 French were killed or died trying to cross the Main. The allied casualties were less than half that number. Dettingen was the last battle in which a British monarch fought on the field.

After this defeat the French withdrew all their troops west of the Rhine. Prince Charles (Karl Alexander) of Lorraine, brother-in-law of Maria Theresa, who commanded the Austrian army, closed up to the river but could not force a passage. Meanwhile, in northern Italy the Austrians, allied with Sardinia (Savoy), held their own against Spain and Naples. *See* Mollwitz; Chotusitz; Toulon II; Velletri; Austrian Succession, War of the.

Devolution, War of. *See* Louis XIV, Wars of.

Dienbienphu (French-Vietnamese War), 1954. With the 1945 surrender of Japan, ending World War II, the Indochinese colony of Vietnam theoretically reverted to French control. But the veteran Marxist Ho Chi-Minh proclaimed a Communist-dominated Vietminh republic as the legal government. Communist China and the Soviet Union supported the Vietminh, while France organized its own government headed by Emperor Bao Dai. By late 1946 the country was torn by civil war. For seven years the military might of France could not stamp out the hard-fighting Vietminh guerrilla forces, which received much aid from Communist China, just across the northern border. Finally, in November 1953, the French commander in chief, Gen. Henri Navarre (who had succeeded Gen. Raoul Salan in the Far East) attempted to lure the guerrillas into a major pitched battle in which European heavy weaponry would prove decisive. Navarre chose to make his stand at Dienbienphu (which translates as "big frontier administrative center"), in a northwest valley 11 miles long (from north to south) and three miles wide. In this entrenched camp on November 20 he placed 20 battalions of infantry and artillery (15,000 men) under the command of Col. (later Gen.) Christian de la Croix de Castries. It was a fatal decision.

The Vietminh saw through Navarre's plan (called Operation Castor). They began a series of diversionary attacks in Laos and elsewhere in Vietnam. These attacks attracted French strength

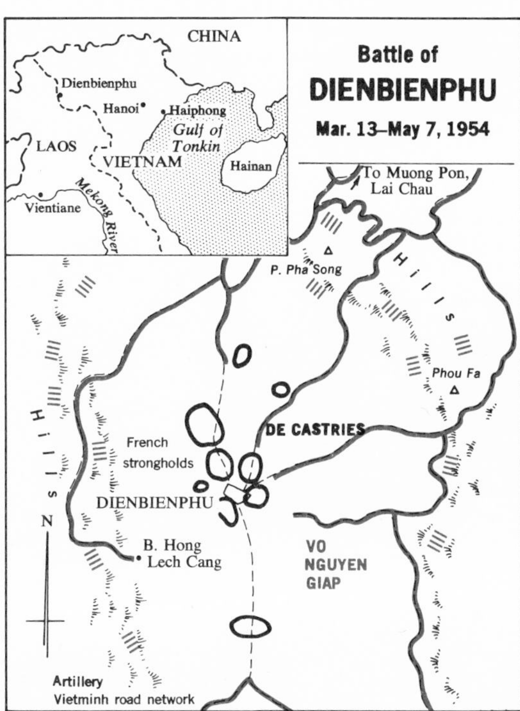

from support of Dienbienphu. The guerrillas then stealthily withdrew from the other fronts to mass in the hills surrounding the fortress—the 308th, 312th, 316th, and 351st divisions. Meanwhile, Gen. Vo Nguyen Giap ringed Dienbienphu with 200 artillery pieces. On March 13, 1954, the Vietminh launched their assault under cover of heavy artillery fire, which soon disabled the two French airstrips. Thereafter the surrounded garrison could be supplied only by air drops. (The return fire from French guns was so ineffective that the artillery commander, Col. Charles Piroth, committed suicide.) Day after day some 70,000 Communist troops tightened their siege by digging trenches toward the fortress. The ten separate French strong points, all having girls' names, fell one by one. Finally, on May 7, the three strong points in the center were overrun and Dienbienphu lay in Vietminh hands. Isabelle, the southernmost position, surrendered the following day. It was one of the greatest victories ever won in colonial warfare against a major power.

The 56-day battle cost the French 2,293 dead and 5,134 wounded. Most of the latter were marched off to prison camps with the able survivors to make a total of 10,000 captured. Vietminh losses were far greater, but they had made their country untenable for the French. Two months later a conference of big powers partitioned Vietnam at the 17th parallel. Territory to the north became the Democratic Republic of Vietnam (North Vietnam), a Communist nation; below the parallel arose the Republic of Vietnam (South Vietnam). *See* South Vietnam; Vietnam War.

Dieppe (World War II), 1942. During the four years between the fall of France (June 1940) and the invasion of Normandy (June 1944), Germany held the western face of Europe from the Arctic Ocean to the Atlantic shores of Spain. Specially trained Allied commando units made repeated nighttime raids against Nazi coastal positions. The largest of these efforts was a daylight "reconnaissance in force" carried out by less than 7,000 men (approximately 5,000 Canadian, 2,000 British) against the French seaport of Dieppe on August 19. Aided by tanks, the assault group gained a foothold on the beach in the face of a strong German defense. After taking heavy casualties during a nine-hour fire fight, the raiders of Gen. John H. Roberts re-embarked as planned. This costly amphibious operation provided valuable lessons that the Allies used later in the war. The Allies lost 98 planes, the Germans 92. Almost half the raiders were lost (the Canadians alone suffered 900 killed and almost 2,000 captured). *See* Normandy; World War II.

Diu (Portuguese Invasion of India), 1509. When the great age of discovery opened, the Moslems held the island and town of Diu on the southern end of the Kathiawar Peninsula of western India. However, a Portuguese fleet commanded by Francisco de Almeida, sailing around the Cape of Good Hope, entered Indian waters in 1509 and on February 2 met the Moslem fleet in a naval battle off Diu. The Portuguese won decisively, establishing their long-time foothold in India. Almeida became his country's first viceroy on the large Asian subcontinent. *See* Goa.

Dodecanese Islands (World War II), 1943. The surrender of the Italian government on September 9, 1943, led British Prime Minister Winston Churchill to order the seizure of the Dodecanese Islands in the lower Aegean Sea. This advance would provide air and sea bases closer to the Balkans and might induce Turkey to enter the war on the Allied side. During the last two weeks in September 1943, Gen. Sir Henry Maitland-Wilson, British commander in the Mediterranean, put a battalion of troops on each of the islands of Cos, Leros, and Samos. Rhodes, the largest island of the group, was strongly held by German forces.

The Nazi army reacted swiftly. On October 3 German parachutists dropped on Cos and recaptured it. Maitland-Wilson sent two more battalions to Leros, which was later strengthened by the British garrison from Samos. On November 12, however, German troops went ashore at both the northern and southern ends of Leros. Several hours later 600 parachutists dropped near the center of the island. In less than four days of fighting the Germans overran Leros, capturing 3,000 prisoners. About 1,000 British and Greek troops were evacuated by sea, but this action resulted in the sinking of six Allied destroyers and two submarines. The battle for the Dodecanese ended Churchill's hope of getting an early foothold in the Aegean. *See* Greece (World War II); Italy, Southern; World War II.

Dogger Bank I (War of the American Revolution), 1781. The entrance of the Netherlands into the war late in 1780 increased the problems of the British navy. Now a fleet had to be maintained on duty in the North Sea. The only battle of the war between Great Britain and Holland took place in this sea at Dogger Bank, a submerged sandbank about 60 miles east of the English coast. Here, on August 15, 1781, the British North Sea fleet of Adm. Hyde Parker (13 ships) encountered a Dutch fleet of equal size under Adm. Zoutman. In a hard fight the Dutch lost one ship and suffered more than 500 casualties. British losses in killed, wounded, and missing were almost as high. Both fleets were so damaged that they put into home ports. *See* Praia; American Revolution.

Dogger Bank II (World War I), 1915. The fourth naval battle of the war began with a German squadron of four cruisers making a surprise sweep across the North Sea. Admiral Franz von Hipper, in command of the attack, reached Dogger Bank, about 60 miles east of England, on the morning of January 24. Here he found the alerted British awaiting him with five battle cruisers and a light cruiser squadron, all under Adm. Sir David Beatty. Hipper promptly reversed his course and headed for his Heligoland base, 180 miles to the east. Beatty pursued. The lead British vessel, the flagship *Lion,* was hit several times and forced out of line. The other British cruisers crippled the *Seydlitz* and sank the slow-sailing *Blücher*. But faulty gunfire and poor communications allowed the remainder of Hipper's squadron to escape. *See* Falkland Islands; Dardanelles; Atlantic Ocean I; World War I.

Dominica. *See* Saintes, Les.

Donauwörth (War of the Spanish Succession), 1704. The Duke of Marlborough (John Churchill), at the head of the allied armies aligned against Louis XIV of France, resolved to take the offensive in 1704. In one of the boldest marches in history, he moved an army of 52,000 men up the Rhine from the Netherlands, beginning on May 19, and then suddenly struck southeast through Germany. Marlborough, aided by Louis William I, margrave of Baden-Baden, arrived on the Danube at Donauwörth, between Ulm and Ingolstadt, on July 1. Here Maximilian II Emanuel, elector of Bavaria, an ally of France, had posted 12,000 men under the Count D'Arco on the fortified hill of the Schellenberg to the northeast. The English duke ordered a frontal assault on the position the following day. In a fierce onslaught, the predominantly English army took the hill at a cost of 5,200 casualties. The Bavarians lost three-fourths of their strength. Marlborough then crossed the river, threatening Augsburg, 25 miles to the south.

Marlborough's invasion had ensured the safety of Vienna from Bavarian-French attack. However, when the French seemed content to block the duke's return up the Danube, he determined to force a decisive battle. Recrossing the Danube, he called for Prince Eugene of Savoy to join him north of the river. *See* Höchstädt I; Gibraltar I; Blenheim; Spanish Succession, War of the.

Doornkop (Jameson's Raid on Transvaal), 1896. To overthrow the regime of Transvaal's president, Oom Paul Kruger, several British leaders in South Africa planned a revolt in Johannesburg. This rebellion was to be supplemented by a raid from Bechuanaland led by Leander Starr Jameson. At the last minute Cecil Rhodes, head of the British South Africa Company in Southern Rhodesia and prime minister of Cape Colony, called off the insurrection within Transvaal. But Jameson foolishly rode south from Mafeking with 470 men on December 29, 1895. He had 140 miles to go to reach Johannesburg. A Boer force under Piet Cronjé intercepted the raiders and defeated them at Krugersdorp, 20 miles to the west, on January 1. Jameson, with the survivors, escaped only to be captured the following day at Doornkop. Handed over to the British for trial, Jameson received a short prison sentence. The embarrassing failure caused Rhodes to resign as prime minister. A congratulatory telegram from Kaiser Wilhelm II to Kruger created a diplomatic crisis between Germany and Great Britain. In South Africa war loomed. *See* Majuba Hill; Bulawayo; Mafeking.

Dornach (Swiss-Swabian War), 1499. The frontier war between the Swiss confederation of cantons and the Holy Roman Emperor Maximilian I had resulted in two major victories for the Swiss in the spring of 1499. The hostile opponents clashed again on July 22 at Dornach, south of Basel, near the Birs River. The sturdy Swiss infantry made their usual relentless assault with pike and halberd, driving the Germans (of the duchy of Swabia) from the field. The battle secured virtual independence for Switzerland and was the last invasion of Swiss soil until the 1700's. *See* Giornico; Calven.

Dorylaeum I (First Crusade), 1097. After the battle at Nicaea, the crusaders marched southeast through Asia Minor in two columns. The first column, consisting chiefly of Normans from France and Italy, was commanded by Bohemond of Taranto. A day's journey behind came the second column, largely Lorrainers and Provençals, led by Raymond IV of Toulouse and Godfrey of Bouillon. The night of June 30, 1097, the first column camped on the ruins of Dorylaeum (Eskişehir). As they were breaking camp the following morning, they were suddenly attacked by a huge army of Seljuk Turks under Kilij Arslan I. Bohemond sent a message for help to the second column and then deployed his knights behind a line of infantry. (A typical headlong crusader charge would have been suicidal against the numerically superior Turks.)

For six hours Bohemond's troops held their ground while mounted Turkish archers swarmed around the camp shooting down men and horses. Sensing that the Christian defenders were beginning to waver, the Turks organized a charge with sabers soon after midday. At that moment knights from the second column rode up to strike the enemy flank and rear. The Turks turned and fled to the north. A Christian pursuit to the limit of their horses' endurance inflicted heavy casualties upon the Asiatics, perhaps as many as 30,000. Christian losses were about 4,000.

The inspired leadership of Bohemond made Dorylaeum a model battle for the crusaders. This victory won the Europeans a healthy respect from their Turkish foes and ensured a relatively peaceful march from here to the plains of Antioch. *See* Nicaea; Tarsus; Antioch I; Crusades.

Dorylaeum II (Second Crusade), 1147. The fall of Edessa (Urfa) to the Turks in 1144 prompted the Christian leaders of Europe to organize the Second Crusade, or General Passage as it was sometimes called. Conrad III, founder of the Hohenstaufen line of Holy Roman emperors, led a large army southeastward, reaching Constantinople in 1147. After crossing the Bosporus, Conrad sent the long train of noncombatants eastward along the Mediterranean coast, while he struck directly overland with his mounted knights and foot soldiers in October 1147. Ten days out of Nicaea, the straggling column of warriors was surprised by a large-scale Turkish attack near Dorylaeum (Eskişehir). The mounted Seljick bowmen decimated the crusader's ranks with their showers of arrows. Only Conrad and some knights fought their way out of the ambush and returned safely to Nicaea. Although most of the noncombatant column, commanded by Bishop Otto of Freising, got through to the Holy Land, Conrad's military strength had virtually disappeared.

Behind the German advance came a French contingent under King Louis VII and Queen Eleanor of Aquitaine. Learning of the disaster suffered by Conrad's force, the French took the coastal road. Beset by winter hardships and Turkish raids, the column reached Antalya (Attalia) in February 1148, too weak to continue. Louis, Eleanor, and most of the knights took ships to Saint Simeon, the port of Antioch. When the remainder of the group sought to continue the overland march in the spring, nearly all perished en route. Thus the great promise of the Second Crusade fizzled out in the wastes of Asia Minor, far short of the Holy Land. *See* Edessa II; Damascus III; Crusades.

Dover I (First Barons' War of England), 1216–1217. In their revolt against King John the English barons asked Louis, son of Philip II of France, to serve as their king. Prince Louis landed in England in May 1216. Combining forces with the rebels, he quickly reduced all the Cinque Ports in the southeast except Dover. Here the royalist garrison under Hubert de Burgh (later earl of Kent) resisted stubbornly.

The following year French reinforcements for Louis crossed the English Channel: 900 troops and supplies carried in 10 warships and 70 small craft. De Burgh sailed out from Dover to intercept the French fleet with 16 large and 20 smaller warships (converted merchantmen). Attacking from upwind, the English gained the upper hand with a shower of crossbow bolts supplemented by lime thrown into the eyes of their opponents. The English sailors then boarded the French vessels and in savage hand-to-hand fighting destroyed or captured three-fourths of the enemy ships. This English naval victory virtually cut the barons' communications with France. When the English success was followed by a second triumph, at Lincoln, in May, Prince Louis had to abandon the siege of Dover. *See* Rochester II; Lincoln II; Barons' Wars.

Dover II (First English-Dutch War), 1652. Three months after the first sea battle between the English and Dutch, the fleets clashed again. The site was off Dover, a few miles south of the scene of the initial engagement, and the English commander was the same, Adm. Robert Blake. For the Dutch, Adm. Maarten Tromp was under suspension and had been replaced by Jan De Witt and Adm. Michel de Ruyter. In this battle the Dutch navy reversed the previous decision. On September 28, 1652, with some 60 ships, the Netherlanders outgunned an equal number of Commonwealth ships, capturing two of them. Two months later the combatants would clash again. *See* Goodwin Sands; Dungeness; English-Dutch Wars.

Dover Strait (Second English-Dutch War), 1666. After the Dutch defeat off Lowestoft, Adm. Michel de Ruyter returned from the West Indies to command the Netherlands navy. At the same time France, under Louis XIV, entered the war on the side of the Dutch. England thus had to split its naval strength. Prince Rupert of Germany, cousin of King Charles II, with 20 ships, guarded the Channel against French intrusion, while the Duke of Albemarle (George Monck) with 80 ships occupied the Strait of Dover. On June 11, 1666, De Ruyter, commanding 100 Dutch warships, engaged Monck and bested him. (The sound of cannon fire rolled up the Thames as far as London.) In the second day of the battle the Dutch maintained their advantage, forcing Monck to withdraw southward. This enabled Rupert's ships to join the fray, and on the third day the two hostile navies battled to a draw. On the fourth day (June 14), however, De Ruyter's guns again proved superior and the beaten English retired into the Thames. English losses in the so-called Four Days' Battle totaled 5,000 killed, 8 ships sunk, and 9 ships captured. The Netherlands lost 2,000 men, including 3 vice-admirals, and 4 ships. But despite their heavier losses, the English resumed the war two months later. *See* Lowestoft; North Foreland II; English-Dutch Wars.

Drepanum (First Punic War), 249 B.C. During the second year of the siege of Lilybaeum, Publius Claudius (Pulcher) took command of the Roman fleet and army pressing against the Carthaginian fortress on Sicily's west coast. In the harbor of Drepanum (Trapani), 18 miles to the north, the Roman fleet of 123 quinqueremes encountered the Carthaginian navy. The experienced seamanship of the Punic sailors proved decisive. Rome lost 93 ships and 8,000 men; several thousand of Claudius' men were taken prisoner. The Carthaginians did not lose a ship. But despite its victory, Carthage could not raise the land siege of Lilybaeum. And more important, the battle of Drepanum was to be the last naval triumph in the long history of the African maritime republic. *See* Lilybaeum; Aegates Islands; Punic Wars.

Dresden (Napoleonic Empire Wars), 1813. While subordinate commanders were being defeated on his northern and eastern fronts, Napoleon I was concentrating on the defense of Dresden to the south. Here Marshal Marquis Laurent de Gouvion Saint-Cyr's XIV Corps stood alone against a 158,000-man allied army under Prince Karl von Schwarzenberg. As the Allies approached the city from across the Bohemian mountains to the south, Napoleon marched one corps 90 miles in three days, two others 120 miles in four days, to build up to 70,000 troops by the morning of August 26, 1813. Early that day, with the allied monarchs (Czar Alexander I of Russia, Francis I of Austria, Frederick William III of Prussia) watching, Schwarzenberg attacked in a great half-circle, both of his flanks secured against the Elbe River, north and south of Dresden. Saint-Cyr's skillful defenses yielded ground slowly and at great cost to the attackers. At 5:30 P.M. the French still held all the city when Napoleon launched a three-pronged counterattack against the now weary allied troops. By nightfall Schwarzenberg had been driven back to his original line.

Early on August 27 Napoleon took the offensive, aiming his heaviest blows at the allied flanks.

By midafternoon Marshal Joachim Murat's cavalry on the north had captured 15,000 Austrians and killed or hopelessly scattered another 9,000. On the southern flank along the Elbe above Dresden, Marshal Édouard Mortier's attack achieved equal success. In the rugged fighting in the center, Gen. Jean Moreau, French victor at Hohenlinden in 1800, who had later joined the Russians, fell mortally wounded. That night the allied sovereigns ordered a retreat back into Bohemia. They had lost more than 38,000 men. Napoleon's losses were less than 10,000. But it was his last major victory on German soil. His exhausted troops could pursue only slowly over narrow mountain roads. And three days later his chief intercepting force met disaster. *See* Katzbach River; Kulm-Priesten; Napoleonic Empire Wars.

Dreux (French Religious Wars), 1562. During the reign of young Charles IX, who was dominated by his mother, Catherine de Médicis, France was torn by a conflict between Catholics and Protestants. The crown's persecution of the Protestants, who were called Huguenots, brought on a religious war that soon broadened into a political struggle for control of the government. The Huguenot army, which drew heavily upon the nobility, was strong in cavalry but weak in infantry. Under the leadership of the Prince de Condé, and Gaspard de Coligny, the admiral of France, the Huguenot army clashed with the royal army in 1562 at Dreux, in north-central France. The mounted Catholic force, representing the crown and the house of Guise, charged the Huguenots but were repulsed, and the constable of France, Duc Anne de Montmorency, was captured. When the Huguenots sought to exploit their success with a vigorous pursuit, however, a Catholic counterattack won the field. The following year Catherine de Médicis quieted this first civil war by issuing the Edict of Amboise, which granted freedom of worship to the Protestant nobility and gentry. *See* Saint-Denis; French Religious Wars.

Drewry's Bluff (American Civil War), 1864. While the Federal commander in chief, Gen. U. S. Grant, directed the main offensive north of Richmond, he ordered the Army of the James to move on the Confederate capital from the southeast. On May 5 this two-corps army, under Gen. Benjamin Butler, moved up the James River to Bermuda Hundred, at the junction of the Appomattox River. During the next two days Butler's men pushed forward to cut the Richmond–Petersburg railway before withdrawing. Although Butler had less than 16,000 men to deploy against the 18,000 Confederates of Gen. Pierre Beauregard, he resumed the offensive on May 12, attacking toward Drewry's Bluff, on the right bank of the James, five miles below Richmond. Butler moved forward with Gen. Quincy Gillmore's X Corps on the left (west), Gen. William Smith's XVIII on the right. He had failed to launch an assault, however, by May 16, when Beauregard suddenly struck the Federal lines with ten brigades, turning the right flank along the river. Butler was forced back to Bermuda Hundred, where he remained but a weak threat. In the futile move toward Drewry's Bluff he had lost 4,160 men. Beauregard's losses were 2,506.

When he learned of Butler's bungled attack, Grant, on May 22, ordered Gen. Smith with 12,500 troops to join him on the Richmond front. This left only a minimum garrison at Bermuda Hundred. Lee, in turn, drew Gen. Robert Hoke's division (7,000 men) from Beauregard for his Army of Northern Virginia. *See* Spotsylvania; North Anna River; American Civil War.

Drogheda (English Civil War), 1649. Although the Roundhead force under Col. Michael Jones had broken the Irish Catholic-Royalist strength at Rathmines, Oliver Cromwell determined to teach the rebels a lesson. As lord lieutenant, commanding 10,000 veterans of the New Model army, Cromwell marched on Drogheda, on the Boyne River in Louth County. Here the Marquis (later 1st Duke) of Ormonde, James Butler, had posted 3,000 Irish Royalists and English volunteers. Cromwell breached the walls with his cannon on September 11 and stormed into the city. Every defender, plus all priests and friars, were put to the sword, a deliberate massacre that ranks with the worst in history. Cromwell then marched south to assault another enemy stronghold at Wexford. *See* Rathmines; Wexford; English Civil War.

Drumclog (Scottish Covenanters' Revolt), 1679. During the reign of England's Charles II, the repressive measures of his secretary of state for Scottish affairs, the Duke of Lauderdale (John Maitland) provoked the abortive Pentland Hills revolt of the Covenanters in 1666. When the Scots obtained no relief, they rose again in 1679. To put down the rebellion, the Viscount Dundee (John Graham of Claverhouse) marched a royal army to Drumclog, Lanark County, in south-central Scotland. Here on June 11 the king's troops were attacked by a Covenanter force led by John Balfour. The Scottish rebels inflicted a stinging defeat upon Dundee. A new royal army would have to take the field to end the uprising. *See* Pentland Hills; Bothwell Bridge.

Dublin (Irish Easter Rebellion), 1916. While Great Britain was deeply involved in World War I, revolutionary groups in Ireland (including some members of the Sinn Fein, a republican movement for self-rule) planned an uprising. Led by

James Connolly and Patrick Pearse, some 1,500 republicans revolted in Dublin, seizing the General Post Office and other central buildings on April 24, 1916. The military arm of the British government quelled the so-called Easter Rebellion in five days of hard street fighting. The last of the insurgents surrendered on April 29. Fifteen were court-martialed and shot, hundreds imprisoned. Among those executed were Connolly, Pearse, and Sir Roger Casement, who had been captured after landing from a German submarine three days before the uprising. *See* World War I.

Dunbar I (English-Scottish Wars), 1296. From his reduction of Berwick upon Tweed, Edward I marched his English army northward to Dunbar, near the mouth of the Firth of Forth. Here the Earl of Athol and other nobles rallied the Scots to repel the invasion. The English forces, under the direct command of John de Warenne, earl of Surrey, crushed the Scottish army on April 27. One account puts the Scottish casualties at 10,000 men (probably too high). The English moved west to seize Edinburgh. On July 2 John de Baliol abdicated the crown of Scotland that Edward had awarded him four years earlier and went into exile. Edward sent the Coronation Stone of Scone back to England and proclaimed himself king of Scotland. *See* Berwick upon Tweed; Stirling Bridge.

Dunbar II (English Civil War), 1650. Unhappy with the English Commonwealth government of Oliver Cromwell, the Scots recognized the exiled pretender Charles II as their king. Cromwell with 16,000 veterans promptly marched north into Scotland where he was confronted by a Scottish army of about 25,000 men, commanded by the able general David Leslie. The Scots outmaneuvered the English army and forced it back upon Dunbar, on the eastern coast. By occupying nearby hills, Leslie hemmed in Cromwell, whose force dwindled to about 11,000. On September 3, 1650, the Scots' Presbyterian ministers ordered Leslie to descend from the hills and attack the embattled English. It was a tragic mistake for the Scots. Cromwell, aided by his generals John Lambert and George Monck (later Duke of Albemarle) fell on the attackers, broke their right flank, and then rolled up the center. The counterattack inflicted 3,000 casualties and took 10,000 prisoners. The English lost only a few men. Despite the defeat, the son of the beheaded English king was crowned Charles II at Scone on January 1, 1651. A decisive battle shaped up. *See* Carbiesdale; Worcester; English Civil War.

Dundalk (English-Irish Wars), 1318. The overwhelming Scottish victory over the English at Bannockburn in 1314 had repercussions in Ireland. Edward Bruce, brother of Robert I of Scotland, invaded the east coast of Ireland the following year. Aided by some native Irish chiefs and a few irresponsible English lords, Edward won control of the Ulster region and on May 1, 1315, at Dundalk, had himself crowned king of Ireland. An attack on English-held Dublin in 1317 failed, however, despite help from Robert. The following year English forces under John de Bermingham (acting for Edward II) clashed with Edward Bruce's army at Faughart, near Dundalk. On October 14 the Scots army of 3,000 men was defeated and Edward Bruce killed. English rule was reimposed over most of the island, but from this time on Ireland became more of a military liability than an asset to the English crown. *See* Bannockburn; Myton.

Dunes, The (Spanish-French Wars), 1658. Although the 1648 Peace of Westphalia closed the Thirty Years' War, it did not end the Spanish-French conflict. Eight years later England entered the war against Spain. The English Commonwealth, in alliance with King Louis XIV, sent 6,000 infantry under Sir William Lockhart to aid the French on the Continent. In May 1658 the allied force of 14,000 men, under the overall command of the French marshal the Vicomte de Turenne, laid siege to Spanish-held Dunkirk. A Spanish army of equal size marched to the relief of the seaport. It was led by Don John of Austria, the Younger; Louis II, the Great Condé, a French nobleman in the service of Spain since 1652; and the Duke of York, the future James II, who commanded a corps of disgruntled English royalists.

On June 14, 1658, the Spanish army, its right on the sea, closed on Dunkirk. Despite the fact that in moving through the coastal dunes they had outmarched their artillery, the Spanish attacked the besiegers, who had turned to meet them. Inland, the Spanish cavalry under Condé penetrated the English-French right flank. But this gain was nullified when Turenne's center and left threw back the attackers. Turenne, one of the ablest generals in history, pressed his troops forward until the entire Spanish line was put to rout. Some 4,000 were killed, wounded, or captured, with English-French losses markedly less. Dunkirk, with its relieving army defeated, surrendered ten days later.

The Treaty of the Pyrenees ended the so-called Spanish Fronde War the following year. England received title to Dunkirk (but sold it to France in 1662). France gained possession of several territories originally in the Spanish Netherlands (Belgium). And the Great Condé was accepted back into French employ by Louis XIV, the Grand Bourbon Sun King, who married the infanta Maria Theresa, daughter of Philip IV of Spain. *See* Valenciennes; Santa Cruz de Tenerife; Maastricht II; Thirty Years' War.

Dungeness (First English-Dutch War), 1652.

The English and Dutch fleets clashed a third time in the Strait of Dover during the first year of the war. This battle was fought off the English headland of Dungeness on November 29, 1652. Admiral Robert Blake again led the Commonwealth navy, opposing the redoubtable Dutch admiral Maarten Tromp, recently reinstated to command. In a two-day action Blake lost 6 of his 40 ships to Tromp's superior force. But despite the hard fighting, the engagement was as inconclusive as the previous ones. *See* Dover II; Portland; English-Dutch Wars.

Dunkirk (World War II). The sudden German victory in Flanders forced the British Expeditionary Force and the French First Army back to the sea at Dunkirk, where 338,000 troops were evacuated to England between May 29 and June 4, 1940. *See* Flanders.

Dunsinane (Rise of Scotland), 1054. The Scottish usurper Macbeth, who had killed Duncan I to become king of Scotland in 1040, came under attack 14 years later by the dead ruler's son Malcolm Canmore. Malcolm's chief strength lay in an army forged by the Danish warrior Siward, called the Strong, the earl of Northumbria. Siward advanced into Scotland and at Dunsinane, in Perth County, defeated Macbeth's supporters. The loser's reported casualties of 10,000 versus 1,500 for the victors is probably no more historically accurate than the story told in Shakespeare's tragedy *Macbeth*. Macbeth fled to the north where he was pursued and slain three years later by the new king, Malcolm III. *See* Carham; Alnwick I.

Dupplin Moor (Scottish Civil War), 1332. Neither Robert I, the Bruce, nor the Earl of Moray, regent for the youthful David II, implemented the Treaty of Northampton by restoring certain Scottish lands to lords designated by the English. Finally, in 1332, Edward de Baliol, son of the former king John de Baliol, led a contingent of so-called disinherited lords in an invasion of eastern Scotland. Landing in Fife County, they met and defeated a larger royalist force at Dupplin Muir on August 11. Baliol had himself crowned king of Scotland. But in acknowledging the overlordship of England's Edward III, he provoked a violent nationalist reaction throughout Scotland. *See* Byland; Halidon Hill.

Dutch War of Louis XIV. The second war fought by Louis XIV of France is often called the Dutch War. *See* Louis XIV, Wars of.

Dybböl (Schleswig-Holstein War), 1864. The duchies of Schleswig (with a large German minority) and Holstein (predominately German) had long been a source of friction between Prussia and Denmark. Early in 1864 Otto von Bismarck, the Iron Chancellor of Prussia's King Wilhelm I, made an alliance with the Austrian Empire of Franz Josef I to settle the Schleswig-Holstein problem. The Prussian general Count Helmuth von Moltke promptly sent a well-trained army into the duchies. The Danish troops of Christian IX fell back to the fortress of Dybböl (Düppel), on the east coast. Under the command of Prince Frederick Charles, nephew of Wilhelm I, the Prussian army invested the fortress on March 30. The last redoubt fell on April 18. Prussian casualties were more than 1,000, Danish losses more than 5,000, including prisoners. The surviving Danes fled to the nearby island of Als (Alsen), while the Prussians pressed into Denmark itself. Christian IX finally yielded the duchies under the terms of the Peace of Vienna, signed on October 30. Prussia absorbed Schleswig, while Austria received the administration of Holstein. As Bismarck had foreseen, this made Austrian Holstein an enclave within Prussian territory—a source of trouble that would lead to war between the allies in two years. Thus Schleswig-Holstein became the first of Bismarck's three wars that would forge a German Empire. *See* Langensalza.

Dyrham (Teutonic Conquest of Britain), 577. Under King Ceawlin, the Anglo-Saxon state of Wessex steadily pushed westward. At Dyrham (Deorham), north of Bath, the Teutonic aggressors met and defeated an army of Britons led by three local kings. All three Briton leaders were killed. Moving on, the men of Ceawlin took Bath and advanced on to the Bristol Channel. The victory at Dyrham thus cut the land communication between the Britons in Wales and those in the southwest, marking a key step in the Teutonic conquest. *See* Mons Badonicus; Degsastan; Chester.

Dyrrachium I (Wars of the First Triumvirate), 48 B.C. Julius Caesar's victory over the Pompeian forces in Spain had been largely offset by defeats handed his lieutenants in Africa and the Adriatic. Now he resolved to attack Pompey directly. Embarking 15,000 of his 25,000 loyal troops, Caesar eluded the stronger Pompeian fleet in the Adriatic and landed on the coast of Epirus on January 4. Marching north, he occupied Oricum and Apollonia. At Dyrrachium (Durrës, in modern Albania), however, he found Pompey entrenched with an army three times as large. Caesar halted his advance, awaiting the reinforcement of his 10,000 additional troops still in Italy. With almost certain victory in his grasp, Pompey refused to attack. Several months later, when the Caesarian reinforcements, under Mark Antony, finally arrived, a major battle took place. Pompey was able to cave in the left (south) of his opponent's line. Caesar lost 1,000 of his veteran legionaries and retired into Thessaly. One of Pompey's commanders in this battle was Titus Labienus, who had deserted Caesar after performing so ably in battles against the Gauls. *See* Ilerda; Bagradas River; Illyria; Pharsalus; First Triumvirate, Wars of the.

Dyrrachium II (Norman-Byzantine Wars), 1081. After driving the Byzantines out of Italy and founding the state of the Two Sicilies, the Norman adventurer Robert Guiscard crossed the Adriatic to Epirus, where he landed on July 17, 1081. He promptly laid siege to Dyrrachium (Durrës), then held by the Byzantine Empire. On October 18 Alexius I Comnenus, the emperor at Constantinople, sent a large force to relieve the besieged city. The vanguard of this army consisted of infantry (including English) armed with five-foot battle-axes. Without waiting for the main body to come up, the infantry rashly attacked the Norman lines. Guiscard counterattacked with a vigorous cavalry charge that cut off and surrounded most of the vanguard on a small hill near the coast. In an action reminiscent of Hastings, the Norman archers and cavalry, making maximum use of missile-and-shock tactics, destroyed the entire infantry corps. The battle illustrated again the inferiority of infantry to feudal cavalry.

After this defeat, the relieving Byzantine army retreated. Guiscard stormed into Dyrrachium the following February and established himself within the boundaries of the empire of Constantinople. The Normans pressed on eastward as far as the Varda River by 1085, when the death of Guiscard ended the Balkan expedition. Guiscard's eldest son, Bohemond of Taranto, later played a major role in the First Crusade. *See* Rome V; Nicaea.

Dyrrachium III (Byzantine-Norman Wars), 1108. To recruit reinforcements for the Christian forces in the Near East, Bohemond of Taranto and Antioch, the greatest soldier of the First Crusade, returned to Europe in 1104. He traveled through France and Spain collecting an army that soon became openly dedicated to fighting against the Byzantine Empire rather than against the Moslems. In 1107 Bohemond's new band of warriors crossed the Adriatic and landed at Dyrrachium (now Durrës in Albania). But the emperor at Constantinople, Alexius I Comnenus, had not been idle. He had assembled an army of Turks to check the invaders. For a year Bohemond maneuvered to slip by the Turkish lines and take the open road to Constantinople. He succeeded only in getting himself surrounded. In 1108 at Devol, outside Dyrrachium, he was forced to surrender in person to Alexius. His life was spared on the condition that he would hold Antioch as a fief of the Byzantine Empire. Bohemond had no intention of fulfilling this promise. He returned to Italy, where he died three years later. *See* Melitene III; Philomelion; Antioch II.

E

East Africa (World War II), 1941. The entrance of Italy into World War II on June 10, 1940, found British Somaliland, in East Africa, surrounded on three sides by Italian forces. On August 15, 1940, 17 battalions of Italian infantry advanced on the port of Berbera and forced Gen. A. R. Godwin-Austen to evacuate the weak British forces by way of the Gulf of Aden. (This was the only Italian victory over Great Britain in the war.) However, Italian dominance of East Africa was short-lived. On February 10, 1941, Gen. Sir Alan Cunningham marched northeast from Kenya into Italian Somaliland with the 11th African and 1st South African brigades. He crossed the Juba River from Kismayu and on February 22 routed a force of 30,000 Italians and colonials from Jelib. In the next three days Cunningham's motorized troops moved 200 miles to occupy Mogadishu, the capital and major seaport of Italian Somaliland. By March 17 they had marched another 740 miles to Jijiga in east-central Ethiopia. (One day earlier the British had reoccupied Berbera.) Driving westward, the fast-moving British took Harrar on March 26, Diredawa on March 29, Addis Ababa on April 6, and then turned north. Meanwhile Gen. William Platt, at the head of the 4th and 5th British Indians, had marched eastward from Kassala, Sudan, in February and attacked Keren in Eritrea. At a cost of 3,000 casualties he took this mountain position on March 27 and turned south to link up with Cunningham's forces. On May 17 the Italian commander in chief in East Africa, the Duke of Aosta (Prince Amedeo Umberto), caught between the two converging British columns, surrendered the remnants of his onetime 220,000-man force. Earlier, on May 5, Haile Selassie had re-entered Addis Ababa. The first lawful sovereign to be driven from his country by the Rome-Berlin Axis, he was the first to return in triumph. *See* Ethiopia; Sidi Barrâni; World War II.

Eastern Solomons (World War II). The second Japanese-American naval battle, on August 24 and 25, 1942, growing out of the fight for Guadalcanal Island. *See* Guadalcanal—Naval Action.

East Indies (World War II), 1941–1942. During the early days of the Pacific War the sudden attacks by Japan in the western Pacific overwhelmed all opposition. To block the Japanese onslaught, Allied leaders set up a unified command called ABDA (Australian, British, Dutch, American) under the British general Sir Archibald Wavell. On January 10, 1942, Wavell arrived at his Bandoeng headquarters near Batavia (now Djakarta) on Java to find his area of responsibility already under heavy assault. The Philippines and Malaya were all but lost and Burma was soon to be invaded. The East Indies, the mostly Dutch-owned island chain protecting Australia, stood in mortal danger.

Japan had already seized some key positions in the resources-rich Indies. Sarawak and Brunei in northern Borneo had been taken between December 16 and 23, 1941. Tarakan, on Borneo's northeastern coast, fell on January 10. Celebes, the island to the east, was invaded on January 11. The thrust through the islands continued, with each new gain serving as a steppingstone to the next point of attack. On January 23 Japanese forces leapfrogged eastward over the large island of New Guinea to take Rabaul on New Britain and Kavieng on New Ireland in the Bismarcks. Swinging back west of New Guinea, they captured Ceram in the Moluccas on January 31.

The ABDA determined to hold the vital central island of Java. But the Japanese soon closed in from three sides. On February 14 enemy paratroops seized Palembang and quickly established an attack base on Sumatra to the west. Southern Borneo was invaded two days later, and now the Java Sea was all that stood against invasion from the north. On the east, the fabled island of Bali was occupied on February 19 and Timor between February 20 and 24. Japan's overwhelming superiority at sea and in the air had doomed the East Indies, and also the ABDA forces seeking to defend Java. General Wavell dissolved the four-nation organization on February 25 and flew out to resume command over India. But the Dutch admiral Conrad Helfrich refused to concede defeat. He sent Dutch, British, and American ships into the Java Sea to stop the two large Japanese invasion convoys that were already nearing Java.

This Allied force met a crushing naval defeat between February 27 and March 1. Meanwhile, the U.S. aircraft tender *Langley,* with a deckload of 32 ready-to-fly P-40's and 32 American pilots sent as last-minute fighter plane reinforcements, was sunk by enemy air attack south of Java on February 27.

The Japanese landed on both the east and west ends of Java on March 1 and in eight days overran the island. On March 9 the Dutch general Heinter Poorten surrendered his remaining force of Allied troops—11,300 Dutch, 5,600 British, 2,800 Australians, and 800 Americans. In the Southwest Pacific only Port Moresby, on the south coast of New Guinea, and command of the Coral Sea stood between Japanese invaders and Australia. *See* Malaya; Java Sea; New Guinea; Coral Sea; World War II.

East Prussia (World War II). The Russia summer offensive of 1944 against Germany pressed across the borders of both East Prussia and prewar Poland in August; German troops resisted stubbornly in their homeland until Königsberg (Kaliningrad) fell on April 9, 1945. *See* Poland–East Prussia.

East Stoke (Yorkist Rebellion against Henry VII), 1487. Two years after Henry VII, the first Tudor king, ascended the throne of England, he was faced with a rebellion. An ambitious priest, Richard Simon (or Symonds), conceived the idea of passing off a young commoner, Lambert Simnel, as the 12-year-old Earl of Warwick (Edward Plantagenet, grandson of the "Kingmaker" of the Wars of the Roses), who was then imprisoned in the Tower of London. Yorkist leaders went along with the imposture, and Lambert was crowned as Edward VI at Dublin (a Yorkist stronghold) in May, 1487. Simon, Lambert, and the Yorkists Lord Francis Lovell and the Earl of Lincoln (John de la Pole) crossed to England on June 4 with an army of several thousand German mercenaries and Irish. On June 16, at East Stoke, Nottinghamshire, the rebels came under attack from a superior force commanded by Henry VII. The insurgents were defeated and put to flight. Lincoln perished, Lovell disappeared, Simon was imprisoned for life, and Lambert was made a servant to the legitimate king.

Because of the heavy Yorkist involvement this uprising is sometimes called the last battle of the Wars of the Roses. The able 24-year administration of Henry VII went far toward healing the scars of the long feudal war. *See* Bosworth Field.

Ebro River (Spanish Civil War), 1938. To take the pressure off the Madrid and Valencia fronts, the Republican government at Barcelona prepared an offensive across the lower Ebro. If successful, the thrust would also restore land communications between Catalonia and the remainder of Republican Spain. The attack was entrusted to Gen. Juan Modesto, commander of the newly organized Army of the Ebro—some 100,000 men. On the night of July 24–25 the Republican army began crossing to the west side of the Ebro against the Nationalist Army of Morocco under Gen. Juan de Yagüe. Taking the enemy by surprise, the government troops scooped out the bulge of the Ebro, capturing 4,000 prisoners. In the center Gen. Enrique Lister took his men 25 miles into Nationalist territory before being checked short of Gandesa. A fierce assault on August 1 was driven back by the rebel troops of Generalissimo Francisco Franco. This stopped the Republican advance. Modesto's men began digging in to protect themselves against the methodical air attacks now launched by the Nationalists. In the fierce August heat of Aragon, Nationalist aircraft dropped an average of 10,000 bombs a day, while their ground forces launched a relentless series of counterattacks. The Republicans gave up a fourth of their captured territory but otherwise held on grimly during the cruel battle of attrition that raged along the stationary front. Late in September, the last of the 4,640 members of the International Brigades, representing 29 different nationalities, were withdrawn from the Republican side (but 6,000 elected to stay to the end, claiming Spanish citizenship).

By October 30 Nationalist strength had increased enough to begin a massive counteroffensive. In a grinding attack the better-armed rebels drove the last Republican from the right bank of the Ebro on November 18. The four-month battle cost the Nationalists 33,000 casualties and 200 aircraft. Across the river the Republican Army of the Ebro lay shattered—30,000 dead, 20,000 wounded, 20,000 captured. The International Brigades that had crossed the river suffered 75 percent casualties. Republican Spain had lost its last major striking power. *See* Teruel; Vinaroz; Barcelona II; Madrid; Spanish Civil War.

Ecnomus (First Punic War), 256 B.C. Four years after its naval victory at Mylae, Rome sent out a large fleet from Sicily to invade Carthage itself. The Roman expedition, commanded by Marcus Atilius Regulus, was challenged by Hanno's Carthaginian fleet off Ecnomus, near Licata, on the south coast of the island. Having the greater number of galleys, about 350, Hanno attacked in a large semicircle. But the 330 Roman vessels fought back hard, using the grappling-and-boarding tactic successfully employed at Mylae. In all, some 300,000 rowers and fighting men took part in the pitched battle. The aggressive Roman fleet shattered the Carthaginian formation, sinking 30 ships and capturing an equal number. Regulus lost 24 vessels but was now free to sail on to Africa. *See* Mylae; Tunis I; Punic Wars.

Ecuador. *See* Latin America.

Edessa I (Persian Wars of the Roman Empire), 260. During the middle years of the third century, the Roman Empire suffered from internal chaos and external enemies—the barbarians in the West and the Persians of the Sassanid dynasty in the East. In an effort to halt the Persian attacks on Armenia and Syria, the emperor Valerian took a Roman army into modern Turkey. At Edessa (Urfa), in the southeast, the legionaries were surprised and defeated by a large Persian force under Shapur I. Valerian was taken prisoner. The first Roman emperor to be taken captive by a foreign foe, Valerian died in captivity some years later. (Nine years earlier Trajanus Decius had become the first emperor to fall fighting the barbarians—the Goths in Thrace.) *See* Philippopolis I; Hormuz; Naissus; Roman Empire.

Edessa II (Crusader-Turkish Wars), 1144. East of the Euphrates River, Edessa (Urfa) had been a Christian state since its capture in 1098 during the First Crusade. The fortress was ruled by Joscelin II in November 1144 when it was suddenly besieged by Zangi (Zengi) the Turkish atabeg, or lord, of Mosul and Aleppo. Believing that Edessa could hold out until spring at least, the other Christian states—Antioch, Tripoli (in Lebanon), Jerusalem—took their time about sending aid. As Joscelin himself was absent, the defense of the city fell to the Roman Catholic Archbishop Hugh. The Turks, whose competence in siegecraft was steadily growing, smashed a breach in Edessa's walls on Christmas Eve and poured into the city. Hugh and most of the other defenders were killed. Two days later the garrison in the citadel surrendered. Zangi ordered the execution of all the Frankish soldiers, selling their women and children into slavery.

Before Zangi could continue his attack to the west, he was assassinated by a servant in 1146. Joscelin attempted to reconquer his city later that year but was beaten back by Zangi's son Nureddin. The mounting Turkish power now gravely endangered all the Christian holdings (called Outremer) in the Near East. Europe would have to send reinforcements in the form of the Second Crusade. *See* Antioch II; Dorylaeum II; Crusades.

Edgehill (English Civil War), 1642. The long-smoldering revolt of the Parliamentarians and Puritans (called the Roundheads) against the Royalist (Cavalier) forces of Charles I broke into open warfare in 1642. Under the command of Robert Devereux, 3rd earl of Essex, the Roundheads raised an army of 20,000 infantry and 5,000 cavalry. Charles, at the head of the Cavalier army of similar size, marched south from Nottingham for the Thames Valley and London, a center of discontent against his regime. At Edgehill in Warwickshire, the Royalist force encountered Essex's army on October 23. In the first battle of the Civil War, Prince Rupert of Germany, nephew of the king, led a Cavalier cavalry charge that routed the two wings of the Roundheads. But in carrying his pursuit too far, he left the Cavalier infantry uncovered. The latter were severely mauled by a Roundhead attack, which captured the royal cannon. Rupert's cavalry returned just in time to prevent a rout. Both sides then withdrew, leaving some 5,000 dead upon the field.

Charles took advantage of the drawn battle by occupying Banbury and Oxford, the latter of which he made his headquarters. He then resumed his march toward London. *See* Newburn; Brentford; English Civil War.

Edington (Danish Invasions of Britain), 878. After more than four months of fugitive warfare following the disaster at Chippenham, Alfred the Great was ready to launch a counteroffensive against the Danes in Wiltshire. His call for a general mobilization in May was enthusiastically received by the Saxons throughout the Essex kingdom. The assembled warriors marched toward the enemy, who were still encamped at Chippenham. The Danes, equally resolute under Guthrum, moved south to meet the English on the bare downs of Edington (then Ethandun). Both sides sent their horses to the rear. For hours sword and ax smote shield as the two armies grappled at close quarters. Finally the Saxons, desperate to survive, gained the upper hand and drove the Danes from the field. Pursuing relentlessly, Alfred penned Guthrum in his camp and took his surrender. Three weeks later the Danish chieftain was baptized and accepted the Peace of Wedmore. The invaders were to be limited to the Danelaw, north of the Thames-Lea line. All southern Britain, including London, came under Alfred's rule.

The battle of Edington was one of the most decisive in English history. It ensured the survival of Wessex, the last remaining kingdom of the Saxon heptarchy. From this base the English, under Alfred's heirs, could expand in the next century and eventually overcome the Danish conquerors. *See* Chippenham; Tettenhall; Danish Invasion of Britain.

Eggmühl (Napoleonic Empire Wars), 1809. A miscalculation by Napoleon I had sent the bulk of his French army southward on April 21, 1809, to shatter the left wing of the Austrian army at Landshut. This left Marshal Louis Davout with only 20,000 men to face the main Austrian army of Archduke Charles Louis, brother of Emperor Francis I, at Eggmühl (Eckmühl), 23 miles to the north. Charles ordered 35,000 troops against Davout on April 22, planning to turn the French left flank along the Danube, southwest of Regensberg (Ratisbon). Although the Austrian attack moved slowly, by 1 P.M. it had begun to overwhelm the French. By this time, however, Napoleon had ordered up Marshal Jean Lannes, who was hurrying north from Landshut with 30,000 troops. Lannes now struck the archduke's left flank, caving it in and capturing Eggmühl. The VII Corps of Marshal François Lefebvre joined in the counterassault from the west. By nightfall the Austrians were thoroughly beaten, losing some 12,000 men, including 5,000 prisoners. French casualties totaled 6,000 in this third major battle in three days.

That night Charles withdrew north of the Danube, leaving only a small garrison south of the river to hold Regensberg. On the following day the French stormed into the city. Charles now retreated eastward along the left (north) bank of the Danube. Northwest of Vienna he was joined by Gen. Baron Johann Hiller's wing, which had finally fought free of French pursuit by successful rear-guard actions, especially at Ebelsberg on May 3. Both armies now raced for Vienna. The French won, Lannes entering the virtually defenseless city on May 10. The Austrians deployed across the Danube, northeast of their capital. *See* Landshut; Aspern-Essling; Napoleonic Empire Wars.

Egyptian Revolt against Turkey (1832–1840). The weakening Ottoman Empire of Turkey faced new trouble in 1832 when Egypt invaded Syria. Egyptian victories led European powers to intervene, thereby limiting Egyptian success. However, Egypt did win its independence of the Turkish sultanate.

Konya	1832
Nizib	1839
Acre IV	1840

El Alamein I (World War II), 1942. The climax of the long, grueling North African campaign took place along a 40-mile line stretching from the Egyptian coastal village of El Alamein inland to the impassable salt marshes of the Qattara Depression. Here Gen. Sir Claude Auchinleck's British Eighth Army, which had been driven back from Mersa Matrûh only two days before, turned on the closely pursuing *Panzerarmee Afrika* of Field Marshal Erwin Rommel. The hastily constructed British defensive line consisted of Gen. Willoughby Norrie's XXX Corps on the right at El Alamein itself and Gen. W. H. E. Gott's XIII Corps inland on the left.

On July 1 the *Afrika Korps* struck the Eighth Army right center with 6,500 infantry and 90 tanks. The three veteran German divisions won some ground but were blocked short of a breakthrough. Auchinleck launched an immediate counterattack on the southern flank of the German salient. On July 10 he switched his attack to the coast road, then back to the desert again. For almost four weeks thrust and counterthrust churned the desert sands with neither side able to drive the enemy from the field. Finally, on July 27, the battle wore itself out and all troops retired behind mines and barbed wire. The British lost 13,000 men but had captured 6,000 Italians and 1,000 Germans. As a bitter reward for halting the fearsome Axis advance, Auchinleck was relieved of his command. On August 15, 1942, Gen. Sir Harold Alexander became commander in chief of the Middle East and Gen. Bernard Montgomery took over the Eighth Army.

The first battle of El Alamein is seldom accorded the recognition it deserves. The successful British attack from this position four months later is often called one of the decisive battles of World War II. But it was the first El Alamein that broke the back of Rommel's offensive 60 miles short of the Nile River, doomed his last attack at Alam Halfa, and gave Alexander and Montgomery breathing time to rebuild the Eighth Army. *See* Mersa Matrûh; Alam Halfa; El Alamein II; World War II.

El Alamein II (World War II), 1942. The greatest battle of the North African campaign came after almost two years of desert warfare, in which Field Marshal Erwin Rommel's *Panzerarmee Afrika* had penetrated Egypt to within 60 miles of the Nile Valley. The last Axis eastward thrust had been blocked at Alam Halfa two months before. Now the initiative passed to Gen. Bernard Montgomery's rebuilt and reinforced British Eighth Army. Both sides were at peak strengths. Eighth Army had 200,000 men, 1,100 tanks, and artillery and air superiority. Rommel's forces, well organized behind mine fields, had 96,000 men (53,000 German, 43,000 Italian) and 500 tanks, of which 200 were German.

On the night of October 23–24, under cover of an 800-gun artillery barrage, Gen. Oliver Leese's XXX Corps (51st Highland, 1st South African, 4th Indian) struck west from the village of El Alamein, spearheaded by the 9th Australian. A second attack at this point was launched the following day by Gen. Herbert Lumsden's X Corps (1st and 10th Armoured, 2nd New Zealand). On the left (south), Gen. Bryan Horrocks' XIII Corps (7th Armoured, 44th and 50th British) carried out secondary attacks. For seven long days the Eighth Army slugged at the Axis defenses, manned chiefly by the veteran *Afrika Korps*—15th and 21st Panzers and 90th Light (motorized). On two of these days, October 27 and 28, Rommel's armor counterattacked fiercely but was beaten back by the Eighth Army with the help of the Royal Air Force. Then on the night of October 30–31, Montgomery launched a second effort, called Operation Supercharge, that on November 2 and again on November 4 punched wide holes in the Axis line. British armor broke out into open desert, squeezing Rommel out of his defen-

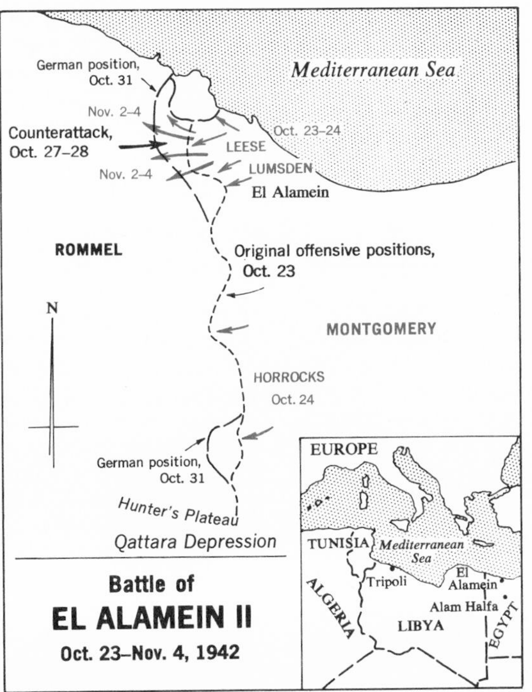

Battle of
EL ALAMEIN II
Oct. 23–Nov. 4, 1942

sive position. The Axis withdrawal, begun the night of November 4–5, continued without letup for 1,500 miles, with Montgomery cautiously but relentlessly in pursuit. The threat to the Nile Valley was wiped away. And with the Anglo-American invasion of Africa in the west on November 8, Allied success in this theater was assured. The victory at El Alamein cost the Eighth Army 13,500 casualties and 600 disabled tanks. German losses were 1,000 killed, 8,000 captured, and 180 tanks destroyed; Italian losses were 1,000 killed, 16,000 captured, and 120 tanks destroyed. One of the prisoners taken was Gen. Ritter von Thoma, commander of the *Afrika Korps*. It was one of the decisive battles of history.

Pressing against the retreating *Panzerarmee,* Montgomery took battle-torn Tobruk on November 13 and Benghazi a week later. El Agheila was captured on November 23. Tripoli fell on January 23, 1943, and on February 13 pursued and pursuer crossed the Tunisian frontier. During this long retreat Rommel lost another 20,000 men, mostly captured. British losses were small. *See* Alam Halfa; Mareth Line; World War II.

Elandslaagte (South African War II). A temporary check by the British, on October 21, 1899, in the successful Boer drive to Ladysmith. *See* Ladysmith.

El Caney (Spanish-American War), 1898. After pushing back the Spanish defenders at Las Guásimas on June 24, the American troop commander in Cuba, Gen. William Shafter, prepared a twin offensive aimed at Santiago. The main effort of his V Corps was to be launched against San Juan Hill, preceded by a secondary assault on El Caney, a small village to the right (northeast). For this the 300-pound Shafter sent forward Gen. Henry Lawton's division (some 6,600 men) early on July 1. The 520 Spanish troops who held the village, under the command of Gen. Joaquin Vara del Rey, fought bravely against the charging Americans. They were finally driven back toward Santiago late in the day, suffering 235 killed (including Vara del Rey) and wounded and 120 captured. American losses were 81 killed and 360 wounded. The capture of El Caney had taken so much longer than planned that Lawton's men were too late to help in the companion attack on San Juan Hill. *See* Santiago de Cuba I; Las Guásimas; San Juan Hill; Spanish-American War.

Ellandun (Rise of Wessex), 825. The kingdom of Mercia (the Midlands), which had established hegemony over Britain south of the Humber River, invaded the kingdom of Wessex in 825. Led by King Beornwulf, the Mercians penetrated to Ellandun, near Swindon, before they encountered the army of Wessex, commanded by King Egbert, grandfather of Alfred, late in the year. In a fierce fight the Wessex warriors checked and then routed the invaders. This battle marked the turning point in the supremacy of Wessex over Mercia in southern Britain. And Egbert, according to many scholars, became the first real king of England. Meanwhile, however, the raids of the Danish vikings were becoming the overriding terror of the age. *See* Winwaed; Hingston Down.

El Mansûra (Seventh Crusade), 1250. The fall of Jerusalem in 1244 prompted the formation of a new crusade in France. Organized by King Louis IX (later Saint Louis) of France, an almost wholly French army of 40,000 men sailed for the advanced Christian base at Cyprus, where it spent the winter of 1248–49. In the following June the crusader army landed on the eastern Nile Delta and quickly routed the Moslem garrison at Damietta. After waiting for the summer flooding of the Nile to recede, Louis marched southward toward the enemy capital of Cairo. On December 14 he reached a canal running east from the Nile, just north of the town of El Mansûra, where the Fifth Crusade had been stopped. Here the Egyptians had established a strong defensive line.

For two months the crusader army was stalled on the north side of the canal. Then on February 8, 1250, Louis launched a two-pronged attack on El Mansûra. He sent his knights four miles to the east where they could cross the canal by a ford. This mounted column was to double back on the south side of the canal to cover the crossing by the infantry. The Count of Artois, brother of the king, led the sweep to the left; Louis followed with the main body of knights. Once across the canal,

Artois, without waiting for the rest of the column, plunged recklessly forward. Catching the Turks by surprise, his bold knights drove them from their camp into the nearby village of El Mansûra. But when the crusaders rode into the town, they became entangled in the narrow streets, making themselves easy targets for Turkish archers shooting from rooftops. Almost the entire vanguard, including Artois and 300 mounted Templars, were killed.

Meanwhile Louis, marching up with the main body, found hard going against the now wide-awake enemy. It was nightfall before the king had secured the half-finished causeway, enabling his foot soldiers to cross the canal. By then a third of the knights had been killed. Although the crusaders clung to their bridgehead south of the canal, they were too weak to advance farther. By the end of February the new Egyptian sultan, Turanshah, had taken over command of the Moslem forces from the hard-fighting Mameluke leader Baybars (Bibars).

When Egyptian ships cut his communications on the lower Nile behind him, Louis had to withdraw. In April he fell back across the canal and started to retreat northward. But pressed hard by the Egyptians and weakened by famine and disease, Louis was forced to surrender his army. All Christians too sick or weak to march were killed by their conquerors. During the negotiations, Turanshah (last of the Ayyubite rulers) was assassinated by the Mamelukes, who took over the Moslem command. The crusaders agreed to hand over Damietta and to pay a ransom of 800,000 pieces of gold. Damietta was evacuated in May. Louis and some of his followers sailed to Acre; the others returned to France. The Seventh Crusade passed into history. *See* La Forbie; Antioch III; Crusades.

El Obeid (War for the Sudan), 1883. Sudan, which had been conquered by Mohammed Ali of Egypt in 1821–22, had long suffered under misgovernment. Finally, in 1881, a Moslem, Mohammed Ahmed, proclaimed himself Mahdi and led a revolt against Egypt, then under a protectorate of Great Britain. To put down the rebellion, Gen. William Hicks, called Hicks Pasha, led an Egyptian expedition into Sudan. At El Obeid, 220 miles southwest of Khartoum, Hicks's army was surrounded by a large Mahdian force on November 1, 1883. The Anglo-Egyptian army, about 10,000 men, fought desperately for three days but were unable to break out of the defile in which they were trapped. By November 4 the Mahdists had massacred the last of the defenders, including Hicks. The British government of William Gladstone resolved to withdraw from Sudan. *See* El Teb; Sudan, War for the.

El Salvador. *See* Chalchuapa.

El Teb (War for the Sudan), 1884. The ferocious revolt of the Mahdists, led by Mohammed Ahmed, against the British protectorate of Egypt, prompted the British government of William Gladstone to order an evacuation of the Anglo-Egyptian forces in Sudan. Because of the vast distances involved, this operation took time. One Egyptian column, led by Valentine Baker, called Baker Pasha, was ambushed at El Teb, near Suakin on the Red Sea, on February 4, 1884. Some 3,500 men tried to fight their way past about 12,000 Mahdists led by Osman Digna. Although the Anglo-Egyptian force inflicted more than 2,000 casualties on the Sudanese, it was virtually wiped out. Baker Pasha was one of the survivors.

When the Mahdists sought to press their advantage, they were repulsed in the second battle of El Teb, on March 29. The victors were some 4,000 Anglo-Egyptian troops led by Gen. Sir Gerald Graham. It was one of the Sudanese's rare setbacks. *See* El Obeid; Khartoum; Sudan, War for the.

Ely I (Norman Conquest of England), 1071. Within four years after the decisive battle of Hastings, William the Conqueror had fastened a firm grip over most of England. The last major English resistance to the Norman conquest came from Hereward the Wake who operated in the East Midlands. Allied with a force of Danes, Hereward raided Peterborough, 75 miles north of London, in 1070. However, in the spring of the following year the Danes withdrew from England following an agreement between their king, Sweyn II, and William. Deprived of allies, Hereward and his rebels took refuge in the so-called Isle of Ely, a rise in the fen country of northern Cambridgeshire. William sent out a Norman force, which besieged Ely and then seized it in the summer of 1071. This ended English resistance, but Hereward escaped to become a semilegendary folk hero. *See* Hastings; Gerberoi.

Ely II (Second Barons' War of England), 1266–1267. The still-belligerent survivors of the barons' defeats collected at the so-called Isle of Ely in the fens of the Ouse River (as had the English refugees of the Norman invasion almost 200 years earlier). Here, under the leadership of John d'Eyvill, they continued to resist the rule of the aged Henry III. However, the king's energetic son Prince Edward marched on Ely and subdued it in the summer of 1267. The remaining members of the refuge acknowledged their submission to the crown. This battle ended the Second Barons' War. Five years later the prince (Longshanks) succeeded to the English throne as Edward I. *See* Axholme; Chesterfield; Radnor; Barons' Wars.

Emesa (Wars of the Roman Empire), 272. While Emperor Aurelian was repulsing the Alamanni from northern Italy, the Roman Empire in the

East fell under the control of Queen Zenobia of Palmyra. At first friendly to Rome, Zenobia now apparently sought to establish a Syrian queendom modeled on Cleopatra's Egypt of earlier times. Aurelian moved eastward and drove the Zenobian forces out of Antioch in 272. When the queen withdrew her army southward up the Orontes River, Aurelian pursued. After a chase of 100 miles, the Romans overtook the Zenobians at Emesa (Homs). Aurelian's legionaries routed the enemy troops. Zenobia fled 75 miles eastward to take refuge within the walls of Palmyra. *See* Pavia I; Palmyra; Roman Empire.

Engano Cape (World War II). One of the distinct naval actions, on October 25, 1944, that went to make up the Japanese-American battle in Leyte Gulf. *See* Leyte Gulf.

England. *See* Danish Invasions of Britain; Great Britain.

English Civil War (1642–1651). Increasing friction between the English crown and Parliament finally flared into open warfare in 1642. In the ensuing civil war, sometimes called the "Great Rebellion," King Charles I was supported by the Anglican episcopacy, while the Presbyterians and other reformers took the side of Parliament. The Royalists, who began the war strong in the north and west of England, lost the north at the battle of Marston Moor in 1644. After the Parliamentarian victory at Naseby the following year, Charles was forced to surrender. The war entered a new phase when the king escaped and made an alliance with the Scots. But the New Model army of Oliver Cromwell put down all Royalist uprisings and repulsed a Scottish invasion. Charles was beheaded in 1649. After opposition in Ireland and a Scottish revolt for Charles II were crushed, the monarchy was abolished and a republic (called the Commonwealth) established under the protectorate of Cromwell. (Two years after the death of Cromwell in 1658, the monarchy was restored under the recalled Charles II.)

Edgehill	1642
Brentford	1642
Grantham	1643
Stratton	1643
Chalgrove Field	1643
Adwalton Moor	1643
Lansdowne	1643
Roundway Down	1643
Newbury I	1643
Cheriton	1644
Selby	1644
Cropredy Bridge	1644
Marston Moor	1644
Tippermuir	1644
Lostwithiel	1644
Newbury II	1644
Inverlochy	1645
Auldearn	1645
Naseby	1645
Alford	1645
Langport	1645
Kilsyth	1645
Philiphaugh	1645
Stow-on-the-Wold	1646
Preston I	1648
Rathmines	1649
Drogheda	1649
Wexford	1649
Carbiesdale	1650
Dunbar II	1650
Worcester	1651

English Civil War, Second. *See* Preston I.

English-Dutch Wars (1652–1674). Commercial rivalry on the high seas led to open warfare between England and the Netherlands in 1652. The fighting, limited to naval action, ended two years later with the Dutch conceding most of the demands of the English Commonwealth government. The second war (1665–1667) was a continuation of the original conflict. England won the colonies of New York, New Jersey, and Delaware before the Treaty of Breda ended the fighting. Five years later the third war (1672–1674) broke out when England supported the French (Louis XIV) invasion of the Netherlands. The Treaty of Westminster, a separate peace between England and Holland, closed the war with no important change from the *status quo*. *See also* Louis XIV, Wars of.

First English-Dutch War	
Goodwin Sands	1652
Dover II	1652
Dungeness	1652
Portland	1653
North Foreland I	1653
Texel I	1653
Second English-Dutch War	
Lowestoft	1665
Dover Strait	1666
North Foreland II	1666
Chatham	1667
Third English-Dutch War	
Southwold Bay	1672
Schooneveldt	1673
Texel II	1673

Eniwetok (World War II). One of the Marshall Islands taken during February 18–22, 1944, by a joint U.S. marine-infantry assault, two weeks after the capture of Kwajalein. *See* Kwajalein-Eniwetok.

Enzheim (Second, or Dutch, War of Louis XIV), 1674. After devastating the Palatinate in the summer of 1674, the marshal the Vicomte de Turenne took his French army back (west) across the upper Rhine. In the fall the army of the Holy Roman Empire (Count Montecuccoli, the Imperial commander, had been temporarily suspended by

Emperor Leopold I) bridged the Rhine near Strasbourg and invaded Alsace. Turenne came up to challenge the Germans at Enzheim, eight miles south of Strasbourg, on October 4. But when the Imperials were reinforced by troops of Frederick William, elector of Brandenburg, Turenne broke off the fight and fell back to middle Alsace. Here he apparently prepared to go into winter quarters but instead planned one of the boldest strokes of his illustrious career. *See* Sinsheim; Turckheim; Louis XIV, Wars of.

Ephesus (Persian-Greek Wars), 499 B.C. Persian rule over the 12 Ionian cities in Asia Minor was challenged by Aristagoras, leader of the chief city of Miletus. Securing the aid of Athens, Aristagoras' allied Greek army attacked and burned Sardis, capital of the Persian province of Lydia. Darius I then sent a Persian army under Artaphrenes the Elder against the rebels. The retreating Greeks were overtaken under the walls of Ephesus, near the west coast, and soundly defeated. Aristagoras fled to Thrace. Athens, which had supplied 20 ships to the rebellion, then withdrew from the war. *See* Lade; Persian-Greek Wars.

Ereğli I (First Crusade), 1101. A second group of reinforcements for the First Crusade reached Asia Minor in the summer of 1101, only to find that the first group had plunged eastward without waiting. Not realizing that the earlier group had been wiped out beyond the Halys (Kizil Irmak) River, the Count of Nevers took his French crusaders along the same route. Halfway across Asia Minor they lost the trail. At Ereğli, southeast of Konya, the Christian column was ambushed by a force of mounted Turkish bowmen from Aleppo. Only Nevers and a few knights escaped the slaughter. The survivors finally reached Antioch after a terrible journey over the Taurus Mountains. *See* Mersivan; Ereğli II; Crusades.

Ereğli II (First Crusade), 1101. Unaware that the first two groups of reinforcements for the First Crusade had been massacred in Asia Minor, a third group set out from Constantinople in the summer of 1101. This force was made up of southern French and of Germans, under the command of the dukes of Aquitaine and Bavaria. Accompanying them was Hugh of Vermandois, younger brother of the French king Philip I. Following the same trail as the French group in front of them, the army reached Ereğli, southeast of Konya. Here, in almost the same spot at which the earlier group had died, they were suddenly attacked by a wandering force of mounted Turkish bowmen from Harran. Only the leaders fought their way free to Tarsus on the Mediterranean coast. Vermandois died of wounds before they could reach Antioch. *See* Ereğli I; Ramleh I; Crusades.

Erie, Lake (War of 1812), 1813. Naval supremacy on Lake Erie safeguarded the British hold on Detroit and kept the Americans on the defensive behind the Maumee River in Ohio. To regain the initiative, in the spring of 1813 the U.S. Navy sent Capt. Oliver Hazard Perry to the mouth of the Sandusky River. Perry hurriedly completed the construction of a ten-vessel flotilla. On September 10 at Put-in-Bay, near the southwestern end of Lake Erie, Perry's little fleet, mounting 55 guns, was attacked by six British vessels, with a total of 65 guns, under the command of Capt. Robert Barclay. The resulting battle

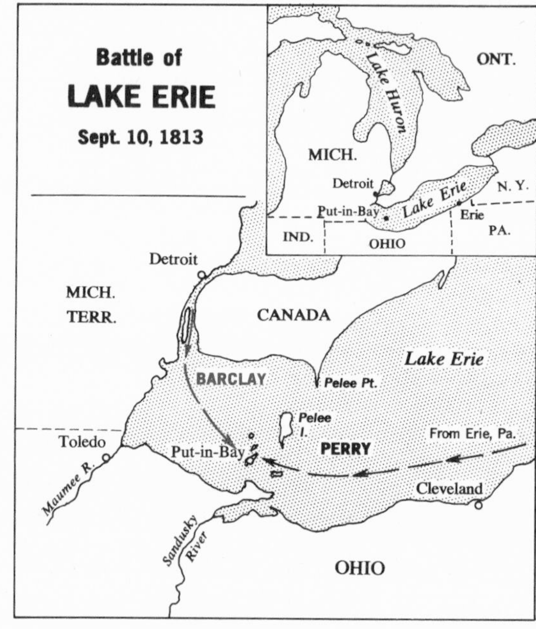

became the bloodiest naval action of the war. Perry's flagship, the *Lawrence,* was sunk early in the fight. But from the *Niagara* the 28-year-old American commander directed the battle which in three hours led to the capture or destruction of the entire British squadron, whose crews suffered 41 killed and 94 wounded. Perry reported the victory laconically: "We have met the enemy and they are ours." The British naval defeat forced their ground troops to evacuate Detroit (September 18) and later Fort Malden (September 24), across the river in Ontario. *See* Frenchtown; Thames River; War of 1812.

Erzincan (Wars of the Seljuk Turks), 1230. In east-central Turkey the Seljuks grew to great power under the sultan Ala ud-Din Kaikobad. This tribe warred against the Persians of Khwarizm along the lower Oxus (Amu Darya). In 1230 Kaikobad's Turks shattered the Persian army of Jalal-ad-Din near Erzincan on the Kara Su (Western Euphrates) River. It was a decisive victory but one that proved disastrous to the Seljuks, for it removed the last army that served as a barrier against the westward flood of the Mongols. Thirteen years later the Mongols swept into Erzincan, forever ending Seljuk rule in eastern Turkey. *See* Manzikert; Baghdad I; Bursa.

Erzurum (Byzantine-Moslem Wars), 928. During the reign of Constantine VII, the Byzantine Empire continued the counteroffensive against the Moslems first launched under Basil I. A brilliant general named John Kurkuas took the Byzantine cavalry into northeast Asia Minor and attacked the strategic fortress at Erzurum. The Moslem garrison was overcome, further crumbling the power of the strife-torn Abbasid caliphate. Kurkuas prepared for new conquests. *See* Samosata; Melitene II; Moslem Conquests.

Erzurum-Erzincan (World War I), 1916. The Turkish victory in Gallipoli released strong forces to deploy against the Russians in the Lake Van–Black Sea area. But before these troops could come into line, Russian Grand Duke Nicholas (demoted from his command on the Eastern Front) struck first in a campaign directed by Gen. Nikolai Yudenich. Driving westward, Yudenich seized Köprukoy on January 17. While the Turks under Abdul Kerim Pasha fell back, the Russians pressed forward to storm and capture Erzurum, 40 miles farther west, during February 12–16. At the same time a Russian column moved northward to capture the Black Sea port of Trabzon (Trebizond) on April 17.

Although Turkish reinforcements were now arriving from Europe, Yudenich continued his offensive. On July 2 he knifed through Bayburt, 60 miles northwest of Erzurum, splitting the Turkish front. He then turned southwest to storm into Erzincan, 96 miles west of Erzurum, on July 25. This battle finished the Turkish Third Army, which had lost 17,000 killed and a similar number captured. Hard-riding Cossack cavalry harried the survivors.

Only on the left flank of the Russian advance could the Turks hold their ground. Here a corps under Gen. Mustafa Kemal (later Kemal Atatürk), attacking eastward, took Muş, 45 miles from Lake Van, and Bitlis, 30 miles closer to the lake, on August 15. But even here the Turkish Second Army was repulsed by Yudenich, and the two villages were retaken by August 24. This ended the formal fighting on the so-called Caucasus front. With the outbreak of revolution in Russia the following March, the czarist armies melted away. The Turks recaptured all their lost territory and were advancing in the Caucasus itself when an armistice was reached on October 31, 1918. *See* Sarikamis; World War I.

Esperance Cape (World War II). The third Japanese-American naval battle, on October 11 and 12, 1942, growing out of the fight for Guadalcanal Island. *See* Guadalcanal—Naval Action.

Essling (Napoleonic Empire Wars). A village across the Danube River from Vienna, seized by Napoleon I on May 21, 1809; the action helped to provoke a major battle with Austria. *See* Aspern-Essling.

Ethiopia (Italian-Ethiopian War II), 1936. On the pretext that Ethiopians had provoked a small border clash at Walwal (Ualual) on December 5, 1935, two Italian armies prepared to invade Ethiopia in a naked aggression to add that nation to Benito Mussolini's African empire. Commanded by Gens. Emilio De Bono and Rodolfo Graziani, one army (250,000 men) marched south from Eritrea, while the second (70,000 men) advanced northwest from Italian Somaliland, on February 3, 1936. A month after the attack, Marshal Pietro Badoglio assumed overall command of the invasion forces. To defend his country, Emperor Haile Selassie could mobilize only scattered tribesmen (perhaps about 250,000) without formal military training or modern arms. The Italians increased their overwhelming military superiority by indiscriminate aerial bombings and by the use of poison (mustard) gas. On May 5, 1936, Italian forces occupied the capital of Addis Ababa, from which the emperor had fled to England. Ethiopian resistance ended, and King Victor Emmanuel III of Italy assumed the title emperor of Ethiopia. Five years later, in World War II, British forces drove out the Italians and restored Haile Selassie to his throne. *See* Aduwa; East Africa.

Eurymedon River (Persian-Greek Wars), 466 B.C. After turning back Persian invaders in four successive battles beginning with Marathon, Athens took the offensive. In 466 B.C. the Athenian general Cimon, son of Miltiades, led an allied Greek expedition to Asia Minor. At the mouth of the Eurymedon River, near the southern coast, the Greeks routed the Persian fleet and scattered their ground forces. This triumph bound the south of Asia Minor to the Athenian confederacy, called the Delian League (because its council and treasury were on the sacred island of Delos). The battle marked the end of the Persian-Athenian conflict and was the last clash between East and West for more than 60 years. *See* Mycale; Cunaxa; Persian-Greek Wars.

Eutaw Springs (War of the American Revolution), 1781. After three narrow defeats in 1781, Gen. Nathanael Greene, American commander in chief in the South, occupied the High Hills of the Santee River in South Carolina. Here he rested his troops and built up his strength to 2,200 men. Greene then moved suddenly against the British army at Orangeburg, S.C. To avoid being cut off from the main British base at Charleston, Lt. Col. Alexander Stuart, who had replaced Lt. Col. Francis Rawdon (later 1st Marquis of Hastings) in command, fell back eastward to Eutaw Springs.

Greene followed and on September 8 launched a bold attack against Stuart, who had some 2,000 men. The American militia in the front line advanced steadily. When the Americans began to falter in the face of heavy fire, the British defenders rushed to counterattack. But the redcoats were promptly driven back by the second American line, composed of North Carolina Continentals. In hard fighting the Americans forced back their opponents, gradually at first and then into full retreat down the Charleston road. At the moment of victory, however, most of the American troops gave up the pursuit to loot the British camp. This gave Stuart time to rally his men for a counterattack. The Americans were driven from the field but managed to re-form in the nearby woods. The short but bitter fight took a high percentage of casualties. Greene lost 139 killed, 375 wounded, and 8 missing. Stuart's losses totaled more than 40 percent of his force—85 killed, 351 wounded, and 430 missing.

Although Greene had technically lost another battle, he had again crippled the British occupation army in the South. From Eutaw Springs, Stuart fell back toward Charleston. This city and Savannah, Ga., now represented the last British holdings in the three southern states. With the main British army in the South, under Gen. Lord Charles Cornwallis, surrendering at Yorktown 6 weeks later, Eutaw Springs became the last pitched battle of the war in this theater. *See* Ninety Six; Yorktown I; American Revolution.

Evesham (Second Barons' War of England), 1265. Unaware that his son's army had been crushed at Kenilworth, Simon de Montfort (earl of Leicester) took his rebel barons across the Severn near Worcester on August 2, seeking to link up with the force of Simon the Younger. Two days later at Evesham on the Avon, Montfort sighted an approaching army. In the rain and half-darkness of a summer storm he mistook the other army for his son's. Prince Edward (later Edward I) entertained no such illusions. His heavy cavalry swept down on the barons and broke their lines. With his ally Roger Mortimer holding the bridge over the Avon, Edward had his opponents caught in an inescapable trap. A terrible massacre took place, in which Montfort was slain and his entire force wiped out. Edward's knights even accidentally wounded King Henry III in their orgy of killing. This battle broke the back of the barons' rebellion, although mopping-up operations continued for more than a year. *See* Kenilworth; Axholme; Chesterfield; Barons' Wars.

Eylau (Napoleonic Empire Wars), 1807. Leaving his winter quarters in East Prussia, the Russian commander, Gen. Levin Bennigsen, launched an offensive westward toward the lower Vistula River early in 1807. Learning of this attack, Napoleon I ordered a counterblow from Warsaw to the north designed to strike the Russians' left (south) flank and cut them off from Königsberg (Kaliningrad). Bennigsen then began pulling back, while the French concentrated against him at Preussisch-Eylau (Bagrationovsk), 23 miles south of Königsberg. On the evening of February 7 Napoleon deployed 45,000 troops on a rough north-south line through the town, facing 67,000 Russians who held a series of low hills to the east. After a heavy artillery duel the following morning, Marshal Pierre Augureau's VII Corps struck the Russian center in a blinding snowstorm. The attack was beaten back with heavy French losses. Meanwhile, however, the III Corps of Marshal Louis Davout began steadily rolling up the Russian left flank. Only the arrival of a Prussian corps of 7000 men under Gen. Anton von Lestocq prevented a complete French breakthrough in this sector. Darkness and exhaustion halted the fighting late in the day.

The indecisive battle cost the French 20,000 casualties. Russian losses were higher, including 11,000 dead. Fearing complete encirclement the next day, Bennigsen withdrew at midnight toward Königsberg, to the north. After driving the Russians out of Ostroleka a week later, Napoleon also pulled back to reorganize and rest for a spring campaign. At the same time he ordered the investment of Danzig to protect his left rear. *See* Pultusk II; Danzig II; Napoleonic Empire Wars.

F

Fair Oaks (American Civil War), 1862. It took Gen. George McClellan more than six weeks to move his 100,000-man Federal army up the peninsula between the York and James rivers to threaten Richmond. On May 20 he reached a position on the Chickahominy River, sending Gen. Erasmus Keyes's III Corps south across the stream, to be followed by Gen. Samuel Heintzelman's IV Corps. The remainder of the Federal force stood north of the Chickahominy, six miles northeast of the Confederate capital at its closest point. Here McClellan remained stationary, waiting for reinforcements, which were being withheld by the Union government to deal with Gen. Thomas (Stonewall) Jackson in the Shenandoah Valley. Meanwhile, the Confederate commander, Gen. Joseph Johnston, built up his defensive force to 60,000 men.

On May 31 Johnston launched a large-scale attack against the exposed III Corps east of Richmond. While Gen. Gustavus Smith on the left (north) demonstrated against the Federals north of the river, Gen. James Longstreet took three columns against Keyes. But Longstreet, instead of attacking toward Fair Oaks with his left-hand force, moved down the center road, delaying the advance from dawn to 1 P.M. Despite the snarled plans, the Confederate general Daniel Hill struck the III Corps at Seven Pines and, when reinforced by other Longstreet units, began driving the Federals back toward the Chickahominy. Witnessing the battle, Gen. Edwin Sumner of the Federal II Corps hurried Gen. John Sedgwick's division across the river to anchor Keyes's right flank at Fair Oaks. This enabled the Federals to limit Longstreet's gains until darkness ended the fighting.

Johnston, twice wounded, was succeeded by Gen. Gustavus Smith, who ordered the attack renewed on the following day (June 1). But the Confederates had lost their opportunity to score a major victory. The Union line held, and when Gen. Robert E. Lee arrived in the afternoon to take over Confederate command, he ordered a withdrawal to the original Confederate positions. Both sides had sent some 41,000 troops into the battle, which is sometimes called Seven Pines. Confederate casualties were 6,134, Federal losses 5,031. *See* Williamsburg; McDowell; Seven Days; American Civil War.

Falaise-Argentan Pocket (World War II), 1944. The American breakthrough at Saint-Lô, and later at Avranches, sent Gen. George Patton's Third Army racing eastward to Le Mans on August 8. From here XV Corps armor turned north toward Argentan. This thrust cut off the rear of the German army group still facing the British Second and Canadian First armies to the north. Patton reached Argentan on August 13, halted briefly on orders of the Twelfth Army Group commander, U.S. general Omar Bradley, and then turned east toward the Seine River. The U.S. V Corps took over Argentan and struck north while Gen. Henry Crerar's Canadian First Army attacked south to Falaise.

The German field marshal Gunther von Kluge now hastily began to withdraw his three armies from impending encirclement. (Field Marshal Walther Model relieved Kluge on August 18.) Fighting desperately, the Nazis held open a ten-mile exit to the east for five days. Although pounded heavily by Allied aircraft and pressed ever tighter on the ground, many of the German forces escaped. On August 19 the Allied pincers snapped shut at Chambois, and three days later the Falaise-Argentan pocket was eliminated. The battle cost the Germans 10,000 dead, 50,000 prisoners, and much of their heavy equipment. The Nazis now fell back to the Seine, closely pursued by Allied armor. *See* Saint-Lô Breakthrough; France, Northern; World War II.

Falkirk I (English-Scottish Wars), 1298. After the crushing English defeat at Stirling Bridge, Edward I turned his whole attention to the war against Scotland. But first he had to end the tense relationship with France's Philip IV. He did this by marrying the king's sister Margaret and betrothing his own son, the future Edward II, to the king's daughter Isabella. Edward then took the field himself against Sir William Wallace, who commanded the Scots. Marching into Stirling County, scene of the 1297 disaster, the English army met Wallace's force at Falkirk on July 22.

The Scots had taken a strong defensive position

built on four solid circles (schiltrons) of spearmen —they had little cavalry and few archers. Edward's armored knights charged the Scottish infantry but were thrown back by the massed spear points. Edward then brought up his Welsh archers. Their showers of arrows from longbows at point-blank range cut gaps in the Scottish ranks. The knights charged into these openings and with lance and sword quickly slaughtered the Scots. Wallace and a few survivors took refuge in dense woods. Edward's men relentlessly hunted down the rebels. Wallace himself was finally captured at Glasgow in 1305. He was hanged, drawn, and quartered at Tyburn. Scotland was incorporated under the English crown, but the people remained unconquered. Robert VIII (called "the Bruce"; later Robert I of Scotland) rallied his countrymen and continued the war. *See* Stirling Bridge; Methven.

Falkirk II ("the Forty-five"), 1746. When the Young Pretender, Prince Charles Edward, invaded England late in 1745, the lack of new recruits forced him to withdraw into Scotland. Here the Highland clans strongly supported the prince's claims for his father as James VIII of Scotland (James III of England). During the long march back into central Scotland, Lord George Murray's tactical skill kept the pursuing English army at bay. When the Jacobites reached Falkirk in Stirling County, they suddenly turned on their tormentors. On January 17, 1746, Murray's 8,000 rebels charged the royal army of similar size under Gen. Henry Hawley. The assault broke the hastily formed English line; 600 royalists were killed and 700 captured, in addition to the loss of all baggage and cannon. Rebel casualties were less than 150.

After their victories at Prestonpans and Falkirk, the rebels seemed invincible in Scotland. But King George's son William Augustus (duke of Cumberland) reorganized the royal forces for a showdown battle. *See* Prestonpans; Culloden Moor; Jacobite Insurrections.

Falkland Islands (World War I), 1914. Following the British naval defeat off Coronel, Chile, the Grand Fleet hurried two battle cruisers and five other cruisers to the South Atlantic. Admiral Sir Frederick Sturdee was coaling this force in the Falkland Islands on December 8 when the squadron of the German admiral Count Maximilian von Spee hove into sight. The five German cruisers and three supply ships turned to flee with the British warships in hot pursuit. In a running fight four German cruisers were sunk: the *Scharnhorst, Gneisenau, Nurnberg,* and *Leipzig.* Spee, his two sons, and 1,800 seamen were lost. The cruiser *Dresden* escaped, only to be found and destroyed three months later off the Juan Fernández Islands in the South Pacific. The British victory in the Falklands, accomplished without the loss of a ship, virtually cleared the outer seas of German surface raiders. *See* Coronel; Dogger Bank II; World War I.

Fallen Timbers (Old Northwest Indian Wars), 1794. American settlement of the Old Northwest territory was long handicapped by hostile Indians —Miami, Shawnee, Potawatomi, Chippewa. In 1790 and again in 1791 expeditions sent into the territory by the United States government had been disastrously defeated by a confederacy directed by Little Turtle. General Anthony Wayne, a Revolutionary War hero, then took over troop command. At the head of 2,000 regulars and 1,000 mounted volunteers, Wayne pressed the Indians back to the Maumee River in northwest Ohio. Here, behind trees blown down in a heavy storm, about 1,300 Indians and perhaps some British made a stand on August 20, 1794 (Little Turtle had been deposed by less able strategists). Wayne fixed the Indian position with his infantry, sending the horsemen around to strike the enemy in the flank. The coordinated attack routed the Indians, killing or wounding several hundred. Wayne lost 33 killed and 100 wounded in the biggest victory ever won against the Northwest Indians. The Treaty of Greenville, signed the following year, ended major hostilities for 17 years. *See* Fort Recovery; Tippecanoe Creek; Indian Wars in the United States.

Farrukhabad (Maratha-British Wars), 1804. The military successes of the British generals Gerard Lake in the north and Arthur Wellesley (later Duke of Wellington) in the center of India virtually crushed Maratha resistance in 1803. But the following year a Maratha chieftain, Jaswant Rao Holkar, renewed the war along the upper Ganges River in the north. Lake, at the head of a small force of British and allied natives, marched to Farrukhabad, 100 miles northwest of Lucknow. On November 14 Lake attacked and routed Holkar's Marathas with a loss to himself of only 2 killed and 20 wounded. Holkar escaped. The recall of Gov.-Gen. Lord Richard Wellesley the following year ended the campaign against Holkar and thus brought to an end the Second Maratha War. *See* Argaon; Kirkee; Maratha-British Wars.

Faubourg Saint-Antoine (French Wars of the Fronde), 1652. When Louis XIV was the ten-year-old king of France, in 1648, the nation became embroiled in a series of uprisings called the Wars of the Fronde. The uprisings were basically a power grab by a clique of nobles, and the fighting was confused and desultory. During the four years of turmoil many of the nobles and generals changed sides, including the two greatest military commanders of the era—Louis II, the Great Condé; and the Vicomte de Turenne. By 1652 the antiroyalists had polarized around Condé, while

Turenne had taken control of the forces loyal to King Louis. On July 2 Turenne pinned Condé against the closed eastern gates of Paris in the Faubourg Saint Antoine, north of the Seine. The royal troops were in the process of annihilating their opponents when Condé's men were suddenly admitted into the city by Anne Marie d'Orleans, called La Grande Mademoiselle. The guns of Paris were then trained on Turenne, thwarting pursuit.

Despite the rebels' escape, this battle ended the Fronde as an internal struggle. Condé went over to the Spanish, who had been at war with France since 1634. King Louis returned to Paris three months later. The chief result of the anarchy of the Fronde period was that it paved the way for the forthcoming absolutism of the great Bourbon "Sun King." *See* Lens; Arras I.

Fehrbellin (Swedish-German War), 1675. During the war of Louis XIV of France against Holland, Charles XI of Sweden took the side of France, while Frederick William, elector of Brandenburg, joined forces with the Dutch. With Frederick William fighting on the Rhine, Sweden launched an invasion of Brandenburg. The elector hurried home, encountering the Swedish army under Marshal Karl Wrangel at Fehrbellin, northwest of Berlin. On June 28 the German army of almost 15,000 men defeated the Swedes, driving them out of Brandenburg. The victors went on to invade Swedish Pomerania, seizing Stettin and Stralsund. It was a serious blow to the military prestige of the northern kingdom. However, supported by France in the 1679 Treaty of St. Germain-en-Laye, Sweden recovered its lost territory. Meanwhile, at sea Charles XI was engaged against Denmark, which had also joined the coalition against Louis XIV. *See* Warsaw I; Jasmund; Northern Wars.

Ferozeshah (Sikh-British War I), 1845. After his victory over the Sikhs at Mudki, Gen. Sir Hugh Gough pressed northward in East Punjab. Reinforced to some 16,000 Anglo-Indian troops, Gough reached Ferozeshah on December 21. Here he made a night attack against the entrenched Sikh camp, held by almost 50,000 warriors. The assault failed, but when a new attempt was made on the following day, the Sikh lines cracked and then collapsed. They fled the field, leaving behind 7,000 casualties. Gough suffered 694 killed and 1,721 wounded in one of the bloodiest combats of the century in the East. *See* Mudki; Aliwal; Sikh-British Wars.

Ferrybridge (Wars of the Roses), 1461. After Edward of York (white rose) had himself proclaimed Edward IV, he mustered a large army and marched northward against the Lancastrian (red rose) forces of the legitimate monarchs, Henry VI and Margaret. The latter army, entrenched behind the Aire River in western Yorkshire, assigned young Lord Clifford to protect the river crossing. The Yorkist advance guard, commanded by Lord Fitzwalter, reached Ferrybridge on March 28, 1461. In a sharp struggle the Yorkists were beaten back. Fitzwalter was killed. Later that day, however, when the main body arrived, a heavier attack carried the bridge. The Yorkists crossed the river, where lay the dead body of Clifford, whose father had been slain at Saint Albans I in the opening battle of the war. The stage stood ready for Edward's showdown battle with the Lancastrians. *See* Saint Albans II; Towton; Roses, Wars of the.

"Fifteen, The." *See* Jacobite Insurrections.

Finisterre Cape I (War of the Austrian Succession), 1747. In the war at sea, Great Britain (George II) strove to block communications between France (Louis XV) and its American possessions. On May 3, 1747, a British fleet of 14 warships intercepted a French convoy, protected by 8 ships of the line, off Cape Finisterre on the northwestern coast of Spain. When Adm. George Anson (later Baron of Soberton) attacked, most of the French merchantmen escaped, but the English determinedly pursued the enemy's ships of the line, which were commanded by Adm. La Jonquière. In the running fight that ensued, all the French warships were sunk or captured. *See* Toulon II; Louisbourg I; Finisterre Cape II; Austrian Succession, War of the.

Finisterre Cape II (War of the Austrian Succession), 1747. The British navy of George II, guarding the sea lanes between France (Louis XV) and its American possessions, intercepted for the second time, in 1747, an enemy convoy off Cape Finisterre on the northwestern coast of Spain. On October 2 Adm. Edward Hawke (later Baron Hawke), with 14 warships, sailed to attack the 9 battleships of Adm. de l'Étenduère. The French commander ordered the 250 merchantmen to scatter while he held off the British fleet. In a heroic defense of eight hours the French lost 6 of their combat vessels but prolonged the action enough so that all the merchant ships made good their escape. This battle, the last naval engagement of the war, gave Great Britain virtual supremacy in the Atlantic Ocean. *See* Finisterre Cape I; Maastricht III; Austrian Succession, War of the.

Finisterre Cape III (Napoleonic Empire Wars), 1805. The Treaty of Amiens, which ended the Second Coalition War against France in 1802, brought only 14 months of peace. Then, in May 1803, Great Britain and France resumed the conflict. Napoleon Bonaparte, now Emperor Napoleon I of France, massed an army at Boulogne but could not implement his threatened invasion of England, chiefly because of the marked superiority of British sea power. This strength was demonstrated on July 22, 1805, off Cape Finisterre, on the northwestern coast of Spain. A British fleet of 15 warships intercepted 20 French and Spanish vessels returning from the West Indies. Rear Admiral Sir Robert Calder, British commander, promptly attacked and took two of the allied ships. The others, under Adm. Pierre de Villeneuve, sailed hurriedly for port. The British pursued but lost contact the next day because of fog and lack of wind. For his failure to win a bigger victory, Calder was censured for errors of judgment. (He was later cleared and promoted to admiral.) Three months later the war at sea would flare into one of the decisive battles of history. Meanwhile Napoleon took the offensive against England's allies on the Continent. *See* Copenhagen I; Ulm; Trafalgar Cape; Napoleonic Empire Wars.

Finland. *See* Scandinavia.

Finland (World War II), 1939–1940. With much of the world at war, the Soviet Union moved to strengthen its northwest frontier. Russia's second largest city, Leningrad, lay only 16 miles from the Finnish frontier, behind which stood the strong Mannerheim Line across the Karelian Isthmus. On a transparent pretext the Red Army invaded Finland on six fronts on November 30, 1939, while the Red Air Force struck at Helsinki. Most of the 26 Soviet attacking divisions (465,000 troops) were concentrated on the Karelian Isthmus between Lake Ladoga and the Gulf of Finland. The Finnish army of nine divisions (130,000 men), commanded by Field Marshal Baron Carl von Mannerheim, fought courageously. They threw back waves of attackers from the Russian Seventh and Thirteenth armies against the Mannerheim Line. In the deep snow and sub-zero temperatures of the Suomussalmi area across the narrow waist of Finland, the Finns annihilated the Russian 163rd and 44th divisions between December 8 and January 11. Finnish casualties were 900 killed, 1,770 wounded.

Badly stung by these defeats, the Russian army under Gen. Kirill Meretskov halted to organize a new offensive. This time the immense Russian superiority in men, guns, and aircraft could not be denied. A powerful attack, directed by Gen. Semyon Timoshenko, began on February 1, 1940. Two Red armies smashed relentlessly at the Mannerheim Line, finally broke through, and captured Viipuri (Vyborg) on March 11. The Finns surrendered the following day. Finnish losses were 25,000 killed and 44,000 wounded. The Red Army lost more than 200,000 in dead alone. But the Soviet Union had won the defensive territory it had demanded. The approaches to Leningrad were further secured when the Baltic countries of Lithuania, Latvia, and Estonia were taken over three months later.

On June 26, 1941, Finland took advantage of Germany's invasion of the Soviet Union four days earlier by launching its own attack. Mannerheim's army quickly reconquered the lost Finnish territory and then aided the German *Wehrmacht* in the long blockade of Leningrad. But again victory was short-lived. In the Red Army's gigantic 1944 offensive Russian troops cracked the Mannerheim Line a second time (in June) and Finland had to accept another humiliating peace (September 19, 1944). Finland then turned on its late ally and on March 3, 1945, formally declared war on Germany. No significant military action resulted. *See* Poland (World War II); Leningrad; World War II.

First Coalition, War of the. *See* French Revolution, Wars of the.

First Triumvirate, Wars of the (53–45 B.C.). The defeat and death of Marcus Licinius Crassus at Carrhae in 53 B.C. left Julius Caesar and Pompey the Great to contend for the rule of Rome. Caesar seized the initiative by crossing the Rubicon River four years later. Eleven battles later Pompey and all his allies were defeated, leaving Caesar the undisputed head of the Roman government.

Carrhae I	53 B.C.
Rubicon River	49 B.C.
Ilerda	49 B.C.
Utica II	49 B.C.
Bagradas River	49 B.C.
Illyria	49 B.C.
Dyrrachium I	48 B.C.
Pharsalus	48 B.C.
Alexandria I	48–47 B.C.
Zela	47 B.C.
Ruspina	46 B.C.
Thapsus	46 B.C.
Munda	45 B.C.

Fisher's Hill (American Civil War), 1864. After his defeat at Winchester, Va., Gen. Jubal Early retreated southward to Fisher's Hill, overlooking Strasburg. Here he deployed his 8,000 Confederate infantry and dismounted cavalry across a four-mile front. General Philip Sheridan, in close pursuit with almost 30,000 men, arrived on September 22. While two Federal corps (VI and XIX) fixed Early's front, Gen. George Crook circled westward with his division. Late in the day Crook struck hard at the Confederate left flank, held by the cavalrymen of Gen. Lunsford Lomax. Sheridan then sent his two corps up the wooded ridge in a frontal assault. Shaken by their defeat three days earlier and by the attack on their left flank, the Confederates fell back in disorder. Early reported 1,235 casualties (of whom 1,100 were captured), not including those of Lomax's cavalry. Federal losses were 528 (including 52 killed).

Early retreated up the valley beyond Harrisonburg. Sheridan withdrew to Winchester, devastating the region as he went. He reported the result with the words, "A crow would have had to carry its rations if it had flown across the valley." But Early was not whipped yet. *See* Winchester III; Cedar Creek; American Civil War.

Fishing Creek (War of the American Revolution). The defeat of Thomas Sumter's force in South Carolina, on August 18, 1780, during the panic-stricken American retreat from Camden. *See* Camden.

Five Forks (American Civil War), 1865. The Federal commander, Gen. U. S. Grant, began stretching his siege lines southwest of Petersburg, Va., by sending the cavalry corps of Gen. Philip Sheridan against the Confederate right flank, on March 29. From Dinwiddie Court House, Sheridan struck northwest toward the important crossroads of Five Forks, defended by Gen. George Pickett with some 19,000 infantry and cavalry. Sheridan, who had 12,000 cavalrymen, called up Gen. Gouverneur Warren's V Corps (about 16,000 men) to attack on his right. On April 1 Sheridan struck the front of Pickett's entrenched position. Although Warren was tardy getting into position, it was his assault late in the afternoon that rolled up the Confederate line. Pickett's army collapsed. Of the 5,200 prisoners taken, Warren's infantry captured 3,200. Yet Sheridan relieved Warren, putting Gen. Charles Griffin in command of the V Corps. The defeat at Five Forks placed Gen. Robert E. Lee's Army of Northern Virginia in such peril that he evacuated Petersburg and Richmond the following night (April 2). *See* Petersburg; Appomattox River; American Civil War.

Flamborough Head (War of the American Revolution), 1779. Following his naval victory at Carrickfergus in 1778, the American captain John Paul Jones put in at Brest, France. Here he obtained command of a rebuilt merchantman which he named the *Bonhomme Richard*. With several smaller vessels Jones sailed for the eastern coast of England. On the afternoon of September 23, 1779, off Flamborough Head in Yorkshire, Jones sighted two English frigates, the *Serapis* and the *Countess of Scarborough*. In a savage battle in which Jones was hampered by the treachery of a captain in his own squadron, the American commander lashed the 42-gun *Bonhomme Richard* along side the *Serapis*. Jones's crew could then fire their muskets from the rigging into the enemy vessel. When the *Bonhomme Richard* caught fire, Capt. Richard Pearson of the *Serapis* asked the Americans to surrender. Jones is reported to have replied: "I have not yet begun to fight." Finally, after three and one-half hours, in what was then full moonlight, the British captain surrendered. Jones quickly transferred his crew and prisoners to the *Serapis*. The burning *Bonhomme Richard* sank the next day. It was the only battle in which a victorious captain lost his own ship and returned to port in a captured vessel. *See* Carrickfergus; American Revolution.

Flanders (World War II), 1940. Germany's ferocious assault on the West began with a right-wing sweep through the Netherlands and Belgium by Field Marshal Fedor von Bock's Army Group "B." Early on May 10, 500 German airborne troops captured two important bridges over the Albert Canal and neutralized the key defensive strong point of Fort Eben Emael. At the same time Field Marshal Walther von Reichenau's Sixth Army of 23 divisions drove through the narrow southern projection of the Netherlands and crossed the Meuse River at Maastricht. On the second day German armor outflanked the fortified city of Liége and then took it from the rear (west). The hard-pressed 17 divisions of Belgium began falling back to the Dyle River line. Here they were joined on May 13 by the British Expeditionary Force (BEF) of nine divisions (Gen. Lord John Gort) and the French First Army (Georges Blanchard). But almost immediately the onrushing *Panzers* forced the Allied armies back to the Schelde River. This line too collapsed, on May 20. The entire Allied First Army Group under the French general Gaston Billotte was being outmaneuvered and outfought.

Meanwhile, a greater Allied disaster was in the making. Bock's smashing westward attack into the Netherlands and Belgium was only a mask for the main German effort southward in the Ardennes. Through this wooded mountainous area, considered impassable by the Allies, Field Marshal Karl von Rundstedt moved his Army Group "A" of 44 divisions on May 10 and 11. Meeting only token opposition, the Germans pushed 70 miles to reach the French frontier on May 12. They established bridgeheads over the Meuse River at Sedan the following day. Led by Gen. Paul von Kleist's three-corps *Panzer* Group, the Germans turned to the west and broke through into good tank terrain. Backing up the armor was Gen. Gunther von Kluge's Fourth Army and Gen. Siegmund List's Twelfth Army. The French Ninth Army (André-Georges Corap), trying to block the armored avalanche, was quickly shattered and its second commander in the battle (Henri Giraud) taken prisoner. General Maxime Weygand now (May 19) replaced Gen. Maurice Gamelin as French commander in chief, but the battle was already lost for the Allies. Through a 50-mile gap in the French lines, *Panzer* spearheads under Gen. Heinz Guderian drove westward 220 miles in seven days, to reach the coast at Abbeville on May 20–21. This armored thrust opened a 60-mile-wide corridor behind the back of the Allied left wing in Belgium. The only strong counter-

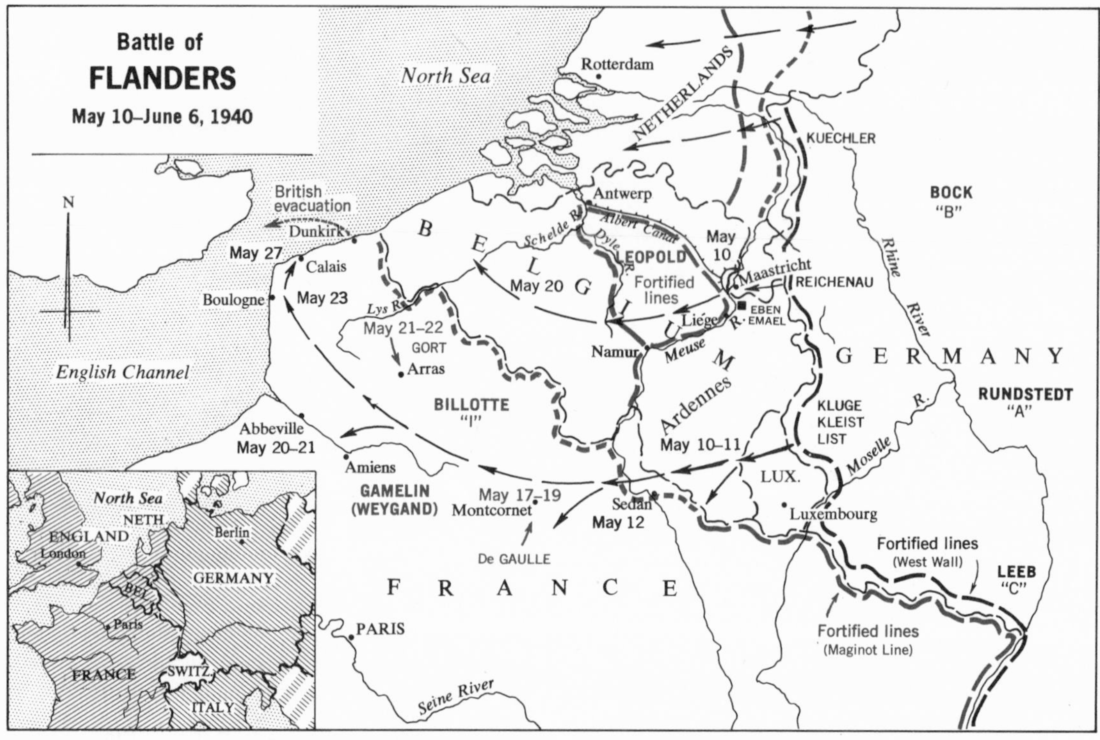

thrust from the south against this corridor of steel came from Gen. Charles de Gaulle's 4th Armored Division at Montcornet between May 17 and 19. On the north Gen. Lord Gort's BEF attacked toward Arras on May 21–22. Both assaults were decisively repulsed.

Kleist's tanks now turned north along the coast to take Boulogne on May 23, and Calais on May 27. The hard-pressed Allies in the northwest were further weakened on May 28 when King Leopold III surrendered his Belgian army to the German Sixth Army and went into internment. Now evacuation by sea was the only hope of escape for the British Expeditionary Force and the remnants of the French First Army of Blanchard. The Allies fell back to their last remaining hold on the coast at Dunkirk, where the British had won temporary superiority in the air.

From May 29 to June 4, 338,000 Allied troops were evacuated to England in almost every type of naval craft imaginable. (Of the 861 vessels employed 243 were sunk.) Another 30,000 men were left on the blood-stained beach, dead or as prisoners. In the 26-day battle of Flanders, the Allies lost more than a million men in prisoners alone; total German casualties were 60,000. The crushing Allied defeat cost 30 French divisions (including almost all their armor in four of the lost divisions), 9 divisions of the BEF, and a group of Free Poles. The door was now wide open for a fresh German onslaught into the heart of France. *See* Netherlands (World War II); France (World War II); World War II.

Fleurus I (Thirty Years' War), 1622. While an allied Catholic army of Spanish and Bavarians was overrunning The Palatinate in 1622, a second Spanish army marched across the Netherlands border to besiege the Dutch city of Bergen op Zoom, on an estuary of the Schelde River. Commanding this Spanish thrust was the Italian-born general Arbrogio di Spinola. Hearing of the new outbreak of hostilities, the Protestant armies of Gen. Count Ernst von Mansfeld and Christian of Brunswick turned northwest from Alsace (where they had retired after the battle of Höchst) toward the Spanish Netherlands. From east of the Rhine another Spanish army, under Gonzales de Córdoba, hurried westward to intercept the allied Protestant force. At Fleurus, in the southwest of present-day Belgium, Córdoba threw up a roadblock. The Protestants reached the town on August 29. Christian promptly charged the Spanish and, although repulsed at first, renewed the attack until he broke through, on the fifth assault. This victory opened the way to Bergen op Zoom, which was relieved early in October.

The battle of Fleurus took a high toll, however. Christian managed to cut his cavalry through the Spanish lines only by sacrificing the bulk of his infantry. He himself lost an arm in the reckless fighting for which he had become famous. *See* Höchst; Stadtlohn; Thirty Years' War.

Fleurus II (War of the Grand Alliance), 1690. When the aggressive Louis XIV of France invaded and devastated the Palatinate in October 1688, the European powers who had created the League of Augsburg two years earlier reorganized as the Grand Alliance. The coalition included England, Holland, Savoy, Sweden, Spain, the Holy Roman Empire, Bavaria, Saxony, and the Palatinate. Both the Grand Alliance nations and France rushed troops into the Spanish Netherlands. Here, at Fleurus, in Hainaut Province, Prince George Frederick of Waldeck took command of an allied army of 40,000 men. He occupied a strong position behind marshy brooks, with both flanks anchored in villages. But the marshal the Duc de Luxembourg, supreme French commander, was one of the top generals of his time. Pressing steadily forward with 45,000 troops, the hunchbacked Luxembourg reached Fleurus on June 30, 1690. After first launching a frontal assault, he sent out his cavalry in a double envelopment of Waldeck's lines. Perfectly executed, the triple assault smashed the allied army, killing 5,000 and capturing another 8,000, plus 48 guns and 150 colors. The French losses were 2,500.

Ten days later Louis XIV won an equally notable victory at sea. *See* Beachy Head; Staffarda; Leuze; Grand Alliance, War of the.

Fleurus III (Wars of the French Revolution), 1794. After the indecisive French victory at Tourcoing in May 1794, the armies of the National Convention and the allies both maneuvered eastward. On June 25 the Revolutionary general Jean Jourdan, at the head of 70,000 troops took Charleroi. But when he moved deeper into the Austrian Netherlands (modern Belgium) on the following day, he was attacked at Fleurus by the allied army, chiefly Austrian, of 50,000 men under the Prince of Saxe-Coburg (Friedrich Josias). The allied commander deployed his assault in five columns. Poor coordination among the columns and a stout French defense, which shook off heavy casualties for six hours, stopped the allied attack in its tracks. Saxe-Coburg fell back across the Meuse, although he had suffered only half as many losses as Jourdan.

The French victory at Fleurus proved to be the turning point in the First Coalition phase of the Revolutionary Wars. Austria evacuated its troops from the Netherlands, which was annexed by France. Holland capitulated that winter. Prussia and Spain dropped out of the war the following year, leaving only Austria, England (which withdrew its continental expeditionary force), and Sardinia (Piedmont) in alliance against the National Convention. *See* Tourcoing; Quiberon; Loano; French Revolution Wars.

Flodden (English-Scottish Wars), 1513. While Henry VIII was invading the France of Louis XII, a Scottish army under James IV crossed the Tweed River into northern England. The English position in Northumberland seemed perilous. James's army numbered almost 50,000 men, and the only experienced English general available was Thomas Howard, earl of Surrey, whose Yorkist family was still under attainder from the Wars of the Roses. Surrey, however, rose to the defense of England. With 25,000 men he marched around the Scottish army, forcing that body to turn and attack him at Flodden on September 9, 1513. The battle was the often repeated performance of the English longbow against the Scottish spear. A murderous storm of arrows cut gaps in the invaders' schiltrons (dense circles of spearmen), which the English cavalry exploited. The axes and bills of the English infantry then slaughtered the surviving Scots in a decisive, hand-to-hand climax. James (husband of Henry VII's daughter Margaret) and most of his nobles lay dead on the last great battlefield won by the longbow. The dead king's year-old-son, James V, inherited the crown of Scotland. And the troublesome border warfare waned for almost 30 years. *See* Guinegate; Solway Moss.

Florence-Fiesole (Wars of the Western Roman Empire), 406. Three years after the Goths had been defeated at Pollentia and driven out of northern Italy, a new barbarian horde swarmed over the Alps. These invaders were Germans, estimated at almost 100,000 men, under the command of an Ostrogoth named Radagaisus. Emperor Honorius holed up in the natural defenses of Ravenna, while the Germans penetrated as far south as the Arno River. Finally the military commander of the Western Roman Empire, Flavius Stilicho, collected an imperial army and attacked Radagaisus' force, which was then besieging Florence. Stilicho managed to drive off the Germans and, pursuing closely, surrounded them at Fiesole, four miles to the northeast. On August 23, 406, the Roman army stormed into the enemy camp and virtually erased all opposition. Radagaisus was captured and executed.

Stilicho's victory bought only four more years of respite for Rome. The able commander was murdered in 408. The following year Alaric again invaded Italy, and now no strong commander stood in the way of the Visigoth king. *See* Pollentia; Rome I; Roman Empire.

Flores (English-Spanish Wars), 1591. Three years after the defeat of the Spanish Armada, a fleet of seven English ships under Lord Thomas Howard (1st earl of Suffolk) sailed into the Azores island group looking for Spanish treasure ships. A Spanish force of 15 fighting ships arrived to drive off the invaders. In the action the English *Revenge*, commanded by Sir Richard Grenville, was crippled and surrounded by Spanish ships. For 15 hours the crew of the *Revenge* fought gallantly against hopeless odds. Two Spanish vessels were sunk in the attack. Finally at daybreak, with Grenville mortally wounded, the *Revenge* surrendered, ending one of history's most dramatic naval battles. The long, undeclared naval war between the two sea powers continued to drag on with neither side gaining a firm advantage. *See* Spanish Armada; Kinsale.

Focsani (Turkish-Russian Wars), 1789. The declining strength of the Ottoman Empire under Sultan Abdul-Hamid I prompted Catherine II, the Great, of Russia and Joseph II of the Holy Roman Empire to wage a new war of aggression in 1789. A combined Russian-Austrian army under Count Aleksandr Suvorov and the Prince of Saxe-Coburg (Friedrich Josias) marched through Bessarabia into Moldavia. On August 1 the allies attacked the Turkish camp at Focsani, in modern Rumania. The Ottomans were thoroughly routed, while the victors pressed deeper (southward) into Turkey. *See* Çeşme; Rimnik.

Fontenoy (War of the Austrian Succession), 1745. In the fifth year of the war Louis XV of France concentrated his forces for a campaign in the southern Netherlands (modern Belgium), which had passed from Spain to Austria after the War of the Spanish Succession in 1714. He assigned Marshal Comte Maurice de Saxe to command the French army. Opposing Saxe were the English and Dutch, allies of Austria, whose chief army of the Holy Roman Empire (Maria Theresa) was engaged in the Second Silesian War with Frederick II, the Great, of Prussia. The Duke of Cumberland (William Augustus), son of Great Britain's George II, commanded the allied force.

Saxe opened the campaign by besieging Tournai, on the Schelde River, with an army of 50,000 men. Cumberland, at the head of an equal number of English, Hannoverians, Dutch, and Austrians, marched to the relief of the city. Five miles to the southeast at Fontenoy, Saxe prepared to receive the attack from a strong defensive position between the Schelde and the Gavrain Wood. To his linear front he constructed four redoubts (a tactic he had learned from a study of the Russian deployment at the 1709 battle of Poltava).

On May 11 the allies attacked. For two hours enfilade fire from the redoubts stopped the Cumberland assault in its tracks. The duke then formed 14,000 infantrymen into a compact wedge. Despite the continued deadly fire, the allies marched between two redoubts straight into the center of the French line, which began to give way. However, Saxe directed a furious counterattack against the flanks of the wedge. In this action his Irish Brigade distinguished itself by its hard fighting. The allied column slowly crumbled and then fell back, losing more than 7,000 in dead and wounded. Under cover of night Cumberland retreated toward Brussels. Tournai surrendered shortly thereafter.

Fontenoy was the last battle for Great Britain in the war. The English army had to be recalled to put down the '45 Rebellion. Saxe pressed on in Flanders to take Brussels, while on the eastern front France's enemy Austria was suffering severe defeats at the hands of Prussia. *See* Cuneo; Hohenfriedeberg; Austrian Succession, War of the.

Forbach. *See* Spicheren.

Formigny (Hundred Years' War), 1450. The renewed French offensive of Charles VII, which had taken Rouen in 1449, pressed the English back to Formigny, 27 miles northwest of Caen. Here reinforcements under Thomas Kyriel and Matthew Gough arrived from England. These troops, added to the survivors of the fallen forts and castles to the east, gave the English command some 5,000 men. On April 15 the Comte de Clermont led a French attack on the English positions at Formigny. The French artillery, placed on both flanks, blasted the mismatched bowmen and billmen, who left their lines only to be overcome by French men-at-arms. Giving no quarter, the French killed almost 4,000 of their English opponents. This decisive battle ended the fighting in northern France. Caen fell without effective resistance in June, as did Cherbourg in August. The long war now moved to the southwest. *See* Rouen III; Castillon; Hundred Years' War.

Fornovo (French Invasions of Italy), 1495. The retreat of the French army of Charles VIII up the Italian peninsula from Naples met no real opposition until the troops reached Fornovo, 70 miles southeast of Milan. Here stood some 30,000 Venetians and Mantuans under the command of Francesco II Gonzaga of Mantua. This force, with a 3- or 4-to-1 superiority in numbers, attacked the withdrawing French on July 6, 1495. Expecting to engage in the supercautious tactics of the usual condottiere (mercenary) warfare, the Italians received an unpleasant surprise when the French heavy cavalry smashed into their ranks, killing and maiming with fierce determination. In ten minutes the Italians broke and fled, leaving 3,500 casualties on the field. French losses numbered only about 100. The polite scufflings of chivalry were over; a new age of deadly warfare had dawned.

Although Charles VIII continued his withdrawal across the Alps, his invasion marked the beginning of more than half a century of French attempts to dominate Italy. In 1499 Charles's successor, Louis XII, led an army into northern Italy which subdued Milan. And two years later the French renewed their attack on Naples. *See* Naples; Barletta.

Fort Caroline (Spanish-French War in Florida),

1565. In the spring of 1564 French Huguenots led by René de Laudonnière established Fort Caroline at the mouth of the Saint Johns River, in modern Florida. The garrison was reinforced by Jan Ribault the following year. To counteract this threat to Spanish possessions in the Americas, Philip II sent out an expedition under Pedro Menéndez de Avilás. Menéndez disembarked on September 7 and 8, 1565, to found Saint Augustine, to the south of the French settlement. Nine days later the Spanish began an overland march to Fort Caroline. On September 20 they stormed the fort, killing 132 defenders in the first hour of the attack. Laudonnière was one of the few survivors of the assault. Ribault was captured and killed the following month. Fort Caroline was renamed San Mateo.

The French retaliated on April 6, 1568. A three-ship expedition under Dominique de Gourgues captured San Mateo and hanged the surviving members of the Spanish garrison.

Fort Clinton and Fort Montgomery (War of the American Revolution). American forts on the Hudson River below West Point, captured by Sir Henry Clinton on October 6, 1777, in a futile diversionary action to relieve the pressure on the British general John Burgoyne at Saratoga. *See* Saratoga.

Fort Dearborn (War of 1812), 1812. With the outbreak of war against Great Britain on June 18, 1812, the United States (President James Madison) ordered an invasion of Upper Canada from Detroit. The American commander in the West, Gen. William Hull, bungled the operation. Fearful that he could not hold Fort Dearborn, on the site of Chicago, against the Indian allies of the British, he ordered the post evacuated. The garrison abandoned the fort on August 15 and set out for Fort Wayne (in present-day Indiana). Along the southern shore of Lake Michigan the garrison fell into the hands of a Potawatomi war party, which killed 12 soldiers, 12 militiamen, and 14 women and children. Another 29 soldiers and 13 women and children were captured. The empty Fort Dearborn was burned to the ground. (A court-martial later sentenced Hull to death for cowardice and neglect of duty, but the sentence was remitted). *See* Detroit; War of 1812.

Fort de Vaux (World War I). A French strong point three miles northeast of Verdun, lost to the Germans on June 6, 1916, despite heroic resistance led by Maj. Sylvain Raynal, and regained by a French counterattack on November 2. *See* Verdun.

Fort Donelson (American Civil War), 1862. The Federal capture of Fort Henry on February 6 forced Gen. Albert Johnston, Confederate commander of the area between Cumberland Gap and Arkansas, to realign his forces. Johnston withdrew his right (east) wing from Bowling Green, Ky., to Nashville, Tenn. At the same time he sent Gen. John Floyd with 12,000 men to reinforce Fort Donelson on the Cumberland River. From Fort Henry, the Federal general U. S. Grant marched 11 miles eastward to invest the Cumberland fort on February 12, with 25,000 men. Meanwhile Com. Andrew Foote came up river with six gunboats in an effort to subdue Donelson by gunfire, as he had Fort Henry. But the Confederate guns were better placed here, and the Federal vessels were repulsed on February 14. Foote received a severe wound.

On February 15 the Confederate defenders struck the right of Grant's line, seeking to force an escape route to the south. The attack, led by Gen. Gideon Pillow, succeeded, but Floyd lost his nerve and ordered the troops back to their original positions. Some of the fort's trenches were already occupied by advancing Federal troops. The Confederate position was now more hopeless than ever. Floyd and Pillow fled across the Cumberland that night, leaving the garrison in charge of Gen. Simon Buckner. The Confederate colonel Nathan Forrest led his cavalry command safely through the Federal lines under cover of darkness. When Buckner asked for terms the following day, Grant demanded and received "unconditional surrender." More than 11,000 Confederates laid down their arms, to add to the 2,000 already lost in killed and wounded. Grant suffered 500 killed, 2,108 wounded, and 224 missing. The fall of forts Henry and Doneson opened the way for Federal troops to move up the Tennessee deep into Confederate territory. Johnston fell back to Corinth, Miss. *See* Fort Henry; Island No. 10; American Civil War.

Fort Douaumont (World War I). A key defensive position north of Verdun captured by a single German company on February 25, 1916, and regained by a French counterattack on November 2. *See* Verdun.

Fort Erie (War of 1812), 1814. After his pursuit of the British army in Ontario was checked in a furious battle at Lundy's Lane on July 25, Gen. Jacob Brown withdrew his American army into Fort Erie. Here, across the Niagara River from Buffalo, N.Y., Gen. Edmund Gaines took charge of a garrison of 2,000 men.

On August 2 the fort came under the siege of Gen. (later Sir) Gordon Drummond's British army of 3,500 men, which had shaken off its heavy losses at Lundy's Lane. Drummond brought up six siege guns on August 13. After a two-day bombardment the British assaulted the fort on August 15 but were repulsed with many casualties. The bombardment was resumed until September 17, when a sudden American sortie led by Gen. Peter Porter destroyed the enemy batteries. Drummond then lifted the siege on September 21. In all, the British lost 609 in killed, wounded, or missing. Total American casualties were 511. Later in the year (November 5), when the United States pulled back behind the Niagara River, Fort Erie was destroyed. *See* Lundy's Lane; Champlain, Lake; War of 1812.

Fort Fisher (American Civil War), 1865. To provide an alternate base for Gen. William Sherman, who was marching northward through the Carolinas, the Federal commander in chief, Gen. U. S. Grant, ordered the capture of Fort Fisher, which guarded the entrance to the Wilmington, N.C., harbor. An 8,000-man force under Gen. Alfred Terry landed near the fort on January 13. The defending Confederate commander, Gen. William Whiting, had some 2,000 troops, plus the division of Gen. Robert Hoke (another 6,000). Terry brought artillery ashore the following day and on January 15 opened a heavy bombardment of the fort. An assault that afternoon stormed the fort, capturing 112 officers and 1,971 men, including the mortally wounded Whiting. Hoke's division was driven off. Federal army losses were 184 killed, 749 wounded, 22 missing. Naval casualties numbered 686. Generals Newton Curtis (wounded four times) and Galusha Pennypacker (also wounded) both won the Medal of Honor for leading the Federal assault brigades. Terry's force opened the port of Wilmington and then became a part of Gen. John Schofield's army, which marched inland to link up with Sherman at Goldsboro, N.C., on March 23. *See* Savannah III; Bentonville; American Civil War.

Fort Frontenac (French and Indian War), 1758. In addition to the attacks on Ticonderoga and Louisbourg in 1758, the British launched a third offensive into the northwest. Lieutenant Colonel John Bradstreet with some 2,000 colonial troops moved up the Mohawk and then westward to Oswego, at the southeastern end of Lake Ontario. Boarding a small fleet, Bradstreet crossed the eastern end of the lake. On August 27 he suddenly swooped down on French-held Fort Frontenac (site of Kingston, Ontario). The surprised and outnumbered garrison surrendered. After destroying supplies and lake shipping, Bradstreet retraced his route.

The fall of Fort Frontenac cut French communications with their posts in the Ohio Valley. On November 25 the garrison at Fort Duquesne, at the forks of the Ohio, blew up the defenses and retreated into Canada. The post was later rebuilt by the British and Americans as Fort Pitt. *See* Louisbourg II; Fort Ticonderoga I; Fort Niagara; French and Indian War.

Fort Henry (American Civil War), 1862. In deference to the proclaimed neutrality of Kentucky the Confederates built Fort Henry on the Tennessee River and Fort Donelson on the Cumberland, just across the state line in Tennessee. Early in 1862 the Federal commander of the Department of Missouri, Gen. Henry Halleck, authorized Gen. U. S. Grant to move up the Tennessee. From February 2 to 5, Grant took 15,000 men in transports to within four miles of Fort Henry. Meanwhile, Com. Andrew Foote took seven gunboats up the river and on February 6 brought the fort under bombardment. The Confederate commander, Gen. Lloyd Tilghman, realizing the weakness of Fort Henry, had already evacuated 2,500 men 11 miles eastward to Fort Donelson. The remaining garrison of 79 artillerymen returned the gunboats' fire only briefly before surrendering the fort. Foote lost 11 killed, 81 wounded, and 5 missing. Confederate casualties were 5 killed, 11 wounded, and 63 missing. Grant promptly began moving his troops, who had arrived after the surrender, overland against Fort Donelson. Foote returned to the Ohio with his flotilla and then entered the Cumberland to support the ground attack. *See* Mill Springs; Fort Donelson; American Civil War.

Fort McHenry (War of 1812), 1814. After burning part of Washington, D.C., the British fleet (ten ships) of Adm. (later Sir) George Cockburn sailed up the Chesapeake Bay toward Baltimore. On September 12 Gen. Robert Ross's army of 4,000 men disembarked at the mouth of the Patapsco, about 14 miles from Baltimore. The fleet moved up the river to where Fort McHenry stood guard over the city. Finding the harbor blocked by sunken hulls, the British ships opened a bombardment on the following night (it was this barrage that prompted a witness, Francis Scott Key, to write the words to "The Star-Spangled Banner"). Unlike Washington, however, Baltimore was stoutly defended under the direction of Gen. Samuel Smith. The 1,000-man garrison inside the fort held on grimly.

Meanwhile Ross's army marched overland toward the fort. The advance was opposed by a 3,200-man militia force under Gen. John Stricker in Godly Wood. Although the Americans were forced back on September 12, they inflicted 346 casualties on the British, many of whom were veterans of the successful Peninsular Campaign in the Napoleonic Wars. One of those killed was Ross. Striker lost 20 killed, 90 wounded, and 200 captured. It was not until the next day (September 13) that the invaders reached the strongly held heights at the edge of the city. When the bombardment of Fort McHenry failed to force an opening that night, the attack on Baltimore was abandoned. The British re-embarked on their transports. On October 14 they sailed out of Chesapeake Bay for Jamaica. *See* Bladensburg; New Orleans I; War of 1812.

Fort Mercer and Fort Mifflin (War of the American Revolution), 1777. After repulsing Gen. George Washington's attack at Germantown on October 4, 1777, Gen. Sir William Howe turned to clearing the Delaware River as a supply route for his British army in Philadelphia. His first move came against Fort Mercer, on the New Jersey side of the river, about ten miles below Philadelphia. On October 22 some 2,000 Hessians under Col. Carl von Donop attacked the fort, garrisoned by Col. Christopher Greene's Rhode Islanders (about 400 men). The assault was beaten off with a loss of 371 attackers. Greene suffered 37 casualties.

The second British attempt was made against Fort Mifflin, on Mud Island, slightly below Fort Mercer. On November 10 the British set up a floating battery north of the island, which bombarded Mifflin for five days. The garrison of 450 men under Col. Samuel Smith and Maj. Simeon Thayer suffered heavily but held on. But when six British warships mounting a total of 238 guns joined the bombardment on November 15, the fort became untenable. That night the 200 able-bodied survivors abandoned Mifflin and crossed to the New Jersey side of the river. British losses were seven killed and five wounded.

Howe now sent Gen. Lord Charles Cornwallis with 2,000 men to make a new assault on Fort Mercer. With the loss of Mifflin, Mercer was doomed. Greene evacuated the fort on November 20 and the Delaware was free for British shipping from Cape May to Philadelphia. *See* Germantown; Monmouth; American Revolution.

Fort Mims (Creek War), 1813. Before the War of 1812 the American-hating Shawnee chief Tecumseh had visited the Creek Indians in the Southeast. Although the Creeks did not join the Indian confederacy at once, they did take the warpath a year after the United States became engaged with Great Britain. Led by a half-breed chief, William Weatherford, called Red Eagle, the Creeks attacked Fort Mims on the east bank of the Alabama River, 35 miles above Mobile, on August 30, 1813. Storming into the fort, the Indians massacred at least 250 of the 550 people in the garrison. Many others were burned to death or died later in captivity (some reports list only 30 survivors). The white frontiersmen in the area immediately flew to arms. *See* Talladega; Indian Wars in the U.S.

Fort Moultrie (War of the American Revolution). A palmetto-log fort on Sullivan's Island whose valiant defense, on June 28, 1776, blocked the first British attack on Charleston, S.C. *See* Charleston I.

Fort Necessity (French and Indian War), 1754. Two years before the Seven Years' War erupted in Europe, hostilities broke out in North America. The focal point was the forks of the Ohio River (now Pittsburgh), where the French had erected Fort Duquesne on the site of a Virginia trading post. A force of 150 Virginia militiamen, under Lt. Col. George Washington, marched toward the disputed fort in 1754. On May 28 Washington routed a small French reconnaissance party, but learning of a larger enemy force advancing toward him, he fell back to a square log enclosure, called Fort Necessity, near present-day Uniontown in southwestern Pennsylvania. Here he was followed and attacked by an army of 600 French and 100 Indians commanded by Capt. Louis Coulon de Villiers. After a day-long battle the Virginians ran short of ammunition and had to surrender, on July 3. The captured militia, including Washington, were released to their homes by the French. *See* Beauséjour; French and Indian War.

Fort Niagara (French and Indian War), 1759. In recognition of his capture of Louisbourg in July 1758, Gen. Jeffrey Amherst was named commander in chief of the British forces in North America for 1759. He led an advance northward from Albany that squeezed the French out of Ticonderoga and Crown Point. This gave the British control of both Lake George and Lake Champlain. Meanwhile he sent Gen. John Prideaux westward to try to take French-held Fort Niagara, located where the Niagara River flows into Lake Ontario. Prideaux laid siege to the fort in June with 2,000 British regulars and 100 Iroquois Indians under Gen. Sir William Johnson. During the investment Prideaux was killed and succeeded by Johnson. On July 24 a force of French and Indians tried to relieve the 600-man garrison but was beaten off with heavy losses. The defenders capitulated the following day. This conquest, with the reinforcement of Oswego on the eastern shore of Lake Ontario, severed the French in Canada from the Ohio Valley. Meanwhile, a third British offensive moved up the Saint Lawrence River. *See* Fort Frontenac; Quebec I; French and Indian War.

Fort Phil Kearny (Sioux War I), 1867. Built along the Bozeman Trail into Montana in 1866, Fort Phil Kearny, Wyo., earned the nickname Fort Perilous for its isolated position along the upper Powder River. On August 2 a woodcutting crew of 32 soldiers and workmen were surrounded outside the fort by some 1,500 Indian warriors led by Red Cloud. Under the leadership of Capt. James Powell, the defenders beat off six attacks by Sioux and Cheyennes before relief arrived from the fort. The successful defense, sometimes called the Wagon Box Fight, was made possible by the new breech-loading rifles and superior marksmanship of the 18th Infantry Regiment soldiers. About 180 Indians were killed or wounded; 7 of Powell's men were killed. The following year the United States ordered the evacuation of Fort Phil Kearny, which was promptly destroyed by the Indians. *See* Massacre Hill; Beecher Island; Sioux Wars.

Fort Pillow (American Civil War), 1864. After the fall of Vicksburg and Port Hudson in July 1863, the Mississippi River became a Federal waterway. To protect river traffic, Federal forces held a string of forts along the banks from Cairo, Ill., to New Orleans, La. One of these was Fort Pillow, 40 miles north of Memphis, Tenn. From nearby Jackson, Tenn., the Confederate cavalry general Nathan Forrest detached a division under Gen. James Chalmers to attack the fort, defended by 262 Negro and 295 white soldiers. Chalmers began an investment of Fort Pillow at dawn on April 12. The Federal commander, Maj. Lionel Booth, was killed by a sniper and replaced by Maj. William Bradford. In midafternoon Bradford refused a surrender ultimatum from Forrest, who had arrived to take personal charge of the attack. The Confederates then assaulted the fort and captured it with a loss of only 14 killed and 86 wounded. The garrison, however, suffered 231 killed, 100 serious wounded, and 226 captured (including 58 Negroes). Southern sources say that these abnormally high casualty figures resulted from a stout defense. But the evidence indicates that most of the garrison were killed after surrendering because of the many Negro soldiers present, thus giving rise to the name Fort Pillow Massacre. *See* Port Hudson; Wilderness; American Civil War.

Fort Recovery (Old Northwest Indian Wars), 1791. The failure of Gen. Josiah Harmar's 1790 expedition against the Indians in the Old Northwest—Miami, Shawnee, Potawatomi, and Chippewa—prompted the United States government to send out a second force the following year. General Arthur St. Clair, governor of the Northwest Territory, left Fort Washington (Cincinnati) in October at the head of 2,000 troops, chiefly ill-trained militia. Moving northward through the Ohio wilderness, the expedition camped at Fort Recovery, 41 miles southwest of Lima, on the evening of November 3. At dawn the next morning the poorly prepared army, weakened by hundreds of desertions, was assailed by a large force of Indians, under Little Turtle. Within two hours 900 Americans lay killed or wounded. St. Clair and the survivors fled to Fort Jefferson, 22 miles away, and then back to Fort Washington. The American commander, who had been court-martialed and exonerated for precipitously abandoning Fort Ticonderoga during the Revolutionary War, resigned from the army the following year. A new expedition against the Indians would have to be organized. *See* Fort Wayne; Fallen Timbers; Indian Wars in the United States.

Fort Saint David (Seven Years' War), 1758. In the third year of the war between Great Britain and France in India, most of the action centered on British-held Fort Saint David, just north of Cuddalore on the east coast. In the spring of 1758 the French commander in the East, the Comte de Lally, launched a siege of the fort. A British fleet of seven warships under Adm. George Pocock sailed to relieve the fort. Off the coast it was intercepted by a French fleet of equal size commanded by the Comte d'Aché, on April 29. In a brisk encounter, no ships were lost, but Pocock's fleet was too crippled to succor the besieged garrison. Fort Saint David, with 500 British and 1,000 native troops, surrendered on June 2.

On August 3 and again on September 10 of the following year the fleets of Pocock and d'Aché clashed off the east coast of India. But these engagements were as inconclusive as the first action —neither side lost a ship. Meanwhile, the French were making a strong effort to capture Madras. *See* Plassey; Madras II; Seven Years' War.

Fort Sitabaldi (Maratha-British War III), 1817. The conflict between the Maratha chief Baji Rao II and the British in India prompted the Rajah of Nagpur (Nappa Sahib) to make war on the Europeans also. On November 24 he attacked Fort Sitabaldi, outside the city of Nagpur, with some 15,000 troops. The British garrison of chiefly Madras and Bengal troops numbered only about 1,300. But in a spirited resistance lasting 18 hours, the defenders beat off every assault. The assailants finally withdrew, after inflicting 300 casualties at great cost to themselves. The British victory ended the uprising. *See* Kirkee; Maratha-British Wars.

Fort Stanwix (War of the American Revolution), 1777. The western prong of the triple British offensive of 1777 aimed at Albany, N.Y., was under the command of Col. Barry St. Leger (temporarily a brigadier general). On July 25 St. Leger left Fort Oswego, N.Y., on Lake Ontario with almost 1,700 British, Tories, and Indians. Moving eastward, he reached Fort Stanwix (Schuyler) on the upper Mohawk River. Here a garrison of 750 Americans under Col. Peter Gansevoort blocked the British advance down the Mohawk. St. Leger laid siege to the fort on August 3. An American relief column of 800 militiamen commanded by Gen. Nicholas Herkimer marched westward from Fort Dayton, 30 miles down the river. Six miles from the fort, at Oriskany, Herkimer's men fell into an ambush on August 6. The Americans were driven back with a loss of 250 men by a mixed force of Loyalists and Indians led by the Mohawk chief Joseph Brant. Among the mortally wounded was Herkimer. British casualties were about 150.

The American commander in chief in New York State, Gen. Philip Schuyler, now sent a second army to relieve the fort. Under the leadership of Gen. Benedict Arnold, 950 volunteers from the main army near Stillwater, N.Y., marched up the

Mohawk. The approach of this column frightened off St. Leger's Indian supporters. The British commander thereupon raised the siege of Fort Stanwix, on August 22, and fell back to Oswego. Arnold relieved the fort two days later and then rejoined the main army opposing Gen. John Burgoyne on the upper Hudson. The rebuff of St. Leger helped seal the doom of Burgoyne at Saratoga two months later. *See* Ticonderoga III; Bennington; Saratoga; American Revolution.

Fort Stedman (American Civil War). The last attempt of Gen. Robert E. Lee to break through the Federal siege lines east of Petersburg, on March 25, 1865. *See* Petersburg.

Fort Sumter (American Civil War), 1861. With the clouds of civil war between the North and the South steadily darkening in the United States, Maj. Robert Anderson, commanding the Federal forts in Charleston (S.C.) harbor, withdrew his 76 troops into Fort Sumter on the night of December 26, 1860. Confederate forces in the city ringed the fort with hostile batteries. Cut off from supplies and reinforcements, Anderson planned to evacuate Fort Sumter on April 15, 1861. But on April 12, three days before the planned evacuation, Confederate guns under the command of Gen. Pierre Beauregard opened fire at 4:20 A.M. During the next 34 hours about 4,000 shells fell in the enclosure, starting fires but doing little damage and inflicting no casualties. Anderson's return fire proved to be equally ineffective. Realizing the hopelessness of his position, the Federal commander agreed to abandon the fort at noon on April 14. Two of his men were killed and another wounded in an accidental powder explosion during the firing of a final salute. The successful Confederate bombardment ignited the fuse that plunged the United States into a savage struggle that would last four years. *See* Philippi, W. Va.; Big Bethel; American Civil War.

Fort Texas (U.S.-Mexican War), 1846. The admission of the former Mexican state of Texas into the United States on December 29, 1845, aggravated already strained relations between the two nations. The situation became worse when both sides claimed the 150-mile-wide strip of territory between the Nueces River and the Rio Grande. In the spring of 1846 Gen. Zachary Taylor, American commander in the Southwest, sent a detachment into the disputed area to build Fort Texas on the Rio Grande (just east of modern Brownsville), opposite the Mexican position at Matamoros on the right bank. A cavalry clash north of the river on April 25 resulted in the death of 11 Americans. Five days later a Mexican force under Gen. Mariano Arista crossed the Rio Grande in strength and on May 3 laid siege to Fort Texas. The American commander, Maj. Jacob Brown, resisted firmly. Four days later Taylor marched his main army to the relief of the beleaguered garrison. After winning battles at Palo Alto and Resaca de la Palma, Taylor relieved the fort on the evening of May 9. Arista fell back across the river to Matamoros. The fort was renamed Brown in honor of its defender. *See* Palo Alto; Resaca de la Palma; Monterrey; U.S.-Mexican War.

Fort Ticonderoga I (French and Indian War), 1758. For a multiple offensive planned in the fifth year of the war, Great Britain sent Gen. James Abercrombie to North America to supplant the unsuccessful 4th Earl of Loudoun (John Campbell). With a force of 12,000 British and colonial troops, Abercrombie moved northward toward the French fort called Carillon at Ticonderoga, early in July. At the approach of Abercrombie's army the French commander, Gen. Marquis Louis de Montcalm, entrenched his 3,000 French and Canadians behind a low ridge in front of the fort. Without waiting for his artillery or making any attempt at a flanking maneuver, Abercrombie launched a frontal assault on the enemy position on July 8. A withering fire repulsed the attack. Five more times the blundering general ordered his men to charge the ridge, and each time they were beaten back with heavy casualties. Abercrombie finally withdrew, after losing 464 killed, 1,117 wounded, and 29 missing. One regiment of British regulars, the 42nd (Black Watch) suffered 50 percent casualties. French losses were less than 400.

Although the other British offensives that summer were successful, the disaster at Ticonderoga prevented a proposed move on Quebec. (Ticonderoga was abandoned by the French the following year in the face of a new British offensive.) *See* Fort William Henry; Louisbourg II; Fort Frontenac; French and Indian War.

Fort Ticonderoga II (War of the American Revolution), 1775. After the opening battle of Lexington and Concord outside Boston, the American colonies took the offensive in New York. On May 9 Ethan Allen crossed Lake Champlain from Vermont with 83 Green Mountain militiamen. Early the following morning he surprised the British post at Fort Ticonderoga on the western shore. One British soldier was wounded before Capt. William Delaplace surrendered the garrison of 42 regular troops "in the name of the great Jehovah and the Continental Congress" as Allen is reputed to have demanded. Two days later another patriot force under Seth Warner seized Crown Point, N.Y., seven miles to the north. The action then shifted back to the Boston area. *See* Lexington and Concord; Bunker Hill; American Revolution.

Fort Ticonderoga III (War of the American Revolution), 1777. In the third year of the war the British general John Burgoyne won his government's approval to launch a three-pronged attack on Albany, N.Y. If successful, this offensive would split off New England from the rest of the American states and go far toward winning the war. Burgoyne himself led the invasion from Canada, which was to press down lakes Champlain and George to the upper reaches of the Hudson River. (Here he was to be joined by a second British force pushing upriver from New York City and a third coming from the west along the Mohawk River.)

On June 17 Burgoyne left Saint Johns (Saint-Jean), Quebec, with 7,700 British, German, Canadian, and Indian troops. Two weeks later he reached the strategic American position at Fort Ticonderoga, at the gateway between lakes Champlain and George. Here the American commander in the north, Gen. Philip Schuyler, had deputized Gen. Arthur St. Clair to hold the fort with some 2,500 men. Unaccountably, the Americans had not fortified the dominant height of Mount Defiance (Sugar Loaf) south of the fort. When Burgoyne's men occupied this hill with two 12-pound guns, St. Clair's position in the fort became untenable.

On the night of July 5 the garrison abandoned Fort Ticonderoga, leaving behind valuable military stores. On the second morning of their retreat to the south, their rear guard was attacked at Hubbardton, Vt. In a sharp 40-minute fight the advancing British and Germans under Gen. Simon Fraser inflicted more than 50 percent casualties on the 600 defenders commanded by Lt. Col. Seth Warner. British losses were 198 killed or wounded. Finally, on July 12, the survivors of St. Clair's force reached Fort Edward on the upper Hudson River. But Schuyler believed this port to be indefensible and fell back to the mouth of the Mohawk. On August 4 the overly cautious commander was replaced by Gen. Horatio Gates, while Burgoyne continued to push southward. *See* Valcour Island; Fort Stanwix; Bennington; American Revolution.

Fort Wagner (American Civil War). The objective of two Federal assaults, on July 11 and 18, 1863, which finally won the fort, in the long campaign against Charleston, S.C. *See* Charleston III.

Fort Washington (War of the American Revolution), 1776. Instead of continuing his northward drive against Gen. George Washington at White Plains, N.Y., the British commander, Gen. Sir William Howe, turned back to attack Fort Washington near the northwestern end of Manhattan Island. Under the direction of Gen. Lord Charles Cornwallis and the German general Baron Wilhelm von Knyphausen, 8,000 British and Hessian troops converged upon the pentagonal earthwork on Washington Heights on November 16, 1776. Here Col. Robert Magaw could deploy less than 3,000 Continentals in an effort to hold an obviously indefensible position. A coordinated assault carried the heights, driving back the Americans into the crowded enclosure. Magaw, who had lost 59 killed and 96 wounded in the outerworks, surrendered his entire surviving force of 2,837. The attack had cost the British 78 killed and 374 wounded. Two days later Cornwallis crossed the Hudson with 4,500 men to attack the companion position of Fort Lee. General Nathanael Greene wisely abandoned the fort without a fight. Washington's entire army now fell back across New Jersey. *See* White Plains; Trenton; American Revolution.

Fort Wayne (Old Northwest Indian Wars), 1790. Three years after the United States Congress had established the Northwest Territory in 1787, settlement was still blocked by hostile Indians—Miami, Shawnee, Potawatomi, and Chippewa—who were encouraged by the British troops stationed in border forts. In the fall of 1790 Gen. Josiah Harmar left Fort Washington (Cincinnati) at the head of an army ordered to subdue the Indian confederacy, which was led by Little Turtle. At modern Fort Wayne, in northeastern Indiana, the American troops came upon an Indian town on October 18. In a sharp struggle Harmar's men were defeated. Four days later the American army suffered a second defeat in the area. With his assignment thoroughly botched, Harmar marched back to Fort Washington. The campaign was a humiliating failure for the young United States government. *See* Fort Recovery; Indian Wars in the United States.

Fort William Henry (French and Indian War), 1757. The only major encounter during the fourth year of the war took place at Fort William Henry, near the southern end of Lake George. Striking south along lakes Champlain and George, Gen. Marquis Louis de Montcalm reached the American fort on August 4, 1757, with 4,000 French and Canadian troops, plus 1,000 Indians. The fort was held by a force of about 1,700 British and colonials commanded by Col. Monro. Taking the fort under fire with his artillery, Montcalm forced a surrender on August 9. Monro, with 1,400 survivors, was disarmed and allowed to retire southward to Fort Edward (Lyman). En route, however, the column was attacked by Montcalm's Indian allies, who killed 50 and carried off another 400 before the French regulars could establish order. *See* Oswego; Fort Ticonderoga I; French and Indian War.

"Forty-five, The." *See* Jacobite Insurrections.

Fort Zealandia (Chinese Pirate Wars), 1661–1662. The chief opposition to the Ch'ing (Manchu) dynasty, established in 1644, came from the Chinese pirate-general Cheng Ch'eng-kung, called Koxinga. Failing to overthrow the new regime, Koxinga turned on the Dutch in Formosa. In 1661 he laid siege to Fort Zealandia, near Tainan on the southwest coast. The fort surrendered the following year. This ended the Dutch rule of Formosa. (In 1683 Formosa was occupied by the Chinese government.) *See* Peking II.

Four Days' Battle. *See* Dover Strait.

Fourth Coalition, War of the. *See* Napoleonic Empire Wars.

France. The major battles and wars fought by the French nation are listed below. For earlier battles *see* Gallic Wars.

Soissons	486
Tolbiacum	496
Vouillé	507
Casilinum	554
Tertry	687
Toulouse I	721
Tours	732
Ravenna III	756
See Charlemagne, Conquests of	
Saucourt	881
Montfaucon	886
Val-'es-Dunes	1047
Gerberoi	1080
Tinchebray	1106
Brémule	1119
Gisors	1197
Château Gaillard	1203–1204
Rouen I	1204
Damme	1213
Muret	1213
Bouvines	1214
Saintes	1242
Courtrai	1302
Mons-en-Pévèle	1304
Cassel	1328
Laupen	1339
See Hundred Years War	
Clermont	1358
Roosebeke	1382
Saint Jacob-en-Birs	1444
Montlhéry	1465
Héricourt	1474
Grandson	1476
Morat	1476
Nancy	1477
Naples	1495
Fornovo	1495
Barletta	1502
Cerignola	1503
Garigliano River	1503
Agnadello	1509
Ravenna IV	1512
Novara I	1513
Guinegate	1513
Marignano	1515
La Bicocca	1522
Pavia V	1525
Boulogne	1544
Saint-Quentin I	1557
Calais II	1558
Gravelines	1558
See French Religious Wars	
Ré, Île de	1627
Castelnaudary	1632
See Thirty Years' War	
Faubourg Saint-Antoine	1652
Arras I	1654
Valenciennes	1656
Dunes	1658
See Louis XIV, Wars of	
See Polish Succession, War of the	
See Austrian Succession, War of the	
Arcot	1751
See French and Indian War; Seven Years' War	
See American Revolution, War of the	
See French Revolution, Wars of the	
See Napoleonic Empire Wars	
See Napoleon's Hundred Days	
Constantine	1837
Isly River	1844
Rome VII	1849
See Crimean War	
Magenta	1859
Solferino	1859
Mentana	1867
See Franco-Prussian War	
Paris III	1871
Tananarive	1895
See World War I	
See World War II	
Dienbienphu	1954
Sinai Peninsula	1956

France (World War II), 1940. After its overwhelming triumph in Flanders, the German army quickly wheeled to the south to knife into France itself. From the coast eastward to the front of the Maginot Line and then south to Switzerland, the Nazis aligned army groups "B," "A," and "C," commanded by Field Marshals Fedor von Bock, Karl von Rundstedt, and Wilhelm von Leeb, respectively. The French commander in chief, Gen. Maxime Weygand, improvised a line running east along the Somme and Aisne rivers and thence within the Maginot fortifications. But this front was longer than the original French frontier. And it could be only weakly held by the 65 divisions that remained after the disaster in Flanders, which had cost France more than a third of its strength (plus the loss of 9 of the 11 divisions of the British Expeditionary Force).

On June 5 the *Panzer*-led German armies, 140 divisions strong, began to grind forward irresistibly on a 100-mile front against the demoralized French. On the west, Bock's Fourth Army (Gunther von Kluge) drove to the Seine River at Rouen on June 9, while his Sixth Army (Walther von Reichenau) thrust down the Oise Valley north of Paris. With the collapse of the French Tenth Army in this sector, the Royal Navy evacuated 136,000

British and 20,000 Polish soldiers to England. In the center Rundstedt's three armies started forward on June 9. The Ninth (Maximilian von Weichs), Second (Strauss), and Twelfth (Siegmund List) were blocked briefly on and below the Aisne, but by June 12 Gen. Heinz Guderian's tanks were crossing the Marne at Châlons, while to the west, Gen. Paul von Kleist's armor was also bridging the Marne at Château-Thierry. When these two *Panzer* groups plunged forward, the French armies were hopelessly fragmented. In the west, Bock's armor raced south from the Seine to reach Cherbourg on June 18 and Brest and Nantes a day later. In the center Kleist's *Panzers* plunged to the Loire (at Nevers) and to Dijon on June 16 and then sped down the Rhone Valley to Lyon. To the east, Guderian's two corps of tanks struck past the rear of the Maginot Line to the Swiss border. The French abandoned their fortified positions on the night of June 14–15, allowing Leeb's First and Seventh armies to pour through into northeast France.

Meanwhile, on June 11, the French government declared Paris an open city and fled to Tours, and later Bordeaux. On June 14 the Nazi Eighteenth Army under Gen. Georg von Kuechler (victors in the Netherlands and the mop-up of Dunkirk) goose-stepped into the French capital. Three days later the aged marshed Henri Pétain, now premier of France, sued for peace. Earlier, on June 10, Mussolini had declared war on France and sent Italian troops toward the Riviera. The formal surrender of France took place at Compiègne on June 22.

Throughout the battle of France (as well as in the earlier fighting in Flanders and the Netherlands), the German *Luftwaffe* had conducted a devastating assault from the sky. Particularly effective were Hermann Goering's tactical fighters and Stuka dive bombers, which had closely supported the German ground attacks. In the five-week conquest of the West the German army lost 27,000 killed, 111,000 wounded, and 18,000 missing. French casualties were not reported, although the Nazis claimed to have taken 1,900,000 prisoners.

The all-victorious German *Wehrmacht* now stood supreme on the continent of Europe west of Russia. Only the island of Great Britain remained in opposition. A proposed German invasion of Britain, Operation Sea Lion, appeared next on the Nazi timetable, but any conquest of Britain would first have to mean winning control of the air. *See* Flanders; Britain (World War II); Normandy; World War II.

France, Northern (World War II), 1944. The Allied victory in the Falaise-Argentan Pocket and U.S. Gen. George Patton's racing armored columns farther east made the battle for Northern France a pursuit of retreating German forces. Allied plans called for trapping and annihilating as many Nazis as possible south of the Seine. This river proved to be a considerable obstacle to the fleeing forces of Field Marshal Walther Model because all its bridges had been destroyed by British and American aircraft.

With his right flank based on the Loire, Patton's Third Army swept past Le Mans on August 14. Three corps then raced northeast toward the Seine on either side of Paris. On August 16 Dreux and Orleans were liberated; Chartres fell on August 18. The XV Corps seized a bridge over the Seine at Mantes, west of Paris, the following day. During the next six days the XV and XII Corps crossed the Seine in force southeast of Paris. On August 23 Free French began an uprising in the capital city. Hurrying to their assistance, the French 2nd Armored Division (Gen. Jacques Leclerc) of the U.S. V Corps entered Paris on August 24. The former German conquerors were driven out 24 hours later. Gen. Charles de Gaulle set up French headquarters in Paris the same day.

Meanwhile on the Allied left, three armies had wheeled to the northeast and were advancing steadily toward the Seine. From the coast inland, they were the Canadian First (Henry Crerar), British Second (Miles Dempsey), and U.S. First (Courtney Hodges). The German units in front of these powerful forces were sent reeling across northern France. Only about 120 German tanks escaped across the Seine.

On the left of the Allied lines, Field Marshal Sir Bernard Montgomery's Twenty-first Army Group drove forward into the Low Countries. The Canadian First Army swept past the channel ports, which were mopped up between September 1 and 30, to reach Bruges, Belgium, on September 9. On the right of the Canadians, the British First Army took Amiens on August 31 (capturing the German army commander Hans Eberback), Brussels on September 3, and Antwerp the following day. Although the Germans had abandoned Antwerp, they clung to the Schelde estuary and thereby blocked use of the port.

Gen. Omar Bradley's Twelfth Army Group made equally good progress on the right side of the Allied line. The U.S. First Army pocketed 25,000 prisoners at Mons on September 3 and then drove into Namur, Liége, and Luxembourg, from September 5 to 10. On the right the U.S. Third Army raced through Reims and Châlons to take Verdun on September 1 and cross the Moselle west of Nancy six days later. On September 11 the U.S. Seventh Army (Alexander Patch), driving up the Rhone Valley, linked up with Patton's forces and entered the Allied line north of Switzerland. Far behind the advance to the German border, the

U.S. general William Simpson's new Ninth Army began the reduction of the German-held ports in Brittany.

Now, however, the Allied advance slowed because of ever-lengthening supply lines and increased German resistance as the Nazi armies fell back on their famed Siegfried Line, or Westwall. Before this battle began, Gen. Dwight Eisenhower had moved SHAEF (Supreme Headquarters, Allied Expeditionary Forces) to the Continent for direct control of operations. Four days later (September 5) Field Marshal Karl von Rundstedt was reinstated as top German commander on the Western Front. Nazi losses in France since D-day totaled 530,000. *See* Falaise-Argentan Pocket; France, Southern; Siegfried Line; World War II.

France, Southern (World War II), 1944. Ten weeks after the overpowering Allied invasion of northern France, a secondary landing was made on the French Mediterranean coast. Called Operation Dragoon (originally, Anvil), the invasion of southern France was designed to open the port of Marseilles. Allied forces were then to drive northward to threaten the flank and rear of the main German armies opposing Gen. Dwight Eisenhower's offensive along the Seine. Most of the Dragoon force consisted of battle-tested U.S. and French units from Italy.

On August 15, preceded by a small (8,000-man) U.S.-British parachutist drop, the Seventh Army under the U.S. general Alexander Patch (of Guadalcanal fame) landed on the beaches between Cannes and Toulon. The U.S. VI Corps (36th, 45th, 3rd Infantry) of Gen. Lucian Truscott established a firm beachhead against light German opposition and moved northwest toward the Rhone Valley.

The French II Corps, landing behind the Americans, struck west toward Toulon and Marseilles. Both these ports were liberated by August 28. When the French I Corps joined in the attack, a new Allied unit was created, the French First Army, under Gen. Jean de Lattre de Tassigny.

Meanwhile the veteran U.S. VI Corps raced northward up the Rhone Valley, pursuing and cutting off large segments of the German Nineteenth Army (Gen. Wiese). Grenoble was taken on August 24, Lyon on September 3. On September 11 the speeding VI Corps linked up with the right flank of Gen. George Patton's U.S. Third Army at Sombernon, northwest of Dijon. In 31 days the Dragoon force had covered some 270 miles and taken 57,000 prisoners of the German Nineteenth Army. In the bypassed triangle of southwestern France another 20,000 German troops (First Army) meekly surrendered. The U.S. Seventh and French First armies now came under Eisenhower's control, organized as the Sixth Army Group under the command of Gen. Jacob Devers. *See* France, Northern; Siegfried Line; World War II.

Franco-Prussian War (1870–1871). The third, and last, of the wars fought by Otto von Bismarck to forge a German empire was aimed at France. The French emperor, Napoleon III, was provoked into a declaration of war on July 15, 1870. Six weeks later the conflict was virtually ended by the overwhelming Prussian victory at Sedan. However, some French troops continued to resist until their government accepted peace terms on March 1, 1871 (the harsh terms helped lead to the revolt of the Paris Commune). The formal treaty signed at Frankfurt am Main on May 10 ceded Alsace and part of Lorraine (including Metz) to Prussia, now called Germany. A German army of occupation was imposed until an indemnity of five billion francs should be paid. (The last of the indemnity was paid off by September 1873.)

Wissembourg	1870
Wörth	1870
Spicheren	1870
Colombey	1870
Mars-la-Tour	1870
Gravelotte	1870
Metz	1870
Sedan	1870
Paris II	1870–1871
Coulmiers	1870
Bapaume	1871
Le Mans	1871
Saint-Quentin II	1871

Frankenhausen (German Peasants' Revolt), 1525. The political unrest of the Reformation produced a series of peasant revolts in Germany. In Thuringia Thomas Münzer led an uprising of Anabaptists against the nobility and clergy. An armed force from the ruling houses of Saxony, Hesse, and Brunswick trapped the rebellious peasants at Frankenhausen on May 15, 1525, and put them to rout. Münzer was captured and immediately hanged. This crushed the revolt. *See* Mühlberg.

Frankfort on the Oder (Thirty Years' War), 1631. The final defeat of Denmark's King Christian IV at Wolgast in 1628 seemed to conclude the Thirty Years' War. But it was the end only for the so-called Danish period of the conflict. The Swedish phase began two years later when King Gustavus II landed in Pomerania at the head of a well-trained army of 13,000 men. Gustavus, an ally of Bourbon France (Louis XIII), had taken up the Protestant cause against the Hapsburg Catholic forces of Holy Roman Emperor Ferdinand II. During the remainder of 1630 the Swedish king augmented his army by vigorous recruiting of Germans.

Meanwhile, John George I and George William, the Protestant electors of Saxony and Brandenburg, respectively, were also arming, determined at last to fight either for the Empire or with the king of Sweden. While they hesitated, Gustavus marched up the Oder in 1631, driving before him the Imperial army of Gen. Albrecht von Wallenstein. This army was now nominally under the command of Field Marshal the Count of Tilly, Wallenstein having been relieved by Ferdinand in August 1630.

By April 13 Gustavus was outside the city of Frankfort. Tilly, busy besieging Magdeburg, could send no relief. The Swedish army stormed into the city, killing, capturing, or scattering the remnants of eight Imperial regiments. The Swedish king's first major victory in Germany enabled him to replenish his supplies, but it had failed to distract the main Imperial army from its assault on Magdeburg, 150 miles to the west. *See* Wolgast; Magdeburg; Thirty Years' War.

Franklin (American Civil War), 1864. With Atlanta lost on September 1, the Confederate commander of the Army of Tennessee, Gen. John Hood, resolved to move northward, striking at Gen. William Sherman's 140 miles of communications back to Chattanooga. Hood marched rapidly, pausing only to jab at Federal detachments in Georgia, at Allatoona on October 5 and at Resaca on October 12. On October 31 the Confederates crossed the Tennessee River in northern Alabama. Sherman, who had been following, now turned back to Atlanta to organize his "march to the sea." General George Thomas, put in charge of containing Hood, ordered Gen. John Schofield to fall back toward Nashville. Hood now hurried into Tennessee to intercept Schofield. The latter withdrew across the Duck River at Columbia on November 27. Hood crossed upriver and both armies raced northward on almost parallel courses. At Spring Hill on November 29 the Confederates just missed blocking off the Federal retreat.

After an all-night march to escape the trap, Schofield reached Franklin, where he entrenched in front of the Harpeth River with some 32,000 troops. Hood closed up rapidly that afternoon (November 30) at the head of 38,000 Confederates who were eager for a battle. His initial assault opened a gap in the center of Schofield's line. But a determined counterattack led by Gen. Emerson Opdycke sealed off the penetration. For almost five hours Hood's men hammered at the Federal defenses without breaking through. By 9 P.M. the fighting had died down. The attackers had lost 6,252 men, including 12 general officers. Among the dead was the veteran division commander Patrick Cleburne. Federal casualties totaled 2,326. East of Franklin the Confederate cavalry of Gen. Nathan Forrest suffered a similar setback at the hands of Federal horsemen under Gen. James Wilson. That night Scholfield crossed the Harpeth to the safety of Nashville's lines, where Thomas assumed command. Hood followed but was too weak to make another assault. *See* Atlanta; Nashville; American Civil War.

Frastenz (Swiss-Swabian War), 1499. The doughty Swiss confederation of cantons fought its third frontier war in 22 years in 1499. It had repulsed Burgundy in the west in 1477 and Milan in the southeast the following year. Now its eastern boundary became disputed with Maximilian I, king of Germany and Holy Roman Emperor. Maximilian's army, composed chiefly of Germans from the medieval duchy of Swabia, occupied the Voralberg province of present-day western Austria. On April 20, 1499, the Swiss infantry came up against the Swabian position at Frastenz. The battle opened when one Swiss wing scaled a cliff left unguarded because it was believed inaccessible. Then the center charged in the customary relentless fashion. The Swabians fled in disorder from the deadly pikes and halberds. Two months later the opponents clashed again 55 miles to the southeast. *See* Giornico; Calven.

Frayser's Farm (American Civil War). The fourth major engagement, on June 30, 1862, in the Seven Days battle east of Richmond. *See* Seven Days.

Fredericksburg (American Civil War), 1862. For more than a month after the battle of Antietam Creek, the Federal general George McClellan remained in place north of the Potomac River. Finally, late in October, he began crossing the river, marching slowly southward. On November 7 President Lincoln, his patience exhausted, replaced McClellan with Gen. Ambrose Burnside. The new commander planned to threaten Richmond by moving to the Rappahannock River at Fredericksburg. He arrived there on November 17 but could not cross because of the lack of a pontoon train. The 400-foot-wide river was finally bridged on the night of December 10. Two days later the Army of the Potomac had moved to Fredericksburg, on the south bank of the Rappahannock, ready to attack Gen. Robert E. Lee's army on the hills overlooking the city. The long delay had enabled the Confederates to assemble a strength of 70,000 men. General James Longstreet's I Corps stood on Marye's Heights on the left (northwest). General Thomas (Stonewall) Jackson's II Corps held the right flank downstream.

On the morning of December 13 Burnside's Army of the Potomac, 120,000 strong, attacked. On the southeast Gen. William Franklin's Left Grand Division (I and VI Corps) drove through Jackson's first and second lines until halted by a vigorous counterattack about 1:30 P.M. The Confederates, in turn, were stopped by a storm of Federal artillery fire. Fighting in this sector then died down. Upstream, Gen. Edwin Sumner's Right

Grand Division (II and IX Corps) had to advance across an open field against Longstreet's artillery and heavy rifle fire. After more than two hours of cruel losses, the attackers withdrew out of range. Burnside then committed Gen. Joseph Hooker's Center Grand Division (III and V Corps) in a renewed assault on Marye's Heights late in the afternoon. Hooker sent three divisions forward, but they were easily repulsed. The day's fighting cost the Army of the Potomac 12,700 killed or wounded. Lee's Army of Northern Virginia, in a strong natural position, suffered 5,300 casualties.

Burnside wanted to launch another offensive the following day but was dissuaded by his Grand Division commanders. On the night of December 14–15 he withdrew across the river. Subsequent efforts to turn Lee's left flank by moving up the Rappahannock failed. On January 25 Burnside was relieved, as were Franklin and Sumner. Hooker became the new commander of the Army of the Potomac. *See* Antietam Creek; Chancellorsville; American Civil War.

Fredrikshald (Great Northern War), 1718. After his return to Sweden in 1714, Charles XII worked feverishly to rebuild his country's military strength. By 1718 the 36-year-old monarch was strong enough to invade Norway, then a possession of Denmark. Late in the year he laid siege to the fortress of Fredrikshald (Halden), near the modern Norwegian-Swedish border. But on December 11, while inspecting the front lines of his troops, Charles was fatally shot. The Swedish army promptly raised the siege.

The crown of Sweden then passed to the late king's sister, Ulrika Eleonora, and her husband, Frederick I of Hesse-Cassel. The new rulers were unable to cope with the coalition formed against their nation: Russia (Peter I), Prussia (Frederick William I), Poland and Saxony (Augustus II), and Denmark (Frederick IV). In 1720 and 1721 Sweden and its adversaries concluded the Great Northern War. Sweden gave up Stettin and western Pomerania to Prussia and its eastern Baltic lands, conquered by Gustavus II a hundred years earlier, to Russia. The chief result of the war was the destruction of Sweden's domination in the Baltic and the accompanying emergence of Russia as a European power. *See* Stralsund II; Great Northern War.

Freeman's Farm (War of the American Revolution). The first battle of Saratoga, on September 19, 1777, which checked Gen. John Burgoyne's advance toward Albany. *See* Saratoga.

Freiberg (Seven Years' War), 1762. By the fall of 1762, except for Prussia and Austria, all the combatants—Russia, Sweden, Great Britain, France—had formally or informally dropped out of the Seven Years' War. Frederick II, the Great, of Prussia and Maria Theresa of the Holy Roman Empire still maintained armies in Saxony. These war-weary forces were reluctant to fight. But on October 29 one last battle took place, at Freiberg, 21 miles southwest of Dresden. The Prussians were under the command of the king's brother, Prince Henry Ludwig, and Gen. Friedrich von Seydlitz. In a minor action with few casualties, the Prussians drove back an Imperial army of Austrians and Saxons. This encounter ended the long, bitter war. In the Treaty of Hubertusburg, signed on February 15, 1763, Prussia retained Silesia, while Saxony remained an electorate of the Holy Roman Empire. *See* Manila I; Burkersdorf; Seven Years' War.

Freiburg (Thirty Years' War), 1644. The Bavarian army of the Holy Roman Empire (Ferdinand III) opened the 1644 campaign by besieging Freiburg in Baden, 80 miles southwest of Stuttgart, on June 27. The Imperial force of 15,000 men, commanded by Field Marshal Baron Franz von Mercy, was too strong for the French marshal the Vicomte de Turenne to attack. He had to await reinforcements from northern France under Louis II, the Great Condé (duc d'Enghien), victor at Rocroi the previous year. When Condé arrived, the united French army crossed the Rhine and on August 3 launched a double attack against Mercy's lines. (Freiburg had surrendered at the end of July.) Turenne with 6,000 men tried to work around to the rear of the Imperials. The steep and wooded hillsides of the Black Forest made progress so slow that the turning movement could not be completed. Nevertheless, Condé launched his frontal assault with 10,000 men at the prearranged hour, 4 P.M. Although checked initially, the French continued to press forward until they seized the entrenchments to their front, by nightfall. Under cover of darkness, Mercy withdrew to a new line of fortifications.

The French waited a day for reinforcements to come up. Then, on August 5, Condé and Turenne renewed their attack on Freiburg. Although faulty coordination made the assault piecemeal, the French battled furiously against a fierce Bavarian defense. At the end of the day Mercy still held the city, though he had lost a third of his force. French casualties were 50 percent.

Despite the costly French failure, Condé and Turenne still had the advantage of superior lines of supply. When, on August 10, they moved to blockade the Imperials, Mercy withdrew in good order and fell back to Rothenburg on the Tauber. Here his Bavarians were screened off by Turenne's cavalry, while Condé cleared the Rhine from Basel to Coblenz. This ended the campaigning in 1644. *See* Tuttlingen; Jankau; Thirty Years' War.

French and Indian War (1754–1763). The American phase of what would become the Seven Years' War in Europe opened with the defeat of

Lt. Col. George Washington's Virginia troops by the French at Fort Necessity in 1754. The following year the French and Indian War formally began. In this conflict American colonial troops fought alongside English regulars against an alliance of French, Canadians, and Indians. The war in the colonies reached a climax with the decisive English victory at Quebec in 1759. Two minor battles followed before the fighting died out. Three years later the 1763 Treaty of Paris ended both the American and European wars. Great Britain stood supreme in North America. For terms of the treaty *see* Seven Years' War.

Fort Necessity	1754
Beauséjour	1755
Monongahela River	1755
George, Lake	1755
Oswego	1756
Fort William Henry	1757
Fort Ticonderoga I	1758
Louisbourg II	1758
Fort Frontenac	1758
Fort Niagara	1759
Quebec I	1759
Quebec II	1760
Montreal	1760

French Religious Wars (1562–1628). A religious-political struggle between Roman Catholics and Huguenots produced a series of civil wars in France. This conflict broke the military power of the Huguenots.

Dreux	1562
Saint-Denis	1567
Jarnac	1569
Moncontour	1569
Coutras	1587
Arques	1589
Ivry-la-Bataille	1590
La Rochelle II	1627–1628

French Revolution, Wars of the (1792–1802). The Legislative Assembly, which had assumed the Revolutionary power in France in 1791, became the target of a Prussian-Austrian alliance the following February. These powers were joined by Sardinia (Piedmont), Great Britain, the Netherlands, Spain, Naples, and the Papal States, to form the First Coalition. The war opened in 1792 with the French victory over Prussia at Valmy. Under the National Convention (1792–1795) France drove first Prussia and then Spain out of the war. The Piedmont, Naples, and the Papal States were overrun. Against Austria (which was acting in behalf of the Holy Roman Empire), Great Britain, and the Netherlands, the Directory (1795–1799) prosecuted the war in Germany, at sea, and, under Napoleon Bonaparte, in Italy and Egypt. Austria left the war in 1797, but Russia joined Great Britain the following year. When Austria, Naples, Portugal, and the Ottoman Empire also entered the conflict, the War of the Second Coalition took shape. Russia withdrew in 1799. This phase ended when the Ottomans, Austria, and Naples (in 1800 and 1801) and Great Britain (in 1802) made peace with France. The French stood supreme on land, Britain on the seas. Meanwhile, Napoleon had become first consul in 1799. Five years later he would be crowned Napoleon I, emperor of France. For subsequent battles *see* Napoleonic Empire Wars.

First Coalition

Valmy	1792
Jemappes	1792
Neerwinden II	1793
Toulon III	1793
Hondschoote	1793
Wattignies	1793
Tourcoing	1794
Ushant II	1794
Fleurus III	1794
Quiberon	1795
Loano	1795
Montenotte	1796
Dego	1796
Mondovì	1796
Lodi Bridge	1796
Mantua	1796–1797
Lonato	1796
Castiglione delle Stiviere	1796
Amberg	1796
Würzburg	1796
Caliano	1796
Bassano	1796
Caldiero I	1796
Arcole	1796
Rivoli Veronese	1797
Saint Vincent Cape II	1797
Malborghetto	1797
Neuwied	1797
Camperdown	1797

French Expedition to Egypt

Pyramids	1798
Nile River	1798
Malta II	1798–1800

Second Coalition

Acre III	1799
Stockach I	1799
Magnano	1799
Cassano d'Adda II	1799
Zurich I	1799
Trebbia River II	1799
Abukir	1799
Novi Ligure	1799
Bergen op Zoom II	1799
Zurich II	1799
Alkmaar II	1799
Stockach II	1800
Montebello	1800
Marengo	1800
Höchstädt II	1800
Hohenlinden	1800

Great Britain Fights On Alone

Alexandria III 1801

Copenhagen I 1801

Frenchtown (War of 1812), 1813. After the loss of Detroit and Fort Dearborn in August 1812, the American forces in the Old Northwest fell back to the line of the Maumee and Wabash rivers. An alarmed U.S. government assigned Gen. William Henry Harrison to retake Detroit. Early in 1813 Harrison launched an offensive around the western end of Lake Erie with a force of Kentuckians commanded by Gen. James Winchester. Winchester reached Frenchtown (later renamed Monroe, Mich.) at the mouth of the Raisin River, 35 miles below Detroit, on January 22. But here he was defeated by a British and Canadian force under Col. Henry Proctor. Some 500 Americans were captured and another 400 killed in the battle or later massacred by Indians.

While Harrison reorganized his army, the British and Indians, under the Shawnee chief Tecumseh, pressed forward to Fort Meigs at the mouth of the Maumee on May 1. After a siege of eight days, stubborn American resistance drove off the attackers. Harrison, however, could not take the offensive as long as the British controlled Lake Erie. *See* Detroit; Erie, Lake; War of 1812.

Friedland (Napoleonic Empire Wars), 1807. The relentless pressure of French marching columns forced the Russian commander, Gen. Levin Bennigsen, back toward his Königsberg (Kaliningrad) base in June 1807. As the Russian army of 60,000 men crossed to the left (west) bank of the Alle River at Friedland (Pravdinsk), it was suddenly confronted by 26,000 French troops under Marshal Jean Lannes. Here, 27 miles southeast of Königsberg, Bennigsen attacked early on June 14. Seizing upon this chance encounter, Napoleon I hurriedly massed his columns to force a major battle. Meanwhile, Lannes, outnumbered more than 2 to 1, fought off the Russian attacks of Prince Pëtr Bagration for nine hours—a tremendous feat of military skill.

By 5 P.M. 80,000 French troops had arrived and deployed west of Friedland. From the south, Marshal Michel Ney's VI Corps jumped off against the Russian left flank and quickly rolled it back along the Alle. Outside Friedland Ney was stopped cold. But Gen. Claude Victor's I Corps rushed up to anchor Ney's left flank. Victor's chief of artillery now pushed forward 30 guns to blast the enemy at a point-blank range of 120 yards. Packed into the tiny village and unable to cross to the west bank in any great number, the Russians suffered cruelly from the volleys of canister and grape. Within two hours all of Bennigsen's troops in Friedland had been killed, captured, or driven into the river.

Darkness ended the fighting with 1,372 French dead, 9,108 wounded, 55 captured. The Russians lost 11,000 dead, 7,000 wounded, and unknown thousands drowned. Bennigsen's army was shattered and in flight, the general himself cowed and broken. (But the battle had an ill omen for France; for the first time the Grande Armée needed important detachments of foreign troops—Poles, Dutch, Saxons, Italians, South Germans—to supplement its French contingents).

As Napoleon's weary troops started slowly in pursuit of the Russians to the northeast, Marshal Nicolas Soult occupied Königsberg on June 16. A week later Czar Alexander I negotiated a truce. On June 25, on a raft in the Niemen River, Napoleon met the czar and King Frederick William III of Prussia to draw up the Treaty of Tilsit. Prussia ceded all territory west of the Elbe (which was formed into the French-dominated Kingdom of Westphalia), and both losers recognized the new Grand Duchy of Warsaw, carved out of their previous dismemberment of Poland. Napoleon stood supreme over all of continental Europe except Scandinavia and Portugal (and soon, Spain). *See* Heilsberg; Saragossa II; Napoleonic Empire Wars.

Fronde, Wars of the. *See* Faubourg Saint-Antoine.

Frontiers of France (World War I), 1914. In the first three weeks of the war the huge German turning movement aimed at Paris crunched through Belgium almost to the French border. On August 20 the German offensive (the Schlieffen Plan) of Field Marshal Helmuth von Moltke ran head on into the initial French offensive (Plan 17), directed by Gen. Joseph Joffre. For five days the hostile armies were locked in combat from the Swiss boundary westward to Mons, Belgium. This struggle along the frontiers facing France—Germany, Luxembourg, Belgium—gave the battle its name. It also introduced the grand tactics of World War I—the simultaneous massing of troops on a scale never before employed. In this battle alone, Germany sent seven armies into action; France, five; and Great Britain (allied with France), one. Across the entire front Germany had a 1½ to 1 superiority in manpower, and on its right wing the advantage stood at almost 2 to 1. From east to west the battle of the Frontiers fell into four separate but interlocking engagements: Lorraine, Ardennes, Charleroi (sometimes called the battle of the Sambre), Mons.

Lorraine. On the extreme eastern end of the front a French advance into Lorraine by the First (Auguste Dubail) and Second (Noël de Castelnau) armies was checked at Sarrebourg and Morhange, respectively. Here the German Seventh (Josias von Heeringen) and Sixth armies, both under Crown Prince Rupprecht of Bavaria, threw back the attack with heavy losses. Then on August 23 Rupprecht launched a counteroffensive toward Epinal. The French fell back to the line of the Moselle—

Épinal, Charmes, Nancy, Toul. Here they held on grimly until the decisive battle of the Marne opened on September 5.

Ardennes. In the center of the front Joffre sent the Third (Gen. Ruffey) and Fourth (Fernand Langle de Cary) French armies into the heavily wooded hills of the Ardennes. This was the key movement of Plan 17—to smash the German center and thus outflank the enemy turning maneuver through Belgium. As the French armies groped through thick fog on the morning of August 21, they struck two German armies on the move toward them. This German force was the pivot of Moltke's right wing in the southern Ardennes, the Fifth Army of Crown Prince Friedrich Wilhelm, who also directed the Fourth Army of the Duke of Württemberg in the northern Ardennes. After two days of furious fighting both French armies retreated, the Third to Verdun, the Fourth to Stenay and Sedan. Friedrich Wilhelm pressed beyond Longwy on August 23, leaving the fortress to be taken by siege troops. A week later Joffre replaced Ruffey as Third Army commander with Gen. Maurice Sarrail. To the west the French Fourth Army checked the German Fourth on the Meuse during August 26–28, but this stout resistance opened a gap of 50 miles between it and the Fifth Army, farther west. Joffre plugged this hole with three corps under Gen. Ferdinand Foch (which, on the eve of the first battle of the Marne, on September 5, became the French Ninth Army).

Charleroi. On the western end of the front the French Fifth Army of Gen. Charles Lanrezac faced the stiffest challenge. To the northeast the German Third Army of Gen. Max von Hausen, which had taken Dinant, Belgium, on August 15, pushed up the Meuse River, threatening the French right flank. To the northwest Gen. Karl von Bülow's German Second Army, dropping off troops to besiege Namur, forced two crossings of the Sambre River between Namur and Charleroi, 21 miles to the southwest, on August 21. A day later Bülow captured Charleroi, which lies on both sides of the Sambre. Here Lanrezac's troops fought fiercely to stop the Germans but failed and had to retreat to the south. This withdrawal opened a ten-mile gap between the French left and the British Expeditionary Force (BEF) just getting into position at Mons. That night (August 22–23) Hausen bridged the Meuse and began striking westward into the right flank of the French Fifth Army (left open by the retirement of the Fourth Army from the Ardennes area). Only a general retreat, started on the night of August 23, extricated Lanrezac's men from a mortal trap. His X Corps alone lost 5,000 men on the Sambre. After a long retreat southward, Lanrezac turned on Bülow and counterattacked sharply toward Guise on August 29. This checked Bülow's advance along the Oise River for 36 hours, but the continuation of the panicky British withdrawal on the left (and the defeat of the Fourth Army on the Meuse to their right) forced the Fifth Army to resume its retreat the next day.

Mons. On the extreme left (west) of the Allied line, 35 miles beyond Charleroi, the four-division BEF (70,000 men, 300 guns) of Field Marshal Sir John French had crossed into Belgium to take up a position at Mons. The British were still moving up behind the 60-foot-wide Mons Canal on August 23 when they were slammed into by the German First Army of Gen. Alexander von Kluck. With 160,000 men and 600 guns, Kluck's army was carrying out the wide turning movement of the Schlieffen Plan through Belgium. Despite the more than 2-to-1 disadvantage in numbers, the BEF held its ground for nine hours before pulling back in the evening. Most of the British defense had rested upon the two divisions of the II Corps (Gen. Horace Smith-Dorrien) west of Mons. In all, the British suffered 4,244 casualties, at a gain of only one day's delay in Kluck's advance.

Thus ended the four-day battle of the Frontiers —a catastrophic defeat for France and its British ally, which left the northern frontier breached at every point of German attack. During the sprawling struggle, about 1,250,000 French troops took part, suffering more than 300,000 casualties. German losses were comparable. For the number of men engaged and for the rate and number of casualties in one four-day span, this was the greatest battle of the war. *See* Namur II; Le Cateau; Marne River I; World War I.

Front Royal (American Civil War), 1862. From his victory at McDowell on May 8, Gen. Thomas (Stonewall) Jackson turned his hard-marching Confederates back into the Shenandoah Valley. Bypassing the main Federal army of Gen. Nathaniel Banks at Strasburg, Jackson crossed Massanutten Mountain and moved quickly down the east side of the valley. En route, he picked up Gen. Richard Ewell's division at Luray, to give him a strength of 16,000 men. On May 23 the entire Confederate force suddenly struck the isolated Federal position at Front Royal, east of Strasburg. In addition to having overwhelming numbers, Jackson's army knew—from reports of the 19-year-old spy Belle Boyd—the exact deployment of the defending Union troops. The Confederates swept into the town, killing, wounding, or capturing 904 of the 1,063-man garrison. Colonel John Kenly, the Federal commander, was wounded and taken prisoner. Confederate losses were less than 50. Many supplies fell into the victors' hands but were lost when a pursuing Federal force routed Jackson's rear guard at Front Royal on May 30. *See* McDowell; Winchester I; American Civil War.

Fuentes de Oñoro (Napoleonic Empire Wars), 1811. The retreat of the French army from the Lisbon area in the spring of 1811 completed the British liberation of Portugal. General Lord Wellington (Arthur Wellesley) then prepared a two-pronged invasion of French-held Spain. To take the southern route to Madrid, he sent an army under Gen. Sir William Carr Beresford (later Lord Beresford). Wellington himself led the approach along the northern route. With some 30,000 British and Portuguese troops he marched eastward to Almeida, near the Spanish frontier. Finding the town strongly held by a French detachment, Wellington began a careful investment. The French commander in this sector, Marshal André Masséna, moved out from his Ciudad Rodrigo base with 30,000 men to relieve Almeida. Wellington took up a strong position at Fuentes de Oñoro, ten miles to the south. Here Masséna attacked on May 5. In a hard-fought battle, the British army held its ground at a cost of 1,500 casualties. Masséna, who suffered a loss of 2,200 men, finally marched back to his base. Wellington promptly seized Almeida and awaited reports from his southern offensive. *See* Bussaco; La Albuera; Napoleonic Empire Wars.

Fulford (Rise of Britain), 1066. The fateful year of 1066 opened for Britain with the death of Edward the Confessor on January 5. His brother-in-law and chief minister became King Harold II the following day. The new ruler was soon faced with two separate attempts to invade England, one in the northeast and one in the south. The first invasion came in the northeast from King Harold III Hardrada of Norway, aided by the English king's exiled half brother Tostig, former earl of Northumbria.

On September 20 the invaders sailed up the Humber and landed at Fulford, two miles south of York. Here they were attacked by troops from Mercia and Northumbria led by the earls Edwin and Morcar. The Norsemen routed their English opponents. Harold II, waiting in London to see which invasion would strike first, now marched quickly northward to try to reverse the Fulford decision. But the losses suffered by the English earls would keep their troops out of this next battle and the even more crucial engagement shaping up at Hastings the following month. *See* Ashingdon; Stamford Bridge; Hastings.

Fürth (Thirty Years' War), 1632. The defeat of the Holy Roman Empire army at Rain and the mortal wounding of its commander, the Count of Tilly, forced Emperor Ferdinand II to recall to service Gen. Albrecht von Wallenstein. From his Bohemian headquarters the coldly efficient Wallenstein assembled a powerful Catholic army of 50,000 men. On May 25 he reoccupied Prague, the Swedish-allied Saxon force under Baron Hans Georg von Arnim falling back into Silesia without a battle by June 7. Wallenstein then marched westward into Germany to link up with the battered army of the Catholic League, now commanded by the elector of Bavaria himself, Maximilian I. The two forces joined up southwest of Nürnberg on July 11. In the latter city Gustavus II, the Swedish king who had united most of Protestant Germany behind him, faced a desperate choice. He had now to remain in the city and risk starvation or to attack the combined Catholic army, which outnumbered his Swedish-German force. Wallenstein, who had assumed supreme field command, crowded his opponent by entrenching on a ridge at Fürth, overlooking the Rednitz River, five miles northwest of Nürnberg.

Gustavus called in all possible reinforcements to bring his army up to about 40,000 men, almost the equal of Wallenstein's. Then, on September 3, the king ordered an assault on the Catholics at Fürth. The attack failed to win the position. It was renewed the following day but was again repulsed. In this two-day battle (sometimes called the Alte Veste) Gustavus lost more than 2,000 men. The defender's losses were somewhat less. The king's position had now become alarming. Finally, on September 18, he risked an attack on the march by abandoning Nürnberg and retreating to the southeast. But Wallenstein did not follow. Instead he headed northeast to plunder Saxony, hoping to split the elector of Saxony, John George I, away from his Swedish alliance. Maximilian took his much smaller force home to Bavaria. *See* Rain; Lützen I; Thirty Years' War.

G

Gaeta (Italian Wars of Independence), 1860–1861. When King Francis II was chased out of Naples on September 7, 1860, he set up the government of the Two Sicilies in Gaeta, on the west coast about halfway to Rome. (Rome itself was garrisoned by French troops in support of Pope Pius IX.) Giuseppe Garibaldi with his thousand Redshirts, plus several thousand other Italians, marched toward Gaeta. The Neapolitan army of Francis tried to hold the line of the Volturno River but was beaten back on October 1. Garibaldi occupied Capua. The Italian army of unification then closed in on Gaeta. Finding the city strongly defended, the Italians began a siege on November 3, directed by the Piedmontese colonel Enrico Cialdini. Offshore the French fleet, although ostensibly neutral, prevented an attack on Gaeta by sea. Finally this fleet withdrew on January 19, 1861. Cialdini then tightened the investment of Gaeta, which capitulated on February 13. Francis abdicated and went into exile, ending the rule of the Neapolitan Bourbons. Cialdini was honored for his victory by being named Duca di Gaeta.

Even before the collapse of the kingdom of the Two Sicilies, both Naples and Sicily (as well as other Italian states) had voted by plebiscite to unite with Piedmont, ruled by Victor Emmanuel II. Now on March 17 the first Italian parliament to be convened proclaimed the kingdom of Italy under Victor Emmanuel II. But Rome, not included in the new nation, continued to be a cause of unrest. *See* Castelfidardo; Aspromonte; Italian Wars of Independence.

Gaines' Mill (American Civil War). A successful Confederate attack on June 27, 1862, the third day of the Seven Days battle east of Richmond. *See* Seven Days.

Galicia (World War I), 1914. The dual monarchy of Austria-Hungary began its World War I operations on two fronts—a secondary attack against Serbia, which was repulsed, and a major effort against Russia from Austria's easternmost province of Galicia. The Austrian commander, Field Marshal Count Conrad von Hötzendorf, concentrated three armies, and later a fourth, northeast of the Carpathian Mountains. Misjudging a simultaneous Russian offensive in this area, Conrad von Hötzendorf sent his First and Fourth armies northward toward the railroad line through Lublin. On August 23 the Austrian First collided with the Russian Fourth at Kraśnik, 28 miles southwest of Lublin. In three days of fighting the Russians were pushed back. Southeast of Lublin the Austrian Fourth Army enjoyed a similar success against the Russian Fifth Army at Komarów, during August 26–September 1.

Meanwhile, to the south, the Austrian Third Army had advanced eastward to the Gnila (Gnilaya) Lipa River, a tributary of the Dniester. But between August 26 and 30 the Austrians were hurled back by the Russian Third and Eighth armies. It was in this area that the Russian commander in Galicia, Gen. Nikolai Ivanov, was making his primary attack. With a numerical advantage of 3 to 1, the Russians pressed on westward, capturing the fortress city of Lemberg (Lvov) on September 3. The Austrian Second Army, arriving from the Serbian front, came into line on the Austrian right (south) flank but was promptly pushed back, as were the Third and Fourth armies to the north. The collapse of the Austrians in this sector opened a 40-mile gap in Conrad von Hötzendorf's line at Rava Russkaya, 32 miles northwest of Lemberg. On September 9 the Russian Fifth Army began pouring through this hole, isolating the Austrian First Army to the northwest. All four Austrian armies now began a general retreat, which did not end until they had reached the slopes of the Carpathians, 100 miles away, on September 26. In all, Conrad von Hötzendorf lost 350,000 men (including 120,000 by capture), which was about two-thirds of his attacking force. This total included 100,000 men shut up in Przemyśl, 54 miles west of Lemberg, which held out until relieved on October 11. (On November 6 Przemyśl again came under Russian siege and this time capitulated, on March 22, 1915, with a loss of 100,000 men and 1,000 guns.) The appalling loss of trained officers in Galicia crippled the Austrian army for the remainder of the war. Russian casualties were heavy too, but their number has never been recorded.

Ivanov's decisive victory in Galicia opened the way for a Russian offensive westward toward Cracow (Kraków), gateway to Silesia. To forestall this threat, the newly organized German Ninth Army was rushed by rail into southern Poland. *See* Gumbinnen; Vistula River–Warsaw; World War I.

Gallic Wars (58–52 B.C.). A member of the First Triumvirate of Rome, Julius Caesar took an army into Gaul to enrich himself and to create a military reputation that would outshine that of his consular rivals, Pompey the Great and Marcus Licinius Crassus. Caesar subdued the barbaric tribes he found in modern France and even crossed the English Channel to defeat a Briton army in 54 B.C.

Bibracte	58 B.C.
Vesontio	58 B.C.
Sambre River	57 B.C.
Morbihan Gulf	56 B.C.
Coblenz	55 B.C.
Verulamium I	54 B.C.
Tongres	54 B.C.
Avaricum	52 B.C.
Gergovia	52 B.C.
Agendicum	52 B.C.
Alesia	52 B.C.

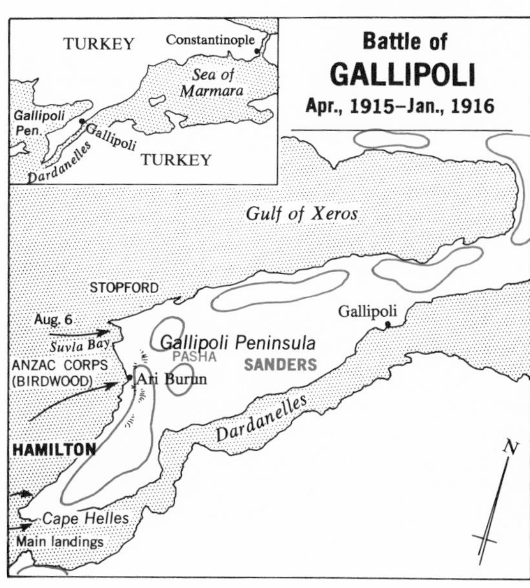

Gallipoli (World War I), 1915–1916. Following the abortive naval attack on the Dardanelles on March 18, 1915, the British and French allies determined to open the precious waterway by a land campaign. While the expedition was being organized, the German general Otto Liman von Sanders, in charge of the Turkish defenses in this area, skillfully deployed the Fifth Army of 60,000 men around the entrances to the Dardanelles. Meanwhile the Allied expedition of Gen. Sir Ian Hamilton staged at Alexandria, Egypt, and then, on April 21, at Lemnos Island. Four days later Hamilton's force (75,000 men) made two amphibious landings at the southern tip of Gallipoli Peninsula, on the European side of the Dardanelles. The main force (Sir Aylmer Hunter-Weston) came ashore in five parties at Cape Helles, on the extreme tip of the peninsula. Although Turkish resistance was only sporadic, poor coordination among the landing parties held the 35,000 invaders on the beaches the first day. Farther up the west coast, the Anzac Corps of 17,000 men (Sir William Birdwood) landed a mile north of its objective at Ari Burun. Pressing inland, the Australian–New Zealand force was soon checked by a Turkish counterattack launched by Col. Mustafa Kemal (later Kemal Atatürk). Here too the Allies were still on the beaches at the end of the first day.

For almost two weeks neither Allied force could push far enough inland to drive the Turks off the heights commanding the beaches. At the same time Liman von Sanders could not drive the invaders into the sea. By May 8 the stalemate was firm, Hamilton having lost almost a third of his army in the total casualties from Cape Helles and Ari Burun, now called Anzac Cove. After considerable controversy (Winston Churchill, who had conceived the operation, was dropped from the cabinet), the British government decided to strengthen the Gallipoli force. The Helles army was increased to four British and two French divisions, the Anzac force to three divisions. Another two divisions (25,000 men) were landed north of Anzac Cove, at Suvla Bay, on August 6.

During the new landing operation, the 35,000 Allied troops at Helles made a secondary attack on the Turkish lines to their front, while Birdwood's 37,000 men drove eastward in the primary offensive. The Turks held firm everywhere. At Suvla Bay, however, the corps of Gen. Sir Frederick Stopford landed without serious opposition and had a golden opportunity to thrust inland behind the Turkish defenses at Anzac Cove. But a three-day hesitation on the beaches allowed the Turks to rush up reinforcements. When Stopford did attack on August 9, he was stopped cold.

The new stalemate dragged on until November 22, when Hamilton was relieved by Gen. Sir Charles Monro. The new commander, who was also directing the Salonika campaign, put Birdwood in charge of Gallipoli. Finally, with the consent of London, the operation was called off. The Suvla Bay and Anzac Cove troops were evacuated by sea on December 20, the Cape Helles force by January 9. Not a single life was lost in the withdrawal. But over all, the mismanaged battle had cost the British and French some 250,000 casualties out of the 410,000 British and 70,000 French landed at Gallipoli. Turkish losses were equally high. However, a stout defense had held the Dardanelles and effectively blocked all aid to Russia by this route. *See* Dardanelles; World War I.

Garigliano River (French-Spanish Wars in Italy), 1503. After a succession of reverses in southern Italy, the French army of Louis XII fell back across the Garigliano River in November 1503. But the Spanish army of Ferdinand (V of Castile, II of Aragon), commanded by the great captain Gonzalo de Córdoba, stayed in pursuit despite the winter weather. On December 28, 15,000 Spanish infantry crossed the Garigliano River at two points and fell on the French camp. As before, the short thrusting sword and the fire of the arquebuses cut down the Swiss pikemen and other foot soldiers of France. The Spanish inflicted several thousand casualties among their more numerous foe, capturing the French artillery train and baggage.

The decisive defeat on the Garigliano forced Louis XII to sue for peace. He acceded to Spanish rule over the kingdom of Naples (Ferdinand added the III of Naples to his titles) in return for continued French control over Milan in the north. *See* Cerignola; Agnadello; Oran I.

Gaugamela (Macedonian Conquests). A plain northeast of Arbela that was the site of the decisive battle between Alexander III, the Great, and the Persian army of Darius III. *See* Arbela-Gaugamela.

Gaul, Caesar's Conquest of. *See* Gallic Wars.

Gaza I (Macedonian Conquests), 332 B.C. Two months after reducing Tyre, Alexander (III) the Great's Macedonian army reached Gaza, 150 miles south on the Mediterranean coast. An important junction of Near East trade routes, Gaza was defended by a Persian garrison commanded by Batis. Alexander laid siege to the city. When the wall surrounding Gaza proved too strong to be breached by ram or bore, the Macedonian conqueror built a 250-foot-high mound at the base of the fortification. From this height the "engines of war" previously used at Tyre catapulted missiles and incendiaries into the city. After three months of bombardment, Gaza yielded to Alexander's assault. The garrison was executed.

The route to Egypt now lay open. Alexander marched unopposed into the Persian-held kingdom, and through the year 332, Macedonian troops occupied the settlements of the lower Nile. On the delta of the great river a new city, Alexandria, was founded. *See* Tyre II; Arbela-Gaugamela; Macedonian Conquests.

Gaza II (World War I), 1917. The British army of Gen. Sir Archibald Murray had no sooner occupied El 'Arish, on December 20, 1916, when it was ordered to invade Palestine. To clear the way, Murray struck at the two Turkish outposts of Magdhaba and Rafa standing between the British and the Palestine frontier, 27 miles to the northeast. In these two actions, on December 23 and January 9, the British (largely Australians and New Zealanders) captured a total of 2,900 prisoners at a loss to themselves of less than 550 casualties.

Extending their railroad and water pipeline, which reached back to the Suez Canal, Murray's army advanced on Gaza early in 1917. Here stood a strong defensive position, manned by about 16,000 Turks under the German colonel Baron Friedrich Kress von Kressenstein. The British attack was entrusted to Gen. Sir Charles Dobell. On March 26 Dobell sent two cavalry divisions under Gen. Sir Philip Chetwode east and north of the town to cut off possible Turkish reinforcements. At the same time the 53rd Infantry Division assaulted the Ali Muntar ridge overlooking Gaza. At first the combined attack went well. But with victory in sight, Chetwode's cavalry mistakenly withdrew. This exposed the right flank of the infantry, forcing a similar withdrawal from Ali Muntar. The attack was resumed on the following day, but now it was too late. The reinforced Turkish garrison drove back the British, inflicting a total of 4,000 casualties. Turkish losses during the two-day battle were 2,400.

On April 17 the Murray-Dobell team made a new attack on the strengthened Turkish lines, which now reached from Gaza southeast to Beersheba. Assaulting, three divisions abreast on a wide front, the British were checked with small gains all along the line. Continuing the offensive resulted only in heavier casualties. On the evening of the third day (April 9) the battle was called off. The British pulled back with a loss of 6,444 men. Turkish casualties numbered only about 2,000.

After the second failure to take Gaza, Murray relieved Dobell. But on June 28 he himself was replaced by Gen. Sir Edmund Allenby from the Western Front. *See* Rumani; Gaza III; World War I.

Gaza III (World War I), 1917. When Gen. Sir Edmund Allenby took over the British army in southern Palestine, he was reinforced to a total of seven divisions (88,000 men, largely Australians and New Zealanders). The Turkish troops that held the 25-mile line from Gaza southeast to Beersheba numbered 35,000. They were advised by Gen. Erich von Falkenhayn, former head of the German armies on the Western Front. Profiting from the failure of two previous British attacks against Gaza, Allenby concentrated five of his divisions against the Turkish left flank at Beersheba. On October 31 the British suddenly struck Beersheba from both west and east. In an all-day battle the Turkish Seventh Army was driven back and the front rolled up westward toward Gaza as far as Tell Esh Sheria. Aiding the

British victory were eight tanks, the only ones employed outside France in the war.

Meanwhile, along the coast, the British holding operation against Gaza was steadily increased in intensity, supported by naval gunfire from ships offshore. This mounting pressure forced the Turks to shift some troops westward to Gaza. Then, on November 6, Allenby struck again on the east front, crumbling the defenses at Tell Esh Sheria and pushing his cavalry toward the coast behind the Turkish Eighth Army. In danger of being cut off, the Gaza defenders evacuated the town the next day and fell back northward to Junction Station, west of Jerusalem. Allenby pursued vigorously, storming into Junction Station on November 14 and into Jaffa, 35 miles northwest of Jerusalem, two days later. Pausing only a few days to regroup, Allenby renewed his northward drive until Jerusalem was outflanked. On December 9 the Holy City fell into British hands without a battle. *See* Gaza II; Megiddo III; World War I.

Gazala (World War II), 1942. On January 21, two weeks after the British Eighth Army had pursued his *Panzerarmee Afrika* back to El Agheila, Libya, the German general Erwin Rommel turned and counterattacked in western Cyrenaica. General Neil Ritchie's British forces retreated or were overrun. In four days the newly arrived 1st Armoured disintegrated under German fire. Benghazi, stocked with supplies for the projected British invasion of Tripolitania, fell on January 29. Six days later the Eighth Army stabilized a defensive line at Gazala, shielding Tobruk. Here it held for almost four months, Gen. W. H. E. Gott's XIII Corps (infantry) on the right along the coast, Gen. Willoughby Norrie's XXX Corps (armor) on the left, inland as far as Bir Hacheim.

On May 26 Rommel's three armored divisions (500 tanks) of his *Afrika Korps* swept around Bir Hacheim 45 miles inland and then turned north, smashing into the British left flank and rear. For two weeks XXX Corps fought furiously but piecemeal and in a disorganized manner. General Frank Messervy of 7th Armoured was twice captured by the Germans and twice escaped. On June 12–13, Gen. Pierre Koenig's Free French were driven out of the inland anchor of Bir Hacheim. Then British armor suffered the greatest defeat in its history, losing 250 of 300 tanks. There followed the so-called Gazala Gallop, as Eighth Army remnants fought their way free and fled back across the Egyptian border. In a major tactical error, Ritchie left the 2nd South African to hold out in Tobruk. This fortress, which had withstood more than seven months of siege a year earlier, now fell in two days.

The long month of fighting and pursuit finally ended on June 25 when the British made a stand at their Mersa Matrûh base. On that day the Middle East commander, Gen. Sir Claude Auchinleck flew up from Cairo, relieved Ritchie of his command, and took personal charge of the Eighth Army. The Gazala defeat and ensuing retreat cost the British about 45,000 casualties, largely prisoners, plus the loss of another 33,000 men in the surrender of Tobruk. Axis losses in killed and wounded were comparable. *See* Sidi-Rezegh; Tobruk III; Mersa Matrûh; World War II.

Gembloux (Netherlands War of Independence), 1578. The third commander that Philip II of Spain sent into the Spanish Netherlands to subdue the bitter revolt was Don John of Austria, the hero of Lepanto II. John occupied Gent (Ghent) in 1576 and Brussels a year later. On January 31, 1578, the Spanish drove the Dutch patriots out of Namur and then pursued vigorously. At Gembloux, ten miles to the northwest, the retreating rear guard was taken in the flank and routed. The main Netherlands force was then assaulted by the Spaniards and destroyed. Almost 8,000 were killed or captured, with a loss of less than 100 to the troops of John. *See* Leyden; Maastricht I; Netherlands War of Independence.

Geok Tepe (Conquest by Russia), 1881. At the conclusion of the Russian-Turkish War of 1877–78, Czar Alexander II sought to subjugate the Tekke tribe, in what is now Turkman S.S.R. A Russian column laid siege to the tribe's fortress of Geok Tepe on September 9, 1878. Despite a bombardment, the Russians were unable to break into the fortress. Three years later a second attempt was made to take Geok Tepe. General Mikhail Skobelev with 10,000 men surrounded the strong point on January 8. After nine days of investment, Skobelev ordered an assault. The Russians stormed into the defenses, killing more than 6,000 of the 30,000-man garrison. Another 8,000 Turcomans fell in the relentless Russian pursuit. This was the last resistance by the Tekkes. *See* Plovdiv; *see also* Philippopolis I and II.

George, Lake (French and Indian War), 1755. The third British offensive against New France in 1755 was under the command of Gen. William Johnson. With 3,500 colonials and 400 Indians, Johnson moved up the Hudson River. At the portage to Lake George he built Fort Lyman (later renamed Fort Edward) and then marched north to Lake George itself. Here on September 8 part of his column was ambushed by a force of 1,400 French and Indians under Gen. Ludwig Dieskau, the French commander at Crown Point. Quickly deploying the remainder of his army, Johnson beat off a heavy attack on his camp. Dieskau was wounded and taken prisoner, and his defeated troops fell back to Fort Ticonderoga. French losses were 400, British casualties 300. Because of dissension among his New England troops, Johnson could not press his advantage. Instead he built Fort William Henry on the site of his camp and then disbanded his army. This ended the multiple British offensive of 1755. *See* Beauséjour; Monongahela River; Oswego; French and Indian War.

Gerberoi (Norman Revolt against England), 1080. After subduing England, William I, the Conqueror, continued to rule over his original dukedom of Normandy. Here, however, his eldest son, Robert II, Curt-hose, three times sought to wrest power from his father. During Robert's second rebellion, in 1080, he was driven from Normandy by forces loyal to William. He took refuge in the castle of Gerberoi, held by his ally King Philip I of France. When William pursued, the two groups of knights clashed outside the walls of the castle. For a time father and son fought in personal combat, with William receiving a wound in the hand. A reconciliation was effected that brought peace for two years.

Robert's last revolt was put down in 1082. Upon the death of his father, Robert finally became duke of Normandy in 1087. He was later involved in a bitter contest with his brother who had assumed the English crown as Henry I in 1100. *See* Ely I; Rochester I; Tinchebray.

Gergovia (Gallic Wars), 52 B.C. To strike at the heart of the widespread Gallic revolt of 52 B.C., Julius Caesar took six Roman legions southward from Avaricum (Bourges). His objective was Gergovia (Clermont) capital of the Arveni and home of Vercingetorix, who had assumed leadership over all the dissident tribes in Gaul. Moving up the Allier Valley, Caesar captured one of the heights outside Gergovia. When his order to seize a second height was carried out with ease, the Roman infantry swept on to assault the town itself. The lack of a coordinated battle plan and the fierce resistance of the Gauls turned the attack into a bloody repulse. Only the firm stand of the Tenth Legion prevented a complete rout. The Romans lost 46 centurions (company commanders) and 700 men. Caesar then gave up the siege and withdrew to the north to link up with the four legions of Titus Labienus in the Seine Valley. *See* Avaricum; Agendicum; Alesia; Gallic Wars.

German States of the Holy Roman Empire. The major battles and wars fought by the Germanic states of the Holy Roman Empire from its origin in 800 to its collapse in 1806 are listed below. Following the establishment of Hapsburg power under Rudolf I (1273–91), Austria dominated the confederation until the rise of Prussia in 1701. For later conflicts *see* Prussia; Germany; Austria.

Louvain	891
Riade	933
Lechfeld	955
Crotone	982
Sant'Angelo	998
Rome V	1084
Legnano	1176
Bornhöved	1227
Cortenuova	1237
Liegnitz I	1241
Marchfeld	1278
Morgarten	1315
Mühldorf	1322
Helsingborg	1362
Sempach	1386
Tannenberg I	1410
See Hussite Wars	
Frastenz	1499
Calven	1499
Dornach	1499
Frankenhausen	1525
Vienna I	1529
Tunis III	1535
Mühlberg	1547
Sievershausen	1553
Keresztes	1596
See Thirty Years' War	
Szentgotthárd	1664
See Louis XII, Wars of	
Fehrbellin	1675
Vienna II	1683
Harkány	1687
Slankamen	1691
Senta	1697
See Great Northern War	
See Spanish Succession, War of the	
Peterwardein	1716
See Polish Succession, War of the	
See Austrian Succession, War of the	
See Seven Years' War	
Focsani	1789
Rimnik	1789
See French Revolution, Wars of the	
See Napoleonic Empire Wars	

Germantown (War of the American Revolution), 1777. After maneuvering Gen. George Washington away from Philadelphia to the northwest, the British commander, Gen. Sir William Howe, turned back to occupy the city on September 26, 1777. To guard his newly won prize, Howe posted 9,000 troops at Germantown. Washington called in reinforcements to build his army up to 8,000 Continentals and 3,000 militia. By October 4 he was strong enough to launch a four-pronged attack against the British lines. The main assault came in the center, with Gen. Nathanael Greene commanding the left column, Gen. John Sullivan the right. On the far left and right Gen. William Smallwood and Gen. John Armstrong, respectively, were to envelop Howe's flanks and close a pincers behind (southeast of) Germantown.

The initial advance of the two center columns

drove into Germantown. But in Sullivan's sector along Skippack Road, 120 red-coated infantry barricaded themselves in the large stone house of Chief Justice Benjamin Chew. This hedgehog position held up the advance of the American reserve forces. Then a division from Greene's column and Gen. Anthony Wayne's troops from Sullivan's command, confused by heavy fog and smoke, fired on each other. Both units broke in panic and the battle was lost. First Sullivan and then Greene began falling back. (Neither of the two pincers movements ever exerted any influence on the battle.) The entire American army retreated with a loss of 152 killed, 521 wounded, and 400 captured. Howe suffered 520 casualties. Washington took up winter headquarters at Valley Forge, where his men suffered terrible hardships. The British spent the winter comfortably 24 miles away in Philadelphia. *See* Paoli; Fort Mercer and Fort Mifflin; American Revolution.

German Vengeance-Weapon Bombardment (World War II), 1944–1945. A week after the Allies stormed ashore at Normandy, Germany began launching "V" (for *Vergeltung,* "vengeance") weapons against England from bases along the Atlantic Coast. The V-1, or buzz bomb, was a pilotless plane loaded with a ton of explosives. The V-2, first launched on September 8, 1944, was a rocket with a similar load of explosives for its warhead. Fortunately for the Allies, both these weapons were still in the early stages of development and had an average accuracy error of over ten miles.

In all, the Nazis unleashed about 8,000 V-1 bombs against England and 10,000 against continental cities, chiefly Antwerp. The number of rockets released totaled 1,200 against England and 1,750 against Antwerp, Liége, and Brussels. England suffered 24,000 casualties in killed and seriously wounded from the V-1, 9,100 from the V-2. Casualties on the Continent numbered about the same.

Although several thousand V-1's were shot down by British fighter planes and antiaircraft fire, the chief defense against such attacks was Allied air harassment of the launching sites. The savage "V" bombardment came to an end on March 29, 1945, when the last of the Nazi bases fell into the hands of Gen. Dwight Eisenhower's ground troops. *See* Britain; Germany—Air Bombardment; Normandy; World War II.

Germany. The overwhelming Prussian victory over France in 1871 gave rise to the German Empire. This entity in turn fought and lost two world wars in the twentieth century. For lists of the battles fought see the wars below. For earlier battles and wars *see* German States of the Holy Roman Empire; Prussia.
See Franco-Prussian War
See World War I
See World War II

Germany—Air Bombardment (World War II), 1942–1945. The German *Luftwaffe* initiated the smashing of enemy cities and long-range strategic targets by aerial bombardment in World War II. Although this policy proved successful early in the war, it failed notably in the battle of Britain, largely because the aerial assault could not be supplemented by an invasion with ground forces. When the Allies took the offensive against Nazi-held Europe, they made devastating use of strategic bombing but only as a preliminary to later attacks on land, which were in turn supported by tactical bombings and strafings.

The major air offensive against Germany began on the night of May 30, 1942. In the first of three successive 1,000-plane raids, British bombers dropped 2,000 tons of bombs on Cologne in 90 minutes. The next night Essen received a similar blow and on June 25, Bremen. During this time the U.S. 8th Air Force was establishing itself in England, and on August 18 it sent its first formation of B-17 Flying Fortresses on a daylight raid against Nazi targets at Rouen, France. This attack set the Allied bombing pattern that was to last throughout the war: the heavy Halifaxes and Lancasters of the Royal Air Force (RAF) Bomber Command concentrated on saturation strikes in night raids; the B-17's of the U.S. carried out precision attacks in day raids.

At first the British method proved more effective. But as the armament of the B-17's was steadily improved and long-range fighter escorts were developed, the 8th Air Force took over an increasingly larger share of the bombing burden. Both offensives struck at the same kind of targets: airfields, transportation and communications centers, and sites of essential war production, such as aircraft factories and fuel plants. Along with improvements in planes and techniques came an increase in the size and destructive power of the bombs. In the spring of 1942 the largest bombs were of the 4,000-lb. type. Two years later 12,000-lb. and even 22,000-lb. bombs were blasting targets all over Hitler's *Festung Europa.* At the same time, Allied planes were carrying increasingly heavier bomb loads. Early in 1942 the average load per aircraft was 2,800 pounds; in 1943 it was 7,500 pounds.

In 1943 the British air chief marshal Arthur Harris, commander of the RAF Bomber Command, launched three major air onslaughts against Germany. From March to July the industrialized Ruhr was the principal target. Between July 24 and August 3 Hamburg suffered four devastating attacks. Then in November Berlin became the primary objective, with 16 large attacks striking the German capital during the next four months.

One of the chief reasons for the shifting of targets was to outwit the resourceful *Luftwaffe* night fighters and massed Nazi antiaircraft fire. The Nazi defense proved particularly deadly the night of March 30–31, 1944, when 795 British aircraft attacked Nürnberg. The Germans shot down 94 planes, to make Nürnberg Britain's costliest single raid of the war.

Meanwhile, the B-17 Flying Fortresses of the U.S. Strategic Air Forces steadily stepped up their daylight attacks, first under Gen. Ira Eaker and then under Gen. Carl Spaatz. The chief targets were the Nazi fighter forces and the German aircraft industry. Throughout 1943 the U.S. bombers were still unescorted by long-range fighters. The climax of these hazardous operations came on October 14, 1943, when 291 Fortresses struck at the Schweinfurt ball-bearing plants: 65 bombers were lost on this "Black Thursday," chiefly to German ME-109's and FW-190's. Earlier, on August 1, 178 U.S. B-24 Liberator bombers based in North Africa made a fierce treetop raid on Ploesti in Rumania, the chief petroleum center of Hitler's Europe. The attack cost 53 airplanes; 310 airmen were killed, 108 taken prisoner in Rumania, and 79 interned in Turkey.

But now hundreds of American long-range fighters were coming off the production line—Thunderbolts (P-47), Lightnings (P-38), and Mustangs (P-51). Their radius of action increased from 475 to 850 miles. By February 23, 1944, Gen. James Doolittle's U.S. 8th Air Force stood ready to force a decision in the air. In a week of concentrated precision bombing the B-17's, accompanied by swarms of deadly, long-range fighters, won control of the air over Germany. From that time on, Allied air superiority became ever greater.

In March 1944 Allied air attacks switched to railway communications in France, Belgium, and western Germany to support the forthcoming cross-Channel invasion, June 6. Sixty-six thousand tons of bombs in three months virtually cut off all railroad communications with the German troops in Normandy. Then, just before D-day, tactical aircraft began destroying bridges and rolling stock. In the later ground offensive against Germany, the U.S. Ninth Air Force (Hoyt Vandenberg) and the British 2d Tactical Air Force (Arthur Coningham) gave close support to Allied troops. As many as 9,000 aircraft a day attacked military targets in the front lines and communication and transportation facilities farther back. Air attacks reached a crescendo between March 21 and 24 during the major Allied crossings of the Rhine. In these four days more than 42,000 sorties were flown against German targets.

The most devastating air attack in history came in back-to-back raids against Dresden, Germany. On the night of February 13, 1945, 723 RAF Lancaster bombers struck the capital of Saxony, followed the next day by 450 Flying Fortresses of the U.S. 8th Air Force. An estimated 135,000 people were killed, leaving insufficient able-bodied survivors to bury the dead.

In all, Allied airmen dropped 2,700,000 tons of bombs on Nazi-held Europe, two-thirds of this amount falling after the Normandy invasion of June 6, 1944. The last major retaliation by the *Luftwaffe* came during the battle of the Ardennes Bulge, when 156 Allied planes were destroyed in a single day (January 1, 1945). But *Luftwaffe* losses were high, and thereafter the German air threat steadily diminished. Hitler's last hope for victory in the air, his new jet-propelled planes, proved indecisive owing to constant Allied harassment of German airfields.

The massive air bombardment of Germany contributed much to the Allied victory. But air force casualties ran high. (Each American heavy bomber carried ten men, each British bomber seven.) The establishment of Allied air superiority over Europe prior to D-day in Normandy cost 140,000 air crew casualties—ten times more than the number of ground troops killed and wounded in the cross-Channel attack itself. *See* Britain; for the most devastating air raids of the Pacific war *see* Japan—Bombardment; World War II.

Germany, East (World War II), 1945. In an overwhelming offensive during January 12–31, three great Russian army groups had smashed almost 300 miles through Poland to cross the prewar German frontier into Pomerania, Brandenburg, and Silesia. (East Prussia had been isolated and was under siege.) On January 31 armored spearheads from Marshal Georgi Zhukov's First White Russian Group reached the Oder River at Küstrin (Kostrzyn), less than 50 miles from Berlin. Here the Russian attack paused to extend both flanks, mop up in the rear, and regroup for a final assault into the German heartland. To the north Zhukov pushed down the Oder's east bank to reach the Baltic, across the river from Stettin (Szczecin), on March 4. The Baltic coast was cleared by joint attack of Zhukov's group and Marshal Konstantin Rokossovski's Second White Russian Group from the east. Rokossovski then turned west to form the right flank of the final offensive. To his left, Gen. Vassili Sokolovski took over the First White Russians at Küstrin, while Zhukov assumed command of the entire Oder-Neisse front.

To the south Marshal Ivan Konev's First Ukrainians had surged through Silesia, except for encircled Breslau (Wroclaw), which held out until May 7. Konev then pushed west, outflanking the upper Oder, to reach the Neisse River. The Russians then stood on an almost straight north-south line from the Baltic to Czechoslovakia. The German defense of this line fell to Ferdinand Schoerner, who was promoted to field marshal in March and given command of all Nazi armies in the east. General Gotthard Heinrici replaced Gestapo chief Heinrich Himmler as commander of the German forces on the Oder east of Berlin.

While German and Russian troops faced each other for ten weeks across the Oder-Neisse line, Allied heavy bombers struck at Nazi targets just behind this front. On March 7 Allied armies in the west crossed the Rhine and began racing through crumbling German defenses. By April 14 only 75 miles separated the two fronts in central Germany.

On that day, following a devastating artillery barrage, Konev's armies stormed across the Neisse River toward Dresden. The Red force soon began moving forward as much as 18 miles in a day. To the north the First White Russians, supported by most of the tactical Soviet air force, burst out of the Küstrin (Kostrzyn) bridgehead. Some 4,000 tanks roared west toward Berlin. Farther north Rokossovski also jumped across the Oder, to set the entire front aflame.

On the left Konev suddenly switched the axis of his advance northward along the Spree River. This attack routed a large German reserve poised to strike at Sokolovski's left flank. By April 18 the Nazi defense line had collapsed. Red armored columns poked into the eastern outskirts of Berlin two days later. By April 25 Zhukov's forces had encircled the city, which fell May 2.

To the north, the Russian armies had marched through Rostock on April 27, on their way west toward a link-up with the Allied field marshal Sir Bernard Montgomery's Twenty-First Army Group. Meanwhile to the south, Konev's troops pushed on to the Elbe River. Here at Torgau, 60 miles south of Berlin, a Russian patrol met a patrol from the American general Omar Bradley's Twelfth Army Group (69th Division of the First Army) on April 25. Nazi Germany had been cut in two. Adolf Hitler committed suicide six days later and the near-paralyzed German government now sought to surrender. On May 4 all north German armies, including those in Denmark and the Netherlands, capitulated. Unconditional surrender of all German forces came on May 8. The greatest military machine in the history of the world had been overwhelmed by an even greater force, forged by mutual need, from the Soviet Union, Great Britain, France, and the United States. *See* Poland–East Prussia; Berlin; Germany, West; World War II.

Germany, West (World War II), 1945. Following the decisive Allied victory in the Rhineland, Gen. Dwight Eisenhower, supreme commander in the west, regrouped his forces for a final assault into the German heartland. For this offensive he had 85 divisions along the Rhine, divided into seven armies and three army groups. In the north, Field Marshal Sir Bernard Montgomery commanded the Canadian First (Henry Crerar), British Second (Miles Dempsey), and U.S. Ninth (Henry Simpson). Gen. Omar Bradley's central army group consisted of the U.S. First (Courtney Hodges) and U.S. Third (George Patton). In the south, Gen. Jacob Devers directed the U.S. Seventh (Alexander Patch) and French First (Jean de Lattre de Tassigny). The Allies had almost complete air supremacy, both strategic and tactical.

Against this mighty array, the German field marshal Albert Kesselring could muster only 60 divisions, so decimated that the total number of Nazi troops equaled about 26 full-strength divisions. Ammunition, fuel, and other supplies were scarce and difficult to distribute under the watchful eyes of Allied airmen. The chief German strength lay in the fanaticism of some units, such as the SS, and in the fact that they were defending the familiar ground of their homeland. Hitler stood ready to relieve the responsible commander each time a crisis occurred.

In the north the British Second Army plunged across the Rhine at Wesel on March 23. The U.S. Ninth began crossing on the right the following day. Aided by a drop of the U.S. 17th and British 6th Airborne divisions, the Allied forces pressed eastward and on March 28, near Haltern, broke out on the North German Plain. Simpson's Ninth then drove along the northern edge of the Ruhr toward Lippstadt.

On the central Rhine both the First and Third armies erupted from their bridgeheads east of the river on March 25. Hodges' forces attacked eastward to reach Marburg on March 28 and then turned north toward Lippstadt. On the right Patton raced through Frankfurt and headed northeast toward Kassel. Farther south, Patch's Seventh Army forced the Rhine at Worms on March 26 and captured Mannheim three days later. The French First Army crossed at Philippsburg on April 1.

On March 28 Eisenhower ordered Bradley's Twelfth Army Group to make the main Allied effort on a three-army front along the axis Kassel–Mühlhausen–Leipzig. (The Ninth Army reverted to Bradley's control on April 1.) Montgomery's armies were ordered to cover the left flank by attacking through the Netherlands and northern Germany. Devers' Sixth Army Group had the mission of protecting the right flank in southern Germany.

First and Third Army armor now plunged northeast, averaging 30 miles a day. On April 1 Hodges' left wing linked up with Simpson's Ninth Army near Lippstadt. The industrially rich Ruhr was thus encircled. Leaving troops to hold the northern face of the pocket, Simpson drove eastward, took Hannover on April 9 and, after a vicious fight at

Magdeburg, reached the Elbe on April 11. On his right Hodges' First Army cleaned out an SS unit at Paderborn, captured Kassel on April 2, and, driving relentlessly forward, took Leipzig on April 19. Six days later a 69th Infantry patrol from the V Corps met a Russian spearhead at Torgau on the Elbe. The Western and Eastern fronts had linked up, shattering Kesselring's defenses and cutting Germany in two.

Meanwhile, the left wing of Patton's Third Army raced eastward to take Mühlhausen on April 4 and cross the Czechoslovakian border on April 17. This advance was halted at Pilsen by Allied directive. Patton's right wing turned south, thrust across the Danube at Ingolstadt on April 25, and plunged into Austria to Linz on May 4.

To the southwest, Patch's Seventh Army cleared Nürnberg on April 20, Stuttgart on April 23, crossed the upper Danube, and took the surrender of Munich on April 30. Berchtesgaden and Salzburg, Austria, fell on May 4. That same day Patch's right wing moved through the Brenner Pass to meet the U.S. Fifth Army advancing northward from Italy. At the extreme southern end of the Allied line, De Tassigny's French First Army took Karlsruhe on April 4, cleared the Black Forest, and pressed southeast along the Swiss border. On May 5 the German forces on the Southern Front capitulated, erasing Allied fears of a guerrilla (Nazi Werewolves) holdout in a Bavarian redoubt.

At the northern end of the Allied line Montgomery's armies also advanced rapidly. Crerar's Canadian First Army moved north toward Emden and Wilhelmshaven to cut off Gen. Johannes Blaskowitz' German troops in Holland. To the right Dempsey's British Second Army drove relentlessly toward the Elbe, routing the sporadic delaying actions fought by Gen. Ernst Busch. Clearing the west bank of the river by April 26, Dempsey plunged across the Elbe to seize Lübeck and Wismar on May 2. Hamburg capitulated the next day. On May 4 all the German troops in the north surrendered to Montgomery.

With Hitler dead in Berlin, Adm. Karl Doenitz had taken over the German reins. Now compressed between the giant pincers of the Allies and Russia, Doenitz sued for peace. The unconditional surrender of Nazi Germany came on May 8. In the 11 months of fighting since D-day the Allies lost 187,000 killed, 546,000 wounded, and 110,000 missing. German losses totaled 80,000 killed, 265,-000 wounded, and 500,000 missing. The Thousand-Year Reich had collapsed in 12 years. *See* Rhineland; Germany—Bombardment; Ruhr Pocket; Germany, East; World War II.

Gettysburg (American Civil War), 1863. The second invasion of the North by Gen. Robert E. Lee's Army of Northern Virginia passed beyond the Potomac on June 24, closing up behind Richard Ewell's II Corps, which was already in the Cumberland Valley of Pennsylvania. On that day Gen. Joseph Hooker's Army of the Potomac also began moving northward into Maryland, shielding both Washington and Baltimore. Displeased by Hooker's performance, President Abraham Lincoln replaced him with Gen. George Meade on June 28. Meanwhile Lee began concentrating his heretofore scattered forecs at Cashtown.

On July 1 the leading elements of Gen. Ambrose Hill's Confederate III Corps bumped into Gen. John Buford's Federal cavalry between Cashtown and Gettysburg. Both sides began building up rapidly. Hill, receiving more and more of his troops, pushed forward to the north-south Seminary Ridge, southwest of Gettysburg. Ewell advanced on the town from the north, driving out the Federal XI Corps of Gen. Oliver Howard. Meade sent Gen. Winfield Hancock forward to organize a Federal position just south of Gettysburg. Hancock hurriedly deployed arriving troops on Culp's Hill and then on Cemetery Ridge to the south (the shank of a four-mile fish hook) as far as, but not including, the terminal hills of Little Round Top and Big Round Top. The first day's fighting at Gettysburg was a Confederate victory. The Federal XI Corps had lost over 4,000 men captured; the I Corps of Gen. Abner Doubleday (who had replaced the slain John Reynolds) had also suffered heavily. But Ewell had stopped short of Culp's Hill, and Lee did not insist that he try to take this northern key to Cemetery Ridge.

On the second day (July 2) Lee sent the I Corps of Gen. James Longstreet against the Federal left (south) flank. The attack was not started until 4 P.M. and then was delivered piecemeal. General Daniel Sickles' Federal III Corps, in a westward-jutting salient, suffered heavily, but quick Federal dispositions held the vital height of Little Round Top. Hill's assault to the left of Longstreet and Ewell's attack against Culp's Hill from the northeast proved equally unsuccessful, although the Confederates charged gallantly all along the line.

During the first two days of the great battle, Lee's knowledge of the enemy had been seriously crippled by the absence of his cavalry leader, Gen. J. E. B. Stuart, who was off on an irresponsible raid to the east. Now the Confederate commander determined to make one more attack, against the center of Meade's position. Under the direction of Longstreet, 15,000 troops—the divisions of Gens. George Pickett, James Pettigrew, and Isaac Trimble—assembled on Seminary Ridge for the assault across the half-mile of open ground to Cemetery Ridge. Longstreet massed 159 guns opposite the Federal line held by the II Corps of Gen. John Gibbon. After an hour's brutal artillery duel with Meade's guns, the Confederates marched eastward in one of the most famous charges in

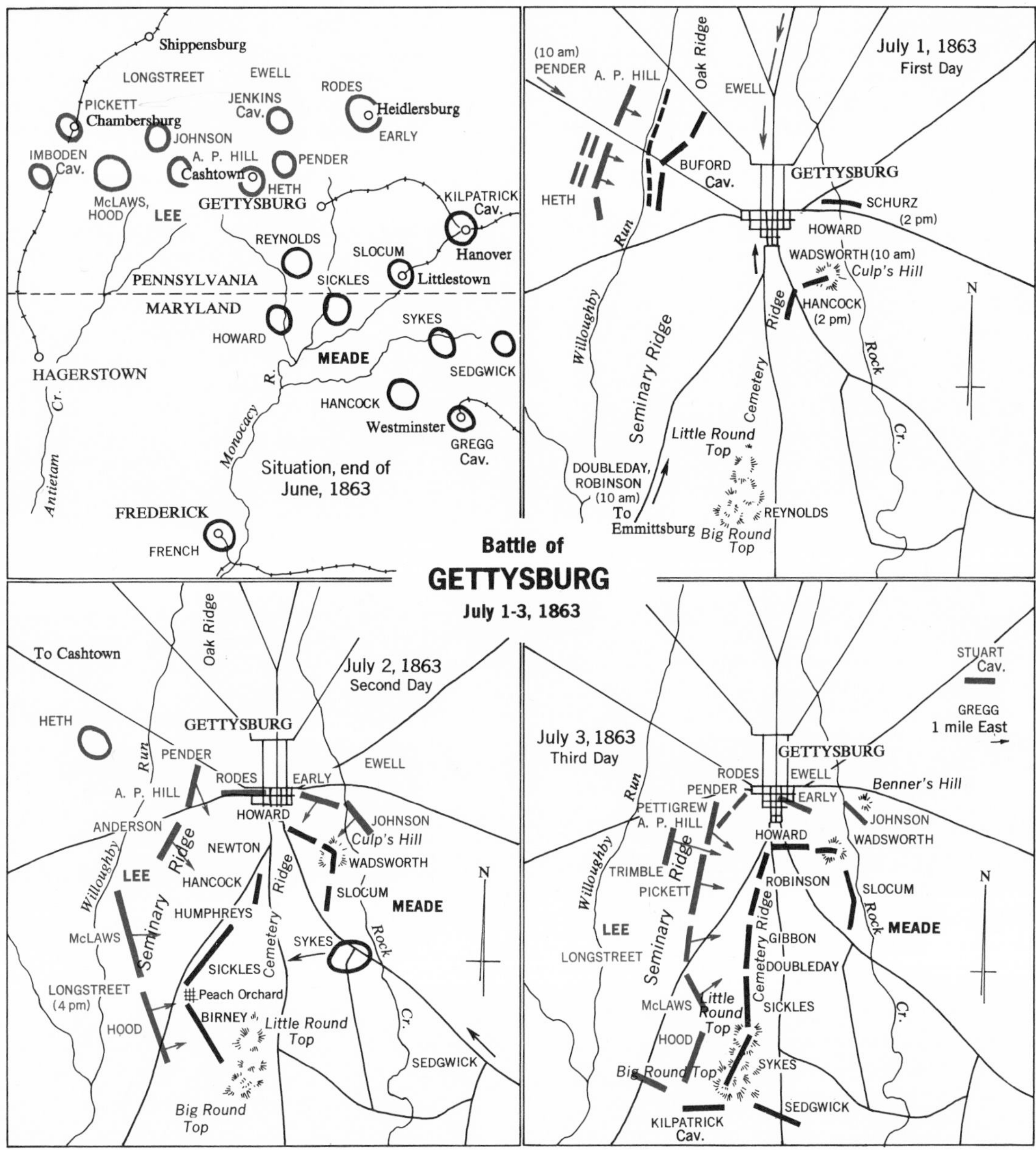

history. Ascending Cemetery Ridge, the Southerners made a small penetration of the Federal position ("the high tide of the Confederacy") before they were beaten back with heavy losses. Nineteen regimental colors were lost to the defenders. Earlier that day Ewell's last attempt to take Culp's Hill had been easily repulsed. Also stopped, by the cavalry of Gen. David Gregg, was Stuart's attack from the north on Meade's communication lines. The battle of Gettysburg was over. During the three days of combat more artillery shells were fired than in all the battles Napoleon ever fought. Of the 88,000 Federal troops engaged, 3,155 were killed, 14,529 wounded, and 5,365 missing. Confederate casualties among Lee's 75,000 troops were 3,903 dead, 18,735 wounded, 5,425 missing.

On July 4 Lee reorganized his battered forces against an expected counterattack. But Meade's men were in no shape to continue the battle. On the night of July 5–6 the Confederate army began its retreat to the south in a driving rain. A slow Federal pursuit enabled Lee to recross the swollen Potomac safely on July 13 and 14. Because the battle of Gettysburg marked the beginning of the end for the Confederate States, it must rank as one of the decisive battles of history. While Lee waited on Seminary Ridge on July 4, Vicksburg, far to the west, fell to Gen. U. S. Grant, splitting the

Confederacy in two along the line of the Mississippi River. *See* Winchester II; Vicksburg; Bristoe Station; American Civil War.

Gibraltar I (War of the Spanish Succession), 1704. Portugal's entry into the war against France in 1703 gave the allies the important naval base of Lisbon. To advance their control of the sea another 300 miles, the English and Dutch resolved to take Gilbraltar, at the entrance to the Mediterranean. Under Adm. Sir George Rooke, assisted by Adm. Sir Cloudesley Shovell, an allied fleet reached the fortress on July 23, 1704. A squadron commanded by Adm. George Byng (later Lord Torrington) bombarded Gibraltar, while Prince George of Hesse-Darmstadt landed a force of 1,800 marines to attack by land. The following day a ship-to-shore assault won the fortress. By August 4 Gibraltar was secure. Allied losses were less than 300. The Spanish promptly launched a counterattack, calling on the French fleet for assistance. But the capture would stand, and the possession of Gibraltar would make Great Britain a Mediterranean naval power ever after. *See* Vigo Bay; Blenheim; Málaga II; Spanish Succession, War of the.

Gibraltar II (War of the American Revolution), 1779–1783. The entrance of Spain (Charles III) into the war on the side of France (Louis XVI) and the United States, on June 16, 1779, made the British base at Gibraltar vulnerable. A combined Spanish and French fleet under Don Alvarez began a loose blockade of the fortress later that year. The garrison commander, Gen. George Eliott (later Baron Heathfield), led a gallant resistance. During the siege British fleets ran the blockade gauntlet several times to succor the defenders. Finally, in September 1782, the allies built up their blockading force to almost 50 ships of the line. Ten fireproof floating batteries, mounting 154 heavy guns and supported by 40 gunboats, formed the nucleus of the attacking force. On land some 33,000 troops under the Duc de Crillon, with 300 pieces of artillery, prepared to launch a ground assault on the 7,000 defenders.

The decisive phase of the siege began on September 9 with a heavy bombardment of Gibraltar by the land artillery. An estimated 7,600 cannon balls and bombs struck the fortress every 24 hours for four days. Then, on September 13, the floating batteries moved into position to add their firepower to the duel. These specially constructed ships proved unequal to the return fire from the besieged artillery. One by one they were blown up, until nine were destroyed, with an estimated loss of 1,500 men. The tenth was boarded and burned by crews from English gunboats. The loss of these batteries led to the collapse of the entire assault. The combined fleets pulled back out of artillery range, still hoping to starve the garrison into submission. But Adm. Lord Richard Howe with 34 British warships arrived the following month and forced his way through the blockade. The provisions, ammunition, and troops brought by Howe enabled Gibraltar to hold out until the end of the war, in 1783, concluded the unsuccessful siege. *See* Ushant I; Saint Vincent Cape I; American Revolution.

Gijón (Spanish Civil War), 1937. The capture of Bilbao and Santander left only Asturias holding out in northern Spain against the Nationalist forces of Generalissimo Francisco Franco. To reduce this Republican stronghold, Gen. Antonio Aranda, on September 1, launched an offensive northward through the Leonese mountains toward Gijón on the Bay of Biscay. For six weeks the Asturians stubbornly held the key mountain passes. Then, on October 15, at the village of Infiesto, Aranda linked up with a Navarrese force under Gen. José Solchaga, which was advancing westward along the coast. This junction made further Asturian resistance hopeless. On October 21 Aranda and Solchago entered Gijón. All the north coast of Spain now lay under Nationalist control. Thousands of executions (including 16 Basque priests) and imprisonments followed. *See* Santander; Teruel; Spanish Civil War.

Giornico (Swiss-Milanese War), 1478. The confederation of Swiss cantons had no sooner repulsed the Burgundian threat from the west than an old menace reappeared. To the southeast the duchy of Milan, victor over the Swiss 56 years before, sent a large army up the Ticino River. A phalanx of Swiss pikemen and halberdiers met the Milanese at Giornico on December 28, 1478. Although markedly outnumbered, the Swiss made their usual relentless attack and cut down the Italians. The decisive victory ended the war with the military reputation of the mountaineer infantry greatly enhanced. *See* Arbedo; Nancy; Frastenz.

Gisors (English-French Wars), 1197. After his return from the Third Crusade, Richard I, Coeur de Lion, carried out a long struggle for northwestern France against Philip II Augustus, beginning in 1194. The only real battle of this war, often interrupted by brief truces, took place at Gisors, 20 miles northwest of Paris. Here the English knights attacked in 1197 and drove the French armored horsemen and their king out of the town on the Normandy frontier. As the see-saw fighting continued, Richard laid siege to the castle of Chaluz in the spring of 1199. Struck by a bolt from a crossbow, England's greatest warrior king died on April 6. The war with France continued under his younger brother John. *See* Alnwick II; Château Gaillard.

Glencoe (William III's Pacification of Scotland), 1692. All the Highland clans were ordered to take an oath of allegiance to William III and Mary before January 1, 1692. When the Macdonald chief was six days late in taking his oath, troops from the rival Campbell clan were sent into Glencoe in western Scotland on February 6. A week of peaceful quartering followed. Then, on the bitterly cold night of February 13, the royal soldiers suddenly fell on the Macdonalds. Most escaped, but 38 were massacred. Although William III had not directly ordered the treacherous attack, he bore the responsibility for the slaughter. *See* Killiecrankie; Limerick.

"Glorious First of June." *See* Ushant II.

"Glorious Revolution, The." *See* Jacobite Insurrections.

Gloucester Cape (World War II). A successful American invasion of Japanese-held New Britain Island, on December 26, 1943. *See* Rabaul.

Gnila Lipa River (World War I). The farthest Austrian advance into Russia, checked and hurled back, during August 26–30, 1914. *See* Galicia.

Goa (Conquest by Portugal), 1510. When the peninsula of India split into five separate Mohammedan kingdoms, Goa on the west coast came under the rule of the Rajah of Bijapur. In 1510 a Portuguese expedition under Affonso de Albuquerque attacked the seaport. Albuquerque, who commanded 1,500 men, forced an entrance into Goa and, despite being heavily outnumbered, routed the Indian defenders. Portuguese losses were less than 100, while Indian casualties totaled several thousand. Goa was made the capital of Portuguese India. During the years, it successfully beat off all attempts by Bijapur to regain possession. *See* Diu; Alcázarquivir.

Goodwin Sands (First English-Dutch War), 1652. The restrictive navigation act passed by the English Commonwealth government of Oliver Cromwell in 1651 led to war with the Netherlands. Before the formal declaration of hostilities, the Dutch fleet of 40 ships under Adm. Maarten Tromp sailed into the Downs roadstead, off the southeast coast of England. On May 19, 1652, the English navy (20 ships) under Adm. Robert Blake attacked the Dutch off Goodwin Sands, sinking two enemy vessels. It was the first battle in an exclusively naval war. *See* Dover II; English-Dutch Wars.

Gorlice-Tarnów (World War I), 1915. By the spring of 1915 the German commander in chief on the Eastern Front, Field Marshal Paul von Hindenburg, had organized still another offensive aimed at knocking Russia out of the war. Under absolute secrecy, the German Eleventh Army was transferred from the Western Front to the Gorlice-Tarnów sector, southeast of Cracow (Kraków). Here it was united with the Austrian Fourth Army, and both forces were placed under the command of Gen. August von Mackensen. Opposite this concentration stood the Russian Third Army, one of the ten armies posted along the frontier from the Baltic Sea to Rumania by Grand Duke Nicholas, uncle of the czar.

Early on May 2, 950 German guns opened a devastating bombardment between Gorlice and Tarnów. German infantry then charged forward against the surprised Russians. At the end of the second day the Russian Third Army was virtually obliterated, 120,000 men being captured. With a clean breakthrough achieved, the Germans plunged on eastward against collapsing resistance. Przemyśl was taken on June 2, Lemberg (Lvov) on June 22. Mackensen, reinforced by the Austrian Third Army and the newly formed German Bug (River) Army, now turned north toward Brest Litovsk, 120 miles east of Warsaw. As the Russian retreat continued all along the front, the Polish capital became increasingly isolated. To complete the conquest, the German Twelfth Army of Gen. Max von Gallwitz marched against the city from the north. (This movement was ordered by Gen. Erich von Falkenhayn, chief of the German general staff, who had taken command of the Gorlice-Tarnów breakthrough.) Warsaw fell during August 4–5. Brest Litovsk on August 25. In September the Russian front was pushed back to a 600-mile line from Lithuania, on the Baltic Sea, southward through the Pripet Marshes to the Rumanian border. The five-month battle cost Russia almost 2,000,000 men, half of them captured. But large forces had escaped the giant German trap. Czar Nicholas II now took personal command of the Russian troops on the Eastern Front, which stood 180 miles east of Warsaw. *See* Vistula River–Warsaw; Naroch Lake; World War I.

Gothic Line (World War II), 1944–1945. Following the storming of the Gustav-Cassino Line and the capture of Rome on June 4, 1944, the Allied Fifteenth Army Group (Sir Harold Alexander) pressed vigorously northward. But during the drive seven divisions (U.S. VI and French corps) were withdrawn to prepare for the amphibious assault against southern France. Meanwhile, Field Marshal Albert Kesselring received eight new German divisions for his Tenth and Fourteenth armies. As a result, both the Allied Fifth Army (Mark Clark) on the left and the Eighth Army (Oliver Leese) on the right encountered harder going.

A stubborn German defense held the road and rail center of Arezzo for a week before withdrawing in the face of a large-scale British assault on July 16. On the right the Polish II Corps pressed up the Adriatic coast to take Ancona. Meanwhile, the Fifth Army had been closing up to the Arno River, capturing Leghorn on July 19 and threatening Pisa and Florence. The Allied forces had now moved more than 250 miles in little more than two months, but by early August they were checked by the outposts of the prepared defenses of the Gothic Line.

Alexander then shifted the weight of his attack to the right. On August 26 ten divisions of the Eighth Army drove at the Gothic Line along a 20-mile front on the Adriatic flank. Progress was slow but steady. Rimini, the eastern anchor of the line, fell on September 20. Meanwhile, the eight divisions of the Fifth Army had taken up the attack on the left. Pisa was captured on September 2 and a thrust was made in the center toward Bologna. The attack carried to within nine miles of Bologna before it was stopped by a German counteroffensive on October 20. By this time Kesselring had managed to seal off the breaches in the Gothic Line, and with the coming of winter the Allies were again blocked in their attempt to end the Italian campaign. From the end of October to April 2, 1945, the only Allied gain was the Eighth Army's push through Ravenna to the southern edge of Lake Comacchio. This period was the longest stalemate in the 20-month Italian campaign.

During the winter lull Alexander replaced Gen. Sir Henry Maitland-Wilson as supreme commander in the Mediterranean. Gen. Mark Clark took command of the Fifteenth Army Group, while both armies also received new commanders—Gen. Lucian Truscott for the Fifth Army and Gen. Richard McCreery for the Eighth. On the German side, Gen. Heinrich Vietinghoff-Scheel, former head of the Tenth Army, succeeded Kesselring as commander of German forces in Italy. *See* Gustav-Cassino Line; Po Valley; World War II.

"Graf Spee" (World War II), 1939. The first real naval battle of World War II was fought in the South Atlantic between Adm. Sir Henry Harwood's British squadron—heavy cruiser *Exeter,* light cruisers *Ajax* and *Achilles*—and the German pocket battleship *Admiral Graf Spee.* In a running battle on December 12, the heavier-gunned and faster German ship crippled the *Exeter* but was itself badly damaged. Captain Hans Langsdorff put his battleship into Montevideo for repairs the following day, but the Uruguayan government gave him only 72 hours to leave port. On December 17 Langsdorff had the *Graf Spee* scuttled outside the harbor. Rather than accept internment with his crew, the German skipper committed suicide. Allied shipping lanes in the South Atlantic were now more secure. *See* Atlantic Ocean II; World War II.

Granada (Spanish-Moslem Wars), 1491–1492. The kingdom of Granada had maintained an independent existence for 244 years when it came under new Spanish attack. Ferdinand (V of Castile, II of Aragon) launched an offensive in 1482 aimed at eliminating the last Moorish holding in Spain.

Nine years later he had reduced all the defensive strong points protecting the Moorish capital. Then on April 26, 1491, Ferdinand led a large Spanish army against Granada itself. In the face of strong Moorish resistance directed by Abu Abdullah Mohammed XI (Boabdil), the Spaniards instituted a siege against the city. Cut off from all sources of supply, the Moslem garrison finally surrendered to King Ferdinand and his wife, Queen Isabella I, who took over Granada on January 2, 1492 (a truly memorable year for the joint kingdom of Castile and Aragon). Thus ended the Moslem conquest of Spain, which had begun 781 years before on the Río Barbate with the defeat of the Visigoths. Spain stood on the threshold of international power. *See* Río Barbate; Baza; Naples.

Grand Alliance, War of the (1688–1697). To curb the aggressive designs of King Louis XIV of France, several European powers formed the League of Augsburg in 1686. This defensive alliance included the Holy Roman Empire (Leopold I) and lesser German states, Spain, Sweden, the Netherlands. When France invaded the Palatinate in September 1688, England and Savoy joined the group to wage the War of the Grand Alliance. The fighting, which spread to North America where it was known as King William's War, was ended by the Treaty of Ryswick in 1697. French aggression was checked but only temporarily. *See also* King William's War; Jacobite Insurrections.

Bantry Bay	1689
Fleurus II	1690
Beachy Head	1690
Staffarda	1690
Leuze	1691
La Hogue	1692

Steenkerke	1692
Lagos I	1693
Neerwinden I	1693
Marsaglia	1693
Namur I	1695

Grandson (Swiss-Burgundian War), 1476. When Charles the Bold of Burgundy conquered Lorraine and marched into Alsace, the Swiss confederation of cantons began mobilizing against him. Charles nevertheless pressed on eastward into Vaud canton, took the surrender of Grandson in February 1476, and then executed the garrison. He was still encamped at Grandson, on the western shore of Lake Neuchâtel, when the first division of Swiss pikemen and halberdiers arrived over Mount Aubert on March 2.

Charles quickly deployed his army of 30,000 well-trained men—Burgundian armored cavalry, English archers, German arquebusiers, Flemish pikemen, and Italian light cavalry. The unyielding Swiss infantry phalanx beat off two heavy cavalry charges. When the Swiss pressed forward, Charles pulled back his center, planning to crush the outnumbered column between his two wings, a tactic similiar to those employed at Marathon and Cannae. However, just as the withdrawal maneuver began, two other Swiss divisions appeared over the hill. Although Charles's army would still have had a numerical advantage, his men lost their nerve. The planned retreat of the center became a flight, which the wings instantly joined. Pressing forward with their traditional steadiness, the Swiss mowed down the rear of the fleeing army and captured the Burgundian camp. Despite the rout, the aggressive Charles was later able to re-form his army and resume his invasion. *See* Héricourt; Morat.

Granicus River (Macedonian Conquests), 334 B.C. After stamping out the revolt in Thebes, Alexander III, the Great, put Greece under the regency of Antipater and turned to the East. He was now ready to act on his dream of conquering Asia. In the spring of 334 B.C. Alexander crossed the Hellespont (Dardanelles) with an army of 30,000 infantry and 5,000 heavy cavalry, supported by a fleet of 160 ships. Ahead of him lay the vast empire of Persia.

To block the invasion, the Persian emperor, Darius III, sent forward some 40,000 Asiatics and Greek mercenaries commanded by Memnon of Rhodes and other satraps of Asia Minor. This hastily assembled force attempted in May to hold the line of the Granicus River, near its mouth in the Propontis (Sea of Marmara). But Alexander forded the stream and in a sharp attack soon dispersed the light Persian cavalry which had been posted in the first defense line. Stripped of its protection, the hired Greek infantry was then methodically annihilated by the heavier, better-armed Macedonians. In all, the invaders' losses were slight compared to the heavy casualties suffered by the army of Darius.

After the battle Alexander began his long march east and south through Asia Minor. Meeting virtually no opposition, he left behind strategically placed garrisons to hold his conquests. Meanwhile Darius was collecting an army to meet the Macedonians at the southern shoulder of Asia Minor. *See* Thebes; Issus; Macedonian Conquests.

Grantham (English Civil War), 1643. One of the Roundhead captains in the inconclusive and crudely fought 1642 battle of Edgehill was a member of Parliament named Oliver Cromwell. After this opening struggle in the Civil War against Charles I, Cromwell spent the winter of 1642–43 raising a cavalry force in the eastern counties. His troop featured tight discipline and religious fervor. In March 1643 Cromwell's 400 cavalrymen encountered an army of Royalist horsemen at Grantham, east of Nottingham in Lincolnshire. Despite being outnumbered 2 to 1, the Roundheads routed the enemy cavalry. It was a minor skirmish but marked Cromwell's first of a long series of victories over the Cavaliers. His troop, later called the Ironsides because of their steel armor as well as their determination, showed to good advantage at Marston Moor the following year. *See* Edgehill; Marston Moor; English Civil War.

Graupius, Mons. *See* Mons Graupius.

Gravelines (Spanish-French Wars), 1558. The French forces of Henry II had suffered a stinging defeat from an invading Spanish-Hapsburg army at Saint-Quentin in August 1557. Turning to the coast, the French partially redeemed their loss by seizing the long-time English stronghold of Calais on January 6, 1558. (Queen Mary's marriage to Philip II of Spain had allied England with the Hapsburgs.) Later that year, however, the French found themselves under new attack from the Spanish and their Imperial allies. The Comte d' Egmont, who had won the victory at Saint-Quentin, took an army of some 10,000 men to Gravelines, on the northwestern coast of France.

Here on July 13, 1558, D'Egmont led a cavalry charge that broke the French lines and then routed the defenders. A thousand or more Frenchmen were killed and an equal number driven into the sea to drown. The Spanish attack was aided by the guns of an English squadron lying off the coast, one of the earliest uses of naval gunfire in a land battle. The following year the Peace of Cateau-Cambrésis was signed between Henry II and Philip II, ending the Valois-Hapsburg wars. France yielded all its conquests except Calais and the Three Bishoprics (Toul, Metz, Verdun). *See* Saint-Quentin I; Calais II.

Gravelotte (Franco-Prussian War), 1870. After two weeks of defeats and retreats, the 113,000-man French army of Marshal Achille Bazaine found its route to the west (toward Verdun) blocked by the First and Second Prussian armies of Gen. (later Count) Helmuth von Moltke. Bazaine then made a stand west of Metz at Gravelotte, his right wing holding Saint-Privat, to the north. On August 18 the combined Prussian armies of almost 190,000 men, under the titular direction of King Wilhelm I, attacked the French positions. At Gravelotte the French held their ground and then threw back the

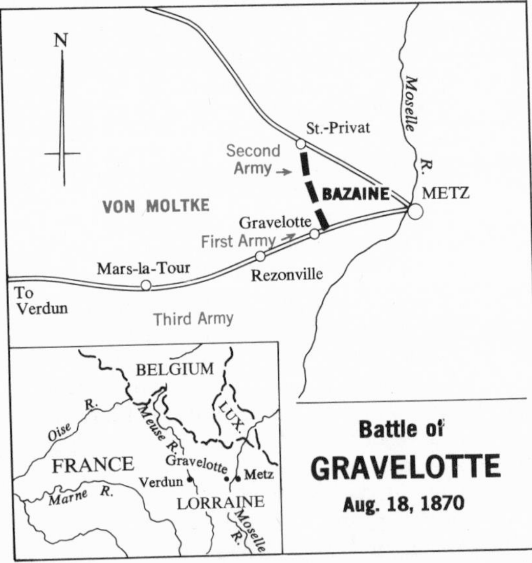

First Army in wild disorder. At Saint-Privat, too, the defenders inflicted cruel casualties on the Prussian Second Army, but here Saxon reinforcements and augmented artillery finally forced the French to yield the town. The Prussians had lost about 20,000 men, the French only about 13,000 plus another 5,000 captured. A more energetic French marshal might have counterattacked to win a decisive battle and perhaps change the course of the war. But Bazaine, at nightfall, withdrew all his troops into the fortress of Metz. It was a fateful decision. *See* Mars-la-Tour; Metz; Sedan; Franco-Prussian War.

Great Bridge (War of the American Revolution), 1775. The first battle of the American Revolution in the South was really only an uprising against the royal governor of Virginia, the Earl of Dunmore (John Murray). Dunmore enraged the planter class by augmenting a small force of British regulars with Negro slaves and indentured servants. With some 1,200 under his command he established his headquarters in Norfolk. In December 1775 Col. William Woodford, at the head of a Virigina regiment of militia plus 200 volunteer riflemen, marched against Norfolk. Dunmore sent out a detachment of 600 men under Capt. Samuel Leslie to block Woodford's advance at Great Bridge across the Elizabeth River, nine miles south of the city.

On December 9 Leslie's mixed group tried to force a crossing of the bridge. They were stopped cold by a withering fire from Woodford's troops on the west bank. The Virginia militia then rushed across the bridge themselves, routing the Royalists, who lost 60 men in killed and wounded. Woodford suffered only a single casualty. Five days later the patriot colonel marched into Norfolk. Dunmore and his supporters fled to British ships in the harbor. On January 1, 1776, Dunmore deliberately burned most of Norfolk by fire from his naval guns. He then left Virginia to join the British fleet. *See* Bunker Hill; Moores Creek Bridge; American Revolution.

Great Britain. The major battles and wars fought by England, Scotland, and Ireland are listed below.

Verulamium I	54 B.C.
Medway River	A.D. 43
Shropshire	50
Verulamium II	61
Mons Graupius	84
Mons Badonicus	c. 500
Dyrham	577
Degsastan	603
Chester	c. 616
Heathfield	633
Heavenfield	634
Maserfield	642
Winwaed	655
Nechtansmere	685
Ellandun	825
See Danish Invasions of Britain	
Brunanburh	937
Stainmore	954
Clontarf	1014
Carham	1016
Dunsinane	1054
Fulford	1066
Stamford Bridge	1066
Hastings	1066
Ely I	1071
Gerberoi	1080
Mynydd Carn	1081
Rochester I	1088
Alnwick I	1093
Tinchebray	1106
Brémule	1119
(The) Standard	1138
Lincoln I	1141
Winchester, England	1141
Wallingford	1153
Alnwick II	1174
Gisors	1197
Château Gaillard	1203–1204

Rouen I 1204
Damme 1213
Bouvines 1214
See Barons' Wars
Saintes 1242
Largs 1263
Radnor 1282
Berwick upon Tweed 1296
Dunbar I 1296
Stirling Bridge 1297
Falkirk I 1298
Methven 1306
Loudon Hill 1307
Bannockburn 1314
Dundalk 1318
Myton 1319
Boroughbridge 1322
Byland 1322
Dupplin Moor 1332
Halidon Hill 1333
See Hundred Years' War
Neville's Cross 1346
Radcot Bridge 1387
Otterburn 1388
Ravenspur I 1399
Homildon Hill 1402
Shrewsbury 1403
Bramham Moor 1408
Sevenoaks 1450
See Roses, Wars of the
East Stoke 1487
Guinegate 1513
Flodden 1513
Solway Moss 1542
Boulogne 1544
Pinkie 1547
Saint-Quentin I 1557
Calais II 1558
Carberry Hill 1567
Langside 1568
Zutphen 1586
Cadiz 1587
Spanish Armada 1588
Flores 1591
Kinsale 1601
Ré, Île de 1627
Newburn 1640
See English Civil War
See English-Dutch Wars
Jamaica 1655
Santa Cruz de Tenerife 1657
Dunes, the 1658
Winnington Bridge 1659
Pentland Hills 1666
Drumclog 1679
Bothwell Bridge 1679
Sedgemoor 1685
See Jacobite Insurrections
See Grand Alliance, War of the
See Spanish Succession, War of the
Passero Cape 1715
Porto Bello 1739
See Austrian Succession, War of the
Arcot 1751
See French and Indian War;
Seven Years' War
Buxar 1764
See American Revolution, War of the
See Mysore-British Wars
See French Revolution, Wars of the
Camperdown 1797
Vinegar Hill 1798
See Maratha-British Wars
See Napoleonic Empire Wars
See War of 1812
See Napoleon's Hundred Days
See Burmese-British Wars
See Afghan-British Wars
Miani 1843
Hyderabad 1843
See Maori-British Wars
See Sikh-British Wars
Boomplaats 1848
See Crimean War
See Indian Mutiny
Taku 1860
Magdala 1868
Kumasi 1874
See Zulu-British War
See South African Wars I
Alexandria IV 1882
Tell el-Kebir 1882
See Sudan, War for the
Bulawayo 1893
Doornkop 1896
See South African Wars II
See World War I
Dublin 1916
See World War II
Sinai Peninsula 1956

Great Northern War (1700–1721). The supremacy of Sweden (Charles XII) in the Baltic region caused three neighboring nations to form a secret alliance in the fall of 1699—Russia (Peter I, the Great), Poland (Augustus II, who was also elector of Saxony), and Denmark (Frederich IV). War broke out the following year. Under the brilliant leadership of the youthful Charles XII, Sweden knocked Denmark out of the war that same year. Augustus II was subdued in 1706. But in turning against Russia, Sweden suffered one of the decisive defeats in history at Poltava. Charles was killed in 1718. His successors accepted peace terms in 1720–21, which greatly reduced Swedish power in the Baltic.

Narva 1700
Klissow 1702
Pultusk I 1703

Thorn	1703
Holowczyn	1708
Liesna	1708
Poltava	1709
Ahvenanmaa	1714
Stralsund II	1715
Fredrikshald	1718

Great Rebellion. *See* English Civil War.

Great Swamp (King Philip's War), 1675. When the Wampanoag chief, King Philip (Metacomet), took the warpath against New England settlers in 1675, he was joined by the Narraganset tribe. To put down the uprising, Governor Josiah Winslow of New Plymouth collected a force of 1,000 men, plus some Indian allies. Marching southwest from Wickford, R.I., Winslow pushed into the Great Swamp where the Narragansets had fortified an island on the present site of South Kingstown. On December 19 the settlers attacked the island and in a desperate fight overran it. The Indian village was set on fire, adding the deaths of women and children to the 100 warriors killed in the assault. Winslow's force lost 80 killed and 150 wounded. Narraganset power was forever broken. *See* Hadley; Indian Wars in the United States.

Greece. In ancient times the city-states of Greece warred against Persia and among themselves before falling under the domination of Macedonia in the fourth century B.C. Two centuries later all of what is now Greece came under the rule of Rome.

See Persian-Greek Wars
See Peloponnesian Wars
See Greek City-States' Wars
See Macedonian Conquests

Ipsus	301 B.C.
Corupedion	281 B.C.
Heraclea	280 B.C.
Asculum I	279 B.C.
Beneventum	275 B.C.

See Hellenistic Monarchies, Wars of the

With the fall of Rome, Greece became part of the Byzantine Empire until overrun by the Ottoman Turks from 1453 to 1456. The modern Greek kingdom won its independence from Turkey in 1829.

See Greek War of Independence

Tyrnavos	1897

See Balkan Wars
See World War I

Sakarya River	1921

See World War II

Greece (World War II), 1940–1941. Jealous of the German victories of his Axis partner, the Italian dictator Benito Mussolini sought conquests in the Balkans. Albania, occupied by Italian forces in April 1939, served as the springboard for the invasion of Greece. On October 28, 1940, six Italian divisions under Gen. Visconti Prasca advanced into northwest Greece on four fronts. For two weeks the invaders drove back the three Greek divisions defending the frontier. But Greek reinforcements, plus the difficult mountainous terrain, halted the advance by November 8. Six days later the Greek commander in chief, Gen. Alexandros Papagos began a counterattack with a force that soon totaled 16 divisions.

Despite some successes that pushed 40 miles across the frontier into Albania itself, the Greek army could win no major victory against the Italian force, now swollen to 26 divisions. On December 6 the Italian chief of staff, Marshal Pietro Badoglio, was replaced by Gen. Count Ugo Cavallero, but the Italian army remained inert. In hard fighting throughout a severe winter the Greeks were aided by five (later seven) squadrons of British aircraft. In March 1941 British ground troops—the New Zealand 2nd and 6th Australian divisions plus the 1st Armoured Brigade—took up positions west of Salonika from the Vardar Valley northwest along the Aliakmon River–Vermion Range.

On April 6 the German Twelfth Army (15 divisions) under Field Marshal Siegmund List invaded southern Yugoslavia and Greece simultaneously. In the first four days of fighting four Greek divisions isolated in eastern Macedonia were destroyed by Germans attacking through the Metaxas Line from Bulgaria. To the west a German corps roared down the Vardar Valley into the Salonika sector, where it encountered the British line on April 9. At the same time an advance by three German divisions to Bitolj (Monastir), in southwestern Yugoslavia, prevented a link-up between troops of the two invaded nations. This armored-infantry advance threatened to cut off the main Greek force of 15 divisions on the Albanian front and to envelop the left of Gen. Sir Henry Maitland-Wilson's British line.

On April 12–13 the Anglo-Greek forces began falling back to a line running west from Mount Olympus. Continued German ground pressure, plus intense aerial attack from some 800 planes, forced a further withdrawal on April 20 to a position west of the historic pass at Thermopylae. On that day, however, the 300,000 Greek troops facing Albania, isolated by the German thrust in their rear, surrendered. The British then began to evacuate the 54,000 men sent to Greece only a month before. Allied vessels managed to embark about 41,000, ending the operation on the night of April 28–29 (26,000 were landed in Crete, the remainder in Egypt). German air attacks sank 26 ships during this operation. Meanwhile, on April 24, King George II surrendered his nation to Germany. Of the 13,000 British and Imperial casualties in Greece, 8,000 were taken prisoner. The six-month battle cost the Italians 125,000 casualties. Hitler reported a loss of 5,500 men in Greece;

Greek losses were not reported although the Germans claimed some 270,000 prisoners.

The defeat in Greece marked the third time in less than a year that British troops had been thrown off the European continent—earlier evacuations had been made in Norway and Flanders. Although Germany had won a decisive victory in Greece, the heavy concentration of Nazi troops in that theater for four to five weeks crucially delayed the scheduled invasion of the Soviet Union. Meanwhile, the sequel to the battle of Greece was taking shape in Crete. *See* Yugoslavia (World War II); Crete; World War II.

Greek City-States' Wars (395–362 B.C.). The victory of Sparta in the Peloponnesian Wars was followed by a period of local conflicts among the city-states of ancient Greece. This period ended with the rise to power of Macedonia.

Haliartus	395 B.C.
Coronea II	394 B.C.
Cnidus	394 B.C.
Naxos	376 B.C.
Leuctra	371 B.C.
Cynoscephalae I	364 B.C.
Mantinea	362 B.C.

Greek War of Independence (1822–1827). The Greek revolt against Turkish rule became so serious that Sultan Mahmud II had to call upon Egypt for help. But when an allied fleet of British, French, and Russian ships destroyed the Egyptian navy and Russia declared war on Turkey, the Greeks were able to win their independence.

Mesolóngion	1822–1826
Navarino	1827

Grenada (War of the American Revolution), 1779. With the entrance of France into the war on the side of the United States early in 1778, the West Indies became a major theater of operations for the rival French and British fleets. On July 2, 1779, the French admiral the Comte d'Estaing landed an expeditionary force on British-held Grenada, southernmost of the Windward Islands. Within two days the French troops had overrun the island. An English fleet of 21 warships under Adm. John Byron arrived on July 6 to counterattack the 25 French ships of the line. Byron was beaten off, with seven of his vessels seriously crippled. But D'Estaing failed to capitalize on his advantage. The British fleet was allowed to withdraw without pursuit. Two months later the French admiral sailed to the coast of Georgia to aid in the siege of Savannah. *See* Newport; Savannah II; American Revolution.

Grochów (Polish Revolt against Russia), 1831. The 1815 Treaty of Vienna placed most of Poland under the control of Russia. Inspired by the Paris revolution of 1830, Polish patriots expelled the Russian garrison of Czar Nicholas I and proclaimed an independent government. A Russian army of about 100,000 men under the German-born general Hans von Diebitsch (Count Ivan Ivanovich) marched toward Warsaw. At Grochów, an eastern suburb on the right bank of the Vistula, the Russians met a somewhat smaller Polish army commanded by Prince Michael Radziwill. In a savage battle that ended in a stalemate on February 20, 1831, Diebitsch lost almost 10,000 men. Polish casualties were only half as many. *See* Ostroleka; Warsaw II; Polish Revolt against Russia.

Grossbeeren (Napoleonic Empire Wars), 1813. When the fighting resumed, after the Austrian declaration of war against France on August 12, 1813, Napoleon I sent Marshal Nicolas Oudinot to take Berlin. With some 66,000 troops Oudinot drove back the outposts of the much larger army of Swedish Crown Prince Jean Bernadotte (former French marshal). On August 23 the French stormed into Grossbeeren, 12 miles south of Berlin. But Gen. Baron Friedrich von Bülow rallied a Prussian force which threw back the French with a loss of 1,500 men. Despite its small scale, this allied victory saved Berlin. Oudinot, with his momentum gone, withdrew in haste to Wittenberg. *See* Bautzen; Dennewitz; Napoleonic Empire Wars.

Gross-Jägersdorf (Seven Years' War), 1757. While Frederick II, the Great, was struggling with Austria (Holy Roman Empress Maria Theresa) on the south and France (Louis XV) on the west, Czarina Elizabeth of Russia sent a ponderous army against Prussia on the east. Under Marshal Count Stepan Apraksin, the Russians crossed the border into East Prussia in the summer of 1757. At Gross-Jägersdorf (now in the U.S.S.R.) a Prussian army of less than 30,000, commanded by Gen. Hans von Lehwald, deployed to stop the invaders. The Russians, with a 3-to-1 superiority, overpowered Lehwald's troops on July 30. But just at the height of the Russian threat, Apraksin's supply organization broke down, some of his men mutinied, and he was forced to move back. This freed Frederick to concentrate against the French who were marching into Saxony. *See* Kolin; Rossbach; Seven Years' War.

Groveton (American Civil War). The opening fight of Bull Run II, on August 26, 1862, in which Gen. Thomas (Stonewall) Jackson's corps overwhelmed the Federal division of Gen. Rufus King; here the Confederate general Richard Ewell lost his leg. *See* Bull Run II.

Guadalajara (Spanish Civil War), 1937. In an effort to complete the encirclement of Madrid, the Nationalists launched a new offensive northeast of the city on March 8. The objective was Guadalajara, 34 miles from the Spanish capital. Two Nationalist armies spearheaded the attack—the right-hand (west) column, led by Gen. José Moscardó, consisted of 22,000 Moroccans, legionaries, and Carlists; the left-hand column was made up of

30,000 Italians under Gen. Mario Roatta. The inexperienced Republican troops of Col. Jurado gave ground before the heavy Nationalist assault. Brihuega, halfway to Guadalajara, fell on March 10 to the Italians. But then the government lines began to stiffen. When Roatta's thrust paused during March 15–17, the Republicans organized a counterattack. On March 18 two divisions, aided by Russian aircraft and tanks, swung over to the offensive. Taken by surprise, the Italians began falling back in a retreat that soon became a rout. Brihuega was retaken. The Republican advance on this front forced Moscardó to withdraw as well. Not all the lost territory was regained, but the Republican counterattack thoroughly destroyed the Nationalist drive on Guadalajara. In the fighting around Brihuega, Roatta lost 2,000 killed, 4,000 wounded, and 300 captured. He was replaced by Gen. Ettore Bastico, veteran of the Ethiopian conquest. Jurado suffered a similar number of killed and wounded. The defeat of the Italians led many observers (but not the Germans) to downgrade motorized troops. *See* Madrid; Málaga III; Bilbao; Spanish Civil War.

Guadalcanal (World War II), 1942–1943. The Japanese southward thrust through the Solomon Islands reached Guadalcanal in July 1942. Here work was begun on an airfield that would seriously threaten the Allied supply line to the Southwest Pacific. To block this advance, the U.S. 1st Marine Division (and two Raider battalions) under Gen. Alexander Vandegrift landed on August 7, 1942, on the north side of Guadalcanal, on Tulagi, and on two smaller islands nearby. Called Operation Cactus, it was the first Allied counteroffensive against Japan in World War II.

In 48 hours the first waves of the 16,000-marine force secured all their objectives, including the still uncompleted airfield near Lunga Point. (The air base was named Henderson Field in honor of a marine major killed at the battle of Midway.) But then the Japanese reacted savagely. Reinforcements poured into Guadalcanal, and strong naval units moved south to bombard U.S. shore positions and attack the Allied fleet that was seeking to protect the American garrison on the island. The result was one of the longest, bloodiest battles of the Pacific War.

While the marines dug in a defensive perimeter (seven miles by four miles) around Henderson Field, elements of what would become the Japanese Seventeenth Army (Haruyoshi Hyakutake) organized a counterattack from the Tenaru River to the east. This thrust was beaten back at the Ilu River on August 20 and 21. By August 20 the first U.S. planes began using the airfield. Fresh landings then doubled the enemy strength to about 6,000. Between September 12 and 14, the reinforced Japanese smashed at the American perimeter, particularly the Lunga River–Bloody Ridge area to the east and south. Again the marines held, but their beachhead stood in grave danger. Japanese warships bombarded the American position and bombers blasted it from the air. The steaming climate, tropical diseases, and relentless jungle warfare took a heavy toll. But perhaps most important of all was the knowledge that despite all the land fighting the struggle would ultimately turn on which side established the air and sea supremacy necessary to win the battle of reinforcements.

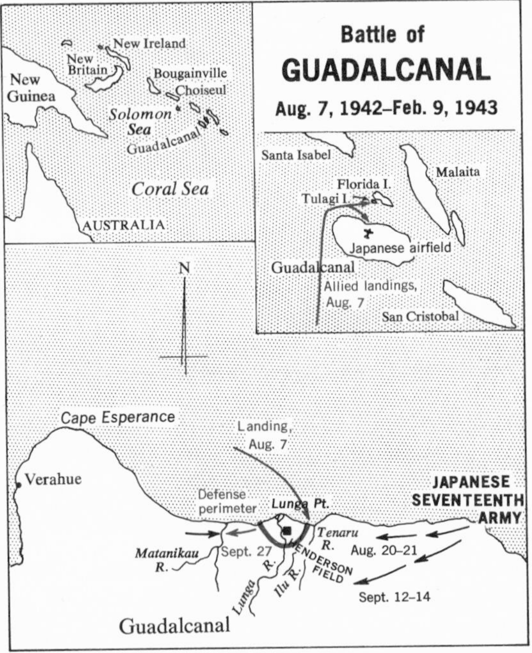

On September 18 the 2nd Marine Division and, later, Army Americal Division began to come ashore. At the same time, however, Japanese troop strength increased so much faster that the 36,000 Nipponese on the island now outnumbered the embattled Americans. A marine attack on the Matanikau River, to the west, on September 27 was defeated with a loss of 60 killed and 100 wounded. The persistent enemy attempts to recapture Henderson Field turned the nights of October and November into a deadly series of hand-to-hand struggles. But each time the defenders held their ground, inflicting casualties as high as 10 to 1. Meanwhile Adm. William Halsey, now in command in the South Pacific, vigorously countered the Japanese air and sea attacks. Finally, on November 15, following the decisive naval battle of Guadalcanal, the enemy went over to the defensive and made no further landings on Guadalcanal. The initiative then passed to the United States. In savage, close-range fighting the Americans gradually pushed back the Japanese. On December 9 command on Guadalcanal passed to the army's

Gen. Alexander Patch; the hard-fighting 1st Marine Division was relieved. With the arrival of the 25th Infantry Division, the U.S. XIV Corps was organized on the island, on January 2, 1943. The almost 50,000 U.S. troops on Guadalcanal now ensured a U.S. victory.

On the nights of February 7–9, swift Japanese destroyers evacuated about 12,000 of their troops from Cape Esperance at the northwest tip of the island. Left behind were 14,000 killed or missing, 9,000 dead of disease or starvation, and 1,000 captured. United States ground forces lost 1,600 killed and 4,200 wounded in action; many others were incapacitated by disease (in November alone malaria disabled 3,200). Nine marines won the Medal of Honor on Guadalcanal. One of the winners, Wildcat pilot Capt. Joe Foss, had become the ranking ace by shooting down 26 enemy planes.

The conquest of Guadalcanal marked the first rollback of Japan's grip on the Pacific islands. It also opened the way for other U.S. victories in the Solomons. *See* Solomon Islands; Guadalcanal—Naval Action; New Guinea; Rabaul; World War II.

Guadalcanal—Naval Action (World War II), 1942. When U.S. marines launched the Allied counteroffensive in the Pacific by landing on Guadalcanal, the Japanese navy reacted ferociously. Japanese naval units dominated the central and northern Solomon Islands and made good use of the protected waterway, nicknamed the Slot, between the two parallel chains of islands. Traffic through here was so heavy it was called the Tokyo Express. The focus of the action was Sealark Channel, north of Guadalcanal, opposite the U.S. beachhead defending Henderson Field. So many ships were sunk in the Channel, it received the name Iron Bottom Bay.

The battle of Guadalcanal began on August 7, 1942, when the supreme Allied commander in the South Pacific, the U.S. admiral Robert Ghormley, landed the 1st Marine Division on the northern side of the island. This landing was carried out by Adm. Richmond Turner's Amphibious Force, protected by a carrier group directed by Adm. Frank Fletcher (of Coral Sea and Midway fame). The Japanese rushed reinforcements to the island, protecting their transports with cruisers, destroyers, and submarines. In turn, the U.S. Navy fought to defend the marine bridgehead on Guadalcanal and to stop enemy troop disgorgements from the Tokyo Express. The resulting struggle for naval supremacy divides into six separate actions.

Savo Island (August 9). In a predawn attack the Japanese admiral Gunichi Mikawa's task force entered Iron Bottom Bay and sank four heavy cruisers (the Australian *Canberra* and the U.S. *Chicago, Quincy, Vincennes*) and killed some 1,000 seamen. Fletcher's carriers had already withdrawn, so the attackers could retreat back up the Slot with only minor damage. Later that day Turner pulled out his Amphibious Force. The Guadalcanal marines were now on their own.

Eastern Solomons (August 24–25). The Japanese admiral Nobutake Kondo attacked with carriers this time. The U.S. carrier *Enterprise* received heavy damage, but the Japanese light carrier *Ryujo* was sunk and 90 planes were shot down. Each side lost a destroyer. The enemy force withdrew. Thereafter Japan sent in reinforcements only at night, but its warships dominated the Solomon waters after dark as completely as U.S. planes controlled the area during the day. In subsequent action submarines sank the U.S. carrier *Wasp* (September 15) and several destroyers.

Cape Esperance (October 11–12). A third Japanese attack came down the Slot to bombard Henderson Field at night. The U.S. admiral Norman Scott's cruisers and destroyers beat back one heavy thrust, but on succeeding nights the airfield suffered severe damage from naval gunfire. In the meantime, thousands of enemy reinforcements were being landed between dusk and dawn. On October 18 Adm. William Halsey replaced Ghormley as supreme Allied commander in the South Pacific.

Santa Cruz Islands (October 26). In his first Guadalcanal action Halsey sent his carriers against the Japanese fleet in the waters east of the Solomons. Two enemy carriers and a cruiser were bombed and about 100 planes shot down. But 74 U.S. planes were lost, the *Hornet* (veteran of Shangri-La and Midway) was sunk, and the *Enterprise* again heavily damaged. There was now not a single U.S. carrier in operation in the entire Pacific.

Guadalcanal (November 13–15). The vicious contest for supremacy in the southern Solomons reached a climax in November when both sides sought to make new troop landings on Guadalcanal at the same time. Admiral Turner, after delivering the last of 6,000 marine and army reinforcements, withdrew his convoy to the southeast. He detached Adm. Daniel Callaghan with five cruisers and eight destroyers. Meanwhile Adm. Raizo Tanaka was moving down the Slot with 11,000 troops in 11 transports and 12 destroyers, preceded by a task force that included two battleships—the *Hiei* and the *Kirishima.* These warships, commanded by Adm. Nobutake Kondo, encountered the American force in Iron Bottom Bay the night of November 12–13. In a furious 30-minute melee Callaghan was killed, three U.S. destroyers were sunk, two cruisers—the *Atlanta* and *Juneau* (with 700 seamen)—were sent to the bottom, and the cruiser *Portland* was disabled. The Japanese returned to the attack the following night and bombarded Henderson Field with some 1,000 shells. At dawn, however, planes from the repaired *Enterprise* and bombers from Henderson

Field and Espiritu Santo, a New Hebrides base, struck at the enemy fleet. The air attack destroyed a cruiser, damaged three others, plus a transport, and sank six transports. That night (November 14) Tanaka doggedly pushed his remaining four transports through to Guadalcanal and unloaded behind the protection of the *Kirishima,* four cruisers, and nine destroyers. The price was high. The battleship and a destroyer were sunk by the U.S. battleship *Washington,* commanded by Adm. Willis Lee. In this action the battleship *South Dakota* was crippled and four destroyers were lost.

Tassafaronga (November 30). The last Japanese effort to land fresh troops on Guadalcanal was weak. Eight destroyers serving as transports were turned back after U.S. forces sank one and severely crippled another. The United States lost the cruiser *Northampton.*

Japan made no further attempt to reinforce its Guadalcanal garrison, although destroyers continued to move in supplies at night. At the end of the victorious American land battle, some 12,000 half-starved Japanese troops were evacuated by daring destroyer runs. In all, the Guadalcanal naval battles cost Japan 1 light carrier, 2 battleships, 4 cruisers, 11 destroyers, and 6 submarines. The Allies lost 2 heavy carriers, 8 cruisers, and 14 destroyers. But the American foothold in the Solomons stood secure. *See* Guadalcanal; Solomon Islands; World War II.

Guam I (World War II), 1941. On the third day of Japan's far-flung attack in the Pacific, 5,400 Japanese troops invaded the unfortified U.S. island of Guam in the Mariana Islands. To defend against this strong amphibious landing, Navy Capt. George McMillin, governor of Guam, had only 430 marines and navy men and 180 Chamorro guards. The unequal battle, on December 10, lasted three hours before McMillin surrendered the island. Seventeen Americans and Guamanians and one Japanese invader were killed. Japan's conquest of the western Pacific rolled on. *See* Pearl Harbor; Philippine Islands; Wake; World War II.

Guam II (World War II). The second of the Japanese-held Mariana Islands to be attacked successfully by U.S. troops, on July 21, 1944. *See* Mariana Islands.

Guatemala. *See* Chalchuapa.

Guilford Courthouse (War of the American Revolution), 1781. When the British commander in the South, Gen. Lord Charles Cornwallis, failed to trap the American army of Gen. Nathanael Greene south of the Dan River, he turned back into North Carolina. Greene collected reinforcements in Virginia until he had 4,400 men. Then, on February 25, 1781, he recrossed the Dan. Moving to Guilford Courthouse, Greene took up a strong position and waited for Cornwallis to attack. The latter marched westward from Hillsboro, reaching the American position in the afternoon of March 15. Greene had deployed his army much as Daniel Morgan had done at Cowpens two months before. His weakest militia (North Carolina) occupied the front line behind a zigzag rail fence. The second line, 300 yards to the rear, was held by a stronger militia force from Virginia. More than 500 yards farther to the rear stood the principal line, the Continentals, drawn up along the brow of the courthouse hill.

Although the British army of 1,900 was heavily outnumbered, the red-coated regulars advanced steadily. They took the two volleys of the militia in the first line and pressed on to the second line. Here the fighting was more severe, but again the relentless British attack overcame American resistance. At the third line the fighting became intense. Finally, rather than risk everything in attempting to win a decisive victory, Greene effected an orderly retreat. Cornwallis won the field, but the price had come high. More than a fourth of his men were casualties—93 dead, 439 wounded. Greene lost 78 killed and 183 wounded, not counting the militiamen who had vanished into the woods. Too weak now to pursue the Americans, Cornwallis turned and marched 200 miles to Wilmington, N.C., to replenish his supplies. He then moved farther north into Virginia. *See* Cowpens; Chesapeake Capes; Hobkirk's Hill; American Revolution.

Guinegate (English-French Wars), 1513. The English Tudor king Henry VIII joined the anti-French Holy League, aimed at Louis XII, in 1511. Two years later he took an army to his English base at Calais, then marched inland to lay siege to the French village of Thérouanne. Here the English received some German reinforcements sent by Holy Roman Emperor Maximilian I. On August 16, 1513, at Guinegate, this force intercepted a French body of cavalry riding to the relief of the besieged village. Before the action became fully developed, the French turned and made a hasty retreat, leaving the famous knight Bayard (Pierre Terrail) and a few other notables as captives of the English. The speedy retreat of the French has given the name "battle of the Spurs" to the engagement. (For another battle of the Spurs *see* Courtrai.) Although the English then took Thérouanne and Tournai, the chief battles of the war were fought in northern Italy and along the English-Scottish border. Henry led his army back to England the following year. *See* Novara I; Flodden.

Guise (World War I). A French counterattack, on August 29, 1914, which temporarily checked the German advance after the battle of the Frontiers. *See* Frontiers of France.

Gujrat (Sikh-British War II), 1849. Following two hard-fought battles against the Sikhs in West

Punjab, Gen. Sir Hugh Gough pressed northeast with his Anglo-Indian army. On February 22 he reached Gujrat near the Chenab River, 68 miles north of Lahore. Here, reinforced to more than 20,000 men, his largest army to date, he opened a heavy bombardment against a Sikh force double in size. Gough's skillfully positioned artillery of 84 guns blasted the enemy for two hours before they bolted their lines. The Anglo-Indian cavalry and infantry took up a vigorous pursuit that virtually destroyed the entire fleeing army. Gough lost 92 killed and 682 wounded. This battle broke Sikh resistance, ending the war, with the Punjab under firm British control. *See* Ramnagar; Chilianwala; Sikh-British Wars.

Gumbinnen (World War I), 1914. The war on the Eastern Front opened on August 17 with the invasion of East Prussia by the 200,000 troops of Gen. Pavel Rennenkampf's First Army of Russia. Advancing on a 35-mile front, the Russians encountered the first elements of the German Eighth Army, commanded by Gen. Max von Prittwitz, at the village of Stallupönen, five miles inside the frontier. A vigorous spoiling attack by Gen. Hermann von François's Prussian I Corps checked the advance on August 17, but that night the Germans had to fall back westward 10 miles toward Gumbinnen (Gusev), 68 miles east of Königsberg (Kaliningrad).

As the Russian offensive ground slowly westward, Prittwitz deployed his army in front of Gumbinnen for a counterattack. François's corps, on the German left (north), launched the assault before dawn on August 20 under a heavy artillery bombardment. Waves of gray-clad infantry rolled against the Russian lines until Rennenkampf's guns had exhausted their ammunition. The German infantry and cavalry then decimated the Russian right wing. Elsewhere, however, the battle took an altogether different turn. In the center Gen. August von Mackensen's German XVII Corps jumped off at 8 A.M., four hours behind François. The Russians, now alerted, unleashed a devastating artillery barrage that checked the assault in this sector and finally drove the attackers into a disorderly retreat of 15 miles. On the southern flank Gen. Otto von Below's I Reserve Corps was four hours later than the XVII Corps in launching its attack. The fighting had barely begun here when the rout of Mackensen's troops forced Below to withdraw as well. This in turn exposed François's corps, on the extreme left, which pulled back that evening to give the Russians a costly but clear-cut victory.

Although Rennenkampf failed to pursue the beaten army, Prittwitz wanted to abandon East Prussia and retire behind the Vistula River. His panic was heightened by the news that Aleksandr Samsonov's Second Army was advancing from the south on a 50-mile front toward the German rear. To preserve the East Prussia front, the German chief of the general staff, Field Marshal Helmuth von Moltke, dismissed Prittwitz. Paul von Hindenburg was called out of retirement to take over the Eighth Army with Gen. Erich Ludendorff, the hero of Liége, as his chief of staff. *See* Tannenberg II; World War I.

Gustav-Cassino Line (World War II), 1943–1944. The Allied offensive in Italy overran the lower quarter of that nation during the early fall of 1943. After taking Naples on October 1, the Fifth Army under the U.S. general Mark Clark thrust north across the Volturno River, between October 12 and 15. But as it approached the Garigliano and the mountains to the north, mud and the increasingly stronger German defenses of Field Marshal Albert Kesselring brought the advance to a halt by mid-November. On the right (Adriatic) side, the British Eighth Army, commanded by Gen. Sir Bernard Montgomery, fought its way across the Trigno and Sangro rivers in November and December before it too was halted, after taking Ortona on December 28.

The Allied armies now faced a formidable belt of fortifications held by the German Tenth Army (Heinrich Vietinghoff-Scheel). Called the Gustav Line, the German defenses stretched across the mountainous spine of Italy from the mouth of the Garigliano River on the west coast to a point north of Ortona on the Adriatic Sea. Manned by nine German divisions with nine others in reserve, the Gustav Line covered the two chief routes to Rome: Highway 7 near the Tyrrhenian coast and Highway 6, which entered the Liri (northern tributary of the Garigliano) Valley at Cassino. General Sir Harold Alexander's Fifteenth Army Group (11 divisions) now faced the heavy task of breaking through this winter line (*Winterstellung*) to Rome, the key objective of the offensive in Italy. The Allies had overwhelming superiority in the air, but the entrenched German positions in the mountains offset much of this advantage. On the ground the Allies were weakened by the loss of seven prime divisions, sent to England for the cross-Channel attack the following year. Also going to England (December 10) for the forthcoming invasion were Gen. Dwight Eisenhower, who was replaced as supreme Mediterranean commander by Gen. Sir Henry Maitland-Wilson, and Montgomery, whose Eighth Army was taken over by Gen. Oliver Leese.

Early in January 1944 the Allied order of battle in Italy stood, from left to right: Fifth Army (six divisions), comprising British X Corps (Gen. Richard McCreery), U.S. II Corps (Gen. Geoffrey Keyes), and Free French Corps (Gen. Alphonse Juin); and Eighth Army (five divisions), comprising British XIII and V Corps. The U.S. VI Corps had been withdrawn from the line to make the Anzio landing, in an effort to outflank the Gustav Line.

Despite the harsh winter weather, Alexander's troops continued to strike at the Gustav Line, particularly in the area dominated by the key height of Monte Cassino. On January 17 the British X Corps forced the passage of the lower Garigliano on the far left but could move no farther. Three days later the U.S. 36th Infantry was thrown back at the Rapido. The other II Corps division, the U.S. 34th, failed to take Cassino early in February. Here the Gustav Line was dominated by 1,100-foot Hill 516, crowned by a Benedictine monastery. On the right of the Fifth Army, the French Corps could make only small gains. On February 16 the New Zealand II Corps (drawn from the Eighth Army) under Gen. Bernard Freyberg struck at Cassino from the north after a heavy bombing of the monastery. This attack also failed.

A third attack on Cassino came on March 15. Freyberg's 2nd New Zealand, 4th Indian, and 78th British divisions gained a foothold in Cassino town but were blocked off the hill by the German 1st Parachute Division. By March 23 the attack had stalled completely, at a cost of 2,400 casualties in the corps. Alexander then shifted most of the Eighth Army from the Adriatic side to the Cassino front, while the Fifth Army concentrated on the lower Garigliano. On May 11th, behind a 2,000-gun barrage, both Allied armies plunged forward (four corps abreast) on a 20-mile front stretching from Cassino southwest to the sea. Hard fighting gradually pushed the Germans back. On May 17 Gen. Wladyslaw Anders' Polish II Corps of the Eighth Army finally took Cassino.

On the far left, the U.S. II Corps drove up the coast to link up on May 25 with the U.S. VI Corps, which had burst out of its Anzio beachhead two days earlier. Meanwhile, the combined assault of the two Allied armies had broken through the entire Gustav Line and a secondary position behind it called the Adolf Hitler Line. Overcoming a last-ditch defense southeast of Rome, the II Corps, led by the U.S. 88th Infantry, drove into the Piazza Venezia in the heart of the city on June 4.

Both Allied armies closely pursued the retreating German Fourteenth (Gen. Mackensen) and Tenth armies. By August 4 the Allies had driven northward some 250 miles to a line Pisa-Florence-Ancona. Here they encountered another prepared German position, the Gothic Line. *See* Salerno; Anzio; Gothic Line; World War II.

Gwalior (Indian Mutiny), 1858. The campaign of Gen. Sir Hugh Rose to suppress the Great Mutiny in north-central India finally reached Gwalior on June 17. Here, 60 miles south of Agra, Rose's column of British and loyal Sepoys encountered a large rebel force led in person by the Rani of Jhansi, who had been driven out of her city ten weeks earlier. In a relentless, three-day battle Rose captured the town. Among the many mutineers slain was the rani. This victory virtually ended the mutiny, except for small isolated suppressions, in the course of which Great Britain took firm control over the entire subcontinent. *See* Jhansi; Indian Mutiny.

H

Haarlem (Netherlands War of Independence), 1572–1573. In the campaign of King Philip II of Spain to subdue a revolt in the Netherlands, his commander, the Duke of Alva, ordered an attack on Haarlem, 12 miles west of Amsterdam, on December 11, 1572. The duke sent his natural son Don Frederic to direct the operation. Frederic bombarded the city and then tried to take it by assault. He failed to gain an entrance despite having 30,000 Spanish, Walloon, and German troops to use against only 4,000 defending Dutch. The garrison maintained its defense by frequent successful sorties against the besieging troops. But starvation took a relentless toll. When the supply of shoe leather, rats, and weeds ran out, Haarlem capitulated, on July 12, 1573. The 1,800 surviving defenders were executed, plus 400 prominent citizens. The besiegers had lost 12,000 men through combat, disease, and capture. (In this ruthless action the Dutch garrison had publicly hanged their prisoners.) *See* Brielle; Alkmaar I; Netherlands War of Independence.

Habbaniya (World War II), 1941. The overwhelming Axis victories early in the war produced, in March 1941, the establishment of a pro-German government in Iraq under Rashid Ali. The rightful Iraqi regent, Emir Abdul-Ilah, fled to the protection of a British warship at Basra, a port on the Persian Gulf. To protect their treaty rights, the British landed a brigade from India at Basra on April 18. Rashid Ali then attacked the British air base at Habbaniya, 40 miles west of Baghdad, on May 2. The assailants numbered about 9,000 men, equipped with 50 guns. To defend the airfield, Air Vice-Marshal Smart had only 250 British infantry, 1,000 Royal Air Force personnel, and about 1,000 native troops. The isolated garrison had no artillery and was further hampered by the need to protect 9,000 civilians. The decisive element, however, proved to be Royal Air Force planes, which kept the Iraqi under frequent attack and finally silenced their artillery completely.

After four days of siege, Rashid Ali's troops began to withdraw. The British force promptly counterattacked and took 400 prisoners and much equipment. On May 7 the Iraqis fell back across the Euphrates River to Al Falluja. The defenders of Habbaniya, now reinforced by a motorized brigade from Haifa (now in Israel), pressed their attack on May 19, captured Al Falluja, and drove into Baghdad on May 30. Rashid Ali fled the country and the regent resumed control of the government the following day.

The British victory in Iraq was followed by the winning of Allied dominance over the entire Middle East. On July 14, 1941, after a month of skirmishing, British and Free French forces ousted the Vichy French regime in Syria (to the west). British casualties numbered about 4,600, French losses about 6,500. Then on August 25 Britain and Russia occupied Iran (to the east) to forestall a possible German coup in that country. British casualties in this operation were 22 killed and 42 wounded. The Iraq triumph was directed by the Middle East commander, Gen. Sir Archibald Wavell; the Syria victory by Wavell and his successor, Gen. Sir Claude Auchinleck; the Iran occupation by Auchinleck. *See* World War II.

Hadley (King Philip's War), 1676. The steady westward expansion by the English colonists in New England led to an Indian uprising in 1675 led by the Wampanoag chief, King Philip (Metacomet). After a year of raiding back and forth, a force of 250 settlers from the Connecticut Valley and 200 allied Mohegan Indians marched into western Massachusetts. Led by Maj. Talcot, the combined army defeated Philip's Indians at Hadley on June 12, 1676. Then, turning eastward, Talcot's men destroyed an enemy force of 250 near Marlborough. Philip himself was hunted down by Capt. Benjamin Church and killed in the Assowamset Swamp on August 11. His wife and nine-year-old child were sold into West Indian slavery. The last of his men surrendered on August 28, ending the war. *See* Indian Wars in the United States.

Haelen (World War I), 1914. While the German armies of Kaiser Wilhelm II pounded at Liége in the opening battle of the war, a cavalry corps under Gen. Georg von der Marwitz crossed the Meuse River to the north. The darkly clad Uhlans rode into Limburg Province, aiming at Louvain. At Haelen the Germans were held up at a bridge defended by Belgian cavalry, commanded by General de Witte. Fighting dismounted, as riflemen, the Belgians beat off repeated German cavalry charges from 8 A.M. to 6 P.M. on August 12, 1914. Marwitz finally withdrew after suffering cruel losses. The victory was hailed throughout the Allied world, but it represented only a temporary check to the massive German sweep through Belgium, which got under way with the fall of the Liége forts four days later. *See* Liége; Namur II; World War I.

Hakata Bay (Mongol Invasions of Japan), 1274. Kublai Khan, Mongol emperor of China and grandson of the great Genghis Khan, turned to foreign invasions after subduing most of the Chinese mainland, including Korea, by about 1270. In 1274 a Mongol-Korean fleet crossed the Sea of Japan, seized the islands of Tsushima and Iki, and then made a landing at Hakata (Hakozaki) Bay in northern Kyushu. Mongol weapons and organization proved far superior to those of the Japanese. But after winning a bridgehead on the island, the invaders returned to Korea because of a storm. The Hojo rulers of Japan, who had succeeded the Minamoto clan, immediately began building fortifications against future invasions. *See* Dan no Ura; Mongol Wars.

Halfaya Pass (World War II). Part of a British counterattack, during June 15–17, 1941, which failed to check the first Axis offensive in North Africa. *See* Salûm–Halfaya Pass.

Haliartus (Greek City-States' Wars), 395 B.C. Nine years after Sparta's victory in the Great Peloponnesian War, conflict broke out between Sparta and Thebes, former allies. Lysander marched a Spartan army into Boeotia to Haliartus. The Boeotians inside Haliartus rushed out to attack the Spartans just as a force of Thebans was approaching to aid the city. Attacked from two sides, the Spartans were routed and Lysander was killed.

Thebes was now joined by Athens, Corinth, and other city-states in a growing revolt (Corinthian War) against Spartan hegemony. *See* Aegospotami; Coronea II; Cnidus; Greek City-States' Wars.

Halidon Hill (English-Scottish Wars), 1333. Taking advantage of the civil war in Scotland between the Royalists of David II and the pretender Edward de Baliol, Edward III laid siege to Berwick upon Tweed. Sir Archibald Douglas, regent for King David, marched a Scottish army to relieve the fortress. On July 19, 1333, the Scots charged the English position at nearby Halidon Hill. Edward III deployed in three divisions of dismounted men-at-arms, each with wings of archers that cut the Scots' force to pieces. The men-at-arms then took to their horses and counterattacked to complete the rout. This deployment, first used at Halidon Hill, became a highly successful English tactic in the later Hundred Years' War.

Following Douglas' defeat (which cost him his life), Berwick surrendered, and young King David fled to France. Edward de Baliol, who had fought on the English side with other "disinherited" lords, did homage to Edward III as the rulers of Scotland. But the kingdom remained unsubdued. *See* Dupplin Moor; Sluys; Neville's Cross.

Hampton Roads (American Civil War), 1862. When Confederate forces seized the Norfolk (Va.) Navy Yard in 1861, they raised the frigate *Merrimac* and rebuilt it into an ironclad ram. Renamed the *Virginia,* the squat ship, which was protected by four inches of iron, carried six 9-inch guns and four of smaller caliber. On March 8 the ironclad sailed into Hampton Roads under Com. Franklin Buchanan with a crew of 350 men. The Federal fleet stationed here was no match for the remade *Merrimac*. The 50-gun *Congress* was forced aground and surrendered. The 30-gun *Cumberland* was rammed and sunk. Other ships were scattered. In the evening the *Virginia* retired. The Confederate plan was to resume the attack the following day under Lt. Catesby ap Roger Jones, who had succeeded the wounded Buchanan.

During the night the new Federal *Monitor* arrived in Hampton Roads from New York. The first specially designed ironclad, it carried two 11-inch guns in a revolving turret protected by 11 inches of iron. (While the *Virginia* was described as a "floating barn roof," the *Monitor* was called a "cheese box on a raft.") Under the command of Lt. John Lorimer Worden, with a crew of 58, the *Monitor* took up a position between the *Virginia* and the crippled Federal fleet. For more than two hours the two ships dueled, in history's first battle between ironclads. Although the *Monitor* proved to be much more maneuverable, it could inflict no important damage on its adversary. About noon a Confederate shell struck the *Monitor's* sight hole, partially blinding Worden and causing the Federal ship to withdraw. The *Virginia* returned to Norfolk. In the two-day naval battle the Federals suffered 409 casualties, the Confederates 21.

When a Federal land attack on Norfolk forced the Confederates to evacuate the city, the *Virginia* was destroyed, on May 9. At the end of the year the *Monitor* went down in a gale off Cape Hatteras, N.C. *See* American Civil War.

Hanau (Napoleonic Empire Wars), 1813. Despite its disastrous defeat at Leipzig, the Grande Armée of Napoleon I shook off allied pursuit by marching westward. On the fifth day of the retreat (October 23) 95,000 French troops reached Erfurt, 65 miles west of Leipzig. The lethargy of the allied pursuit was based largely on the knowledge that Bavaria had switched its allegiance and that Gen. Karl Wrede's army now stood directly astride Napoleon's route of withdrawal into France. On October 30 the French army reached Hanau on the Main River, 11 miles east of Frankfort. Here Wrede had concentrated 43,500 Bavarian and partisan troops. Unhesitatingly, Napoleon's advance guard struck the roadblock with cavalry, artillery, and bayonets. Before such a determined onslaught, the Bavarian defenses collapsed with a loss of 10,000 men. The French, who suffered half as many casualties, entered Hanau the following day. On November 1 Napoleon crossed the Rhine at Mainz. For the first time in 20 years French soldiers prepared to defend their own soil.

Napoleon's withdrawal behind the borders of France isolated many strong points still holding out in Germany. Although some of these, such as Hamburg, held by Marshal Louis Davout, defied capture, others fell to hard-pressing allied forces. Marshal Marquis Laurent de Gouvion Saint-Cyr surrendered Dresden on November 11 to the Austrians. Danzig, under Gen. Comte Jean Rapp, capitulated to Prussia on December 30. *See* Leipzig; Brienne; Napoleonic Empire Wars.

Hara Castle (Japanese Persecutions of Christians), 1637–1638. The Tokugawa shogunate, which came to power in 1600, persecuted Christians ruthlessly. By 1637 the largest remaining Christian settlement was on Shimabara Peninsula in western Kyushu. When these people revolted late that year, Shogun Iemitsu moved in a large body of Imperial troops. Some 37,000 rebels, chiefly Christians, sought refuge in Hara Castle. After a siege of three months the castle fell early in 1638. All those who had survived the siege were killed. This massacre erased almost the last traces of Christianity in Japan. *See* Toyotomi Castle.

Harfleur (Hundred Years' War), 1415. Civil strife in France between the Burgundians and the Orleanists, who included the mad Charles VI, prompted England's Henry V to lead a new expedition across the Channel. Aligning himself with the Burgundian faction, Henry landed an army of about 10,000 men at the mouth of the Seine in mid-August 1415. He laid siege to Harfleur, then the chief port of northwestern France, on August 19. The garrison's stout defense, plus an epidemic of dysentery in the English ranks, prolonged the siege until September 22. On that date Harfleur surrendered. Henry expelled the French inhabitants and encouraged English immigration in an attempt to turn the city into a continental base similar to Calais. With his army reduced to little more than 5,000 men by sickness, casualties, and the garrison left at Harfleur, Henry marched northward toward Calais. (France regained Harfleur in 1435, lost it five years later, and took permanent possession in 1449.) *See* Margate; Agincourt; Hundred Years' War.

Harkány (Austrian-Turkish Wars), 1687. The failure of Mohammed IV's Turkish army at Vienna in 1683 marked a turning point in the long border conflict. A German-Austrian army under Charles V of Lorraine and Louis William I of Baden-Baden marched into Hungary and seized Buda on the Danube in 1686. Meanwhile Peter I, the Great, of Russia laid siege to Azov, and a Venetian army commanded by Gen. Francesco Morosini overran the Peloponnesus, in present-day Greece. The Turks fell back into southern Hungary, where Charles V, titular duke of Lorraine, attacked them at Harkány, just southwest of the site of the decisive battle won by Suleiman the Magnificent over the Hungarians in 1526. In this "second battle of Mohács," on August 12, 1687, the Western army reversed the previous decision, thoroughly routing the Ottomans. The panic-stricken Turkish soldiers fled across the Danube and promptly deposed Mohammed IV, who was succeeded by Suleiman III. But the tide of war continued to flow against the Ottoman Empire. *See* Vienna II; Slankamen.

Harlem Heights (War of the American Revolution). A British reconnaissance in force against George Washington's position in northern Manhattan, on September 16, 1776, which led Sir William Howe to try a flanking maneuver to the east. *See* White Plains.

Harpers Ferry (American Civil War), 1862. When Gen. Robert E. Lee took his Confederate army into Maryland during September 4–6, he sent Gen. Thomas (Stonewall) Jackson to seize Harpers Ferry. The capture of this Potomac River crossing would give Lee a protected line of communications down the Shenandoah Valley. On September 13 Jackson moved on Harpers Ferry from the west with the divisions of Gens. Ambrose Hill and Alexander Lawton. The Federal commander, Col. D. S. Miles, withdrew his 12,000-man garrison into the angle formed by the Potomac and Shenandoah rivers. Across the Shenandoah to the east Gen. John Walker's Confederate division took up a position on Loudon Heights. A third Confederate force, two brigades of Gen. Richard Anderson's division (under the overall command of Gen. Lafayette McLaws), occupied Maryland Heights north of the Potomac.

Jackson's ring of artillery, on high ground overlooking Harpers Ferry, opened its bombardment on September 14. That night Col. Benjamin Davis and Amos Voss led 1,200 Federal cavalrymen safely out of the besieged position through McLaws' lines to the north. Miles made no attempt to follow with his infantry. When the Confederate bombardment resumed on the morning of September 15, Miles surrendered the garrison. (He was accidentally killed during the capitulation.) Jackson promptly started his troops on a forced march northward toward Sharpsburg where the remainder of Lee's army was preparing to resist the attack of Gen. George McClellan's 75,000 troops of the Army of the Potomac. *See* Bull Run II; Antietam Creek; American Civil War.

Hastenbeck (Seven Years' War), 1757. While Frederick II, the Great, of Prussia was fighting the Austrian armies in Bohemia, his English ally was organizing an Anglo-Hannoverian force on the Weser River in the west. Under William Augustus, Duke of Cumberland (son of George II), an army of 36,000 men guarded Hannover against French invasion. This mission was put to the test by King Louis XV, who sent a French army of 74,000 men under the Marquis de Courtanvaux (Louis Le Tellier, later duc d'Estrées) toward Hannover. On July 26, 1757, the invading column struck Cumberland's position at Hastenbeck, three miles southeast of Hameln. In a fierce, confused struggle each commander believed himself to be beaten. But the French won the day when the English duke precipitately withdrew his troops to the Elbe.

Six weeks later Cumberland signed the Convention of Kloster-Zeven, dissolving his army and abandoning Hannover and Brunswick to the French. The British government repudiated the agreement, the king himself relieving his son of command. But the damage was done. Frederick's western flank lay exposed to attack by France (and it would be two years before Great Britain could field another army in Europe). Meanwhile a fresh disaster struck Frederick in East Prussia. *See* Kolin; Gross-Jägersdorf; Rossbach; Seven Years' War.

Hastings (Norman Conquest of England), 1066. While Harold II was routing the Norse invasion at Stamford Bridge in the north, England suffered the long-dreaded Norman invasion in the south. Under the Norman duke, William, 7,000 warriors sailed across the English Channel in 450 flatboats to land at Pevensey in Sussex on September 28. For the next two weeks William organized his army and raided the countryside for supplies. Meanwhile, Harold hurriedly marched the 200 miles from York to London in seven days, built up his force to 7,000 men, and then, on the evening of October 13, deployed his Saxons on the slope of Senlac Hill eight miles north of Hastings, barring the direct route to London. The next morning William, the future Conqueror, attacked at the present-day town of Battle.

The battle of Hastings proved to be a deadly struggle between the infantry of Harold and the feudal cavalry (and archers) of the Normans. Standing firm on a deep front of 1,100 yards, the ax- and spear-wielding Saxons threw back the first charge of William's armored knights. When the Norman left began retiring in disorder, the English infantry started down the hill in pursuit but were promptly cut to pieces by William's disciplined knights in the center. By energetic leadership, Harold re-formed his main line of defense

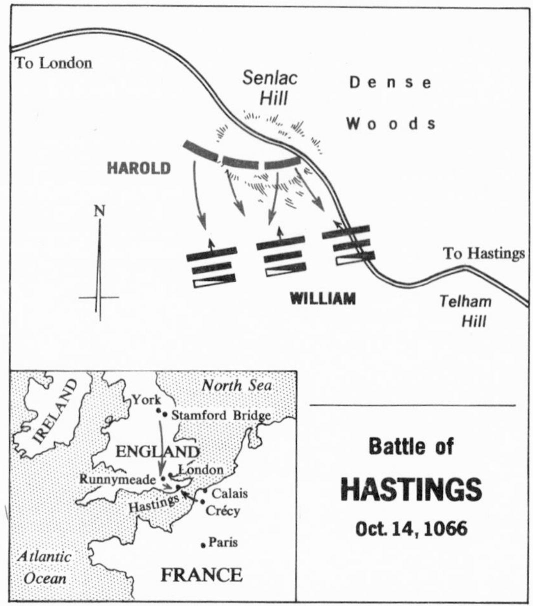

before the second Norman attack could be launched. Now the fight settled down to a steady pounding of the Saxon mass by William's cavalry. Hour after hour Harold's foot soldiers held their ground and, despite cruel losses from showers of arrows, inflicted heavy casualties on the horses and men of the invaders.

Toward evening the battle turned. William feigned a general withdrawal of his cavalry. This apparent opening was more than the long-frustrated Saxon foot soldiers could resist. They broke ranks to charge in pursuit. Halfway down the hill the Norman knights wheeled about to slaughter the onrushing infantry. Although Harold's bodyguard (the housecarls) remained unconquered, this force too dissolved when the king himself fell mortally wounded from an arrow in the eye. The battle was over. Both sides lost at least a quarter of their troops.

William, who had three horses killed under him in the fighting, camped on the battlefield, where he later ordered the building of Battle Abbey. The way was now open to London, and after a cautious advance to the capital, William the Conqueror was crowned king of England at Westminster Abbey on Christmas Day. Thus Hastings came to be the most decisive battle ever fought on English soil; only the World War II battle of Britain rivals it in importance in English history. *See* Val-'es-Dunes; Stamford Bridge; Ely I.

Havana (Seven Years' War), 1762. The so-called Family Compact brought Spain (Charles III) into the war on the side of France (Louis XV) early in 1762. It was disastrous for the Spanish. On March 5 the British admiral Sir George Pocock, veteran of the war in India, sailed from England with 19 warships carrying 10,000 troops. He entered the harbor of Havana, Cuba, on June 5, landed the expeditionary force, and established a blockade, which trapped 12 Spanish vessels in the port. Ashore, the British troops under the Earl of Albemarle (George Keppel) suffered more from disease than from Spanish weapons. Morro Castle, guarding the harbor, surrendered on July 30. Two weeks later Havana fell to the 2,500 able-bodied British who remained from the original force. The conquest of Cuba cut the communications between the rich Spanish colonies in the Americas and the mother country. At the peace table the following year, however, Cuba was ceded back to Spain in exchange for West and East Florida. *See* Manila I; Freiberg; Seven Years' War.

Heathfield (Teutonic Conquest of Britain), 633. In the early seventh century the northern kingdom of Northumbria dominated the other six Anglo-Saxon states (together, the seven were called the Heptarchy) of Britain. Its king, Edwin, who was a convert to Christianity, stood as probably the strongest ruler in English history up to that time. In 633, however, King Penda of Mercia (the Midlands), the champion of paganism, made an alliance with Cadwallon (Caedwalla), the Christian king of North Wales (Gwynedd), aimed at breaking Edwin's power. The armies of the strange alliance attacked the Northumbrians near Doncaster at Heathfield (Hatfield Chase), 45 miles east of Manchester. In a fierce battle Edwin's army was defeated and he was killed. His severed head was exhibited on the walls of his captured capital of York. *See* Chester; Heavenfield.

Heavenfield (Teutonic Conquest of Britain), 634. A year after losing their king (Edwin) at the battle of Heathfield, the Northumbrians rallied behind Edwin's nephew Oswald. One of the two armies that had united to defeat them was the Britons, under Cadwallon (Caedwalla). The Northumbrians caught up with this force at Heavenfield, near the Roman Wall. Without their Mercian allies, the Britons were totally defeated and Cadwallon was killed. Heavenfield was the last full-scale battle between an exclusively Briton army and their Saxon conquerors.

Eight years later Oswald turned his Northumbrians against Mercia, but the results were disastrous. *See* Heathfield; Maserfield.

Hedgeley Moor (Wars of the Roses), 1464. The overwhelming victory of Edward IV's Yorkists (white rose) at Towton in 1461 seemed to extinguish Lancastrian (red rose) hopes of restoring Henry VI to power in England. But the exiled monarch's unyielding wife, Queen Margaret, fought on from friendly courts in Scotland, Burgundy, and France. In 1462 and again in 1463 she tried, but failed, to establish a solid Lancastrian base in the far north. Then in 1464 the Lancastrian Henry Beaufort, duke of Somerset, who had been pardoned and befriended by Edward IV, returned to his original cause and raised a revolt in Northumberland. He was joined by Sir Ralph Percy, who was also on parole from the Yorkist king.

At Hedgeley Moor near Alnwick the rebels encountered a strong Yorkist force commanded by Lord Montagu, brother of Warwick the Kingmaker. In a pitched battle on April 25, 1464, the Lancastrian rebels suffered a stinging defeat. Percy was killed. Somerset escaped, but he and other survivors were closely pursued by the victorious Montagu. *See* Towton; Hexham; Roses, War of the.

Heilsberg (Napoleonic Empire Wars), 1807. Before Napoleon I could launch his spring offensive in East Prussia, his French forces came under attack by the Russian army of Gen. Levin Bennigsen, on June 5, 1807. But strong resistance all along the line blunted and then turned back the Russian advance in two days. Napoleon now seized the initiative and advanced northeastward up the left bank of the Alle River. Bennigsen fell back to his strongly fortified camp at Heilsberg (Lidzbark Warmiński). Marshal Joachim Murat, directing the French advance guard of cavalry and Marshal Nicolas Soult's IV Corps, ordered an attack against the bulk of the 90,000-man Russian army on June 10. The premature assault was beaten back with some 8,000 casualties on each side. Faced with relentless French pressure all along the line, however, Bennigsen withdrew to the north two days later. *See* Danzig II; Friedland; Napoleonic Empire Wars.

Heligoland Bight (World War I), 1914. The first naval battle of World War I resulted from a British squadron's raid on the German ships in the Heligoland Bight off the northwest coast of Germany. During the night of August 27–28 the English commodore Sir Reginald Tyrwhitt sailed from Harwich, England, to the Bight with the light cruisers *Arethusa* and *Fearless* and two destroyer flotillas. At dawn Tyrwhitt's ships attacked, supported by a cruiser force under Adm. Sir David Beatty, which had moved down from the main British fleet at Scapa Flow. Royal Navy guns sank three German light cruisers and one destroyer and crippled three other cruisers. More than 1,000 Germans were killed or drowned and 200 taken prisoner. The British ships withdrew late the same day without the loss of a ship and at a cost of 33 killed and 40 wounded. As a consequence of this battle, Kaiser Wilhelm II ordered Adm. Alfred von Tirpitz to "avoid any action which might lead to heavy losses." *See* Coronel; World War I.

Hellenistic Monarchies, Wars of the (301–146 B.C.). The death of Alexander III (the Great) in 323 B.C. foreshadowed the end of the great Macedonian Empire he had created. Following the battle of Ipsus in 301 B.C., the empire was carved into four major states—Macedonia, Egypt, Thrace (which included most of Asia Minor), and the Seleucid kingdom in Syria. These states, called the Hellenistic monarchies, warred among themselves until the Roman Republic established its rule over the entire area. *See also* Macedonian Wars.

Ipsus	301 B.C.
Corupedion	281 B.C.
Pergamum	230 B.C.
Sellasia	221 B.C.
Raphia	217 B.C.
Panion	200 B.C.
Cynoscephalae II	197 B.C.
Thermopylae II	191 B.C.
Magnesia	190 B.C.
Pydna	168 B.C.
Corinth	146 B.C.

Helsingborg (Danish-German War), 1362. King Waldemar IV of Denmark, after freeing his country from foreign rule, challenged the strong Hanseatic League of North German cities. In 1362 his Danish warships encountered the German fleet off Helsingborg (Hälsingborg) on the southwestern coast of Sweden. Waldemar's vessels won a decisive victory, and in the peace treaty that followed he canceled many of the Hansa trading privileges in Denmark. (During 1368–70, however, the Hanseatic League regained its dominance over Denmark and the Baltic.)

Hennersdorf (War of the Austrian Succession), 1745. Despite two earlier defeats by Frederick II, the Great, of Prussia in 1745, the armies of the Holy Roman Empire (Francis I and Maria Theresa) launched a two-pronged attack aimed at Berlin. From Saxony, Marshal Rutowski moved northeast, while Prince Charles of Lorraine (brother of the emperor) marched northward through Bohemia. To meet this threat, Frederick hurried back from Silesia. He intercepted the Austrian army of Prince Charles on the Saxon-Silesian border at Hennersdorf (in present-day southwestern Poland) on November 24. Catching their opponents on the march, the Prussians scattered the Austrian column. A vigorous pursuit forced Charles to fall back into Bohemia. Meanwhile, a second Prussian army, under Field Marshal Leopold I of Anhalt-Dessau, was moving up the left bank of the Elbe against the Saxon prong of the Imperial offensive. *See* Soor; Kesselsdorf; Austrian Succession, War of the.

Heraclea (Rise of Rome), 280 B.C. Rome's conquest of central Italy early in the third century B.C. brought the aggressive republic into contact with the Greek city-states (Magna Graecia) at the southern end of the peninsula. Friction developed almost immediately. The Italiotes of Tarentum (Taranto) called on Greece for help, and in 281 B.C. King Pyrrhus of Epirus landed on the western coast of Lucania with 25,000 men and 20 elephants (an innovation in Italian warfare). The following year some 35,000 Roman troops under P. Laverius Laevinus marched into Lucania and crossed the Siris (Sinni) River in the face of the enemy. Pyrrhus then attacked. The Romans fought back furiously and inflicted heavy casualties on the Epirot phalanx. But Pyrrhus' cavalry proved superior and finally routed the legionaries. The Romans lost about 7,000 men, plus 2,000 captured, the Epirots 4,000. *See* Pandosia; Vadimonian Lake; Asculum I; Roman Republic.

Heraclea Pontica (Moslem-Byzantine Wars), 806. Under the Abbasid dynasty, a new series of Arabian raids into Asia Minor brought on another war with the Byzantine Empire in 804. Under the personal direction of Harun al-Rashid, the caliph of the *Arabian Nights,* the Moslems pushed northward through Ancyra (Ankara). The Imperial army of Nicephorus I continued to fall back from the hard-driving Arab cavalry. Finally, in 806, Harun's forces stormed into Heraclea Pontica (Ereğli), on the Black Sea, and captured it. Constantinople had to accept a humiliating peace. (Nicephorus was killed in battle against the Bulgars five years later.) *See* Zab al Kabir; Amorium; Moslem Conquests.

Heraclea Propontis (Civil Wars of the Roman Empire), 313. A few months after Constantine I's triumph over Valerius Maxentius in Italy, he formalized his alliance with Licinianus Licinius through the Edict of Milan. The Edict affirmed the principle of liberty of conscience, granted Licinius the eastern half of the Roman Empire, and foreshadowed the end of Valerius Maximinus' power in Syria and Egypt. Maximinus promptly invaded the Balkan Peninsula. With some 70,000 men, he seized Byzantium (later Constantinople) and moved on Heraclea Propontis (on the Sea of Marmara). Licinius, at the head of a 30,000-man Illyrian army, marched to the relief of Heraclea. Eighteen miles outside the city, Maximinus attacked on April 30. His larger force gained an initial advantage, but in a fierce struggle the tactical skill of Licinius and the steadiness of his troops gradually won the upper hand. At the end the Illyrians stood complete victors. Maximinus fled to Cilicia, where he died the following year.

Licinius and Constantine divided the Roman Empire between them. The victor of Heraclea took the East, Constantine the West. But the corulers had to test their respective combat strengths before settling down to a period of peace. *See* Saxa Rubra; Cibalae; Roman Empire.

Herat I (Mongol Conquest of Central Asia), 1220–1221. From their chilling devastation of the Khwarizm cities of Bukhara and Samarkand, which are now in Uzbek S.S.R., the Mongols of Genghis Khan plunged southwest into present-day Afghanistan. The thriving city of Herat, on the trade route from India to Mesopotamia and Europe, surrendered almost immediately to Tului, youngest son of the Conqueror. But the Moslem residents soon rebelled, killed the newly appointed Mongol governor, and threw out the occupying force. A stronger Mongol army returned to take the city under attack. For six months Herat resisted siege—the Mongols were fearsome horsemen in the open but weak in the equipment and skill necessary to reduce a fortified city. Finally, however, Herat was forced to capitulate again, in 1221. Virtually every man, woman, and child fell to the sword as an example to others who might be tempted to resist a Mongol army. *See* Samarkand; Merv; Mongol Wars.

Herat II (Persian-Afghan War), 1837–1838. The aggressive Shah Mohammed sent a Persian army to attack Herat, in northwestern Afghanistan, late in 1837. When the garrison resisted capture, the Persians settled down to a siege of the ancient city on the trade route from India. On June 4 of the following year a large-scale assault was beaten back with a loss of more than 1,500 Persians. Faced with probable defeat and strong British pressure, Mohammed withdrew his army four months later.

The succeeding shah, Nasir ud-Din, took Herat in 1856 when the Afghan commandant died, but was forced out by British arms the following year. *See* Kabul II.

Héricourt (Swiss-Burgundian Wars), 1474. The Duke of Burgundy, Charles the Bold, marched his army of conquest into Lorraine in 1474. Alarmed at the threat to their borders, the Swiss sent out a strong phalanx armed with the usual pikes and halberds. On November 13, 1474, at Héricourt, near Belfort, France, the two armies clashed head on. The tough, merciless Swiss infantry cut the Burgundian force to pieces and occupied the town. In two years, however, Charles would return to invade Switzerland itself. *See* Saint Jacob-en-Birs; Montlhéry; Grandson.

"Herrings, Battle of the." *See* Rouvray.

Hexham (Wars of the Roses), 1464. When a new uprising by Lancastrian (red rose) rebels against Yorkist Edward IV (white rose) was defeated at Hedgely Moor in April 1464, Henry Beaufort, the duke of Somerset, escaped capture. Taking refuge in nearby Hexham, also in Northumberland, Somerset began reorganizing his followers. On May 15, however, the Lancastrian camp received a surprise attack from a Yorkist army under Lord Montagu, brother of Warwick the Kingmaker and the victor of the previous month's battle. The rebels were virtually annihilated, and Somerset himself was captured and beheaded.

Edward IV then instituted a wave of executions that wiped out most of the nobles sympathetic to the Lancastrian cause. Bamborough Castle, the last rebel stronghold in the north, surrendered on July 10. The pathetic old king, Henry VI, was taken and imprisoned in the Tower of London. In Wales the Castle of Harlech held out until 1468; then it, too, capitulated. (One of the paroled prisoners was Henry of Richmond, 12-year-old nephew of the Lancastrian rebel Jasper Tudor and the future Henry VII.) Despite the loss of her last foothold on the island, Queen Margaret remained defiant in exile. And when the Yorkist party began quarreling within itself, new hope sprang up for the enthronement of her son Edward. *See* Hedgeley Moor; Banbury; Roses, Wars of the.

Himera (Wars of Sicily), 480 B.C. In a clash between Sicilian city-states, Theron of Agrigentum seized Himera on the north coast. The ousted Himeran leader Terillos then called for help from the city-state of Carthage on the north African coast. Hamilcar responded with a fleet which blockaded Himera. At this point Gelon of Syracuse came to the aid of Theron and the Agrigentines with a powerful naval force. The Syracusans overwhelmed the Carthaginians; Hamilcar was killed.

The victory of Syracuse made that state dominant in Sicily. Carthage, severely depleted in strength, did not rebuild its naval power until the end of the century. *See* Cumae; Selinus-Himera.

Himera River (Wars of Sicily), 311 B.C. Between 319 and 313 B.C. Agathocles, with aid from Carthage, became undisputed leader of Syracuse. After extending his authority over neighboring cities, Agathocles turned on his ally and sought to oust Carthage from its control over western Sicily. In 311, however, at the mouth of the Himera River on the south coast, Agathocles was defeated by the Carthaginians, commanded by Hamilcar (the second Carthaginian general by this name). Hamilcar followed up this victory (sometimes called the battle of Mount Ecnomus) by laying siege to Syracuse itself. But the wily Syracusan leader eluded the besiegers and sailed to North Africa to carry the war to Carthage. Although he won some success there, he was unable to take the enemy capital. After more than two years, Agathocles returned to Syracuse in 307 and the following year made peace with Carthage. *See* Crimisus River; Messina I.

Hingston Down (Danish Invasions of Britain), 837. Fortunately for Britain, the rise to power of Wessex in the south came just in time to form a West Saxon base of resistance to the savage raids of the Danish Vikings. In 837 the Britons of Cornwall joined the Vikings in an attack on southwestern Britain. However, King Egbert of Wessex, grandfather of Alfred, met the allied force at Hingston Down near Callington and defeated them. The Danes withdrew and Cornwall was forcibly added to Wessex rule. *See* Ellandun; Aclea; Danish Invasions of Britain.

Hippo Regius (Wars of the Western Roman Empire), 430. In the confused civil strife that shredded the Western Roman Empire in the fifth century,

Bonifacius served as governor of Africa. To cement his position, he asked for help from the Vandals of Spain. It was one of the most disastrous invitations in history. The Vandal king, Genseric (Gaiseric), landed on the Algerian coast with 50,000 men and promptly turned on his host. Overrunning much of North Africa, the Vandals laid siege to Hippo Regius (Bône), capital of the Roman government. Bonifacius, with control of the sea, managed to keep the city provisioned. During the siege, one of those who died was the bishop Saint Augustine. After 14 months the Vandals abandoned the siege, but the Roman victory was transient. Within five years the Vandal kingdom in Africa was firmly established. *See* Rome I; Châlons-sur-Marne II; Roman Empire.

Hira (Moslem Conquest of Persia), 633. The first Moslem attack against the powerful Persian empire of the Sassanians was little more than the usual border raid. Under Khālid ibn-al-Walīd, later to become one of the great generals of Islam, a force of Arab horsemen swooped down on the village of Hira, just west of the lower Euphrates River. After extracting a very small tribute, the Arabs withdrew (Khālid to make a forced march across the Syrian desert to Ajnadain). At that time the Persian ruler was Rustam, the regent for the youthful Yazdegerd III. Rustam sent out a counter raiding force. The following year, these Persian cavalrymen routed a band of Arabs in the so-called Battle of the Bridge. Hira again came under Persian control. It was, however, the last Persian victory over the Arabs. In a few months the new military power of the Moslems would destroy two armies of the Byzantine Empire and overrun both Palestine and Syria. Persia would have to deal with its western neighbor on a live-or-die basis. *See* Ajnadain; Yarmuk River; Kadisiya; Moslem Conquests.

Hobkirk's Hill (War of the American Revolution), 1781. When Gen. Lord Charles Cornwallis marched to Wilmington, N.C., after his narrow victory at Guilford Courthouse on March 15, 1781, he left Lt. Col. Francis Rawdon (later 1st Marquis of Hastings) in charge of British forces in South Carolina. The American general Nathanael Greene promptly moved southward against Rawdon. By April 25 Greene, with 1,551 men, had reached Hobkirk's Hill, a sandy ridge about a mile north of Camden. Rawdon marched out of the town and launched an attack against the southeastern corner of the hill. Knowing that the British had only 900 troops against him, Greene counterattacked the advancing foe, planning to envelop both flanks. But Rawdon lengthened his line by quickly bringing up reserve units. The American thrust then faltered, and when their cavalry sweep against the enemy rear failed, Greene's entire army began falling back. Effective rear-guard action discouraged the British from pursuing. American losses were 19 killed, 115 wounded, and 136 missing. Rawdon suffered 258 casualties, including 38 killed. Although he had won the battle, the British commander found that his line of communications to the south had been cut by the patriot irregulars of Francis Marion. Rawdon thereupon retreated to Monk's Corner, 35 miles north of Charleston. *See* Guilford Courthouse; Ninety Six; American Revolution.

Hochkirch (Seven Years' War), 1758. While Frederick II, the Great, was checking the Russian offensive in Brandenburg, the army of his brother Prince Henry stood in grave danger in Saxony. Here the marshal Count Leopold von Daun was on the move with a 90,000-man army of the Holy Roman Empire (Maria Theresa). Hurrying southward, the Prussian king joined Henry to make a force of 37,000. He encamped at Hochkirch, about 40 miles east of Dresden, on October 13, planning to attack the following day. Deceived by the sight of Imperial campfires, Frederick failed to implement basic security measures. That night Daun led his men through the intervening woods and assaulted the Prussian camp from all sides at dawn. The surprise was complete. In a savage struggle only the iron discipline of Frederick's troops prevented total destruction. The Prussians finally fought their way clear, leaving behind more than 10,000 casualties and 100 guns. Daun's losses, more than 7,500, were too heavy for him to pursue. This was the last pitched battle of the 1758 campaign. *See* Zorndorf; Bergen; Kay; Seven Years' War.

Höchst (Thirty Years' War), 1622. After defeating one Protestant force on the Neckar River, the Catholic armies in The Palatinate raced northward to the Main. Here they sought to intercept the Protestant army of Christian of Brunswick before it could cross the river and link up with the veteran mercenary army of Gen. Count Ernst von Mansfeld. The allied Catholic armies—the Spanish led by Gonzales de Córdoba and Bavarians commanded by Field Marshal the Count of Tilly—reached the Main on June 22 just as Christian was bridging the river at Höchst, west of Frankfort. The young Protestant leader, with about 12,000 men and very little artillery, was in a desperate situation. The Catholic force was larger and had the advantage of position. However, Christian gallantly held a small bridgehead south of the river while his main body forced a crossing in the face of heavy musket and artillery fire. The passage cost him 2,000 troops and most of his baggage, but he succeeded in pressing past the Catholic armies to join Mansfeld's force. Although Córdoba and Tilly claimed a victory, chiefly on the basis of far fewer casualties, they failed signally to stop the reckless Brunswick prince.

The battle of Höchst proved to be virtually

meaningless. Although the combined Protestant forces now numbered 25,000 men, almost equaling the Catholic armies, they soon withdrew to the west side of the Rhine. This withdrawal doomed the cause of the elector Frederick V in his Palatinate. Heidelberg, after a siege of 11 weeks, capitulated on September 19. On November 5 Sir Horace Vere, commanding a small force of English in the Rhine Valley, abandoned Mannheim. He held on to the small fortress of Frankenthal, the last outpost of Protestantism in The Palatinate. But this too was surrendered the following year. *See* Wimpfen; Fleurus I; Thirty Years' War.

Höchstädt I (War of the Spanish Succession), 1703. The only battle of 1703 took place in Bavaria. Duc Claude de Villars, the ablest marshal in the service of Louis XIV, joined with the elector of Bavaria, Maximilian II Emanuel, to make a thrust along the Danube toward Vienna. At Höchstädt, between Ulm and Ingolstadt, an Austrian army sent out by Holy Roman Emperor Leopold I dug in to block the offensive. Villars came on strong and on September 30 attacked the Imperials. The French routed their opponents, inflicting 11,000 casualties at a cost of only 1,000 to themselves. The route to Vienna now lay open, but Villars could not obtain the cooperation of other French marshals, and the opportunity to knock the empire out of the war was lost. *See* Landau; Donauwörth; Spanish Succession, War of the.

Höchstädt II (Wars of the French Revolution), 1800. After his victory over the Austrians at Stockach in May 1800, Gen. Jean Moreau marched his French Army of the Rhine from Baden into Bavaria. Falling back before the French, Gen. Baron Paul Kray von Krajowa retired to Ulm, on the Danube. But Moreau suddenly swung left (east) and struck for the river below Ulm. On June 19 his 60,000-man army attacked Höchstädt, 30 miles downstream. Although Kray von Krajowa had a numerical superiority of at least 10,000, he was caught off balance. After 18 hours of disorganized fighting Moreau captured the town, securing a firm hold on the left bank of the Danube. The French took several thousand prisoners; the number of killed and wounded on both sides was small considering the large numbers of troops involved. This victory forced Kray von Krajowa to evacuate Ulm and retreat eastward behind the Inn River. Moreau crossed the Danube and occupied Munich in July. But then operations ceased while Napoleon Bonaparte, taking advantage of his triumph at Marengo in Italy, held truce talks with the Austrian government. *See* Stockach II; Marengo; Hohenlinden; French Revolution Wars.

Hohenfriedeberg (War of the Austrian Succession), 1745. One of the major powers opposing Empress Maria Theresa of the Holy Roman Empire dropped out of the war on April 22, 1745. When Charles Albert, who was elector of Bavaria and also imperial pretender Charles VII, died, his son and successor, Maximilian III Joseph, agreed to support Francis Stephen, husband of the empress, for the crown. In return, Austria restored all territory taken from Bavaria. This event again isolated Frederick II, the Great, and his Prussian army—he could expect no help from France, which was busy in a campaign in Flanders.

Determined to prosecute the Second Silesian War, Prince Charles of Lorraine, brother-in-law of Maria Theresa, marched across the Sudetic Mountains toward Frederick. The Imperial army, numbering 85,000 Austrians and Saxons, moved into Silesia to oppose the 65,000 Prussians concentrated near Strzegom (Striegau), 35 miles southwest of Breslau (Wroclaw) in present-day Poland. On June 4 the Saxon force in the Imperial vanguard was suddenly struck by Frederick's army at Hohenfriedeberg. The fast-firing, tightly disciplined Prussians routed the Saxons before the main Austrian force could come to its assistance. The Prussians then fell on the Austrians and after desperate fighting put them to flight as well. Prince Charles withdrew into Bohemia with several thousand killed and wounded and even more captured. Prussian losses totaled about 2,000. It was one of Frederick's greatest victories. The Prussian king now pursued the retreating Imperial army. *See* Fontenoy; Soor; Austrian Succession, War of the.

Hohenlinden (Wars of the French Revolution), 1800. After Napoleon Bonaparte's victory at Marengo in northern Italy on June 14, 1800, France and Austria held intermittent truce talks for almost six months. Meanwhile, the French Army of the Rhine under Gen. Jean Moreau held up in Munich, which it had taken in July. To the east the demoralized Austrian army of Gen. Baron Paul Kray von Krajowa stood behind the Inn River. Holy Roman Emperor Francis II now replaced Kray von Krajowa with his own 18-year-old brother, Archduke John, and built up the Austrian army to some 130,000 men. Napoleon too had been active. From Paris he reinforced Moreau's army to a strength of 119,000. Then, late in the year, he broke off peace talks and launched Moreau toward Vienna. At the same time Archduke John crossed the Inn to strike the French left flank.

The two hostile forces bumped into each other at Hohenlinden, 20 miles east of Munich, on December 3. In a wildly disorganized battle the tactics of the subordinate French commanders proved decisive. The Austrians were thrown back with almost 20,000 casualties. Moreau advanced cautiously eastward until December 8, then suddenly drove the retreating Austrians 189 miles toward Vienna in 15 days. Meanwhile another French army, under Gen. Jacques Macdonald, marched from Switzerland into the Tyrol. On Christmas Day Francis II signed the Armistice of Steyer. When a third French army, commanded by Gen. Guillaume Brune, began pushing the Austrians out of northern Italy in January, the emperor was ready for peace. The Treaty of Lunéville, signed on February 9, 1801, took Austria out of the Second Coalition (and virtually destroyed the last bonds of the Holy Roman Empire). As only England remained in the struggle against France, the fighting was limited to Egypt and the high seas. *See* Höchstädt II; Alexandria III; French Revolution Wars.

Holowczyn (Great Northern War), 1708. After his conquest of Poland, including the formal deposition of Augustus II in favor of Stanislas Leszczyński, Charles XII of Sweden delayed a year before turning east against his last remaining foe, Peter I, the Great, of Russia. During this time he wrested increased toleration for Protestants from Holy Roman Emperor Joseph II. On New Year's Day, 1708, with the largest army he had ever commanded (24,000 cavalry, 20,000 infantry), the Swedish king crossed the Vistula and struck for Moscow.

It was six months before the Russians tried to block the invasion, at Holowczyn, west of Mogilev on the Dnieper. On July 4 Charles XII attacked the Russian army of Gen. Prince Aleksandr Danilovich Menshikov, which was anchored on the small village, and split it in two. (It would be the last pitched battle won by the daring Swedish king.) The Russians troops fell back but scorched the earth as they did so. The Swedes pressed on eastward, but as supplies grew short Charles suddenly turned south toward the Ukraine. Here he planned to link up with the Cossack hetman, Ivan Mazepa. But the change in direction exposed the flank of a large Swedish supply column moving to Charles's aid from Riga. *See* Thorn; Liesna; Great Northern War.

Holy Roman Empire. For battles and wars fought by the member states of the Holy Roman Empire (800–1806) *see* German States of the Holy Roman Empire; Italy.

Homildon Hill (English-Scottish Wars), 1402. While England was preoccupied with the Hundred Years' War in France and civil unrest at home, the defense of the Scottish border fell chiefly on the Percy family of Northumberland. Sir Henry Percy (Hotspur), son of the first Earl of Northumberland, had been defeated and captured (but later ransomed) on one Scottish raid into northern England in 1388. Now in 1402 a new foray, led by Archibald, 4th earl of Douglas, penetrated as far south as Durham County. On the raiders' return north, the Percys, aided by George Dunbar, earl of March, intercepted them at Homildon (Humbledon) Hill in September. Instead of the headlong charge so frequently employed by feudal forces, the English first softened up their opponents with arrows from the deadly longbows. Then a cavalry attack routed the Scots with heavy losses. Otterburn was avenged and Douglas taken prisoner. King Henry IV demanded that the Scottish noble be turned over to him. This order created a rift between the Percys and the crown. *See* Otterburn; Ravenspur I; Shrewsbury.

Hondschoote (Wars of the French Revolution), 1793. During the near collapse of the armies of the National Convention in 1793, the allies drove into northwestern France. But instead of pressing on toward an undefended Paris, the Anglo-Hannoverian force turned off to besiege Dunkirk in August. From the French capital Lazare Carnot hurried westward to take charge of the Revolutionary troops. On September 6 he sent Gen. Jean Houchard with 40,000 men against the allied army at Hondschoote, in southwestern Belgium. In a three-day battle the poorly organized French drove back the enemy by sharpshooting from behind hedgerows and dikes. The victory raised the siege of Dunkirk. Houchard failed to pursue vigorously, however, and a week later suffered a defeat at Courtrai (Kortrijk). He was then arrested and guillotined on November 16. Meanwhile, a second French army had blocked the Austrian advance on Paris. *See* Neerwinden II; Toulon III; Wattignies; French Revolution Wars.

Honduras. *See* Chalchuapa.

Hong Kong (World War II), 1941. The British crown colony off the southeastern coast of China became one of the original targets of the Japanese onslaught in the Pacific and the first British possession to fall. On December 8 the Japanese 38th Division struck at the British line on the mainland, which was defended by three battalions. Heavily raided from the air and under constant attack on the ground, Gen. C. M. Maltby withdrew his troops to the island on the night of December 12–13. Here stood another three British battalions. Six days later Japanese forces crossed the mile-wide waterway to invest Hong Kong itself. The unequal fight continued on the island for a week. Finally, on Christmas Day, the British governor, Mark Young, surrendered the island to the Japanese. Almost 11,000 men, more than half of them Imperial troops, became prisoners of war. Japanese casualties were 2,745. *See* Pearl Harbor; Malaya; Philippine Islands; World War II.

Hormuz (Wars of Sassanian Persia), 226. The Arsacid dynasty had ruled Parthia for about 475 years and had warred with Rome for much of that time. During the reign of Artabanus V, however, a hostile Persia developed under the leadership of Ardashir (Artaxerxes). In 226 the two rival armies clashed at Hormuz, near modern Bandar

Abbas on the Strait of Ormuz. The Parthians were crushed and Artabanus was killed. Ardashir I moved to establish the Sassanian dynasty, which would rule Persia until conquered by the Arabs in 641. Under the Sassanids, Persia became an even stronger menace to the Roman Empire. *See* Edessa I.

Horseshoe Bend (Creek War), 1814. The U.S. militia general Andrew Jackson carried the war against the Indians into the upper Creek country in the spring of 1814. With the aid of Gen. John Coffee and 3,000 militiamen, Jackson marched against a large war party of Creeks and allied Cherokees who had taken up a fortified position in the Horseshoe Bend (Tohopeka) of the Tallapoosa River in eastern Alabama. On March 27 the Americans attacked, killing almost 900 Indian warriors and capturing 500 women and children. American losses came to 51 killed and 148 wounded. Five months later most of the Creeks signed the Treaty of Fort Jackson. Meanwhile, as the War of 1812 continued, Jackson became a major general in the regular army, in charge of the Mobile–New Orleans military district. *See* Talladega; New Orleans I; Indian Wars in the U.S.

Hoxne (Danish Invasions of Britain), 870. The increasingly bold Danish raiders were challenged by Edmund, the king of East Anglia, in 870. In a pitched battle at Hoxne, in northern Suffolk County, the Saxons were overpowered by the Viking invaders. Edmund was captured and reportedly beheaded when he refused to renounce Christianity. He was later given the name "the Martyr" and interred at Bury Saint Edmunds. Now Wessex was the only remaining Saxon hope to arrest the fierce warriors from the Continent. *See* York; Ashdown; Danish Invasions of Britain.

Hubbardton (War of the American Revolution). A rear-guard action fought on July 7, 1777, during the American retreat from Fort Ticonderoga. *See* Fort Ticonderoga III.

Huesca (Spanish-Moslem Wars), 1096. Although southern Spain lay under firm Moslem control during the rule (1086–1106) of the Berber Yusuf ibn-Tashfin, fighting between Spaniards and Moors continued in the northeast. In 1096 Pedro I of Aragon and Navarre attacked the fortress city of Huesca, which had been held by the Moors since the eighth century. The Spaniards stormed into the city and captured it. Pedro promptly made it the capital of his kingdom. *See* Zallaka; Saragossa I.

Hundred Years' War (1337–1453). Despite a series of short wars, England and France remained deadlocked over England's tenure in Aquitaine, the claims of English kings to the throne of France, and France's alliance with Scotland. To enforce English demands on Philip VI, Edward III began ravaging northwestern France in 1337, thus launching what came to be called the Hundred Years' War. The first battle to be fought resulted in the English naval victory at Sluys (Sluis) three years later. Although truces periodically interrupted the fighting, the war dragged on for 113 more years, in France and along the English-Scottish border. England made an alliance with Portugal and later with Burgundy; France won the support of Castile. In 1453 the last of the English troops were expelled from what is now France (except for Calais). This ended the war, despite the absence of any formal peace treaty between the two governments, then ruled by Henry VI of England and Charles VII of France. Two years later the Wars of the Roses broke out in England.

Sluys	1340
Crécy	1346
Calais I	1346–1347
Winchelsea	1350
Poitiers	1356
Auray	1364
Nájera	1367
La Rochelle I	1372
Châteauneuf-de-Randon	1380
Margate	1387
Harfleur	1415
Agincourt	1415
Rouen II	1418–1419
Beaugé	1421
Cravant	1423
Verneuil	1424
Orleans	1428–1429
Rouvray	1429
Jargeau	1429
Patay	1429
Rouen III	1449
Formigny	1450
Castillon	1453

Hungarian Revolt (1848–1849). Hungarian dissatisfaction with the strife-torn rule of the Austrian emperor Ferdinand I broke into open revolt in 1848. Aided by an army from Russia (Nicholas I), the Austrian government, then ruled by Franz Josef I, crushed the uprising the following year.

Schwechat	1848
Kápolna	1849
Timisoara	1849

Hungary. The major battles fought by Hungary during its existence as an independent kingdom are listed below. In the sixteenth century the kingdom was divided between Ottoman Turkey and Austria. For this period *see* German States of the Holy Roman Empire. From 1867 until 1918 Hungary was the junior partner in a dual monarchy with Austria. An independent nation since that time, it was the site of a nationwide battle in World War II (see the following entry).

Mohi	1241
Kressenbrunn	1260
Marchfeld	1278

Nicopolis 1396
Varna I 1444
Kossovo II 1448
Belgrade I 1456
Belgrade II 1521
Mohács 1526
Szigetvár 1566
Keresztes 1596
See Hungarian Revolt
See World War I
See World War II

Hungary (World War II), 1944–1945. During the Russian autumn offensive of 1944, a wide sweep by the left (south) flank army of Gen. Fedor Tolbukhin carried up the Danube River to Belgrade on October 20. Inside this arcing thrust the Second Ukrainian Army of Gen. Rodion Malinovski plunged into "Hungary" from the south. The defending German force, called Army Group South, under Gen. Friessner (and later Woehler), fought desperately to hold a pocket protecting Budapest and the Lake Balaton oil fields to the southwest. Meanwhile another Russian force had driven through passes in the Carpathians in the rear of the Hungarian capital. By Christmas Eve, Budapest was encircled, but it continued to resist.

Hitler ordered much of the *Wehrmacht's* meager reserve force used in a futile counterattack to relieve the city. Pest, on the Danube's east bank, fell on January 18, 1945, Buda, on the west bank, on February 18. The route to Austria was now open to Malinovski's Second Ukrainian Army. Russia reported the death of 49,000 Germans and the capture of 110,000 in the Budapest fighting. *See* Balkans; Austria (World War II); World War II.

Hürtgen Forest (World War II). A part of the Siegfried Line defenses won by the U.S. First Army in fierce fighting in November 1944. *See* Siegfried Line.

Hussite Wars (1420–1434). The Bohemian followers of John Hus rose in anti-Catholic revolt when their leader was executed for heresy in 1415. Under the generalship of Jan Zizka, the so-called Hussites repelled every attempt of King Sigismund of Bohemia to subdue them. They marched into Germany itself before an internal struggle between extreme Taborites and moderate Utraquists led to their downfall.

Prague I 1420
Kutná Hora 1422
Německý Brod 1422
Ústí nad Labem 1426
Český-Brod 1434

Hwai-Hai (Chinese Civil War), 1948–1949. The Nationalist disasters at Kaifeng and Tsinan were only preliminary to the battle that began taking shape in east-central China between the Lunghai Railway and the Hwai River. Here Gen. Liu Chih had massed half a million troops, including Generalissimo Chiang Kai-shek's prize Armored Corps led by Chiang's second son, Gen. Chiang Wei-kuo. From the north and west, Gen. Ch'en Yi, one of Mao Tse-tung's top commanders, concentrated half a million troops of the Communist People's Liberation Army (PLA). Fighting began on November 7 in what was to be one of the great battles of modern history. PLA columns methodically isolated the battleground and then chopped up the encircled Nationalist units one by one. Chiang Kai-shek rushed in thousands of reinforcements in a futile effort to turn the tide.

Sixty-five days of fighting ended on January 12, 1949, with 550,000 Nationalist troops annihilated—5 army groups, 7 other full-strength divisions, the Armored Corps, and miscellaneous units (including the last of the 39 American-equipped divisions). Liu Chih and Chiang Wei-kuo escaped by plane from Hsuchang (Hsuchow). Two top Nationalist commanders were killed and two others captured. To the north, Tientsin fell on January 15, Peking (then called Peiping) six days later. Eastward from Hwai-Hai, the road lay open to Chiang's capital of Nanking. *See* Tsinan; Nanking III; Chinese Civil War.

Hydaspes River (Macedonian Conquests), 326 B.C. After the crushing defeat inflicted on Darius III in the battle of Arbela-Gaugamela, Alexander the Great occupied the rich Persian cities of Babylon, Susa, and Persepolis. From 330 to 327 he marched his disciplined veterans through what are now Iraq, Iran, part of the U.S.S.R., Afghanistan, and West Pakistan. Alexander received acknowledgment as the new master of all the ancient kingdoms—Media, Parthia, Bactria, and others.

In 326 B.C. the Macedonian conqueror, after pressing through the Hindu Kush Mountains, reached the Indus River Valley. Here on the Hydaspes (now Jhelum) tributary of the great river, an Indian king, Porus, blocked Alexander's advance with some 50,000 troops. Leaving the bulk of his army (about 40,000) on the west bank of the river, Alexander made a night march 18 miles upstream, where he crossed the river on crude pontoons with a detachment of 14,000 picked cavalry and infantry. The following day he attacked the flank of Porus' position. After eight hours of hard fighting (the Macedonian horses were terrified by the enemy's 200 elephants), Alexander's battle-wise soldiers routed the Indians, killing 12,000 and taking 9,000 prisoners, including King Porus. The Macedonians lost 980 men in their last battle of Asian conquest.

Alexander wanted to push on, but his army rebelled and refused to go farther. The young war lord bowed to the wishes of his men. He sent Nearchus with a fleet of boats down the Indus River to return by way of the Arabian Sea to the Persian Gulf. Alexander took the rest of the troops across the Desert of Gedrosia to Susa and then Babylon, where he established his headquarters. On June 13, 323 B.C., Alexander died, after an 11-day fever, at the age of 32. Although his dream of a great Graeco-Persian Empire was only partly realized, Alexander had won a secure place in history as one of the great military commanders of the world. *See* Arbela-Gaugamela; Crannon; Macedonian Conquests.

Hyderabad (British Conquest of Sind), 1843. After his victory against overwhelming numbers of Baluchistanis at Miani in February, Gen. Sir Charles James Napier gathered reinforcements and pushed down the Indus River. On March 24 he attacked Hyderabad, capital of the Sind, defended by Shir Mohammed with 20,000 troops. Although his army numbered less than 6,000 Anglo-Indians, Napier stormed into the city under cover of artillery fire. The Baluchistanis were routed, ending their resistance. The Sind then came under British control. *See* Miani; Mudki.

I

Ia Drang River (Vietnam War). The second phase of an American offensive during November 14–24, 1965, against North Vietnamese regular troops near the Cambodian border. *See* Chu Pong–Ia Drang River.

Ilerda (Wars of the First Triumvirate), 49 B.C. When Pompey the Great fled from Rome to Greece, Julius Caesar moved to conquer Spain, Pompey's now-leaderless province. On the way Caesar stopped to take the surrender of the free city of Massilia (Marseilles). But finding the people devoted to Pompey, he placed the city under siege and entered Spain with an army of 40,000 men. Here Pompey's lieutenants—Lucius Afranius, M. Terentius Varro, and Marcus Petreius—commanded some 70,000 troops. Caesar attacked the enemy camp at Ilerda (Lérida), along the Segre River, a northern tributary of the Ebro. He was driven off. But after winning the support of the local Spaniards, Caesar forced the Pompeians out of their camp. In a brilliant series of marches and countermarches he maneuvered the enemy into a weak defensive position and then encircled them. The distraught Pompeians surrendered without further resistance.

When Massilia capitulated, Caesar was free to return to Italy and prepare his campaign against Pompey. *See* Rubicon River; Utica II; Illyria; Dyrrachium I; First Triumvirate, Wars of the.

Ilipa (Second Punic War), 206 B.C. Continuing his three-year conquest of Spain, the brilliant Publius Cornelius Scipio (later Africanus) finally encountered the main Carthaginian army at Ilipa in the southern part of the peninsula (60 miles north of modern Seville). The Roman army of 48,000 men took a defensive position against some 75,000 Carthaginians commanded by Hasdrubal, son of Gisco, and by Mago, brother of Hannibal (the other brother, Hasdrubal Barca, had already been killed in Italy). After refusing battle for several days, Scipio caught the Africans by surprise with a dawn attack on their camp. But this factor was less important than the ingenious tactics employed by the Roman. Placing his doubtful Iberian allies in a refused center, Scipio used his best troops (the legions and his cavalry) to strike at the enemy's two flanks. The attack crushed in both Carthaginian wings, forcing the strong center opposite the Romans to fall back without giving battle. Scipio followed up his triumph with a methodical pursuit that destroyed the African army in detail.

The victory at Ilipa (also called Silpia) ended the Carthaginian hold on Spain. This battle, plus the decisive defeat handed the Punic forces in Italy the year before, opened the way for Scipio to carry the war to the African homeland. *See* New Carthage; Metaurus River; Utica I; Punic Wars.

Illyria (Wars of the First Triumvirate), 49 B.C. While Julius Caesar was conquering Spain, the province of the fugitive Pompey, Caesar's lieutenant P. Cornelius Dolabella assembled an expeditionary force to invade Illyria. In crossing the Adriatic the Caesarian fleet was attacked by the Pompeian navy under Marcus Octavius (Pompey himself was in Greece). Dolabella, after losing a major part of his fleet, withdrew. The defeat isolated a Caesarian garrison on the island of Krk (Veglia). Gaius Antonius surrendered this force to Pompey's followers. *See* Ilerda; Bagradas River; Dyrrachium I; First Triumvirate, Wars of the.

Imphal (World War II). A town in northeastern India, isolated by a Japanese attack in March 1944 and under siege for three months before being relieved. *See* Burma II.

Inchon (Korean War), 1950. The United States Eighth Army and the South Korean forces, all under Gen. Walton Walker, finally checked the Communist conquest of the Korean peninsula at the Pusan Perimeter, in the southeast, in August 1950. Meanwhile, the United Nations supreme commander, Gen. Douglas MacArthur, prepared to strike at the right rear of the invading North Korean army. On September 15 the newly organized X Corps (1st Marine and 7th Infantry divisions) under Gen. Edward Almond made an amphibious landing at Inchon, the port of the South Korean capital of Seoul, on the west coast. Preceded by two days of naval bombardment, the 1st Marine Division of Gen. Oliver Smith seized the tiny offshore island of Moontip (Wolmi-do) in the morning and then stormed the beaches later that day. Forcing their way inland against surprisingly weak North Korean resistance, the marines captured Kimpo Airfield, to the north, on September 17—the same day the 7th Infantry began coming ashore. Seoul came under attack as the American X Corps deepened and widened its beachhead.

At the same time (September 16) the Eighth Army, now 140,000 strong, broke out of the Pusan Perimeter and headed northwest toward Seoul. The thinly stretched North Korean lines began to crumble. On September 26 the two American forces linked up near Osan, cutting off elements of eight Communist divisions in the southwest. Two days later the battered city of Seoul was liberated, except for isolated pockets of street fighting.

Moving rapidly northward, American and South Korean forces reached the vicinity of the 38th parallel on October 1. The first ROK (Republic of Korea) unit crossed the troublesome boundary that day. Walker's troops, under the authorization of the United Nations, did so eight days later. *See* Pusan Perimeter; North Korea; Korean War.

Indian Mutiny (1857–1858). Tightening British rule, the breaking down of cherished traditions, and the fear of forcible conversion led to widespread unrest against the British East India Company. On May 10, 1857 trouble began with a riot by Sepoy troops in a Meerut brothel. The troops then stormed the jail, releasing 85 of their comrades who had refused to use Enfield rifle cartridges, which they believed to be greased with pork and beef fat, forbidden to Moslems and Hindus, respectively. (The cartridge paper had to be bitten before it was inserted in the muzzle.) The rebellion soon spread throughout the Ganges Valley in northern India, where four-fifths of the East India Company army consisted of native troops. After more than a year the mutiny was suppressed. On September 1, 1858, the rule of India was transferred from the East India Company to the crown. Reforms were instituted, and in 1876 Queen Victoria was proclaimed Empress of India.

Cawnpore I	1857
Delhi II	1857
Lucknow	1857–1858
Arrah	1857
Cawnpore II	1857
Jhansi	1858
Gwalior	1858

Indian Peninsula. The major battles and wars fought by what are now the nations of India and Pakistan are listed below.

Peshawar	1001
Somnath	1024
Taraori	1192
Indus River	1221
Delhi I	1398
Meerut	1399
Diu	1509
Goa	1510
Panipat I	1526
Panipat II	1556
Talikota	1565
Madras I	1746
Arcot	1751
See Seven Years' War	
Panipat III	1761
Buxar	1764
See Mysore-British Wars	
See American Revolution, War of the	
See Maratha-British Wars	
Miani	1843
Hyderabad	1843
See Sikh-British Wars	
See Indian Mutiny	
See World War I	
See World War II	

Indian Wars in the United States (1637–1890). Beginning in colonial times, the steady westward march of American settlers brought on conflicts with Indian tribes. Except for Blue Licks, the battles listed below are those fought independently of the French and Indian War and the American Revolution.

The Colonial Era

Stonington (Pequot War)	1637
Great Swamp (King Philip's War)	1675
Hadley (King Philip's War)	1676
Bushy Run (Pontiac's Rebellion)	1763
Point Pleasant (Lord Dunmore's War)	1774

United States-Indian Wars

Blue Licks (American Revolution)	1782
Fort Wayne (Old Northwest Indian Wars)	1790
Fort Recovery (Old Northwest Indian Wars)	1791
Fallen Timbers (Old Northwest Indian Wars)	1794
Tippecanoe Creek (Tecumseh's Confederacy)	1811
Fort Mims (Creek War)	1813
Talladega (Creek War)	1813
Horseshoe Bend (Creek War)	1814
Bad Axe (Black Hawk War)	1832
Ash Hollow (Sioux Wars)	1855
Killdeer Mountain (Sioux Wars)	1864
Sand Creek (Cheyenne and Arapahoe Wars)	1864
See Sioux Wars	
Beecher Island (Cheyenne and Arapahoe Wars)	1868
Washita River (Cheyenne and Arapahoe Wars)	1868
Salt River (Apache Wars)	1872

Lava Beds (Modoc Rebellion) 1873
See Sioux Wars
Bear Paw Mountains
(Nez Percé War) 1877
Wounded Knee Creek
(Ghost Dance War) 1890

Indus River (Mongol Conquest of Central Asia), 1221. The Mongol conquest of the once powerful Khwarizm Empire in less than two years left Genghis Khan with only one remaining foe in central Asia. This was the late Shah Mohammed's son Jalal-ad-Din, who had raised a new army of opposition in northern Afghanistan. In the autumn of 1221 the Great Khan with 40,000 mounted warriors pushed through Bamian Pass, in the Hindu Kush range, in pursuit of the redoubtable Moslem sultan. Jalal-ad-Din with some 30,000 men retreated to the banks of the Indus River. Here he turned to make a stand with his back to the river, his right flank protected by a bend in the Indus and his left wing anchored against a mountain ridge.

When the Mongols approached, the Moslem sultan opened the battle with a cavalry charge by his right wing. When the attack gained ground, he sent his center forward as well, reinforcing both sections with detachments from his guarded left flank. This was a fatal mistake, for Genghis Khan had ordered a general named Bela to take 10,000 Mongols over the seemingly impassable ridge on Jalal's left. The flanking force debouched from the heights just as the Moslems appeared on the point of a decisive triumph. At the same time the Great Khan himself led a counterattack on the other side of the battlefield. The double envelopment shattered the Moslem army, which was then methodically cut to pieces. Most of the vanquished who fled the scene of destruction drowned in the waters of the Indus. Jalal-ad-Din escaped by swimming his horse to the far bank, but he was now a ruler without a country or an army. The Mongol horde stood unchallenged from Tibet to the Caspian Sea. *See* Bamian; Kalka River; Mongol Wars.

Ingaví (Bolivian-Peruvian War), 1841. The Chilean victory of Yungay in 1839 broke up the Confederation of Bolivia and Peru. Agustín Gamarra of Peru, who had served in the Chilean army, then became president of Peru. Two years later Gamarra took an army of 5,000 Peruvians southward into Bolivian territory. At the mountain of Ingaví (Yngaví), south of La Paz, the invaders were met by the Bolivian army of President José Ballivían, some 4,000 strong. On November 20 the hostile forces fought a pitched battle resulting in the rout of the Peruvian army. Gamarra was killed. This battle ended the invasion and the war. *See* Yungay.

Inkerman (Crimean War), 1854. To break the British-French siege of Sevastopol, Russian Prince Aleksandr Menshikov prepared a large-scale sortie toward the east. At dawn on November 5, the Russians thrust out of the city against the thin allied line near the mouth of the Chernaya River. The British general Lord Raglan (Fitzroy Somerset) and the French commander, Gen. Aimable Pélissier, rallied their troops to make a stand at Inkerman. In a savage hand-to-hand struggle the Russians were finally repulsed by the smaller allied army. Menshikov retired behind Sevastopol's defenses having lost about 12,000 men. Raglan's casualties were 2,500; Pélissier's, about 1,000. The siege continued. *See* Sevastopol I; Crimean War.

Inverlochy (English Civil War), 1645. The same issues that had plunged England into civil war in 1642 also divided Scotland. Acting in behalf of King Charles I, the Marquis of Montrose (James Graham) had led the Highland clans to victory at Tippermuir, setting up the occupation of Perth and Aberdeen in the fall of 1644. Turning to the west in the winter, Montrose, with only about 1,500 Royalists, challenged an army of Lowland Covenanters and Campbells almost double his force. On February 2, 1645, at Inverlochy near the head of Loch Linnhe, Montrose met and defeated this enemy force with heavy loss. The beaten commander, the Marquis of Argyll (Archibald Campbell, 8th earl of Argyll), took refuge on a ship in Loch Linnhe. This battle ended the power of the Campbell clan for many years. Montrose then turned back to the east to continue his campaign. *See* Tippermuir; Auldearn; English Civil War.

Ioannina (First Balkan War), 1912–1913. Less than two months after the outbreak of the war, Bulgaria and Serbia, both of which had won clear-cut victories over Turkey, agreed to an armistice, on December 3, 1912. However, both Montenegro and Greece fought on. Greek troops sent out by King George I had invested Ioannina (Janina), near the Albanian frontier. Although cut off from outside relief, the Turkish garrison resisted stoutly. Finally the Ottomans of Mohammed V were forced to capitulate, on March 5, 1913. The war was concluded by an armistice in April. *See* Shkodër II; Adrianople VII; Balkan Wars.

Ipsus (Breakup of Alexander's Empire), 301 B.C. The death of Alexander III (the Great) in 323 B.C. left the loosely tied Graeco-Persian Empire without an undisputed leader. His generals—the Diadochi—soon began a bloody struggle for power that raged throughout western Asia, Egypt, Macedonia, and Greece. This confused fighting took the life of Alexander's illegitimate half brother (Philip III), mother (Olympias), wife (Roxana), young son (Alexander IV), and regent (Perdiccas). It also cost the lives of many of the Diadochi.

The see-saw warfare was finally forced to a climax by a one-eyed general who assumed the title King of Macedonia as Antigonus I (Cyclops) in 306. Gathering a force of 30,000 men, Antigonus marched into Asia Minor in an attempt to reunite Alexander's empire under his leadership. At the village of Ipsus in 301 the Macedonians encountered an allied force of similar size under Cassander, who also claimed to be king of Macedonia, Lysimachus of Thrace, and Seleucus I (Nicator) of Babylon. The Macedonians were thoroughly beaten. Antigonus was killed and his son Demetrius I (Poliorcetes) could collect only 8,000 survivors after a flight of 200 miles.

The distribution of spoils after the battle of Ipsus shattered Alexander's old empire beyond recovery. Seleucus took Syria, founding the Seleucidae dynasty of western Asia that was to endure until brought down by the Romans in 64 B.C. Lysimachus became ruler of Thrace and most of Asia Minor. Cassander won control of Macedonia, which continued to dominate all of Greece. Ptolemy I, who had not taken an overt part in the coalition, received a free hand in Egypt. *See* Hydaspes River; Corupedion; Hellenistic Monarchies, Wars of the.

Isandhlwana (Zulu-British War), 1879. Acknowledging the strength of the Zulu nation in southeast Africa, Great Britain recognized Cetewayo as king in 1872. Seven years later, however, the Zulus began building up their military strength. A British regiment of 1,800 men sent to disarm the Zulus was surrounded at the great rock of Isandhlwana on January 22, 1879, by 20,000 native warriors. Although the Zulu impis (regiments) had only throwing spears (assagais) for weapons against artillery and rifles, they killed all but 55 of the British troops. Cetewayo prepared to invade Natal. *See* Rorke's Drift; Zulu-British War.

Island No. 10 (American Civil War), 1862. When the Southern general Leonidas Polk was forced to withdraw from western Kentucky after the fall of Fort Donelson, the Confederate command in the West resolved to hold the Mississippi River farther downstream at New Madrid, Mo., and at Island No. 10, near the corner of Tennessee. General John McCown was put in command of both positions. To attack this double block of the Mississippi, Gen. Henry Halleck, commander of the Federal Department of Missouri, ordered Gen. Pope to organize a corps and move against New Madrid. Pope reached the Missouri village on the river on March 3. Ten days later he had completed preparations for a siege. As soon as Pope opened a bombardment of the defenses, however, McCown evacuated New Madrid and crossed the river into upper Tennessee. McCown was relieved and replaced by Gen. William Mackall.

Pope pressed his offensive by cutting a canal through the swamps, enabling two gunboats to run past the Confederate batteries on Island No. 10. On April 7, protected by the fire of the gunboats, four regiments crossed the Mississippi to Tiptonville, Tenn. This thrust bottled up the Confederates on a peninsula formed by a bend in the river. Mackall promptly surrendered 3,500 men on the mainland and Island No. 10. Another 500 Confederates escaped eastward. This victory opened the Mississippi to Federal navigation as far south as Fort Pillow, Tenn. It also propelled Pope into national prominence and led to his appointment by President Abraham Lincoln to head the Army of Virginia two months later. *See* Fort Donelson; Shiloh; American Civil War.

Isly River (French-Algerian War), 1844. Although France held most of the Algerian coast beginning in 1830, the interior remained under the rule of Abd-el-Kader. Twice the Arab leader fought the French and repulsed their southward thrusts, during 1832–34 and 1835–37. When a third conflict broke out, late in 1840, a large French expeditionary force under Marshal Thomas Bugeaud marched against Abd-el-Kader. Driven westward across the Moroccan border, the rebel chief secured the help of Sultan Abd-er-Rahman. On August 14, 1844, the two native leaders with some 40,000 men, chiefly cavalry, made a stand along the Isly River in northeastern Morocco. Bugeaud with 8,000 infantry and cavalry, supported by artillery, beat back every Algerian assault. The French cavalry then counterattacked, driving their opponents from the field with some 1,500 dead. Abd-el-Kader surrendered three years later to the French general Louis Lamoricière, leaving France in control of most of Algeria. *See* Constantine.

Isonzo River I–XI (World War I), 1915–1917. Although a member of the Triple Alliance, Italy stayed neutral at the outbreak of the war in 1914. Lured by Allied promises of Austrian territory, the Italian government of King Victor Emmanuel III renounced its alliance with Austria-Hungary and Germany on May 3, 1915, and declared war on the Dual Monarchy 20 days later. (War was not declared against Germany until August 28, 1916.) The 484-mile frontier with Austria generally followed the southern slopes of the Alps, affording little opportunity for Italian offensive action. Only in the east along the Isonzo River could the Italians find terrain suitable to attack. Here, on a 60-mile front at the head of the Adriatic Sea, Gen. Count Cadorna massed 35 Italian divisions. To hold the Isonzo, the Austrian commander in chief, Field Marshal Count Conrad von Hötzendorf, assembled 14 divisions (later increased to 22) under Archduke Eugene and Gen. Svetozar Borojević von Bojna.

The opening Italian attack on the Isonzo defenses got under way on June 23. It was the first of 11 distinct battles waged along this river during the next 27 months. Content to maintain a defensive posture on this front, the Austrians held on grimly, leading to staggering losses on both sides. Although always outnumbered, Eugene's troops had the advantage of favorable terrain and superior artillery. Cadorna's total gains at the end of the 11 battles were a meager 10 to 12 miles. For their persistent courage in the face of repeated rebuffs, the Italian soldiers in the Second (on the left flank) and Third (to the south) armies gained the admiration of the world.

Isonzo I (June 23–July 7, 1915).

Isonzo II (July 18–August 3, 1915).

Isonzo III (October 18–November 3, 1915).

Isonzo IV (November 10–December 2, 1915).

These four battles cost the Italians 66,000 killed, 190,000 wounded, and 22,500 captured. Austrian casualties totaled 165,000.

Isonzo V (March 9–17, 1916). Pressed by the Allies for a diversionary offensive, Cadorna attacked again despite the additional handicaps of snow, rain, and fog. He accomplished nothing before he had to call a halt in order to meet an Austrian offensive in the Trentino aimed at Asiago, and ultimately Padua.

Isonzo VI (August 6–17, 1916). After having blocked the Austrians in the Trentino with troops taken from the Isonzo, Cadorna rushed his forces back to the embattled river line. Against the now weakened enemy position, the Italians won their first success of the war. Gorizia was captured on August 9 and a bridgehead secured across the Isonzo. But the lack of reserve strength and stiffened Austrian resistance prevented a breakthrough.

Isonzo VII (September 14–17, 1916).

Isonzo VIII (October 10–12, 1916).

Isonzo IX (November 1–4, 1916). Changing his tactics to sharp stabs at the enemy line, Cadorna reduced the number of his casualties from that in the three battles listed above but still scored no significant gain.

Isonzo X (May 12–June 8, 1917). Strengthened over the winter by fresh troops and increased armament, the Italians renewed the offensive, gaining a few yards of ground. But an Austrian counterattack during June 4–8 drove back Cadorna's armies to their starting point.

Isonzo XI (August 19–September 12, 1917). Built up to a peak strength of 51 divisions, aided by 5,200 guns, Cadorna sent the Second (Luigi Capello) and Third (Duke of Aosta) armies on still another assault on the Austrian defenses. The massive attack dented the enemy lines, but the Italian infantry outran their artillery and supplies and could not capitalize on their advantage.

This action closed the fruitless, bloody battles of the Isonzo River. In answer to Austrian pleas, Germany had sent an army to the northern flank aimed at aiding their allies in a powerful turning assault against Cadorna's Isonzo armies. This assault, which came in October at Caporetto, is sometimes called the Twelfth Battle of the Isonzo. *See* Asiago; Caporetto; World War I.

Israeli-Arab War (1967). The third war in 19 years between Israel and its Arab state neighbors was fought June 5 to 10, 1967. Despite an Israeli victory in 1948–49 and again in 1956, no peace terms were negotiated and tension in the Middle East remained high. The United Arab Republic (Egypt), under President Gamal Abdel Nasser, Jordan, and Syria steadily built up their military forces, as did Israel. On May 17, 1967, Nasser demanded and received the withdrawal of the United Nations Emergency Forces from the Gaza Strip. Five days later he closed the Gulf of Aqaba to Israeli shipping (Israel had long been denied use of the Suez Canal).

Fighting broke out on the morning of June 5. Israel, led by Premier Levi Eshkol, Defense Minister Moshe Dayan, and Chief of Staff Yitzhak Rabin, seized the initiative in the early hours of the conflict. Israeli planes attacked the U.A.R., Jordan, and Syria, claiming 374 enemy aircraft destroyed, chiefly on the ground. Free from enemy air attacks, Israeli armored columns plunged into the Gaza Strip, fanned westward into the Sinai Peninsula in a three-pronged advance toward the Suez Canal, and raced southward to Sharm el Sheikh at the entrance to the Gulf of Aqaba. After three days of fighting, the Egyptian army was in flight on all fronts; a small naval force captured Sharm el Sheikh on June 7. Meanwhile, to the east, Israeli forces occupied the Old City of Jerusalem on June 7 and began attacking the Jordanian army west of the Jordan River. On the same day, King Hussein of Jordan agreed to the cease-fire proposed by the United Nations. Egypt accepted the cease-fire on June 8 and Syria accepted on the following day, but Israeli forces continued their drive toward Damascus.

Finally, on June 10, both sides ceased formal warfare although minor skirmishes continued for several days. The war cost the lives of many thousands of Arab soldiers and civilians and 679 Israeli soldiers. *See* Jerusalem IX; Sinai Peninsula.

Issus (Macedonian Conquests), 333 B.C. A year and a half after his invasion of the Persian Empire, Alexander III, the Great, had conquered Asia Minor. In October 333 he reached the Asian mainland and turned south down the Syrian coast. Here at the village of Issus, a thoroughly alarmed Darius III took the field himself at the head of an army greatly outnumbering the 35,000 Macedonians. Darius posted his motley army behind the shallow Pinarus River in the rear of Alexander's force. The Persian king's maneuver, however, wedged his Asiatics and Greek mercenaries into a mile-wide coastal plain between foothills and the sea, thus surrendering his numerical advantage.

Alexander the Great charged across the stream to lessen the effects of Persian missiles. In the hard fighting that followed, a breach was made in the left of Darius' line. The Macedonian heavy cavalry quickly penetrated the gap, striking in flank the hired Greek phalanx at the center. The Persian line wavered and then broke. Darius fled the field, followed by his rank and file except for the Greek mercenaries, who died where they stood. Alexander ordered a vigorous pursuit, which resulted in the slaying of tens of thousands of the retreating enemy. Macedonian losses were estimated at 450.

After this monumental defeat, Darius offered to surrender all of Asia west of the Euphrates River and to pay a tribute of 10,000 talents. But Alexander demanded unconditional surrender, hoping to fuse the entire civilized world into one huge empire under his leadership. The march through Syria continued. *See* Granicus River; Tyre II; Macedonian Conquests.

Italian-Turkish War (1911–1912). Claiming that Turkey obstructed its peaceful penetration of Tripoli, the Italian government of Victor Emmanuel III declared war on September 29, 1911. No major battles were fought. Italy occupied Tripoli and Rhodes (plus other Dodecanese islands). One week after the First Balkan War broke out on October 8, 1912, Sultan Mohammed V accepted peace terms. Italy gained Tripoli and Cyrenaica and later officially received the Dodecanese.

Italian Wars of Independence (1821–1870). The peninsula of Italy, dominated by Austria and divided into nine separate states, had long sought freedom from foreign rule and unification into a single nation. An independence movement against the Bourbon monarchy of Naples failed in 1821. An attempt to throw off the Austrian yoke during 1848–49 also failed. A third attempt, launched in 1859 with the support of France, finally succeeded, chiefly through the efforts of Italian heroes Giuseppe Garibaldi, Conte Camillo di Cavour, and Victor Emmanuel II of Sardinia (Piedmont), who became the first king of a united Italy in 1861. The province of Venetia was annexed in 1866. Four years later Rome at last came under the control of an all-Italian government and was made the capital.

Rieti	1821
Custoza I	1848
Novara II	1849
Rome VII	1849
Venice	1849
Magenta	1859
Solferino	1859
Calatafimi	1860
Milazzo	1860
Castelfidardo	1860
Gaeta	1860–1861
Aspromonte	1862
Custoza II	1866
Vis	1866
Mentana	1867

Italy. The major battles and wars of what is now the nation of Italy are listed below. For earlier conflicts *see* Roman Republic; Roman Empire.

Pavia II	476
Ravenna I	491–493
Rome III	536–537
Rome IV	546–547
Taginae	552
Casilinum	554
Pavia III	569–572
Ravenna II	729
Ravenna III	756
Pavia IV	773–774
Apulia	875–880
Taormina	902
Crotone	982
Sant'Angelo	998
Dyrrachium II	1081
Rome V	1084
Legnano	1176
Cortenuova	1237
Benevento	1266
Tagliacozzo	1268
Messina II	1284
Campaldino	1289
Curzola	1299
Alghero	1353
Pulj	1379
Chioggia	1379
Salonika I	1430
Negroponte	1470
Shkodër I	1478
Naples	1495
Fornovo	1495
Lepanto I	1499
Barletta	1502
Cerignola	1503
Garigliano River	1503
Agnadello	1509
Ravenna IV	1512
Novara I	1513
Marignano	1515
La Bicocca	1522
Pavia V	1525
Rome VI	1527
Preveza	1538
Cyprus	1570–1571
Lepanto II	1571
Candia II	1646–1669

See Louis XIV Wars
See Polish Succession, War of the
See Austrian Succession, War of the
See French Revolution, Wars of the; Napoleonic Empire Wars; Napoleon's Hundred Days
See Italian Wars of Independence

Chernaya River	1855
Aduwa	1896
See Italian-Turkish War	
See World War I	
Ethiopia	1936
Albania	1939
See World War II	

Italy, Southern (World War II), 1943. The Allied invasion of the European continent took place less than three weeks after the conquest of Sicily. On September 3 two divisions of Gen. Sir Bernard Montgomery's British Eighth Army crossed the Strait of Messina and landed at Reggio Calabria on the toe of the Italian boot (Operation Baytown). Meeting little opposition from the disorganized Italian Army (which was trying to surrender to the Allies), Montgomery pushed his XIII Corps north through Calabria, the 5th British Division along the west coast, the 1st Canadian along the east coast.

The British thrust, making good progress over narrow, hilly roads, helped convince Marshal Pietro Badoglio to surrender the Italian government on the evening of September 8. The next morning the Allied Fifth Army swarmed ashore at Salerno, 150 miles to the north. A week later the XIII Corps, driving north against withdrawing German forces (under Gen. Herr), made contact with the right flank of the Fifth Army near Vallo, thus uniting the Allied forces on the west coast of Italy.

Meanwhile, on September 9, the British admiral Sir Andrew Cunningham's fleet had landed the British V Corps at Taranto inside the Italian heel. Here the 1st Airborne Division captured the great naval base and then struck across the heel toward the important airfields at Foggia, 110 miles to the north. This drive gathered momentum on September 22, when the British 78th Division landed at Bari on the east coast. Foggia was taken five days later. A Commando strike 50 miles up the coast at Termoli on October 3 ensured Allied use of the great complex of airfields in the Foggia area.

The advance of the British Eighth Army on the Adriatic Coast and in the interior now merged with the U.S. general Mark Clark's Fifth Army in a drive northward on the German Gustav Line protecting Rome. *See* Sicily; Salerno; Gustav-Cassino Line; World War II.

Ituzaingó (Uruguayan War of Independence), 1827. When Argentina broke away from Spain and when Brazil became independent of Portugal, the territory in between was incorporated in Brazil as the Cisplatine Province. The people in this area sought the help of Argentina in securing their freedom from Brazil. In the revolt that ensued, an army of independence under Carlos de Alvear was formed of both Argentines and Uruguayans. On February 20, 1827, this force fought the army of Brazil at Ituzaingó, in what is now northeastern Argentina. The Brazilians, commanded by the Marquês de Barbacena, were decisively beaten. Great Britain then intervened and helped set up Uruguay as an independent nation the following year. *See* Montevideo.

Iuka (American Civil War), 1862. After the Federal victory at Shiloh, Gen. Henry Halleck pressed as far south as Corinth, Miss., before dispersing his armies all the way from Memphis to Chattanooga. Called to Washington in July, he was replaced by Gen. U. S. Grant. On September 13 the Confederate general Sterling Price moved his 14,000-man army from Tupelo to Iuka, astride Grant's communication lines with Gen. Don Carlos Buell in eastern Tennessee. Grant promptly launched an attack against Price, sending Gen. Edward Ord with 8,000 men eastward along the railroad to Iuka, while Gen. William Rosecrans with 9,000 troops circled southward to cut off the expected Confederate retreat. Late in the afternoon of September 19 Rosecrans was within two miles of Iuka when he was suddenly struck by Price's left (south) wing under Gen. Henry Little. In two hours of fierce fighting the attack was stopped. Little and 263 others were killed, among the 1,516 Confederate casualties. Rosecrans lost 782 men. When Price learned that Ord was prepared to join in the attack the following day, he withdrew southward under cover of darkness. Rosecrans and Ord returned to Corinth. *See* Shiloh; Corinth, Miss.; American Civil War.

Ivry-la-Bataille (French Religious Wars), 1590. The eight religious (and political) wars that had convulsed France since 1562 reached a climax in the fight to succeed the Catholic Valois king Henry III. The Catholic army, or Holy League, commanded by the Duc de Mayenne (Charles de Lorraine) of the Guise family, had failed to defeat the Huguenots under Henry of Navarre (later Henry IV) at Arques in 1589. Now, six months later, the two hostile armies faced each other at Ivry-la-Bataille, on the Eure River 40 miles west of Paris. De Mayenne commanded a force of 25,000 men; half of his 21,000 infantrymen carried pikes. Henry's army was only half as large, but it had a higher percentage of musketeers and a better-trained cavalry arm. It also had a marked advantage in deployment. On March 14, 1590, De Mayenne ordered an advance, which was quickly thrown into confusion by enemy musket volleys and fierce cavalry counterattacks. Henry's troops soon routed their foe, inflicting

4,000 casualties at a loss to themselves of only 500. It was the decisive battle of the French Religious Wars.

The victor immediately marched on Paris but failed to take it, as De Mayenne and the Spanish Duke of Parma came to the assistance of the city. Three years later, however, when Henry formally adopted Catholicism, Paris opened its gates and acknowledged him as its king. Thus, as Henry IV, the former Huguenot launched the Bourbon line of kings. When De Mayenne also swore allegiance to the new sovereign, the Holy League fell apart. Henry then ended the religious wars on April 15, 1598, with the Edict of Nantes, which granted equal political rights and some religious freedom to the Huguenots. *See* Arques; La Rochelle II; French Religious Wars.

Iwo Jima (World War II), 1945. The frequent bombing runs of U.S. B-29 Superfortresses between the Marianas and Japan focused attention on the tiny volcanic island of Iwo Jima, lying only 700 miles south of Tokyo. Iwo-based Japanese radar and fighters plagued the U.S. 20th Air Force. The capture of Iwo would eliminate this menace and provide fighter protection for heavy bombers over the Japanese homeland. In addition, the island could serve as a convenient emergency landing strip for crippled or fuelless B-29's on their 1,500-mile flight back to Saipan and Tinian

Japan also appreciated the importance of Iwo. In the eight square miles of the sulfurous island Gen. Tadamichi Kuribayashi packed 21,000 troops and the heaviest firepower and strongest defenses of the Pacific War—1,500 fortified caves, hundreds of ferroconcrete pillboxes, blockhouses, and trenches, and miles of interconnecting tunnels. To attack this formidable array, the marine general Harry Schmidt's V Amphibious Corps readied the 4th and 5th Marine divisions for an assault on the southeast beaches.

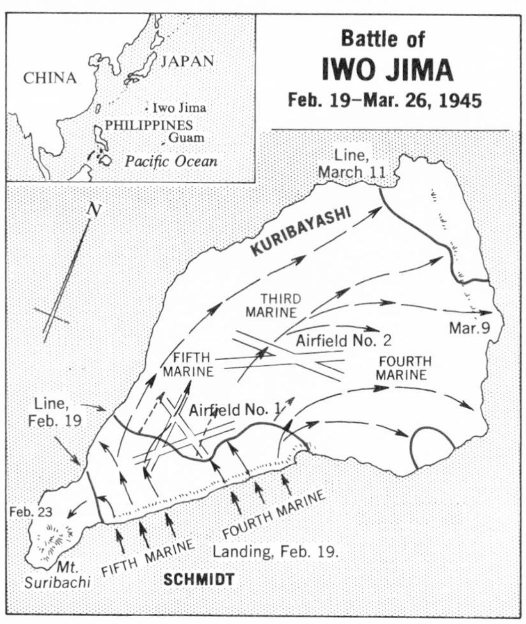

On February 19, after weeks of intensive aerial bombardment and three days of naval shelling, the invasion took place. On the left (south) the 5th Marine Division (Keller Rockey) fought its way across Iwo's narrow neck the first day, isolating the Mount Suribachi defenses on the southern tip of the island. On the right the 4th Marine Division (Clifton Gates) reached the edge of Airfield Number One, nailing down the north flank of the landing beach. But a constant hail of Japanese artillery and small-arms fire took a frightful toll that first day—more than 2,400 marines had been hit, including some 600 killed.

On the second day the 5th Marine Division turned left and attacked toward Suribachi. Despite continued stiff resistance, this division pressed forward until, on February 23, the assault carried to the top of Suribachi's 550-foot peak. Here at 10:30 A.M. a small American flag was raised on a pipe by Lt. Harold Schrier's patrol. At 2:30 P.M. the mountain slopes were clear and a larger (96 x 56 in.) flag was raised on the top. The photograph of the event, taken by Joe Rosenthal, soon became the most dramatic battle picture in American history.

To the north, the 4th Marine Division had taken Airfield Number One and wheeled right up the east coast. Now the 5th Marine Division turned 180 degrees from Mount Suribachi and attacked up the west coast. Between these two units, the reserve 3rd Marine Division (Graves Erskine) occupied the center of the advance through Airfield Number Two on February 24. In this northern half of Iwo the Japanese fanatically held on to cross-island defense lines keyed on the Motoyama Plateau. On March 9 the 3rd Marine Division reached the sea in the northeast. A week later the 4th Division had crushed al' resistance on the right (east) flank. It was not until March 26, however, that the 5th Division could report all opposition eliminated on the left.

The battle of Iwo Jima cost the Marine Corps more than 6,821 dead and over 18,000 wounded. Twenty-six men won the Medal of Honor (12 of them posthumously) on the island where, Adm. Nimitz said that "uncommon valor was a common virtue." Almost every Japanese defender had been killed. But the conquest began paying dividends even before the fighting ended. On March 4 the first fuelless B-29 landed on Airfield Number One on its way back to the Marianas. It was the first of 2,251 Superfortresses, carrying 24,761 crewmen to make use of Iwo Jima's emergency landing fields. *See* Mariana Islands; Okinawa; World War II.

J

Jackson (American Civil War). The second action, on May 14, 1863, of Gen. U. S. Grant's Vicksburg campaign, in which he split the Confederate forces and defeated Gen. Joseph Johnston's army. *See* Vicksburg.

Jacobite Insurrections (1689–1691; 1715; 1745). The deposition of James II of England and the enthronement in 1689 of his son-in-law and daughter, William of Orange (William III) and Mary, were accomplished without bloodshed, in what has been called "the Glorious Revolution." Partisans (Jacobites) of James and his heirs, however, remained powerful and disturbing influences in Ireland and Scotland for generations.

Opposition to James began soon after his accession in 1685 as it became apparent that he intended to rule as absolute monarch and to restore Roman Catholicism. When a son (James Edward) was born to James in 1687, eminent citizens invited William and Mary to save England from what they feared would be a succession of Catholic tyrants. William landed at Torbay on Nov. 5, 1688, and the following February he and Mary were proclaimed king and queen. James fled to France, but reappeared shortly in Ireland, where he had no difficulty in assembling an army. At the same time, the Viscount Dundee was rallying Scots Highlanders to the service of the deposed king. The Scots ambushed and routed a royalist force at Killiecrankie Pass in July 1689, but Dundee was killed in the battle and the Scot's revolt soon died out. In Ireland the growing strength of James's army prompted William to take the field himself. His forces completely crushed the Jacobites at the Boyne River on July 1, 1690. James took refuge again in France and died there in 1701.

In 1715 royalist forces quickly put down an insurrection of Jacobites in northern England and Scotland that sought to enthrone James II's son, James Edward (the Old Pretender), in place of the Hannoverian king, George I. In 1745, while the British government was preoccupied with the War of the Austrian Succession, the clans rallied again around the Old Pretender's son, Charles (the Young Pretender; "Bonnie Prince Charlie"). The rebels twice defeated a royalist army before they were routed and the Young Pretender was forced to flee to France. These two insurrections are known as "the Fifteen" ('15) and "the Forty-five" ('45) or, collectively, as "the Rebellion."

Resistance to the Glorious Revolution

Londonderry	1689
Killiecrankie	1689
Boyne River	1690
Aughrim	1691
Limerick	1691
Glencoe	1692
"The Fifteen"	
Sheriffmuir	1715
Preston II	1715
"The Forty-five"	
Prestonpans	1745
Falkirk II	1746
Culloden Moor	1746

Jadar River (World War I), 1914. To crush Serbia and thus open the Berlin–Baghdad railroad, Austria launched a two-pronged invasion across Serbia's northern frontier on August 12. Under the supreme command of Gen. Oskar Potiorek, part of the Austrian Second Army struck from the north while the Fifth and Sixth crossed the Drina River from the west. The Serbian general Radomir Putnik promptly moved his Second and Third armies against the chief danger point—the advance of the Austrian Fifth Army. In a fierce, five-day battle along a 30-mile front on the Jadar River, beginning on August 16, the Serbs struck at the hinge between the enemy VIII and XIII corps and drove them back. To the north the IV Corps of the weakened Second Army was also repulsed, while to the southwest the Austrian Sixth Army failed to make any headway. Potiorek then recalled his poorly coordinated and now exhausted armies. He had suffered 40,000 casualties. The first invasion of Serbia had resulted in a colossal failure. *See* Rudnik Ridges; World War I .

Jalula (Moslem Conquest of Persia), 637. The Persian army beaten at Kadisiya was rallied by Emperor Yazdegerd III six months later at the entrance to the mountains 50 miles north of

Madain. After looting the rich capital of Ctesiphon, the Arabian army of Sa'd ibn-Abi-Waqqās rode north in pursuit. At Jalula the Moslem cavalry began the slashing attacks that had proved so effective against the heavier-armed but demoralized Persians. Again Yazdegerd's horsemen broke and fled, losing heavily in the rout. The Moslems pushed on to invade and occupy central Persia. It would be four years before Yazdegerd could organize another army to defend his country against the invaders. *See* Kadisiya; Nihawand; Moslem Conquests.

Jamaica (English-Spanish Wars), 1655. After its discovery by Columbus in 1494, the island of Jamaica in the West Indies became a possession of Spain. In 1655, however, a joint army-navy expedition from England launched a campaign of conquest. Under Gen. Robert Venables and Adm. William Penn, the English landed on the island on May 11. In a short struggle they ousted the Spanish garrison. The capture of Jamaica led to declared war between England and Spain, which was already locked in arms against France on the Continent. *See* Santa Cruz de Tenerife.

Jankau (Thirty Years' War), 1645. While prolonged peace negotiations were going on in Munster and Osnabruck, fighting erupted again on the eastern front early in 1645. Field Marshal Lennart Torstenson, who commanded the Swedish army on the Elbe, suddenly struck southward toward Prague. Holy Roman Emperor Ferdinand III called for help from Maximilian I, elector of Bavaria, who sent his cavalry under Gen. Johann von Werth to reinforce the Imperial army.

On March 6 the combined Bavarian-Austrian army intercepted Torstenson at Jankau, near Tabor, 35 miles southeast of Prague. Here rough, wooded terrain prevented a formal battle alignment. In a series of small independent actions the Imperial army could not utilize its superiority in numbers against the hard-fighting Swedes. Count von Goetz, the Austrian cavalry commander, was outmaneuvered and slain. When his horsemen bolted, the Imperial infantry followed. Now Werth's Bavarian cavalry was left alone to battle the Swedes. Although the Bavarians fought gallantly, they were beaten back with heavy loss of life. The survivors fled into Prague. Emperor Ferdinand abandoned his Bohemian capital to seek safety in Vienna. But when Torstenson sought to take Prague by siege, he found the countryside too barren to support his army. He thereupon withdrew down the Elbe Valley.

Thus the battle of Jankau won no advantage for the anti-Hapsburg forces of Sweden and France. It was a cruel loss to the Empire, however. The heavy casualties suffered by the Bavarian cavalrymen broke the backbone of the army (as Rocroi two years previously had destroyed the superb Spanish infantry of the Hapsburgs). Meanwhile, Bavaria itself was reinvaded by a French army. *See* Freiburg; Mergentheim; Thirty Years' War.

Japan. The major battles and wars fought by what is now the nation of Japan are listed below.

Dan no Ura	1185
Hakata Bay	1274
Kyushu	1281
Kamakura	1333
Sekigahara	1600
Toyotomi Castle	1614–1615
Hara Castle	1637–1638
Tokyo	1868

See Chinese-Japanese War I
See Russian-Japanese War
See Chinese-Japanese War II
See World War I
See World War II

Japan—Bombardment (World War II), 1944–1945. Japan, the ultimate target of the Allied offensive in the Pacific, first came under air attack in a nuisance raid by carrier-based U.S. Army bombers in April 1942. Later B-29 Superfortress bombers from China struck the enemy homeland. It was not until B-29's began operating from Saipan and other Mariana bases on November 24, 1944, however, that Japanese targets suffered heavy damage. The B-29's belonged to XXI Bomber Command (Haywood Hansell, and later Curtis LeMay), which was part of the 20th Air Force, commanded by Chief of the Army Air Forces Henry Arnold from Washington, D.C.

For more than three months high-level (25,000 feet) raids continued. Then on March 9, 1945, 234 B-29's came down to 7,000 feet to drop 1,667 tons of incendiary bombs on Tokyo. The fire bombing burned out almost 16 square miles in the heart of the city, destroyed 250,000 homes, and killed 83,793 people. It ranks as the second most lethal air raid in history (surpassing the later Hiroshima and Nagasaki atomic bomb attacks but not the double raid on Dresden, Germany). Similar raids struck Nagoya, Osaka, Kobe, and Yokohama. By mid-June these five major cities lay in ruins, with a total of almost 100 square miles burned out.

After the Allied victory over Germany on May 8, the bombardment of Japan increased in tempo. The 8th Air Force was redeployed from Europe to Okinawa. With the 20th Air Force (now under Gen. Nathan Twining) in the Marianas, the 8th formed the U.S. strategic air arm under Gen. Carl Spaatz. By July 1,200 bombing sorties a week were being carried out against Japan. In all, long-range strategic bombings killed 260,000 Japanese and left more than 9,000,000 homeless. Bomber combat losses were 343 aircraft and 243 in crew.

In February 1945 land-based bomber attacks began to be supplemented by carrier aircraft strikes of the U.S. fleet, later reinforced by a British task force. Beginning on July 10, Adm. William Halsey's U.S. Third Fleet steamed boldly into Japanese coastal waters to fire its naval guns at targets on shore.

Meanwhile, the U.S. had developed the atomic bomb and on July 27 demanded Japan's immediate surrender as an alternative to the use of this terrible new weapon. The ultimatum was rejected. On August 6 a B-29 bomber (*Enola Gay*) from Tinian dropped a single atomic bomb on Hiroshima, shattering three-fifths of the city and killing 71,379 inhabitants out of a population of about 300,000.Three days later another atomic bomb was dropped on Nagasaki, with only slightly less destruction and casualties.

While Japan was being blasted from the air and sea, U.S. submarines were conducting an equally devastating underwater offensive against enemy merchant ships. Of the 8.5 million tons of Japanese shipping sunk during the war, 5 million (1,113 ships) fell to submarines. The cost was 45 U.S. submarines.

Although the Soviet Union had declared war on Japan on August 8 and invaded Manchuria, this action proved to be inconclusive. More important was Halsey's return strike at Honshu with the Third Fleet on August 9 and an 800-plane B-29 raid five days later. Finally, after three and one-half years of war, on August 15 (Tokyo time), 1945, Japan accepted unconditional surrender. The war in the Pacific, and all of World War II, was over. *See* Shangri-La; Iwo Jima; Okinawa; Germany—Air Bombardment; World War II.

Jarama River (Spanish Civil War). A local Nationalist success southeast of Madrid, during February 6–28, 1937, which further tightened the siege of Madrid. *See* Madrid.

Jargeau (Hundred Years' War), 1429. When the French army under Joan of Arc drove off the English besiegers of Orleans on May 8, 1429, the Hundred Years' War reached a turning point. Aided by the Comte de Dunois and other military commanders, Joan moved to clear the line of the Loire, held by English detachments commanded by the Duke of Suffolk (William de la Pole). On June 12 Joan's French, now fighting determinedly, stormed the fortress of Jargeau, ten miles east of Orleans. The English, becoming rapidly demoralized, yielded, and Suffolk was taken prisoner. Three days later Meung fell; Beaugency came under siege on June 16 and surrendered three days later. Meanwhile John Talbot, earl of Shrewsbury, collected the remaining English forces and began falling back toward the Seine. The major French counteroffensive was under way. *See* Orleans; Patay; Hundred Years' War.

Jarnac (French Religious Wars), 1569. The peace that ended France's second civil war between the Huguenots and the Catholic royalists of Charles IX lasted less than a year. Urged on by his mother, Catherine de Médicis, and the house of Guise, the king sent an army into western France to quell Protestant unrest there. Commanded by Charles's younger brother, the Duc d'Anjou (later Henry III), and by the Seigneur de Tavannes, the royal cavalry defeated the Huguenots at Jarnac, on the Charente River, on March 13, 1569. The rebel commander, the Prince de Condé, was killed. Huguenot leadership then fell entirely on Gaspard de Coligny, admiral of France, who continued the third civil war against the crown. *See* Saint-Denis; Moncontour; French Religious Wars.

Jasmund (Swedish-Danish Wars), 1676. The historical enmity between Sweden and Denmark prompted the two maritime nations to take opposite sides in the French war against Holland. Sweden (Charles XI) aligned itself with Louis XIV, while Denmark (Christian V) fought on the side of the Dutch, who in turn sent a squadron of ships to the Baltic to help the Danes. The first major sea battle of the war took place off Jasmund Peninsula on Rügen Island, on May 25, 1676. The Danish admiral Niels Juel handed the Swedish fleet a resounding defeat. The following year the two hostile navies would clash again. *See* Fehrbellin; Köge Bight; Northern Wars.

Java Sea (World War II), 1942. By February 25, 1942, Japan had overrun most of the western Pacific southward to Java. The ABDA (Australian, British, Dutch, American) efforts to block the onrushing Japanese had failed utterly, and the Allied organization was dissolved. Now the only obstacle to Japan's invasion of the island of Java was a weak Allied naval force commanded by the Dutch admiral Karel Doorman. On the afternoon of February 27, Doorman's 14-ship fleet steamed north from Java into the Java Sea to intercept a superior Japanese naval force commanded by Adm. Sokichi Takagi. In a savage seven-hour battle, Doorman was killed, and his flagship, *De Ruyter,* and another Dutch light cruiser (*Java*) were sunk. Also lost were two British (*Electra, Jupiter*) and one Dutch (*Kortenaer*) destroyers, with the British heavy cruiser *Exeter* (veteran of the *Graf Spee* battle) badly damaged. One Japanese destroyer was crippled.

The remaining Allied vessels now attempted to escape the deathtrap of the Java Sea and make for Australia. The American heavy cruiser *Houston* (the ship President F. D. Roosevelt had used on four cruises before the war) and the Australian light cruiser *Perth* raced for Sunda Strait, at the western end of Java. Here they were met by a strong force of Japanese warships, and both cruisers were sunk on the night of February 28–March 1. More than half the *Houston*'s 1,000 men and half the *Perth*'s crew of 680 were killed or drowned.

The damaged *Exeter,* escorted by the British destroyer *Encounter* and the American destroyer *Pope,* also tried to escape through Sunda Strait. But they too were intercepted and sunk by a superior force of Japanese warships, on March 1. More than 800 survivors were taken captive by the Japanese. Only four American destroyers safely slipped by the enemy by navigating the narrow Bali Strait at the eastern end of Java. Not an Allied vessel remained afloat in the Java Sea and the loss of Java Island was now inevitable. South of Java the carnage continued, with the loss of the U.S. oiler *Pecos,* two U.S. destroyers, *Pillsbury* and *Edsall,* as well as other vessels fleeing the doomed island. *See* East Indies; Coral Sea; World War II.

Jemappes (Wars of the French Revolution), 1792. Inspired by the surprising rebuff of the Prussian invasion at Valmy, the Revolutionary French National Convention ordered an offensive in Flanders during the autumn of 1792. General Charles Dumouriez, the victor of Valmy, took an ill-organized army of 40,000 men northward. At Jemappes, just west of Mons in modern Belgium, he came upon an entrenched army of 14,000 Austrians under Duke Albert of Saxe-Teschen. A sudden French attack routed the Austrian force on November 6, in the first infantry battle of the War of the First Coalition. Saxe-Teschen resigned his command, while the French pressed on to take Brussels and all of the Austrian Netherlands. *See* Valmy; Neerwinden II; French Revolution Wars.

Jena-Auerstedt (Napoleonic Empire Wars), 1806. While the huge Prussian army (130,000 men) of King Frederick William III lumbered westward through Saxony in October 1806, French troops of Napoleon I were also on the move. Marching at the rate of 25 miles a day, three columns of the Grande Armée crossed the southeastern end of the hilly Thuringian Forest, to appear suddenly on the left flank and rear of the Prussian army on October 10. As the Prussians faced about to meet the sudden attack, King Frederick deployed his troops westward toward Weimar and divided his forces—Prince Friedrich of Hohenlohe-Ingelfingen concentrated 48,000 men between Jena and Weimar; the Duke of Brunswick (Karl Wilhelm Ferdinand) assembled 63,000 men at Auerstedt, 11 miles to the north. Both Prussian armies now faced their own lines of communication to the east.

At daybreak on October 14 Napoleon threw his main body of 56,000 men against Hohenlohe-Ingelfingen. In bitter fighting, the Prussians counterattacked in parade-ground formations, firing volleys on command. Their ranks crumpled under heavy musket and artillery fire, chiefly from the V Corps of Marshal Jean Lannes. About noon,

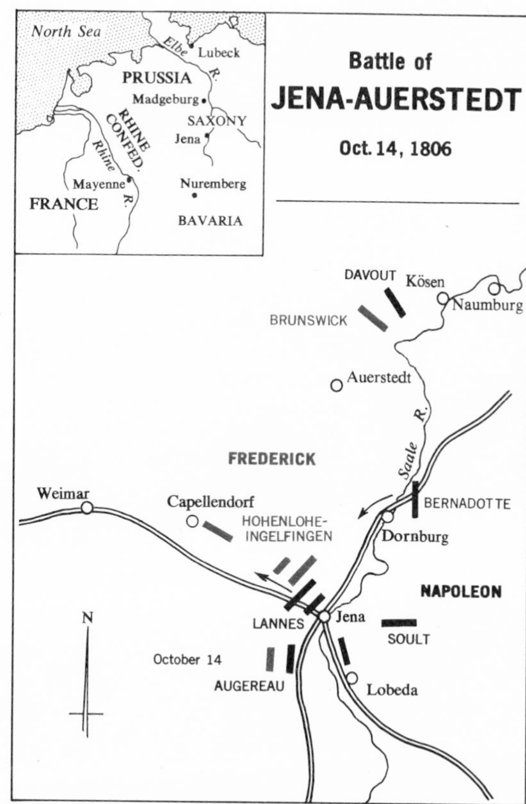

after cruel losses the Prussian (and Saxon) line began to waver. Napoleon then sent in the corps of Marshals Nicolas Soult (IV) and Pierre Augereau (VII) to join Lannes in a furious assault. Hohenlohe-Ingelfingen's troops fell back, their lines broken by stabbing French cavalry attacks. By evening Napoleon had pushed into Weimar. He had lost about 5,000 men. Prussian and Saxon casualties were 11,000 killed and wounded, 15,000 captured.

Meanwhile, the isolated northern wing of Napoleon's army, 26,000 men of the III Corps under Marshal Louis Davout, had also attacked toward Weimar at dawn. At Auerstedt the French bumped into Brunswick's main Prussian army. When Davout continued to press forward, the duke dissipated much of his superior strength in piecemeal counterattacks. A fatal wound felled the duke, who was replaced in command by King Frederick himself. Fighting in poor order, the Prussians fell back on both flanks, allowing the hard-driving French to move their artillery far enough forward on the wings to enfilade the entire line. By 1 P.M. Davout's attack was tearing apart the Prussian front. The French poured into Auerstedt, while the beaten army fled westward. Davout's fight had cost him 8,000 men, but he had killed or wounded 12,000 of the enemy and taken 3,000 prisoners and 115 guns. He would be made Duc d'Auerstedt for his masterful triumph over an army of more than twice the strength of his own.

The double victory of the French placed them closer to Berlin than the scattered pieces of King Frederick William's Prussian army. Napoleon started an immediate thrust northeast toward Berlin, while the defeated Prussians fell back toward the Baltic Sea. *See* Saalfeld; Lübeck; Napoleonic Empire Wars.

Jenkins' Ear, War of (1739). A series of clashes at sea, particularly off the American coast, led to declared war between Great Britain and Spain. After the British capture of the Spanish settlement of Porto Bello, the conflict merged into the larger War of the Austrian Succession. *See* Porto Bello.

Jerusalem I (Babylonian Conquest), 586 B.C. Through the victory of Nebuchadnezzar II (Nabuchodonosor) over the Egyptians at Carchemish in 605, the kingdom of Judah came under Babylonian rule. Eight years later King Jehoiachin, the prophet Ezekiel (Ezechiel), and other Judahite leaders were taken captive to Babylonia. Nebuchadnezzar then installed his uncle, the 21-year-old Zedekiah (Sedecias), on the throne of Judah in 597. When Zedekiah later fomented a revolt against Babylonia, Nebuchadnezzar marched an army into Palestine and besieged Jerusalem. After 16 months the city was completely out of food. The Jewish soldiers tried to escape by night toward Jericho but were pursued and killed. Zedekiah was forced to watch the slaying of his sons. Then his eyes were put out. The city was destroyed and for the second time many Jews (4,600 in all), and Zedekiah in chains, were carried into Babylonian exile. This battle ended the kingdom of Judah. *See* Carchemish; Tyre I.

Jerusalem II (Revolt of the Maccabees), 168–165 B.C. During Syrian rule over Judea, Antiochus IV (Epiphanes) sought to Hellenize the Jews. He destroyed the wall of Jerusalem, looted the Temple, and erected an altar to Zeus. This provoked a Jewish revolt led by Mattathias of the Hasmonaeans and his five sons, who took refuge in the nearby mountains. After several skirmishes the Jews, under the direction of Judas (the third son), drove off the Syrian army. With the liberation of Jerusalem, Judas (who received the surname Maccabaeus, perhaps meaning "the Hammerer") reconsecrated the Temple in 165 (commemorated by the Jewish Feast of Dedication, or Hanukkah).

Fighting between Jew and Syrian continued for another quarter of a century. Judas Maccabaeus was killed in 160. It was not until 141 B.C. under the leadership of his brother Simon that Judea achieved a troubled independence, which would last only 75 years. *See* Jerusalem III.

Jerusalem III (Conquest by Rome), 66–63 B.C. After only 75 years of freedom the ancient Jewish capital became a battleground again when civil war broke out among the members of the ruling Maccabees (Hasmonaean) family. This was unfortunate timing on the part of the Jews. The decline of the Egyptian and Syrian monarchies had created a political vacuum in western Asia that Rome was rapidly filling. The Roman general Pompey the Great intervened in the Palestinian dispute by laying siege to Jerusalem in 66 B.C. After holding out for three years, the city surrendered. Judea then came under the Roman governor of Syria. The establishment of Roman hegemony over the old Hellenistic monarchies was now complete. *See* Roman Republic.

Jerusalem IV (Jewish Wars of the Roman Empire), A.D. 70. The bloody reconquest of Judea by the Roman legions under Titus Flavius Vespasian had reached the walls of Jerusalem by A.D. mid-68. Vespasian began siege operations, but when civil war erupted in Rome, he took his time about reducing the Jewish city. In December 69 Vespasian was called to Italy to take charge of the empire. His son Titus took command of the 60,000 troops surrounding Jerusalem. Titus began prosecuting the siege vigorously. But this only increased Jewish resistance, led by the fanatical Zealot sect. In the spring Titus finally penetrated the northern suburb of Bezetha. Then in one of the most desperate struggles in history, the Romans fought their way into the city, street by street, building by building. On August 29 the fortified Temple was burned out. Nine days later the rest of the devastated city fell into Roman hands.

The Hebrew historian Josephus reported that 1,100,000 people perished in the siege. But this figure may be exaggerated even for the four-year campaign of reconquest. It is known that thousands of survivors were sold into slavery. By calculated policy, Rome always punished political rebels far more ruthlessly than barbarian opponents. *See* Jotapata; Cremona I; Roman Empire.

Jerusalem V (Byzantine-Persian Wars), 615. Eleven years after Emperor Mauricius had helped Khosrau (Chosroes) II gain the throne of Persia, the Byzantine ruler was assassinated (602). To avenge the murder of his benefactor, Khosrau declared war on the Byzantine Empire. Under the capable leadership of a general named Shahrbaraz, Persian troops overran Mesopotamia and Asia Minor to reach the Bosporus, opposite Constantinople, in 608. The Byzantine capital proved to be unyielding, but elsewhere Imperial resistance was feeble. The Persians reduced Antioch in 611 and Damascus three years later. In 615 Khosrau's troops stormed into Jerusalem. A reported 50,000 were killed and another 35,000 marched back to Persia as prisoners. The city was sacked and the True Cross carried off to Ctesiphon. Moving on, the Persians took Alexandria and subjugated Egypt by 619. The Asian empire of Darius I had been restored. Meanwhile, however, the miserable Byzantine assassin-emperor Phocas had been replaced by Heraclius, who was busy rebuilding his armed forces. *See* Melitene I; Nineveh II.

Jerusalem VI (Conquest by Moslems), 637. Following their great victory on the Yarmuk River, one Arabian army pressed northward to Damascus while a second Moslem force launched an attack against Jerusalem. With no Byzantine army to defend them, the residents, under the patriarch Sophronius, rallied behind the city's walls. The strength of the Moslem armies lay in their hard-riding cavalry, which could do little against a fortified city except surround it. For four months the Arabs, under the personal direction of the caliph Omar I, besieged Jerusalem. Finally, realizing the hopelessness of their isolated position, the defenders surrendered the city to Omar. Within the next year all of Palestine lay under Moslem rule. *See* Yarmuk River; Aleppo; Moslem Conquests.

Jerusalem VII (First Crusade), 1099. Early in January 1099 the First Crusaders began the long march south from Antioch toward Jerusalem under Raymond IV of Toulouse, Robert of Normandy, Godfrey of Bouillon, Robert of Flanders, and Tancred of Taranto. (Tancred's uncle Bohemond stayed behind to rule Antioch, while Baldwin of Boulogne remained at his new county of Edessa.) On June 7 the Christian army of 1,200 knights and 11,000 foot soldiers reached Jerusalem, held by a Moslem garrison under the jurisdiction of the caliph of Cairo (Al-Musta' li) since the displacement of the Seljuk Turks the year before.

Finding the city stoutly defended behind strong walls, the crusaders began constructing three giant siege towers. On the night of July 13 they began filling in the ditch at the base of the walls, despite the shooting of arrows and hurling of stones by the defenders. The following night they moved up the towers—Raymond's at Mount Sion in the south, Godfrey's against Herod's Gate in the north, and Tancred's at the northwest, near the Holy Sepulcher. Raymond's assault force in the south met strong opposition and was checked at the walls. In the north, however, Godfrey's men fought their way across his flying bridge and got inside the walls, opening the Gate of Saint Stephen. The knights of Godfrey and Tancred poured into the city, launching a wholesale massacre of Moslems and Jews. Tancred seized the Temple in the southeast. Here the defenders, with their rear now exposed, fell back to the Tower of David and surrendered to Raymond. One account reports the death of 70,000 non-Christians by nightfall of July 15.

The objective of the crusade had been achieved. Jerusalem and all its holy places were in Christian hands. But the fighting was not over, for a large Egyptian army was already on the march into Palestine. *See* Antioch I; Ashkelon I; Crusades.

Jerusalem VIII (Crusader-Turkish Wars), 1187. The catastrophic Christian defeat at Tiberias (Hattin) erased the only army that could have defended Jerusalem against the forthcoming assault by Saladin's Turks. Nevertheless, the city's citizens determined to resist. With King Guy of Lusignan already a prisoner of the Turks, the command of the Holy City fell to Balian of Ibelin, who had barely escaped the same fate on July 4. To conduct the defense, Balian knighted all boys of noble birth over the age of 15 as well as 30 selected burgesses. Everyone else worked feverishly to strengthen Jerusalem's walls.

On September 20 Saladin appeared before the city and laid siege to it. Nine days later his engineers had battered a breach in the wall. Moslem attempts to penetrate the opening were repulsed by gallant fighting on the part of the defenders. But the shortage of fighting men and the absence of any reserve whatsoever doomed the Holy City. Balian asked for terms and Saladin agreed to ransom captives at the rate of ten dinars for a man, five for a woman, and one for a child.

On October 2 the Moslems poured into the city and expelled all the Franks. Those that could pay the ransom became free; the others were sold as slaves. Jerusalem reverted to Moslem control. The Christian castles in the interior fell like tenpins. A year later Saladin dismissed his victorious army, convinced that his countercrusade was ended. But the Frankish hold on Tyre spurred Europe to still another crusade. *See* Tiberias; Acre I; Crusades.

Jerusalem IX (Israeli-Arab War), 1948. The periodic guerrilla warfare between Jews and Arabs in Palestine broke into open conflict on May 15, 1948, when the new Jewish state of Israel came into existence as a result of the partition of Palestine by the United Nations. Arab troops from Egypt, Jordan, Syria, Lebanon, and Iraq marched to the aid of the irregular bands of Arabs already fighting against Jewish forces in Israel. The Jewish military organization was the Hagana, which had operated as an underground defense organization during Great Britain's mandate over Palestine (from 1922 until May 14, 1948). Most of the Jewish settlements fought off the Arab attackers. But the Arabs cut the major supply road from Tel Aviv to Jerusalem and took the latter city under siege. A trickle of supplies was transported into Jerusalem over a newly constructed secondary route called the Burma Road. Jewish military defenses within Jerusalem came under the command of Col. David Shaltiel of the Hagana (who was replaced by Col. Moshe Dayan on August 4), while the chief civil officer was Dov Joseph (later to become military governor).

Arab attacks in the eastern part of Jerusalem

soon isolated the Old City. On May 28 the Jewish defenders in this section surrendered to Abdullah el Tel, local commander of the Arab Legion: 340 Jewish soldiers were taken prisoner. About 1,300 people, chiefly women, children, and the aged, took refuge in the New City.

On June 11 the United Nations secured a cease-fire in Israel, but negotiators failed to find a formula for peace and the battle was resumed on July 9. A second truce was effected in Jerusalem on July 17 and in the rest of Israel two days later. By then the Arabs had suffered an estimated 5,000 casualties out of their total force of about 25,000 in Israel. After this time Jerusalem was shelled periodically, and sporadic fighting broke out in other parts of the country. But hostilities gradually died down by the end of the year. The failure of the United Nations to establish mutually acceptable peace terms was dramatized on September 7 when the chief mediator, Count Bernadotte of Sweden, was assassinated in Jerusalem, allegedly by a Jewish terrorist group (the Stern Gang, or Lohmei Herut Yisrael). One of the major points at issue was the United Nations resolution calling for the internationalization of Jerusalem. This plan was thwarted on February 2, 1949, when the city was officially incorporated into the state of Israel and in 1950 was made the national capital. During the first six months of 1949 Israel negotiated armistice agreements with each of the neighboring Arab nations. But no Arab state would officially recognize Israel by signing a formal peace treaty. In Jerusalem the boundary between Israel and Jordan remained where the fighting was stopped by the second truce—that is, along a line roughly dividing the Old City (held by Jordan) from the New. *See* Sinai Peninsula.

Jhansi (Indian Mutiny), 1858. During the early days of the Great Mutiny in India, rebel troops had seized the town of Jhansi, 130 miles south of Agra. General Sir Hugh Rose, at the head of several thousand British and loyal Indian troops, arrived outside the town the following March and placed it under siege. On April 1 Rose fought a pitched battle against a rebel relief force led by Tantia Topi. Using his cavalry to maximum advantage, Rose drove off the mutineers, who left 1,000 dead on the field. On the following day Rose assaulted Jhansi and carried it. Tantia Topi, who had fled into the jungle, was captured a year later by Sir Robert C. Napier and hanged. *See* Cawnpore II; Gwalior; Indian Mutiny.

Jidda (Establishment of Saudi Arabia), 1925. During World War I, Sherif Husein ibn-Ali proclaimed Arabian independence and in 1916 became the first king of the Hejaz. By 1924, however, he had provoked the opposition of the Wahabi sect in Nejd. Led by Abdul-Aziz ibn-Saud, the Wahabis forced Husein to abdicate in favor of his son Ali on October 3. Ten days later ibn-Saud occupied Mecca and in January 1925 laid seige to the last Hejaz stronghold, Jidda, the port of Mecca, 46 miles to the west on the Red Sea. After a year-long siege, Jidda surrendered on December 23. (Ali ibn-Husein had abdicated four days before.) On January 8, 1926, the victorious ibn-Saud proclaimed himself king of the Hejaz and Nejd. The name Saudi Arabia was adopted for the kingdom in 1932.

Johannesburg (South African War II), 1900. With the Orange Free State conquered and annexed, Gen. Lord Frederick Roberts sent his British army across the Vaal River into the Transvaal, the last Boer stronghold. General Louis Botha, in command of the Boer forces in the Transvaal, fell back northward. On May 17 a fast-moving British cavalry column under Sir Bryan Mahon pushed into Mafeking, ending the 217-day siege. Two weeks later British troops stormed into Johannesburg. Continuing his offensive, Roberts drove 34 miles north to take the Transvaal capital of Pretoria on June 5. Five days later Gen. Sir Redvers Buller forced the passes of the Drakensberg Mountains in the southeast and invaded Transvaal from Natal. The two armies linked up at Vlakfontein on July 4. This ended formal Boer resistance. Transvaal was annexed on September 3, while its president, Oom Paul Kruger, fled to Europe.

The Boers, however, refused to surrender. Led by Botha, Jacobus De La Rey, Christiaan DeWet, James Hertzog, Jan Christiaan Smuts, and others, they prolonged the war another 20 months by guerrilla raids on the British army of occupation. Finally Gen. Lord Kitchener crushed resistance by erecting barbed wire fences, blockhouses, and concentration camps. On May 31, 1902, the hard-fighting commandos at last accepted British sovereignty at Vereeniging, 35 miles south of Johannesburg. *See* Bloemfontein; Mafeking; South African Wars.

Jotapata (Jewish Wars of the Roman Empire), A.D. 68. To suppress the Jewish revolt, which had already defeated one Roman army, Emperor Nero sent out an unknown senator, Titus Flavius Vespasian. The new general marched into the rebellious province at the head of an army of 60,000 men in A.D. 67. There followed one of the bloodiest campaigns of the Roman Empire. Although the Jews lacked the arms and training of the legionaries, they fought with a fanaticism that made them feared opponents. In northern Palestine the Jewish historian Flavius Josephus (originally named Joseph ben Matthias) directed the defense of the Galilean fortress of Jotapata. When Vespasian found the place too strong to storm, he laid siege to it. After 47 days of bitter struggle, Josephus surrendered the fortress early in 68 and became a willing prisoner of the Romans. Jotapata was sacked.

Vespasian marched on southward, reconquering, town by town, the desperately resisting Jews. By the end of May he had forced his way past Jericho and soon began besieging Jerusalem. But when Rome itself erupted into civil war, Vespasian contented himself with a holding action. *See* Bezetha; Bedriacum; Jerusalem IV; Roman Empire.

Junín (Peruvian War of Independence), 1824. After liberating Chile, José de San Martín prepared an expedition to Peru, the stronghold of Spanish rule in the New World. The invasion army was carried northward in the ships of Thomas Cochrane (called Lord Cochrane), former British admiral. After landing at Callao in 1820, San Martín marched to Lima, both cities having been evacuated by the Spanish viceroy José de La Serna. On July 28, 1821, the independence of Peru was proclaimed. Simón Bolívar and his able general Antonio de Sucre arrived in 1822. San Martín surrendered the patriot leadership to Bolívar. The war was then carried to the royalists in the highlands. On August 6, 1824, Bolívar and Sucre reached Junín, 95 miles northeast of Lima. Here the republicans decisively defeated the Spanish army of La Serna, which was commanded by Gen. José Canterac. Sucre pushed on after the royalists. *See* Maipo River; Ayacucho.

Jutland (World War I), 1916. The British blockade of Germany was proving so strangling that Adm. Reinhard Scheer resolved to take the offensive in the hope of weakening the grip of the enemy's Grand Fleet in the North Sea. Early on May 31 he sent Adm. Franz von Hipper with five battle cruisers north along the coast of Jutland, while he followed by 50 miles with the High Seas Fleet—16 new and 8 old battleships. The two German groups also included 11 light cruisers and 63 destroyers. The British Grand Fleet, which could decode German radio dispatches, was already at sea, steaming eastward in two divisions. The southern fleet, under Adm. Sir David Beatty, consisted of 6 battle cruisers and 4 battleships. Seventy miles to the north came the main force of 3 battle cruisers and 24 battleships, commanded by Adm. Sir John Jellicoe. In addition to the 37 large ships, the two British groups included 34 lighter cruisers and 80 destroyers.

At 3:25 P.M. the battle cruiser squadrons of Hipper and Beatty sighted each other. Hipper reversed course, steaming southward to close the gap with the High Seas Fleet. Beatty turned with him. The two forces, on parallel courses, dueled for an hour, to the advantage of the Germans, who sank the battle cruisers *Indefatigable* and *Queen Mary*. When Scheer's main fleet hove into sight, Beatty doubled back to the north. Both German

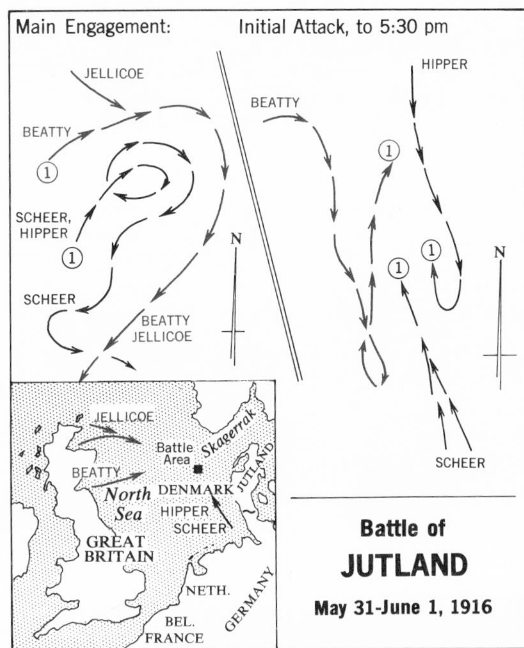

Battle of
JUTLAND
May 31-June 1, 1916

groups followed. This soon brought them within range of Jellicoe's Grand Fleet, which was steaming southeastward. As the two main fleets approached each other, Jellicoe deployed eastward to get between the Germans and the Jutland coast. The main engagement began about 6 P.M. Hipper's flagship, the *Lützow,* was knocked out of action, the British cruiser *Invincible,* sunk. As the British fleets crossed his van (called "crossing the T"), Scheer turned back southwest under cover of a smoke screen and destroyer torpedo attacks. Firing continued until darkness.

The British now held a distinct advantage, standing between the German High Seas Fleet and its base. About 10 P.M., however, Scheer turned his ships to the southeast and began forcing his way through the British light forces at the rear of Jellicoe's line. In a confused four hours of night fighting, the German ships broke through and made good their escape by morning. In this action the Germans lost the crippled *Lützow* and the battleship *Pommern.* The British Grand Fleet then returned to its bases.

The indecisive battle of Jutland (called battle of the Skagerrak by Germany) involved a total of more than 250 ships. In addition to the major ship sinkings, Great Britain lost three light cruisers and eight destroyers, Germany four cruisers and five destroyers. In tonnage, however, British losses were almost twice those of Scheer. Germany claimed a victory but never again sought an open battle. Jutland may have been the last of the great naval battles fought exclusively with surface ships. *See* Dogger Bank II; Atlantic Ocean I; World War I.

K

Kabul I (Moslem Conquest of the East), 709. The Afghan city of Kabul, commanding the mountain passes into India, was captured by the first Arabian invasion of the East in 664. Lost during later civil strife among the Moslems, it was retaken by Mohammed ibn-Kasim (Qasim) in a new thrust in 709. Mohammed pushed on to the lower Indus River and then turned north to the Punjab. This conquest established Mohammedanism in the modern nation of Pakistan. *See* Carthage III; Río Barbate; Kashgar; Moslem Conquests.

Kabul II (Afghan-British War I), 1842. To forestall possible Russian designs in Afghanistan, a British expedition from India marched to Kabul in 1839 and deposed the amir, Dost Mohammed Khan. A former king friendly to Great Britain, Shah Shuja, was enthroned. Afghan resentment built up to the point that the British agreed to withdraw. On January 6, 1842, Gen. W. G. K. Elphinstone left Kabul with 4,500 Anglo-Indian troops, plus 12,000 civilians. Delayed by bad weather, the column was attacked by Afghans led by Akbar Khan, son of Dost Mohammed Khan. All the retreating force were killed except for a single survivor, who reached Jalalabad on January 13. Among the slain was Shah Shuja. The Afghans pressed on eastward but were stopped at Jalalabad by a sturdy Anglo-Indian defense under Sir Robert Sale.

A punitive expedition under Gen. Sir George Pollock marched from India toward Kabul. On September 14 Pollock defeated Akbar Khan and occupied Kabul. Some Afghans were arrested and part of the city was destroyed. But on insistence from London, Pollock withdrew the following month. Dost Mohammed Khan resumed his rule over Afghanistan. *See* Herat II; Miani; Peiwar Pass; Afghan-British Wars.

Kadesh (Egyptian-Hittite Wars), 1288 B.C. The earliest battle of which details of tactics and formations are known took place on the Orontes River in western Syria. Four years after ascending the throne of Egypt, Ramses II sought to restore his country's crumbling empire by marching against the Hittite kingdom in Asia Minor, which had been expanding southward along the eastern Mediterranean coast. The pharaoh advanced on Kadesh up the west bank of the Orontes, where his army of 20,000 men was suddenly assaulted by 16,000 Hittites under Muwatallish. The main weight of the attack came from 2,500 chariots, each of which carried three men. Only the personal leadership of Ramses enabled the Egyptians to cut their way out of the trap. When the Hittites paused to loot the fallen, the Egyptians regrouped and launched a counterattack that drove to the gates of Kadesh. But the city held and the battle ended in a stalemate. After 17 years of indecisive warfare, peace was restored between the two kingdoms. Egypt regained only southern Palestine. *See* Megiddo I; Samaria.

Kadisiya (Moslem Conquest of Persia), 637. The growing power of the Arabian Moslems made certain a showdown clash with the empire of Sassanian Persia, to the east. The Persians moved first. In the spring of 637, Rustam, regent for Yazdegerd III, took an army of about 100,000 men across the Euphrates River to Kadisiya (al-Qādisīyah), near the present Hilla, in Iraq. Expecting the Persian attack, Caliph Omar I sent forth 30,000 Arabian cavalrymen under Sa'ad ibn-Abi-Waqqās.

The battle began with the usual series of cavalry rushes by the Arabs. But the huge Persian force held its ground and then counterattacked with elephants, which terrified the Arabian horses. Sa'ad was barely able to prevent a rout at the end of the first day's combat. Fighting resumed the second day, and although the slashing Moslem attacks inflicted heavier casualties than were received, no decision was reached. On the third day Sa'ad was reinforced by some veterans of the Syrian campaign who knew how to fight elephants with arrows and javelins. The beasts were wounded and then stampeded back through the Persian lines, opening holes for the Arabian cavalry to charge through. The Moslems pressed home their attacks throughout the day and during the night (called the "Night of the Clangor"). At daybreak a sandstorm began blowing in the faces of the stubborn Persians. Rustam sought personal safety by swimming across a canal running to the Euphrates. He was caught and beheaded. The Persian army then disintegrated, taking terrible losses from the Arabians, who gave no quarter. Moslem losses in the battle totaled 7,500 killed. In the booty captured by the Arabs was the jewel-encrusted sacred banner of Persia.

Sa'ad crossed the Euphrates in pursuit. Yazdegerd offered to yield all territory west of the Tigris. When the Arabs scoffed at this, the Persian emperor abandoned his capital at Ctesiphon, which was promptly occupied and sacked. He later made two other attempts to halt the Moslem invaders, but the decisive battle of the Arabian-Persian War had already been fought at Kadisiya. *See* Hira; Jalula; Moslem Conquests.

Kaifeng (Chinese Civil War), 1948. While the People's Liberation Army (PLA) was tightening its encirclement of Mukden in southern Manchuria, Mao Tse-tung launched a second Communist offensive in east-central China. In mid-April 1948 Yenan, the long-time Communist headquarters in Shensi Province (which the Nationalists had occupied with great but meaningless fanfare the previous March) was retaken. PLA commanders Ch'en Yi, Liu Po-ch'eng, and Ch'en Keng then shifted 200,000 men eastward against the Lunghai line in northern Honan Province. The target here was the city of Kaifeng, defended by some 250,000 troops loyal to Generalissimo Chiang Kai-shek. But sheer numbers were misleading. Many Nationalist troops were defecting to the Communists. On June 19 the PLA stormed into Kaifeng, capturing huge stores of military equipment (much of it American-supplied). Within a week the Communists abandoned the city, emphasizing their aim of destroying enemy forces rather than occupying territory. *See* Mukden II; Tsinan; Chinese Civil War.

Kalka River (Mongol Invasion of Europe), 1223. While the Mongol horde of Genghis Khan overran the Khwarizm Empire of central Asia, a detached army under Subotai plunged around the southern end of the Caspian Sea into European Russia. A hasty coalition of Russian princes from the Ukraine assembled an army, which included Turkish Cumans, to oppose the invaders. The western force deployed along the Kalka (Kalmius) River, north of the Gulf of Taganrog. Composed almost entirely of 80,000 poorly organized foot soldiers, the Russian force was no match for the smaller but hard-hitting Mongol cavalry. Subotai's mounted archers cut down their opponents with arrows and then swept through the decimated Russian ranks with sword and lance. Although gaining a total victory, the Mongols did not press their advance. Instead they rode back eastward to rejoin the main army of Genghis Khan in central Asia. But the easy triumph was not forgotten. In 15 years the Asiatics would return, intent on permanent conquest. *See* Merv; Indus River; Kiev I; Mongol Wars.

Kamakura (Japanese Civil Wars), 1333. The feudalistic military government of Japan under the Minamota and, later, the Hojo clans ruled from Kamakura, in southeastern Honshu. Beginning about 1185 Kamakura grew steadily until it had a population of almost one million. In 1331 the city became the prime objective of Daigo II, who headed a revolt against the Hojo dictatorship. After two years of fighting, Kamakura fell to Daigo's forces, in 1333. The victor restored imperial rule to Japan. Kamakura, virtually destroyed in the battle, was soon outstripped by the rise of Kyoto and Tokyo and never regained its former glory.

Daigo's imperial restoration failed to unite Japan, however. Instead the country became split between a northern and a southern dynasty, and in the next two centuries almost continual civil strife blocked national progress. *See* Kyushu.

Kandahar (Afghan-British War II), 1880. The hostility of the Afghan amir Shere Ali to the British was largely responsible for the second war between the two nations. After winning one battle late in 1878, British troops under Gen. Sir Frederick Roberts marched from India to occupy Kabul on October 7, 1879. Shere Ali, who had died earlier in the year, was replaced by a nephew, Abd-er-Rahman Khan. But in the south Ayub Khan, son of the late ruler, revolted and overwhelmed a small British garrison at Maiwand, west of Kandahar, in July 1880. Roberts promptly marched 313 miles in 22 days to reach Kandahar. Here on September 1, with 10,000 men, he defeated Ayub, inflicting 2,000 casualties and destroying the rebel army. The British again withdrew from Afghanistan. Abd-er-Rahman Khan consolidated his power, driving Ayub into exile. *See* Maiwand; Afghan-British Wars.

Kandurcha (Conquests of Tamerlane), 1391. From his Tatar capital of Samarkand, the Mongol conqueror Tamerlane (Timur Lenk, or Timur the Lame) took his army through Persia and then turned northward to plunge into the Caucasus. His objective was the army of the Mongol Golden Horde, commanded by his erstwhile ally Toktamish. Tamerlane pursued the enemy khan into the steppes of Russia. Finally, in 1391, at an uncertain placed called Kandurcha, the two armies met in a cavalry battle that probably involved a total of 100,000 horsemen. Tamerlane won a decisive victory. After dethroning Toktamish, the Mongol victor rode back to complete his conquest of Persia, and later to invade India. The overwhelming defeat forever crippled the Golden Horde. *See* Delhi I; Mongol Wars.

Kápolna (Hungarian Revolt), 1849. To put down the revolt in Hungary against the Austrian Empire, newly enthroned Franz Josef I sent out an army commanded by Prince Alfred zu Windisch-Graetz. The prince occupied Budapest on January 5 and then pressed northeast toward Eger. At Kápolna the Hungarians, under Polish patriot Gen. Henryk Dembiński, attempted to make a stand on February 26. Throughout that day the rebels held their ground, but when the Austrian army resumed its attack the next day, the Hungarians fell back in disorder.

However, Gen. Arthur von Görgey, who had become commander in chief of the rebels, reorganized the rebel army and, in a series of small actions, liberated almost all of Hungary by the end of April. On May 21 he reoccupied Budapest. *See* Schwechat; Timisoara; Hungarian Revolt.

Kappel (Swiss Religious Wars), 1531. The civil unrest caused by the Reformation led the Catholic (largely the rural) cantons of Switzerland to form an army. This force was attacked at Kappel, in Zurich canton, by a smaller army of local Protestants. The Protestant charge, on October 11, 1531, was ill-advised and resulted in a crushing defeat. One of those killed was the reformer Ulrich Zwingli, who was chaplain to the Zurich troops.

Kars I (Crimean War), 1855. The concentration of British and French troops against Sevastopol in the Crimea left other Russian forces free to fight Turkey. In 1855 Czar Alexander II, who had succeeded his father, Nicholas I, on March 2, sent a Russian army southward in the Caucasus. The Turkish troops of Sultan Abdul Medjid I fell back into Armenia. At Kars, Ottoman troops under the British general Sir William P. Williams made a spirited resistance. But on November 28 the Russians stormed into the city, whose defenders were weakened by starvation. At this point, however, the threatened intervention of Austria forced the czar to halt the offensive. He signed preliminary peace terms with Turkey, France, and Great Britain on February 1, 1856. *See* Sevastopol I; Crimean War.

Kars II (Russian-Turkish War), 1877. While the major Russian offensive of Czar Alexander II against Turkey took place in the Balkans, a second column thrust through the Caucasus. Commanded by Gen. Count Mikhail Loris-Melikov, this army reached Kars in Armenia. On November 17 the Russians assaulted Kars, which was defended by some 24,000 Turks. After a savage encounter, the Ottomans surrendered. They lost almost 7,000 in killed and wounded; all the others became prisoners. Russian casualties were little more than 2,000.

General Ahmed Mukhtar Pasha, the Turkish commander of Sultan Abdul-Hamid II on this front, fell back to Erzurum, on the upper Kara Su (western Euphrates). The Turks had to withdraw from this point the following year. However, the last battle of the war would take place in the Balkans. *See* Shipka Pass; Plovdiv; Russian-Turkish War.

Kashgar (Moslem Invasion of China), 736. Early in the eighth century a new Arabian thrust to the East carried the Moslem army of Qutayba as far as Kashgar, in western Sinkiang, China. In 736 Hsüan Tsung of the T'ang dynasty led a large force of Chinese and Turkish allies to this key oasis and communications center. The Arabs of the Hisham caliphate were defeated and driven back. This battle checked the Moslem advance to the East at about the same time that other Arab armies were being halted in western Europe and Asia Minor. *See* Kabul I; Tours; Acroïnum; Moslem Conquests.

Kasserine Pass (World War II). Part of the battle for Tunisia, during February 14–22, 1943, in which American troops met German *Panzer* divisions for the first time and suffered a sharp setback. *See* Tunisia.

Katzbach River (Napoleonic Empire Wars), 1813. When the Prussian general Gebhard von Blücher broke the French-allied armistice by an attack westward from Breslau (Wroclaw) on August 14, 1813, Napoleon I concentrated against the Prussians. With 150,000 troops against Blücher's 95,000, the French stopped the advance and then counterattacked on August 21. The Prussians hastily withdrew behind the Katzbach (Kocaba) River, northwest of Breslau. Seeing a greater threat from an Austrian attack on his southern front, Napoleon turned the Prussian sector over to Marshal Jacques Macdonald. Disobeying his commander, Macdonald recklessly began crossing the Katzbach in three widely separated columns on August 26. Blücher wheeled about and in a blinding rainstorm routed the French with his superior cavalry and artillery. Macdonald lost 15,000 men and 100 guns. Blücher was later made Prince of Wahlstatt for his victory here. More important, the victory gave new confidence to Blücher's Army of Silesia. Meanwhile, Napoleon prepared to defend against a large-scale attack on Dresden. *See* Grossbeeren; Dresden; Napoleonic Empire Wars.

Kay (Seven Years' War), 1759. The third Russian offensive of the war ordered by Czarina Elizabeth got under way in the summer of 1759. Under Field Marshal Count Pëtr Saltykov (Soltikov), 70,000 Russians ploughed westward, crossing the Brandenburg border near Züllichau. The Prussian commander of Frederick II, the Great, on this front was Gen. Richard von Wedell. Hurrying forward, Wedell rashly attacked the Russians at Kay, west of Züllichau, with only 26,000 men. The result was a stinging defeat, on July 23, which cost the Prussians 6,000 casualties. Wedell fell back beyond the Oder River, while Saltykov turned north to move down the right bank toward Frankfurt. Frederick rushed north to take over the defense of Brandenburg. His plight was made more desperate when the Austrian commander, the Count von Daun, sent 35,000 Imperial troops from Saxony to join the Russians. *See* Zorndorf; Kunersdorf; Seven Years' War.

Kazan (Conquest by Ivan IV), 1552. The khanate of the Golden Horde, which had ruled most of present-day Russia since the thirteenth century, established its capital at Kazan in 1438. This city, near the upper Volga where the great river turns south, became a prime objective of the first Russian czar, Ivan IV, the Terrible. In his first campaign of expansion, Ivan marched eastward and attacked the Tatar city in 1552. It fell to the Russian feudal cavalry, which then wheeled southward down the Volga. *See* Astrakhan I.

Kenesaw Mountain (American Civil War), 1864. In his drive southward toward Atlanta, Ga., the Federal commander, Gen. William Sherman, repeatedly maneuvered to force the Confederate army of Gen. Joseph Johnston to fall back. By May 25 Johnston had retreated 90 miles to Dallas–New Hope Church. After four days of skirmish and maneuver Sherman again refused to make a frontal attack. Instead, he leapfrogged his three armies eastward to Kenesaw Mountain where Johnston's right flank stood, blocking Federal use of the railroad. On June 27 Sherman changed his tactics to assault Kenesaw Mountain. The attack was made on the north by the left flank Army of the Tennessee under Gen. James McPherson. In the center Gen. George Thomas (Army of the Cumberland) and on the right Gen. John Schofield (Army of the Ohio) conducted a holding operation. The blow fell on the corps of Gen. William Loring, who had succeeded the slain Gen. Leonidas Polk. (The corps of Gen. William Hardee, opposite Thomas, and Gen. John Hood, on the extreme Confederate left, were little engaged.) For two hours the Federals gallantly stormed the heights, only to be stopped cold with 2,000 killed or wounded and 50 missing. Because of the cramped front, Sherman, whose 100,000-man force was almost double that of Johnston, could employ only some 16,000 in the attack. This gave the Confederates a slight local superiority, which, coupled with their strong entrenchments, led to their loss of only 270 killed or wounded and 172 missing.

Sherman now changed back to a campaign of maneuver. McPherson was shifted to the southwest flank, forcing Johnston to retreat southward once more. *See* Resaca; Atlanta; American Civil War.

Kenilworth (Second Barons' War of England), 1265–1266. Simon de Montfort (earl of Leicester) made himself the strongest man in England by his victory over King Henry III at Lewes. In little more than a year, however, the barons had become divided by factional disputes, while at the same time Henry's son, Prince Edward, was building up the royalist party. Montfort also found himself in a poor military position, with his forces split by the Severn Valley, which was held by Prince Edward's knights. Montfort sought to cross the river to the east. But before he could do so, his son's army on the other side was attacked by Edward's knights at Kenilworth in Warwickshire, on July 31, 1265. The royalists' surprise assault took the town, capturing most of the barons' troops. Young Simon took refuge in the castle. Here he held out while his father was defeated and slain at Evesham the following month. With the elder Montfort out of the way, the royalists besieged Kenilworth Castle. The garrison held out until December 14, 1266, before finally surrendering. Meanwhile the younger Montfort had escaped to Axholme. *See* Lewes; Evesham; Axholme; Barons' Wars.

Kerbela (Moslem Civil Wars), 680. The death of the first Ommiad caliph, Muawiyah I, led to a new civil war. He had proclaimed his son Yazid I as his successor. However, the Kufans of Iraq nominated Husain, son of Ali, to rule Islam. Advancing from Mecca, Husain was treacherously deserted by the Kufans at Kerbela (Karbala), 55 miles southwest of Baghdad. Virtually defenseless, Husain was attacked and slain by the supporters of Yazid on October 10, 680. This betrayal and defeat permanently split off the Shiite branch of Islam, which commemorates Husain's death each year in the month of Muharram. *See* Siffin; Zab al Kabir; Moslem Conquests.

Kerenski Offensive. *See* Lemberg II.

Keresztes (Turkish-Austrian Wars), 1596. Peace between Austria and the Ottoman Turks, which had been signed in 1533 (four years after the great siege of Vienna), was broken in 1593. For the next 13 years sporadic fighting took place in the so-called Long War. The chief battle took place at the fortress of Keresztes, near Eger (Erlau) in north-central Hungary. Here Prince Sigismund Bathory of Transylvania and Archduke Maximilian of Austria commanded the Christian defenses. For three days, October 24–26, 1596, the Turkish army of Mohammed III attacked before finally storming into Keresztes and routing the defenders. But the declining Turkish Empire did not press its advantage, and after ten more years of border warfare the succeeding sultan, Ahmed I, agreed to peace terms. Austria received recognition as an equal (thereby becoming free of tribute) in return for surrendering claims to Transylvania, which the Turks gave to István (Stephen) Bocskay. *See* Lepanto II; Khotin I.

Kernstown I (American Civil War), 1862. When the Federal general George McClellan began organizing his campaign to thrust up the peninsula against Richmond, Federal troops were ordered from the lower Shenandoah Valley to support the offensive. Learning of this troop movement, the Confederate general Thomas (Stonewall) Jackson advanced northward from Mount Jackson by forced marches, determined to hold Gen. Nathaniel Banks's command in the valley. A cavalry skirmish at Kernstown, four miles south of Winchester, on March 22 led Jackson to believe that only a rear guard opposed him. On the following day he stormed into Kernstown with 4,200 men only to find it held by 9,000 men of Gen. James Shields's division. The Confederates were thrown back, suffering 700 casualties. Federal losses were 590. Although the attack was repulsed, its boldness led Federal officers to overestimate Jackson's strength. The flow of Federal troops to the East was reversed. *See* Ball's Bluff; Yorktown II; McDowell; American Civil War.

Kernstown II (American Civil War), 1864. After his unsuccessful raid to Washington, D.C., the Confederate general Jubal Early returned to the Shenandoah Valley at Berryville, Va. Ten miles to the west Gen. George Crook's Federal Army of West Virginia was encamped at Kernstown, south of Winchester. Early sent forward a division under Gen. John Breckinridge. After cavalry skirmishes on July 23, Breckinridge launched a general attack the following day. Crook's two-division force was routed and fled northward across the Potomac River with a loss of 1,185 men, including 479 captured. This Confederate victory convinced the Federal commander in chief, Gen. U. S. Grant, that he must deny the Shenandoah Valley to the enemy. Gen. Philip Sheridan was detached from the Richmond offensive to take charge of the projected campaign. *See* Monocacy River; Winchester III; American Civil War.

Kesselsdorf (War of the Austrian Succession), 1745. The first prong of the Holy Roman Empire (Francis I and Maria Theresa) offensive against Prussia came to grief in November 1745 when Frederick II, the Great, turned back the Austrian column of Prince Charles of Lorraine at Hennersdorf. Meanwhile a second Prussian army under Field Marshal Leopold I of Anhalt-Dessau hurried up the left bank of the Elbe from Magdeburg. This movement was designed to intercept the second prong of the Imperial offensive—a march through Saxony by Marshal Rutowski from the Main Valley. The Old Dessauer came upon Rutowski at Kesselsdorf, ten miles west of Dresden, on December 15. The Prussians promptly attacked and routed the Saxons and their allies. The Imperial offensive had been thoroughly repulsed.

Ten days later, and after four serious defeats in seven months, Maria Theresa accepted the Treaty of Dresden. The treaty confirmed Frederick's possession of Silesia, first granted by the Treaty of Breslau (Wroclaw) three years earlier. The Second Silesian War thus ended. But in Italy and Flanders the War of the Austrian Succession continued. *See* Hennersdorf; Rocourt; Austrian Succession, War of the.

Kettle Creek (War of the American Revolution), 1779. The British conquest of Georgia early in 1779 led to heavy partisan warfare in the interior. A group of 700 Tories under Col. Boyd of North Carolina marched southward to join the British army at Augusta, Ga., which had been occupied on January 29. Passing through South Carolina, Boyd's Loyalists plundered the countryside. A patriot militia force of 300 men under Col. Andrew Pickens set out in pursuit. On February 14 Pickens' men overtook the Tories and surprised them at Kettle Creek in Georgia, 50 miles northwest of Augusta. Attacking the enemy encampment from all sides, the militia killed more than 40, including Boyd, and captured 75. (Five of the prisoners were later tried and hanged.) The defeated army broke up, 300 getting through to Augusta and the rest returning to their homes. Pickens lost 9 killed and 23 wounded. *See* Port Royal Island; Briar Creek; American Revolution.

Khartoum (War for the Sudan), 1884–1885. To carry out the Anglo-Egyptian evacuation of the Sudan, the British government of William Gladstone sent out Gen. Charles Gordon. Called "Chinese" Gordon for his exploits in the Far East during 1860–65, Gordon was a powerful military figure in Great Britain. Arriving in Sudan on February 18, 1884, Gordon decided not to abandon the country to the Mahdian dervishes of Mohammed Ahmed. He asked his government for reinforcements instead. While London hesitated, Gordon evacuated some 2,500 women, children, and wounded from Khartoum, at the junction of the White Nile and Blue Nile. On March 12, however, he was trapped in a fort north of the city (now North Khartoum) by an overwhelming number of Mahdists. For ten months Gordon directed the Egyptians in a spirited defense of Khartoum. A relief expedition under Gen. Sir Garnet Wolseley left Cairo in October. But on January 26, 1885, the Mahdists stormed into the fortifications, killing Gordon and every defender. Wolseley's advance guard arrived two days later. They prudently withdrew back into Egypt. *See* El Teb; Abu Klea; Atbara; Sudan, War for the.

Khojend (Mongol Conquest of Central Asia), 1219. Genghis Khan began his invasion of the Khwarizm Empire of central Asia by sending an army under his eldest son, Juji (Juchi), on a wide sweep to the southwest, through the Tien Shan mountains. As Juji's detached column of cavalry penetrated the lofty mountain chain, it encountered the Moslem army of Khwarizm commanded by the reigning shah, Mohammed. The two forces clashed in a long valley along the headwaters of the Jaxartes River (Syr Darya) early in 1219. After a murderous struggle in which each side lost tens of thousands of troops, both armies pulled back.

Juji then debouched from the mountains through another valley. Receiving 5,000 additional men from his father, he moved down the Jaxartes to the walled city of Khojend (Leninabad). A Mongol attack drove out the garrison, which was commanded by a Turkish lieutenant of the shah named Timur Malik. But the stubborn Malik held up the Mongol advance for another month from an island position in the river. When his position was finally overrun, he alone managed to escape with his life. Juji then pressed on southward toward Samarkand. *See* Peking I; Bukhara; Mongol Wars.

Khotin I (Polish-Turkish Wars), 1621. When Moldavia revolted against Ottoman Turkish rule and allied itself with Poland (Sigismund III), Sultan Osman II marched into the Ukraine in 1621. At Khotin (Hotin), on the right bank of the Dniester, he was blocked by a large Polish army under Gen. Jan Karol Chodkiewicz. During the battle the ailing, old Chodkiewicz died, handing over command to Prince Stanislaw Lubomirski. Although the Turks held a large numerical advantage, the decaying Janizary corps broke under Polish attack and fled the field. Osman retreated to Constantinople, hoping to rebuild his army. But before he could do so the Janizaries revolted and killed him. *See* Keresztes; Candia II.

Khotin II (Polish-Turkish Wars), 1673. During the Cossack revolt against King Michael Wisniowiecki of Poland, the Ottoman Turks of Mohammed IV joined the rebels. Marching rapidly, the Turks swept through Kamenets Podolski in the Ukraine in 1672. The Polish king sued for peace, but his diet refused to ratify the treaty. John III Sobieski then rallied the Polish forces and counterattacked at Khotin, on the right bank of the Dniester. John's army routed the Turks, and when John continued the offensive to Lublin, Mohammed agreed to accept a truce in 1676. The Turks waived tributary payments in return for a hold on part of the Ukraine (which was lost to the Russians during the next five years). *See* Szentgotthárd; Vienna II.

Kiev I (Mongol Invasion of Europe), 1240. Fifteen years after his easy victory on the Kalka River in 1223, the Mongol general Subotai led a second invasion of Russia. On this thrust he shared command with Batu Khan, grandson of the great Genghis Khan. The invaders found a land divided among independent duchies, which often quarreled among themselves. Militarily, the Russians could offer only foot soldiers armed with axes and spears to oppose hard-riding Mongol cavalry equipped with bows as well as swords. The duchies fell like tenpins. Their cities, guarded by log stockades, were set afire and the helpless inhabitants massacred. The invaders reached Kiev, the great metropolis of southern Russia, in 1240. But instead of the expected strong resistance, the Mongols found only a disorganized force, deserted by its local prince. The barbarians stormed into the city on December 6, plundering and killing at will. Kiev was burned to the ground.

While Subotai and Batu Khan spurred on westward, the khanate of the Golden Horde was organized to rule from a headquarters on the lower Volga. For almost two centuries most of Russia south of Novgorod lay under Asiatic suzerainty. *See* Kalka River; Neva River; Cracow; Mongol Wars.

Kiev II (World War II). The largest pocket created by the rapid German advance into western Russia; more than 600,000 Russian troops were killed or captured between September 19 and 26, 1941. *See* Soviet Union (World War II).

Killdeer Mountain (Sioux Wars), 1864. During three years of the Civil War, Gen. Alfred Sully had the responsibility of protecting settlers and emigrants west of the Missouri River in the Dakotas. In 1864 he marched from Sioux City, Iowa, northwest toward an Indian concentration on the Knife River, a western tributary of the Missouri. On July 28 his column of 2,200 armed men reached Killdeer Mountain (Tahkahokuty), in the Badlands. Here stood some 5,000 Sioux. Using artillery and cavalry charges with great skill, Sully drove the Indians off the height, inflicting about 100 casualties. Sully lost 15 killed or wounded. *See* Indian Wars in the United States.

Killiecrankie (Resistance to the Glorious Revolution), 1689. After the deposition of England's James II, the Viscount Dundee (John Graham of Claverhouse) raised the standard of the fallen king among the Highlanders of Scotland. To put down the rebellion, Gen. Hugh Mackay took 4,000 troops, loyal to William III and Mary, into the Grampian Mountains of Perth County. Dundee, with a smaller force, ambushed the government troops at Killiecrankie Pass on July 27, 1689. More than half of Mackay's army was killed or captured. But among the victor's much smaller losses was Dundee himself. A colonel named Cannon took over the rebel troops. But when he led a disastrous attack the following month on Dunkeld, also in Perth County, the revolt began petering out. *See* Londonderry; Boyne River; Glencoe; Jacobite Insurrections.

Kilsyth (English Civil War), 1645. Despite the rising tide of losses suffered by Charles I's Cavaliers in England, their counterparts in Scotland continued to overwhelm all opposition. The successful Marquis of Montrose, (James Graham), after repulsing the Covenanters at Alford, marched southwest into Stirling County. Here his defeated opponent Gen. William Baillie was joined by another Covenanter force under the Marquis of Argyll (Archibald Campbell 8th earl of Argyll). On August 15, 1645, the two hostile forces fought a decisive battle at Kilsyth. Montrose's army overwhelmed the Covenanters, destroying virtually the entire enemy infantry force of several thousand men. The brilliant Royalist general now stood supreme in Scotland. But the almost total Roundhead success over the Cavaliers in England during the summer of 1645 freed the regular Scots army (under Gen. David Leslie) for return to the homeland. Montrose soon faced his greatest military challenge. *See* Langport; Alford; Philiphaugh; English Civil War.

Kimberley (South African War II), 1899–1900. When Gen. Piet Cronjé launched the war on the western front, he attacked Mafeking, while sending a second Boer column against Kimberley. The latter, a diamond center near the Orange Free State border, came under attack on October 14. Although outnumbered, the garrison fought off the assault, which was then turned into a siege. The defenders, including Cecil Rhodes, resisted investment until Kimberley was relieved on February 15, 1900, by a cavalry column under Gen. Sir John French. Casualties to the garrison totaled 180 killed and wounded. *See* Mafeking; Ladysmith; Poardeberg; South African Wars.

King George's War (1744–1748). The third French and English conflict in North America was part of the larger War of the Austrian Succession in Europe. Its colonial name came from the reigning British monarch, George II. The chief battle in America was the English capture in 1745 of Louisbourg on Cape Breton Island, which was returned to France by the concluding Peace of Aix-la-Chapelle (Aachen) in 1748. *See* Louisbourg I; Austrian Succession, War of the.

King Philip's War (1675–1676). An uprising by the Wampanoag Indians, which took the name of their chief, King Philip, against the New England colonists. The Wampanoags were joined by the Narraganset tribe. Both Indian groups were virtually annihilated by colonial military action.

Great Swamp 1675
Hadley 1676

Kings Mountain (War of the American Revolution), 1780. Following his clear-cut victory at Camden, S.C., in August 1780, the British general Lord Charles Cornwallis marched north to Charlotte, N.C. To protect his left flank, he sent Maj. Patrick Ferguson with a Loyalist force of some 1,100 men on a raid to the west. Ferguson's advance stirred up the frontiersmen in the mountains of western Carolina and eastern Tennessee. Carrying their rifles and their own rations, 900 of these men gathered under the leadership of militia colonels Isaac Shelby, John Sevier, and William Campbell. They started in pursuit of Ferguson, who turned back and then took up a strong position on Kings Mountain, S.C., near the border of North Carolina. On October 7 the frontiersmen surrounded the Loyalists on the northeastern hump of the mountain. Well-aimed rifle fire took a heavy toll of the defenders, whose bayonets could not drive back the patriots. When Ferguson was killed, the surviving 698 Tories surrendered; 157 had been killed and 163 wounded so severely they were left on the field. Nine of the prisoners were tried for treason and hanged. Patriot losses were 28 killed and 62 wounded.

After the battle most of the frontiersmen returned to their homes. But the American victory served an important purpose—Cornwallis abandoned his invasion of North Carolina and fell back to Winnsboro, S.C. *See* Camden; Cowpens; American Revolution.

King William's War (1689–1697). Hostility between the New England colonists and the French and Indians became a formal conflict when England declared war on France (Louis XIV) in 1689. The only major battle in North America was fought at Port Royal in Nova Scotia in 1690. Named for King William III of Great Britain, the colonial war ended with the 1697 Peace of Ryswick, which concluded the larger, European phase, called the War of the Grand Alliance. *See* Port Royal I; Grand Alliance, War of the.

Kinsale (Irish Rebellion against Elizabeth I), 1601. The periodic discontent of Ireland merged into the Spanish-English struggle in the 1590's. Supported by Spain, Hugh O'Neill (earl of Tyrone) led an insurrection against English rule in 1598. Queen Elizabeth's favorite, Robert Devereux (2nd earl of Essex), rushed to Ireland the next year but failed to put down the uprising. (He returned to London, plotted against the crown, and was executed in 1601.) Charles Blount (Lord Mountjoy) was then put in charge of the English forces. The new commander had the revolt under control when 4,000 Spanish soldiers landed at Kinsale on the south shore of Ireland in 1601. When Mountjoy prevented a union of the allies, the Spanish were forced to surrender before the end of the year. The English general then turned back to the rebels and compelled the submission of Tyrone himself. *See* Flores.

Kirkee (Maratha-British War III), 1817. The Second Maratha War in the early 1800's resulted in the deposition of all tribal chiefs except Baji Rao II, who retained rule at Poona. In 1817 this chief too came in conflict with the British. He attacked a British army of four regiments (three of them native) at Kirkee, a suburb of Poona 80 miles southeast of Bombay, on November 5. The Maratha horsemen were routed with a loss of more than

500 men. British casualties were only 75. The rule of Baji Rao, seventh and last peshwa of the Marathas, was ended the following year at Sholapur when the last of his followers were routed. The British took over Poona. *See* Farrukhabad; Fort Sitabaldi; Maratha-British Wars.

Kirk-Kilissa (First Balkan War), 1912. With the outbreak of the First Balkan War, Sultan Mohammed V of Turkey ordered a rash offensive against Bulgaria in Thrace. The Bulgarian troops of Czar Ferdinand I met the Turkish army at Kirk-Kilissa (Kirklareli), 35 miles east of Adrianople (Edirne), on October 25. The Ottomans were thrown back with heavy losses. Meanwhile, a second Turkish army was in action against Serbia in Macedonia. *See* Kumanovo; Lüleburgaz; Balkan Wars.

Kirovabad (Russian-Persian War), 1826. In the long and troublesome frontier conflict between Russia and Persia, Czar Nicholas I opened a new agression in 1825. The following year a Russian army under Gen. Ivan Paskevich (later Count of Erivan and Prince of Warsaw) attacked a large Persian force at Kirovabad (Gandzha), 110 miles south of Tiflis. Paskevich won decisively over the troops of Shah Fath-Ali, to launch a bright military career. By the Treaty of Turkmanchai, signed in 1828, the sultan ceded most of Persian Armenia to Russia. *See* Grochów; Herat II.

Klissow (Great Northern War), 1702. After knocking Denmark out of the war and routing the Russian army of Peter I, the Great, at Narva in 1700, King Charles XII of Sweden turned against his third enemy, Poland. The Polish king, Augustus II (who was also elector of Saxony), had sent a Saxon army northward to besiege Riga in 1700. These troops fled at the approach of the Swedish army on June 17, 1701. Charles followed in close pursuit, marching across the border into Poland itself.

In the following spring the Swedish king occupied Warsaw where he later installed his own ruler, Stanislas Leszczyński, on the throne. The Poles and Saxons continued to fall back. Finally, at Klissow, 110 miles southwest of Warsaw, they made a stand. On July 13 Charles, with only 12,000 men, attacked the combined army of twice that size. Under the force of the Swedish assault the Poles crumbled, and then the Saxons. With a clear field ahead, Charles pushed on 45 miles to seize Kraków (Cracow) on the Vistula. He then doubled back north seeking out Augustus. *See* Narva; Pultusk I; Great Northern War.

Klokotnitsa (Bulgarian-Greek Wars), 1230. After the fall of Constantinople to the Latin knights of the Fourth Crusade, the Byzantine Empire broke up into several states. One of these was Epirus, which, under the leadership of Theodore Angelus, began warring on its neighbors. Theodore's aggressions brought him into conflict with John Asen II of Bulgaria. The rival armies clashed in 1230 at Klokotnitsa on the Maritsa River in southern Bulgaria. The Bulgars swept the field, taking Theodore prisoner. John Asen went on to seize all of western Thrace and Macedonia. He allowed Theodore's brother Manuel to rule Epirus and Thessalonia but only as his vassal. *See* Constantinople V; Trnovo; Adrianople V.

Knoxville (American Civil War), 1863. While the main Federal and Confederate armies in Tennessee faced each other at Chattanooga, Gen. Ambrose Burnside occupied Knoxville on September 2 with the Federal IX and, later, the XXIII Corps. On November 17 Gen. James Longstreet was detached from the Confederate army of Gen. Braxton Bragg and sent against Knoxville. With two infantry divisions totaling 10,000 men and with 5,000 cavalrymen under Gen. Joseph Wheeler, Longstreet closed on Knoxville. Unable to besiege the city, he organized a dawn attack by Gen. Lafayette McLaws' division on November 29. The objective of the Confederate assault was a northern salient of the defenses called Fort Sanders (Loudon). In bitter cold weather the attackers were repulsed with a loss of 813 men. Federal losses were 113.

This failure, coupled with the news of Bragg's defeat at Chattanooga four days earlier, discouraged Longstreet. When he learned that a Federal relief column was en route from Chattanooga, the Confederate commander retreated northeast to winter quarters at Greenville. In the spring Longstreet's corps rejoined Gen. Robert E. Lee's army in Virginia. *See* Chattanooga; Wilderness; American Civil War.

Köge Bight (Swedish-Danish Wars), 1677. The naval war between Sweden (Charles XI) and Denmark (Christian V) continued into 1677 as part of the larger conflict between Louis XIV of France and Holland. Aided by a squadron of Dutch ships, the Danish admiral Niels Juel challenged Sweden's fleet under Evert Horn in Köge (Kjöge) Bight, south of Copenhagen, on June 30. The Danes again won a clear-cut victory, capturing or sinking 11 of the Swedish ships-of-the-line. *See* Jasmund; Northern Wars.

Kolin (Seven Years' War), 1757. After the Prussian victory outside Prague in May, Frederick II, the Great, tightened his siege of the Austrian-held city. To relieve the beleaguered garrison of Prince Charles of Lorraine (Karl Alexander), a second army of the Holy Roman Empire (Empress Maria Theresa) moved into Bohemia from Austria. The commander, Field Marshal Count Leopold von Daun, advanced to Kolin on the Labe (Elbe) River, 35 miles east of Prague, with 53,000 Imperial troops. Frederick's blue-clad Prussian army of more than 60,000 men outnumbered each of the opposing forces. But instead of taking advantage of this superiority, plus his favorable interior-line position, the king divided his army. With only 35,000 Prussians he marched on Daun, who was entrenched outside Kolin.

On June 18 Frederick ordered a hasty attack against the Austrian right wing. As the Prussians maneuvered in full view of the enemy, their flanks were severely harassed by Imperial pandours, the irregular light troops of Croatia. These strikes broke up the Prussian offensive into a series of piecemeal attacks, which the Imperials repulsed with heavy casualties in five hours of fighting. Frederick finally pulled back with a loss of more than a third of his force and most of his artillery. Daun suffered 8,000 casualties. This heavy defeat forced the Prussian king to raise the siege of Prague and evacuate Bohemia; he fell back into Saxony. But now Austria's two major allies, France and Russia, were also on the move against Prussia. *See* Prague IV; Hastenbeck; Gross-Jägersdorf; Seven Years' War.

Konya (Egyptian Revolt against Turkey), 1832. As a reward for his aid to Mahmud II of Turkey during the Greek War of Independence, Mehemet (Mohammed) Ali, viceroy of Egypt, demanded possession of Syria. When this was refused, Mehemet sent his son Gen. Ibrahim Pasha into Syria at the head of a large Egyptian army. The invaders occupied Acre, Damascus, and Aleppo during the summer of 1832, then invaded Anatolia. A Turkish army under Reshid Pasha marched out to block the Egyptians at Konya, near the center of Anatolia. But on December 21 the Ottomans were overwhelmed by Ibrahim's army. Only the intervention of Russia (Nicholas I) at Constantinople prevented a complete defeat for Mahmud II. The following year France (Louis Philippe) also took a hand in the Near East, persuading the Turks to surrender Adana and Syria. Ibrahim became the Egyptian governor of Syria. *See* Navarino; Nizib; Egyptian Revolt against Turkey.

Korean War (1950–1953). With the defeat of Japan in World War II, the vanquished Japanese troops in Korea surrendered—those north of the 38th parallel to the Soviet Union, those to the south to the United States. This artificial line soon became a sealed political boundary. Supported by Communist China and the Soviet Union, the northern half of Korea became the Democratic People's Republic, which claimed authority over the entire peninsula. South of the parallel, the Republic of South Korea came into being on August 15, 1949. American troops withdrew that summer. Secretly armed with Chinese and Russian equipment, the 127,000-man army of North Korea suddenly struck across the 38th parallel on the morning of June 25, 1950. The 98,000 troops of South Korea, advised by a 500-man American military group, were caught unprepared. On June 26 President Harry Truman ordered Gen. Douglas MacArthur to send help to South Korea from the U.S. occupation forces in Japan. The United Nations voted to provide military aid the following day. Under the blue and white banner of the United Nations, the United States and, to a lesser extent, 15 other nations battled the North Koreans and later a force of 750,000 "volunteer" Chinese Communists for three years. Finally an armistice on July 27, 1953, ended open hostilities, with a heavily manned border along the 38th parallel still dividing Korea in half. Peace negotiations dragged on with no settlement reached for years. It became the longest armistice in history.

The Korean War cost the United Nations 447,697 dead, 547,904 wounded and missing. Of this total the United States suffered 29,550 dead, 106,978 wounded and missing; South Korea 415,004 dead, 428,568 wounded and missing. Communist casualties were estimated at 520,000 for North Korea, 900,000 for Communist China. The United Nations fought its first war with severely limited objectives. But it did save South Korea by repulsing Communist aggression.

Pusan Perimeter	1950
Inchon	1950
North Korea	1950
Thirty-Eighth Parallel	1951–1953

Kossovo I (Turkish Conquest of Serbia), 1389. Under the leadership of Murad I the Ottoman Turks had become a formidable power in southeastern Europe late in the fourteenth century. From Adrianople in 1365 to Cernomen on the Maritsa River in 1371 and on to Sofia in 1385, they had marched relentlessly against the Serbian states. In 1389 the Serbian prince Lazar I assembled an estimated 20–25,000 troops—Serbs, Bosnians, Albanians, Bulgars, Wallachians—to stop the Turkish advance. Lazar's army met Murad's invaders at Kossovo in southern Yugoslavia on June 20 (traditionally June 15), one of the bench mark dates in Balkan history. In a bloody struggle, the heavy mailed cavalry of the Turks (called the spahis), plus the infantry corps of Janizaries, won a decisive victory. Lazar was captured and killed. Serbia became a vassal state of the Turks, and in later battles against Christian Europe, Lazar's son Stephan Lazarevich loyally supported his new masters.

During the battle of Kossovo, Murad was murdered by a Serb posing as a traitor. He was succeeded by his son Bajazet I (Bayazid), the first Turk to take the title sultan. *See* Maritsa River; Nicopolis.

Kossovo II (Turkish-Hungarian Wars), 1448. Four years after suffering a crushing defeat at Varna from the Ottoman Turks, János Hunyadi led a new Hungarian army of 24,000 men into Serbia. The hard-fighting Transylvanian knights penetrated as far as Kossovo, in what is now southern Yugoslavia, near the site of the decisive Serbian defeat of 1389. Here Murad II came up hurriedly with his well-organized and larger Turkish army. Hunyadi placed his German infantry, armed with handguns and pikes, in the center opposite the Janizary infantry, which carried crossbows. On the wings the Hungarian cavalry, called hussars, deployed against the Turkish mounted spahis. The first clash, on October 16, 1448, brought no decision, although both sides lost heavily. On the following day, however, the Hungarian cavalry gave way before the heavier-mailed horsemen of the Ottomans. Hunyadi then had to withdraw his vulnerable center and retreat. Almost half of the original Hungarian force and a third of the Turks lay dead on the bloody field.

Murad's third major victory over Christian Europe left no strong rival to contest the Balkans with the Ottoman Empire. Only the Albanian guerrilla fighter Scanderbeg (George Castriota) still resisted Turkish rule, and his efforts were doomed to failure. With the Balkans conquered, the great Byzantine capital of Constantinople stood in imminent danger. *See* Varna I; Constantinople VII.

Kovel-Stanislav (World War I), 1916. Continued German attacks against Verdun in the west and Austrian pressure on the Italian front led Czar Nicholas II to launch a second Russian offensive to aid his French and Italian allies. Only one Russian field commander, Gen. Aleksei Brusilov, in charge of the Southwest Army Group, stood ready to attack. Quietly concentrating four armies (Eighth, Eleventh, Seventh, and Ninth, from north to south) from the Pripet Marshes 300 miles south to Rumania, Brusilov jumped off on June 4. The Austrian armies in the Ukraine, under the supreme command of Field Marshal Count Conrad von Hötzendorf, were caught by surprise and fell back. Lutsk fell on June 6. Four days later the Russians had advanced 50 miles toward the vital transportation center of Kovel at the northern end of Brusilov's front. In the south Czernowitz (Chernovtsy) in Bucovina was taken on June 17. By the end of the month Russia had inflicted 700,000 Austrian-German casualties in its greatest success of the war.

Although Czar Nicholas II rushed all available reserves to Brusilov, the Germans and Austrians were able to move faster along their superior lateral railroad lines. The German commander in chief on the Eastern Front, Field Marshal Paul von Hindenburg, transferred 15 German and 8 Austrian divisions from other sectors to shore up his crumbling lines. In the north Gen. Alexander von Linsingen took command of the defenses in front of Kovel and in bitter fighting slowed and then checked the Russian offensive in July. In the south Brusilov penetrated as far west as Stanislav. But here too the Austrian-German line began solidifying. By September 20 the battle, often called the Brusilov Offensive, had ended. Russia had exhausted its supply of manpower, armament, and ammunition. Each side lost more than 1,000,000 men, about one-half of those lost to each army were prisoners or deserters.

This last great battle on the Russian front had far-reaching consequences. Austria was so weakened that it submitted completely to German direction from this time forward. Rumania, heartened by the initial Russian success, entered the war on the Allied side with disastrous results. And inside Russia discontent with the czarist government increased so rapidly as to bring on open revolution the following year. *See* Naroch Lake; Lemberg II; World War I.

Kraśnik (World War I). The opening Austrian attack in Galicia, which pushed back a secondary Russian offensive, on August 23–25, 1914. *See* Galicia.

Kressenbrunn (Bohemian-Hungarian Wars), 1260. Despite the shattering defeat suffered from the Mongols at Mohi in 1241, Béla IV worked valiantly to rebuild Hungary. Unfortunately for Béla, his reign coincided with that of Ottokar II of Bohemia, who was leading his nation to the height of its medieval power. The long hostility between the two kings reached a climax at Kressenbrunn in 1260. Béla marched his Hungarian army up to the east bank of the March River in Moravia just as Ottokar's Bohemians reached the west bank. Neither army was capable of fording the river in the face of an enemy. Ottokar courteously allowed the Hungarians to cross the March unhindered. He then directed a fierce attack that virtually destroyed the Hungarian army. Béla was forced to withdraw and surrender the province of Styria. *See* Mohi; Marchfeld.

Kula Gulf (World War II). The site of two Japanese-American naval battles in July 1943. *See* Solomon Islands.

Kulevcha (Russian-Turkish War), 1829. The Russian armies of Prince Aleksandr Menshikov opened the campaign of 1829 by seizing the fortress of Silistra on the right bank of the Danube. Then a force under Gen. Count Hans von Diebitsch marched southward toward the Balkan Mountains. At Kulevcha, 40 miles west of Varna, the Russians trapped a Turkish army of some 40,000 men in a large defile on June 11. In a savage struggle, the Turkish commander, Mustafa Reshid Pasha, lost about 5,000 men before he could extricate his troops. This Russian victory opened the route through the mountains for Diebitsch. Pressing forward in the deepest penetration of Turkish territory so far achieved, Diebitsch seized Adrianople on August 20. (Meanwhile a second Russian army, commanded by Gen. Ivan Paskevich—later Count of Erivan and Prince of Warsaw—drove through the Caucasus.) With the Russians only 130 miles away from Constantinople, Sultan Mahmud II accepted the Treaty of Adrianople on September 14, ceding to Czar Nicholas I all territory as far as the southern mouth of the Danube. *See* Varna II; Konya.

Kulikovo (Rise of Russia), 1380. In the century after the death of their great leader Alexander Nevski, the Russians remained under the suzerainty of the Mongolian Tatars of the southeast. But Russia's growing strength made this domination increasingly hard to bear. Finally, in 1380, the grand duke of Vladimir and Moscow, Demetrius Donskoi, organized his fellow princes in a revolt against their Tatar masters. From Moscow the newly assembled Russian army moved south to Kulikovo, near the source of the Don. Here they met the Mongol horde on September 8 and won an overwhelming victory. The battle of Kulikovo shattered the Tatar military reputation and marked the beginning of eventual Russian liberation. (A century later Ivan III, the Great, would rule as the first true national sovereign of Russia.) *See* Peipus Lake; Kandurcha.

Kulm-Priesten (Napoleonic Empire Wars), 1813. Following its major defeat at Dresden, the allied army of Prince Karl von Schwarzenberg began withdrawing through the Erz Gebirge into Bohemia on the night of August 27, 1813. Napoleon I thereupon sent a French army of 32,000 men under Gen. Dominique Vandamme to intercept the eastern wing of the retreating enemy in the mountains. On August 30 Vandamme reached Kulm, 25 miles south of Dresden. But here he found the Russian general Count Aleksandr Ostermann-Tolstoy blocking his route at Priesten with 44,000 troops. Vandamme held his ground in a sharp struggle. But during the action a Prussian force of 10,000 under Gen. Count Friedrich Kleist von Nollendorf suddenly debouched from a side road into the French rear at Kulm. Only half the French army escaped the accidental trap, which cost the allies 11,000 casualties. Vandamme himself was captured. This victory restored allied morale, which had been badly shaken at Dresden. *See* Dresden; Dennewitz; Napoleonic Empire Wars.

Kumanovo (First Balkan War), 1912. While one Turkish army of Sultan Mohammed V was being repulsed in Thrace, a second force was opposing the Serbians in Macedonia. Here an army of King Peter I Karageorgevich met the Turks at Kumanovo, 15 miles northeast of Skoplje, on October 24. In a three-day battle the Ottomans were beaten and driven back. Pressing southward, the Serbs seized Monastir (Bitolj) on November 18 before agreeing to an armistice on December 3. Meanwhile, the Sultan's armies suffered a severe defeat at the hands of the Bulgarians. *See* Kirk-Kilissa; Lüleburgaz; Balkan Wars.

Kumasi (British-Ashanti Wars), 1874. The tribal kingdom of Ashanti (a land now part of Ghana) warred intermittently with the British Gold Coast in West Africa during the nineteenth century. In the second of these conflicts, begun in 1873, the British general Sir Garnet Wolseley (later Lord Wolseley) led an expedition of 2,500 troops against the Ashanti capital of Kumasi (Coomassie), 115 miles northwest of Accra. On February 4 of the following year Wolseley stormed into the city. The chieftain, Kofi Karikari, accepted British peace terms.

In the fourth war, Gen. Sir Francis Scott duplicated Wolseley's feat on January 18, 1896. The area was then made a British protectorate. The Gold Coast area became the British dominion of Ghana in 1957 and a republic in 1960.

Kunersdorf (Seven Years' War), 1759. The third Russian offensive of the war sent out by Czarina Elizabeth marched across the Brandenburg frontier in the summer of 1759. Overpowering a Prussian army at Kay, Field Marshal Count Pëtr Saltykov (Soltikov) with 55,000 men reached the Oder opposite Frankfurt. From Saxony, Russia's ally Austria of the Holy Roman Empire (Maria Theresa) marched 35,000 troops northward to effect a junction with Saltykov. The harassed Prussian king, Frederick II (the Great), rushed into Brandenburg where he assembled an army of 50,000 men. He tried to prevent the Imperial army from joining forces with the Russians, but the two Austrian noblemen commanders, Count Hadik von Futak and Baron Gideon von Laudon, slipped past the Prussians. The combined army of 90,000 entrenched itself among the sandhills of Kunersdorf (Kunowice), four miles east of Frankfurt.

On August 11 Frederick crossed the Oder with 43,000 men. The following day he attacked the formidable allied force, seeking to envelop both enemy flanks. In the wooded and broken ground the Prussian columns became disorganized. Instead of a coordinated assault, the offense degenerated into piecemeal attacks, which the Russians and Austrians repulsed with heavy casualties. The Prussian cavalry of Gen. Friedrich von Seydlitz rode into the fray but failed to reverse the slaughter of the blue-clad infantry. In six hours the Prussians lost more than 20,000 men and 178 guns. It was Frederick's most crushing defeat. Casualties in the Austro-Russian army totaled 15,700.

If the allies had followed up their overwhelming victory, all Prussia might have been overrun. Frederick had only 3,000 effectives and for a time even resigned his military command. But the allies quarreled between themselves until supply shortages forced the Russian army to return home. In the south the Austrian marshal Count Leopold von Daun captured Dresden on September 4. But otherwise he too failed to capitalize on the calamitous Prussian defeat. *See* Kay; Maxen; Seven Years' War.

Kursk (World War II). A Russian salient west of Kursk, which the defenders held against converging German attacks between July 5 and 13, 1943, in the largest tank battle in history. *See* Soviet Union (World War II).

Kut-al-Imara I (World War I), 1915. The campaign against Turkey in Mesopotamia (now Iraq) began with a British force from India occupying Basra, at the junction of the Tigris and Euphrates rivers, on November 22, 1914. Under the command of Gen. Sir John Nixon, the Anglo-Indian corps pushed up both rivers to take Amara, 100 miles north on the Tigris, on June 3, 1915, and Nasiriya, a similar distance northward on the Euphrates, on July 25. Turkish opposition was so negligible that Nixon decided to send a reinforced division northward toward Baghdad. Marching up the Tigris with 11,000 men, Gen. Sir Charles Townshend encountered a strong Turkish position at Kut-al-Imara. Here stood 10,500 troops under Gen. Nur-ud-din. Maneuvering to attack from the north, Townshend routed the Turks on September 28. In the confusion, however, most of the defeated troops escaped northward to Ctesiphon. After reorganizing and resupplying his army, Townshend set out for Baghdad, 100 miles to the northwest. *See* Ctesiphon III; World War I.

Kut-al-Imara II (World War I), 1915–1916. After his defeat at Ctesiphon, the British general Sir Charles Townshend withdrew down the Tigris River to Kut-al-Imara. Here he chose to risk a Turkish siege rather than retreat farther. On December 8, 1915, the pursuing Turks under Gen. Nur-ud-din closed in on the river village with some 12,000 men. Townshend's force of 12,000 Anglo-Indians fortified the small tongue of land formed by the U-turning Tigris and awaited relief. From Basra, the British commander in Mesopotamia, Gen. Sir John Nixon, sent out a column under Gen. Sir Fenton Aylmer. Aylmer, struggling against floods and determined Turkish resistance between January 18 and 21, was forced to turn back with a loss of 6,000 men. In a second attempt, on March 8, Aylmer was again repulsed. This time he suffered almost 3,500 casualties. On April 1 Gen. Sir Percy Lake, who had succeeded Nixon, dispatched a third relief force up the river. Commanded by Gen. Sir George Gorringe, the British broke through the first Turkish line, only to be thrown back on April 22. By now, suffering and sickness in the besieged fortress had become acute. To save the 10,000 surviving members of the garrison (including 2,000 English), Townshend surrendered Kut-al-Imara on April 29. The British defeat was complete. Four months later, however, Gen. Sir Frederick Maude arrived to instill new life into the British forces in Mesopotamia. *See* Ctesiphon III; Baghdad IV; World War I.

Kutná Hora (Hussite Wars), 1422. After the repulse of his army from Prague in 1420, Sigismund, king of Hungary and Bohemia and Holy Roman Emperor, took personal charge of the crusade against Jan Zizka's Taborite heretics. He arrived in Bohemia late in 1421 at the head of a large army, including tens of thousands of Germans. But meanwhile Zizka, with a maximum of only 25,000 men at his disposal, had welded a tight military organization featuring wheeled artillery and the tactical use of baggage wagons as mobile forts. The two hostile forces met at Kutná Hora (Kuttenberg), 45 miles southeast of Prague, on January 6, 1422. Zizka's brilliant defense behind his ring of wagon-forts stopped Sigismund's army with heavy losses. Then a fierce Bohemian charge routed the invaders with still greater casualties. Sigismund fell back to make another stand. *See* Prague I; Německý Brod; Hussite Wars.

Kwajalein-Eniwetok (World War II), 1944. Following the U.S. conquest of the Gilbert Islands in November 1943, Adm. Chester Nimitz ordered an attack on the Marshall Islands, 600 miles to the northwest. On February 1, 1944, the marine general Holland Smith's V Amphibious Corps stood ready to strike at Kwajalein Atoll in the center of the archipelago. Preceded by a heavy air and naval bombardment, the U.S. 7th Infantry Division (Charles Corlett) landed on the islet of Kwajalein itself, while the 4th Marine Division (Harry Schmidt) stormed ashore on the twin islet of Roi-Namur, 45 miles to the north. One marine regiment took Roi the first day; another regiment overran Namur, to the east, by noon of the second day. Almost 3,500 Japanese were killed and 264 captured. Marine losses were 190 dead and 547 wounded. Meanwhile the 7th Infantry (victor on Attu) was crushing all Japanese resistance on Kwajalein Islet. Here in three days more than 3,800 enemy troops were killed, at a loss of 177 Americans killed and 1,000 wounded. By February 4 Kwajalein was secure.

The rapid conquest of Kwajalein prompted Nimitz to go after Eniwetok, 400 miles to the northwest, two months ahead of schedule. On February 18 the independent 22nd Marine Regiment (John Walker) attacked the islet of Engebi. The next day the 27th Infantry's 106th Regiment (Thomas Walker) struck at Eniwetok Islet itself. By February 22 the whole of Eniwetok had been cleared. The remaining islands of the Marshalls were occupied soon thereafter. The Japanese commander, Adm. Musashi Kobayashi, lost 9,000 men in a futile defense of the islands. Total American casualties were 640 killed and 1,885 wounded.

The next series of islands to come under attack in the Central Pacific was the Marianas. *See* Tarawa-Makin; Mariana Islands; Truk; World War II.

Kyushu (Mongol Invasions of Japan), 1281. Seven years after sending out the first invasion of Japan, the Chinese Mongol emperor Kublai Khan, grandson of the great Genghis Khan, tried again. The invasion fleet, carrying an estimated 50,000 warriors, crossed the Sea of Japan and for the second time seized the islands of Tsushima and Iki. After landing on northern Kyushu, the Mongols pushed inland. But the walls and other fortifications the Hojo leaders had constructed in western Japan effectively checked all Mongol attempts to make a breakthrough. Meanwhile, at sea the mobility of the smaller Japanese ships enabled the defenders to take a heavy toll of the Mongol-Korean vessels. After almost two months of deadlocked fighting on land, a severe storm wrecked much of the invading armada. The few thousand surviving Mongols then withdrew back to Korea. The death of Kublai in 1294 ended the Mongol threat to Japan. *See* Hakata Bay; Kamakura; Mongol Wars.

L

La Albuera (Napoleonic Empire Wars), 1811. When Gen. Lord Wellington (Arthur Wellesley) opened an offensive from Portugal into French-held Spain, he himself directed the attack along the northern route to Madrid. To the south, the British thrust fell to the command of Gen. Sir William Carr Beresford (later Lord Beresford). With some 35,000 Spanish, Portuguese, and British troops, Beresford circled toward the French fortress of Badajoz. Fitfeen miles to the southeast he was attacked by 30,000 French troops under Marshal Nicolas Soult on May 16, 1811. In a bitter battle, Beresford's allied troops bolted the field, but his 9,000 British infantry held their ground against heavy odds and finally beat off the French assault. Soult withdrew to Badajoz, suffering almost 8,000 casualties. All but 5,000 of the British contingent were killed, wounded, or captured. Although Wellington had also won his battle, both victory margins were so narrow that he had to reorganize his forces for a new invasion of Spain early the following year. *See* Fuentes de Oñoro; Ciudad Rodrigo; Tarragona; Napoleonic Empire Wars.

La Bicocca (French Wars in Italy), 1522. France, which had regained Milan after the battle of Marignano (Melegnano) in 1515, soon faced a new challenge in northern Italy. The Hapsburg king Charles I of Spain became Holy Roman Emperor Charles V in 1519. He claimed Milan (as well as the duchy of Burgundy). Francis I, the Valois king of France who had vainly sought the imperial crown, retaliated by claiming Spanish Navarre and Naples. Charles's lansquenets (troops, largely German, copying the pike tactics of the Swiss but adding the refinement of arquebusiers) drove the French out of Milan and several other cities in Lombardy. The French made a stand at La Bicocca, a few miles northeast of Milan, on April 27, 1522. Here their Swiss mercenaries made a headlong charge against the Imperial troops entrenched behind hedges. Despite heavy musket fire, which took a cruel number of casualties, the Swiss pressed on to the main line of resistance. But here they could not surmount a slope defended by a forest of pikes. With their customary stubbornness, the mountain men persisted until 3,000 of them lay dead at the foot of the rampart. The French commander had to withdraw his army from Lombardy. And in the following month even the valuable seaport of Genoa had to be surrendered.

The battle of La Bicocca proved inconclusive in the dynastic wars of Italy: two years later Francis I sent another army across the Alps to make good the 1522 French losses. But for the Swiss it was a turning point in their military history. At the insistence of their common soldiers, the officers had come forward to lead the hopeless charges against the Imperial entrenchments. Almost all of these commanders fell. (According to some reports, one of them was the semilegendary Arnold von Winkelried of Unterwalden; most authorities, however, place Arnold's heroism at Sempach in 1386). From this day forward the Swiss were no longer regarded as the best shock troops in Europe. The German lansquenets and the Spanish sword-and-buckler men now rated higher. *See* Marignano; Pavia V.

La Coruña (Napoleonic Empire Wars), 1809. After the inglorious Convention of Cintra (Sintra) allowed the French army to evacuate Portugal unmolested in the summer of 1808, the British government of George III sent out Gen. Sir John Moore to take over command of its expeditionary force at Lisbon. Moore seized the initiative and marched boldly northeast into Spain, to Salamanca and then to Valladolid, 100 miles north of Madrid. His advance, however, was carefully watched by Napoleon I, who had taken direct command at Madrid following French disasters at Bailén, in Spain, and at Vimeiro, in Portugal.

On Christmas Day 1808 Napoleon suddenly struck westward from Madrid with 50,000 men, cutting off Moore's communications with Portugal. The outnumbered and outmaneuvered British commander turned left and headed for the northwest coast of Spain, 250 miles away. The French army gave chase. At Astorga, near León, Napoleon relinquished command of the pursuit to Marshal Nicolas Soult. Moore's retreat through the Cantabrian Mountains in midwinter, harassed by Soult's advance guard, inflicted cruel hardships on the British troops.

Finally, on January 14, 1809, Moore's men reached the harbor at La Coruña only to find their prearranged evacuation by a British fleet delayed by contrary winds. Two days later Soult, with 20,000 men, attacked the British, now reduced to 14,000 hardy survivors. In a savage battle the French were thrown back with a loss of 2,000 men. The embarkation was free to proceed without further hindrance, but the British victory cost the life of Moore; his second-in-command, Gen. Sir David Baird, lost an arm in the battle. General John Hope completed the evacuation on January 18. *See* Vimeiro; Oporto; Napoleonic Empire Wars.

Lade (Persian-Greek Wars), 494 B.C. The revolt of the Ionian Greeks against the Persian rule of Darius I ended disastrously on land in 499 B.C. At sea, the Persian fleet under Artaphrenes the Elder began a blockade of Miletus, the leading Ionian city of Asia Minor. In an effort to raise the blockade, an allied Greek fleet of 353 Lesbian, Samian, and Chian ships attacked the Persian galleys off the island of Lade in 494 B.C. Originally outnumbered, the Greek fleet was further weakened by the last-minute desertion of the Samians and some Lesbians. The Persians won a decisive victory, then landed and sacked Miletus. With the Ionian revolt crushed, Darius turned to attacks on Athens and Eretria for having aided the rebel cities. *See* Ephesus; Marathon; Persian-Greek Wars.

Ladysmith (South African War II), 1899–1900. With the outbreak of war on October 12, the Boer commander in chief, Gen. Petrus Joubert, sent a force under Gen. Piet Cronjé to attack Mafeking and Kimberley in the west. He himself launched a thrust into Natal, aimed at capturing the seaport of Durban. Defending against the Boer attack was Gen. Sir George White with 10,000 British troops. The well-armed Boer army, in superior numbers, pressed southeast to Dundee, 120 miles from Durban, on October 20. Here at Talana Hill the British were driven back with almost 500 casualties. On the following day the Boers were checked at Elandslaagte along the Dundee–Ladysmith railroad. But the repulse was only temporary. The British, fighting a strong rear-guard action, were steadily squeezed back toward Ladysmith. At Nicholson's Nek on October 30, two battalions were surrounded and taken prisoner. During this struggle, the outgunned defenders were aided by the arrival of two large naval pieces brought up from Durban by Sir Hedworth Meux (Lambton). Two days later White fell back into Ladysmith. Here he was promptly besieged by Joubert's army.

Although the Boers could bombard the town at will, the garrison fought off all attempts to penetrate the defenses. After 119 days of siege, Ladysmith was relieved by an army under Gen. Sir Redvers Buller, on February 28. The long conflict cost White almost 900 battle casualties, plus many more who died of disease. *See* Mafeking; Kimberley; Colenso; South African Wars.

La Forbie (Sixth Crusade), 1244. In a treaty signed between the irrepressible Frederick II, of Germany and the Holy Roman Empire, and his Turkish counterpart Malik al-Kamil, the sultan of Egypt, Jerusalem and several other holy places were turned over to the Christians on February 18, 1229. A ten-year truce bound the agreement. The expiration of the truce led to no immediate outbreak of hostilities, for both Christians and Moslems were divided by internal dissensions.

For the next five years only raiding disturbed the peace of the Holy Land. Then the Frankish barons of Outremer made a gigantic blunder. They allied themselves with the sultan of Damascus in his civil war with the sultan of Egypt, who promptly countered this stroke by hiring 10,000 nomadic Khwarismians from northern Syria to join his army at Gaza. En route south, the savage nomads swooped down on the virtually defenseless Jerusalem on June 11, 1244. For more than two months they slaughtered and pillaged, besieging the several walled convents of the city. A truce finally released 6,000 survivors to make their way westward to the coast. Only 300 ever reached Jaffa.

Meanwhile the Christian army at Acre began marching southward in company with their new allies, the Turks of Syria. The Egyptian army, reinforced by the ruthless Khwarismians, waited at Gaza. The two opponents clashed at La Forbie, a few miles to the north, on October 17, 1244. Early in the battle the Syrian allies took flight, leaving the Christians greatly outnumbered by the Egyptian force. The Moslem horsebowmen cut the Franks to pieces. Several thousand perished in the sands of La Forbie while hundreds became prisoners. Of more than 600 knights from the military orders—Hospitallers, Templars, Teutonics—only 62 fought their way out. The Christian hold on Outremer had again been reduced to a thinly populated coastline strip. But with the loss of Jerusalem for the second time, a new crusade began forming in France. *See* Damietta; El Mansûra; Crusades.

Lagos I (War of the Grand Alliance), 1693. Although the French fleet had been decisively crippled in the 1692 battle of La Hogue, English and Dutch ships were still not immune from attack. In 1693 Adm. Sir George Rooke with a squadron of allied warships was escorting 400 merchantmen to the Mediterranean when the convoy was suddenly attacked on June 27, off Lagos in southern Portugal. The French admiral the Comte de Tourville, commanding a force double the 20 allied ships, pressed his advantage ruthlessly for two days. At least 100 merchant vessels and 2 or 3 English and Dutch fighting ships were destroyed before Rooke could extricate the convoy. Despite the costly losses the defeat failed to weaken England's naval superiority over the fleets of Louis XIV. *See* La Hogue; Neerwinden I; Grand Alliance, War of the.

Lagos II (Seven Years' War), 1759. In the fourth year of the war, King Louis XV's government ordered the French fleet to concentrate at Brest for a planned invasion of England. From Toulon, Com. de la Clue sailed westward with 12 ships of the line. On August 7 he slipped past Gibraltar but was almost immediately spotted and pursued by the English fleet under Adm. Edward Boscawen. Five of the French vessels turned northward to put in at Cadiz, Spain. The remaining 7 were soon overtaken by Boscawen's 14 warships. A running fight ensued. The French ship at the rear was forced to surrender, two escaped into the Atlantic, and the other four were run ashore on the coast of Lagos Bay. Here the English followed on August 18 and, despite the neutrality of Portugal, captured two and burned the other two ships. The destruction of De la Clue's fleet forced the French to limit their offensive planning to an invasion of Scotland by the Brest fleet. *See* Hastenbeck; Minden II; Quiberon Bay; Seven Years' War.

La Hogue (War of the Grand Alliance), 1692. Dissatisfied with the French naval operations so far in the war, Louis XIV urged his admiral the Comte de Tourville to defeat the combined English and Dutch fleets. Such a victory would open the way to a French invasion of England (William III and Mary). Tourville sailed from Brest with 44 ships, expecting strong reinforcements from the Toulon fleet. Although the ships from Toulon did not arrive, Tourville attacked the allied navy on May 19, 1692, at La Hogue, a roadstead off Pointe Barfleur on the northeast coast of the Cotentin Peninsula in northwest France. By skillful seamanship the French warships held their own that day against the British and Dutch fleet, which numbered more than twice as many ships, under the English admirals Edward Russell (later Earl of Orford) and Sir John Ashby and the Dutch commander Adm. Philips van Almonde. That night Tourville began a withdrawal to the west, but when the tide changed the French vessels became separated. The allies pursued vigorously. Twenty French ships rounded Cape La Hague to find shelter at Saint-Malo. But of the others, which tried to escape eastward, 15 were destroyed during the next four days—3 at Cherbourg, including the flagship *Royal Sun,* and 12 at La Hogue by allied ships under Adm. Sir George Rooke. Each of the lost ships carried at least 60 guns. Tourville made his escape.

The battle of La Hogue proved to be the decisive naval action of the war. From this point on

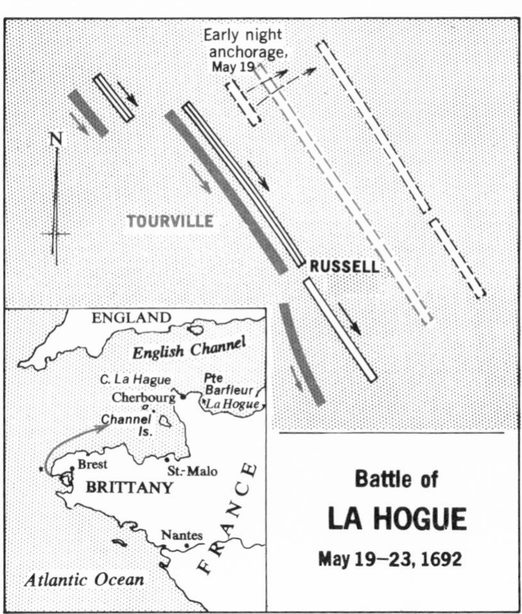

Battle of LA HOGUE
May 19–23, 1692

the French were reduced to privateering and commerce raiding. In fact, France has never been able to match the naval strength of Great Britain since that time. *See* Beachy Head; Steenkerke; Lagos I; Grand Alliance, War of the.

Laing's Nek (South African War I), 1881. When the Boers in the Transvaal revolted to establish their own republic, they besieged the small British garrisons in the area. From Natal, Gen. Sir George Colley marched inland with a column of 1,000 men. At the pass of Laing's Nek, in the Drakensberg Mountains, Petrus Joubert blocked the way with a detachment of Boer troops. On January 28 Colley attacked the strong position and was thrown back with a loss of almost 200 men. Boer casualties were 14 killed and 27 wounded. *See* Ulundi; Majuba Hill; South African Wars.

Lake. For battle sites beginning with this word, see name of lake. For Lake Champlain, for example, see Champlain, Lake.

Lamian War. *See* Crannon.

Landau (War of the Spanish Succession), 1702. Except for the war in northern Italy, the chief theater of operations in 1702 was along the Rhine in The Palatinate. Here Louis William I, margrave of Baden-Baden, commanded an army of the Holy Roman Empire (Leopold I). Opposing this Imperial force was a French army under the aged marshal Nicolas de Catinat. The margrave crossed to the west side of the Rhine near Speyer, then turned left to Landau on July 29. Catinat was too weak to send aid, and on September 12 the Landau garrison capitulated. But now the elector of Bavaria, Maximilian II Emanuel, entered the war on the side of Louis XIV of France. Louis William withdrew up the Rhine. A new French army, led by Duc Claude de Villars, marched up the opposite bank, crossed over at Friedlingen, and inflicted a minor defeat on the Badeners in a cavalry attack. The engagement is notable chiefly as the first victory in the brilliant military career of Villars. Both sides then went into winter quarters. *See* Luzzara; Vigo Bay; Höchstädt I; Spanish Succession, War of the.

Landeshut (Seven Years' War), 1760. The campaign of 1760 opened with Frederick II, the Great, in grave danger of being crushed by three columns converging on Prussia: the Russians from East Prussia and two Austrian armies from Saxony and Silesia. Fortunately for Prussia, its opponents failed to coordinate their offenses. The first enemy commander to take the field was the Baron Gideon von Laudon, the Austrian general of the Holy Roman Empire (Maria Theresa). Laudon maneuvered the Prussian army of Baron Heinrich de La Motte-Fouqué out of Landeshut (Kamienna Góra), the Silesian fortress in the Sudetic Mountains. Frederick ordered his subordinate to retake Landeshut. La Motte-Fouqué made the attempt with his 13,000-man force on June 23. But Laudon's 31,000 Imperials overwhelmed the Prussians, virtually destroying the entire army. Frederick himself then turned his back on his other enemies and marched into Silesia. Meanwhile, on the western front another Prussian general held off a French army. *See* Maxen; Liegnitz II; Warburg; Seven Years' War.

Landshut (Napoleonic Empire Wars), 1809. The French victory at Abensberg on April 20, 1809, split the two wings of the large Austrian army of Archduke Charles Louis (brother of Emperor Francis I). Charles pulled his main force eastward to Eggmühl (Eckmühl), between the Danube and Isar rivers. His left wing, commanded by Gen. Baron Johann Hiller, fell back southward across the Isar River to Landshut. Not realizing that Hiller's command represented only 36,000 men, Napoleon I sent most of his strength southward in pursuit. Led by Marshal Jean Lannes, the French overtook and smashed Hiller's rear guard in the suburbs of Landshut, north of the river, on the evening of April 21. Then, charging across a burning bridge over the Isar, they stormed into the city. The Austrians resisted desperately but were forced to retreat hurriedly farther south when the French IV Corps of Marshal André Masséna approached Landshut down the right bank of the Isar. In all, Hiller lost 9,000 men, plus most of his baggage and artillery. Meanwhile, 23 miles to the north, Marshal Louis Davout's III Corps faced the bulk of the Austrian army. *See* Abensberg; Eggmühl; Napoleonic Empire Wars.

Langensalza (Seven Weeks' War), 1866. The carving up of Schleswig-Holstein in 1864 led to war between Prussia and Austria two years later, just as foreseen by Otto von Bismarck, the Iron Chancellor of Prussia's Wilhelm I. Hannover, along with Bavaria, Saxony, and most of the other German states, sided with Austria. The Prussian chief of the general staff, Gen. Helmuth von Moltke (later Count von Moltke), sent the bulk of his forces against Austria in Bohemia while dispatching one army to deal with the allies of Franz Josef I. This army, under Gen. Eduard Vogel von Falkenstein, marched into Saxony. On June 27 the Prussian advance guard attacked the Hannoverian army commanded by King George V at Langensalza, 19 miles northwest of Erfurt. The Prussians were repulsed with more than 2,000 casualties. But when Vogel von Falkenstein brought up the rest of his 50,000 troops, the greatly outnumbered Hannoverians surrendered two days later. George V abdicated and Hannover was absorbed by Prussia. The victors turned on the other south German allies of Austria, but before another battle could be fought here the war was decided in Bohemia. *See* Dybböl; Münchengrätz; Sadowa; Seven Weeks' War

Langport (English Civil War), 1645. After decisively routing the Cavalier army at Naseby, Sir Thomas Fairfax and Oliver Cromwell took a strong detachment of the Roundhead's New Model army into the Royalist stronghold in the southwest. Here Gen. Lord George Goring attempted to defend Bridgwater by bringing on a battle at Langport on July 10, 1645. But his cavalry force was ridden down by Cromwell's horsemen. Some of the Royalists were killed; by far the greater number surrendered. The Roundheads pressed through Somersetshire and turned north into Gloucestershire. Charles I's ablest commander, his nephew Prince Rupert of Germany, held Bristol, England's second largest city at that time. At the approach of the Parliamentary army, however, Rupert surrendered the city, on September 11. Now only one more battle remained for Charles. *See* Naseby; Stow-on-the-Wold; English Civil War.

Langside (Scottish Rebellion against Mary), 1568. When Mary, Queen of Scots, escaped from her imprisonment at Lochleven, she rallied many Catholic Scottish supporters to her cause. An army of 6,000 men under the 5th Earl of Argyll (Archibald Campbell) assembled at Langside, a southern suburb of Glasgow. This force was challenged by an equal number of Protestants commanded by the Earl of Moray (James Stewart), the regent for young James VI. The two armies clashed on May 13, 1568. A cavalry charge routed the queen's troops, who fled the field. Mary escaped to Cumberland in England, where she was kept under guard by Elizabeth I until she was executed in 1587. *See* Carberry Hill; Cadiz.

Lansdowne (English Civil War), 1643. During the second year of the Civil War the Cavalier forces in the west, commanded by Gen. Sir Ralph (later Lord) Hopton, won a narrow victory at Stratton and then marched toward Bath. A few miles to the east, at Lansdowne, they were blocked by Gen. Sir William Waller's Roundhead army. On July 5 the Cavaliers charged Waller's positions and after a sharp struggle routed the heavily armored London cavalrymen, who were called the Lobsters. Although Hopton captured the enemy's artillery and baggage, the attack cost so many casualties in his own ranks that he retired to Devizes in Wiltshire. *See* Stratton; Roundway Down; English Civil War.

Laon (Napoleonic Empire Wars), 1814. The Allied thrust to Paris down the Marne Valley had been deflected northward beyond the Aisne River early in March 1814. Napoleon I with less than 47,000 troops pushed the much larger army of the Prussian field marshal general Gebhard von Blücher back to Laon, 77 miles northeast of Paris. Here the French emperor attempted a turning movement from the right (east) by Marshal Auguste Marmont's 9,500-man VI Corps. But now Blücher, with his army reinforced to 85,000 men, turned to fight. On March 9 he sent Gen. Count Hans Yorck (York) von Wartenburg against Marmont. Caught unprepared, the French commander fell back with heavy losses. Below Laon, Napoleon held his ground throughout the following day, then withdrew without being pursued. The two-day battle cost 6,000 French casualties to 4,000 allied losses. *See* Craonne; Reims; Napoleonic Empire Wars.

Largs (Norse Invasion of Scotland), 1263. A Norwegian invasion fleet under Haakon IV was shipwrecked at Largs on the southwest coast of Scotland. To protect the survivors, the Norwegian king sent out another landing party. A Scottish army under Alexander III attacked the combined force of invaders on October 2 and routed them. The Scandinavian survivors took to their ships, abandoning the invasion project. *See* Alnwick II; Berwick upon Tweed.

La Rochelle I (Hundred Years' War), 1372. England's control of the seas, established in the 1340 battle of Sluys (Sluis), received a severe blow in 1372. The Earl of Pembroke, carrying reinforcements to Aquitaine, sailed into the Bay of Biscay with a fleet of armed merchantmen. Off La Rochelle the English vessels were intercepted by a fleet of Castilian galleys on June 22. (Castile had become France's ally after the battle of Nájera.) Making good use of superior maneuverability, the Spanish galleys destroyed the English sailing ships. Pembroke became a prisoner of war. It was one of the worst defeats suffered by England in the long war. *See* Sluys; Winchelsea; Nájera; Châteauneuf-de-Randon; Margate; Hundred Years' War.

La Rochelle II (French Religious Wars), 1627–1628. During the reign of Louis XIII, the Huguenots revolted again under the religious and political persecutions of the Catholic crown. Cardinal Richelieu, chief minister of the king, took under siege the chief Huguenot stronghold of La Rochelle, on the Bay of Biscay, in 1627. Behind strong defenses the garrison held out subbornly against the royal troops. England, under Charles I, promised aid to La Rochelle, but three expeditions failed to succor the city. Meanwhile Richelieu ruthlessly prosecuted the siege, and after 14 months the starving garrison capitulated on October 28, 1628. With this victory Richelieu began a subjugation of the Huguenots that reduced them from an armed political party to a small, tolerated religious sect. *See* Ivry-la-Bataille; Ré; Castelnaudary; French Religious Wars.

La Rothière (Napoleonic Empire Wars), 1814. Three days after being driven out of La Rothière in northeast France, the Prussian field marshal General Gebhard von Blücher counterattacked with some 53,000 troops. Napoleon I, with some 40,000 inexperienced French troops, planned a withdrawal. But the order was delivered too late. Blücher assaulted head on, on February 1. In savage fighting the French held their ground until nightfall and then skillfully disengaged. Each side lost about 6,000 men. Although a second large allied army under Prince Karl Schwarzenberg threatened Paris from the southeast, Napoleon resolved to concentrate against Blücher first. *See* Brienne; Champaubert-Montmirail; Montereau; Napoleonic Empire Wars.

Las Guásimas (Spanish-American War), 1898. With the outbreak of war against Spain on April 21, the United States began assembling an expeditionary force at Tampa, Fla. Under the command of the 300-pound Gen. William Shafter, a force of about 17,000 regulars and volunteers sailed for Cuba on June 14 on 32 transports. The V Corps expedition arrived off Santiago de Cuba six days later. Shafter began disembarking on June 22 at Daiquirí, 14 miles east of Santiago, and later at Siboney, farther west. The Spanish commander, Gen. Arsenio Linares, offered no resistance on the beaches. Instead, the defenders chose to hold Las Guásimas, a fortified gap through the hills leading to Santiago. On June 24 Gen. Joseph Wheeler (a Confederate veteran of the American Civil War), who was the senior commander ashore, led an attack westward against the 250-foot-high ridge, defended by about 1,500 Spaniards. The 1,000 Americans in the assault were to be aided by some 800 Cubans under Gen. Calixto García, but the rebels provided scant support. In a sharp fight the Spanish were driven back with a loss of 10 killed and 25 wounded. Wheeler's casualties were 16 killed and 52 wounded. Shafter then held up the advance to prapare a major thrust toward Santiago. *See* Santiago de Cuba I; El Caney; Spanish-American War.

Las Navas de Tolosa (Spanish-Moslem Wars), 1212. Five years after his crushing defeat at Alarcos, King Alfonso VIII of Castile, in 1200, denounced the truce he had made with the Almohad empire in Spain and Northwest Africa. Both Christians and Moors began to prepare for a showdown battle. Pope Innocent IV ordered a crusade against the infidel, which helped end the longtime civil struggles among the Christian states of Spain. Kings Sancho VII, the Strong, of Navarre and Pedro II of Aragon, grandson of Alfonso, allied their armies with the Castilian monarch at Toledo. At the head of the largest military force ever assembled in Christian Spain, perhaps 100,000 men, Alfonso marched south.

Meanwhile, Mohammed I of Granada, son of al-Mansur, the Almohad victor of Alarcos, had assembled an army estimated at several hundred thousand warriors. At the approach of the Christians, Mohammed abandoned his outposts in the Guadiana Valley and fell back south of the Sierra Morena range. Alfonso found the passes too strongly guarded to penetrate, but a local shepherd guided the army through an open defile. The Christians suddenly appeared in front of the Moslems on the *nava,* or small plain, north of Jaén. Neither side made a move for two days. Then on July 16 Alfonso launched a fierce frontal attack with his cavalry. The king placed himself with the Castilian troops in his own center; on his left rode Archbishop Rodrigo of Toledo, the knights of the orders of Santiago (founded 1171) and Calatrava (established 1164), and Pedro of Aragon; Sancho the Strong commanded the right flank. Violent fighting raged back and forth across the plain. Slowly the heavier armor and swords of the knights pushed back both wings of the Moslem line. Toward the end of the day Mohammed's mounted center, which had held fast and inflicted severe casualties, counterattacked. When the charge was turned back by the knights, their ranks stiffened by infantry spearmen, Moorish resistance collapsed. Alfonso's whole army swept forward, turning the battle into a massacre. An estimated 150,000 Moors fell to Christian sword and spear.

The battle destroyed the flower of the Moorish army and ended raids into Christian territory. Within 50 years the Almohad dynasty would disintegrate. The kingdom of Castile now ruled the key central plateau of Spain, but disputes among the rival Christian kingdoms blocked the union of the country for another 250 years. *See* Alarcos; Muret; Cordova.

Laswari (Maratha-British War II), 1803. During the first six weeks of the Second Maratha War, British Gen. Gerard Lake in northern India took Aligarh, Delhi, and Agra. He then marched against the Maratha stronghold at Laswari, 78 miles southwest of Delhi. On November 1, 1803, Lake's British and allied native troops, some 10,000 men, defeated a much larger Maratha army and captured Laswari. British casualties numbered several hundred, Maratha losses several thousand. Meanwhile, the younger brother of Gov.-Gen. Lord Richard Wellesley (Arthur Wellesley, the future Duke of Wellington) was winning comparable victories in central India. *See* Aligarh; Assaye; Farrukhabad; Maratha-British Wars.

Latin America. The military history of Latin America includes Mexico, Central America, South America, and Cuba.

Spanish Conquest and Rule

Tenochtitlán	1520–1521
Otumba	1520
Cajamarca	1532

Napoleonic Empire War

Buenos Aires	1806–1807

Wars of Independence

The ferment of the Napoleonic era caused the Spanish provinces of La Plata to set up a separatist government in 1810. Two nations grew out of this territory. Paraguay declared its independence from Spain in 1811 and from Buenos Aires two years later. Argentina organized an independent government based on Buenos Aires in 1816. The first of the South American provinces to seek independence from Spain by military action was New Granada in the northwest. Beginning in 1810 patriots tried four times under the leadership of Simón Bolívar to throw off the Spanish yoke before they were successful. Then three battles freed New Granada, or Great Colombia, which in time subdivided into four nations: Colombia in 1819, Venezuela in 1829, Ecuador in 1830, and Panama (from Colombia) in 1903.

Boyacá	1819
Carabobo	1821
Pichincha	1822

In Mexico a similar revolutionary movement, during 1810–15, was crushed.

Calderón Bridge	1811

But a second attempt succeeded in securing independence, on February 24, 1821. Meanwhile, Chile was liberated after three battles.

Rancagua	1814
Chacabuco	1817
Maipo River	1818

In Peru the two foremost republicans, Simón Bolívar and José de San Martín, joined forces to free that country from Spanish rule.

Junín	1824
Ayacucho	1824

One of the victorious generals, Antonio de Sucre, with Simón Bolívar, organized the independence of Bolivia in 1825 without a battle. During this time Brazil became independent of Portugal

(1822), while the states of Central America threw off the Spanish yoke (1823). The tenth South American nation to win its independence was Uruguay.

Ituzaingó 1827

Wars and Revolutions

Yungay (Peru, Bolivia, Chile) 1839
Ingaví (Peru, Bolivia) 1841
Montevideo (Uruguay) 1843–1851
See U.S.-Mexican War
Monte-Caseros (Argentina) 1852
Calpulalpam (Mexico) 1860
Puebla II (Mexico with France) 1862–1863
Querétaro (Mexico with France) 1867
Aquidaban River (Paraguay, Uruguay, Argentina, Brazil) 1870
Tacna (Chile, Peru, Bolivia) 1880
Chalchuapa (Central America) 1885
See Spanish-American War
Columbus, N.M. 1916
Carrizal 1916

Castro Revolt in Cuba

Moncada Fortress 1953
Sierra Maestra 1958
Santa Clara–Santiago 1958

Latin War. *See* Trifanum.

Lauffeld (War of the Austrian Succession), 1747. While the war in Italy dragged on with neither side able to gain an advantage, the French forces of Louis XV pushed steadily forward through the Austrian Netherlands. A new British army under the Duke of Cumberland (William Augustus), son of King George II, joined the Austrian-Dutch forces in 1747 after quelling the '45 Rebellion in Britain. With Gen. Count Leopold von Daun, Cumberland managed to isolate a French detachment of 30,000 men at Lauffeld in northeast Belgium, just west of Maastricht. An allied victory seemed certain. But Marshal Comte Maurice de Saxe, French field commander, marched some of his battalions 50 miles in two days to concentrate a relieving force against the English-Dutch-Hannoverian-Austrian army. On July 2 Saxe attacked. He broke the allied lines, inflicting some 6,000 casualties. As the vanquished forces withdrew, Saxe sent a corps westward to besiege Bergen op Zoom. *See* Rocourt; Bergen op Zoom I; Austria Succession, War of the.

Laupen (Swiss-Burgundian Wars), 1339. In an open aggression against the Swiss, an army of 15,000 Burgundians marched eastward and laid siege to Laupen, 10 miles southwest of Bern. The local Swiss, supported by a force from the three forest cantons (Uri, Schwyz, and Unterwalden) under Rudolph von Erlach, moved to relieve the city. They took up a position on a slope, where the Burgundians, commanded by Count Gerard of Vallangin, sought to dislodge them by massing their feudal cavalry on the right of their line. The battle opened on June 21, 1339, with the count's horsemen charging the Swiss wing to their front. At the same time the two centers and farther wings locked together in infantry combat. Here the Burgundians, although greatly superior in numbers, were no match for the halberds and pikes of the fierce mountaineers. They fell back in great disorder. The victorious Swiss columns then wheeled to the left to attack the enemy cavalry, which had almost ridden down the foot soldiers opposing them. This flank assault routed the Burgundian knights, driving them from the field. The siege of Laupen was raised.

Laupen was one of the first battles on the European continent to demonstrate the power of well-trained infantry against the now fading strength of mounted knights. Bannockburn (1314) had signaled the start of this trend; Crécy in 1346 confirmed the first revival of infantry since Roman times. *See* Morgarten; Sempach.

Lava Beds (Modoc Rebellion), 1873. While the Indians on the Great Plains continued to war against the white men, the Modoc Indians in the Far West also took the warpath in an effort to avoid resettlement on a reservation. Under chief Captain Jack, the Modocs, after an orgy of murder and pillage, found refuge in the natural defenses of the Lava Beds near Tule Lake in northern California. Here 75 warriors, with about 150 women and children, held the so-called Modoc Line. In January 1873 Gen. Edward Canby sent 400 men, including parts of the 1st Cavalry and 21st Infantry regiments, to dislodge the Indians from their well-defended positions. The Modocs repulsed the two-column attack, killing 16 men and wounding 53 others. Canby called off the attack, while he built up his force to 1,000 men. In peace talks on April 11 Canby and a preacher, Eleazer Thomas, were treacherously slain by the Indians.

Three days later a new assault force under Gen. Jefferson Davis, covered by mortar fire, fought its way into the Lava Beds. In six weeks of bitter fighting, the Modocs were finally overpowered on June 1, at a cost of 82 lives to the attackers. Captain Jack and three others were captured, tried, and executed, largely on the testimony of Hooker Jim, a Modoc who turned state's evidence. The surviving Modocs were moved eastward to Indian Territory (now Oklahoma). *See* Indian Wars in the United States.

Le Cateau (World War I), 1914. After the defeat of the British Expeditionary Force (BEF) at Mons in the battle of the French Frontiers, on August 23, Field Marshal Sir John French led his troops southward in the general Anglo-French retreat. The massive German right (west) wing rolled forward into France on a front 75 miles wide. At the extreme left of Gen. Joseph Joffre's five French armies, French with five and a half British divisions stood in constant danger of being overlapped by the wide-swinging German First Army of Gen. Alexander von Kluck. This threat materialized on August 26 when the Germans caught up with French's left flank corps, the II, at Le Cateau, 18 miles north of Saint-Quentin. Separated by the Oise River from the I Corps (Gen. Sir Douglas Haig) on his right, Gen. Horace Smith-Dorrien had no alternative but to stand and fight. It became the biggest battle fought by the British army since Waterloo, a century before.

For 11 hours the three and a half divisions of the II Corps fought tenaciously against waves of gray-clad attackers from Kluck's army. Finally, after darkness fell, the British managed to disengage and continue their southward retreat to Saint-Quentin on the Somme. At Le Cateau the II Corps lost 8,077 men and 36 guns. (In the first five days in action the British suffered almost 15,000 casualties.) But the strong delaying action enabled the BEF to extricate itself from the scythelike German sweep into western France. To support the weak Allied left, Joffre now shifted the Army of Lorraine, under Gen. Michel Joseph Maunoury, westward to Amiens, as the new French Sixth Army on the extreme west of the line. *See* Frontiers of France; Marne River I; World War I.

Lechfeld (Wars of the German States), 955. Twenty years after the Magyars of modern Hungary had been repulsed at Riade by Henry I, they resumed raiding into eastern Germany. Henry's son Otto I, the Great, recruited a large army of mail-clad cavalry from all the duchies under his rule and marched against the invaders. At Lechfeld, south of Augsburg, in Bavaria, the Germans crushed the Magyars with heavy losses in a savage ten-hour battle. The decimated barbarians fell back across modern Austria to beyond the Leitha River. This battle ended the Magyar menace, for they became Christianized in 970. Earlier, in 962, big, red-headed Otto had himself crowned Holy Roman Emperor. *See* Riade; Crotone.

Legnano (German Invasion of Italy), 1176. Frederick I, called Frederick Barbarossa (Red Beard), Holy Roman Emperor and king of Germany and Italy, spent 30 years (1154–84) of his reign trying to subdue the cities of northern Italy. The chief battle came in 1176 when the Italian cities, organized in the Lombard League and supported by the papacy, assembled an army of infantrymen at Legnano, northwest of Milan. On May 29 this force engaged the mounted German knights of Frederick. The infantry won a decisive victory, forcing the emperor to flee Italy in disguise. Legnano marks the first major triumph of infantry over feudal cavalry in the Middle Ages. It would be many years before weapons and tactics equalized the fight between foot and mounted foes, but the slowly emerging strength of the *bourgeoisie* foreshadowed the downfall of the armored knight. *See* Cortenuova.

Leipzig (Napoleonic Empire Wars), 1813. After failing a second time to take Berlin, Napoleon I began withdrawing west of the Elbe River on September 24, 1813. He planned to use Leipzig on the Elster River as his major forward base. But his strategy collapsed quickly when the Prussian general Gebhard von Blücher forced a crossing of the Elbe at Wartenburg on October 3, and Swedish Crown Prince Jean Bernadotte (former French marshal) bridged the river farther downstream. These two commanders began a descent on Leipzig from the north, while Prince Karl von Schwarzenberg, masking Dresden, approached with an Austrian army from the south. By October 15 Napoleon had massed 122,000 of his available 175,000 troops in the Leipzig area. The allies had almost half their 200,000 men converging on Leipzig in an ever tightening arc.

Early on October 16 Schwarzenberg sent the Russian general Mikhail Barclay de Tolly with 78,000 men against Napoleon's southern defenses. When the disorganized attack petered out at noon, the French counterattacked and drove back the allies viciously. On the north Blücher's 54,000 Prussians failed to dislodge Marshal Auguste Marmont's VI Corps, which had less than half the enemy's strength. By nightfall the French held the advantage on both fronts, but their limited successes foretold glum developments in the near future.

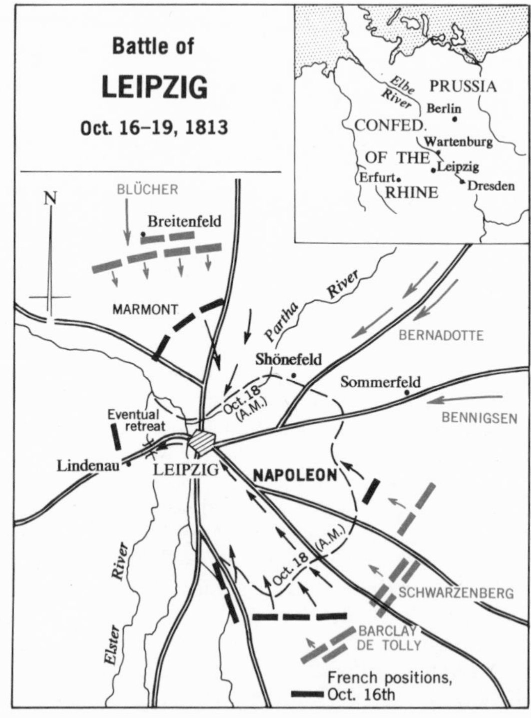

There was little fighting the second day (October 17). Napoleon completed the withdrawal of his 175,000 troops within the Leipzig perimeter. On the allied side, Bernadotte arrived from the north with 85,000 troops, while Gen. Levin Bennigsen (made a count during the battle) closed in from the east with a Russian army of 70,000 men. On October 18 the 355,000 allies launched a massive concentric attack against the French. Nine hours of murderous assaults gained little ground but convinced Napoleon that he could not stand such a battle of attrition. During the night and in the early morning hours of October 19, he withdrew across the Elster toward Erfurt. A premature demolition of the single bridge over the river stranded 20,000 French who were fighting a rearguard action in the city. The explosion cost the life of Polish Prince Józef Poniatowski (a marshal of France) and resulted in the capture of the French generals Jacques Lauriston and the Comte Reynier. In all, the so-called battle of the Nations cost the French at Leipzig 38,000 killed and wounded and 15,000 prisoners (plus another 15,000 wounded who were in the city's hospitals before the battle started). Allied casualties were estimated at more than 52,000. The battered French army retreated southwest toward Frankfort on the Main, followed by the allied armies. *See* Dennewitz; Hanau; Napoleonic Empire Wars.

Le Mans (Franco-Prussian War), 1871. One of the several civilian armies that took the field against Prussia after the French disaster at Sedan was commanded by Gen. Antoine Chanzy at Le Mans. A well-trained Prussian army under Prince Frederick Charles, nephew of King Wilhelm I, moved against Le Mans, 117 miles southwest of Paris, early in 1871. Although the French had many more men, they were no match for the Prussians. In a three-day battle beginning on January 10, the German regulars inflicted 10,000 casualties and destroyed the French army as a fighting unit. Now, except for the Paris garrison, only one patriot force, in northern France, remained to contest the Prussian armies of occupation. *See* Bapaume; Saint-Quentin II; Paris II; Franco-Prussian War.

Lemberg I (World War I). The capital of the Austrian province of Galicia, Lemberg (now (Lvov) fell to the Russians on September 3, 1914; it was regained by a German-Austrian counteroffensive on June 22, 1915. *See* Galicia; Gorlice-Tarnów.

Lemberg II (World War I), 1917. The forced abdication of Czar Nicholas II on March 13 elevated Aleksandr Kerenski to nominal control of the Russian government. Russian forces on the Eastern Front rapidly disintegrated, the Germans (Paul von Hindenburg) making no move that would serve to unify the demoralized enemy. Kerenski, however, was under heavy Allied pressure to take the offensive. Finally, on July 1, the Russian leader yielded, ordering Gen. Aleksei Brusilov, now chief of staff, to launch an attack westward toward Lemberg (Lvov). With three armies, composed chiefly of Finns, Poles, and Siberians, Brusilov advanced as much as 30 miles. But before he could reach Lemberg, the Germans counterattacked his right (north) flank on July 19. The Russian forces promptly collapsed. Within two weeks they were driven back to the Galicia frontier in hopeless confusion. This so-called Kerenski Offensive was the last Russian effort of the war. *See* Kovel-Stanislav; Riga II; World War I.

Leningrad (World War II), 1941–1944. The gigantic German invasion of the Soviet Union smashed forward on three fronts—north, center and south—in the summer of 1941. On the northern front the principal objective was the key Baltic port of Leningrad, the second largest city in Russia. To secure this goal Field Marshal Wilhelm von Leeb grouped two German armies in East Prussia—the Sixteenth and Eighteenth—plus the Third Panzer Group of Gen. Erich Hoeppner. On June 22 this force lunged northeast into Lithuania, crossed the Niemen River, and captured the capital of Vilnius four days later. Racing ahead, Gen. Erich von Manstein's *Panzer* corps seized bridges over the Dvina River almost 200 miles farther north in Latvia. Riga, the Latvian capital, fell on July 1. While tanks sped on toward Lake Ilmen, German infantry marched into Estonia. In August Leeb's left wing completed the conquest of the Baltic States up to Narva on the Estonian-Russian border. The Estonian capital of Tallin fell on August 30. The right wing was sweeping through Pskov, Staraya Russia, and Novgorod, while Hoeppner's armor pressed north to Luga, only 90 miles from Leningrad.

Meanwhile Finland had declared war on the Soviet Union on June 26 and was working closely with the Nazis. The main Finnish force of 12 divisions under Field Marshal Baron Carl von Mannerheim, plus two German divisions, threatened Leningrad from the north by driving down the Karelian Isthmus. But progress here was slow and Viipuri (Vyborg) was not taken until August 30.

Pressed from both south and north, the Russian general Kliment Voroshilov pulled back what forces he could (about 200,000) inside the city and put the entire population to work constructing defenses. General M. Khozin then took over as commandant of Leningrad. By September 4 the city was under fire but its defenses held.

Leningrad's 3 million people suffered terrible privations during the long siege that followed. Thousands were killed and wounded by artillery shells. More died of starvation and the cold. In winter some food, fuel, and military supplies were slipped through the German blockade over frozen Lake Ladoga.

A Russian attack against the Sixteenth Army at Lake Ilmen in February 1942 failed to drive away the besieging Germans. During the summer, Manstein, who had moved south to conquer the Crimea, was ordered back to this front. He employed the same assault tactics successfully used at Sevastopol but could not penetrate the Leningrad defenses. In January 1943 Gens. Leonid Govorov and Kirill Meretskov led another assault on the Nazi vise but failed to break through. Meanwhile, the German failure to capture the city and the relentless pressure of Russian counterforces resulted in frequent changes in the German top command. Leeb was replaced by Field Marshal Ernst Busch early in 1942 and Busch, in turn, by Field Marshal Georg Kuechler later that summer.

In mid-January 1944 four Russian armies launched a major offensive aimed at breaking the Leningrad siege—Govorov (Leningrad Army), Meretskov (Volkhov Army), Markian Popov (Second Baltic Army), Ivan Bagramian (First Baltic Army). Attacking along a 120-mile front from Lake Ilmen north to Leningrad, Meretskov fought his way into Novgorod on January 15 and 10 days later, aided by Govorov, cleared the east bank of the Volkhov River. The Moscow road to Leningrad was open at last, ending a siege of 31 months. Continuiing to press the erstwhile besiegers westward, the Red armies took Luga on February 14 and Staraya Russia, south of Lake Ilmen, on February 18. Finally, in March, German Field Marshal Walter Model, now in charge of Army Group North, managed to check the Russian advance along the Estonian border at the line Narva–Lake Peipus–Pskov.

The routing of the Germans from Leningrad isolated the Finnish army in the north. In February Finland became the first German satellite to publicly try to break away when it asked for armistice terms from the Soviet Union. Govorov, now promoted to marshal, took command of the drive to knock Finland out of the war, while armistice negotiations proceeded.

On June 10 Govorov's Leningrad Army attacked up the Karelian Isthmus as Russia had done almost five years earlier. In 10 days the Mannerheim Line was again breached as far back as Viipuri (Vyborg). At the same time Meretskov's renamed Karelian Army drove up the railroad toward Murmansk, taking Petrozavodsk on June 29. The front then became quiet while an armistice was arranged. On September 19, for the second time in the war, Finland accepted Russian peace terms.

Meanwhile, southwest of Leningrad, Gen. Lindemann had taken command of German Army Group North during four months of relative inaction. But the quiet was deceptive. Govorov was withdrawing his victorious army from the Karelian Isthmus and wheeling westward. He struck the German left flank north of Lake Peipus, captured Narva on July 26, and plunged into Estonia. At the same time Gen. Ivan Maslennikov's Third Baltic Army was attacking south of Lake Peipus. On July 24 Pskov fell, the last important city in Russia proper to be liberated, opening the way for a Soviet thrust into southern Estonia.

Farther to the south a wider and more devastating Soviet sweep was in progress. Bagramian, assisted by Gen. Andrei Yeremenko, swung northward from Vilnius (taken on July 13) in Lithuania toward the Gulf of Riga. The Russian advance reached Jelgava (Mitau) on August 1 and threatened to splinter the Eighteenth and Sixteenth German armies, now commanded by Gen. Ferdinand Schoerner. In the north Govorov continued his advance through Estonia, capturing the capital of Tallin on September 23 and clearing the entire state by the end of the month. Meanwhile, German troops around the Gulf of Riga counterattacked fiercely to hold open a corridor to the west. Finally, on October 14, Red armies smashed into the city of Riga. But by that time Schoerner (who was later relieved) had managed to withdraw the bulk of his force (12 understrength divisions) to the Kurland (Courland) Peninsula, which juts into the Baltic Sea. Here the three Russian Baltic armies closed them in with a ring of steel. The once-powerful German Army Group North had now been reduced to impotency. Although the trapped force could be supplied only by sea, it held out until the following spring. Then, as part of their overwhelming April offensive that extended deep into central Europe, Russian troops wiped out the last pocket of Nazi resistance in Latvia. *See* Soviet Union (World War II); Moscow; Crimea; Finland (World War II); White Russia; Germany, East; World War II.

Lens (Thirty Years' War), 1648. Action on the Netherlands-French front, which had been relatively quiet after the shattering Spanish defeat at Rocroi in 1643, erupted again in 1648 during the last months of the prolonged peace negotiations. Archduke Leopold William, younger brother of Holy Roman Emperor Ferdinand III, took the offensive. At the head of a rebuilt Austrian-Spanish army, Leopold marched into northwest France toward Arras. In command of the French army on this front was Louis II, the Great Condé, serving the youthful Louis XIV. At Lens, 11 miles northeast of Arras, Condé deceived the Hapsburg army of some 15,000 into thinking he was continuing to retreat. Then he doubled back on August 2 to strike Leopold's column on the march. Although Condé's force was slightly inferior in numbers, the surprise attack of the French overwhelmed the invading army. Almost the entire Hapsburg force was killed, wounded, or captured. This "second Rocroi," plus the earlier loss of Bavaria and the siege of Prague, induced Ferdinand to sign the Treaty of Westphalia on October 24.

Thus ended the Thirty Years' War, one of the most ruinous conflicts in history. The Swedish army alone was charged with destroying 1,500 towns and 18,000 villages. Some of the German states lost more than half their people. Total deaths in Germany have been estimated at 7,500,000, or more than a third of the prewar population. Bands of armed soldiers roamed the countryside for years after, living on the plunder of already impoverished peasants and townspeople. The war accomplished very little. Sweden had become a major power in northern Europe, while the religious and secular hold of the Holy Roman Empire over the German states had been greatly weakened. For France and Spain, however, there was no peace. *See* Rocroi; Zusmarshausen; Arras I; Thirty Years' War.

Lepanto I (Turkish-Venetian Wars), 1499. Late in the fifteenth century the city-republic of Venice wielded so much power that Rome and other Italian states called in the Ottoman Turks as military allies. Under Sultan Bajazet II, the Turks had built up a powerful naval arm. The Ottoman fleet attacked and defeated the Venetian navy off Lepanto (Návpaktos) in southwestern Greece on July 28, 1499. It was the first great sea victory won by the Turks. Venice sued for peace and agreed to give up some of its Grecian trading stations. In the long run, however, the Christian states of Europe would regret their encouragement of Turkish aggression. *See* Shkodër I; Chaldiran; Belgrade II.

Lepanto II (Defeat of Turkish Fleet), 1571. When the Ottoman Turks of Selim II attacked the Venetian-held island of Cyprus in 1570, much of Christian Europe became aroused. On May 20, 1571, Pope Pius V and Philip II of Spain formed a Holy League in support of Venice against the Turks. Don John of Austria, 24-year-old half brother of the Spanish ruler, began assembling an allied fleet at Messina. It consisted of 316 ships, including 208 galleys and 6 double-size galleys called galleasses. The ships carried 30,000 veteran troops and 50,000 mariners. (Each galley carried about 350 men.) Before this armada was ready for battle, Cyprus fell on August 3. But Don John sought out the Turkish fleet off Lepanto (Návpaktos), in southwestern Greece, on October 7. The Ottoman navy, commanded by Ali Pasha, consisted of 250 galleys, including some speedy half-size galleys called galiots, all rowed by slaves chained to benches. Some 16,000 Turkish soldiers of an 88,000-man force stood ready to fight from the decks.

The two hostile forces, both deployed in crescent

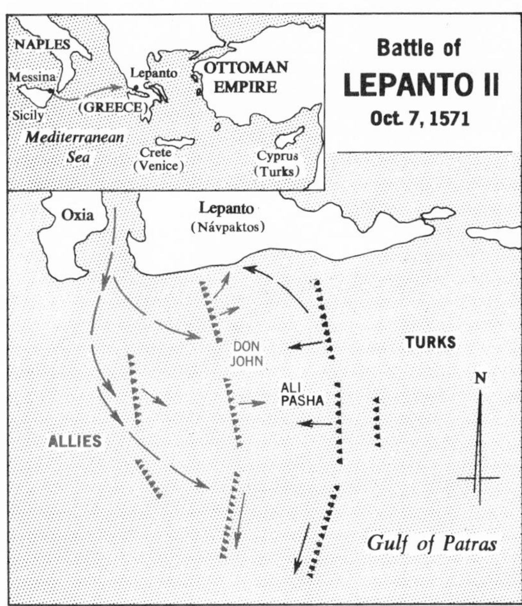

formations, locked together in a furious fight, dominated by ramming and boarding tactics. During three hours of close combat that resembled a land battle, Don John's troops, aided by heavy arquebus fire, gradually gained the upper hand. Some 130 Turkish galleys were captured and another 80 burned or sunk. Ali Pasha, who fell in the battle, lost 25,000 soldiers and mariners killed and 5,000 taken prisoner. Allied losses amounted to 17 ships and 7,500 killed, but twice this number of Christian galley slaves were freed.

Although the Turks soon rebuilt their fleet, they never again achieved the mastery of the Mediterranean that they had held before the battle of Lepanto. The victory of the Spanish and Venetian fleets thus ranks as the greatest naval engagement since the battle of Actium in 31 B.C. Lepanto was also the last great naval battle fought by oar-driven ships. Some of the fruits of the victory were lost, however, when the allies began quarreling among themselves—Spain wanted to attack the Moslems in Africa; Venice wanted to regain Cyprus. In 1573, however, Venice made a separate peace with Selim II, relinquishing its claim to Cyprus. *See* Cyprus; Keresztes.

Leuctra (Greek City-States' Wars), 371 B.C. After 33 years of sporadic warfare, Athens and Sparta agreed to peace terms in 371 B.C. The third member of the truce talks, Thebes, insisted on signing in behalf of all Boeotia. This position by the Theban leader, Epaminondas, caused the negotiations to break down. In July a Spartan force of 10,000 men under King Cleombrotus I marched into Boeotia to punish the Thebans. At Leuctra, ten miles short of the capital, Epaminondas arranged a force of 6,000 Thebans in a new oblique position. Concentrating his heaviest power on the left—48 ranks deep—Epaminondas refused his right flank. The Spartans, organized in the usual line of eight ranks, could not withstand the massed Theban attack on their own right. This wing gave way, collapsing on its center and rolling up the entire Spartan line. The Spartans turned and fled, leaving 2,000 dead on the field, including their king.

The battle of Leuctra shattered Spartan military prestige and ended its chance of establishing hegemony over Greece. Thebes now stood supreme, but its leadership, like that of Athens and Sparta before it, was to be constantly challenged by the fractiousness of neighboring city-states. *See* Naxos; Cynoscephalae I; Mantinea; Greek City-States' Wars.

Leuthen (Seven Years' War), 1757. Frederick II, the Great, was still in Saxony, where he had repulsed the French at Rossbach, when he learned of the Prussian defeat at Breslau (Wroclaw) suffered by his subordinate August Wilhelm, duke of Brunswick-Bevern, on November 22, 1757. Retracing his route, the Prussian king again marched 170 miles in 12 days to reach Liegnitz (Legnica) with only 13,000 effectives. Here he was joined by a motley army of 30,000 men—the leaderless survivors of the Breslau disaster (Brunswick-Bevern had been captured), garrison troops, and raw recruits. Despite the quality and size of his army, Frederick resolved to liberate Breslau immediately. Marching eastward to Leuthen, he found the road blocked by an army of 72,000 Austrians, commanded by prince Charles of Lorraine (Karl Alexander), brother-in-law of Holy Roman Empress Maria Theresa, and by Marshal Count Leopold von Daun.

On the morning of December 5, Frederick approached the Austrians, who were deployed from north to south along a five-mile front. Behind the cover of wooded hills the Prussians swung sharply to their right (south). This brought them opposite the extreme Austrian left, which was organized behind an abatis. His intentions still concealed from the enemy, Frederick ordered up a battery of ten fortress guns, the heaviest concentration of front-line artillery used up to that time. The battle opened with the Prussian artillery blasting the Austrian defense works into splinters. Then the blue-clad infantry rushed forward in an oblique formation, the battalions echeloned to the left so that that wing was refused. The deployment gave the Prussians a heavy superiority at the point of contact. As more and more battalions came into action, the Austrian line was rolled up on itself. At Leuthen village the white-coated Imperial infantry tried to change their front from west to south, but they were overwhelmed. At the same time their cavalry buckled and fled from a charge by

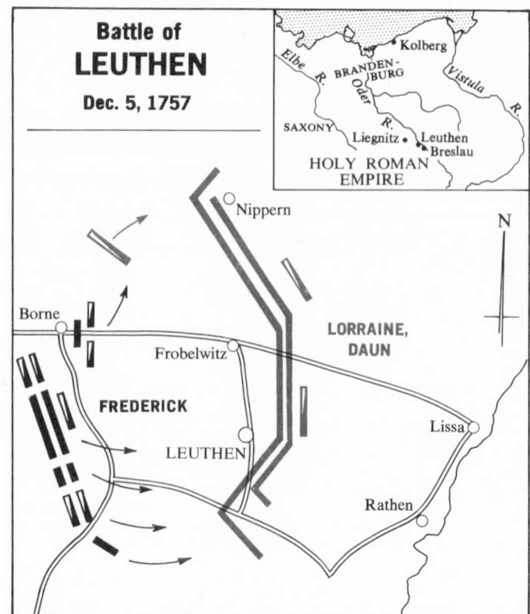

Gen. Hans von Zieten's horsemen. Before dusk ended the combat, 6,000 Austrians were dead or wounded and more than 20,000 had surrendered. Prussian losses in killed and wounded also totaled 6,000.

Frederick's clear-cut victory at Leuthen led to the recapture of Breslau five days later. This closed the fighting for 1757. In a spectacular six-week campaign the Prussian king had overrun Saxony, repulsed the French, and smashed the Austrians so completely that they would not take the field again until late the following summer. *See* Breslau; Rossbach; Olmütz; Seven Years' War.

Leuze (War of the Grand Alliance), 1691. The undefeated general who directed Louis XIV's attack on the Spanish Netherlands was the marshal the Duc de Luxembourg. The year after his clear-cut victory over the Alliance army in 1690, Luxembourg pressed westward from Fleurus. Mons fell in April. Then, 15 miles farther west, Luxembourg again encountered the Dutch and German army, under Prince George Frederick of Waldeck, at Leuze. On September 20 the French attacked and for the second time in the war administered a stinging defeat to the German prince. William III, king of England and stadholder of Holland, now arrived to take command of the Alliance armies. *See* Fleurus II; Steenkerke; Grand Alliance, War of the.

Lewes (Second Barons' War of England), 1264. The royalist forces of Henry III and Prince Edward (later Edward I) received their first setback of the war when they failed to take the Cinque Ports early in May 1264. They then withdrew to Lewes, near the Sussex coast. From London the rebel barons of Simon de Montfort (earl of Leicester) and Gilbert de Clare (earl of Gloucester), marched to attack. Halting nine miles to the north of Lewes, the Montfortians offered to negotiate peace terms. When the king refused, the rebels closed onto the down northwest of the royalist camp on the night of May 13. On the following day Henry's troops attacked the rebels. Prince Edward's knights penetrated the center of the barons' lines but then found themselves beset by both wings of Montfort's armored cavalry. The outmaneuvered royalists were overwhelmed. Before the survivors could escape from the field, Henry, his brother Richard, and Edward were all taken prisoner. King Henry agreed to concessions that secured his release, but Montfort, not the throne, now stood as the greatest power in England. *See* Rochester III; Kenilworth; Barons' Wars.

Lexington and Concord (War of the American Revolution), 1775. During the increasing bitterness between the American colonies and Great Britain, the Continental Congress began organizing the colonial militia. In Massachusetts a military depot was established at Concord, 21 miles from the New England headquarters of the British occupation force at Boston. General Thomas Gage, the British commander in chief in America, resolved to destroy the depot and capture the rebel leaders Samuel Adams and John Hancock. On the night of April 18, 1775, Gage sent 700 troops under Lt. Col. Francis Smith to accomplish the double mission. When the detachment crossed the Charles River, patriots Paul Revere and William Dawes rode rapidly ahead alerting the countryside. The British column reached Lexington, 16 miles from Boston, at dawn. Here they found 70 armed minutemen under Capt. John Parker drawn up on the village common. Although there was no official command, Smith's men opened fire, killing eight and wounding ten of the militiamen. One British soldier was wounded. This was the opening battle of the American Revolutionary War.

Moving on to Concord, a British platoon was attacked at North Bridge, suffering 14 casualties. Early in the afternoon the red-coated column reformed to return to Boston. But now some 4,000 American militiamen had assembled along the road. Firing from behind trees, rocks, and fences, the colonials harassed the return march all the way back to Charlestown. Before they could come under the protective bombardment of their ships in the harbor, the British suffered 73 killed, 174 wounded, and 26 missing. American casualties totaled 95—49 killed, 41 wounded, 5 missing. The colonial militia then closed in around Boston, launching a siege that would last almost a year. Meanwhile other patriots attacked British posts in upper New York. *See* Ticonderoga II; Bunker Hill; American Revolution.

Leyden (Netherlands War of Independence), 1574. The second commander sent out by Philip II of Spain to crush the revolt in the Netherlands was Don Luis de Requeséns. The new Spanish general continued the Duke of Alva's program of pressing southward through the coastal provinces, seeking to cut off the interior from the sea. In 1574 he sent a force of 8,000 men under Gen. Valdez to take Leyden (Leiden) on the Oude River. On May 26 Valdez began surrounding the city with 62 fortified strong points, then settled down to starve the inhabitants into submission.

William I (the Silent) of Orange, leader of the Dutch resistance, ordered the dikes cut south of the city on August 3. He then sent the Dutch fleet of "Sea Beggars" under Louis de Boisot (Sieur de Ruart) over the flood waters to relieve the city. Fighting off the Spanish inland fleet, Boisot's shallow-draft vessels pressed northward and by October 2 were able to throw food into the starving city. The next day Valdez raised the siege and withdrew. The battle had cost the Spanish almost 10,000 men, and it was to be the last major siege operation conducted in the northern provinces that make up the modern Netherlands (but not in the southern provinces—modern Belgium). *See* Alkmaar I; Walcheren; Gembloux; Netherlands War of Independence.

Leyte (World War II), 1944. The road for Gen. Douglas MacArthur's long-promised return to the Philippines became open in September 1944. Striking northward, MacArthur's troops had captured Morotai, between New Guinea and Mindanao, while Adm. Chester Nimitz' III Marine Corps had conquered Peleliu and Angaur islands in the Central Pacific to the east. When the U.S. Third Fleet (William Halsey) found little Japanese opposition on Mindanao (September 9–10), the United States decided to bypass the southern Philippines in favor of a direct assault on Leyte, in the center of the island group. The invasion was assigned to the Sixth Army under Gen. Walter Krueger. The XXIV Corps (7th, 77th, and 96th Infantry divisions) of Gen. John Hodge was transferred from Nimitz' to MacArthur's command to augment the newly organized X Corps (1st Cavalry and 24th Infantry divisions) of Gen. Franklin Sibert. Opposing Krueger's two corps was the Japanese Thirty-fifth Army (Sosaku Suzuki), responsible for defending Mindanao and the Visayan Islands of the central Philippines.

Admiral Thomas Kinkaid's U.S. Seventh Fleet carried the Sixth Army to Leyte under an air umbrella furnished by naval aircraft and Gen. George Kenney's Southwest Pacific Air Forces. On October 17 and 18 U.S. Rangers seized the small islands guarding the eastern entrance to Leyte Gulf. After a two-hour naval bombardment on October 20, four infantry divisions landed on the east coast of Leyte between Tacloban and Dulag, 17 miles to the south. Both the two divisions of the X Corps on the right and the 96th and 7th divisions of the XXIV Corps on the left fought their way inland during the first four days, providing a beachhead large enough to accommodate new airfields. By November 2 the Sixth Army controlled Leyte Valley from Carigara on the north coast to Abuyog in the southeast. On the left the 7th Infantry crossed the island to Baybay on the west coast. But thereafter, progress was slowed by heavy rains and stout Japanese resistance in the mountainous interior. In addition, the Japanese commander in the Philippines, Gen. Tomoyuki Yamashita, was pouring in reinforcements from nearby islands. Some 45,000 Japanese troops landed at Ormoc on the west coast between October 23 and December 11, despite the decisive defeat handed their fleet in the naval battle of Leyte Gulf.

To stop the Japanese build-up, Krueger launched a two-pronged offensive against the Ormoc Valley in November. On the right (north) the X Corps, soon reinforced by the 32nd Infantry division, attacked Limon, the northern gateway to the valley. The village fell, after hard fighting, on December 10. Meanwhile, on the left, the 11th Airborne division joined the XXIV Corps, freeing the 7th Infantry for a second thrust across the island, this time at Balogo, on November 22. Two weeks later the struggle for Ormoc itself began when the 77th Infantry landed at Ipil, three miles to the south. By December 10 Ormoc was taken and contact established with the 7th Division, which in turn had linked up with the 11th Airborne. The two corps then drove up both ends of Ormoc Valley to meet at Libungao on December 20. The last Japanese port on Leyte, Palompon on the northwest coast, was seized Christmas Day. The following day Gen. Robert Eichelberger's Eighth Army assumed command on the island (XXIV Corps was assigned to the Okinawa invasion). It took another four months before all pockets of resistance were eliminated on Leyte and the nearby coast of Samar, to the northeast.

The battle of Leyte was a major victory for the United States. Japanese determination to hold the island enabled U.S. forces to inflict irreplaceable losses in ships and aircraft. In addition, the Niponnese ground troops lost six divisions totaling more than 70,000 men. American casualties were 15,584, including 3,584 killed. *See* Philippine Islands; New Guinea; Peleliu-Angaur; Leyte Gulf; Luzon; World War II.

Leyte Gulf (World War II), 1944. The U.S. invasion of Leyte on October 20 threatened to sever Japan's vital oil supply from the East Indies. In a desperate effort to hold the Philippines, Adm. Soemu Toyoda ordered the Japanese fleet to take the offensive according to a clever plan. The resulting battle became one of the largest and most complex engagements in naval history.

On October 22 Adm. Jisaburo Ozawa left Japanese waters for the Philippines with a force of four carriers, two battleships, three cruisers, and eight destroyers. This so-called Northern Force was to serve as bait to draw Adm. William Halsey's Third Fleet away from Leyte Gulf. (In anticipation of losing this entire force, Toyoda held his six largest carriers back in Japan.) At the same time two other Japanese task forces were converging on the Philippines from the west. The plan called for these forces to drive off Adm. Thomas Kinkaid's Seventh Fleet and then to annihilate the unprotected U.S. assault forces in Leyte Gulf. The left hook of the attack, the Center Force, was directed by Adm. Takeo Kurita. With 5 battleships, 12 cruisers, and 15 destroyers, Kurita headed for the Sibuyan Sea and San Bernardino Strait, planning to enter Leyte Gulf from the north. The right hook of the attack was actually two groups—Adm. Shoji Nishimura (two battleships, one cruiser, four destroyers) and Adm. Kiyohide Shima (three cruisers, four destroyers). This Southern Force approached Leyte Gulf from the south through the Sulu and Mindanao seas.

The chief weakness of the U.S. naval forces protecting the Leyte invasion was the command setup. Halsey's Third Fleet (16 carriers, 6 battleships, 15 cruisers, 58 destroyers) was directed by Adm. Chester Nimitz, commander in chief of the Pacific Fleet. On the other hand, Kinkaid's Seventh Fleet (16 escort carriers, 6 battleships, 11 cruisers, 86 destroyers) was part of Gen. Douglas MacArthur's Southwest Pacific Command.

The battle opened on October 23, two days ahead of the Japanese timetable, when Kurita's Center Force was attacked by two U.S. submarines off Palawan in the South China Sea. The *Darter* and *Dace* sank two cruisers (including the flagship, *Atago*) and crippled a third. The following day carrier planes from the Third Fleet made five air strikes against the Center Force in the Sibuyan Sea. Five warships suffered damage, and the superbattleship *Musashi* capsized with a loss of half its 2,200-man complement. Kurita, complaining to his superiors by radio about lack of air cover, turned back west. Meanwhile, east of the Philippines, 76 planes from Ozawa's Northern Force struck the Third Fleet and destroyed the carrier *Princeton,* but at a cost of 56 Japanese planes. Halsey then took the bait and steamed north, uncovering the Leyte beachhead.

On the following day, October 25, the battle of Leyte Gulf fragmented into three separate engagements.

Surigao Strait. To block the southern entrance into Leyte Gulf, Kinkaid gave Adm. Jesse Oldendorf command of the Seventh Fleet's fighting ships. During the early morning darkness of October 25, Oldendorf ambushed the Japanese Southern Force as it emerged from Surigao Strait.

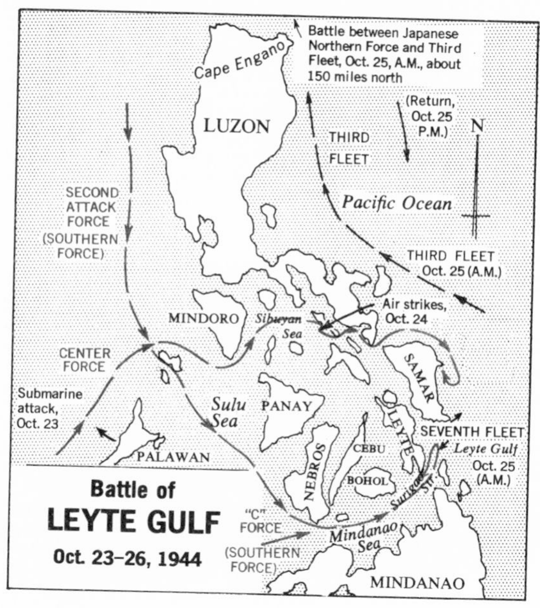

Battle of LEYTE GULF Oct. 23–26, 1944

American PT boats, destroyers, and capital ships destroyed six of Nishimura's seven ships in less than two hours. Shima, steaming 40 miles behind with his seven-ship force, reversed his course and withdrew, losing only a light cruiser. In what may have been the last line battle of naval history, the United States suffered one damaged destroyer.

Cape Engaño. At dawn on October 25, after the Seventh Fleet's night victory in Surigao Strait, Halsey's Third Fleet located the Japanese Northern Force off Cape Engaño of northeastern Luzon. Five fierce U.S. air strikes sank all four of Ozawa's bait carriers, plus a destroyer. Just as the Third Fleet's fighting ships were on the verge of annihilating the entire enemy force, Halsey received distress calls from Leyte Gulf and stopped the attack. Kurita's Center Force had reversed course again, passed through San Bernardino Strait, and was threatening to destroy the near-defenseless amphibious forces in the Gulf. Halsey turned around and started a 300-mile race to the south.

Samar. When Kurita debouched from San Bernardino Strait on the morning of October 25, he turned south toward Leyte Gulf. Halfway down the east coast of Samar Island, he encountered a Seventh Fleet force of six escort carriers and seven destroyers and destroyer escorts under Adm. Clifton Sprague. The American ships tried to flee from the stronger, faster enemy force. Despite the desperate maneuvers of his screening vessels, plus fierce attacks by carrier planes, Sprague's force stood in danger of total destruction. But after two hours of heavy shelling, Kurita suddenly called off the chase and retired northward toward San Bernardino Strait. Only the carrier *Gambier Bay* and three escorting ships had been sunk, while the Japanese had lost three cruisers. Kurita's extraordinary withdrawal probably prevented a major disaster to the thin-skinned assault shipping of the Seventh Fleet. On October 26 the battle of Leyte Gulf ended with U.S. carrier planes sinking an additional cruiser from Kurita's fleeing Center Force in the Sulu Sea.

Japan failed utterly to attain its main objective of destroying the amphibious shipping in Leyte Gulf. The battle cost the Nipponese more than 300,000 tons of combat ships—three battleships, four carriers, ten cruisers, and nine destroyers—and ruined their fleet's capacity to fight another naval battle. The United States lost 37,000 tons of fighting ships—one light and two escort carriers, two destroyers and one destroyer escort. One of the escort carriers, the *St. Lo* (as well as three other damaged carriers), was the victim of the first *kamikaze* (divine wind) attacks by Japanese pilots who suicidally dive-bombed their planes into American ships. The way was now open for further Allied conquests in the Philippines and on islands even closer to Japan. *See* Leyte; Luzon; Iwo Jima; World War II.

Liaoyang (Russian-Japanese War), 1904. After crossing the Yalu River on May 1, the Japanese army in southern Manchuria pressed steadily northwest to the railroad running north from Port Arthur. During this march Field Marshal Marquis Iwao Oyama built up his invading force to seven well-armed divisions. When Oyama turned north along the railroad, he began encountering stiffened Russian resistance, directed by Gen. Aleksei Kuropatkin. At Liaoyang, 35 miles south of Mukden, the Russians had amassed about 100,000 men, an army comparable in size to Oyama's. Beginning on August 25, the two hostile armies clashed on a broad front. The battle quickly deteriorated into a series of local encounters. For six days the Japanese gained little ground in a violent slugging match. Then on September 1 the Russians counterattacked for two days. Oyama checked the enemy offensive only by committing all his reserves. At this point Kuropatkin gave up the battle and withdrew northward. In the first great land battle of the war the Japanese suffered 23,500 casualties, the retreating Russians 16,500. *See* Yalu River II; Shaho River; Russian-Japanese War.

Liége (World War I), 1914. The greatest war in history up to that time began with a German invasion of Belgium as a route of attack against France. Belgium, ruled by King Albert I, had remained neutral while the great powers of Europe armed for all-out war. When the German armies of Kaiser Wilhelm II crossed the border for a right-wing sweep toward Paris, however, the Belgians resisted fiercely despite tremendous odds. The first German attack struck Liége, the gateway to Belgium, on the left bank of the Meuse River, on August 4, 1914. Here Gen. Otto von Emmich's specially organized German Army of the Meuse (six brigades) pushed between the forts east of the river to enter the city on August 7. The citadel surrendered to Gen. Erich Ludendorff the same day. But 11 of the 12 forts ringing the city, under the command of Gen. Gérard Leman, held out until blasted into submission by 420- and 305-mm. siege mortars during August 13–16. Leman was taken prisoner. On the following day the German First, Second, and Third armies under Field Marshal Helmuth von Moltke began their gigantic turning movement (the Schlieffen Plan) through Belgium. To avoid being cut off, the Belgian army pulled back to Antwerp. This movement left Brussels to be occupied without resistance by the 320,000 men of Gen. Alexander von Kluck's First Army, beginning on August 20. *See* Haelen; Namur II; World War I.

Liegnitz I (Mongol Invasion of Europe), 1241. The powerful right hook that the Mongols had thrown against Poland shattered the army of Boleslav V at Cracow in March 1241. (Meanwhile, the main body of Asiatics was knifing into Hungary.) Pushing on westward from Cracow through Breslau (Wroclaw), the Mongol army of Kaidu, grandson of Genghis Khan, encountered a second Christian army at Wahlstatt, near Liegnitz (Legnica), on April 9. This European force, commanded by Henry II, duke of Silesia, consisted of German infantry, mounted Teutonic knights, and the remnants of the Polish force defeated at Cracow the previous month. Strong in numbers but lacking cohesion and able leadership, the European army disintegrated before the hard-hitting attacks of the Mongol horse archers. When the Asiatics drew their swords and charged Henry's decimated ranks, the rout became total. The duke and his barons died to a man. With the right flank now secure, Kaidu's Mongols crossed the central Carpathians to join the main body in Hungary. *See* Cracow; Mohi; Mongol Wars.

Liegnitz II (Seven Years' War), 1760. The defeat suffered by a subordinate at Landeshut in June 1760 prompted Frederick II, the Great, to march his Prussian army into Silesia. He reached Liegnitz (Legnica) on August 15, but here his 30,000-man army was all but surrounded by some 90,000 troops, consisting of an army of Russians (Empress Elizabeth) and two Austrian armies of the Holy Roman Empire (Maria Theresa). The Prussians, exhausted by hard marching and short of supplies, tried to slip away to the north on the night of August 15. In the dark they slammed against an Austrian army under Baron Gideon von Laudon, which was moving to close the last escape route. In a wild melee Frederick's men cut the Austrian column to pieces, inflicting 10,000 casualties and capturing 82 guns. The Prussian king resumed his retreat unmolested by his enemies. But while Frederick was still in Silesia, Berlin was raided by Cossacks and burned, during October 9–12. Frederick hurried north but turned left to Torgau when he learned that the major Austrian forces were concentrating there. *See* Landeshut; Torgau; Seven Years' War.

Liesna (Great Northern War), 1708. To avoid the scorched-earth program of the Russians of Peter I, the Great, Charles XII of Sweden turned away from the Moscow road to march into the Ukraine. It was a fateful decision. His allies, the Cossacks of hetman Ivan Mazepa, proved to be far weaker than the Swedish king had anticipated. And even more serious was the increased danger to the Swedish supply column that was moving from Riga southward to Charles's aid. Under Gen. Adam Lewenhaupt, the hundreds of heavily loaded wagons now had to move many miles beyond their planned junction with the Swedish army.

The Russians advanced to strike the exposed flank of the supply column near the course of the Dnieper. In September 1708 a series of hit-and-run attacks gradually began to wear down the 11,000-man escort Lewenhaupt commanded. Outnumbered 4 to 1, the Swedes on October 9 finally had to destroy their artillery and supplies near the village of Liesna and cut their way out. Only about half the force escaped their Russian tormentors to join Charles in the Ukraine. Russian losses probably totaled 10,000. *See* Holowczyn; Poltava; Great Northern War.

"Light Brigade, Charge of the." *See* Balaclava.

Ligny (Napoleon's Hundred Days), 1815. Less than a year after accepting exile on Elba, Napoleon Bonaparte landed back in France, on March 1, 1815. The French, unhappy with the restored Bourbon rule and knowing of the discord at the Congress of Vienna, rose to his support. King Louis XVIII fled to Belgium, while Austria, Great Britain, Prussia, and Russia united to send huge armies against the quickly rearming French nation. Requiring an early military success, Napoleon sent his hastily mobilized army northward. Crossing the Belgian frontier on June 14, he seized Charleroi, thereby driving a wedge between the Anglo-Dutch army of the Duke of Wellington (Arthur Wellesley) to the west and the Prussian army of Field Marshal Gen. Gebhard von Blücher to the east. This bold stroke caught the allied commanders still assembling their forces.

On June 16 Napoleon ordered Marshal Michel Ney, in command of the French left wing, to take Quatre Bras, on the road to Brussels. Napoleon himself, with 77,000 troops, struck the slightly larger army of Blücher at Ligny. In a savage, no-quarter assault the French dislodged the Prussians from Ligny. As darkness ended the fighting, Blücher pulled back to the north with a loss of 28,000 men, including some 12,000 who deserted during the night. French casualties totaled 11,500. Napoleon had achieved his objective of forcing Blücher away from Wellington. *See* Tolentino; Quatre Bras; Wavre; Waterloo; Napoleon's Hundred Days.

Lille (War of the Spanish Succession), 1708. After his clear-cut victory at Oudenarde, the Duke of Marlborough (John Churchill) sent Prince Eugene of Savoy southward to besiege the French fortress of Lille in Flanders. Eugene arrived outside the walls on August 12, 1708, and started investing the city, while Marlborough covered the siege. Both Marshal Louis Joseph (duc de Vendôme) and the Duke of Berwick (James Fitz-james, natural-born nephew of Marlborough) came up with a relieving force but were unable to penetrate the English-Dutch-German screen. Meanwhile, inside the city the aged but valiant Marshal Duc Louis de Boufflers, with a garrison of 15,000 men, fought off a succession of bloody assaults. The siege settled down to a battle of supply lines. When Marlborough opened and then successfully defended a line of communications to Oostende, on the North Sea, the doom of Lille was sealed. The city surrendered on October 25, although the citadel held out until December 8. In all, the French lost about 7,000 men, the allies half that number.

Marlborough followed up his victory at Lille by recapturing Bruges before the end of the year and Gent (Ghent) early in January. These victories completely reversed the military situation. Louis XIV wanted peace now, but as no acceptable terms were offered, the war dragged on. *See* Oudenarde; Tournai; Spanish Succession, War of the.

Lilybaeum (First Punic War), 250–241 B.C. The Roman offensive in Sicily finally reduced the Carthaginian hold to the west coast of the island. Here stood the fortress of Lilybaeum, defended by a 10,000-man garrison. A strong Roman force attacked the stronghold and, when the Carthaginians resisted, laid siege to it. The legionaries invested the outer walls but could not break through the inner ramparts. Meanwhile, the superior Punic sailors eluded the blockading Roman vessels to resupply the garrison. Publius Claudius (Pulcher) took command of the siege the following year. After his fleet was virtually annihilated in the naval battle off Drepanum (Trapani), the siege became limited to the Roman land forces. Beginning in 247, the defense of the fortress was directed by Hamilcar Barca, the able father of the brilliant Hannibal, from his headquarters on Mount Eryx (Monte San Giuliano), 22 miles to the north. Lilybaeum held out until a severe naval defeat in the Aegates Islands caused Carthage to accept peace terms in 241. *See* Panormus; Drepanum; Aegates Islands; Punic Wars.

Limerick (Resistance to the Glorious Revolution), 1691. After defeats on the Boyne River and at Aughrim, the Irish rebellion against the English rule of William III began to peter out. The last stronghold held by the Jacobite rebels was Limerick, a seaport on the Shannon River which, under the Earl of Lucan (Patrick Sarsfield), had broken a siege by the English king in 1690. In the summer of 1691 royalists commanded by William's lieutenant in Ireland, Gen. Godert de Ginkel (later Earl of Athlone), instituted a new siege. Lucan again directed the defense, but this time the city's situation was hopeless. On October 3 the garrison surrendered. Under the terms of the so-called pacification of Limerick, the Irish supporters of the deposed James II were allowed to take an oath of allegiance to William III and Mary or to leave the country. Some toleration was granted Roman Catholics. Thus another English-Irish conflict came to an end. *See* Aughrim; Glencoe; Jacobite Insurrections.

Lincoln I (The English Anarchy), 1141. In the confused fighting of the Anarchy period, Stephen of Blois struggled hard to hold the English crown against the claims of his cousin Maud (Matilda). In besieging Lincoln castle, which had been lost to Ranulf, earl of Chester, late in 1140, Stephen was attacked by a relieving force of Maud's supporters. Led across the Trent River by Robert, earl of Gloucester (half brother of Maud), and Ranulf, the rebels defeated the royalists and took Stephen captive on February 2, 1141. During the latter's imprisonment at Bristol, Maud was enthroned in Winchester. But her rule proved to be brief. *See* Standard, The; Winchester, England.

Lincoln II (First Barons' War of England), 1217. The barons who had rebelled against King John continued their revolt against his son and successor, Henry III. In the southeast one baronial group, commanded by Prince Louis of France, pretender to the English throne, campaigned against Dover. Another group of rebels laid siege to Lincoln in the Midlands. Here, however, William Marshal (1st earl of Pembroke and Strigul), regent for the young Henry, marched 400 knights to the relief of the city. The royalists broke through the siege lines to enter Lincoln on May 20, 1217. All day the dismounted royalists fought in the streets against some 600 baronial and French knights led by the Count of Perche. Although a total of only three knights (including Perche) were killed, many of the unarmored retainers were slaughtered. Finally almost half the rebel knights surrendered, in what was derisively called "the Fair of Lincoln." This victory, coupled with a royalist naval victory off Dover, persuaded many barons to give up the revolt. *See* Rochester II; Dover I; Sandwich I; Barons' Wars.

Linköping (Swedish-Polish Wars), 1598. Sigismund III, who became king of Poland in 1587, inherited the crown of Sweden five years later. His attempts to re-establish Catholicism in Sweden led to a revolt by Protestant forces under his uncle Charles. The royal army clashed with the rebels at Linköping, 110 miles southwest of Stockholm, in 1598. Sigismund was thoroughly beaten. Charles became hereditary prince of Sweden, deposed his nephew, and in 1604 ascended the Swedish throne as Charles IX. *See* Polotsk; Riga I.

Lippe River (Germanic Wars of the Roman Empire), 11 B.C. To safeguard the development of Gaul, the Roman emperor Augustus (Octavian) found it necessary to stop the Germanic tribes from raiding westward across the Rhine. In the spring of 11 B.C. Augustus sent an army under his stepson Drusus to subdue the Germans. Drusus crossed the Rhine and successfully ascended the valley of the Lippe. He marched far to the north, meeting little opposition. On its return to the Lippe, however, Drusus' army was surrounded by a huge force composed of several Germanic tribes. The destruction of the Roman army seemed so certain that the Germans were reported to have apportioned the spoils of conquest in advance. But Drusus was an able, aggressive commander. He struck hard at the encirclement, broke through the enemy lines, and routed them with heavy losses. After constructing a fort near the Lippe at Aliso, Drusus returned to Gaul.

Two years later Drusus took another successful pacifying expedition into Germany. On his way back he was killed in a fall from his horse. In 8 B.C. an older brother, Tiberius (later emperor), accepted the submission of the German tribes without a battle. *See* Actium; Teutoburger Wald; Roman Empire.

Lisbon (Portuguese-Moslem Wars), 1147. Two different crusades merged in Portugal in the spring of 1147. A fleet of the Second Crusade, sailing down the west coast of Europe, put in at Oporto on the Douro River. Here the crusaders found the Christian Alfonso I, who had become the first king of an independent Portugal, preparing an attack on the Moorish stronghold of Lisbon. The Crusaders agreed to help the Portuguese. Additional naval strength came from a squadron of English, Flemish, and Frisian ships, which had also been on the way to the Holy Land. The combined force moved south to the mouth of the Tagus River and laid siege to the Lisbon fortress by sea and land. After four months of heavy fighting, the Moorish garrison surrendered. The victors, lacking a single supreme commander, ignored the surrender agreement and executed most of the Moslem prisoners. Alfonso made Lisbon the capital of his young kingdom. Unfortunately for the Second Crusade in the Near East, most of the members of the fleet from the north settled down in Portugal. Only a few ships pushed on across the Mediterranean. *See* Ourique; Santarém I.

Little Bighorn River (Sioux War II), 1876. Despite the check received by Gen. George Crook's troops on the Rosebud River, two other army columns pushed into the Sioux country of southeastern Montana. The commanders, Gen. Alfred Terry and Col. John Gibbon, planned to link up on the Little Bighorn River on June 26. Lieutenant Colonel George Custer with 600 troopers of the 7th Cavalry was detached from Terry's force to make a preliminary reconnaissance. Force marching 83 miles in 24 hours, Custer reached the river on June 25. Here at noon he divided his force into three groups. It was a tragic decision. Across the river stood a Sioux and Cheyenne village with 3,000 to 3,500 warriors led by Sitting Bull, Crazy Horse, and Gall.

Major Marcus Reno with three troops of cavalry moved across the river upstream to attack from the south. On his left rode Capt. Frederick Benteen, also with three troops. Custer himself took five troops downstream. (One troop stayed behind to guard the pack train.) Reno, on the west side

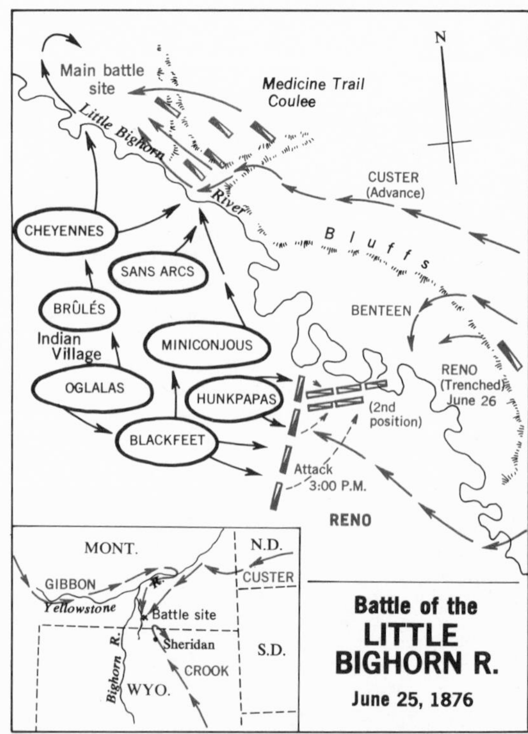

of the Little Bighorn, met a superior force of Indians and was driven back across the river to a defensive position on high bluffs. Here he was later joined by Benteen's troopers. Together they stood off a persistent attack for the remainder of the day and all of June 26, at a cost of 53 killed and 52 wounded.

Meanwhile downstream, opposite the flank and rear of the village, Custer was suddenly assaulted by Indians pouring across the river both north and south of him. Many of them were Gall's warriors who had just routed Reno's force. In one desperate hour Custer and all his 211 men were completely overwhelmed. Not a man survived what has come to be known as "Custer's Last Stand." Terry and Gibbon came up with their columns on June 27 to relieve the beleaguered Reno-Benteen force. It was the U.S. Army's worst defeat in the long bloody history of Indian warfare. *See* Rosebud River; Wolf Mountain; Indian Wars in the United States.

Loano (Wars of the French Revolution), 1795. The first battle of the war in Italy took place in the fall of 1795. Defeated in the Netherlands the previous year, Holy Roman Emperor Francis II concentrated his Austrian army in northern Italy, hoping to drive out the French invasion forces. But at Loano on the Italian Riviera the French commander, Gen. Barthélemy Schérer, met and defeated the Austrians on November 24. From Paris, Napoleon Bonaparte, who had routed a mob with artillery (October 5) and subsequently became head of the Army of the Interior, ordered Schérer to launch a grand-scale offensive in Italy. When Schérer balked, the Corsican general himself took command. *See* Fleurus III; Montenotte; French Revolution Wars.

Lobositz (Seven Years' War), 1756. The rise of Prussia during the War of the Austrian Succession (including the first two Silesian Wars) provoked a new alignment of European powers. Great Britain (George II), fearing a French attack on Hannover, formed an alliance with Frederick II, the Great, of Prussia. In opposition stood a coalition of Austria and the Holy Roman Empire (Maria Theresa), France (Louis XV), Russia (Elizabeth), Sweden, and Saxony. Knowing of the ring organized against him, Frederick struck first. On August 29, 1756, he marched into Saxony, thus launching the Third Silesian War, better known as the Seven Years' War (in North America the conflict between Great Britain and France, called the French and Indian War, was already two years old). It was the first true world war.

The Prussian army occupied Dresden on September 2, while the 18,000-man Saxon force fell back 11 miles to the southeast, to Pirna on the Elbe River. To aid the distressed Saxons, Field Marshal Count Maximilian von Browne hurried up from Bohemia with an Austrian army of 30,000 men. Frederick moved farther up the Elbe to meet him with an army of equal size. The two forces clashed at Lobositz (Lovosice), in northwestern Bohemia, on the morning of October 1. A thick fog and rough ground broke the battle into a series of battalion-sized engagements. In this type of fighting the discipline and tenacity of the Prussian troops proved superior. The Austrians were beaten back with a loss of 3,000 men. Frederick's casualties were as heavy.

The Prussian victory at Lobositz sealed the doom of the Saxon army at Pirna. They surrendered on October 15 and were immediately impressed into Prussian service. This ended the fighting for 1756. War was now officially declared all around and Frederick prepared to take the offensive again the following year. *See* Minorca I; Oswego; Prague IV; Seven Years' War.

Lodi Bridge (Wars of the French Revolution), 1796. After knocking the kingdom of Sardinia (Piedmont) out of the war in April 1796, Napoleon Bonaparte turned his French army northeast against the 24,000-man Austrian army of Gen. Baron Jean de Beaulieu. On May 7 he crossed to the north side of the Po, while Beaulieu with 24,000 troops fell back northeast beyond the Adda River. The road was now open to Milan, but first Napoleon wanted to safeguard his right flank. Veering eastward, he entered Lodi on May 10, setting up a battery of 30 guns to blast the Austrian defenses across the Adda. Late in the day Gen. André Masséna's division charged across the 200-yard-long wooden bridge. Austrian cannon and musket fire riddled the cramped column on the narrow bridge. But the inspired assault swept forward, despite some 400 casualties, to bayonet the defenders away from their guns. When other columns forded the Adda above and below Lodi, Beaulieu fell back toward Mantua. In all, each side suffered about 2,000 casualties. Napoleon then marched 20 miles northwest to enter Milan in triumph. Six days later he set up the Lombard Republic. *See* Mondovì; Mantua; Lonato; French Revolution Wars.

Lódź (World War I), 1914. Following the collapse of the German drive on Warsaw in September and October and in anticipation of a Russian attack into Silesia, the German commander in chief on the Eastern Front, Field Marshal Paul von Hindenburg, moved the German Ninth Army northward by rail to the Posen-Thorn (Poznań-Toruń) area. Here, under the immediate command of Gen. August von Mackensen, the Germans attacked southeast toward Warsaw on November 11. South of the Vistula River, Mackensen struck hard at the Russian First Army of Gen. Pavel Rennenkampf and drove it back. Keeping up their pressure, the Germans advanced 50 miles in four days. By November 16 Mackensen had penetrated deeply between the Russian First Army and the Second Army to the south.

The Russian high command had indeed launched an invasion of Silesia on November 14. Two days later it was recalled, and the Fifth Army rushed northward to aid the Second Army, now threatened with encirclement in front of Lódź. Marching 70 miles in 48 hours, the Fifth checked Mackensen's right flank on November 19. In confused fighting the German XXV R Corps, east of Lódź, was surrounded and only barely fought its way free. Finally, on December 6, the Russians abandoned Lódź to straighten their line below Warsaw. Although the German attack had failed to crush the Russian Second Army, it had successfully eliminated the threat to Silesia. *See* Vistula River–Warsaw; Masurian Lakes II; World War I.

Loja (Spanish-Moslem Wars), 1486. The Spanish counteroffensive against the Moorish kingdom of Granada began with the conquest of the key western strong point of Alhama de Granada in 1482. Later King Ferdinand V of Castile (II of Aragon) moved against the second Moorish fortress to the west, Loja, but was beaten off. In 1486, however, Ferdinand returned to the attack. His Spanish troops stormed into Loja and reduced it. Now the Moors' capital of Granada lay only 21 miles away. But to the south the Moslems still held the seaport of Málaga. *See* Alhama de Granada; Málaga I.

Lonato (Wars of the French Revolution), 1796. When Napoleon Bonaparte pushed the Austrian army of Gen. Baron Jean de Beaulieu beyond (east of) the Adige River on May 30, 1796, he sent a French force southwestward to besiege Mantua. But before he could take the surrender of the fortress on the Mincio River, Field Marshal Count Dagobert von Wurmser debouched from the Alps with a fresh army of 50,000 Austrians, divided into three columns. Napoleon abandoned the line of the Adige and stripped the force around Mantua to concentrate most of his 43,000 troops at Lonato, near the southern end of Lake Garda. Here he deployed against the right-flank column of the Austrian army, which had been threatening the French line of communications back to Milan while moving down the western side of Lake Garda. On August 3 Napoleon attacked this force, which was led by Gen. Quasdanovitch, and put it to route before the slow-moving Wurmser could come to its aid from the east. Quasdanovitch retreated up the lake. *See* Mantua; Castiglione delle Stiviere; French Revolution Wars.

Londonderry (Resistance to the Glorious Revolution), 1689. The aggressive Catholicism of James II led to his deposition as king of England in 1688. The throne then passed to his son-in-law and daughter, William III of Orange and Mary. In the following spring James landed in Ireland, immediately enlisting the support of the Duke of Tyrconnel (Richard Talbot) and many other Irish. From Dublin James's Catholic army (called Jacobites) marched northward to lay siege to the royalist town of Londonderry on April 17. The Protestant garrison of several thousand men under Maj. Henry Baker held out stubbornly for 105 days. Finally on July 30 a naval expedition commanded by Col. Percy Kirke broke the boom laid across the Foyle River and brought relief to the starving survivors. Thereupon James abandoned the siege. Three days later the ex-king received another setback when his followers were routed at Newton Butler after a foolhardy attack on the royalist town of Enniskillen. Meanwhile England had become embroiled in the War of the Grand Alliance against France. *See* Bantry Bay; Killiecrankie; Boyne River; Jacobite Insurrections.

Long Island (War of the American Revolution), 1776. After abandoning Boston in March 1776, Gen. Sir William Howe prepared a British expedition against New York City. Anticipating the enemy's move, Gen. George Washington shifted his American army southward to defend the strategic port. Between August 22 and 25, Howe, with the aid of a British fleet under his brother Adm. Lord Richard Howe, landed 20,000 troops on the southwestern end of Long Island. Here the American general Israel Putnam commanded a force of some 7,000 men. On the British left (west) Gen. James Grant faced the American right wing under Gen. William Alexander, known as Lord Stirling. To the east, the German general Philip von Heister, commanding a force of Hessian mercenaries, opposed Gen. John Sullivan. On the night of August 26 Howe unleashed his main effort, a wide circling movement to the right led by Gen. Sir Henry Clinton. On the following morning Clinton struck the left rear of the American position, caving it in. Only desperate rear-guard fighting enabled the American army to fall back behind the defenses on Brooklyn Heights. But they suffered 1,500 casualties, including 200 killed, to the British 400. Both Sullivan and Stirling were captured.

Howe's army pressed forward all along the line but did not assault the Brooklyn breastworks. Instead, the British commander began a siege operation. However, on the night of August 29 Washington skillfully withdrew Putnam's army to Manhattan Island. Two weeks later Washington made a second retreat, to Harlem Heights at the northern end of the island. This move prevented his being outflanked when the British crossed the East River to land at Kip's Bay on September 15. *See* Bunker Hill; Valcour Island; White Plains; American Revolution.

"Long War." *See* Keresztes.

Lookout Mountain (American Civil War). The second action in the battle of Chattanooga, on November 24, 1863, in which Gen. Braxton Bragg's Confederates unexpectedly lost the key height south of the city. *See* Chattanooga.

Loos (World War I). The British contribution (September 25–October 8) to the Allied offensive in Artois. *See* Artois-Loos.

Lorraine (World War I). The easternmost part of the massive battle fought along the French frontier during August 20–24, 1914, in which the first French and German offensives of the war met head on. *See* Frontiers of France.

Lose-coat Field (Wars of the Roses), 1470. The royalist defeat at Banbury in 1469 had placed King Edward IV under the firm control of his younger brother the Duke of Clarence and of the Earl of Warwick, the Kingmaker. Edward, however, only waited for an opportunity to reassert his royal power. Under the pretext of suppressing a small uprising in Lincolnshire, the king ordered an army into the field early in 1470. On March 12 the royal troops suddenly confronted the rebels at Empingham in Rutlandshire. The surprised insurgents hurriedly fled the field, shedding their coats to speed their escape (hence the name of the battlefield). Robert Welles, their leader, was captured. Before his beheading, he implicated Warwick and Clarence in the Lincolnshire conspiracy. Both of these men promptly fled to the Continent to make an alliance with the exiled Lancastrian (red rose) Queen Margaret and her son Edward. *See* Hexham; Ravenspur II; Roses, Wars of the.

Lostwithiel (English Civil War), 1644. Despite the overwhelming defeat at Marston Moor, which cost him the entire north of England, King Charles I continued to defy the Roundheads. From his Oxford headquarters he marched westward in pursuit of the 3rd Earl of Essex (Robert Devereux), who was invading the Royalist stronghold of Cornwall. On September 2, 1644, Charles's Cavalier army fell on the rear of Essex's force and quickly surrounded it at Lostwithiel, 30 miles west of Plymouth. The Roundhead commander and most of his cavalry cut their way out. But virtually all the infantrymen, about 8,000, and the artillery fell into the king's hands. Charles now wheeled about and marched toward London. *See* Marston Moor; Newbury II; English Civil War.

Loudon Hill (English-Scottish Wars), 1307. After spending the winter of 1306–07 in exile, the Scottish leader Robert I, the Bruce, self-proclaimed king, returned to renew the war against England. The Scots rallied to his command at Loudon Hill in Ayr County of southwestern Scotland. Here the English army, under the Earl of Pembroke, marched in May. Recklessly the English mounted knights charged the massed Scottish spearmen. The Scots held their ground, repulsing the onslaught with heavy losses.

The defeat enraged the English king, Edward I. Although confined to a litter by old age and infirmities, he took personal charge of the campaign. On July 7, however, he died at Burgh-by-Sands, near the Solway Firth. His son assumed the crown as Edward II, but the new king withdrew the army and abandoned the war against Scotland for seven years. *See* Methven; Bannockburn.

Louis XIV, Wars of (1667–1714). During his 72-year reign over France, King Louis XIV fought four major wars.

1. War of Devolution (1667–1668). France, without fighting a battle, occupied and retained 12 fortified towns on the border of the Spanish Netherlands (modern Belgium). These included Lille, Tournay, and Oudenarde.

2. The Second, or Dutch, War (1672–1679). Angered at the opposition of the Netherlands during the War of Devolution, Louis XIV marched against the Dutch. Under William III of Orange (later William III of England) the Netherlands won the support of the Elector of Brandenburg (Frederick William), the Holy Roman Emperor (Leopold I), and Spain (Charles II). The war raged in the Low Countries, along the Rhine, and in the Mediterranean Sea. In a series of treaties between 1678 and 1679, Louis was the major victor, gaining part of Flanders and Franche-Comté. To these territories Louis XIV added Lorraine, Luxembourg, Trier, and Strasbourg by occupation, during 1680–84, in the so-called War of the Reunions.

Maastricht II	1673
Sinsheim	1674
Seneffe	1674
Enzheim	1674
Turckheim	1675
Sasbach	1675
Stromboli	1676
Augusta	1676
Mons I	1678

3. War of the Grand Alliance (1688–1697); also called War of the League of Augsburg, or King William's War. *See* Grand Alliance, War of the.

4. War of the Spanish Succession (1701–1714); also called Queen Anne's War. *See* Spanish Succession, War of the.

Louisbourg I (King George's War), 1745. To guard the entrance to the Saint Lawrence River, France, under Louis XV, fortified Louisbourg on Cape Breton Island, between 1720 and 1740. It was believed to be the strongest fortress in the Western Hemisphere. However, during the War of the Austrian Succession—called King George's (II) War in America—the British determined to capture it. An English fleet under Com. Peter Warren, in cooperation with a land force of New Englanders under Col. William Pepperell, made an assault on Louisbourg beginning on April 30, 1745. On June 17 the combined operation seized the fortress from the French garrison. This capture endangered the French position in North America, but it was offset by British losses in India. By the 1748 Treaty of Aix-la-Chapelle (Aachen), Louisbourg was returned to France, Madras to Great Britain. *See* Madras I; Maastricht III; Louisbourg II; King George's War.

Louisbourg II (French and Indian War), 1758. As part of their multiple offensive in the fifth year of the war, a British expedition set out for the French fortress of Louisbourg located on Cape Breton Island. Commanded by Gen. Jeffrey Amherst (and including Gen. James Wolfe among its officers) the expedition was supported by a fleet of 40 ships under Adm. Edward Boscawen. On June 8 Amherst, with 9,000 British regulars and 500 colonials, landed southwest of the fort and began an investment. Fighting their way overland, the attackers closed in on the garrison of 3,000 French regulars, plus some Indians and armed civilians. On June 18 the British artillery was brought ashore to aid in the siege. Finally, on July 26, the French surrendered the fortress. It was the first major British victory of the war. However, a second notable success would follow in August. *See* Fort Ticonderoga I; Fort Frontenac; French and Indian War.

Louvain (Wars of the German States), 891. Under the Carolingian dynasty, the East Frank, or German, kingdom of the Holy Roman Empire suffered like the rest of West Europe from savage raids by Northmen. In 891 the raiders penetrated up the Schelde and Dyle rivers as far as Louvain. Here Arnulf, the *de facto* Frank ruler, launched a counterattack that overwhelmed the Northmen with heavy losses. *See* Montfaucon; Riade.

Lowestoft (Second English-Dutch War), 1665. Commercial and colonial rivalry provoked a second naval war between England and the Netherlands in March 1665. The first major battle of the conflict was fought three months later off Lowestoft, eastern England, in the North Sea. On June 13 the English fleet of 150 ships, under the Duke of York (brother of Charles II and future James II), engaged a Dutch force of comparable size directed by Adm. Opdam. During the furious battle the two flagships fought each other, with the *Royal Charles* sinking its opposite number. Opdam was killed. Finally the bombardment by the 5,000 English naval guns proved superior and forced the Dutch to withdraw under cover of a squadron commanded by Adm. Cornelis Tromp, son of the veteran admiral killed in the First English-Dutch War. English personnel losses included Adm. Sir John Lawson and two other lords. The Hollanders returned to the offensive the following year. *See* Texel I; Dover Strait; English-Dutch Wars.

Lübeck (Napoleonic Empire Wars), 1806. The double French victory at Jena-Auerstedt on October 14, 1806, shattered the Prussian army of King Frederick William III and placed Napoleon I between the Prussians and Berlin. The French emperor immediately sent Marshal Louis Davout northeast across the Elbe. Brushing aside weak rear-guard opposition, Davout marched 150 miles in ten days to enter Berlin on October 24. Another French column pushed on 50 miles to the northeast to overtake and capture 16,000 Prussians, under Prince Friedrich of Hohenlohe-Ingelfingen, at Prenzlau four days later. Stettin fell on October 29. Meanwhile to the west the ablest Prussian commander still in the field, Gen. Gebhard von Blücher, fell back to Lübeck, which he entered on November 5. Hard on his heels, the French marshals Nicolas Soult and Jean Bernadotte stormed into the city the following day. Blücher escaped to nearby Ratkow with part of his 10,000-man force. Here he surrendered on November 7. Prussia lay prostrate at Napoleon's feet, but without resting, he now turned east where Czar Alexander I was mobilizing Russian troops in support of the fleeing King Frederick. *See* Jena-Auerstedt; Pultusk II; Napoleonic Empire Wars.

Lucknow (Indian Mutiny), 1857–1858. At the outbreak of the Great Mutiny in May, 1,700 English and loyal Indian troops fortified the residency in Lucknow, 270 miles southeast of Delhi. Here they took refuge on July 1 upon the approach of a mutineer force. Under Sir Henry Lawrence, the garrison held out against some 60,000 rebels. On September 25 a British army of some 3,000 men commanded by Gens. Sir Henry Havelock and Sir James Outram fought their way into the residency from Cawnpore. The week's march through hostile Oudh had cost the relief column more than 500 casualties. Inside Lucknow the garrison had lost almost as many troops in defending against periodic Indian assaults. Among the dead was Lawrence.

But now the mutineers tightened their siege. Havelock died of exhaustion, leaving Outram in command. On November 19 a second relief force under Sir Colin Campbell, new commander in chief for India, reached Lucknow after a fighting march. Campbell reinforced the garrison and then moved southwest to put down a new threat at Cawnpore. Outram continued to hold the beleagured residency for four more months. Finally, on March 21, 1858, Lucknow was liberated by Campbell after a new three-week campaign. The rebel chief, Nana Sahib, disappeared into the jungle. *See* Delhi II; Arrah; Cawnpore II; Indian Mutiny.

Ludford (Wars of the Roses), 1459. The Earl of Salisbury, after his Yorkist (white rose) victory over the Lancastrians (red rose) at Blore Heath, linked up with Richard of York's main force at Ludford (Ludlow). The rebels then advanced to Worcester. Encountering a superior army under King Henry VI, the Yorkists fell back to Ludford. The Lancastrians pursued and at nightfall on October 12, 1459, only the Teme River separated the two antagonists. During the night, however, Yorkist morale collapsed and many men deserted. When Henry began organizing his attack in the morning, he found the rebel army in flight. Richard returned to Ireland, and Salisbury and his son Warwick to Calais. But the Yorkist leaders remained adamant in their opposition to the crown and now prepared a general muster of rebels. *See* Blore Heath; Sandwich II; Roses, Wars of the.

Lugdunum (Civil Wars of the Roman Empire), 197. The three military claimants to the throne of the Roman Empire had been reduced to two in 196 with the victory of Septimius Severus at Byzantium. But while Severus was consolidating his position in the East and later in Rome, Clodius Albinus of Britain assembled a force of 50,000 men in Gaul. Organizing an army of equal size around his Pannonian legions, Severus crossed the Alps into modern France. North of Lugdunum (Lyons), the two huge armies clashed in a decisive battle. The legions of Britain and Gaul were thoroughly beaten. Severus ordered the beheading of Albinus and returned to Rome in triumph. *See* Byzantium I; Ctesiphon II; Roman Empire.

Lüleburgaz (First Balkan War), 1912. The attack of Mohammed V in Thrace had been checked by Bulgarian troops on October 22 at Kirk-Kilissa. Bulgaria, ruled by Czar Ferdinand I, then took the offensive. At Lüleburgaz, 86 miles northwest of Constantinople, the Bulgarians attacked on October 28. In a fierce three-day battle the Turks were routed, falling back to Çatalca (Chatalja), a fortified line across the pensinsula protecting Constantinople. The Bulgarians pursued and assaulted the lines on November 17 and 18 but were beaten back. Pressured by Russia (Nicholas II) not to take the Turkish capital, Czar Ferdinand agreed to an armistice on December 3. *See* Kirk-Kilissa; Adrianople VII; Balkan Wars.

Lundy's Lane (War of 1812), 1814. After the American victory at the Chippewa River in Ontario on July 5, 1814, the British army fell back northward to the vicinity (westward) of Niagara Falls. At Lundy's Lane the British commander, Gen. (later Sir) Gordon Drummond, deployed 3,000 troops along the roadway. The American general Jacob Brown pursued with 2,600 effectives. On July 25 Gen. Winfield Scott led the attack on the British position. The resulting five-hour battle, lasting into the night, was the fiercest land action of the war. Brown finally pulled back with 171 killed, 572 wounded, and 110 missing. British losses were 84 killed, 559 wounded, and 235 captured or missing. The Americans withdrew into Fort Erie, which they had taken earlier in the month. Now it was the turn of the British to pursue. *See* Chippewa River; Fort Erie; War of 1812.

Lusitanian War. *See* Numantia.

Lutter am Barenberge (Thirty Years' War), 1626. The coordinated attack of the Protestant (anti-Hapsburg) forces against the Catholic armies of Field Marshal the Count of Tilly and Gen. Albrecht von Wallenstein in the spring of 1626 got off to a bad start. General Count Ernst von Mansfeld, in attempting to cross to the left bank of the Elbe, was blocked by Wallenstein at Dessau and his 12,000-man army shattered, on April 25. Meanwhile Christian IV of Denmark and Norway was advancing up the Weser River with some 15,000 troops. After the defeat of Mansfeld, Wallenstein detached 8,000 of his men to supplement Tilly's 18,000-man army of the Catholic League. Upon hearing of this, Christian turned around and headed back toward his Brunswick base of Wolfenbüttel. Tilly took up the pursuit. By August 27 Christian was overtaken at Lutter am Barenberge, 20 miles short (south) of his base. Wheeling about, the Danish king deployed his army, including 20 cannon, across the road of his retreat.

Tilly flung the mass of his superior infantry against the roadblock. In a furious fight the Bavarians gradually forced back the Danes (and German volunteers). When his men seized the enemy's cannon, Tilly's victory was secure. Christian's troops bolted northward, leaving 6,000 dead on the field and another 2,500 captured. With more than half of his army gone, Christian fell back all the way to the North Sea coast near the estuary of the Elbe. The following year Wallenstein moved down the Elbe to drive Christian across the border into Holstein. In 1628 the Danish king would make one more try at invading Germany. *See* Dessau Bridge; Stralsund I; Wolgast; Thirty Years' War.

Lützen I (Thirty Years' War), 1632. Following the indecisive battle of Fürth, outside Nürnberg, Gen. Count Albrecht von Wallenstein marched his Catholic army of the Holy Roman Empire (Ferdinand II) northeast into Saxony. By plundering this state, he hoped to force the elector of Saxony, John George I, to disavow his alliance with Gustavus II of Sweden. But the Swedish king dared not risk this possibility. He turned his army of 16,000 men to the north and marched in pursuit of Wallenstein. At Lützen, 15 miles southwest of Leipzig, he found the Imperial commander had deployed an army of 15,000 men to oppose his advance. (Count Gottfried zu Pappenheim with another 10,000 Imperials was hurrying south from Halle.)

On the foggy morning of November 16, 1632, the Swedish-German army attacked Wallenstein's position, which was anchored on Lützen village on the right flank. Here Wallenstein himself commanded against Bernhard, duke of Saxe-Weimar. On the opposite wing, Gustavus opposed the Imperial general Heinrich Holk. At about ten o'clock Gustavus led a charge on this flank that forced back Holk's cavalry. But Pappenheim rode up with his cavalry in time to check the Swedish surge. In the bitter fighting, however, Pappenheim was killed. The next commander to fall was King Gustavus, shot through the head, side, arm, and back. Duke Bernhard, who had been holding his ground against Wallenstein's counterassaults on the Lützen side, took over supreme command. The

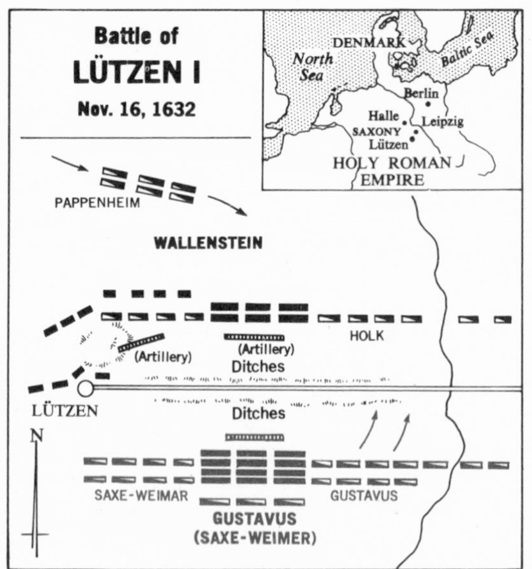

now heartbroken Protestants fell on their opponents so furiously that they drove them from the field. Abandoning his artillery, Wallenstein, under cover of the fog and gathering darkness, withdrew northward to Halle, leaving more than 3,000 men dead on the field. About 1,500 Swedes were killed. It was Wallenstein's first major setback of the war. He later retired into Bohemia, while the disorganized Protestant forces sought a new leader.

The battle of Lützen is associated with the death of a third leading figure of the Thirty Years' War. On November 29 Frederick V, former elector palatine and "Winter King" of Bohemia, who had played a major part in launching the war, died a broken, defeated man at the age of 36. *See* Fürth; Nördlingen I; Thirty Years' War.

Lützen II (Napoleonic Empire Wars), 1813. The great disaster suffered by Napoleon I in his retreat from Moscow in 1812 gave new hope to the reluctant allies of France. Prussian forces under Gen. Count Hans Yorck (York) von Wartenburg concluded an agreement of neutrality with Russia on December 30. This was followed by a declaration of war against France on March 16, 1813, by King Frederick William III. Sweden, under the former French marshal Crown Prince Jean Bernadotte, joined the anti-Napoleon alliance built around Great Britain (George III) and Russia (Alexander I). The Prussian and Russian monarchs set up headquarters in Dresden, putting the Prince of Sayn-Wittgenstein-Ludwigsburg, assisted by Gen. Gebhard von Blücher, in charge of the allied army.

To hold off the mounting allied attack, Napoleon hurriedly deployed 120,000 troops behind the Elbe and lower Saale rivers. Taking the initiative, the French emperor crossed the Saale on April 30. His V Corps under Gen. Jacques Lauriston captured Leipzig on May 2. That same day the allies struck the French right rear at Grossgörschen and four other villages southeast of Lützen. Napoleon promptly concentrated his forces against the bulk of Wittgenstein's army of 73,000 men. In a bitter day-long battle, the French III (Michel Ney), XII (Nicolas Oudinot), and VI (Auguste Marmont) Corps threw back the assault, inflicting 20,000 casualties. The allies fell back to the east. But Napoleon's 22,000 casualties and lack of cavalry prohibited a vigorous pursuit. *See* Berezina River; Bautzen; Napoleonic Empire Wars.

Luzon (World War II), 1945. The U.S. land victory on Leyte and naval victory in Leyte Gulf opened the way for Gen. Douglas MacArthur's full-scale liberation of the Philippines by way of Luzon, the chief island of the group. As a preliminary to the invasion of Luzon, Eighth Army (Robert Eichelberger) units landed on the island of Mindoro, to the south, on December 15, 1944. Infantrymen quickly established a beachhead in the San Jose area large enough to accommodate two airfields. From here Gen. George Kenney's aircraft began hammering at Japanese installations on Luzon. On Luzon itself Gen. Tomoyuki Yamashita organized his Fourteenth Army into three main defensive groups: Shobu (140,000 men) in the north, Kembu (30,000) in the center, and Shimbu (80,000) in the south.

While carrier planes from the Third Fleet (William Halsey) struck at Japanese air bases throughout the area, the Seventh Fleet (Thomas Kinkaid) transported Gen. Walter Krueger's Sixth Army toward northwestern Luzon. During this invasion period *kamikaze* attacks sank 20 U.S. ships and heavily damaged 24 others. On January 9 Krueger landed at Lingayen Gulf, two corps abreast. (It was the same invasion route taken by the Japanese three years earlier.) The landing order of battle was I Corps of Gen. Innis Swift on the left (east)—43rd and 6th Infantry divisions; XIV Corps of Gen. Oscar Griswold on the right—37th and 40th Infantry divisions.

The assault pushed rapidly inland (68,000 men landed the first day) to a maximum penetration of 40 miles by January 20. By then the I Corps's drive to the east was receiving bitter opposition from the Shobu Group, despite reinforcement by the 158th Regiment on January 11, the 25th Infantry Division six days later, and, before the end of the month, the 32nd Infantry Division. During this fighting, U.S. Rangers made a daring raid behind enemy lines to release several hundred Allied prisoners at Cabanatuan. On the right XIV Corps thrust rapidly southward across the Central Plain, reached Clark Field on January 23, and a week later had secured that major base, as well as pushing 25 miles farther south to Calumpit. Farther to the right on the west coast, the XI Corps of Gen. Charles Hall had landed at San Antonio on January 29, against the Kembu Group. Aided by Filipino guerrillas, the 38th and 24th Infantry divisions sealed off Bataan Peninsula. (By February 21 Bataan had been freed; the island of Corregidor, at the mouth of Manila Bay, fell to a combined amphibious and airborne assault five days earlier.)

On February 2 Krueger launched his reorganized XIV Corps on a dash to Manila. The 1st Cavalry Division raced into the outskirts of the capital on the night of February 3–4, liberating 3,500 Allied internees at Santo Tomas University. The 37th Infantry fought its way into the northwestern edge of Manila the following night and freed another 1,300 Allied prisoners from Bilibid Prison. The Japanese then fell back behind the Pasig River and began a fanatical, month-long resistance that destroyed much of the city and cost some 16,000 Nipponese deaths. Manila finally fell on March 4. Assisting in the capture was the 11th Airborne from the Eighth Army, which had landed southwest of the city on January 31 and pushed to the southern suburb of Paranaque four days later before being abruptly checked by strong enemy defenses. This division rescued civilian internees at Los Banas later in February.

During this time the I Corps in the north was pressing north and east against tough Shobu Group defenses in mountainous terrain. On February 14 the 6th Infantry drove through Bongabon to the east coast and then was transferred south to the Manila front. To the left, the 25th, 32nd, 33rd, and, later, the 37th Infantry divisions, plus Filipino army units, made only slight gains despite weeks of savage fighting. Baguio, the Philippine summer capital, fell on April 27, the key communications center of Sante Fe on May 27. The 37th Division then began a thrust down Cagayan Valley, which on June 26 met a force attacking south from Aparri (seized five days earlier). This offensive split the Shobu Group into two pockets, incapable of any major counterattack.

To the south, on the front east of Manila, the XI Corps had assumed control on March 15. Here the 6th and 43rd Infantry and 1st Cavalry were held up from any major advance by the strong Shimbu Line in the Sierra Madre Mountains. Slowly but relentlessly the Americans pushed back the Japanese, until by July 1 only the 38th Infantry was left in central Luzon to continue the reduction of a shrinking enemy pocket.

Meanwhile, in southern Luzon, the 1st Cavalry (transferred from the Manila front) and 11th Airborne of the XIV Corps drove southeast toward and down the Bicol Peninsula. Here the 158th Regimental Combat Team had seized Legaspi on April 1. One month later the two forces met near Naga. Mopping-up ended resistance in the XIV Corps zone on June 1.

On July 1 the Eighth Army assumed control on Luzon, freeing Krueger's Sixth Army for the projected invasion of Japan that fall. Three days later MacArthur declared Luzon secure. But when the war ended on August 15, the 6th, 32nd, 37th, and 38th divisions of the XIV Corps were still containing more than 50,000 Japanese troops that Yamashita surrendered from northern and eastern Luzon. *See* Leyte; Southern Philippines–Borneo; World War II.

Luzzara (War of the Spanish Succession), 1702. After the capture of his marshal, the Duc de Villeroi, at Cremona, King Louis XIV sent Marshal Louis Joseph, duc de Vendôme to command the French forces in northern Italy. Meanwhile, the victor of Chiari and Cremona, Prince Eugene of Savoy, continued to harass the French holdings in Lombardy and Emilia with his Austrian army of the Holy Roman Empire (Leopold I). During the summer of 1702 Vendôme took up a strong position at Luzzara, 18 miles north of Reggio nell'Emilia. Here on August 15 Eugene led a fierce assault. Despite a stubborn resistance, the French were eventually driven from their lines. Both sides lost several thousand men, but the battle produced no advantage. Eugene soon left Italy to join the Duke of Marlborough (John Churchill) in central Europe, and the capable Vendôme thwarted all further Imperial advances in Italy until 1706. *See* Cremona II; Landau; Cassano d'Adda I; Spanish Succession, War of the.

Lycia (Moslem-Byzantine Wars), 655. Successful everywhere with their superb cavalry, the Moslems turned to the sea and constructed a fleet of swift galleys, called dromons. Under Abdullah ibn-Sa'd, governor of Egypt, the new fleet captured Cyprus in 648 and Rhodes in 654. The Byzantine emperor Constans II sent out his ships to re-establish Constantinople's command of the Mediterranean. The two hostile navies met off the Lycian coast (Dhat al-Sawari) of southern Asia Minor. Despite their maritime inexperience, the Arabian sailors won a resounding victory, their first at sea. Now the Byzantine capital itself stood in danger. But a civil war of succession among pretending caliphs postponed an attack on Constantinople for almost 20 years. *See* Alexandria II; Basra; Constantinople III; Moslem Conquests.

Lynchburg (American Civil War), 1864. From Staunton, Va., which he reached on June 6, Federal Gen. David Hunter pressed on southeast toward the important rail center of Lynchburg, Va. To block this dangerous advance, Gen. Robert E. Lee sent Gen. John Breckinridge with two brigades westward, followed by the corps of Gen. Jubal Early. Hunter attacked Lynchburg on June 18 but was repulsed by Breckinridge's troops, plus Early's advance guard. Learning of the strong force massing against him, Hunter retreated into present-day West Virginia and then moved north by rail and water. Early marched into the Shenandoah Valley to launch his raid on Washington, D.C. *See* Piedmont; Monocacy River; American Civil War.

Lys River (World War I), 1918. When his first major offensive of the year failed to break through between the British and French armies along the Somme River, the German commander, Gen. Erich Ludendorff, launched a second attack along the Lys River in Flanders. On April 9, behind a heavy bombardment, Gen. Ferdinand Quast's Sixth Army struck westward from Armentières, south of the river. Here a Portuguese division in the center of Gen. Henry Horne's British First Army was overrun, forcing back the entire line for five miles. On the following day Gen. Friedrich Sixt von Armin's German Fourth Army joined the attack north of Armentières. Lacking reserves, which had been pulled southward to the Lys River, the British Second Army of Gen. Sir Herbert Plumer was thrown back. Messines Ridge was lost. The two German drives linked up on April 11 for a concerted attack toward the sea. But the British field marshal Sir Douglas Haig rushed in all available manpower, including some French troops sent northward by the Allied commander in chief, Gen. Ferdinand Foch. Gallant defensive fighting by the British finally stalled the German attack by April 29. The offensive had gained an average of ten miles.

Although Ludendorff had won a second tactical success, he had failed to achieve a breakthrough. Instead, he now held an awkward salient south of Ypres at a cost of 350,000 casualties. Allied losses, almost all British, totaled 305,000. *See* Somme River II; Aisne River III; World War I.

M

Maastricht I (Netherlands War of Independence), 1579. The fourth commander that Philip II of Spain sent out to subdue the revolt in the Spanish Netherlands was Alessandro Farnese, duke of Parma. A brilliant general as well as a shrewd statesman, Parma began by attacking the rebel city of Maastricht, on the Maas (Meuse) River in the southeast, on March 12, 1579. The garrison, numbering only 2,000 soldiers and armed townspeople, held out against the 20,000 Spanish troops by flooding the approaches. But Parma pressed the assault by ringing the city with 11 strong points and four months later stormed into Maastricht. Enraged at the loss of 4,000 men during the siege, the Spanish slaughtered double that number of inhabitants. *See* Gembloux; Antwerp I; Netherlands War of Independence.

Maastricht II (Second, or Dutch, War of Louis XIV), 1673. Exercising his definition of *droit de dévolution,* Louis XIV of France claimed and occupied several fortified towns along the border of the Spanish Netherlands in 1667 and 1668. The occupation constituted the first "war" initiated by the Grand Bourbon Monarch. When Holland supported Spain in this so-called War of Devolution, Louis resolved to humble the United Provinces of the Netherlands. In 1672, with his able generals the marshal the Vicomte de Turenne and Louis II, the Great Condé, Louis marched into Holland at the head of 100,000 men to launch his second war. Only the dramatic opening of the dikes by William III of Orange saved Amsterdam from capture. Meanwhile, under the direction of the Marquis de Vauban, who devised the modern system of military defense, a French force laid siege to Maastricht, in the southeast, on June 16, 1673. One of the strongest fortresses in Europe, Maastricht fell in just 13 days to Vauban's engineering skill. His maze of parallels and approaches negated the defenses of the city. *See* Dunes; Southwold Bay; Sinsheim; Louis XIV, Wars of.

Maastricht III (War of the Austrian Succession), 1748. The all-victorious French conqueror of the Austrian Netherlands, Marshal Comte Maurice de Saxe, pressed his offensive in 1748 by besieging the southeastern Dutch city of Maastricht on the Maas (Meuse). As in all previous battles, the English-Dutch-Hannoverian-Austrian coalition proved inadequate against the able Saxe. Maastricht capitulated on May 7. A large Russian army, sent out by Empress Elizabeth, now arrived on the lower Maas to aid the allies against the French. But the new force arrived too late. Both France (Louis XV) and the Holy Roman Empire (Francis I and Maria Theresa) were weary of the war, especially in Italy, where 1745–47 maneuver-and-skirmish tactics had produced no decision. On October 18 all the belligerents signed the Treaty of Aix-la-Chapelle (Aachen). The only significant winner was Prussia, whose earlier conquest of Silesia had signaled the rise of a new European power. Within eight years most of the combatant nations, but in a different alignment, would be at war again. *See* Bergen op Zoom I; Finisterre Cape II; Austrian Succession, War of the; Seven Years' War.

McDowell (American Civil War), 1862. After his defeat at Kernstown, the Confederate general Thomas (Stonewall) Jackson withdrew up the Shenandoah Valley to Swift Run Gap. The Federal general Nathaniel Banks, with superior forces (15,000 men), pursued cautiously as far as New Market. Learning of a Federal plan to have Gen. John Frémont's army in West Virginia link up with Banks, Jackson determined to strike the former first. Leaving a holding force at Swift Run Gap on April 30, he set out with about 6,000 men to cross the Shenandoah Valley in front of Banks. In four days the Confederates marched 92 miles and covered 25 more by rail. Picking up 3,000 men from Gen. Edward Johnson's division at West View, Jackson reached McDowell on May 8. Here he was attacked by the brigades (3,000 men) of Gens. Robert Schenck and Robert Milroy from Frémont's army. The outnumbered Federals were defeated and driven back across Bull Pasture River, although they inflicted 498 casualties at a loss of 256 to themselves. Jackson pursued the vanquished troops northward as far as Franklin, W. Va., then marched back to the Shenandoah to resume his campaign of tying down Union forces there. *See* Kernstown I; Front Royal; American Civil War.

Macedonian Conquests (338–322 B.C.). While the city-states of ancient Greece warred among themselves, Philip II built Macedonia into a military power. The Macedonians subdued all of Greece and then under Alexander III, the Great, conquered eastward as far as the Indus River.

Chaeronea I	338 B.C.
Thebes	335 B.C.
Granicus River	334 B.C.
Issus	333 B.C.
Tyre II	332 B.C.
Gaza I	332 B.C.
Arbela-Gaugamela	331 B.C.
Megalopolis	331 B.C.
Pandosia	331 B.C.
Hydaspes River	326 B.C.
Crannon	322 B.C.

Macedonian Wars (215–146 B.C.). For more than a hundred years after the death of Alexander III, the Great, Macedonia remained a strong military power. Then a series of four wars with the growing republic of Rome brought total defeat and the end of Macedonian independence. The First Macedonian War (215–205 B.C.), in which Philip V tried to help Hannibal and the Carthaginians, produced no pitched battle. The Fourth War 149–148 B.C.) was in actuality only a revolt that was quickly quelled by Rome.

Second Macedonian War

Cynoscephalae II	197 B.C.

Third Macedonian War

Pydna	168 B.C.

Madagascar (World War II), 1942. Japan's sweeping conquests early in 1942 challenged Great Britain's control of the Indian Ocean. In this contest the western key to the Indian Ocean was the valuable harbor of Diego Suarez, on the island of Madagascar (off the eastern coast of Africa). At that time Madagascar was ruled by the Vichy French under Gov.-Gen. Armand Annet. To forestall Japanese seizure of the island, Britain sent out an expeditionary force under Adm. Neville Syfret and Gen. Sturges. On May 5 two British brigades landed on the northwest coast. Fighting their way across the narrow northern tip of Madagascar, the British captured Diego Suarez (Antsirane) on May 7.

During negotiations with the French for administration of the island, the British battleship *Ramillies* was torpedoed in the harbor. Negotiations broke down. The British then ordered Gen. William Platt, commander in East Africa, to occupy the rest of the island. Amphibious assaults took Majunga on the west coast on September 10 and Tamatave on the east side on September 18. Inland, the capital of Tananarive fell on September 23. The French withdrew southward, but on November 5 Annet capitulated. He was interned at Durban, South Africa. The Free French of Gen. Charles de Gaulle took over the island on January 8, 1943. Great Britain's occupation of Madagascar gained a valuable naval base and ensured Allied communications with the Near and Far East. Total British casualties were less than 500. *See* Ceylon; World War II.

Madras I (War of the Austrian Succession), 1746. When the War of the Austrian Succession spread to the subcontinent of India, the great Mogul Empire, with its capital at Delhi, was already disintegrating. In a country swept by anarchy and bloodshed, only England and France remained as challengers for domination. The French moved first in the person of Marquis Joseph Dupleix, governor of Pondicherry on the Carnatic coast in the southeast. He persuaded the Nawab of the Carnatic to remain neutral while he attacked the English settlement 80 miles to the north at Madras, on September 5, 1746. After a five-day attack aided by a sea bombardment by Adm. the Comte de la Bourdonnais, the city surrendered. Some of the defenders, including a 21-year-old clerk named Robert Clive, escaped to nearby Fort Saint David. The French retained possession of Madras until the 1748 Treaty of Aix-la-Chapelle (Aachen) prescribed that the city be returned to Great Britain in exchange for Louisbourg in Nova Scotia. *See* Louisbourg I; Arcot; Austrian Succession, War of the.

Madras II (Seven Years' War), 1758–1759. Following their capture of Fort Saint David from the British in June 1758, the French in India attacked northward from their Pondicherry base on the east coast. Their objective was the chief British post at Madras. On December 16 the Comte de Lally with several thousand European and native troops invested the city and Fort Saint George. The garrison, with a comparable force under Col. Stringer Lawrence, resisted stoutly. After the first of the year De Lally stepped up the bombardment, preparing to launch an assault. However, the arrival of a British fleet in the harbor on February 16 forced the French to raise the siege. In all, the attackers lost 400 Europeans, the defenders more than 1,000 British and sepoys. *See* Fort Saint David; Wandiwash; Seven Years' War.

Madras III (War of the American Revolution), 1782. The English-French maritime phase of the war reached halfway around the world early in 1782. Admiral Pierre André de Suffren with a squadron of 12 French warships sailed into the Bay of Bengal, seeking to land 3,000 troops on the east coast of India. Off Madras stood a British fleet of 9 ships of the line commanded by Adm. Sir Edward Hughes. On February 17 the aggressive Suffren in his flagship, *Héros,* led an attack upon the British vessels. Despite a brisk action, neither side could gain an advantage, and after two hours the battle was broken off. Hughes retired to Trincomalee on Ceylon for repairs, while Suffren landed his troops near Porto Novo to help in the siege of Cuddalore, which the British surrendered on April 4. *See* Praia; Trincomalee I; American Revolution.

Madrid (Spanish Civil War), 1936–1939. The longest and bloodiest battle of the war began with a Nationalist attempt to march on Madrid from Pamplona. Under Col. Francisco Garcia Escámez a body of Nationalist rebels moved southward on July 19, 1936. Militia forces of the Republican government in Madrid held the mountain passes in the Sierra de Guadarrama, protecting the Spanish capital. On July 22 the Nationalists captured Alto de León, northwest of the city, and three days later Somosierra Pass to the north. In both struggles the Republicans had the advantage in numbers but were defeated by superior rebel artillery. Nevertheless, the government continued to hold the heights of the Guadarrama, blocking any farther Nationalist advance.

With the fall of Toledo on September 27, the Nationalists, under Gen. Emilio Mola, pressed toward Madrid from the south, southwest, and west. In this October campaign Mola sent forward four columns, claiming to have a "fifth column" of Nationalist supporters already in the city. By November 6 the attackers had closed in enough to deploy for an assault. On that day the Republican Prime Minister, Francisco Largo Caballero, evacuated the city for Valencia. Madrid's defenses were entrusted to Gen. José Miaja. The following dawn Mola sent Gen. José Varela with 20,000 troops, chiefly Moroccans and legionaries, against the southwest side of the city. Varela had the support of Italian mechanized forces and the German Condor Legion, which included aircraft. Miaja relied on the poorly armed urban militia and the XI International Brigade, some 1,900 Germans, French, Poles, and others, commanded by the Hungarian Lazar Stern, who called himself Emilio Kleber. (It was the first of six such brigades to fight on the government side.) Miaja also had some Soviet tanks and aircraft. In bitter fighting the Republicans held their ground for a time. But on November 16 Varela forced a crossing of the Manzanares River and during the next week captured 75 percent of the University City. During this struggle Buenaventura Durruti, the last of the classical Spanish anarchists, was killed while leading a column of 3,000 followers in defense of the city. By November 23 both sides were so exhausted they turned to digging trenches and building fortifications. Madrid had held, but it was now hemmed in on the north and west and subjected to brutal bombings by German, Italian, and Nationalist aircraft.

In an effort to tighten the siege of the city, Varela employed 17,000 infantry and cavalry, beginning on December 13, in an attack aimed at cutting the Corunna Road leading 25 miles northward to El Escorial. The battle reached its peak during January 3–15, when the Nationalists took and held a ten-kilometer section of the road. Each side lost about 15,000 men in this struggle, which only confirmed the military stalemate.

On February 6, 1937, the Nationalists launched a new offensive southeast of Madrid in the Jarama

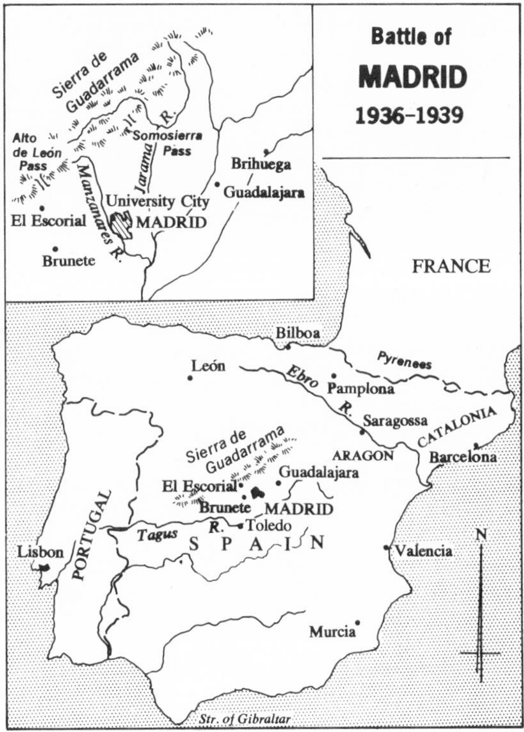

Valley, seeking to cut the high road to Valencia. The Republicans, commanded by Gen. Sebastían Pozas, were driven back east of the river, which the Nationalists under Gen. Luis Orgaz forced on February 11. Four days later Miaja took charge of the government troops on this front as well. By the end of the month the fighting had died down, with the Republican lines bent back but still in possession of the Valencia Road. Their casualties were 20,000; Nationalist losses totaled about 25,000.

After stopping the Nationalist offensive aimed at Guadalajara in March, the Republicans prepared an attack of their own. On July 6, 50,000 government troops struck southward toward Brunete, 15 miles west of Madrid, trying to cut off the besiegers in front of the capital. Miaja's men captured Brunete and drove a five-mile salient into the Nationalist lines before Varela rallied his forces and drove the Republicans back almost to the starting point by July 25. The attack cost the Republicans 25,000 casualties and 100 of their 150 aircraft. Varela lost about 10,000 men and 23 planes.

The deadlocked Madrid front then turned quiet. Nationalist generalissimo Francisco Franco, content to hold in place outside the city, concentrated on mopping up northern Spain and pushing eastward into Aragon and Catalonia throughout 1937 and 1938. When Barcelona fell on January 26, 1939, Madrid's hopes for a Republican victory collapsed almost completely. These defeats were followed on February 27 by an international setback—Great Britain and France recognized the Franco regime as the legitimate government of Spain. Meanwhile, the grinding siege of the Republican forces and civilians in Madrid went on. By early 1939 more than 400 people a week were dying of starvation. Then, late in February, Col. Segismundo Casado, commander of the Republican Army of the Center in the city, led an anti-Communist revolt against Miaja and the Juan Negrín government. Unable to prevent a civil war within the Civil War, Negrín and other leaders flew to France on March 6. For six days Republican forces battled each other in Madrid, until finally the Communists were defeated. On March 19, Franco, who had watched his enemies tear each other to pieces in the capital, agreed to start peace negotiations with Casado. When truce talks faltered over the generalissimo's demand for unconditional surrender, the Nationalists launched their first offensive against Madrid in almost two years, on March 26. The Republican lines quickly disintegrated. Thirty thousand defenders south of the city surrendered the first day. More thousands simply threw away their arms and went home. On March 31 Nationalist troops marched into Madrid, ending the Civil War and putting Franco in complete charge of the destiny of Spain. (Valencia had fallen without a struggle on March 30.) *See* Toledo II; Málaga III; Guadalajara; Barcelona II; Spanish Civil War.

Mafeking (South African War II), 1899–1900. When war broke out between the South African Republic and Great Britain, the Boer commander in chief, Gen. Petrus Joubert, launched an offensive in western Transvaal under Gen. Piet Cronjé. On October 13 Cronjé, with about 5,000 men, attacked Mafeking on the Bechuanaland border of Transvaal, 160 miles west of Pretoria. Although the garrison commander, Col. Sir Robert Baden-Powell, could muster only 700 troops, augmented by 600 armed townspeople, he beat off the assault. Cronjé then instituted a siege of Mafeking. Leaving a lieutenant in charge, Cronjé took half his troops away to fight elsewhere. The still-outnumbered garrison held on grimly until relieved by a column of British cavalry under Sir Bryan Mahon on May 17, 1900. The 217-day siege cost the Boer attackers about 1,000 casualties; Baden-Powell lost 273 men. *See* Majuba Hill; Doornkop; Kimberley; South African Wars.

Magdala (British Invasion of Ethiopia), 1868. Ras Kassa, who seized the throne of Ethiopia as Theodore in 1855, ruled ruthlessly. In 1864 he imprisoned the British consul Charles Cameron. Two years later a British envoy sent to negotiate the release of Cameron was also thrown into prison at Magdala, in the north-central part of the country. Early in 1868 Gen. Sir Robert Napier (later Lord Napier), at the head of a punitive expedition of Anglo-Indians, marched into Ethiopia. Recruiting strength from dissident local chiefs, Napier stormed into Magdala on April 13. The defeated garrison fled, Theodore committing suicide. After releasing the prisoners, Napier destroyed the fortress and then withdrew. Ethiopia lapsed into anarchy. *See* Alexandria IV; Aduwa.

Magdeburg (Thirty Years' War), 1631. The invasion of Germany by Gustavus II of Sweden and the uncertain alignment of John George I and George William, the Protestant electors of Saxony and Brandenburg, respectively, made desperate the situation of Field Marshal the Count of Tilly's Catholic army in north-central Germany. Tilly was now the top military commander of the Holy Roman Empire of Ferdinand II. In March 1631 he had sent his lieutenant, the cavalry general Count Gottfried zu Pappenheim, to besiege Magdeburg, the key fortress on the Elbe. Now, despite Gustavus' march up the Oder to Frankfort, Tilly resolved to press home the attack on Magdeburg. The city of 30,000 inhabitants was held by a small but determined garrison under the Hessian soldier Dietrich von Falkenberg.

In April Tilly took over personal command of the siege with 22,000 men. By May 18 the Catholic lines of investment had been pushed close enough to make a direct assault on the city. For two days Falkenberg's men beat off the Imperials. But early in the morning of May 20 the attackers forced an entry in two places and stormed into the city. Falkenberg was killed. The long-frustrated Imperial army plunged into an orgy of plunder and slaughter, completely beyond Tilly's control. Near noon a series of fires broke out that soon engulfed Magdeburg in a sea of flame. Victor and vanquished fled for their lives. For three days the wind-swept fire remained unchecked, reducing the city to blackened rubble. Only about 5,000 of the inhabitants survived.

The destruction of the city shocked Europe and gave rise to the Protestant war cry "Magdeburg quarter!" (meaning no quarter for the defeated). The United Provinces of the Netherlands promptly joined France in subsidizing the German campaign of Gustavus. And George William finally entered the struggle, also on the side of the Swedish king. For Tilly the ruin of Magdeburg was also a strategic disaster. It deprived him of his only north German base and forced him to move against Gustavus without a supply or communications center. *See* Frankfort on the Oder; Werben; Thirty Years' War.

Magenta (Italian Wars of Independence), 1859. After the failure of the revolutionary movements of 1848–49, most liberal Italians put their hopes of unification on the kingdom of Sardinia (Piedmont), ruled by Victor Emmanuel II. On December 10, 1858, the king's chief minister, Conte Camillo di Cavour, formally enlisted the help of Louis Napoleon III of France for a forthcoming war of liberation from Austria. The following spring an army of Piedmontese and French pushed eastward across the Ticino River into Austrian-held Lombardy. Led by the French marshal Comte Marie Patrice de MacMahon, the allies encountered a superior Austrian army under Gen. Count Eduard von Clam-Gallas at Magenta, 14 miles west of Milan. In a confused fight on June 4 the Austrians, numbering more than 50,000 men, were driven back with losses of several thousand. Allied casualties were also high. For his part in the battle, MacMahon was made duke of Magenta. *See* Venice; Solferino; Italian Wars of Independence.

Magersfontein (South African War II), 1899. From his victory at the Modder River on November 28, Gen. Lord Paul Methuen pressed on toward besieged Kimberley. At Magersfontein he found that the Boer general Piet Cronjé had halted his retreat to take up a strong defensive position. Methuen deployed his 1st Division for attack on December 11, sending the Highland Brigade on a flanking maneuver. The Highlanders, however, came under heavy fire while still in column and suffered more than 700 casualties, including their brigadier. The entire attack against the 9,000 entrenched Boers then bogged down. Methuen withdrew after suffering more casualties. It was the second British defeat of the three "Black Week" disasters. *See* Modder River; Stormberg; Colenso; South African Wars.

Magnano (Wars of the French Revolution), 1799. When the European powers of the Second Coalition launched a multiple offensive against the armies of the French Directory early in 1799, northern Italy again became a prime theater of operations. On April 5 an Austrian army under Gen. Baron Paul Kray von Krajowa moved on Magnano, ten miles south of Verona. Here the French, commanded by Gen. Barthélemy Schérer, suffered a signal defeat. They fell back westward to the Adda River near Milan, where Gen. Jean Moreau took over command. The Austrians, now reinforced by a Russian army, pressed in pursuit. *See* Stockach I; Cassano d'Adda II; French Revolution Wars.

Magnesia (Wars of the Hellenistic Monarchies), 190 B.C. After being repulsed at Thermopylae in his bid to conquer Greece, Antiochus III, the Great, of Syria pulled back to Asia. The following year, 190 B.C., the Roman navy, aided by the Rhodes fleet, defeated the Syrian fleet off Crete and then Rome launched its own invasion of Asia. A force of 40,000 legionaries under Lucius Cornelius Scipio and his brother Publius Cornelius Scipio Africanus landed on the central western coast of Asia Minor near Magnesia (ad Sipylum). Antiochus quickly moved to repel the invaders. His army of 80,000 men struck the Roman left and penetrated to the camp site. But on the other flank the Syrians were driven back by the Roman cavalry under Eumenes II of Pergamum. At this crucial point the Asian elephants stampeded and smashed through their own phalanx. Taking advantage of the broken ranks in front of them, the Roman legions attacked fiercely, putting the larger Syrian force to rout. As usual, the fleeing foot soldiers fell easy prey to the pursuers and suffered a loss of half their force. Roman losses totaled only 300. The victory substantiates Scipio Africanus' reputation as Rome's greatest general up to the time of Julius Caesar.

Antiochus accepted Rome's peace terms the following year. He paid a large indemnity, gave up his remaining war vessels, and surrendered Asia Minor, which was divided between Pergamum and Rhodes. Armenia and Bactria took this opportunity to break away from the Seleucid Empire. *See* Thermopylae II; Hellenistic Monarchies, Wars of the.

Maida (Napoleonic Empire Wars), 1806. In reshuffling the map of Europe after his overwhelming victory at Austerlitz in December 1805, Napoleon I of France deposed the king of Naples, Ferdinand IV (later Ferdinand I of the Two Sicilies). He installed his older brother, Joseph Bonaparte, on the throne early the following year. The new king soon had to send a French army, under Gen. Jean Reynier, southward into Calabria where Great Britain had landed an expeditionary force. On July 6 the British force of about 5,000 men commanded by Gen. John Stuart attacked the French at Maida. A fierce bayonet assault routed Reynier's army. But when Marshal André Masséna began concentrating fresh French forces against him, Stuart had to re-embark his troops, in September. Naples came completely under Bonaparte's control. But meanwhile, new fighting had broken out in Germany. *See* Austerlitz; Saalfeld; Napoleonic Empire Wars.

Maipo River (Chilean War of Independence), 1818. To suppress the newly established revolutionary government of Chile, the Spanish governor of Peru sent an army southward. Some 6,000 royal troops reached the Maipo River, south of Santiago, in central Chile. Here stood about 9,000 Chilean patriots commanded by José de San Martín. On April 5 the two forces fought a pitched battle. The royalists under Gen. Manuel Osorio suffered a crushing defeat, 1,000 being killed and more than 2,000 captured. Chilean casualties were little more than 1,000. This victory secured the independence of Chile. *See* Chacabuco; Junín.

Maiwand (Afghan-British War II), 1880. The British occupation of Kabul in 1879 pacified northern Afghanistan. But in the south Ayub Khan, son of the former amir, Shere Ali, was blocked off from rule by the British. Ayub organized a revolt and on July 27 stormed the small British garrison at Maiwand, west of Kandahar. Despite a brave resistance, more than 950 Anglo-Indian troops were killed and another 160 wounded. The few survivors barely escaped to Kandahar. *See* Peiwar Pass; Kandahar; Afghan-British Wars.

Majuba Hill (South African War I), 1881. After his repulse at Laing's Nek on January 28, Gen. Sir George Colley reorganized his British force. Moving forward again, he occupied Majuba Hill, which commanded the vital pass through the Drakensberg Mountains. Taking advantage of faulty British deployment, the Boer general Petrus Joubert made a dawn attack on February 27. The British were swept off the hill, suffering 280 casualties, including the slain Colley, out of their 550-man force. This battle ended the war, with independence won for the South African Republic. *See* Laing's Nek; Doornkop; Mafeking; South African Wars.

Makin Island (World War II). One of the Gilbert Islands taken by American infantry during the marine assault on Tarawa, during November 20–23, 1943. *See* Tarawa-Makin.

Málaga I (Spanish-Moslem Wars), 1487. Having reduced the Moorish strong points west of Granada, Ferdinand (V of Castile, II of Aragon) then turned southward to the coast. Here stood Málaga, a seaport and vital shipping point for the Moslem kingdom of Granada, 60 miles to the northeast. With a large Spanish army, Ferdinand laid siege to the city on April 17, 1487. The Moorish garrison resisted successfully for a time but was finally forced to surrender, on August 18. Ferdinand's troops entered Málaga and sold most of the Moslem captives into slavery. Granada now lay open to attack from the west. Ferdinand, however, postponed such a dangerous assault by first moving against the strong points east of the city. *See* Loja; Baza.

Málaga II (War of the Spanish Succession), 1704. When the Anglo-Dutch fleet and landing party seized Gibraltar on August 4, 1704, the Spanish (Philip V) immediately tried to win back the fortress. To aid this counterattack, a French fleet of 52 ships under Adm. Comte de Toulouse (natural son of Louis XIV) sailed westward. It was intercepted off the coast of Málaga, 66 miles short of Gibraltar, by Adm. Sir George Rooke's English and Dutch force, numbering 58 ships. On August 24 the two hostile fleets clashed in a melee of ship against ship. Although no vessels were lost, the allies suffered some 1,500 casualties, their opponents twice that number. The French finally withdrew, giving Rooke the strategic victory of preventing the junction of the two enemy fleets. This battle safeguarded the possession of Gibraltar, which became secure on March 10 of the following year, when a final French naval assault was beaten back by the English admiral Sir John Leake off Marbella. The focus of fighting in Spain now shifted eastward to Barcelona. *See* Gibraltar I; Barcelona I; Cassano d'Adda I; Spanish Succession, War of the.

Málaga III (Spanish Civil War), 1937. While the fighting raged around Madrid early in 1937, three Nationalist rebel columns converged on Málaga, on the Mediterranean coast, 66 miles northeast of Gibraltar. Pressing in from the west was the so-called Army of the South under Gen. Gonzalo Queipo de Llana. From Granada, Col. Antonio Muñoz marched a column against the northeastern side of Málaga. To the north, between the two Spanish armies, stood nine mechanized battalions of Italian Black Shirts commanded by Gen. Mario Roatta. The offensive got under way on January 17.

Although the Republican commander at Málaga, Col. Villalba, had 40,000 troops to defend the city, all were poorly organized militiamen. These government troops fell back steadily before the three enemy columns, which reached the outskirts of Málaga on February 3. Three days later Republican resistance collapsed. The survivors fled up the coast toward Almería, their retreat cruelly harassed by Nationalist tanks and aircraft. Generalissimo Francisco Franco stood unchallenged in Málaga. *See* Madrid; Guadalajara; Spanish Civil War.

Malakhov (Crimean War). A key defensive strong point at the southeastern end of Sevastopol, whose capture by the French on September 8, 1855, led to the fall of the city. *See* Sevastopol I.

Malaya (World War II), 1941–1942. The broad-scale Japanese attack in the Pacific assigned the largest number of troops to the invasion of the upper Malay (Kra) Peninsula. Beginning on December 8, the first day of the Pacific war, Japan landed seaborne forces at Singora, Patani (both in southern Thailand), and Kota Bharu on the west coast of Malaya, and Alor Star and Penang Island on the east coast. Rapid advances overran airfields and gave Japanese planes complete superiority in the air. Under the British general A. E. Percival, the hard-pressed 9th and 11th Indian divisions could offer no more than delaying actions. By the end of December three Japanese divisions had forced their way 150 miles down the peninsula to the vicinity of Ipoh, 200 miles north of the great naval base at Singapore.

In January Gen. Tomoyuki Yamashita's Twenty-fifth Army, now four divisions, continued to push forward, supplemented by amphibious landings behind the British lines. The superior Japanese force drove back the outnumbered British, despite the help provided by the addition of the 8th Australian and 18th Indian divisions. By January 27 the Japanese were pressing hard against an ever shrinking bridgehead at the southern tip of the Malay Peninsula. Four days later the British withdrew across the causeway over Johore Strait (1,100 yards wide) to the island of Singapore. The battle of Malaya had ended in a thorough British defeat. The attempt to blow up the causeway behind the retreating troops was only partially successful—a dark omen for the Singapore battle that was to follow. *See* Hong Kong; "Prince of Wales"–"Repulse"; Singapore; World War II.

Malborghetto (Wars of the French Revolution), 1797. Napoleon Bonaparte's defeat of the Austrian army at Rivoli Veronese in January 1797 virtually completed his conquest of northern Italy. He then marched 43,000 French troops eastward across the Alps to carry the war to Austria itself. To block this offensive, Archduke Charles Louis, brother of Holy Roman Emperor Francis II and victor over the French in Germany the previous autumn, deployed 33,000 Austrian infantry to hold the mountain passes. The French pressed relentlessly forward. On March 23 Gen. André Masséna's division routed the Austrian defenders at Malborghetto in the Carnic Alps. The archduke fell back and on April 18 agreed to a preliminary peace at Leoben, where Napoleon had penetrated to within 100 miles of Vienna.

On the same day Austria suffered a heavy defeat in the Rhineland at the hands of another French army. The truce agreement of Leoben was then converted into the Treaty of Campo Formio, signed on October 17, under the terms of which Austria accepted territory in northern Italy, chiefly Venice, in exchange for recognition of the newly created Cisalpine Republic at Milan and the cession of Belgian provinces to France. Napoleon now began to plan for his invasion of Egypt, to take place the following year. *See* Rivoli Veronese; Neuwied; Pyramids; French Revolution Wars.

Maldon (Rise of England), 991. During the reign of Ethelred II, the Unready, Vikings from Denmark and Norway resumed their devastating raids on the coasts of England. One group of Danish raiders landed at Maldon in Essex in August and demanded tribute. The Alderman of Essex, Byrhtnoth, refused. In the battle that followed, Byrhtnoth was killed and most of his men were slain. The victorious Danes plundered the countryside at will.

In an effort to buy off the raiders, Ethelred paid heavy tribute to both King Earl Haakon of Norway and King Sweyn I, Forkbeard, of Denmark. The payments were in vain. Ethelred was forced to flee to Normandy, while first Sweyn and then his son Canute were acknowledged kings of England. *See* Tempsford; Brunanburk; Stainmore; Pen; Danish Invasions of Britain.

Maloyaroslavets (Napoleonic Empire Wars), 1812. Although Napoleon I had captured Moscow in September 1812, he had neither destroyed the Russian army nor persuaded Czar Alexander I to accept peace. On October 19 he evacuated Moscow and sent a strong force southwest toward Kaluga under the command of his stepson, Eugène de Beauharnais. Detecting the French route, Field Marshal Mikhail Kutuzov hurried to intercept Eugène at Maloyaroslavets, 75 miles southwest of the Russian capital. On October 24 the retreating column of 15,000 men found some 20,000 Russians holding the small village and the single bridge over the steep-banked Luzha. Unable to maneuver, Eugène made a head-on assault. In a bitter battle the two armies fought most of the day for control of the bridge. Finally, after Maloyaroslavets had changed hands seven times, the French drove off Kutuzov's troops. The action cost Eugène 5,000 casualties; Russian losses were about 6,000. More important, however, was the strategic effect of the battle. Napoleon, fearing increased enemy resistance along this route, swung Eugène to the north and made the Moscow–Smolensk road the main avenue of retreat. *See* Borodino; Berezina River; Napoleonic Empire Wars.

Malplaquet (War of the Spanish Succession), 1709. After taking the surrender of Tournai on September 3, 1709, the Duke of Marlborough (John Churchill) marched southeast to besiege Mons. South of the city, the duke and his second-in-command, Prince Eugene of Savoy, found their army of 100,000 men opposed by a French army of 90,000 under Marshal Duc Claude de Villars, assisted by the aged Marshal Duc Louis de Boufflers. For two days the two largest armies heretofore assembled in the Western world faced each other. During this time the French threw up a series of palisades, abatis, and other entrenchments just north of the village of Malplaquet (now in northern France). On September 11 the allied army of English, Dutch, Germans, and Austrians attacked. As at Blenheim five years before, Marlborough assaulted both French wings. On his left the Dutch were held with fearful slaughter, but on the right Eugene gradually forced his way through dense woods. After seven hours of fighting the duke struck in the center with a force of more than 30,000 cavalrymen. In a cruel struggle the French horsemen were slowly pushed back. The French army then withdrew in good order all along the line, under the direction of Boufflers, who had succeeded the wounded Villars.

Malplaquet was the bloodiest battle of the war and the entire century. (No greater slaughter would take place until Napoleon's victory at Borodino 103 years later.) The allies lost 24,000 men in killed and wounded (Eugene was wounded), the French half that number. Few prisoners were taken in the savage struggle. Mons capitulated on October 20, but the heavy allied losses precluded any further offensive that year. As it turned out, Malplaquet proved to be the last great battle fought by Marlborough, who never lost an engagement and never failed to take a town he had besieged. The following two years became campaigns of maneuver and minor sieges on the western front with neither side winning an advantage. At the end of 1711 Marlborough was dismissed. Meanwhile, the allies suffered another defeat in Spain. *See* Tournai; Brihuega; Spanish Succession, War of the.

Malta I (Siege by Turks), 1565. In the steadily growing Moslem domination of the Mediterranean Sea, the island of Rhodes was lost by the Knights of Saint John of Jerusalem (the Hospitalers) in 1522. Eight years later Holy Roman Emperor Charles V settled the Knights on Malta. The island soon became a headquarters for Spanish pirates. Then in May 1565 the Ottoman Turkish navy of Suleiman I, the Magnificent, laid siege to Malta. A Mohammedan landing party captured the fortress of Saint Elmo, but Valletta, on the northeast coast, held out valiantly. Through the summer the Turks pressed to complete the conquest, but each assault was beaten back. Finally, in September, the Turks had to raise the siege. In all, 9,000 men (of whom only hundreds survived) successfully resisted a force of some 40,000. *See* Rhodes; Preveza; Szigetvár.

Malta II (Wars of the French Revolution), 1798–1800. When Napoleon Bonaparte dashed across the Mediterranean to invade Egypt in the summer of 1798, he seized the island of Malta on the way, on June 12. General Vaubois was left with 3,500 troops to hold the island, which had previously been governed by the Order of the Knights of Malta. With the shattering of the French fleet in the Mediterranean at the battle of Nile on August 1, however, local maritime supremacy passed to Great Britain. The following month a British naval force under Adm. Lord Keith blockaded Malta and landed troops on the island. Here Capt. Alexander Ball took command of an attack that reconquered all of Malta except the port city of Valetta, where Vaubois stubbornly resisted. The British laid siege to Valetta but failed to win its surrender until September 5, 1800, when starvation forced the garrison to capitulate. Meanwhile the main theater of action had shifted back to the European Continent. *See* Pyramids; Nile River; Abukir; French Revolution Wars.

Malta III (World War II), 1941–1942. The tiny Mediterranean island of Malta (95 sq. mi.) provided Great Britain a vital air and naval base during the North African campaign, from December 1940 to May 1943. Malta-based aircraft helped defend British convoys moving through the Mediterranean and at the same time attacked Axis ships operating between Sicilian-Italian ports and Tripoli. As a result the island came under heavy enemy air attack for more than 20 months. When Axis troops held airfields in Cyrenaica, Libya, from April to November 1941 and February to November 1942, Malta was often paralyzed by repeated German and Italian air attacks. As many as 300 bombers a day, directed by the German air marshal Albert Kesselring, blasted the island, strangling the Royal Air Force, dispersing naval units, and forcing the inhabitants to go underground. By May 1942 the 2,470 Axis air raids on Malta made it probably the most bombed area in the world. With the supplying of the island reduced to a trickle of food, fuel, ammunition, and fighter aircraft, Malta stood in imminent danger of collapse.

In March 1942 four merchant ships carrying 26,000 tons of supplies left Alexandria, Egypt, for Malta, convoyed by strong Royal Navy units. All four were sunk. In the spring the British carrier *Eagle* and the U.S. carrier *Wasp* flew in 126 Spitfires, which quickly halted daylight raids (37 Axis planes were shot down the first day with the loss of 3 Spitfires). But an attempt to resupply the island in June resulted in the loss of 15 of 17 merchantmen. At this point the Malta governor, Gen. William Dobbie, was replaced by Field Marshal Lord Gort.

A last, desperate try to save Malta, Operation Pedestal, came in August. Fourteen heavily loaded merchant ships steamed into the Mediterranean, escorted by a task force under the British admiral E. N. Syfret—4 carriers, 14 battleships and cruisers, and 40 destroyers. The Axis rushed to the attack with 21 submarines, 23 E-boats, and 540 aircraft. The carrier *Eagle* and two cruisers (*Manchester, Cairo*) were sunk, and several other warships were damaged in the furious battle that followed. Nine of the supply ships failed to reach the island, but the five others got through, including the badly crippled U.S.S. *Ohio,* the only tanker in the convoy. Despite the heavy losses, the relief was sufficient to revitalize Malta. Three months later the British conquest of North Africa eliminated much of the air offensive against the island. Malta was finally secure. *See* Sidi Barrâni; El Alamein II; World War II.

Malvern Hill (American Civil War). The last engagement, on July 1, 1862, in the Seven Days battle east of Richmond, which also closed out the fighting in the fruitless Peninsular Campaign to capture the Confederate capital. *See* Seven Days.

Manila I (Seven Years' War), 1762. The bitterly fought Seven Years' War (French and Indian War in North America) began drawing to a close halfway around the world from where it began. Spain's entrance into the conflict on the side of France early in 1762 made vulnerable its hold on Manila in the Philippine Islands. This was particularly true since the British victory in India had freed new forces for an attack on Spanish possessions in the Far East. In the fall a combined British expedition under Adm. (later Sir) Samuel Cornish and Gen. (later Sir) William Draper sailed from India to Luzon. On October 5 the British entered Manila harbor and forced the city to surrender. This was the next-to-last battle of the war. In the peace treaty signed the following year, Manila was restored to Spain. *See* Havana; Freiberg; Seven Years' War.

Manila II (Spanish-American War), 1898. Following his destruction of the Spanish fleet in Manila Bay on May 1, the American admiral George Dewey blockaded the city of Manila and awaited troop reinforcements from the United States. The first contingent of soldiers arrived on June 30. By July 25 Gen. Wesley Merritt commanded 10,700 men, deployed south of Manila. Also ready to attack the city was a force of 10,000 Filipino guerrillas under Gen. Emilio Aguinaldo, who had proclaimed an independent Philippine republic on July 1. On August 9 Dewey and Merritt demanded that the Spanish governor-general Fermin Jaudenes surrender the city. When Jaudenes refused, the American troops assaulted the city on August 13 and occupied it, receiving little resistance from the 13,000-man garrison. Formal Spanish capitulation came the following day. Unknown to the participants in the almost bloodless battle, Spain and the United States had agreed on an armistice two days before (August 12).

The Filipino troops of Aguinaldo, frustrated in their ambitions to capture Manila and further enraged by their failure to secure immediate independence, launched a three-year Philippine insurrection against American occupation forces on February 4, 1899. *See* Manila Bay; Santiago de Cuba I; San Juan Hill; Philippine Insurrection against the U.S.; Spanish-American War.

Manila Bay (Spanish-American War), 1898. With the outbreak of war between the United States and Spain, American Com. George Dewey sailed from China toward the Philippines on April 27. His squadron of four cruisers and two gunboats entered Manila Bay on the evening of April 30. At daybreak the following morning Dewey steamed directly at the ten Spanish vessels of Adm. Patricio Montojo anchored off Cavite Point, about seven miles from Manila. When his formation moved within range of the enemy fleet, Dewey said to Capt. Charles Gridley, commander of the flagship *Olympia:* "You may fire when you are ready, Gridley." For almost seven hours the American squadron raked the Spanish fleet until every enemy vessel was destroyed, captured, or put out of action. The battle cost the lives of 381 Spaniards. None of the American ships was damaged and only eight seamen were wounded. Lacking the troops to conduct a landing operation, Dewey imposed a blockade on Manila and awaited army reinforcements. *See* Manila II; Santiago de Cuba I; Spanish-American War.

Mannerheim Line (World War II). The chief Finnish defensive position, across the Karelian Isthmus, was twice breached by Russian armies during World War II, in February 1940 and June 1944. *See* Finland (World War II).

Mantinea (Greek City-States' Wars), 362 B.C. The defeat of Sparta at Leuctra led to confused fighting in the Peloponnesus for eight years. Finally, in 363, Thebes sent its resourceful commander Epaminondas to establish control over the peninsula. Athens hurriedly sent troops to aid Sparta. The following year Epaminondas met the allied forces at Mantinea. Using the same oblique order as at Leuctra, the Thebans struck the first blow with their left wing, which had the heaviest concentration of force. This assault smashed the Mantineans on the allied right and then rolled up the Spartan center against the Athenians at the far end of the line. In the pursuit of the crushed coalition, Epaminondas suffered a mortal wound. This loss, coupled with the death of Pelopidas two years earlier at Cynoscephalae, left Thebes leaderless. But the overall political situation in Greece was even worse. The city-states now had no single power able to establish unity and enforce a peace. Local conflicts broke out that so weakened the democracies that they became easy prey to outside domination. *See* Leuctra; Cynoscephalae I; Chaeronea I; Greek City-States' Wars.

Mantua (Wars of the French Revolution), 1796–1797. From his conquest of Milan (except for the citadel), Napoleon Bonaparte turned eastward against the Austrian army of Gen. Baron Jean de Beaulieu, which stood across the Mincio River. On

May 30 Napoleon with 31,000 men outmaneuvered the 29,000 Austrian troops to cross the Mincio at Borghetto virtually unopposed. This thrust split the army of Beaulieu, who retreated northward up the Adige River with half of his force. The remaining Austrians joined the garrison in Mantua, to give its commander, Gen. Campo d'Irles, 13,000 men and 500 cannon. By June 4 Napoleon had begun to invest the fortress with some 9,000 men under Gen. Jean Serurier. When the Milan citadel capitulated on June 29, the French heavy guns were moved to the lower Mincio to help prosecute the siege of Mantua. However, the advance of the field marshal Count Dagobert von Wurmser into northern Italy at the head of a large new Austrian army forced Napoleon to lift the siege on July 31. Mantua was victualed. But when Wurmser was driven back at Lonato and Castiglione delle Stiviere, Napoleon resumed the siege on August 24, against a garrison now strengthened to 15,000 men. On September 13 Wurmser, who had suffered two more defeats at Caliano and Bassano, threw himself and his 12,000 remaining troops into Mantua. Two days later the Austrian commander made a sortie to the east in an effort to widen his hold, but he was beaten back with a loss of 4,000 men and 24 cannon by the French generals André Masséna and Charles Kilmaine.

When a new Austrian offensive into northern Italy was shattered at Rivoli Veronese on January 14, 1797, Mantua was cut off from all hope of relief. On February 2 Wurmser surrendered to Serurier. Some 16,000 men and 1,500 guns were taken. During the siege 18,000 Austrians and 7,000 French had died, chiefly from disease.

With his conquest of northern Italy virtually complete, Napoleon now marched eastward against Austria itself. *See* Lodi Bridge; Rivoli Veronese; Malborghetto; French Revolution Wars.

Manzikert (Byzantine-Turkish Wars), 1071. Much of the military manpower of the Byzantine Empire came from the Isaurians and Armenians of Asia Minor. When the aggressive Seljuk Turks began raiding into Asia Minor, the Byzantine emperor Romanus IV Diogenes beat them off, during 1067–71. In the latter year Romanus took an army of 40,000 well-trained Byzantines to relieve the Armenian village of Manzikert (Malazkirt). Northwest of Lake Van near the present Turkish-Iranian border, he encountered a force of 70,000 mounted Turks, commanded by Alp Arslan, second sultan of the Seljuk Turks. Alp Arslan offered to negotiate, but Romanus refused and led a headlong charge into the center of the Turkish line. The Byzantine assault drove back the Turks until dusk, when Romanus called off the attack. As soon as the Byzantine withdrawal began, the Turks wheeled about and counterattacked. Now the tide of battle abruptly changed. Despite a heroic defense, Romanus soon found his army surrounded. In a futile stand in the darkness, the Byzantine army was destroyed. Romanus became a prisoner. Released for ransom, he was murdered in a court intrigue before the end of the year. Alp Arslan was himself assassinated the following year.

The decisive Turkish victory at Manzikert erased the once-powerful standing army of the Byzantines. With no force to stop them, the Seljuks swept on to take Antioch, Damascus, and Jerusalem. This cut off Constantinople's recruiting ground and ensured the eventual downfall of the Byzantine Empire. *See* Dyrrachium II; Nishapur; Philomelion.

Maori-British Wars (1843–1870). Disputes over land ownership between New Zealand natives and British settlers led to two different uprisings by the Maoris. The first, during 1843–48, was suppressed largely through the efficient management of Sir George Grey. The second, during 1860–70, was put down only with the help of British and Australian troops. Both wars were simply local guerrilla actions. The chief Maori leader was Te Kooti. Sir Donald McLean helped introduce a lasting peace, but the Maoris lost their land as completely as had the Indians in the American West.

Maratha-British Wars (1779–1818). A series of three conflicts between the British in India and the Maratha people of the Deccan—1779–1781; 1803–1804; 1817–1818. Only the second and third wars produced pitched battles.

Aligarh	1803
Laswari	1803
Assaye	1803
Argaon	1803
Farrukhabad	1804
Kirkee	1817
Fort Sitabaldi	1817

Marathon (Persian-Greek Wars), 490 B.C. After defeating the Ionian Greeks in Asia Minor, Darius I of Persia sent his son-in-law Mardonius to invade European Greece in 492. Thrace and Macedonia were subdued before a storm wrecked the Persian fleet, forcing Mardonius to return to Asia. Two years later a second Persian expedition crossed the Aegean Sea. Artaphrenes the Younger and Datis, nephew of Darius, conquered Eretria, on the island of Euboea, in seven days. A Persian force of 15,000 soldiers under Datis then landed near Marathon, 24 miles northeast of Athens. The Greek general Miltiades rallied some 10,000 Athenian and 1,000 Plataean citizen-soldiers to attack the heretofore invincible Persians near the east coast, on September 12, 490 B.C.

Miltiades arranged the Greek infantry (hoplites) in a long line across the two-mile-wide plain of Marathon. With swords, spears, and shields, the

Greeks rushed at the invaders. The Greek center was beaten back by the more lightly armed Persians. But the Athenian flanks, which had been carefully strengthened by Miltiades, penetrated both wings of the enemy defense line and then wheeled inward to envelop the Persian center. This tactic routed Datis' army, which fell back to its ships. After finding the city of Athens to be strongly defended, the Persians returned to Asia. The Greeks lost 192 men (including the titular commander, or polemarch, Callimachus), the Asiatics 6,400. The first major assault from the East had been decisively repulsed in a single afternoon. Because the determined defense of the Greeks proved that Europe could resist military encroachments from Asia, the battle of Marathon is often considered the first of the great decisive battles of the world. *See* Lade; Thermopylae I; Salamis; Persian-Greek Wars.

Marchfeld (German-Bohemian Wars), 1278. The first Hapsburg ruler of Germany and the Holy Roman Empire, Rudolph I, encountered strong opposition in the East from the Bohemian king Ottokar II, the Great. Bohemia then stood at the height of its power in the Middle Ages. Ottokar, who also claimed the duchy of Austria, refused to recognize Rudolph. After years of quarreling, the armies of the two rivals met on the plain of Marchfeld (Durnkrut), north of the Danube from Vienna. Allied with the Germans was a Hungarian force under Ladislas IV. In a pitched battle of knights on August 26, the Bohemians were defeated and Ottokar was killed. The dead king's seven-year-old son, Wenceslas II, succeeded to the Bohemian throne under German regency. The house of Hapsburg would stand supreme in the Danube Valley until 1918. *See* Kressenbrunn.

Marengo (Wars of the French Revolution), 1800. The well-planned French offensive in northern Italy during the spring of 1800 forced Austrian commander Gen. Baron Michael von Melas to concentrate his forces at Alessandria. Here the swift-moving columns of Napoleon Bonaparte, now first consul of the French government, converged to force a major battle. On the evening of June 13 the French reached Marengo, two and a half miles southeast of Alessandria. Melas, however, did not wait to be attacked. With 31,000 troops he lashed out at the French the following morning. Napoleon, caught by surprise, could deploy only 23,000 men to resist the advance of the white-coated Austrians. Covered by the fire of 80 guns, Melas' infantry pounded at Marengo for five hours. About 2 P.M. the French line, held by the corps of Gen. Jean Lannes on the right (northeast) and Gen. Claude Victor on the left (southwest), began to give way. Napoleon threw in all available reserves, but an hour later his battered forces had been driven back almost four miles to San Giuliano.

At this point the Austrians seemed to have won a clear victory. As his troops pressed forward, the 71-year-old Melas turned the command over to a subordinate and retired to Alessandria. But the slow Austrian pursuit enabled Napoleon to reorganize his forces, and when a fresh corps under Gen. Louis Desaix arrived from the southeast, the French launched a counterattack late in the

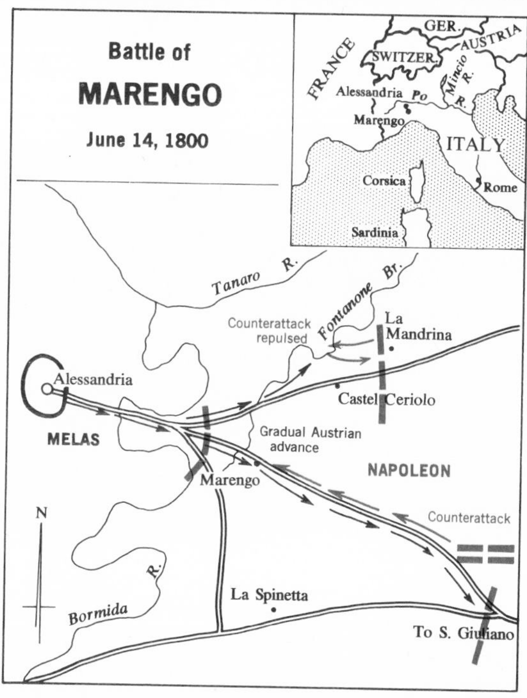

afternoon. Desaix was killed almost immediately, but his 6,000 men gave new hope to Napoleon's army. Now it was the Austrians' turn to be surprised. The fury of the French counterattack checked their advance and bent them back toward Marengo. Slashing assaults by the French cavalry under young Gen. François E. Kellermann (son of the Valmy hero) soon turned the white-coated retreat into a rout. Nightfall ended the battle. In all, the French suffered 5,835 casualties, the Austrians 9,402.

In Alessandria, the shaken Melas agreed to a truce on the following day and withdrew all his troops east of the Mincio River and north of the Po. Although Napoleon's victory had been narrowly won, it was received in France with great enthusiasm. The young Corsican hurried to Paris to take over both military and civilian authority. After prolonged negotiations with Austria, he would break the truce for a thrust from Germany aimed at Vienna. *See* Montebello; Höchstädt II; French Revolution Wars.

Mareth Line (World War II), 1943. At the end of its 1,500-mile retreat across Libya, Field Marshal Erwin Rommel's *Panzerarmee Afrika* halted inside the Tunisian frontier. Here the Axis forces dug in behind the Mareth Line, originally constructed by the French against possible Italian attack from Libya. From the east, Gen. Sir Bernard Montgomery's pursuing British Eighth Army closed up slowly, hampered by long communication lines. Rommel used this breathing time to turn to the west and drive back the First Allied Army, during February 14–22, which had marched into western Tunisia in November. With the Axis rear temporarily safe as a result of this quick thrust, Rommel returned to face his old antagonist, the Eighth Army. On March 6 the 10th, 15th, and 21st Panzer divisions lunged out of the Mareth Line, aiming at the British supply dumps at Médenine. By nightfall the Germans had lost 52 of their 140 attacking tanks and pulled back. Montgomery's troops lost no tanks and suffered only 130 casualties. This was the last attack of the "Desert Fox" in Africa; six days later Rommel flew back to Germany.

Meanwhile the Eighth Army had been resupplied, as well as reinforced by Free French forces under Gen. Jacques Leclerc. On March 20 a heavy artillery barrage opened the attack on the 20-mile-long Mareth Line. Under cover of a frontal assault by the XXX Corps near the coast, Gen. Bernard Freyberg's New Zealand Division (part of X Corps) on the left made a wide flanking movement of 200 miles. By March 26 the New Zealanders had turned the line's inland anchor at El Hamma, opening the way for the British 1st Armoured into the German rear. Unable to defend against both this attack and a renewed frontal assault, the Italian general Giovanni Messe withdrew his combined German-Italian First Army northward to the Gabès–Gafsa road. The Axis forces lost 7,000 prisoners in the battle of the Mareth Line.

On April 6 Montgomery's Eighth Army attacked the Gabès position and drove the Axis farther north, taking 2,000 prisoners in the first six hours of fighting. The following day a British patrol met a patrol from the U.S. II Corps, which was pushing east from Gafsa. Having started about 2,000 miles apart, the two Allied armies were now joined for the climax to the battle of Tunisia, the last engagement in North Africa. *See* El Alamein II; Northwest Africa; Tunisia; World War II.

Margate (Hundred Years' War), 1387. During a short period of French ascendancy in the Hundred Years' War, Louis I, duc d'Anjou and regent for Charles VI, planned to invade England. His strongest asset was a combined French-Castilian fleet, which had upset England's mastery of the Channel in the 1372 battle of La Rochelle. On March 24, 1387, this fleet encountered the navy of Richard II off Margate in southeastern England. The English warships, commanded by the Earls of Arundel and Nottingham, won a decisive victory, capturing or destroying 100 of the French-Castilian vessels. This battle ended the invasion threat to England, but it so enhanced the reputation of Arundel that his party became a menace to Richard II. *See* La Rochelle I; Radcot Bridge; Hundred Years' War.

Margus (Civil Wars of the Roman Empire), 285. The Roman empire had been ruled for more than a century by a succession of military despots when a vacancy on the throne brought on a decisive clash between two pretenders: Carinus, son of a former emperor (Carus) and commander of the legions of the West; and Diocletian, a veteran officer proclaimed emperor by the troops in the East. The two rival armies met at Margus on the Morava River in Moesia (eastern Yugoslavia). In a pitched battle, Carinus' legions all but routed the forces of Diocletian, which had been weakened by fighting against Persia and the exhausting move to Moesia. At the crucial moment, however, Carinus was slain by one of his own officers. This action enabled Diocletian to win an uphill victory and become undisputed ruler of Rome. Diocletian's 20-year reign inaugurated the line of "later emperors," which survived until the division of the empire in 395. The first task of the new emperor was to resume the struggle with Sassanian Persia. *See* Palmyra; Carrhae II; Roman Empire.

Mariana Islands (World War II), 1944. The U.S. conquest of the Gilbert and Marshall islands broke Japan's outer defensive ring in the Central Pacific and opened the way for an attack on the Mariana Islands, 1,300 miles to the northwest. From air bases on these islands, B-29 Superfortresses could bomb the Japanese homeland as well as the Philippines, both targets being 1,500 miles away. The Marianas were also important as the headquarters of Japan's Central Pacific fleet, commanded by Adm. Chuichi Nagumo, who had led the attack on Pearl Harbor. Thus a U.S. attack here might provoke the decisive naval battle sought by Adm. Chester Nimitz, the American commander in chief in the Central Pacific. The Mariana group was held by the Japanese Thirty-first Army, commanded by Gen. Hideyoshi Obata.

By June 15, 1944, the marine general Holland Smith's V Amphibious Corps stood ready to invade Saipan, the northernmost of the three major islands. Two marine divisions abreast assaulted the western side of the island on a four-mile front—the 2nd Division (Thomas Watson) on the left, just below the coastal city of Garapan, and the 4th Division (Harry Schmidt) extending to the southern end of the island. Despite fierce resistance from 30,000 enemy troops (Yoshitsugu Saito), the marines had fought their way almost a mile inland by nightfall. While both divisions pressed eastward, the 27th Infantry Division (Ralph Smith) landed the night of June 16–17. The infantrymen swung right to take Aslito (Isely) Airfield the following day. (Army P-47 Thunderbolts began using the field on June 23.) During the next four days of bitter fighting, the V Corps cleaned out most of the southern half of the island.

The three divisions then wheeled to the left—the 2nd Marine on the west coast (the left wing), 27th Infantry in the center, 4th Marine on the east coast. The attack to the north began on June 23 against continued savage resistance. When the 27th Infantry advance lagged behind that of the two flanks, Gen. Holland Smith relieved Gen. Ralph Smith. Under Gen. Sanderford Jarman and later Gen. George Griner, the army division pulled abreast of the two marine units by July I. While the 2nd Marine Division captured Garapan, the other two divisions punched toward Marpi Point at the northern tip of the island. On July 6 both Nagumo and Saito committed suicide. The leaderless Japanese troops then launched savage *banzai* attacks, which cost them nearly 2,500 dead. Two days later, on July 9, resistance on Saipan ended with a mass suicide of Japanese soldiers and civilians off Marpi Point. Only 1,000 enemy prisoners survived the Saipan conquest. United States casualties were 10,347 marines and 3,674 soldiers, including 3,426 dead.

On July 21 the United States switched its attack on the Marianas to Guam, at the southern end of the island chain. The marine general Roy Geiger, commander of the new III Amphibious Corps, sent the 3rd Marine Division (Allen Turnage) ashore north of Apra Harbor, while the 1st Brigade (Lemuel Shepherd) and the 77th Infantry Division (Andrew Bruce) attacked south of Apra. Both assaults struck the west side of the island, the same place as the Japanese conquest of Guam on December 10, 1941. Guam was defended by some 19,000 troops under Gen. Takeshi Takashina.

The southern beachhead had been pressed inland a mile by nightfall of the first day. But it took the 3rd Marine Division in the north four days of the hardest fighting on the island to push a mile inland and link up the two beachheads. On the night of July 25–26 the Japanese mounted fierce counterattacks, which were beaten back only by narrow margins. The 1st Brigade then completed the mop-up of Orote Peninsula between the two landing beaches. Meanwhile, on July 31, the 3rd Marine and the 77th Infantry divisions, left to right abreast, struck northeast. A week later the 1st Brigade came into the line on the left, adding impetus to an already steady advance. On August 10 the assault reached the northern tip of the island, returning Guam to U.S. control. The reconquest cost 7,800 American casualties—6,716 marines, 839 soldiers, and 245 sailors, including 1,023 dead.

Three days after the invasion of Guam, Tinian came under attack by the marines' V Amphibious Corps under Gen. Harry Schmidt, who had replaced Gen. Holland Smith, newly promoted to commander of the General Fleet Marine Force Pacific. Tinian, three and a half miles south of Saipan, had enough level ground to provide the best B-29 air bases in the Pacific. It was defended by 9,000 Japanese soldiers and sailors under a drunken admiral, Kakuji Kakuda. On July 24 the 2nd Marine Division made a feint at landing near Tinian Town on the southwest coast, while the 4th Marine Division (now Clifton Cates) stormed ashore in the northwest. By evening Cates' marines had carved out a mile-deep beachhead. That night more than 1,200 Japanese died trying to wipe out the lodgment. The next day the 2nd Marine Division of Gen. Watson landed at the same beach, cleaned out the northern end of the island, and then turned right to attack down the east coast abreast of the 4th Marine Division. The fastest marine advance of the war up to that time overran Tinian by July 31. United States casualties were the lightest of the Marianas battle—327 killed and 1,771 wounded. Virtually all Japanese not killed by the marine attack died in fruitless *banzai* charges or committed suicide.

The battle of the Marianas resulted in the death of more than 40,000 enemy troops and provoked the Japanese Navy into a disastrous counterattack in the Philippine Sea to the west. And on November 24 the first B-29 raid on Japan came from Saipan bases in the Marianas. *See* Tarawa-Makin; Kwajalein-Eniwetok; Philippine Sea; Peleliu-Angaur; World War II.

Marignano (French Wars in Italy), 1515. Like his two predecessors—Charles VIII and Louis XII—Francis I sent a French army across the Alps into northern Italy. Aligned against him were Pope Leo X, Maximilian I of the Holy Roman Empire, Ferdinand of Spain and Naples, the Swiss cantons, Milan, and Florence. Only the Swiss, however, fielded a large enough force, some 25,000 men, to challenge the French force of comparable size.

The two hostile armies met at Marignano (Melegnano), ten miles southeast of Milan, on September 15, 1515. The Swiss marched to attack in their customary three echelons of pikemen. But their headlong valor proved inferior to French cannon, which tore gaping holes in the Swiss ranks while Francis himself led a furious cavalry counterattack. The Swiss were repulsed only to regroup and renew their assault again and again. At midnight the battle waned, to be resumed at dawn. Finally, after 28 hours of deadly combat, the heretofore invincible Swiss withdrew their last 3,000 men from the corpse-strewn field. Cannon and entrenched arquebusiers had clearly surpassed pikes and halberds. Even the victors lost a third of their force. For his bravery on the field, Duc Charles de Bourbon was created constable of France. This was the last battle between French and Swiss troops until the French Revolutionary Wars.

The French recovered Milan, while both the papacy and the Holy Roman Empire agreed to peace terms. But seven years later war in Italy flared anew. *See* Novara I; La Bicocca.

Maritsa River (Turkish Conquest of Balkans), 1371. The steadily growing power of the Ottoman Turks in the Balkans prompted Serbia to launch a large-scale counteroffensive. Three Serbian princes, descendants of the great Stephen Dushan, organized an army and marched into Turkish territory. On September 26, 1371 the Christian force met the Turks, commanded by Murad I, near Cenomen on the Maritsa (Meric) River. The Turkish army now featured a body of heavy cavalry known as spahis and an infantry corps of Janizaries, made up of well-trained youthful captives. Many of the latter were former Christians who had been converted (often involuntarily) to Mohammedanism. Murad's army overwhelmed the Serbs, killing two of the three princes. The Turkish ascendancy remained unchecked. *See* Adrianople VI; Kossovo I.

Marj-Dabik (Turkish-Egyptian Wars), 1516. Two years after his first invasion of Persia, Selim I, the Grim, sultan of the Ottoman Turks, again marched toward the Euphrates River. But this time Kansu al-Gauri, the Mameluke sultan of Egypt, came to the aid of his Persian ally, Shah Ismail I. The Mameluke army met the Turks at Mari-Dabik (Dolbek), north of Aleppo in Syria, on August 24, 1516. Superior Turkish tactics and armament, especially artillery, crushed the Egyptian force, whose sultan fell in the battle. Selim quickly seized Aleppo, Damascus, and all of Syria. When the new Egyptian sultan, Tuman Bey, refused to accept Turkish suzerainty, the Ottomans marched toward the Nile. *See* Chaldiran; Cairo.

Marne River I (World War I), 1914. The massive battle along the French frontiers during August 20–24 opened the way for five German armies in the center and on the right to penetrate deep into France, from Verdun westward to Amiens. The greatest danger to commander in chief Gen. Joseph Joffre's Allied line above Paris came from his extreme left, where Gen. Alexander von Kluck's German First Army was invading western France. Unable to check the overpowering enemy advance, the French Sixth Army of Gen. Michel Joseph Maunoury fell back until on August 30 it was within 30 miles of Paris. Here it came under control of the city's military governor, Gen. Joseph Simon Gallieni. To the right of the French Sixth was the British Expeditionary Force (BEF), five and one-half divisions under Field Marshal Sir John French. After his defeats at Mons, Belgium, and again at Le Cateau on August 26, the British commander had retreated precipitously through Compiègne, heedless of exposing the allied French units on his flanks. Turning eastward, Sir John withdrew across the Marne on September 3. The other three French armies facing north—Fifth (Charles Lanrezac, replaced by Louis Franchet d'Esperey on September 3), Fourth (Fernand Langle de Cary), and Third (Maurice Sarrail)—yielded ground grudgingly but steadily to the pounding advance of four other German armies.

Then, on August 31, Kluck turned his forward rush from south to southeast. The historic German maneuver (Schlieffen Plan) had called for Kluck's force to make a sweeping encirclement of the French armies from the west and south of Paris. But now believing the enemy all but beaten, he launched an inner wheel north of the French capital to roll up the left of the Allied line. (Chief of the German general staff Helmuth von Moltke approved the change of direction.) Reaching the Marne on September 3, Kluck crossed it only a day behind the BEF and the French Fifth Army. Pressing his weary troops on to the south, Kluck stood halfway to the Seine, directly east of Paris, by the evening of September 5. The next morning, on orders from Moltke who was concerned about the exposed right flank of the German advance, the First Army began to withdraw to the north. It was too late. Maunoury and Gallieni launched a surprise counteroffensive the same morning (September 6) against the IV Reserve Corps of Gen. Hans Gronau, along the Ourcq River.

Despite the exhaustion and heartbreak of 12 consecutive days of retreat, the French troops on

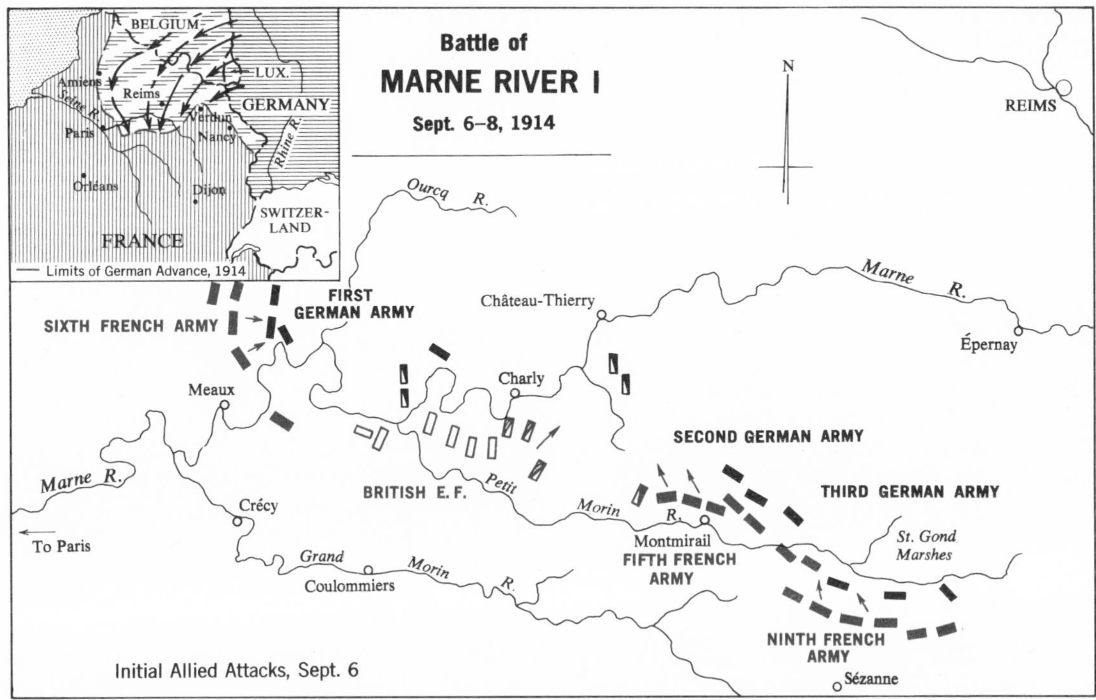

the left maintained their discipline and will to fight. When Kluck's inner wheel provided an opportunity to counterattack, they responded nobly. On the left Maunoury's Sixth Army of 150,000 men struck hard at Kluck's exposed flank, while Franchet d'Esperey's Fifth turned on its pursuers, driving a wedge in the 30-mile gap that had opened up between the German First and Second (Karl von Bülow) armies. The British, who had also turned around under Sir John French's reluctant order, also moved into this gap. On the right of the French counteroffensive, Gen. Ferdinand Foch's newly created Ninth Army hit at the junction between the German Second and Third (Max von Hausen) armies, then grimly held on against furious counterattacks below the Saint Gond marshes.

For three bloody days (September 6–8) the battle swayed back and forth along a 100-mile front. On the west Kluck's army swung about viciously to meet Maunoury's flank attack. The hard-fighting French barely held their ground. Vital reinforcements arrived from Paris by taxicab. These were the 6,000 troops of the IV Corps, one of the two corps Joffre shifted from the Moselle front for the battle. Detraining in Paris, they were rushed into action by a fleet of 600 taxis, which made two 36-mile trips to the lines at the Ourcq River, north of the Marne. To the east Franchet d'Esperey launched an energetic night attack on September 8–9, driving back the right flank of the German Second Army. This forced Kluck to withdraw northward to protect his left rear against the British, who were now recrossing the Marne. On September 9 the entire German line began a fighting retreat of 40 miles back to the Aisne River, from in front of Verdun westward to Noyon. Casualties totaled about 5 percent on each side for those engaged—900,000 Germans (44 infantry and 7 cavalry divisions in 5 armies) and 1,082,000 French and English (56 infantry and 9 cavalry divisions in 6 armies). Moltke was relieved and replaced by Gen. Erich von Falkenhayn on September 14.

A vital contribution to the French victory came from the eastern end of Joffre's line. Here the French First (Auguste Dubail) and Second (Noël de Castelnau) armies stubbornly held the fortress cities—Épinal, Charmes, Nancy, Toul—along the Moselle River. Despite the transfer of two corps to the Marne front, this right wing for 18 days fought off the almost constant hammerings of two German armies under Crown Prince Rupprecht of Bavaria—his Sixth and the Seventh of Gen. Josias von Heeringen. Moltke finally called off the German attack on September 9. In between the two fronts, the French Third and Fourth armies successfully contained the penetration from Verdun to the upper Marne by the German Fifth and Fourth (the Duke of Württemberg), both directed by Crown Prince Friedrich Wilhelm.

The French victory along the 300-mile Marne front fell short of the major triumph that could have been achieved by piercing the German lines (in large part caused by Sir John French's hesitant counterattack). Nevertheless, the battle must be ranked as one of the decisive engagements of history. It clinched the complete and equal failure of the two offensive strategies designed to bring the war to a quick close—the German Schlieffen Plan and the French Plan 17. Thus the first battle of the Marne determined that World War I would last a long time. *See* Le Cateau; Aisne River I; World War I.

Marne River II (World War I), 1918. Despite the limited successes of his first four offensives, the German commander, Gen. Erich Ludendorff, launched still another all-out assault on the Western Front on July 15. This attack, from both sides of Reims, was scheduled to reach the Marne River, east of Paris. On the German left (east) flank the First Army (now under Gen. Bruno von Mudra) and Third Army (Karl von Einem) made only small gains before being stopped at 11 A.M. by the French First Army of Gen. Henri Gouraud. West of Reims, however, Gen. Max von Boehn's Seventh Army smashed forward to the Marne between Château-Thierry and Épernay. A bridgehead nine miles long and four miles deep was seized south of the river before the advance was halted on July 17 by the French Ninth Army (Marie Mitry), which had moved up to the east of the shaken Sixth Army (Jean Degoutte). In the defense of this sector the American 3rd Division played a strong role. In all, 52 German divisions were held in check by 36 Allied divisions—23 French, 9 American, 2 British, 2 Italian. This so-called Champagne-Marne offensive was the last major German drive on the Western Front. Ludendorff's five separate attacks had cost him more than 800,000 casualties and so weakened his armies that the initiative now passed to the Allies.

On the day after the German offensive stalled, July 18, the Allied commander in chief, Gen. Ferdinand Foch, launched a massive counterattack against the Marne salient. On the east and south the French Fifth (Henri Berthelot) and Ninth armies made secondary assaults. On the west the main attack came from the Sixth and Tenth (Charles Mangin) armies. Supplementing the four French armies were 14 Allied divisions—8 American, 4 British, 2 Italian. Mangin jumped off early in the morning, followed by the other armies in a counterclockwise direction. Aided by 350 tanks, the two western armies advanced from two to five miles on the first day. When their continued thrust into the salient threatened to cut the vital Soissons–Château-Thierry road, Ludendorff began to withdraw from the Marne. Soissons was liberated on August 2. By August 3 the Germans had fallen back to a line along the Vesle and Aisne rivers at the base of the former salient. An American attack on August 6 found the enemy solidly entrenched. This closed the battle, which had begun with a German offensive and ended with an Allied victory. On August 6, also, Foch became marshal of France. *See* Noyon-Montdidier; Amiens; World War I.

Marsaglia (War of the Grand Alliance), 1693. Although the Spanish Netherlands remained the war's main theater of operations, the duchy of Savoy, south of Switzerland, became the scene of a second battle in 1693. The French general Nicolas de Catinat had routed the army of Savoy, under the duke Victor Amadeus II, three years earlier. Now the duke organized a new force that included Austrian, Spanish, and English troops. On October 4 this allied army engaged Catinat at Marsaglia, near the Po. But again the duke's men were no match for the well-trained French army. They were driven across the river with the loss of several thousand men. Three years later Savoy became the first member of the Grand Alliance to make a separate peace with Louis XIV, on May 30, 1696. The French returned their conquests in exchange for the Duke of Savoy's neutrality. *See* Staffarda; Neerwinden I; Namur I; Grand Alliance, War of the.

Mars-la-Tour (Franco-Prussian War), 1870. The retreat of the French forces of Marshal Achille Bazaine continued after the battle of Colombey on August 14. Bazaine, more demoralized than his troops, fell back across the Moselle, pursued by the Prussian armies of Gen. (later Count) Helmuth von Moltke. Between Metz and Verdun the Prussian Second Army of Prince Frederick Charles attempted to contain the withdrawing French at Mars-la-Tour and nearby Vionville. In a battle on August 16 Bazaine's men scored an early advantage, but the lethargic commander allowed the enemy to build up against him and block his route to the west. Each side suffered more than 15,000 casualties. Bazaine now turned back toward Metz. *See* Colombey; Gravelotte; Franco-Prussian War.

Marston Moor (English Civil War), 1644. For the first two years of the Civil War the Cavaliers of Charles I held their own or gained narrow victories over the Roundhead armies of the Parliamentarians. In the summer of 1644, however, York, the center of Royalist strength in the north, came under vigorous siege from a combined force of Scots and Roundheads. After securing his Oxford headquarters against another Roundhead threat, Charles sent his nephew Prince Rupert of Germany to relieve the hard-pressed Yorkist forces of William Cavendish, marquis of Newcastle. Rupert, with a strong cavalry detachment, arrived just in time to relieve York. The besiegers retired westward seven miles to Marston Moor. Here the Scots of Alexander Leslie (Lord Leven) and the Roundheads of Lord Fairfax were reinforced by a third Parliamentarian force, the heavy cavalry, called Ironsides, under Oliver Cromwell and Gen. Lord Manchester (Edward Montagu). The com-

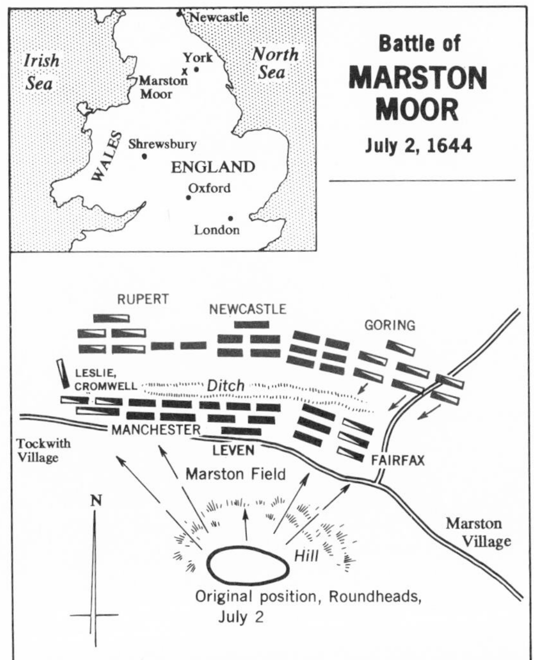

bined Parliamentarian armies totaled 20,000 infantry and 5,000 horsemen.

Prince Rupert, believing he was under royal orders to destroy the enemy, marched after the Roundheads. Even with the support of Newcastle's men and a cavalry force under Gen. Lord George Goring, the Cavalier strength numbered only 11,000 infantry and 7,000 horsemen. On July 2 Rupert's pursuit came upon the Roundhead positions. After a day of inconclusive skirmishing the prince began to disengage his forces, planning to make a general attack the following day. But at six o'clock in the evening the entire Roundhead line swept forward. On the Cavalier left Goring's cavalry repulsed the assault and even managed a successful counterattack. But elsewhere the Cavaliers were overwhelmed, chiefly at the hands of Cromwell's cavalry and the Scottish horsemen commanded by Gen. David Leslie. Newcastle lost almost his entire force and fled into exile. Rupert's heretofore invincible cavalry, which he had unwisely deployed by squadrons instead of as a unit, was shattered. This largest battle of the war was also the bloodiest —4,000 dead lay upon the field when nightfall mercifully ended the no-quarter fighting.

Marston Moor cost the king both his northern army and the north. York surrendered on July 16 and the city of Newcastle on October 16. Although Rupert could collect only remnants of the Cavalier force, Charles remained undaunted. From Oxford he marched westward in pursuit of an invading Roundhead army. Meanwhile, fighting also broke out in Scotland. *See* Cropredy Bridge; Tippermuir; Lostwithiel; English Civil War.

Martinique (Seven Years' War), 1762. The sea power of Great Britain, which had consistently overshadowed that of the French navy during the first four years of the war, grew even stronger after the conquest of Canada in 1760. Early in 1762 Adm. George Rodney, with some army veterans of the Canadian fighting, attacked the French island of Martinque in the West Indies. The island defenders were quickly overwhelmed, surrendering on February 12. This victory made possible the securing of all the smaller Windward Islands. Martinque, however, was restored to France by the Treaty of Paris the following year. *See* Quiberon Bay; Seven Years' War.

Maserfield (Teutonic Conquest of Britain), 642. King Oswald of Northumbria, who had avenged his uncle Edwin's death at Heavenfield, sought to punish the other aggressor, Mercia, eight years later. He took his army to Maserfield (Oswestry), near the present Welsh border. Here he fought a pitched battle against the Mercians of King Penda. But for the second time Penda crushed a Northumbrian army. Oswald was slain and decapitated like his uncle before him. It would be another 13 years before Penda was again challenged—this time by a brother of Oswald. *See* Heavenfield; Winwaed.

Massacre Hill (Sioux War I), 1866. To protect the Bozeman Trail, leading from Wyoming into Montana Territory, from the attacks of the Plains Indians, the United States constructed Fort Phil Kearny (nicknamed Fort Perilous) along the upper Powder River in 1866. Here the 18th Infantry Regiment of Col. Henry Carrington sought to safeguard white emigrants in northern Wyoming. On December 21 a wood train of wagons was suddenly attacked by some 2,000 Sioux led by Crazy Horse and Red Cloud. To protect the train, which stood about five miles from the fort, Capt. William Fetterman led a counterattack with 2 other officers and 79 men. Unaware of the Indians' strength, Fetterman and his command were surrounded beyond Lodge Trail Ridge on a height later called Massacre Hill. Despite a desperate resistance, every soldier was killed. About 60 of the attackers were slain. The Indians then besieged the fort itself. But a veteran frontiersman, John "Portugee" Phillips, slipped through the Indian lines to ride 236 miles to Fort Laramie, Wyo., to obtain reinforcements. The siege was broken. *See* Platte Bridge; Fort Phil Kearny; Sioux Wars.

Masurian Lakes I (World War I), 1914. The overwhelming German victory at Tannenberg during August 26–30 crushed one arm of the Russian pincers movement against East Prussia. Field Marshal Paul von Hindenburg, with his chief of staff, Gen. Eric Ludendorff, then turned the German Eighth Army back to face the second arm—the Russian First Army of Gen. Pavel Rennenkampf.

For this attack Hindenburg's army was reinforced by two corps sent eastward from the French frontier by the chief of the German general staff, Field Marshal Helmuth von Moltke. (These two corps, arriving too late for the battle of Tannenberg and unneeded for the forthcoming struggle, would be sorely missed by the German offensive toward the Marne on the Western Front.) During the destruction of the Russian Second Army at Tannenberg, Rennenkampf's First Army had remained out of contact to the northeast, where it was inching its way through the Insterburg Gap between Königsberg (Kaliningrad) and the Masurian Lakes. Informed of Samsonov's defeat, Rennenkampf pulled back to the Masurian Lakes, anchoring his left (south) here and organizing a cordon defense northward to the Baltic Sea.

On September 5 the German Eighth Army began hammering at the Russian line, with the heaviest attacks coming in the south. When this offensive threatened to outflank the Russians, Rennenkampf ordered a general withdrawal late on September 9. To protect his left flank from the rapid drive of Gen. Hermann von François's I Corps, which covered 77 miles in four days, Rennenkampf made a counterattack against the German center on September 10. This checked Ludendorff's advance for 48 hours and enabled many Russian troops to escape envelopment—some retreating forces fell back 55 miles in one 50-hour period. By September 13 the German pursuit began to slacken. East Prussia had been cleared of the invader at a cost of only 10,000 casualties. Russian losses were about 125,000. General Ivan Jilinsky, who had misdirected the Russian invasion of East Prussia, was replaced by Gen. Nikolai Russki, one of the victorious generals on the Galician front. *See* Tannenberg II; Galicia; Vistula River–Warsaw; World War I.

Masurian Lakes II (World War I), 1915. During the first winter of the war the German commanders on the Eastern Front, Field Marshal Paul von Hindenburg and his chief of staff, Gen. Erich Ludendorff, planned a knockout blow against Russia. The chief attack was to come from two German armies in East Prussia against the Russian Tenth Army (Gen. Sievers) standing north of the Masurian Lakes. On February 7 the German Eighth Army (Otto von Below) struck eastward in a heavy snowstorm against the Russian left (south) flank. Caught by surprise, the Russians began falling back, only to be assaulted from the right (north) on the following day by the newly formed German Tenth Army (Hermann von Eichhorn). All four Russian corps seemed in grave danger of destruction. But the stubborn resistance of the XX Corps in the Forest of Augustow enabled the other three to escape. When this force finally surrendered on February 21, it brought the number of Russian casualties up to 200,000, half of whom were prisoners. German combat losses were light, but many units suffered severely from exposure, in what is sometimes called the Winter Battle of Masuria. *See* Masurian Lakes I; Gorlice-Tarnów; World War I.

Matapan (World War II), 1941. During the battle for Greece, a British naval force under Adm. Henry Pridham-Whippell encountered an Italian fleet (Arturo Riccardi) off Cape Matapan in the Greek Peloponnesus. In a day and night battle on March 28, eight British capital ships—three battleships, four cruisers, and an aircraft carrier—sank three Italian 8-inch cruisers, one or two smaller cruisers, and two destroyers, and damaged a battleship. More than 900 Italian seamen were rescued from the water. British casualties were two naval aircraft. This action helped to maintain Allied naval supremacy in the eastern Mediterranean. *See* Taranto; Greece (World War II); World War II.

Maxen (Seven Years' War), 1759. When Austria and Russia failed to crush all Prussian resistance after their overwhelming triumph at Kunersdorf, Frederick II, the Great, took new heart in the fall of 1759. He slowly rebuilt the Prussian army. Then he saw an opportunity to cut off the Austrian army of Field Marshal Count Leopold von Daun (in the service of Holy Roman Empress Maria Theresa) in Saxony. The Prussian king sent Gen. Friedrich von Finck with 12,000 men to work around behind Daun, who was in Dresden. But the Austrian general withdrew southward ten miles to Maxen. Here he surrounded Finck with 42,000 Imperial troops. After two days of attempting to break out, the Prussian surrendered his army on November 20. (Finck was later court-martialed by Frederick, convicted, and imprisoned.) But Daun failed to capitalize on his victory and soon went into winter quarters for the year. *See* Kunersdorf; Landeshut; Seven Years' War.

Mecca (Mohammed's Conquest of Arabia). 630. When Mohammed's opponents broke the 628 Treaty of Hudaybiya, the Moslems resumed the civil war in Arabia. Their growing power made ultimate victory a certainty. Mohammed himself led an attack from Medina, 210 miles south to Mecca. Storming into the city of his birth in January 630, the Prophet won over the inhabitants, destroying a reported 360 pagan idols. Mecca was then enshrined as the Holy City of Islam. During the remaining two years of his life, Mohammed, by sword and persuasion, succeeded in stamping out virtually all paganism in Arabia. The job was completed about 633 under the caliphate of Abu-Bakr, one of the fathers-in-law of the Prophet. *See* Medina; Hira; Ajnadain; Moslem Conquests.

Mechanicsville (American Civil War). The first major action of the Seven Days battle east of Richmond, on June 26, 1862, in which the Confederate attack was checked. *See* Seven Days.

Médenine (World War II). A sudden attack by three German *Panzer* divisions from behind the Mareth Line, on March 6, 1943, which was repulsed by the British Eighth Army. *See* Mareth Line.

Medina (Mohammed's Conquest of Arabia), 627. Alarmed at the growing strength of Mohammed's Islamic movement in Medina, his opponents organized an attack on the city. Abu Sufyan of the Koreish tribe led a force of 10,000 men to Medina, which was defended by the Prophet and some 3,000 followers. Fighting behind a trench dug around the city, the Moslems repulsed every Koreish attack for 20 days. The besiegers then gave up the attack and dispersed. The following year Mohammed secured the right to make a pilgrimage to Mecca (Treaty of Hudaybiya). From this time on the initiative in the Arabian civil war passed to the Moslems. Two of the converts during this period were destined to become great Islamic generals—Khālid ibn-al-Walīd, the conqueror of Syria, and Amr ibn-al-As, victor in Egypt. *See* Ohod; Mecca; Moslem Conquests.

Medway River (Roman Conquest of Britain), A.D. 43. Almost a hundred years after Julius Caesar invaded Britain and then withdrew, Emperor Claudius I sent several Roman legions under Aulus Plautius to make a second attempt to conquer the island. The expedition landed on the southeast coast and pushed inland to the Medway River, a southern tributary of the Thames. Here the Romans encountered a Briton force, under Caractacus, which was prepared to resist. Plautius sent a detachment of German auxiliaries across the river to attack the Britons' horses and thus disable their war chariots. On the second day a future Roman emperor, Vespasian, forded the river farther upstream with a legion and struck the Britons in the flank. The legionaries routed their less disciplined foe. Plautius then moved forward to occupy Camulodunum (Colchester), northeast of London. Claudius himself landed in Britain and declared that island to be a province of Rome.

Plautius extended the conquest by seizing Lindum (Lincoln), to the north; Deva (Chester), in the northwest; and Isca Silurum (Caerleon), in the west on the Welsh border. Although Caractacus continued to harass the marching legions, he was powerless to prevent the subjugation of Britain. *See* Verulamium I; Shropshire.

Meerut (Conquests of Tamerlane), 1399. Following his destruction of Delhi, the Mongol conqueror Tamerlane (Timur Lenk, or Timur the Lame) crossed the Jumna River and marched 40 miles northeast to Meerut. Heavily fortified, Meerut was considered to be impregnable. The Mongol leader started mining operations, but on January 9, 1399, his impatient troops stormed the city by means of ladders. The Indian garrison was massacred and the mines were used to destroy the fortifications. Now satisfied, Tamerlane cut his way out to the Indus River, ready to renew his thrust to the east. *See* Delhi I; Baghdad II.

Megalopolis (Macedonian Conquests), 331 B.C. While Alexander the Great was busy conquering Persia, the restless Greeks in the Peloponnesus organized a revolt against Macedonian rule. Sparta, led by King Agis III, secured the alliance of Achaea, Elis, and Arcadia. But the city of Megalopolis, capital of the Arcadian confederation, refused to join the rebellion. Agis then attacked the reluctant ally and was holding the city under siege when Antipater, Alexander's governor of Greece, arrived with a superior Macedonian army. As in the revolt of Thebes (335 B.C.), the rebels were thoroughly beaten. Agis was killed. This ended Greek resistance until the death of Alexander III spurred a new uprising eight years later. *See* Thebes; Arbela-Gaugamela; Crannon; Macedonian Conquests.

Megiddo I (Egyptian Invasion of Asia), 1479 B.C. The first of the great conquerors, King Thutmose III of Egypt, fought the earliest battle of which a partial account exists. In the spring of 1479 B.C. Thutmose marched an Egyptian army around the eastern end of the Mediterranean to put down a revolt in northern Palestine. The rebel army, led by the king of the Syrian city of Kadesh, moved southward to Megiddo, which commanded the pass leading into the Plain of Esdraelon. Deploying his army in three groups, the Egyptian king led a dawn attack that promptly routed the Syrian-Palestinian force drawn up southwest of Megiddo. The defeated allies fled within the walls of the city. But the Egyptians, instead of pressing their advantage, stopped to loot the enemy camp. Thutmose then invested Megiddo and took its surrender after seven months of siege.

Megiddo, often referred to as the site of the Armageddon battlefield described in the Bible, was the first of at least 15 successful campaigns carried out by Thutmose during his 54-year reign. The booty and tribute collected from the vanquished were used to decorate Egyptian temples. *See* Kadesh.

Megiddo II (Egyptian Conquest of Judah), 609 B.C. In a desperate effort to aid the collapsing Assyrian Empire, Necho II marched up from Egypt with an army of reinforcements. Necho arrived too late to save his Assyrian ally, but at Megiddo, in northern Palestine on the ancient road from Egypt to Mesopotamia, he encountered the

Judahite army, commanded by King Josiah. The Judahites were crushed and Josiah was killed by an arrow. Four years later, however, the Egyptians were driven out of Asia by the neo-Babylonian Empire of Chaldea. *See* Nineveh I; Carchemish.

Megiddo III (World War I), 1918. The capture of Jerusalem in December 1917 opened the way for a renewed British offensive in Palestine. But German attacks on the Western Front forced the British to recall most of the troops in Gen. Sir Edmund Allenby's Palestinian command. During the spring and summer Allenby trained green replacements from India to build back his army to 60,000 men. At the same time he raided east of the Jordan River several times. In these strikes he was aided by the Arab force of Col. Thomas Edward Lawrence, which continually harassed Turkish communication lines. The Turkish commander, the German general Otto Liman von Sanders, was misled by this activity on his left front. He had deployed a third of his 30,000 troops (the Fourth Army) east of the Jordan when Allenby struck on the Turkish right (coastal) flank.

Allenby, who had secretly massed most of his infantry along the coast north of Jaffa, attacked early on September 19 on a 65-mile front. The thinly stretched Turkish line collapsed in three hours. Allenby rushed his cavalry corps through the gap toward Megiddo, then wheeled the horsemen to the right behind the enemy Eighth and Seventh armies. With their route to the north blocked, the Turks fled eastward across the Jordan, leaving 25,000 prisoners in British hands. This retreat caused the Turkish Fourth Army on the eastern flank to withdraw also. As the Turks scrambled northward toward Damascus, they were harassed by British cavalry and aircraft and by raiding Arabs. Liman von Sanders had no opportunity to make a stand. His *Asienkorps* of German troops joined the retreat. Damascus fell on October 2, and Aleppo, more than 200 miles to the north, on October 28. Two days later the Turkish government asked for and received an armistice. The battle of Megiddo had resulted in the capture of 75,000 prisoners at a cost to the British of 5,600 casualties. In all, the Palestine campaign resulted in more than 550,000 British casualties, of which 90 percent were nonbattle. *See* Gaza III; World War I.

Melitene I (Byzantine-Persian Wars), 578. When Tiberius II Constantinus came to the Byzantine throne in 578, he inherited the fourth war that the Sassanid king of Persia, Khosrau (Chosroes) I, was waging against Constantinople. Tiberius took command of the Imperial forces at Melitene (Malatya), just west of the Euphrates River. Here the Persians, who had earlier ravaged Syria, were checked. Although the battle was inconclusive, Khosrau suffered heavy losses and withdrew under cover of night. Another truce was arranged. *See* Callinicum; Jerusalem V.

Melitene II (Byzantine-Moslem Wars), 934. Six years after the reconquest of Erzurum, the Byzantine Empire continued the offensive against the Moslems in Asia Minor. Constantine VII again sent out the able general John Kurkuas. Taking the experienced Byzantine cavalry across the upper Euphrates, Kurkuas attacked and captured the outpost of Melitene (Malatya). The inability of the crumbling Abbasid caliphate to reinforce its frontier had enabled Constantinople to regain control of the upper Euphrates and Tigris rivers. *See* Erzurum; Candia I; Moslem Conquests.

Melitene III (First Crusade), 1100. In securing their position in the Near East, the First Crusaders had established a reputation of invincibility among their Turkish opponents. This aura did not last long, however. In 1100 Bohemond of Taranto marched out from Antioch toward Melitene (Malatya) to answer an appeal for help from the Armenian garrison. En route, his knights were ambushed by a Turkish force. Most of the crusaders were killed. Bohemond was taken prisoner and held for ransom until 1103. *See* Ashkelon I; Mersivan; Crusades.

Mentana (Italian Wars of Independence), 1867. The question of control of Rome, which had troubled the young kingdom of Italy since its formation in 1861, seemed on the way to settlement when the last of the French troops withdrew late in 1866. However, this only provided an opportunity for the ardent Italian patriot Giuseppe Garibaldi to organize a new march on Rome. Knowing that the papal forces of Pius IX were too weak to defend the city, Louis Napoleon III returned a French force to Rome in October 1867. Garibaldi, who had been disavowed by King Victor Emmanuel II, pressed on with this invasion of the Papal State.

On November 3 at Mentana, northeast of Rome, the insurgents encountered a combined force of French and papal troops. The Garibaldians were thoroughly beaten, largely through the efforts of hard-fighting papal Zouaves and the French use of breech-loading, center-fire rifles, called *chassepots* (for their inventor). Garibaldi was captured and sent to the island of Caprera. Three years later the Franco-Prussian War forced Louis Napoleon III to withdraw all his troops from Rome, on August 19, 1870. The city was promptly stormed by Italian patriots. On October 3 Rome was annexed to Italy and made the capital of the kingdom. *See* Vis; Italian Wars of Independence.

Mergentheim (Thirty Years' War), 1645. Despite the peace negotiations being conducted in Westphalia, the second big battle of 1645 began taking shape in Bavaria. From the Rhine the French marshal the Vicomte de Turenne had marched and plundered his way to Heilbronn and then to Rothenburg and later to Mergentheim. Here on the Tauber River, 20 miles south of Wurzburg, Turenne's veteran Weimar army demanded to be put into rest quarters.

While the invaders were thus partially dispersed, a joint Bavarian-Austrian army under Field Marshal Baron Franz von Mercy and Gen. Johann von Werth, the latter of whom had just returned almost alone from the Imperial disaster at Jankau, moved to attack. Before dawn on May 2 Mercy and Werth struck the surprised French camp. They routed the defenders and seized all the artillery and baggage. Turenne, with only a third of his force collected, fell back toward the Rhine. But now he was reinforced by a fresh French army under Louis II, the Great Condé (duc d'Enghien). Together the French commanders prepared a new drive to the Danube. *See* Jankau; Nördlingen II; Thirty Years' War.

Mersa Matrûh (World War II), 1942. Following its long retreat from Gazala-Tobruk in Libya, the British Eighth Army, now under the personal direction of the Middle East commander, Gen. Sir Claude Auchinleck, halted at the Egyptian base of Mersa Matrûh. General Holmes's X Corps hastily occupied the coastal town; Gen. W. H. E. Gott's XIII Corps took up positions nine miles inland. On June 26, Field Marshal Erwin Rommel's *Panzerarmee Afrika,* in close pursuit, knifed into the weak British center between the two corps. With only 2,500 German infantry and 60 tanks, the spearhead *Afrika Korps* routed four British divisions, equipped with 150 tanks, in three days. The Eighth Army fell back 120 miles to El Alamein with a loss of 6,000 prisoners and 40 tanks. The Nile Valley and the Suez Canal seemed in great danger of Axis capture. *See* Gazala; Tobruk III; El Alamein I; World War II.

Mersivan (First Crusade), 1101. During the summer of 1101 an army of reinforcements for the First Crusade reached Asia Minor. United under the supreme command of the veteran Count Raymond IV of Toulouse, the German, French, and Lombard force set out along the route of the First Crusade. But upon hearing that Bohemond of Taranto, the ruler of Antioch, was held prisoner by the Turks of Sivas, the crusaders turned northeast to rescue him. Against the advice of Raymond, the army crossed the Halys (Kizil Irmak) River, pressing deep into enemy territory. At Mersivan the Turks suddenly attacked. Their mounted bowmen, keeping at a distance and thus neutralizing the European's swords and lances, methodically cut down the Christians. The entire column, including clergy, women, and children, was wiped out, except for Raymond and a handful of knights who cut their way to safety at Sinope on the Black Sea. *See* Melitene III; Ereğli I; Crusades.

Merv (Mongol Conquest of Central Asia), 1221. In the third year of his conquest of central Asia, the Mongol leader, Genghis Khan, sent his youngest son, Tului, westward into modern Turkmen S.S.R. Tului took his column of cavalry to the ancient city of Merv (Mary), on the Murghab River. Here the Moslem garrison successfully fought off Mongol attacks for 22 days. Finally, however, Tului tricked some of the city's leaders into opening a gate in the walls. The Mongols poured through, massacred the inhabitants, and converted Merv into a burned-out wasteland. Meanwhile, the Great Khan himself had turned south in pursuit of Jalal-ad-Din, who had replaced his dead father, Mohammed, as shah of the rapidly disintegrating Khwarizm Empire. *See* Herat I; Bamian; Mongol Wars.

Mesolóngion (Greek War of Independence), 1822–1826. Early in 1822 a Greek assembly declared independence from the Turkish government of Mahmud II. After a series of uprisings and massacres on both sides, a Turkish army of 30,000 men overran all of the Greek peninsula north of the Gulf of Corinth. While the provisional government fled to the islands, a determined garrison held on to the key fortress of Mesolóngion (Missolonghi) on the north side of the Gulf of Patras, guarding the entrance to the Gulf of Corinth. In January 1823 the Turks had to fall back from the stout defense led by Alexandros Mavrokordatos. The Greeks, however, were unable to take the offensive because of factional strife between patriot groups. (In 1824 one of the most famous defenders of Mesolóngion, George Gordon, Lord Byron, died of malaria.)

Unable to put down the rebellion with Turkish troops, Sultan Mahmud called on his ally Mehemet (Mohammed) Ali, viceroy of Egypt. In February 1825 an Egyptian army under Gen. Ibrahim Pasha, son of Mehemet Ali, landed on the Peloponnesus from Crete and soon subdued the peninsula. In April, a Turkish army commanded by Reshid Pasha began a new investment of Mesolóngion from the north. A year later, on April 23, 1826, the fortress finally fell to the Turks. The Greek defeat led France, Great Britain, and Russia to intervene in the war. *See* Navarino; Greek War of Independence.

Messina I (First Punic War), 264 B.C. Early in the third century B.C. the seaport of Messina (Messana) in northeast Sicily, across the strait from Italy, was seized by Syracuse-hired mercenaries from Campania. The mercenaries called themselves Mamertines, or "sons of Mars." About 270 B.C., Syracusans, under Hiero II, and the Carthaginians from western Sicily launched independent attacks on Messina. Carthage won the race and occupied the city. The Mamertines called on Rome for aid, and in 264 a Roman army secured the city, expelling the Carthaginians. Disturbed by this strong new neighbor, Hiero attacked Messina a second time. Again he was driven off and, when pursued by the aggressive Romans, sued for peace. Syracuse became an ally of Rome in the latter's First Punic War with Carthage, which was precipitated by the battle over Messina. Messina itself became a free city under Roman protection. *See* Mylae; Ecnomus; Punic Wars.

Messina II (Aragonese Conquest of Sicily), 1284. After 14 years of the harsh French rule of Charles I of Anjou, the island of Sicily in 1282 revolted in a brutal insurrection called the Sicilian Vespers. (The outbreak began at Palermo with the ringing of church bells for vesper service on March 31, 1282.) To aid the rebels, the Italian naval officer Ruggiero di Lauria, serving Pedro III of Aragon, assembled a fleet of Sicilian and Spanish vessels. On October 2, 1284, this fleet engaged the French vessels of Charles northwest of Messina. Admiral Lauria's ships won an overwhelming victory. Charles was driven from Sicily, which came under Aragonese rule. Pedro III took the title Peter I of Sicily. *See* Tagliacozzo; Alghero.

Messines (World War I), 1917. To break out of the Ypres (Ieper) salient, now held for more than two and a half years, the British field marshal Sir Douglas Haig planned a major offensive. But first he had to oust the Germans from the commanding Messines Ridge to the south. An attack by the British became imperative in the spring to keep the Germans occupied while Gen. Henri Pétain worked to restore French morale after the disastrous losses in Aisne River II. By June 7 Haig was ready. His engineers had planted 19 mines, containing almost a million pounds of high explosives, under Messines Ridge. The mines were exploded early in the morning, accompanied by a heavy artillery bombardment. Nine divisions in Gen. Sir Herbert Plumer's Second Army rushed forward to seize the ridge. At the same time Gen. Hubert Gough's Fifth Army moved up to exploit the opening, along with the First French Army of Gen. François Anthoine. East of the key height enemy resistance soon stiffened. The German commander in Flanders, Crown Prince Rupprecht of Bavaria, ordered Gen. Friedrich Sixt von Armin's Fourth Army to fall back and then to counterattack. This maneuver limited the British advance, which was called off on June 14. *See* Ypres II; Aisne River II; Ypres III; World War I.

Metaurus River (Second Punic War), 207 B.C. Ten years after invading Italy at the head of a strong Carthaginian army, Hannibal realized that to win a decisive victory he needed major reinforcements. He ordered his younger brother Hasdrubal to join him from Spain with as many men as possible. The Roman commander in Spain, Publius Cornelius Scipio (later Africanus), guarded the eastern passes of the Pyrenees to block just such a junction of enemy forces. But in the summer of 208 B.C. Hasdrubal eluded the Roman roadblock by crossing the mountains far to the west. After wintering with Gallic allies at Auvergne in central France, Hasdrubal marched through the Alps in the spring, probably along the same route taken by Hannibal in 218. Anti-Roman Ligurians and Gauls swelled his ranks. Hasdrubal crossed to the east side of the peninsula and then turned south along the Adriatic coast. He sent a message to Hannibal to unite with him south of the Metaurus River (near the present Ancona). The message never reached his brother; it was intercepted by the Romans.

To defend Rome against the suddenly awesome threat of two Carthaginian armies in Italy, the Senate elected two new consuls. The veteran Marcus Livius Salinator was ordered to stop Hasdrubal in the north, while Gaius Claudius Nero was sent south to Apulia with the mission of blocking any attempt by Hannibal to move out of Lucania. The Barca brothers stood within 200 miles of each other when Nero received Hasdrubal's intercepted message. He promptly made a decision that turned the whole course of the war. With 7,000 picked men, he slipped out of the lines facing Hannibal and made a remarkable six-day forced march to reinforce Livius in the north (the first recorded military operation in which a commander took advantage of an interior position by attacking one enemy before the other could come to the rescue). Although Nero moved with great

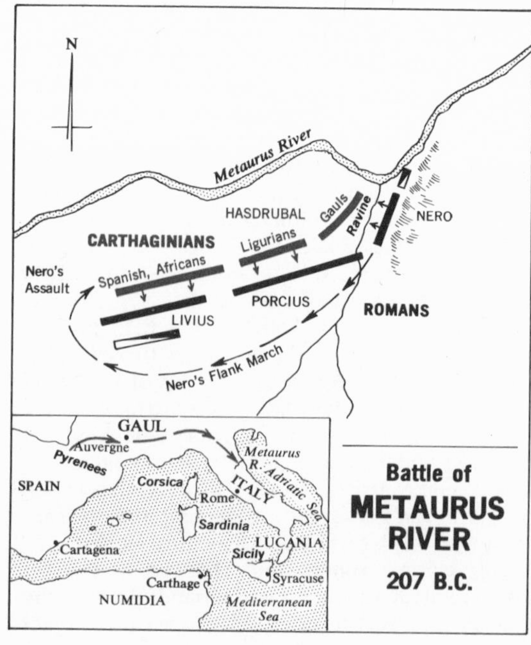

Battle of METAURUS RIVER 207 B.C.

secrecy, Hasdrubal became suspicious that the Romans had united against him. The Carthaginian pulled back to the Metaurus River, but before he could cross, the legions attacked.

The Roman army made a violent assault on Hasdrubal's line. But despite a numerical advantage, the Romans were checked by the skillfully deployed Carthaginians. Then Nero made a second decisive maneuver. He withdrew from his position on the right wing and quickly marched his 7,000-man force around the rear of the Roman line. Before the Carthaginians could change front, Nero struck their right flank and crushed it. The entire Roman army moved in and methodically annihilated Hasdrubal's force where it stood. Among the 10,000 slain was the commander himself. About 2,000 Romans were killed.

As soon as the battle was over, Nero reassembled his troops and launched another six-day forced march back to Apulia. His weary men re-entered Canusium (Canosa di Puglia) before they were missed. Hannibal's first news of the crushing defeat came when his brother's severed head was thrown into the Carthaginian camp.

The Roman victory at the Metaurus ranks as one of the decisive battles in history. Although Hannibal remained in Italy another four years, his ultimate defeat was assured. Rome's stubborn resistance and the brilliant leadership of Nero combined to defeat one of the world's greatest military commanders. It was now certain that Rome, and not Carthage, would win supremacy in the West. *See* Capua; Zama; Punic Wars.

Methven (English-Scottish Wars), 1306. Robert VIII (called "the Bruce") had taken little or no public part in Sir William Wallace's guerrilla warfare against the English forces of Edward I. But with the capture and execution of Wallace in 1305, "the Bruce" assumed leadership of the Scots nationalistic movement. He had himself crowned at Scone as Robert I in 1306. Edward, enraged, sent an English army into Perth County in central Scotland. At Methven, northwest of Perth, the English routed Bruce's small band of rebels on June 19. Bruce fled to Rathlin Island off the coast of Ireland. But supposedly encouraged by watching the persistence of a spider building a web, he returned early the next year to resume the war. *See* Falkirk I; Loudon Hill.

Metz (Franco-Prussian War), 1870. Following the battle of Gravelotte on August 18, the French marshal Achille Bazaine foolishly withdrew some 170,000 troops into the nearby fortress of Metz on the Moselle River. The entire army was promptly besieged by the Prussian army of Prince Frederick Charles, nephew of Wilhelm I. When Louis Napoleon III tried to lead a relief force to the Moselle on August 31, Bazaine ordered a sortie from Metz. The French gained some ground but were driven back into their lines the following day with a loss of more than 3,000 men. Prussian casualties were less than 3,000. The disaster at Sedan ended all hope of immediate relief. But Paris still held out and new French armies were building in the provinces when Bazaine cravenly surrendered Metz on Ocober 27. About 170,000 troops and 1,500 guns fell into the hands of the Prussians. (After the war the new Third Republic court-martialed Bazaine and convicted him of treason; he received a sentence of 20 years' imprisonment.) *See* Gravelotte; Sedan; Paris II; Franco-Prussian War.

Meuse River–Argonne Forest (World War I), 1918. With the elimination of the Saint-Mihiel salient, the Allied commander in chief, Marshal Ferdinand Foch, stood ready to launch two all-out attacks against the Germans on the Western Front. The offensive was planned as a huge pincers: British and French armies attacking from the west, the American Expeditionary Force from the south. On September 26 Gen. John Pershing's First Army jumped off, three corps abreast—III, V, and I—from the Meuse River westward to the far side of the Argonne Forest. A few minutes earlier the French Fourth Army (Henri Gouraud) had begun its advance on the left (west). Holding a defensive zone almost 12 miles deep were the German armies of Gen. Max von Gallwitz on the east, those of Crown Prince Friedrich Wilhelm on the west.

In hilly, tangled terrain, German resistance held the French army to a gain of nine miles during the first five days of the assault. The Americans pushed five miles along the heights of the Meuse but only two miles in the more difficult Argonne. After a pause of three days, the Americans resumed the attack on October 4. For the next four weeks a series of grueling frontal attacks gradually pushed back the German defenders. This was the fighting that produced the famed Lost Battalion (Charles Whittlesey) of the 77th Division and the exploits of Sgt. Alvin York (132 prisoners captured). On October 12 Pershing divided his command. General Hunter Liggett took over the First Army, while Gen. Robert Bullard assumed charge of the new Second Army, which was making a secondary attack east of the Meuse. Finally, on October 31, the Argonne Forest was cleared, marking a ten-mile American advance. At the same time Gouraud's French Fourth Army had reached the Aisne River, 20 miles from its starting point.

On November 1 the Americans and French resumed their offensive against the German armies, which were now under Gen. Wilhelm Groener, who had replaced Gen. Erich Ludendorff as chief operations officer on the Western Front. By the time of the armistice, on November 11, the Allied units

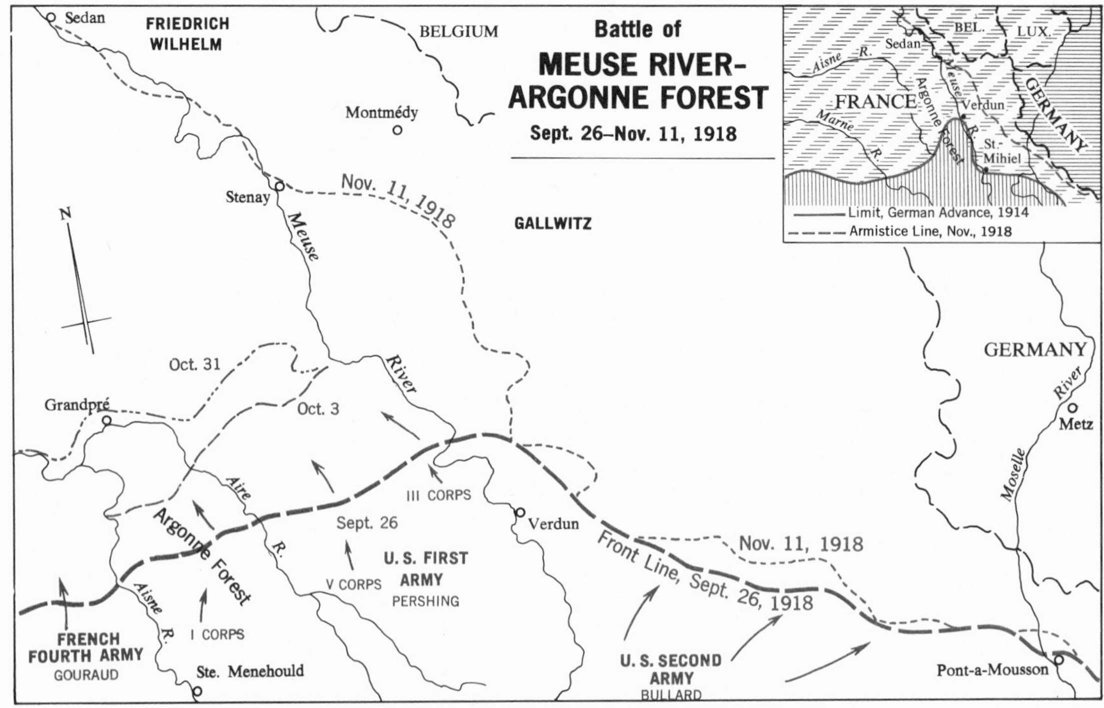

had moved forward another 21 miles to reach Sedan on the east and to within 6 miles of Montmédy, on the west. The battle cost the Germans 100,000 casualties; American losses were 117,000. Meanwhile the western arm of the pincers had been equally effective. *See* Marne River II; Saint-Mihiel; Cambrai–Saint-Quentin; World War I.

Mexico. *See* Latin America.

Miani (British Conquest of Sind), 1843. Hostility between the amirs of Sind (now in West Pakistan) and the British in northwest India erupted into open warfare in 1843. At Miani (Meeanee), six miles north of Hyderabad on the Indus River, Gen. Sir Charles James Napier with 2,800 Anglo-Indian troops encountered 20,000 Baluchistanis. On February 17 the Baluchistanis attacked and almost overran Napier's position before being finally beaten off with 5,000 casualties. The British lost 256 killed and wounded. Napier pressed on southward. *See* Kabul II; Hyderabad.

Midway (World War II), 1942. Japan's sweeping conquests in the Pacific early in 1942 brought the front line to Midway Island, 1,000 miles west of Hawaii. Late in May the Japanese admiralissimo Isoroku Yamamoto sent a diversionary naval force to the Aleutian Islands, while Adm. Chuichi Nagumo, who had led the attack on Pearl Harbor, took a four-carrier striking force followed by an invasion fleet—a total of about 88 ships—to Midway. Anticipating such an attack, the U.S. Pacific commandant, Adm. Chester Nimitz, quickly assembled two task forces east of Midway—Number 16 commanded by Adm. Raymond Spruance and Number 18 directed by Adm. Frank Fletcher. The chief American strength lay in the large carriers *Enterprise, Hornet,* and *Yorktown,* plus aircraft based on Midway itself.

On June 3 U.S. Midway-based planes attacked part of the Japanese fleet more than 500 miles west of Midway. The blow was unsuccessful. The following morning 108 Japanese planes struck hard at Midway, inflicting much damage and destroying 15 of the 25 marine fighters defending the island. Meanwhile 10 U.S. torpedo bombers struck at the Japanese fleet—the first of three successive attacks by planes from Midway. No hits were scored and 7 planes were shot down. In the second strike 8 of 27 Marine dive bombers were lost with again no damage inflicted. Finally 15 B-17 bombers attacked, and for the third time the enemy carriers escaped unhurt. American torpedo bombers from all three carriers then hit at the Japanese fleet. Little was accomplished and 35 of the 41 bombers were shot down. But this attack opened the way for a devastating assault by 54 dive bombers from the *Enterprise* and *Yorktown* (the *Hornet* bombers missed the target). Three of the heavy carriers—*Akagi, Kaga,* and *Soryu*—their decks loaded with aircraft about to take off, were sunk within five minutes, changing the whole course of the war. The fourth carrier, *Hiryu,* was destroyed in a second attack that afternoon. Before that, however, planes from the *Hiryu* had mortally wounded the *Yorktown*. Deprived of their

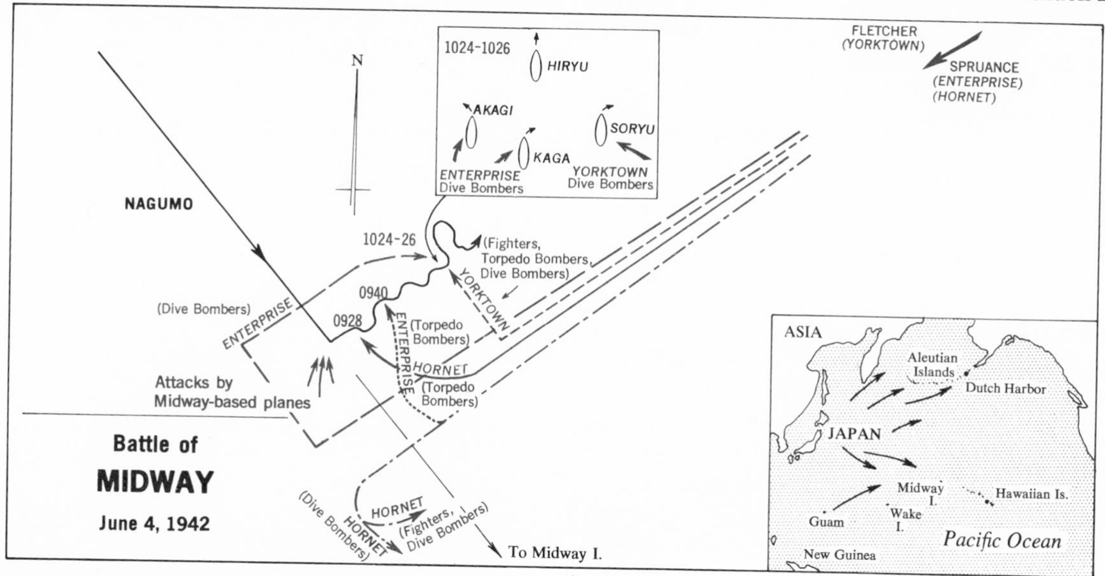

precious carriers, the Japanese began withdrawing on June 5. The American forces were too weakened to pursue, but they did sink a heavy cruiser, the *Mikuma,* the following day. In the hard-fought four-day battle, the United States lost 150 planes, 307 men, and the destroyer *Hammann,* in addition to the *Yorktown* (finished off by a submarine attack on June 6). Japan lost 275 planes with much higher personnel casualties (probably 4,800). And the many carrier pilots lost when their ships were sunk were virtually irreplaceable.

The battle of Midway was the turning point in the Pacific naval war. Together with the earlier Coral Sea battle, it ended six months of Japanese ascendancy and made possible a U.S. counteroffensive, beginning in the Solomon Islands two months later. It was small comfort to Japan that the minor attack on the Aleutians had been successful in the meantime. *See* Coral Sea; Aleutian Islands; Solomon Islands; World War II.

Milazzo (Italian Wars of Independence), 1860. The thousand Redshirts of Giuseppe Garibaldi, augmented by local volunteers, had driven the Neapolitan troops of Francis II out of northwestern Sicily by the summer of 1860. Marching eastward, the Italian independence fighters deployed against the fortified seaport of Milazzo (Mylae) 17 miles west of Messina. (The offshore waters of Mylae had been the scene of a naval battle in the First Punic War.) On July 20 Garibaldi's men routed the royal troops, who fell back to Messina. A month later the Redshirts crossed the strait to the mainland and marched on Naples. The army of Francis II dissolved, the last of the Bourbon rulers of the kingdom of the Two Sicilies fleeing to Gaeta on September 7. Garibaldi next prepared to liberate Rome. *See* Calatafimi; Castelfidardo; Italian Wars of Independence.

Mill Springs (American Civil War), 1862. Although the border state of Kentucky proclaimed its neutrality early in the Civil War, both North and South maneuvered for a dominant position in the area. From Cumberland Gap a Confederate force under Gen. Felix Zollicoffer moved west to Mill Springs and then crossed to the north side of the Cumberland River at Beech Grove. Here Gen. George Crittenden took command of the Confederate troops in eastern Kentucky. Under the direction of Gen. Don Carlos Buell, based at Louisville, a Federal army of 4,000 men under Gen. George Thomas marched south from Lebanon to attack the Confederate position.

Learning of the Federal advance against him, Crittenden moved forward (north) on the night of January 18, 1862, with 4,000 troops. Leading elements of the two hostile forces struck head on early the following morning at Logan Cross Roads. Zollicoffer was killed during a hot fight in which Thomas threw forward enough reserves to break the Confederate left. Crittenden fell back, abandoning Beech Grove, and retreating across the Cumberland that night. The withdrawal cost him most of his heavy equipment. Confederate losses were unreported, but the defeat led many to desert. It was the most severe setback suffered by the South up to that time. Thomas suffered 39 killed and 207 wounded. The action in Kentucky now shifted westward to the river forts on the Tennessee and Cumberland rivers. *See* Fort Henry; American Civil War.

Minden I (Germanic Wars of the Roman Empire), A.D. 16. Seven years after the massacre of

Varus' Roman legions in the Teutoburger Wald, Emperor Tiberius sent an avenging force into Germany. The main body of Romans, eight legions commanded by Germanicus Caesar, nephew of the emperor, descended the Ems River and then struck eastward. The Romans crossed the Weser at Minden. On the plains east of the river Germanicus encountered a coalition of Germanic tribes under Arminius, the conqueror of Varus. This time the legionaries were prepared. They thoroughly routed the Germans, wounding Arminius, who barely escaped with his life.

On the return march of the Romans, Arminius abandoned his heretofore successful guerrilla tactics and attacked the column in the open. He was driven off with even greater losses. Minden was the last great battle fought by two exceptionally able commanders. Germanicus died suddenly at Antioch in A.D. 19. Arminius was slain in tribal warfare two years later. *See* Teutoburger Wald; Roman Empire.

Minden II (Seven Years' War), 1759. Following their victory at Bergen in April 1759, the French advanced northward toward Hannover. The commander, the marshal Duc Louis de Contades, had some 60,000 troops, largely of inferior quality. To block this advance, the Prussian general in the west, the field marshal Ferdinand, duke of Brunswick, ally of Frederick II (the Great), resolved to hold Minden, on the Weser River. Ferdinand could muster only 45,000 men, including six English infantry regiments and a cavalry detachment under Gen. Lord George Sackville.

As the French approached on August 1, Ferdinand took the offensive. As a result of a misunderstanding, the British infantry, followed by Hanoverian foot soldiers, attacked the French cavalry. The surprise tactic, combined with the methodical advance of the redcoats, who halted only to unleash volleys of fire by platoons, demoralized and then broke the French lines. With a major victory in his grasp, Ferdinand ordered his cavalry forward for the crushing blow. Sackville refused to obey (for which he was later court-martialed and cashiered from the army of George II). This enabled Contades to effect an orderly withdrawal although he lost 7,000 men and 43 guns. The Anglo-Hannoverian army suffered less than 3,000 casualties, half of them from the ranks of the gallant British infantry. This battle ended the last serious French threat to Hannover—and to Prussia. But on the eastern front Frederick's forces stood in grave danger of collapsing before a dual Russian-Austrian offensve. *See* Bergen; Kunersdorf; Seven Years' War.

Minorca I (Seven Years' War), 1756. Without a declaration of war, King Louis XV of France sent the Toulon fleet with 15,000 troops aboard to attack the British-held island of Minorca in the Mediterranean. Under the admiral the Marquis de la Galissonière, the French expedition landed in April 1756. Louis, duc de Richelieu, the troop commander, promptly began an investment of the important harbor city of Port Mahón, defended by less than 3,000 English soldiers under Gen. William Blakeney.

The British government of King George II sent Adm. John Byng with 13 warships and 4,000 troops to try to relieve the island. On May 20 Byng launched an attack against the 12 French ships of the line blockading the harbor. Suffering from a faulty tactical disposition and a lack of resolute leadership, Byng's squadron was firmly repulsed. With all their supplies and reinforcements still on board, the English fleet withdrew to Gilbraltar. Here Byng was relieved by Adm. Edward Hawke. Byng was later court-martialed and shot on the quarterdeck of his flagship. Port Mahón surrendered on June 28 and Minorca came under French control. The island was restored to Great Britain at the end of the Seven Years' War, which had now formally begun. *See* Calcutta; Lobositz; Seven Years' War.

Minorca II (War of the American Revolution), 1782. During the combined Spanish-French siege of Gibraltar, the European allies launched a secondary attack on the British-held island of Minorca in the western Mediterranean. From Cadiz, Spain, an allied fleet sailed on July 22, 1781, to land 14,000 Spanish and French troops on the western end of Minorca. The invaders, commanded by Louis De Crillon (Duc de Mahon), quickly overran the island except for the naval base at Port Mahon, on the eastern side. Here the British general James Murray, with less than 1,000 men, withstood a siege of six months. Disease and combat casualties steadily weakened the garrison, however, and on February 5, 1782, the city surrendered. By that time Murray had only 660 men fit for duty. The peace treaty signed the following year ceded Minorca to Spain. *See* Gibraltar II; Yorktown I; American Revolution.

Minsk (World War II). A pocket created by the link-up of two German *Panzer* groups east of the city, in which 300,000 Russians were killed or captured between June 27 and July 2, 1941. *See* Soviet Union (World War II).

Missionary Ridge (American Civil War). The third, and decisive, action in the battle of Chattanooga, on November 25, 1863, in which Gen. U. S. Grant's Federals ascended the height, despite their officers' commands to halt, and captured it. *See* Chattanooga.

Mithridatic Wars (88–66 B.C.). In a series of three wars, Mithridates VI Eupator, king of Pontus, fought against the armies of Rome. The first war ended with peace terms favorable to Rome. Mithridates resisted invasion in the second war, in which no real battle took place. In the third war, however, he was defeated and driven out of Pontus to the Crimea by Pompey the Great.

First Mithridatic War

Athens-Piraeus	86 B.C.
Chaeronea II	86 B.C.
Orchomenus	85 B.C.

Third Mithridatic War

Cyzicus II	73 B.C.
Tigranocerta I	69 B.C.
Nicopolis-in-Armenia	66 B.C.

Mobile Bay (American Civil War), 1864. To subdue the important Confederate port of Mobile, Ala., the Federal government sent out a joint army-navy expedition. Under the command of Gen. Gordon Granger, 5,500 troops of the XIII Corps landed on the western end of Dauphine Island in Mobile Bay on August 3. During the next 20 days Granger successively reduced the forts of Gaines, Powell, and Morgan, at the entrances to Mobile Bay, capturing 1,464 prisoners and 104 guns with little loss of life on either side. Meanwhile Adm. David Farragut ran his Federal fleet of 18 ships past the guns of the forts on August 5, to attack the ironclad *Tennessee* and three wooden gunboats, all commanded by the Confederate admiral Franklin Buchanan, in Mobile Bay. In a naval battle that lasted less than two hours the *Tennessee* was incapacitated. The wounded Buchanan then surrendered. There were 312 Confederate casualties among the 470 men in action. Federal losses were 319 out of the 3,000 engaged. When his ship, the *Tecumseh,* was sunk by a mine early in the battle, Farragut is reported to have said, "Damn the torpedoes," ordering the assault continued. The city of Mobile did not fall, however, until April 12, 1865, after Gen. Robert E. Lee's surrender at Appomattox. *See* Atlanta; Appomattox River; American Civil War.

Modder River (South African War II), 1899. In an effort to relieve besieged Kimberley, Gen. Lord Paul Methuen marched the 1st British Division northward into the Orange Free State. At the Modder River, an eastern tributary of the Vaal, he encountered a Boer force of almost 9,000 men under Gen. Piet Cronjé. Methuen attacked early on November 28. Although the British found the Boers in greater strength than expected, they persisted in the assault, finally turning the enemy position before nightfall. The victory cost Methuen 24 officers and 460 men. Boer casualties were about the same. Cronjé withdrew westward to Magersfontein. Methuen pursued. *See* Kimberley; Magersfontein; South African Wars.

Moesia (Dacian Wars of the Roman Empire), A.D. 89. During the reign of Emperor Domitian the scattered tribes of Dacia (modern Rumania) were united under the strong leadership of Decebalus. In 85 Decebalus suddenly crossed the Danube to the south side and seized the Roman province of Moesia. Domitian hurried out from Rome to regain control of Moesia. He put Cornelius Fuscus in charge of the Roman legions in the area. But Fuscus was defeated and killed while trying to cross the Danube to invade Dacia, in the spring of A.D. 87. Two years later a Roman army under Calpurnius Julianus struck north across the Danube and defeated the Dacians. Decebalus then formed an alliance with the Germanic tribes of the Marcomanni and Quadi. Rather than risk further fighting, Domitian negotiated a peace with Decebalus that aroused bitter opposition in Rome. *See* Sarmizegetusa; Roman Empire.

Mogilev (Napoleonic Empire Wars), 1812. During prolonged but insincere negotiations between Napoleon I of France and Alexander I of Russia, both sides mustered enormous armies for the inevitable conflict. On June 22, 1812, the French emperor with 430,000 troops crossed the Niemen River to strike eastward along the axis Grodno–Minsk–Orsha. The czar's 420,000 men, prepared to trade space for time, began falling back, offering little resistance to the French columns thrusting deeply into their country. On July 8 the III Corps of Marshal Louis Davout on the right wing pushed into Minsk. This advance threatened to isolate the Second Russian Army of Prince Pëtr Bagration to the south from the main body of Gen. Mikhail Barclay de Tolly, which stood north of Davout. On July 23 Bagration struck northward at Davout, who had now seized Mogilev on the Dnieper River. Although the 48,000-man army of Bagration had a 2-to-1 superiority in numbers, it failed to dislodge the French from a strong position south of the city. After losing 4,000 men, the prince countermarched to cross the Dnieper below Mogilev. Davout's casualties totaled about 1,000. *See* Smolensk I; Napoleonic Empire Wars.

Mohács (Turkish Conquest of Hungary), 1526. After the fall of Belgrade in 1521, all of southeastern Europe lay open to the Ottoman Turks. Suleiman I, the Magnificent, took the road with an army of almost 100,000 men in 1526. Louis II of Hungary and Bohemia hurriedly assembled an army of 20,000 men on the Danube at Mohács (near the present border of Yugoslavia). Some assistance came from Sigismund I of Poland. The Turks arrived on August 29. Louis unwisely launched a headlong assault on the invading army, despite the poor discipline among his knights and peasants. The Turks, with sound deployment and superior artillery, cut the Christian force to pieces. On the following day an Ottoman counterassault swept the field. Among the 10,000 Western dead lay Louis, seven bishops, and several hundred nobles. The battle of Mohács broke Hungary's hold on central Europe.

Suleiman, after plunging on to take Budapest,

appointed a Transylvanian, John Zápolya, to rule the Magyars. But the Hapsburg Ferdinand I (later Holy Roman Emperor) claimed the throne of Hungary, resulting in years of civil war. When Ferdinand drove out Zápolya in 1528, the Turkish army returned. *See* Belgrade II; Vienna I.

"Mohács, Second Battle of." *See* Harkány.

Mohi (Mongol Invasion of Europe), 1241. While a northern column of Mongols cleared the right flank in Poland, the main body of Asiatics crossed the eastern Carpathian Mountains. Debouching into Hungary, the Mongols, under Sutotai's command, began ravaging the countryside. Hurriedly, the Hungarian king, Béla IV, assembled a mounted army of archers and lancers on the Danube, probable 100,000 men. Faced with the most formidable foe yet encountered in Europe, the Mongols cautiously withdrew eastward across the Sajó River, a northwest tributary of the Theiss (Tisza). Béla rashly pursued. On the night of April 10–11, the Mongol general Sutotai sent out detachments to recross the Sajó both above and below the Hungarian position at Mohi. At dawn Mongol missile fire opened on the Hungarian center across the river. Then the two flanking detachments struck Béla's wings and rear. Under cover of this combined assault, the main body of Asiatics, led by Batu Khan, grandson of the great Genghis, forded the Sajó for a frontal attack. By noon the Hungarian army, with 70,000 dead, had ceased to exist.

Béla fled toward the Adriatic closely followed by one band of Mongols, while other bands devastated the prostrate kingdom as far west as Pest, on the Danube, which they crossed on Christmas Day 1241. But except for a westward raid into Austria, this was the high-water mark of the invasion. Learning that Ogadai (Ogotai), son and successor to Genghis as the chief khan, had died in the east, the Mongol invaders rode home to Karakorum to elect a new leader. Except for the Golden Horde on the lower Volga, the Mongols vanished forever from Europe. *See* Leignitz I; Baghdad I; Mongol Wars.

Molino del Rey (U.S.-Mexican War), 1847. Truce negotiations between the United States and the Mexican president Antonio de Santa Anna collapsed on September 7. On the following day Gen. Winfield Scott resumed his attack against the defenses south of Mexico City. The main Mexican fortification was the rocky, walled hill of Chapultepec, three miles to the southwest. Before assaulting this position, Scott sent Gen. William Worth with 3,450 men to carry out a diversionary attack against Molino del Rey, believed to contain a gun foundry, just southwest of Chapultepec. On September 8 Worth launched his strike. He found the complex of buildings held in force. It took the Americans all day to overrun Molino del Rey, in the course of which they inflicted 2,700 casualties on the defenders, including 700 captured. But Worth's losses were so high—117 killed, 653 wounded, 18 missing—that he withdrew southward to the suburb of Tacubaya that evening. Scott now prepared a large-scale offensive against Chapultepec itself. *See* Contreras-Churubusco; Chapultepec; U.S.-Mexican War.

Mollwitz (War of the Austrian Succession), 1741. With the death of Holy Roman Emperor Charles VI, the male line of the Austrian Hapsburgs became extinct. By the terms of a previous agreement (Pragmatic Sanction), Charles's daughter, Maria Theresa, archduchess of Austria, queen of Bohemia and Hungary, and wife of Francis of Lorraine (future Francis I), ascended the throne. Her right to rule was promptly challenged by the claims of three men—Charles Albert, elector of Bavaria; Philip V, king of Spain; and Augustus III, king of Poland (and elector of Saxony). The situation was complicated by the claim of Frederick II, the Great, of Prussia (formerly the electorate of Brandenburg) to the Austrian hold on Silesia, which included the valley of the Oder. On December 16, 1740, Frederick marched across the border into Silesia with 30,000 well-trained Prussian troops (the inheritance of his father, Frederick William I). He soon occupied most of the province. This power grab launched the First Silesian War.

Early in 1741 Maria Theresa sent out an Austrian army of 20,000 men under Field Marshal Count Wilhelm von Neipperg to oust the Prussians. At Mollwitz (in present-day southwestern Poland), Neipperg challenged Frederick on April 10 on a snow-covered field. Frederick, who commanded a force of equal size this day, had a superiority in infantry but Neipperg an advantage in cavalry. The Prussians also had 60 field guns to the Austrians' 18. When the Prussian artillery opened the battle, Neipperg's cavalry charged Frederick's horsemen stationed on the right and routed them. Frederick, who had stationed himself on this flank, was swept out of the battle. But when the Austrians tried to ride down the enemy infantry, they found the Prussians drawn back at an angle that gave the foot soldiers a murderous field of fire. Five times the Austrians charged and each time they were repulsed by accurate musket fire, directed by Field Marshal Count Kurt von Schwerin. Then the Prussian infantry moved forward, firing at twice the rate of the enemy. (This rate was made possible by the use of an iron ramrod, as opposed to the wooden one that was in general use at the time.) The Austrian opposite wing (Neipperg's left) was overlapped and the entire line rolled up. Neipperg withdrew under the cover of darkness, leaving

5,000 dead, wounded, and captured on the field. Frederick suffered only half as many casualties.

The battle of Mollwitz was the only major action of 1741, but it led to a larger war. France (Louis XV), Spain (Philip V), and Bavaria (Charles Albert, who claimed to be Emperor Charles VII) joined Prussia, while Great Britain (George II), Holland, and Sardinia (Savoy) allied themselves with Austria and the Holy Roman Empire. The War of the Austrian Succession then began with a Franco-Bavarian army invading Bohemia, where Gen. Comte Maurice de Saxe seized Prague on November 26. In reply, an Austrian army under Field Marshal Count Ludwig Khevenhüller prepared to move into Bavaria. *See* Chotusitz; Austrian Succession, War of the.

Monastir (First Balkan War). A Turkish-held city, now called Bitolj, seized by the Serbians on November 18, 1912, during the First Balkan War. *See* Kumanovo.

Moncada Fortress (Castro Revolt in Cuba), 1953. Little more than a year after Fulgencio Batista had seized dictatorial powers in Cuba (1952), a revolutionary movement developed in Oriente, the easternmost province on the island. Led by Fidel Castro and his brother Raúl, the rebels made their first strike on July 26, 1953. Early in the morning 166 men slipped into Santiago to seize Moncada Fortress. The rebels inflicted 50 casualties on the government soldiers in the garrison at a cost to themselves of only 7 killed or wounded. But because of poor planning they failed to capture the armory. Short of ammunition and guns, the rebels withdrew. In the pursuit that followed, 70 were captured or killed. Both Castro brothers were captured and received prison sentences. Although the rebels were thoroughly defeated, the battle gained the movement national prominence, martyrdom, and the name "26 of July Movement" for the revolution. *See* Sierra Maestra.

Moncontour (French Religious Wars), 1569. The third civil uprising of the Huguenots against Charles IX went badly for the rebels. After suffering a defeat at Jarnac, the Huguenots found themselves pressed in Poitou by the Catholic forces of the Duc d'Anjou, younger brother of the king (and the future Henry III). They sought to hold Moncontour, 27 miles northwest of Poitiers, but the position was weak. On October 3, 1569, D'Anjou, aided by the Seigneur de Tavannes, charged the Huguenot army and routed it with heavy losses. This royalist victory enabled the Catholic forces to march on Poitiers, held under Huguenot siege by Gaspard de Coligny, the admiral of France. The Huguenot commander had to withdraw in the face of the relief expedition headed by Henry I de Lorraine, duc de Guise.

Peace was restored the following year at Saint Germain. The Huguenots obtained conditional freedom of worship in return for surrendering La Rochelle, Montauban, and other centers of resistance in western and southern France. But two years later King Charles gave in to the insistence of his mother, Catherine de Médicis, and the house of Guise by ordering the Saint Bartholomew's Day massacre of Huguenots. Beginning on August 23 and 24, 1572, in Paris (where De Coligny was killed), the terror spread over the country for a month. Thousands of Protestants were slain. The massacre led to a fourth Huguenot uprising (1572–73) against Charles and three more against his successor, Henry III, in 1574–76, 1577, and 1580. All were inconclusive, with no decisive battle fought. The eighth, and final, civil war broke out in 1587. *See* Jarnac; Coutras; French Religious Wars.

Mondovì (Wars of the French Revolution), 1796. After Napoleon Bonaparte consolidated the French victory at Dego in northwestern Italy, on April 15, 1796, he stood squarely between the Austrian army of Gen. Baron Jean de Beaulieu and the Sardinian troops of King Victor Amadeus II. He then turned westward to concentrate against Sardinia (Piedmont). On April 21 he attacked the Italians in front of Mondovì and drove them beyond the town. With almost 36,000 men Napoleon now closely pursued the retreating force, which had been reduced to half of its original 25,000. To prevent an advance on his capital at Turin, King Victor asked for terms on April 23. Five days later he surrendered, giving Napoleon control of Piedmont. The victorious general now turned back (eastward) on the Austrian army. With his ally knocked out of the war, Beaulieu pulled back from the Genoese coast and crossed to the north bank of the Po River on May 2. *See* Dego; Lodi Bridge; French Revolution Wars.

Mongol Wars (1214–1402). Led by the Genghis (Jenghiz) Khan and his descendants, the Mongols swept out of their homeland to invade China, Japan, India, Persia, the Near East, and Europe. In the next century a second Mongol conqueror, Tamerlane (Timur Lenk, or Timur the Lame), invaded Russia, India, and the Near East.

Era of Genghis Khan

Peking I	1214
Khojend	1219
Bukhara	1220
Samarkand	1220
Herat I	1220–1221
Merv	1221
Bamian	1221
Indus River	1221
Kalka River	1223
Kiev I	1240

Cracow	1241
Liegnitz I	1241
Mohi	1241
Baghdad I	1258
Ain Jalut	1260
Mongol Invasions of Japan	
Hakata Bay	1274
Kyushu	1281
Tamerlane's Conquests	
Kandurcha	1391
Delhi I	1398
Baghdad II	1401
Angora	1402

"Monitor" vs. "Merrimac." *See* Hampton Roads.

Monmouth (War of the American Revolution), 1778. The fourth year of the war opened with France (Louis XVI) aligning itself with the United States on February 6, 1778. With the mighty French fleet expected to sail to America, Gen. Sir Henry Clinton, who succeeded Gen. Sir William Howe as British commander in the United States, feared for his position in Philadelphia. On June 18 Clinton evacuated the city and began marching eastward across New Jersey. The American commander in chief, Gen. George Washington, seized this opportunity to end the long agony of his army at Valley Forge. He broke camp the following day and started in pursuit of the British. General Charles Lee, with 6,400 men, was sent on ahead to strike Clinton's column of 13,000 troops while the latter were on the march. Lee overtook the British rear guard, under the command of Gen. Lord Charles Cornwallis, at Monmouth, N.J., on June 28. But he deployed carelessly, and when Clinton faced his army about and concentrated against him, Lee ordered a precipitate retreat. Only the arrival of Washington with the main body (7,000 men) prevented a disaster. The American army re-formed quickly and beat back repeated British assaults. Nightfall finally ended the longest battle of the war and the last major engagement in the North. American casualties totaled 360, the British two less.

That night Clinton marched away to Sandy Hook, N.J., where he embarked his army on June 30 and sailed to New York City. Washington led his army northward, crossed the Hudson, and occupied White Plains, N.Y., on July 20. Thus both armies stood in the same positions they had held two years before. Lee was court-martialed for misbehavior and suspended from command. *See* Fort Mercer and Fort Mifflin; Newport; Savannah I; American Revolution.

Monocacy River (American Civil War), 1864. When the Federal force of Gen. David Hunter was driven away from Lynchburg, Va., on June 18, the Confederate general Jubal Early marched unopposed into the Shenandoah Valley. With 10,000 infantry and 4,000 cavalry, Early hurried northward down the valley. He reached Winchester on July 2, crossed the Potomac into Maryland, and raided eastward. At the Monocacy River, southeast of Frederick, Early's men ran into a 6,000-man blocking force under Gen. Lewis Wallace, on July 9. The Confederate commander sent a flanking force across the river to strike the Federal left. Wallace was simply overpowered, losing 1,880 men (including 1,188 missing). He fell back to Baltimore, while Early, who had suffered less than 700 casualties, pressed on to Washington, D.C.

Finding the defenses of the nation's capital too strong to assault, Early withdrew on the night of July 12. He crossed the Potomac at Leesburg to re-enter the Shenandoah Valley via Snicker's Gap. *See* Lynchburg; Kernstown II; American Civil War.

Monongahela River (French and Indian War), 1755. Major General Edward Braddock of Great Britain arrived in Virginia in 1755 and promptly launched a multiple offensive against New France. Early in June Braddock himself, at the head of 1,400 British regulars and 450 colonials under Lt. Col. George Washington, marched into southwestern Pennsylvania. His objective was French-held Fort Duquesne, at the forks of the Ohio (now Pittsburgh). Braddock crossed the Monongahela about eight miles from the fort on July 9. Here his column was suddenly attacked from the front and both flanks by a mixed force of 900 French and Indians commanded by Capt. Jean-Daniel Dumas. Fighting from an exposed position while their enemies fired from behind trees and other concealment, the British suffered 50 percent casualties before they were able to retreat. Braddock was mortally wounded. Washington took charge of the withdrawal, leading the survivors back to Fort Cumberland, Md., a week later. *See* Beauséjour; George, Lake; French and Indian War.

Mons I (Second, or Dutch, War of Louis XIV), 1678. After six years of fighting that had raged in the Low Countries, along the Rhine, and in the Mediterranean, all the allied nations were as ready as Louis XIV for peace. On August 10, 1678, France agreed to terms with William III's Holland and then in succession with Spain, the Holy Roman Empire, Denmark, and Brandenburg. But William III of Orange (later William III of England) believed himself to be betrayed by the Dutch merchants in the truce signed between Holland and France. Four days later, his army still intact, William attacked the French troops near Mons, in the Spanish Netherlands. Although naturally caught by surprise, the French rallied behind Marshal the Duc de Luxembourg, the successor to the Vicomte de Turenne, and Louis II, the Great Condé. At the end of a hard day's fighting, William was repulsed with the loss of several thousand men.

This was the opening of a remarkable military career for Luxembourg, who was destined to become one of the few active generals in history who never lost a major battle. Despite the treacherous assault at Mons, the peace continued in force for ten years. From 1680 to 1684, however, Louis XIV, in the so-called War of the Reunions, seized without a battle such border territories as Lorraine, Luxembourg, Trier, and Strasbourg. *See* Augusta; Louis XIV, Wars of.

Mons II (World War I). The westernmost part of the massive battle fought along the French frontier during August 20–24, 1914, in which the first French-British and German offensives of the war met head on. *See* Frontiers of France.

Mons Badonicus (Teutonic Conquest of Britain), c. 500. After the withdrawal of the Roman legions early in the fifth century, Britain was flooded by invading bands of Jutes, Angles, and Saxons. The history of Britain is obscure during this bloody barbarian conquest. Apparently the only major opposition to the invaders came from the so-called King Arthur. This almost completely legendary figure is believed to have collected a group of Roman Britons that came to be known as knights and fought the barbarians in 12 battles. It is easy to believe that early cavalry would overpower the dismounted invaders. The greatest of Arthur's battles is called that of Mons Badonicus (Mount Badon), an uncertain site that may be Badbury, near Swinton in north-central England. Arthur's knights are reported to have checked the Teutons' westward surge for two generations at the beginning of the sixth century. But the barbarian flood could not be stopped for long. During this century seven separate Anglo-Saxon kingdoms—the heptarchy—slowly emerged in what is now England. *See* Mons Graupius; Dyrham.

Mons-en-Pévèle (French-Flemish Wars), 1304. The startling victory of its foot soldiers over the flower of French chivalry at Courtrai in 1302 brought only two years of peace to Flanders. In 1304, King Philip IV, the Fair, of France sent another feudal army northward to discipline the rebellious Flemings. The two armies met at Mons-en-Pévèle on August 18. This time the Flemings did not have the advantage of fighting from a strong defensive position. And although the French mailed cavalry charged as headlong as it had at Courtrai, this time it broke the ranks of the Flemish pikemen. Pressing their opening, the French knights used their swords and lances to scatter the overwhelmed infantry and then cut them down in flight. Some 6,000 Flemings fell, reversing the earlier decision and once more asserting the medieval supremacy of mounted knights over foot soldiers. In a treaty the following year, Philip gained Lille, Douai, and other French-speaking towns but allowed Flanders to remain independent. *See* Courtrai; Cassel.

Mons Graupius (Roman Conquest of Britain), A.D. 84. With the bloody revolt of A.D. 61 suppressed, most of Britain became subservient to Roman rule. During the reign of Emperor Domitian, however, the Caledonians of modern Scotland revolted against the Roman military governor, Gnaeus Julius Agricola. The legions marched northward and at Mons Graupius (probably Mount Killiecrankie in central Scotland) encountered 30,000 rebels under Calgacus. The Caledonians attacked fiercely but were bloodily repulsed by the heavier-armed and better-drilled legionaries of Agricola. Some 10,000 Caledonians were killed at a cost of 360 Romans.

This battle ended all organized resistance to Roman rule. For almost 300 years Britain remained one of the most peaceful of Rome's 45 provinces. To guard against barbarian incursions from the north, Emperor Hadrian in 122 ordered the building of a 73-mile wall across the island between the Tyne and the Solway. Twenty years later, under Emperor Antoninus, a second wall was constructed farther north across the narrower Forth–Clyde waist of Britain. But this barrier stretched the occupying forces too thin and it was abandoned in 186. *See* Verulamium II; Mons Badonicus.

Montebello (Wars of the French Revolution), 1800. When Napoleon Bonaparte took over the French government as first consul late in 1799, the Consulate armies in northern Italy seemed hopelessly beaten. Only Genoa remained in French hands, and the garrison here, under the redoubtable general André Masséna, lay directly in the path of the main Austrian offensive, commanded by Gen. Baron Michael von Melas. Napoleon hurriedly concentrated forces in Switzerland during the winter of 1799–1800. But instead of moving directly to relieve Genoa, he sent several French columns through the Alpine passes into the flank and rear of Melas' Austrians. This movement came too late to save Genoa, which Masséna was forced to evacuate on June 4. But on the following day the French push through the Lombardy plain reached Milan. General Jean Lannes, who commanded the advance guard, pressed on to occupy Pavia and cross the Po River. Fifteen miles south of Pavia, at Montebello, the French encountered the Austrian rear guard under Gen. Karl Ott, who had marched northward from his conquest of Genoa.

On June 9 Ott, with 17,000 men and 35 guns, met Lannes head on. The French, outnumbered 3 to 1, fell back, but Gen. Claude Victor's corps of 6,000 men arrived just in time to check the Austrian assault. Lannes swung over to the attack and in a sharp fight routed Ott, who suffered 4,000 casualties. French losses totaled 500. (Lannes later became Duc de Montebello.) Melas continued to concentrate his forces at Alessandria, while Napoleon's columns converged on the same place. *See* Novi Ligure; Marengo; French Revolution Wars.

Monte-Caseros (Argentine Civil War), 1852. During its early years of independence, Argentina was torn by civil strife. Then in 1829 Juan de Rosas, governor of Buenos Aires, established order in his province, and six years later over most of the country. The dictatorial rule of Rosas and his Gaucho party, particularly the attempts to conquer Uruguay, finally led to internal opposition. Supported by Uruguay and Brazil, Justo de Urquiza assembled a rebel army. On February 3, 1852, at Monte-Caseros, about 300 miles up the Uruguay River, some 20,000 rebels decisively defeated the slightly larger army of Rosas. Urquiza became the chief executive of Argentina, while Rosas fled into exile. *See* Montevideo.

Montenotte (Wars of the French Revolution), 1796. Napoleon Bonaparte took over his first major command, the Army of Italy, on March 27, 1796, on the Riviera between Nice and Genoa. The 27-year-old general had only 40,000 troops and 60 guns. In the Ligurian Hills to the north stood 55,000 enemy soldiers and 150 guns—on the right (east) 30,000 Austrians, commanded by Gen. Baron Jean de Beaulieu; on the left (west) 25,000 Italians of the kingdom of Sardinia (Piedmont), under Victor Amadeus II. On the night of April 11–12 Napoleon launched a sudden attack into the hills against the Austrian right wing. The continued assault the following morning carried the heights of Montenotte, inflicting 2,500 casualties on the enemy. This victory effectively cut communications between the two allied armies. *See* Loano; Dego; French Revolution Wars.

Montereau (Napoleonic Empire Wars), 1814. After smashing the allied advance toward Paris in the Marne Valley during February 10–15, 1814, Napoleon I hurried southward to the Seine River. Here Austrian Prince Karl von Schwarzenberg's main allied army was threatening the French capital from the southeast. Marching some units 60 miles in 36 hours over muddy roads, Napoleon checked the allied advance at Mormant, 30 miles from Paris, on February 17. This action, plus the news of the Prussian defeat to the north, prompted Schwarzenberg to order a retreat. He left Crown Prince Eugene of Württemberg to hold the key village of Montereau, at the junction of the Seine and Yonne. On February 18 the French cavalry advance under Gen. Étienne Gérard reached Montereau, blasted it with artillery, and then swept through the town, capturing the stone bridges over both rivers. The allied garrison lost 5,000 men and 15 guns. French casualties were only half as large. Schwarzenberg now fled eastward to Troyes. *See* Champaubert-Montmirail; Bar-sur-Aube; Napoleonic Empire Wars.

Monterrey (U.S.-Mexican War), 1846. General Zachary Taylor's American army halted at Matamoros after crossing the Rio Grande into Mexico on May 18. With the arrival of supplies and reinforcements Taylor began a march up the river on July 6. At the mouth of the San Juan River he turned southwest toward Monterrey, on August 19, with some 6,000 troops (half of whom were short-term volunteers). A month later he reached the outskirts of the Mexican city. On September 20 Taylor led the attack on Monterrey from the east, while sending Gen. William Worth with a strong detachment to make an assault from the west. Worth captured the key defensive position of Federation Hill on September 21 and Independence Hill the following day. Meanwhile, Taylor thrust into the city on September 21 and in hard fighting drove the garrison into the Citadel (Black Fort). Blockaded on all sides, Gen. Pedro de Ampudia surrendered three days later, his troops laying down their arms on September 25. In all, the Americans lost 488 men, including 120 killed; the defenders suffered 367 casualties.

Taylor now granted an eight-week armistice, to the annoyance of President James Polk, who had sent out another invading army to Santa Fe where it split into two columns—one moved west to California and the other south to Chihuahua, Mexico. *See* Resaca de la Palma; San Pasqual; Chihuahua; U.S.-Mexican War.

Montevideo (Uruguayan Civil War), 1843–1851. The independence of Uruguay was won at the battle of Ituzaingó in 1827, chiefly by the "thirty-three immortals." Soon factional strife developed between two of these heroes, Manuel Oribe, who headed the Blancos party, and José Rivera, leader of the Colorados. With the support of the Argentine dictator Juan de Rosas, Oribe marched against Montevideo, held by the forces of Riviera, early in 1843. Failing to take the city on February 16, the Blancos settled down to a siege. One of the leading defenders of Montevideo was the Italian patriot Giuseppe Garibaldi.

The loose siege dragged on until an Argentine revolt under Justo de Urquiza weakened the Blancos' outside support. Finally, on October 8, 1851, Urquiza led a combined force of Colorados, Brazilians, and Paraguayans to Montevideo. In a sharp fight Oribe was beaten and the eight-year siege lifted. *See* Ituzaingó; Monte-Caseros.

Montfaucon (Rise of France), 886. Despite an occasional setback, such as at Saucourt, the Northmen continued to raid far up the rivers of western Europe. In 885 a large band moved up the Seine toward Paris. Stopped by a stubborn defense behind the walls of the city, the Northmen began a siege of Paris. The West Frankish king, Charles the Fat, a Carolingian, refused to take the field against the invaders. But the Count of Paris, Eudes (Odo), a member of the later Capetian dynasty, launched a gallant offensive against the Northmen. At Montfaucon, northwest of Verdun, he fought a great battle with the invaders in 886 and routed them. Thousands of the enemy were killed. The victory raised the siege of Paris. Charles the Fat was deposed the following year for his failure to defend the kingdom. *See* Saucourt; Louvain.

Montiel (Castilian Civil War), 1369. The aptly named Pedro the Cruel kept his crown of Castile and León in 1367 only with the help of the Anglo-Gascon army of England's Edward the Black Prince. When Edward quarreled with Pedro and withdrew across the Pyrenees, the Spanish kingdom again erupted in revolt. For the second time Henry of Trastamara, half brother of Pedro, and the French general Bertrand Du Guesclin assembled an army of rebels. This force encountered Pedro's royalists at Montiel, in present-day Ciudad Real province of south-central Spain. In a wild melee, the rebels won a decisive victory, Henry personally killing Pedro. He then proclaimed himself Henry II of Castile and León. Du Guesclin (created Duke of Molinas by Henry) returned to France to resume harassment of the English armies in Aquitaine. But to the south France had made a firm ally, and when the two fleets combined, a new challenge developed to England's command of the seas. *See* Nájera; La Rochelle I; Aljubarrota.

Montijo (Spanish-Portuguese Wars), 1644. After 60 years of domination, Portugal threw off Spanish control in 1640. But the new Portuguese monarch, John IV, first king of the house of Braganza, suffered from frequent Spanish plots to unseat him. Finally, in 1644, a Portuguese army under Gen. Mathias d'Albuquerque invaded western Spain. On May 26 Albuquerque's troops met and defeated a Spanish army of Philip IV at Montijo, 18 miles northeast of Badajoz. (Most of the Spanish military strength had been siphoned into central Europe by the Thirty Years' War.) The victory brought peace to John IV for the rest of his reign (until 1656), but his successors, Alfonso VI and Peter II, had to resist new aggressions from their eastern neighbors until 1668, when King Charles II of Spain formally recognized Portuguese independence. *See* Alcántara; Rocroi.

Montlhéry (French-Burgundian War), 1465. The long-time enmity between the duchy of Burgundy and the kingdom of France reached a climax in the respective reigns of Charles the Bold and Louis XI. In 1465 Charles joined the dukes of Alençon, Berry, Bourbon, and Lorraine in the anti-French League of Public Weal. The army of this league met the royal troops of Louis at Montlhéry, 15 miles south of Paris, in July of that year. Louis's army received a stinging defeat, forcing him to accept the Treaty of Conflans. However, the wily French monarch largely ignored the terms of the treaty and soon broke up the league by diplomatic maneuvers. *See* Héricourt.

Montmirail (Napoleonic Empire Wars). One of the villages between the Marne and Seine rivers where Napoleon I maneuvered brilliantly during February 10–15, 1814, to check temporarily the allied invasion of France. *See* Champaubert-Montmirail.

Montreal (French and Indian War), 1760. General Jeffrey Amherst (later Lord Amherst), British commander in North America, organized a multiple offensive in 1760 designed to conquer Montreal, the last major French holding in Canada. Amherst himself moved from Oswego down the Saint Lawrence with 10,000 men. From Crown Point Gen. William Haviland brought 3,400 men up the Richelieu River. At the same time Gen. James Murray advanced up the Saint Lawrence from Quebec at the head of 2,500 troops. The three columns converged on Montreal on September 6. Two days later the French governor-general, Marquis de Vaudreuil-Cavagnal, surrendered Montreal and the entire province of New France (soon to be the British colony of Canada). French outposts to the south quickly came under British-American possession. The most important of these, Detroit, surrendered to Maj. Robert Rogers on November 29.

In the Treaty of Paris, which ended the French and Indian War (as well as the Seven Years' War, its European counterpart) in 1763, France ceded to Great Britain Canada and all territory east of the Mississippi except New Orleans, which, with the territory west of the river had been deeded to Spain the previous year. Havana was restored to Spain by Great Britain in exchange for West and East Florida. *See* Quebec II; French and Indian War.

Mookerheide (Netherlands War of Independence), 1574. During the savage struggle between the Dutch provinces and the Spain of Philip II, William I (the Silent) of Orange symbolized the resistance of the Netherlanders. In 1574 his brothers Louis and Henry of Nassau held the Dutch village of Mookerheide on the Meuse, in the southeast. But on April 14 a well-armed Spanish force of some 5,000 men attacked the village and routed the Dutch patriots, who had a superiority in numbers but who were poorly armed and ill-trained. Several thousand Dutch were killed, including the two brothers of William. *See* Walcheren; Leyden; Netherlands War of Independence.

Moores Creek Bridge (War of the American Revolution), 1776. The British offensive in the

South opened in North Carolina, where Gen. Sir Henry Clinton landed an expeditionary force near Cape Fear early in 1776. To link up with Clinton's troops, a band of 1,800 Loyalists (Tories) led by Gen. Donald McDonald and Col. Donald McLeod marched toward the coast. At Moores Creek Bridge, near Wilmington, the advance of the predominately Scottish Loyalists was blocked by 1,100 patriot militiamen commanded by Col. James Moore. When the Loyalists tried to force a crossing of the stream on February 27, they were repulsed by a sharp fire from the east bank. The patriots then counterattacked, crossed Moores Creek, and totally routed the enemy force. Thirty of the Scots were killed or wounded and 850 captured. The patriots suffered only two casualties. When he learned of this defeat, Clinton abandoned his plans to occupy North Carolina and switched his attack to Charleston, S.C. *See* Great Bridge; Charleston I; American Revolution.

Morat (Swiss-Burgundian War), 1476. Despite his rout at Grandson, Charles the Bold of Burgundy took his army of 20,000 mercenaries deeper into Switzerland. In Fribourg canton he laid siege to Morat on the eastern shore of Lake Morat. The Swiss infantry, perhaps 35,000 strong, marching to the relief of the village, passed unnoticed across the left front of the Burgundian lines on June 22, 1476. Attacking unexpectedly near the center of Charles's position, the Swiss pikemen and halberdiers struck through to the lake, splitting the enemy force in two. The battle quickly became a slaughter as the hard-fighting mountaineers smashed their opponents in detail. South of Morat village, a force of 6,000 Italian infantrymen penned against the lake died where they stood. Charles withdrew into Lorraine, but the confederation of cantons sent an army in pursuit. *See* Grandson; Nancy.

Morbihan Gulf (Gallic Wars), 56 B.C. In his third summer of campaigning against the Gauls, Julius Caesar moved into Brittany to put down a rebellion of the Veneti. A seafaring people, the Veneti had a fleet of 200 high, flat-bottomed boats. To combat this force, the Romans quickly constructed their own warships in the mouth of the Loire. Under Decimus Junius Brutus, this fleet sailed along the southern coast of Brittany to the Gulf of Morbihan. Here Caesar's vessels encountered the Veneti in the first naval battle of the Atlantic. Using sickles attached to the ends of long poles, the Romans cut down the rigging on the enemy ships, thus immobilizing the entire fleet. The legionaries then boarded the ships one by one, killed the crews, and destroyed the vessels.

The loss of their fleet erased the Veneti's desire to continue the war. Caesar seized their capital of Vannes and executed or sold into slavery the tribal officials. The Roman legions spent that winter near the northwestern coast of France. *See* Sambre River; Coblenz; Gallic Wars.

Morgarten (Swiss-Austrian Wars), 1315. In 1314 the crown of the Holy Roman Empire was claimed by both Louis IV of Bavaria and Frederick the Handsome of the house of Hapsburg. The Swiss cantons supported Louis IV. To crush this opposition, Frederick's brother, Archduke Leopold I of Austria, marched into Switzerland with an army of 15,000 knights and infantrymen. The Swiss army, numbering only 1,500 foot soldiers, laid an ambush at Morgarten, a narrow pass between Lake Aegeri and a mountainside.

When the half-mile-long Austrian column reached the pass on November 15, 1315, a Swiss party on the heights opened the battle by rolling an avalanche of boulders and tree trunks down the precipitous slope. The Swiss soldiers, wielding halberds and morning stars (reinforced clubs), then fell on the disorganized Austrian knights at the head of the column. The attack drove the heavy cavalry back against its own infantry in a helpless tangle of men and horses. Advancing in a relentless phalanx, the Swiss methodically cut down the Austrians or else hurled them into the lake. The butchery ended only when the last Austrian had fled back up the road. Morgarten, a victory won by a wise choice of battleground, launched the Swiss reputation as one of the best infantry forces of the Middle Ages. *See* Muhldorf; Laupen.

Morotai (World War II). An island in the Molucca group, held by the Japanese and successfully invaded by Allied troops on September 15, 1944, as part of the battle for New Guinea. *See* New Guinea.

Mortimer's Cross (Wars of the Roses), 1461. The overwhelming victory of Queen Margaret's army at Wakefield on December 30, 1460, gave the Lancastrians (red rose) the upper hand. A march on London to free King Henry VI from Yorkist (white rose) control was begun. In the west, however, the Yorkists rallied behind the late Richard's eldest son, Edward (later Edward IV). At Mortimer's Cross in Herefordshire Edward's force encountered the army of Welsh Lancastrians under the earls of Pembroke and Wiltshire on February 2, 1461. Edward's men-at-arms attacked and routed their foes. In the tradition of the no-quarter practice begun at Wakefield, many of the defeated were beheaded, including Owen Tudor, grandfather of the future Henry VII. Edward marched east to join the earl of Warwick, who was blocking Queen Margaret's advance on London. *See* Wakefield; Saint Albans II; Roses, Wars of the.

Mortlack (Danish Invasion of Scotland), 1010. The Danish raids on the east coast of Scotland threatened to turn into a permanent lodgment in 1010. Under Sweyn I, Forkbeard, the invaders flooded modern Banff County. King Malcolm II ordered every available man out to stop them. A pitched battle took place at Mortlack. After a desperate struggle the Scots gained the upper hand and, pressing their advantage, drove the Danes back to their ships. In later years a monument was erected in Dufftown to commemorate this decisive victory.

With the Danish danger out of the way, Malcolm turned to unifying the Scottish nation. His success in laying the foundations of modern Scotland soon led him into conflict with the Northumbrians of England. *See* Maldon; Nairn; Clontarf; Carham; Danish Invasions of Britain.

Moscow (World War II), 1941–1942. In the overpowering Nazi invasion of the Soviet Union, the initial German drive toward Moscow had halted near Smolensk throughout September. During this time Field Marshal Fedor von Bock's Army Group Center sent two armies southward to close a gigantic pincers with Army Group South, at Kiev. On October 2 the reassembled force of 60 divisions resumed its attack in an attempt to make the last 200 miles into the capital by winter.

On the right Gen. Heinz Guderian's Second Panzer Group plunged through Orel on October 8 and Chern on October 24 and then ground on toward Tula, 100 miles directly south of Moscow. In the center, the Third and Fourth Panzer groups under Gens. Hermann Hoth and Erich Hoeppner (assigned from the Leningrad front) powered a huge pincers movement at Vyazma. About 600,000 Russians were killed or captured in this encirclement between October 2 and 13. Third Panzer armor (now commanded by Hans Reinhardt), backed up by the Ninth Army, then swung north and west of the city, taking Kalinin on October 15. In the center Gen. Gunther von Kluge's Fourth Army smashed straight at the capital, now only 40 miles away. The Russian government (but not Premier Josef Stalin) moved 550 miles southeast to Kuibyshev on the Volga.

At this point, however, stiffening Russian resistance and roads made muddy by heavy rains slowed the German advance. Kluge's attack picked up speed again when frost hardened the ground in mid-November. But on November 20 the full fury of the Russian winter virtually paralyzed men and machines. A last-gasp effort came on December 2. The 2nd Panzer Division ploughed to within sight of the Kremlin (ordered blown up by Hitler to signal the overthrow of Communism) but could move no farther. An infantry division (258th) of the Fourth Army fought its way into the suburbs of Moscow but was thrown back by armed factory workers in two days of heavy fighting, with many casualties. In the fighting since November 16 the Soviet Union claimed to have killed 85,000 Germans.

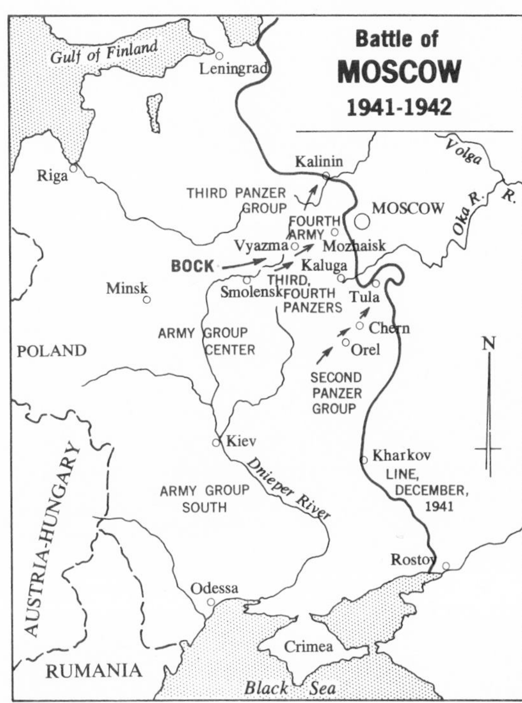

Despite the absence of cold-weather clothing and equipment, Hitler forbade the German troops to withdraw. This order caused terrible suffering and thousands of casualties from the cold. The German plight worsened on December 6 when Gen. Georgi Zhukov, who had replaced Semën Timoshenko on this front, launched a counteroffensive with 100 fresh divisions. (Timoshenko took over the southern front.) South of Moscow, a Red army led by ski troops struck at Guderian's Tula salient on December 9. In five days 30,000 Germans were killed and much heavy equipment lost. Guderian was relieved by Gen. Rudolf Schmidt.

Pressing westward, the Russians captured Kaluga on December 26, lost it, and then recaptured the city four days later. Mozhaisk, 60 miles straight west of the Russian capital, fell to Zhukov's counterattack on January 18. North of Moscow, Kalinin had been retaken after heavy street fighting, on December 15. Kluge, now commanding the central German armies, fell back to Vyazma, in the south, and Rzhev, in the north, both 125 miles from Moscow. (Gen. Gotthard Heinrici took over the Fourth Army.) Along this line Kluge organized a series of hedgehog positions that managed to resist further Russian advances. But the severe cold caused more casualties than did enemy action, reducing some corps to a third of their fighting strength and ending German offensive power in this sector.

The battle of Moscow was Germany's first major defeat on land in World War II and the turning point on the entire central front. After holding in place through the rest of 1942, the *Wehrmacht* began falling back in March 1943 under heavy and repeated Russian blows. *See* Soviet Union (World War II); Leningrad; Crimea; Ukraine; World War II.

Moselle River (World War I). Before and during the first battle of the Marne, the French right wing barred the almost continuous German thrust at France's eastern door, during August 21–September 7, 1914, making possible the decisive action on the Paris front. *See* Marne River I.

Moslem Conquests. Beginning with Mohammed, the Arabs carried the sword of Islam for about 350 years. From Arabia the Moslems overran the Middle East, North Africa, Portugal, Spain, and part of France before being checked. The Turks then became the most militant arm of Mohammedanism. For later battles and wars *see* Mongol Wars; Portugal; Spain; Turkey.

Badr	624
Ohod	625
Medina	627
Mecca	630
Hira	633
Ajnadain	634
Pella	635
Damascus I	635
Yarmuk River	636
Kadisiya	637
Jalula	637
Jerusalem VI	637
Aleppo	638
Nihawand	641
al-Fustât	641
Alexandria II	642
Tripoli I	643
Lycia	655
Basra	656
Siffin	657
Constantinople III	673–678
Kerbela	680
Carthage III	698
Kabul I	709
Río Barbate	711
Constantinople IV	717–718
Covadonga	718
Toulouse I	721
Tours	732
Kashgar	736
Acroïnum	739
Zab al Kabir	750
Heraclea Pontica	806
Amorium	838
Samosata	873
Apulia	875–880
Taormina	902
Erzurum	928
Melitene II	934
Simancas	934
Zamora	939
Candia I	960–961
Adana	964
Aleppo-Antioch	969
Damascus II	976
Crotone	982

Mount Ecnomus. *See* Himera River.

Mount Tifata (Marius-Sulla Civil War), 83 B.C. The successful conclusion of the First Mithridatic War did not enable Lucius Cornelius Sulla to return to Rome in triumph. Instead, he had to fight his way back at the head of an army. In the spring of 83 B.C. Sulla landed at the Adriatic port of Brundisium (Brindisi). Advancing cautiously toward the capital, Sulla encountered an army of the popular party under Consul Caius Norbanus at Mount Tifata, east of Capua. The veteran legions of Sulla routed the enemy force and occupied Capua, where they spent the winter. The following year (82 B.C.) Sulla resumed his march on Rome. On the way he cut to pieces a recruit army under the younger Gaius Marius. (Marius committed suicide.) Sulla then entered Rome but found a larger force massed against him at the Colline Gate. *See* Orchomenus; Colline Gate; Roman Republic.

Mount Vesuvius (Third Servile War), 73–71 B.C. During its rise to world domination, Rome acquired a vast number of slaves, many of whom received harsh treatment. In 135–32 B.C. the slaves in Sicily revolted in the First Servile War. They were ruthlessly put down. The Second Servile War (103–99), also in Sicily, followed the same pattern. The most serious uprising occurred in 73 B.C., when the Thracian slave and gladiator Spartacus seized Mount Vesuvius. Thousands of fugitive slaves rallied to this sanctuary, which was turned into an armed camp. Twice Marcus Licinius Crassus led a Roman army against the rebels and, although victorious both times, failed to crush the uprising. Finally, in 71 B.C., Pompey (later called the Great) returned from quelling another revolt in Spain to take up the attack. Spartacus was killed and his routed force hunted down and executed. Pompey now became known as Pompey the Great. *See* Colline Gate; Roman Republic.

Mudki (Sikh-British War I), 1845. The opening conflict of the war found the British commander, Gen. Sir Hugh Gough, marching into the East Punjab to try to contain the Sikh invasion. Gough, who had some 12,000 Anglo-Indian troops, was surprised at Mudki on December 18 by about 30,000 Sikhs. After an initial setback, the Anglo-Indian army drove the enemy from the field, capturing almost half their 40 guns. The victory cost Gough 870 casualties, including the slain Sir Robert Sale, a hero of the First Afghan War. *See* Hyderabad; Ferozeshah; Sikh-British Wars.

Mühlberg (German Reformation Wars), 1547. During the political and religious unrest of the Reformation, the Spanish Hapsburg ruler of the Holy Roman Empire, Charles V, sought to unite Germany and re-establish Catholicism, at least in part. Much of his opposition came from the Schmalkaldic League, headed in the north by the Protestant princes John Frederick I, elector of Saxony, and Philip, landgrave of Hesse. Unhappily for the Protestant cause, members of the League could not agree on a combined military effort. Charles subdued the princes in southern Germany and then marched to Saxony. His troops, under the Spanish Duke of Alva, forced a crossing of the Elbe River and attacked the elector's army at Mühlberg, about 35 miles east of Leipzig, on April 24, 1547. Some 13,000 Imperial troops thoroughly defeated a slightly smaller Saxon force. John Frederick was captured and Philip surrendered soon after. Some of their lands were given to princely lines favorable to the Holy Roman Empire. But the Reformation forces were too strong to remain dormant. *See* Frankenhausen; Sievershausen.

Mühldorf (Holy Roman Empire Civil War), 1322. Upon the death of Henry VII of Luxemburg in 1313, both Louis IV of Bavaria and Frederick the Handsome of Hapsburg claimed to be Holy Roman Emperor. A long period of civil war ensued. Finally, in 1322, the quarrel reached a climax at Mühldorf on the Inn River, 45 miles east of Munich. Here the Imperial troops of Louis met and defeated Frederick's knights. The Hapsburg duke was captured and imprisoned until 1325 when he became joint emperor with Louis, as Frederick III. *See* Morgarten.

Mukden I (Russian-Japanese War), 1905. Following the drawn battle of the Shaho in 1904, the Japanese field marshal Marquis Iwao Oyama built up his Manchurian army to 300,000 men. On February 21, 1905, he launched an offensive northward toward Mukden on a front of 47 miles. The defending Russian forces of Gen. Aleksei Kuropatkin, in about equal numbers, fought back stubbornly. Day after day the Japanese offensive ground slowly forward. Maneuver gave way to a simple battle of attrition. On March 6 Oyama pushed both his flanks forward in a massive encirclement of Mukden. Four days later the pincers closed north of the city. But Kuropatkin had escaped the trap by withdrawing his army still farther north. Mukden had fallen to the Japanese in a two-and-a-half-week battle that cost the victors 50,000 casualties. Russian losses were almost twice as high. Although he had saved the bulk of his troops, Kuropatkin was relieved. The gesture was meaningless, for the decisive theater of action now became the sea. *See* Shaho River; Tsushima Strait; Russian-Japanese War.

Mukden II (Chinese Civil War), 1947–1948. Late in 1947 the Communist People's Liberation Army (PLA) had overrun almost all of Manchuria. Their next target became Mukden, the chief city of southern Manchuria. By December 23 five PLA columns, supported by artillery, were converging on the city. The Nationalist leader, Generalissimo Chiang Kai-shek, sent Gen. Wei Li-huang to Mukden on February 1, 1948, as head of the Northeastern Bandit-Suppression Headquarters. But five more of Mao Tse-tung's columns were added to the Communist offensive, bringing their strength in this area up to 200,000 men.

The encirclement slowly tightened. On September 12, 30,000 PLA troops began cutting the Liaosi corridor, the only land route still open from Manchuria. In October, Gen. Liao Yao-hsiang tried to lead three Nationalist armies and miscellaneous other units out of the trap. By the end of the month this entire force was wiped out or captured by Gen. Lin Piao's besiegers. Meanwhile, Wei Li-huang escaped by plane. On November 1 the surviving Mukden defenders—the Fifty-third Army and the 207th (Youth) Division—surrendered the city. Mukden's seaport of Yunghow capitulated four days later. All of Manchuria lay under Communist control. *See* Sungari River; Kaifeng; Chinese Civil War.

Mulhouse (World War I), 1914. As the German armies opened the war against France by plunging into neutral Belgium, the French commander in chief, Gen. Joseph Joffre, launched an offensive in the northeast. On August 7, 1914, he sent the VII Corps under General Bonneau over the Vosges Mountains into Alsace, which had been under German rule since 1871. Bonneau's troops fought their way into Altkirch at a cost of 100 casualties and on the following day entered Mulhouse (Mulhausen) without firing a shot. However, as the French proceeded with their liberation, the German Seventh Army (Josias von Heeringen) at Strasbourg rushed up reinforcements. Early on August 9 the Germans counterattacked. The French held Mulhouse for 24 hours, then, fearing envelopment, withdrew southwest to within ten miles of Belfort. Charging Bonneau with a lack of aggressiveness, Joffre relieved him from command. A three-corps Army of Alsace, under Gen. Paul Pau, was organized on the French extreme right flank. *See* Liége; Frontiers of France; World War I.

Münchengrätz (Seven Weeks' War), 1866. At the outbreak of war between Prussia (Wilhelm I) and Austria (Franz Josef I) in June 1866, Gen. Helmuth von Moltke (later Count von Moltke), chief of the Prussian general staff, sent four armies plunging southward. One force was to deal with the armies of Hannover and Austria's other allies in southern Germany. The other three armies began converging on Bohemia. From the vicinity of Torgau, the Army of the Elbe, 45,000 men under Gen. Karl Herwarth von Bittenfeld, moved on Dresden. The outnumbered Saxon corps withdrew into Bohemia to link up with the Austrian army of the north, which was assembling there under Gen. Ludwig von Benedek.

The Army of the Elbe then joined forces with the Prussian First Army of Prince Frederick Charles, nephew of Wilhelm I. This combined force of 140,000 men pushed through the passes in the Bohemian mountains northeast of Prague. At Münchengrätz (Mnichovo Hradiště) the Prussians met a forward Austrian corps commanded by Gen. Count Eduard von Clam-Gallas on June 28. In a sharp skirmish the Austrians suffered 300 killed and wounded, plus 1,000 captured. Clam-Gallas retreated to Gitschin (Jičin), where the Prussians drove him back again, inflicting greater casualties. Clam-Gallas was relieved, while Benedek ordered a general withdrawal toward the upper Labe (Elbe), between Sadowa and Königgrätz (Hradec Králové). *See* Langensalza; Sadowa; Seven Weeks' War.

Munda (Wars of the First Triumvirate), 45 B.C. Returning to Rome after his decisive victory at Thapsus, Julius Caesar took four simultaneous triumphs (ceremonials). He stood master of the Western World except for Spain. Here Gnaeus Pompey, son of the late Pompey the Great, had been fomenting rebellion against Roman rule. The situation became more troublesome when another of Pompey's sons, Sextus, and a former disciple of Caesar's, Titus Labienus, fled to Spain after their defeat in North Africa. Caesar took an army to Spain early in 45 B.C. to reinforce his hard-pressed lieutenants there. After a difficult march he encountered the enemy's main body at Munda, in the southern part of the province, on March 17. Although the Pompeians had a larger force, they could not stand up under Caesar's skillful maneuvering and vigorous attacks. The legionaries swept the field, killing or capturing 20,000 opponents. Labienus was killed, Gnaeus Pompey captured and executed. Sextus escaped to refuge in northern Spain. The Caesarians lost only 1,000 men.

The battle of Munda ended Spanish resistance to Roman rule. Caesar returned to Rome in September, where he was made sole consul for ten years. He now planned an expedition to conquer Persia. But Munda would be his last victory. Discontent with his authoritarian status led to his assassination on March 15, 44 B.C. (the Ides of March in the Roman calendar). *See* Thapsus; Mutina; First Triumvirate, Wars of the.

Muret (Albigensian Crusade in France), 1213. The crusade called for by Pope Innocent III against the Albigenses, or Catharist heretics, pitted the nobles of northern France against those of the south. Simon IV de Montfort led the Catholic crusaders of the north; Raymond VI, count of Toulouse, commanded the Albigenses. The fighting was savage. In a battle at Muret in September 1213 the southern army was decisively beaten, breaking the back of their resistance. The Aragon king, Pedro II, who had fought so ably at Las Navas de Tolosa in Spain and now had supported his brother-in-law Raymond, fell in the struggle, marking the end of Aragon's interests north of the Pyrenees. Philip II Augustus of France had remained aloof from the conflict. However, Montfort's victory opened the way for bringing southwestern France under French rule. *See* Las Navas de Tolosa; Bouvines.

Murfreesboro. *See* Stones River.

Mursa (Civil Wars of the Roman Empire), 351. While Constantius II was campaigning against Persia in the East, his brother Constans, ruler of the western half of the Roman Empire, was dethroned by Flavius Popilius Magnentius. Constans was killed in the struggle early in 350. Constantius then abandoned the Persian War and marched into the Balkans. At Mursa (Osijek), near the confluence of the Drave and Danube in modern Yugoslavia, Constantius' army of 40,000 men encountered a force of 50,000 troops under Magnentius. On September 28, 351, the two opponents clashed in a bitter struggle that resulted in a victory for Constantius, although he lost almost 15,000 men. Magnentius, despite suffering fewer casualties (12,000), had to fall back to Aquileia, at the head of the Adriatic. Constantius pursued inexorably the following year, forcing his foe to retreat across northern Italy into Gaul. Finally, in 353, deserted by his remaining troops, Magnentius committed suicide. The unity of the Roman Empire had been re-established once again. *See* Singara; Argentoratum; Roman Empire.

Muthul River (Roman Conquest of Numidia), 108 B.C. Several Italians were killed at Cirta (Constantine) when Jugurtha usurped the throne of Numidia about 111 B.C. Although Jugurtha's grandfather Masinissa had been a valuable Roman ally in the Second Punic War, Rome sent a punitive expedition into Numidia. The legionaries were humiliated by the fierce African tribesmen in the so-called Jugurthine War. Finally Quintus Metellus (Numidicus) took over the Rome expeditionary force. In a pitched battle along the Muthul River, in 108 B.C., Metellus routed the Numidians, but Jugurtha escaped to carry on guerrilla war against Rome. The Senate then authorized Gaius Marius to raise an army of volunteers from the poor. This was the beginning of professional armies in Rome. In 105 B.C., Lucius Cornelius Sulla, acting for Marius, captured Jugurtha. The rebel king was taken to Italy where he died in prison. Numidia was divided between two other descendants of Masinissa. *See* Numantia; Roman Republic.

Mutina (Wars of the Second Triumvirate), 43

B.C. The assassination of Julius Caesar on March 15, 44 B.C., led to a fierce power struggle among a number of Romans—Mark Antony, a trusted lieutenant in several Caesarian battles; Decimus Brutus, another war veteran, who had become governor of Cisalpine Gaul; Marcus Brutus, who had received the rule of Macedonia; G. Cassius Longinus, who was assigned to Syria; Marcus Lepidus, governor of Transalpine Gaul; and G. Julius Caesar Octavianus, called Octavian, the 19-year-old great nephew, adopted son, and legal heir of the slain Caesar.

Claiming a mandate from the Roman people, Antony took a force to Cisalpine Gaul. His four legions surrounded Decimus Brutus in Mutina (Modena), 200 miles north of Rome. He then laid siege to the town. On April 14, 43 B.C., Antony was attacked by three armies sent out by the Senate, commanded by Octavian and the consuls Aulus Hirtius and Vibius Pansa. Antony's forces held their ground; Pansa was fatally wounded. A second attack, a week later, raised the siege, but Hirtius fell in this action.

Antony fled westward to Gaul, where he made an alliance with Lepidus. Octavian went to Rome in July and forced the senate to name him a consul. He thereupon switched his support to Antony. In November, Octavian, Antony, and Lepidus received legal approval to form a Second Triumvirate. Opponents were ruthlessly executed (including the great orator Marcus Tullius Cicero and his brother Quintus Tullius Cicero). Decimus Brutus was killed by Gauls in the north. With Rome under firm control, the triumvirs turned to the East, where Marcus Brutus and Cassius had joined forces in Macedonia. *See* Munda; Philippi; Second Triumvirate, Wars of the.

Mycale (Persian-Greek Wars), 479 B.C. After the decisive naval victory at Salamis in 480 B.C., a Greek naval force under the Spartan king Leotychides sailed across the Aegean Sea to take the island of Samos. The Persian fleet then withdrew to the mainland of Asia Minor, beaching their ships at Cape Mycale. The Greeks stormed ashore, whereupon the Persians burned their ships before the Greeks could seize them. The 60,000-man Persian force was now trapped, however, between the Spartans on the coast and a group of Ionians inland. In a joint Greek-Ionian attack, the entire enemy army was destroyed. The peril of Persian domination of Greece had now been ended, and the remaining initiative in this war passed to the Greeks. *See* Salamis; Plataea I; Eurymedon River; Persian-Greek Wars.

Myitkyina (World War II). A key Japanese-held airfield in northern Burma, captured by American and Chinese troops on May 17, 1944. *See* Burma II.

Mylae (First Punic War), 260 B.C. During the years that Rome was building the strongest army in the world, Carthage ranked as the greatest maritime nation. To compete at sea, Rome constructed a new fleet of quinqueremes (five banks of oars), which relied on grappling irons and boarding bridges, rather than the traditional ram, for offensive power. The first clash between the Roman and Carthaginian navies occurred off the Lipara Islands, north of Sicily, in 260. Rome lost 17 ships.

Later in the year Gaius Duilius (Nepos) replaced Gnaeus Cornelius Scipio as commander of the Roman navy and challenged Hanno's Carthaginian fleet again, at Mylae (now Milazzo), 17 miles west of Messina. This time Rome's new naval tactics proved successful. Although Duilius had fewer galleys, the Romans proved superior at hand-to-hand fighting once an enemy ship had been boarded. In what was to become Rome's first sea victory, Carthage lost 50 ships, 3,000 men killed, and 7,000 taken prisoner. This decisive Roman triumph protected the republic's hold on Messina and thwarted Carthage's attempted invasion of Italy. (To honor the victorious general a Duilian Column was erected in the Forum at Rome.) *See* Messina I; Ecnomus; Punic Wars.

Mynydd Carn (Welsh Civil War), 1081. Wales was already torn by civil war among various petty princes when the Norman invasion began pressing in from the east. Finally, in 1081, Gruffydd ap Cyan of Gwynedd and Rhys ap Tewdwr of Deheubarth allied their armies against the forces of rival princes. At the battle of Mynydd Carn, near Saint Davids in the southwest, the two allies won a total victory. This helped stabilize Wales under the leadership of the provinces of Gwynedd and Deheubarth until Wales became an English principality in 1284. *See* Ely I; Rochester I.

Myriocephalon (Byzantine-Turkish Wars), 1176. In an effort to repel the Seljuk Turks from his eastern frontier, the Byzantine emperor Manuel I Comnenus, grandson of Alexius I, marched into Asia Minor in 1176. The Byzantine army, now composed largely of mercenaries, reached the fortress Myriocephalon in ancient Phrygia. Here, in a long defile, Manuel was surrounded by a large force of Turkish mounted bowmen from Iconium, under Kilij Arslan II. The Imperial army suffered a crushing defeat on September 17 and was forced to fall back on Constantinople. The Turkish victory at Myriocephalon dealt a heavy blow to Byzantine prestige in the Near East. This in turn seriously weakened the positions of the Frankish crusaders in Syria and Palestine. *See* Philomelion; Erzincan.

Mysore-British Wars (1767–1799). The establishment of the British East India Company led to a series of four wars with the native Mohammedan state of Mysore during 1767–99. The first conflict (1767–69) produced no real battle and ended with Haidar (Hyder) Ali, the maharaja of Mysore, securing a treaty favorable to his people. Each of the three following wars (1780–84; 1790–92; 1799) produced a major battle.

Porto Novo 1781
Seringapatam I 1792
Seringapatam II 1799

Mytilene (Great Peloponnesian War), 427 B.C. Believing that Sparta would supply aid, the island of Lesbos revolted against Athenian domination in 428. Cleon, who had succeeded Pericles in Athens, sent a fleet under Paches to put down the rebellion. Paches reached Lesbos and landed 1,000 hoplites at the chief city of Mytilene before the dilatory Spartan vessels could interfere. In May of the following year Mytilene surrendered. In retaliation for the earlier massacre at Plataea, all the male inhabitants of the city were condemned to death. Only the leaders were executed, however. *See* Plataea II; Pylos-Sphacteria; Peloponnesian Wars.

Myton (English-Scottish Wars), 1319. A year after Robert I, the Bruce, captured Berwick upon Tweed, the last English hold on Scotland, Edward II took the fortress under siege. Thereupon the Scottish king sent a diversionary force under Sir James Douglas raiding southward into Yorkshire in northeast England. The archbishop of York, William Melton, hastily assembled an army, which met the raiders at Myton, near the Swale River. On September 20, 1319, Douglas' Scots routed the English army. Because the defeated force contained many priests and monks, the Scots called the battle "the chapter of Myton." Douglas' victory produced the desired effect. Alarmed by the apparently strong force in his rear, Edward II ordered the siege of Berwick to be abandoned. *See* Bannockburn; Boroughbridge.

N

Näfels (Austrian-Swiss Wars), 1388. In 1388 Austria invaded Switzerland for the third time in the fourteenth century. The much stronger Austrian army penetrated into Glarus canton. But at Näfels, in a battle reminiscent of Morgarten in 1315, the Swiss laid an ambush on April 9. As the invading column reached the foot of a mountain, it was disorganized by an avalanche of boulders rolled down the slope. The Swiss then rushed to attack with their deadly halberds and pikes. After routing the enemy cavalry, the fierce-fighting mountaineers assaulted and drove off the Austrian infantry as well. Six years later the Duke of Austria signed a 20-year truce with the confederation of Swiss cantons. Switzerland became a dependent of the Holy Roman Empire, thus achieving virtually complete independence. *See* Sempach; Arbedo.

Nairn (Danish Invasion of Scotland), 1009. The savage Danish raids on the coast of Britain struck Scotland early in the eleventh century. Sweyn I, Forkbeard, landed a force of Danes on the coast of Moray Firth and laid siege to Nairn. Under their king, Malcolm II, a Scots army marched toward the coast to raise the siege. The Danes turned on the relieving force and drove it back. Malcolm was wounded in the hard fighting. The invaders withdrew at the end of the summer but returned in greater force the following year. *See* Maldon; Mortlack; Danish Invasions of Britain.

Naissus (Gothic Invasion of the Roman Empire), 269. In the spring of 268 the Roman Empire was threatened by the greatest barbarian offensive up to that time. More than 300,000 Goths and others swarmed over the eastern European provinces of Rome. One force of Goths pressed past the Black Sea to reach Asia Minor. Another force advanced into the western Balkans, where a continuation of the drive would split the empire in two. Claudius II, a veteran officer who had become emperor that year, marched into modern Yugoslavia to head off the invaders. At Naissus (Nis) the Roman legions fought a pitched battle with a huge force of barbarians in 269. The hard-pressed Romans finally crushed the Goths when Claudius launched an attack with a 5,000-man reserve against the enemy rear. An estimated 50,000 Goths fell in this battle.

Claudius received the honorary title Gothicus for his successful rout of the barbarians. But before he could follow up his victory he died of the plague, the next year. *See* Philippopolis I; Edessa I; Placentia; Roman Empire.

Nájera (Hundred Years' War), 1367. The long struggle between England and France crossed the Pyrenees into Spain in 1367. Pedro the Cruel, king of Castile and León, was finding it necessary to defend his crown against his half brother, the count of Trastamara (later Henry II of Castile). Trastamara enjoyed the support of a French army commanded by Bertrand du Guesclin. In his capacity as prince of Aquitaine, Edward, the Black Prince, of England allied himself with Pedro. The two armies clashed at Nájera (or Navarrete), between Logrono and the Castilian capital of Burgos, on April 3, 1367. Edward's skillful generalship (so often demonstrated in France) and the fighting qualities of his Anglo-Gascon-Spanish army led to a rout of the rival French-Spanish force. Pedro's claim to his throne was protected, but the English intervention proved to be a failure in the long run. A quarrel over money with Pedro led the Black Prince to withdraw his army, and two years later the unpopular Castilian king again came under attack. *See* Auray; Montiel; Hundred Years' War.

Naklo (Rise of Poland), 1109. The Polish state, which had emerged in the tenth century under the Piast dynasty, received some of its most enlightened rule from Boleslav III, the Wrymouth. In 1109 Boleslav attacked the Pomeranians at Naklo, in north-central Poland. He soundly defeated them and thus gained access to the Baltic Sea. (Later that year he checked the German advance of Holy Roman Emperor Henry V near Breslau.) Poland held this gain little more than a hundred years, however. In the thirteenth century the crusading order of Teutonic Knights cut their way through Prussia, establishing Christianity with the sword. This conquest blocked the Polish kingdom's access to the sea. *See* Cracow.

Nam Dong (Vietnam War), 1964. To protect

against guerrilla attacks by the Viet Cong (VC), the government of South Vietnam established armed camps throughout the country. One of these was Nam Dong in the northwest, near the Laos and North Vietnam borders. Here stood 311 Vietnamese troops, 60 Nung soldiers, and an American Special Forces team of 12 men commanded by Capt. Roger Donlon. About 2 A. M. on July 6 Nam Dong came under severe attack by 800 to 900 Viet Cong guerrillas. Under a heavy mortar barrage the Communist forces overran the South Vietnamese at the edge of the camp to reach the center of the perimeter defenses. In a vicious fight the VC attack was repulsed at daylight. Two Americans were killed, eight others wounded, including Donlon, who suffered multiple wounds. Although the battle of Nam Dong was only one of many similar encounters in South Vietnam, it is notable for the award of the Medal of Honor to Donlon. It was the first time the highest United States decoration was awarded in the Vietnam War. *See* South Vietnam; Van Tuong Peninsula; Vietnam War.

Namur I (War of the Grand Alliance), 1695. At the junction of the Sambre and Meuse rivers, the city of Namur was a key point in the control of the Spanish Netherlands. Fortified by the Dutch engineer Baron Menno van Coehoorn, the city resisted for 36 days before surrendering on June 5, 1692, to the French siege tactics of the Marquis de Vauban. The siege cost the French 2,600 in killed and wounded, while the garrison suffered twice that number of casualties.

Three years later, however, the situation had changed. The French marshal the Duc de Luxembourg had died undefeated and had been replaced by the less able marshal the Duc de Villeroi. And the Alliance commander, William III, king of England and stadholder of Holland, still maintained an army in the field despite a steady string of reverses. Early in July William, assisted by Coehoorn, attacked Namur. Steadily pressing their assault, the Alliance troops finally forced a capitulation on September 1, although the operation cost the attackers 18,000 casualties to less than half that number for the French.

With the war virtually deadlocked, Louis XIV arranged the Treaty of Ryswick with the Grand Alliance in 1697. But no lasting settlement was effected, and four years later a more serious conflict, the War of the Spanish Succession (Queen Anne's War), broke out. *See* Marsaglia; Neerwinden I; Chiari; Grand Alliance, War of the.

Namur II (World War I), 1914. In the third week of the war the German Second Army of Gen. Karl von Bülow marched up the Meuse River into southern Belgium. On August 20 the German advance reached Namur, at the confluence of the Sambre and Meuse rivers, the last fortress city barring the way into France. While Bülow pushed on across the Sambre above Namur, he dropped off troops to besiege the city. The main Belgium army had fallen back to Antwerp to avoid being cut off, leaving only 37,000 men to hold Namur against a German force of more than 100,000 with 400 to 500 pieces of artillery. Most of the city's defense rested upon its circle of forts, similar to those which the Germans had battered into submission at Liége the week before. In fact many of the 420- and 305-mm. siege mortars used against Liége were now moved to Namur. Their two-ton shells, in conjunction with the bombardment of other heavy guns for five days, forced the capitulation of the city on August 25. Five thousand defenders became prisoners of war. Meanwhile, the mammoth German offensive (the Schlieffen Plan) rolled headlong into the French and British armies that were launching Attack Plan 17 along the northern border of France. *See* Liége; Antwerp II; Frontiers of France; World War I.

Nancy (Swiss-Burgundian War), 1477. Driven out of Switzerland in 1476, Charles the Bold of Burgundy took up a strong position at Nancy, capital of Lorraine. The Swiss infantry marched to the attack on January 5, 1477. While the main body moved up for a frontal assault, the vanguard circled to the left to come in on the Burgundian flank. In a coordinated rush the Swiss fell on Charles's troops, wielding their deadly pikes and halberds. The Burgundian army was destroyed, its leader killed. The battle of Nancy ended the power of Burgundy. Louis XI of France incorporated the duchy into his nation. Only Flanders remained apart, under its ruler, Marie (daughter of Charles), who preserved its independence by hurriedly marrying Prince Maximilian of Hapsburg, son of Holy Roman Emperor Frederick III. *See* Morat; Giornico.

Nanking I (Overthrow of Mongols), 1356. Most of China was ruled by the Mongols after Genghis Khan's invasion in 1214, which captured Peking. This so-called Yuan dynasty (1260–1368) gradually disintegrated into anarchy in the fourteenth century. Finally a monk turned warrior, Chu Yüan-chang, organized a rebel force against the Mongol government. In 1356 he stormed and took Nanking (Chiangning), in what was the turning point in the revolution. Chu, who later took the title Hung Wu, steadily pressed the Mongols out of China. By 1368 his Ming dynasty, with its capital at Nanking, stood secure. It would last until 1644. *See* Peking I; Peking II.

Nanking II (Chinese-Japanese War II). The Japanese capture of Nanking on December 13, 1937, was followed by widespread atrocities that became known as the "rape of Nanking." *See* China I.

Nanking III (Chinese Civil War), 1949. The crushing Nationalist defeat at Hwai-Hai in January, coupled with the earlier loss of Manchuria, left Generalissimo Chiang Kai-shek virtually powerless to defend the rest of China against the Communist People's Liberation Army (PLA) of Mao Tse-tung. When the last attempt to negotiate a peace treaty failed on April 20, PLA columns marched southward across the Yangtze River. The Nationalist government fled from Nanking to Canton, later to the World War II capital of Chungking, and then to Chengtu. On April 22 the Communists stormed and captured Nanking. Shanghai, to the east, fell on May 27. All resistance now collapsed before the marching feet of the PLA. On October 1 the Chinese People's Republic formally took over the reins of government at Peking (renamed from Peiping). Chiang Kai-shek and the remaining leaders of the rump Kuomintang dictatorship, which had ruled for 21 years, flew to Formosa in December. The civil war was ended, with the Communists in firm control of the Chinese mainland. *See* Mukden II; Hwai-Hai; Chinese Civil War.

Naples (French Invasions of Italy), 1495. The troubled Italian peninsula suffered a new invasion late in the fifteenth century. Charles VIII of France, claiming hereditary rights to Naples through the house of Anjou, crossed the Alps in the autumn of 1494 with an army of 30,000 men, which included heavy cavalry and mobile artillery. Aligned with Lodovico Sforza of Milan, the French king met little opposition. He routed the Medici from Florence, advanced on Rome, and then marched into Naples on February 22, 1495, expelling the Spanish (Aragonese) administration of Ferdinand (Ferrante) II.

However, when Charles returned to France later that year, an anti-Valois coalition quickly formed against the French conquerors in Italy. Making up this so-called Holy League were Milan, Venice, Pope Alexander VI, Ferdinand (V of Castile, II of Aragon), and Maximilian I of the Holy Roman Empire. Its army was led by Gonzalo de Córdoba, a veteran of Spanish fighting against the Portuguese and Moors. The League's army retook Naples, forcing the French to retreat up the peninsula. *See* Granada; Fornovo.

Napoleonic Empire Wars (1803–1814). During the Wars of the French Revolution, France had held its own against both the First and Second Coalitions of European powers. Napoleon Bonaparte, who had risen to first consul in 1799 and then emperor of France in 1804, ruled an empire already embroiled in a new conflict. Great Britain, which had resumed the war in 1803, was joined by Austria (for the Holy Roman Empire), Russia, Sweden, and later Naples. In this War of the Third Coalition, Spain sided with France. Austria was knocked out of the war in 1805, and the Holy Roman Empire was dissolved the following year (Francis II becoming Francis I, emperor of Austria). That summer Prussia joined the Third Coalition. Napoleon successfully prosecuted the war against Prussia and Russia during 1806–1807. But when he occupied Spain in 1808, France soon became engaged in a two-front war—in the Iberian Peninsula, and against Austria, which resumed the fighting in 1809. While the long Peninsular War dragged on in the West, Austria was again defeated. But the French invasion of Russia in 1812 became a terrible disaster for the Napoleonic armies. Thereafter French power steadily declined. During the Fourth Coalition (or the Wars of Liberation), during 1813–1814, Napoleon's armies were beaten on every front by troops from Russia, Prussia, Sweden, Austria, Great Britain, Spain, and several German states. The victorious allies entered Paris on May 31, 1814. Meanwhile Napoleon had abdicated and gone into exile on Elba. For the battles fought on his return see Napoleon's Hundred Days; see also French Revolution Wars.

Third Coalition

Finisterre Cape III	1805
Ulm	1805
Trafalgar Cape	1805
Caldiero II	1805
Oberhollabrunn	1805
Austerlitz	1805
Cape Town	1806
Buenos Aires	1806–1807
Maida	1806
Saalfeld	1806
Jena-Auerstedt	1806
Lübeck	1806
Pultusk II	1806
Eylau	1807
Danzig II	1807
Heilsberg	1807
Friedland	1807
Copenhagen II	1807
Peninsular War—First Phase	
Saragossa II	1808–1809
Bailén	1808
Vimeiro	1808
La Coruña	1809
Oporto	1809
Talavera de la Reina	1809
Fourth Austrian War	
Sacile	1809
Abensberg	1809
Landshut	1809
Eggmühl	1809
Aspern-Essling	1809
Raab	1809
Wagram	1809
Peninsular War—Second Phase	
Bussaco	1810

Fuentes de Oñoro 1811
La Albuera 1811
Tarragona 1811
Ciudad Rodrigo 1812
Badajoz 1812
Salamanca 1812

Invasion of Russia

Mogilev 1812
Smolensk I 1812
Borodino 1812
Maloyaroslavets 1812
Berezina River 1812

Fourth Coalition

Lützen II 1813
Bautzen 1813
Vitoria 1813
Grossbeeren 1813
Katzbach River 1813
Dresden 1813
Kulm-Priesten 1813
Dennewitz 1813
Leipzig 1813
Hanau 1813
Brienne 1814
La Rothière 1814
Champaubert-Montmirail 1814
Montereau 1814
Bar-sur-Aube 1814
Craonne 1814
Laon 1814
Reims 1814
Arcis-sur-Aube 1814
Paris I 1814
Toulouse II 1814

Napoleon's Hundred Days (1815). While the Congress of Vienna debated the settlement of the Napoleonic Empire Wars, the exiled emperor returned from Elba in 1815. France rose in his support, King Louis XVIII fleeing to Ghent. Although his lieutenant Joachim Murat was defeated in Italy, Napoleon threatened to regain all his former European conquests until he was stopped at Waterloo, Belgium, on June 18. This ended the historic Hundred Days, which began with his re-entry into Paris on March 20. Napoleon again abdicated and was exiled to Saint Helena. The Quadruple Alliance—England, Austria, Prussia, and Russia—stood supreme in Europe.

Tolentino 1815
Ligny 1815
Quatre Bras 1815
Wavre 1815
Waterloo 1815

Naroch Lake (World War I), 1916. In response to appeals from France, Czar Nicholas II of Russia resolved to launch a diversionary offensive on the Eastern Front. The czar, who had assumed personal command of the Russian armies in the previous September, chose to attack the German lines at Naroch Lake in White Russia, north of the Pripet Marshes. On March 18 he sent the Tenth Army against the Germans, who were under the overall command of Field Marshal Paul von Hindenburg. Well-aimed machine-gun and artillery fire cut the Russian attackers to pieces. When a spring thaw turned the battlefield into a sea of mud, the czar's troops became hopelessly bogged down by March 26. The poorly organized offensive cost the Russians 100,000 casualties without a single offsetting gain. *See* Gorlice-Tarnów; Kovel-Stanislav; World War I.

Narva (Great Northern War), 1700. The strong position of Sweden in the Baltic region led to a coalition late in 1699 of three neighboring nations —Russia (Peter I, the Great), Poland (Augustus II, who was also elector of Saxony), and Denmark (Frederick IV). Although Sweden's Charles XII was only 17 years old at the time, he proved to be an able military commander. On August 4 of the following year the young king landed an expeditionary force just north of Copenhagen. Denmark sued for peace and withdrew from the war immediately, on August 18, 1700.

Charles then turned against Russia, which was besieging the Swedish-held city of Narva in modern Estonia, near the Gulf of Finland. On November 30 he landed a Swedish army of 8,000 men nearby and promptly attacked the Russian entrenchments, manned by some 40,000 troops. The Swedish assault, under cover of a snowstorm, carried past the Russian outpost into the center of their lines. Within three hours the huge Russian army abandoned its positions and fled, leaving behind an estimated 10,000 dead. Swedish losses were less than 1,000.

After the resounding victory at Narva, Charles marched southwest toward Riga, which was under siege by the Saxons. He arrived at the Latvian city on June 17, 1701. The Saxons withdrew into Poland with the Swedes in close pursuit. *See* Klissow; Great Northern War.

Naseby (English Civil War), 1645. Although the battle of Marston Moor in 1644 had been a clear-cut defeat of Charles I and his Cavaliers, the victorious Roundheads had not capitalized on their advantage. The Royalists had rebounded to more than hold their own by the end of the year. Parliament then reorganized its forces into the New Model army, with a total strength of 22,000 men. Sir Thomas Fairfax became commander in chief, but Oliver Cromwell, as leader of the steel-clad cavalry called the Ironsides, was the strongest man in the army. The new military force was soon put to the test.

In the spring of 1645 Charles I marched out from his Oxford headquarters, seeking to re-establish himself in the north. He took and sacked Leicester. Fairfax and Cromwell hurried to inter-

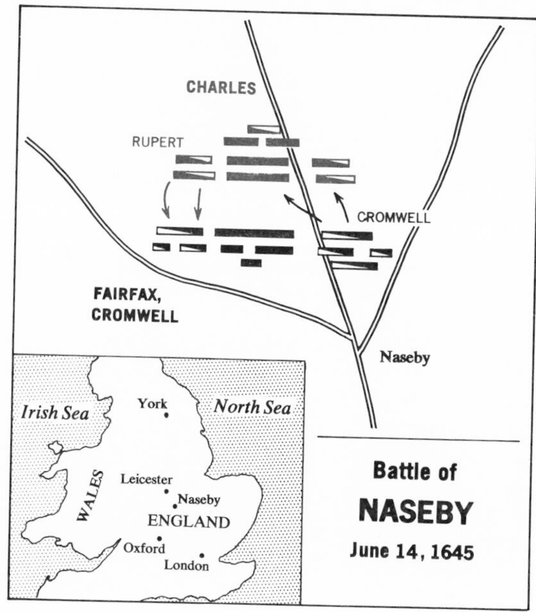

Battle of NASEBY June 14, 1645

cept with about 14,000 men of the New Model army. Charles turned to meet the challenge in the hunting country about Naseby, in Northamptonshire. The two forces slammed together on June 14. Despite being outnumbered by almost 2 to 1, the king's cavalry commander (and nephew), Prince Rupert of Germany, led a·charge which broke the Parliamentary left. But repeating his mistake at Edgehill three years before, Rupert pursued too far, taking his force out of the main action, while the Cavalier left flank and center were being overwhelmed by Cromwell's hard-fighting Puritans. All the Royalist infantrymen were killed or captured (some 3,500), the artillery was seized, and the baggage train lost. Charles escaped with Rupert's cavalry, but his cause fell at Naseby. The war would continue with minor sieges and maneuvers (and even two Royalist victories in Scotland), but the Cavaliers were never again able to take the open field against the New Model army. *See* Marston Moor; Newbury II; Alford; Langport; English Civil War.

Nashville (American Civil War), 1864. When the Federal general John Schofield successfully retreated into Nashville, Tenn., after his victory at Franklin, he came under the command of Gen. George Thomas. The Confederate general John Hood pursued but halted southeast of the city without attacking. He deployed his 31,000 troops and waited for Thomas to come after him. Thomas, with 49,000 men available, prepared for two weeks and then launched a classic assault against the Confederate lines on December 15. Early in the morning the Federals opened the battle with a secondary attack against Hood's right (east), held by Gen. Benjamin Cheatham's corps. Then Thomas struck hard at the Confederate left. Leading the attack was the XVI Corps of Gen. Andrew Smith, followed by the IV Corps of Gen. Thomas Wood on Smith's left, and still later by the XXIV Corps of Schofield on Smith's right. This weight caved in the Confederate corps of Gen. Alexander Stewart. Fortunately for Hood, nightfall halted the fighting and gave him time to reorganize his lines. That night Cheatham moved from the Confederate right to the left of Gen. Stephen Lee's center corps, which had seen little action that day.

The Federal army held its ground during the night, moved up to the new Confederate positions on the morning of December 16, and then about 3:30 P.M. launched a furious attack. On the left, Thomas was stopped. But on the far right (west) Gen. James Wilson's dismounted cavalry penetrated Hood's left rear, threatening to block the Confederate line of retreat. This attack collapsed the entire defensive position. Hood was driven from the field in disorder. Only darkness and a heavy rain enabled the Confederates to fall back southward without being overwhelmed by the Federal pursuit. The defeat cost Hood about 1,500 in killed and wounded and 4,462 captured. Thomas' casualties were 387 killed, 2,562 wounded, and 112 missing.

On December 25 Hood retreated across the Tennessee River into Mississippi. He was relieved of command at his own request the following month. It was a useless gesture—the Confederate Army of Tennessee had ceased to exist as an effective combat force. *See* Franklin; Savannah III; American Civil War.

Nations, Battle of the. *See* Leipzig.

Naulochus (Wars of the Second Triumvirate), 36 B.C. When Parthia cost Mark Antony his military reputation and Cleopatra subverted his political standing, Rome began falling under the firm control of the 27-year-old Octavian. The greatest military menace to this triumvir was the powerful fleet assembled by Sextus Pompey, son of Pompey the Great. Octavian ordered the construction of a new navy under Marcus Vipsanius Agrippa. Late in July the new galleys carried an army of Octavian loyalists to Sicily. This action forced young Pompey to fight a showdown naval battle off Naulochus, a port in northeast Sicily. The two fleets, each of 200 ships, battled ferociously on September 3. Agrippa's newer vessels gradually gained the upper hand. Pompey fled the scene with only 17 surviving ships. (He was captured and executed in Asia Minor the following year by Antony's troops.)

Marcus Lepidus, the third triumvir, moved to Sicily from his African domain. When he unwisely tried to secure the island for himself, his troops revolted. Octavian promptly put him under house arrest until his death in 13 B.C. Now only Antony stood between Octavian and supreme mastery of the Roman world. *See* Perusia; Phraaspa; Actium; Second Triumvirate, Wars of the.

Naupactus (Great Peloponnesian War), 429 B.C. Early in the war the Athenian navy under Phormio instituted a blockade of the Gulf of Corinth. Twice in 429 the Peloponnesian fleet, commanded by Cnemus, tried to drive off the blockaders. Both times the outnumbered triremes of Athens defeated their less skillful opponents off Naupactus (Návpaktos, called Lepanto by the Italians). *See* Plataea II; Mytilene; Peloponnesian Wars.

Navarino (Greek War of Independence), 1827. When the Turkish sultan Mahmud II called in Egyptian troops and warships to quell the Greek revolt in 1825, the other powers in Europe became alarmed. Great Britain, France, and Russia sent a total of 24 ships to aid Greece. Under the command of the English admiral Sir Edward Codrington, the allied fleet entered the harbor of Navarino (Pylos) in the southwestern Peloponnesus on October 20, 1827. Here stood the entire Egyptian fleet of Mehemet (Mohammed) Ali, plus a number of Turkish vessels. Firing broke out. The much superior allied ships blasted more than 50 Egyptian-Turkish ships to the bottom and ran others aground. Codrington lost less than 300 men, while the defenders' casualties totaled over 4,000. This was the last pitched battle fought between wooden sailing ships (and the last cooperative military effort among Great Britain, France, and Russia until the World War I Dardanelles campaign).

Russia (Nicholas I) declared war on Turkey the next year. Mehemet Ali was persuaded to withdraw his Egyptian forces from Greece. As a result of the London Protocol signed on March 22, 1829, Greece was recognized as a separate kingdom, under Otto I of Bavaria, in 1832. *See* Mesolóngion; Varna II; Greek War of Independence.

Naxos (Greek City-States' Wars), 376 B.C. The growing rivalry between Thebes and Sparta gave Athens the opportunity to support Thebes by reviving a maritime league against the ancient Spartan foe. In 376 part of the resurgent Athenian navy, commanded by Chabrias, encountered a Spartan fleet off the island of Naxos, in the mouth of the Aegean Sea. The 80 Athenian triremes inflicted a severe defeat on the Spartans, destroying 49 of the 60 enemy vessels engaged in the battle.

But Athens was reluctant to push its naval advantage. The rising power of the Theban army under the energetic commanders Pelopidas and Epaminondas had become a new danger. In 371 Athens and Sparta agreed to yet another truce. *See* Coronea II; Cnidus; Leuctra; Greek City-States' Wars.

Nechtansmere (Northumbian Invasion of Scotland), 685. Under King Ecgfrith the aggressive Anglo-Saxon kingdom of Northumbria pushed steadily northward into modern Scotland. Finally King Bruide rallied the Picts and made a stand at Nechtansmere, near Forfar in present Angus County. On May 20 the Picts routed the invaders and killed Ecgfrith. The battle checked the expansion of Northumbria at the Firth of Forth. It would be more than 300 years, however, before the Scots reacquired territory to the south. *See* Winwaed; Carham.

Neerwinden I (War of the Grand Alliance), 1693. In the fourth summer of the continental war, William III, king of England and stadholder of Holland, continued in direct command of the Alliance armies. At the small village of Neerwinden, northwest of Liége, the king-general took up a strong position with both flanks behind small streams. The undefeated French marshal of Louis XIV, the Duc de Luxembourg, marched some 40,000 veteran troops to Neerwinden. Luxembourg opened the battle on July 29 with an attack on the center of William's lines. Although the Alliance men held, William had to reinforce the position from the wings to withstand the powerful French assaults. This was the opportunity Luxembourg had anticipated. Now he launched a double attack against both of William's weakened flanks. The fierce French onslaught buckled the Alliance line. Thousands of Dutch, Germans, and Spanish were driven into the Landen and Geete streams to drown.

Before William could extricate his army, he lost 18,000 men—killed, wounded, and captured—plus 104 guns. French casualties were less than half this total. Although the war in the Spanish Netherlands dragged on for another four years, Neerwinden was the last major battle for Luxembourg. The French marshal died in 1693 without ever experiencing defeat. Meanwhile, the war continued in Savoy. *See* Steenkerke; Marsaglia; Grand Alliance, War of the.

Neerwinden II (Wars of the French Revolution), 1793. With the execution of King Louis XVI on January 21, 1793, the National Convention stood as undisputed master of France. Aligned against the Revolutionary government were Austria, Sardinia (Piedmont), Prussia, Great Britain, Holland, and Spain. Despite the odds against France, Gen. Charles Dumouriez launched an offensive aimed at Holland. At Neerwinden, 22 miles northwest of Liége, he encountered the Austrian army under the Prince of Saxe-Coburg (although actual command was exercised by Charles Louis, archduke of Austria, and the chief of staff, Baron Karl Mack von Leiberich). Here on March 18 the French were checked and then soundly defeated. Dumouriez, the victor in the first two battles of the war, went over to the allies. The Austrians retook Brussels and drove the French out of the Austrian Netherlands (modern Belgium). *See* Jemappes; Hondschoote; Toulon III; French Revolution Wars.

Negroponte (Venetian-Turkish Wars), 1470. When the Byzantine Empire fell into decay, the aggressive city-state of Venice took over many of the important commercial centers in the Aegean Sea. One of the most valuable of these posts, occupied in 1366, was the island of Negroponte (Euboea), northeast of Attica, the largest island of Greece. After the fall of Constantinople to the Ottoman Empire in 1453, Negroponte became a prime object of Turkish aggression. Mohammed II, the Conqueror, built up the Turks' first navy, and in 1470 he attacked Negroponte by sea. In the first naval victory of their history, the Ottomans stormed and captured the Greek island. It would remain under Turkish rule for more than 350 years. *See* Constantinople VII; Shkodër I.

Německý Brod (Hussite Wars), 1422. After his disastrous defeat at Kutná Hora, Sigismund, king of Hungary and Bohemia and Holy Roman Emperor, withdrew 15 miles to the southeast. Jan Zizka, the blind military genius of the Taborite Hussites, pursued with mobile artillery and wagon-forts. Taking advantage of his interior lines, Zizka met the German crusaders at Německý Brod (Deutsch-Brod) on January 10, 1422. Again the Bohemians won decisively, even though they numbered less than half the 23,000 troops Sigismund threw into the battle. Leaving more than 50 percent of his men dead on the field, Sigismund fled, narrowly avoiding capture.

This battle ended the first crusading attempt to subdue the Hussites. Three later crusades failed even to come to grips with the fierce-fighting Bohemians. Meanwhile, however, in a bloody civil war among the Hussites, the extreme Taborites maintained their superiority over the more moderate Utraquists. During this internal struggle Zizka died, on October 11, 1424. Taborite leadership then fell to the married priest Andrew Procop, called the Great. *See* Kutná Hora; Ústí nad Labem; Hussite Wars.

Netherlands (World War II), 1940. Following the German conquest of Norway, Adolf Hitler launched a ferocious assault on the West. The first victim was the Netherlands. The right wing of the huge German attack, Field Marshal Fedor von Bock's Army Group "B," drove across the Dutch and Belgian borders early in the morning of May 10. Simultaneously 16,000 German airborne troops (4,000 of them parachutists) under Gen. Kurt Student landed in Rotterdam and other key areas. On the third day of the attack the 11 German divisions of Gen. Georg von Kuechler's Eighteenth Army had smashed westward 100 miles to link up with the airborne forces. The 10 divisions of the Dutch army were thus defeated before they could be aided by the French Seventh Army (Henri Giraud), which was racing up through Belgium.

On May 14 the Netherlands government capitulated. Queen Wilhelmina fled to England and Gen. Henri Winkelman surrendered his thoroughly beaten forces. On the day of surrender German *Luftwaffe* bombers raked defenseless Rotterdam, the Dutch reporting 30,000 civilian casualties. Dutch military casualties (excluding prisoners) totaled about 10,000. Stronger in everything but numbers, the invading Germans lost far fewer men; for example, only 180 in the airborne assault on Rotterdam. The German Eighteenth Army took the surrender of some French Seventh Army units on May 17 and then turned south to aid in the attack on Belgium. *See* Norway (World War II); Flanders; World War II.

Netherlands War of Independence (1567–1648). To throw off Spanish rule, the seven Protestant provinces in the north (modern Netherlands) revolted against King Philip II in 1567. The rebels won their first battle five years later. They declared their independence in 1581 but did not win recognition until the end of the Thirty Years' War in 1648. Meanwhile the southern provinces (modern Belgium) remained loyal to Spain.

Brielle	1572
Haarlem	1572–1573
Alkmaar I	1573
Walcheren	1574
Mookerheide	1574
Leyden	1574
Gembloux	1578
Maastricht I	1579
Antwerp I	1584–1585
Zutphen	1586
Turnhout	1597
Nieuwpoort	1600
Oostende	1601–1604
Breda	1625

Neuve-Chapelle (World War I), 1915. Early in 1915 the French field marshal Joseph Joffre requested that British units relieve the two French corps in the Ypres (Ieper) salient, on the Western Front. The British commander, Field Marshal Sir John French, resolved to make a strong attack before releasing the French troops. On March 10 he launched one of the war's first massive artillery barrages, against the German-held village of Neuve-Chapelle, followed by an assault by the British First Army under Gen. Sir Douglas Haig. The attack carried the village the first day. However, the German commander, Gen. Erich von Falkenhayn, rushed 16,000 reserve troops to the area, and these began slowing the British advance on the second day. By March 13 the Germans had contained the breakthrough short of a key ridge east of Neuve-Chapelle. Field Marshal French, who had suffered 13,000 casualties, then released the French corps to Joffre for his projected Artois offensive. But the first punch was thrown by Falkenhayn against Ypres. *See* Ypres I; Ypres II; Artois II; World War I.

Neuwied (Wars of the French Revolution), 1797.

During the spring of 1797 one Austrian army of Holy Roman Emperor Francis II was being driven back from Italy through the Alps toward Vienna. At the same time another Austrian army stood in the Rhineland. Here the Austrians, under Gen. Werneck, faced a large French force commanded by Gen. Louis Hoche. On April 18 the French attacked Werneck's army at Neuwied, seven miles northwest of Coblenz, and routed it. The Austrians fell back eastward across the Lahn River with a loss of several thousand men and most of their artillery. On the same day at Leoben, Austria, Austrian Archduke Charles Louis accepted a truce from Napoleon Bonaparte. This led to the Treaty of Campo Formio and peace between Austria and the French Directory six months later. *See* Malborghetto; French Revolution Wars.

Neva River (Rise of Russia), 1240. Early in the thirteenth century the Swedes pressed forward into the northwestern part of what is now Russia. In 1240 Alexander, the Russian prince of Novgorod, gathered an army to meet the invaders on the Neva River, near the present site of Leningrad. The Russians threw back the Swedes in a decisive battle, thereby blocking any further advance. To commemorate this great victory, the Novgorod prince took the name Alexander Nevski. *See* Novgorod; Adrianople III; Peipus Lake.

Neville's Cross (English-Scottish Wars), 1346. While the English king Edward III was fighting the Hundred Years' War in France, David II of Scotland returned from exile to head an invasion of England. The Scots army pressed southward into Durham County before it was challenged by a British force commanded by Henry de Percy of Alnwick and Ralph de Neville. The Scots then took up an immobile defensive position at Neville's Cross. Using missile-and-shock tactics with an attack first by archers and then by spearmen, the English overwhelmed the invaders from the north on October 17. David became a prisoner. He was held for a ransom of 100,000 marks to be paid over the next ten years, a sum that sorely burdened his countrymen. But even with their king in enemy hands, Scottish resistance was too tough for England to overcome and in the next generation Scotland took the offensive. *See* Halidon Hill; Crécy; Otterburn.

Newburn (British Bishops' Wars), 1640. The Scottish rejection of Anglican episcopacy led to the First Bishops' War against the English forces of Charles I in 1639. Each side raised an army, but a temporizing agreement was reached later that year before a battle could be fought. In 1640, however, the Scots reaffirmed their opposition and sent an army under the veteran European campaigner Field Marshal Alexander Leslie (later Lord Leven) across the Tweed River into Northumberland. Charles countered by sending William Seymour, duke of Somerset northward at the head of a royal army. The two forces met at Newburn on the Tyne River on August 28. The Scots, stiffened by battle-hardened soldiers from the Thirty Years' War, opened a cannonade that soon routed the royalist army. Charles averted further trouble by agreeing to subsidize the Scottish troops until a permanent settlement could be reached (the Treaty of Ripon). *See* Edgehill.

Newbury I (English Civil War), 1643. After three narrow Cavalier victories in the west during the second year of the Civil War, Charles I ordered an attack on the Roundhead city of Gloucester in August 1643. But the city held out, and early in September a superior Roundhead army under Robert Devereux, 3rd earl of Essex, arrived to raise the siege. Charles then resolved to make another advance on London. As the king headed for the capital, Essex raced to intercept the Cavalier thrust. The marching routes of the two armies intersected at Newbury, in Berkshire, 53 miles west of London. Here on September 20 the hostile forces battled furiously. Prince Rupert of Germany, nephew of the king, led a successful cavalry charge against the Roundhead horsemen. But the Parliamentarian pikemen and musketeers held their ground, inflicting heavy casualties on Cavalier infantry and horsemen alike. Despite the even fighting, Charles withdrew to Oxford that night, leaving many of his nobles dead on the field. London remained securely in Roundhead hands. *See* Roundway Down; Cheriton; English Civil War.

Newbury II (English Civil War), 1644. Following his signal victory over the Roundheads of the Earl of Essex (Robert Devereaux) in Cornwall, Charles I marched back eastward. The Parliamentarian commanders—Essex, Lord Manchester (Edward Montagu), Sir William Waller, and Oliver Cromwell—hurriedly joined forces to block the route to London. At Newbury, 53 miles west of London, Charles' Cavaliers encountered the combined Roundhead armies on October 27, 1644. The king tried to fight his way through the enemy lines but failed. That night he began withdrawing to his Oxford headquarters, successfully eluding all Roundhead attempts to cut him off.

Although the second battle of Newbury was again a drawn contest, it marked a milestone in Parliamentarian warfare. Essex and Manchester were relieved, with Sir Thomas Fairfax and Oliver Cromwell taking command of a reorganized, all-purpose New Model army of 22,000 men for the fourth year of the war. *See* Lostwithiel; Naseby; English Civil War.

New Carthage (Second Punic War), 209 B.C. After his disastrous defeat on the Trebbia River in northern Italy in 218, Publius Cornelius Scipio joined his brother Gnaeus Cornelius Scipio in Spain, where the Romans carried the war to

Carthage's colony. Here the Scipio brothers won some success in their drive south from the Ebro River. But in 212 B.C. Hannibal's two brothers, Hasdrubal and Mago, led two Carthaginian armies in a counteroffensive against the Romans. Both Scipio brothers were killed and the legionaries driven back to the Ebro. Two years later P. C. Scipio's son, the 27-year-old Publius Cornelius Scipio (later Scipio Africanus), landed with a new Roman force, determined to avenge his father's death.

In 209 young Scipio led a quick march halfway down the Spanish east coast to the enemy stronghold of New Carthage (Cartagena). Caught by surprise, the Carthaginian armies in the interior could not reach their capital in time to reinforce it. In seven hours Scipio's legions stormed the city and conquered it. New Carthage was the first of the young general's triumphs over the Barca brothers. *See* Trebbia River I; Ilipa; Punic Wars.

New Georgia Island (World War II). Held by the Japanese, it was invaded by American troops on July 2, 1943, and the key Munda airfield was captured on August 5. *See* Solomon Islands.

New Guinea (World War II), 1942–1944. In the ferocious Japanese surge through the southwestern Pacific, Nipponese troops seized Lae and Salamaua on northeastern New Guinea's Huon Gulf on March 8, 1942. This advance anchored Japan's conquest of the East Indies and threatened the important base of Port Moresby, in southeastern New Guinea—the last defensive post protecting Australia. The fierce two-day battle of the Coral Sea, May 7 and 8, forced Japan to withdraw an invasion convoy headed for Port Moresby. But the Japanese were determined to fight for New Guinea, and as a result the turkey-shaped island became a bloody battleground for almost two and one-half years.

On July 21 and 22 amphibious troops of the Japanese Eighteenth Army (Matazo Adachi) landed at Gona and Buna, more than a hundred miles east of their Lae-Salamaua bridgehead and about halfway along the northern Papuan coast to Milne Bay at the eastern end of the island. From their new bases the Japanese launched a double offensive against Port Moresby. On August 26, 1,900 troops stormed ashore at Milne Bay, where two Australian brigades, together with U.S. engineers, were building airstrips for the U.S. general George Kenney's newly organized Southwest Pacific Air Command. The Allied defenders fought fiercely, killed 600 invaders, and forced the remainder to evacuate ten days later.

Meanwhile, on July 22, two Japanese regiments from Gona-Buna began marching south along the Kokoda Trail over the 13,000-foot Owen Stanley Range. On August 12 they occupied Kokoda village, and by September 17 the head of this column had reached the village of Ioribaiwa, only 32 miles from Port Moresby. But here the 7th Australian Division, defending along the trail, halted the advance. The Australian general Edmond Herring then counterattacked back up the rugged Kokoda track. In some of the world's worst terrain for combat, the Australians gradually forced the Japanese out of the mountains into the wild swamps of kunai grass around Gona and Buna. Here the 7th Division and other Australian units were joined by the U.S. 32nd and, later, 41st Infantry divisions. In savage jungle warfare the Allies drove the enemy out of Gona on December 10, 1942, and out of Buna on January 3, 1943. The last Japanese resistance in this sector at Sanananda Point, was overcome on January 23. This action completed the liberation of Papua, at a cost of 8,546 U.S. and Australian casualties (another 2,334 Americans were disabled by disease). Japanese losses were about 12,000 killed and 350 captured (4,000 escaped to New Britain or the Huon Gulf area). But more important, the Papua victory marked the beginning of Gen. Douglas MacArthur's long-term counteroffensive in the Southwest Pacific. A major part of that counteroffensive was contributed by the U.S. I Corps, commanded by Gen. Robert Eichelberger, which later grew into the Sixth Army under Gen. Walter Krueger.

In the spring of 1943 Eichelberger's troops, supported by Adm. Thomas Kinkaid's Seventh Fleet, began a long, hard fight to drive the Japanese off the north coast of New Guinea. From Gona, on the coast, and Wau, inland, U.S. and Australian units pushed west and north toward the Salamaua-Lae area. On the night of June 29–30 a regiment of the U.S. 41st Infantry division landed at Nassau Bay, just short of Salamaua. Aided by the 5th Australian, this unit drove on Salamaua and captured it on September 12. Meanwhile, Lae was enveloped. On September 4 the 9th Australian Division (of El Alamein fame) made an amphibious landing ten miles east of the village, while the U.S. 503rd Parachute Regiment and the 7th Australian landed by air in the Markham Valley to the west. Lae fell on September 16. Six days later a brigade of the 9th Australian landed on the coast at Finschhafen, on the Huon Peninsula 50 miles above Lae. The capture of Finschhafen on October 2 led to the later Allied conquest of the entire Huon Gulf area.

On January 2, 1944, the 32nd Infantry landed at Saidor, 100 miles to the west, and secured an airstrip there. This jump bypassed some 12,000 Japanese still on the north coast of the Huon Peninsula. No more than 4,400 of the isolated Japanese survived. The 32nd then bounded farther west to take Mindiri on March 5. Late in April brigades from the 5th and 11th Australian divisions leapfrogged the Americans to the Astrolabe Bay area, taking Bogadjim, Madang, and Alexishafen, during April 24–26. Meanwhile, Krueger's Sixth Army made a successful 400-mile amphibious leap westward to the Hollandia area on April 22. The U.S. 24th Infantry landed at Tanahmerah Bay, while the 41st Infantry (minus the 163rd Regiment) went ashore at Humboldt Bay, 25 miles to the east. These two divisions linked up on April 26. At the same time the 163rd Regiment seized Aitape, 125 miles farther east. This triple landing bypassed some 50,000 troops of the Japanese Eighteenth Army in the Wewak sector. Efforts to break out of the Aitape trap were repulsed by U.S. troops of the XI Corps under Gen. Charles Hall. More than 8,800 Japanese were killed, at a U.S. loss of 450 dead and 2,500 wounded.

On May 17 the Sixth Army leaped westward another 125 miles to the Maffin Bay area, landing at Arara, and on the offshore island of Wakde the following day. At Wakde the Japanese fought tenaciously against the 163rd and 158th regiments, the 6th Infantry Division, and elements of the 31st and 33rd Infantry divisions. The island was won in four days, but Maffin Bay was not secured until late June. Total U.S. casualties in this area were 455 killed and 1,500 wounded. Almost 4,000 Japanese were killed.

During the struggle for Wakde, the 41st Infantry bounded forward another 200 miles on May 27 to Biak Island, which dominated the entrance to Geelvink Bay, near the western end of New Guinea. This island was held by 10,000 Japanese, who successfully blocked the first American attempt to dislodge them. Early in June enemy transports landed an additional 1,000 troops, but U.S. air and sea attacks mauled the remainder of the Japanese convoy, sinking two destroyers and shooting down 50 planes. Cut off from further reinforcements, the Japanese on Biak grudgingly gave ground to the 41st and later the 24th Infantry. By June 20 U.S. I Corps had taken most of the island, although some points resisted until August. The capture of Biak cost the U.S. 474 killed and 2,400 wounded. More than 6,100 Japanese were killed and 450 captured. The smaller island of Noemfoor, 70 miles to the southwest, was taken during July 1–6 by the 158th Infantry Regiment and the 503rd Parachute Regiment. American losses were 70 killed and 350 wounded; 2,000 Japanese were killed and 250 captured. On July 30 and 31 the 6th Infantry occupied Sansapor on the Vogelkop Peninsula at the northwestern end of New Guinea. This completed MacArthur's arduous 1,500-mile leapfrogging operation across the entire northern coast of the island. Some 135,000 Japanese troops were cut off and left behind.

One more major operation would close the New Guinea struggle and open the battle to liberate the Philippines. During the succession of Japanese defeats in New Guinea, other Japanese forces had established a strong base to the northwest on Halmahera Island in the Moluccas. MacArthur now sent the XI Corps (Charles Hall) past Halmahera to the northern Molucca island of Morotai. Aided by strong air and naval support from the Seventh (Thomas Kinkaid) and Fifth (William Halsey) fleets, the landing took place on September 15. The 31st and part of the 32nd Infantry quickly carved out a divisions perimeter to protect the construction and use of airfields strategically located midway between western New Guinea and Mindanao in the southern Philippines. (At the same time Adm. Chester Nimitz' drive across the Central Pacific was opening the eastern door to the Philippines with the conquest of Peleliu-Angaur.) On Morotai the United States lost 45 killed and 95 wounded, the Japanese 325 killed or captured. The last New Guinea action was anticlimactic. The Asia and Mapia (Saint David) islands, 150 miles north of the Vogelkop Peninsula, were taken for communications bases by the U.S. Eighth Army (Robert Eichelberger) in its first operation, during November 15–20.

The two-year battle for New Guinea was one of the most trying in U.S. history. In addition to an entrenched and numerically superior enemy, Allied troops had to combat rugged terrain, an unfavorable climate, tropical disease, and long, tenuous communication lines. But the conquest of the world's second largest island was essential to the Allied offensive against Japan. The Southwest Pacific air forces now had bases from which to strike deep with the enemy's defensive lines. And MacArthur stood ready to fulfill his promised return to the Philippines. *See* East Indies; Coral Sea; Rabaul; Solomon Islands; Bismarck Sea; Peleliu-Angaur; Leyte; World War II.

New Hope Church (American Civil War). A four-day skirmish at Dallas, Ga., between the Federal forces of Gen. William Sherman and the Confederate army of Gen. Joseph Johnston, from May 25 to 28, 1864; the fighting, 30 miles northwest of Atlanta, cost each side about 2,000 casualties. *See* Kenesaw Mountain.

New Madrid (American Civil War). A Confederate strong point in southern Missouri on the Mississippi River, evacuated on March 13, 1862, during the Federal general John Pope's campaign against Island No. 10. *See* Island No. 10.

New Market (American Civil War), 1864. To increase the pressure on the Confederate armies, the Federal commander in chief, Gen. U. S. Grant, ordered Gen. Franz Sigel to attack up the Shenandoah Valley. The Confederate cavalry of Gen. John Imboden fell back fighting to New Market. Here he was reinforced by two brigades under

Gen. John Breckinridge, plus 247 cadets from Virginia Military Institute. As Sigel approached New Market early on May 15 with 5,150 men, Breckinridge moved out to the attack. The Federals were forced back until about 4 P.M., when Sigel ordered a general retreat northward to Strasburg. He had suffered 831 casualties. Confederate losses were 577 (including 10 killed and 47 wounded among the cadets, whose professor-leader, Scott Shipp, was killed). Grant replaced Sigel with Gen. David Hunter. *See* Spotsylvania; Piedmont; American Civil War.

New Orleans I (War of 1812), 1815. The southernmost of the three British offensives against the United States in 1814 was directed toward New Orleans, the chief port on the Gulf of Mexico and the entrance to the strategic Mississippi Valley. A British fleet of more than 50 ships entered Lake Borgne, east of New Orleans, on December 13, to disembark 7,500 troops under Gen. Sir Edward Pakenham. Many of these soldiers were veterans of the successful Peninsular Campaign in the Napoleonic Wars. The American commander in this area, Gen. Andrew Jackson, was fortifying Baton Rouge at the time, expecting the British to move up the Mississippi River. Now he hurried to New Orleans at the head of some 5,000 troops. The British advance guard had pushed to within seven miles of the city when Jackson checked the thrust with a night attack on December 23–24. He then fell back two miles to Chalmette where the Americans began building breastworks of logs and cotton bales along dry Rodriguez Canal. The flanks of this position stood anchored in a cypress swamp on the left and the east bank of the Mississippi on the right.

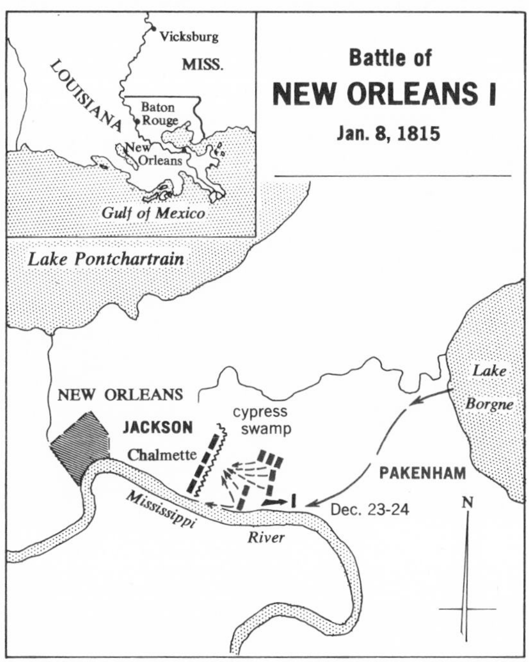

On January 8 Pakenham, with his main body of 5,300 men, made a head-on assault against the American line. The British, advancing in close ranks on a narrow front, made an inviting target for Jackson's artillery and his 4,500 infantry, which included expert Kentucky and Tennessee riflemen. Stopped by the withering fire in their faces, the redcoated regulars reorganized for a second assault. This too failed to gain the American position. In 30 minutes the attackers lost 2,036 men in killed and wounded; Pakenham and two other generals were slain. Jackson lost only 8 killed and 13 wounded. The British retreated to their ships, where they learned that the war had ended two weeks before with the signing of the Peace of Ghent on December 24.

The peace treaty did little more than close the War of 1812. Most of the issues that had brought on the conflict had already disappeared with the overthrow of Napoleon I in Europe. Although the battle of New Orleans cannot be ranked as a decisive engagement, it did have important long-range results. It was the greatest land victory of the war and, as such, restored American military pride, much injured by earlier fiascoes. It demonstrated that U.S. troops could hold their own against strong European forces. And it projected Andrew Jackson into national prominence and eventually into the Presidency. For the British it was the most crushing defeat suffered since Bannockburn (1314) and Castillon (1453). *See* Champlain, Lake; Fort McHenry; War of 1812.

New Orleans II (American Civil War), 1862. Dominance of the seas enabled the Federal government to mount an attack against New Orleans while the Confederates still held Port Hudson, Vicksburg, and other points up the Mississippi River. On April 18 Adm. David Farragut led a 16-ship fleet mounting 200 guns, plus a mortar flotilla, to the mouth of the Mississippi. Here the 19 mortar boats of Com. David Porter took under fire Fort Jackson on the west bank and Fort Saint Philip, on the east side. The 13-inch mortars did little damage to the forts, which were under the command of Gen. Johnson Duncan. After six days of futile bombardment, which caused less than 50 Confederate casualties, Farragut changed his tactics. At 2 A.M. on April 24 he began running his fleet past the forts, completing the operation by dawn with the loss of only three small gunboats. The weak Confederate river fleet was encountered and annihilated. As Farragut's ship approached New Orleans, 80 miles upriver, the Confederate commander in the city, Gen. Mansfield Lovell, evacuated his 4,000 militia without a fight. New Orleans surrendered on April 25. The entire attack had cost Farragut 36 killed and 135 wounded.

Meanwhile Gen. Benjamin Butler had landed about 15,000 Federal troops on the Gulf Coast near Lake Pontchartrain. He now marched toward New Orleans, bypassing forts Jackson and Saint Philip, 90 miles to the south. The garrisons in the two Confederate forts, about 250 men each, then mutinied, forcing a surrender on April 28. Three days later Butler marched into New Orleans to launch his efficient but controversial occupation of the city. *See* Shiloh; Chickasaw Bluffs; American Civil War.

Newport (War of the American Revolution), 1778. In July 1778, five months after France (Louis XVI) entered the war on the side of the United States, a French fleet of 12 warships under the Comte d'Estaing arrived off the American coast. To capitalize on the naval power of the new ally, the American commander in chief, Gen. George Washington, planned a joint operation against the British base at Newport, R.I. This city, occupied since December 1776, was held by Gen. Sir Robert Pigot with some 3,000 British troops.

D'Estaing arrived off Newport on July 29, but it was a week before the American troop commander, Gen. John Sullivan, was ready to launch his attack with some 10,000 men, chiefly militia. Sullivan pressed toward the city from the northeast, building a series of parallels toward the British defenses. To raise the siege, a British fleet of eight ships of the line, under Adm. Lord Richard Howe (brother of Gen. Sir William Howe), appeared off Newport on August 9. For two days the rival fleets maneuvered for advantage. Then a violent storm crippled ships on both sides. Howe returned to New York for repairs, while D'Estaing sailed for Boston to refit and then to the French base on Martinique, on August 21. When the French left, Sullivan's militia began deserting wholesale. A week later he was forced to abandon the siege and fight his way out. In all, the Americans lost 30 killed, 137 wounded, and 44 missing. British casualties totaled 260. *See* Ushant I; Grenada; American Revolution.

Newtown (War of the American Revolution), 1779. During most of the war the American frontier settlements of western Pennsylvania and New York suffered terribly from Indian raids encouraged by the British and Tories. To reduce the terror, Gen. George Washington sent out a punitive expedition of 1,400 troops, commanded by Gens. John Sullivan and James Clinton, in the spring of 1779. The Americans destroyed hostile Indian villages and devastated cropland. On August 29 they came upon a force of 1,500 Tories and Indians on the Chemung River near Newtown, six miles southeast of Elmira, N.Y. The British ranger captain Walter Butler (son of Col. John Butler who founded Butler's Rangers) and Mohawk chief Joseph Brant attempted to make a stand on a steep hill. But they were routed by a hard-driving attack, which left a dozen dead on the field. American losses were 3 killed and 39 wounded. This was the only formal resistance to Sullivan's retaliatory expedition. *See* Paulus Hook; American Revolution.

Nicaea (First Crusade), 1097. The first Turkish-held city to be attacked by the First Crusaders was Nicaea (Iznik) on Lake Ascania, just east of the Sea of Marmara, in Asia Minor. The crusaders were commanded by a council of European lords that included the Norman prince Bohemond of Taranto, his nephew Tancred, Baldwin of Boulogne, Raymond IV of Toulouse, Godfrey of Bouillon, Robert of Normandy, Robert of Flanders, Hugh of Vermandois, and Stephen of Blois. They took the fortress under siege in May 1097. When the Sultan of Nicaea, Kilij Arslan I, returned from Armenia to relieve the city, his Turkish cavalry was beaten back by the heavier-armored European knights. Pressing their siege, the crusaders breached the outer walls on June 18. But when they began their assault the following day, the knights found that the Turkish garrison had wisely surrendered during the night to the Byzantine emperor Alexius I Comnenus. Although superficially allied with the Latin invaders, the Byzantines took no active part in the war to free the holy places of the East from the infidel Moslems. A week later the frustrated crusaders set off southeast across Asia Minor. *See* Dorylaeum I; Crusades.

Nicaragua. *See* Chalchuapa.

Nicholson's Nek (South African War II). A British rear-guard action, on October 30, 1899, along the road of retreat, in the face of the Boer thrust to Ladysmith. *See* Ladysmith.

Nicopolis (Turkish Conquest of the Balkans), 1396. Following the crushing defeat the Ottoman Turks dealt Serbia at Kossovo in 1389, Bajazet (Bayazid) I overran Bulgaria. For the next 450 years this troubled land would be an outlying province of the Ottoman Empire. Christian Europe now became alarmed at the formidable Mohammedan menace in the southeast. Pope Boniface IX proclaimed a crusade against the infidel, and King Sigismund of Hungary assembled a great army of knights at Buda on the Danube in the spring of 1396. Estimated by some authorities to be about 50,000, the force included Hungarians, Poles, Germans, Italians, English, plus some 2,000 French under John the Fearless of Nevers. Sigismund's army marched down the Danube, pillaging the countryside as it went. The so-called Crusaders halted at Nicopolis (Nikopol), Bulgaria, then held by the Ottomans, and besieged it uncertainly for two weeks in September 1396.

Meanwhile Bajazet hurried westward from his siege of Constantinople, collecting his Christian levies from the Balkans along the way. On September 25 the Turkish army reached the plain four miles south of Nicopolis. Without a battle plan, the French knights led the charge of Sigismund's army. They broke through the first Ottoman line but were then engulfed in a fierce counterattack. Pressing their charge, Bajazet's troops drove into and then routed the disorganized European host. One of the Ottoman leaders was the Serbian vassal Stephen Lazarevich. Thousands of the Christian army were killed on the field, struck down in flight, or drowned trying to cross the Danube. An estimated 10,000 were taken prisoner and then executed. John of Nevers and a few nobles were spared and later ransomed. Sigismund and a handful of other nobles escaped in a galley, which passed down the Danube, into the Black Sea, and through the Bosporus and Dardanelles to the safety of the Mediterranean.

Thus the great crusade ended in complete disaster. The only Christian gain was the temporary raising of the siege of Constantinople, which had been under land blockade since 1391. Only the invasion of Asia Minor by Tamerlane at this time saved Europe from further Ottoman conquests. *See* Prague I; Kossovo I; Salonika I; Angora.

Nicopolis-in-Armenia (Third Mithridatic War), 66 B.C. Rome's abrupt recall of the successful L. Licinius Lucullus from Armenia gave Mithridates VI Eupator the opportunity to rebuild his forces. In 68 and 67 B.C. the energetic king reestablished himself in Pontus. The following year, however, Pompey the Great landed in Asia Minor and began driving Mithridates to the east. At Nicopolis in Armenia Minor the Roman legions outflanked the enemy army to occupy high ground along the route of retreat. The Pontines imprudently made their evening camp below the Roman position. During the night Pompey's men rushed the opposing camp and annihilated Mithridates' force. The king escaped around the eastern end of the Black Sea to the Crimea. (Three years later Mithridates, Rome's most formidable opponent since Hannibal, committed suicide.) Moving on to Artaxata, Pompey took the surrender of Tigranes the Great, son-in-law of Mithridates, who was allowed to continue his rule over Armenia, but only as a vassal of Rome. The Mithridatic Wars were over. *See* Tigranocerta I; Mithridatic Wars.

Nieuwpoort (Netherlands War of Independence), 1600. The ten-year campaign of Maurice of Nassau, leader of the northern Dutch provinces in their revolt against Spain, reached a climax in 1600. With some 11,000 men (almost all infantry), Maurice deployed among the sand dunes of Nieuwpoort, ten miles southwest of Oostende. Here he encountered a Spanish army of equal size, commanded by Albert, archduke of Austria. The two forces slammed together on July 2 in the greatest pitched battle of the war. Albert's troops, spread in four great blocks of infantrymen, found the broken ground more suitable to the smaller-sized, checkerboard arrangement of the Dutch. The heavier musket fire of the Dutch, plus their greater mobility, slowly gained the upper hand, and by the end of the day they had broken the Spanish lines, inflicting heavy casualties. Despite the clear-cut Netherlands victory, Maurice could not prevent the Spaniards from investing Oostende the following year. *See* Turnhout; Oostende; Netherlands War of Independence.

Nihawand (Moslem Conquest of Persia), 641. Four years after his Persian armies had been decisively beaten at Kadisiya and Jalula, Yazdegerd III organized a new force to make a final stand against the conquering Moslems of Arabia. He and his son Firuz III built up an army of almost 100,000 men at Nihawand (40 miles south of Hamadan in modern Iran). To the attack came a much smaller force of Arabian cavalry under Sa'd ibn Abi-Waqqās, the Moslem general of Caliph Omar I. The new Persian army, like its predecessors, could not stand up against the swift, slashing attacks of the desert horsemen. Sa'ad's Arabians swept the field, inflicting heavy casualties. Yazdegerd fled to a mountain refuge. The Arabian conquest of Persia was complete. With the murder of Yazdegerd ten years later and the flight of Firuz to China, the Sassanian dynasty ended.

In the east, the all-victorious Arabs pushed on to the borders of India within two years. In the west, Syria had been taken and the invasion of Egypt was already under way. *See* Jalula; al-Fustât; Moslem Conquests.

Nile River (Wars of the French Revolution), 1798. Although Great Britain had won the only two naval battles fought early in the war (Ushant II and Saint Vincent Cape II), its naval forces were markedly inferior in strength to the combined navies of France, Spain, and Holland. Thus, in the summer of 1798, Napoleon Bonaparte was able to dash across the Mediterranean to Egypt, occupying Malta on the way. Doggedly, Adm. Sir Horatio Nelson with 13 British ships set out to hunt down the French fleet. He found the 13 French ships (plus 4 frigates) of Adm. François-Paul Brueys anchored in a two-mile line in Abukir (Aboukir) Bay, at one of the mouths of the Nile River, on August 1.

Late in the afternoon Nelson attacked the enemy line, sending four ships inshore along one side while he led the attack down the offshore side in his flagship, the *Vanguard*. Thus each French vessel was subjected to a simultaneous cannonade from both sides. The British swept past the surprised line before Brueys could re-form the French into a better battle position. In the all-night battle every French warship but two was captured

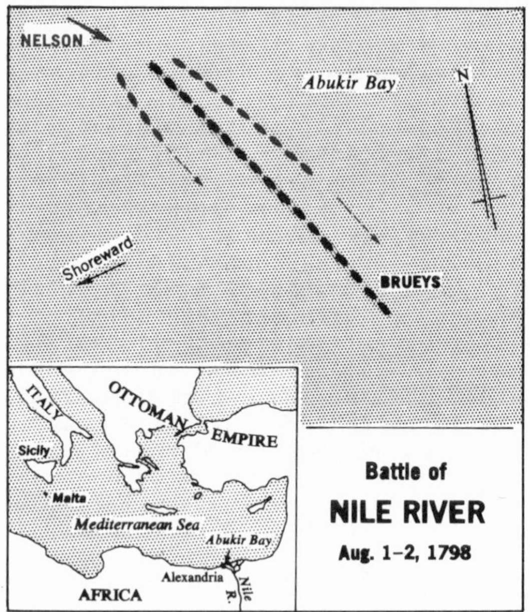

Ninety Six

Battle of
NILE RIVER
Aug. 1-2, 1798

or destroyed including the flagship, *L'Orient,* on which Brueys was killed. (The victorious British admiral was made Baron Nelson of the Nile.) Nelson's overwhelming victory cut Napoleon's communications with France and doomed the projected French conquest of the Middle East. Thus it ranks as one of the decisive battles of the 23-year French Revolutionary Wars. *See* Ushant II; Pyramids; Saint Vincent Cape II; Acre III; French Revolution Wars.

Ninety Six (War of the American Revolution), 1781. Despite his defeat at Hobkirk's Hill on April 25, 1781, the American general Nathanael Greene maintained the offensive in South Carolina. His next move was against the British post at Ninety Six in the western part of the state. Here stood a stockade defended by 550 Tories under the command of Lt. Col. John Cruger. Greene with 984 Continentals, plus a few militiamen, reached the fort on May 22. Finding the defenses strong, the Americans began an investment by constructing parallels toward the chief redoubt at the eastern end. On June 8 the American colonel Henry (Light-Horse Harry) Lee arrived with his Legion from Augusta, Ga., which he had taken two days earlier. Lee's men began a series of parallels on the western side of the fort. But progress was slow, and when Greene learned that the British commander in the South, Lt. Col. Francis Rawdon (later 1st Marquis of Hastings), was marching to the relief of Ninety Six with 2,000 regulars, he ordered an assault on June 18. The Americans stormed the fort from both east and west but were beaten off with 57 killed, 70 wounded, and 20 missing. Tory losses were 27 dead and 58 wounded. There was now no time to continue the siege or to launch another assault. Greene marched away to the northeast, on June 20. Rawdon arrived the following day. Again Greene had lost a battle but scored an advantage. The British could not hope to hold Ninety Six against another offensive. They evacuated the fort and retired southeast to Orangeburg, S.C. *See* Hobkirk's Hill; Eutaw Springs; American Revolution.

Nineveh I (Fall of Assyria), 612 B.C. The alliance of Cyaxares of Media and Nabopolassar of Babylonia's Chaldean dynasty foreshadowed the doom of the great Assyrian Empire. In 612 B.C. the new allies attacked the Assyrian capital of Nineveh on the Tigris River. The Assyrians, under Sin-shar-ishkun, resisted furiously but were overwhelmed, and their king was killed. Nineveh was destroyed, never to be rebuilt.

In an attempt to keep the kingdom alive, Ashur-uballit, an Assyrian general, set up headquarters in Harran, 250 miles to the west. But Nabopolassar doggedly followed up his Nineveh victory and in 610 captured Harran. Assyria had ceased to exist. *See* Samaria; Megiddo II.

Nineveh II (Byzantine-Persian Wars), 627. While Emperor Heraclius was rebuilding the army of the Byzantines, the Persian host of Khosrau (Chosroes) II stood on the Bosporus, a mile from Constantinople. Only the Imperial fleet prevented an investment of the city by the Persians and their temporary allies, the Avars of the Balkans. At last, in 623, Heraclius took the offensive. He crossed over to Asia Minor, plunged through Armenia in 624 to destroy the great Persian fire temple, and then turned south into Mesopotamia. One by one, he recovered the lost fortresses that had been the outposts of the Roman, and then the Byzantine, Empire. The outmaneuvered Persian army finally made a stand on the Tigris near the ruins of Nineveh, on December 12, 627. In a fierce, all-day battle the well-trained Imperial cavalry gradually gained the upper hand over the more numerous, but less disciplined, Persian horsemen. Although Khosrau's men still held their ground at nightfall, they fell back under cover of darkness. Heraclius marched resolutely on the Sassanian capital of Ctesiphon. Before he could reach it, Khosrau fled. The Persian king was deposed and executed the following year. The True Cross was surrendered to the Byzantines, who restored it to Jerusalem. During the next five years, anarchy in the Persian capital ensured a peace favorable to Constantinople: the Persians evacuated Egypt and restored the original frontiers. Heraclius had completed one of the most successful campaigns in military history. *See* Jerusalem V; Viminacium; Ajnadain.

Nishapur (Rise of the Seljuk Turks), 1038. The Ghaznevid dynasty ruled the Moslems of southwestern Asia early in the eleventh century with the help of a Turkish border tribe called the Seljuks, named in honor of their first chieftain. However, in 1038 two grandsons of Seljuk, Tughril Beg and Chagar Beg, prepared an ambush for the army of the Ghaznevid prince at Nishapur, in the northeastern corner of present-day Iran. The warlike Seljuks defeated the Persians and within a few years overran most of the Iranian plateau. Leaving his brother in charge of their conquests, Tughril Beg marched westward. He reached Baghdad in December 1055. The city surrendered without a fight when the Seljuk chief, now proclaimed sultan, promised to support the caliph of Baghdad as the true Moslem leader. The new power in the Near East would soon challenge the Byzantine Empire. *See* Manzikert.

Nizib (Egyptian Revolt against Turkey), 1839. After taking Syria away from Mahmud II of Turkey in 1832, Mehemet (Mohammed) Ali, viceroy of Egypt, kept threatening to break completely from the Ottoman government. Finally, in 1839, the Turkish sultan marched an army into northern Syria to end the rebellion. At Nizib the 30,000 Turks encountered a strong Egyptian-Syrian force under Gen. Ibrahim Pasha, son of Mehemet Ali, on June 24. Ibrahim's superior artillery so shattered the Turkish ranks that an infantry attack drove them from the field in complete disorder. One of the witnesses to the Turkish rout was a young Prussian captain, Helmuth von Moltke, military advisor to Constantinople. *See* Konya; Acre IV; Egyptian Revolt against Turkey.

Nola (Second Punic War), 215 B.C. The great slaughter at Cannae was the last unqualified victory of Hannibal in Italy. When Rome refused to collapse following that defeat, the Carthaginian army was forced to seek secondary objectives. From his headquarters at Capua, Hannibal marched toward Naples. A conquest of that port might help to open a sea lane back to Africa. But at Nola, 16 miles northeast of Naples, Marcus Claudius Marcellus organized a strong Roman defensive position. Hannibal attacked the village but was repulsed. His cavalry, invincible in the open, was helpless in an attack on a fortified position. Lacking the equipment to conduct a siege, Hannibal turned back. Nola was his first defeat, and Marcellus became the first Roman commander to rebuff the wily Carthaginian. *See* Cannae; Capua; Syracuse III; Punic Wars.

Nördlingen I (Thirty Years' War), 1634. For almost two years after the Swedish victory at Lützen, the Thirty Years' War had a period of relative quiet on the battle fronts. No outstanding figure rose to the leadership of the Protestant cause to replace the killed Gustavus II. The military command passed to two men: the German Bernhard, duke of Saxe-Weimar and the Swedish field marshal Gustaf Horn. On the Catholic side, Gen. Count Albrecht von Wallenstein, the Holy Roman Empire commander, was assassinated by his own men on February 25, 1634. Emperor Ferdinand II then put the direction of the Imperial forces under his son Archduke Ferdinand (and future Ferdinand III), assisted by Gen. Matthias Gallas.

In 1634 the Imperial troops of young Ferdinand took the offensive. Marching up the Danube Valley through Regensberg and Donauwörth, the army of 15,000 men laid siege to Nördlingen, held by a strong Swedish garrison. Here on September 2 Archduke Ferdinand was joined by his cousin, also named Ferdinand, the cardinal-infante of Spain, at the head of 18,000 highly trained Spanish infantry and cavalry. Of the combined force of 33,000, 13,000 were horsemen. The Catholic army deployed south of the city, turning about to await the attack of Horn's outnumbered (16,000 infantry, 9,000 cavalry) Protestants who were marching up to relieve the city. On the night of September 5–6 Horn circled wide to the right (east) to launch a dawn attack aimed at the commanding ground on the left flank of the Catholic position. In a fierce struggle the Swedes took the hill only to lose it to a vigorous Spanish counterattack. For seven hours Horn sent his men again and again to try to take the hill, but each attack fell short. Finally, at midday, the Swedish commander notified Saxe-Weimar that he was withdrawing across the rear of the Protestant lines. Here Saxe-Weimar's men had also been battling furiously against a superior foe.

The two Ferdinands, directing the Imperialist-

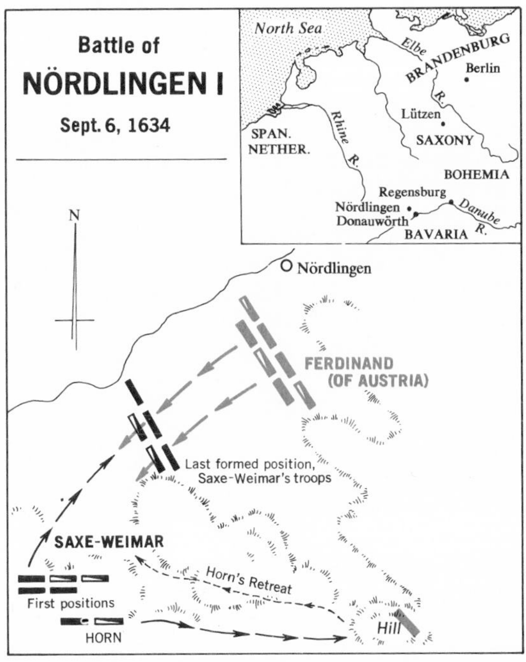

Spanish forces, saw Horn's men begin their withdrawal. Seizing the opportunity, the Catholic armies abandoned their positions in front of the town and charged straight ahead. Saxe-Weimar's lines buckled and then broke, allowing the attackers to pour through against the flank of Horn's weary column. A fearful slaughter followed. At the end of the day the victorious Archduke Ferdinand reported 17,000 enemy dead and another 4,000 captured, including Horn.

The Hapsburg victory at Nördlingen put the Holy Roman Empire in its most dominant position since the early days of the war. Its victorious armies now divided: Ferdinand, the cardinal-infante of Spain, marched for the Rhine and the Spanish Netherlands, where he was governor-general; Ferdinand of Austria struck across Franconia and Württemberg. The defeated Saxe-Weimar withdrew 150 miles across the Rhine. Here he was later named commander in chief of the anti-Hapsburg forces by Cardinal the Duc de Richelieu of France, who now took over control of the war, relegating the Swedes to a lesser role in the conflict from this point on. France declared war on Spain on May 21, 1635. Thus the long struggle changed complexion after Nördlingen. With Catholic France (Louis XIII) aligned against Catholic Spain (Philip IV) and the Catholic Emperor, the Bourbon versus Hapsburg (Austrian and Spanish) conflict overshadowed the religious issue that had launched the war. To counterbalance the active involvement of France, Emperor Ferdinand II promulgated the Peace of Prague on May 30, 1635. Saxony, Brandenburg, and most of the other Protestant German states now changed sides to fight as allies of Bavaria, Austria, and the other Catholic states of the Empire. *See* Lützen I; Wittstock; Thirty Years' War.

Nördlingen II (Thirty Years' War), 1645. After being routed at Mergentheim early in May 1645, the French marshal the Vicomte de Turenne took his Weimarian-French army into Hesse-Cassel. Here he was joined by the Army of France under Louis II, the Great Condé. The two commanders combined forces under Condé, as they had done at Freiburg the previous year, and reinvaded Bavaria. The Bavarian-Austrian army of the Holy Roman Empire (Ferdinand III) fell back to the village of Allerheim, southeast of Nördlingen. Under the command of Field Marshal Baron Franz von Mercy and Gen. Johann von Werth, the Imperial army entrenched itself, barring the way to the Danube.

On August 3 Condé led his 12,000 men in a gallant assault on the enemy positions. The Bavarians and Austrians, also totaling about 12,000, resisted with a tenacity reminiscent of the first battle of Nördlingen 11 years earlier. At the height of the struggle Mercy fell mortally wounded. With his fall the Imperials began to lose ground, until they were finally driven back toward the Danube with losses of more than 5,000. But the French, suffering comparable casualties, were too crippled to pursue. When Condé became ill, his army returned to France. Left alone, Turenne had to retire to Philippsburg.

The second battle of Nördlingen (and the third major engagement of the year) closed the fighting in 1645. The campaigns of the next two years were limited to maneuver and countermaneuver as the armies searched for food in a land almost completely devastated. The year 1648 finally brought an end to the fighting, although not until three more battles had taken place. *See* Mergentheim; Zusmarshausen; Thirty Years' War.

Normandy (World War II), 1944. Both the Allies and Germany realized that the decisive struggle in the West must come from a U.S.-British invasion of western Europe. For two years the Allies worked on invasion plans and built up supplies and fighting strength in the United Kingdom. By May 1944, 800,000 combat troops alone (47 divisions) stood ready in the British Isles. The commander in chief was the U.S. general Dwight Eisenhower, who directed SHAEF (Supreme Headquarters, Allied Expeditionary Forces). The British general Sir Bernard Montgomery commanded the ground forces for the cross-Channel attack.

The landing site, a well-guarded secret, was to be a 50-mile stretch of the Normandy coast from Caen westward to a beach at the base of the Cotentin Peninsula. From east to west five beaches were to be assaulted by infantry divisions: Sword (British 3rd), Juno (Canadian 3rd), Gold (British 50th), Omaha (U.S. 1st and part of 29th), and Utah (U.S. 4th). Guarding this section of the heavily fortified Atlantic Wall was the German Seventh Army of Gen. Friedrich Dollman and part of German Army Group B, commanded by Field Marshal Erwin Rommel (Rommel's other army—the Fifteenth, commanded by Gen. Hans von Salmuth—stood north of the Seine River). The chief German commander in the West was Field Marshal Karl von Rundstedt, who had 36 infantry and 6 *Panzer* divisions in the coastal area facing England.

The invasion came on June 6, 1944. It was the greatest amphibious landing in history. The assaulting force was carried to Normandy by a fleet of more than 4,000 ships under command of the British admiral Sir Bertram Ramsay. From the air, 4,900 fighter planes and 5,800 bombers under the British air chief marshal Trafford Leigh-Mallory smashed at the German coastal defenses with 14,600 sorties in the first 24 hours. On the night before, the U.S. 82nd and 101st Airborne divisions had parachuted behind Utah Beach to capture exits into the Cotentin Peninsula; the British 6th Airborne had dropped at the east boundary of Sword Beach to seize bridges over the Orne River and the Caen Canal, in order to protect the left flank. At dawn the first infantry waves of Operation Overlord fought their way ashore through prepared defenses in the face of heavy German fire. Supported by naval bombardment and close air support, the sea-borne assault clawed out five beachheads by nightfall of D-day. On the left (east) the three landings of Gen. Miles Dempsey's Second British Army stood secure. At Gen. Omar Bradley's U.S. First Army front, the 1st Division hold on Omaha Beach was precarious, but the Utah force had pushed inland five miles. Allied casualties totaled 11,000 (including some 2,500 dead)—far less than had been feared.

During the next six days the invading forces linked up their beachheads to form a lodgment 80 miles long and an average of 10 miles deep. At the same time, eight more combat divisions landed and the success of the invasion was assured. Caught by surprise, the top German commanders reacted slowly; they feared that the main landing was still to come farther north in the Pas-de-Calais area.

On the left flank of the beachhead strong German *Panzer* units held the British Second Army out of Caen for weeks. On the right three corps of the U.S. First Army defended the

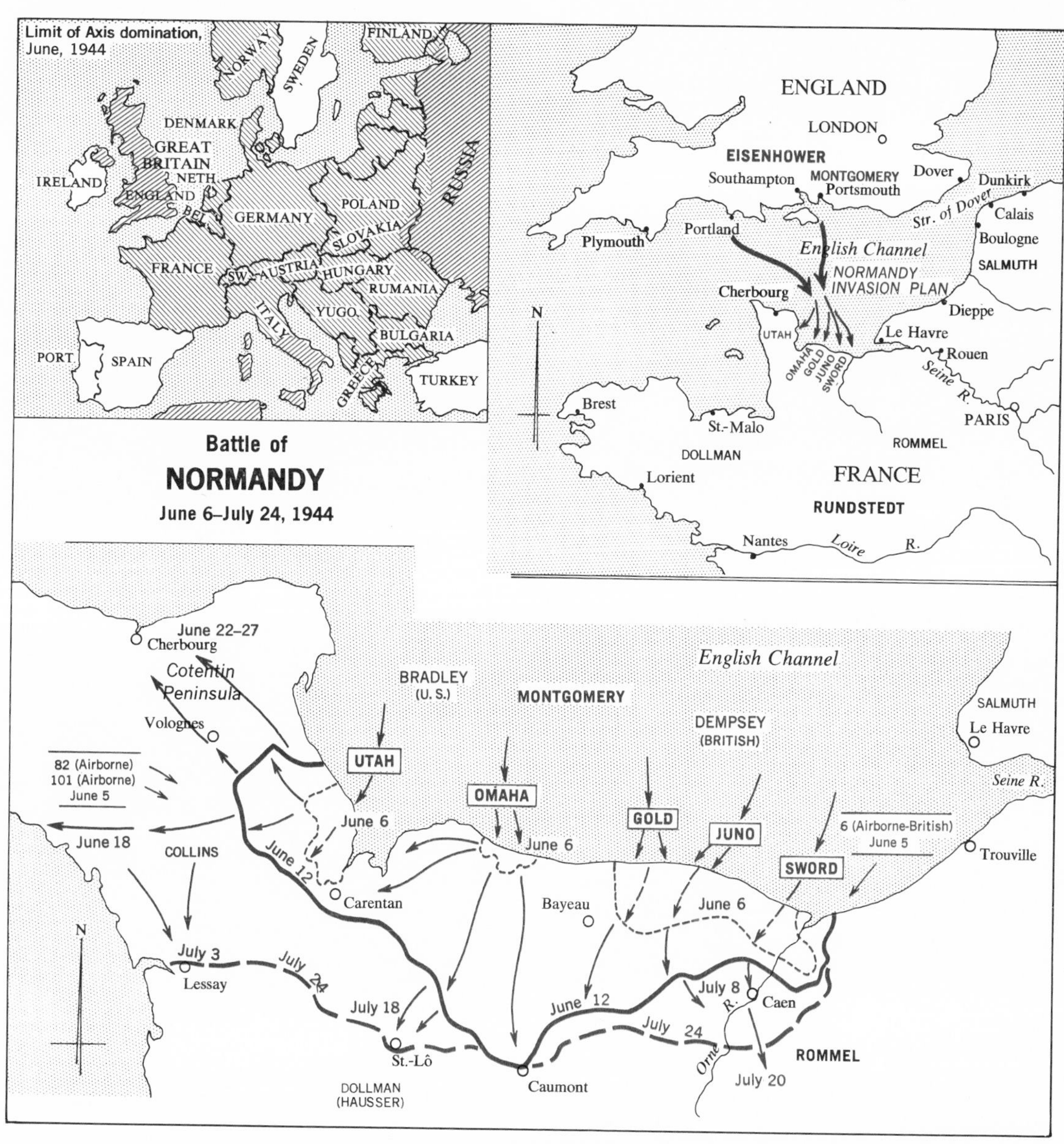

Battle of NORMANDY
June 6–July 24, 1944

perimeter from Caumont to Carentan. North of Carentan, Gen. J. Lawton Collins' VII Corps thrust westward across the base of the Cotentin Peninsula. After five days of violent fighting through hedgerows, the Americans reached the Atlantic coast on June 18. Turning north, the 9th, 79th, and 4th Infantry divisions reached the outer defenses of Cherbourg in two days. A six-day attack, from June 22 to 27, finally forced the surrender of the stubborn Nazi garrison. Although German demolitions severely wrecked unloading piers, the Allies soon had a major port to help supply the rapidly swelling forces in the Normandy beachhead. (Cherbourg beaches came into use on July 16, piers on August 7.)

Elsewhere the battle of Normandy became a slug-fest. The Allies poured in men and supplies, seeking to build up strength to break out of the lodgment. The Germans rushed up reinforcements, particularly *Panzer* units, in a desperate effort to contain the beachhead. On June 28 the German Seventh Army commander, Dollman, was killed and replaced by SS Gen. Paul Hausser. Then on July 3 Hitler relieved Von Rundstedt; Field Marshal Gunther von Kluge, who had won success on the Russian front, became chief commander in the West.

On July 3 the U.S. First Army launched a southward attack that spread across most of its front. But the Germans fought back fiercely and only limited gains were achieved. The U.S. force took Lessay, in order to anchor the right flank, and Saint-Lô, near the center of the American sector, fell on July 18. The five divisions attacking this town suffered 11,000 casualties in 12 days. Meanwhile on the left, the British Second Army finally captured the part of Caen west of the Orne River on July 8. A second attack carried through the town to the south on July 20. Although the beachhead forces now held only about one-fifth of the area assigned to them, by July 24 they were ready to try for a major breakthrough. The first 48 days of fighting in France cost the Allies 122,000 casualties; German losses numbered 117,000. *See* Dieppe; Saint-Lô Breakthrough; World War II.

Northampton I (Second Barons' War of England), 1264. Less than 50 years after the close of the First Barons' War against the English crown, a new revolt broke out. This rebellion was spearheaded by Simon de Montfort, earl of Leicester and brother-in-law of Henry III. Montfort raised an army in London and in the Cinque Ports in the southeast, while his son Simon occupied Northampton, 60 miles northwest of London. To subdue the revolt, Henry and his son, Prince Edward (later Edward I), mustered a royalist force at Oxford. Marching on Northampton, Henry attacked the castle on April 6. The garrison surrendered the following day, before the elder Montfort could arrive from London with reinforcements. Young Montfort and several other barons became prisoners of the crown. The senior Montfort turned back and laid siege to Rochester Castle in Kent. *See* Sandwich I; Bedford; Rochester III; Barons' Wars.

Northampton II (Wars of the Roses), 1460. The landing of Richard Neville, Earl of Warwick at Sandwich in June 1460 gave the rebel Yorkists (white rose) the strength to force a decisive battle with the royalists of Henry VI. The king began mustering his Lancastrian (red rose) forces at Northampton, 60 miles northwest of London. But before Henry could complete his mobilization or his entrenchments, Warwick attacked the royal camp on July 10, 1460. At the opening assault Lord Grey of Ruthin (later Earl of Kent), who commanded one Lancastrian wing, turned coat and helped the attacking men-at-arms over the breastworks. The Duke of Buckingham and most of the Lancastrian nobles perished. Henry's troops bolted, leaving the king to fall into the hands of the Yorkists.

Henry was taken to London and placed on the throne, under complete Yorkist control. In November he disinherited his young son Edward, the Prince of Wales, naming as his successor Richard of York, who now returned from exile in Ireland. Many hailed this compromise as the end of the war. But those who made the settlement reckoned without the indomitable spirit of Henry's wife, Queen Margaret, who began assembling an army from her refuge in Wales. *See* Sandwich II; Wakefield; Roses, Wars of the.

North Anna River (American Civil War), 1864. When the prolonged struggle at Spotsylvania produced no breakthrough, the Federal general U. S. Grant again shifted the Army of the Potomac south and east, on the night of May 20–21. Alert to the danger to his right flank, the Confederate general Robert E. Lee moved on the same night to a position behind the North Anna River. Here he deployed his three corps (about 50,000 men) in a strong V-shaped position. Grant's four corps, which almost doubled Lee's strength, arrived opposite the Army of Northern Virginia on May 23. On the left (west), Gen. Horatio Wright's VI Corps was crossing the river when it was attacked by Gen. Ambrose Hill's III Corps. In a sharp struggle that cost each side more than 600 casualties, Wright forced his way across the river and Hill retired to his entrenchments. On the far eastern flank, Gen. Winfield Hancock's II Corps encountered opposition from the Confederate II Corps of Gen. Richard Ewell and crossed only part of his command that day.

On the following day (May 24) Hancock completed his crossing, while on the Federal right center Gen. Gouverneur Warren's V Corps also moved south of the river to a position east of Wright. On Grant's left center, however, Gen. Ambrose Burnside (IX Corps) remained north of the river, finding the apex of the Confederate position (Gen. Richard Anderson's I Corps) too strong to attack.

Grant was now vulnerable to attack, with his army split into three widely separated parts. But fortunately for the Federals, the Confederate high command could not take advantage of their favorable disposition—Lee and Hill were sick, Ewell was exhausted from trying to fight on one leg, and Anderson (filling in for the wounded Gen. James Longstreet) inexperienced. After two days of light skirmishing Grant again marched by his left flank, on the evening of May 26, toward Cold Harbor, ten miles northeast of Richmond. Lee moved with him, keeping the Confederate army in front of the Confederate capital. *See* Spotsylvania; Cold Harbor; American Civil War.

Northern Wars (1656–1721). The aggressive Swedish monarchy had become the strongest power in the Baltic area in the seventeenth century. In 1656 Charles X Gustavas invaded Poland and captured Warsaw in what was called the First Northern War. After small conflicts against Brandenburg and Denmark, Sweden brought on the Great Northern War. *See* Great Northern War.

Warsaw I	1656
Fehrbellin	1675
Jasmund	1676
Köge Bight	1677

North Foreland I (First English-Dutch War), 1653. The fifth engagement of the first naval war between England and the Netherlands again found Adm. Maarten Tromp directing the Dutch fleet. Gen. George Monck (later duke of Albemarle) commanded the Commonwealth ships in place of Adm. Robert Blake, who had been wounded in the previous battle. For two days, June 2 and 3, 1653, the hostile navies fought off North Foreland on the southeast coast of England. Although the English gained a slight advantage, losses on both sides were small. One of those killed was Gen. Richard Deane, a veteran Commonwealth commander who had signed the death warrant for King Charles I. A more conclusive battle would take place within two months. *See* Portland; Texel I; English-Dutch Wars.

North Foreland II (Second English-Dutch War), 1666. Less than two months after its clear-cut defeat in the Strait of Dover, the English navy was refitted and back at sea. The Dutch fleet under Adm. Michel de Ruyter was engaged for the third time in the war, off North Foreland, southeastern England, the scene of an inconclusive battle 13 years earlier in the first naval war between these sea powers. On August 4, 1666, the two hostile fleets clashed fiercely. This time the English admiral the Duke of Albemarle (George Monck) reversed the previous decision by trouncing the Hollanders. But expert Dutch seamanship effected an orderly withdrawal. The war now stagnated while Charles II of England, Jan De Witt, grand pensionary of the Netherlands, and Louis XIV of France wrangled over peace terms. *See* Dover Strait; Pentland Hills; Chatham; English-Dutch Wars.

North Korea (Korean War), 1950. After crossing the 38th parallel early in October, the American Eighth Army of Gen. Walton Walker and South Korean units drove steadily northward. The shaken North Korean Communist army offered only local resistance. On the left (west) the United Nations supreme commander, Gen. Douglas MacArthur, sent the I Corps (Frank Milburn) forward along the axis Kaesong-Sariwon-Pyongyang. The North Korean capital of Pyongyang fell on October 19 and 20. On the east coast the X Corps (Edward Almond), operating independently of the Eighth Army, landed behind the driving South Korean (ROK) units, which reached the Yalu River boundary of Manchuria, some 100 miles upstream, on October 26. Both the I and X corps now struck northward, scattering North Korean forces to their front. The reduction of North Korea seemed assured, with all United Nations troops ordered to close up to the Yalu. Some 135,000 Communist prisoners were entering United Nations stockades, to add to the 200,000 already killed, wounded, or missing.

Just when the only remaining military problem appeared to be that of adequate logistic support, a new danger appeared. Late in October, so-called volunteer units of Chinese Communists (which had secretly crossed to the south side of the Yalu) entered the fighting north of the Chongchon River near the dividing line between the two American corps at the center of the peninsula. The ROK II Corps, the first to suffer attack from the Chinese, on the night of October 25–26, was driven south of the Chongchon. Only a fourth of the ROK 7th Division's 3,500 men escaped the Chinese onslaught. Six days later (November 1) the first Russian-built MIG-15 jet planes appeared over North Korea to contest American control of the air.

When the Chinese failed to press their advantage, MacArthur chose to weaken his already overextended communication lines by a final thrust to the Yalu all along the front, beginning on November 24. On the following night 300,000 Chinese troops (later identified as the Third and Fourth Field armies, commanded by Gens. Chin Yi and Lin Piao, respectively) smashed at the weak hinge between Walker's Eighth Army on the left (west) and Almond's X Corps on the right. The attack of some 180,000 Chinese caved in Walker's inland flank. In hard fighting the entire I, IX (John Coulter), and ROK II corps fell back, losing much of their artillery. On December 1, 3,000 of the 7,000 men in the U.S. 2nd Infantry Division were killed or wounded in a Communist ambush near the Chongchon River. Pyongyang was given up on December 5. The 50-mile retreat continued until a line was stabilized near the 38th parallel by the end of the month.

Meanwhile to the east, the 1st Marine Division (Oliver Smith) was cut off at the Choshin Reservoir on November 27 by another 120,000 Chinese. In a courageous retreat the marines fought their way to the coast at Hungnam, where they were evacuated by ship on December 15. Smith's men, who even brought out their dead, suffered 7,500 casualties (half from frostbite) while inflicting an estimated loss of 37,000 on the enemy. Other elements of the X Corps were taken aboard ship here and at Wonsan to the south.

The massive intervention of the Chinese Communists had completely reversed the United Nations advance through North Korea. By the year's end the Chinese, oblivious to a staggering number of casualties, had driven southward to the vicinity of the 38th parallel. *See* Inchon; Thirty-Eighth Parallel; Korean War.

Northwest Africa (World War II), 1942. The first large-scale Allied counteroffensive against the Axis in World War II came in North Africa. On the east Gen. Bernard Montgomery's British Eighth Army hurled back the Nazi *Panzerarmee Afrika* at El Alamein, beginning on October 23, 1942. Then, on the west, a force of 107,000 Anglo-Americans in 650 ships invaded French Northwest Africa on November 8. Called Operation Torch, it was the biggest amphibious attack in history up to that time. Under command of the American general Dwight Eisenhower, the Allied forces made three landings—at Casablanca, on the west coast of Morocco; Oran, in western Algeria; and Algiers, midway along the Algerian coast.

Algiers fell first. On the evening of the invasion the French general Alphonse Juin surrendered the city to the American general Charles Ryder, who commanded a British force and regimental combat teams from the U.S. 9th and 34th divisions (32,000 men).

At Oran the French forces resisted the landing for two days. But on November 10 the American general Lloyd Fredendall's 1st Infantry and 1st Armored divisions (31,000 men) took the city's surrender.

On the Moroccan coast the French resident-general August Nogues directed a spirited opposition to the landings in the Casablanca area. French warships in the harbor fiercely engaged the American fleet protecting the invasion and lost seven ships, three submarines, and a thousand casualties. On land, the American general George Patton's 3rd and 9th Infantry and 2nd Armored divisions (34,000 men) consolidated their lodgments and three days later accepted the French surrender.

Meanwhile Adm. Jean François Darlan, the most powerful French figure in North Africa, ordered a general cease fire on November 10. Originally, the Allied candidate to head the French in North Africa had been Gen. Henri Giraud, who had escaped German captivity in France. Darlan, however, commanded more strength, and on November 13 he became the chief French official in Africa. On the Continent, Germany marched into unoccupied (Vichy) France upon learning of the Anglo-American invasion. (Darlan was assassinated on December 24, whereupon Giraud did become the top French military leader in Africa.)

On the fighting front, the Algiers landing force, by prearrangement, was christened the British First Army, under command of Gen. Kenneth Anderson. This unit (in division rather than army strength) moved east to occupy Bougie on November 11, Bône (by parachutists) on November 12, and then crossed the frontier into Tunisia three days later. To the south an American parachute detachment occupied Tebessa, Algeria, on November 15 and pushed on to reach Gafsa, in west-central Tunisia, on November 17.

But the Axis had won the race for Tunisia. Protected by air forces operating from Sicily, German and Italian troops poured in by air and sea. (Tunisia was beyond the range of the 14 British fighter squadrons based at Gibraltar that had supported the Allied landings in Algeria and Morocco.) By the end of November 15,000 Axis troops (including the 10th *Panzer* Division) and 100 tanks had taken up positions in Tunisia. *See* Mareth Line; Tunisia; World War II.

Norway. *See* Scandinavia.

Norway (World War II), 1940. After the quick conquest of Poland the huge German war machine remained motionless for more than six months. Then it struck northward in the world's first large-scale combined operation of army, navy, and air force. Adolf Hitler wanted to ensure the flow of Swedish iron ore into Germany and to thwart a potential Allied operation in Scandinavia. On April 9 German troops occupied Denmark. That same day six Nazi battle groups simultaneously invaded neutral Norway's six major ports along a thousand miles of coastline. The attackers were parachutists, airborne infantry, and assault troops smuggled into the harbors in the holds of merchant ships. In addition to complete surprise, the 25,000 invading Germans were aided by well-trained Nazi underground groups and by Norwegian fifth column traitors, chiefly Maj. Vidkun Quisling. Within 48 hours the Germans won control of all six ports: from north to south, Narvik, Trondheim, Bergen, Stavanger, Kristiansand, and Oslo.

The capital fell to less than 1,500 airborne Germans who had landed at nearby Fornebu Field under command of Gen. Nikolaus von Falkenhorst, overall German commander in Norway. Parts of the stunned and disorganized Norwegian army surrendered, while others under King Haakon VII retreated inland and attempted resistance from forest and mountain.

The Allies launched a hastily improvised counterinvasion between April 14 and 19, with the two largest landings in mid-Norway, at the small ports of Namsos and Andalsnes, which bracketed Trondheim, and in the far north around Narvik. But the Allies had no large port or airfield to funnel in reinforcements and heavy equipment, and they could not provide air cover against the incessant attacks by the German *Luftwaffe.* Within two weeks superior German striking power forced the 30,000 Allied troops in the Trondheim area (directed by Gen. H. R. S. Massy from London) to begin evacuation, and by May 3 all of central Norway was in Nazi hands.

The counterlandings near Narvik, commanded by Adm. Lord Cork, were more successful. Here, for six weeks, 20,000 Allied troops besieged the port, which was held by 6,000 German soldiers and sailors. Finally, on May 28, Gen. Sir Claude Auchinleck's ground forces fought their way into the city, driving the Nazi defenders into the mountainous interior. But by then the ever-growing Allied disaster in northern France forced a complete retreat from Norway. The last troops in Narvik re-embarked for Great Britain on June 9. One of those who escaped was the Norwegian king, who set up an exile government in London.

Only at sea did the Nazis pay a stiff price for their conquest. A major loss was indirect—the formerly neutral 1,000-ship fleet of Norwegian merchantmen now joined the Allies. Direct German losses included an 8-inch cruiser, 2 light cruisers, 10 destroyers, 11 transports, 8 submarines, and 11 auxiliary vessels. Allied losses, mostly British, were also heavy (aircraft carrier *Glorious,* cruisers *Effingham* and *Curlew,* 9 destroyers, and 6 submarines). But the Allies could more easily rebuild their naval strength, while the German losses seriously weakened Hitler's chances of ever invading England. (On the ground Germany lost 5,300 in killed and wounded.)

In all other respects Germany gained immensely from the conquest of Norway (and Denmark). The Nazi northern flank was secured, the resources of Scandinavia were ensured for German consumption, and important submarine and air bases were acquired for attack against Great Britain and its shipping lifeline. *See* Poland (World War II); Netherlands (World War II); Atlantic Ocean II; World War II.

Notium (Great Peloponnesian War), 407 B.C. The naval supremacy in the Aegean Sea that Alcibiades had won for Athens in 410 did not last long. While Alcibiades was away collecting money, his ships were attacked off Notium in Asia Minor by a Peloponnesian fleet commanded by the able Lysander. Fifteen Athenian galleys were lost. The defeat led to the overthrow of Alcibiades, who was replaced by Conon. Lysander too was relieved, but because his appointment had expired. *See* Cyzicus I; Arginusae Islands; Peloponnesian Wars.

Novara I (French Wars in Italy), 1513. Despite their victory at Ravenna in 1512, the French of Louis XII were driven out of Milan the following month by the re-formed League of Cambrai. This alliance, once founded with the help of France, now consisted of Spain (including Naples), the Holy Roman Empire, the papacy, the Swiss cantons, England, and several Italian city-states. In 1513 the French army of 10,000 under Louis de La Trémoille still held Novara, 28 miles west of Milan, the second most important city of the duchy. The Swiss army of some 13,000 attacked the French camp on June 6, catching the defenders by surprise. A deadly battle ensued in which the Swiss pikemen finally gained the upper hand, but at heavy loss to themselves. La Trémoille suffered 50 percent casualties. Hundreds of German mercenaries fighting in the French ranks surrendered only to be executed by the Swiss after the battle. This loss forced Louis XII to withdraw from Italy, but new troubles awaited him at home before peace was finally achieved in 1514. *See* Ravenna IV; Guinegate; Marignano.

Novara II (Italian Wars of Independence), 1849. The unsatisfactory armistice of 1848 between Austria and Sardinia (Piedmont) lasted less than seven months. On March 12, 1849, Charles Albert, king of Sardinia, denounced the truce. The Austrian army in Lombardy, under Field Marshal Joseph Radetzky, promptly seized the fortress of Mortara. This brought on a major battle between Radetzky and the Piedmontese troops of Charles Albert at Novara, 28 miles west of Milan, on March 23. As at Custoza the previous summer, the Austrian regulars proved far superior to the undisciplined Italian army. The Piedmontese were thoroughly routed. A week later Bresica, 54 miles northeast of Milan, was ruthlessly subdued by the Austrian general Baron Julius von Haynau. Charles Albert abdicated in favor of his son Victor Emmanuel II (later to become the first king of Italy). A peace treaty signed on August 9 provided for the payment to Austria of an indemnity of 65 million francs. Meanwhile, two new republics had been set up in Rome and Venice. *See* Custoza I; Rome VII; Venice; Italian Wars of Independence.

Novgorod (Rise of Russia), 862. At the end of the eighth century, Scandinavian vikings called Varangians, or Rus, pushed south from the Baltic toward the Black Sea. The Slavic settlements in the path of the conquerors were thoroughly overrun. In 862 the Scandinavian chieftain Rurik (Riurik or Rorik), a semi-legendary figure, led the storming and capture of Novgorod in northwest Russia. The first of the so-called Russian princes, Rurik founded a royal house that ruled for more than 700 years. Novgorod and Kiev, which fell to the Vikings soon after, became the great trading centers of early Russia. *See* Adrianople III; Neva River.

Novi Ligure (Wars of the French Revolution), 1799. Successive defeats by the Russian (Count Aleksandr Suvorov) and Austrian (Baron Michael von Melas) armies of the Second Coalition had driven the French Directory forces out of northern Italy by the summer of 1799, except for a bridgehead at Genoa. The Paris government then sent out Gen. Barthélemy Joubert with reinforcements to take over the shattered commands of Gens. Jean Moreau and Jacques Macdonald. Joubert deployed 35,000 French troops in the Ligurian hills north of Genoa to try to block the advance of Suvorov, who headed the allied army.

On August 15 Suvorov sent his superior allied army against the French entrenched at Novi Ligure, between Genoa and Alessandria. In 16 hours of fierce fighting the Russians and Austrians carried the fortified heights, although they lost 8,000 men in the attack. The French suffered 11,000 casualties; Joubert and four of his division commanders lay dead on the field. Moreau and Gen. Laurent de Gouvion Saint-Cyr collected the defeated remnants and escaped into the mountains near the Italian-French border. In a devastating four-month campaign the allies had overturned all of Napoleon Bonaparte's 1796 victories in northern Italy. Napoleon himself returned to France from Egypt within a month. *See* Trebbia River II; Abukir; Montebello; French Revolution Wars.

Noyon-Montdidier (World War I), 1918. To maintain the German initiative, Gen. Erich Ludendorff organized a fourth offensive in 1918. His primary objective was to threaten Paris by linking up the Amiens salient with the Aisne-Marne salient to the south. On June 9 he sent the Eighteenth Army of Gen. Oskar von Hutier southward from the Noyon-Montdidier sector. The attack pushed back the French Third Army (Georges Humbert). On the following day Gen. Max von Boehn's Seventh Army surged westward from Soissons against the French Tenth Army of Gen. Charles Mangin. The two attacking forces were scheduled to converge on Compiègne. Hutier advanced six miles in his drive, but Boehn was held to small gains. By June 13 the entire offensive had stalled, with heavy losses to the Germans. The French deep-zone defenses had not only stopped the enemy but had also reduced their own casualties. *See* Somme River II; Aisne River III; Marne River II; World War I.

Numantia (Roman Subjugation of Iberia), 142–133 B.C. When Rome chased Carthage out of Spain in the Second Punic War (218–01 B.C.), it took over administration of the entire peninsula. But the Iberians offered periodic resistance to Roman rule, and in 143 this opposition flared into open conflict, called the Lusitanian War. The revolt, led by the Lusitanian (Portuguese) shepherd Viriathus, centered on the fortified city of Numantia in north-central Spain. Although Viriathus was assassinated four years later, the Iberians threw back every attempt by the Roman legions to take the city. Finally, in 134 B.C., Scipio Aemilianus, grandson of Scipio Africanus and conqueror of Carthage, took over command of the siege. Fifteen months later (133 B.C.) Numantia fell. For his success in crushing the revolt, Scipio received the surname "Numantinus." *See* Ilipa; Carthage I; Roman Republic.

O

Oberhollabrunn (Napoleonic Empire Wars), 1805. After taking the surrender of a large Austrian army at Ulm in October 1805, Napoleon I wheeled about to march down the Danube Valley with some 116,000 French troops. The only resistance to the French advance came from the Russian army of Gen. Mikhail Kutuzov, which had come to the aid of the demoralized Austrian commanders of Holy Roman Emperor Francis II. Pressing relentlessly forward, Napoleon seized Vienna on November 13 and then turned north, hoping to trap Kutuzov's army of 40,000 men in lower Austria. However, at Oberhollabrunn (Hollabrunn), 25 miles north of Vienna, the Russian prince Gen. Pëtr Bagration threw up a strong roadblock with 7,000 troops. On November 16 Marshal Joachim Murat, with cavalry, Marshal Jean Lannes' V Corps, and part of Marshal Nicolas Soult's IV Corps slammed against the Russian position. All day Bagration fought a magnificent delaying action, finally pulling back after dark after losing half of his division. The temporary check to the French advance enabled Kutuzov to withdraw safely to the east of Brünn (Brno). *See* Ulm; Caldiero II; Austerlitz; Napoleonic Empire Wars.

Ocean Pond. *See* Olustee.

Oenophyta (First Peloponnesian War). The second half of the Tanagra-Oenophyta battle in 457 B.C., in which Athens defeated Thebes. *See* Tanagra-Oenophyta.

Ohod (Mohammed's Conquest of Arabia), 625. A year after Mohammed's initial military victory at Badr, his followers clashed again with the Koreish tribe led by Abu Sufyan. At Ohod, northwest of Medina, a thousand Moslems fought their second battle against a force three times their size. This time Islam was defeated; 70 died on the field and the Prophet himself was wounded. Mohammed retired to Medina, but his opponents did not attack the city for another two years. *See* Badr; Medina; Moslem Conquests.

Okinawa (World War II), 1945. The last and greatest land battle of the Pacific War took place on Okinawa, a 794-square-mile island lying less than 400 miles below southern Kyushu. This largest island in the Ryukyu chain formed the last steppingstone to Japan in the long U.S. advance across the Central and Southwest Pacific. From here was to come the planned invasion of Japan's home islands—Kyushu in November 1945, Honshu in March 1946 (an attack negated by the Japanese surrender on August 15, 1945).

To defend Okinawa against the onrushing Americans, Gen. Mitsuru Ushijima deployed more than 100,000 troops of the Thirty-second Army, the great majority of them dug in behind the Naha–Shuri–Yonabaru Line across the southern one-fifth of the island. The Japanese planned to fight to the death behind this line, giving their *kamikaze* suicide pilots time to destroy Adm. Raymond Spruance's Fifth Fleet protecting the invasion.

Under the overall command of Adm. Chester Nimitz, the amphibious attack forces were brought to Okinawa under Adm. Richmond Kelly Turner (who had directed such operations since Guadalcanal, 30 months earlier). The assault was assigned to the newly organized Tenth Army, commanded by Gen. Simon Buckner, Jr., veteran of the Aleutian counteroffensive in 1943. On March 26 the 77th Infantry Division (Andrew Bruce) seized the Kerama and Keise Islands, off the southwestern coast of Okinawa. The invasion itself would come six days later on the Hagushi beaches of western Okinawa, ten miles above the main Japanese defense line. Here Marine general Roy Geiger's III Amphibious Corps would make up the north wing of the assault—6th Marine Division (Lemuel Shepherd) on the left, 1st Marine Division (Pedro del Valle) on the right, and 2nd Marine Division (Thomas Watson) feinting a landing on the southern tip of the island. The Tenth Army's south (right) wing consisted of Gen. John Hodge's XXIV Corps—7th Infantry (Archibald Arnold) and 96th Infantry (James Bradley) divisions, left to right.

On April 1 Buckner's army hit the beaches and moved quickly inland against only light opposition. By nightfall 50,000 troops occupied a beachhead eight miles long and three to four miles deep. Two days later the 1st Marine Division had consolidated a corridor to the east coast across

Okinawa's two-and-a-half-mile waist. To their left, the 6th Marine Division had swung north, sweeping up both coasts. On April 8 the 6th reached the rugged Motobu Peninsula, jutting westward into the East China Sea. It took 12 days to clear this strong center of resistance. But by April 20 the northern fourth-fifths of Okinawa's 65-mile length was secure.

During the conquest of the Motobu Peninsula, the offshore island of Ie Shima was invaded by the 77th Infantry Division on April 16. In a savage four-day struggle the soldiers captured the island, killing some 4,700 Japanese. United States losses were 258 dead and 879 wounded. One of those killed, on April 18, was the American war correspondent Ernie Pyle.

Meanwhile, on the southern end of the island, XXIV Corps found much harder going. After moving eastward across the width of Okinawa in the first two days, the infantrymen turned 90 degrees to the south, 7th on the left flank, 96th on the right. By April 8 Japanese resistance had greatly increased, and three days later the XXIV Corps was stopped by the outerworks of the Naha–Shuri–Yonabaru Line. Hodge then sent the 27th Infantry Division (George Griner) in on the west coast to the right of the 96th. On April 19, XXIV Corps launched a major assault, three divisions abreast, on a five-mile front. But in 12 days of vicious, see-saw fighting less than two miles were gained. The III Amphibious Corps was then ordered into line to form the right wing, 6th Marine Division on the west coast, the 1st inland. On the left flank, the 7th retained its position on the east coast; the 77th moved in on its right to relieve the battered 27th and 96th divisions.

On May 4 and 5 Ushijima sent a heavy counterattack against the Tenth Army's left flank. The effort was disastrous for the Japanese, who had to leave their strong entrenchments and fight in the open—6,227 were killed. The XXIV Corps suffered 714 casualties. Six days later Buckner resumed the offensive despite drenching spring rains (the refreshed 96th had relieved the 7th on the far left). In grim, grueling warfare, both U.S. corps fought into and through Japanese defense lines. On May 23 the 6th Marine Division stormed into Naha to turn the enemy's west flank. The 1st Marine Division in the center took Shuri Castle on May 29. On the right the XXIV Corps punched relentlessly southward, outflanking the line on the east.

On June 4 the 6th Marine Division made a shore-to-shore amphibious assault on Oroku Peninsula, in the southwest. The peninsula was conquered in ten days of savage fighting, while the 8th Regiment (Col. Clarence Wallace) of the 2nd Marine Division joined the main thrust to the southern tip of Okinawa. During this last, bitter

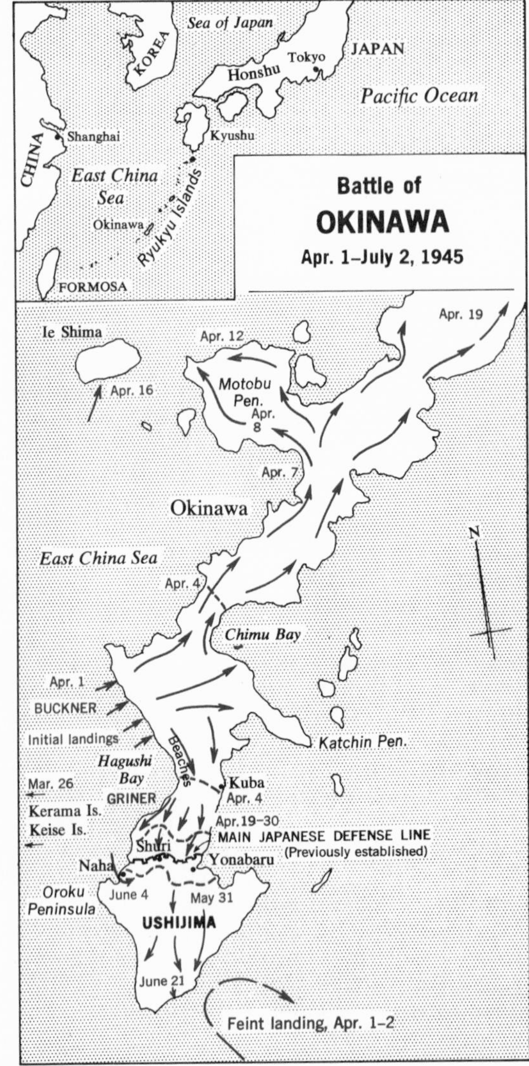

advance Buckner was killed by enemy artillery, on June 18, and replaced by Geiger of the marines. Three days later, on June 21, the Tenth Army reached the southern coast and then turned back to mop up remaining pockets of resistance. The land battle officially ended on July 2.

The Japanese Thirty-second Army was wiped out—more than 100,000 killed and 10,000 captured. United States casualties were also heavy—2,938 marines dead or missing and 13,708 wounded, 4,675 army dead or missing and 18,099 wounded.

At sea and in the air the battle was as vicious as on the ground. On April 7 the world's mightiest battleship, the *Yamato,* steaming south toward the fray, was sunk by U.S. carrier planes in the East China Sea. Also destroyed were a Japanese light cruiser and four destroyers. Before the battle of Okinawa ended, another nine Japanese ships were sunk. The Nippon navy was virtually extinct. Japanese aircraft assaulted the Tenth Army and its offshore shipping throughout the land battle. Bombers did little damage, but in some 1,900 attacks *kamikazes* dived through air defenses to sink 36 U.S. ships and damage another 368. These attacks killed 4,907 navy men and wounded another 4,824. But during the three-month battle some 7,800 Japanese planes were destroyed, at a cost of 763 U.S. aircraft. Japanese air power had become a shadow.

From Okinawa the Allies now prepared for the projected invasion of Japan. General Joseph Stilwell took over the Tenth Army, which, with the U.S. First Army (being redeployed from Europe), came under the overall command of Gen. Douglas MacArthur. Admiral Nimitz continued in control of all naval units. But the ground assault on Japan became unnecessary when the U.S. aerial bombardment forced the Nipponese government to accept unconditional surrender six weeks after the battle of Okinawa ended. *See* Iwo Jima; Japan—Bombardment; World War II.

Olmütz (Seven Years' War), 1758. The third year of the war in Europe opened with an invasion of Moravia by Frederick II, the Great. His Prussian army of 40,000 men reached the Imperial strongpoint of Olmütz (Olomouc) on the March River in May 1758. The invaders laid siege to the city but lacked sufficient numbers to invest it completely. As a result, the marshal Count Leopold von Daun, the Austrian commander of Holy Roman Empress Maria Theresa, was able to keep open supply and communications lines to the city. Meanwhile Imperial irregular troops harassed the Prussian supply route, which stretched 90 miles from Olmütz back to the Silesian border. In June a large convoy en route to the siege lines was attacked and destroyed. Frederick then raised the seven-week siege on July 1. During the time the Prussian king was engaged in Moravia, two of his subordinate commanders were fighting the French and the Russians. *See* Leuthen; Crefeld; Zorndorf; Seven Years' War.

Oltenița (Crimean War), 1853. The rivalry between Russia (Nicholas I) and Turkey (Abdul Medjid I) in southern Europe developed into open conflict in 1853. Turkey declared war on October 4 and sent an army under Gen. Omer Pasha northward across the Danube River. At Oltenița, where the Arges flows into the Danube, the Ottomans met a Russian force that had occupied Wallachia (modern Rumania) earlier that year. Making use of his superior numbers, Omer overwhelmed the Russian army on November 4, driving it northward. This was the first Turkish victory over Russia in more than a hundred years of intermittent warfare. But the advantage was short-lived. *See* Sinope; Crimean War.

Olustee (American Civil War), 1864. To secure a base in northern Florida, a Federal division under Gen. Truman Seymour landed at Jacksonville on February 7, 1864. Meeting no opposition, the 5,100 troops pressed 45 miles inland to Olustee. Reaching this village on February 20, Seymour was attacked by a Confederate brigade under Gen. Joseph Finegan in midafternoon. Although two Federal regiments were quickly routed, a third held in place until Seymour could withdraw under cover of darkness. The defeat cost the Federals 203 killed, 1,152 wounded, and 506 missing, plus the loss of six guns. Confederate casualties, in what is sometimes called the battle of Ocean Pond, totaled only 934. Seymour fell back to Jacksonville. *See* American Civil War.

Omdurman (War for the Sudan), 1898. During his two-and-a-half year campaign to reconquer Sudan, Gen. Horatio Herbert (later Lord) Kitchener had methodically pressed up the Nile, building a railroad as he went. At every point that the Mahdists offered resistance, they were beaten off with heavy losses. Finally, at the end of August 1898, Kitchener arrived at Omdurman, on the left bank of the Nile opposite Khartoum, where Gen. George "Chinese" Gordon had fallen more than thirteen years before. Here the Mahdists had established their capital, under The Khalifa (Abdullah et Taaisha), who had succeeded the original Mahdi (Mohammed Ahmed) in 1885. Now with 26,000 troops, about a third of them British, Kitchener attacked Omdurman on September 2. The Mahdists, in superior numbers, fought fiercely but in a few hours were completely routed by the Anglo-Egyptian army. With a loss of 15,000 men, about a third of their force, the Sudanese dervishes fled, relentlessly pursued by detachments of Kitchener's army, which had suffered only 500 casualties. The Khalifa escaped into Kordofan Province, where he was hunted down and killed the next year (November 24) by Sir Francis Reginald Wingate. A key Mahdist lieutenant, Osman Digna, was captured on January 19, 1900.

The battle of Omdurman completed the reconquest of Sudan. On January 19, 1899, Great Britain and Egypt established a ruling condominium, later called the Anglo-Egyptian Sudan. The crisis with France, which had penetrated the upper Nile at Fashoda (Kodok), was settled two months later. *See* Atbara; Sudan, War for the.

Oostende (Netherlands War of Independence), 1601–1604. From his severe defeat at Nieuwpoort, Albert, archduke of Austria, took his Spanish army ten miles northeast to Oostende. Failing to take the Netherlands (now Belgian) city by storm on July 5, 1601, the Spaniards began constructing siege lines. Although Maurice of Nassau, commander of the northern Dutch provinces in their revolt against Spain, could provide no relief, the Oostende garrison held out stubbornly. The following year King Philip III of Spain sent out Ambrogio di Spinola to take direct charge of the siege. Finally, in 1604, after three years of privation, Oostende surrendered.

The war dragged on for five more years without a major battle. From 1609 to 1621 the Twelve Years' Truce halted fighting, which was then resumed, but again no conclusive engagement took place. Maurice's younger half brother Frederick Henry (later Prince of Orange) liberated more Dutch cities during 1625–47, while on the seas Adm. Maarten Tromp established the Netherlands' superiority over Spanish warships. Finally the Treaty of Westphalia, which ended the Thirty Years' War in 1648, gave recognition to the United Provinces of the Netherlands. The southern provinces (modern Belgium) remained under Spanish rule. *See* Nieuwpoort; Breda; Netherlands War of Independence.

Oporto (Napoleonic Empire Wars), 1809. The evacuation of the British army at La Coruña, Spain, in January 1809 left only two small forces opposing the French in the Lisbon area—a British garrison in the city and an embryonic Portuguese army under Gen. William Carr Beresford (later Lord Beresford). The French marshals Nicolas Soult and Claude Victor soon overwhelmed the Spanish guerrilla forces in western Spain. In March Soult thrust into Portugal and successfully stormed the city of Oporto, 170 miles northeast of Lisbon. Thousands of the inhabitants died in the ruthless assault. But before the French could move on the Portuguese capital, Gen. Sir Arthur Wellesley (later Duke of Wellington) returned in April to take command of the British troops there, which were quickly built up to a strength of 30,000. Wellesley marched northward, crossed the Douro River at night, and on May 12 surprised Soult in Oporto. The British attack carried the city at a cost of only a few casualties. In the evacuation of Oporto and retreat into the mountains of the north, the French lost several thousand men. Now emboldened, Wellesley directed a second British invasion of Spain. *See* La Coruña; Talavera de la Reina; Napoleonic Empire Wars.

Oran I (Spanish Conquest from Moors), 1509. During the reign of Ferdinand V of Castile (II of Aragon), the war against the Moors was carried across the Mediterranean to North Africa. A crusading expedition organized by the able Cardinal Jiménez de Cisneros landed in present-day Algeria near Oran. Under the command of Pedro Navarro (who later gained more fame in Italy), the Spaniards seized the heights overlooking the city on May 17, 1509. Using their pikes, they then escaladed the walls of the city and stormed into Oran. The Moslems were no match for the deadly sword-and-buckler fighting of the Spanish infantry, soon to be the best foot troops in Europe. Thousands of Moors were either killed or captured.

The expedition went on to take Tripoli the following year. This ended the crusade, with the Moslem rulers obliged to pay tribute to the Spanish crown. *See* Garigliano River; Ravenna IV.

Oran II (World War II), 1940. After the surrender of France, the French fleet, fourth largest in the world, became a great prize. A major segment of the fleet lay at the Algerian port of Mers-el-Kebir, at Oran—two modern battle cruisers (*Dunkerque* and *Strasbourg*), two battleships, several light cruisers, and a number of destroyers, submarines, and auxiliary vessels. On July 3 British Naval Task Force H (6 capital ships, 11 destroyers) under Adm. Sir James Somerville approached the harbor and demanded that the French ships join the Royal Navy, sail to North America, or be scuttled. When the French admiral Marcel-Bruno Gensoul refused the ultimatum, British ships, supported by naval aircraft, opened a crushing 10-minute bombardment. Some 1,000 French sailors were killed. The only large French ship to escape destruction was the *Strasbourg*. This decisive naval action against a late ally enabled Great Britain to maintain her supremacy in the western Mediterranean.

Most of the remaining French fleet was scuttled at Toulon on November 27, 1942, to prevent its seizure by Germany following the Nazi take-over of Vichy France. *See* France (World War II); Dakar; World War II.

Orchard Knob–Indian Hill (American Civil War). The opening action of the battle of Chattanooga, on November 23, 1863, in which the Federal forces of Gen. U. S. Grant captured the heights leading to Missionary Ridge. *See* Chattanooga.

Orchomenus (First Mithridatic War), 85 B.C. After driving the Pontic army from Chaeronea, the Roman legions of L. Cornelius Sulla pursued the Asiatics six miles north to Orchomenus. Here the Pontic commander, Archelaus, launched a cavalry charge that drove back the Romans. But Sulla personally rallied his legionaries and in a vicious counterattack routed the enemy force. With the destruction of the Pontic expeditionary force, Mithridates VI Eupator disowned his field commander. Archelaus then joined the Romans.

Sulla, supported by a fleet under L. Licinius Lucullus, took his army to Asia for an attack on Pontus itself. But here he found a hostile Roman army commanded by G. Flavius Fimbria, a supporter of his rival Gaius Marius. Sulla also learned that in Rome his opponents in the popular party of Marius had seized control of the government. Suddenly the aggressive Mithridates seemed less of a threat than the situation at home. Sulla accepted the peace offer of the Pontic king in 84 B.C.—the evacuation of his conquests, surrender of 80 warships, and an indemnity of 3,000 talents. Turning to the army of Fimbria, Sulla won his fellow Romans over to his side. Fimbria committed suicide. Sulla was now ready to return to the civil war in Italy. *See* Chaeronea II; Mount Tifata; Cyzicus II; Mithridatic Wars.

Oriskany (War of the American Revolution). The defeat of an American column seeking to relieve Fort Stanwix, on August 6, 1777. *See* Fort Stanwix.

Orleans (Hundred Years' War), 1428–1429. After their overpowering victory at Verneuil in 1424, the English and their Burgundian allies held almost all of France north of the Loire River. The Duke of Bedford (John of Lancaster), commander in France and regent for his young nephew Henry VI, next sent Thomas de Montacute (4th earl of Salisbury) with 5,000 men, to capture Orleans. This city, on the right (north) bank of the Loire, guarded the chief passage of the river and was the largest stronghold still loyal to the dauphin Charles (later Charles VII). On October 23, 1428, Salisbury laid siege to Orleans by taking a strong point on the south bank and a fortification on the island of Tourelles in the river. From here his siege cannon could fire into the city's streets. North of the river he established an arc of six stockaded posts. Salisbury was killed by a cannon ball on November 3 and was succeeded by William de la Pole, duke of Suffolk. The investment of Orleans proceeded leisurely, unhampered by French countermeasures, except for a futile attempt to halt an English supply convoy in the battle of the Herrings, at Rouvray, on February 12, 1429.

Meanwhile, the incomparable Joan of Arc had suddenly appeared at the French court at Chinon and won the confidence of the irresponsible young

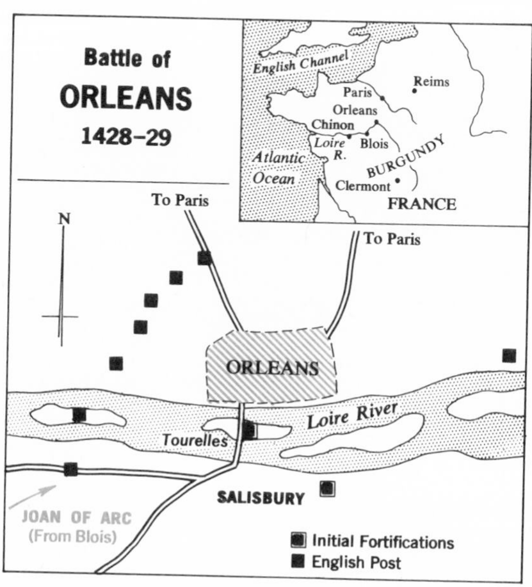

Charles. Finally given a command for the relief of Orleans, the 17-year-old girl marched from Blois on April 25 at the head of a small but dedicated French force. Arriving at Orleans, 35 miles away, she persuaded the Comte de Dunois and other French commanders to attack the English bridgehead south of the river and the Tourelles. In a desperate fight on May 7 Joan's troops, supplemented by a sally from the Orleans garrison, drove the English out of their positions, killing 300 and capturing another 200. The next day the badly demoralized English burned their stockades north of the river and abandoned the siege.

The battle of Orleans was the turning point in the Hundred Years' War. Inspired by Joan of Arc, a wave of nationalistic feeling swept through France. From this time on the French marched to a steady succession of victories that ousted their erstwhile conquerors. *See* Verneuil; Rouvray; Jargeau; Hundred Years' War.

Ostroleka (Polish Revolt against Russia), 1831. The revolutionary army of Poland had checked the Russian troops sent out by Czar Nicholas I at Grochów, on February 20, in the first battle of the war. A second battle developed from Polish efforts to unite with Lithuania. At Ostroleka on the Narew River, 62 miles northeast of Warsaw, the Polish army met a large Russian force commanded by the German-born general Hans von Diebitsch (Count Ivan Ivanovich). On May 26 the Poles suffered a severe defeat. Now Warsaw alone stood in defiance of the Russian government. *See* Grochów; Warsaw II; Polish Revolt against Russia.

Oswego (French and Indian War), 1756. The third year of the war in North America (the opening year for its European counterpart, the Seven Years' War) found a new French commander in the field, Gen. Marquis Louis de Montcalm. His opposite number, the British and colonial commander in chief, the Earl of Loudoun (John Campbell), was also newly arrived. It was a quiet year of combat except for one daring French stroke. Montcalm, from his Fort Frontenac headquarters at the northeastern end of Lake Ontario, sent an expedition across the eastern end of the Lake to Oswego, N.Y., the only English hold on the Great Lakes. The French landed on August 11 and laid siege to the village. After three days of bombardment in which the commandant was killed, the colonial garrison surrendered. Forts Oswego and Ontario were destroyed. The French returned to their base, preparing to strike the following year in eastern New York. (Oswego was recovered by Gen. Sir William Johnson in 1759 and Fort Ontario was rebuilt.) *See* George, Lake; Fort William Henry; French and Indian War.

Otterburn (English-Scottish Wars), 1388. The long years of minor border skirmishing erupted into open warfare again in 1388 when a Scottish force under James Douglas, (2nd earl of Douglas), aided by some French, invaded northern England. An English army of Northumberland was mustered by Sir Henry Percy (Hotspur) to repel the invaders. Commanding a markedly larger force (about 9,000 men), Percy attempted a rash night assault on the Scottish camp at Otterburn on August 15. Although Douglas was killed, the unyielding Scots spearmen threw back the attack, causing some 2,000 casualties. Percy became a prisoner of war but was later ransomed. The battle became celebrated in two popular ballads, the Scottish *Otterburn* and English *Chevy Chase*. For the next 14 years Scottish raiders dominated the English border. *See* Neville's Cross; Homildon Hill.

Otumba (Spanish Conquest of Mexico), 1520. When Hernando Cortes was driven out of Tenochtitlán on June 30, 1520, he retreated eastward to Lake Texcoco. On the northern shore at Otumba his force of 200 Spaniards and several thousand Indian allies was intercepted by a huge army of Aztecs on July 8. In a savage battle, Cortes finally routed his attackers with heavy losses. The Spanish conquistador then returned to Tenochtitlán to lay siege to that city. *See* Tenochtitlán; Cajamarca.

Oudenarde (War of the Spanish Succession), 1708. Following up the French successes of 1707, Louis XIV sent his marshal Louis Joseph, duc de Vendôme to reoccupy Bruges and Gent (Ghent) in the spring of 1708. From Gent, Vendôme marched up the Schelde toward Oudenarde (Audenaarde). Aroused by these losses of key points, the Duke of Marlborough (John Churchill) hurried westward from Brussels at the head of almost 80,000 English, Dutch, and German troops. He reached and crossed the Schelde on July 11 below Oudenarde, after marching 50 miles in 65 hours. Here the allied army encountered Vendôme's force of nearly 100,000 men. Before the surprised French could deploy properly, their left flank was engaged by Marlborough's right, under Prince Eugene of Savoy. The duke himself held the center against the French, while sending a Dutch force under Marshal Overkirk wide to the left (west) to hit the French in flank. By sundown the two allied wings had almost closed around half the French army. More than 7,000 surrendered and another 6,000 were killed or wounded. The allies suffered 3,000 casualties.

The battle at Oudenarde restored the allies' initiative in Flanders. Vendôme fell back to Gent while Marlborough turned south to attack Lille. *See* Toulon I; Lille; Spanish Succession, War of the.

Ourcq River (World War I). The opening French counterattack northeast of Paris, on September 6, 1914, in the first battle of the Marne. *See* Marne River I.

Ourique (Rise of Portugal), 1139. During the Spanish wars of liberation against the Moors, Alfonso VI of Castile and León created the title Count of Portugal to reward the crusader knight Henry of Burgundy in 1094. Henry's son Alfonso Henriques shook off León's domination and then launched his own campaign against the infidel. In 1139 he attacked the Moslem fortress of Ourique, 30 miles southwest of Beja, in the southwest corner of modern Portugal. The young count won a smashing victory. He then proclaimed himself Alfonso I, king of an independent Portugal. Four years later he was so recognized by Castile and by the papacy in Rome. Meanwhile Alfonso continued his well-planned campaign to drive the Moors out of his new country. *See* Lisbon.

P

Paardeberg (South African War II), 1900. While the British continued to fight in Natal to relieve Ladysmith, Gen. Lord Roberts launched an offensive toward besieged Kimberley in western Orange Free State. The Boer commander on this front, Gen. Piet Cronjé, entrenched his army of 5,000 men south of the town. But Roberts sent a cavalry column under Gen. Sir John French on a wide encircling maneuver. French fought his way into Kimberley on February 15, ending the four-month siege. With his rear now threatened, Cronjé moved to Paardeberg, 23 miles southeast, on the Modder River. Here he was fiercely attacked by four brigades under Gen. Lord Kitchener, on February 18. More than 1,000 British fell in the futile attempt to dislodge the Boers from a dry river bed. Roberts then called off the assault, surrounded the Boer position, and opened up with a steady artillery bombardment. Finally, on February 27, Cronjé surrendered his surviving 4,000 troops. It was the first important British victory of the war. On the following day Gen. Sir Redvers Buller, on his fourth attempt, fought his way into Ladysmith, relieving that town from its own four-month siege. The advantage in South Africa had at last passed to the British. *See* Ladysmith; Vaal Krantz; Kimberley; Bloemfontein; South African Wars.

Palmyra (Wars of the Roman Empire), 272–273. The Roman victory at Emesa had routed the main rebel army of Queen Zenobia of Palmyra. When Zenobia fled to the safety of the walled city of Palmyra, Emperor Aurelian followed with his legions and laid siege to the city. Early in 273 Aurelian was reinforced by a second Roman army under Marcus Aurelius Probus. Zenobia, realizing that her city was doomed, attempted to escape. She was captured, however, and Palmyra fell to the besiegers. Aurelian put a governor over Palmyra and started back to Rome. The citizens of the city immediately revolted and set up their own government. The Roman emperor marched back to Palmyra, slaughtered the inhabitants, and reduced the city to ruins.

The Roman emperor then hurried to Gaul to put down a revolt by the legions of Esuvius Tetricus. Upon his return to Rome, Aurelian celebrated a triumph (adorned by Zenobia and Tetricus) and received the title *Restitutor Orbis,* "Restorer of the World." *See* Emesa; Margus; Roman Empire.

Palo Alto (U.S.-Mexican War), 1846. The immediate cause of the war between the United States and Mexico was a dispute over the 150-mile-wide strip of land between the Neuces River and the Rio Grande. When both sides sent troops into the disputed area, hostilities erupted. On May 3 a Mexican force under Gen. Mariano Arista laid siege to American-held Fort Texas (where Maj. Jacob Brown was in command) on the left bank of the Rio Grande near present-day Brownsville. General Zachary Taylor, American commander in the Southwest, set out from Point Isabel on May 7 with 2,300 men to relieve the fort. At Palo Alto, ten miles to the northeast, his route was blocked by some 6,000 Mexican troops commanded by Arista. The first pitched battle of the war opened at 2 P.M. on May 8. The superior firepower of American rifles and artillery broke up a Mexican cavalry attack and firmly held off all enemy attempts to utilize their advantage in manpower. After five hours Arista fell back, having suffered 300 to 400 casualties. American losses were 9 killed, 45 wounded. *See* Fort Texas; Resaca de la Palma; U.S.-Mexican War.

Panama. *See* Latin America.

Pandosia (Macedonian Conquests), 331 B.C. The Greeks in the southern Italian city of Tarentum (now Taranto), called Italiotes, had long warred with the Italian state of Lucania, to the west. In 338 B.C. Archidamus III of Sparta sought to aid the Italiotes but was killed. Alexander I of Epirus, uncle of Alexander III, the Great, then sailed across the Ionian Sea to help Tarentum. At first he won some success against the Lucanians and made an alliance with Rome. But at the battle of Pandosia (331 or 330 B.C.), in western Lucania, he was assassinated, and the Italiotes were eventually driven back to Tarentum.

The Greek city-states in Italy maintained distant but satisfactory relations with the burgeoning Roman republic until early in the third century B.C. Then it was Tarentum again that provoked a fatal conflict. *See* Megalopolis; Heraclea; Macedonian Conquests.

Panion (Wars of the Hellenistic Monarchies), 200 B.C. After re-establishing the Seleucid Empire, Antiochus III, the Great, turned south to renew hostilities with his long-time enemy—Egypt. To strengthen his maritime power, Antiochus allied himself with Philip V of Macedonia. A proposed joint offensive against Egypt was thwarted in 201 when the Macedonian fleet was defeated and turned back off the Island of Chios. Antiochus proceeded nevertheless with his ground attack, and at Panion in Palestine his Syrian army encountered the Egyptians, now ruled by ten-year-old Ptolemy V, son of Ptolemy IV. The Egyptian army (with some Greeks in support), commanded by Scopas, suffered a stinging defeat. Antiochus took over all of the Asian territory held by Egypt. Only the threatened intervention of Rome prevented an invasion of the African kingdom.

Peace terms between Syria and Egypt were settled in 195, with Antiochus' daughter (later Cleopatra I) betrothed to Ptolemy. The marriage two years later did not prevent Egypt from joining Rome in an attack on Syria in 190. *See* Raphia; Thermopylae II; Hellenistic Monarchies, Wars of the.

Panipat I (Mogul-Afghan Wars), 1526. A descendant of Tamerlane, Baber, began raiding into India in 1519. Six years later he crossed the Indus River with an army of about 2,000 Moguls (Mongols), determined to make a permanent conquest. At Panipat, 53 miles north of Delhi, Baber encountered a much larger Afghan army (including elephants) under Ibrahim Lodi. On April 20, 1526, the Mogols totally defeated the Afghans, killing Ibrahim and ending the Lodi dynasty. Baber occupied Delhi and Agra, founding the great Mogul dynasty of northern India that remained in power until 1761 (and survived in part until 1857). *See* Panipat II.

Panipat II (Mogul-Afghan Wars), 1556. During the rule of the third Mogul emperor of northern India, Akbar the Great, the Hindus revolted, seizing Delhi. Akbar, at the head of an army of 20,000 loyal followers, met a much larger force of Hindus at Panipat, 53 miles north of Delhi. On November 5, 1556, the Mogul army repulsed an elephant-led attack and then utterly routed the rebels. Delhi was regained and the entire empire re-established by this victory. *See* Panipat I; Talikota.

Panipat III (Afghan-Maratha Wars), 1761. The aggressive amir of Afghanistan Ahmad Shah Durrani repeatedly invaded the Punjab in order to add to his great wealth, which included the Koh-i-noor diamond. Beginning in 1758, however, the Maratha tribe pushed into the region, taking Delhi, en route,. from its Mohammedan ruler. From his Kandahar capital, Ahmad collected a huge army and marched eastward. At Panipat, 53 miles north of Delhi, the Afghans met an army of equal size composed of Marathas and Sikhs, probably more than 70,000. On January 14, 1761, the two forces clashed in a murderous battle that took a huge loss of life on both sides. The Marathas were shattered, their power broken. Later, a mutiny in Afghanistan caused Ahmad to return home, leaving northwestern India in utter chaos. *See* Buxar.

Panormus (First Punic War), 251 B.C. Early in the First Punic War (262 B.C.) a Roman army had taken the port of Acragas (Agrigentum) on the southwest coast of Sicily by routing the Carthaginian garrison commanded by Hanno. Rome then turned to warfare at sea and in Africa for eight years. After the disastrous defeat in Tunis, however, the Italian republic launched a new offensive to drive Carthage out of Sicily. In 254 a Roman army seized Panormus (Palermo) on the northwest coast, which served as Carthage's capital in Sicily.

Three years later Hasdrubal, son of Hanno (and son-in-law of Hamilcar Barca), attempted to recover the city, then defended by a Roman army under Lucius Caecilius Metellus. At the approach of the Carthaginians, Roman light troops came out to attack. Hasdrubal drove them back with an attack by his elephants. However, when the elephants continued to charge, they were driven into a large ditch surrounding the city and many were killed. Metellus then sortied from the city with his legionaries and routed the Carthaginians. The battle cost Hasdrubal his entire force of elephants in Sicily. Rome now moved on the last Punic stronghold in Sicily, Lilybaeum (Marsala). *See* Tunis I; Lilybaeum; Punic Wars.

Paoli (War of the American Revolution), 1777. During the first eight days after the American defeat on Brandywine Creek, both Gen. George Washington's Continentals and Gen. Sir William Howe's British army marched and countermarched in the vicinity of Philadelphia. By September 19 Washington stood east of the Schuylkill River, still covering the U.S. capital (although Congress fled to Lancaster, Pa., the same day and on October 4 moved on to York). West of the river, at Paoli, the American commander in chief had posted Gen. Anthony Wayne with 1,500 men and four fieldpieces to threaten Howe's flank and rear. On the following night four British regiments under Gen. Lord Charles Grey slipped up on Wayne's division. Before daylight on September 21 Grey led a vicious bayonet assault on the American camp. Wayne's men were routed with a loss of almost 300 in killed and wounded. The attackers suffered only eight casualties. With his lines of communication thus cleared, Howe maneuvered Washington away from Philadelphia and then suddenly wheeled about to march into the city on September 26. *See* Brandywine Creek; Germantown; American Revolution.

Paraguay. *See* Latin America.

Paris I (Napoleonic Empire Wars), 1814. When Napoleon I tried to halt the allied drive on Paris by attacking their rear to the east, he miscalculated his enemy's determination. Under Prince Karl von Schwarzenberg, four allied columns, ignoring their disrupted communications, converged on the French capital. Here Napoleon's older brother, Joseph, who had failed to hold Spain earlier, botched the job of strengthening the city's defenses. Marshal Auguste Marmont fell back into Paris with a few thousand beaten remnants of the Grande Armée. To these he could add only 20,000 regulars and National Guardsmen. The allies, in overwhelming strength, struck the eastern outskirts of the city before daylight on March 30. Joseph cravenly fled before noon. Marmont, aided by Marshal Édouard Mortier, fought back courageously, but when the invaders captured Montmartre, turning the left of the French line, the battle was lost. At 2 A.M. on March 31 the city was abandoned. The assault cost the allies 8,000 casualties, the French half as many. Napoleon, who had been massing troops at Fontainebleau, to the southeast, raced to a point 11 miles south of Paris where he learned of the loss of the city.

But the thoroughly beaten French could resist no longer. Unable to rally his men for an assault on Paris, Napoleon abdicated in favor of his three-year-old son on April 6. The allied leaders insisted on unconditional abdication and exile to the island of Elba in the Mediterranean. The defeated emperor accepted on April 11. On the previous day Marshal Nicolas Soult had lost the last battle of the long war at Toulouse. *See* Arcis-sur-Aube; Toulouse II; Tolentino; Ligny; Napoleonic Empire Wars.

Paris II (Franco-Prussian War), 1870–1871. The overwhelming defeat and capture of Napoleon III at Sedan on September 2 doomed the Second Empire of France. Two days later the Third Republic, dominated by Léon Gambetta and Gen. Louis Trochu, was proclaimed at Paris. But the new government was unable to change the course of the war. The German armies of the Prussian king Wilhelm I swept on to invest Paris—the Army of the Meuse (Crown Prince of Saxony) on the north, the Third Army (Crown Prince Frederick William) on the south. The encirclement was completed near Versailles on September 20. Although Trochu had more troops available inside the city than the 146,000 men Gen. Helmuth von Moltke had for the attack, the French general passively accepted the siege. On October 8 Gambetta made a dramatic escape from Paris by balloon to rally support in the provinces. The fortress of Metz, 178 miles northeast of Paris, held out against a similar siege until October 27, when Marshal Achille Bazaine suddenly surrendered the 170,000-man garrison. Bazaine was later court-martialed, convicted, and imprisoned for treason; Moltke was made a count for his part in the action.

On November 29 Trochu launched his first attempt to break through the Prussian lines. Called the Great Sortie, the attack carried across the Marne River to the southeast before it was repulsed. French casualties numbered 5,236; Prussian, 2,091. Again on December 21 the French thrust at the siege lines, this time in the Le Bourget region of the northeast. Trochu's men were forced back with a loss of more than 2,000; Prussian casualties were less than 500. The Prussian guns ringing Paris opened a bombardment of the city on December 27. The approximately 12,000 shells that fell during the next three weeks took 97 lives and wounded 278 others. By mid-January French resistance had been crushed in the provinces. With only an eight-day supply of food remaining, Paris capitulated on January 28. The siege had cost 28,450 French military casualties, of which less than 4,000 had been killed. The provisional republican government accepted peace terms on March 1. Meanwhile, on January 18, in the Hall of Mirrors at Versailles, Wilhelm I had been proclaimed emperor of Germany. The three successful wars in six years, engineered by Otto von Bismarck, the Iron Chancellor, had forged an empire based on the kingdom of Prussia. *See* Sedan; Metz; Coulmiers; Paris III; Franco-Prussian War.

Paris III (Revolt of the Paris Commune), 1871. On March 1, the National Assembly of the Third Republic voted to end the Franco-Prussian War, accepting peace terms which included a humiliating two-day occupation of Paris by the Prussians and removal of the seat of government to Versailles. The whole city of Paris, including most members of the National Guard (which was composed almost entirely of Parisian workingmen), was united in revolt against the Assembly. The new government took steps to suppress the rebels, who favored continuation of hostilities. On March 18 Adolph Thiers, chief executive officer of the Third Republic, dispatched troops to disarm the National Guard and to seize guns on Montmartre, the center of resistance. There and throughout the city, however, most of the regular troops refused to use force, and fraternized with the insurrectionists. Thiers fled to Versailles and ordered his troops to retire from Paris, leaving the city in control of the National Guard's Central Committee. The Committee ruled Paris until March 28, when it resigned in favor of a popularly elected Commune.

Early in May, the Germans began releasing thousands of French prisoners of war, many of whom were to assist in the recapture of Paris. On May 21, the reorganized French Army, under the marshal Comte de MacMahon, began a final assault on the city. Some 30,000 National Guardsmen and the unorganized but courageous citizenry fought from behind street barricades. In seven days of savage fighting, called Bloody Week, the 130,000 government troops cleared Paris block by block. Retaking the city cost the government the lives of 83 officers and 790 men, but the Communards lost between 20,000 and 30,000 men, most of whom were summarily executed. (Only 2,500 had died in the terror of the French Revolution almost a hundred years earlier.) During the military trials which took place after the fighting, another 10,000 to 20,000 Communards were imprisoned and a small number of them were also executed. More damage was inflicted on the city than in any war (the Tuileries Palace was destroyed). The Third Republic had paid a high price for its security. *See* Paris II.

Paris IV (World War II). The capital of France was liberated from German control by a combination of Free French inside the city and the French 2nd Armored Division in two days of fighting on August 24–25, 1944; 3,200 Germans were killed and wounded, 20,000 captured; French military casualties were 42 killed and 77 wounded; 127 civilians were killed, 714 wounded. *See* France, Northern.

Parma (War of the Polish Succession), 1734. The war, which opened with the Russian siege of Danzig in 1733, shifted to Italy as the main theater of operations in 1734. Here Russia's ally, Austria (Holy Roman Emperor Charles VI), became pitted against France, Spain, and Savoy (Sardinia). The Austrian army in Italy suffered from a lack of aggressive direction from Vienna and from weak leadership on the field. At Parma, 75 miles southeast of Milan, the Austrians fought an indecisive battle on June 29 against a French force under Marshal François Coigny (the 80-year-old marshal Duc Claude de Villars, French hero of the War of the Spanish Succession, had died in the field). Field Marshal Count Claudius Mercy, the Austrian commander, was killed. No other leader could revitalize the Imperial troops, who were later maneuvered out of Milan and the Po Valley by the French (Louis XV) and out of the Neapolitan provinces by the Spanish (Philip V) by the end of 1735. When the Treaty of Vienna ended the war in 1738, Austria retained Milan but lost Naples and Sicily (Kingdom of the Two Sicilies) to the Spanish Bourbon monarch Charles IV, son of Spain's Philip V. Meanwhile, fighting also broke out along the upper Rhine. *See* Danzig I; Philippsburg; Polish Succession, War of the.

Passchendaele (World War I). The final action of the third battle of Ypres, on November 6, 1917, in which the Canadians captured the village of Passchendaele—a name sometimes given to the battle itself. *See* Ypres III.

Passero Cape (War of the Quadruple Alliance), 1718. Philip V, the Bourbon king who had won the throne of Spain despite the long War of the Spanish Succession, launched his own campaign of aggression only three years after peace had been achieved. In 1717 he seized Sardinia and in the following July invaded Sicily. To preserve the peace settlements, Great Britain, France, Holland, and Austria (for the Holy Roman Emperor Charles VI) formed the Quadruple Alliance. George I of Great Britain sent Adm. Sir George Byng (later Lord Torrington) to the Mediterranean with a fleet of 21 ships. On August 11 Byng attacked the Spanish fleet of 22 vessels off Cape Passero on the southeast coast of Sicily. In a running fight northward the English destroyed or captured 15 of the enemy ships. Don Antonio Castañeta, the Spanish commander, was killed.

The only battle of the war was this naval action. In the Treaty of the Hague two years later, Philip renounced his Italian conquests, Austria gained Sicily in return for surrendering its claims to the Spanish throne, and Savoy (Victor Amadeus II) received title to Sardinia. *See* Denain; Porto Bello; Quadruple Alliance, War of the.

Patay (Hundred Years' War), 1429. In the face of the fierce French counteroffensive Joan of Arc was commanding along the Loire, John Talbot, earl of Shrewsbury, began an English withdrawal toward the Seine. Joan sent her aroused Orleanist French army in pursuit. At Patay, in a confusing region of hedgerows and forests, the French, under Estienne de Vignolles La Hire, attacked the flank of the English column on June 18. The surprise assault gave Shrewsbury's archers no time to employ their deadly longbows. The French men-at-arms overran the column and then routed a force of knights under Sir John Fastolf, which had come up to reinforce their stricken colleagues. Shrewsbury was captured. More than a third of his 5,000-man army had been destroyed and the rest widely dispersed.

The battle of Patay hastened the revival of the French and the corresponding collapse of the English forces north of the Loire. Under the prodding of Joan of Arc, the French court traveled to Reims where the dauphin was crowned Charles VII on July 17, 1429. Joan was captured at Compiègne by Burgundians on May 23 the following year. Ransomed by the English, she was burned at the stake in Rouen on May 31, 1431. But the nationalistic forces she set in motion continued unabated. Burgundy became reconciled to Charles VII in 1435 (Treaty of Arras). Paris was liberated a year later. The French steadily squeezed out their erstwhile conquerors. Gascony, except for Bordeaux and Bayonne, was liberated by 1442. In the north, Rouen, the key to Normandy, came under French attack. *See* Jargeau; Rouen III; Hundred Years' War.

Paulus Hook (War of the American Revolution), 1779. The success of his attack on Stony Point,

N.Y., in July 1779 prompted the American commander in chief, Gen. George Washington, to launch a similar assault farther down the Hudson River. His objective was Paulus Hook, a sandy projection into the river opposite New York City and the last major British outpost in New Jersey. On the night of August 18, Maj. Henry (Lighthorse Harry) Lee of Virginia led a force of 300 men across the intervening salt marshes and out onto the promontory. In a sudden bayonet attack the Americans overwhelmed the 250-man garrison of the British major William Sutherland. Fifty defenders were killed and 158 taken prisoner. Only Sutherland and 40 Hessians who resisted from a blockhouse escaped capture. Lee had to evacuate Paulus Hook hurriedly before Gen. Sir Henry Clinton could launch a counterattack across Upper New York Bay. This battle ended military operations in the North for 1779, except for an American campaign against the Indians. *See* Stony Point; Newtown; American Revolution.

Pavia I (Alamanni Invasion of the Roman Empire), 271. Following his repulse of the Alamanni at Placentia, Emperor Aurelian moved to expel the barbarians from the Roman Empire. He marched his legionaries 30 miles westward to Pavia (Ticinum). Here the Romans fought a pitched battle against the Germanic invaders. The barbarians were soundly defeated and withdrew across the Alps. To shorten Rome's far-flung frontiers, Aurelian now ordered the abandonment of the old province of Dacia. The new boundary was fixed on the Danube. Aurelian also ordered the construction of large defensive walls around the city of Rome. He then moved east to put down a rebellion in Syria. *See* Placentia; Emesa; Roman Empire.

Pavia II (Wars of the Western Roman Empire), 476. In its dying days the Western Roman Empire had ten different emperors between 455 and 475. The tenth ruler during this time was the youthful Romulus Augustulus who was raised to the throne (then at Ravenna) through a military coup carried out by his father, Orestes. Orestes, a former officer in Attila's army, was almost immediately challenged by another barbarian leader, Odoacer (Odovacar) of the Heruli tribe. The two opposing forces clashed at Pavia, in northern Italy on August 27 and 28, 476. Odoacer triumphed, killing Orestes in the two-day battle. The victor then marched southeast to Ravenna and deposed the ironically named Romulus Augustulus on September 4. This date marks the actual end of the Western Roman Empire. Odoacer sent the insignia of imperial power to the emperor of the East at Constantinople, determining to rule the last fragment of Roman territory as a province of Leo II. *See* Rome II; Ravenna I.

Pavia III (Lombard Invasion of Italy), 569–572. Italy lay exhausted from the Byzantine-Gothic Wars and was beset by famine and pestilence when the Lombards swarmed across the Alps in 568. Led by Alboin, the Lombards laid siege to Pavia the following year. In Constantinople Justin II remained indifferent, sealing the fate of the city. After three years of hardship and starvation the inhabitants yielded to the invaders. Pavia became the capital of the new Lombard kingdom of Italy.

The Lombard invasion was stopped short of Ravenna, Rome, and Naples. Always at odds with the papacy in Rome, the Lombard kingdom fell a hundred years later when the Roman Catholic Church secured military aid from the evolving Carolingian dynasty of the Franks. *See* Casilinum; Ravenna III.

Pavia IV (Conquests of Charlemagne), 773–774. Five years after becoming king of all the Franks, Charlemagne marched into Italy to aid Pope Adrian I against the Lombards. Crossing the Graian Alps in two columns, Charlemagne outflanked the Lombard army of King Desiderius at the Mount Cenis pass. The Frankish cavalry of 4,000 men swept down the Po Valley to Pavia, where the Lombard king took refuge behind the strong walls of the city. Lacking machinery to break through Pavia's defenses, Charlemagne deployed his troops around the city in September 773, planning to starve out the enemy. During the wait the Frankish king rode on to Verona and then to Rome itself, to visit the Pope, in the spring. Finally in June 774, Desiderius surrendered the city and his kingdom, agreeing to enter a monastery in France. Charlemagne proclaimed himself "king of the Lombards."

The Frankish king made a quick return trip to northern Italy during the winter of 775–76 to quell a rebellion against his rule in Treviso. Thereafter the Lombard kingdom vanished from history. *See* Ravenna III; Roncesvalles; Charlemagne, Conquests of.

Pavia V (French Wars in Italy), 1525. In October 1524, two years after being driven out of Italy, Francis I took another large French army across the Alps. He retook Milan from the Hapsburg army of Holy Roman Emperor Charles V that month. Marching 20 miles to the south, the French laid siege to Pavia. To relieve the city, Fernando de Avalos (Marquis de Pescara) and the renegade Duke Charles de Bourbon (formerly constable of France) brought up an Imperial army of equal size (about 20,000 men), chiefly Spanish.

On February 21, 1525, this force charged the French siege lines only to be beaten back by heavy artillery fire. Francis launched a cavalry counterattack to follow up this advantage, but the Spanish infantry held its ground. The battle reached a crucial point when Pescara deployed a corps of 1,500 expert arquebusiers on the flank of the

French lines. From here, concentrated musket fire riddled the ranks of the French and their allied Swiss infantry. When the Spanish charged a second time, they swept the field. Francis himself was taken prisoner and sent to Madrid. Here he concluded peace the following year, surrendering French claims to Italy. Thus Pavia became the decisive battle of the Italian wars in the first half of the sixteenth century. *See* La Bicocca; Rome VI.

Peach Tree Creek (American Civil War). A gallant but futile Confederate attack on July 20, 1864, designed to break up Gen. William Sherman's drive on Atlanta. *See* Atlanta.

Pea Ridge (American Civil War), 1862. General Samuel Curtis, who had taken command of the Federal Army of the Southwest in Missouri, launched an offensive on February 10, 1862, toward Springfield. Here Gen. Sterling Price's Confederate force had wintered after the Southern victory at Wilson's Creek the previous August. Price evacuated the city and retreated into the Boston Mountains of northwestern Arkansas. Curtis pursued with some 11,000 Federal troops. Price's 8,000 men were now reinforced by Gen. Ben McCulloch's division and other units sent forward by Gen. Earl Van Dorn, Confederate commander in chief west of the Mississippi River. With an army built up to 17,000 men, Van Dorn marched northward to meet Curtis. The Union general took up a defensive position near Pea Ridge, overlooking Little Sugar Creek to the south.

Early on March 7 Van Dorn launched a diversionary attack to the west while concentrating his main effort against the Federal left at Elkhorn Tavern. In a day of hard fighting, the Confederate attacks on both flanks gained ground but failed to break through the Federal defenses. McCulloch was killed. On the second morning Curtis counterattacked the nearly exhausted Confederate forces. He sent two divisions under Gen. Franz Sigel to drive Van Dorn's eastern wing from the Elkhorn Tavern–Pea Ridge area. Another assault, on the west flank, also broke through the Confederate lines. Van Dorn retreated southward to the Arkansas River. He was then ordered eastward to help in the defense of the Mississippi River. The battle of Pea Ridge cost the Confederates 800 casualties, the Federals 1,384. It was one of the most important victories of the Union in the Trans-Mississippi theater. *See* Wilson's Creek; American Civil War.

Pearl Harbor (World War II), 1941. The surprise Japanese attack on Pearl Harbor, Hawaii, brought the United States into World War II more than two years after the conflict had flamed across Europe, Africa, and the Middle East. In the midst of Japanese-American negotiations to preserve the peace, Adm. Chuichi Nagumo, on November 26, 1941, led a fleet of six aircraft carriers with supporting battleships and cruisers out of the Kurile Islands toward Hawaii. Concealed by the fog and gales of the northern Pacific latitudes, Nagumo's fleet approached the target undetected. About 275 miles north of Hawaii, the Japanese carriers launched 360 bombers and fighters, on December 7.

The principal target, the great U.S. naval base of Pearl Harbor on Oahu Island, lay open and unsuspecting on a quiet Sunday morning. At nearby airfields stood rows of aircraft arranged for training purposes, not combat. The first wave, of 183 aircraft, struck at 7:55 A.M., the second wave, of 170 planes, at 8:40. For two hours hostile planes blasted and raked the anchored Pacific Fleet of the United States. Five midget (two-man) submarines penetrated the harbor, but they did little damage and all were destroyed.

The attack, concentrated on the 8 battleships in the harbor, blew up the *Arizona,* capsized the *Oklahoma,* and sank the *West Virginia* and *California* at their moorings. The other 4 battleships suffered damage, while 11 other vessels were sunk or crippled. The U.S. Pacific Fleet was disabled. In addition, 247 planes were destroyed or severely damaged, most of them on the ground. Military casualties were 2,330 killed and 1,145 wounded. The Japanese lost 28 planes. The U.S. military commanders in Hawaii, Adm. Husband Kimmel and Gen. Walter Short, were relieved from duty.

Simultaneously with the attack on Pearl Harbor (December 7, Greenwich time), the Japanese bombed the Philippine Islands and Hong Kong and landed troops in Malaya. The Japanese had become masters of the western Pacific. *See* Guam I; Wake; Philippine Islands; Hong Kong; World War II.

Peipus Lake (Rise of Russia), 1242. Two years after a Swedish invasion from the north had been repulsed, the Russian city of Novgorod was threatened from Riga, to the southwest. This aggression came from the Livonian Brothers of the Sword, a branch of the crusading Teutonic Knights of Germany. The Novgorod prince Alexander Nevski marched out to meet the new invaders on the frozen waters of Lake Peipus. In a strange battle on ice, the Russians defeated and drove back the Livonian knights. Alexander, one of Russia's greatest heroes, became grand duke of Kiev four years later and the strongest prince in the land. Technically, however, he served as a vassal of the Mongols throughout his reign. (His son Daniel founded Moscow in 1295.) *See* Neva River; Kiev I; Kulikovo.

Peiwar Pass (Afghan-British War II), 1878. The increasingly friendly relations between the Afghan amir Shere Ali and Russian Czar Alexander II led to a second war between Great Britain (Queen Victoria) and Afghanistan. A British-Indian force of 3,200 men marched out of India toward the hostile country. On December 2, 1878, the expedition was beset at Peiwar Pass (Kotal) by an army of 18,000 Afghans armed with 11 artillery pieces. Gen. Sir Frederick Roberts, the British commander, skillfully turned the Afghan position and routed them with heavy losses, including all their artillery. The next year Roberts pushed on to Kabul, occupying that city in October. *See* Kabul II; Maiwand; Afghan-British Wars.

Peking I (Mongol Conquest of China), 1214. After cementing his rule over all of Mongolia, Genghis (Jenghiz) Khan, born Temujin, turned eastward from his capital at Karakorum to invade China. Penetrating the Great Wall in three places, the Mongol horde descended on Peking (then called Yen-king, and later Khanbalik). After a long and obstinate siege, the city fell to Genghis Khan in 1214. The Mongols overran most of North China, taking Honan in 1233 and thus ending the Kin Tatar dynasty. Extending their rule over South China, the Mongols under Kublai Khan, grandson of the great conqueror, unseated the house of Sung and founded the Yüan dynasty in 1280, with the capital at Peking. (This dynasty ruled China until replaced by the Mings in 1368.) Following his conquest of China, Genghis Khan had turned westward to attack the Khwarizm Empire of Persia in 1219. *See* Khojend; Bukhara; Nanking I; Mongol Wars.

Peking II (Fall of the Ming Dynasty), 1644. The Chinese pirate-general Li Tzŭ-ch'êng had become so powerful by 1644 that he marched into Peking and seized the capital. The emperor hanged himself, thus ending the Ming dynasty. But the Ming general Wu San-Kuei refused to give up. He called in the army of the Manchus from Mukden, led by the regent, Dorgun. The combined force expelled the pirates from Peking. The Manchus then set up the youthful Shun Chih as the first of the Ch'ing dynasty, which was to rule China until 1912. *See* Nanking I; Fort Zealandia.

Peking III (Boxer Rebellion), 1900. The steady grab of Chinese territory by European powers in the 1890's led to strong antiforeign feeling in north China. Encouraged by Dowager Empress Tz'ŭ Hsi, a band of youths formed a secret organization whose name was translated as the Society of Harmonious Fists, the so-called Boxers. Outbreaks of violence prompted the British admiral Sir Edward Hobart Seymour to lead an international expedition to Tientsin, where the invaders were fired upon by the Taku forts. The Boxers in Peking promptly arose, killed the German minister, the Baron von Ketteler, and laid siege to the foreign legations, on June 20. A six-nation expeditionary force (including the U.S. 14th Infantry Regiment) finally landed at Tientsin on July 14. Marching 80 miles northwest, the expedition fought its way into Peking to relieve the legations on August 14. On September 7 of the following year the Boxer Protocol, signed by 12 nations, made peace with China. *See* Taku.

Peleliu-Angaur (World War II), 1944. After the U.S. victories in the Mariana Islands and the Philippine Sea, Adm. Chester Nimitz needed only one more central Pacific steppingstone to the Philippines—the Palau Islands, 550 miles to the east, in the western Carolines. By mid-September the marine general Roy Geiger's III Amphibious Corps (temporarily commanded by Gen. Julian Smith) stood ready to invade the island of Peleliu and the smaller island of Angaur, eight miles to the south. Peleliu, six miles long and two miles wide, held more than 10,000 Japanese troops, strongly entrenched in 500 fortified caves and many other strong points, nearly all interconnected by tunnels. The defenders were ably led by Gen. Sadae Inoue.

On the morning of September 15 Gen. William Rupertus' 1st Marine Division landed on the southwest corner of Peleliu, three regiments abreast. Despite a heavy air and naval bombardment, the Japanese resisted savagely. It took four days for the marines to clear the southern end of the island, containing the airfield. (The airfield was opened on September 26.) The marines then turned left to attack northward up the length of Peleliu. Here they were stopped by heavy artillery and small-arms fire from Umurbrogol Mountain (later called Bloody Nose Ridge).

Meanwhile, on September 17, the 81st Infantry Division of Gen. Paul Mueller stormed ashore at Angaur, which was defended by some 1,400 Japanese. In three days the island was overrun (although pockets in the northwest resisted until October 13). Geiger, in charge of the III Corps again, ordered the 321st Regiment to Peleliu, while the 323rd occupied Ulithi without opposition. On September 24 the 321st infantrymen joined the marine attack by assaulting Bloody Nose Ridge from the west. By nightfall of September 27 the Japanese holding this high ground had been encircled. On October 15 command on Peleliu passed to Mueller. The 321st (and later the 323rd) Regiment's grim, yard-by-yard reduction of Bloody Nose Ridge continued until the last defender was overcome on November 25.

The Palau conquest cost the highest casualty rate (almost 40 percent) of any amphibious attack in American history. The 1st Marine Division lost 6,526 men, of whom 1,252 were killed; the 81st Infantry Division suffered 1,393 casualties, including 208 dead. Japanese casualties, including reinforcements from nearby islands, stood at 13,600 killed and 400 captured. Inoue was one of the prisoners.

Simultaneously with the invasion of the Palaus, Gen. Douglas MacArthur had taken Morotai in the Moluccas, opening the southern door to the Philippines. Now his right flank in the central Pacific was secured by Peleliu, Angaur, and Ulithi. *See* New Guinea; Mariana Islands; Leyte; Philippine Sea; World War II.

Pella (Moslem Conquest of Syria), 635. After the Moslem victory at Ajnadain, Khālid ibn-al-Walīd led his Arabian horsemen northward past Jerusalem toward Damascus. In northern Palestine the retreating Byzantine army made a stand at Pella (Marj al-Saffar) on January 23, 635. But for the second time the hard-riding Arabian cavalry routed their opponents. It was the first victory under the caliphate of Omar I. Khālid then pressed on toward Damascus. *See* Ajnadain; Damascus I; Moslem Conquests.

Peloponnesian Wars (458–404 B.C.). The rise of Sparta in the Peloponnesus produced a natural rivalry with Athens for supremacy in ancient Greece. The First Peloponnesian War led to a 30-year peace treaty between the two strong city-states in 446. But 15 years later a new and larger conflict, called the Great Peloponnesian War, broke out. It ended with the defeat and surrender of Athens, leaving Sparta the dominant power in Greece.

First Peloponnesian War	
Aegina	458–457 B.C.
Tanagra-Oenophyta	457 B.C.
Coronea I	447 B.C.
Great Peloponnesian War	
Plataea II	429–427 B.C.
Naupactus	429 B.C.
Mytilene	427 B.C.
Pylos-Sphacteria	425 B.C.
Delium	424 B.C.
Amphipolis	422 B.C.
Syracuse I	415–413 B.C.
Cynossema	411 B.C.
Cyzicus I	410 B.C.
Notium	407 B.C.
Arginusae Islands	406 B.C.
Aegospotami	405 B.C.

Pelusium (Persian Conquest of Egypt), 525 B.C. Before Cyrus the Great could complete the establishment of the powerful Persian Empire, he was killed in 529 B.C. His son and successor, Cambyses II, carrying on the aggressions of his father, marched across the desert of Syria to invade Egypt. In 525 B.C. at Pelusium (22 miles southeast of Port Said) the Persians crushed an Egyptian army commanded by Psamtik (Psammetichos) III. Moving on to Memphis, Cambyses took the surrender of the pharaoh after a short siege. Egypt as far south as Nubia then became a Persian province. *See* Babylon; Persian-Greek Wars.

Pen (Rise of England), 1016. The death of the Danish king Sweyn I, Forkbeard, who had claimed the throne of England, and the reluctance of Ethelred II, the Unready, to assert his power left English rule confused early in 1016. Even before Ethelred's death, his aggressive son Edmund (Ironside) had rallied Saxon forces around him and claimed the crown. At the same time Sweyn's son Canute landed in England, also claiming the right to rule. The two forces clashed at Pen, in Somersetshire. Edmund's Saxons won the battle, and upon the death of his father, the young warrior became Edmund II of England. Canute, however, refused to concede. *See* Maldon; Ashingdon; Danish Invasions of Britain.

Peninsular Campaign (American Civil War). A four-month campaign, from April to July 1862, up the peninsula between the York and James rivers, in which the Federal commander, Gen. George McClellan, failed to capture Richmond. *See* Kernstown I; Yorktown II; Williamsburg; Fair Oaks; Seven Days.

Peninsular War (Napoleonic Empire Wars). In 1807 and 1808, during the height of the empire of Napoleon I, French troops occupied Portugal and Spain. Spanish patriots resisted, especially at Saragossa and Bailén. To encourage this opposition to France, Great Britain sent an army under Gen. Sir Arthur Wellesley (later Duke of Wellington) to the Iberian Peninsula. After five years of fighting, the French army was driven out of the peninsula into southern France, where it was broken at Toulouse in 1814. *See* Napoleonic Empire Wars.

Pentland Hills (Scottish Covenanters' Revolt), 1666. The restoration of Charles II to the English throne meant the triumph of Episcopalianism and corresponding restrictions for Scottish Covenanters. During the Second Dutch War Col. James Wallace led a Covenanter revolt against the rule of the Duke of Lauderdale (John Maitland), English secretary of state for Scottish affairs. General Thomas Dalyell (or Dalzell) took a royalist army into the Pentland Hills of southeastern Scotland. On November 28, 1666, Dalyell quelled the rebellion by routing the Scots army. *See* Drumclog.

Pequot War (1636–1637). A brief conflict between the Pequot Indians and the American colonists in New England. *See* Stonington.

Pergamum (Wars of the Hellenistic Monarchies), 230 B.C. During the third century B.C., when Egypt and the Seleucid Empire were almost continually at war for supremacy in western Asia, two new kingdoms developed in Asia Minor. About 279 B.C. a band of Gauls (Celts) swarmed into the central part of the peninsula and established the kingdom of Galatia. They were checked from expanding farther by Antiochus I (called Soter) of the Seleucids, whose elephants terrified the invaders. A few years later much of western Asia Minor, led by Eumenes I, broke away from the Seleucids to set up the independent state of Pergamum. The Galatians, now firmly established in their capital of

Ancyra (Ankara), began exacting tribute from the new kingdom. However, Eumenes' successor, Attalus I, refused to continue the tribute and in 230 near the city of Pergamum fought a decisive battle against the Galatians. Attalus crushed his opponent's army. He then established his rule over all of Asia Minor west of Mount Taurus as Attalus I Soter (Savior). *See* Corupedion; Sellasia; Hellenistic Monarchies, Wars of the.

Perryville (American Civil War), 1862. During the summer of 1862 the Federal army of Gen. Don Carlos Buell was shifted from Shiloh eastward toward Chattanooga. But on August 28 the Confederate general Braxton Bragg left that city and began marching northward through eastern Tennessee into central Kentucky. This maneuver forced Buell to fall back almost to the Ohio River. At the same time, farther to the east, the Confederate general Edmund Kirby-Smith also invaded Kentucky, winning a battle at Richmond and occupying Lexington. When Bragg seized Mun fordsville on September 17, Buell retreated into Louisville. Here he received reinforcements that brought his strength up to almost 60,000 men.

On October 1 the Federal commander began marching southeast against Bragg's army of 22,500 then at Bardstown. The Confederates fell back toward Perryville. On October 8 a battle developed, for which neither side was prepared. Bragg, misjudging the situation, had sent a corps eastward to aid Kirby-Smith, leaving himself only 16,000 men at Perryville. Buell's forces were also too dispersed for effective combat. General Thomas Crittenden's corps stood in supporting distance but stayed out of the action, leaving the bulk of the fighting to the corps of Gens. Charles Gilbert and Alexander McCook—some 39,000 men. The day of confused combat cost Buell 845 killed, 2,851 wounded, and 515 missing. Confederate losses were 510 killed, 2,635 wounded, 251 missing. Bragg's army, along with Kirby-Smith's army, now began a long retreat southward to Murfreesboro, Tenn. When Buell failed to pursue, he was replaced by Gen. William Rosecrans. *See* Richmond, Ky.; Stones River; American Civil War.

Persian-Greek Wars (499–401 B.C.). When the 12 Ionian cities of Asia Minor revolted against Persian rule in 500 B.C., Athens and Eretria came to their aid. The Persians crushed the revolt and then carried the war to the city-states in Europe. This conflict died out in 466 B.C., only to be resumed by Spartan interference in a Persian civil war, which led to the Greek defeat at Cunaxa and the retreat of Xenophon's Ten Thousand.

Ephesus	499 B.C.
Lade	494 B.C.
Marathon	490 B.C.
Thermopylae I	480 B.C.
Salamis	480 B.C.
Plataea I	479 B.C.
Mycale	479 B.C.
Eurymedon River	466 B.C.
Cunaxa	401 B.C.

Peru. *See* Latin America.

Perusia (Wars of the Second Triumvirate), 41–40 B.C. While Mark Antony was in Egypt, his wife, Fulvia, and his brother Lucius Antonius (Antony) led a revolt of Italian landowners against Octavian. (Fulvia may have aimed merely to draw Antony away from Cleopatra.) At one point Octavian, who was the only resident ruler of the Second Triumvirate, had to flee Rome. But in 41 B.C. Octavian loyalists under M. Vipsanius Agrippa trapped the rebel force in Perusia (Perugia), 85 miles north of the capital. The rebels capitulated the following March. Fulvia died a few months later.

In November 40 B.C. Antony returned briefly to Brundisium (Brindisi) to cement the triumvirs' pact by marrying Octavian's sister Octavia. He assumed jurisdiction over Greece and western Asia. Octavian took command of all Gaul. Marcus Lepidus, the weakest member of the trio, was assigned to Africa.

Two primary objectives now obsessed the chief triumvirs—the reduction of Sextus Pompey's fleet and the invasion of Parthia. *See* Philippi; Phraaspa; Naulochus; Second Triumvirate, Wars of the.

Peshawar (Ghaznevid Invasions of India), 1001. The Moslem sultan Mahmud of Ghazni (now in Afghanistan) was one of the most aggressive rulers of his day. In 1001 he led 10,000 of his Afghan troops through the Khyber Pass into modern Pakistan. At Peshawar he encountered a force of some 40,000 Punjabis and 300 elephants, commanded by the rajah Jaipal of Lahore. The hard-riding Afghan cavalry routed their more numerous opponents and went on to plunder the region. It was the first of 17 raids Mahmud made into the Indian peninsula during the next 29 years. *See* Somnath.

Petersburg (American Civil War), 1864–1865. The Federal commander, Gen. U. S. Grant, changed his tactics after the costly failure of his frontal attack at Cold Harbor. In a brilliant maneuver he marched the Army of the Potomac (under Gen. George Meade) east of Richmond, crossed the James River, and closed in on the rail center of Petersburg, 23 miles south of the Confederate capital. The swift Federal move put the XVIII Corps of Gen. William Smith in front of Petersburg on June 15. Smith attacked westward late that afternoon with 13,700 troops. He deployed so cautiously, however, that the 3,000 Confederate defenders of Gen. Pierre Beauregard managed to prevent a breakthrough into the city.

Two more Federal corps arrived the following day (June 16)—the II under Gen. Winfield Han-

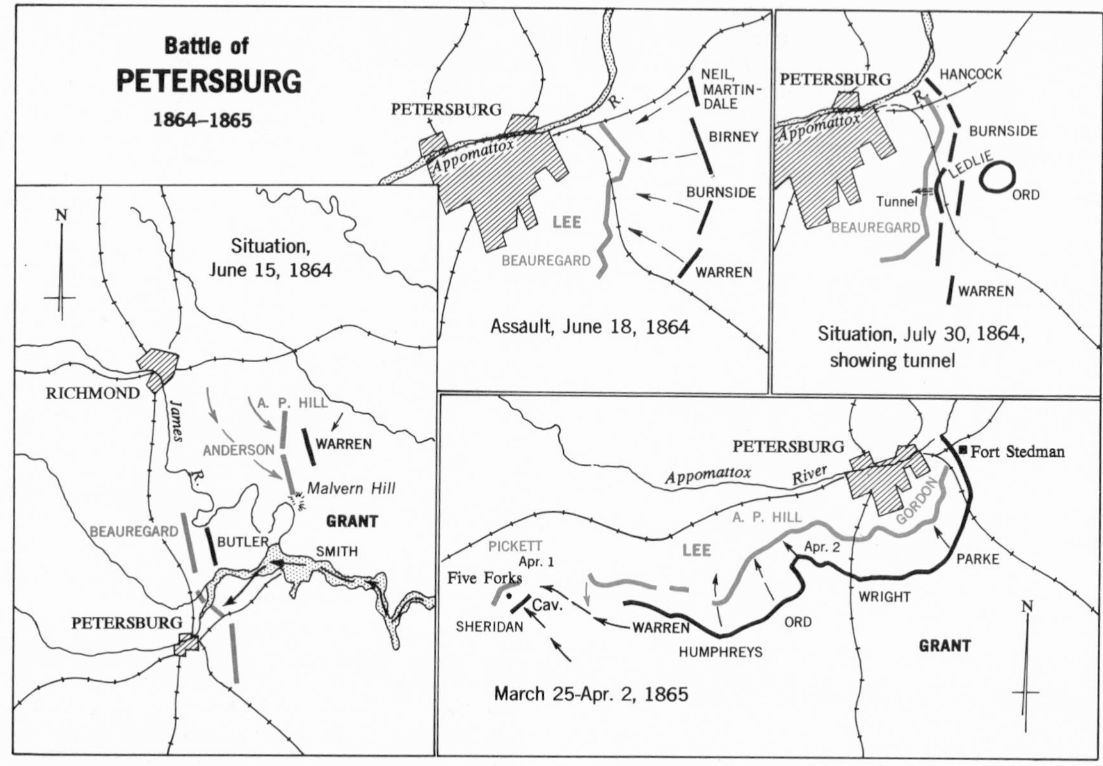

cock (later succeeded by Gen. David Birney) and the IX commanded by Gen. Ambrose Burnside—to give the attackers a strength of 48,000 men. But again Beauregard, now reinforced to 14,000 men, held off the Federals and continued to do so on June 17. By June 18 Grant had 95,000 troops available. He launched a major assault early that morning. The 20,000 Confederate defenders fought back grimly as Gen. Robert E. Lee hurried the rest of his Army of Northern Virginia into the entrenchments. By the end of the day Lee had 38,000 men in position. Grant's hopes for a quick capture had evaporated. In the three-day assault the Federals lost 1,688 killed, 8,513 wounded, and 1,185 captured or missing. Confederate casualties were unreported but were certainly far less severe.

The Petersburg front now settled down to prolonged trench warfare. To penetrate the Confederate line, a Federal group of former coal miners under Lt. Col. Henry Pleasants tunneled 511 feet under the enemy entrenchments, planting a mine of 8,000 pounds of powder in the sector commanded by Burnside. The mine was exploded at 4:40 A.M. on July 30, blowing a crater 170 feet long, 60 to 80 feet wide, and 30 feet deep. The explosion killed or wounded 278 Confederates and created a 500-yard gap in their lines. Burnside sent in the division of Gen. James Ledlie to exploit the opportunity. But the attack was poorly organized and became worse when Ledlie cowered drunk in a dugout. Finally more than 20,000 Federals joined in the assault. The Confederates, under the direct command of Beauregard, reacted quickly and slaughtered many attacking troops trapped in the crater. Meade called off the operation after suffering 3,798 casualties. (Burnside resigned from the army.) Total Confederate losses were about 1,500.

The siege of Petersburg dragged on month after month. Grant tested Lee's defenses around Richmond north of the James and extended the siege lines south and southwest of the beleaguered city. But Lee's troops threw back every attempt to break through. Meanwhile, although Gen. Jubal Early's raid had temporarily threatened Washington, D.C., the Confederates had lost the Shenandoah Valley to Gen. Philip Sheridan. They also had suffered through Gen. William Sherman's capture of Atlanta and subsequent march to the sea, as well as the shattering of Gen. John Hood's Army of Tennessee at Nashville. During the winter of 1864–65 rain and mud curtailed operations on both sides. Then on March 25 Lee launched what was to be his last offensive. Gen. John Gordon led his division in a fierce attack against Fort Stedman, at the northern end of the Federal line. But the Federal general John Parke, who had taken over the IX Corps, repulsed the drive, which cost the Confederates more than 4,400 casualties. Federal losses were about 2,000.

Grant, with 125,000 troops at his command, now seized the initiative. South of the city, he pushed the siege lines farther and farther westward until Lee's Petersburg defenses stretched so far they could not be held in strength by the remaining 57,000 Confederates. A defeat at Five Forks, 11 miles to the southwest, on April 1, convinced the besieged commander that he must evacuate Petersburg and Richmond. Confirming evidence came the following day, when Gen. Horatio Wright's VI Corps made a decisive penetration of the Confederate position between Petersburg and Five Forks. In this fighting the veteran commander of the Confederate III Corps, Gen. Ambrose P. Hill, was killed. On the night of April 2–3 the 30,000 Confederate defenders abandoned their lines and began retreating westward along the Appomattox River. Federals occupied both Petersburg and Richmond the following day. The ten-month siege, which broke the back of Lee's army, cost the Federals 42,000 casualties, the Confederates 28,000. *See* Cold Harbor; Nashville; Five Forks; Monocacy River; American Civil War.

Peterwardein (Austrian-Turkish Wars), 1716. Two years after a new war between Venice and the Ottoman Empire broke out in 1714, Austria of the Holy Roman Empire intervened in behalf of the Italian city. Acting for Emperor Charles VI, Eugene, prince of Savoy, marched into the Balkans at the head of an army of 40,000 men, many of them combat veterans of the War of the Spanish Succession. At Peterwardein, along the Danube in present-day Yugoslavia, Eugene encountered a 100,000-man Turkish army of Ahmed III. The two forces clashed on August 5, 1716. The experienced Imperial troops dealt the Ottomans a crushing defeat. At a cost of some 3,000 casualties, Eugene's troops killed or wounded 20,000 Turks and captured 200 artillery pieces. Pursuing the fleeing enemy, the Imperial army seized Belgrade during the summer of 1717. In the Treaty of Passarowitz, signed the following year, the Ottoman Empire surrendered additional territory in the Balkans. *See* Senta.

Pharsalus (Wars of the First Triumvirate), 48 B.C. Following his defeat at Dyrrachium, Julius Caesar with 20,000 faithful troops retreated 200 miles to the southwest. Pompey with a force twice as large followed at a distance, reluctant to provoke a battle. By the time the antagonists reached eastern Thessaly, both armies were exhausted, the men irritable and pressing for a decisive action. On the plains of Pharsalus, on August 9, Pompey finally gave combat after linking up with the legion of Metellus Pius Scipio, who had moved from Syria to Macedonia. Caesar too had been reinforced—by the troops of Domitius Calvinus. The open field gave Caesar the opportunity to employ his proven tactical genius. When Pompey's strong cavalry

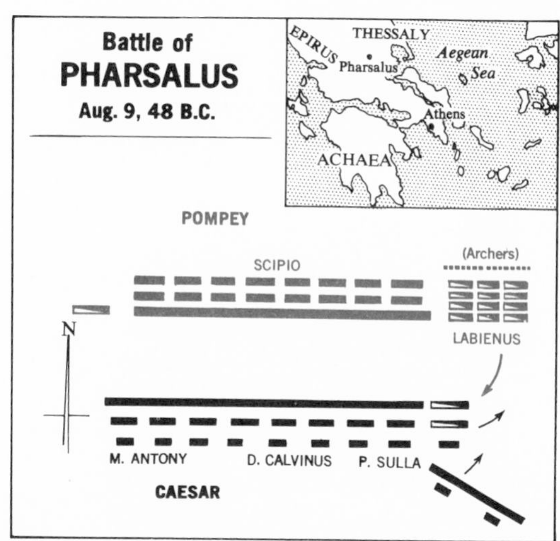

force, under Titus Labienus, began to sweep around Caesar's right wing, it was attacked in the flank and routed by a reserve specially deployed for such a purpose. A vigorous Caesarian attack (Mark Antony commanded the left wing) shattered the enemy's lines and put them to flight. Pompey, one of the first to retreat, escaped to the coast and took a ship to Egypt, where he was murdered. He left 6,000 dead on the field; many more surrendered. Caesar reported his dead at 200 privates and 30 centurions (company commanders) but probably lost about 1,200 men.

The battle of Pharsalus and subsequent death of the once brilliant commander Pompey the Great did not end Rome's civil war. But it did virtually ensure Caesar's ultimate triumph. The Roman senate gave Caesar a five-year term, as consul. *See* Dyrrachium I; Alexandria I; First Triumvirate, Wars of the.

Philiphaugh (English Civil War), 1645. The Cavalier commander in Scotland, the Marquis of Montrose (James Graham), had secured the entire country for Charles I by the summer of 1645. But the shattering of Cavalier forces in England had freed the regular Scottish army for Roundhead service in the homeland. A strong cavalry detachment under Gen. David Leslie now rode northward to challenge Montrose's forces, encamped at Philiphaugh in Selkirk County. On September 13 Leslie led 4,000 battle-hardened Covenanters into the Cavalier camp. The Royalists, taken by surprise, suffered a disastrous defeat. Montrose, with only a few surviving followers, fled to the Continent. And the king's cause in Scotland was extinguished. *See* Kilsyth; Langport; Stow-on-the-Wold; English Civil War.

Philippi (Wars of the Second Triumvirate), 42 B.C. Soon after seizing office, the Second Triumvirate of Mark Antony, Octavian, and Marcus Lepidus was endangered by a huge army of opposition assembled in Macedonia by the so-called republican leaders M. Junius Brutus and G. Cassius Longinus. Allied with the republicans was Sextus Pompey, second son of Pompey the Great, who commanded the largest fleet then in existence. Antony and Octavian sent Lepidus to recover Sicily from Pompey, while they crossed the Adriatic in the summer of 42 B.C. to engage Brutus and Cassius. At Philippi, ten miles from the Aegean coast in central Macedonia, the triumvirs' army of 20 legions encountered a force of almost equal size (100,000 men) under the two republican leaders. The battle opened October 27 with Brutus aligned against Octavian on the triumvirs' left (north), Cassius against Antony on the right. Brutus' troops threw back Octavian's legions and penetrated their camp. On the southern flank, however, Antony, who had learned his tactical skill from Julius Caesar, defeated Cassius. At the end of the day's fighting Cassius, believing the false report that Brutus had also been defeated, committed suicide. This freed Antony to come to the aid of Octavian. In a second battle, November 16, the combined Triumvirate force then overpowered Brutus, who also committed suicide.

Octavian returned to Rome, while Antony stayed to establish control over the eastern provinces. This assignment took him to Egypt in 41 B.C., where he remained a year with Cleopatra VII. *See* Mutina; Perusia; Second Triumvirate, Wars of the.

Philippi, W. Va. (American Civil War), 1861. With the outbreak of hostilities at Fort Sumter in April, both the North and South hurried to field armies in the northwestern corner of Virginia. General George McClellan with 20,000 Federal troops of the Department of the Ohio (River) pushed eastward toward Cumberland, Md. At the same time 5,000 Confederate troops under Gen. Robert Garnett stationed at Beverly probed northward. An advance element of this army reached Philippi, in what is now West Virginia, on June 3. That night a Federal force made an enveloping attack that routed the Confederates and inflicted 15 casualties. Two Federal soldiers were wounded. This action, sometimes called the Philippi Races, was the first land battle of the war. *See* Fort Sumter; Rich Mountain; American Civil War.

Philippine Insurrection against the United States. 1899–1902. When the United States declared war on Spain on April 21, 1898, Filipino discontent against Spanish rule coalesced into open rebellion. General Emilio Aguinaldo, who had returned from exile to lead the insurrection, proclaimed himself president of the Philippine republic on July 1. Filipino patriots stood ready to aid the successful American assault on Manila on August 13 but were blocked off by the troops of Gen. Wesley Merritt. Aguinaldo then took up a position outside the city.

Under terms of the Treaty of Paris, signed on December 10, 1898, the Philippine Islands were ceded by Spain to the United States. Frustrated in their desire for immediate independence, Filipino patriots attacked the American forces occupying Manila on February 4, 1899. The assault was repulsed. But U.S. troops then had to take the offensive in guerrilla warfare that flamed throughout the islands. Marching northward from Manila, the Americans attacked and captured the rebel capital of Malolos on March 31. Aguinaldo withdrew to Tarlac, 65 miles north of Manila. When this city fell to the Americans in November, Filipino forces began disintegrating. Aguinaldo fled to northeastern Luzon where he continued to harass American occupation troops until captured by a ruse carried out by Col. Frederick Funston on March 23, 1901. Resistance finally ended a year later. *See* Manila II.

Philippine Islands (World War II), 1941–1942. One of the principal objectives of the sweeping Japanese offensive in the western Pacific was the island of Luzon, the largest and most important in the Philippine Archipelago. Here was stationed the vast majority of the U.S. Far East forces under supreme Philippine commander Gen. Douglas MacArthur—11,000 U.S. soldiers and marines, 8,000 air corps personnel; 12,000 Philippine Scouts; and 100,000 Philippine soldiers, largely untrained and poorly equipped. Here also, in Manila Bay, was the base of Adm. Thomas Hart's U.S. Asiatic Fleet. The U.S. Army Air Corps, under Gen. Lewis Brereton, had some 275 planes, but only 35 B-17 Flying Fortresses and 107 P-40 Tomahawks and Kittyhawks could be considered modern combat aircraft.

On December 8 a noontime raid on Clark Field, the key air corps base 50 miles northwest of Manila, knocked out 15 of the 17 Flying Fortresses standing on the ground. That night Hart withdrew his fleet south to Borneo to take it out of the range of Japanese bombers. The Japanese invasion began two days later when 4,000 men landed at Aparri and Vigan, at the northern end of Luzon. Another landing came on December 14 at Legaspi, on the southern end of the island. But these were only probing attacks. The main enemy assault was made on December 22 by Gen. Masahura Homma's Fourteenth Army (43,000 men) at Lingayen Gulf on the west coast, 125 miles north of Manila. Under complete air superiority, Homma quickly linked up with the Aparri-Vigan invaders from the north and then drove south to the plains leading to Manila. The sudden thrust led MacArthur on December 23 to order a withdrawal to the rugged Bataan Peninsula, on the west coast between Manila Bay and the South China Sea. The importance of this decision became evident the following day when 9,500 Japanese soldiers landed at Lamon Bay, 60 miles southeast of Manila, placing the Philippine capital in a giant pincers. During the next seven days American and Philippine units fought gallant delaying actions to hold off the onrushing invaders while their comrades retreated from both north and south into Bataan. Manila, heavily bombed for two days, was declared an open city on December 26 to prevent further destruction. (It was occupied on January 2.)

By New Year's morning 1942 both Gen. Jonathan Wainwright's northern force and the southern unit (George Parker, later replaced by Albert Jones) had fallen back to the Bataan Peninsula. The two Calumpit bridges over the Pampanga River were blown up in the faces of the pursuing Japanese. MacArthur and the Philippine president, Manuel Quezon, set up headquarters on Corregidor Island, the "Rock" off Bataan's southern coast in the mouth of Manila Bay. The withdrawal had been accomplished without the loss of a major unit. Personnel losses totaled about 13,000, many of them Filipino desertions. MacArthur's 80,000 remaining American and Filipino troops now prepared to withstand new attacks on the last defensive position on Luzon, at Bataan and Corregidor.

During the early fighting on Luzon, 5,000 Japanese assault troops landed on the large island of Mindanao, at the southern end of the archipelago, on December 20. They overran the strategic port of Davao later that day. Leapfrogging farther south to Jolo Island and North Borneo, the Japanese completely severed the route between the Philippines and the rapidly building Allied base in Australia. Further conquests in the Philippines were stalled by the heroic defenders on Luzon. But after Bataan was evacuated on April 10, the Japanese quickly occupied strategic coastal positions throughout the Visayan Island group in the central Philippines with virtually no opposition.

When Wainwright surrendered Corregidor Island on May 6, he was forced to order capitulation of all Philippine forces. On May 10 Gen. William Sharp at Malaybalay, Mindanao, surrendered his Visayan-Mindanao command. Four days later Col. John Horan gave up his guerrilla regiment in the mountains of northern Luzon. Panay, the last of the Visayan forces (under Gen. Bradford Chynoweth) to resist, capitulated on May 18. Although all the Philippines were now officially surrendered, guerrilla activity by Filipinos and Americans never ceased. For more than two years underground forces harassed the Japanese occupation troops and supplied information to the mounting Allied counteroffensives in the Pacific—the Southwest Command under MacArthur and the Central Command of Adm. Chester Nimitz. *See* Pearl Harbor; Bataan-Corregidor; Leyte; World War II.

Philippine Sea (World War II), 1944. The U.S. invasion of the Mariana Islands on June 15, 1944, brought the Japanese fleet out fighting for the first time since the naval battles of Guadalcanal in the fall of 1942. Determined to force a showdown battle, Adm. Soemu Toyoda ordered a combined force of 9 carriers (Jisaburo Ozawa) and 18 battleships and cruisers (Matome Ugaki) to attack the U.S. warships protecting the landing on Saipan. (Toyoda had succeeded Mineichi Koga, killed in an air crash in March.) Here Adm. Raymond Spruance, commander of the Fifth Fleet, organized defensive preparations and sent the 15 fast carriers of Task Force 58 (Marc Mitscher) west to intercept the combined Japanese fleet, 90 miles away.

The battle of the Philippine Sea (between the Marianas and the Philippines) opened early on June 19 with an attack on Task Force 58 by Japanese land-based planes from Guam and Truk. Hellcat fighters from Mitscher's carriers destroyed 35 enemy fighters and bombers. The remainder of the air battle was fought by 430 Japanese carrier planes attacking the 450 planes of Task Force 58 in four fierce waves. At the end of the eight-hour Japanese onslaught only 100 of Ozawa's planes returned to their carriers. The rest had been destroyed in the most decisive aerial combat in history. Thirty American planes were lost in what the flyers called "The Marianas Turkey Shoot." No serious damage was inflicted on the Fifth Fleet. Meanwhile two U.S. submarines had slipped through the screen protecting the Japanese carriers. With a single torpedo the *Albacore* sank the 33,000-ton *Taiho,* Japan's biggest flattop, with a loss of 1,650 seamen. Three torpedoes from the *Cavalla* exploded the 22,000-ton carrier *Shokaku,* again with heavy loss of life.

That night (June 19) the Japanese fleet fled northwest with the U.S. carriers in pursuit. On the evening of June 20, Mitscher launched 209 aircraft to strike again at the enemy warships, now 300 miles away. These planes destroyed the carrier *Hiyo* and 40 of the 75 Japanese planes sent up to intercept them. Twenty U.S. planes were shot down and 80 more were lost returning to their carriers after dark. But 51 of the aviators were rescued from the water. The battle of the Philippine Sea ended that night. Although six of Ozawa's carriers escaped, almost all of Japan's trained pilots had been killed, and the amphibious landings in the Marianas had been protected. *See* Guadalcanal—Naval Action; Mariana Islands; Leyte Gulf; World War II.

Philippopolis I (Gothic Invasion of the Roman Empire), 251. While Rome was beset by military anarchy in the middle of the third century, the Goths were overrunning the empire in eastern Europe. From Dacia the barbarians swarmed south across the Danube into Moesia and Thrace. In 251 Emperor Trajanus Decius marched into Thrace to relieve the besieged city of Philoppopolis (Plovdiv). But the Roman legions were beaten back. The

Goths then stormed into the city and sacked it. An estimated 100,000 people were killed in the siege and subsequent massacre.

Decius pressed his campaign against the Goths, but before the year was over he was killed in combat. He thus became the first Roman emperor to fall fighting the barbarians. It was a harbinger of future misfortune for the empire. *See* Aquileia I; Edessa I; Naissus; Roman Empire.

Philippopolis II (Fourth Crusade), 1208. Two years after he had turned back the Latin army of Emperor Baldwin I of Constantinople in 1205, the Bulgarian ruler Kaloyan died and was succeeded by his nephew Boril. With the Bulgars now under weaker leadership, the new Latin emperor, Henry of Flanders, brother of Baldwin, resolved to mount a second attack up the Balkan Peninsula. From the site of their previous defeat at Adrianople (Edirne), the Latin crusaders (chiefly Franks) rode up the Maritsa Valley to Philippopolis (Plovdiv), in west-central Bulgaria. Here they encountered Boril's army, which was ill-prepared to meet the charge of the Latin knights. Boril was soundly defeated and fell back to his capital of Trnovo, north of the Balkan Mountains. Five years later he was forced to make peace with Henry at Constantinople. *See* Adrianople IV; Trnovo; Crusades.

Philippsburg (War of the Polish Succession), 1734. The limited War of the Polish Succession had opened with the Russian siege and capture of Danzig. The fighting then shifted to Italy, where Austria (of Charles VI's Holy Roman Empire) was outmaneuvered by France (Louis XV), Spain (Philip V), and Sardinia (Savoy). Meanwhile less important action took place along the upper Rhine. The only real battle was fought for the fortress of Philippsburg, east of the river near Karlsruhe. Here the Imperial army was besieged in 1734 by a French force under the Duke of Berwick, (James Fitz-james), one of Louis XIV's top commanders in the earlier War of the Spanish Succession. The duke was killed by a cannon ball on June 12, but his troops went on to storm the fortress successfully after Gen. Comte Maurice de Saxe had thwarted the efforts of Prince Eugene of Savoy to relieve Philippsburg. This was the last time the aged Eugene took the field. The able ally of the Duke of Marlborough (John Churchill) and opponent of Berwick in the previous war, Eugene died two year later. The fall of Philippsburg had no decisive result. After years of negotiation, the 1738 Treaty of Vienna restored the *status quo* along the Rhine and secured Augustus III on the throne of Poland. *See* Parma; Danzig I; Polish Succession, War of the.

Philomelion (Byzantine-Turkish Wars), 1116. Ten years after the crushing Byzantine defeat at Manzikert in 1071, Alexius I Comnenus ascended the Imperial throne at Constantinople. He was to become a great general, diplomat, and ruler. In the west he rebuffed the advances of Cumans, Patzinaks, and Normans against the Byzantine Empire. After allowing the First Crusaders to pass through the eastern part of his territory, he resumed the war against the Seljuk Turks in Asia Minor. In 1116 the largely mercenary army of Alexius met the Turks at Philomelion (Aksehir) in central Asia Minor. In one of the rare comebacks of the time, the Byzantine cavalry routed the mounted Seljuk bowmen. The Turks accepted truce terms the following year, agreeing to stay east of a north-south line running from Sinope through Ankara (Ancyra) and Philomelion. *See* Manzikert; Dyrrachium III; Myriocephalon.

Phraaspa (Wars of the Second Triumvirate), 36 B.C. After establishing a working relationship with Octavian, the other chief triumvir, Mark Antony returned to the East. He resumed preparations for invading Parthia, a plan carried forward from the days of Julius Caesar. But now Antony had a new dependent to share any spoils obtained in the conquest. At Antioch he married Cleopatra VII early in 36 B.C., although he was still wed to Octavia, sister of Octavian.

Antony marched his infantry directly toward Parthia in the following spring, sending two legions with his siege train and his Armenian and Pontine allies through the valley of the Araxes (Araks) River. Without waiting for his second section, Antony attacked the Parthian capital of Phraaspa. He was repulsed. Meanwhile, the Parthian king, Phraates IV, ambushed the other Roman army at Gazaca and annihilated it late in August.

Antony besieged Phraaspa but with the loss of his heavy equipment could not breach the walls of the city. At the onset of winter he gave up the siege and made a forced retreat of 24 days back to Armenia. The hardships of the march, coupled with Parthian harassing attacks by horse-archers, brought the losses of the Roman expedition to a total of about 30,000. Antony returned to Alexandria and Cleopatra, a move that alienated most of Rome. *See* Perusia; Naulochus; Actium; Second Triumvirate, Wars of the.

Piave River (World War I), 1918. Despite the overwhelming defeat at Caporetto, the Italian armies of Gen. Armando Diaz held on grimly behind the Piave River late in 1917. The fierce defense of Monte Grappa, near the western end of the line, gave the heights the name "Sacred Mountain." Meanwhile Diaz rebuilt his armies up to 57 divisions, including five Anglo-French divisions from the Western Front. (During the winter two Italian divisions were transferred to France; six Anglo-French divisions were returned to that area.) North of the Piave the German troops were also recalled to the Western Front. But the Austrian armies were reinforced to 58 divisions in one more effort to knock Italy out of the war. For this offensive the Austrian command was divided between Gen. Svetozar Borojević von Bojna on the left (east) and Field Marshal Count Conrad von Hötzendorf, recently demoted from Austrian chief of staff, on the right, in the Trentino.

The main Austrian attack got under way on June 15. On the right Conrad von Hötzendorf registered a small gain, only to be checked hard the following day by a counterattack by the Italian Sixth and Fourth armies, which included the Anglo-French troops. Thereafter, both the Austrian Tenth and Eleventh armies did little more than hold in place. On the lower Piave, however, Borojević von Bojna forced a crossing of the river with the Sixth and Fifth armies and advanced as much as three miles. For the next eight days a fierce struggle took place south of the river—the Austrians fighting to enlarge their bridgehead, the Italian Eighth and Third armies striving desperately to contain it. Unable to draw reinforcements from Conrad von Hötzendorf's stalemated sector, Borojević von Bojna was finally forced to withdraw north of the river on the night of June 22–23. This ended the Austrian offensive, which turned out to be the last such effort of the war for the Dual Monarchy. The defeat cost the two Austrian commanders a total of 150,000 casualties, including 24,000 captured. *See* Caporetto; Vittorio Veneto; World War I.

Pichincha (Ecuadorian War of Independence), 1822. When Simón Bolívar moved east from Colombia to attack the Spaniards in Venezuela, he sent a second army southwest into Ecuador. Led by the able patriot Antonio de Sucre, the revolutionaries attacked a royalist force at Pichincha, northwest of Quito, on May 24, 1822. The patriots were completely victorious. Moving on to occupy Quito, Sucre assured the independence of Ecuador, which accepted Bolívar as president. *See* Carabobo; Junín.

Piedmont (American Civil War), 1864. Dissatisfied with the performance of Gen. Franz Sigel at New Market, the Federal commander in chief, Gen. U. S. Grant, put Gen. David Hunter in charge of Federal forces in the Shenandoah Valley. From Strasburg, Hunter marched southward toward Staunton on May 26, directing Gen. George Crook to meet him there after taking a more westward route. At Harrisonburg Hunter circled to the east to avoid the Confederate defenses organized by Gen. William (Grumble) Jones. Jones took 5,000 men to intercept the Federals at Piedmont, seven miles southwest of Port Republic. Early on June 5 Hunter's superior force struck hard at Jones's division. By midafternoon the Confederate defenses collapsed. Jones was killed. In all, the Confederates lost about 600 in killed and wounded and 1,000 prisoners. Hunter, who suffered 780 casualties, occupied Staunton the following day. Crook arrived on June 8. *See* New Market; Lynchburg; American Civil War.

Pilsen (Thirty Years' War), 1618. The long-smoldering feud between Catholics and Protestants in Bohemia finally flared into a war that would last 30 years and devastate central Europe. The struggle began when the Bohemian Protestants called in outside help against their Catholic king, Ferdinand of Austria (future Ferdinand II of the Holy Roman Empire). Military assistance for the rebels came from Charles Emmanuel, duke of Savoy, and Frederick V, elector palatine. Their army of 20,000 men under the German mercenary general Count Ernst von Mansfeld crossed the Bohemian border and marched on Pilsen (Plzeň), a Catholic stronghold 52 miles southwest of Prague. On November 1, 1618, Mansfeld attacked and after 15 hours of fighting captured the town.

Mansfeld's victory checked Catholic plans to seize Prague. After wintering in Pilsen, the German general resumed the offensive the following year. *See* Sablat; Thirty Years' War.

Pinkie (English-Scottish Wars), 1547. After the death of Henry VIII early in 1547, English policy called for the marriage of ten-year-old Edward VI with five-year-old Mary, Queen of Scots. When the pro-French party in Scotland objected, the Duke of Somerset (Edward Seymour), English protector of the boy king, and the Duke of Northumberland (John Dudley), marched an army toward Edinburgh. The Scottish army under the Earl of Huntly (George Gordon) charged the invaders at Pinkie, east of the city, but were checked and then routed by an English cavalry attack on September 10, 1547. Somerset occupied Edinburgh but did not follow up the victory, partly because of domestic strife in England. The city was abandoned three years later. *See* Solway Moss; Boulogne; Carberry Hill.

Pirot (Serbian-Bulgarian War), 1885. After their repulse at Slivnica on November 19, the Serbian troops of King Milan I fell back northwest behind their border to Pirot. The defeated army, now numbering about 40,000 men, was pursued by a Bulgarian force of comparable size, commanded by Alexander I. On November 26 the Bulgarians stormed into Pirot only to be thrown back the next day. Alexander rallied his troops and retook the town by evening. The intervention of Austria (Franz Josef I) halted fighting on November 28. Serbian losses were about 2,000, Bulgarian casualties slightly more. A peace treaty signed on March 3, 1886, ended the war with the *status quo* re-established. *See* Slivnica; Balkan Wars.

Placentia (Alamanni Invasion of the Roman Empire), 271. A year after Aurelian became emperor of Rome, northern Italy was invaded by a host of Alamanni supported by Jutungi and Vandals. Aurelian hurried an army northward. The Romans reached Placentia (Piacenza) on the Po, 40 miles southeast of Milan, just ahead of the barbarians. In a fierce encounter the Alamanni and their allies were driven back. But the Roman victory only checked the invasion. The decisive battle had yet to be fought. *See* Naissus; Pavia I; Roman Empire.

Plassey (Seven Years' War), 1757. While Great Britain and France fought a mortal struggle in Europe and North America, the nawab of Bengal took the side of France in India. Siraj-ud-daula (Surajah Dowlah) had assembled an army of 50,000 men, which dominated the province. However, his cruel rule provoked many Indians to support a rebel chieftain named Mir Jafar for the Bengalese throne. Robert Clive, the British commander in India, resolved to exploit this discontent. Aligning himself with Mir Jafar, Clive organized an army of 3,000 men, of whom less than a third were British. Clive marched to Plassey, 80 miles north of Calcutta. Here, from a grove of trees beside

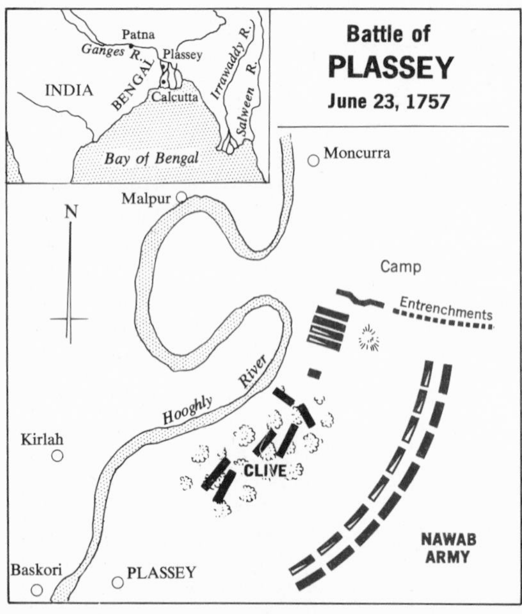

the rain-swollen Hooghly River, he faced the Nawab's army, which with some French auxiliaries outnumbered his force 17 to 1.

On June 23 a four-hour cannonade ensued. Then, worried by treachery in his own ranks, the nawab began to withdraw. Clive's army immediately attacked, inflicting a total of 500 casualties. The Indian force fled in panic, leaving the British supreme on the field. The victory, at a cost of 65 men killed, wounded, or missing, made Clive master of Bengal and marked the beginning of the British Empire in the East. A few days later Siraj-ud-daula was assassinated, and the British ally Mir Jafar ascended the throne of Bengal. *See* Calcutta; Fort Saint David; Seven Years' War.

Plataea I (Persian-Greek Wars), 479 B.C. Following the rout of his Persian fleet at Salamis in 480 B.C., Xerxes returned to Asia, turning over the command of his land forces to his brother-in-law Mardonius. In August of the following year Mardonius withdrew from Athens into Boeotia. At Plataea, near the Attica border, he encountered a strong force of allied Greeks commanded by the Spartan general Pausanias. In a fierce struggle the swords and spears of the Greek hoplites proved to be superior. Mardonius was killed. With his death, the Persians panicked and became easy prey for the attacking Greeks. Giving no quarter, Pausanias' warriors annihilated almost the entire enemy force. This decisive battle, coupled with a simultaneous Greek victory at Mycale in Asia Minor, ended the several Persian attempts to subdue Greece. *See* Salamis; Mycale; Persian-Greek Wars.

Plataea II (Great Peloponnesian War), 429–427 B.C. The 30-year treaty between Athens and Sparta brought only 15 years of peace before a new conflict erupted between the two leading Greek city-states. The renewed hostilities, called the Great Peloponnesian War, began at Plataea, an ally of Athens. In 431 a band of Thebans entered the city by treachery. Themselves tricked into surrendering, the Thebans were then killed. This incident, added to complaints by Megara and Corinth, induced Sparta to take the Peloponnesian League into war with Athens. In 429 Archidamus II marched a Spartan force to Plataea and besieged the city, which was defended by 400 Plataeans and 80 Athenians (most of the noncombatants were sent out of the city). The garrison repulsed numerous assaults, and during the long months of siege half of the defenders escaped through the enemy's lines. By 427, however, starvation forced Plataea to capitulate. The Spartan victors charged the survivors with treasons and put to death 200 Plataeans and 25 Athenians. *See* Coronea I; Naupactus; Mytilene; Peloponnesian Wars.

Platte Bridge (Sioux War I), 1865. The massacre of the Indians encamped at Sand Creek, Colo., in November 1864 provoked most of the Plains tribes into widespread retaliation. Some 3,000 Cheyenne, Sioux, and Arapahoe warriors converged on the Platte Bridge Station of the Oregon Trail, in present-day Wyoming, during the following summer. Led by a chief called Roman Nose, the Indians ambushed a supply wagon train bound for the station on July 25. A party of 25 cavalrymen under Lt. Casper Collins rode out to protect the train. This was just the opportunity the Indians had been awaiting. As the troop crossed the bridge, it was cut off and surrounded. Eleven of the cavalrymen, including Collins, were killed before they could fight their way back to the fort, in a four-hour battle. The supply train was overwhelmed and its guard annihilated. The town of Caspar, Wyo., which later developed on this spot, was named (although misspelled) for Casper Collins who had led the brave but fruitless rescue attempt. *See* Sand Creek; Massacre Hill; Sioux Wars.

Plattsburg (War of 1812). Occupied by the British offensive into upper New York State on September 6, 1814, but relinquished when the American victory on Lake Champlain five days later forced a general British retreat to Canada. *See* Champlain, Lake.

Pleasant Hill (American Civil War). The second day of fighting in the battle of Sabine Crossroads, on April 9, 1864, after which both Federals and Confederates began to retreat. *See* Sabine Crossroads–Pleasant Hill.

Plei Me (Vietnam War), 1965. In one of the largest Communist offensives of the war a combined force of 6,000 Viet Cong and North Vietnamese regular troops attacked Plei Me, 20 miles from the Cambodian border, on October 19. A triangular-shaped fort, Plei Me was held by 400 South Vietnamese troops (Montagnards) assisted by 12 U.S. Special Forces officers and men. For seven days waves of Communists assaulted the fort under cover of mortar and recoilless rifle fire. To bolster the besieged garrison, 250 Vietnamese Rangers were dropped inside Plei Me by helicopter on the second day of the attack. A relief force sent out from II Corps headquarters at Pleiku was checked by a Communist ambush. Assisted by 600 sorties by U.S. Skyraiders and supplied by parachute drop from transport planes, the defenders of Plei Me held out until October 27, when elements of the U.S. 1st Cavalry Division (Airmobile) landed by helicopter north of the fort and raised the siege. The Communist army withdrew westward into Cambodia with a loss of 850 killed and 1,700 wounded. Nine of the Special Forces men had been killed or wounded. *See* South Vietnam; Van Tuong Peninsula; Chu Pong–Ia Drang River; Vietnam War.

Plevna (Russian-Turkish War), 1877. The Russian army of Grand Duke Nicholas, after capturing the Danubian fortresses of Svištov (Sistova) and Nikopol (Nicopolis) from the Turkish garrisons, pressed southward into modern Bulgaria. On July 20 the Russians reached the major Ottoman fortress of Plevna, which was commanded by Marshal Osman Nuri Pasha with about 30,000 men. A reckless attack led by Gen. Nicolas Krüdener's corps was beaten back with a loss of almost 2,000 men. Ten days later Krüdener attacked again, but for the second time had to fall back, losing more than 7,000 men in this assault.

The Russian army of investment, now 90,000 strong, launched a new assault on September 11

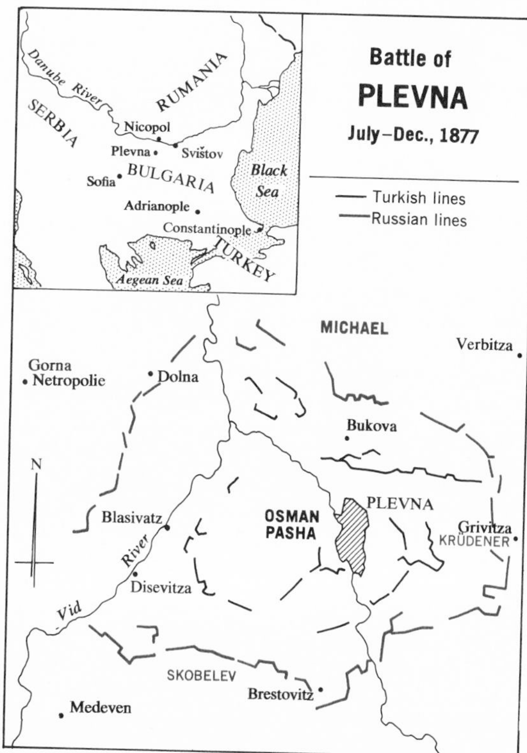

under the command of Grand Duke Michael, younger brother of Nicholas and Czar Alexander II. A force led by Gen. Mikhail Skobelev captured two redoubts on the southwest, but a Turkish counterattack regained the positions the second day. In all, the Russians lost 20,000 men in the futile two-day battle. Turkish casualties were about 5,000. The firm Ottoman resistance aroused the admiration of most of the civilized world. However, the impossibility of obtaining relief doomed the garrison, which was now encircled by 100,000 Russians. Command of the besiegers passed to the future Rumanian king Carol I, assisted by the competent engineer officer Gen. Frants Totleben.

Realizing the hopelessness of his position, Osman tried to break out on December 10. With 25,000 troops, accompanied by 9,000 sick and wounded in carts, the Turkish commander cut his way across the Vid River. But Russian reinforcements plugged the gap and forced the garrison back across the river. Osman received a serious wound. The Turks, who had lost 5,000 men in the sortie, withdrew into Plevna and surrendered that evening, ending the 143-day siege. Some 2,000 Russians had fallen during the futile breakout, making their total casualties for the siege some 38,000.

As the Russians resumed their advance in the Balkans, a second army was thrusting through the Caucasus. Sultan Abdul-Hamid II, whose troops were holding fast only at Shipka Pass, appealed to the other European powers for mediation. He was rebuffed. *See* Svištov; Shipka Pass; Kars II; Russian-Turkish War.

Plovdiv (Russian-Turkish War), 1878. The Russian victories at Plevna in December 1877 and Shipka Pass early in January 1878 riddled the Turkish front in the Balkans. Sofia fell to the armies of Czar Alexander II, also in January. From here Gen. Osip Gurko marched southeast to Plovdiv (Philippopolis), on the Maritsa River. Attacking on January 17, Gurko's troops stormed into the fortified city, routing the outnumbered defenders of Gen. Suleiman Pasha. The Turks lost 5,000 in killed and wounded and 2,000 prisoners. Russian casualties were only about 1,300.

Pressed by the continuing Russian advance, Suleiman withdrew down the Maritsa Valley, abandoning Adrianople (Edirne) to a column led by Gen. Mikhail Skobelev. By the end of the month the armies of Sultan Abdul-Hamid II had retreated almost to Constantinople. At this point an alarmed Great Britain sent a fleet to the Turkish capital to force mediation. Russia agreed to an armistice on January 31 and signed the Treaty of San Stefano on March 3. *See* Pleona; Shipka Pass; Geok Tepe; Russian-Turkish War.

Point Pleasant (Lord Dunmore's War), 1774. To put down Indian raids in western Virginia, Col. Andrew Lewis marched to Point Pleasant (now W.Va.), where the Kanawha River flows into the Ohio. Here his 1,100 men linked up with another force commanded by Virginia's colonial governor, Lord Dunmore (John Murray). On the night of October 9 a large war party of Shawnees under Chief Cornstalk crossed the Ohio to attack the encampment at dawn. It was one of the fiercest battles fought in the Indian wars east of the Mississippi. The colonial troops resisted grimly, and by the end of the day the Indians gave up the assault, withdrawing northward across the Ohio that night. Almost 50 Virginians were killed and 100 wounded. Indian losses were unknown but believed to be unusually heavy. This battle broke the back of the Indian power in the western lands of the colonies. *See* Blue Licks; Indian Wars in the United States.

Poitiers (Hundred Years' War), 1356. The English king Edward III resumed the war in the summer of 1356 by sending his eldest son, Edward, the Black Prince, on a ruthless raid into the heart of France. From the English territories of Gascony and Aquitaine, the younger Edward pillaged northeast toward Orleans. However, when he turned westward to Tours, the Black Prince's 7,000-man force was taken in pursuit by a French army of 16,000 men under King John II, the Good. The English hurried toward the coast but, burdened by their plunder, were outmarched by the French. At Maupertuis, seven miles southeast of Poitiers, Prince Edward was forced to halt and make a defensive stand among vineyards and hedgerows on September 17. The site favored the employment of his corps of 2,000 longbowmen.

The French armored knights dismounted and advanced on foot. English arrows took a heavy toll, but the French pressed relentlessly forward. Seeing that his position was soon to be overrun, Prince Edward ordered a countercharge by his infantry, who were armed with spears and axes. At the same time a detachment of archers and mounted men-at-arms circled around and struck the left flank of the advancing column. The coordinated attack broke and then routed the French army. Unable to move fast in their heavy mail, 2,000 knights, the flower of French nobility, were slaughtered. King John and 2,000 others became prisoners of war. Prince Edward completed his withdrawal to Bordeaux, where his royal captive was sent to England.

In 1359 King Edward returned to the war in France and marched almost to Paris before he was forced to turn back. Much of the land was so devastated it could not support an army. Although it had been demonstrated that French military power was inferior to that of England, it was equally clear that France refused to be conquered. As a result, the Peace of Bretigny was signed in 1360. Edward received full sovereignty to Aquitaine, Calais, and Ponthieu. King John's ransom was fixed at three million gold crowns (half a million pounds sterling). The future Charles V, the Wise, acted as regent for his captive father. The treaty brought only four years of peace, however. *See* Calais I; Auray; Hundred Years' War.

Poland. The kingdom of Poland, which arose in the Middle Ages, was dismembered during 1772–95 by three partitions among Russia, Prussia, and Austria. Regaining its independence in 1918, it was the site of the first great land battle of World War II (see following entry).

Naklo	1109
Cracow	1241
Tannenberg I	1410
Varna I	1444
Polotsk	1579
Linköping	1598
Khotin I	1621
Riga I	1621
Beresteczko	1651
Warsaw I	1656
Khotin II	1673
Vienna II	1683
See Great Northern War	
See Polish Succession, War of the	
See Polish Revolt against Russia	
See World War I	
Warsaw IV	1920
See World War II	

Poland (World War II), 1939. The German invasion of Poland on September 1 opened World War II. In addition to new armament and equipment the war introduced a new type of swift, mechanized attack, called blitzkrieg, or lightning war, in which an entire nation could become a single battlefield. The Nazi army launched the invasion with 58 divisions, 14 of which were armored (the *Panzers*) or motorized. In contrast, Poland's Marshal Edward Smigly-Rydz could mobilize only 30 divisions and a single motorized brigade.

The attack was made by five powerful armies from three directions—Third Army (Georg von Kuechler) from East Prussia in the north; Fourth Army (Gunther von Kluge) from Pomerania in the west; and Eighth (Johannes von Blaskowitz), Tenth (Walther von Reichenau), and Fourteenth (Siegmund List) from Silesia in the southwest. General Fedor von Bock commanded the northern army group, Gen. Karl von Rundstedt the army group to the south. In the first two days more than 1,400 attacking German aircraft destroyed the Polish air force of less than 900 planes, mostly on the ground.

Poland was quickly overrun, with large segments of its troops encircled and annihilated. Racing 140 miles the first week, armored spearheads of the Tenth Army reached the southern Warsaw suburbs on September 8 and began smashing the city with bombers and heavy artillery. Five days later the Third Army closed the pincers on Warsaw from the north. On September 17 the Fourth and Fourteenth armies closed an outer pincers far to the east. On the same day the Russian army marched into eastern Pöland, covering 110 miles in two days to reach the old Curzon Line of 1919.

Beleaguered Warsaw surrendered on September 27. The next day Germany and Russia partitioned Poland. A few Polish leaders escaped to Paris and then to London to set up a government-in-exile under Gen. Wladyslaw Sikorski. German losses were 10,600 killed, 30,300 wounded, and 3,400 missing. About 450,000 Poles became prisoners of war; other casualties could not be determined. Russia then turned its attention to Finland, while Germany feinted in the west and then attacked Norway in the spring.

The Nazi invasion of Russia in June 1941 quickly overran eastern Poland. In a 1944 counteroffensive Russian troops recrossed the old Polish border on January 4. *See* Finland (World War II); Norway (World War II); Soviet Union (World War II); Poland–East Prussia; World War II.

Poland–East Prussia (World War II), 1944–45. The great Russian winter offensive of 1943–44 had pushed the German army back inside Poland's 1939 borders. Then, in the summer of 1944, Poland became, for a second time, one of the despoiled battle sites of the war. The fighting opened simultaneously on two fronts—in the north between the Baltic and the Pripet Marshes and in the south between the Pripet and the Carpathian Mountains.

The northern front was given the name Fatherland Line by the Germans because it protected the home territory of the Reich. Here Gen. Ivan Chernyakhovski's Third White Russian Army drove across the Niemen (Nemunas) River of Lithuania–White Russia in three places. The right (northern) prong captured Kaunas (Kovno) on August 1 and pressed toward the eastern border of East Prussia. The center prong, which had bridged the river at Grodno on July 26, drove toward Suwalki and the southeastern edge of East Prussia. On the left (south) Chernyakhovski had joined with Gen. T. F. Zakharov's Second White Russian Army to take Bialystok on July 18.

Zakharov then pivoted northwest and he, too, pushed against East Prussia. But the Nazi defenders of the historic German province, under Field Marshal Ernst Busch, resisted stubbornly. Farther south Gen. Konstantin Rokossovski's First White Russian Army drove across the Bug River on July 22 and wheeled north to storm into the old fortress city of Brest Litovsk six days later. Rokossovski then suddenly lunged toward Warsaw, passing through Siedlce to reach the capital's eastern suburb of Praga on July 31. This Russian thrust to the Vistula ignited an underground uprising within Warsaw. The revolt was ruthlessly suppressed and three elite SS (*Schutzstaffel*, or Protective Corps) rushed to Warsaw to hurl back Rokossovski's spearhead. But Marshal Georgi Zhukov, who had taken over the First White Russian Army, came up to the line of the Vistula on this front.

South of the Pripet Marshes, the Russian left wing had launched the summer offensive on July 16, with Marshal Ivan Konev's First Ukrainian Army attacking on a 125-mile front between Luck (Lutsk) and Tarnopol. On July 20 Konev entered Rawa Ruska, routing the forces of Field Marshal Walther von Model, now commanding the German armies in this sector. Farther south, Gen. Ivan Petrov had joined in the attack to take Stanislav and press westward. Lvov, now pinched out, fell on July 27. The Konev-Petrov team, plunging on westward, crossed the San at Jaroslaw and Przemyśl on July 28. The momentum of the drive carried the First Ukrainian Army to a bridgehead across the Vistula at Baranow, south of Warsaw, on August 1.

The Soviet summer offensive, which began in White Russia and the Ukraine, had rushed 450 miles to the Vistula in five weeks. But the German armies rallied to hold the river line for six months. The fighting then shifted south across the Carpathians.

On January 12, 1945, Russia opened its final great offensive along 750 miles of front. Spearheading the overwhelming infantry attacks were huge Stalin tanks (mounting 122-mm. cannons), now being delivered to combat units in great numbers. On the south three armies of Marshal Konev (the strongest Russian force, with 32 infantry divisions, 8 armored corps) came hurling out of the Baranow bridgehead over the Vistula River. The left wing wheeled southwest toward Kraków, while the center drove westward for Oppeln. Racing an average of 18 miles a day, Konev's armor reached these cities on January 19 and 26, respectively. This drive toward the upper Oder sliced off the key industrial area of Upper Silesia.

Meanwhile Konev's right-flank army had pivoted north from the Vistula bridgehead to enflank the German forces that were opposing Zhukov's First White Russians in the center. Zhukov had launched his attack across the Vistula on January 14. Warsaw was bypassed and fell on January 17. In six days Russian armor roared 150 miles west between the Vistula and Warta rivers, bypassing the fortified communications centers of Thorn (Torún) and Posen (Poznán). The crumbling German forces in this area were being commanded now by the Nazi Gestapo chief Heinrich Himmler. By January 30 Zhukov was crossing the Brandenburg frontier less than 100 miles from Berlin. Konev's forces pulled abreast on the left. In less than three weeks the Red armies had raced forward almost 300 miles to penetrate prewar German territory.

On the right Rokossovski, now commanding the Second White Russian Army Group, plunged northwest to reach the Baltic west of Danzig (Gdansk) on January 26. This offensive ripped a huge hole in the German front and isolated the German defenders of East Prussia. Rokossovski then turned east. He slugged his way into Gdynia on March 28 and into Danzig two days later.

Meanwhile, the pocket of East Prussia pressed by Rokossovski on the southwest had been under siege on the south and east by the Third White Russian group. On February 1 Gen. Chernyakhovski split the pocket by knifing to the Baltic between Elbing (Elblag) and the provincial capital of Königsberg (Kaliningrad). Chernyakhovski was killed in action on February 18. His replacement, Marshal Aleksandr Vasilievsky, relentlessly compressed the German defense line. A German bridgehead at Braunsberg caved in on March 20, and on April 9 the Königsberg garrison of 90,000 surrendered. The battle of Poland–East Prussia was over; but the battle for East Germany had already begun. *See* White Russia; Germany, East; Warsaw VI; World War II.

Polish Revolt against Russia (1831). Patriots in Russian-ruled Poland rose in revolt against Czar Nicholas I in 1831. But with the Russian capture of Wąrsaw the uprising was crushed.

Grochów 1831
Ostroleka 1831
Warsaw II 1831

Polish Succession, War of the (1733–1735). When the throne of Poland became vacant, Spain, France, and Sardinia (Savoy) supported the claim of Stanislas Leszczyński, while Russia and Austria nominated a rival candidate, Augustus, son of the late ruler, Augustus II. War broke out in Poland and then spread to Italy and to the Rhine River. The Treaty of Vienna, signed in 1735 and ratified three years later, ended the fighting with the Russian-Austrian candidate installed as King Augustus III of Poland.

Danzig I 1733–1734
Parma 1734
Philippsburg 1734

Pollentia (Wars of the Western Roman Empire), 402. Honorius, who had inherited the Western Roman Empire from his father, Theodosius I, the Great, faced a formidable challenge to his rule from Alaric, king of the Visigoths. Alaric invaded Italy from the northeast and headed for Milan, where Honorius had established his capital. The emperor fled to Ravenna, leaving the defense of Italy to Flavius Stilicho, son of a Vandal chieftain. Stilicho called in Roman troops from Britain and the Rhine and marched to the relief of Milan. Alaric turned southward, raiding deeply into the peninsula. Stilicho followed and at Pollentia (Pollenza) attacked the Gothic camp on April 6, 402, while the invaders were celebrating Easter. The Goths fought back savagely, but Stilicho pressed his charge relentlessly and overwhelmed the enemy encampment. Thousands of Goths were killed; among the prisoners taken was Alaric's wife.

Alaric fell back to the north, again pursued by Stilicho. The imperial army drove the Goths into the Alps. Although Stilicho was unable to destroy the invader's main force, he won enough time to concentrate against a new German invasion. *See* Aquileia II, Florence-Fiesole; Roman Empire.

Polotsk (Polish-Russian Wars), 1579. Under the leadership of Ivan IV, the Terrible, Russia cleared the Volga of Tatars and then turned westward to encroach upon the White Russian lands of Poland and Lithuania. In 1563 Ivan had seized Polotsk on the right bank of the Dvina River. But Stephen Báthory, who ascended the throne of Poland in 1575, rallied his countrymen and four years later attacked and regained Polotsk. He marched on to Pskov, driving the Russian army before him. Finally, in 1582, peace was restored between Poland (and Sweden) and Russia, with Ivan forced to yield the territory he had taken to Stephen

Báthory's field commander, Jan Zamojski. (Polotsk did not return to Russian control until 1772.) *See* Astrakhan II; Linköping.

Poltava (Great Northern War), 1709. The invasion of Russia by Charles XII of Sweden had turned into a near disaster by the winter of 1708–09. His supply column from Riga had been virtually destroyed en route, and the anticipated heavy reinforcements from the Cossacks of hetman Ivan Mazepa turned out to be less than 2,000 men. A severe winter in the Ukraine reduced the Swedish effectives to less than 20,000. Nevertheless, in May Charles resumed the offensive, laying siege to the city of Poltava on the right bank of the Vorskla River (a tributary of the Dnieper), 85 miles southwest of Kharkov. But now the marked advantage the Swedes had heretofore enjoyed over the Russians had vanished. Charles had little artillery remaining and only a small amount of powder. At the same time Peter I, the Great, had assembled an army of 60,000 Russians to try to raise the siege of Poltava. In June the czar sent all but 10,000 of his troops across the Vorskla to the west side, north of the city and the Swedish siege lines. Here the Russians entrenched themselves behind several redoubts, which were covered by artillery fire.

The Swedish army could not withstand a countersiege and on July 8 launched an all-out attack on the Russian positions. Charles, who had been wounded in the foot a few days before, was carried into action on a litter. Gunfire from the redoubts failed to halt the valiant Swedish assault. The Russian lines quivered but did not break, and their artillery and musket fire took a terrible toll. When the attack showed signs of faltering after two hours of furious combat, Peter sent his great numbers forward in a sweeping counterblow. Overlapped on both wings, the Swedes began falling back, at first stubbornly and then in wild disorder. The Russians pressed ahead, squeezing the Swedes into the narrow angle formed by the Vorskla and Dnieper rivers. The entire invading army was killed or captured except for Charles and some 1,500 followers who escaped southward into Turkish territory.

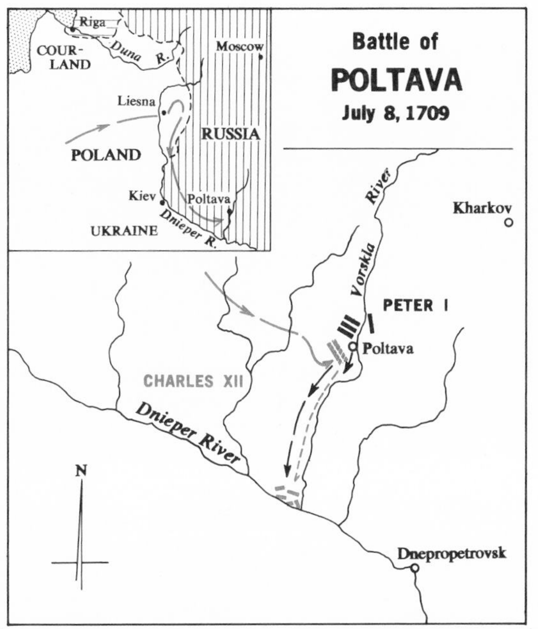

The Russian victory at Poltava ranks as one of the decisive battles of history. It ended forever Swedish military power. Conversely, the battle marked the beginning of Russian ascendancy in eastern Europe. While Charles XII had been subduing Poland, Peter I had founded Saint Petersburg (Leningrad), his "window to Europe," on the Gulf of Finland. The victory over the Swedish monarch not only preserved this maritime outlet but vanquished his chief rival for supremacy in the Baltic. *See* Liesna; Ahvenanmaa; Great Northern War.

Pondicherry (Seven Years' War), 1761. Following their victory at Wandiwash early in 1760, the British forces in India steadily pushed the French back to their main base at Pondicherry on the east coast. By August Lt. Col. (later Sir) Eyre Coote with more than 6,000 English and sepoy troops began the investment of Pondicherry. With the British navy patrolling the seas, Coote could expect ample reinforcements and supplies. The Comte de Lally's 3,000 French and native defenders, however, could not hope for succor from the outside. It was not until December that Coote's artillery was ready to open a breaching fire. Two weeks later a hurricane wrecked the battery. But on January 10, 1761, the bombardment was renewed, and five days later the garrison capitulated. When he returned to Paris, De Lally was wrongly charged with treason and beheaded in 1766. Meanwhile, however, Pondicherry was restored to France by the Treaty of Paris, which ended the Seven Years' War in 1763. *See* Wandiwash; Seven Years' War.

Port Arthur I (Chinese-Japanese War I), 1894. Continuing their combined sea-land offensive, the Japanese launched an attack on the Chinese naval base of Port Arthur on November 21. After an initial naval bombardment, a Japanese force under Gen. Count Iwao Oyama stormed ashore. The Chinese garrison of some 9,000 men offered only a feeble resistance, then withdrew up the Liaotung Peninsula. *See* Yalu River I; Weihaiwei; Chinese-Japanese War I.

Port Arthur II (Russian-Japanese War), 1904–1905. The first great war of the twentieth century opened with a sneak attack by Japanese ships on the Russian fleet anchored off Port Arthur, on the night of February 8–9. Two battleships and a cruiser suffered hits from the attacking flotilla of

Adm. Heihachiro Togo. The Japanese admiral settled down to a blockade of the port, while war was officially declared two days later. Inside the harbor Adm. Stepan Makarov took charge of the Russian fleet and sortied vigorously against the besiegers. Then on April 13 his flagship, the *Petropavlosk,* struck a mine and sank with the loss of 600 lives, including the "Cossack Admiral." For several months thereafter the Russian fleet stayed within the harbor.

Under the protection of Togo's naval guns, five Japanese divisions landed above Port Arthur on May 5. General Count Maresuke Nogi, in command of the invading force, sent the bulk of his troops under Gen. Yasukata Oku to attack the Russian defenses on the heights of Nanhan. Here the Russians, directed by Gen. Anatoli Stësel and supplemented by accurate artillery fire, repulsed one assault after another on May 26. Finally the Japanese pulled back to allow their own artillery and naval guns to blast Nanhan. On the following day a new attack carried the hill. At least one-sixth of the 3,000 defenders lay dead. The victory cost the attackers 4,500 casualties, but they had now penned up the Russians in Port Arthur. By

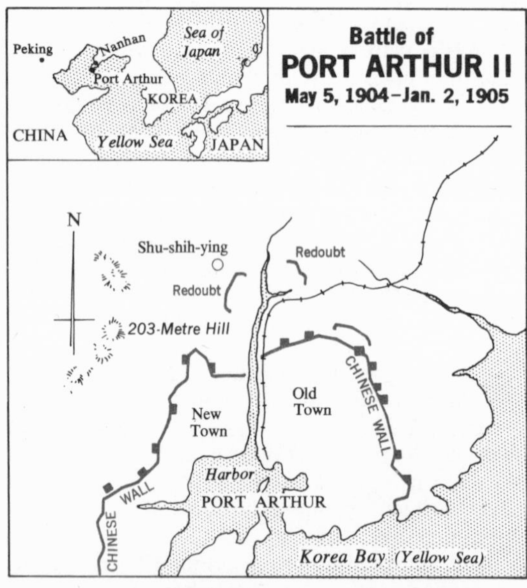

June 1 Nogi's investment lines were complete. He had more than 80,000 men; the defenders numbered less than 42,000.

When Japanese siege guns began shelling the Russian ships in the harbor, the harassed fleet, now led by Adm. Vitheft, slipped past Togo's blockade into the Yellow Sea. But on August 10 the pursuing Japanese warships overtook the Russian vessels and forced them back into the dubious safety of Port Arthur. Vitheft was killed in the sea battle. This defeat thwarted an attempted junction with the Russian ships similarly blockaded at Vladivostok.

Meanwhile Nogi pressed a relentless ground attack against the formidable Russian defenses in the hills outside Port Arthur. Despite casualties and illnesses that incapacitated more than 13,000 a month, the Japanese persisted until December 5, when they captured the key height known as 203-Metre Hill. This position allowed accurate artillery fire to be laid against the trapped Russian fleet in the harbor. The four surviving battleships were promptly sent to the bottom. Finally, on January 2, 1905, Stësel surrendered Port Arthur to the Japanese, who had suffered 58,000 killed and wounded and 34,000 sick in the seven-month siege. During this time other Russian forces had been consistently overpowered by the invading Japanese armies. *See* Yalu River II; Mukden I; Tsushima Straït; Russian-Japanese War.

Port Gibson (American Civil War). The first unsuccessful Confederate attempt, on May 1, 1863, to halt Gen. U. S. Grant's thrust into Mississippi that resulted in the siege of Vicksburg. *See* Vicksburg.

Port Hudson (American Civil War), 1863. As part of the Federal campaign to clear the length of the Mississippi River, Gen. Nathaniel Banks moved up from New Orleans with 20,000 troops. On May 26 Banks's XIV Corps closed in on the Confederate strong point of Port Hudson, La., 25 miles north of Baton Rouge. On the following day the Federals attacked the port, held by some 16,000 men under Gen. Franklin Gardner, but were repulsed. Banks then laid siege to Port Hudson. On June 11 and June 14 he made two more unsuccessful assaults. Although the garrison suffered terrible deprivation, it held out until July 9, when it learned that Vicksburg, upriver, had fallen, thus rendering Port Hudson untenable. Total Confederate losses were 7,200, including 5,500 who surrendered. The siege cost the Federals 3,000 in killed, wounded, and missing. The Mississippi River was now in complete possession of the Union, and the Confederate States were cut in two. *See* New Orleans II; Chickasaw Bluffs; Vicksburg; American Civil War.

Portland (First English-Dutch War), 1653. The fourth clash in the naval war between the English Commonwealth and the Netherlands took place off Portland on the southern coast of England. The Dutch commander was again Adm. Maarten Tromp, this time reinforced by the ships of Michel de Ruyter. For the English it was the fourth action for Adm. Robert Blake, who was aided by Gens. George Monck (later duke of Albemarle) and Richard Deane. The battle opened on February 18, 1653. On this day only some of the 70 Commonwealth ships took part, and they were worsted by the Dutch, who were intent on protecting a convoy of 200 merchantmen. The English pursued the enemy eastward. On the following day, off the Isle of Wight, the English destroyed or captured 5 of the 80 Dutch warships. The Netherlands broke off the engagement on February 20, having lost a total of 10 combat vessels and 40 merchant ships. English ship losses were comparable but Blake suffered a serious wound. *See* Dungeness; North Foreland I; English-Dutch Wars.

Porto Bello (War of Jenkins' Ear), 1739. During the reign of George II, increasing naval friction between Great Britain and the Spain of Philip V led to war. In 1731 at Havana an English sailor, Robert Jenkins, reputedly had an ear cut off by a Spanish captain named Fandino. This incident provided the immediate cause of hostilities, which were not formally declared until October 19, 1739. Sir Robert Walpole sent a British fleet of six ships under Adm. Edward (Old Grog) Vernon into the Caribbean Sea. On November 22 Vernon attacked and captured the Spanish settlement of Porto Bello on the Isthmus of Panama. A later assault on Cartagena, on the northwest coast of Colombia, was repulsed, however. Thereafter, the War of Jenkins' Ear merged into the larger War of the Austrian Succession. *See* Passero Cape; Mollwitz.

Porto Novo (Mysore-British War II), 1781. Seeing an opportunity to strike at the British East India Company, Haider (Hyder) Ali, the maharaja of Mysore, resumed hostilities in 1780 in alliance with France, which was then engaged with Great Britain in the War of the American Revolution. Mysorean troops invaded the Carnatic on the southeastern coast, destroying the British posts. From Madras Gov.-Gen. Warren Hastings sent out an army under the command of Gen. Sir Eyre Coote. The able Coote brought Haidar to battle at Porto Novo, 125 miles south of Madras, on July 1, 1781. The English and allied Indian army routed their opponents, restoring British control. Haidar died the next year. His son Tipu Sahib continued to oppose the British but avoided a pitched battle for the remainder of this Mysore war, officially ended in 1784. *See* Seringapatam I; Madras III; Mysore-British Wars.

Port Republic (American Civil War). The second half of the last battle, on June 9, 1862, fought by the Confederate general Thomas (Stonewall) Jackson against Federal forces in the Shenandoah Valley. *See* Cross Keys–Port Republic.

Port Royal I (King William's War), 1690. The European struggle against King Louis XIV of France, called the War of the Grand Alliance, became a small English-French conflict in North America known as King William's War. The chief English offensive, under Sir William Phips, was directed against Port Royal (later renamed Annapolis Royal), on the western coast of Nova Scotia. In the spring of 1690 Phips attacked the fortress with an army composed largely of Massachusetts militiamen. The French garrison surrendered on May 11. Phips then launched an attack against Quebec on the Saint Lawrence but was rebuffed. Meanwhile, the French retook Port Royal the following year and retained it by the terms of the Peace of Ryswick, signed in 1697. *See* Port Royal II; King William's War.

Port Royal II (Queen Anne's War), 1710. The French stronghold of Port Royal, on the western coast of Nova Scotia, had twice changed hands in King William's War (War of the Grand Alliance in Europe), which took place during 1689–97. In the following English-French conflict, Queen Anne's War (War of the Spanish Succession), it again came under attack, in 1704 and 1707. A third English expedition, commanded by Col. Francis Nicholson and Sir Charles Hobby, launched a new assault in 1710. Finally, on October 16, the fortress surrendered. Coming permanently under British rule, it was renamed Annapolis Royal in honor of the British monarch. *See* Port Royal I; Queen Anne's War.

Port Royal Island (War of the American Revolution), 1779. With the British capture of Savannah, Ga., late in 1778, the war in the southern states became a series of probing actions for the next six months. In the first of these battles Gen. Augustine Prevost, British commander in Georgia, sent 200 men, under Maj. Gardiner, to seize Port Royal Island at the mouth of the Broad River in South Carolina. From his headquarters at Purysburg, S.C., Gen. Benjamin Lincoln, American commander in the South, ordered Gen. William Moultrie to check the British advance. Moultrie, at the head of 300 militia, occupied the town of Beaufort on the island. On February 3, 1779, Gardiner tried to oust the Americans but was repulsed with heavy losses in less than an hour. The British retreated to their ships, giving up the invasion effort. American losses were 8 killed and 22 wounded. *See* Savannah I; Kettle Creek; American Revolution.

Portugal. The major battles and wars fought by the nation of Portugal are listed below.

Ourique	1139
Lisbon	1147
Santarém I	1171
Alcácer do Sal	1217
Aljubarrota	1385
Ceuta	1415
Tangier	1437
Diu	1509
Goa	1510
Alcázarquivir	1578
Alcántara	1580
Montijo	1644

See Spanish Succession, War of the
See Napoleonic Empire Wars—Peninsular War

Santarém II 1834
See World War I

Po Valley (World War II), 1945. After a five-month winter stalemate on the Italian front, the U.S. general Mark Clark's Fifteenth Army Group stood ready to resume the offensive against Gen. Heinrich Vietinghoff-Scheel's German Tenth and Fourteenth armies. The Allied plan was to break through the mountainous heights of the Gothic Line and destroy the German forces on the plains south of the Po River.

The offensive opened on April 9 with a three-corps attack by the British Eighth Army on the east (Adriatic) flank. Despite stubborn German resistance, Gen. Richard McCreery's Eighth Army V Corps fought its way up Highway 16 into the Argenta Gap on the right, while the Polish II Corps on the left captured Imola, on the road to Bologna, on April 14. The same day Gen. Lucian Truscott's U.S. Fifth Army took up the attack, the II Corps driving north toward Bologna while the IV Corps struck west of the city. (The 92nd Infantry Division held the long front stretching westward to the Ligurian Sea.) Led by the 10th Mountain Division, the Americans broke into open country northwest of Bologna on April 20. The half-encircled city fell to the Poles the next day.

Both Allied armies now raced northward, trapping thousands of Germans in the rear. On April 23 the U.S. 10th Mountain forced the Po southeast of Mantua. As other Allied units closed up to the river, the two German armies fled across the Po. Under devastating air attack, Vietinghoff-Scheel's forces lost most of their heavy equipment. North of the Po the pursuit became a rout as Allied columns knifed northward toward the foothills of the Alps. Behind the collapsing German front Italian partisans rose up. They seized control in Genoa, Milan, and Venice. (On April 28 one partisan band captured and executed the erstwhile Italian dictator Mussolini and his mistress.)

The Fifth Army entered Verona on April 26 and Milan three days later. On the right, the Eighth Army, driving around the head of the Adriatic, linked up with Tito's Yugoslav partisans on May 1. Meanwhile Vietinghoff-Scheel had formalized the wholesale German capitulations. On April 29 he had unconditionally surrendered the German forces in Italy to Field Marshal Sir Harold Alexander, effective May 2. (At that time Alexander commanded combat units from eight different nations.) Almost a million Germans laid down their arms, ending the 20-month Allied campaign in Italy. It was the first of the large-scale Nazi surrenders, between May 2 and 8, 1945, that ended the war in Europe.

Although Italy was always a secondary theater in World War II, it drained away vital German strength, much as the fighting in Spain had sapped the French Empire of Napoleon 135 years earlier. In all, Allied casualties in Italy numbered almost 350,000. The German total of killed, wounded, and missing was higher. *See* Gothic Line; Germany, East; Germany, West; World War II.

Prague I (Hussite Wars), 1420. The betrayal and execution for heresy of John Hus at the Council of Constance in 1415 provoked an anti-Roman Catholic uprising among his followers in Prague. Pope Martin V proclaimed a crusade against the rebellious Bohemians. In response Sigismund, king of Hungary and Bohemia and Holy Roman Emperor, sent imperial troops to Prague. Sigismund had raised a huge army but organized it no better than the force that had been mauled by the Turks at Nicopolis in 1396. The Bohemians rallied behind Jan Zizka, leader of the Taborite, or extreme, faction of the Hussites. They closed the gates of the city and entrenched themselves outside the walls on the Hill of Witkov. When Sigismund's host attacked on July 14, 1420, Zizka thoroughly repulsed them with only 9,000 men. It was the first demonstration of Zizka's military genius, which would become the terror of eastern Europe during the next four years. And Sigismund would find the gates of Prague closed to him for 16 years. *See* Kutná Hora; Hussite Wars.

Prague II (Thirty Years' War), 1648. While peace negotiators worked in Westphalia to end the long, bitter conflict, the Holy Roman Empire of Ferdinand III faced a new danger in Bohemia. A Swedish army under the marshal Count Johan von Königsmarck marched on Prague during the summer of 1648 and called for a surrender. There were virtually no Imperial troops to send to the aid of the city. But Prague, which had capitulated without a fight twice before in the war (1620 and 1635), now arose in fierce resistance. Townspeople, students, and religious joined to repel the Swedish besiegers. For more than three months Prague grimly held out with no prospect of relief. Finally the signing of the Treaty of Westphalia, on October 24, ended the war and saved the city. Nine days later the Swedes withdrew. Meanwhile, the last pitched battle of the war had taken place in northwest France. *See* Zusmarshausen; Lens; Thirty Years' War.

Prague III (War of the Austrian Succession), 1744. The Austrian conquest of Bavaria and the expulsion of France from Germany worried Frederick II, the Great, of Prussia. Fearing that Maria Theresa, disputed empress of the Holy Roman Empire, would next try to retake Silesia from him, Frederick concluded a new alliance with Louis XV of France and Charles Albert, elector of Bavaria, who claimed to be Emperor Charles VII of the Holy Roman Empire. At the head of 80,000 men, the Prussian king marched through

Saxony and invaded Bohemia, thus launching the Second Silesian War.

On September 2 he reached Prague. After six days of attack the Austrian garrison surrendered. Frederick penetrated farther up the Vltava (Moldau) toward the border of present-day Austria. But no French army moved to aid him, and the Bavarians were too weak to stop the Imperial forces (which now included Saxony) from concentrating against Frederick. When Prince Charles of Lorraine, brother-in-law of Maria Theresa, arrived with the Austrian army from the Rhine, Frederick turned back north. His retreat harried by Prince Charles and Hungarian irregulars, the king abandoned Prague and pulled back into Silesia with heavy losses. Meanwhile, the first serious fighting of the war was taking place in Italy. *See* Chotusitz; Dettingen; Velletri; Austrian Succession, War of the.

Prague IV (Seven Years' War), 1757. In the second year of the war Frederick II, the Great, concentrated his Prussian forces for an attack on Prague. Here Prince Charles of Lorraine, brother-in-law of Holy Roman Empress Maria Theresa, had deployed 66,000 Imperial troops. When Frederick arrived at the Bohemian city on May 5, 1757, with 64,000 men, he found the defenses too strong to assault. Moving up the Moldau River that night, the Prussians crossed over to strike the Austrian right flank the following morning. A faulty reconnaissance sent the attackers floundering through moss-grown bogs where they were shattered by Austrian guns. Among the thousands who fell was Field Marshal Count Kurt von Schwerin, able veteran of the War of the Austrian Succession.

Despite the bloody repulse, Frederick re-formed his lines and attacked a second time, his left flank protected by Gen. Hans von Zieten's wide cavalry sweep. As the Prussian infantry advanced, Zieten drove off the Austrian horsemen, to fall on the flank and rear of the enemy foot soldiers. This coordinated assault crumbled the Imperial lines. Prince Charles fell back behind the defenses of Prague, leaving 10,000 dead and wounded on the field (including Field Marshal Count Maximilian von Browne), plus more than 4,000 prisoners. Some 16,000 Austrians retreated 20 miles to the southeast to join a second Imperial army under Field Marshal Count Leopold von Daun. The Prussians, who also lost 14,000 in killed, wounded, and missing, took up a siege of Prague. *See* Lobositz; Kolin; Seven Years' War.

Praia (War of the American Revolution), 1781. The third European nation, after France and Spain, to enter the war against Great Britain was the Netherlands, on December 20, 1780. To protect the Dutch settlement at the Cape of Good Hope against possible British attack, a French squadron of five warships led a convoy out of Brest on March 22, 1781. Under the command of Adm. Pierre André de Suffren, the French squadron reached the Portuguese-owned Cape Verde Islands on April 16. Here, in the harbor of Praia (Porto Praya) on São Tiago Island, Suffren encountered a British fleet of 5 warships and 35 transports commanded by Com. George Johnstone. The British expeditionary force was en route to the Cape, as the French government of Louis XVI had anticipated. Unhesitatingly, Suffren sent his convoy on to the south while he sailed into the neutral port, guns blazing. Before the British commander could form his ships into battle order, Suffren's flagship, *Héros,* led the French ships back out to sea. Johnstone was trapped. He could not pursue without abandoning his transports. And when he did get all his ships under way again, he found that Suffren had beaten him to the Cape by two weeks, thus making the Dutch position too strong to attack. Johnstone returned to England, while Suffren went on to contest British control of the Bay of Bengal. *See* Madras III; American Revolution.

Prairie Grove (American Civil War), 1862. After their victory at Pea Ridge in March, Federal forces held a firm grip on northwestern Arkansas. General James Blunt's division of 7,000 men stood at Prairie Grove, about 15 miles south of Fayetteville. To destroy this isolated force, the Confederate general Thomas Hindman left Van Buren, Ark., on December 3 with 11,000 Confederates. By the evening of December 6 Hindman was ready to attack Blunt, when he learned that a second Federal force of 3,000 men under Gen. Francis Herron was marching down from Missouri. Leaving a cavalry screen opposite Blunt, Hindman circled to the east to get between the two enemy armies. The following morning the Confederates struck the lead elements of Herron's column and drove them back. Instead of following up his advantage against Herron, who had just completed a 125-mile march, Hindman took up a defensive position. Herron's tired troops made three unsuccessful attacks against the entrenched Confederates. But now Blunt, who had heard the battle sounds to his rear, came up to strike Hindman's left flank. Only a fierce cavalry counterattack enabled the Confederates to hold their position. That night Hindman withdrew to the south. He had lost 1,317 men. The combined Federal losses were 1,251. *See* Pea Ridge; American Civil War.

Preston I (English Civil War), 1648. For two years after the Cavalier collapse ended the Civil War, all England and Scotland lay in the grip of the New Model army, the military arm of the Roundheads. King Charles I was in semi-exile on the Isle of Wight. Then in the spring of 1648 a series of uprisings against the army shook Britain. In this so-called Second Civil War the Royalists, Parliament, London, the Presbyterians, the Scots army, and many of the common people were aligned against the rule of Oliver Cromwell and his lieutenants Lord Thomas Fairfax and Henry Ireton. But the army was invincible. It ruthlessly suppressed all opposition, and when 20,000 Scots invaded northern England, it marched to meet them at Preston in Lancashire. Although Gen. David Leslie remained in nominal charge of the invaders, the tactical command lay with James Hamilton (1st duke of Hamilton). During August 17–20 the disorganized and poorly led Scottish force was attacked and destroyed piecemeal by 8,500 well-trained veterans of Cromwell. Hamilton was captured and executed. This ended the Second Civil War. Cromwell, as military dictator, stood supreme. Charles was brought to trial and beheaded on January 30, 1649. Only Ireland remained in opposition to the new Commonwealth government of England. *See* Stow-on-the-Wold; Rathmines; English Civil War.

Preston II ("the Fifteen"), 1715. Unhappy with the Hannoverian king George I, supporters of the Old Pretender, James Edward (as James III), rose in revolt in northern England in the fall of 1715. Their leader, the Earl of Derwentwater (James Radcliffe), failed to link up with a similar Jacobite uprising in Scotland. But reinforced by Scots to some 4,000 men, the rebels marched on Preston, in Lancashire, and occupied it. A royal army under Gen. Charles Wills attacked the city on November 13 (the same day the Scottish rebels were checked at Sheriffmuir). The Jacobites resisted stoutly but on the following day surrendered. The uprising collapsed with this battle. Derwentwater and 29 others were executed the following year. But the failure of the British government to break up the Highland clans of Scotland led to the more serious "Forty-five" Rebellion 30 years later. *See* Sheriffmuir; Prestonpans; Jacobite Insurrections.

Prestonpans ("the Forty-five"), 1745. Despite the crushing of the '15 Rebellion, the Highland clans of Scotland remained opposed to the 1707 union of Scotland and England and to the Hannoverian kings George I and II. When the Young Pretender, Prince Charles Edward, landed in the Western Isles of Scotland (from France) on July 25, 1745, the clans flew to arms to support the prince's claims for his father as James III of England and James VIII of Scotland. Lord George Murray collected an army of 2,000 Scottish Jacobites at Glenfinnan in southeast Scotland. He marched southward to Prestonpans, where the rebels were intercepted by a royal army of 3,000 men under Gen. Sir John Cope. On September 21 the Highlanders charged and routed the government force. More than a thousand royalists were captured and hundreds killed or wounded. Murray's losses numbered less than 150.

The master of most of Scotland, Prince Charles Edward crossed the border into England, taking Carlisle, Penrith, Lancaster, and Preston. He penetrated as far as Derby in central England, 125 miles from London, before the lack of new recruits forced him to retrace his march. *See* Preston II; Falkirk II; Jacobite Insurrections.

Preveza (Christian-Turkish Naval Wars), 1538. The growing sea power of the Ottoman Turks worked a particular hardship on the maritime economy of Venice. In 1538 Holy Roman Emperor Charles V, Pope Paul III, and Venice combined in a Holy League to deal with the Turks. A Christian fleet commanded by Andrea Doria of Genoa sailed to the west coast of Greece in 1538. Here lay the Ottoman navy of Suleiman I, the Magnificent, under the direction of the able Barbary pirate Barbarossa II (Khaireddin). The two hostile fleets fought a sharp engagement off Preveza at the entrance to the Ambracian Gulf. After losing seven galleys without inflicting a single loss on the Turks, Doria withdrew. Two years later the Venetians gave up the unequal struggle, surrendering their last trading station on the Peloponnesus. *See* Tunis III; Malta I.

Priesten (Napoleonic Empire Wars). A small village in the mountains south of Dresden where a Russian army checked a French pursuit on August 30, 1813, following Napoleon's victory at Dresden. *See* Kulm-Priesten.

"Prince of Wales"–"Repulse" (World War II), 1941. When the outbreak of war in the Pacific became imminent, the British Admiralty sent the 35,000-ton battleship *Prince of Wales* and the 33,000-ton battle cruiser *Repulse* to Singapore. To defend against the Japanese invasion of the upper Malay Peninsula, which began on December 8, Adm. Tom Phillips took the two large ships and four destroyers into the South China Sea. Two days later Japanese bombers and torpedo bombers, based near Saigon, attacked the capital ships, 84 bombers striking in waves of about 9 planes each. Unprotected by fighter planes of their own, the warships could offer only unequal battle. Mauled by successive torpedo hits, the *Repulse* sank in an hour and a half, the *Prince of Wales* an hour later. Admiral Phillips and a thousand men were lost. Four enemy planes had been shot down. Japanese naval power stood supreme in the Pacific Ocean west of Hawaii. *See* Pearl Harbor; Malaya; Singapore; World War II.

Princeton (War of the American Revolution), 1777. When the British commander, Gen. Sir William Howe, learned that his Hessian mercenaries had lost Trenton during the last week of 1776, he sent Gen. Lord Charles Cornwallis to try to retake the city. On January 2 Cornwallis confronted the 5,200-man American army of Gen. George Washington east of Trenton. He postponed an attack, however, until the following day. That night Washington took his outnumbered Continentals around the left flank of Cornwallis to fall on the British rear guard at Princeton commanded by Col. Charles Mawhood. In the morning Washington drove the enemy back toward New Brunswick. British losses were about 400, including prisoners; the Continentals suffered 40 killed or wounded. The outmaneuvered Cornwallis wheeled about to advance on Princeton, but Washington slipped away to the north. When the Americans took up a strong position in the hills around Morristown, Howe ordered his troops back into winter quarters. Washington's lightning strokes at Trenton and Princeton had liberated all but the eastern part of New Jersey. Congress returned to Philadelphia from Baltimore. *See* Trenton; Brandywine Creek; American Revolution.

Prussia. For the battles and wars fought by the Prussians until their rise to power in 1701 *see* German States of the Holy Roman Empire. Prussia steadily increased in power until it launched a three-war campaign of aggression, during 1864–1870, which forged the German Empire of the Second Reich. For later conflicts *see* Germany.

See Great Northern War
See Spanish Succession, War of the
See Austrian Succession, War of the
See Seven Years' War
See French Revolution, Wars of the;
Napoleonic Empire Wars;
Napoleon's Hundred Days
Dybböl 1864
See Seven Weeks' War
See Franco-Prussian War

Przemyśl (World War I). A fortified city in southeastern Poland held by Austria-Hungary; the only land fortress to suffer prolonged siege in the war, it resisted Russian capture during September 24–October 11, 1914, but capitulated after a second siege that lasted from November 6, 1914 to March 22, 1915; three months later Russian forces were driven from the city. *See* Galicia; Gorlice-Tarnów.

Puebla I (U.S.-Mexican War), 1847. While Gen. Winfield Scott's army was establishing control over Mexico City, a Mexican army struck at the American line of communications leading back to Veracruz. At Puebla, 65 miles to the east, Gen. Joaquin Rea surrounded the American garrison on September 14 and demanded its surrender. The beleaguered commander, Col. Thomas Childs, refused, even though most of his 2,300 troops consisted of wounded and convalescents. Childs's position became more desperate when Gen. Antonio de Santa Anna, who had fled from Mexico City and renounced the presidency, arrived with about 8,000 additional troops. On October 1, however, Santa Anna left Puebla, weakening the will of the besiegers. Eleven days later an expedition from Veracruz led by Gen. Joseph Lane forced the Mexicans to raise the siege. This was the last conflict of the war. On February 2 the Treaty of Guadalupe Hidalgo brought peace between the United States and Mexico. *See* Chapultepec; U.S.-Mexican War.

Puebla II (French-Mexican War), 1862–1863. During the American Civil War, the Mexican government of Benito Juárez suspended payment on foreign debts. French, British, and Spanish troops occupied Veracruz on December 17, 1861. Great Britain and Spain withdrew the next spring, but Louis Napoleon III determined to establish a Mexican government under French hegemony. A French army of 7,500 men under the Comte de Lorencez marched inland. On May 5, 1862, Lorencez attacked Puebla, which was defended by some 12,000 Mexicans, commanded by Gen. Ignacio Zaragoza. The French were repulsed with more than 400 casualties. Mexican losses were 215 killed and wounded. Lorencez was replaced by Gen. Élie Forey.

In 1863 the French army, reinforced by troops from abroad and by Mexican Conservatives, launched a new drive into the interior. Puebla came under attack on May 4 by a force under Forey. The garrison, led by Gen. Jesús Gonzales Ortega, resisted stubbornly. However, four days later a Mexican relief column under Ignacio Comonfort was ambushed and routed by a French detachment commanded by Gen. Achille Bazaine. Comonfort was killed. With all hope gone Gonzales Ortega surrendered Puebla on May 17. The victorious French pushed on into Mexico City on June 7. Archduke Ferdinand Maximilian of Austria was installed as emperor. *See* Calpulalpam; Querétaro.

Pulj (Venetian-Genoese Wars), 1379. The maritime rivalry between Venice and Genoa brought on a new war (often called the War of Chioggia) between the two Italian sea powers in 1379. A Genoese fleet of 22 galleys under Luciano Doria sailed up the Adriatric to attack the Venetian navy based at Pulj (Pola) on the Istrian Peninsula (now in Yugoslavia). The Venetian navy, under Vittorio Pisano, sallied out and captured the attackers' flagship, killing Doria. Undaunted, the Genoese fought back fiercely, sinking 15 out of the 20 Venetian galleys. Pisano retreated into the harbor with his surviving vessels. *See* Curzola; Chioggia.

Pultusk I (Great Northern War), 1703. After his victory at Klissow and subsequent capture of Kraków (Cracow) in 1702, King Charles XII of Sweden wintered in Poland. The following spring he turned back north seeking out another Saxon army. (Augustus II, the elector of Saxony and deposed king of Poland, was in hiding.) At Pultusk, 32 miles north of Warsaw, the Swedes came upon a force of some 10,000 Saxons, about the size of their own army. When Charles launched his attack on April 21, the enemy force held only momentarily before taking to their heels. The Saxons lost only 600 killed and 1,000 captured. The Swedish king then turned northwest to the great Polish fortress of Thorn (Toruń). *See* Klissow; Thorn; Great Northern War.

Pultusk II (Napoleonic Empire Wars), 1806. While Napoleon I shattered the Prussian armies in the fall of 1806, King Frederick William III fled eastward to Russia with some 10,000 troops still intact. Here the Prussians received the support of Czar Alexander I, who was mobilizing a 100,000-man army to hold Russian Poland. Boldly the Grande Armée marched eastward, Marshal Joachim Murat's cavalry reaching Warsaw on November 26. Crossing the Vistula downstream (northwest) of the Polish capital with the bulk of his army, Napoleon closed up to the left of Murat's thrust in December. The 50,000 Russian troops (plus the Prussian corps) in the area, commanded by Gen. Levin Bennigsen, steadily gave ground back to the Narew River. Here on December 26 Marshal Jean Lannes with 20,000 men lunged forward to Pultusk, 32 miles north of Warsaw. In a sharp fight Bennigsen's 37,000 defenders held the town until nightfall. Then, claiming a major victory, the Russian general fell back to Ostroleka and later northward toward Königsberg (Kaliningrad), on the Baltic. French accounts report 5,000 Russian casualties at a loss of only 1,500 to themselves. The Russians claim to have inflicted 8,000 casualties on the attackers of Pultusk. Both sides now halted operations to go into winter quarters. *See* Lübeck; Eylau; Napoleonic Empire Wars.

Punic Wars (264–146 B.C.). A fight over Messina in 264 B.C. brought on the first of three Punic Wars between the two largest powers in the Mediterranean—Rome and Carthage. In each conflict Rome was the victor, the third ending in the extinction of Carthage.

First Punic War

Messina I	264 B.C.
Mylae	260 B.C.
Ecnomus	256 B.C.
Tunis I	255 B.C.
Panormus	251 B.C.
Lilybaeum	250–241 B.C.
Drepanum	249 B.C.
Aegates Islands	241 B.C.

Second Punic War

Saguntum	219–218 B.C.
Trebbia River I	218 B.C.
Trasimeno Lake	217 B.C.
Cannae	216 B.C.
Nola	215 B.C.
Syracuse III	214–212 B.C.
Capua	212–211 B.C.
New Carthage	209 B.C.
Metaurus River	207 B.C.
Ilipa	206 B.C.
Utica I	203 B.C.
Zama	202 B.C.

Third Punic War

Carthage I	149–146 B.C.

Pusan Perimeter (Korean War), 1950. Spearheaded by tanks, the army of North Korea crossed the 38th parallel at 11 points on June 25 and plunged southward into the Republic of Korea. Caught unprepared, the South Korean army of Gen. Chae Byong Duk reeled back from the 200-mile border. The capital of Seoul fell in three days as the North Koreans under Gen. Chai Ung Chai bridged the Han River on June 30 and pressed forward down the length of the peninsula, the I Corps on the west, II Corps to the east. Under the auspices of the United Nations, Gen. Douglas MacArthur flew in United States troops from Japan to aid the South Koreans. The first American ground forces (700 men from the 24th

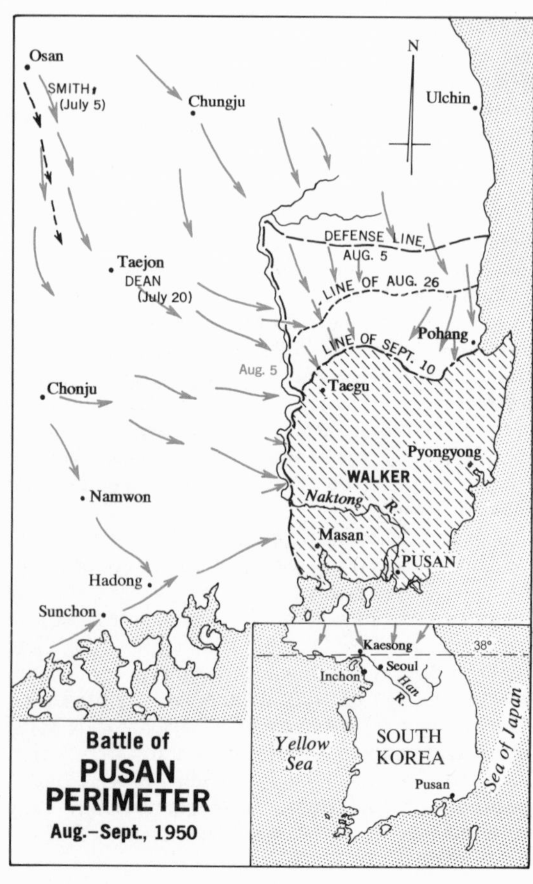

Battle of PUSAN PERIMETER Aug.–Sept., 1950

Infantry Division under Col. Charles Smith) took up positions at Osan, 30 miles south of Seoul, on July 5. Without effective antitank weapons, the combined American–South Korean forces could not halt the armored thrusts of the Russian-made T-34 tanks employed by the North Koreans. About 150 Americans were killed, wounded, or missing in the first Communist attack.

As more United States units arrived by air and sea, Gen. William Dean of the 24th Division committed them in a series of delaying actions along the vital Seoul-Taejon-Pusan axis. But the retreat continued. Taejon fell on July 20. Dean himself was wounded and later captured. Meanwhile, on July 13 Gen. Walton Walker had assumed command of the United States Eighth Army in Korea, which soon included the 1st Cavalry and 25th Infantry (and later the 2nd Infantry) divisions, as well as marines. Despite American dominance of the air and sea, the Eighth Army and South Korean units were pushed back to the Naktong River by August 5. Pohang, 63 miles northeast of Pusan, fell on August 11. In a perimeter around the key port of Pusan, in the southeast, the Eighth Army dug in for a desperate defense.

The North Koreans, who had suffered an estimated 58,000 casualties in their drive southward, hammered at the perimeter defenses and managed to secure several bridgeheads across the Naktong, in the west. Taegu, 55 miles to the northwest, and Masan, 29 miles west, were seriously threatened. But Walker made maximum use of his interior-line position to shift reserves to trouble spots. By the end of August all Communist penetration attempts had been checked or eliminated. At that time Walker commanded 91,500 Republic of Korea (ROK) troops, 87,000 Americans, and 1,500 British. In September the fighting at the edge of the perimeter showed a gradual diminishment of North Korean offensive power. Meanwhile in Japan, MacArthur organized an amphibious strike behind the Communist lines in the Seoul area. *See* Inchon; Korean War.

Pydna (Third Macedonian War), 168 B.C. When King Philip V of Macedonia died in 179 B.C., his son Perseus succeeded to the throne. Carrying on the national grudge against Rome, Perseus precipitated the Third Macedonian War eight years later. In 171 at Larissa, in eastern Thessaly, a Macedonian army under Perseus repulsed a large force of Romans but did not follow up its advantage. Two years later Lucius Aemilius Paulus (Macedonicus) led a Roman army into Macedonia. On June 22, 168 B.C., Perseus attacked the invaders at Pydna, on the west shore of the Gulf of Salonika. The first surge of the Macedonian phalanx drove the Romans back. But the fighting over rough ground gradually fragmented the phalanx. Taking advantage of the Macedonian disarray the legionaries launched a fierce counterattack that cut their opponents to pieces. The long-famous Macedonian phalanx was totally annihilated, in its last battle. In all, some 20,000 were killed and 11,000 taken prisoner. More than 100 Romans were killed.

The following year Perseus was dethroned and taken as a captive to Rome. Macedonia was divided into four weak republics and forced to pay tribute to Rome. The mighty empire forged by the military genius of Philip II and Alexander the Great had come to an end. (A pretender to the now-extinct Macedonian throne, Andriscus, revolted in 149, to cause the so-called Fourth Macedonian War. The uprising was crushed the following year, Andriscus executed, and Macedonia made a Roman province.)

To nail down its conquest of all of Greece, the Roman army marched into Aetolia, which had been allied to Macedonia, and executed 500 rebels. Moving on to Achaea, the Romans whisked off 1,000 hostages, including the historian Polybius, to Italy. *See* Cynoscephalae II; Corinth; Macedonian Wars.

Pylos-Sphacteria (Great Peloponnesian War), 425 B.C. The Athenian general Demosthenes sailed a fleet south to the Peloponnesus in 425 where he seized and began fortifying the promontory of Pylos on the southwest coast. The alarmed Spartans immediately isolated Demosthenes by occupying the offshore island of Sphacteria. The Spartan force was in turn blockaded by the Athenian fleet. When the double siege threatened to last indefinitely, the Athenian leader Cleon put himself in direct command and quickly captured the island of Sphacteria. The 120 Spartans taken prisoner in the assault were held as hostages to guard against a future invasion of Attica. But the prolonged fighting in the Peloponnesus forced the Athenians to call off Demosthenes' expedition. *See* Mytilene; Delium; Peloponnesian Wars.

Pyongyang (Chinese-Japanese War I), 1894. The war opened with a Japanese attack on Pyongyang (now in North Korea), then held by China under the name Heijo. Some 12,000 Chinese troops occupied the city. On September 16 Gen. Marquis Michitsura Nodzu led an assault by 14,000 Japanese soldiers. Better armed and better disciplined, Nodzu's army routed the Chinese with heavy losses. The Japanese suffered only 650 casualties. *See* Yalu River I; Chinese-Japanese War I.

Pyramids (Wars of the French Revolution), 1798. After driving the Austrian armies out of northern Italy, Napoleon Bonaparte turned across the Mediterranean to strike at the British in India by way of Egypt, then part of the Turkish Empire. On May 19, 1798, he sailed from Toulon at the head of an expeditionary force of 36,000 men. Stopping at Malta on June 10, he seized that island from the Order of the Knights of Malta and then went on to land in Egypt, west of Alexandria, on July 1. The following day the French invaders seized Alexandria from the Mameluke ruler, Ibrahim Bey. Ibrahim crossed to the east of the Nile and prepared to flee into Syria. But the Mameluke military commander, Murad Bey, determined to block the French advance toward Cairo by holding Embabeh, north of the Pyramids, on the left bank of the Nile. Although he had 40,000 troops at his command, Murad could count on only the 6,000-man Mameluke cavalry.

On July 21 Napoleon moved southward on the Egyptian position along the river, while sending a strong flanking column westward to envelop the enemy's left. To avoid being pocketed against the Nile, Murad launched an all-out cavalry assault to his front. The Mameluke horsemen fought fiercely, but they were no match for French muskets and artillery. When the counterassault failed, the entire Egyptian army collapsed. The French flanking column closed in to take Embabeh, cutting off large numbers of the disorganized Egyptian infantry. Murad fell back to the south unmolested, while Napoleon, who had suffered only about 300 casualties, crossed the river the next day to occupy Cairo.

The invasion of Egypt seemed completely successful. But on August 1 the protecting French fleet was shattered by a British attack at the mouth of the Nile. Cut off from Europe by sea, Napoleon turned eastward to attack the Ottoman Empire in Syria. *See* Malborghetto; Malta II; Nile River; Acre III; French Revolution Wars.

Q

Quadruple Alliance, War of the (1718). A coalition formed by Great Britain, France, the Netherlands, and Austria that successfully checked Spanish aggression in the Mediterranean Sea. *See* Passero Cape.

Quatre Bras (Napoleon's Hundred Days), 1815. When Napoleon Bonaparte returned from exile to lead the revived French armies in the spring of 1815, he struck northward across the Belgian frontier. Here his objective was to drive a wedge between the Prussian army of Field Marshal Gen. Gebhard von Blücher on the right (east) and the Anglo-Dutch army of the Duke of Wellington (Arthur Wellesley) on the west. While Napoleon himself attacked Blücher, Marshal Michel Ney led the French left wing up the Brussels road toward Quatre Bras on June 16. Ney, with 25,000 troops, drove the Anglo-Dutch army of Prince William of Orange back into the town early in the afternoon. But just when the French seemed on the verge of sweeping aside the 36,000 enemy troops, Wellington rushed up the English division of Gen. Sir Thomas Picton. The allied line stiffened. Ney, through a misunderstanding with Napoleon, failed to use the I Corps on his right and thus threw away his chance of winning a decisive victory. Darkness halted the fighting with the French suffering 4,300 casualties, the allies 4,700. In the morning Wellington pulled back his army toward Waterloo. *See* Ligny; Waterloo; Napoleon's Hundred Days.

Quebec I (French and Indian War), 1759. While an overland expedition was clearing the French from western New York in 1759, the British launched the biggest attack of the war, against Quebec, 300 miles up the Saint Lawrence River. A combined force of 9,000 soldiers under Gen. James Wolfe and a fleet of 20 ships (Adm. Charles Saunders) moved up the river gateway to New France early in the summer. On June 27 troops were landed without opposition on Île d'Orléans, just downstream from Quebec. Wolfe also sent a force to occupy Pointe Levi (Levis), on the right bank of the river opposite the city. Part of the fleet carried some troops beyond Quebec on July 18 in order to threaten French communications upriver. But further progress seemed blocked by a stout defense which Gen. Marquis Louis de Montcalm organized with 14,000 men (despite the interference of the incompetent governor-general, the Marquis de Vaudreuil-Cavagnal).

Wolfe had landed a detachment under Gen. George Townshend on the north bank of the Saint Lawrence River, below the city. On July 31 Townshend launched an attack from this direction. But at the Montmorency River, a northern tributary of the main stream, the British were repulsed with a loss of almost 500 men. This position was abandoned on September 3.

Encouraged by a probing attack above the city in August, Wolfe slipped past Quebec with 4,500 men in small boats on the night of September 12. Landing two miles upriver, Wolfe's men found a trail up the cliffs that debouched them onto a plateau called the Plains of Abraham. As the mist cleared on the morning of September 13, Montcalm marched out from the city with a force of

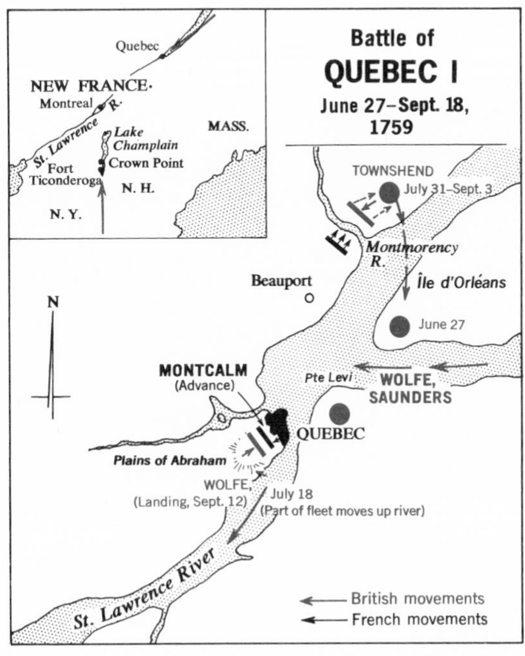

equal size. Both armies deployed in the formal European military style of the eighteenth century. As the French advanced, massed volleys of one-ounce balls from British muskets (the closest fired at a distance of 40 yards) shattered their ranks. In 15 minutes more than 1,400 killed and wounded fell, including the fatally wounded Montcalm. British losses in killed and wounded totaled only 660. Wolfe, wounded three times, died on the field.

After their bloody repulse on the Plains of Abraham the French retreated into Quebec itself. Behind strong fortifications, and still having a superiority in numbers, the garrison might have held out indefinitely. But Vaudreuil-Cavagnal fled, eventually to Montreal, and on September 18 the city surrendered.

The battle of Quebec was the turning point in the French and Indian War. It led to the British conquest of all Canada and determined that North America would be essentially an English rather than a French continent. Thus it ranks as one of the decisive battles of history. *See* Fort Niagara; Quebec II; French and Indian War.

Quebec II (French and Indian War), 1760. After the loss of Quebec to the British in September 1759, the governor-general of New France, the Marquis de Vaudreuil-Cavagnal, retreated up the Saint Lawrence River to Montreal. The following spring he sent out Gen. Duc François de Lévis with 8,500 men with orders to retake the Canadian capital. As Lévis approached the city, Gen. James Murray, who had succeeded the slain general James Wolfe as British troop commander in Canada, marched out to meet the attackers. On April 27 the two armies clashed southwest of Quebec. Outnumbered 2 to 1, Murray was defeated with a loss of a third of his force. He fell back into the city and barely managed to hold Quebec until a British fleet arrived with reinforcements and supplies the following month. Lévis then retreated back to Montreal, most of his Canadian militia and Indians deserting en route. In July Murray moved upriver to take part in the multiple British offensive against Montreal. *See* Quebec I; Montreal; French and Indian War.

Quebec III (War of the American Revolution), 1775. In the first year of the war the American Continental Congress authorized a two-pronged invasion of British-held Canada. General Richard Montgomery, moving northward from Ticonderoga, took Saint Johns (Saint-Jean) on the Richelieu River on November 2, 1775, and occupied Montreal eleven days later. Marching down the Saint Lawrence River, he reached Quebec with 300 men on December 3. Here, on the Plains of Abraham, he joined a band of 600 hardy colonials, under Col. Benedict Arnold, who had cut their way 350 miles through the Maine wilderness to Quebec the previous month. The combined American armies launched an attack against the city early in the snowy morning of December 31—Arnold striking the Lower Town on the north, Montgomery on the south. The British defending force of 1,800 men, commanded by Gen. Sir Guy Carleton, decisively repulsed the rash assault. Montgomery was killed and Arnold wounded. In all, almost 100 Americans were killed or wounded and another 300 taken prisoner. British losses were 5 killed and 13 wounded. The colonials remained outside Quebec for the remainder of the winter but in April ended the disastrous expedition by falling back to Lake Champlain. *See* Valcour Island; American Revolution.

Queen Anne's War (1701–1713). The War of the Spanish Succession in Europe spread to North America where the fighting between French and English was called Queen Anne's War, for the reigning British monarch. The only major battle in the colonies took place at Port Royal in 1710. Three years later the Treaty of Utrecht ended both the European and American phases of the war. *See* Port Royal II; Spanish Succession, War of the.

Queenston Heights (War of 1812), 1812. The western prong of the multiple American offensive against British Canada ended in the craven surrender of Detroit on Aug. 16, 1812. The middle prong got off to a better start when Gen. Stephen Van Rensselaer invaded Ontario, across the Niagara River from New York State, on October 13. Van Rensselaer's attack carried Queenston Heights and killed the British commander, Gen. Sir Isaac Brock (who had been knighted for his victory at Detroit). The British, however, rallied some 1,000 men and counterattacked the 600 Americans on the heights. Expected American reinforcements did not appear because the New York militia refused to leave the state. Van Rensselaer, his army shattered, fell back across the border and retired from command. His successor, Gen. Alexander Smyth, made a feeble effort to force the Niagara River on November 28 before he was relieved.

Meanwhile the eastern, and largest, prong of the offensive got under way from Plattsburg, N.Y. Under the command of Gen. Henry Dearborn, the expedition moved up Lake Champlain with Montreal its objective. But at the Canadian border, on November 19, Dearborn's militia troops balked at going any farther, and he was forced to return to Plattsburg. *See* Detroit; Frenchtown; War of 1812.

Querétaro (French-Mexican War), 1867. With the French army of Louis Napoleon III in control of Mexico, through Napoleon's puppet Archduke Ferdinand Maximilian of Austria, the Mexican government of Benito Juárez fled across the U.S. border. Here Gen. Mariano Escobedo organized a new Mexican army. Re-entering his country in 1865, Escobedo fought his way southward against the French–Mexican Conservative forces of Miguel

Miramón. Then, under pressure from the United States, Napoleon withdrew his army from Mexico on March 12, 1867. Escobedo pushed forward, hurriedly trapping Maximilian and Miramón in Querétaro, 160 miles northwest of Mexico City. On May 14 the republicans stormed into the town, taking Maximilian and Miramón captive. Both were executed. Juárez restored order and on December 19 was elected president of Mexico. *See* Puebla II.

Quiberon (Wars of the French Revolution), 1795. In northwestern France the peasants of the department of Vendée remained largely Royalist (supporters of the executed Louis XVI), opposing the National Convention in a series of uprisings beginning in 1793. On June 27, 1795, a British fleet landed 3,600 French émigrés at the base of the Quiberon Peninsula of southern Brittany. Here the expeditonary force was strengthened by thousands of Royalists. However, Gen. Louis Hoche marched a Revolutionary army into the region and in a series of engagements during July 16–21 captured 6,000 of the poorly led rebels. Among the prisoners, about 700 were identified as émigrés and promptly executed. Only about 1,800 managed to re-embark for England. This victory of Hoche's broke the back of the Vendée uprisings, which were completely suppressed by March 5 of the following year. *See* Fleurus III; Loano; French Revolution Wars.

Quiberon Bay (Seven Years' War), 1759. Despite the ruin of their Toulon fleet at Lagos Bay in August, the French of Louis XV continued their plan to invade Scotland. On November 14, 1759, Marshal de Conflans (a sea officer despite his title) sailed from Brest with 21 ships of the line. On the same day Adm. Edward Hawke sailed from England with a fleet of 23 warships. To elude the English navy, De Conflans moved southeast along the underside of the Brittany peninsula. On November 20 he put into Quiberon Bay. Despite the dangerous shoals, made more treacherous by a strong wind and heavy sea, Hawke followed. The chase now ended in a wild melee. Seven French warships were captured or destroyed. Seven others escaped up the mouth of a small river, where the last one did not work itself free for two years. The remainder found refuge southward at Rochefort. The heavy losses, plus the hopelessly divided condition of the French fleet, ended the government's hope of carrying the offensive to Great Britain. Hawke lost only two vessels, which were wrecked on the shoals. *See* Lagos II; Martinique; Warburg; Seven Years' War.

R

Raab (Napoleonic Empire Wars), 1809. Learning of Napoleon I's victory on April 22 at Eggmühl (Eckmühl), Eugène de Beauharnais, viceroy of Italy and stepson of the emperor, launched a complementary offensive in northeastern Italy from behind the Adige River. His opponent, Archduke John, brother of the Austrian emperor Francis I, fearing to be cut off from the main Austrian army in the Danube Valley, fell back eastward. John's 40,000-man army yielded the line of the Isonzo in May and withdrew into Hungary. Fortified by the news of Napoleon's check at Aspern-Essling, John attempted to make a stand at Raab (Györ), 70 miles southeast of Vienna, on June 14. But Beauharnais, with an army of comparable size, struck hard, inflicting more than 5,000 casualties on the Austrians. French losses were less than 3,000. Although John held his ground until nightfall, he withdrew under cover of darkness, crossed the Danube, and moved upstream. At Pressburg (Bratislava), however, 30 miles from Vienna, he was stopped by French troops. Meanwhile, Beauharnais besieged and took Raab on June 25 and then linked up with Napoleon's army at Vienna. *See* Sacile; Eggmühl; Aspern-Essling; Wagram; Napoleonic Empire Wars.

Rabaul (World War II), 1943–1944. In Japan's sweeping Pacific conquests early in 1942, the Australian base of Rabaul on northern New Britain Island became an early victim. The battle opened with heavy air attacks from Truk (in the Carolines) and from Adm. Chuichi Nagumo's carriers (back from Pearl Harbor). On January 23 Japanese troops landed at Rabaul and at the neighboring base of Kavieng on New Ireland Island (both islands parts of the Bismarck Archipelago). The small Australian garrisons were quickly overwhelmed. Japan then developed Rabaul, and to a lesser extent Kavieng, into a formidable naval and air base anchoring its Southwest Pacific line.

When the Allies launched their counteroffensive in that area, it was decided to bypass and isolate Rabaul. The first step came during June 22–30, 1943, when the U.S. 112th Cavalry and 158th Infantry regiments seized the Woodlark and Trobriand islands in the Solomon Sea to the south. From these bases, plus new airfields acquired in the advance up the Solomon Islands ladder, Allied aircraft smashed repeatedly at Rabaul. U.S. carrier-based planes of Adm. William Halsey's Third Fleet joined in this long-term reduction.

On December 15, 1943, the 112th Combat Team bounded to Arawe, on the southwest coast of New Britain. But this was only preliminary to a major amphibious landing by the U.S. 1st Marine Division (William Rupertus) at Cape Gloucester, 75 miles to the northwest, on December 26. On the fourth day the marines captured the Cape Gloucester airstrip and by January 16, 1944, had dug in an impregnable perimeter around the field, opening it to Allied planes. From here the 1st Marine Division leapfrogged almost halfway up the north coast to seize Talasea between March 6 and 8. In all, the marines killed 5,000 and captured 500 of Gen. Iwao Matsuda's 10,000 Japanese on New Britain, at a cost of 310 dead and 1,083 wounded. General Douglas MacArthur's Southwest Pacific Command (including Adm. Thomas Kinkaid's Seventh Fleet) now had access to the straits between New Britain and New Guinea. Meanwhile Maj. Gregory (Pappy) Boyington had become the top marine ace of World War II. He destroyed 28 enemy planes before being shot down and captured near Rabaul on January 2.

Elsewhere the Allies completed the encirclement of Rabaul. The 3rd New Zealand Division took the Green Islands, 115 miles east of Rabaul, on February 15. Two weeks later the U.S. 1st Cavalry Division landed at Los Negros in the Admiralties to the west. Early in March these troops occupied Manus, thus controlling the Admiralties and cutting off Japanese communications with Rabaul to the southeast. In the Admiralties' fighting, 3,300 Japanese were killed or captured, while 300 Americans lost their lives. On March 20 the U.S. 4th Marine Regiment occupied Emirau Island in the Bismarcks, 70 miles north of Kavieng. The construction and use of airfields on all these conquered islands reduced Rabaul and Kavieng to impotency. More than 100,000 Japanese at these two bases were left to die on the vine as the Allied offensive moved west and north. *See* Solomon Islands; New Guinea; Tarawa-Makin; World War II.

Race to the Sea (World War I). A series of

flanking maneuvers by both the German and the Allied armies that extended the Western Front from Noyon northward to the North Sea in September and October 1914; the term is a misnomer in that the objective was not to reach the coast but to turn each other's flank. *See* Aisne River I; Ypres I.

Radcot Bridge (Revolt against Richard II), 1387. A clique of English barons called the Lords Appellant, holding most of the nation's military power, dominated the court of Richard II. To counteract this force, Robert de Vere (Earl of Oxford) mustered an army of 4,000 royalists in the west and marched toward London. At Radcot Bridge, over the upper Thames in Oxfordshire, Oxford encountered the baronial cavalry commanded by Henry Bolingbroke (Earl of Derby and later Henry IV) and Thomas of Woodstock (Duke of Gloucester). After a short skirmish, the royalists broke and fled. Oxford escaped and went into exile. The battle left Richard II at the mercy of the militant barons. Twelve years later he was mortally challenged by Bolingbroke for the crown of England. *See* Margate; Ravenspur I.

Radnor (English Conquest of Wales), 1282. The Welsh leader Llewelyn ab Gruffydd, who had opposed Henry III in the Second Barons' War, also resisted the rule of the king's son and successor, Edward I. In 1282 Edward marched into the hills of eastern Wales. He encountered the Welsh at Radnor and defeated them. Llewelyn was killed. His brother David was hanged and quartered the following year. (During this campaign the English learned the deadly efficiency of the Welsh longbow). Wales came under the administration of the English crown. Edward's fourth son, later Edward II, was named Prince of Wales. He thus became the first heir to the English throne to receive that title. *See* Ely II; Berwick upon Tweed.

Rain (Thirty Years' War), 1632. The victory of Gustavus II of Sweden at Breitenfeld and his subsequent sweep into The Palatinate gave the Protestant forces a dominant position in Germany. The Swedish king now commanded a powerful army of his own (including some Scots and Germans), plus more than 60,000 troops that the Protestant German princes put at his disposal. After wintering at Frankfort on the Main, Gustavus set out on March 2, 1632, for Bavaria. Here Field Marshal the Count of Tilly was hurriedly reorganizing the army of the Holy Roman Empire (Ferdinand II). When Gustavus crossed the Danube at Donauwörth on April 7, Tilly fell back eastward beyond the Lech River, 22 miles north of Augsburg. The Swedish army of 25,000 men reached the left (west) bank of the river opposite the village of Rain a week later. On April 15 Gustavus opened a heavy artillery bombardment on Tilly's troops, which numbered about 20,000. Under cover of this fire the Swedes forced a crossing of the river and charged the Imperial positions. Tilly, who was mortally wounded, could not prevent the Catholic army from bolting the field, leaving their artillery and baggage to the enemy.

The remnants of the demoralized Catholic forces were collected by Maximilian I, elector of Bavaria. Emperor Ferdinand then recalled to command Gen. Count Albrecht von Wallenstein, who had been dismissed two years earlier after fighting the battles of Dessau Bridge, Stralsund, and Wolgast. Meanwhile, on April 24 Gustavus entered Augsburg and in mid-May, Munich. In June he set up headquarters in Nürnberg, preparing to organize the Protestant princes of Germany into a cohesive union. *See* Breitenfeld I; Fürth; Thirty Years' War.

Ramadi (World War I), 1917. Following his capture of Baghdad, the British commander in Mesopotamia, Gen. Sir Frederick Maude, consolidated his position during the summer. When cooler weather arrived, he resumed his offensive against the Turks in modern Iraq. Maude marched his Anglo-Indian army 60 miles westward to Ramadi where a strong Turkish garrison held the right bank of the Euphrates River. In a two-day attack, September 28–29, the British overwhelmed the enemy force, taking most of them prisoner. Maude returned to Baghdad where he died of cholera on November 18. His successor, Gen. Sir William Marshall, was ordered to send two divisions to Gen. Sir Edmund Allenby in Palestine, thus limiting Marshall's future operations. *See* Baghdad IV; Sharqat; World War I.

Ramillies (War of the Spanish Succession), 1706. In the sixth year of the war the major scene of combat shifted to the Spanish Netherlands. Here King Louis XIV of France ordered Marshal the Duc de Villeroi to attack eastward from the Dyle River to the Meuse, between Namur and Liége. En route, the French were intercepted by the allied English-Dutch-German army under the Duke of Marlborough (John Churchill). On May 23 Marlborough deployed his 50,000 men in the path of Villeroi's movement, near the village of Ramillies. The English duke feigned an attack on the French left (north), then struck hard on the other flank, south of Ramillies. Marlborough's 25,000-man cavalry force rode down the French horsemen, who numbered about the same, wheeled to their right, and rolled up the entire rear of the French line.

Meanwhile, the allied infantry made a frontal assault on Ramillies. This twin onslaught shattered the 50,000-man army of Villeroi (who was thereafter replaced by Marshal Louis Joseph, duc de Vendôme, transferred from Italy). Some 15,000 were killed, wounded, or captured. The allied losses were only a third as great. This victory led to the surrender of Brussels, Antwerp, and most of modern Belgium. The French position seemed desperate, but as after Blenheim two years earlier, the allies could not coordinate a decisive stroke against Louis XIV. *See* Blenheim; Turin; Stollhofen; Spanish Succession, War of the.

Ramleh I (First Crusade), 1102. The massacre in Asia Minor of all three armies of reinforcement for the First Crusade forced King Baldwin I of Jerusalem to defend the Holy Land with the few troops who had elected to stay in the East after the Christian conquest of 1099. Determined to oust the crusaders, the Caliph of Cairo sent an army into Palestine in 1101. King Baldwin turned back this threat at Ramleh (Er Ramle), a key fortress on the road from Jerusalem to the coast. The following year a second and larger army of Arab light horse and Sudanese infantry marched north from Egypt. Baldwin met the attack at Ramleh again. But with only 500 knights in his assault Baldwin was driven back. At the end of the day he and the other leaders sought refuge in a tower. The king escaped during the night to return the following day with a relief force, which routed the Moslems. But meanwhile, Stephen of Blois, Conrad, the German constable of the Holy Roman Empire, and the others in the tower had been killed.

Three years later the Caliph of Cairo sent up another army. Although large in numbers, it was poorly trained and equipped. King Baldwin again repelled the invaders at Ramleh. *See* Jerusalem VII; Ereğli II; Dyrrachium III; Antioch II; Crusades.

Ramleh II (Crusader-Turkish Wars), 1177. When the competent Turkish general Saladin made himself master of Egypt in 1169 and of Damascus in 1174, the Christian states of the Near East stood in grave danger of going under. The end seemed at hand in the autumn of 1177 when Saladin marched a great army of Mamelukes up from Egypt, brushing aside a force of Knights Templars at Gaza. Baldwin IV, the 17-year-old king of Jerusalem, hurried into the fortress at Ashkelon with 500 knights. Saladin had enough troops to invest Ashkelon with part of his force while moving on to the undefended Holy City with the rest of his army.

But young King Baldwin, although handicapped by leprosy, proved to be a skillful warrior. He sent a message to the bypassed Templars at Gaza ordering an attack on the rear of the besiegers of Ashkelon. During the ensuing struggle outside the walls, Baldwin broke through the lines with his knights. Picking up reinforcements on the way, he rode hard after Saladin. Baldwin's cavalry struck the rear of the Turkish column outside Ramleh (Er Ramle) on the road from Jaffa to Jerusalem. The sudden charge disrupted the Mamelukes. They panicked and fled back toward Egypt, barely safeguarding the life of their leader. It was a vital triumph for the Christians, who now had obtained a few years' respite from the mighty Saladin. *See* Ashkelon II; Tiberias; Crusades.

Ramnagar (Sikh-British War II), 1848. When the Sikhs tried to throw over the regency of Sir Henry Lawrence, imposed after their defeat in the first war, the scene of conflict shifted from East to West Punjab. General Sir Hugh Gough, again in command of Anglo-Indian forces, marched up to the Chenab River, 55 miles northwest of Lahore. On November 22 he tried to force a crossing against some 35,000 Sikhs deployed opposite Ramnagar. Heavy artillery fire and fierce resistance on the ground hurled back the attackers with heavy losses. *See* Sobraon; Chilianwala; Sikh-British Wars.

Rancagua (Chilean War of Independence), 1814. The first revolutionary government of Chile was established by José de Carrera, who overthrew Spanish control in 1811. However, the opposition of another rebel, Bernardo O'Higgins, led to dissension among the Chileans. This division enabled the Spanish viceroy to field an army against the revolutionaries. At Rancagua, 48 miles south of Santiago, in central Chile, the royal troops met the rebels on October 1. In a two-day battle in which Carrera offered only belated support to O'Higgins, the Spaniards won decisively. Santiago was taken and the royal government re-established. *See* Chacabuco.

Raphia (Wars of the Hellenistic Monarchies), 217 B.C. When Antiochus III took the throne of the Seleucid Empire in 233 B.C., he inherited little but the capital of Antioch. The Damascene and three Syrian wars with Egypt (280–41) had gradually whittled down the western part of the empire founded by Seleucus I Nicator. Most of the eastern part had broken away as the kingdom of Parthia, isolating the state of Bactria, still farther east.

Determined to rebuild his empire, Antiochus marched against the Egyptian Empire of Ptolemy IV. At Raphia (Rafa), on the Palestine-Egyptian frontier, Antiochus with 20,000 men met 25,000 Egyptian troops and drove them back. In the pursuit the Syrian phalanx became disorganized. The Egyptians then counterattacked and completely routed the Syrians. Antiochus lost 14,000 killed and 4,000 captured. This battle ended the Fourth Syrian War.

Antiochus was an able leader, however. He rebuilt his army and during the next four years won back much of Asia Minor. Turning eastward he re-established Seleucid hegemony over Parthia and Bactria during 209–04. These successes won him the title Antiochus the Great. Only his defeat by Egypt remained to be avenged. *See* Pergamum; Sellasia; Panion; Hellenistic Monarchies, Wars of the.

Rathmines (English Civil War), 1649. While England and Scotland were torn by the great Civil War, Ireland also suffered from an internecine conflict. Here the Marquis (later Duke) of Ormonde (James Butler), led the Royalist-Catholic forces against the Roundhead army of Col. Michael Jones. At the end of July 1649 Ormonde had encamped before the Parliamentary city of Dublin. While Ormonde prepared an attack, Jones made a sudden sortie from the city on August 2. The English rolled up Ormonde's advance column south of Dublin and then fell on the surprised Irish camp at Rathmines. Jones's men routed the Royalists completely, killing and capturing several thousand of the enemy and seizing Ormonde's artillery. Despite this victory, Oliver Cromwell continued his plans to subdue Ireland personally. *See* Preston I; Drogheda; English Civil Wars.

Rava Russkaya (World War I). A Russian victory, on September 9, 1914, which opened a 40-mile gap in the Austrian lines and resulted in a deep advance into Galicia. *See* Galicia.

Ravenna I (Gothic Conquest of Italy), 491–493. After the Heruli chieftain Odoacer (Odovacar) had deposed Romulus Augustulus, the last ruler of the Western Roman Empire, in 476, Italy lay at the mercy of the barbarians. Odoacer had himself proclaimed king and sought to reign from the former Roman capital of Ravenna. But general lawlessness ruled the land. Then in 489 Theodoric the Great, king of the Ostrogoths, invaded northeast Italy upon the advice of the Byzantine emperor, Zeno the Isaurian.

Odoacer, failing to stop the Ostrogoth invaders at Aquileia and Verona, retired to Ravenna. Theodoric promptly besieged his enemy here for three years. Then, under the protection of a truce, the Ostrogoth entered the city and treacherously executed the Heruli king. Theodoric and his successors ruled the Italian peninsula until overthrown by the Byzantine emperor Justinian half a century later. *See* Pavia II; Rome III.

Ravenna II (Wars of the Byzantine Empire), 729. When the Byzantine emperor Leo III, the Isaurian, outlawed image worship in the Roman Catholic Church in 726, his beliefs brought him into conflict with Pope Gregory II. To enforce his papal edict, Leo sent an army to Ravenna in northeast Italy. Here Pope Gregory had assembled an armed force to defend both his tolerance of images and his secular rule in Italy. After a sharp struggle the Byzantines were driven back to their ships and forced to re-embark for Constantinople. This battle widened the breach between the Byzantine Empire and the Church. *See* Constantinople IV; Ravenna III.

Ravenna III (Frankish Invasion of Italy), 756. The Lombard kingdom that had become established in northern Italy in 572 stood at odds with the papacy in Rome most of the time. Under King Aistulf, the Lombards seized Ravenna in 751. This ancient city was technically the Italian capital of the Byzantine Empire. But after years of neglect by Constantinople, it now lay between the contention of Lombardy and Rome. Alarmed at the growing power of Aistulf, Pope Stephen II asked aid from Pepin III, the Short (son of Charles Martel and farther of Charlemagne), king of the Franks. In 756 Pepin marched across the Alps and with a minimum of military action chased the Lombards out of Ravenna. He then gave the pope the conquered territory. This "Donation of Pepin" was the foundation of the Papal State and the tacit recognition of the papacy as the temporal successor to the Roman Empire in Italy. *See* Pavia III; Ravenna II; Pavia IV.

Ravenna IV (French-Spanish Wars in Italy), 1512. When the League of Cambrai broke up and turned against the France of Louis XII, Pope Julius II held Ravenna, on the northeastern coast of Italy. The French army, under Louis' nephew the Duc de Nemours (Gaston de Foix), moved east from Milan to besiege Ravenna. To relieve the city, the Spanish king Ferdinand, who also ruled Naples, sent out an army commanded by the Conde de Alvetto (Pedro Navarro) and the Marquis de Pescara (Fernando de Avalos). On April 11, 1512, the Spanish took the French siege lines under heavy fire with cannon and arquebuses mounted on wheels. For three hours the French infantry held their positions despite the deadly fusillade. Meanwhile, on a flank, Nemours deployed 24 French cannon, which began raking the Spanish lines with a murderous return fire. Then the French lansquenets (a phalanx of hired German pikemen and musketeers) charged, supported by a cavalry assault. The battered sword-and-buckler men of Spain were virtually annihilated. But Louis's victory in one of the bloodiest battles of the century only increased his troubles. Nemours had fallen at his moment of triumph. And the Holy Roman Empire of Maximilian I and the Swiss cantons now joined the coalition against France. *See* Agnadello; Oran I; Novara I.

Ravenspur I (Deposition of Richard II), 1399. While Richard II of England was leading his second expedition in Ireland, his exiled rival, Henry Bolingbroke of Lancaster, sailed across the Channel from France. Henry landed at Ravenspur, at the mouth of the Humber in Yorkshire, July 4, 1399. He met no organized resistance. Joined by most of the northern barons, Henry marched on London. Richard, hurrying back, could not halt what had now become an irresistible advance. The king gave himself up in mid-August and submitted to imprisonment in the Tower, where he was (probably) murdered the following year. The victor had himself crowned as Henry IV. *See* Radcot Bridge; Homildon Hill.

Ravenspur II (Wars of the Roses), 1471. When the Earl of Warwick (Richard Neville, the Kingmaker), and George, Duke of Clarence (younger brother of King Edward IV) landed at Devonshire in September 1470, the southern counties joined their cause. Marching to London, Warwick freed the hapless Lancastrian (red rose) Henry VI from the Tower and recrowned him on October 13. Meanwhile Edward fled to the Burgundy court of Charles the Bold on September 29. Here Edward's brother-in-law outfitted him with 1,200 Flemish and German mercenaries and enough ships to return to England in force.

Edward's Yorkist (white rose) expeditionary force eluded the Warwick-Lancastrian fleet in the English Channel and landed at Ravenspur in Yorkshire on March 14, 1471. The fighting monarch dispersed the weak attempts to resist his small but well-disciplined force. When the Earl of Northumberland (John Neville), with a 4-to-1 superiority in numbers, blocked his advance southward, Edward skillfully maneuvered around him and marched into London. The unfortunate Henry VI went back to the Tower on April 11. But Warwick had been busy assembling his own army, and a showdown battle loomed between Edward's Yorkists and the turncoat Kingmaker, who was now leading the Lancastrians. *See* Lose-coat Field; Barnet; Roses, Wars of the.

Ré, Île de (English-French Wars), 1627. During the Huguenot uprising in France against King Louis XIII and his minister Cardinal Richelieu, England sought to aid the besieged Protestant stronghold of La Rochelle on the west coast of France. In 1627 Charles I sent George Villiers, 1st duke of Buckingham, with an expedition to seize the Île de Ré, offshore in the Bay of Biscay. The English landed on the island in July but were held up by the citadel. When French reinforcements under Comte Henri de Schomberg arrived in October, Buckingham was forced to abandon the siege. His retirement cost hundreds of lives both on the island and at sea. Two later English expeditions failed, and La Rochelle fell to Richelieu in October 1628. Charles then concluded peace with France the following year. *See* La Rochelle II.

Reading (Danish Invasions of Britain), 871. Beginning with the battle of Ashdown in January, the year 871 became a long series of conflicts between the Danes and the West Saxons of Wessex under Ethelred I and his brother Alfred. In an effort to win a decisive battle, the brothers led an attack against the Danish camp at Reading, 40 miles west of London. The Wessex warriors charged bravely, but were unable to break into the enemy entrenchments. They were repulsed and driven from the field with heavy losses. It was now the Vikings' turn to take the offensive. *See* Ashdown; Wilton; Danish Invasions of Britain.

"Rebellion, The." *See* Jacobite Insurrections.

Redan (Crimean War). A strong defensive position on the south of Sevastopol that fell to the British on September 8, 1855; although the position was recaptured by the Russians, the battle led to the evacuation of the city three days later. *See* Sevastopol I.

Reims (Napoleonic Empire Wars), 1814. After his setback at Laon on March 10, 1814, Napoleon I fell back to Soissons, on the middle Aisne River. Two days later he learned that an allied force had recaptured Reims, 40 miles to the east. With less than 30,000 men the French emperor marched across the entire front of the Prussian field marshal Gen. Gebhard von Blücher's army, which was three times the size of the French army, to fall on Reims on March 13. His sudden attack routed the 13,000 Prussians and Russians under Gen. Saint-Priest. The city was recovered at a loss of less than 1,000 casualties. Allied losses were 6,000. This victory, however, was the last of the campaign for the energetic French commander. He stood 83 miles northeast of Paris between two allied armies, each of which was much larger than his own fought-out army. *See* Laon; Arcis-sur-Aube; Napoleonic Empire Wars.

Remagen (World War II). The capture of the only standing bridge over the Rhine River, the Ludendorf, at Remagen, on March 7, 1945, by the U.S. 9th Armored Division, opened the way for the Allied advance into the heart of Germany. *See* Rhineland.

Resaca (American Civil War), 1864. After the Federal capture of Chattanooga in November 1863, there was no action on this front for more than five months. During this time Gen. William Sherman replaced Gen. U. S. Grant, who moved to Virginia to oversee the offensive against Richmond. Sherman built up a force of 98,000 men, divided into three armies: the Tennessee (James McPherson), the Cumberland (George Thomas), and the Ohio (John Schofield). The Confederate commander, Gen. Joseph Johnston, who had replaced Gen. Braxton Bragg, stood on Rocky Face Ridge with some 50,000 troops, protecting Dalton, Ga.

On May 7 Sherman began his advance on Atlanta. A turning movement to the southwest maneuvered Johnston out of his strong position on Rocky Face on May 12 and 13. The Confederate commander retired southward to Resaca where he took up another good position. Sherman attacked here on May 14 on a broad front north and west of the town—Schofield on the left, Thomas in the center, McPherson on the right. Johnston, reinforced to 60,000 by the addition of Gen. Leonidas

Polk's corps, beat off the assaults. But when Sherman again threatened to circle westward and get in his rear, Johnston retreated farther south the following night. *See* Chattanooga; Kenesaw Mountain; American Civil War.

Resaca de la Palma (U.S.-Mexican War), 1846. After the American victory at Palo Alto on May 8, Gen. Zachary Taylor pushed on southward to the relief of besieged Fort Texas on the Rio Grande. Four miles short of his goal, Taylor found the route blocked a second time by the Mexican general Mariano Arista. The Mexican army of 5,700 men occupied a strong position in a dry river bed. Without waiting for reinforcements, the American general deployed his 1,700 troops in a facing ravine called the Resaca de la Palma. The battle opened at 2 P.M. on May 9 with a heavy fire fight, in which American rifles and artillery proved superior. The battle blazed until late in the afternoon, when the Mexican army broke in disorder, fleeing across the Rio Grande. Taylor's troops pursued closely. Many Mexicans drowned in the river in addition to the 262 killed, 355 wounded, and some 150 captured or missing. American losses were 39 killed, 83 wounded. Fort Texas was relieved several hours later.

Taylor, who became a national hero with his victory at Resaca de la Palma, crossed the Rio Grande on May 18 to occupy Matamoros, which Arista had evacuated the previous day. Here the Americans halted to await reinforcements before carrying the war deeper into Mexico. *See* Fort Texas; Palo Alto; Monterrey; U.S.-Mexican War.

Reunions, War of the. *See* Louis XIV, Wars of; Mons I.

Reval (Wars of Scandinavia), 1219. The Danish conquest of German Baltic lands which began under Canute VI continued under his brother and successor, Waldemar II. In a battle at Reval (now Tallin) in modern Estonia, the Danes were hard pressed by an army of Germans. At a critical moment a red and white flag (the Dannebrog, which became the national banner of Denmark) miraculously came into the possession of Waldemar, or appeared in the sky according to one account. Rallying under the new banner, the Danes threw back their opponents and went on to seize all of Estonia. *See* Viborg; Bornhöved.

Rheinfelden (Thirty Years' War), 1638. After remaining on the defensive west of the Rhine for more than three years, the Protestant German army (in the pay of France) under Bernhard, duke of Saxe-Weimar, swung over to the attack early in 1638. Saxe-Weimar invested Rheinfelden on the upper Rhine, a few miles east of Basel (now in Switzerland), and then began crossing the river. He had about half of his troops across on March 2 when the bridgehead was struck by a Bavarian army of the Holy Roman Empire (Ferdinand III) hurrying up from the Black Forest. The attack, led by Gen. Johann von Werth (Jean de Weert), placed Saxe-Weimar in a precarious position. But under cover of night the duke took his forward troops up the Rhine a few miles, crossed over to the left bank, and on the following morning moved back down the river to Rheinfelden, where Werth had crossed over. The counterthrust caught the Imperials by surprise. All who did not flee were captured, including Werth. Saxe-Weimar's biggest loss was the mortal wounding of the Huguenot general the Duc de Rohan. The Franco-German army now moved on the key Rhine fortress of Breisach, gateway to Germany. *See* Wittstock; Breisach; Thirty Years' War.

Rhineland (World War II), 1945. Before the last of the German attackers had been driven out of the Ardennes bulge, the Allies had resumed their offensive against the Siegfried Line. Progress was so slow, however, that a large-scale effort became necessary to effect a breakthrough to the Rhine Valley.

On February 8 the Canadian First Army (Henry Crerar) launched Operation Veritable, a major attack southeast from Nijmegen, Holland, between the Meuse and the Rhine. The latter was reached on February 14. A converging thrust by the U.S. Ninth Army (William Simpson), called Operation Grenade, crossed the Roer River on February 23. The two advances linked up at Geldern, Germany, on March 3. Two days later the Allies had pressed to the Rhine from opposite Düsseldorf northward, leaving only a small German bridgehead at Xanten-Wesel. The Canadians eliminated this pocket on March 10. Meanwhile, to the south, the left wing of the U.S. First Army (Courtney Hodges) attacked toward Cologne on February 23 to cover the Ninth Army's right flank. This offensive swept across the Rhine plain, while the U.S. Third Army of Gen. George Patton punched its way through the Siegfried Line north of the Moselle River.

On the central front the rest of the First Army and the Third Army, both under the group command of Gen. Omar Bradley, launched a broad attack on March 5 toward the middle Rhine (Operation Lumberjack). By March 10 the Americans had closed to the river from Coblenz northward through Bonn and Cologne (which fell March 7), to link up with the Canadians at Wesel.

The rapid advance to the Rhine yielded a surprising and rich dividend. On March 7 the U.S. 9th Armored Division discovered the railroad bridge at Remagen still standing. (It was the only Rhine bridge not demolished by the Germans.) In a daring gamble, leading elements dashed across the Rhine and seized a bridgehead on the east bank. Gen. Dwight Eisenhower, supreme Allied commander in Europe, ordered the new breakthrough hurriedly reinforced. Despite German counterattacks and determined efforts to wreck the bridge, Hodges rushed three corps (III, V, VII) across the river by bridge, pontoon, and ferry. By March 21 the bridgehead had grown to 20 miles long and 8 miles deep. (The Remagen success caused the Allies to shift the main axis of their attack from Field Marshal Sir Bernard Montgomery's northern group of armies to Bradley's central force.)

During the Remagen bridgehead build-up, the U.S. general Jacob Devers' Sixth Army Group launched its own advance to the Rhine (Operation Undertone). It took the form of a huge pincers movement against SS Gen. Paul Hausser's Seventh and First German armies. On March 15 the right wing of Patton's Third Army attacked south across the Moselle River into the Saar. Two days later Gen. Alexander Patch's U.S. Seventh Army began hammering through the Siegfried Line, headed northeast. By March 21 the joint U.S. offensive had crushed all German opposition west of the Rhine except for a shrinking foothold around Landau. Then on March 22 Patton's 5th Infantry Division wheeled from south to east and plunged across the Rhine at Oppenheim. Encouraged by light opposition in this area, the VIII Corps bridged the river at Boppard, 40 miles to the north, on March 24. Germany's last natural defensive barrier had now been breached in three places on Bradley's front.

The Rhineland battle inflicted a major defeat on three Nazi army groups—Johannes Blaskowitz in the north, Walther Model in the center, Hausser in the south. Some 60,000 Germans were killed or wounded and almost 250,000 captured. This heavy toll, plus the loss of much heavy equipment, ruined the Nazi chances of holding the Allied armies at the Rhine. Americans killed in action totaled 6,570; British and Canadian deaths were markedly fewer. *See* Siegfried Line; Ardennes II; Germany, West; World War II.

Rhodes (Capture by Turks), 1522. The steady westward march of the Ottoman Turks made precarious the Christian hold on Rhodes, at the eastern end of the Mediterranean. Conquered by the Knights of Saint John of Jerusalem (the Hospitalers) in 1310, the island withstood a three-month siege by the Ottomans in 1480. In 1522, however, with Rhodesian pirates threatening his communication lines with Egypt, Suleiman I, the Magnificent, launched an iron-handed siege of the island, on July 28. The Knights resisted valiantly, but no help came from the West, and on December 21 the famine-stricken garrison surrendered. The Turks had lost heavily through disease and battle casualties (perhaps 60,000 men), but persistent sea blockade, plus effective artillery and the first use of bombs, made possible their strategic victory. (In 1530 Holy Roman Emperor Charles V reestablished the Knights of Saint John on Malta.) *See* Belgrade II; Mohács; Baghdad III.

Riade (Wars of the German States), 933. The Magyars of modern Hungary temporarily ended their terrorizing of central Europe with a truce negotiated by Henry I, the Fowler, in 924. Henry, the first of the Saxon kings in Germany, used the nine-year respite to strengthen fortifications in Saxony and Thuringia. He broke the truce in 933 by swooping down on the Magyars at Riade, on the Saale River a few miles south of Merseberg. The mail-clad German cavalry crushed the more lightly armored horsemen of the barbarians. The first severe defeat of the Magyars, it stopped further raids for 20 years. *See* Louvain; Lechfeld.

Richmond, Ky. (American Civil War), 1862. During the summer of 1862 both the Federal and Confederate armies in the West shifted forces into eastern Tennessee and Kentucky, to open up a new front in that region. On August 14 Gen. Edmund Kirby-Smith marched northward from Knoxville with a Confederate force of 9,000 men. Rather than attack the 8,000 Federal troops of Gen. George W. Morgan at Cumberland Gap, Kirby-Smith bypassed that position and moved into eastern Kentucky. This maneuver forced Morgan to evacuate Cumberland Gap. Pressing on northward, Kirby-Smith found Richmond held by 6,500 inexperienced Federal troops, sent forward from Louisville. This force, commanded by Gens. Mahlon Manson and Charles Cruft, checked the Confederate advance just south of Richmond on August 29. On the following morning Kirby-Smith's army, now closed up, launched a vigorous assault. In hard fighting the Federals were driven back into Richmond, where Gen. William Nelson could not rally them. Nelson was wounded and Manson wounded and captured as the defeated army retreated toward Louisville. In all, there were 206 Federals killed, 844 wounded, and 4,303 missing (most of whom were captured). Kirby-Smith, who had suffered 78 killed and 372 wounded, moved to Lexington, then turned southwest to link up with Gen. Braxton Bragg's army at Perryville. *See* Shiloh; Perryville; American Civil War.

Rich Mountain (American Civil War), 1861. During the opening weeks of the Civil War, both North and South maneuvered armies in western Virginia to try to establish domination of this area, in which the sympathies of the populace leaned toward the Union. General Robert Garnett, in command of the Confederate forces at Beverly (in present-day West Virginia), posted Lt. Col. John Pegram with two regiments at Rich Mountain in Randolph County. To attack this position, Gen. George McClellan, commander of the Department of the Ohio (River), sent out four regiments under Gen. William Rosecrans. On July 11 the Federals circled around the left (south) of Pegram's position, cutting off his line of retreat. After a short but hopeless battle, Pegram surrendered 553 officers and men the following evening. Federal casualties totaled 46. Pegram was later exchanged and served the South until killed in 1865. Garnett was killed during the retreat of his main army, which began after he had learned of the loss of Rich Mountain. The Federal victory here skyrocketed the reputation of McClellan, especially following the Northern disaster at Bull Run. *See* Philippi, W. Va.; Bull Run I; Cheat Mountain; American Civil War.

Riel's Rebellion. *See* Batoche.

Rieti (Italian Wars of Independence), 1821. Discontented with their tyrannical king, Ferdinand IV, a liberal group in Naples forced him to flee in 1820. Ferdinand IV (who was Ferdinand III of Sicily and Ferdinand I of the Two Sicilies) sought help from the Austrian army in Italy. The Neapolitans in turn relied on a rebel force of about 10,000 men under Guglielmo Pepe. At Rieti, 42 miles northwest of Rome, the Neapolitans were overwhelmed on March 7, 1821, by a greatly superior Austrian army. Pepe was banished from the kingdom under penalty of death. The Austrians marched into Naples and restored Ferdinand to the throne on March 23. *See* Tolentino; Custoza I; Italian Wars of Independence.

Riga I (Swedish-Polish Wars), 1621. Despite his crushing defeat at Linköping in 1598, Sigismund III, king of Poland, never relinquished his claim to the throne of Sweden. At the outbreak of the Thirty Years' War in 1618, Sigismund sided with the Catholic-Hapsburg forces of the Holy Roman Empire. Gustavus II of Sweden, still not an active participant in the bitter conflict itself, marched on the Polish-held port of Riga. Arriving in August 1621, the Swedish force invested the city but failed to take it from the hard-fighting garrison. Nevertheless, Gustavus persisted in his attack and on September 11 forced a breach in the city's walls. Pressing forward, the Swedes entered Riga to take its surrender four days later. With the Poles ousted, the city was granted self-government. Nine years later Gustavus landed a Swedish army on the coast of Pomerania to enter the Thirty Years' War on behalf of the anti-Imperial Protestant forces. *See* Linköping; Khotin I; Frankfort on the Oder.

Riga II (World War I), 1917. The collapse of the Russian attack on Lemberg (Lvov) led the German field marshal Paul von Hindenburg to conclude that one more offensive would overthrow the shaky provisional government of Aleksandr Kerenski and thereby knock Russia out of the war. On September 1 the German Eighth Army (Oskar von Hutier) stormed across the Dvina River into Riga. Within two days the feeble Russian resistance inside the city had been crushed. The Germans threatened a march on Petrograd (Leningrad) to the northeast. But the capture of Riga produced the desired results. The defeated Russian commander, Gen. Lavr Kornilov, led an abortive counterrevolutionary movement during September 8–14. Then in the so-called October Revolution (November 7 and 8, new-style calendar), Kerenski was deposed, and the Bolsheviks of Nikolai Lenin and Leon Trotsky seized power. Hostilities on the Eastern Front ceased on December 2. When Russian negotiators stalled for better peace terms, the Germans resumed the offensive on February 18, 1918, but only to force a formal capitulation to the treaty terms signed at Brest Litovsk on March 3. Russia was at last out of the war, freeing masses of German troops for action on the Western Front. *See* Lemberg II; Somme River II; Russian Civil War; World War I.

Rimnik (Turkish-Russian Wars), 1789. In the second war that Catherine II, the Great, waged against the Ottoman Empire, Russia was joined by the Holy Roman Emperor Joseph II. After defeating the Turkish army of Sultan Abdul-Hamid I at Focsani in August 1789, the Russian-Austrian army pressed deeper into Moldavia. At Rimnik the allies, about 25,000 strong, encountered a much larger Turkish force on September 22. The commanders, Count Aleksandr Suvorov and the Prince of Saxe-Coburg, launched a powerful attack that virtually wiped out the sultan's troops. As a reward for the victory, Catherine gave Suvorov the title Count Rimniksky. Crushed by defeat, Abdul-Hamid died before the end of the year. His successor, Selim III, signed a peace treaty at Jassy three years later, which pushed back the Turkish frontier in Europe to the Dniester River. *See* Focsani.

Río Barbate (Moslem Conquest of Spain), 711. The Moslem westward sweep across North Africa was completed during 708–11 by the Arab general Musa ibn-Nusayr. Musa sent his conquerors 13 miles across the Strait of Gibraltar into Spain. Tariq led the invaders, a force of 7,000 Arab and Berber horsemen. At Wadi Bekka, on the Barbate River near Cape Trafalgar, King Roderick of the Visigoths attempted to stem the powerful Moslem force, then reinforced to 12,000 warriors. Roderick's 15,000 defenders proved to be no match for the swift, slashing charges of Tariq's cavalry. They were soundly defeated after an hour's fighting on July 19. Roderick, last of the Gothic kings, was either slain or drowned in the Guadalquivir River trying to escape. The Moslems rode on to take Cordova (the Moor capital-to-be), Toledo (the Visigoth capital), and half of the Iberian Peninsula by the end of the summer. Musa himself crossed over to Spain the following year and began attacking the strongholds bypassed by Tariq. He took Mérida on June 1, 713, Seville by the end of June, and later Saragossa and other cities of central and northeast Spain. The Visigoth kingdom vanished into history. *See* Carthage III; Covadonga.

Río Salado (Spanish-Moslem Wars), 1340. The long Christian counteroffensive against the Moors in Spain had reached Tarifa in 1292 before it slowed down again. In 1340, however, Alfonso XI of Castile (which now included León) found himself threatened by an army of Moslems from both southern Spain and Africa. With the aid of Portugal's Alfonso IV, the Castilian king made a stand on the Río Salado near Tarifa on October 30. In one of the most decisive battles of the centuries-old conflict, the Christians beat off and then routed their Moslem attackers. Alfonso IV of Portugal, related by marriage to Alfonso XI, fought so heroically as to earn the nickname "the Brave." The African threat to Spain came to an end. Alfonso XI then pressed on to the Moorish stronghold at Algeciras. *See* Cordova; Algeciras.

Rivoli Veronese (Wars of the French Revolution), 1797. As the second year of Napoleon Bonaparte's campaign in northern Italy opened, the Austrians made a fourth attempt to relieve the beleaguered fortress of Mantua. This time Gen. Josef Alvinczy (Baron von Borberek) with 28,000 troops struck southward from Trent down the Adige Valley in the main attack. Napoleon hurriedly sent the divisions of Gens. Barthélemy Joubert and André Masséna 14 miles north of Verona to Rivoli. Here on January 14 the outnumbered French smashed the Austrian thrust in one of the hardest battles of the war. Napoleon lost 2,200 men, but his troops inflicted 3,300 casualties on the enemy and took 7,000 prisoners. In a vigorous pursuit of the fleeing Austrians on the following day, Joubert captured another 6,000.

Meanwhile Masséna marched southward all night to surround and capture a second Austrian column, now isolated outside Mantua. For his two-day success in this operation Masséna was created Duc de Rivoli. The shattering of this Austrian offensive doomed the long-besieged fortress at Mantua. *See* Arcole; Mantua; Malborghetto; French Revolution Wars.

Roanoke Island (American Civil War), 1862. To invade North Carolina, Gen. Ambrose Burnside embarked three Federal regiments on 65 vessels at Annapolis, Md. Supported by a naval task force of 19 warships under Capt. Louis Goldsborough, the expedition entered Pimlico Sound, approaching Roanoke Island from the west. Under the covering fire of the Federal warships, Burnside landed his troops late on February 7. On the following day he defeated a Confederate force under Gen. Henry Wise and took 2,500 prisoners. Another 149 Confederates were killed, wounded, or missing in the combined sea and ground action. Federal casualties were 14 in the naval force and 264 among the ground troops.

Leaving a garrison on Roanoke, Burnside occupied New Bern on March 14 and Beaufort on April 26. On July 3 Burnside and 7,500 men from his command were ordered to Fort Monroe, Va., to reinforce Gen. George McClellan's army. Gen. John Foster was left in charge of the relatively static North Carolina operation. *See* American Civil War.

Rochester I (Norman Rule of Britain), 1088. The rough rule of William II, Rufus, who had succeeded his father, the Conqueror, in 1087, provoked a revolt of the barons. One of the leaders of the rebellion was the king's uncle Bishop Odo of Bayeux. Captured by William's army, the bishop ostensibly began arranging the surrender of other rebels in Rochester Castle in Kent. Instead, he joined forces with the garrison. William laid siege to the castle and forced its capitulation. Odo was sent into exile. *See* Ely I; Alnwick I.

Rochester II (First Barons' War of England), 1215. Despite the signing of the Magna Carta on June 15, 1215, relations between King John and his barons steadily worsened. On September 30 the barons obtained possession of Rochester Castle in Kent. In the first battle of the civil war that followed, John laid siege to the castle early in October. The garrison surrendered seven weeks later, on November 30, when the castle was successfully mined. John's royalist knights pushed on against rebel strongholds in the east until the barons' candidate for the English crown, Louis, son of Philip II of France, landed in Kent in May of the following year. The war now turned against John, but before a decisive battle could be joined the king died, on October 28, 1216. The royalists promptly crowned his young son as Henry III. Although the succession took much of the steam out of the barons' cause, the civil war continued. *See* Bouvines; Dover I; Lincoln II; Barons' Wars.

Rochester III (Second Barons' War of England), 1264. Following its victory over the barons and the capture of young Simon de Montfort at Northampton, the royalist army of Henry III and Prince Edward marched into Kent. Here Simon de Montfort (earl of Leicester), who had marched out from London, and Gilbert de Clare (earl of Gloucester), who had moved up from Tonbridge, had linked up at Rochester. The rebels had captured the town and were storming the outworks of the castle when the royalists arrived on April 18. The Montfortians raised the siege and fell back into London. Only the timely arrival of Henry had saved the royalist garrison in the castle. Henry's army pushed on south to Tonbridge, threatening the rebels' hold on the Cinque Ports. *See* Northampton I; Lewes; Barons' Wars.

Rocourt (War of the Austrian Succession), 1746.

When Frederick II pulled Prussia out of the war in December 1745, Prince Charles of Lorraine of the Holy Roman Empire (Francis I and Maria Theresa) took an Austrian army into the Netherlands to oppose France (Louis XV). However, this allied gain was offset by the earlier withdrawal of British troops to put down the "Forty-five" Rebellion at home. Now Marshal Comte Maurice de Saxe, the able French field commander, pressed forward to Rocourt (Raucoux), just north of Liége on the Meuse. Here on October 11, 1746, Saxe met and defeated an Austrian-Dutch force under Prince Charles. The Imperials suffered a loss of 5,000 men. Saxe continued his advance. Meanwhile, the war in Italy had moved no closer to a decision. *See* Kesselsdorf; Finisterre Cape I; Lauffeld; Austrian Succession, War of the.

Rocroi (Thirty Years' War), 1643. As the war moved into its 26th year, the major military action shifted from Germany to what is now northeast France. About the same time a new generation assumed direction of the conflict. In France, both Cardinal the Duc de Richelieu and King Louis XIII were dead. Cardinal Jules Mazarin now served as chief minister to the five-year-old Louis XIV. On the military front the French commander was 22-year-old Louis II Condé (duc d'Enghien), who would become known as the Great Condé. In charge of the opposing Spanish army was Gen. Francisco de Melo, acting for King Philip IV.

In the spring of 1643 Melo crossed the modern boundary between Belgium and France to lay siege to Rocroi, west of the Meuse River. Condé, who had 15,000 infantry and 7,000 cavalry, promptly marched to the relief of the city. On May 19 he came upon the superior Spanish army (18,000 infantry, 8,000 cavalry) drawn up south of Rocroi. Both sides deployed their horsemen on the wings, infantry in the center. Condé opened the battle on his right flank by charging and routing the Spanish cavalry to his front. On the other wing, however, the Spanish cavalry pushed back the French horsemen opposite them. Condé then wheeled to his left and began recklessly cutting a right-angle swath through the enemy lines of infantry. This tactic isolated the elite Spanish foot soldiers (about 8,000) in the front ranks from the less well-trained Italians, Germans, and Walloons in the rear. The latter troops soon gave way and Condé broke through to the opposite wing, where he came upon the rear of Melo's cavalry. These horsemen, still fully engaged with the French to their front, could not withstand the pincers assault. They fled from the field. The Spanish infantry, now completely encircled, fought off all French attacks. But late in the day the tercios crumbled before the continuing onslaughts from all sides. They died almost to the man. So perished the flower of the Spanish army, probably the best-trained infantry troops in the world at that time.

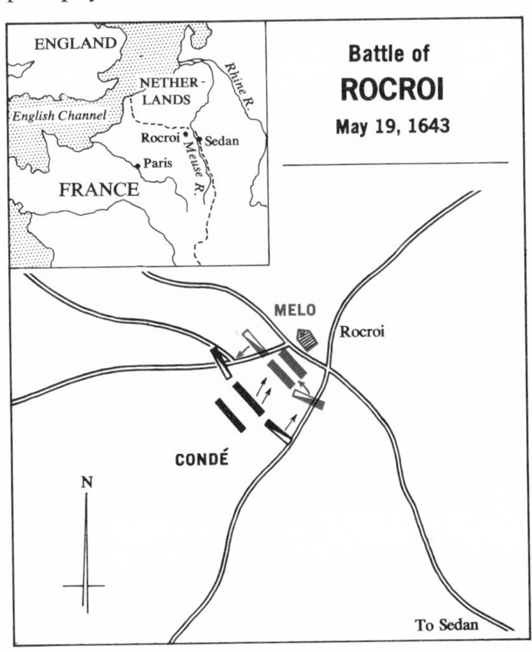

The battle was a turning point in Spanish military history. Of 18,000 foot soldiers, 7,000 were captured and 8,000 killed. Spain would never again produce infantry troops the equal of those who fell under the relentless French attack at Rocroi. Condé, who suffered 4,000 casualties, entered the city in triumph the following day. But while the victory on this front put France in the ascendancy, the fighting in Germany provided no such clear-cut decision. *See* Breitenfeld II; Tuttlingen; Lens; Thirty Years' War.

Roman Empire. When Octavian assumed the title of Augustus in 27 B.C., he founded the Roman Empire on the foundations of the ancient republic. Under the rule of the successors of Augustus, Rome reached its greatest power, stretching from Britain as far eastward as Babylonia and from the North Sea to the Nile River. Beginning in the third century, Rome suffered an almost steady decline. In 395 it was divided between the Western and Eastern empires, a temporary arrangement that became permanent in 474 with the formal rise of the Byzantine Empire at Constantinople. Invaded by successive waves of barbarians during the fifth century, the foreshortened Western Roman Empire fell in 476 with the defeat and death of Romulus Augustulus. *See also* Byzantine Empire; Roman Republic.

Lippe River	11 B.C.
Teutoburger Wald	A.D. 9
Minden I	16
Medway River	43
Shropshire	50
Artaxata	58

Tigranocerta II	59
Verulamium II	61
Arsanias River	62
Bezetha	66
Jotapata	68
Bedriacum	69
Cremona I	69
Jerusalem IV	70
Treves	70
Mons Graupius	84
Moesia	89
Sarmizegetusa	106
Caesarea	135
Ctesiphon I	165
Aquileia I	166–167
Byzantium I	194–196
Lugdunum	197
Ctesiphon II	197–198
Philippopolis I	251
Edessa I	260
Naissus	269
Placentia	271
Pavia I	271
Emesa	272
Palmyra	272–273
Margus	285
Carrhae II	296
Verona	312
Saxa Rubra	312
Heraclea Propontis	313
Cibalae	314
Adrianople I	323
Byzantium II	323–324
Chrysopolis	324
Singara	348
Mursa	351
Argentoratum	357
Amida I	359
Tigris River	363
Châlons-sur-Marne I	366
Adrianople II	378
Aquileia II	394

Western Roman Empire

Pollentia	402
Florence-Fiesole	406
Rome I	410
Hippo Regius	430
Châlons-sur-Marne II	451
Aquileia III	452
Rome II	455
Pavia II	476

Roman Empire, Eastern. The eastern part of the Roman Empire, with its capital at Constantinople; it is better known as the Byzantine Empire. *See* Byzantine Empire.

Roman Republic. The major battles and wars fought by the republic of Rome are listed below. For later conflicts *see* Roman Empire.

Veii	405–396 B.C.
Allia	390 B.C.
Trifanum	338 B.C.
See Samnite Wars	
Vadimonian Lake	283 B.C.
Heraclea	280 B.C.
Asculum I	279 B.C.
Beneventum	275 B.C.
See Punic Wars	
Telamon	225 B.C.
Clastidium	222 B.C.
Cynoscephalae II	197 B.C.
Thermopylae II	191 B.C.
Pydna	168 B.C.
Corinth	146 B.C.
Numantia	142–133 B.C.
Muthul River	108 B.C.
Arausio	105 B.C.
Aquae Sextiae	102 B.C.
Vercellae	101 B.C.
Asculum II	90–89 B.C.
See Mithridatic Wars	
Mount Tifata	83 B.C.
Colline Gate	82 B.C.
Mount Vesuvius	73–71 B.C.
Jerusalem III	66–63 B.C.
See Gallic Wars	
See First Triumvirate, Wars of the	
See Second Triumvirate, Wars of the	

Rome I (Wars of the Western Roman Empire), 410. With the murder of Flavius Stilicho, his top military commander, Emperor Honorius was powerless to defend the Western Roman Empire. Taking advantage of this weakness, the Visigoth king, Alaric, burst into northern Italy from Illyricum and took the unguarded Via Flaminia toward

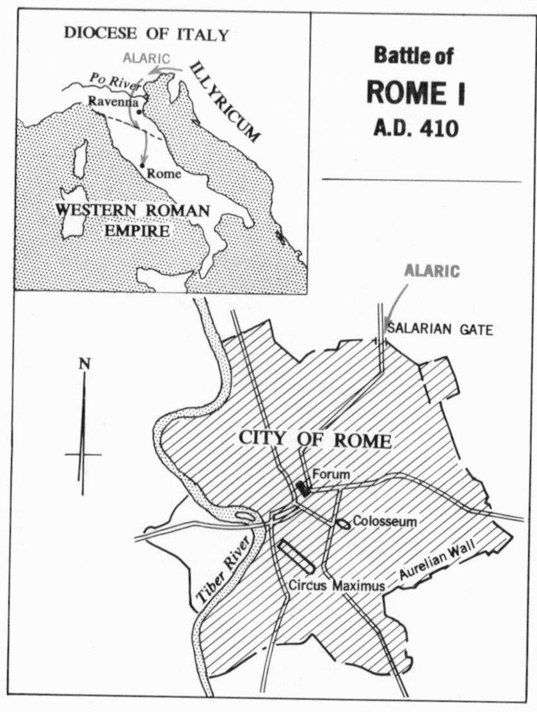

Rome. Honorius fled to refuge in Ravenna. For the first time since Hannibal, an enemy army stood outside the gates of the world's leading city.

Honorius sought to reach a settlement, while Alaric laid siege to Rome. Faced with starvation, the city government agreed to pay Alaric tribute and to meet his other demands. But the Imperial court at Ravenna was unyielding. When negotiations finally broke down, the barbarians stormed through the Salarian Gate of the Aurelian Wall, on the north side, entering Rome on August 24, 410. An orgy of massacre and pillage followed. The fall of Rome, which had resisted all invaders for 800 years, reverberated throughout the stricken empire. Alaric moved on to southern Italy, planning a conquest of Sicily and Africa. But he died suddenly before the end of the year.

The sack of Rome illustrated the weakening bonds of the Western Empire. Barbarian invasions and civil strife had resulted in the loss of Britain, the Rhineland, much of Gaul, and Spain. The next disaster would take place in Africa. *See* Florence-Fiesole; Hippo Regius; Roman Empire.

Rome II (Wars of the Western Roman Empire), 455. Despite the continued incursions of barbarians into the empire, the Roman court seemed concerned largely with internal conspiracies. Flavius Aëtius, the last great military commander of Rome, was personally slain by Emperor Valentinian III on September 21, 454. Six months later Valentinian himself was murdered, and a Roman senator named Petronius Maximus took the throne. His rule was to be brief. Genseric (Gaiseric), the Vandal king who had won North Africa 20 years before, arrived at the mouth of the Tiber with a large fleet of ships. Meeting little opposition, Genseric reached Rome on June 2. For the next 14 days the city was plundered far more savagely than in Alaric's sacking in 410. The thorough work of the Vandals provided a new and lasting word for destructiveness. Maximus was either killed by the Romans, whom he had failed to protect, or by the ferocious invaders.

The Western Roman Empire was now mortally wounded and its greatest city prostrate. (The Suevian barbarian Ricimer stormed Rome in 472, but by then the city was virtually defenseless.) Although the Western Empire would linger on another 20 years, the only real question had become when and where it would end. *See* Aquileia III; Pavia II; Roman Empire.

Rome III (Wars of the Byzantine Empire), 536–538. Two years after rewinning the Vandal kingdom of North Africa for the Byzantine Empire, Justinian I, the Great, launched the reconquest of Rome, now held by the Ostrogoths. He sent Belisarius, the victor at Carthage, with 11,000 Imperial cavalrymen to Italy. Landing in Sicily late in 535, Belisarius quickly brought the island under control. Leaving an occupation force of 2,500 men, he crossed the Strait of Messina in May 536 and entered Italy. Riding rapidly northward, Belisarius seized Naples. Then, before the confused Ostrogoth army could mass against him, the Byzantine general slipped his army into Rome itself on December 10, 536. But Vitiges (Witiges), the Gothic leader, now hurried to besiege the city in March 537 with a force of some 30,000 men. For more than a year Belisarius was penned up in the former capital of the world. Finally the arrival of reinforcements from Constantinople enabled the Byzantine army to burst out of the Aurelian Wall and pursue the Goths into northern Italy early in 538.

During the next two years Belisarius, with fewer then 20,000 fighting men, warred against Vitiges and the Goths in northern Italy. He also had to defend the Po Valley against the incursions of Burgundians and ax-throwing Franks from across the Alps. Then, in the spring of 540, Belisarius tricked the Visigoths into admitting him to their (and the last Roman) capital of Ravenna. He promptly took Vitiges prisoner, ending the war, with the Italian peninsula back under the rule of the Eastern Roman Emperor. (In Ravenna Belisarius recaptured the crown of the Roman emperor Valens, lost to the Visigoths in the battle of Adrianople in 378.) *See* Carthage II; Rome IV.

Rome IV (Wars of the Byzantine Empire), 546–547. In 541, a year after Belisarius had reconquered the Italian peninsula for the Byzantine Empire of Justinian I, the Ostrogoths again went on the offensive. Under the capable Christian leader Totila (Baduila), the Goths routed a Roman army at Faenza, 19 miles southwest of the capital at Ravenna, in 542. They then swept southward, bypassed Rome, and penetrated as far as Naples by 543. When Totila laid seige to Rome in the autumn of 545, Justinian scraped together an army, and sent Belisarius back to Italy. But the new force was too small to raise the siege of Rome. Belisarius had to pull back; Totila stormed into the city on December 17, 546, and sacked it.

In February of the following year Totila was maneuvered away from the city, and Belisarius promptly reoccupied it. But to carry the war against the Goths in the north, the Imperial forces had to abandon Rome to its own fate. The Goths promptly occupied it again, as the darkness of the early Middle Ages settled over the former capital of the Caesars. *See* Rome III; Taginae.

Rome V (Capture by Normans), 1084. The long feud between Holy Roman Emperor Henry IV and the papacy took a violent turn in 1084. The German ruler marched into Rome and deposed Pope Gregory VIII. To redeem his throne, the pope called upon the Norman adventurer Robert Guiscard. At the head of a motley army that included Moslems, Guiscard stormed into the city, driving out Henry's Germans. Gregory resumed his rule. But the new conquerors got out of hand and sacked Rome so savagely that the pope was forced into virtual exile at Salerno. *See* Dyrrachium II.

Rome VI (Spanish Sack of Rome), 1527. When Francis I reinvaded Italy with a French army in 1524, Pope Clement VII changed sides and supported the French. It was a mistake. The decisive French defeat at Pavia the following year left Italy at the mercy of the victorious Spanish king and Holy Roman Emperor Charles V. The hastily formed anti-Hapsburg League of Cognac—the pope, Francis, Francesco Sforza of Milan, and the rulers of Venice and Florence—proved helpless against the Spanish army, which was now the best in Europe. Commanded by the renegade French duke Charles de Bourbon, the Spaniards swept down the peninsula and attacked Rome. Although the duke fell in the assault, his army stormed into the city on May 6, 1527. The victorious Spaniards and their German mercenary allies, totaling 30,000 men, then sacked the city in a manner reminiscent of the barbarian pillages 1,100 years earlier. Thousands of Romans were massacred. The pope was captured. After his release Clement fled to Orvieto, but he returned the following year to accept a peace with Charles that restored the papal states. In 1530 he crowned Charles king of Lombardy. Meanwhile, the site of the Valois-Hapsburg wars shifted to western Europe. *See* Pavia V; Saint-Quentin I.

Rome VII (Italian Wars of Independence), 1849. During the war between Austria, the ruling power in Italy, and Sardinia (Piedmont), a republic of Rome was proclaimed on February 9, 1849, by Giuseppe Mazzini and others. Pope Pius IX had fled earlier from Rome to Gaeta. On April 24, 1849, a French expeditionary force sent out by the Second Republic landed at Civitavecchia, 39 miles northwest of Rome, to restore papal rule. Under the command of Gen. Nicolas Oudinot, son of a Napoleonic general of the same name, some 6,000 French attacked Rome five days later. Inside the city patriots organized by Giuseppe Garibaldi fought off the invaders during April 29–30. Reinforced, Oudinot launched another assault on June 3 but was again repulsed. He then clamped a tight siege on the city. Finding his position in Rome hopeless, Garibaldi made terms with the French commander on June 30. Two days later, with his 5,000 rebels, Garibaldi marched out of the city, only to be struck by another enemy. Austrian troops pursued the Italians and eventually killed, captured, or dispersed the entire force. (Garibaldi escaped.) Now only the new republic of Venice remained to challenge Austrian domination of Italy. *See* Novara II; Venice; Italian Wars of Independence.

Roncesvalles (Conquests of Charlemagne), 778. Tempted by dynastic quarrels among the Arabs in Spain, Charlemagne led an army of Christian Franks across the Pyrenees in the spring of 778. He entered Pamplona and then pushed down the Ebro to Saragossa. Finding the city defended behind high walls by Abd-er-Rahman I, Charlemagne settled down to a siege. When he learned that the Saxons were in revolt east of the Rhine, the Frankish king abandoned the siege and began the return march to Gascony. In August the head of the column recrossed the Pyrenees. But the baggage train and strong rear guard were ambushed by mountain Basques (who were also Christians) at the pass of Roncesvalles. Not a Frank escaped. Among the dead was the paladin Roland, prefect of the Breton March. The defeat later sparked a great body of medieval literature, including the epic *Chanson de Roland*. *See* Pavia IV; Süntelberg; Charlemagne, Conquests of.

Roosebeke (French-Flemish Wars), 1382. The long-standing Flemish discontent with French rule, which had erupted in three battles early in the century, broke out again in 1381 during the reign of Charles VI. Economically allied with England and burdened with heavy taxes, the people of Flanders took up arms under the leadership of Philip van Artevelde. The following year a large number of peasants and townspeople massed at Roosebeke in East Flanders. Here on November 27 they were attacked by a strong force of mounted French knights commanded by the Count of Flanders, Louis II de Male. Ill-trained and poorly armed, the Fleming infantry was wedged together by repeated cavalry charges and then cut down with sword and lance. It was a one-sided slaughter equaled only by Cannae and Adrianople II. Van Artevelde lay among the slain. A severe repression followed. A year later, on the death of the Count of Flanders, the region passed to the rule of Burgundy, which stamped out the last vestiges of revolt by 1385. *See* Cassel; Clermont.

Rorke's Drift (Zulu-British War), 1879. After their overwhelming victory over the British at Isandhlwana on January 22, 1879, the Zulus under Cetewayo pressed into northern Natal that night. At Rorke's Drift (a ford on a tributary of the Tugela River) an outpost of 140 British troops resisted the advance of 4,000 Zulu warriors. Led by John Chard of the Royal Engineers, the garrison used its rifle and artillery fire effectively against the thrown spears (assagais) of the attackers. After an all-night assault, on January 22–23, the native troops withdrew, leaving 400 dead on the field. The heroic garrison, which suffered 25 casualties, later received 11 Victoria Crosses for the battle. *See* Isandhlwana; Ulundi; Zulu-British War.

Rosebud River (Sioux War II), 1876. The rush of gold seekers to the Black Hills in 1874 and 1875 aroused the fury of the Sioux (Dakota confederacy), the largest group of Plains Indians. To put down the uprising, Gen. George Crook marched out of Fort Laramie, Wyo., in late May 1876. On the Rosebud River, in southeastern Montana, Crook's 1,200 men encountered some 1,500 Sioux and Cheyenne warriors on June 17. Led by Crazy Horse, the Indians held their ground, killing 10 and wounding 34. They then made good their escape, while Crook had to fall back for new supplies. Meanwhile, two other army columns had taken the field in Montana. *See* Little Bighorn River; Indian Wars in the United States.

Roses, Wars of the (1455–1485). Two years after its Hundred Years' War with France dragged to a close in 1453, England became torn by civil war. The reigning monarch, King Henry VI of the house of Lancaster, was a weak, incapable ruler who suffered from periods of insanity. To fill the vacuum of government leadership, a power struggle developed between the house of Lancaster (red rose) and the rival house of York (white rose) headed by Richard Plantagenet, the third duke of York. This struggle flared into open warfare at Saint Albans in 1455.

Six years later Henry VI was deposed, and the Yorkist claim to the throne was fulfilled with the crowning of Richard's son as Edward IV. Henry's wife, Queen Margaret, however, in the interests of her son Edward, secured Scottish and French aid and kept on fighting for the Lancastrian cause. When the former Yorkist general, the Earl of Warwick (Richard Neville), changed sides, Henry VI was recrowned in 1470. Edward IV rallied the Yorkists and in the battle of Tewkesbury captured Queen Margaret and killed young Edward. Henry VI died mysteriously soon thereafter.

This ended the main phase of the war. But when Edward IV died 12 years later, his 13-year-old son and successor, Edward V, was overthrown by the boy's uncle, the Duke of Gloucester (and third son of Richard Plantagenet), who assumed the crown as Richard III. In the culminating battle at Bosworth Field in 1485, Richard III was killed and the throne won by the Earl of Richmond, who became Henry VII. The new king adopted the symbol of a red and white rose and established the Tudor dynasty, which would rule England for more than a hundred years.

Saint Albans I	1455
Blore Heath	1459
Ludford	1459
Sandwich II	1460
Northampton II	1460
Wakefield	1460
Mortimer's Cross	1461
Saint Albans II	1461
Ferrybridge	1461
Towton	1461
Hedgeley Moor	1464
Hexham	1464
Banbury	1469
Lose-coat Field	1470
Ravenspur II	1471
Barnet	1471
Tewkesbury	1471
Bosworth Field	1485

Rossbach (Seven Years' War), 1757. Frederick II, the Great, faced his greatest peril in the summer of 1757. Prussia and its English ally had suffered successive defeats in the south (from Austria), west (from France), and east (from Russia). As the hostile ring tightened about him, the Prussian king rallied his forces and struck out to the west where the advance of 30,000 French and 11,000 Imperial troops of the Holy Roman Empire posed the greatest threat. In 12 days Frederick marched 170 miles to confront the invaders of Saxony at Rossbach, 26 miles southwest of Leipzig. The Prussians, reduced to 21,000 effectives by the forced march, camped northeast of the village.

On November 5 the allied commanders, the Prince de Soubise and the Prince of Saxe-Hildburghausen, resolved to crush Frederick with a large-scale turning movement against the Prussian left flank. Anticipating the maneuver, Frederick deployed a small masking force to his front while his main body executed a leftward turning movement of its own behind a cover of hills. The ponderous allied columns, somewhat disorganized by a too-hasty march, suddenly received the full force of the Prussian blow on their right flank. Behind the fire of 18 heavy guns, Gen. Friedrich von Seydlitz' cavalry, followed by seven battalions

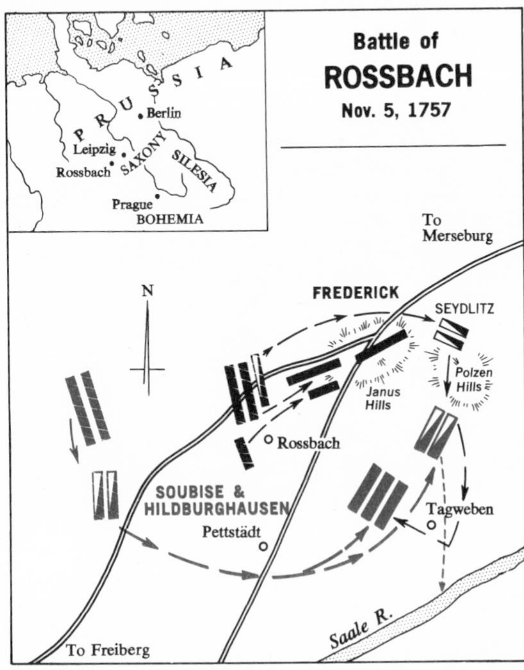

of infantry, routed the enemy cavalry and then swooped down on the startled allied infantry. In 40 minutes the Prussian horsemen gunned and sabered the French and Imperials into wild flight. Most of the Prussian foot soldiers were still coming up when Soubise fled the field with 7,500 casualties, chiefly prisoners. The victors lost less than 600 men. Frederick's spectacular victory at Rossbach broke the advance from the west. From this time forward, France would be kept in check by a subordinate Prussian commander, the Duke of Brunswick. But Frederick was still in grave danger on other fronts. *See* Hastenbeck; Gross-Jägersdorf; Breslau; Seven Years' War.

Rouen I (English-French Wars), 1204. England's war with Philip II Augustus of France for possession of Normandy had dragged on inconclusively for six years under Richard I, Coeur de Lion. However, when John succeeded to the English crown the French rapidly gained the upper hand. The fall of Château Gaillard in March 1204 cost the English army its chief defensive bastion in Normandy. Philip's knights pressed on to Rouen, the most important city in the duchy. A sharp attack captured the fortress on June 24. The French had now pushed the English out of all the territory north of the Loire. *See* Château Gaillard; Damme.

Rouen II (Hundred Years' War), 1418–1419. The crushing defeat at Agincourt in 1415 left France barren of military and spiritual strength. Henry V of England beat off an attempt to regain the port of Harfleur (1416–17), then overran most of Normandy. He took Caen in 1417, Falaise and Cherbourg in 1418. In the summer of 1418 the English moved against Rouen, the chief city of northwestern France. Rouen resisted capture and girded itself for a siege under the command of Guy de Boutillier. Noncombatants were expelled from the city. The English refused passage through their siege lines, forcing the 12,000 refugees to endure terrible hardships for months in the no man's land between the two forces. When the Duc de Burgundy (Jean sans Peur) made only a half-hearted attempt to raise the siege, Rouen surrendered on January 19, 1419. The English pressed on toward Paris.

On September 19 Burgundy was assassinated by the Orleanist (Armagnac) supporters of the insane Charles VI and the dauphin Charles (future Charles VII). Burgundy, under Philip the Good, then made an alliance with England, resulting in the Treaty of Troyes on May 21, 1420. The dauphin was disinherited. Henry V was to be regent of France and would succeed Charles VI on the latter's death. Paris and all northern France came under the control of England and its Burgundian allies. *See* Agincourt; Beaugé; Hundred Years' War.

Rouen III (Hundred Years' War), 1449. In the 20 years after the French victory at Orleans, the armies of Charles VII steadily squeezed the English out of France. During this time English forces sent over by Henry VI stubbornly held on to Rouen, the key to Normandy. In 1449, however, the residents of the city, encouraged by French troops in the neighborhood, revolted. Unable to put down the uprising, the Duke of Somerset (Edmund Beaufort) withdrew his garrison to the castle. On October 29 he was forced to surrender this stronghold to the French. Rouen, which had served as the English administrative center for northern France since 1419, was finally free. *See* Patay; Formigny; Hundred Years' War.

Roundway Down (English Civil War), 1643. The Cavalier-Roundhead struggle in the west was closely contested during the second year of the Civil War. When the Royalist commander, Gen. Sir Ralph (later Lord) Hopton, took refuge in Devizes early in July 1643, he was promptly besieged by the Parliamentarian commander, Gen. Sir William Waller. From Oxford, Prince Maurice of Germany, nephew of King Charles I (and younger brother of the Cavalier cavalry leader, Prince Rupert), rode to the relief of the city at the head of a strong force of horsemen. On July 13 Maurice attacked the besiegers at Roundway Down, a Wiltshire hill outside Devizes. His charge swept the Roundheads off the height, and they were taken in the rear by Hopton's infantry surging out from the town. The Roundheads lost more than a thousand men in killed and captured.

Prince Rupert pressed this advantage by seizing Bristol, the second largest city in the kingdom, on July 25. King Charles then ordered a joint attack on Gloucester, the lone Roundhead stronghold between Bristol and the Royalist-held city of York. *See* Lansdowne; Newbury I; English Civil War.

Rouvray (Hundred Years' War), 1429. During the English siege of Orleans, Sir John Fastolf left Paris with an armed supply convoy for the troops of the Duke of Suffolk (William de la Pole), which were investing the French city on the Loire. Both English forces were under the direction of the Duke of Bedford (John of Lancaster), English commander in France and regent for his young nephew Henry VI. Fastolf's convoy was escorted by 1,000 archers and some 1,200 Burgundian militia. At Rouvray on February 12, 1429, the column came under attack by an army of 4,000 Orleanist French (loyal to the dauphin Charles, later Charles VII) and Scots commanded by the Comte de Clermont. Fastolf made good use of a tactic developed by the Hussites in Bohemia and later widely used in the American West: He formed his wagons in a circle, placing the archers on top of the vehicles and the spearmen in between.

The French charged bravely but were beaten

off with heavy casualties by the novel English defense. Fastolf took the convoy safely on to Orleans. Because the supplies consisted chiefly of barrels of salt fish, the military action at Rouvray is often called the battle of the Herrings. The French defeat seemed to destroy all hope of raising the siege of Orleans, the largest city remaining in their hands, but at Domremy a 17-year-old peasant girl was hearing mystical voices urging her to save France. *See* Orleans; Jargeau; Hundred Years' War.

Rubicon River (Wars of the First Triumvirate), 49 B.C. The breakup of the First Triumvirate came with the slaying of M. Licinius Crassus at Carrhae in 53 B.C. This left the rule of Rome to Pompey the Great, who had remained in the capital, and Julius Caesar, who was busy suppressing the Gauls across the Alps. Pompey seized the opportunity to become virtual dictator. At his behest the senate ordered Caesar to disband his army upon the successful completion of the Gallic campaign. Caesar, however, refused and, during the night of January 10–11, led the Thirteenth Legion south across the Rubicon River near Ravenna on the Adriatic coast. There was no resistance from Pompey's outposts. As the river marked the limit of Caesar's jurisdiction, the crossing was a declaration of war against the government in Rome.

The Rubicon proved to be far more a political than a military action. Within 60 days Rome capitulated to Caesar's handful of men, supported at a distance by the veteran troops in Gaul, who remained loyal to Caesar. Pompey fled to Greece to organize resistance there. Caesar is reported to have said: "I am going to Spain [Pompey's province] to fight an army without a general, and thence to the East to fight a general [Pompey] without an army." *See* Carrhae I; Alesia; Ilerda; First Triumvirate, Wars of the.

Rudnik Ridges (World War I), 1914. Little more than two weeks after being expelled from Serbian soil the Austrian commander, Gen. Oskar Potiorek, launched a second invasion, on the night of September 7–8. This time the Austrian Fifth Army attacked from the north, the Sixth from the west. Behind the Save and Drina rivers, the three Serbian armies of Gen. Radomir Putnik battled desperately to check the invaders. Finally, on September 17, Potiorek halted the offensive to regroup the forces in his bridgeheads into Serbia.

Recognizing the weakness of his existing front, Putnik made a general withdrawal to a more defensible line farther east. On November 5 the Austrians launched their third advance, doggedly driving back the Serbs. Valjevo fell on November 15. Potiorek then shifted the weight of his attack to the north, threatening the Serbian capital of Belgrade. Rather than risk the safety of his armies, Putnik evacuated the city to solidify his right flank. The Austrians occupied Belgrade on December 2. To the south they now held a position beyond the Kolubra River, with a thinly stretched supply line extending back through mountainous terrain.

Putnik, who had deployed his Second, Third, and First armies on a north-south line along the Rudnik Ridges, chose December 3 to launch a head-on counterattack. Inspired by the appearance of 70-year-old King Peter I at the front, the Serbs rushed forward furiously. After five days the Austrians had had enough. Potiorek again ordered a retreat, the Fifth Army falling back through Belgrade, the Sixth through Šabac. The pursuing Serbians reoccupied Belgrade on December 15. Once more Austrian invasion plans had been completely wrecked. Each side suffered 100,000 in killed alone. *See* Jadar River; Serbia (World War I); World War I.

Rufiji River (World War I), 1917. The Allied conquest of German Southwest Africa in mid-1915 enabled most of the South African troops to concentrate against the German colony of East Africa (Tanganyika). But here the German general Paul von Lettow-Vorbeck proved a crafty guerrilla fighter. For more than two years he eluded the forces of first Gen. Jan Christiaan Smuts and then Gen. Sir Jacob Louis van Deventer. Finally, on November 28, 1917, Deventer surprised the main German army of 5,000 men just south of the Rufiji River. The Allied army of Belgians, Portuguese, Indians, South Africans, and, chiefly, Nigerians took the surrender of the greatly outnumbered Germans. Lettow-Vorbeck escaped, however, and with a handful of men eluded capture during a 1,600-mile pursuit. He finally capitulated on November 25, 1918, with 1,300 men. *See* Windhoek; World War I.

Ruhr Pocket (World War II), 1945. One of the prime Allied objectives in their sweep across western Germany was the industrial center of the Ruhr, along the middle Rhine. General Dwight Eisenhower's forces closed to the Rhine in March 1945. The mission of holding the west bank opposite the Ruhr, from Bonn north to Duisburg, was then assigned to the U.S. Fifteenth Army (Leonard Gerow). Fifteen miles south of Bonn, Gen. Courtney Hodges' U.S. First Army struck east from its Remagen bridgehead on March 25. Reaching Marburg three days later, the VII Corps suddenly wheeled north toward Lippstadt. Meanwhile, along the north side of the Ruhr, the XIX Corps of Gen. William Simpson's Ninth Army was driving up the Lippe River, also headed for Lippstadt. On April 1 the two American columns, the Ninth's 2nd Armored Division and the First's 3rd Armored Division linked up, encircling the Ruhr.

Trapped inside the pocket of some 4,000 square miles was Field Marshal Walther Model with most of his Fifth Panzer and Fifteenth armies, plus an additional 100,000 miscellaneous troops. Unable to break out, the Nazis nevertheless resisted fiercely, hoping to slow down the main Allied offensive. But the U.S. general Omar Bradley, now directing both the Ninth and First armies, ordered the eastward drive continued, leaving only two corps from each army to reduce the pocket. In the north Simpson's XVI and XIX (in part) corps pressed inward toward the Ruhr River; Hodges' III and XVIII Corps hammered at the eastern and southern sides. By April 14 the shrinking pocket had been split in two by a north-south attack. During the next four days German troops began to surrender wholesale, while Model reportedly committed suicide. Resistance ended on April 18 with the final capitulation of 317,000 prisoners, including 30 generals—the greatest Nazi mass surrender in World War II. *See* Rhineland; Germany, West; World War II.

Rumani (World War I), 1916. When Turkey entered the war on the side of the Central Powers, Great Britain established a protectorate over Egypt, chiefly to guard the Suez Canal. It was a prudent move. A Turkish force of 20,000 men, commanded by the German colonel Baron Friedrich Kress von Kressenstein, crossed the Sinai Desert and attacked the canal on February 2, 1915. The invaders were finally forced to withdraw by the guns of British and French warships. Almost a year later the British in Egypt stood ready to mount their own offensive toward the east. Led by Gen. Sir Archibald Murray, an army composed largely of Australian and New Zealand troops advanced slowly along the shoreline, building a railroad and water pipeline as they went.

The Turks of Kress von Kressenstein harassed the operation but did not make a major attack until the British march column reached Rumani on August 4, 1916. Maneuvering inland, the Turks tried to turn the British right flank. But Murray, anticipating the enemy movement, pivoted his troops to the south and on the following day struck the Turkish column in its own right flank. The fierce British attack inflicted 6,000 casualties, including 4,000 captured. Murray's losses totaled 1,130. This setback, coupled with a desperate need for water, forced the Turks to withdraw.

Pressing doggedly eastward, the British reached El 'Arish, 27 miles from the border of Palestine, on December 20. From here they could defend against further attacks against the Suez Canal; or they could move against the Turks in Palestine. *See* Gaza II; World War I.

Rumania (World War I), 1916–1917. After two years of indecision the government of King Ferdinand I took Rumania into the war on the Allied side on August 27, 1916. The following day the First, Second, and Fourth armies attacked northwest through the Transylvanian Alps. The Third Army stood in the south to defend the line of the Danube River against Bulgaria. Both the war declaration and the offensive were poorly timed. Other fronts were quiet, permitting Germany and its weak Austrian partner to concentrate against Rumania. In the northwest mountains the Rumanian armies advanced more than 40 miles in two weeks against the Austrian First Army (Baron Artur Arz von Straussenburg). But poor communications on a 200-mile front and stiffened Austrian resistance brought the attack to a standstill by September 18.

Meanwhile in the southeast disaster threatened. From Bulgaria the German field marshal August von Mackensen marched into Dobruja at the head of the Army of the Danube—Bulgars, Turks, and a few Germans. Pressing northward between the Danube and the Black Sea, Mackensen took Turtucaia on September 6 and Silistra three days later. On September 16, however, he was checked south of Rumania's single Black Sea port of Constanța by an allied force under the Russian general Zaionchovsky—a Russian corps, the remnants of Gen. Alexandru Averescu's Rumanian Third Army, and a division of Serbian volunteers. Three Rumanian divisions were recalled from Transylvania to bolster this line. On October 20 Mackensen, reinforced by two more Turkish divisions, renewed the attack. Zaionchovsky's line cracked open as the Army of the Danube poured through. Constanta fell on October 23, shutting off all possible Allied aid. Leaving a holding force here, Mackensen moved west along the Danube to assist in a combined attack on Bucharest.

During this disaster in Dobruja, an equally serious threat was developing in the west. The former German chief of staff Gen. Erich von Falkenhayn had arrived to take charge of the German Ninth Army opposite the left flank of the Rumanian advance into Transylvania. On September 18 Falkenhayn began a series of sharp counterattacks that forced back, in turn, the First, Second, and Fourth Rumanian armies. Drawing more reinforcements, Falkenhayn stepped up his offensive on November 10, aided by the Austrian First Army on his left (north). The Rumanians gave way all along the line. As the German Ninth Army advanced on Bucharest from the west, Mackensen crossed the Danube on November 23 and attacked toward the capital from the south.

Rumania made one more try to avert defeat. On December 1 Averescu, collecting what troops he could from the Bucharest area, struck hard at the gap between Falkenhayn and Mackensen. He took 3,000 prisoners on the left flank of the Danube Army, but then had to fall back hurriedly when the German Ninth Army closed in on his right flank and rear. Completely demoralized, the Rumanians now evacuated Bucharest, on December 6, and fled northward to escape the converging German thrusts. By January 7 the Rumanian army, reduced to about 150,000 men, accompanied by King Ferdinand, had retreated behind the Seret (Sereth) and Pruth rivers in Moldavia. Here they held out, receiving some assistance from Russia. Germany had won all the vital granaries and oil fields at a cost of 60,000 combat casualties. Rumanian losses were almost 400,000. A truce was finally signed on December 6, 1917, and a definitive peace treaty on May 7, 1918. *See* Salonika II; World War I.

Ruspina (Wars of the First Triumvirate), 46 B.C. Returning to Rome after the Zela victory in Asia, Julius Caesar spent three months tightening his grip on the government. Late in 47 B.C. he was forced to sail for North Africa where Sextus, son of the late Pompey the Great, and Juba I, king of Numidia, stood in defiance of Caesar's rule. Landing on the northeast coast of Tunisia, Caesar pushed his army inland from Ruspina (Monastir). He soon (January 3) found his three Roman legions perilously enveloped by hard-hitting Numidian cavalry under the command of Titus Labienus, Caesar's able lieutenant of the Gallic Wars. But the great tactical skill of Caesar again won the day. Forming his infantry so that alternate units faced to the rear and the wings faced outward, the Roman commander ordered an attack. The legionaries shattered the enemy circle in every place at once. Somewhat more cautiously, Caesar now moved south toward Thapsus. *See* Bagradas River; Zela; Thapsus; First Triumvirate, Wars of the.

Russia. The major battles and wars fought under the name of Russia and later the U.S.S.R. are listed below.

Novgorod	862
Adrianople III	972
Kalka River	1223
Neva River	1240
Kiev I	1240
Peipus Lake	1242
Kulikovo	1380
Kandurcha	1391
Kazan	1552
Astrakhan I	1554–1556
Astrakhan II	1569
Polotsk	1579
Beresteczko	1651
Azov	1696
See Great Northern War	
See Polish Succession, War of	
See Austrian Succession, War of	
Çeşme	1770
Focsani	1789
Rimnik	1789
See French Revolution Wars; Napoleonic Empire Wars; Napoleon's Hundred Days	
Kirovabad	1826
Varna II	1828
Kulevcha	1829
See Polish Revolt against Russia	
Timisoara	1849
See Crimean War	
See Russian-Turkish War, 1877–1878	
Geok Tepe	1881
See Russian-Japanese War	
See World War I	
See Russian Civil War	
Vyborg	1918
Warsaw IV	1920
See World War II	

Russian Civil War 1918–1920. The Bolshevik Revolution, which put Nikolai Lenin at the head of the new Communist (Red) government of Russia in November 1917, soon led to civil war with counterrevolutionary forces (White). The situation was aggravated by the Treaty of Brest Litovsk, signed with Germany on March 3, 1918, which took Russia out of World War I at great cost in territory. Poland, Finland, the Ukraine, the Caucasus, and the Baltic provinces (Latvia, Lithuania, Estonia) were surrendered. Many opposed to the harsh treaty terms joined with anti-Communists, provincial nationalists, and Allied troops to wage war on the Soviets on five fronts. The White armies were finally defeated without a major pitched battle by the Red forces molded by Leon Trotsky, who organized and directed a total of several million Soviet soldiers in all. Much of Trotsky's success was due to the confusion and lack of cooperation among the White armies and the passive support given the Reds by the great masses of Russian people.

1. In Siberia, Adm. Aleksandr Kolchak set up a White government at Omsk. He was supported by the Czechoslovak Legion, 40,000 former prisoners and deserters of the Austrian army. Kolchak captured Kazan in August 1918. But his forces gradually melted away before he could cross the Volga River. He was captured and executed in February 1920.

2. American, British, and French troops landed at Murmansk, in the north, in June 1918 and, under the command of the British general Frederick Poole, seized Archangel on August 1 and 2. After sporadic fighting against the Reds, the allied troops were withdrawn late in 1919. There were 500 American casualties in the 339th Infantry Regiment.

3. General Anton Denikin took over command of all White forces in the Caucasus in the fall of 1918. He advanced to Orel, 205 miles from Moscow, before being driven back into the Crimea. General Baron Pëtr Wrangel took over command. But in November 1920 the survivors

were evacuated to Constantinople. The chief Red commander on this front was Semën Budënny.

4. From the Baltic provinces Gen. Nikolai Yudenich struck at Petrograd (Leningrad) in 1919 but was turned back only ten miles short of the city and fled into exile. Estonia, Latvia, and Lithuania were all subdued between February and July 1920.

5. In the Ukraine, Gen. Pavel Skoropadski led an independence movement that collapsed when German troops were withdrawn in November 1918. *See* Vyborg; Warsaw IV; Soviet Union.

Russian-Japanese War (1904–1905). The aggressive policy of Russia (Nicholas II) in the Far East led to increasing friction with Japan (Emperor Mutsuhito). Prolonged negotiations between the two countries collapsed when the Japanese admiral Heihachiro Togo sent his torpedo boats to attack the anchored Russian fleet at Port Arthur, on February 8, 1904. Two days later war was declared. The Japanese won a succession of victories before U.S. President Theodore Roosevelt mediated truce talks. The peace terms signed at Portsmouth, N.H., on September 5, 1905, acknowledged Japan's foremost interest in Korea. Russia ceded its lease on the Liaotung Peninsula and the southern half of Sakhalin. Both powers promised to evacuate Manchuria in favor of China. Japan, which had signed a treaty with Korea in 1904, steadily increased its control until formally annexing that former kingdom in 1910.

Port Arthur II	1904–1905
Yellow Sea	1904
Yalu River II	1904
Liaoyang	1904
Shaho River	1904
Mukden I	1905
Tsushima Strait	1905

Russian-Turkish War (1877–1878). The third war between Russia (Alexander II) and Turkey (Abdul-Hamid II) in the nineteenth century grew out of an earlier conflict between the Ottomans and Serbia. The year after the Turks crushed Serbian resistance in 1876, Russia entered the war in behalf of its fellow Slavs. Turkey, driven back in the Balkans and in the Caucasus, accepted the Treaty of San Stefano on March 3, 1878. Montenegro, Serbia, and Rumania secured their independence. Bulgaria became an autonomous state. Russia received territory in Armenia and a large indemnity. The Berlin Conference during June 13–July 13 modified some of these agreements and gave the administration of Cyprus to Great Britain.

Svištov	1877
Plevna	1877
Kars II	1877
Shipka Pass	1877–1878
Plovdiv	1878

S

Saalfeld (Napoleonic Empire Wars), 1806. The treaty signed between Napoleon I and King Frederick William III of Prussia after the French victory at Austerlitz late in 1805 was short-lived. In the summer of the following year Napoleon formed the south and central states of Germany into the Confederation of the Rhine, in direct opposition to Prussia's territorial interests. Frederick William occupied Saxony and on October 7 demanded that France withdraw west of the Rhine. From his headquarters at Würzburg, Napoleon promptly marched northeast to meet the Prussian army, which was already on the move. He sent three strong columns over the southeastern end of the hilly Thuringian Forest to threaten the enemy's left (south) and rear, on October 8. Unaware of the swift French advance, Prince Louis Frederick (Ferdinand), son of Prince Augustus Ferdinand and nephew of Frederick II (the Great), pushed forward across the Saale River with 9,000 Prussian and Saxon troops. On October 10 the prince suddenly found himself under an enveloping attack by Marshal Jean Lannes's V Corps. Driven back under the walls of Saalfeld, Louis led a desperate cavalry charge against the 5,500 French. The counterattack was crushed and the prince killed. Almost a third of the Prussian army was lost at a cost of 200 French casualties. Lannes crossed the Saale to join in Napoleon's wide sweep against Jena. *See* Austerlitz; Maida; Jena-Auerstedt; Napoleonic Empire Wars.

Sabine Crossroads–Pleasant Hill (American Civil War), 1864. In the last major campaign west of the Mississippi River, the Federal commander, Gen. Nathaniel Banks, led a naval-land expedition up the Red River toward Shreveport, La., beginning on March 10. On April 8 the Federal army approached the road junction of Mansfield, where the Confederate general Richard Taylor had resolved to halt his 200-mile retreat before the superior enemy force. To defend this position, about 40 miles south of Shreveport, Taylor deployed 5,300 infantry and 3,000 cavalry a few miles to his front, at Sabine Crossroads. Although neither commander expected to fight here, advance guards drew both armies into battle late that day. In a fierce encounter Banks's men were driven back in disorder.

That night the Federals withdrew 15 miles southward to Pleasant Hill. Taylor pursued and on the next afternoon attacked Banks, who had assembled reserves to give him a strength of more than 12,000. Taylor, though reinforced to a slight superiority, was defeated this time. In the two-day battle he suffered 2,500 casualties. General Edmund Kirby-Smith, Confederate commander west of the Mississippi, ordered a withdrawal to Mansfield. But when he discovered that Banks was already in retreat, Kirby-Smith sent Taylor to harass the Federal column.

Banks, who had lost more than 3,500 men in two days, abandoned the attempt to take Shreveport. He fell back down the Red River, accompanied by the gunboats of Adm. David Porter. At Alexandria he was forced to fight a series of skirmishes, during May 1–8, before extricating both his army and the river fleet. Banks was relieved later that month. The campaign had also produced such friction in Confederate ranks that Smith relieved Taylor. So ended the fighting in the Trans-Mississippi Department, which, after the fall of Vicksburg on July 4, 1863, had become a minor theater of the war. *See* Port Hudson; Fort Pillow; American Civil War.

Sablat (Thirty Years' War), 1619. The terrible Thirty Years' War began inauspiciously, late in 1618, with the capture of the Catholic city of Pilsen (Plzeň) by a Protestant army of mercenaries under the command of the German general Count Ernst von Mansfeld. The following year Mansfeld marched on the Catholic stronghold of Budweis (České Budějovice), 75 miles to the southeast. En route, the larger part of his 20,000-man column was cut off near the village of Sablat by a royal force sent out by the Bohemian king, Ferdinand (later Ferdinand II, Holy Roman Emperor) and commanded by the Comte de Bucquoy. After seven hours of fighting on June 10, 1619, Mansfeld withdrew at nightfall, having lost his baggage train and 1,500 dead or captured.

This initial Catholic victory widened the gap between the hostile camps. The Catholic League of Germany under Maximilian I of Bavaria took the side of Ferdinand, as did Spain, which stood ready to invade Protestant Germany from Flanders. The Bohemians, on the other hand, named a new king, the Protestant elector palatine, Frederick V. The decisive battle for Bohemia lay just ahead. *See* Pilsen; White Mountain; Thirty Years' War.

Sacile (Napoleonic Empire Wars), 1809. In the fourth war between Austria and France since 1792, both sides mobilized for decisive action along the Danube River in southern Germany and Austria. It was in the secondary theater of northern Italy, however, that the first battle took place. Here Eugène de Beauharnais, viceroy of Italy and stepson of Napoleon I, commanded an army of 37,000 French and Italians. In opposition stood an Austrian army of 40,000 under Archduke John, brother of Emperor Francis I. On April 16, 1809, the two hostile forces clashed in a disorganized scuffle at Sacile in northeastern Italy, near the head of the Adriatic. When an Austrian flank movement threatened the French line of retreat, Eugène fell back behind the Piave River, and later the Adige. No action followed until Napoleon's thrust to Vienna later that month forced Archduke John to retreat into Hungary. Eugène pursued. *See* Abensberg; Raab; Napoleonic Empire Wars.

Sackets Harbor (War of 1812), 1813. During much of 1813 the British and Canadians fought the Americans in New York State for control of Lake Ontario. The most determined British assault was made by Sir George Prevost, governor general of Canada, on Sackets Harbor at the eastern end of the lake. On May 28 and 29 Prevost's expeditionary force assaulted the American garrison of 600 men commanded by Gen. Jacob Brown. But Brown's men held their ground and finally forced the invaders to withdraw. Meanwhile, another battle was shaping up at the western end of the lake. *See* Queenston Heights; Stony Creek; War of 1812.

Sadowa (Seven Weeks' War), 1866. The Prussian offensive against Austria, engineered by chief of the general staff, Gen. Helmuth von Moltke (later Count von Moltke), got under way in June 1866. Making the first large-scale military use of the telegraph and railroads in Europe, Moltke sent three armies southward to converge on Gitschin (Jičin) in northeastern Bohemia. The First Army of Prince Frederick Charles, with the Army of the Elbe (Karl Herwarth von Bittenfeld) on its right, crossed the Bohemian Mountains to engage the Austrian advance guard at Münchengrätz (Mnichovo Hradiště) and Gitschin late in June. Faced with this forward concentration of 125,000 Prussians, the Austrian commander, Gen. Ludwig von Benedek, began to withdraw his 205,000 troops to the southeast toward Königgrätz (Hradec Králové), on the upper Labe (Elbe) River. But the retreat was so leisurely that the Prussian First Army caught up with the Austrians at Sadowa, some 65 miles east of Prague, on July 3 before Benedek could cross the river.

The Prussian plan was to fix the enemy until the Second Army of Crown Prince Frederick William (later Frederick III) could come up on the left (east) flank from Silesia. However, the rash attack of Gen. Eduard von Fransecky's 7th Division brought on a major battle on the morning of July

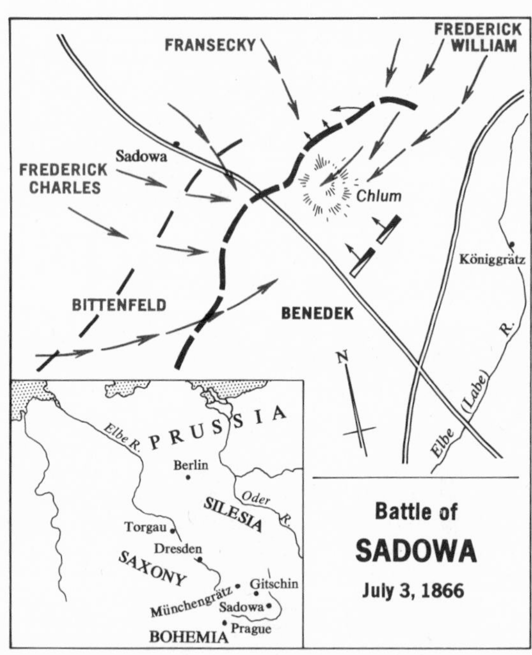

Battle of SADOWA
July 3, 1866

3. Taking advantage of their superiority in numbers, the Austrians battered the attackers along the entire seven-mile arc of the front. His orders delayed by a broken telegraph line, the crown prince and his army of almost 100,000 men did not arrive until afternoon. Hurrying forward, he struck the right flank of the Austrian line a massive blow that carried the hill at Chlum, the key to the Austrian defensive position. When Benedek's cavalry counterattacks failed, the battle was lost. Under cover of heavy artillery fire, the beaten Austrians (including 25,000 Saxons) withdrew. They had lost 40,000 men, half of them prisoners. Prussian casualties totaled 9,000. A major factor in the Prussian victory was the use of the needle gun, a center-fire, breech-loading rifle that gave a rapid rate of fire and could be loaded from a prone position (which was impossible for the Austrian muzzle-loaders).

The battle of Sadowa, which engaged the largest number of troops yet found on a European battlefield, bankrupted the military resources of Franz

Josef I. A preliminary peace treaty was signed on July 26, the definitive terms on August 23. Thus ended the second of the three wars by which Iron Chancellor Otto von Bismarck forged the empire of Germany. And Sadowa became one of the decisive battles of history. *See* Münchengrätz; Seven Weeks' War; Franco-Prussian War.

Saguntum (Second Punic War), 219–218 B.C. Soon after Carthage ceded Sicily to Rome at the end of the First Punic War, the African republic began establishing a colony in eastern Spain. For 20 years New Carthage, as the colony was called, flourished under Hamilcar Barca, who was succeeded by his son-in-law Hasdrubal and then by his son Hannibal in 221. A covenant with Rome (signed 226) limited Carthaginian expansion to the region south of the Ebro River. Within this sphere of influence stood the fortress of Saguntum, which was allied to Rome. In the summer of 219, Hannibal, with an army composed largely of Spanish recruits, attacked the fortress but was driven off. He then laid siege to the city and after eight months took its surrender.

The conquest of Saguntum provoked the Second Punic War between Rome and Carthage. To forestall a Roman invasion of Carthage, Hannibal resolved to attack the homeland of the Italian republic. In May 218 the able Carthaginian general began a long, hazardous march from New Carthage at the head of a loyal but wildly assorted army of 46,000 Africans and Iberians.

Hannibal crossed the Pyrenees and entered southern France. Hearing of the march, the Roman general Publius Cornelius Scipio took a fleet to Marseille (Marseilles) during the summer, but he was too late to intercept the fast-moving Carthaginians. Hannibal crossed the Rhone and struck northeast into the Alps. In an astonishing feat of strength and skill, Hannibal led his army over the crest of the Alps in 15 November days despite heavy snows and extreme cold. Rome now revised its strategy. A planned invasion of Carthage was canceled. Publius Scipio returned to Italy to defend the Roman outposts in the Po Valley, while his brother Gnaeus Cornelius Scipio led an expedition to Spain. *See* Aegates Islands; Trebbia River I; Punic Wars.

Saint Albans I (Wars of the Roses), 1455. The periodic fits of insanity suffered by King Henry VI led to a power struggle between the houses of Lancaster (red rose) and York (white rose) to dominate the government of England. In the spring of 1455 Richard of York raised an army of 3,000 men in the north and with the earls of Salisbury and Warwick (father and son, both named Richard Neville), marched toward London. King Henry, Queen Margaret, and the dukes of Somerset (Edmund Beaufort) and Buckingham (Humphrey Stafford) at the head of a slightly smaller force moved out from London to intercept the rebels. They reached Saint Albans, 20 miles to the northwest, and halted there. On May 22, 1455, Richard of York assaulted the Lancastrians in Saint Albans with archery and cannon, while Warwick led a group of mounted knights around the town and attacked from the rear. The envelopment routed the royalist knights. Three hundred men perished, including the lords Somerset and Thomas de Clifford and many other Lancastrian nobles. The king submitted to Yorkist control, while Margaret and her two-year-old son Edward fled into exile.

Saint Albans was the opening battle in a 30-year war between York and Lancaster. Although the struggle left little mark on the common people, the nobility fought so implacably that their ranks became severely depleted. *See* Blore Heath; Roses, Wars of the.

Saint Albans II (Wars of the Roses), 1461. From its victory at Wakefield, Queen Margaret's Lancastrian army (red rose) began an advance on London to free King Henry VI from Yorkist (white rose) control. The Earl of Warwick (Richard Neville) moved out to Saint Albans, 20 miles northwest of the capital. Here his Yorkist army from Calais blocked the royal advance and awaited reinforcements from Edward of York, who was marching eastward from his victory at Mortimer's Cross. But before Edward could arrive, Queen Margaret launched a surprise attack on February 17. The Lancastrians stormed into the town and killed half the Yorkist troops. Warwick and the Duke of Norfolk (John Mowbray VI) barely escaped, abandoning King Henry under a tree. Sir Thomas Kyriel, a redoubtable veteran of the Hundred Years' War, who was charged with the king's safekeeping, was captured and beheaded.

Led by their reunited king and queen, the Lancastrians could have entered London unopposed. Instead they marched off to the north. This proved to be a decisive mistake. Warwick, his shattered army now strengthened by the forces of the tardy Edward of York, fell back to London. Here the young Yorkist noble had himself proclaimed King Edward IV, on March 4, 1461. But he knew that to enforce his claim he needed to crush the Lancastrians. Edward promptly marched northward seeking out the army of Henry and Margaret. *See* Wakefield; Mortimer's Cross; Ferrybridge; Roses, Wars of the.

Saint-Denis (French Religious Wars), 1567. Four years after the end of the first uprising, a new civil war broke out between the Protestant Huguenots and the Catholic crown of France. Charles IX, who ruled under the domination of his mother, Catherine de Médicis, and the house of Guise, sent an army to Saint-Denis, seven miles northeast of Paris. Under the command of the

Duc de Montmorency, the royal cavalry defeated the heavily outnumbered Huguenot force led by the Prince de Condé, and Gaspard de Coligny, admiral of France. But the battle took the life of Montmorency and had no real effect on the steadily worsening civil strife. The Peace of Longjumeau, signed on March 23 of the following year, proved to be equally indecisive. *See* Dreux; Jarnac; French Religious Wars.

Saintes (English-French Wars), 1242. Civil unrest in France prompted Henry III to invade the nation of Louis IX in an attempt to win back the Angevin lands lost during the reign of his father, King John. Making an alliance with the French rebels, the counts of La Marche and Toulouse, Henry landed at Saintonge, on the Bay of Biscay, with an army built around a corps of 700 crossbowmen. He received little military help from his French allies, however, when Louis IX marched to repel the English expedition. The French royalist army pushed across the Charente River at Taillebourg on July 20, putting the English in an untenable position. The two armies clashed at Saintes the following day; Henry was defeated. Although it was a minor battle, the English king realized his position had become hopeless. He retreated into Gascony and abandoned the war against Louis. In 1259 the Treaty of Paris confirmed the English loss of northwestern France, but Henry retained a claim to Gascony. *See* Bedford; Courtrai.

Saintes, Les (War of the American Revolution), 1782. Following the decisive French-American victory over Great Britain at Yorktown in 1781, the scene of the American phase of the war shifted to the West Indies. Here a French fleet of 33 warships under the Comte de Grasse began escorting an invasion convoy of 150 vessels toward British-held Jamaica in the following spring. At the three little islands called Les Saintes, between Guadeloupe and Dominica, de Grasse encountered a British fleet of 37 ships of the line commanded by Adm. George Rodney. On April 9 the two fleets engaged in a long-range gun duel with no advantage to either side. In maneuvering during the next two days, collisions among the French fleet put three vessels out of action. Then, early in the morning of April 12, a favorable wind brought on a major battle. (Earlier that day French and British ships had clashed off Ceylon, half a world away at Trincomalee.) The fleets had nearly passed each other on opposite tacks when a change of wind enabled the British to break the French line of battle in two places. De Grasse failed to re-form his line and, after a day-long battle, surrendered his flagship, *Ville de Paris,* to Adm. Lord Hood, in the *Barfleur*. Meanwhile Rodney, in the *Formidable,* directed the taking of four other French ships. The remainder of the French vessels scattered. Most of them later reassembled at Haiti, but the defeat ended all hopes of attacking Jamaica.

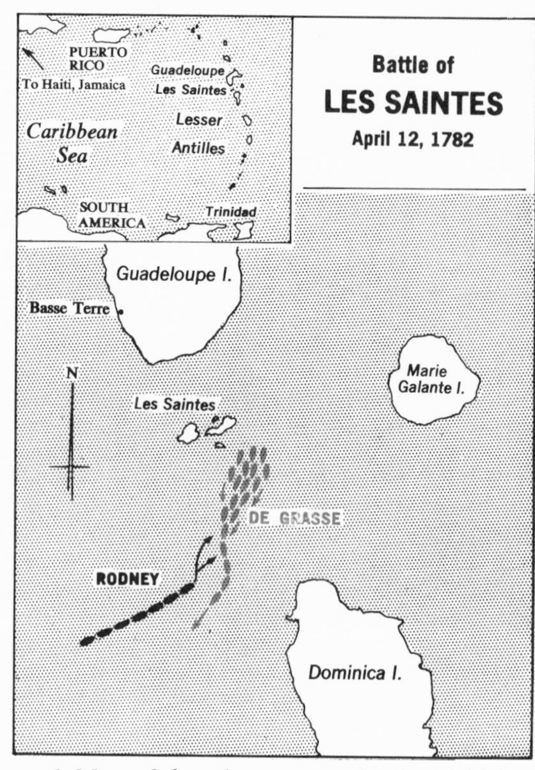

The battle of Les Saintes (or Dominica) was the largest maritime struggle in a century. But Rodney drew much criticism for not aggressively pursuing the beaten fleet and thereby winning an even greater victory. Instead, he put in at Jamaica with his notable prisoner, De Grasse, the first French naval commander ever to be taken in combat. This battle ended the fighting in the Western Hemisphere. Only in India and its nearby waters did the war continue. *See* Yorktown I; Trincomalee I; American Revolution.

Saint Jacob-en-Birs (Swiss-French Wars), 1444. During a period of civil strife among the Swiss cantons, the French dauphin of Charles VII, the future Louis XI, invaded Switzerland with an army of 15,000 Orleanist (Armagnac) mercenaries. A Swiss phalanx of less than 1,000 men, armed with the customary pikes and halberds, marched out to meet the invaders. Obsessed with a belief in their invincibility, the Swiss crossed the Birs just south of Basel and attacked the much larger army at Saint Jacob on September 24, 1444. The force of their assault broke the French center, but then they were surrounded. Forming a hedgehog, the stubborn Swiss fought off numerous cavalry charges interspersed with missile bombardments. It was not until the end of the day that the last defender fell. But the victory cost Louis 2,000 dead. He abandoned the invasion and turned back into Alsace. Although defeated, the Swiss enhanced their military reputation for fielding armies of courageous men who chose annihilation to retreat. *See* Arbedo; Héricourt.

Saint Johns (War of the American Revolution). A British-held fort (Saint-Jean) taken on November 2, 1775, after a 55-day siege, by the American general Richard Montgomery in his march to Montreal. *See* Quebec III.

Saint-Lô Breakthrough (World War II), 1944. During the first seven weeks of the Normandy invasion, Allied forces had built up according to plan. But fierce German resistance had contained the beachhead just south of a line from Caen through Caumont and Saint-Lô to Lessay, about 20 miles inland from the landing beaches. To break out of the rugged hedgerow country, which restricted the use of armor, the British general Sir Bernard Montgomery and the U.S. general Omar Bradley prepared Operation Cobra.

The attack jumped off on July 25 behind a bomb carpet in which Allied planes dropped 4,200 tons of bombs in an area 2,500 by 6,000 yards, west of Saint-Lô ("shorts" caused 558 U.S. infantry casualties). Gen. J. Lawton Collins' VII Corps of the U.S. First Army launched the assault. Although suffering more than 1,000 casualties the first day, Collins committed two mobile columns on July 26. While the left held off savage German counterattacks, the right fought its way into Coutances on July 28 and two days later plunged to Avranches, at the northern base of the Brittany Peninsula. On August 1 the U.S. Third Army under Gen. George Patton became operational. Patton's armor struck quickly through the gap at Avranches. The VIII Corps knifed into Brittany and then sliced the region off by reaching Nantes on August 10. (The major ports—Brest, Lorient, Saint-Nazaire—held out and were bypassed.) Three other corps raced south and east toward the rear of Gen. Paul Hausser's German Seventh Army.

On August 6 German armor at Mortain launched a powerful counterattack westward toward Avranches. It was aimed at cutting off Patton's columns from the rear. But Gen. Courtney Hodges' U.S. First Army parried the blow after two days of bitter fighting. On August 8 Patton turned his XV Corps northward toward Argentan. This move threatened to crush the entire German army group of Field Marshal Gunther von Kluge against the anvil of the British Second and Canadian First armies, which were still holding the Allied base line from Caen to Caumont. *See* Normandy; Falaise-Argentan Pocket; World War II.

Saint-Mihiel (World War I), 1918. The newly arrived and activated American First Army of Gen. John Pershing formally took over the Saint-Mihiel sector on August 30. This was a salient jutting to the Meuse River southeast of Verdun that the Germans, now under the supreme command of Gen. Erich Ludendorff, had carved out in 1914. After the two successful Allied offenses on the Marne River and east of Amiens during the summer, the Germans began withdrawing from the salient on September 11. They were too late. Early the following morning 16 American divisions attacked, aided by French artillery and tanks and an air force of mixed units commanded by the U.S. colonel William Mitchell. Two American corps, the I and IV, struck the south face of the salient, while the French II Colonial Corps hit the nose and the American V moved in from the west. Within 36 hours the surprised Germans were driven from the salient with a loss of 15,000 prisoners and more than 250 guns. Pershing suffered 7,000 casualties.

The American attack could have carried deeper into the German lines, but the offensive had been deliberately limited by the Allied commander in chief, Marshal Ferdinand Foch. Pershing's troops were now moved westward to the Argonne Forest to begin a major offensive. *See* Marne River II; Amiens; Meuse River–Argonne Forest; World War I.

Saint-Quentin I (Spanish-French Wars), 1557. The Valois-Hapsburg struggle in northern Italy made the Spanish Hapsburg Charles V of the Holy Roman Empire the dominant figure in Italy by 1525. The chief site of hostilities then shifted to western Europe. In 1552 the French Valois king Henry II seized the Three Bishoprics—Toul, Metz, and Verdun. But when fighting erupted again in 1557, the Flemish Comte d'Egmont, in the service of Charles's successor, Philip II, marched into northern France with a largely Spanish army reinforced by some English. The French, under the constable Duc Anne de Montmorency, hurried a relieving army toward Saint-Quentin on the Somme River. On August 10, 1557, however, the French were intercepted in a narrow defile and subjected to a series of hard-hitting cavalry attacks. Almost two-thirds of the 20,000-man force was killed, wounded, or captured. One of those captured, and held prisoner for three years, was the French Admiral Gaspard de Coligny. D'Egmont's smaller Hapsburg army suffered far fewer casualties. *See* Pavia V; Calais II; Gravelines.

Saint-Quentin II (Franco-Prussian War), 1871. Although the French people had bravely taken up arms after the defeat of their army at Sedan, the civilian units were no match for the well-trained Prussian forces of occupation. One by one the provincial armies collapsed before they could seriously challenge the Prussian siege of Paris. The last remaining French army in the field, along the upper Somme River, was commanded by Gen.

Louis Faidherbe. This force of about 40,000 men encountered a smaller Prussian army, commanded by Gen. Auguste von Goeben, at Saint-Quentin on January 19. The French were decisively beaten, losing more than 3,000 in killed and wounded and some 9,000 prisoners. German casualties were little more than 2,000. The defeat at Saint-Quentin ended all hope of relieving the Paris garrison, which surrendered nine days later. *See* Bapaume; Le Mans; Paris II; Franco-Prussian War.

Saint-Quentin III (World War I). The right flank objective of the last major Allied offensive of the war; it started on September 29, 1918, and forced the Germans out of Saint-Quentin on October 1, opening the way to a large-scale breakthrough. *See* Cambrai–Saint-Quentin.

Saint Vincent Cape I (War of the American Revolution), 1780. When Spain entered the war on June 16, 1779, on the side of France and the United States, Spanish King Charles III sent a fleet to cooperate with the French navy in laying siege to the British base at Gibraltar. To relieve the fortress, a British fleet of 20 warships under Adm. George Rodney sailed from England on December 29. Passing Cape Saint Vincent, on the southwest coast of Portugal, Rodney encountered a Spanish fleet of 11 ships of the line commanded by Adm. Don Juan de Langara. Believing the approaching vessels were merely a supply convoy, the Spanish admiral did not try to escape until it was too late. Rodney sent his ships to attack on January 16. In a brief contest, one Spanish warship was blown up and six were captured, with no loss to the British. Rodney took the captured vessels and the supply ships he was convoying into Gibraltar. This aid helped the fortress endure a siege (loosely maintained) of more than three and a half years. *See* Gibraltar II; American Revolution.

Saint Vincent Cape II (Wars of the French Revolution), 1797. The second naval battle of the war took place early in 1797 after Great Britain had been driven out of the Mediterranean and now faced the hostile fleets of France, Spain, and the Netherlands. On February 14, the British admiral Sir John Jervis with 15 ships of the line was sailing 25 miles off Cape Saint Vincent on the southwest coast of Portugal. Here he encountered a Spanish fleet of 27 vessels under Don José de Córdoba, sailing for Cadiz, Spain, in two sections. The main Spanish section of 18 ships turned northward. Without waiting for orders, Com. Horatio Nelson (later Lord Nelson) doubled back to lead the attack against this larger group. Four Spanish ships with 3,000 prisoners were taken without the loss of a British vessel and only 300 casualties. For this notable victory Jervis was made Earl of Saint Vincent and Nelson a Knight of the Bath. *See* Ushant II; Camperdown; Nile River; French Revolution War.

Saint-Vith (World War II). A sturdy roadblock by the U.S. 7th Armored Division, between December 17 and 23, 1944, that delayed the German advance along the northern side of the Ardennes bulge. *See* Ardennes II.

Saipan (World War II). The first of the Japanese-held Mariana Islands to be captured by U.S. troops in fighting between June 15 and July 9, 1944. *See* Mariana Islands.

Sajó, The (Mongol Invasion of Europe). *See* Mohi.

Sakarya River (Greek-Turkish War II), 1921. With the support of the victorious Allies of World War I, Greek troops occupied Smyrna (Izmir) on May 15, 1919. Turkey, under Sultan Mohammed VI, stood in such danger of dismemberment that a strong nationalist movement developed, under Mustafa Kemal (Kemal Pasha), who later came to be known as Kemal Ataturk. When this group established a provisional government at Angora (Ankara) in 1920, the Greek army of Alexander I advanced inland, on June 22. Two days later the invaders pushed into Alasehir, 75 miles to the east. Here the offensive was halted for peace negotiations in Constantinople (later Istanbul). When the nationalists refused to abide by the sultan's concessions the Greeks, now ruled by Constantine I, renewed their attack on March 23, 1921. At İnönü, 150 miles west of Angora, the invaders were temporarily checked by a force under İsmet Paşa, who took the name of the town for his surname. By August 24 the Greeks had advanced to the Sakarya River, within 70 miles of Angora. A desperate Turkish defense led by Mustafa Kemal and İsmet Paşa finally threw back the invaders on September 16.

On August 18 of the following year the Turks launched a counteroffensive, which steadily drove back the Greeks. By September 9, Smyrna was liberated and the Greek army expelled from the mainland. The Treaty of Lausanne, signed in 1923, ended the undeclared war. Greek claims to Anatolia were denied and the Turkish border in Europe was fixed at the Maritsa River. Meanwhile, Mohammed VI abdicated, ending seven centuries of Ottoman rule. Mustafa Kemal became the first president of the new republic.

Salado, Río. *See* Río Salado.

Salamanca (Napoleonic Empire Wars), 1812. After reducing the French-held fortresses of Ciudad Rodrigo and Badajoz, near the Spanish-Portuguese border, early in 1812, Gen. Lord Wellington (Arthur Wellesley) thrust boldly into northern Spain. With some 40,000 British, Portuguese, and rebel Spanish troops, Wellington maneuvered for weeks to gain an advantage over the French army of similar size commanded by Marshal Auguste Marmont. Finally the two hostile forces clashed on July 22 at Salamanca, 107 miles northwest of Madrid. Wellington's troops scored a signal victory, inflicting 12,000 casualties at a cost to themselves of 5,000 men. Marmont was wounded. His successor, Gen. Comte Bertrand Clausel, skillfully pulled back the defeated army.

Wellington promptly marched for Madrid, while King Joseph Bonaparte, older brother of Napoleon I, fled with his government beyond the Ebro River. But the British stay in the Spanish capital was short-lived. The French marshal Nicolas Soult, marching up from Andalusia with superior numbers, threatened to isolate Wellington in Madrid. To protect his lines of communications, the British commander fell back to the Portuguese frontier. *See* Badajoz; Vitoria; Napoleonic Empire Wars.

Salamis (Persian-Greek Wars), 480 B.C. The Persian invasion of Greece under Xerxes began more auspiciously than had that of Xerxes' father, Darius I, ten years earlier at Marathon. On land, the Persians overran most of Greece as far south as the Isthmus of Corinth. At sea, Xerxes' navy of almost 600 galleys bottled up the 366 triremes (three banks of oars) of the Greek fleet in the Saronic Gulf. While the Persian army watched from the shore in September, the Greek commander Themistocles lured Xerxes' fleet into the cramped waters off Salamis. With Persian maneuverability seriously hampered, the Greek triremes, under the Spartan Eurybiades, attacked furiously. By ramming and boarding tactics, the Athenians sank more than 200 (perhaps 300) of the enemy galleys at a cost of 40 of their own vessels.

In this first decisive naval battle of history the Persian fleet was driven from the shores of Europe. Xerxes now had to postpone further ground attacks until the following year, giving the Greek city-states time to unite against him. The Great King himself returned to Asia, leaving 80,000 men under his brother-in-law Mardonius. *See* Thermopylae I; Plataea I; Mycale; Persian-Greek Wars.

Salem Church (American Civil War). A part of the battle of Chancellorsville, on May 3 and 4, 1863, in which the Federal east wing was defeated and driven northward across the Rappahannock River. *See* Chancellorsville.

Salerno (World War II), 1943. Although the British Eighth Army had invaded the Italian mainland in the south on September 3, the main Allied thrust was directed at Salerno on the west coast. The ultimate objective was the key port of Naples. On the eve of the September 9 landing the Italian government of Marshal Pietro Badoglio surrendered to the Allied supreme commander, Gen. Dwight Eisenhower. But German troops under Field Marshal Albert Kesselring seized control of strategic points in Italy and poured southward to stop the Allied thrust up the boot. (On September 12, Nazi commandos under Capt. Otto Skorzeny rescued the imprisoned Benito Mussolini, who was then installed as puppet head of German-occupied Italy.)

The Allied Fifth Army under the U.S. general Mark Clark made the amphibious assault on Salerno (Operation Avalanche) at dawn on September 9, 1943. The U.S. VI Corps, commanded by Gen. Ernest Dawley (later relieved by Gen. John Lucas), landed on the right (southern) flank. In the first three days the 36th and 45th Infantry divisions took Paestum and pushed ten miles inland. On the left the British X Corps (56th and 46th divisions) under Gen. Richard McCreery captured Battipaglia, near the center of the beachhead, and the town of Salerno, along the northern flank.

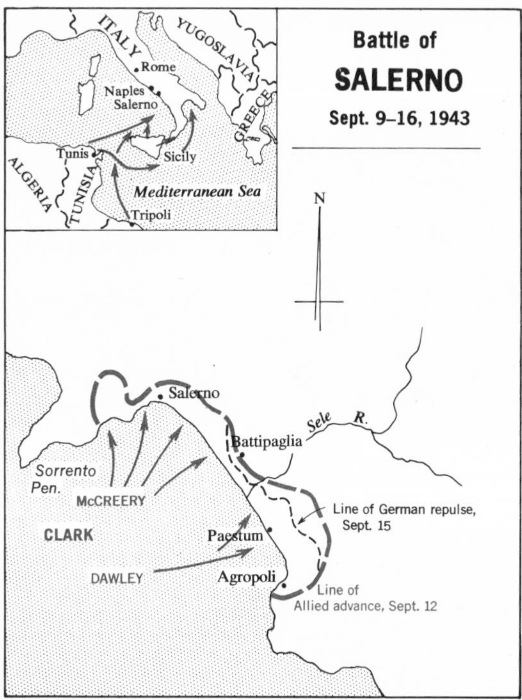

On September 12, however, the Germans launched a furious counterattack. Strong armored units recaptured Battipaglia and on the third day of the assault pressed to within two miles of the coast in some places. On September 14 Allied planes made 2,000 air strikes against the attacking Nazis, while the guns of Allied warships added to the bombardment. The British general Sir Harold Alexander, in charge of Allied ground forces in Italy, rushed in the U.S. 82nd Airborne and the British 7th Armoured divisions. By the evening of September 15 the counterattack was stopped and Kesselring began pulling back his forces. The next day Gen. Sir Bernard Montgomery's British

Eighth Army, moving up from southern Italy, established contact with the hard-pressed Fifth Army. The Salerno landing was finally secure.

Reinforced by the U.S. 3rd Division, Gen. Clark's troops then broke out of the beachhead toward Naples. That port city fell to the Fifth Army on October 1. It soon became the key base for supplying the Allied northward drive up the Italian boot. *See* Italy, Southern; Gustav Cassino-Line; World War II.

Salonika I (Turkish-Venetian Wars), 1430. The crushing defeat at Angora in 1402 paralyzed the Ottoman Empire until the strong ruler Murad II rebuilt the sultanate during the 1420's. During this time the Venetians had taken over the defense of Salonika, the key to the Vardar Valley, from the Byzantine Empire as part of a mutual pact against the Turks. In resuming the Ottoman advance in Europe, Murad attacked Salonika on March 1, 1430. The 1,500-man Venetian garrison could not hold off the determined Turkish assault. Salonika fell and the surviving defenders were either executed or sold into slavery. Islam was again on the march in southeastern Europe. (Salonika would remain in Turkish hands until 1912.) *See* Angora; Varna I.

Salonika II (World War I), 1915–1918. When Bulgaria mobilized in September 1915 for concerted action with Austria-Hungary and Germany against Serbia, the Allies rushed a British and French division to Salonika, Greece, on October 3. Nine days later the French general Maurice Sarrail began marching northward to the aid of Serbia. But the relief was too little and too late. The Bulgarian Second Army of Gen. Nicolas Jekov, driving steadily westward, cut the railroad from Salonika on October 23. Screening off the Allied advance, the Bulgarians pressed deeper into Serbia. Sarrail, who now commanded two more French divisions, fell back to Lake Dojran on the Greek border. With Serbia defeated, mounting Bulgarian pressure and the wavering attitude of the Greek government (King Constantine I) compelled Sarrail to withdraw to Salonika on December 3. Although the port facilities were small and the climate unfavorable, the Allies decided to hold Salonika (soon called the Bird Cage). Sarrail's Armée d'Orient was increased to about 250,000 men by mid-1916, including the reconstituted Serbian army from Corfu.

In the summer of 1916 Sarrail began to advance northward toward the Macedonian frontier of Greece. But a counterattack by the German Eleventh Army, on the west, and the Bulgarian First, Second, and Fourth armies, aligned eastward, limited the Allied advance. The new front became stabilized by August 27. To help Rumania, which had entered the war on the Allied side, Sarrail launched a new offensive in September. Bitolj (Monastir) in Serbia was taken on November 19. But again German-Bulgar resistance firmly checked the offensive by French, British, Russian, Italian, and Serbian troops. The Central Powers suffered 60,000 casualties, the Allies 50,000. With Rumania knocked out of the war, the Salonika front again quieted down.

In March 1917 another Sarrail offensive proved to be inconclusive. Now Allied pressure finally forced the abdication of pro-German Constantine from the Greek throne, on June 12. His second son, Alexander, came to power, and two weeks later Greece entered the war on the Allied side. But there was little to be gained as long as the quarrelsome Sarrail remained in command. He was finally relieved, on December 22, 1917, by the French general Marie Guillaumat. The new commander reorganized the Salonika force, which now numbered over 350,000 combat troops. When Guillaumat was recalled to the Western Front in July 1918, Gen. Louis Franchet d'Esperey took over the Allied army.

By late summer of 1918 Germany had virtually abandoned the Salonika front to Bulgaria. The Bulgarian troops were suffering from short supplies and poor morale. When Franchet d'Esperey began a well-organized offensive on September 14, the Bulgarians quickly collapsed. The general Allied assault was launched by, from left (west) to right, the French (in part), Serbians, French (in part), British, and Greek armies. By September 17 the attackers had advanced 20 miles in the center. The battered Bulgarians were split and in full retreat from Albania to the Struma (Strymon) River. Passing through the infantry, the French cavalry took Skoplje on September 29. The isolated German Eleventh Army (stripped of all German troops except the staffs) surrendered. With the road to Sofia opened, Bulgaria signed an armistice on September 30. King Ferdinand abdicated four days later as Allied columns raced through the Balkans.

The drawn-out Salonika battle wasted a great deal of Allied manpower and supplies desperately needed on the Western Front. Casualty figures will never be definitely known. However, it is clear that malaria weakened Allied ranks far more than did enemy action. For example, the British reported 481,000 cases of illness in contrast to 18,000 wounded during the campaign. During the summer of 1916, the French had 35,122 hospital cases, of which only 672 were combat casualties. *See* Serbia (World War I); Rumania (World War I); World War I.

Salt River (Apache Wars), 1872. When the Apaches of Arizona took the warpath in 1872, they were pursued by Col. George Crook. Choosing a winter campaign, Crook marched from Camp Date Creek through the Tonto Basin. In a canyon along Salt River, in the south-central part of present-day Arizona, the column of regular cavalry and infantry caught up with the Indians. Here and farther downriver at Turret Butte, Crook's men destroyed the force of outlaw Apaches on December 26. Returned to reservations the following year, the Apaches resumed hostilities in 1885. Their leader, Geronimo, surrendered to Crook's successor, Gen. Nelson Miles, in 1886, ending the Apache wars. *See* Washita River; Lava Beds; Indian Wars in the United States.

Salûm–Halfaya Pass (World War II), 1941. General Erwin Rommel's first North African offensive, starting from El Agheila on March 24, swept across Cyrenaica (except Tobruk) and into Egypt during April 1941. Desperate for a British victory, the Middle East commander in chief, Gen. Sir Archibald Wavell, at the insistence of Prime Minister Winston Churchill, launched a premature counterattack in an effort to relieve besieged Tobruk. Called Operation Battleaxe, the two-division attack by Gen. Noel Beresford-Peirse took place at the coastal town of Salûm and inland at Halfaya Pass in northwestern Egypt during June 15–17. It was beaten back with more than 1,000 casualties and the loss of 100 tanks, or about half the British armored strength. Four days later Wavell was replaced. He was sent to India in a trade of assignments with Gen. Sir Claude Auchinleck, who earlier had been at Narvik in the Norwegian campaign. The battle of Salûm–Halfaya Pass is also notable for the first World War II appearance of the German 88-mm. gun as a deadly antitank weapon. *See* Tobruk II; Sidi-Rezegh; World War II.

Samar (World War II). A naval action off the east coast of Samar Island between Japanese and American forces on October 25, 1944, that constitutes part of the battle of Leyte Gulf. *See* Leyte Gulf.

Samaria (Fall of Israel), 722 B.C. To preserve some of its autonomy, the kingdom of Israel in northern Palestine agreed to pay tribute to the powerful Assyrian Empire. During the reign of King Hoshea (Osee), however, this tribute was withheld. An Assyrian army under Shalmaneser V marched into Israel in 724 B.C. and laid siege to the capital of Samaria, 36 miles northwest of Jerusalem. The thick walls of the city held out the invaders for a time. But in the third year of the siege, Sargon II, who had succeeded to the Assyrian throne upon the death of Shalmaneser, burst into Samaria and took its inhabitants prisoner. Hoshea and more than 27,000 of his people were exiled to Media. The kingdom of Israel ceased to exist. *See* Nineveh I; Jerusalem I.

Samarkand (Mongol Conquest of Central Asia), 1220. The fall of Bukhara early in 1220 left the Khwarizm city of Samarkand in an untenable position. To the east and south stood some 50,000 Mongols under the command of Genghis Khan's eldest son, Juji (Juchi). To the west, the Great Khan himself, after the sack and burning of Bukhara, began moving on the ancient city. Samarkand's governor tightened the defenses and prepared to withstand a siege with some 50,000 warriors. Once the Mongol horde had surrounded the city, however, traitors opened the gates, hoping to appease the fierce invaders. The treachery served no purpose. The Mongols methodically slaughtered and sacked, only slightly less devastatingly than at Bukhara a few weeks before. The barbarian tide prepared to move on. Meanwhile, Mohammed, the shah of Khwarizm, fled to an island in the Caspian Sea, closely pursued by two of the Khan's divisions. He escaped capture but died of exhaustion and hardship. *See* Khojend; Bukhara; Herat I; Mongol Wars.

Sambre. *See* Charleroi, under Frontiers of France.

Sambre River (Gallic Wars), 57 B.C. During the winter of 58–57 B.C., Julius Caesar rested and reinforced his Roman army in Burgundy. In the spring he marched northwest with eight legions to try to put down the Belgic confederacy of Gallic tribes. Along the Aisne River, Caesar took the surrender of the Suessiones and Bellovaci without a battle. Farther north, however, the Nervii headed a tribal coalition that was determined to resist the Roman advance. On the near side of the Sambre, Caesar made camp. He sent his cavalry across the river to feel out the enemy position. The Gauls quickly routed the Roman horsemen and then swarmed across the Sambre to attack the main force of legionaries. In a fierce, hand-to-hand struggle, the Roman left and center threw back the attackers. On the right, however, two legions (Seventh and Twelfth) were surrounded and in danger of annihilation. Caesar then rode out in front of the line and took personal charge of the battle. This action rallied the Romans. A counterattack broke the enemy lines, sending them back across the river. Of some 50,000 Gauls who launched the attack, few more than 500 survived.

Another tribe, the Aduatuci, had been moving west from the Rhine to reinforce the Nervii. Caesar now turned his legions toward this group. Near modern Namur the Aduatuci offered a false surrender. The Romans discovered the trick, killed 4,000, and sold other thousands into slavery. Caesar then established winter quarters along the Loire between what is now Orleans and Angers. *See* Vesontio; Morbihan Gulf; Gallic Wars.

Samnite Wars (343–290 B.C.). A series of three wars in which the growing republic of Rome established its supremacy over central Italy. The First Samnite War produced no real battles and ended inconclusively. After subduing the Samnites, Rome turned on their Gallic and Etruscan allies and crushed them at Vadimonis Lake.

Second Samnite War

Caudine Forks	321 B.C.
Bovianum	305 B.C.

Third Samnite War

Camerinum 298 B.C.
Sentinum 295 B.C.

Samosata (Byzantine-Moslem Wars), 873. After many years of being on the defensive against Moslem attacks in Asia Minor, the Byzantine Empire swung over to the offensive in 873. Directed by the first of the Macedonian emperors, Basil I, the Imperial cavalry drove eastward to take Samosata (Samsat) on the upper Euphrates River. This battle marked the beginning of a Byzantine military revival, just at the time the Moslem world was wracked by internal conflict. *See* Amorium; Apulia; Moslem Conquests.

Sand Creek (Cheyenne and Arapahoe War), 1864. The killing of an emigrant party near Denver in the fall of 1864 climaxed a growing hostility between Indians and settlers in the West. Colorado settlers demanded prompt retaliatory action. A fanatical militia colonel, John M. Chivington, assembled 900 men and marched against a camp of Cheyenne and Arapahoe Indians on Sand Creek, in present Kiowa County. Many of the Indian warriors were away negotiating a peace treaty with the United States government. On November 29 Chivington swooped down on the unsuspecting Indian village, which was ruled by Black Kettle. Some 300 were killed, including 225 women and children. Ten soldiers lost their lives. The Sand Creek massacre, as it came to be called, provoked the Plains Indians into a long and savage struggle against the white settlers and the U.S. Army in the West. *See* Platte Bridge; Indian Wars in the United States.

Sandwich I (First Barons' War of England), 1217. During the summer of 1217 the royalist forces of young Henry III steadily gained the upper hand in their civil war against the barons who supported Prince Louis of France for the crown of England. In August reinforcements for the rebels sailed from France across the Strait of Dover, under the command of Eustace the Monk. This French fleet was intercepted off Sandwich (in Kent) by English ships commanded by Hubert de Burgh (later earl of Kent). In a naval battle on August 24 the French troopships escaped, but the supply vessels were captured by the English. Also captured was Eustace, who was promptly beheaded.

Short of supplies and cut off from French bases by the English command of the sea, the barons sought peace. The war officially ended on September 12 with the signing of a treaty at Kingston-on-Thames. Under the general amnesty, Louis retired to France. *See* Lincoln II; Bytham; Barons' Wars.

Sandwich II (Wars of the Roses), 1460. After the ignominious Yorkist (white rose) flight at Ludford in the autumn of 1459, the Lancastrians (red rose) sought several times to seize Calais from the rebel Earl of Warwick (Richard Neville). Each attempt failed, however, largely because of superior leadership on Warwick's part. Then in the summer of 1460 the Yorkists swung over to the offensive. On June 20 Warwick crossed the English Channel with a body of troops. Landing at Sandwich, one of the Cinque Ports of southeastern England, he routed a Lancastrian force opposing the invasion. With the bridgehead secured, the main force of Yorkists landed and marched northwest. *See* Ludford; Northampton II; Roses, Wars of the.

San Jacinto River (Texan War of Independence), 1836. After storming the Alamo on March 6, the Mexican general Antonio de Santa Anna marched eastward to Galveston Bay. Here Gen. Sam Houston had assembled a small army of Texan-Americans to block the path of the invading force. On April 21 Houston met Santa Anna's 1,200 Mexicans along the western bank of the San Jacinto River, near its mouth. Although badly outnumbered, the Texans routed the enemy. Santa Anna was captured. He agreed to recognize the independence of Texas (an agreement later repudiated by the Mexican Congress).

On October 22 Sam Houston became the first president of the Republic of Texas. A formal petition for annexation to the United States was refused on August 25, 1837. However, Texas was admitted to the United States on December 29, 1845, thereby worsening relations with Mexico. *See* Alamo; Fort Texas; Texan War of Independence.

San Juan Hill (Spanish-American War), 1898. Following the successful capture of Las Guásimas on June 24, the American troop (V Corps) commander in Cuba, the 300-lb. Gen. William Shafter, organized a two-column attack westward against Spanish-held Santiago de Cuba. The right column, commanded by Gen. Henry Lawton, would lead off with an assault against the inland village of El Caney. Lawton's division would then move south toward the coast to join in the major assault on San Juan Hill. To defend against the expected attack, the Spanish general Arsenio Linares had posted 520 troops at El Caney and 10,400 men on the heights of San Juan, which included the smaller Kettle Hill to the northeast.

The offensive got under way on the morning of July 1. On the right Lawton ran into trouble at El Caney, took all day to capture the hamlet, and rejoined the main body only after an all-night march. Despite the continued absence of this support, the main body of 8,400 Americans, under the command of Shafter himself, pressed forward toward San Juan Hill. The right flank, composed in part of the dismounted 1st U.S. Volunteer Cavalry Regiment (the Rough Riders, under Col. Leonard Wood and Lt. Col Theodore Roosevelt), was commanded by Gen. Samuel Sumner because of Gen. Joseph Wheeler's illness. The left was led by Gen. Jacob Kent. The column struggled forward slowly (their position readily apparent because of the use of black-powder ammunition in contrast to the smokeless powder fired by the Spaniards), sparked by the determination of the regular troops. Finally an assault ordered by subordinate commanders overran both Kettle and San Juan hills. Here the Americans, who had suffered 1,572 casualties, dug in, while the Spaniards fell back to the outskirts of Santiago.

The precarious American position improved greatly after Adm. William Sampson's ships destroyed the Spanish fleet outside Santiago harbor on July 3. After prolonged negotiations, Linares formally surrendered Santiago's 12,000 defenders and another 12,000 troops in outlying detachments on July 17. Shafter's army, beginning to suffer severely from disease, began re-embarkation for the United States on August 4. *See* Las Guásimas; El Caney; Santiago de Cuba I; Manila II; Spanish-American War.

San Pasqual (U.S.-Mexican War), 1846. Six weeks after the United States declared war on Mexico, Col. Stephen Watts Kearny left Fort Leavenworth, Kans., on June 29 with the U.S. "Army of the West," a force of about 1,700 men. Marching into New Mexico, Kearny reached Sante Fe on August 18. Finding no opposition from the Mexican settlers, on September 25 he pushed on toward California with 100 dragoons (mounted infantry). At San Pasqual, 40 miles northeast of San Diego, the Americans ran into a roadblock manned by Mexican-Californian troops. On December 6 Kearny's men routed the enemy, at a cost to themselves of 18 killed and 13 wounded. Mexican losses were probably less. Kearny reached San Diego six days later. Despite all the military and political maneuvering in California, the fight at San Pasqual was the only pitched battle of the war in that area. California became a part of the United States in the Treaty of Guadalupe Hidalgo, signed February 2, 1848. *See* Monterrey; Buena Vista; Chihuahua; U.S.-Mexican War.

Santa Clara–Santiago (Castro Revolt in Cuba), 1958. When the government offensive against the "26 of July Movement" rebels in the Sierra Maestra failed in the summer of 1958, Fidel Castro swung over to the offensive. From Oriente Province in the east, two columns, led by Ernesto "Che" Guevara and Camillo Cienfuegos, passed through Camagüey Province into Las Villas. Here in the autumn they began operations to cut the island in two. Gaining recruits as they marched, the rebels converged on Santa Clara, in the center of the province, on December 28. Meanwhile, Castro, aided by another column under his brother Raúl, began overrunning the plains of Oriente, closing in on Santiago. With both Santa Clara and Santiago on the verge of surrender, Fulgencio Batista fled into exile on December 31, ending his more than six years of dictatorship. Santa Clara capitulated on January 1. Santiago surrendered the next day to Castro, who was aided by Eulogio Cantillo, government general who had turned his coat. Pressing westward, Castro marched into Havana on January 8. Cuba was secure and the first strong Communist government in the Western Hemisphere established. *See* Sierra Maestra.

Santa Cruz de Tenerife (English-Spanish Wars), 1657. The undeclared war between England and Spain become official following the English capture of Jamaica in 1655. Two years later the leading admiral of the Commonwealth, Robert Blake, sailed a fleet into the Canary Islands. Here on April 20, 1657, he attacked a Spanish force of 16 ships defending the strongly fortified city of Santa Cruz on Tenerife Island. In a brilliant exploit, Blake sank every Spanish vessel and destroyed the city. He lost one ship and 50 seamen. This was Blake's last battle. Coupled with his heroic work in the First Dutch War, Santa Cruz earned Blake a rank among English admirals close to that of Lord Nelson. *See* Jamaica; Dunes, the.

Santa Cruz Islands (World War II). The fourth Japanese-American naval battle, on October 26, 1942, growing out of the fight for Guadalcanal Island. *See* Guadalcanal—Naval Action.

Santander (Spanish Civil War), 1937. After capturing Bilbao in March, the Nationalist Army of the North, under Gen. Fidel Dávila, opened a campaign against Santander, to the west. On August 14, 106 battalions began a relentless drive north and west through the Cantabrian Mountains. To defend the port city on the Bay of Biscay, Gen. Mariano Gamir Ulíbarri commanded some 50,000 Republican troops. But they were poorly trained and weakly armed. Battered by artillery and aerial bombardment, the Republicans fell back steadily, offering no solid resistance. On August 23 most of the Basque forces withdrew from the battle, surrendering to the Italian general Ettore Bastico. Two days later Dávila entered Santander to complete the conquest. Ulíbarri and other Republican leaders fled by air to France. *See* Bilbao; Saragossa III; Spanish Civil War.

Sant'Angelo (German Invasion of Italy), 998. As his father, Otto II, before him, the Holy Roman Emperor Otto III took a German army to Rome. Here he found that the Roman duke Crescentius the Younger had ousted Pope Gregory V and installed John XVI as an antipope. The German emperor attacked the duke's forces and cooped him up in a castle at Sant'Angelo on the Garigliano River near Cassino. Otto stormed the castle, captured Crescentius, and executed him. Gregory V, the first German pope, was restored. *See* Crotone; Rome V.

Santarém I (Portuguese-Moslem Wars), 1171. Portugal's first king, Alfonso I, spent more than 40 years in a hard, grinding campaign to liberate his country from the Moors. In 1171, 24 years after his capture of Lisbon, he advanced 43 miles up the Tagus to attack the enemy stronghold at Santarém. After a sharp battle he took the city and began the usual practice of replacing the Moors with Christian settlers. A Moslem attempt to regain Santarém was beaten back in 1184. *See* Lisbon.

Santarém II (Portuguese Civil War), 1834. Two years after nine-year-old Maria II succeeded her father, Pedro I, as ruler of Portugal in 1826, her regent uncle, Dom Miguel, usurped the throne. A five-year civil war followed, while Maria fled to England and then Brazil. Finally loyalist troops began getting the upper hand. They were led by the Duque de Saldanha, assisted by the British naval officer Sir Charles Napier (cousin of Gen. Sir Charles James Napier). On February 18, 1834, the loyalists forced a showdown battle with the rebels at Santarém, 43 miles up the Tagus River from Lisbon. Dom Miguel was decisively defeated and forced to relinquish all claims to the Portuguese throne.

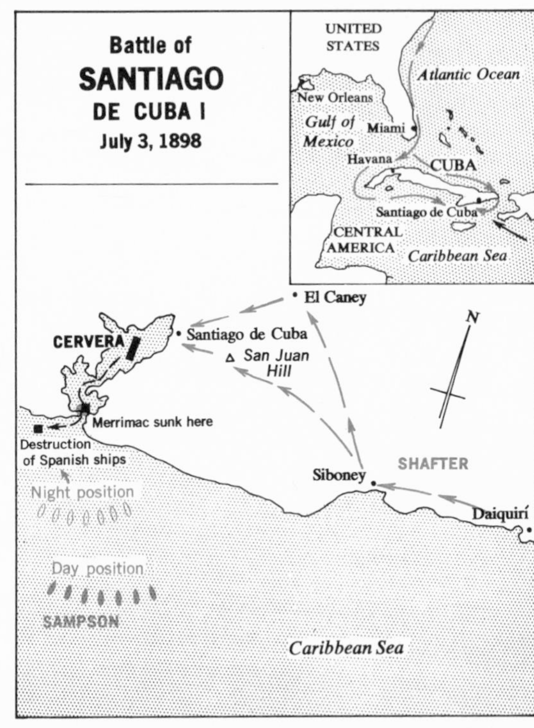

Santiago de Cuba I (Spanish-American War), 1898. When war broke out between the United States and Spain on April 21, the Spanish fleet of Adm. Pascual Cervera stood among the Cape Verde Islands. Eight days later Cervera steamed for the Caribbean Sea. At the same time Adm. William T. Sampson took the American Atlantic fleet toward the same area. A second American task force, the Flying Squadron commanded by Com. Winfield Scott Schley, also joined the hunt for the Spanish ships. On May 29 Schley located Cervera's fleet of four cruisers and three destroyers in the harbor of Santiago de Cuba on the southeastern coast of the island. Sampson arrived on June 1 to assume command of the blockade with five battleships and two cruisers. Two days later Lt. Richard Hobson scuttled the American collier *Merrimac* at the mouth of the harbor in a futile attempt to bottle up the Spanish fleet inside.

While U.S. ground forces landed east of Santiago and pressed slowly toward the city, Sampson held his ships in a tight semicircular array six miles offshore (three miles at night). Finally, on July 3, Cervera's fleet tried to run the blockade. As the Spanish ships steamed out of the harbor and turned west along the coast, they came under the concentrated fire of Sampson's guns. Within four hours every fleeing ship was sunk or forced ashore in flames. Spanish losses were 323 killed, 151 wounded, and 1,813 captured, including Cervera. American casualties were one killed and two wounded.

This defeat, coupled with the continuing land siege of the city by the troops of Gen. William Shafter, sealed the fate of the 12,000 Spanish troops in Santiago. The city's commander, Gen. Arsenio Linares, surrendered the garrison, plus 12,000 men in nearby Spanish detachments, on July 17. Except for an almost bloodless occupation of Puerto Rico by Gen. Nelson Miles on July 25, the war in the Caribbean was over. *See* Las Guásimas; El Caney; San Juan Hill; Manila II; Spanish-American War.

Santiago de Cuba II (Castro Revolt in Cuba). Attacked by the rebel forces of Fidel Castro, the city was captured on January 2, 1959. *See* Santa Clara–Santiago

Saragossa I (Spanish-Moslem Wars), 1118. With the border between Christian and Moslem through central Spain fairly stabilized for a century, most of the fighting took place in the northeast. In 1096 Pedro I of Aragon and Navarre had established his capital at the recently conquered city of Huesca. His younger brother Alfonso I, the Warrior, carried the war farther south. In 1118 he stormed and captured Saragossa on the Ebro River. He transferred the Aragonese capital here, where it remained until the fifteenth century. *See* Huesca; Alarcos.

Saragossa II (Napoleonic Empire Wars), 1808–1809. After knocking Austria, Prussia, and Russia out of the war in 18 months, during 1805–1807, Napoleon I of France had to contend only with Great Britain in his drive for mastery of Europe. To shut off British trade with the Continent, the

French emperor occupied Portugal late in 1807 and in May of the following year tricked King Charles IV into abdicating the throne of Spain. He then called up his older brother, Joseph, from Naples to become king of Spain. Most of the Spanish people immediately rose in revolt, launching the so-called Peninsular War. When the city of Saragossa, on the Ebro River 170 miles northeast of Madrid, resisted the new ruler, Marshal François Lefebvre took the city under siege, in June 1808. The garrison fought back stubbornly, and when a major French army capitulated at Bailén in July, the siege was raised.

After Marshal Jean Lannes routed a Spanish force at Tudela on November 23, the defeated troops returned to Saragossa. In December the French, commanded by Marshals Bon Adrien de Moncey and Édouard Mortier, returned to attack Saragossa. Again the Spanish garrison resisted, under the leadership of Gen. José de Palafox y Melzi (later Duke of Saragossa). One of the heroic figures of the defense was the semilegendary Maid of Saragossa who took her wounded lover's place on the ramparts (commemorated in Byron's *Childe Harold*). The besiegers persisted, however. Lannes took over the French command on January 22, 1809, and on February 20 his troops stormed into the city and took its surrender. *See* Friendland; Bailén; Napoleonic Empire Wars.

Saragossa III (Spanish Civil War), 1937. From Catalonia the Republican Army of the East, under Gen. Sebastián Pozas, launched an offensive westward into Aragon in late summer 1937. In a loosely planned attack, the Republicans hoped to reach Saragossa on the Ebro River by advancing on a wide front from the French border south to Teruel. The execution proved to be even more flawed than the plan. Beginning on August 24, the attackers won some local successes both north and south of the Ebro. But the Nationalist general Muguel Ponte at Saragossa directed a firm resistance on his central front, as well as at Huesca to the north and Teruel to the south. By the end of September the entire Republican campaign in Aragon had collapsed with little to show for the heavy casualties suffered. *See* Santander; Gijón; Spanish Civil War.

Saratoga (War of the American Revolution), 1777. Despite the defeat of his raiding party at Bennington in August 1777, the British commander, Gen. John Burgoyne, resolved to push on southward to Albany, N.Y. He made this decision even though he now knew that the other two prongs of the triple British offensive had failed to get off their mark—Gen. Sir William Howe from New York City and Col. Barry St. Leger from Fort Oswego, N.Y. On September 13, with his army reduced to about 6,000 men, Burgoyne crossed to the west bank of the Hudson River. Ten miles south of Saratoga (Schuylerville), and still 22 miles short of Albany, the British found the American army entrenched on Bemis Heights. General Horatio Gates, who had arrived on August 19 to take over command of the American forces from Gen. Philip Schuyler, had about 7,000 troops with fresh militiamen pouring in almost daily.

Burgoyne sought to outflank the American position by sending Gen. Simon Fraser with 2,000 men to seize high ground on the left (west) of Gates's position, on September 19. This American wing was commanded by Gen. Benedict Arnold, aided by Gen. Daniel Morgan and Col. Henry Dearborn. In a fierce fight in the woods around Freeman's Farm the British advance was checked. In this first battle of Saratoga, Burgoyne lost 600 in killed, wounded, or captured. Of the 3,000 Americans engaged, 319 were casualties.

After the battle of Freeman's Farm, both sides held their respective positions. Two weeks later

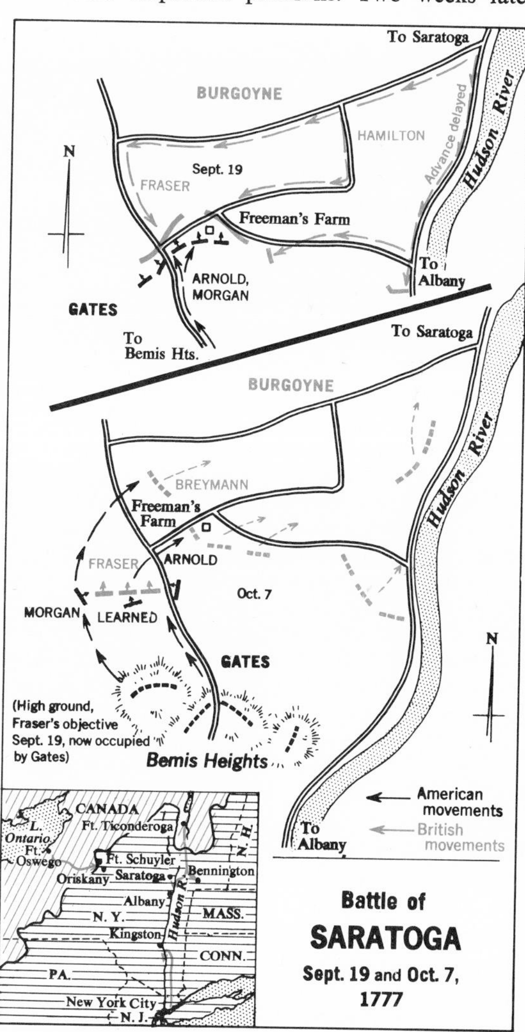

Battle of SARATOGA Sept. 19 and Oct. 7, 1777

Gen. Sir Henry Clinton, the British commander in New York City, began moving up the Hudson River in an effort to take some pressure off Burgoyne. On October 6 he seized forts Clinton and Montgomery. By October 16 his ships had penetrated as far northward as Kingston. But here he turned back to New York when he learned of the British surrender on October 17.

Meanwhile Burgoyne made one more desperate effort to break out toward Albany. On October 7 with 1,600 picked men he made a reconnaissance in force against the American left. From his army on Bemis Heights, which now numbered 11,000 men, Gates sent Morgan and Gen. Ebenezer Learned to repel the advance. West of Freeman's Farm the Americans checked and then threw back the British attack. General Simon Fraser, the reconnaissance commander, fell mortally wounded. At this point Gen. Benedict Arnold took charge of the American left wing and led a fierce counter-assault against the redcoats. The Continentals swept forward to capture a key redoubt defended by Col. Heinrich Breymann's German mercenaries. Breymann was killed and Arnold himself wounded in the leg. In this second action at Saratoga, called the battle of Bemis Heights (also known as the second battle of Freeman's Farm or the battle of Stillwater, a town three miles to the south), the British suffered 600 casualties. American losses were 150.

The loss of Breymann's redoubt exposed Burgoyne's west flank. That night (October 7) he withdrew a mile to the north. On the following night he retreated seven miles farther, to the heights of Saratoga. Here his encirclement became complete on October 13 when John Stark led 1,100 New Hampshire militia across the Hudson to take up a position in the British rear. Burgoyne then asked Gates for surrender terms. And on October 17 the British formally surrendered, 5,728 men laying down their arms.

The British capitulation at Saratoga was the turning point in the American Revolution. It cemented American determination to win their full freedom. And it encouraged France to come into the war on the side of the new United States, on February 6, 1778. Spain and then Holland followed suit, turning the revolution into a world war. Thus the American victory at Saratoga ranks as one of the decisive battles in military history. *See* Fort Ticonderoga III; Bennington; American Revolution.

Sardis (Persian Conquest of Lydia), 546 B.C. Cyrus the Great founded the powerful Persian Empire in 550 B.C. by overthrowing and capturing Astyages, king of Media and son of Cyaxares. Four years later Cyrus marched against the Asia Minor kingdom of Lydia, ruled by Croesus. The Lydian army moved eastward to meet the 20,000-man army of Cyrus. When the summer passed without a decisive battle, Croesus withdrew to his capital of Sardis. Cyrus unexpectedly crossed the plateau of Cappadocia during the winter to surprise the Lydians outside the walls of their capital. Cyrus launched his attack in three waves—armored spearmen, javelin men, and archers. Croesus' forces crumbled under this coordinated onslaught, the survivors fleeing into Sardis. (Reportedly, the Lydian cavalry had bolted at the sight of Persian camels.) Cyrus laid siege to the city and then in a bold surprise stroke penetrated the walls and took Sardis without destroying it. Croesus was captured. The kingdom of Lydia passed into history, while the Persian Empire expanded to include all Asia Minor. *See* Tyre I; Babylon.

Sarikamiş (World War I), 1914–1915. Hostilities between Russia and Turkey began on October 29, 1914, with Turkish warships, including the German cruisers *Goeben* and *Breslau,* bombarding the Black Sea ports of Odessa and Sevastopol. Russia declared war four days later. On land, fighting was generally limited to the isolated Caucasian front. Here the Turkish commander, Gen. Ahmet İzzet Paşa, at the head of 95,000 troops, sought to draw the Russian army away from its bases at Ardahan and Kars and then destroy it. As expected, the Russian general Myshlayevski began advancing southwest from Kars in December 1914. He had reached Sarikamis, 30 miles deep into Asia Minor, when he encountered the Turks on December 29. In five days of fighting in bitter cold weather the 60,000 Russians overwhelmed their more numerous foe. The routed Turkish army fell to a mere 18,000 in the defeat and disorganized two-week retreat to Lake Van that followed.

Later that year (1915) the two antagonists traded indecisive blows north of Lake Van. General Nikolai Yudenich, who had taken command of the Russian forces on this front, suffered a repulse to his advance guard at Malazgirt (formerly Manzikert). But when the Turkish general Abdul Kerim Pasha pressed forward, he was outflanked and defeated at Karakilisse (Karaköse). *See* Erzurum-Erzincan; World War I.

Sarmizegetusa (Dacian Wars of the Roman Empire), 106. The Dacians of modern Rumania, who had warred against the Roman Empire in A.D. 89, revolted again during the reign of Trajan. In 102 Trajan took seven legions across the Danube from Moesia. North of the Iron Gate, he defeated the Dacians under Decebalus in a bitter battle. Decebalus accepted peace terms, but during the next two years rebuilt his army in preparation for a new conflict. In 105 Trajan returned at the head of another strong Roman army. He pushed steadily northward despite fierce resistance. By the time he reached Sarmizegetusa, the Dacian capital (southeast of modern Lugoj), the Romans had broken the army of Decebalus. The Dacian scorched-earth policy, coupled with the vigorous Roman offensive, had depopulated the country. Decebalus committed suicide. Trajan then declared Dacia to be a province of Rome. *See* Moesia; Roman Empire.

Sasbach (Second, or Dutch, War of Louis XIV), 1675. After his brilliant victory at Turckheim early in 1675, the French marshal the Vicomte de Turenne crossed the Rhine into Baden in the spring. Here his long duel of maneuver continued against Count Montecuccoli, commander of the Holy Roman Empire (Leopold I) forces. Finally, on July 27, Turenne's French trapped the Germans into a hopeless position at Sasbach, east of the Rhine near the Swiss border. But when the veteran French commander was killed by a cannon ball early in the battle, his lieutenants lost their advantage. The French inflicted double their casualties on the Imperials but at the end of the day were sent fleeing back across the Rhine. Montecuccoli pursued into Alsace. Now Louis XIV, in desperation, brought the aged Louis II, the Great Condé, out of retirement to command the French army. Condé blocked off the invaders and forced Montecuccoli to retreat back into Baden. But the loss of Turenne meant the loss of French initiative in the war, except for naval warfare in the Mediterranean. *See* Turckheim; Stromboli; Mons I; Louis XIV, Wars of.

Sassanian Persia. The last native dynasty of Persian kings, which came to power in A.D. 226, took its name from Sassan, grandfather of its founder, Ardashir I. A strong rival of the Byzantine Empire, the dynasty was finally eliminated by the Arabs in 641.

Hormuz	226
Edessa I	260
Carrhae II	296
Singara	348
Amida I	359
Tigris River	363
Amida II	502
Dara	528
Callinicum	531
Melitene I	578
Jerusalem V	615
Nineveh II	627
Hira	633
Kadisiya	637
Jalula	637
Nihawand	641

Saucourt (Rise of France), 881. One of the great horrors of the ninth century was raids by bands of Northmen. The fierce warriors from Scandinavia controlled the seas of western Europe and frequently sailed inland up the great rivers to pillage settlements. They often struck and retired in safety before an armed force could move against them. In 881, however, Louis III of the West Franks (France) managed to fight a pitched battle with a large force of Northmen at Saucourt, south of the mouth of the Somme River. The Carolingian king repulsed the invaders with heavy losses. But even such a thorough defeat did not end the raids. *See* Montfaucon.

Savage's Station (American Civil War). The third engagement, on June 29, 1862, in the Seven Days battle between Federals and Confederates east of Richmond. *See* Seven Days.

Savannah I (War of the American Revolution), 1778. Frustrated in the North by George Washington's generalship, the British commander Gen. Sir Henry Clinton shifted his campaign to the southern states late in 1778. He hoped to take advantage of the strong Loyalist sentiment in the area. On December 27 a British fleet under Com. Hyde Parker landed 3,500 British troops, commanded by Col. Archibald Campbell, at the mouth of the Savannah River, 15 miles below the town of Savannah, Ga. Campbell moved upriver, while the American general Robert Howe marched out from Savannah with 700 Continentals and 150 militia to oppose the invaders. Howe secured his flanks against adjoining swampland. But on December 29 a British detachment found a path through the swamp and came in behind the American right wing. Campbell then launched a coordinated attack on the American front and rear. Howe's men were routed, abandoning 48 cannon, 23 mortars, and many barrels of powder. In the short battle and wild retreat 83 were killed or drowned, 453 captured. The British lost only three killed and ten wounded.

The American retreat continued northward across the state border into South Carolina. The British occupied Savannah. General Augustine Prevost, the royal governor of East Florida, arrived to administer Georgia, which now lay under complete British control. *See* Charleston I; Port Royal Island; American Revolution.

Savannah II (War of the American Revolution), 1779. In their attempt to regain Savannah, Ga., the Americans secured the cooperation of the French fleet under the Comte d'Estaing. On September 12, 1779, D'Estaing landed 3,500 troops on the Savannah River, eight miles below the town. Here the French army was joined by the specially recruited 200-man legion of Gen. Count Casimir Pulaski. Four days later the American commander in the South, Gen. Benjamin Lincoln, arrived with 600 Continentals and 750 militia. The allied force then launched a siege against Savannah, held by 3,200 British and Loyalists under Gen. Augustine Prevost.

The besiegers began to work their way forward by parallels, but progress was slow against the strongly entrenched garrison. A five-day bombardment, October 4–8, had little effect. On the morning of October 9 the allies stormed the fortifications. It was the fiercest fight since Bunker Hill, especially at the Spring Hill redoubt southwest of the city. Here the attack of Col. John Laurens of South Carolina almost carried the earthwork, but it was beaten back after an hour with 173 dead. West of Spring Hill, Pulaski fell mortally wounded. The assault failed at every point. American and French losses were 244 killed and 584 wounded, a fifth of those engaged and almost half of those in the Spring Hill area. British casualties totaled 155 killed, wounded, and missing.

Two weeks after the battle D'Estaing re-embarked his troops and sailed for France. With the withdrawal of this fleet the siege was raised. Lincoln marched back to Charleston, S.C. *See* Savannah I; Briar Creek; Charleston II; American Revolution.

Savannah III (American Civil War), 1864. Satisfied that there was no Confederate threat to his rear following his capture of Atlanta, Federal general William Sherman destroyed the military potential of the city on November 12. With 62,000 Federal troops and rations for 20 days he set out southeast for Savannah, Ga., three days later. He moved in two wings: the right, or Army of Tennessee, under Gen. Oliver Howard, was made up of the XV and XVII Corps; the left, or Army of Georgia, under Gen. Henry Slocum, consisted of the XIV and XX Corps. Screened by the cavalry of Gen. Hugh Kilpatrick, Sherman's army destroyed all railroads and other resources in a swath 50 to 60 miles wide. The only strong Confederate opposition came from the harassing flank and rear attacks of Gen. Joseph Wheeler's cavalry.

Sherman reached Savannah, 225 miles from Atlanta, on December 10, thus opening communications with the Federal fleet offshore. His controversial "march to the sea" had succeeded. The city itself, under the command of Gen. William Hardee, refused to surrender. Sherman brought in siege guns from the fleet, but Hardee abandoned Savannah and retreated northward on December 21. *See* Franklin; Atlanta; Fort Fisher; Bentonville; American Civil War.

Savo Island (World War II). A Japanese naval victory on August 9, 1942, over American ships protecting an amphibious landing on Guadalcanal. *See* Guadalcanal—Naval Action.

Saxa Rubra (Civil Wars of the Roman Empire), 312. Early in 312 Constantine I routed the forces of Valerius Maxentius, his fellow pretender to the throne of the Roman Empire, in the Po Valley. With some 50,000 loyal troops he then marched on his rival in Rome. Leaving the protection of Rome's walls, Maxentius advanced to meet Constantine nine miles north of the capital at Saxa Rubra. Before the battle of October 28, Constantine is reported to have seen a flaming cross in the sky and the words *in hoc signo vinces* ("by this sign thou shalt conquer").

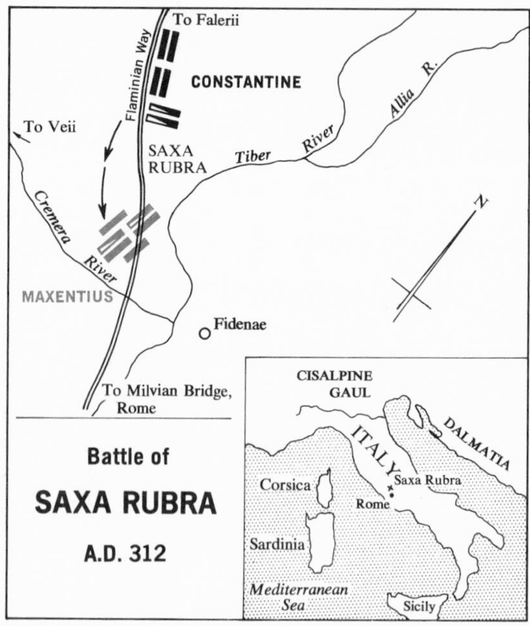

Battle of SAXA RUBRA A.D. 312

When the two contending armies collided, Constantine's cavalry scattered the enemy horse on both wings. His combined attack then shattered Maxentius' unprotected infantry. Some died where they stood. Many others, attempting to escape eastward on the Milvian Bridge (Pons Milvius) over the Tiber River, were drowned. Among the dead in the river was Maxentius.

The supernatural manifestation before the battle led Constantine to become the first Roman emperor to accept Christianity. Now only two men remained to challenge his supremacy—Licinianus Licinius, a temporary ally in Illyria, and Valerius Maximinus in the East. *See* Verona; Heraclea Propontis; Roman Empire.

Sayler's Creek (American Civil War). A Federal attack on the Confederate rear guard as it retreated up the Appomattox River on April 6, 1865. *See* Appomattox River.

Scandinavia. The major battles and wars fought by the modern nations of Denmark, Finland, Norway, and Sweden are listed below. *See* Danish invasion of Britain.

Saucourt	881
Montfaucon	886
Louvain	891
Swold	1000
Stiklestad	1030
Viborg	1157
Reval	1219
Bornhöved	1227
Largs	1263

Helsingborg	1362
Brunkeberg	1471
Linköping	1598
Riga I	1621
See Thirty Years' War	
See Northern Wars	
See Louis XIV, Wars of	
See Great Northern War	
Copenhagen I	1801
Copenhagen II	1807
Dybböl	1864
Vyborg II	1918
See World War II	

Schooneveldt (Third English-Dutch War), 1673. In the second year of the third naval war, England's object was to destroy the Dutch fleet and thus open the way for an allied English-French assault on the Netherlands coast. This amphibious attack would supplement the overland thrust of Louis XIV's army on the Continent. Commanded by Prince Rupert of Germany, cousin of Charles II, the English (54 ships) combined with the French (27 ships), under Adm. the Comte Jean d'Estrées, and sailed for the coast of Holland. On June 7, 1673, the able Dutch admiral Michel de Ruyter with 55 ships-of-the-line sailed out of the Schelde estuary to attack the invaders off Schooneveldt. In a sharp engagement De Ruyter checked the allied navies and then withdrew. A week later, on June 14, the Dutch returned to the attack and again held their own against a superior force. After this engagement the English and French returned to their ports to refit and resupply. De Ruyter had successfully blocked an invasion for another two months. *See* Southwold Bay; Texel II; English-Dutch Wars.

Schwechat (Hungarian Revolt), 1848. As part of the general revolutionary fervor that swept across Europe in 1848, Hungary rose in revolt against the Austrian Empire of Ferdinand I. A rebel force marched on Vienna, capital of the empire, where revolutionaries inside the city threw up barricades in sympathy. Prince Alfred zu Windisch-Graetz, imperial commander in Bohemia, who had crushed a revolt in Prague earlier in the year, led an army of Austrian regulars against the rebels. At Schwechat, a suburb southeast of Vienna, the prince routed the Hungarians on October 30. In conjunction with Gen. Josip Jelačić od Bužima (Jellachich), governor of Croatia, Windisch-Graetz bombarded Vienna into submission the following day. A month later Ferdinand was persuaded to abdicate in favor of his nephew Franz Josef I. *See* Kápolna; Hungarian Revolt.

Second Coalition, War of. *See* French Revolution, Wars of the.

Second Triumvirate, Wars of the (43–31 B.C.). A year after the assassination of Julius Caesar in 44 B.C., the rule of Rome passed to a Second Triumvirate—Mark Antony, Marcus Lepidus, and Caesar Octavianus, called Octavian. The triumvirs subdued all opposition but then quarreled among themselves. Octavian defeated both his rivals to become the first emperor of Rome, under the name of Augustus, in 27 B.C.

Mutina	43 B.C.
Philippi	42 B.C.
Perusia	41–40 B.C.
Phraaspa	36 B.C.
Naulochus	36 B.C.
Actium	31 B.C.

Sedan (Franco-Prussian War), 1870. When Marshal Achille Bazaine withdrew 170,000 French troops into the fortress of Metz on August 19, he dealt a mortal blow to the hopes of Napoleon III of repelling the Prussian invaders. The only French army now in the field was that of the Comte de MacMahon at Châlons-sur-Marne. Taking personal charge, the French emperor marched these 130,000 troops northeast, determined to relieve Metz even at the expense of uncovering Paris. But the hour was too late for France. General (later Count) Helmuth von Moltke, chief of the Prussian general staff, had already blockaded Metz with one Prussian force, while forming a new Army of the Meuse (under the Crown Prince of Saxony) for an attack toward Châlons. This thrust deflected the emperor's army northward, away from Metz, on August 29. Instead of turning back

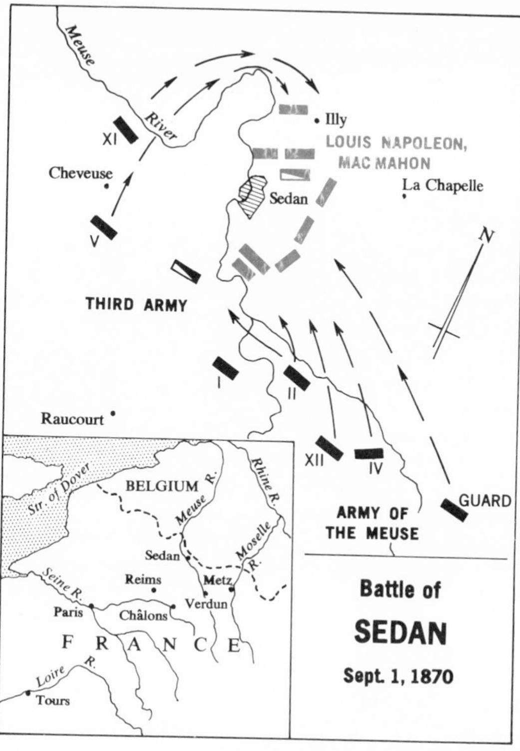

Battle of SEDAN
Sept. 1, 1870

to defend Paris, the French retired into the small border fortress of Sedan. Here, to the north, moved the Third Prussian Army (under Crown Prince Frederick William), which Moltke had recalled from a march on Paris. The trap snapped shut when the two Prussian armies closed on Illy from both north and south. On September 1 the French made a desperate effort to fight their way out, but the Prussian lines of encirclement held fast at a cost of almost 9,000 killed and wounded. French casualties were 3,000 killed, 14,000 wounded, and 20,000 taken prisoner. Both Napoleon III and MacMahon (who was wounded) surrendered their swords. On the following day Gen. Emmanuel de Wimpffen, who had succeeded MacMahon, completed the capitulation of the 82,000 beleaguered French troops. It was one of the most crushing defeats in French history. The victorious Prussians marched southward on Paris. *See* Metz; Paris II; Franco-Prussian War.

Sedgemoor (Monmouth's Revolt against James II), 1685. The accession of the English Catholic king, James II (younger brother of Charles II), in February 1685 provoked an immediate Protestant revolt. It was engineered by the Duke of Monmouth, natural son of Charles II and thus nephew of the English monarch. On June 11 Monmouth landed at Lyme Regis in Dorsetshire, where hundreds flocked to his cause. James, still at the height of his power, sent the Earl of Feversham (Louis Duras) westward to put down the revolt. Feversham's chief military strength came from the Household Cavalry and a regular regiment of dragoons, commanded by Col. John Churchill (later Duke of Marlborough). While Monmouth was collecting an army of six or seven thousand peasants and miners in the West Country, he learned of bad news from Scotland. Here his ally Archibald Campbell, 9th earl of Argyll, had landed to stir up a Covenanter revolt. But the uprising never came off, and Argyll was captured and sentenced to beheading.

Realizing his desperate plight, Monmouth risked everything in a night attack on the royal army encamped at Sedgemoor in Somersetshire. On July 6 the rebels surprised the Feversham troops, but Churchill quickly restored order and brought the attackers under heavy artillery fire supplemented by cavalry charges. Although the rebels fought tenaciously, they were all killed or captured. Monmouth escaped the slaughter but was hunted down a few days later and beheaded. The last of the rebellion was stamped out by Chief Justice George Jeffreys, who sentenced more than 200 prisoners to hang and exiled another 800 to Barbados in a series of decrees called the Bloody Assizes. Sedgemoor was the last formal military action in England until the German naval attacks and Zeppelin raids of World War I. *See* Bothwell Bridge; Londonderry.

Sekigahara (Unification of Japan), 1600. After many years of struggle for unity, Japan moved toward a centralized government under the dictatorship of Toyotomi Hideyoshi in the sixteenth century. When Hideyoshi died in 1598, a new scramble for power began among four regents of his youthful son. Finally Gen. Iyeyasu (Ieyasu) seized control in 1600. His rivals united against him, organizing an army of some 100,000. On September 16 Iyeyasu, with a force almost as large, met the enemy army at Sekigahara in central Honshu. In a great battle Iyeyasu won overwhelmingly, inflicting tens of thousands of casualties on the rebels. This victory crushed virtually all opposition. Three years later Iyeyasu, who had established his headquarters in present-day Tokyo (Edo), received a commission as shogun. This was the founding of the Tokugawa shogunate that lasted until 1867. *See* Toyotomi Castle.

Selby (English Civil War), 1644. After the Cavalier victory at Adwalton Moor in 1643 (the second year of the Civil War), William Cavendish, marquis of Newcastle, controlled most of Yorkshire for Charles I. Early the following year, however, his position was threatened by a large army of Scots that had begun a relentless march into northern England. Newcastle faced the Scots, sending Lord John Belasyse southward to hold off another Roundhead army commanded by Lord Ferdinando Fairfax and his son Sir Thomas. At Selby, on the Ouse River south of York, Belasyse was attacked and routed by the Fairfaxes on April 11. The Cavalier force lost more than a thousand men and all its artillery and baggage. With his rear thus exposed, Newcastle turned York into a strong point, which soon came under Scottish-Roundhead siege. *See* Adwalton Moor; Marston Moor; English Civil War.

Selinus-Himera (Carthaginian Invasion of Sicily), 409 B.C. Soon after the Sicilians had repulsed the threat of Athenian imperialism at Syracuse, they resumed their own civil wars. This quarreling gave Carthage the opportunity to avenge its defeat of 480 B.C. at Himera. In 409 the energetic Hannibal (not to be confused with the famed general of the Punic Wars) landed some 50,000 Carthaginian troops at Selinus on the south coast. After nine days of siege the hopelessly outnumbered garrison surrendered. (A relieving force of Syracusans under Diocles arrived too late to aid the city.) The Carthaginians razed Selinus and carried the survivors into captivity.

Hannibal then turned to Himera on the north coast and laid siege to that city. Again Diocles came out from Syracuse to aid his fellow Sicilians. Arriving in the harbor with 25 ships, the Syracusans managed to rescue half of Himera's inhabitants. But when they returned three days later, they found that Hannibal had stormed the city and sacked it. Some 3,000 prisoners were executed in revenge for the death of Hannibal's grandfather, Hamilcar, at the first battle of Himera. *See* Himera; Syracuse II; Acragas.

Sellasia (Wars of the Hellenistic Monarchies), 221 B.C. In the century after Alexander the Great's death, 12 cities of the northern Peloponnesus banded together in the Achaean League for mutual protection. In the 220's B.C., however, a strong Spartan king, Cleomenes III, threatened to conquer the entire peninsula. The leader of the Achaean League, Aratus of Sicyon, appealed for aid to the Macedonian king Antigonus III (Doson), who sent a phalanx of 10,000 men. In a hard-fought battle at Sellasia, 12 miles north of Sparta, the allied force crushed the Spartan army. Cleomenes fled to Egypt. But the victory proved to be a mixed blessing for the Achaeans. Antigonus seized the opportunity to establish firm control over most of the Peloponnesus, which he welded together into a new Hellenic League. *See* Hellenistic Monarchies, Wars of the.

Sempach (Swiss-Austrian Wars), 1386. In the long hostility between Austria and the Swiss cantons, Leopold III made a new invasion of Switzerland in 1386. Near the village of Sempach the Austrian duke dismounted the 1,500 men-at-arms in his front column and attacked on foot on July 9. The Austrians drove through the Swiss vanguard of Lucerners. But just when victory seemed certain, the main body of Swiss came up. Leopold then dismounted his second column, but before these knights could deploy, the Swiss swarmed into them, wielding their deadly halberds and pikes. At this point the third Austrian column turned and rode off the field, leaving the first two columns to their fate. In the face of the typical relentless attack of the Swiss, Leopold and virtually all his dismounted knights perished.

The battle of Sempach provides the story of Arnold von Winkelried, the Swiss hero who single-handedly gathered enough Austrian lances into his body to give his countrymen an opening to exploit. However, some accounts ascribe this action to the battle of La Bicocca in 1522. *See* Laupen; Näfels.

Seneffe (Second, or Dutch, War of Louis XIV), 1674. Having successfully blocked the broad-scale invasion by Louis XIV, William III of Orange (later William III of England) marched south from Holland to support his Spanish ally (Charles II) in what is now Belgium. Here Louis II, the Great Condé, at the head of a large French army was pushing back the weak Spanish forces along the border. On August 8, 1674, the Dutch army came into action in Brabant Province. It was to be William's first great land battle and the last for the veteran French nobleman. After a strong probing attack against Condé, William realized the impenetrability of the enemy position and began to withdraw. This movement exposed a Dutch-Spanish flank, which Condé immediately assaulted at Seneffe, six miles southwest of Nivelles. After a fierce struggle lasting almost 17 hours, both sides disengaged their forces, unable to gain an advantage. At least one-seventh of the total troops involved were killed. The site of fighting now shifted back eastward to the Rhine. *See* Sinsheim; Enzheim; Louis XIV, Wars of.

Senta (Austrian-Turkish Wars), 1697. While the Holy Roman Empire was engaged in the War of the Grand Alliance in the west, the Ottoman Empire under Mustapha II rebuilt its forces in southeastern Europe. To meet this new threat, Emperor Leopold I sent out a well-trained Imperial army commanded by Eugene, prince of Savoy. On September 11, 1697, Eugene met the Turkish army at Senta (Zenta), 80 miles northwest of Belgrade, on the Tisza River. In one of the most decisive battles of the long Christian-Moslem struggle, the Imperial army inflicted a crushing defeat on the Turks, who suffered 20,000 casualties. This battle ended the fighting for a time. The Treaty of Karlowitz, signed in 1699, ceded Turkish-held territory to Austria, Venice, and Poland. The peace was supposed to last for 25 years, but when Venice and Turkey became involved in a war in 1714, Austria came to the aid of the Italian city. *See* Azov; Peterwardein.

Sentinum (Third Samnite War), 295 B.C. Despite the setback at Camerinum in 298 B.C., Rome carried the war to its opponents—the Samnites, Gauls, Lucanians, and Etruscans. In 295 Quintas Fabius Maximus took five legions across the Apennines to the town of Sentinum (Sassoferrato), about 35 miles inland from the Adriatic Sea. Here he encountered a coalition army under the Samnite Gellius Equatius. The war chariots of the Gauls gave the coalition an initial advantage against the Roman left wing. But on the right the Samnites were driven back, enabling Fabius to attack the Gauls in flank. After a savage struggle the entire enemy line collapsed, giving Rome complete victory. The Romans lost 8,200 men, but they killed about 25,000 (including the Samnite commander) and captured another 8,000.

The Roman triumph at Sentinum proved decisive. Samnium accepted peace terms as an autonomous ally. Of the original coalition, only the Gauls and the Etruscans stood in the way of total Roman supremacy in central Italy. *See* Camerinum; Vadimonis Lake; Samnite Wars.

Sepeia (Rise of Sparta), 494 B.C. After more than two centuries of conflict, only the Greek city-state of Argos remained to challenge Sparta for supremacy in the Peloponnesus. Then in 494 B.C. a Spartan army under Cleomenes I surprised the Argive armed force (reputedly while the latter was eating) at Sepeia. The Spartans won decisively and established undisputed dominion over the Peloponnesus. In the next 36 years Sparta's continued growth brought it into direct conflict with Athens for hegemony in Greece. *See* Aegina; Peloponnesian Wars.

Sepoy Mutiny or **Sepoy Rebellion.** *See* Indian Mutiny.

Serbia. A Balkan power for a time in the Middle Ages, Serbia lost its independence to the Ottoman Empire of Turkey after 1389. For battles and wars under Turkish rule, *see* Turkey. Serbia won its freedom in 1878. A major battleground of World War I (see the following entry), it became part of Yugoslavia in 1918.

Adrianople VI	1365
Maritsa River	1371
Kossovo I	1389
Nicopolis	1396
Kossovo II	1448

See Balkan Wars
See World War I

Serbia (World War I), 1915. The first three Austrian drives into Serbia had been thoroughly repulsed in 1914. Preoccupied with the Russian front, Austria made no new effort to conquer its smaller neighbor for almost a year. Then, in the autumn of 1915, Bulgaria joined the Central Powers, and a massive three-nation offensive with 300,000 troops was prepared to crush Serbia from both the north and the east. German Field Marshal August von Mackensen took charge of three invading armies: in the north stood the Austrian Third Army (stiffened by three German divisions) west of Belgrade and the German Eleventh Army east of the city; to the northeast was the Bulgarian First Army. A fourth army, the Bulgarian Second, under the command of King Ferdinand's general staff, was poised in the southeast to cut the Salonika–Belgrade railroad, thus isolating Serbia from Allied aid. To defend his nation against such a coordinated onslaught, Gen. Radomir Putnik could field only five armies totaling little more than 200,000 men. He deployed his First and Third armies along the northern frontier; the Timok, Second, and Macedonian armies faced east.

The fourth invasion of Serbia got under way on October 6, the Austrians crossing the Save River, the Germans the Danube. Belgrade, pinched out between these two forces, fell on October 9. As the two Serbian armies on this front fell back, fighting desperately, the Bulgarian First Army thrust westward across the frontier on October 11. Within a week Mackensen had all his armies advancing in line. The poorly armed Serbs were steadily pushed back from both the north and the east, although they withdrew only grudgingly and in good order. In the south the Second Bulgarian Army (Nicolas Jekov) reached Kumanovo on October 23, cutting the railroad from Salonika and blocking off the weak (and late) Allied force advancing from Greece.

By mid-November the Serbians faced either complete surrender or withdrawal through the snow-covered mountains of neutral Albania. The hardy fighters chose to withdraw, and in one of the epic retreats in history 100,000 Serbians reached the Adriatic Sea. Here they were picked up by the French navy and transported to the island of Corfu in January 1916. Later they would join the Allies on the Salonika front and help liberate their homeland in 1918. Mackensen halted his advance on the Albanian and Greek borders on December 4. The offensive had killed, wounded, or captured more than 100,000 Serbian soldiers. Serbia was knocked out of the war and the railroad opened from Berlin to Constantinople. King Nicholas of Montenegro, who had supported Serbia, fled to Italy when the Austrians overran his country. *See* Rudnik Ridges; Salonika II; World War I.

Seringapatam I (Mysore-British War III), 1792. The Third Mysore War began in 1790 with the invasion of Travancore by Tipu Sahib, the sultan of Mysore. Lord Cornwallis, the British governor-general of India, came to the aid of Travancore, which was under the protection of the British crown. In March 1792 British and allied native troops invested Seringapatam, the fortress-capital of Mysore. Tipu capitulated on March 19, ceding half of his territory and paying a large indemnity. This ended the Third Mysore War. *See* Porto Novo; Seringapatam II; Mysore-British Wars.

Seringapatam II (Mysore-British War IV), 1799. Tipu Sahib, the sultan of Mysore who had fought two previous wars against the British in India, launched his third conflict (and the Fourth Mysore War) in 1799. The British governor-general, Lord Richard Wellesley (brother of the Duke of Wellington), promptly ordered an attack on Tipu's capital of Seringapatam. On May 4 Gen. George Harris led a force of British and allied native troops in an assault on the Mysore island fortress. The garrison was overpowered and Tipu killed. This victory ended the war and established British supremacy in southern India. *See* Seringapatam I; Mysore-British Wars.

Servile Wars. *See* Mount Vesuvius.

Sevastopol I (Crimean War), 1854–1855. After routing the Russian army of Prince Aleksandr Menshikov at the Alma River, the British-French force pressed on to Sevastopol. The Crimean fortress came under bombardment on October 17, but the allied commanders—Gen. Lord Raglan (Fitzroy Somerset) and Gen. François Canrobert—had too few men to take the city by storm. They settled down to a siege, Adm. Sir Edmund Lyons (later Lord Lyons) bringing up a squadron of British ships to close off the harbor. The Russians, under the direction of engineer officer Count Frants Totleben, threw up strong fortifications.

To relieve the city, Russian forces of Czar Nicholas I attacked the allies at Balaclava on October 25. Eleven days later Menshikov's besieged garrison made a sortie at Inkerman. Both assaults were beaten off. A third Russian attack, on the Chernaya River on August 16 of the following year, also failed to dislodge the allies. Meanwhile, both defenders and besiegers suffered terrible hardships. Inside the city allied artillery shells struck civilians and soldiers alike during the 322-day battle. In the siege lines there was a scarcity of fuel, clothing, and supplies. The sick and wounded received little attention until Florence Nightingale organized relief work and nursing at the British base at Üsküdar (Scutari), across the Bosporus from Constantinople.

In the spring of 1855 the allies launched several violent assaults upon Sevastopol but each time were repulsed. Finally, on September 8, the French, now under the command of Gen. Aimable Pélissier, successfully stormed Malakhov, the fortification at the southeastern end of the city. (Pélissier was later made Duc de Malakoff.) Meanwhile, the British under Gen. James Simpson (the successor of Raglan, who had died) took the Redan fortification on the south, but then lost it, suffering more than 2,000 casualties. Nevertheless, Prince Mikhail Gorchakov, who had earlier succeeded Menshikov, abandoned Sevastopol on September 11, blowing up the defenses and sinking the ships in the harbor.

The fall of the city virtually ended the war, although the main Russian armies stood undefeated. Czar Alexander II, who had come to rule upon the death of his father, Nicholas I, on March 2, signed the final peace terms at the Congress of Paris on March 30, 1856. The war had not settled the growing "eastern question." But it had checked Russian influence in southeastern Europe and preserved the integrity of Turkey. *See* Alma River; Balaclava; Inkerman; Chernaya River; Kars I; Crimean War.

Sevastopol II (World War II). The chief city of the Crimea, which resisted German capture in the fall of 1941, came under tight siege on June 3, 1942, and was forced to surrender on July 1; it was liberated by a Russian offensive on May 9, 1944. *See* Crimea.

Seven Days (American Civil War), 1862. Continuing his overcautious deployment east of Richmond, the Federal commander, Gen. George McClellan, moved the bulk of his army (60,000 men) south of the Chickahominy River. Only the V Corps of Gen. Fitz-John Porter was left north of the stream. When the Federal army seemed to be settling down for a siege of the Confederate capital, Gen. Robert E. Lee began planning to attack McClellan. Leaving only 25,000 men to hold off the Federals east of the city, Lee shifted 65,000 troops northward to strike the exposed 30,000 men of Porter across the Chickahominy. On June 25 Gen. Joseph Hooker's division of Gen. Samuel Heintzelman's Federal IV Corps made a probing attack at Oak Grove in the Fair Oaks–Seven Pines region south of the river. It was a minor action (626 Federal, 441 Confederate casualties), except for opening what was to become the major Seven Days battle. It was also the last Federal offensive in this week-long engagement.

By the following day (June 26) Lee was ready to envelope Porter's separated wing. General Thomas (Stonewall) Jackson, just arriving from the Shenandoah Valley with 18,000 men, was to strike the Federal right flank from the north, while three other Confederate divisions assaulted from the west. When Jackson failed to come up, Gen. Ambrose Hill attacked alone with his division from Mechanicsville at 3 P.M. Trying to cross Beaver Dam Creek, Hill was bloodily repulsed. Nightfall ended the fighting, with 1,400 Southern casualties out of the 16,350 actually engaged. Porter, who had fought his corps well, lost only 361 men. Anticipating that Lee would continue the offensive the next day, McClellan ordered the V Corps to fall back southeast to Gaines' Mill.

On June 27 Lee renewed the attack on Porter, with the divisions of Gens. Daniel Hill, Jackson, Ambrose Hill, and James Longstreet deployed in a semicircle from northeast to southwest. But again Jackson moved slowly, delaying the assault to the afternoon. It was not until evening that Porter's lines southeast of Gaines' Mill broke before the overwhelming numbers of Confederates. That night Porter retreated across the Chicka-

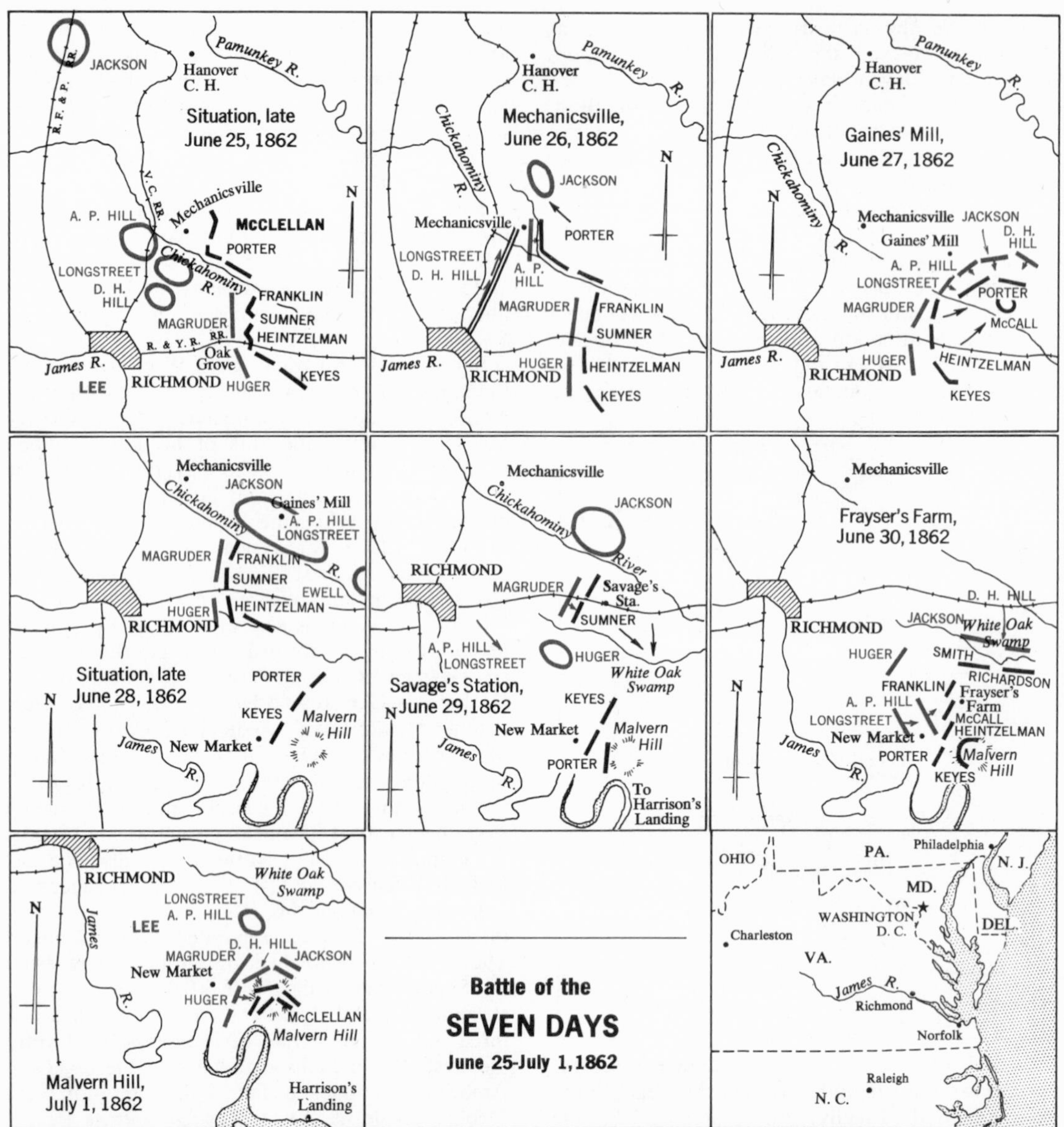

hominy to the south. In this third day of the battle Lee's casualties totaled 8,751; Federal losses, almost all in Porter's corps, were 6,837.

McClellan now decided to withdraw all five of his corps southward, changing his base from White House, on the Pamunkey tributary of the York, to Harrison's Landing on the James. Most of June 28 was spent marching toward the new base. When Lee became certain of the direction of McClellan's movement, he ordered a pursuit. On June 29 Gen. John Magruder, whose demonstrations had deceived McClellan for three days, attacked eastward against the Federal rear guard at Savage's Station, on the Richmond and York River Railroad. He was to be supported by Jackson's assault from the north. But for the third time in this battle the hero of the Shenandoah Valley campaign procrastinated. This enabled Gen. Edwin Sumner's Federal II Corps to hold off Magruder until the entire rear guard could pull back through White Oak Swamp. The day's fighting cost 1,590 Federal and 625 Confederate casualties.

Lee's plans for a coordinated offensive against the retreating Federals misfired again on June 30. Of the six divisions ordered against McClellan's west flank and rear, only those of Longstreet and Ambrose Hill launched an assault, and then not until late afternoon. Both attacking units struck Gen. George McCall's division of the V Corps at Frayser's Farm, south of Glendale and the White

Oak Swamp. The Federal division collapsed and McCall was captured. But neighboring Union troops, aided by early darkness, sealed off the Confederate penetration. Federal losses were 2,853, Confederate casualties 3,615. That night McClellan finally got his entire army atop Malvern Hill, overlooking the James River.

The Federal position on Malvern Hill was the strongest yet occupied in the seven days of combat. Nevertheless, Lee attacked it directly early on July 1, only to call off the assault when Federal artillery fire dominated the battlefield. Late in the afternoon the Confederate commander ordered a new attempt. But the Federal defenders easily beat back a piecemeal attack, first by Daniel Hill, then by Jackson, and finally by Gen. Benjamin Huger (Ambrose Hill and Longstreet never got into the fight). When darkness ended the battle, the Confederates had lost 5,355 men, the Federals 3,214.

This action closed the Seven Days battle, which cost a total of 36,000 casualties, 20,000 of them Confederate. McClellan continued his retreat to Harrison's Landing the next day. Lee moved his army back to Richmond. In August the Federal army was recalled to the Washington area, ending the unsuccessful Peninsular Campaign. It would be two years before Richmond would again be seriously threatened. *See* Fair Oaks; Cedar Mountain; American Civil War.

Sevenoaks (Cade's Rebellion), 1450. In the spring of 1450 Jack Cade, a dissident of mysterious origin, led a revolt in Kent (southeastern England) against government corruption and oppressive taxes. King Henry VI sent out royal troops under the Duke of Buckingham (Humphrey Stafford) to put down the uprising. On June 18 at Sevenoaks, 20 miles southeast of London, Buckingham's force fought a pitched battle with a much larger number of Cade's rebels. The royalists were routed and Buckingham was killed.

Cade then marched on London with several thousand men. Entering the city on July 3, he forced the drumhead trial and execution of Lord Say, the treasurer, and William Crowmer, sheriff of Kent. When the rebels turned to pillaging, they lost the support of the city's residents. Repulsed at London Bridge on July 5, the rebels disbanded. Cade was hunted down and mortally wounded a week later.

Seven Pines. *See* Fair Oaks.

Seven Weeks' War (1866). In dividing up the spoils of the 1864 conquest of Schleswig and Holstein, the Prussian chancellor, Otto von Bismarck, deliberately placed the Austrian Empire of Franz Josef I in an untenable position. On June 14, 1866, Austria declared war against a well-prepared Prussia. Three battles and exactly seven weeks later the thoroughly beaten Austrians accepted preliminary peace terms. Franz Josef ceded slices of territory and was forced out of German affairs. Prussia enlarged its boundaries and became the dominant state in the new North German Confederation headed by the King of Prussia (Wilhelm I).

Langensalza	1866
Münchengrätz	1866
Sadowa	1866

Seven Years' War (1756–1763). The undeclared war between France and Great Britain that began in North America in 1754 and was called the French and Indian War helped provoke a general conflict in Europe two years later. Called the Seven Years' War, or the Third Silesian War, it found Austria (acting for the Holy Roman Empire), Russia, France, Sweden, and Poland aligned against Prussia, Great Britain, and Portugal. While Frederick II, the Great, was the focal point of fighting in Europe, England and France battled at sea and in India and the West Indies. Spain entered the war on the side of France in 1762 only to be defeated by England in Cuba and in the Philippines. Russia and Sweden dropped out of the conflict the same year. The Treaty of Paris in 1763 ended the Seven Years' War as well as the French and Indian War. Great Britain received Minorca, Canada, and Florida. France ceded Louisiana to Spain; Prussia retained Silesia. *See also* French and Indian War.

Minorca I	1756
Calcutta	1756
Lobositz	1756
Prague IV	1757
Kolin	1757
Plassey	1757
Hastenbeck	1757
Gross-Jägersdorf	1757
Rossbach	1757
Breslau	1757
Leuthen	1757
Olmütz	1758
Fort Saint David	1758
Crefeld	1758
Zorndorf	1758
Hochkirch	1758
Madras II	1758–1759
Bergen	1759
Kay	1759
Minden II	1759
Kunersdorf	1759
Lagos II	1759
Maxen	1759
Quiberon Bay	1759
Wandiwash	1760
Landeshut	1760
Warburg	1760
Liegnitz II	1760
Torgau	1760
Pondicherry	1761

Martinique 1762
Burkersdorf 1762
Havana 1762
Manila I 1762
Freiberg 1762

Shaho River (Russian-Japanese War), 1904. Although the battle of Liaoyang was almost a stalemate of exhaustion, the Russian commander, Gen. Aleksei Kuropatkin, withdrew his army northward toward Mukden early in September 1904. Japanese field marshal Marquis Iwao Oyama followed. At the Shaho River, 15 miles south of Mukden, the Russians halted their retreat. In mid-October Kuropatkin lashed out at his pursuers. As at Liaoyang two months earlier, the long front of more than 40 miles broke down into a series of fierce local engagements, which lasted until autumn rains halted the fighting. Both sides dug in behind barbed wire for the winter. *See* Liaoyang; Mukden I; Russian-Japanese War.

Shanghai (Chinese-Japanese War II). A three-month battle in which the Japanese finally conquered the city on November 8, 1937. *See* China I.

Shangri-La (World War II), 1942. During the early months of the Pacific war, the Allies suffered an unbroken string of defeats at the hands of the Japanese. To boost morale and to take the offensive, even if only briefly, the U.S. admiral William Halsey led Naval Task Force 16 across the North Pacific to within 650 miles of Japan. On April 18 Col. James Doolittle and 15 other pilots in B-25 Mitchell bombers took off from the flight deck of the carrier *Hornet*. Thirteen bombers raided Tokyo and one each struck Nagoya, Osaka, and Kobe. All planes got through to their targets, and though the attack did little damage, it cheered the Allies and caused consternation in Japan.

One plane landed in Vladivostok, where it was impounded by the Russians. The other 15 were abandoned in midair or crashed in China. Of the 80 air corps men, three were killed and eight captured. The eight prisoners were tried for "inhuman" acts and all found guilty; five received life imprisonment sentences and three were beheaded. To preserve the secrecy of the carrier launching, the United States announced that the army planes had been based at Shangri-La, a mythical country described in James Hilton's novel *Lost Horizon*. *See* Japan—Bombardment; World War II.

Sharqat (World War I), 1918. Late in the war the British high command resolved to resume the offensive in Mesopotamia with the objective of securing the oil fields at Mosul. On October 23 the British commander, Gen. Sir William Marshall, sent an Anglo-Indian corps northward up the Tigris River from Baghdad. Under the leadership of Gen. Sir Alexander Cobbe, the mounted British troops covered 77 miles in 39 hours to reach the Little Zab River. The Turkish commander, Gen. Ismail Hakki, planned to make a stand here with his Sixth Army. But when Cobbe maneuvered to threaten his rear, Hakki fell back to a position north of Sharqat, 60 miles from Mosul. Pressing forward, the British attacked on October 29. With a loss of only 1,886 men, Cobbe took 11,300 prisoners and 51 guns. Although his lines still stood intact, Hakki surrendered with another 7,000 men on the following day. An Indian cavalry division occupied Mosul on November 14.

The battle of Sharqat ended the fighting in Mesopotamia. The campaign had cost Great Britain and India 92,500 casualties, of whom 28,621 were killed or died of disease. Turkish losses are unknown except for the 45,000 men that were captured. The final British victory was due more to the conquest of Palestine than any triumph in Mesopotamia. *See* Ramadi; Megiddo III; World War I.

Sheriffmuir ("the Fifteen"), 1715. Dissatisfaction with the 1707 union between England and Scotland, plus the unpopularity of Hannoverian King George I, led to a Jacobite rebellion in Scotland in 1715. Declaring for the Old Pretender (James Edward), John Erskine (6th or 11th earl of Mar), began raising a force of 10,000 Highland men at Perth on September 6. At about the same time a second Jacobite uprising took place in northern England. The two rebel armies failed to effect a junction, and at Sheriffmuir, in southern Perth County, Mar was challenged by a royalist army of 3,300 men under Archibald Campbell, 3rd duke of Argyll. On November 13 Argyll checked the rebel advance despite his great inferiority in numbers. After the indecisive action, the Jacobite force disintegrated during its retreat. Mar abandoned the rebellion. He fled to France the following February with the Old Pretender, who had landed in Scotland on Christmas Day after his followers had been hopelessly dispersed at Preston as well as at Sheriffmuir. *See* Preston II; Jacobite Insurrections.

Shiloh (American Civil War), 1862. The Federal offensive in the West became more coordinated on March 11, when President Abraham Lincoln put Gen. Henry Halleck in overall command. Halleck sent Gen. U. S. Grant with 42,000 men to Pittsburg Landing on the west side of the Tennessee River near the border of Mississippi. He then ordered Gen. Don Carlos Buell to move from Nashville, Tenn., to link up with Grant. Meanwhile Gen. Albert Johnston, in charge of Confederate armies in the West, concentrated some 40,000 troops at Corinth, Miss. Seizing the initiative, Johnston marched 25 miles northward to Pittsburg Landing, arriving there on April 5.

Early the following morning the Confederates attacked Grant's six divisions, which were encamped with little thought to defense or security.

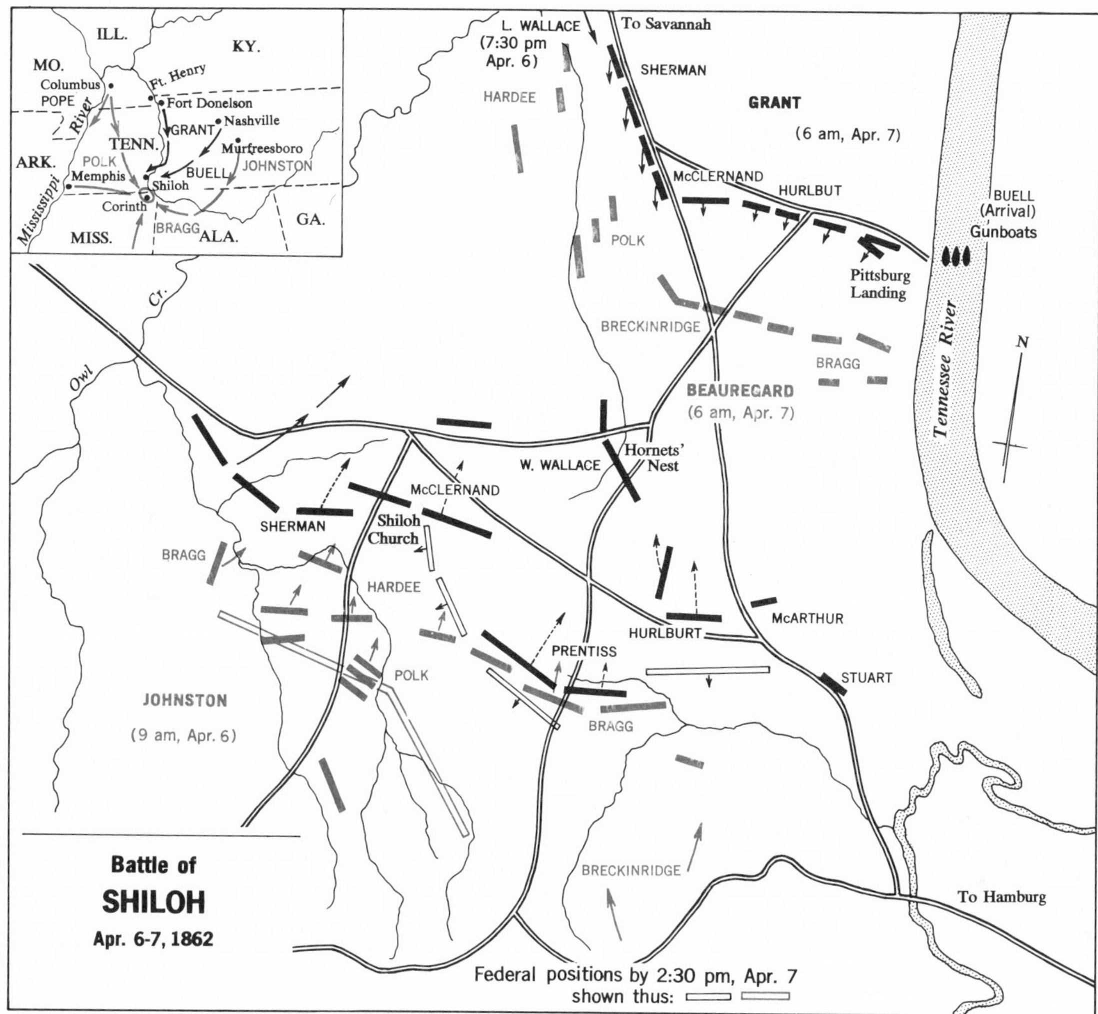

The corps of the Confederate generals Leonidas Polk (I), Braxton Bragg (II), and William Hardee (III) struck the divisions of Gen. William Sherman and Gen. Benjamin Prentiss in a furious onslaught that drove the Federals back two miles. The attack also engulfed the divisions of the Federal generals John McClernand, Stephen Hurlburt, and William Wallace. Grant hurried forward from Savannah, Tenn., to take charge of the defense of the landing area, but the fiercely fighting Confederates slowly closed toward the river. The action was so intense all along the front that Johnston's corps commanders, including Gen. John Breckinridge of the reserve corps, took charge of whatever units were available, regardless of organization. Johnston himself was killed about 2:30 P.M. Pierre Beauregard succeeded to the command. On the Federal side W. Wallace fell mortally wounded, while at 5:30 P.M. Prentiss surrendered with 2,200 men after a spirited fight to hold a patch of woods called the Hornets' Nest. About 6 P.M. Beauregard halted the attack, expecting to complete the Confederate victory the following day. However, that night Gen. Lewis Wallace's division tardily came up on the Federal right (northwest), while three of Buell's divisions finally began arriving from the east to strengthen Grant's command. They came into line on the left nearest the river.

At dawn the next day (April 7) Grant launched a counteroffensive that had spread all along the line by 10 A.M. The fresh Union troops swung the balance against the weary and now outnumbered Confederates. Slowly the Southerners gave ground, fighting as desperately as on the previous day, particularly around Shiloh Church. At 2:30 P.M. Beauregard ordered a retreat. The Confederates turned and marched back to Corinth. Grant's troops occupied the camps they had held before the battle. On April 8 a belated Federal pursuit was checked by the cavalry of Gen. Nathan Forrest.

The narrow Union victory at Shiloh prepared

the way for the conquest of the entire length of the Mississippi. Federal casualties were 1,754 killed, 8,408 wounded, 2,885 missing. Confederate losses totaled 10,697—1,723 killed, 8,012 wounded, 959 missing. *See* Island No. 10; New Orleans II; Iuka; American Civil War.

Shipka Pass (Russian-Turkish War), 1877–1878. During the 143-day Russian siege of Plevna, a second army of Czar Alexander II pushed into the Balkan Mountains of central Bulgaria. Some 7,000 men under Gen. Fëdor Radetski reached Shipka Pass on August 21, when they were attacked by a much larger Turkish army commanded by Gen. Suleiman Pasha. The Ottoman assault drove back the Russians until reinforcements for Radetski arrived. A counterattack won back the lost ground. Fighting died out on August 26 with both sides holding their original positions. Russian losses totaled 4,000; Turkish casualties were more than twice as heavy. On September 16 Suleiman made a new attempt to clear the pass, but he was beaten back.

With the fall of Plevna on December 10, the Russian army received further reinforcements, bringing its strength up to more than 50,000. General Osip Gurko, who had assumed command, launched an offensive on January 8, 1878. In bitter fighting the Russians carried the Turkish entrenchments, forcing a surrender the following day. The Turks lost 4,000 in killed and wounded and 36,000 prisoners. Gurko's casualties were about 5,000. *See* Plevna; Kars II; Plovdiv; Russian-Turkish War.

Shkodër I (Venetian-Turkish Wars), 1478. One of the last European powers to resist Turkish aggression in the Balkans was Venice. The Italian city-state held trading stations along the Greek and Albanian coasts. These outposts came under attack from the Ottoman Turks of Mohammed II, the Conqueror, who had built up a strong navy after taking Constantinople in 1453. Shkodër (Scutari), a fortified town in northwestern Albania, suffered a heavy bombardment in the summer of 1478. Twice the Turks launched assaults against the town, but both times the Venetians beat them off. Mohammed finally gave up the siege but was awarded Shkodër by the Treaty of Constantinople, which Venice signed the following year. Less than 500 men marched safely out of the battered Albanian town. *See* Negroponte; Lepanto I.

Shkodër II (First Balkan War), 1913. The first of the Balkan powers to declare war on Turkey in 1912 was Montenegro, followed by Bulgaria, Serbia, and Greece. Under King Nicholas I, Montenegrin troops laid siege to the Turkish-held city of Shkodër (Scutari), now in northwestern Albania. Bulgaria and Serbia agreed to an armistice with Mohammed V on December 3, but Montenegro and Greece continued the war. On April 22, 1913, the besiegers stormed into the city, despite the protests of their allies who had assigned Shkodër to Albania. Two weeks after Austria (Franz Josef I) intervened, Nicholas yielded the city. *See* Lüleburgaz; Ioannina; Balkan Wars.

Shrewsbury (Percy Revolt against Henry IV), 1403. Four years after ascending the throne of England, Henry IV faced a large-scale rebellion, chiefly from the Percys of Northumberland and Owen Glendower's Welsh faction. Without waiting for his father to recruit additional troops, Sir Henry Percy (Hotspur) marched south toward Shrewsbury. Here he planned to destroy a small royalist force commanded by Henry (Prince Hal), the Prince of Wales. King Henry IV arrived just in time to intercept the rebels at Hateley Field, three miles north of the city, on July 21, 1403. (Glendower was still at Carmarthen in southern Wales.) Percy took up a strong defensive position that offset the numerical superiority of the combined royalists. Prince Hal led the charge, which resulted in desperate fighting until Percy fell mortally wounded. Percy's troops then broke and fled. Many leaders, including his uncle, Thomas Percy (earl of Worcester), were captured and executed. (Hotspur appears as a soldier in Shakespeare's *Henry IV,* Part I.) The elder Henry Percy (earl of Northumberland) received a pardon but only waited for a new opportunity to overthrow Henry IV. *See* Homildon Hill; Bramham Moor.

Shropshire (Roman Conquest of Britain), A.D. 50. For seven years after Roman legions invaded Britain for the second time, Caractacus carried on guerrilla warfare against the intruder. Finally, in A.D. 50, a force of legionaries under Ostorius Scapula cornered the rebel chieftain on a hill in Shropshire near the Welsh border. The Roman attack routed the Britons, but Caractacus escaped once again. He fled north to the Brigantes tribe and sought to arouse new opposition to the occupying forces. However, the tribal queen handed him over to the Romans.

Caractacus, with his wife, daughter, and brothers, was taken to Rome and paraded through the streets in chains. After the exhibition, Emperor Claudius I freed the entire family. Britain, however, was to make one more cataclysmic attempt to throw off Roman rule. *See* Medway River; Verulamium II.

Sicily (World War II), 1943. The Allied clean sweep of North Africa in May 1943 opened the Mediterranean for thrusts against Sicily and the Italian mainland. Anglo-American forces under the U.S. general Dwight Eisenhower began mounting an amphibious operation (called Husky) to make the first strike at the Axis homeland. On the night of July 9–10 a fleet of 3,000 ships and landing craft approached the southern shore of Sicily carrying 14,000 vehicles, 600 tanks, 1,800 guns, and 160,000 men of the Fifteenth Army Group under the British general Sir Harold Alexander. For the previous week the island had been heavily bombed by the British air marshal Arthur Tedder's Allied air force. Now elements of the British 1st Airborne and U.S. 82nd Airborne divisions parachuted in ahead of the amphibious assault, creating confusion and damage among the 350,000 Axis defenders—three German infantry and four Italian infantry divisions and six Italian coast defense divisions, all under the command of the Italian general Alfred Guzzoni.

Protected by 3,680 aircraft (against an Axis total of 1,400), the Allied amphibious force hit along 100 miles of beach at dawn. The British general Sir Bernard Montgomery's Eighth Army landed on the southeast corner of Sicily—Gen. Miles Dempsey's XIII Corps (5th and 50th Infantry) on the right, Gen. Oliver Leese's XXX Corps (51st Infantry, 1st Canadian) on the left. To the west Gen. George Patton's U.S. Seventh Army (1st, 3rd, 45th Infantry, 2nd Armored) struck near the center of Sicily's southern coast. Both armies were supplemented by Commando or Ranger units. By nightfall all seven assault infantry divisions had carved out their assigned beachheads.

On the right the Eighth Army captured the port of Syracuse on July 12 and Augusta two days later. It then drove north toward Catania, midway up the east coast. But here Axis defenses on the commanding slopes of 11,000-foot Mount Etna brought the advance to a halt. At this time German reinforcements were rushed to Sicily, with German Gen. Hube taking charge of all Nazi troops. On the left the Seventh Army captured the port of Licata on D-Day and then beat off a strong German armored attack at Gela, with the help of naval gunfire under the supreme Allied naval commander, the British admiral Sir Andrew Cunningham. The U.S. 3rd Infantry, 82nd Airborne, and 2nd Armored, forming a provisional corps under Gen. Geoffrey Keyes, then cleared the southwestern coast and drove across the island through hilly terrain to take Palermo on the north coast on July 22. Meanwhile, Gen. Omar Bradley's II Corps smashed through the center of Sicily to San Stefano. The main U.S. thrust then turned east in two drives—along the coast and 20 miles inland along the lateral Nicosia–Randazzo highway. This attack pinched the German defenses at Mount Etna, enabling the British to take Catania on August 5. Bradley's troops took Troina on August 6 and Randazzo on August 13 and raced into the key port of Messina at the northeastern end of the island on August 17. The Eighth Army arrived there from the south only hours later. Meanwhile, some 40,000 German (including the crack 1st Parachute) and 60,000 Italian troops were evacuated across the narrow Strait of Messina to the mainland of Italy.

The capture of Messina ended the 38-day battle. Axis casualties totaled 167,000, of whom 37,000 were Germans. The Allies lost 31,158 in killed, wounded, and missing, of whom 11,923 were Americans. The war now stood at the threshold of Italy itself. This swelling threat, plus devastating Allied bombings, ended the Fascist regime. Benito Mussolini resigned on July 25 and was succeeded by Marshal Pietro Badoglio. But the swift German take-over of the Italian Peninsula thwarted Allied plans for a quick conquest. *See* Tunisia; Italy, Southern; Salerno; World War II.

Sidi Barrâni (World War II), 1940. The three-year North African campaign opened in September 1940 when the Italian Tenth Army under Marshal Rodolpho Graziani invaded Egypt from Libya. At Sidi Barrâni, 60 miles into Egypt, the Italian army set up a series of fortified camps in the desert. Eighty miles to the east, the British Western Desert Force (sometimes called Army of the Nile and later renamed the XIII Corps and finally the Eighth Army) under Gen. Sir Richard O'Connor was based at Mersa Matrûh, the terminus of the railway and road leading out from Alexandria. In a surprise march O'Connor's army of 36,000 (chiefly the 4th Indian Infantry and 7th Armoured divisions) circled south of the Italian defenses and attacked the Sidi Barrâni encampments from the flank and rear (west) on December 9. In three days of fighting the British army routed 75,000 Italian troops, capturing 38,000 prisoners. British casualties numbered about 600. The first Axis threat to the Suez Canal was smashed.

O'Connor immediately pressed the 7th Armoured westward across the Libyan frontier toward Bardia. The 4th Indian Infantry was ordered to Eritrea by Gen. Sir Archibald Wavell, head of the Middle East Command. *See* Bardia; East Africa; World War II.

Sidi-Rezegh (World War II), 1941. The second British offensive in Libya was ordered by a new Middle East commander, Gen. Sir Claude Auchinleck, and directed by a new combat leader, Gen. Alan Cunningham (hero of East Africa), head of the recently formed (September 26, 1941) Eighth Army of 118,000 men. The opposing force was the Axis *Panzergruppe* (100,000 men), commanded by Gen. Erwin Rommel and comprised of the three-division German Afrika Korps and eight Italian divisions. The attack, called Operation Crusader, was launched on November 18 by Gen. A. R. Godwin-Austen's XIII Corps (infantry) on the right along the coast and Gen. Willoughby Norrie's XXX Corps (armor) swinging wide into the desert on the left (south). The initial attack of British armor reached Sidi-Rezegh, the key to besieged Tobruk, on November 19. But

Rommel beat back an attempted link-up with the Tobruk garrison and then counterattacked fiercely on November 22, driving to the British rear at the Egyptian frontier three days later.

When Cunningham wanted to fall back to Mersa Matrûh, Auchinleck relieved him and appointed Gen. Neil Ritchie to command of the Eighth Army. For two weeks the scattered British units stubbornly held their ground and even opened a corridor to Tobruk on November 29. Then, on the night of December 7–8, Rommel, short of supplies, began to fall back across Cyrenaica. The British occupied Gazala on December 15 and Benghazi on December 25. The pursuit finally ended at El Agheila on January 6. Axis casualties during the seven-week battle and pursuit were more than 33,000; the Eighth Army lost 17,700.

The British did not follow up their important victory at Sidi-Rezegh, largely because scheduled reinforcements had to be diverted to the Far East against Japan. Meanwhile Rommel had received additional tanks and air support during his long retreat, and two weeks later he struck back savagely. *See* Salûm–Halfaya Pass; Gazala; Tobruk III; World War II.

Siegfried Line (World War II), 1944. The swift Allied advance across northern France, southern Belgium, and Luxembourg brought Gen. Dwight Eisenhower's SHAEF (Supreme Headquarters, Allied Expeditionary Forces) armies up to the German frontier. Here stood the famous Siegfried Line, or Westwall, a formidable series of prepared positions, now hastily refurbished and occupied by retreating Nazi troops from the west and fresh units from inside Germany. As the Allied forces closed to the line, stiffening German resistance and overextended supply lines braked their offensive.

General Eisenhower now had seven armies on line from the North Sea to Switzerland. From north to south they stood: Field Marshal Sir Bernard Montgomery's Twenty-First Army Group, consisting of the Canadian First (Henry Crerar) and British Second (Miles Dempsey); Gen. Omar Bradley's Twelfth Army Group, consisting of the U.S. Ninth (Henry Simpson), U.S. First (Courtney Hodges), and U.S. Third (George Patton); and Gen. Jacob Dever's Sixth Army Group, consisting of the U.S. Seventh (Alexander Patch) and French First (Jean de Lattre de Tassigny). Opposing this force, Field Marshal Karl von Rundstedt, the German commander in the West, had 63 divisions divided into six armies. The Fifteenth (Zangen), First Parachute (Kurt Student), and Seventh (Ernst Brandenberger), under Field Marshal Walther Model, held from the North Sea to the Moselle River. To the south, ahead of the Siegfried Line in Alsace-Lorraine, were the First (Knobelsdorff), Fifth Panzer (Hasso von Manteuffel), and Nineteenth (Wiese), all under Gen. Hermann Balck.

For three months in the fall of 1944 the Allied armies hammered at the German Westwall in some of the hardest fighting of the war. In the north Montgomery sought to establish an airborne bridgehead over the lower Rhine and thus enflank the northern end of the Siegfried Line. In Operation Market-Garden three airborne divisions—U.S. 82nd and 101st and British 1st—parachuted into the area from Nijmegen north to Arnhem on September 17. Their objective was to seize seven bridges and open a corridor 60 miles long into Holland. At the same time the XXX Corps (Bryan Horrocks) of the British Second Army plunged north to link up with the airheads. The Nazi First Parachute Army reacted violently, however. The British ground attack was opposed at every step and could not reach the hard-pressed 1st Airborne at Arnhem before this northernmost airhead was caved in on September 25 by Nazi counterattacks. Only one-fourth of the 10,000 British parachutists got back safely—1,100 were killed and 6,500 captured. German losses were 3,300 killed and wounded. (It took seven more months to capture Arnhem.)

The Canadian army on the left was more successful. After a bitter struggle this force seized South Beveland (October 30) and Walcheren Island (November 3), both at the mouth of the Schelde River. By November 9 the entire Antwerp port area was cleared at a cost of 27,633 Canadian casualties; 12,500 Germans were captured. Beginning on November 26, Antwerp became a key source of supplies, despite a four-month harassing bombardment by Nazi flying bombs and rockets.

On the central front the U.S. First Army reached the Siegfried Line at Aachen on September 12. After hard fighting, the XIX and VII corps forced their way into Aachen on October 13. Eight days of vicious house-to-house combat cleared the first German city to fall to the Allies. In November the Ninth Army, which had moved into line on the left, joined with the First in a hard attack against the German defenses on a 25-mile sector east of Aachen. Here the V Corps fight through the Hürtgen Forest became one of the bloodiest engagements of the campaign. By December 1 the advance had penetrated to the Roer River, 25 miles from Cologne. Meanwhile to the south, the Third Army had thrown back a counterattack by the German Fifth Panzer and First armies south of Metz during September 18–October 1. Resuming the offensive, Patton encircled Metz on November 18 and in a huge half-turn to the north forced the Germans back to the Westwall along the Saar River.

The two Allied armies on the southern end of the line made the biggest advance of this period. The U.S. Seventh Army drove to the Vosges Mountains, seized the Saverne Gap, and then plunged into Strasbourg on November 23. Patch also wheeled his forces northward, pressing up against the Siegfried Line from Strasbourg past the Karlsruhe corner to his boundary with Patton near Bitche. At the same time the French First Army advanced through Belfort and Mulhouse on November 22 to the Rhine River at the Swiss border. In the center of De Tassigny's area, however, the German Nineteenth Army stubbornly held a westward jutting salient around Colmar.

During the late autumn of 1944 the Allies took some 75,000 Nazi prisoners and advanced closer to the Rhine. But a skillful German defense along the Siegfried Line held Eisenhower's armies to disappointing gains. And the Allied strategy of a broad-front attack had left some sectors dangerously weak in reserves, particularly in the Ardennes. *See* France, Northern; Ardennes II; German Vengeance-Weapon Bombardment; World War II.

Sierra Maestra (Castro Revolt in Cuba), 1958. After serving almost two years in prison for their abortive attack on Moncada Fortress in Santiago, Fidel and Raúl Castro received an amnesty from the Cuban government of Fulgencio Batista. The rebels then fled to Mexico to train a revolutionary army near the capital. On December 2, 1956, the Castros, now joined by an Argentine Marxist and physician named Ernesto "Che" Guevara, returned to Cuba. When the landing in Oriente Province failed to incite a general uprising, the rebels escaped into the nearby Sierra Maestra. There followed months of guerrilla warfare against the armed forces of Gen. Eulogio Cantillo. Finally, with 1,000 men, Cantillo launched an offensive against the mountain hideout of the rebels in the summer of 1958. Although Castro could muster only 300 men, he turned back three separate government attacks into the Sierra Maestra, during June 28–29, July 11–21, and July 28–August 3. Finding the government troops reluctant to fight, Castro launched his own offensive with the men of the "26 of July Movement." *See* Moncada Fortress; Santa Clara–Santiago.

Sievershausen (German Reformation Wars), 1553. When the Spanish Hapsburg Charles V of the Holy Roman Empire smashed the Schmalkaldic League of Protestants at Mühlberg in 1547, he had the help of Maurice, duke of Saxony. But soon thereafter Maurice changed sides. While Charles was busy warring against Henry II of France in the west, Maurice secured the release of his cousin John Frederick I, elector of Saxony, and his father-in-law, Philip, landgrave of Hesse. In 1552 Maurice won from Charles the Convention of Passau, obtaining partial religious toleration for the German states. The following year he attacked Albert Alcibiades, margrave of Brandenburg and ally of Charles. At Sievershausen, 15 miles east of Hannover, on July 9, 1553, Maurice's Saxons routed the Brandenburg army, but the victorious duke received a mortal wound. Two years later Charles signed the Peace of Augsburg, granting the Protestant princes of Germany territorial rights and religious toleration. *See* Mühlberg.

Siffin (Moslem Civil Wars), 657. The fourth caliph of Islam, Ali, had no sooner put down a revolt in Basra than Muawiyah, the governor of Syria, opened a new rebellion. Ali promptly marched from Al Kufa to Siffin, in Syria. For more than three months his loyal troops fought periodically against the forces of Muawiyah. When neither side could gain an advantage, a truce was declared and the quarrel submitted to arbitration in August 657. But no agreement was reached. The conflict dragged on until January 661, when Ali was assassinated. Muawiyah then became undisputed ruler and the first in a long line of Ommiad (Omayyad) caliphs. His reign was one of violent conquest in both Asia and Africa. *See* Basra; Constantinople III; Kerbela; Moslem conquests.

Sikh-British Wars I and **II** (1845–1846, 1848–1849). The first conflict between the Sikh sect in the Punjab and the British developed from a dispute over the Sutlej River area of northwestern India in 1845. After three months of fighting, the Sikhs ceded their claims to the territory and recognized British supremacy in Kashmir.

Mudki	1845
Ferozeshah	1845
Aliwal	1846
Sobraon	1846

Unhappy with the 1846 settlement, the Sikh chiefs led a rebellion against British rule two years later. Defeated again, they acceded to the British annexation of the Punjab in 1849. After this the Sikhs remained loyal allies of the British.

Ramnagar	1848
Chilianwala	1849
Gujrat	1849

Silesian Wars (1740–1742; 1744–1745; 1756–1763). The first and second Silesian wars were part of the War of the Austrian Succession; the third was an alternate name for the Seven Years' War (called the French and Indian War in North America). *See* Austrian Succession, War of the; Seven Years' War.

Silistra (Crimean War), 1854. The second battle of the war to take place in the Balkans found the Russian forces of Nicholas I on the offensive against the Turkish armies of Abdul Medjid I. Under Field Marshal Ivan Paskevich, prince of Warsaw, the Russians crossed the Danube on March 20 and soon invested the Ottoman fortress of Silistra on the south bank in what is now northeastern Bulgaria. The garrison held out stubbornly, even though no Turkish relief party was sent to their aid. Finally, on June 9, Paskevich abandoned the siege, having lost about 10,000 men. The successful Turkish resistance had aroused the admiration of other European powers, and when Russia refused to evacuate the Danube principalities, Great Britain and France declared war. The site of the war then shifted, first to the Baltic and then to the Crimea. *See* Oltenița; Bomarsund; Alma River; Crimean War.

Silpia. *See* Ilipa.

Simancas (Spanish-Moslem Wars), 934. Despite the illustrious reign of the Ommiad caliph Abd-er-Rahman III in Spain, the Christian states in the northwest gradually gained strength. King Ramiro II of León initiated the long counteroffensive against the Moslems by attacking Simancas, eight miles southwest of Valladolid. The armored Leonese cavalry routed the Moslems, in the first Christian victory south of the Pyrenees since Covadonga in 718. *See* Covadonga; Zamora; Moslem Conquests.

Sinai Peninsula (Israeli-Egyptian War), 1956. Eight years of border clashes between the new state of Israel and its Arab neighbors flared into open conflict in the fall of 1956. The event was preceded by an increase in Middle Eastern tension when the Egyptian president, Gamal Abdel Nasser, nationalized the Suez Canal on July 26. Great Britain and France took the lead in calling for international control of the vital waterway. Then on October 29 the small but well-trained Israeli army of Premier David Ben-Gurion suddenly struck across the Egyptian border into the Sinai Peninsula. The two ill-prepared Egyptian divisions in this region could offer only slight resistance to the ten attacking brigades commanded by Gen. Moshe Dayan. While the Israelis thrust toward the canal, Anglo-French air forces began bombing Egyptian airfields on October 31. This was in preparation for the dropping of airborne troops five days later. This force seized Port Fuad and Port Said at the northern end of the canal.

World opinion was outraged. Although Great Britain and France claimed only to be enforcing a cease-fire between Israel and Egypt, many believed that their joint objective was the establishment of control over the Suez Canal. The Israeli invasion had already halted on November 4, with the entire Sinai Peninsula conquered at a cost of 1,000 casualties, including 172 killed. Egyptian losses included thousands of prisoners and hundreds of tanks, self-propelled guns and trucks. Faced with strong criticism in the United States and the United Nations, Britain and France called off their show of force in the canal zone. A United Nations police force hurried to the area to prevent further hostilities. The Anglo-French troops were withdrawn in December. Three months later the Israeli army pulled out of the Sinai Peninsula. The Suez Canal remained firmly in Egyptian hands. *See* Jerusalem IX; Israeli-Arab War.

Singapore (World War II), 1942. The overwhelming Japanese victory on the Malay Peninsula forced Gen. A. E. Percival's British troops to retreat across Johore Strait to the 220-square-mile island of Singapore. On January 31 the last of the routed forces cleared the 70-foot-wide causeway, which was then dynamited but only partially destroyed. Percival had about 85,000 British, Indian, and Australian troops (only 70,000 were armed and many of those were not combat soldiers) to defend the 30-mile perimeter of the island. The huge guns of the Singapore naval fortress were designed to repulse a sea attack. Their flat trajectories were useless for artillery bombardment against a land attack on the unfortified northern end of the island.

General Tomoyuki Yamashita, conqueror of Malaya, brought up heavy siege guns to the southern tip of the peninsula. These guns began blasting the island on February 5. On the nights of February 8 and 9 some 5,000 Japanese amphibious forces crossed the narrow waterway and gained bridgeheads on both the northwest and northern sides of the island. Their engineers quickly repaired the damaged causeway, enabling tanks and 25,000 reinforcements to pour ashore. Japanese ground troops pushed steadily toward Singapore City, while supporting artillery and aircraft raked the island. On February 13, 3,000 noncombatants slipped off Singapore in small boats, hoping to reach Java. Almost all were killed or captured by an intercepting Japanese naval force. Meanwhile, Japanese spearheads penetrated deeply into the British lines, splitting the weary defenders into isolated groups. With the water supply shut off and food, ammunition, and gasoline dangerously low, Percival surrendered the island on February 15. Taken prisoner were 32,000 Indian, 16,000 British, and 14,000 Australian troops. In the two battles of Malaya and Singapore, Great Britain lost 138,000 men, including 130,000 prisoners. Total Japanese casualties were 9,800. Great Britain's Prime Minister Winston Churchill described it as "the worst disaster and largest capitulation in British history." The fall of the supposedly impregnable Singapore fortress shocked the Allied world. More important, it doomed the Dutch East Indies and opened the door to Japanese invasion of the Indian Ocean. *See* Malaya; East Indies; Ceylon; World War II.

Singara (Persian Wars of the Roman Empire), 348. During the early years of his reign, Constantius II, Roman Emperor of the East, was enmeshed in a long series of conflicts with the Sannanian Persian Empire of Shapur (Sapor) II. Most of the fighting took place in Mesopotamia, between the Euphrates and Tigris rivers. Although the fighting was often bloody, it dragged on for more than 20 years with neither side able to gain the upper hand. In 348 Constantius marched on the outpost of Singara. Meeting a force of Shapur's Persians, the Roman army put the enemy to rout and pursued energetically to the foot of the heights overlooking Singara. Here the weary victors camped for the night, unaware that Shapur had posted the main Persian body in the hills above them. During the night the Persians fell on the legionaries' bivouac and inflicted a terrible slaughter. It was the worst setback suffered by Constantius in the East.

The Persians, however, were unable to capitalize on their triumph at Singara. Two years later they failed (for the third time) to take the key fortress of Nisibis (Nusaybin), on the Syrian frontier. The three-month siege cost Shapur some 20,000 men.

Constantius had single-mindedly campaigned against Persia despite the great unrest in the European part of the empire, ruled by his two brothers, Constantine II and Constans. When the brothers quarreled in 340, Constantine II was killed by Constans. The latter was himself slain early in 350 by Flavius Popilius Magnentius, who usurped the Western throne. Constantius then abandoned the Persian war to deal with the hostile ruler in the West. *See* Chrysopolis; Mursa; Roman Empire.

Sino-Japanese Wars. *See* Chinese-Japanese Wars.

Sinope (Crimean War), 1853. Although Turkey (Abdul Medjid I) opened the war with a victory over Russia along the Danube on November 4, the contest at sea took a different turn. Czar Nicholas I sent a Russian fleet across the Black Sea. On November 30 the Russian vessels trapped nine Turkish ships in the harbor at Sinope. A heavy, no-quarter bombardment totally destroyed the Ottoman squadron and harbor installations. More than 4,000 Turks were killed. The battle aroused the indignation of Great Britain and France, who promptly ordered their fleets into the Black Sea to protect Turkish shipping. The war would soon widen. *See* Oltenița; Silistra; Crimean War.

Sinsheim (Second, or Dutch, War of Louis XIV), 1674. When Louis XIV of France marched on Holland in 1672, Spain (Charles II), Brandenburg (Frederick William), and the Holy Roman Empire (Leopold I) sent troops in support of William III's beleaguered Netherlanders. Along the upper Rhine, Louis' great commander, the marshal the Vicomte de Turenne encountered a wily old opponent he had first fought against more than a quarter of a century earlier—the Austrian general Count Montecuccoli, who had led the Imperial armies in the latter days of the Thirty Years' War. These two generals relied more on maneuver than on battle. But in 1674 Turenne suddenly crossed the Rhine at Philippsburg and fell on an Imperial force at Sinsheim, 20 miles to the east, on June 16. Although the surprised Charles V, titular duke of Lorraine, had some 10,000 men—the equal of Turenne's French attackers—he was routed with a loss of almost a third of his force. Montecuccoli was too far down the Rhine to aid his ally. Turenne then laid waste The Palatinate, to destroy his enemy's source of supply, before withdrawing to the Rhine. Meanwhile another battle shaped up in the Spanish Netherlands. *See* Maastricht II; Seneffe; Enzheim; Louis XIV, Wars of.

Sioux Wars I and II (1865–1868; 1875–1877). The Sand Creek Massacre in 1864 led to an uprising of Plains Indians from 1865 to 1868. The Sioux joined the other tribes on the warpath when the United States began building forts along the Bozeman Trail from Fort Laramie, Wyo., to Bozeman, Mont., thus giving the conflict the name Sioux War. In the Treaty of Fort Laramie, signed on April 29, 1868, the government agreed to abandon the Bozeman Trail and the Sioux accepted a permanent reservation in Dakota Territory.

Platte Bridge	1865
Massacre Hill	1866
Fort Phil Kearny	1867

The Sioux again took the warpath in 1875 when the Black Hills gold rush and an extension of the Northern Pacific Railroad violated their reservation. After their major victory over Lt. Col. George Custer at the Little Bighorn River, the Sioux and their allies were hunted down and crushingly defeated within seven months.

Rosebud River	1876
Little Bighorn River	1876
Wolf Mountain	1877

Skagerrak. *See* Jutland.

Slankamen (Austrian-Turkish Wars), 1691. The Ottoman Empire of southwestern Europe suffered a string of reverses at the hands of the Holy Roman Empire under Leopold I: Vienna, 1683; Harkány, 1687; Belgrade, 1688. However, under Vizier Mustafa Kuprili, brother of Sultan Ahmed II, the Turks rallied to drive the Austrians out of Bulgaria, Serbia, and Transylvania, and retook Belgrade in 1690. As a result, a new Imperial army was formed under Louis William I, margrave of Baden-Baden. In 1691 the margrave marched down the Danube to Slankamen, opposite the mouth of the Tisza, northwest of Belgrade. Here on August 19 the Imperials, numbering about 20,000, encountered a Turkish army twice as large. In a major battle the Ottomans were routed and the vizier was slain on the field. The government at Vienna could not press its advantage, however, because in the west it had become involved with France in the War of the Grand Alliance. *See* Harkány; Fleurus II; Azov.

Slivnica (Serbian-Bulgarian War), 1885. Seven years after winning its independence from Turkey, Serbia went to war with Bulgaria. The new nation was demanding compensation for the Bulgarian annexation of Eastern Rumelia. Under King Milan I, some 25,000 Serbian troops invaded Bulgaria to meet a smaller army commanded by Stefan Stambolov for Alexander I of Bulgaria (Prince Alexander Joseph, cousin of Czar Alexander III of Russia). The two forces battled at Slivnica (Slivnitza), 19 miles northwest of Sofia for three days beginning on November 17. On the first day Stambolov made a spoiling attack that checked the Serbian advance until more Bulgarian troops could come up. Aided by reinforcements, the Bulgarians then beat off Serbian assaults on November 18 and 19. By midafternoon of the last day, Milan's attackers were repulsed so thoroughly that they retreated in disorder, pursued by the Bulgarians. The Serbians lost about 2,000 men, the Bulgarians approximately 3,000. *See* Pirot; Balkan Wars.

Sluys (Hundred Years' War), 1340. The first two years of the Hundred Years' War found Edward III of England ravaging northern and western France without provoking a battle from Philip VI. Then, urged on by the Flemings, who were natural allies of the English because of the interdependence of the wool trade, Edward determined to invade Flanders. In 1340 he took an English fleet of 200 ships to Sluys (Sluis), an inlet near the present Dutch-Belgian border (then the port of Bruges), where the French navy guarded the approach to the Continent. In a nine-hour battle on June 24 the English attacked the 166 French ships at their moorings. Making good use of his shipboard longbowmen, Edward, from the *Thomas,* directed the destruction of most of the French, and some hired Genoese, vessels. The French admiral, Hugues Quierat, was killed.

Following this victory, the English expeditionary force landed and laid siege to Tournai. But the archers were ineffective against the stone walls of the city and Tournai resisted capture. Edward reembarked for England with no profit from his naval triumph except temporary mastery of the English Channel. *See* Halidon Hill; Crécy; Hundred Years' War.

Smolensk I (Napoleonic Empire Wars), 1812. The invasion of Russia by Napoleon I in June 1812 forced the armies of Czar Alexander I to fall back for a month without giving battle. A small engagement at Mogilev on July 23 resulted in a defeat for the Second Russian Army of Prince Pëtr Bagration. Bagration then withdrew northeast toward Smolensk to link up with the First Army commanded by Gen. Mikhail Barclay de Tolly. On August 17 Napoleon's advance elements struck Smolensk. In four hours of hard fighting the French cleared the suburbs up to the city's ancient fortifications by nightfall. The thrust cost the French almost 9,000 casualties, the Russians slightly more. Some 50,000 men took part on each side. Fearing that Napoleon might launch a drive across the Dnieper above the city and thus threaten Russian communications back to Moscow, Barclay de Tolly evacuated Smolensk that night. A week later Gen. Mikhail Kutuzov (later made Prince of Smolensk) took over supreme Russian command. *See* Mogilev; Borodino; Napoleonic Empire Wars.

Smolensk II (World War II). A pocket created by the link-up of German forces east of the city, in which more than 100,000 Russians were killed or captured, between July 16 and August 6, 1941. *See* Soviet Union (World War II).

Sobraon (Sikh-British War I), 1846. After three successive defeats, all the Sikh invaders still in East Punjab had been forced back to the Sutlej River opposite Sobraon. Here they made a stand, halfway between Aliwal, where they had been driven across the river, and Lahore, 45 miles to the northwest. On February 10 the 25,000 Sikhs came under attack by a 15,000-man Anglo-Indian army under Gen. Sir Hugh Gough. Feinting at the enemy right flank, Gough struck hard at the Sikh left. The defenders were driven out of their entrenchments, and as their line was rolled up, they plunged into the river. An estimated 8,000 were killed in combat or drowned in the Sutlej trying to escape. Gough, who had won two of the previous victories, suffered some 2,300 casualties in this last battle of the war. *See* Aliwal; Ramnagar; Sikh-British Wars.

Sofia (Byzantine-Bulgarian Wars), 981. While the Byzantine Empire was preoccupied with internal troubles and a counteroffensive against the Moslems in the east, a strong Bulgarian power built up in the Balkans. Tsar Samuel, an able commander, stretched his empire from the Black Sea to the Adriatic and from the Danube southward into the Peloponnesus. Determined to strike down this growing menace from the north, Emperor Basil II marched out from Constantinople at the head of a large Byzantine army. He encountered Samuel's force near Sofia, the future capital of Bulgaria, in 981. Basil was defeated and forced to return to his capital. He would not take the field against the Bulgars for another 15 years. *See* Adrianople III; Balathista.

Soissons (Rise of France), 486. Five years after succeeding his father as king of the Salian Franks, Clovis I organized a military campaign from his capital of Tournai (now in Belgium). Marching southward, he encountered a rival army under Syagrius, the last Roman governor of Gaul, at Soissons on the Aisne River. The fierce, ax-throwing Franks overwhelmed the opposition. Syagrius was killed. Clovis then took over all of Gaul between the Somme and the Loire rivers, to firmly establish the Merovingian dynasty. *See* Tolbiacum.

Solferino (Italian Wars of Independence), 1859.

After the narrow defeat at Magenta on June 4, the Austrian army fell back eastward across Lombardy. At Solferino, five miles in front of the Mincio River, the Austrians halted to entrench themselves on a series of hills. Emperor Franz Josef arrived to take personal command over Gen. Count Eduard von Clam-Gallas' army of about 100,000 men. The French and Piedmontese army of comparable size, which had doggedly pursued, deployed to attack on June 24. This force too was personally led by monarchs—Louis Napoleon III of France and Victor Emmanuel II of Piedmont. In actual command were the French generals Comte Marie Patrice de MacMahon, Emmanuel de Wimpffen, Adolphe Niel, and Achille Baraguay d'Hilliers.

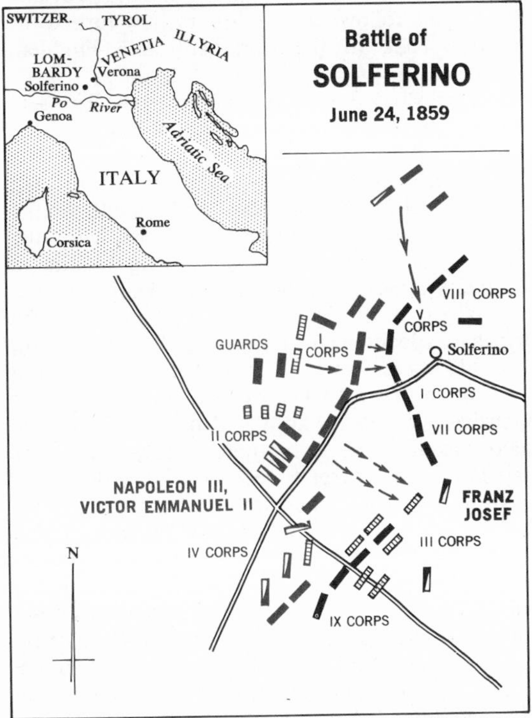

The allied assault broke the Austrian center only after bloody fighting that lasted most of the day. Franz Josef ordered a withdrawal across the Mincio, leaving behind 20,000 killed, wounded, and missing. Many Austrian casualties were caused by the French use of newly developed rifled artillery. Allied losses were almost as high, including nearly 4,000 of the 25,000-man Piedmontese corps. Sickened by the slaughter he had seen, Louis Napoleon abandoned his Piedmont allies and signed a truce with Austria. Lombardy was ceded to France, which in turn allowed it to be annexed by Piedmont. In exchange France received Nice and Savoy. The defection of France jolted, but did not quell, Italian hopes of liberation and unification. (The heavy casualties here and at Magenta three weeks earlier helped lead to the establishment of the International Red Cross in 1864.) *See* Magenta; Calatafimi; Italian Wars of Independence.

Solomon Islands (World War II), 1942–1944. Japan's overwhelming string of conquests in the western Pacific stretched through the East Indies and northern New Guinea by early March 1942. The Japanese then leaped to the Solomon Islands, which, with New Guinea, helped to enclose the Coral Sea northeast of Australia. The Solomons group of seven large and many small islands stretches 600 miles northwest-southeast in two parallel chains. Japanese troops began the Solomons battle on March 13 by seizing Buka, at the northern end of the archipelago. Bougainville was invaded on April 7, Tulagi on May 3. On July 6 the Japanese landed on Guadalcanal, near the southern end of the Solomons, and began constructing an air base there (later called Henderson Field). This was the high tide of Japanese penetration of the Southwest Pacific.

Now, after eight months of almost solid defeat and retreat (except at Midway), the United States and its Pacific Allies stood ready to seize the initiative. On August 7, 1942, the U.S. 1st Marine Division landed on Guadalcanal and Tulagi. Japan's navy reacted vigorously, leading to a series of six naval engagements in the waters around the Solomons. Although suffering heavy losses, Adm. William Halsey's South Pacific fleet eventually beat back the Japanese efforts to retake the island. At the same time U.S. marines (and later infantry) stubbornly defended Henderson Field and later managed to drive the Japanese off the island.

On February 21, 1943, two weeks after the conquest of Guadalcanal, the U.S. 43rd Infantry Division seized Russell Island to the northwest. This move launched the long, hard climb up the Solomons ladder. (On April 18 Adm. Isoroku Yamamoto, supreme Japanese commander in the Pacific, was shot down and killed over Bougainville by U.S. P-38's; Adm. Mineichi Koga succeeded him.) On June 30 the U.S. 43rd Infantry took Rendova Island, off the coast of New Georgia in the central Solomons, and two days later invaded New Georgia itself, seeking control of the vital Munda airfield. The Japanese then stepped up their night-running "Tokyo Express" to bring in supplies and reinforcements to Gen. Noboru Sasaki. This brought on a clash with the U.S. Third Fleet in Kula Gulf, between New Georgia and Kolombangara Island, on July 6 and again on July 12 and 13. The United States lost the cruiser *Helena* and two destroyers. Three Japanese warships were sunk, but fresh enemy troops were landed on New Georgia. The United States then rushed in the 25th and 37th Infantry divisions, plus two marine Raider battalions and a New Zealand brigade. This

XIV Corps, under the U.S. general Oscar Griswold, finally captured Munda airfield on August 5 and during the next two months completed the occupation of the New Georgia group and neighboring islands of Kolombangara and Vella Lavella. In naval action in the central Solomons the Japanese lost three destroyers in Vella Gulf on August 6 and 7 (two more were sunk later by Allied aircraft), and another one during the evacuation of Vella Lavella on October 6 and 7. The Allies lost the destroyer *Chevalier* in the latter engagement. On the ground the Allies lost 1,150 killed and 4,100 wounded. Japanese casualties were about 10,000.

The Allies pressed on up the Solomons ladder. On October 27 the 3rd New Zealand Division landed on the Treasury Islands and secured them in 11 days. In a feint to the east, a U.S. marine battalion made an amphibious attack against Choiseul Island. Then, on November 1, the 3rd Marine Division (Allen Turnage) bypassed the Shortland Islands and landed at Empress Augusta Bay on the west coast of Bougainville. The marines quickly secured a large enough beachhead to accommodate an airfield. The Japanese Seventeenth Army counterattacked savagely by land, sea, and air. But the U.S. 37th Infantry Division began landing on November 8 to help defend the 10-square-mile beachhead (now held by the I Marine Corps under Gen. Alexander Vandegrift) against increasingly strong Japanese assaults. By December 10 Navy Seabees (Construction Battalion) had completed an airstrip. When the U.S. Americal Division arrived on December 28, the marines were relieved. The division had lost 423 killed and 1,418 wounded in destroying a force of some 4,000 Japanese.

The last enemy effort to smash the lodgment on Bougainville, now grown to 22 square miles, came between March 8 and 25, 1944, against what then was the XIV Corps (Oscar Griswold). Some 5,000 Japanese were killed before the attack was repulsed, with a loss of 263 U.S. troops. Allied sea and air superiority now prevented further Japanese reinforcement or resupply. And the remaining Japanese on the island were soon too weak to threaten the U.S. beachhead.

The last naval engagement in the Solomons area had been fought on November 25 between Buka and Rabaul. Three of five Japanese destroyers were sunk by the five "Little Beaver" destroyers of Capt. Arleigh (Thirty-One-Knot) Burke. The Tokyo Express had run its last trip out of Rabaul.

The victory at Empress Augusta Bay ended the bitter two-year struggle for the Solomon Islands. Before the fighting had concluded here, the Allied offensive in the Pacific had already moved hundreds of miles west and north. *See* Guadalcanal; Guadalcanal—Naval Action; New Guinea; Rabaul; Tarawa-Makin; World War II.

Solway Moss (English-Scottish Wars), 1542. To safeguard his northern boundary, Henry VIII of England sought to force James V of Scotland to give up his pro-Catholic, pro-French policies. When this failed, border warfare between the two nations broke out again. A Scottish invasion of northwestern England was checked at Solway Moss in Cumberland. Here on November 24, 1542, the invaders, some 10,000 strong, were subjected to an English counterattack. The English, markedly outnumbered but taking advantage of poor leadership and weak organization on the part of their enemy, utterly smashed the Scottish army. News of the overwhelming defeat hastened the death of James, who was succeeded on the throne by his infant daughter Mary Stuart, Queen of Scots. A peace treaty between England and Scotland became effective the following year. Henry now turned his attention back to the Continent. *See* Flodden; Boulogne.

Somme River I (World War I), 1916. The second of the two great battles of the year on the Western Front was an offensive planned by the French field marshal Joseph Joffre. Joffre had originally scheduled the main attack south of the Somme River by 40 French divisions, with the British under Gen. Sir Douglas Haig making a secondary attack north of the river. (Haig had succeeded Sir John French as commander of the British Expeditionary Force on December 19, 1915.) However, the long, bitter fighting at Verdun used up so many French divisions that, when the offensive got under way, the British launched the major assault on a 15-mile front, aimed at Bapaume. The weaker French attack (16 divisions) on a 10-mile front had Peronne for its objective. Both armies were subordinated to the French general Ferdinand Foch.

The artillery bombardment began on June 24, but bad weather delayed the infantry attack until July 1. On the right (south) the French Sixth Army of Gen. Marie Émile Fayolle, astride the Somme, made an immediate penetration of the German lines, commanded in this area by Gen. Fritz von Below. To the north, however, Gen. Sir Henry Rawlinson's British Fourth Army ran into a storm of machine-gun fire from well-prepared positions. Pressing their attack in dense formations, the British suffered 57,450 casualties, chiefly in the section from Fricourt northward. It was the heaviest loss suffered in one day by any British army in history. To compensate for the setback on his left, Haig sent the newly organized Fifth Army of Gen. Sir Hubert Gough forward on the right to hold the gains made by his southernmost corps (XIII) and the French. The German chief of staff, Field Marshal Erich von Falkenhayn, partly countered this move by concentrating north of the Somme, turning over the command south of the river to Gen. Max von Gallwitz. For ten weeks the Allies

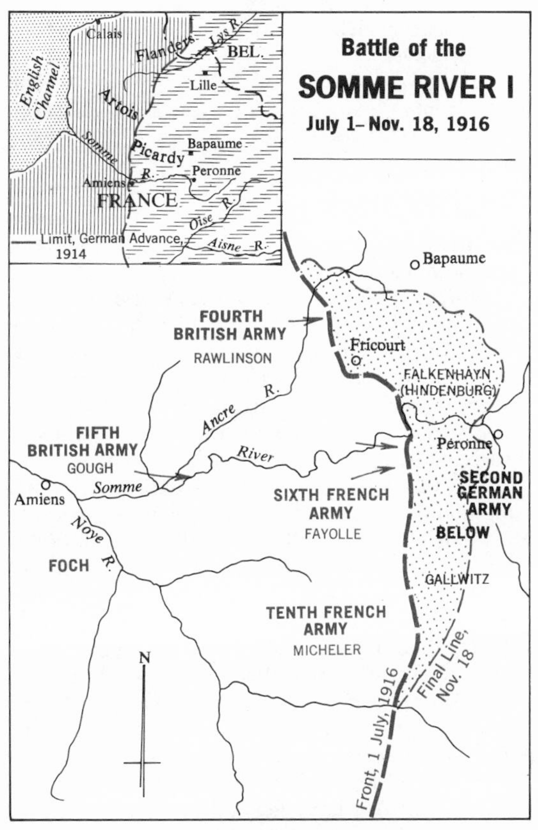

hammered unmercifully at the German lines and gradually pushed back the defenders with heavy casualties on both sides. To the south, Fayolle's French also made small but costly gains. On August 29 Falkenhayn was replaced by Field Marshal Paul von Hindenburg and chief operations officer Gen. Erich Ludendorff.

Haig tried to force a breakthrough opposite the center of the British line by employing tanks for the first time in battle, on September 15. Due to mechanical breakdowns, only 18 of 36 took the field. Their shock tactics deepened the Allied penetration to a total of seven miles but failed to rout the enemy. The battle resumed as one of attrition only—no more than 125 square miles were conquered. It finally ended in miserable weather on November 18, with a combined total of 1,265,000 casualties—650,000 German, 420,000 British, 195,000 French. The following month both Joffre and Foch were retired. General Robert Nivelle took over command of the French armies on the Western Front on December 12. *See* Verdun; Arras II; World War I.

Somme River II (World War I), 1918. Reinforced by troops from the now peaceful Russian front, the German commander, Gen. Erich Ludendorff, resolved to gain a major victory in the West before a decisive number of American troops could arrive. On March 21 he launched the first of five successive offensives against the Allied lines. Preceded by a bombardment of 6,000 guns and a heavy gas attack, three armies struck westward along a 50-mile front south of Arras held by the British armies of Field Marshal Sir Douglas Haig. From north to south the attacking German armies were the Seventeenth (Otto von Below), Second (Georg von der Marwitz), and Eighteenth (Oskar von Hutier). A total of 71 German divisions drove ahead under cover of artillery fire, smoke, and fog. On the south the 15 British divisions of Gen. Hubert Gough's Fifth Army gave way. The following day (March 22) Gough ordered a withdrawal behind the Somme River. (He was later replaced by Gen. Sir Henry Rawlinson.) This retreat uncovered the right flank of Gen. Sir Julian Byng's Third Army (14 divisions), which also began pulling back.

As the German attack rolled forward 14 miles the first four days, Ludendorff shifted his main weight south of the Somme, where Hutier was making the largest gains. Here the French general Marie Émile Fayolle took charge of a mixed force of French and British units. Hutier pressed forward to take Montdidier on March 27, but now his troops were near exhaustion and supplies were slow in reaching the front lines. On April 4 the attack ended after a gain of 40 miles. The aim of driving a wedge between the British and French and forcing the former back to the sea almost succeeded. Ludendorff's first offensive of the year had taken 70,000 prisoners, captured 1,100 guns, and inflicted almost 160,000 additional casualties. But the German losses in killed and wounded were nearly as severe. During the battle the distraught Allies had made Gen. Ferdinand Foch chief coordinator of troops on the Western Front. On April 14 he became actual commander in chief. *See* Somme River I; Cambrai; Lys River; World War I.

Somnath (Ghaznevid Invasions of India), 1024. Among the 17 raids conducted by the Moslem sultan Mahmud of Ghazni (part of modern Afghanistan) into the Indian peninsula, one (the 12th) penetrated as far as Somnath on the southern coast of Kathiawar. The holy city was sacked and from one of the temples the "Gates of Somnath" were carried off. (Some gates were brought back to India in 1842 by the Earl of Ellenborough, then British governor-general of the dominion, but were found to be not the originals). During his rule, 997–1030, Mahmud expanded the Afghan kingdom from the Tigris to the Ganges and northward to the Amu Darya (Oxus). He was concerned chiefly with booty and with enforcing conversion to Mohammedanism. *See* Peshawar.

Soor (War of the Austrian Succession), 1745. After Frederick II, the Great, and his Prussian army had inflicted a major defeat on the Austrians in the spring of 1745, the victor agreed to recognize Francis I as joint ruler with his wife, Maria Theresa, of the Holy Roman Empire. But the empress insisted on reclaiming Silesia and sent an army northward under Prince Charles of Lorraine, brother of Francis. The Imperials, 30,000 strong, encountered Frederick, with a smaller army, at Soor (Sohr) in northeastern Bohemia on September 30. An Austrian attack endangered Frederick's position. But the Prussians, fighting with machine-like precision (two volleys for every one returned), changed front in the face of the enemy and gradually drove them back. Prince Charles retreated, losing 5,000 men in killed, wounded, and captured. Prussian losses were only half as large. Maria Theresa would not give up, however, and ordered a new advance up the Elbe aimed at Berlin. *See* Hohenfriedeberg; Hennersdorf; Austrian Succession, War of the.

South African Wars I and **II** (1880–1881, 1899–1902). There were two distinct wars for control of the interior of South Africa fought between Great Britain and the Dutch Boers who had settled north of the Vaal River. In 1877 Great Britain annexed the Transvaal. Three years later the Boers revolted and in two battles repulsed British attempts to subdue them. On April 5, 1881, Great Britain recognized the South African Republic.

Laing's Nek	1881
Majuba Hill	1881

Long-standing hostility between the Boers and the British became hardened when the discovery of gold in Transvaal's Witwatersrand brought in many new settlers, largely British. Cecil Rhodes, who was Prime Minister of Cape Colony (1890–96) to the south, and the British South Africa Company of Southern Rhodesia, to the north, aggressively sought a single union of all South Africa. Then the abortive Jameson Raid by British adventurers in 1895–96 worsened relations to the point that both sides prepared for war. The Orange Free State, between Cape Colony and the Transvaal, allied itself with Boer President Oom Paul Kruger on October 11, 1899. War began the following day. By July 4, 1900, the British had decisively defeated the two landlocked republics. But guerrilla warfare continued until Gen. Lord Kitchener stifled resistance by erecting a line of blockhouses across the land and herding some 120,000 Boers into concentration camps. By the Treaty of Vereeniging, signed May 31, 1902, both the Orange Free State and the Transvaal became a part of British South Africa. The Union of South Africa was established six years later and approved in 1910.

Mafeking	1899–1900
Kimberley	1899–1900
Ladysmith	1899–1900
Talana Hill	1899
Elandslaagte	1899
Nicholson's Nek	1899
Modder River	1899
Stormberg	1899
Magersfontein	1899
Colenso	1899
Spion Kop	1900
Vaal Krantz	1900
Paardeberg	1900
Bloemfontein	1900
Johannesburg	1900

Southern Philippines–Borneo (World War II), 1945. With Leyte secure and victory on Luzon assured, Gen. Douglas MacArthur ordered the liberation of the southern Philippines by Gen. Robert Eichelberger's Eighth Army. The technique was to be a series of 38 rapid, amphibious thrusts, most of them by regimental combat teams (RCT), staged by Adm. Daniel Barbey's Seventh Amphibious Force. The battle began on February 28 when the 186th RCT of the 41st Infantry Division landed on Palawan, at the western end of the archipelago. Panay, to the northeast, fell to the 40th Infantry Division on March 18. The 40th Infantry then hopped eastward to northern Negros on March 29. Although the 503rd Parachute RCT came ashore to help on April 8, Japanese troops resisted here until mid-May. Meanwhile, the Americal Infantry Division seized Cebu between March 26 and May 2 and cleared southern Negros and Bohol in April. By the end of May the central islands had been secured, often with the help of Filipino guerrillas.

Mindanao, the second largest island in the Philippines, was invaded on March 10 at Zamboanga, in the southwest, by the 41st Infantry (minus the 186th RCT). From here, shore-to-shore landings in April liberated the Sulu Archipelago, opening the way to Borneo. On April 17 the X Corps (24th and 31st Infantry divisions) invaded Mindanao. Although X Corps was reinforced by the 108th RCT of the 40th Infantry Division and elements of the 41st, pockets of the Japanese Thirty-fifth Army were still holding out in eastern Mindanao when the war ended on August 15. The last Mindanao landings in July was the 52nd separate amphibious assault carried out by Eichelberger's troops since Christmas 1944. At the time of Japan's surrender, some 100,000 of the original Philippine garrison of 450,000 troops were still at large. In all, the liberation of the Philippines cost the U.S. ground forces 62,143 casualties, including 13,700 killed.

As an adjunct to the Philippine campaign, MacArthur assigned the Australian general Thomas Blamey the mission of invading Borneo, to shut off Japan's oil supply from the East Indies. Supported by U.S. and Australian air and sea forces, the 9th Australian Division began the seizure of the offshore island of Tarakan on May 1. On June

10 the 9th Australian landed at Brunei and Sarawak in northwest Borneo, while the 7th Australian recaptured Balikpapan on the east coast on July 1. Further operations in the East Indies were obviated by Japan's surrender on August 15. *See* East Indies; Leyte; Luzon; World War II.

South Mountain (American Civil War). The opening action in the battle of Antietam Creek, in which Gen. George McClellan's Federal right wing forced its way through Turner's Gap on September 14, 1862. *See* Antietam Creek.

South Vietnam (Vietnam War), 1961—. Following the French defeat at Dienbienphu in May 1954, an international conference at Geneva, Switzerland, divided Vietnam at the 17th parallel. North of this line the area became the Communist Democratic Republic, or North Vietnam, ruled by President Ho Chi-Minh from the capital of Hanoi. To the south, the Republic of Vietnam, with its capital at Saigon, came into existence in 1955. Communist guerrillas, called Viet Cong, soon began to war against the South Vietnamese government of President Ngo Dinh Diem. Although only some 25,000 guerrillas were in the field, President Diem's armed forces steadily lost ground. To aid the struggling republic, the United States began supplying economic assistance and in 1961 sent a 685-man advisory mission to South Vietnam. In 1962 the number of advisors and technicians grew to 11,000. But still the Communist forces, drawing most of their support from North Vietnam, plus some aid from Communist China and the Soviet Union, kept the initiative. On November 2, 1963, Diem was overthrown and killed in a military coup. Thereafter a succession of unstable governments made the military situation even worse. The number of U.S. troops was increased to 16,000 in 1963, with many of them taking a more active role in fighting the guerrillas. In 1964 United States strength in South Vietnam grew to about 23,000. On August 5 American aircraft for the first time bombed North Vietnam. On February 8, 1965, bombings began on a regular basis. But Viet Cong attacks also increased in strength, from battalion to regimental size.

The first U.S. combat unit, the 3,500-man 9th Marine Brigade, landed at the major northern base of Danang in March 1965. Four months later (July 28) President Lyndon Johnson publicly announced that "We will stand in Vietnam." To confirm that decision, the number of American soldiers sent to South Vietnam was increased to 190,000 by the end of the year. These troops included the following units: 1st Cavalry Division (Airmobile) near An Khe; the 1st Infantry Division and the 173rd Airborne Brigade at Bien Hoa; the 1st Brigade of the 101st Airborne Division at Phan Rang; and the Third Marine Amphibious Force at Danang and Chu Lai. These forces, plus South Korea's Tiger Division at Qui Nhon and 5,000 marines at Tuy Hoa, a Royal Australian regiment of 1,200 men, and a New Zealand artillery battery, all came under the supreme American commander, Gen. William Westmoreland, who had his headquarters in Saigon. For the first time in history helicopters (about 1,800) played a major battle role, serving both transportation and weaponry functions. Adding to the increased U.S. punch was the Seventh Fleet just offshore, and the planes of the 2nd Air Division (later designated the Seventh Air Force), supplemented by B-52 heavy bombers of the 3rd Air Division based on Guam.

At the same time the South Vietnamese army of Premier Nguyen Cao Ky (who took office June 19, 1965) grew to about 600,000 men, plus 6,500 American advisors. The South Vietnamese were organized into four corps areas, numbered from north to south, with the III Corps area including Saigon. In opposition stood some 215,000 Viet Cong and an estimated 10,000 North Vietnamese regulars.

In 1965 the United States suffered 6,928 combat casualties in Vietnam, including 1,241 killed. South Vietnamese losses were 11,327 killed and 23,009 wounded. These figures brought the total battle casualties since January 1, 1961 to the following:

	Killed	*Wounded*
United States	1,484	7,337
South Vietnam	30,427	63,009
Viet Cong	104,500	250,000

On December 24, 1965, President Johnson halted American bombing of North Vietnam targets in an effort to bring about truce negotiations. When no peace agreement was reached, the bombing was resumed, on January 31, 1966. During 1966 the United States increased its number of troops in South Vietnam to 389,000. Most of this additional strength came from the newly landed 25th, 4th, and 9th Infantry divisions. South Vietnamese forces grew to about 750,000 fighting men during the year. And the Philippines contributed 2,000 troops. But at the same time Communist forces, which numbered about 250,000 first-line troops at the beginning of the year, also increased steadily. An average of about 7,000 new men a month were added—4,500 by infiltration from the North (mostly down the Ho Chi-Minh Trail), the rest by draft from Viet Cong–controlled areas.

In 1966 ground action the U.S. and South Vietnamese forces sought to seek out and destroy Communist forces. The largest of these attacks, called Operation Hastings, saw 5,000 U.S. marines and a South Vietnamese force of equal size overwhelm the 324th North Vietnamese Division (8–10,000 men) just south of the demilitarized zone along the 17th parallel, on July 15–August 5. The marines, who suffered "moderate" casualties (about

10 percent) counted 882 enemy dead, estimated another 1,000 dead, and captured 15. American pilots flew 1,209 supporting sorties, the highest number of strikes in any operation in the war up to that time.

The biggest American operation of the Vietnamese War in 1966 was launched on October 15 against the Communist-held War Zone C, 45 to 65 miles northwest of Saigon near the Cambodian border. In this attack, called Operation Attelboro, some 25,000 U.S. combat troops killed a reported 1,101 enemy soldiers, chiefly from the Viet Cong 9th Division and the 101st North Vietnamese Regiment. American casualties were described as "light." The operation ended on November 25.

The war in the air escalated on June 29, 1966, when U.S. carrier- (A-4 Skyhawks and F-4 Phantoms) and land- (F-105 Thunderchiefs) based bombers destroyed most of the North Vietnamese petroleum storage tanks near Haiphong and Hanoi. For the remainder of the year U.S. planes struck hard at enemy targets in North as well as South Vietnam. The increased tempo of air warfare was illustrated in the number of U.S. planes lost, chiefly to ground fire. At the end of 1965, 165 American aircraft had been shot down. At the end of 1966 the total number of planes lost in combat was 468, plus 4 helicopters, over North Vietnam and 150, plus 251 helicopters, over South Vietnam.

During 1966, the first full year of warfare for the American troops, the United States suffered 5,047 combat deaths in Vietnam. Communists killed were estimated at 55,000. Some 20,000 Communists defected to South Vietnam.

In 1967, for the first time, U.S. troops invaded the Communist-held Mekong Delta, south of Saigon. On January 6, some 4,000 marines landed by sea and air (Operation Deckhouse Five) in an area believed to contain about 100,000 Viet Cong. Two days later a larger U.S. offensive struck the so-called Iron Triangle, a Communist stronghold 20 to 30 miles north of Saigon. In this three-week attack, called Operation Cedar Falls, some 30,000 U.S. troops penetrated the triangle from three sides. American units included the 1st and 25th Infantry divisions, the 196th Light Infantry Brigade, the 173rd Airborne Brigade, and the 11th Armored Cavalry Brigade. The third U.S. offensive of the year, and the largest to that time, was an invasion of War Zone C, a 1,000-square-mile Communist stronghold 75 miles northwest of Saigon. Called Operation Junction City, the assault of 30,000 troops under Gen. Jonathan Seaman began February 22.

The U.S. Army has designated three distinct campaigns in Vietnam (with at least one more to be specified): Advisory Campaign, from March 15, 1962, to March 7, 1965; Defense, from March 8, 1965, to December 24, 1965; and Counteroffensive, from December 25, 1965, to June 30, 1966. *See* Nam Dong; Van Tuong Peninsula; Vietnam War.

Southwold Bay (Third English-Dutch War), 1672. Less than six months after the end of the Second English-Dutch War, Charles II signed an alliance with Jan De Witt, head of the Netherlands government, aimed at curbing the power of Louis XIV of France. Then, two years later, on June 1, 1670, the English king reversed himself and signed a secret pact with Louis (the Treaty of Dover). As a result the third war broke out between England and Holland, on March 17, 1672.

The Dutch admiral Michel de Ruyter put to sea with 91 ships-of-the-line. On June 7 he surprised the combined English and French fleet of 101 ships at Southwold (Sole) Bay, 90 miles north of the Thames's mouth. In getting under way, the allies, commanded by the Duke of York (future James II), became split; the French, under Adm.

the Comte d'Estrées, sailed south and east, the English north and west. The Dutch turned to fall furiously on the English ships before the French could enter the action. Both sides suffered cruel losses—for example, York twice had to abandon crippled flagships. Finally De Ruyter drew off, with neither side holding an advantage. However, the Dutch action checked a planned French invasion of their coast.

On land, the troops of Louis XIV were moving swiftly into southern and eastern Holland. But when Amsterdam opened its dikes on June 25, a seemingly certain French conquest was permanently blocked. Then, on July 8, William of Orange (later William III of England) took over the Netherlands government. This strengthened Dutch resistance. *See* Chatham; Schooneveldt; English-Dutch Wars.

Soviet Union (World War II), 1941–1944. Following a successful seven-week campaign in the Balkans, Germany stood master of all Western Europe except for the island of Great Britain. With this fighting limited to the air and sea, the all-victorious German ground forces were free for the long-planned drive to the East (*Drang nach Osten*) against an erstwhile ally, the Soviet Union. On June 22, 1941, Adolf Hitler launched Operation Barbarossa, the greatest ground attack in history, with 138 divisions, 19 of them armored. On the left Field Marshal Wilhelm von Leeb's Army Group "C" (30 divisions) attacked from East Prussian through the Baltic States toward Leningrad. On the right Field Marshal Karl von Rundstedt's Army Group "A" (57 divisions) drove southeast from southern Poland and Rumania into the Ukraine. Army Group "B" (51 divisions) in the center carried the heaviest weight of armor. Here, from the vicinity of Warsaw, Field Marshal Fedor von Bock hurled his four armies north of the Pripet Marshes straight toward Moscow.

To defend against this onslaught, the Soviet Union had 148 divisions spread along the 1,500-mile frontier from the Baltic to the Black Sea. The Russian army groups were commanded by (from north to south) Gens. Kliment Voroshilov, Semën Timoshenko, and Semën Budënny. The ensuing struggle became history's greatest land battle.

Germany's basic tactic was to encircle huge segments of the Russian forces with fast-moving Panzer units and then annihilate pockets of resistance with infantry. Under this plan the Russian army would be destroyed before it could retreat behind the Ural Mountains. During the early weeks of the huge, sprawling battle, the Nazis struck and shattered most of the divisions emplaced along the frontier. This furious ground attack was supported by thousands of tactical aircraft, in which Germany had a marked superiority in both type and numbers. In the first two months of the invasion the *Luftwaffe* destroyed some 4,500 Russian planes; almost 2,000 Nazi aircraft were lost.

All three German army groups raced hundreds of miles deep into Russia and captured about a million prisoners by the end of September. Yet none of the drives reached their primary objectives, and the Soviet Union began throwing 210 reserve divisions into the battle to further slow the Nazi advances.

In the north Leeb's armies advanced rapidly through the Baltic States to close in on Leningrad in ten weeks.

The center advance toward Moscow smashed through Russian Poland and into White Russia (Byelorussia) north of the Pripet Marshes. By July 2 the *Panzers* of Gens. Heinz Guderian and Hermann Hoth had bypassed a large Russian force in the Bialystok-Slonim area. The German armor raced on to form a pincers at Minsk, 200 miles inside the Soviet Union, on June 27. In six days German infantry killed or captured almost 300,000 prisoners in this trap. But many other Russian soldiers escaped to fight again farther east.

Continuing their drive along the Minsk–Moscow highway, the *Panzers* crossed the Dnieper River on July 10 and reached Smolensk six days later. Here, 400 miles into the Soviet Union, another large pincers closed, with 100,000 Russians killed or captured by August 6. But again enough Red soldiers escaped to build up a defense line along the Desna River, 200 miles from Moscow. At this point Hitler ordered Bock to halt, while Guderian's Second Panzer Group and Gen. Maximilian von Weich's Second Army were turned south toward Kiev on the southern front. The advance on Moscow was not resumed until October 2.

Meanwhile, on the southern front, Rundstedt's three armies, led by Gen. Paul von Kleist's First Panzer Group, slanted southeast across Russian Poland and into the Ukraine. By the end of July German armor had routed Budënny's numerically larger forces south of Kiev and was sweeping toward the Black Sea. Two weeks later this attack reached the mouths of the Bug and Dnieper rivers, trapping many Russians who had been defending against the slower-moving advance from Rumania across the lower Prut and Dniester rivers.

Early in September Guderian's *Panzers* and Weich's Second Army wheeled south from the central advance. At the same time, about 350 miles away, Kleist's armor turned to the north, forming a gigantic pincers in the Kiev area on both sides of the Dnieper. The encirclement succeeded and by September 26 more than 600,000 Russian troops had been killed or captured (Kiev had fallen on September 19). Budënny's defeat here was the worst suffered by a Russian commander in World War II.

With the return of Kleist's First Panzer Group from the Kiev pincers, Rundstedt's Army Group "A" launched a multi-pronged offensive in southern Russia where Red Marshal Timoshenko now commanded. On the left Gen. Walther von Reichenau's Sixth Army struck west toward Voronezh on the upper Don but was held up by stubborn Russian resistance near Kursk. In the center the Seventeenth Army advanced to the Donets, taking Kharkov on October 29. The Don, however, was still 125 miles away. In the far south the Eleventh Army, commanded by Gen. Erich von Manstein, sent down from the Leningrad sector, made better progress. It took the Black Sea port of Odessa on October 16 and pierced the Perekop Isthmus into the Crimea.

Meanwhile Kleist's tanks lunged forward toward the Maikop oil fields beyond the Don. Rostov, the gateway to the Caucasus on the lower Don, fell on November 22. But a week later the Russian army counterattacked across the frozen river and recaptured the city. When Hitler insisted that Rostov be held, Rundstedt resigned, on December 1. Instead the German southern armies, now under Reichenau, fell back 50 miles to the Mius River, where they held throughout the winter and made ready for a new assault on the Caucasus the following year.

The six-month invasion of the Soviet Union had penetrated 550 miles and occupied more than 500,000 square miles of Russian territory. Germany reported 770,000 men lost in killed, wounded, and missing. (U.S. estimates placed this figure much higher.) Russian casualties were three times as large, plus more than 1,000,000 prisoners claimed by the Nazi armies.

In 1942 the major German offensive took place on the southern front. Here 66 German and 17 satellite (Rumanian, Hungarian, Italian) divisions jumped off in June. The Crimea was cleared in a month, but the drive for the Caucasus' oil fell short. And at Stalingrad, the high-water mark of the German advance, the Nazis lost one of the great decisive battles in history. By the time these battles were closed by a Soviet winter offensive, the *Wehrmacht* had suffered some 1,200,000 casualties and had lost much heavy equipment—planes, tanks, guns. Russian losses were probably less severe.

In 1943 the German armies suffered even greater defeats at the hands of increasingly strong Soviet attacks. In the south, the site of the heaviest fighting, the Russians cleared the Ukraine. The northern (Leningrad) front remained relatively quiet. But in the center Timoshenko, now returned to command on the Moscow front, employed four great armies to hammer westward, with the main axis of advance (*schwerpunkt*) the Moscow–Minsk highway. In this sector, German Army Group Center under Field Marshal Gunther von Kluge (who had replaced Bock during the battle of Moscow) abandoned its Rzhev-Vyazma salient, 125 miles west of Moscow, in March. The new German positions stood in defense of the key road and rail center of Smolensk.

Two hundred miles to the southeast, German Army Group Center struck at the 150-mile-wide Kursk salient that jutted 100 miles into the Nazi lines, on July 5. For eight days Kluge's 38 German divisions (17 of them armored) smashed from both north and south at the Soviet armies holding the salient—Gen. Konstantin Rokossovski along the northern edge, Gen. Nikolai Vatutin at the southern edge. In the bitter fighting Soviet antitank artillery knocked out as much as 40 percent of the German armor, which included the new Mark VI Tiger tanks.

On July 12 a new element entered the battle when Gen. Markian Popov's army attacked the overlapping German wedge at Orel, 100 miles to the north. Popov's advance, coupled with furious Russian resistance in the Kursk salient, forced Kluge to call off the largest tank battle (almost 3,000 involved) in history, on July 13. Kluge's attack, the last German offensive on the central Eastern Front, cost 100,000 men and maimed most of his *Panzer* and motorized divisions. The Orel salient itself became indefensible when Popov's attack spread to other Red armies along almost 1,000 miles of front. Kluge abandoned Orel on August 5. Popov then drove 75 miles westward to Bryansk by September 20 and pressed on into White Russia. To the north, Gens. Vassili Sokolovski and Andrei Yeremenko battered their way into Smolensk on September 25. Then, in a two-pronged offensive, Sokolovski pushed toward Vitebsk, while on his right flank Yeremenko drove through Velikie Luki and Nevel (October 5) toward Polotsk. Meanwhile, to the south, Rokossovski fought his way into Gomel late in November.

In 1944 the Red armies completed the liberation of (south to north) the Crimea, Ukrainia, White Russia, and Russia proper. When Russian troops liberated Bessarabia and plunged into Galati, Rumania, on August 27, only the Baltic States of the Soviet Union remained in German hands. And here the last of the Nazi invaders did not surrender until the spring of 1945. Although all Soviet casualty figures are estimates, it is believed that approximately 6,750,000 Russians lost their lives in the struggle against Germany.

On August 8, 1945, the Soviet Union entered the Pacific theater of action by declaring war on Japan. Russian armies began marching into Manchuria, but six days later the Japanese government accepted the Allied surrender terms and World War II was over. *See* Yugoslavia (World War II); Greece (World War II); Leningrad; Moscow;

Crimea; Caucasus; Stalingrad; Ukraine; White Russia; World War II.

Spain. The major battles and wars fought by what is now the nation of Spain are listed below.

Saguntum	219–218 B.C.
New Carthage	209
Ilipa	206
Numantia	142–133
Ilerda	49
Vouillé	A.D. 507
Río Barbate	711
Covadonga	718
Roncesvalles	778
Simancas	934
Zamora	939
Toledo I	1085
Zallaka	1086
Huesca	1096
Saragossa I	1118
Alarcos	1195
Las Navas de Tolosa	1212
Cordovo	1236
Messina II	1284
Río Salado	1340
Algeciras	1344
Nájera	1367
Montiel	1369
Aljubarrota	1385
Toro	1476
Alhama de Granada	1482
Loja	1486
Málaga I	1487
Baza	1489
Granada	1491–1492
Naples	1495
Barletta	1502
Cerignola	1503
Garigliano River	1503
Oran I	1509
Ravenna IV	1512
See Latin America	
La Bicocca	1522
Pavia V	1525
Rome VI	1527
Saint-Quentin I	1557
Gravelines	1558
Lepanto II	1571
See Netherlands War of Independence	
Alcántara	1580
Cadiz	1587
Spanish Armada	1588
Flores	1591
See Thirty Years' War	
Montijo	1644
Arras I	1654
Jamaica	1655
Valenciennes	1656
Santa Cruz de Tenerife	1657
Dunes	1658
See Louis XIV, Wars of	
Passero Cape	1718
Porto Bello	1739
See Polish Succession, War of the	
See Austrian Succession, War of the	
See Seven Years' War	
See American Revolution, War of the	
See French Revolution, Wars of the	
See Napoleonic Empire Wars—Peninsular War	
See Carlist Wars	
Alcolea	1868
See Spanish-American War	
Anual	1921
See Spanish Civil War	

Spanish-American War (1898). The 1895 Cuban insurrection against the rule of Spain (Queen Maria Christina, regent for her son Alfonso XII) gradually built up strong sympathetic interest in the United States. On February 15, 1898, the American battleship *Maine* mysteriously exploded in Havana harbor, killing 260 officers and men. President William McKinley yielded to public opinion, which had been inflamed by a sensational press, and on April 11 asked Congress for authority to end the civil war in Cuba. Congress recognized the independence of Cuba on April 19 and demanded Spanish withdrawal. Spain broke off diplomatic relations with the United States. War was formally declared by Congress on April 25, retroactive to April 21. The United States overwhelmed the Spaniards on both land and sea. Hostilities ended on August 12, with the peace treaty signed on December 10. Spain relinquished Cuba, ceded Puerto Rico and Guam, and turned over the Philippines to the United States for $20 million. The United States had suddenly become a world power (but was faced with a three-year fight to put down the Philippine insurrection).

Manila Bay	1898
Santiago de Cuba I	1898
Las Guásimas	1898
El Caney	1898
San Juan Hill	1898
Manila II	1898

Spanish Armada (English-Spanish Wars), 1588. English aid to the Netherlands provinces in their revolt against Spain prompted the Spanish king, Philip II, to prepare a huge invasion fleet. Called the Invincible Armada, the fleet was to secure control of the English Channel and then transport a Spanish army under the Duke of Parma (Alessandro Farnese) from the Netherlands to England. Delayed for a year by Sir Francis Drake's daring raid on Cadiz in 1587, the Armada finally sailed in May 1588. It consisted of 130 ships (including 20 galleons, 44 armed merchantmen, and 8 Mediterranean galleys), carrying 2,500 guns and 30,000 men, two-thirds of them soldiers. Under the command of the Duke of Medina-Sidonia (Alonso de Guzmán), the Armada suffered chiefly from a lack of experienced naval leadership and from a weakness in long-range guns.

Meanwhile, Elizabeth I had organized a land army to repel the invasion and had ordered to sea the English navy under the command of Lord Charles Howard of Effingham, assisted by Drake, Sir John Hawkins, and Martin Frobisher. The core of the fleet consisted of 34 ships carrying 6,000 men. Another 163 privately owned vessels also put to sea, but half of these were too small or too weakly armed to be important.

Delayed by storms, the Armada did not approach the southern coast of England until July 19. Maneuvering to the windward (west) of the invader, on July 21, the English navy began bombarding the seven-mile crescent of Spanish ships, taking advantage of the English superiority in long-range guns. Off Portland Bill on July 23, the Isle of Wight on July 25, and into the Channel, the

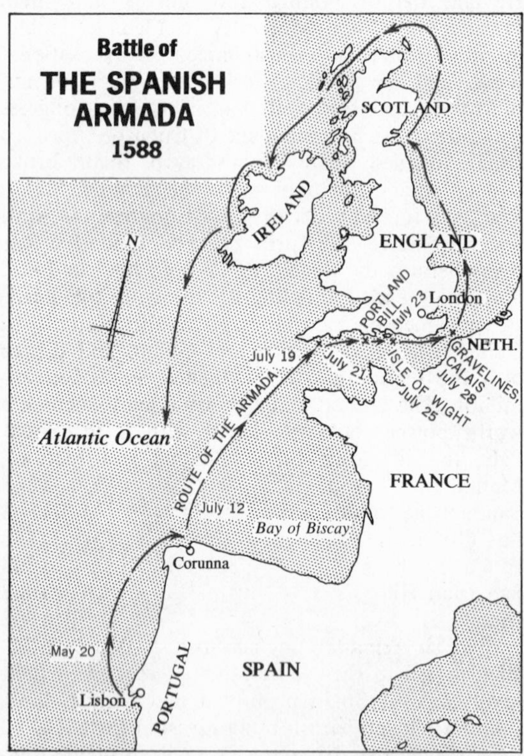

English guns raked the Spanish ships, causing serious casualties among the crews, with only small losses to themselves. On July 28 the Spanish commander put in at Calais. The next night the English sent eight vessels armed with explosives as fire ships into the crowded harbor. These sixteenth-century torpedoes, plus the collisions caused by chaotic maneuvering to escape the assault, took a heavy toll of the Armada. Medina-Sidonia hurriedly put to sea again. At Gravelines, 15 miles southwest of Dunkirk, his rendezvous with Parma's troops misfired, in large part because of the blockade carried out by the small Dutch fleet. With no alternative, the Spanish turned and fought their tormentors for eight hours on July 29. Three of the Armada's ships were sunk and another four or five driven on the banks. Both sides had by then exhausted their ammunition. With a change in the wind, the Spanish broke off the battle, sailing northward into the North Sea and around the north of Scotland. Battered by storms, little more than half of the original force reached Iberian ports in September and October.

In all, England had inflicted far fewer casualties on the Armada than had storms and shortages of food and water. But the moral impact of the heroic defense against the mightiest empire since Roman times raised England to a first-class naval power. The fighting also marked a distinct change in naval tactics: the increasing effectiveness of long-range gunfire clearly outmoded the old, close-in, boarding style of warfare at sea. Thus the defeat of the Spanish Armada ranks as one of the decisive battles of history. *See* Cadiz; Flores.

Spanish Civil War (1936–1939). The republican government of Spain, established after the forced abdication of Alfonso XIII in 1931, suffered violent agitation from both the Left and the Right, plus strong separatist movements among the Basques and Catalans. In the elections of February 16, 1936, the Leftist parties, combined in a Popular Front, won decisively over the Right. Then on July 18 conservative army chiefs at Melilla in Spanish Morocco launched a revolt against the government that soon spread to garrison towns inside Spain. Most of the army and air force troops supported the insurrection, as did the Carlists and large contingents of Moors from the Army of Africa. The rebel Nationalists, led by Gen. Francisco Franco and Gen. Emilio Mola, set up a junta at Burgos, in north-central Spain, on July 30. More than 50,000 Italian and 10,000 German "volunteers" fought alongside the Nationalists. The Soviet Union supplied equipment and advisors to the loyalist Republican forces of the government, which consisted chiefly of determined, but poorly organized and ill-armed militia, plus 20,000 regular soldiers and six international brigades. In a two-and-a-half-year war the Nationalists won control of Spain. The cost in lives was 611,000—110,000 Nationalists killed in action, 86,000 executed; 175,000 Republicans killed in action, 40,000 executed; 200,000 civilian deaths.

Toledo II 1936
Madrid 1936–1939
  Corunna Road 1936–1937
  Jarama River 1937
  Brunete 1937

Málaga III	1937
Guadalajara	1937
Bilbao	1937
Santander	1937
Saragossa III	1937
Gijón	1937
Teruel	1937–1938
Vinaroz	1938
Ebro River	1938
Barcelona II	1938–1939

Spanish Fronde War. A name given to the French-Spanish War which sprang up during the Thirty Years' War. *See* Arras I; Valenciennes; Dunes, The; Thirty Years' War.

Spanish Succession, War of the (1701–1714). When the childless King Charles II of Spain neared death, most of the powers of Europe became preoccupied with the successor to the soon extinct Spanish house of Hapsburg. Louis XIV of France claimed the throne for his grandson Philip, duke of Anjou. Upon the death of Charles II in 1700, the duke was proclaimed Philip V of Spain. England, the Netherlands, and the Holy Roman Empire (Leopold I) formed a new Grand Alliance and declared war on France on May 4, 1702. The coalition was bolstered by Prussia in 1702 and Portugal and Savoy (which changed sides) in 1703. The War of the Spanish Succession was closed by a series of treaties in 1713 and 1714. Philip V was recognized as king of Spain and the colonies, but the Spanish Netherlands (modern Belgium) were transferred to Austria. The North American phase of the conflict was called Queen Anne's War. *See also* Queen Anne's War.

Chiari	1701
Cremona II	1702
Luzzara	1702
Landau	1702
Vigo Bay	1702
Höchstädt I	1703
Donauwörth	1704
Gibraltar I	1704
Blenheim	1704
Málaga II	1704
Cassano d'Adda I	1705
Barcelona I	1705
Ramillies	1706
Turin	1706
Almansa	1707
Stollhofen	1707
Toulon I	1707
Oudenarde	1708
Lille	1708
Tournai	1709
Malplaquet	1709
Brihuega	1710
Denain	1712

Sphacteria (Great Peloponnesian War). An island off the coast of Greece captured by Athens in the battle of Pylos-Sphacteria in 425 B.C. *See* Pylos-Sphacteria.

Spicheren (Franco-Prussian War), 1870. With the outbreak of war against Prussia on July 15, a French corps along the border raided into Saarbrücken and captured the city on August 2. But it was almost immediately forced to fall back by one of the three large Prussian armies Gen. (later Count) Helmuth von Moltke, chief of the general staff, had launched against the forces of Napoleon III. On this front Gen. Karl von Steinmetz' army marched into the Saar. At Spicheren, Steinmetz deployed 27,000 troops in an attack against a French army of 24,000 under Gen. Charles-Auguste Frossard on August 6. The French were routed in a confused fight, which cost the Prussians almost 5,000 casualties. The French lost about 4,000 in killed and wounded in a battle sometimes called Forbach, a village to the west. From Spicheren the beaten army retreated toward Metz, 32 miles to the west. On the same day another French force suffered defeat at Wörth, 40 miles to the southeast. *See* Wörth; Colombey; Franco-Prussian War.

Spion Kop (South African War II), 1900. After three months of being besieged and defeated by the Boers of Transvaal and the Orange Free State, Great Britain sent two new commanders to South Africa: Gen. Lord Frederick Roberts and Gen. Lord Kitchener. The former commander in chief, Gen. Sir Redvers Buller, retained direction of the Natal front. On January 19 Bullers launched a second attempt to relieve Ladysmith. With 20,000 men he fought his way across the Tugela River. On the third day of the offensive Gen. Sir Charles Warren's 5th Division captured the key height of Spion Kop, 24 miles southwest of Ladysmith. But the slopes were too steep to bring up artillery, and a Boer counterattack, commanded by Gen. Louis Botha, regained the hill on January 23. On the following day Buller admitted defeat and fell back across the Tugela. He had lost 87 officers and more than 1,600 men. Boer losses were markedly fewer. The Natal campaign was still deadlocked. *See* Ladysmith; Colenso; Vaal Krantz; South African Wars.

Spotsylvania (American Civil War), 1864. Disengaging from the deadlocked position in the Wilderness, Gen. U. S. Grant's 101,000 Federal troops began moving southeast on the night of May 7. The objective of the Army of the Potomac (George Meade) was New Spotsylvania Court House, a key road junction on the way to Richmond. Only a faster march by Gen. Robert E. Lee's I Corps (commanded by Gen. Richard Anderson in the absence of the wounded Gen. James Longstreet) blocked the Federal advance, on the afternoon of May 8. Lee then brought up the remainder of his 56,000-man Army of Northern

Virginia. As both sides concentrated for a major battle, Grant sent his cavalry (under Gen. Philip Sheridan) on a dashing, but inconclusive, raid against Richmond.

As Grant's army closed up to the entrenching Confederates, the II Corps of Gen. Winfield Hancock threatened Lee's left (west) flank, under Anderson's command. But Hancock was recalled in favor of a frontal assault against the center, held by Gen. Richard Ewell's II Corps. On May 10 the corps of Gen. Gouverneur Warren (V) and Gen. Horatio Wright (VI), who had replaced the slain Gen. John Sedgwick, hammered twice at the left half of Lee's line. The attacks were beaten off, but more than 1,000 Confederates were taken prisoner. The following day Grant wired that he would "fight it out on this line if it takes all summer."

Grant spent May 11 massing for a decisive blow against the center of Lee's line—a horseshoe-shaped salient still held by Ewell. At 4 A.M. on May 12, Gen. Ambrose Burnside's IX Corps struck the east face of the salient, followed by the attacks of Hancock's corps in the center and Wright's on the west. In a day-long battle the so-called Bloody Angle or Mule Shoe was reduced. Ewell's battered corps yielded 2,000 prisoners and 20 guns. During the next six days Grant probed Lee's right flank and then the left but always found the Confederates well entrenched. Worried about a possible Federal thrust to the southeast, Ewell attacked northward on May 19, but found the Federal lines strongly held. On the following night Grant did indeed begin shifting his weight south and east toward Richmond.

In the bloody fighting around Spotsylvania, particularly the attacks of May 10 and 12, the Army of the Potomac suffered more than 17,000 casualties. Lee's losses, reduced by fighting from entrenchments, probably totaled 9–10,000. Meanwhile other Federal offensives had been checked southeast of Richmond and in the Shenandoah Valley. *See* Wilderness; Drewry's Bluff; New Market; Yellow Tavern; North Anna River; American Civil War.

Spring Hill (American Civil War). A marching encounter, on November 29, 1864, in which the Confederate Army of Tennessee failed to intercept the Federal retreat northward to Franklin. *See* Franklin.

"Spurs, Battle of the." *See* Courtrai; Guinegate.

Stadtlohn (Thirty Years' War), 1623. A year after coming to the aid of the United Dutch Provinces at Fleurus, the reckless Christian of Brunswick had collected a new army of 15,000 men. In the summer of 1623 he reopened his campaign against the Catholic Hapsburgs by marching eastward from the Netherlands into the Lower Saxon Circle, between the Weser and Elbe rivers. Here he asked the Protestant mercenary army of Gen. Count Ernst von Mansfeld to join him. Mansfeld, however, remained on the Rhine. Now Christian found himself threatened by Field Marshal the Count of Tilly, at the head of the Catholic League army (chiefly Bavarians), who had crossed the Saxon border on July 13. Christian began withdrawing toward the Netherlands, crossing the Weser on July 27 and the Ems a few days later. But Tilly's better-organized troops were gaining steadily on the retreating Protestants.

Finally, on August 6, less than ten miles from the safety of the Dutch border, Christian was forced to turn and fight at the little village of Stadtlohn in Westphalia. Although Christian held a strong position on a hill, he was outnumbered and subjected to increasingly heavy attacks by Tilly. The steady Catholic pressure soon broke the cavalry on the two wings of Christian's army. When the horsemen bolted, the Protestant infantry turned to flee also but were cut off by a bog in their rear. Tilly's men swept forward to kill some 6,000 and capture another 4,000. Among Christian's losses were 50 of his leading officers and all his artillery and ammunition. He escaped behind the Netherlands border later that night with only 2,000 cavalrymen.

The battle of Stadtlohn finished Christian, the "mad Halberstadter," as an effective commander of Protestant forces. Three days later, all hope abandoned, the elector palatine (and briefly king of Bohemia), Frederick V, signed an armistice with Tilly's superior, Ferdinand II, Holy Roman Emperor. But peace for Germany was short-lived. Foreign powers intervened, and in the following year England, France, the United Provinces of the Netherlands, Sweden, Denmark, Savoy, Venice, and Brandenburg (George William) all joined an anti-Hapsburg alliance aimed at Spain and the Holy Roman Empire. *See* Fleurus I; Breda; Dessau Bridge; Thirty Years' War.

Staffarda (War of the Grand Alliance), 1690. Savoy, the Alpine duchy south of Switzerland that had joined the League of Augsburg in 1687 and the Grand Alliance two years later, found itself under severe French attack in 1690. Louis XIV sent out a French army under Gen. Nicolas de Catinat. On August 18 Catinat met the troops of Savoy, under the duke Victor Amadeus II, at Staffarda, on the upper reaches of the Po. The French overwhelmed their opponents and proceeded to overrun most of the duchy. But the war's chief theater of operations continued to be the Spanish Netherlands. *See* Fleurus II; Leuze; Marsaglia; Grand Alliance, War of the.

Stainmore (Rise of England), 954. During the reign of the West Saxon king Edwy (Edwig), the Norsemen made an attempt to throw off English rule. Led by Eric Bloodaxe, exiled king of Norway, the rebels attacked a Saxon army at Stainmore, near Edendale, in Westmoreland County. The Saxons, led by an English earl from Northumbria, crushed the Norsemen. Eric Bloodaxe was killed. This battle marked the end of the viking kingdom of York. *See* Brunanburh; Maldon.

Stalingrad (World War II), 1942–1943. In 1942 the German offensive in Russia was concentrated on the southern front. On the left, Field Marshal Fedor von Bock (Army Group "B") had as his principal target the strategic city of Stalingrad (later Volgograd). Southward, on the right, Army Group "A" aimed at gaining the rich oil fields of the Caucasus. Bock launched the attack on June 22 from the line of the upper Donetz (Izyum, Kharkov, Kursk). The left wing advanced to the Don at Voronezh on July 1 but could not hold the city—a failure that was to prove disastrous three months later. Bock was replaced by Field Marshal Maximilian von Weichs on July 13.

Farther south, however, Gen. Hermann Hoth's Fourth Panzer Army raced 100 miles to the Don and then turned southeast to slant down the corridor between the Donetz and the Don. This drive helped Gen. Paul von Kleist's First Panzer Army cross the lower Don in its advance into the Caucasus. Meanwhile Gen. Friedrich von Paulus marched the German Sixth Army eastward from the Don bend toward Stalingrad on the right (west) bank of the Volga.

On August 24 the German ground forces pressed into the western outskirts of the city. But the Sixty-second Red Army, supplemented by civilians, fought a desperate block-by-block and house-by-house defense under the direction of Gen. Vassil Chuikov. By September 22 the Germans had reached the center of the city, now reduced to rubble by intense artillery bombardment.

Throughout the early weeks of the battle Gen. Georgi Zhukov reinforced the Stalingrad garrison from across (east of) the Volga just enough to prevent the Germans from reaching the river in force. At the same time the Russians strengthened their flanks above and below the city. On November 19, over ground hardened by frost, the Russian general Konstantin Rokossovski attacked north of the city, and two days later his armor bridged the Don River at Kalach. Through this opening Gen. Nikolai Vatutin routed three successive satellite armies—Third Rumanian, Eighth Italian, and Second Hungarian. A counterattack by two armored divisions (Panzer Corps "H") proved futile. South of the city, Gen. Andrei Yeremenko lunged forward on November 20 and in five days routed the Fourth Rumanian Army of 15 divisions. Some 65,000 prisoners were taken. The two Russian drives now pushed forward to link up west of Stalingrad. Hitler refused to let the Sixth Army withdraw, and on November 23 the Russian ring

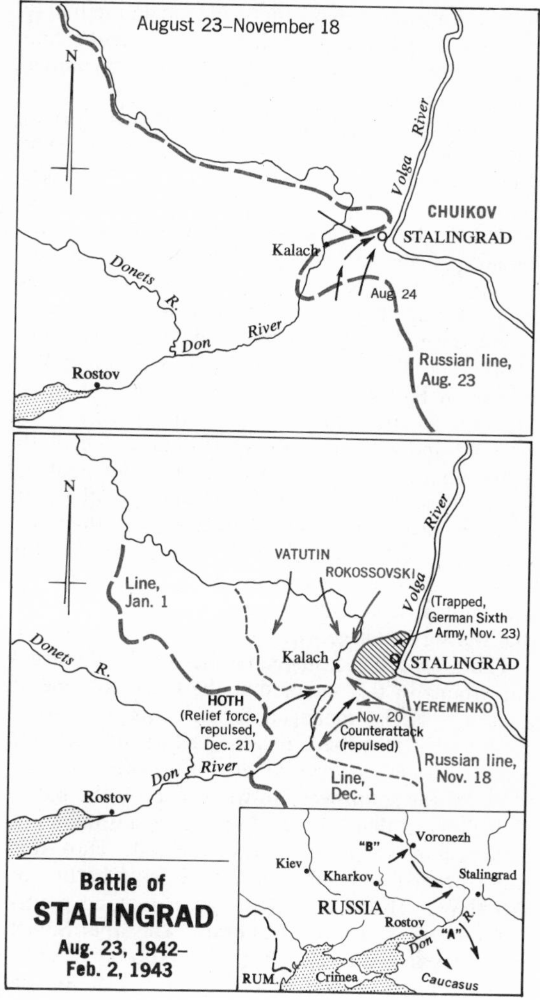

closed around some 300,000 German and satellite troops (22 divisions).

The original pocket was 25 miles long east to west and about half as deep. The only communication with German headquarters was by radio and airplane. Reich Marshal Hermann Goering promised that his *Luftwaffe* would fly in an average of 300 tons of supplies a day. But bad weather and strong Russian air defenses kept German supplies well below this subsistence minimum. Although Hitler continued to refuse permission for the Sixth Army to leave the Volga, he did allow Gen. Erich von Manstein to organize a relief force (called Army Group Don) in an attempt to break through the Russian ring of steel. Gen. Hermann Hoth's Fourth Panzer Army led the attack, which began on December 12 from a point 60 miles southwest of Stalingrad. The German *Panzers* advanced steadily until December 21, when they stood only 30 miles from Paulus' force. But here the attack bogged down, and two days later it was called off.

The Red armies around the cauldron immediately renewed their offensive, which in six weeks had cost the German army 300,000 men, 2,000 tanks, and 4,000 guns on the Stalingrad front.

The Sixth Army was now doomed. A formal demand for surrender came on January 8, but Hitler refused permission. Two days later the Russians, behind a heavy artillery barrage, assaulted the trapped Germans from three sides. By January 16 the last major airfield was taken and the pocket reduced to 15 miles long by 9 miles deep. During the next eight days Russian armor knifed through and split the pocket into two segments. The Russians again demanded surrender, and again Hitler ordered a fight to the last man. Desperately short of supplies and weakened by the cold and relentless Russian attacks, the Sixth Army finally caved in. One of the half-pockets was itself split in two, and on January 31 the first segment surrendered. Two days later the other two segments capitulated. By now only about 91,000 men remained alive. Leading them into captivity was Paulus, who had been promoted to field marshal during the siege.

The long-delayed surrender held so many Russian troops in this sector that the German general Paul von Kleist managed to extricate his Army Group "A" from the Caucasus just in time to prevent a similar debacle there. But the German forces in the south were so weakened by the battle of Stalingrad that they could never again launch a major offensive on the Eastern Front. Thus this battle proved to be one of the decisive battles of World War II and one of the great turning points in military history. *See* Caucasus; Ukraine; Soviet Union (World War II); World War II.

Stallupönen (World War I). The first action on the Eastern Front, on August 17, 1914, in which a German corps made a spoiling attack against the Russian advance into East Prussia. *See* Gumbinnen.

Stamford Bridge (Rise of Britain), 1066. The news of the English defeat at Fulford on September 20 reached King Harold II in London where he had been watching to see which of two expected invasions would strike first, the Norwegian in the north or the Norman in the south. Harold immediately took the old Roman road to York at the head of his loyal Danish household troops (housecarls). His rapid five-day march took by surprise the Norse invaders camped by Stamford Bridge over the Derwent, eight miles northeast of York. King Harold III Hardrada of Norway and the English renegade Tostig had no time to form their troops before the English Harold charged the encampment on September 25.

At first the Norsemen held their ground, but then, deceived by a feigned withdrawal, they launched a premature counterattack. The English wheeled about and dealt them a severe repulse. Harold Hardrada was killed by an arrow in the throat. Harold II halted the battle to offer peace to his half brother Tostig. When the offer was refused, the English infantry charged again, overpowering the Norsemen. Nearly all the invaders were killed, including Tostig. The few who survived fled Britain in their ships. It was the last time that a Scandinavian army seriously threatened England.

At the moment of victory, however, came news from the south that the Norman duke, William, had landed at Pevensey. The second invasion of the year now endangered the reign of Harold II. *See* Fulford; Hastings.

Standard, The (English-Scottish Wars), 1138. Upon the death of Henry I in 1135, the English crown had two claimants—his daughter Maud (Matilda) and his brother-in-law Stephen of Blois. During the period of weak rule, often called the Anarchy, that followed, David I, king of Scotland, seized the opportunity to invade Northumberland. The brutal conduct of the Scots spurred a determined defense, organized by Archbishop Thurstan of York. At Cowton Moor, north of Northallerton, the English rallied around a cart carrying the banners of Saint Peter of York, Saint John of Beverley, and Saint Wilfrid of Ripon, thereby giving the name Standard to the battle. In a murderous encounter the Englishmen of the north, aided by William, count of Aumale, threw back the Scots with heavy losses on August 22. Despite the victory, Stephen had to yield the earldom of Northumberland to David's son Henry the following year in order to concentrate his forces against the rebellion of Maud's followers. *See* Brémule; Lincoln I.

Stara Zagora (Byzantine-Bulgarian Wars), 1189. The First Bulgarian Empire, which had been erased by Byzantium in 1018, reawakened under John I and Peter Asen during the 1180's. Operating from Trnovo (Tirnovo), in northern Bulgaria, the brothers made an alliance with the Cumans, a Turkish race of southeastern Europe, in 1186. The Byzantine emperor, Isaac II Angelus, agreed to let them alone north of the Balkan Mountains. But when the Asens began raiding into Thrace and Macedonia, Isaac marched out from Constantinople to put down the rebels. His Byzantine army encountered the Bulgars near Stara Zagora (called Berrhoe), on the south slope of the Balkan Mountains. The Bulgars threw back the Byzantines, securing the Second Bulgarian Empire. *See* Balathista; Adrianople IV.

Steenkerke (War of the Grand Alliance), 1692. The French troops of Louis XIV opened the 1692 campaign in the Spanish Netherlands by taking Namur on June 5, after a 36-day siege. This victory, which seemed to open the way to Brussels, prompted the Alliance armies to take the offensive. William III, king of England and stadholder of Holland, fresh from his conquests in Ireland, had now taken direct command against the all-victorious French marshal the Duc de Luxembourg. On August 2 William marched all night to surprise the French encamped at Steenkerke, in Hainaut Province. At dawn on the following day William's vanguard of 15,000 men swept into the French position, inflicting heavy casualties. Luxembourg, however, cooly reorganized his troops under fire and rushed in reinforcements. His Swiss contingent battled fiercely against the eight English regiments of Gen. Hugh Mackay before finally giving way. But now the crack Household troops of France came up and counterattacked the tiring English infantry. In a bloody contest fought with short-range gunfire and cold steel, William's men were gradually beaten back. By noon the Alliance attack had collapsed and the whole army was in retreat.

The battle cost William some 8,000 men, half of them English (which was half of the English force on the Continent), including two generals. French losses were slightly less severe. *See* Leuze; Neerwinden I; Grand Alliance, War of the.

Stiklestad (Wars of Scandinavia), 1030. The Christian king Olaf II of Norway, who had wrested his country from Danish and Swedish control, was forced into exile in 1028. Two years later, with a loyal force from Sweden, he landed northeast of Trondheim in an attempt to regain control of Norway. In a battle at nearby Stiklestad he was defeated and killed by anti-Christian Norwegians supported by some Danes. Olaf became a national hero and the patron saint of Norway with his canonization in 1164. *See* Swold; Viborg.

Stillwater. *See* Saratoga.

Stirling Bridge (English-Scottish Wars), 1297. Almost immediately after Edward I of England had proclaimed himself king of Scotland, a strong nationalistic spirit swept through the northern nation. An outlaw knight, Sir William Wallace, rallied a group of Scots in the southwest and began a series of forays against the English occupying forces. Edward, busy warring against France, assigned the Earl of Surrey to put down the rebellion. Surrey took the surrender of a rebel force at Irvine in July, but Wallace and Andrew of Moray continued their depredations in central Scotland. Surrey marched against the rebels at Stirling with a large force. Incautiously, he ordered his army to cross the long, narrow bridge over the Forth River, near the Abbey of Cambuskenneth, on September 11. Wallace, watching the operation from an ambush, waited until about 5,000 English had crossed over the river and Stirling Bridge was crowded with troops. He then fell on the vanguard with his full force, wiping out the entire bridgehead. The remainder of the English army fell back and, when closely pursued, evacuated most of Scotland as far south as the Tweed. Edward I would have to begin his conquest all over again. *See* Dunbar I; Falkirk I.

Stockach I (Wars of the French Revolution), 1799. On Christmas Eve, 1798 the European enemies of France formed the Second Coalition against the Directory. It consisted of Russia (Paul I), Great Britain (George III), Austria (Francis II), and Naples, Portugal, and the Ottoman Empire. As part of the Coalition's grand strategy, Archduke Charles Louis, brother of Holy Roman Emperor Francis II, marched an Austrian army of 60,000 men against the 40,000 French troops in Baden, Germany, commanded by Gen. Jean Jourdan. At Stockach on March 25, 1799, the archduke defeated the French and drove them back to the Rhine. Jourdan, with a loss of 5,000 men, then retreated across the river and yielded his command to Gen. André Masséna. Meanwhile, taking advantage of Napoleon Bonaparte's excursion into the Middle East, the Austrians also launched a new offensive in northern Italy. *See* Abukir; Magnano; Zurich I; French Revolution Wars.

Stockach II (Wars of the French Revolution), 1800. When the Consulate, with Napoleon Bonaparte as first consul, replaced the Directory as the government of France late in 1799, the French armies returned to the offensive. On the western front Gen. Jean Moreau's 50,000-man Army of the Rhine marched across that river into Baden, Germany, at the end of April 1800. A somewhat larger Austrian force under Gen. Baron Paul Kray von Krajowa moved forward to block the French advance through the Black Forest. The two hostile armies clashed at Stockach, in southeastern Baden, on May 3. The French won a resounding victory, capturing thousands of Austrians. Each side lost about 2,000 in killed and wounded. Kray von Krajowa fell back toward Ulm, closely pursued by Moreau. Meanwhile Napoleon himself was direcing a large-scale attack in northern Italy. *See* Abukir; Montebello; Höchstädt II; French Revolution Wars.

Stollhofen (War of the Spanish Succession), 1707. Despite the near collapse of his French empire after the 1706 battle of Ramillies, Louis XIV rallied his forces to reverse the tide the following year. While the northern front in the Spanish Netherlands bogged down in stalemate, the French forces aborted an allied attempt in Spain to substitute Archduke Charles of Austria for Philip V. Picking up the French initiative, the marshal Duc Claude de Villars marched to the Rhine. Here on the middle Rhine Louis William I, margrave of Baden-Baden, held the celebrated Lines of Stollhofen, a supposedly impregnable position between

Karlsruhe and Strasbourg. In a surprise night attack on May 22, Villars stormed and took the entrenchments, capturing 50 artillery pieces. The loss of this key defensive position opened Germany to large-scale French raids. Meanwhile, most of the allied strength was concentrated on an attack from northwest Italy on Toulon. *See* Ramillies; Almansa; Toulon I; Spanish Succession, War of the.

Stones River (American Civil War), 1862–1863. Following the stalemated battle of Perryville, the Confederate general Braxton Bragg retreated from Kentucky to concentrate at Murfreesboro, Tenn. The Federal commander, Gen. William Rosecrans, who had replaced Gen. Don Carlos Buell, moved to Nashville. On December 26 Rosecrans marched his army of 45,000 southeast toward Murfreesboro. Approaching the town on December 30, he found the Confederate corps of Gens. William Hardee and Leonidas Polk posted on the west side of Stones River, in front of Murfreesboro.

Each side launched an attack on December 31 against the opponent's right flank. Bragg's offensive, led by Hardee's corps and Gen. John Wharton's cavalry, got off the mark first, driving Gen. Alexander McCook's corps back three miles before Rosecrans could stabilize a line, almost perpendicular to his original front. The Federal attack east of Stones River was recalled to strengthen the line against Hardee's assault on the west flank, as well as against Polk's less successful thrust in the center where Gen. Philip Sheridan's division of Gen. George Thomas' corps fought stubbornly to prevent a Confederate breakthrough. Fortunately for the Federals, Gen. John Breckinridge kept the 8,000 Confederate troops east of Stones River out of this action, expecting Rosecrans to renew the attack on this flank. Finally Bragg got Breckinridge to move westward, in the afternoon, to bolster the now faltering Confederate offensive. As these fresh troops arrived, Polk sent them piecemeal against what was now the Federal left flank. Each assault was repulsed with heavy losses by Thomas' corps. Darkness ended the fighting that day with the Federal army compressed into a tight semicircle, its back to Stones River.

Both armies remained in position on January 1. On the following day Rosecrans sent part of Gen. Thomas Crittenden's corps east of Stones River. This move was countered by Breckinridge, who had recrossed the stream. The Confederates made a sharp attack late in the afternoon in an attempt to dislodge the Federal bridgehead but were beaten back with 1,700 casualties. When Rosecrans stubbornly held in place on January 3, Bragg decided to abandon the attack. That night he began a retreat to Tullahoma, 36 miles to the south. Rosecrans occupied Murfreesboro (a name sometimes given to this battle) but pursued no farther. There would not be another battle on this front for more than nine months. Federal casualties at Stones River totaled 12,906, out of the 41,400 troops engaged. Of the 34,739 Confederate effectives, 11,739 were casualties. *See* Perryville; Chickamauga; American Civil War.

Stonington (Pequot War), 1637. An uprising by the Pequot Indians in New England in 1636 led to a punitive expedition by American colonists the following year. On June 5 a militia force of 70 men, accompanied by 100 Mohican and Narraganset allies, under Capt. John Mason, attacked and burned out the stockaded Indian village near Stonington in southeastern Connecticut. The surviving Pequots from among the original party of 600 men, woman, and children fled west, where they were intercepted and slaughtered near present-day Southport by a colonial force from Plymouth Plantation and Connecticut, on July 13. This forever destroyed the power of the Pequot tribe. *See* Indian Wars in the United States.

Stono Ferry (War of the American Revolution), 1779. Despite the disastrous American defeat at Briar Creek, Ga., on March 3, 1779, Gen. Benjamin Lincoln, American commander in the South, marched against Augusta again in April. To draw Lincoln out of Georgia, the British general Augustine Prevost marched from Savannah toward Charleston, S.C. Here Gen. William Moultrie hastily threw up fortifications on the neck of land between the Ashley and Cooper rivers above the city. When he found the town defended and learned that Lincoln was marching back, Prevost began withdrawing on May 12. He fell back to James Island, south of the city, and then to Johns Island, leaving a strong rear guard on the mainland at Stono Ferry. Early on June 20 Moultrie led 1,200 men, largely militia, in an attack on the enemy position, manned by 900 British, Hessians, and Tories. The inexperienced Americans were no match for the regulars, who beat them back with a loss of 146 killed or wounded and 155 missing. British losses were 26 killed, 163 wounded. The attack, however, persuaded Prevost to abandon completely his incursion into South Carolina. *See* Briar Creek; Savannah II; American Revolution.

Stony Creek (War of 1812), 1813. To gain control of Lake Ontario, the United States organized a joint military and naval command under Gen. Henry Dearborn and Capt. Isaac Chauncey early in 1813. Some 1,600 American troops raided York (Toronto) on April 27, burning the public buildings. Returning to Niagara on May 8, the raiding force squeezed the British garrison out of Fort George. The British general John Vincent fell back westward, pursued by 2,000 Americans. Near the western end of Lake Ontario, ten miles from Hamilton, Vincent made a stand on Stony Creek. Although he was outnumbered almost 3 to 1, the

British commander sharply repulsed the American army, capturing Gens. William Winder and John Chandler. The defeated force withdrew to Fort George. *See* Sackets Harbor; Erie, Lake; Chrysler's Farm; War of 1812.

Stony Point (War of the American Revolution), 1779. The fifth year of the war in the North opened when Gen. Sir Henry Clinton, British commander in New York City, sent a large force up the Hudson River. On June 1 the expedition seized the uncompleted American fort at Stony Point, a rocky promontory in the river opposite Peekskill. A garrison of almost 700 men under Lt. Col. Henry Johnson was assigned to strengthen and hold the fort. Six weeks later the American commander in chief, Gen. George Washington, ordered Gen. Anthony Wayne to retake the fort. Wayne with 1,350 men launched a surprise bayonet attack on the night of July 15. In a fierce fight the Americans won Stony Point by dawn of the following day. They killed 63 defenders, wounded 70, and captured 543. Wayne lost 15 killed and 80 wounded. Because of its nearness to New York City, Washington had the fort dismantled, withdrawing Wayne's men on July 18. He then planned a similar attack in New Jersey. *See* Monmouth; Paulus Hook; American Revolution.

Stormberg (South African War II), 1899. As part of Gen. Sir Redvers Buller's three-pronged offensive in December, a British column from Cape Colony moved toward Stormberg (the other two objectives were Ladysmith and Kimberley). In this sector the Boers had penetrated to within 70 miles of Queenstown. On December 10 Gen. William Forbes Gatacre with 3,000 troops made a night march against the Boer position. Misled by guides, the British blundered into a murderous enemy fire. Before they could withdraw, 89 were killed or wounded and more than 600 became prisoners. It was the first of three defeats that made up British "Black Week." *See* Modder River; Magersfontein; Colenso; South African Wars.

Stow-on-the-Wold (English Civil War), 1646. After nearly four years of bitter civil warfare, almost all of England and Scotland lay under the grip of the Roundheads' New Model Army. The last remaining force of Charles I in the field was commanded by Gen. Lord Jacob Astley. On March 26, 1646, this Cavalier army of about 1,500 men was cornered at Stow-on-the-Wold, 50 miles northwest of the king's headquarters at Oxford. After a brief fight Astley surrendered. The king abandoned Oxford and on May 5 surrendered himself to the Scottish army, under Gen. David Leslie, at Newark. This ended the king's part of the fighting, but two years later the second phase of the conflict, often called the Second Civil War, broke out. *See* Langport; Philiphaugh; Preston I; English Civil War.

Stralsund I (Thirty Years' War), 1628. The great design of Holy Roman Emperor Ferdinand II in 1628 was to secure a port on the Baltic and thus establish a Hapsburg line across central Europe from Bohemia northward along the Oder. To effect this plan, Gen. Albrecht von Wallenstein sent an Imperial army to take Stralsund, a port on the Pomeranian coast opposite the island of Rügen. Wallenstein's army arrived outside the walls of the Hanseatic city in February. When Stralsund resisted, the Imperials instituted a siege. Gustavus II, king of Sweden, supplied maritime aid in return for the use of Stralsund as a potential base for a Swedish landing in Germany. Thus fortified, the city held on stubbornly. Wallenstein himself arrived on July 6 and promptly ordered two assaults on the Baltic defenses. Both attacks were beaten off, and on July 28 he returned to Prague. A week later the siege was abandoned.

The victory at Stralsund did little to strengthen the anti-Hapsburg forces, except morally. And even morale was placed in the balance when King Christian IV of Denmark and Norway made one more attempt to invade Mecklenburg. *See* Lutter am Barenberge; Wolgast; Thirty Years' War.

Stralsund II (Great Northern War), 1715. In 1714, fourteen years after he had left Sweden at the head of a conquering army and five years after his crushing defeat at Poltava, in Russia, Charles XII returned to claim his throne. Swedish fortunes, depressed by Russia (Peter I), Denmark (Frederick IV), Poland (Augustus II), and Prussia (Frederick William I), stood at low ebb. The Pomeranian port of Stralsund on the Baltic lay under siege by a combined Prussian-Danish army. Charles, desperately trying to rebuild Swedish military strength, sought to recapture the island of Rügen, which the besiegers had taken earlier to give them a commanding position over the town. The Swedish counterattack was beaten off, Charles withdrawing to his homeland. The Stralsund garrison surrendered soon thereafter. *See* Ahvenanmaa; Fredrikshald; Great Northern War.

Stratton (English Civil War), 1643. In the second year of the Civil War between the Cavaliers of Charles I and the Roundheads (Parliamentarians), the action opened in southwestern England. Here the Cornishmen, largely loyal to the crown, augmented the Cavalier army under Gen. Sir Ralph (later Lord) Hopton. The Roundhead force in this area, commanded by Gen. Sir William Waller, featured London cavalrymen so heavily armored they were called Lobsters. At Stratton in Cornwall, Hopton's men fiercely assaulted a hill held by the Roundheads on May 16. The charge carried the hill and put the Lobsters to flight. Stratton was the first of three narrow victories in the west won by the Royalists that year. *See* Grantham; Lansdowne; English Civil War.

Stromboli (Second, or Dutch, War of Louis XIV), 1676. The Spanish-held island of Sicily revolted against the rule of Charles II in July 1674. Louis XIV of France, as part of his long anti-Hapsburg campaign, promptly took the island under his protection and sent the Marquis Duquesne into the Mediterranean at the head of a French fleet. Spain appealed to William III of Orange (later William III of England) for naval aid. The veteran commander Adm. Michel deRuyter responded with 22 ships, including 4 fire ships. Early in January 1676, supplemented by a single Spanish vessel, De Ruyter took up a position between the Lipara Islands and the north coast of Sicily. On January 8 Duquesne sailed out from Messina to attack with 20 ships of the line and 6 fire ships. The two hostile fleets clashed off the island of Stromboli. The French attack soon became disorganized, enabling De Ruyter to pull back from the superior force aligned against him. With neither side gaining an advantage, the battle broke off—Duquesne returning to Messina and De Ruyter putting in at Palermo. Three months later the battle would resume. *See* Sasbach; Augusta; Louis XIV, Wars of.

Sudan, War for the (1881–1899). The Sudanese, who had long suffered under Egyptian misrule, revolted in 1881 under the leadership of Mohammed Ahmed, who proclaimed himself the Mahdi, or ruler of the faithful. Great Britain was drawn into the struggle through its loose protectorate over Egypt. Within four years the Mahdists had expelled almost all the Anglo-Egyptians from the Sudan. A two-and-one-half-year campaign of reconquest, led by Gen. Horatio Herbert (later Lord) Kitchener, finally brought peace to the Sudan. An Anglo-Egyptian condominium ruled the land until 1956, when Sudan became a republic.

El Obeid	1883
El Teb	1884
Khartoum	1884–1885
Abu Klea	1885
Atbara	1898
Omdurman	1898

Sungari River (Chinese Civil War), 1947. In northern Manchuria, Communist troops, now called the People's Liberation Army (PLA), prepared an offensive southward against the Nationalist armies of Generalissimo Chiang Kai-shek. In January three PLA columns crossed the frozen Sungari River, headed southward toward Changchun. At the end of two weeks' fighting, they were driven back across the river. On February 21 the thrust was repeated; and again it was beaten back. A third attack across the Sungari, during March 8–15, was repulsed. But by now the Nationalists retained only a small bridgehead north of the river. In May the largest attack the Communists had mounted so far in the war sent four columns (270,000 men) plunging across the Sungari into central Manchuria. By the end of June this offensive too was checked, 150 miles from the Sungari, but the casualty cost to the Nationalists was extremely high. Chiang's garrisons in Changchun, Yungki, and Mukden had been virtually isolated by wrecked communication lines between the cities. The initiative in Manchuria now came into the permanent possession of Mao Tse-tung's Communists. *See* Szepingkai; Mukden II; Chinese Civil War.

Süntelberg (Conquests of Charlemagne), 782. During his long campaign against the pagan Saxons of the Weser-Elbe district of Germany, Charlemagne sent out a Frank army to capture the enemy chieftain, Wittekind (Witukind). Led by trusted lieutenants, the Franks located a large body of Saxons on a ridge north of the Weser River in modern Hannover. In a brave but foolish charge up the slope, the Franks were cut to pieces by the fierce-fighting Saxons. Charlemagne then took personal command of the campaign. Although ranging up and down the Weser Valley, the enraged king failed to capture Wittekind. At Verden, on the Aller River, he had 4,000 Saxon prisoners executed when they refused to reveal their leader's hiding place. Charlemagne stayed on in Germany, gradually winning over the Saxons by sword and persuasion. Finally, in 785, Wittekind surrendered himself for baptism and submission at Paderborn. Charlemagne's 13-year struggle to establish Frankish rule over the Saxons was at an end. *See* Roncesvalles; Tisza River; Charlemagne, Conquests of.

Suomussalmi (World War II). Part of the battle of Finland, in which two Russian divisions were wiped out; December 8, 1939–January 11, 1940. *See* Finland (World War II).

Surigao Strait (World War II). A part of the Japanese-American naval battle in Leyte Gulf, on October 25, 1944, confined exclusively to surface action. *See* Leyte Gulf.

Svištov (Russian-Turkish War), 1877. The tinderbox Balkan Peninsula burst into flame in 1876 with the Serbian declaration of war on Turkey. The Ottoman forces of Abdul-Hamid II soon routed the weak Serbian army. But Russia, stirred by Pan-slavism, declared war on Turkey on April 24, 1877. Grand Duke Nicholas, younger brother of Czar Alexander II, marched the Army of the Danube into modern Rumania. On the night of June 26 a Russian advance guard of 15,000 men under Gen. Mikhail Dragomirov slipped across the Danube in boats. A swift attack toward the Turkish fortress of Svištov (Sistova), 14 miles east of Nikopol (Nicopolis), followed. The surprised Ottoman garrison yielded the fort the following day to an assault led by Gen. Mikhail Skobelev. Total Russian casualties were less than a thousand.

The Russians then moved upriver to seize Nikopol on July 16 after a two-day bombardment.

Grand Duke Nicholas now stood ready to attack the major Turkish stronghold of Plevna, 24 miles to the southwest. *See* Plevna; Russian-Turkish War.

Sweden. *See* Scandinavia.

Switzerland. The major battles fought by the Swiss people are listed below.

Morgarten	1315
Laupen	1339
Sempach	1386
Näfels	1388
Arbedo	1422
Saint Jacob-en-Birs	1444
Héricourt	1474
Grandson	1476
Morat	1476
Nancy	1477
Giornico	1478
Frastenz	1499
Calven	1499
Dornach	1499
Novara I	1513
Marignano	1515
La Bicocca	1522
Kappel	1531
Zurich I	1799
Zurich II	1799

Swold (Wars of Scandinavia), 1000. The Danish viking Sweyn I, Forkbeard, who had raided Great Britain in 994, joined his fleet with the Swedish ships of Olaf Skutkonung in 1000. In a semi-legendary naval battle off Swold Island in the Baltic Sea the allied vessels surprised the ships of King Olaf I of Norway. The Norwegian ships were destroyed. Olaf I is reported to have jumped overboard and disappeared. Norway was divided between Denmark and Sweden until the appearance of Olaf II in 1016. *See* Stiklestad; Nairn.

Syracuse I (Great Peloponnesian War), 415–413 B.C. During the brief Peace of Nicias in the Great Peloponnesian War, Athens decided to attack Syracuse, a burgeoning Sicilian city-state friendly to the allies of the Spartan League. In the summer of 415 B.C., 134 war galleys sailed for Syracuse under the combined leadership of three Athenian generals. But Alcibiades, the ablest of the three and the nephew of Pericles, was recalled to Athens while en route, on a charge of sacrilege. Then Lamachus fell in an early skirmish, leaving Nicias, a cautious and inexperienced leader, the sole commander of the invasion.

In the fall the Athenian fleet occupied the harbor of Syracuse and landed more than 20,000 troops to lay siege to the city. As was the ancient custom, the attacking force began construction of a double encircling wall—the inner wall designed to hold in the besieged, the outer wall placed to hold out any force attempting to bring relief; the attackers held the ground between the two walls. More Athenian troops landed in the spring of 414.

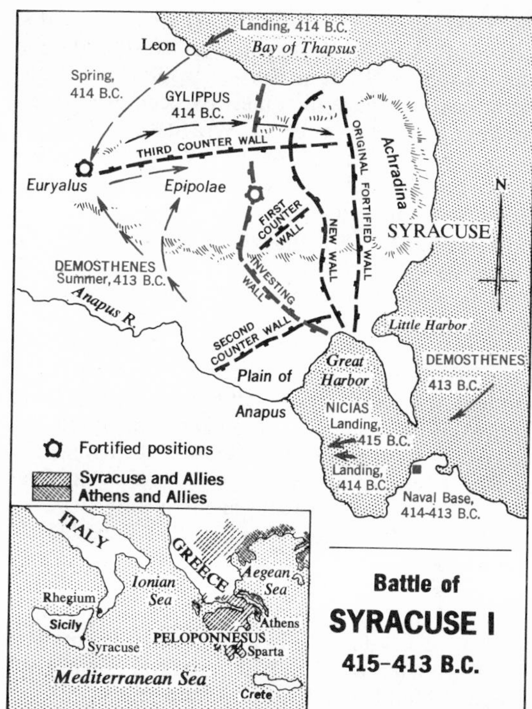

Battle of SYRACUSE I 415–413 B.C.

Syracuse seemed to be doomed, but Nicias pushed his construction so sluggishly that a Spartan force of more than 2,000 under Gylippus was able to reinforce the city through an unfinished section of the walls. Gylippus, with the Syracusan commander Hermocrates, then seized the high ground behind the city (the Epipolae) in 414 and began building counter walls. This construction blocked the circumvallation of the city and squeezed the Athenians into the low ground near the harbor. More reinforcements reached Syracuse from Corinth, Thebes, and other Peloponnesian cities.

Athens countered in the spring of 413 by sending the veteran general Demosthenes with 5,000 troops and 70 galleys to strengthen Nicias. Demosthenes launched a massive night attack against the Epipolae and its western terminus at Euryalus. Most of the high ground had been taken when the Athenian surge suddenly collapsed. In the retreat back to the harbor the attackers suffered heavy losses. Demosthenes wanted to call off the siege, but Nicias vacillated throughout the summer. Meanwhile the Athenian fleet of 160 ships was gradually being destroyed by a series of naval actions offshore. When it became too late to escape by sea, the Athenians sought to withdraw into the interior of the island. Attacked while on the march, the last survivors of Athens' 40,000-man force were killed or captured. Demosthenes and Nicias were executed and the 6,000 prisoners sold into slavery.

This fierce two-year battle proved to be one of

the most decisive in history. It forever ended Athenian hopes of expanding westward—the domination of Western Europe would be left for Rome and Carthage to contest two centuries later. In Greece, the disaster at Syracuse contributed much to the eventual defeat of Athens in the Great Peloponnesian War. *See* Cumae; Amphipolis; Cynossema; Peloponnesian Wars.

Syracuse II (Carthaginian Invasion of Sicily), 387 B.C. Following their conquests of Selinus, Himera, and Acragas, the Carthaginians prepared to assault Syracuse, largest and richest of the Sicilian cities. However, a plague swept through the invaders, forcing the commanding general, Himilco, to accept peace terms in 404. This gave Dionysius the Elder time to organize the Syracusan forces and even to take the offensive against nearby Carthaginian-held towns. In 398–97 he swung over to the west coast and reduced the enemy's stronghold of Motya on the island of San Pantaleo. In this attack Dionysius employed catapults, a new engine of war for Sicily, and large movable towers, to cope with high-placed defense points.

The see-saw fighting in Sicily turned in favor of Carthage later in 387. After a naval victory off Catania, Himilco laid siege to Syracuse with some 50,000 Carthaginans. When another epidemic killed off thousands of the besiegers, Dionysius launched a land-sea counterattack, aided by a relieving force of 30 Spartan triremes. The Syracusans surprised the enemy fleet while most of the crews were ashore and destroyed every Carthaginian vessel. Meanwhile Dionysius' ground attack stormed through the besiegers' lines and put the Carthaginians to flight. Himilco and his chief officers abandoned their army and fled the island. Himilco later committed suicide. Despite the crushing defeat, Carthage continued to resist subsequent attempts by Dionysius to throw the invaders off the island. *See* Acragas; Crimisus River.

Syracuse III (Second Punic War), 214–212 B.C. After Marcus Claudius Marcellus repulsed Hannibal at Nola, he was sent to Sicily, where Syracuse had headed a revolt against Roman rule. The key to the island, Syracuse was the ancient city on the east coast that had successfully resisted all previous attacks, including those of Athens and Carthage itself in previous centuries. Syracuse seemed even more impregnable now. Its garrison, commanded by Hippocrates, knew that a defeat would bring them execution as traitors to Rome. And much of the city's defenses rested upon ingenious new military engines developed by the Greek physicist Archimedes.

With 25,000 men, Marcellus attacked Syracuse by land and sea. Stubborn resistance by the city's defenders, plus the effective use of slings, catapults, and derricks devised by Archimedes, turned back the assault. Marcellus then organized siege lines, at the same time subduing other pockets of revolt in Sicily. What threatened to become a long siege shifted abruptly when the Romans on land gained an entrance to the upper part of the city during a Syracusan festival. Forcing their way through the opening in ever greater numbers, the Roman legions cut a path to the harbor where they destroyed the defenses holding off their fleet. Syracuse was conquered. One of those killed in the widespread slaughter was the 75-year-old Archimedes, the greatest scientist of the Hellenistic age. The city and all of Sicily now lay under Roman rule. *See* Nola; Capua; Punic Wars.

Szentgotthárd (Austrian-Turkish Wars), 1664. With the Peace of Westphalia ending the Thirty Years' War, the dukedom of Austria (under the Holy Roman Empire) concentrated on defending its eastern border against the Ottoman Turks. A new war erupted in 1663 when the grand vizier of Sultan Mohammed IV, Ahmed Kuprili, marched into Hungary with a Turkish army. A French contingent under Charles V, titular duke of Lorraine, reinforced the Imperial army commanded by Field Marshal Count Raimund Montecuccoli. The Austrian general took up a strong position at Szentgotthárd (Saint Gotthard) behind the Rába River in western Hungary. The Turks attacked on August 1, 1664. In a fierce fight they were beaten back and forced to withdraw. Nine days later at Vasvar the Ottomans signed a 20-year peace treaty with representatives of the Holy Roman Empire of Leopold I, which allowed the local estates to elect the prince of Transylvania. *See* Candia II; Khotin II.

Szepingkai (Chinese Civil War), 1946. After Generalissimo Chiang Kai-shek's troops occupied Mukden on March 15, the Nationalist armies were scheduled to move northward. To forestall this expected advance into central Manchuria, Communist forces of Mao Tse-tung, on March 18, seized Szepingkai (Ssupingchieh), a key junction on the South Manchuria Railway about 70 miles north of Mukden. On April 16 the Nationalist New First Army under Gen. Sun Li-jen attacked the Communist position at Szepingkai. It was the first pitched battle of what would become a savage civil war. In five weeks' fighting, the Nationalist army of 70,000 men drove out the Communists, reported to number 110,000 troops, on May 20. Marching 70 miles farther north, the Nationalists occupied Changchun five days later. But meanwhile the last of the Soviet Union's troops had evacuated northern Manchuria, on May 3, leaving Mao's forces in firm control beyond Changchun.

On June 7 Communist negotiator Chou En-lai and Chiang agreed on an armistice, which lasted until June 30. During this time the U.S. general George C. Marshall made one last attempt to effect a permanent truce but failed. *See* Sungari River; Chinese Civil War.

Szigetvár (Turkish Invasion of Europe), 1566. The long, intermittent war for Hungary carried on by the Ottoman Turkish sultan Suleiman I, the Magnificent, against the Holy Roman Empire continued when Ferdinand I was succeeded by Maximilian II. In 1566 Suleiman invaded Hungary again, laying siege to Szigetvár in the southwest on August 5. The 3,000-man garrison, led by Miklós Zrinyi, a Croatian noble, resisted stoutly. During the fighting the 72-year-old Suleiman died of natural causes, but the vizier kept his death a secret. On September 7 the Turks finally stormed into the city. Zrinyi and the surviving defenders fell in a futile effort to stem the attack. Suleiman's death was then announced. His 46-year reign had made the Turkish Empire the greatest power in the Middle East—if not in all of Europe. His successor, Selim II, obtained a favorable peace settlement from Maximilian two years later. *See* Vienna I; Astrakhan II.

T

Tacna (War of the Pacific), 1880. A quarrel over the rich nitrate deposits in the Bolivian littoral led the government of President Hilarión Daza to declare war on Chile on April 5, 1879. Chile, under the presidency of Aníbal Pinto (and later Domingo Santa María), was well prepared. When the Peruvian president Mariano Prado refused to declare his neutrality, Chile declared war on that country as well. This launched the five-year War of the Pacific. With an army and navy superior to that of its combined enemies, Chile marched into the littoral. At Tacna on May 26, 1880, the Chileans, under Gen. Manuel Baquedano, dealt a decisive defeat to the allied forces commanded by then Bolivian president Narciso Campero. The victors pressed northward, while a second army landed near Callao, Peru, and occupied Lima the following year. This virtually knocked Peru out of the war. And on October 20, 1883, Miguel Iglesias, then president of Peru, signed the treaty of Ancón with Chile, ceding its own nitrate province of Tarapacá.

With the loss of its ally, Bolivia was helpless. Campero agreed to the Treaty of Valparaiso on April 4, 1884. By its terms, Bolivia ceded its nitrate-rich littoral and lost its access to the Pacific. Chile had now become the dominant power in western South America.

Taginae (Wars of the Byzantine Empire), 552. Having reconquered Italy in 540 and then lost it again to the Ostrogoths, Emperor Justinian I of the Byzantine Empire ordered a new campaign in 551. He sent an army of 20,000 men under Narses, an aged eunuch, up the Balkan Peninsula and around the head of the Adriatric into northern Italy. At the Apennine village of Taginae (Tadinum), near the Flaminian Way, Narses encountered the main body of Goths commanded by their Christian king Totila (Baduila). The two armies fought a pitched battle here in July 552. The Goths were routed, largely by Imperial archers. Totila lay among the 6,000 killed. It was the first recorded success in the coordinated employment of pike and bow.

This battle proved decisive. Narses methodically marched through Italy, destroying the last remnants of Gothic power. Rome was liberated by the end of the year, and in 553 all the peninsula again came under the jurisdiction of Constantinople. The wizened little Narses faced only one more threat—from the Franks—to his Byzantine province. *See* Rome IV; Casilinum.

Tagliacozzo (German Invasion of Italy), 1268. Two years after Charles I of Anjou had established himself as king of the Two Sicilies, he was threatened by a German army of the Holy Roman Empire. The invaders were led by Conradin, the 16-year-old son of the late Conrad IV, and by Frederick, duke of Austria. On August 23, 1268, the two forces met at Tagliacozzo in central Italy. Charles's army (aided by the papacy) routed the Germans with a circling movement, capturing and then beheading both Conradin and Frederick. The death of Conradin ended the Hohenstauffen dynasty, which had dominated Germany and the Holy Roman Empire for 130 years. The ruthless Charles now stood supreme in southern Italy and Sicily. *See* Benevento; Messina II.

Taierhchwang (Chinese-Japanese War II). The scene of the first major Chinese victory over the Japanese, in fighting between March 31 and April 9, 1938, in the four-year "incident" preceding World War II. *See* China I.

Taku (Western Attacks on China), 1860. In forcing trade concessions from China, the Western Powers often resorted to naked aggression. One of the strongest Chinese defenses was a series of forts at Taku, on the mouth of the Hai River, which guarded the approach to Tientsin, 37 miles to the west. On June 25, 1859, a British gunboat flotilla, supplemented by a marine landing party, was firmly repulsed. A second attempt to take the forts came on August 21, 1860. General Sir James Hope Grant, at the head of a 17,000-man British-French force, stormed the forts after a heavy naval bombardment. The defenses were taken and Tientsin opened to trade. Grant then marched 80 miles northwest to occupy Peking on October 12. The government of Emperor Hsien Fêng agreed later that month to the Peking conventions, which increased the indemnities to be paid to Great Britain and France. *See* Peking III.

Talana Hill (South African War II). A British defeat near Dundee, on October 20, 1899, in the successful Boer thrust to Ladysmith. *See* Ladysmith.

Talavera de la Reina (Napoleonic Empire Wars), 1809. After driving the French army of Marshal Nicolas Soult out of Portugal in May 1809, the British general Sir Arthur Wellesley determined to reinvade Spain. At the head of 20,000 British troops, and receiving the cooperation of a Spanish army of similar size under Gen. Cuesta, Wellesley marched up the Tagus Valley. He reached Talavera de la Reina, some 70 miles southwest of Madrid, in July. But here his supplies gave out, while a French army of 50,000 men under Marshal Claude Victor began moving in on the British position. At the same time Soult's reorganized army approached from the north. Without waiting for Soult's arrival, Victor attacked on July 28. The Spaniards proved to be of little value in a set-piece battle, leaving some 16,000 British to oppose an assaulting force of 30,000 French. In a fierce seesaw struggle, Victor's army was thrown back with a loss of 7,300 men and 20 guns. Wellesley suffered almost 5,400 casualties.

Victor withdrew toward Madrid. Wellesley, too crippled to pursue or to meet Soult, retreated down the Tagus River into Portugal. (He was later created Viscount Wellington for his Talavera victory.) Soult brushed past guerrilla resistance to overrun all of southwestern Spain except Cadiz. *See* Oporto; Bussaco; Napoleonic Empire Wars.

Talikota (Mogul-Hindu Wars), 1565. For more than two centuries the Hindu kingdom of Vijayanagar in southern India stood as a barrier against the advance of Mohammedans from the north. Then, during the reign of the Mogul emperor Akbar the Great, Moslem sultans from the Deccan organized a coalition against the Hindus. In 1565 the army of this confederation met the army of Vijayanagar at Talikota in southeastern Bombay province. The Mohammedans won an overwhelming victory, which destroyed the Hindu kingdom. *See* Panipat II.

Talladega (Creek War), 1813. After the Creek massacre of Fort Mims, Ala., on August 30, 1813, Gen. Andrew Jackson assembled a force of Tennessee militia in order to put down the Indian uprising. On November 9 his deadly-shooting frontier riflemen surrounded a Creek war party at Talladega in east-central Alabama. More than 500 Indian warriors were killed at a cost of nominal militia casualties. *See* Fort Mims; Horseshoe Bend; Indian Wars in the U.S.

Tanagra-Oenophyta (First Peloponnesian War), 457 B.C. The Athenian naval victory over Aegina alarmed Sparta. A Spartan army marched across the Corinthian Isthmus to re-establish the Boeotian League under Thebes, as a buffer against further Athenian aggressions. At Tanagra, 14 miles east of Thebes, the Peloponnesian allies attacked a force of some 14,000 Athenians, which was supplemented by a body of Thessalian cavalry. Both sides lost heavily in a bitter battle, that turned against the Athenians when the Thessalians deserted.

Despite their victory, the Spartans returned home because of their many casualties. Myronides then rallied the Athenians and two months later crushed the Thebans and their allied armies at Oenophyta. This victory restored the hegemony of Athens over central Greece. But Athenian supremacy continued to be challenged by neighboring city-states, despite the enlightened leadership provided by Pericles. *See* Aegina; Coronea I; Peloponnesian Wars.

Tananarive (French Conquest of Madagascar), 1895. France had sought to conquer Madagascar from the Hova people since the early 1600's. After several attempts to establish itself on the island, the French government of the Third Republic launched a major expedition in 1895. Under the command of Gen. Jacques Duchesne, some 15,000 troops landed at Majunga, on the northwestern coast, in February. Stymied by disease and transportation troubles, Duchesne finally sent a column southeast into the interior toward the capital of Tananarive. By September 30 the French had arrived outside the city and opened a bombardment. The Hova queen, Ranavalona III, surrendered at once. The following year Joseph Gallieni took over as governor of the newly proclaimed colony. Native resistance was suppressed and order established.

Tangier (Portuguese Invasion of Africa), 1437. When John I of Portugal conquered Ceuta in present-day Spanish Morocco in 1415, he had been accompanied by his son and heir, Edward (Duarte). Later, as king, Edward tried to enlarge the Portuguese holding by attacking the Moslem city of Tangier, an Atlantic port 25 miles to the west of Ceuta. His army suffered a disastrous defeat at the hands of the Moors. To make peace, Edward was forced to yield his younger brother Frederick to the Moors as a hostage and promised to surrender Ceuta. Edward reneged on giving up Ceuta; his brother remained a prisoner of the Moors and died in captivity five years later.

Edward's son, Alfonso V, pressed the Moslems so hard in Africa that Tangier finally fell to Portugal in 1471. But he suspended further campaigns across the Strait of Gibraltar in favor of a war against Castile. *See* Ceuta; Toro.

Tannenberg I (Rise of Poland), 1410. By the start of the fifteenth century the Teutonic Knights ruled most of Prussia and the Baltic States from their capital at Marienburg (Malbork). In 1410, however, the Polish king Ladislas II (or V) Jagello organized an army to challenge their power. The Poles, aided by Bohemian mercenaries under Jan Ziska, Russians, and Lithuanians, met the main body of knights at Tannenberg (Stebark) in northeast Poland on July 15. King Ladislas's army won an overwhelming victory. Thousands of knights were killed, and the Teutonic Order never recovered its former glory.

Tannenberg II (World War I), 1914. Three days after the Russian victory at Gumbinnen on August 20, the German Eighth Army in East Prussia received two new leaders: Gen. Paul von Hindenburg as commander in chief, Gen. Erich Ludendorff as chief of staff. Fortunately for Germany, the Russian First Army, under Gen. Pavel Rennenkampf, did not follow up its original triumph. This gave the new German commanders time to concentrate against the Russian Second Army, which was moving up from the south. Under Aleksandr Samsonov, this force of five corps crossed the frontier to strike the German XX Corps of Gen. Friedrich von Scholtz on August 22 and drive it back to Tannenberg. The Eighth Army was already turning away from Rennenkampf and moving southward against Samsonov (a plan worked out by Col. Max Hoffmann, deputy chief of operations). The XVII Corps (August von Mackensen) and I Reserve Corps (Otto von Below) marched against the right flank of the Russian Second Army, while the I Corps (Hermann von François) traveled by rail to come in on the left flank. On August 26 the gigantic double envelopment got under way (helped in part by the auditing of Russian wireless messages which were being sent in the clear).

Unaware of the concentration against him, Samsonov resumed his clumsy attack the same day on a 70-mile front. The action opened on his right (northeast) flank where his detached VI Corps, marching to close up to the main body, blundered into Mackensen's XVII Corps. Toward the end of a day of confused fighting, Below's corps came up to support Mackensen. The Russians were badly mauled and fell back, exposing Samsonov's center. Here the Russian commander had made little progress in the heavy fighting. Despite the tightening pincers against him, he ordered fresh attacks the following day (August 27). But now François had come up on the west, and early that morning he drove back the Russian left wing with a devastating artillery bombardment. The two huge armies, totaling some 300,000, now flailed at each other across a 40-mile front.

On August 28 François again pressed his corps eastward, turning the Russian left flank under another heavy artillery barrage. Meanwhile, Below thrust toward the open Russian flank at Allenstein (Olsztyn), as Mackensen pursued Samsonov's broken wing (the VI Corps). At his Neidenburg

headquarters, Samsonov abandoned his ever diminishing control of the battle. Jumping on a horse, he rode to the front in a hopeless attempt to rally his troops by personal command. That night he ordered a general retreat of the Second Army.

The next two days, August 29 and 30, the Russians floundered eastward through marshes and dense woods. The two center corps, which had penetrated deepest into East Prussia, had the farthest to go to escape the tightening German vise. Both units fell apart, while the commanders, Gens. Martos and Kliouev, were captured. Samsonov killed himself in flight. The entire Second Army was virtually wiped out in one of the great disasters in military history—92,000 were taken prisoner, 30,000 were killed or missing, and some 400 (of 600) guns were lost. German casualties totaled 13,000 killed, wounded, and missing. Hindenburg now turned the Eighth Army back to face Rennenkampf, who had made almost no move to save Samsonov's army from extinction. *See* Gumbinnen; Masurian Lakes I; World War I.

Taormina (Moslem Conquest of Sicily), 902. Beginning in 827 the Moslems of North Africa began a slow, step-by-step conquest of Sicily. The great port of Syracuse finally fell in 878. But the Byzantine garrison at Taormina, on the east coast, continued to hold out. It was not until 902 that a new Moslem attack captured the city, which was promptly burned. All Sicily now lay under Moslem rule, with all Christians who could escaping across the Strait of Messina to southern Italy. *See* Apulia; Erzurum; Moslem Conquests.

Taranto (World War II), 1940. In the struggle to control the eastern Mediterranean Sea, the first major victory was won by the British admiral Sir Andrew Cunningham. On the evening of November 11 he sent 21 planes from the carrier *Illustrious* to attack the Italian fleet at Taranto, in the boot heel of Italy. A deadly torpedo assault crippled three Italian battleships and two cruisers and sank two auxiliary ships. Two British planes were lost. This action disabled half the Italian battle fleet for several months and cost Fleet commander Adm. Domenico Cavagnari his job. *See* Matapan; World War II.

Taraori (Moslem Invasions of India), 1192. The Persian sultan Mohammed of Ghor, after seizing power in Ghazni (part of modern Afghanistan) in 1173, launched a series of invasions of India soon afterward. He subdued Sind in 1182 and the Punjab in 1187. Four years later he was turned back by a Hindu army on the Saraswati (Sarsuti) River. However, in 1192 the Moslem sultan returned to the attack. Near the site of his earlier defeat, at Taraori, 14 miles from Thanesar, Mohammed's mounted archers crushed a Hindu army. The defenders handicapped themselves by a disunited command and caste restrictions that produced clumsy tactics. Mohammed of Ghor plunged on to occupy Delhi and make all northwestern India tributary to him.

Ghor survived the Mongol conquests of Genghis Khan but was obliterated by Tamerlane in 1383. Delhi, ruled for more than three centuries by a dynasty of slave kings, also suffered terribly from Tamerlane's invasion. *See* Somnath; Indus River; Delhi I.

Tarawa-Makin (World War II), 1943. The U.S. offensive against Japan in the Central Pacific began with an attack on the Gilbert Islands, about 2,400 miles southwest of Hawaii. Here the Japanese under Adm. Keiji Shibasaki had heavily fortified the Tarawa chain of atolls, particularly the islet of Betio, and Makin, 100 miles to the north. The V Amphibious Corps (Marine Gen. Holland M. Smith) launched the attack on November 20 when the 2nd Marine Division (Julian Smith) stormed ashore at Betio. Ferocious strikes by carrier aircraft and heavy naval shelling preceded the landing. But the 4,800 Imperial Japanese marines on the islet were well protected by pillboxes, blockhouses, and ferroconcrete bombproofs. The invading U.S. marines suffered a continuous blast of artillery, machine-gun, and small-arms fire. Of the 5,000 assault troops, 1,500 were killed or wounded the first day in securing two small beachheads, neither more than 250 yards deep. Despite additional heavy casualties the second day, the marines fought a corridor across the islet and captured the air strip (later named Hawkins Field). The battle then became a brutal struggle to clear Betio's 291 acres yard by yard. At the end of the fourth day Tarawa was won at the cost of 991 dead and 2,311 wounded. Almost 4,700 Japanese were killed.

To the north during the same four days, Gen. Ralph Smith's 27th Infantry Division had attacked and captured Makin Island, defended by some 900 Japanese troops and laborers. The 165th Regiment, which carried out the conquest of the main islet of Butaritari, lost 66 dead and 152 wounded. Some 440 enemy troops were killed. Heavier U.S. casualties were suffered by the supporting fleet—the escort carrier *Liscome Bay* was torpedoed and sunk with a loss of almost 650 of her 900-man crew.

Adm. Chester Nimitz had successfully taken the first U.S. step in the Central Pacific toward the Japanese homeland. From Hawkins Field and other air bases in the Gilberts, American planes now began to hammer at the next objective, the Marshall Islands. *See* Rabaul; Kwajalein-Eniwetok; World War II.

Tarragona (Napoleonic Empire Wars), 1811. Most of the fighting during the early years of the Peninsular War took place in Portugal and western Spain. Here the French armies of Napoleon I vied with the English under the Gen. Lord Wellington (Arthur Wellesley) and his Spanish and Portuguese allies. In the east, however, the French marshal Louis Suchet kept a firm grip on Barcelona and northern Catalonia and Aragon. In May 1811 he thrust southward to besiege Tarragona. The Spanish garrison resisted stubbornly but was gradually pushed back from one defense line to another. By June 21 Suchet had secured a lodgment in the lower town. A week later his besieging army stormed into the upper town and took the surrender of Tarragona. Suchet then pressed farther south. In 1812 he took Valencia, which he held for more than a year. Only the collapse of King Joseph Bonaparte's French government at Madrid forced Suchet to evacuate his conquests in eastern Spain. *See* La Albuera; Ciudad Rodrigo; Napoleonic Empire Wars.

Tarsus (First Crusade), 1097. Before leaving Asia Minor in the summer of 1097, the crusaders again split into two columns. The main body took the longer but safer northern route across the Anti-Taurus range to Antioch. However, first Tancred, a Norman lord from Italy, and then Baldwin of Boulogne marched directly southeast through Cilicia. Tancred reached Tarsus with 100 knights and 200 infantry. The Turkish garrison made the mistake of leaving the protection of the city's walls to attack the outnumbered European army in the open. Tancred's knights cut the Turks to pieces. When Baldwin arrived, he found Tancred in possession of Tarsus. In command of a larger force, he made Tancred move on to the east. To hold the city, the French lord shut the gates against another group of 300 Normans from Italy which was attempting to join Tancred. That night the Turks returned to massacre the Normans camped outside the city's walls.

Baldwin and Tancred made their peace later that year. Tancred linked up with the main body in front of Antioch, while Baldwin marched eastward to seize Edessa (Urfa). Here he made himself lord of the county of Edessa in March 1098. *See* Dorylaeum I; Antioch I; Crusades.

Tassafaronga (World War II). The sixth, and last, Japanese-American naval battle, on November 30, 1942, growing out of the fight for Guadalcanal Island. *See* Guadalcanal—Naval Action.

Telamon (Conquest of Cisalpine Gaul), 225 B.C. The inexorable northward expansion of Rome brought a new revolt by the Po Valley Celts, called the Cisalpine Gauls. Swarming southward through ancient Etruria, they annihilated a Roman army sent out to stop them at Clusium (Chiusi), only 85 miles north of Rome. The Gauls then swung southwest to the coast, but at Cape Telamon were caught between two other Roman armies. Despite a desperate resistance, the invading force was cut to pieces. Rome then sent its legions northward to carry the war to the Gallic homeland. *See* Clastidium; Roman Republic.

Tell el-Kebir (Egyptian Revolt), 1882. After shelling and occupying Alexandria in July, Great Britain landed an army in lower Egypt to put down the nationalist revolution led by Col. Arabi Pasha. General Sir Garnet Wolseley (later Lord Wolseley) with 17,000 men marched inland. At Tell el-Kebir, a village near Zagazig, stood Arabi's Egyptian army, some 22,000 strong. Making a night march across the desert, the British attacked on September 13. Wolseley's troops routed the rebels, inflicting heavy casualties at a cost to themselves of only 300 killed and wounded. Wolseley pushed on south to occupy Cairo two days later. Arabi was captured and sent into exile, ending the revolt. The joint British-French control over Egypt was abolished. Only Great Britain remained as protector. *See* Alexandria IV.

Tempsford (Rise of England), 918. For ten years after his victory over the Northumbrian Danes at Tettenhall, Edward the Elder, son of Alfred the Great, methodically reduced the Danelaw. In this conquest the Wessex king received strong support from his sister Ethelfleda, "the Lady of the Mercians." Finally, in 918, Edward stormed and took the Danish fortress at Tempsford, near Bedford. The Danish leader, Guthrum II, was killed and all resistance in East Anglia broken. Later that year when Ethelfleda died, Edward united Wessex and Mercia under one Saxon crown. *See* Tettenhall; Brunanburh; Danish Invasions of Britain.

Tenochtitlán (Spanish Conquest of Mexico), 1520–1521. The Spanish conquistador Hernando Cortes, with 600 men, landed on the east coast of Mexico and marched into the interior in 1519. On November 8 he entered Tenochtitlán (now Mexico City), the Aztec capital. Although the Aztec emperor, Montezuma II (Moctezuma), was friendly, he was held as a hostage by the Spaniards. When the Aztecs, led by Guatemotzin (nephew of Montezuma), revolted the following year, Cortes had to fight his way out of the city, on the night of June 30. He suffered severe losses in what the Spaniards called *La Noche Triste* ("the night of sadness"). Montezuma was killed in the struggle.

After defeating a large Indian army at Otumba, Cortes returned to Tenochtitlán on May 26, 1521, and laid siege to it. The city was successfully stormed on August 13 and destroyed. Guatemotzin, who had become Aztec emperor, was captured and later killed. This virtually ended resistance to the Spanish conquest of Mexico. *See* Otumba.

Tertry (Rise of France), 687. After the death of Clovis I in 511, the Frankish kingdom suffered a long nightmare of civil strife among his Merovingian descendants. During this troubled time, the mayors of the palaces of Austrasia and Neustria gradually accumulated more and more power. In 687 Pepin of Herstal, also called Pepin II, the mayor of Austrasia, challenged the Neustrians of Thierry III at Tertry (Testry), in the Somme department of northern France. The Austrasians won the field, capturing Thierry. This minor battle had more important consequences than the usual conflict among the Franks: Pepin provided a unifying influence that he was able to hand down to his son Charles Martel, who was the ruler during the Arab invasion of southern France that began in 718. *See* Vouillé; Toulouse I; Tours.

Teruel (Spanish Civil War), 1937–1938. With the completion of the conquest of northern Spain, Generalissimo Francisco Franco turned his Nationalist forces toward Madrid and the Republican-held territory to the east and south. But the government, now moved from Valencia to Barcelona, struck first. The Republican armies of the East (Hernández Sarabia) and the Levante (Leopoldo Menéndez) launched a joint offensive on December 15 against Teruel, 138 miles east of Madrid. In bitter cold weather Hernández Sarabia's troops surrounded the city by nightfall. But the garrison commander, Col. Rey d'Harcourt, with 4,000 men (half of them civilians), held out grimly in the southern part of Teruel. Two weeks later Franco sent Gens. José Varela and Antonio Aranda on a counteroffensive to try to relieve the city. The Republican lines bent under their combined assault but did not break. Snow and cold hampered both sides. Finally, on January 8, Rey d'Harcourt surrendered to the Republicans besieging his now greatly reduced force.

At this point, however, the victorious government troops were themselves besieged in Teruel. The fierce struggle continued. Then, on February 7, a swift Nationalist cavalry attack drove back the Republicans north of the city, taking 7,000 prisoners and inflicting 15,000 other casualties. This was the turning point in the battle. Ten days later Gen. Juan de Yagüe's Moroccan troops crossed the Alfambra River and marched southward along its east bank, cutting off Teruel from the north. By February 20 the city was encircled except for the Valencia road to the southeast. Hernández Sarabia withdrew, leaving 10,000 dead in the city and losing 14,500 prisoners to the Nationalists. The government offensive of Premier Juan Negrín and War Minister Indalecio Prieto had ended in utter failure. *See* Gijón; Saragossa III; Vinaroz; Spanish Civil War.

Tettenhall (Rise of England), 910. Upon the death of Alfred the Great in 899, his son Edward succeeded to the crown of Wessex. With his sister Ethelfleda, "the Lady of the Mercians," Edward was forging a strong English kingdom when the Danes broke the peace in 910. The king marched his army northward into Staffordshire. On August 5 the Saxons fought a pitched battle at Tettenhall against the Northumbrian Danes. Edward, now called the Elder, won a decisive victory and soon thereafter established his rule as far north as the Humber. *See* Edington; Tempsford; Danish Invasions of Britain.

Teutoburger Wald (Germanic Wars of the Roman Empire), A.D. 9. Under the reign of Emperor Augustus (Octavian), Rome seemed to have successfully suppressed the half-wild Germanic tribes east of the Rhine. To keep the peace, Publius Quintilius Varus maintained a strong base in modern Westphalia with three legions of infantry and about 800 cavalry. In the autumn of A.D. 9 Varus was beguiled into making a march to the east to put down a local insurrection. This move was anticipated by the Cherusci chief Arminius (Hermann), who was serving as an auxiliary in the Roman army while at the same time arousing the Germans to revolt. The unsuspecting Varus marched into the Teutoburger Wald (Teutoberg Forest), between the Ems and Weser rivers. Here the maneuverability of his troops was severely limited by thick woods, marshes, and gullies. The heavy baggage train further slowed the pace. Arminius slipped away, almost unnoticed.

Near present-day Detmold the marching column was suddenly assaulted by a large force of Germans led by Arminius. At the first shower of enemy darts the lightly armed Roman auxiliaries (chiefly Germans themselves) deserted en masse. But the well-disciplined legions held their ground despite heavy casualties from the all but invisible tribesmen. When Varus attempted to resume his march the following day, he again suffered savage attacks. His cavalry, attempting to break free, was disorganized by the rough terrain and slaughtered in detail. By the end of the day only a handful of Roman infantry survived. The third day saw the end of the bloody ambush, with the last of the 20,000 Romans succumbing to Arminius' men. Varus committed suicide to avoid capture.

The massacre in the forest has sometimes been called one of the decisive battles of history. Although it only temporarily distressed the Roman Empire, it did force Augustus to accept the Rhine as the northern limit of his domain. This boundary would serve generally until the fifth century, when the Germans themselves poured westward across the river to help shatter the collapsing empire of Rome. *See* Lippe River; Minden I; Roman Empire.

Tewkesbury (Wars of the Roses), 1471. The defeat and death of the earl of Warwick (Richard Neville) at Barnet crippled, but did not destroy, the hope of Queen Margaret, wife of Henry VI, to place her Lancastrian (red rose) son Edward on the throne of England. From Weymouth she marched hurriedly northward toward the Welsh border where new allies could be recruited. Perceiving her plan, Edward IV led his Yorkist (white rose) army westward in an attempt to cut off the Lancastrians. Margaret's troops were commanded by the 4th Duke of Somerset (Edmund Beaufort), whose father and elder brother had already given their lives in the long, savage civil war. The Lancastrians, by marching 40 miles on the last day, reached their objective first. But Edward pressed forward to bring on the battle of Tewkesbury, at the confluence of the Avon and Severn rivers, on May 4.

Seeing an opening in Edward's ranks, Somerset left a strong defensive position on the Lancastrian left to attack the Yorkist center. His penetration was quickly contained and then taken in the flank by 200 of Edward's spearmen. Somerset was driven back in disorder, leaving his Lancastrian flank unguarded. The Yorkist men-at-arms rushed forward to roll up the enemy center. Here the 18-year-old Edward, Prince of Wales, fought bravely but was overcome and killed. The entire Lancastrian army now disintegrated, never to reassemble. Somerset and other nobles who survived the fighting were later beheaded. Queen Margaret gave herself up. The victorious Edward IV returned to London. His younger brother, the Duke of Gloucester (and future Richard III), visited the Tower on the night of May 21. The next day the old, hapless Lancastrian king, Henry VI, was found dead. Now the only surviving claimant to the crown of

England was the 14-year-old exile Henry Tudor, earl of Richmond. *See* Barnet; Bosworth Field; Roses, Wars of the.

Texan War of Independence (1836). The Mexican state of Texas proclaimed its independence in 1836. Although defeated in their first battle, the Texans won their independence two months later.

Alamo	1836
San Jacinto River	1836

Texel I (First English-Dutch War), 1653. After five inconclusive battles in English waters, the Commonwealth navy took the offensive in the First Dutch War. Under Gen. George Monck (later duke of Albemarle) an English force had sailed across the North Sea to engage the fleet of Adm. Maarten Tromp off the Dutch island of Texel. On July 30, 1653, the two navies battled without a decision. But on the following day Monck, reinforced by fresh ships, resumed the attack and defeated the Netherlanders. Tromp, who was killed in the fray, lost 20 of 100 ships through capture or sinking. English ship losses were comparable, but their personnel casualties were less than 400, a fourth of the Dutch total. This was the last battle of the war, peace being signed the following spring. *See* North Foreland I; Lowestoft; English-Dutch Wars.

Texel II (Third English-Dutch War), 1673. After being checked off Schooneveldt in June, the allied English and French navies returned to the Netherlands coast in August. Their mission was to land a body of troops to support the overland invasion of Louis XIV against William of Orange (later William III of England). The English (60 ships) under Prince Rupert of Germany (cousin of Charles II), and the French (30 ships), under Adm. the Comte Jean d'Estrées, arrived off the island of Texel on August 20. Here Adm. Michel de Ruyter, who had successfully maintained the Dutch maritime strength in two wars, met the allies again. With only 70 ships-of-the-line, the Dutch maneuvered so skillfully that much of the allied superiority was nullified. The furious battle continued until almost nightfall, when De Ruyter withdrew. Although no decisive victory was gained, the Dutch clearly removed the threat of a coastal invasion. Peace between England and Holland was concluded on February 7, 1674, although the Dutch-French war continued for another four years. *See* Schooneveldt; Maastricht II; English-Dutch Wars.

Thames River (War of 1812), 1813. The American naval victory on Lake Erie on September 10, 1813, opened the way for Gen. William H. Harrison to take the offensive against Upper Canada. With 4,500 troops, Harrison crossed the western end of Lake Erie to land in Ontario on September 27. The British commander, Gen. Henry Proctor, evacuating Detroit and Fort Malden, fell back northeast, over the protests of his Indian allies, who were led by the Shawnee chief Tecumseh. On October 5 Harrison overtook the British-Indian army on the north bank of the Thames River in southeastern Ontario. In a sharp encounter the Americans won the battle, largely through the attack of a mounted Kentucky regiment led by Col. Richard Johnson (later a vice president of the U.S.). At a cost of 15 killed and 30 wounded, the victors took 477 prisoners, plus another 48 killed or wounded. Among the slain lay Tecumseh. His death ended the effective Indian alliance with the British. The Old Northwest now stood secure except for Fort Michilimackinac in Michigan Territory, which stayed in enemy hands until the end of the war. *See* Erie, Lake; Chateaugay River; War of 1812.

Thapsus (Wars of the First Triumvirate), 46 B.C. During the three months after the battle at Ruspina, both Julius Caesar and the Pompeians strengthened their respective armies for the expected decisive struggle in North Africa. Caesar requisitioned enough troops to make 10 legions. The Pompeian force grew to the equivalent of 14 legions, under the command of four bitter enemies of Caesar: his former lieutenant Titus Labienus; Metellus Pius Scipio, one of the defeated leaders at Pharsalus; Sextus Pompey, son of the late Pompey the Great; and Juba I of Numidia, victor over Rome at the Bagradas River three years earlier. The battle took place near Thapsus, on the northeast coast of what is now Tunisia, on April 6. Caesar's tactical genius and the valor of his well-trained legionaries combined to crush the enemy coalition. Young Pompey and Labienus fled to Spain; Juba and Metellus Scipio committed suicide. At Utica Marcus Porcius Cato, the Younger, learned of the Caesarian victory and he too committed suicide. Only Spain remained to challenge the absolute rule of Caesar, who now received appointment from the Roman senate as dictator for ten years. *See* Ruspina; Munda; First Triumvirate, Wars of the.

Thebes (Macedonian Conquests), 335 B.C. Two years after his decisive triumph over the Greek city-states at Chaeronea, Philip II was assassinated. His son Alexander III, the Great, succeeded to the Macedonian throne. During a campaign against a barbarian force in the Balkans, Alexander was rumored to have been slain. Athens and Sparta immediately agreed to join Thebes in a revolt against Macedonian rule. Incited by Demosthenes, the Thebans surrounded the Macedonian occupation force in the city's acropolis, the Cadmea. Alexander suddenly appeared at Thebes with a relieving force. A Macedonian captain (later general), Perdiccas, led an assault into the city, which was supplemented by a sortie from the Cadmea. The Thebans were quickly overpowered.

To teach his subjects a lesson, Alexander ordered the execution of 6,000 inhabitants and the destruction of every building in the city except the former home of Pindar, the poet. With his Grecian holdings now secure, Alexander was free to launch his assault on the Persian Empire. *See* Chaeronea I; Granicus River; Macedonian Conquests.

Thermopylae I (Persian-Greek Wars), 480 B.C. Nine years after their repulse at Marathon the Persians renewed their attack on Greece. Xerxes, son of Darius I, led a 100,000-man force across the Dardanelles (then called the Hellespont) on a bridge of boats. Marching through Thrace and Macedonia, Xerxes turned left into Thessaly. At Thermopylae Pass, the gateway to Boeotia (and Attica), the Greeks took up a strong defensive position in the spring of 480 B.C. But the line was turned after three days of fighting, when the traitor Ephialtes showed the Persians a flanking route through another pass. To give the main body of 5,000 Greek hoplites time to withdraw to the south, Leonidas I of Sparta, with 300 of his men, fought a desperate rear-guard action against overwhelming odds. The defenders of Thermopylae died to the last man, but they held off the Persians long enough for their comrades to escape.

The Greeks then abandoned Attica to Xerxes (who razed Athens) and retired behind a wall built across the Isthmus of Corinth. The Persians followed to Salamis, which overlooks the Saronic Gulf. Here in September they saw their campaign hopes crushed in the naval battle of Salamis. *See* Marathon; Salamis; Persian-Greek Wars.

Thermopylae II (Wars of the Hellenistic Monarchies), 191 B.C. Antiochus III, the Great, of Syria saw that to the west the Roman victory over Macedonia at Cynoscephalae in 197 B.C. had left Greece seemingly powerless to resist seizure. Ignoring Roman interests in that land, the Seleucid monarch invaded Greece, where he won support only from the Aetolians. But Rome reacted quickly, landed an army in Epirus, and soon drove the Syrian army back to Thermopylae. Here 40,000 legionaries under Manius Acilius Glabrio and Marcus Porcius Cato attacked Antiochus, who held a strong defensive position with a smaller force. The Romans struck hard at a post held by 2,000 Aetolians and captured it. This exposed the main Syrian force to a Roman attack on the flank. In a fight reminiscent of the historic Persian-Greek battle at the pass almost 200 years earlier, the Syrians suffered a disastrous defeat. Antiochus (with his Carthaginian aide, Hannibal) re-embarked for Asia with only 500 survivors. *See* Cynoscephalae II; Panion; Magnesia; Roman Republic.

Third Coalition, War of. *See* Napoleonic Empire Wars.

Thirty-Eighth Parallel (Korean War), 1951–1953. The intervention of massive forces of Chinese Communist "volunteers" (actually the Third and Fourth Field armies) had driven the United Nations (UN) forces of Gen. Douglas MacArthur back to the 38th parallel by the end of 1950. Here Gen. Matthew Ridgway, in command of the American Eighth Army (since the death of Gen. Walton Walker in an automobile accident on December 23), deployed his three corps—from left (west) to right—across the width of the Korean peninsula: I (Frank Milburn), IX (John Coulter), and later the X (Edward Almond) farther east. On the far right three South Korean corps—I, II, and III—held the east end of the line. In all, Ridgway had 365,000 men from 18 different nations. In opposition stood 485,000 Communists composed of Gen. Lin Piao's Chinese and the North Koreans of Premier Kim Il Sung.

Early on January 1, 1951, the Communist troops, mostly Chinese, struck at the United Nations position following an all-night mortar and artillery barrage. The heaviest attack came against the I and IX corps, which were slowly forced back. Despite cruel casualties, the Communist attack rolled forward. Ridgway evacuated Inchon and the South Korean capital of Seoul on January 4. On the east, the X Corps gave up Wonju on January 10 in its retreat southward. Finally a stubborn United Nations defense, aided by strong air support, stabilized a line across the peninsula, about 75 miles south of the 38th parallel, on January 24.

The next day Ridgway launched a counteroffensive to the north. Day by day the United Nations troops slugged their way forward across a front suddenly turned fluid. In a battle aimed at attrition more than position, the UN troops drove back the Communist forces. In the west, Inchon and Kimpo Airfield (base of the F-86 Sabrejets, which had wrested control of the skies from the Russian-built MIG-15's) were recovered on February 10. Seoul was bypassed on the east and taken without a fight on March 14—the fourth time the now shattered city had changed hands. About this time Gen. Peng Teh-huai relieved Lin Piao as supreme Chinese commander in Korea. Late in March Ridgway's men recrossed the 38th parallel (except on the far left). This advance led to an irrevocable disagreement between MacArthur, who wanted to attack Chinese bases in Manchuria, and President Harry Truman, who insisted on limiting the war. On April 11 Truman relieved MacArthur. Ridgway became supreme commander, with Gen. James Van Fleet taking over the Eighth Army.

Meanwhile the Communist enemy built up personnel, armor, and artillery strength for their own offensive from the Iron Triangle. This open plateau—Chorwon, Kumhwa, Pyongyang—was a key road hub and staging area near the center of the peninsula, 20 to 30 miles north of the 38th parallel. On the night of April 22–23 the Chinese–North Korean forces launched a major offensive which hit hard in the Seoul area and extended eastward all the way to the Sea of Japan. For a week some 350,000 Communist troops pressed the offensive, with most of the attacks coming at night. Van Fleet was forced to give ground, but by the 1st of May had stabilized a line which covered Seoul in the west and then ran northeast to a point above the 38th parallel. The Communists then halted the attack to regroup and to replenish their heavy casualties. On the night of May 15–16, however, a second offensive smashed against the right (eastern) half of the UN line. The ROK III Corps in the center was annihilated, forcing the UN X Corps to withdraw south of the 38th parallel. Only determined resistance by the U.S. 2nd Infantry and 1st Marine divisions (reinforced by the U.S. 3rd Infantry Division) enabled Van Fleet to check the offensive, on May 20, after five days of savage fighting.

On the very next day the Eighth Army launched a counteroffensive all along the line. The exhausted, overextended Communist troops gave ground slowly but steadily. All the territory lost in the enemy's two spring attacks was rewon by the UN forces. By June 11 the Chorwon-Kumhwa base of the Iron Triangle was reached. To the east the so-called Punchbowl near Sohwa was being cleared. By June 15 the front line ran 20 miles north of the 38th parallel, except in the extreme west. During the almost constant fighting since April 22, the Communists are believed to have suffered upwards of 200,000 casualties. United Nations losses were markedly lower.

Hostilities ceased on July 10, 1951, in favor of peace talks. When these negotiations collapsed in August, Van Fleet resumed his limited, chopping-up offensive. But generally, both sides spent most of their time improving their defensive positions. When peace talks resumed at Panmunjon, all offensives gradually settled down to active but small-scale defensive operations. During the winter the 40th and 45th Infantry divisions replaced the 24th and 1st Cavalry. Throughout 1952 and the first half of 1953, patrolling, outpost skirmishing, and artillery and air attacks (almost exclusively by American planes) kept the war going and added to the casualty toll without altering the general tactical deployment. During this time Gen. Mark Clark replaced Ridgway as United Nations supreme commander. General Maxwell Taylor succeeded to command of the Eighth Army. Both sides continued to augment their forces until the United Nations strength stood at 768,000 men, that of the Communists well over a million.

After months of negotiations, blocked chiefly by the United Nation's demand for voluntary repatriation of war prisoners, sick and wounded prisoners were exchanged in Operation Little Switch, between April 20 and 26, 1953. Finally, on July 27, an armistice was signed that ended all overt fighting. The Eighth Army then turned to strengthening its defensive line along the war-torn 38th parallel between the Koreas, pending the settlement of a firm peace. *See* North Korea; Korean War.

Thirty Years' War (1618–1648). One of the most savage conflicts in history, the Thirty Years' War grew from a revolt in Bohemia into a European struggle between Catholic and Protestant powers. This predominantly religious phase may be subdivided into two distinct periods: Bohemian (1618–1625) and Danish (1625–1629). The war then developed into a political struggle against the house of Hapsburg first by Sweden and then France. These campaigns of conquest, fought almost exclusively on German soil, may also be subdivided into two periods: Swedish (1630–1635) and Swedish-French (1635–1648). Until 1637 the war found Ferdinand II, the Catholic Hapsburg Emperor of the Holy Roman Empire, and Philip IV of Spain aligned against Christian IV of Denmark and Norway and Gustavus II (Gustavus Adolphus) of Sweden. Ferdinand III, who succeeded his father, contended against the successors of Gustavus and the French armies sent out by the cardinals the Duc de Richelieu and Jules Mazarin. The Treaties of Westphalia, signed in 1648, granted indemnities to Sweden and France, recognized the republics of the United Netherlands and Switzerland, and provided more religious toleration for Protestants. Germany lay prostrate, denuded of manpower and wealth.

Bohemian Period

Pilsen	1618
Sablat	1619
White Mountain	1620
Wiesloch	1622
Wimpfen	1622
Höchst	1622
Fleurus I	1622
Stadtlohn	1623

Danish Period

Dessau Bridge	1626
Lutter am Barenberge	1626
Stralsund I	1628
Wolgast	1628

Swedish Period

Frankfort on the Oder	1631
Magdeburg	1631
Werben	1631
Breitenfeld I	1631
Rain	1632
Fürth	1632

Lützen I	1632
Nördlingen I	1634
Swedish-French Period	
Wittstock	1636
Rheinfelden	1638
Breisach	1638
Breitenfeld II	1642
Rocroi	1643
Tuttlingen	1643
Freiburg	1644
Jankau	1645
Mergentheim	1645
Nördlingen II	1645
Zusmarshausen	1648
Prague II	1648
Lens	1648

The continuation of the fighting between Spain and France (later joined by England) resulted in three more battles, often called the Spanish Fronde, before peace was achieved in the 1659 Treaty of the Pyrenees.

Arras I	1654
Valenciennes	1656
Dunes, the	1658

Thorn (Great Northern War), 1703. The last major obstacle to the conquest of Poland by Charles XII of Sweden was the strong fortress of Thorn (Toruń), on the Vistula 110 miles northwest of Warsaw. After his victory over a Saxon army at Pultusk in April 1703, the Swedish king marched on Thorn with 10,000 troops. The defending garrison numbered about 5,000 men. (The deposed—by Charles—king of Poland and elector of Saxony, Augustus II, was in hiding.) Despite a gallant defense, for a short time, Thorn fell to the Swedish besiegers on September 22.

The following year, with all Poland at his feet, Charles forced the election of Stanislas Leszczyński to the throne. He then proceeded to a methodical conquest of all opposition in both Poland and Saxony, including the ouster of a Russian army (1705–06) sent by Peter I, the Great, to harass Charles. On September 24, 1707, at Altranstädt, in Saxony, the hapless Augustus II officially renounced his claim to the crown of Poland and his anti-Swedish alliance. Charles was now ready to turn on his last remaining foe, Russia. *See* Pultusk I; Holowczyn; Great Northern War.

"Three Emperors, Battle of the." *See* Austerlitz.

Three Henrys, War of the. *See* Coutras.

"Three Kings, Battle of the." *See* Alcázarquivir.

Tiberias (Crusader-Turkish Wars), 1187. While the Frankish leaders of Christian Palestine and Syria (which together were called Outremer) quarreled among themselves, the able Turkish general Saladin grew stronger. In 1183 he took over Aleppo from a rival Turkish chieftain and three years later he absorbed Mosul. Now Egypt and Syria were firmly united under one Moslem ruler. The first consequence of divided Frankish rule in the face of Saladin's power came in Galilee in May 1187. Led by the Grand Master of the Temple, 143 Templar and lay knights charged a Mameluke army of 7,000 cavalrymen at the Springs of Cresson. All but the Grand Master and two other knights perished on the field.

On July 1 Saladin crossed the Jordan River and, with a powerful army of 60,000 Turks, laid siege to the fortress of Tiberias, on the western shore of the Lake of Galilee. To relieve Tiberias, the Franks assembled the largest Christian army to appear in the Near East. Carrying a part of the True Cross as their standard, the Frankish leaders—Reynald of Chatillon (prince regent of Antioch), Raymond III of Tripoli, in Lebanon, and King Guy of Lusignan of Jerusalem—moved eastward from Acre with 10,000 infantrymen, 1,200 mounted knights in armor, and some 2,000 light cavalry. On the march of July 3 the crusader column suffered terribly from the heat, lack of water, and harassing raids by mounted Turkish bowmen. Late in the day King Guy of Jerusalem halted the army only three miles short of the Sea of Galilee, at waterless Hattin—his men thirsty, exhausted, and demoralized.

At dawn on July 4 Saladin's rested and watered army attacked the Christian camp from all sides, filling the air with arrows. King Guy's infantry defied his order to stand fast and surged toward the sea. They were surrounded on a hilltop (called

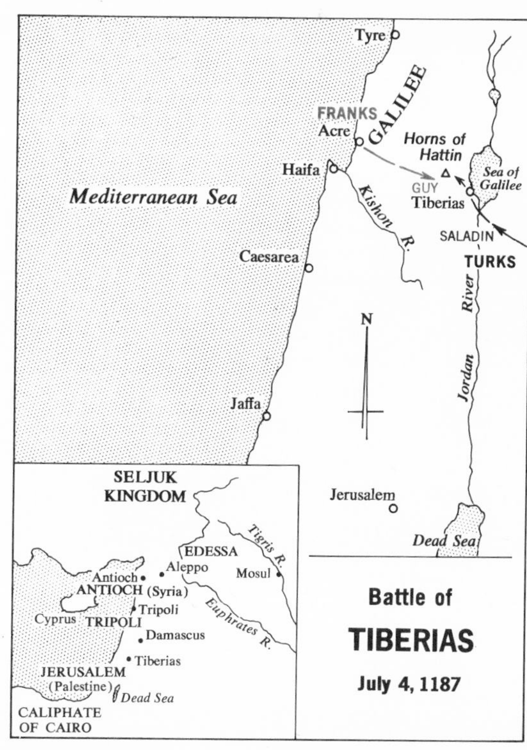

Battle of TIBERIAS July 4, 1187

the Horns of Hattin), where Turkish mounted archers inflicted heavy casualties before the whole group surrendered. Without water they could not continue the battle. The knights and their horses, also suffering from thirst and now without the protection of infantry, became encircled and thus easy targets for Turkish arrows. Only Raymond of Tripoli, Balian of Ibelin, Reynald of Sidon, and a few others cut their way free. The relic of the True Cross was captured by the Moslems, along with King Guy, his brother Amalric (later Amalric II of Jerusalem), Reynald of Chatillon (who was beheaded), and most of the other nobles of the land. The most important captives were held for ransom; some warriors were executed; most of the foot soldiers were sold as slaves.

The fortress of Tiberias capitulated the following day. Saladin then marched to the coast to shut off the crusaders' sea communications. Within two months, Acre, Jaffa, Ashkelon, and Gaza had fallen to the Turks. Only Tyre and, of course, Jerusalem held out (plus Tripoli, in Lebanon, and Antioch, which were protected by truces scrupulously observed by Saladin). As the Holy City refused to surrender, the Moslem general now moved his army there. *See* Ramle II; Jerusalem VIII; Crusades.

Tigranocerta I (Third Mithridatic War), 69 B.C. When the Roman army of L. Licinius Lucullus drove Mithridates VI Eupator out of Pontus in 73 B.C., the Asian monarch took refuge with his son-in-law Tigranes the Great of Armenia. Lucullus doggedly pursued and four years later besieged Tigranocerta (Siirt), the fortified capital of Armenia, on a tributary of the Tigris River. To relieve the city, Tigranes assembled some 100,000 Pontic and Armenian troops to attack the 10,000 Roman besiegers. In a pitched battle outside the walls of the capital, the Asiatic superiority in numbers was more than offset by the stern discipline of the legionaries and the able leadership of Lucullus. Maneuvering to high ground in the rear of Tigranes, the Romans charged and dispersed the enemy cavalry. Then falling upon the unescorted Asian infantry, Lucullus put them to rout as well.

The Roman commander tried to continue his campaign, but his troops refused to enter the mountains of Armenia. Meanwhile, Lucullus, despite his brilliant victories, had fallen into disfavor at home. Urged on by the rising orator M. Tullius Cicero, the Roman government recalled Lucullus. Pompey the Great was sent to Asia to conclude the war. *See* Cyzicus II; Nicopolis-in-Armenia; Mithridatic Wars.

Tigranocerta II (Parthian Wars of the Roman Empire), A.D. 59. When he was driven out of Artaxata in A.D. 58, Tiridates I fled southwest to Tigranocerta (Siirt). The victorious Roman general, Gnaeus Domitius Corbulo, spent the winter near the remains of the ancient Armenian capital and then marched in pursuit. Tiridates used troops sent forward by his brother, the Parthian king Vologesus I, to harass the Roman column, but he could not halt it. Corbulo pressed steadily forward to enter and occupy Tigranocerta that autumn. Here Corbula installed Tigranes, a friend of Rome, on the throne of Armenia. This arrangement brought only two years of peace with Parthia, however. *See* Artaxata; Arsanias River; Roman Empire.

Tigris River (Persian Wars of the Roman Empire), 363. When Julian became undisputed emperor of Rome upon the death of Constantius II, he was already famous for his reconquest of Gaul and his public espousal of paganism (hence the name "Apostate"). The most serious threat to his reign lay to the East, where Shapur (Sapor) II of Sassanian Persia was systematically seizing Amida, Singara, and other Roman outposts in Mesopotamia. Julian assembled an army in Syria and early in 363 began to drive back the Persian invaders. Reaching the Tigris River, he forced a crossing in the face of strong Persian opposition. The emperor evidently planned to assault the enemy capital of Ctesiphon but then switched his objective to the Persian army. While moving northward up the left bank of the Tigris, the Roman army fell under heavy attack by superior enemy forces. Julian suffered a mortal wound and died in camp.

The Roman soldiers proclaimed one of their generals, Jovian, the new emperor. Jovian accepted peace terms from Shapur, which ceded all Roman claims to territory east of the Tigris. He died, however, early in 364, before he could return to Europe. *See* Argentoratum; Amida I; Châlons-sur-Marne I; Roman Empire.

Timisoara (Hungarian Revolt), 1849. The military success of the Hungarian rebels under Gen. Arthur von Görgey led their diet to proclaim a republic on April 13, 1849. This alarmed the Russian czar Nicholas I, who sent troops to support the Austrian Empire of Franz Josef I. In June a Russian army under Field Marshal Ivan Paskevich (Prince of Warsaw) pressed into Hungary from the north, while Gen. Baron Julius von Haynau invaded from the west with an Austrian army. Hungarian resistance slowly crumbled. On August 9 a rebel army commanded by the Polish patriot Gen. Henryk Dembiński made a stand at Timisoara (Temesvár) in southwestern Rumania against the Austrians. The Hungarians suffered a total rout and were never able to take the field again. Four days later Görgey surrendered the remaining rebel army to the Russians at Világos. Dembiński and Lajos Kossuth, governor-president, fled to Turkey.

Görgey was interned by the Austrians. But nine rebel generals were hanged and four shot at Arad by the bloodthirsty Haynau. Hungary was stripped of its historic identity and absorbed into the Austrian Empire. (After the Austrian defeat in the Seven Weeks' War in 1866, however, Hungary became a part of the dual monarchy of Austria-Hungary). *See* Kápolna; Hungarian Revolt.

Tinchebray (Norman Civil War), 1106. The rule of William II, Rufus, ended with his death on a hunting expedition in 1100. Henry Beauclerc, the younger brother, claimed the crown, but it took him six years to crush out all opposition in England. In Normandy, however, the older brother, Robert II, duke of Normandy, remained defiant. The English king, now Henry I, crossed the Channel with an army and attacked the Norman rebels at Tinchebray on September 28. In the greatest battle since Hastings, Henry's knights won a decisive victory. Robert was captured and imprisoned in England until his death 28 years later. England and Normandy were united again under a single ruler. *See* Alnwick I; Brémule.

Tinian (World War II). The third and last of the Japanese-held Mariana Islands to be successfully invaded by U.S. troops, on July 24, 1944. *See* Mariana Islands.

Tippecanoe Creek (Tecumseh's Confederacy), 1811. The steady westward sweep of white settlement in the Old Northwest Territory provoked the Shawnee chief Tecumseh to organize a defensive Indian confederacy. Alarmed frontiersmen then demanded the destruction of the Indian capital of Prophetstown, at the junction of Tippecanoe Creek and the Wabash River. On September 26, 1811, William Henry Harrison, governor of Indiana Territory and a captain in the regular army, marched northward from Vincennes, Ind., with an army of 1,000 men. Covering 150 miles in six weeks, Harrison encamped a mile below the Indian village on November 6. At dawn the next day the camp was attacked by the Indians under the command of "the Prophet" (Tenskwatawa), brother of Tecumseh who was temporarily absent. In a furious day-long battle Harrison's troops beat back the assault. After destroying the village on November 8, the Americans retired to Fort Harrison, 65 miles above Vincennes. The battle on the Tippecanoe broke the back of Indian resistance in the Old Northwest but only increased American hostility to the British government in Canada, which had lent support to the uprising. This British aid to the Indians was one of the causes of the War of 1812 that broke out the following year. *See* Detroit; Thames River; Indian Wars in the United States.

Tippermuir (English Civil War), 1644. With the main Scottish army, commanded by the Earl of Leven (Alexander Leslie) and his brother Gen. David Leslie, fighting in England on the side of the Roundheads, Scotland itself became a power vacuum. A former Covenanter, the Earl (later Marquis) of Montrose (James Graham), commissioned by King Charles I, rallied the Highland clans to the Cavalier cause in 1644. To oppose this force, Lord Elcho (David Wemyss, later 2nd earl of Wemyss) organized a Covenanter army of 5,000 men. The two antagonists clashed at Tippermuir, in east-central Scotland, on September 1. Although the Scottish Royalists were greatly outnumbered, Montrose led them to an overwhelming victory, killing 2,000 of the Covenanters. The able general moved forward to occupy nearby Perth two weeks later, and then Aberdeen. *See* Marston Moor; Inverlochy; English Civil War.

Tisza River (Conquests of Charlemagne), 795–796. The barbarian Avars had long worried Charlemagne with their threat to eastern Bavaria and to northeastern Italy. The great king had personally led a Frankish expedition to the Avar stronghold along the Danube in 790 but had failed to subdue the fierce and elusive tribe. Finally, in 795, he sent out a column of troops from Bavaria and another from Italy. Joining forces beyond the upper Danube, the Franks forced their way across the Tisza (Theiss) River, a northern tributary of the Danube, to the Avar stronghold, a settlement enclosed by a huge ring of earthworks. Eric of Friuli led the Frankish charge that routed the barbarian defenders. The spoil amounted to 15 cartloads of treasure, which the Avars had accumulated during two centuries of raids against Constantinople and western Europe. The Avars vanished from history. And a grateful Pope Leo III crowned Charlemagne Emperor of the West (later Holy Roman Emperor) at Saint Peter's in Rome, on Christmas Day 800. *See* Süntelberg; Charlemagne, Conquests of.

Tobruk I (World War II), 1941. Continuing the first British offensive in Libya, Gen. Sir Richard O'Connor's XIII Corps pressed westward from Bardia on January 4, 1941. Three days later the British reached Tobruk and promptly laid siege to the Italian-held city, which guarded the best harbor in Libya. Then, on January 21, the 6th Australian and the 7th Armoured divisions assaulted the fortress, defended by 32,000 Italian troops commanded by Gen. Petassi Manella. (This force was part of Marshal Rodolpho Graziani's Tenth Army.) The initial attack split the perimeter defenses. By the evening of the second day Tobruk was in British hands, with only small losses. Manella and 25,000 of his men were taken prisoner. Continuing his Libyan advance, O'Connor pressed westward toward Benghazi. *See* Bardia; Beda Fomm; World War II.

Tobruk II (World War II), 1941. Gen. Erwin

Rommel's first Axis offensive in North Africa began on March 24, 1941, at El Agheila, Libya. Meeting thin British resistance, he drove eastward rapidly, recapturing an evacuated Benghazi on April 4 and reaching Tobruk four days later. This latter fortress was garrisoned chiefly by the 9th Australian Division of Gen. Morshead. Rommel's troops stormed Tobruk during April 10–14 and again on April 30 but were beaten back each time. Meanwhile the Axis counterattack carried eastward to the Egyptian frontier on April 28. For 240 days the Tobruk garrison resisted siege, as the Royal Navy brought in supplies and replaced the Australians with the 70th Infantry. Finally, on November 29, a British Eighth Army victory at Sidi-Rezegh relieved Tobruk. *See* Salûm–Halfaya Pass; Sidi-Rezegh; World War II.

Tobruk III (World War II), 1942. In Gen. (later Field Marshal) Erwin Rommel's second offensive in Libya, his *Panzerarmee Afrika* smashed through the British defenses at Gazala and drove the Eighth Army back across the Egyptian border. Urged on by Prime Minister Winston Churchill, Gen. Neil Ritchie unwisely left behind a force of 35,000 men, chiefly the 2nd South African Division, to hold Tobruk. On June 17 Rommel captured the key point of Sidi-Rezegh and then turned northwest to attack Tobruk itself. After a two-day assault by the 15th and 21st Panzer divisions, Gen. Klopper surrendered 33,000 men and a huge accumulation of supplies. The staggering defeat opened the way for an Axis drive in Egypt and cost Ritchie his job.

Following the decisive British victory at El Alamein in the fall of 1942, the Axis *Panzerarmee* retreated across Libya, passing through Tobruk without a fight on November 13, 1942. *See* Gazala; Mersa Matrûh; El Alamein II; World War II.

Tokyo (Japanese Revolution), 1868. A long-standing cleavage between proforeign and antiforeign parties in Japan brought on civil war in 1868. The uprising, led by men wanting to restore the central power of the emperor, forced the resignation of Hitotsubashi, last of the Tokugawa shoguns. This ended almost 700 years of feudal military government. On July 4 the last of the shogunate followers were defeated in Tokyo, then called Edo. The new emperor, Mutsuhito (Meiji), moved the capital from Kyoto to renamed Tokyo. *See* Chinese-Japanese War I.

Tolbiacum (Rise of France), 496. While the Merovingian king Clovis I was attempting to unite all the Franks under one rule, his reign was threatened by an invasion from what is now Germany. The savage Alamanni tribe was once again swarming across the Rhine toward Lorraine. Clovis marched eastward to meet the invaders at Tolbiacum (Zülpich), near Cologne. In the fierce struggle that followed, the Alamanni seemed to have the edge over the ax-wielding Franks. But then Clovis personally led a charge that routed the invaders. The Alamanni were driven back across the Rhine for the last time.

It has been reported that Clovis had sworn to become a Christian, the religion of his wife Clotilda, if he were victorious in this battle. True or not, Clovis and several thousand of his soldiers were baptized on Christmas Day 496 by Remigius, bishop of Rheims (Reims). *See* Soissons; Vouillé.

Toledo I (Spanish-Moslem Wars), 1085. The Christian counteroffensive against the Moslems in Spain, which began in the north in 934, pressed slowly but steadily forward. In 1083 Alfonso VI, the Valiant, of Castile and León captured Madrid and two years later launched an attack against the Moorish stronghold of Toledo in central Spain. The assault succeeded. The Moors were expelled and the city became the capital of the united kingdoms of Castile and León (until the Spanish capital passed to Madrid in 1560). When the Almoravids of northwestern Africa swept into Spain the following year, only Castilian Toledo and Aragonese Saragossa were able to hold the line of Christian Spain. *See* Zamora; Zallaka.

Toledo II (Spanish Civil War), 1936. When the hastily armed militia of the Republican government had seemingly routed the rebel (Nationalist) garrisons in Madrid, they hurried 40 miles southwest to Toledo on July 20. The city promptly fell to the Republicans except for the Alcázar, the palace-fortress that commanded Toledo and the Tagus River. Here Col. José Moscardo had assembled about 1,300 men—members of the Civil Guard, army officers, Falangists, and cadets from the Military Academy. Unable to dislodge this force from behind their barricades, the militia settled down to a siege of the Alcázar. Two months later the Nationalist armies of Col. José Varela pushed two columns up the Tagus Valley, choosing to relieve the Alcázar rather than to make an immediate assault on Madrid. In a four-day march Varela swung north of Toledo and cut the road to Madrid on September 26. The Nationalists then stormed into the city, the better-trained Moroccan troops routing the militia and relieving the fortress the following day. A massacre of all suspected Republicans followed. Madrid would be the next, and most important, target of the Nationalist forces. *See* Madrid; Málaga III; Spanish Civil War.

Tolentino (Napoleon's Hundred Days), 1815. When Napoleon Bonaparte landed in France from Elba early in 1815, one of the first to declare for the returned emperor was Marshal Joachim Murat, a brother-in-law and former king of Naples. Murat hurried to Italy to regain his former kingdom. He put himself at the head of an Italian army. Despite Napoleon's warning not to fight a major battle at this time, Murat challenged a large Austrian army under Gen. Bianchi at Tolentino, 100 miles northeast of Rome, on May 3. Murat's Italians were badly beaten and dispersed beyond recall. Murat fled to France. After the defeat of Napoleon at Waterloo, Murat was captured and executed on October 13. The Bourbon monarch Ferdinand was restored to the throne at Naples as Ferdinand IV (and the following year to the kingdom of the Two Sicilies as Ferdinand I). *See* Paris I; Ligny; Waterloo; Napoleon's Hundred Days.

Tongres (Gallic Wars), 54 B.C. During the winter after his invasion of Britain, Julius Caesar had to encamp his Roman legions over a wide area of Gaul because of a grain scarcity. In modern Belgium the Eburonian chief Ambiorix took advantage of this disposition to attack an isolated detachment at Tongres (Tongeren). Although the assault failed, the Roman commander, Titurius Sabinus, agreed to accept the Gauls' offer of safe passage to the nearest Roman station, at Namur, 50 miles away. While the column of 9,000 men was on the march, it was suddenly attacked by an overwhelming number of Eburones. The entire force, including Sabinus, was slaughtered.

Ambiorix pressed on to besiege the Namur encampment, commanded by Quintus Cicero. He was driven off, however, by a relief force led by Julius Caesar himself. The Roman commander then decided to spend the rest of the winter with his army in Gaul, rather than return to Italy as was his custom. *See* Verulamium I; Avaricum; Gallic Wars.

Torgau (Seven Years' War), 1760. The long campaign of maneuver and combat in 1760 headed toward a climax in the autumn. Field Marshal Count Leopold von Daun, at the head of 65,000 Austrian and other troops of the Holy Roman Empire (Maria Theresa), moved to Torgau on the Elbe. When he learned of the approach of a large Prussian army under Frederick II, the Great, Daun organized a fortified camp south and west of the city. The Prussian king marched up from the south with 44,000 men. Despite the Imperial advantage in numbers and position, Frederick resolved to attack on November 3. He sent Gen. Hans von Zieten to charge the enemy front, while he circled wide to the left (west) to come in on Daun's rear with the main assault. Zieten rode forward with his cavalry but soon encountered Austrian light troops in front of the main defensive position. In overcoming this opposition, he failed to launch his attack at the prearranged time of 2 P.M. As a result, when Frederick struck the enemy position, he met the full force of the Austrian artillery and musket fire. Out of 6,000 blue-clad grenadiers in the initial assault, only 600 survived volleys of grape and case shot from 400 enemy guns. But the king recklessly poured in reserves. Finally, at sunset, this continued pressure, plus the belated attack of Zieten, forced an entry into the Austrian lines. As the savage fighting raged on in the darkness, Daun pulled his army back into the city and later across the Elbe.

Frederick had taken Torgau, but it had cost him 13,120 casualties, almost a third of his force. The Austrians lost 4,200 in killed and wounded and 7,000 prisoners. Both sides were too crippled to renew hostilities that year. And with the bloody memory of Torgau still fresh in the minds of the commanders, the campaign of 1761 became one of maneuver and countermaneuver. *See* Liegnitz II; Burkersdorf; Seven Years' War.

Toro (Castilian Civil War), 1476. The death of Henry IV of Castile in 1474 led to a dynastic war for the vacant throne. Henry had designated his sister Isabella I, called the Catholic, to succeed him. But the widowed queen, Juana of Portugal, claimed the crown for her daughter (probably illegitimate), also named Juana. The daughter's interests were supported by some Spanish nobles and by her uncle and husband, Alfonso V of Portugal. To support Juana's claim, an army of perhaps 8,000 men, led by Alfonso, marched to Toro on the Duero River in northwestern Spain. Meanwhile, Isabella's husband, Ferdinand V (also called the Catholic), the future Ferdinand II of Aragon, raised an army and moved on Toro. In a sharp two-hour attack on March 1, 1476, Ferdinand's troops routed the Portuguese and Castilian rebels. Isabella's crown rested securely.

The succession of Ferdinand to the throne of Aragon in 1479 united that state with Castile and markedly strengthened Spanish rule. A stepped-up campaign against Moorish-held Granada became one of the early objectives of the new union. *See* Alhama de Granada.

Toronto (Canadian Rebellion), 1837. Long-standing grievances between the British-appointed governors and the popularly elected assemblies finally erupted into rebellion in 1837. In Lower Canada, where the uprising was confined to the Montreal area, the rebels were quickly routed, their leaders fleeing to the United States. In Upper Canada, William Mackenzie collected an army of 800 insurgents. On December 5 he attacked Toronto, seeking to set up a provisional government. But the rebels were driven off by a force under Lt. Gov. Sir John Colborne. Mackenzie fled to Buffalo, N.Y., where his rebel activities provoked tense relations between Canada and the United States for a time. Although Mackenzie's mission failed, it dramatized abuses in the British government of Canada and paved the way toward the achievement of dominion status for Canada 30 years later. *See* Batoche.

Toulon I (War of the Spanish Succession), 1707. The victory of Prince Eugene of Savoy at Turin in 1706 prompted the allied commander, the Duke of Marlborough (John Churchill), to launch an attack on the French port of Toulon the following year. Eugene and the army of the Holy Roman Empire, under Victor Amadeus II, duke of Savoy, marched southwest along the Mediterranean coast. They were supplied and supported by a strong English fleet commanded by Adm. Sir Cloudesley Shovell. When the land force reached Toulon, Shovell landed thousands of marines, sailors, and cannon to assist the attack. But the French were determinedly massing to defend their great port.

On July 17 the joint expedition launched its critical attack against the city. But through lack of enterprise, the assault faltered and then collapsed. The Imperials retreated into Italy, while Shovell, after destroying several French ships in the harbor, also withdrew. On his return to England he was shipwrecked and lost, along with three of his warships. Thus ended the fighting in 1707—a year of defeats for the allies at the hands of a resurgent France. *See* Turin; Stollhofen; Oudenarde; Spanish Succession, War of the.

Toulon II (War of the Austrian Succession), 1744. The first sea battle of the war grew out of a British (George II) attempt to cut the naval communications between France (Louis XV) and northern Italy. Late in 1743 the English admiral Thomas Matthews blockaded the Mediterranean port of Toulon with 29 vessels. On February 19 the French admiral De Court sailed from Toulon with 15 ships of his own fleet and 12 warships from the navy of France's ally, Spain (Philip V). Three days later the two hostile fleets clashed in a confused and contradictory fight. Subordinate commanders on both sides refused to obey the orders of their superiors. After inflicting the greater damage, the Franco-Spanish fleet broke off the action, losing only one ship (to Capt. Edward Hawke, who was later to gain wider fame). Matthews and three of his captains were court-martialed and cashiered from the service. *See* Velletri; Finisterre Cape I; Austrian Succession, War of the.

Toulon III (Wars of the French Revolution), 1793. After the French defeat at Neerwinden on March 18, 1793, and the defection of the able general Charles Dumouriez, the National Convention troops were driven out of the Austrian Netherlands and to the northeast, back across the Rhine. In the south, the key naval base of Toulon opened its gates to a contingent of British, Spanish, and Royalists on August 29. But just when the situation looked blackest for France, Georges Danton's Committee of Public Safety took charge. A new vigor possessed the nation and the army. At Toulon a French army under Gen. Dugommier laid siege to the garrison, commanded by British general Lord Mulgrave (Sir Henry Phipps). By December 18 all the land defenses had been taken, forcing Mulgrave to evacuate by sea. Much of the assault's success was due to the actions of a young artillery captain named Napoleon Bonaparte. *See* Neerwinden II; Hondschoote; French Revolution Wars.

Toulouse I (Moslem Invasion of France), 721. The hard-hitting Moslem cavalry, which had overrun all of Spain except the northwest corner, soon rode across the Pyrenees into southern France. Toulouse fell in 718 and Narbonne a year later. In 721, however, Duke Eudes (Odo) of Aquitaine rallied the Franks and challenged the invaders near Toulouse. The Moslem horsemen were severely beaten by ax-wielding infantry; their leader, al-Samh ibn-Malik, was killed. This Frankish victory checked the raiders' advance for a time. But a more formidable Moslem invasion would be launched 11 years later. *See* Covadonga; Tours; Moslem Conquests.

Toulouse II (Napoleonic Empire Wars), 1814. With Spain liberated from the French armies of Napoleon I by the end of 1813, the victorious general Lord Wellington (Arthur Wellesley) marched across the western Pyrenees into France itself. (In the east Marshal Louis Suchet withdrew across the Pyrenees in March 1814.) Pressing northward, Wellington drove the French commander Marshal Nicolas Soult away from Bayonne. On March 12, 1814, the 25,000-man British and Spanish army occupied Bordeaux, while Soult fell back eastward across the Garonne River. Wellington pursued. Bridging the river on April 10, the English general attacked Soult at Toulouse. The French army of some 30,000 men beat back a premature assault by Spanish troops north of the city. But a British attack led by Gen. Sir William Carr Beresford (later Lord Beresford) drove the French out of the city. Soult retreated with a loss of 3,000 troops. Wellington's casualties totaled 4,600, including about 2,000 Spanish.

This was the last battle of the Peninsular War and, in fact, the last for the First French Empire. Napoleon I abdicated unconditionally the following day, accepting exile on the island of Elba. *See* Vitoria; Paris I; Tolentino; Ligny; Napoleonic Empire Wars.

Tou Morong (Vietnam War), 1966. As the 1966 monsoon season approached, a large Communist force threatened to overrun the outpost of Tou Morong in the central highlands province of Kontum. To relieve the somewhat isolated outpost, which was held by a South Vietnamese unit, Gen. Willard Pearson, commander of the U.S. 1st Brigade of the 101st Airborne Division, launched a three-pronged offensive. On June 5 three attacking battalions converged on Tou Morong. They were the 1st Battalion of the U.S. 327th Infantry, from the northeast; a South Vietnamese Ranger battalion, from the northwest; and the 42nd Battalion of the South Vietnamese regular army (ARVN), from the southwest. During this maneuver phase of Operation Hawthorne, as the offensive was called, the Allied forces encountered little opposition. But at 0200 hours on June 7 a North Vietnamese force struck hard at the American-held position north of Tou Morong. The Communists were beaten off in a seven-hour battle, leaving 85 dead around the perimeter. The Allied troops, aided by two more American battalions—from the 502nd Infantry and the 5th Cavalry—then began encircling the 24th North Vietnamese Regiment in that area. In the next six days and nights of heavy jungle fighting more than 1,200 Communist troops were killed and wounded. The Americans and South Vietnamese, who had been supported by 27,000 rounds of artillery and 473 air sorties, suffered only one dead to every ten enemy killed. The operation to relieve Tou Morong had been turned into a major victory over the Communists in northern Kontum Province. *See* South Vietnam; Vietnam War.

Tourcoing (Wars of the French Revolution), 1794. To open the third year of the war, both sides launched offensives in the northwest. From the Austrian Netherlands the allied commander, the Prince of Saxe-Coburg (Friedrich Josias), marched into Flanders. At Tourcoing, eight miles northeast of Lille, he bumped head on into the French army of Gen. Charles Pichegru, sent northward by the National Convention's defense minister, Lazare Carnot. On May 18, 1794, the allied army divided into five columns, in an attempted encirclement of the Revolutionary forces. But delays in maneuvering and stubborn French resistance immobilized all but the two center columns. Isolated from the flanking units, the allied center was overwhelmed by a vigorous French counterattack, which inflicted 5,500 casualties. The French pressed on to take Charleroi, in modern Belgium, on June 25, leading to a decisive battle between the French and allied armies. *See* Wattignies; Fleurus III; French Revolution Wars.

Tournai (War of the Spanish Succession), 1709. During the winter of 1708–09, peace negotiations broke down when the allies demanded that Louis XIV of France drive his grandson Philip V from the throne of Spain. The war resumed in the spring. The Duke of Marlborough (John Churchill) determined to march the allied army of 100,000 men to Paris. Barring his way was the strongly fortified city of Tournai, on the Schelde River, in the Spanish Netherlands (now Belgium), and the French army of 90,000 commanded by Marshal Duc Claude de Villars. Fearing to bypass Tournai, Marlborough, assisted by Prince Eugene of Savoy, invested the city on June 27. Villars was unable to relieve the fortress and it fell on September 3. French losses totaled about 3,000. The allies—English, Dutch, German—then moved southeast to Mons. The fall of Tournai preserved Marlborough's record of never failing to take a city he had besieged. *See* Lille; Malplaquet; Spanish Succession, War of the.

Tours (Moslem Invasion of France), 732. The fierce Moslems, who had conquered Spain by 713, began raiding northward into France five years later. In the summer of 732 Abd-er-Rahman, the Arabian emir of Spain, led a huge invasion army across the western Pyrenees. At the Garonne River, Duke Eudes (Odo) of Aquitaine tried to check the Moslem flood, but his Franks were easily brushed aside. Abd-er-Rahman pressed on toward the Loire River at the head of more than 60,000 hard-riding cavalrymen.

Fortunately for the Franks, Charles Martel (the Hammer) had continued the unifying program of his father, Pepin II, among the Austrasian and Neustrian Franks. Now he hurriedly assembled Frankish infantry and deployed them in a solid square between Tours and Poitiers, directly in the path of the oncoming Moslem cavalry. The invaders rushed forward, relying on the tactics that had won them so many victories during their century of conquest—slashing attacks, an overwhelming number of horsemen, and a wild fervor that could be stopped only by killing. Despite the

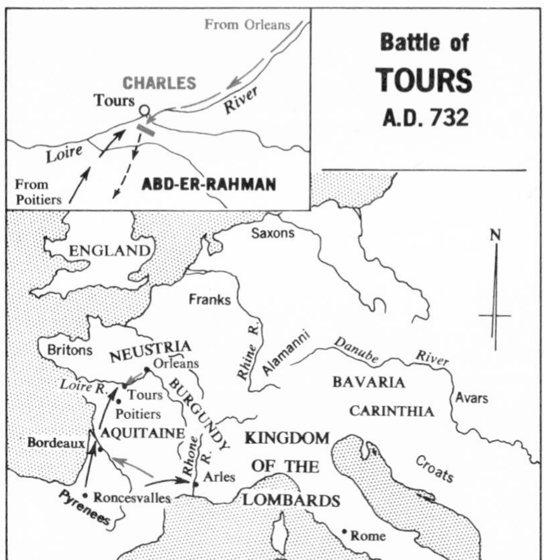

ferocity of the assault, the Frankish square stood firm while the foot soldiers chopped down men and horses with their swords and axes. It was one of the rare times in the Middle Ages when infantry held its ground against mounted attack. The Moslems struck again and again—for two days according to Arab sources, seven days by Christian accounts. Finally the fall of Abd-er-Rahman himself took the steam out of the Moslem onslaught. Under cover of night the invaders began to fall back. Not wishing to trust his undisciplined Franks to a pursuit, Charles Martel permitted the Moslems to withdraw unhindered. But a pursuit was unnecessary. The sharp setback, the death of their leader, and frightful casualties combined to mark Tours as the high-water mark of the Moslem invasion of western Europe. They continued to retreat southward, recrossing the Pyrenees, never to return, in 759. The victory of Charles Martel on this field is often called one of the most decisive battles of history. *See* Covadonga; Toulouse I; Moslem Conquests.

Towton (Wars of the Roses), 1461. To enforce his claim to the English crown, Edward IV marched a large Yorkist (white rose) army northward to attack the Lancastrian (red rose) forces of the legitimate King Henry VI and Queen Margaret. On March 28, 1461, Edward's army, ably commanded by the Earl of Warwick (Richard Neville), defeated the Lancastrians at Ferrybridge, to force the Aire River in western Yorkshire. The following day the Yorkists launched an attack against the royalists, who occupied a strong position on a slope at Towton, their right flank secured by Cock Creek. With a blinding snowstorm at their back, attacking spearmen reached the opponents' front lines unobserved. At the same time the favorable wind enabled the Yorkist archers to kill and maim at a range beyond the reach of Lancastrian arrows. To end this double dilemma, the 20,000 royalists left their positions to charge downhill on their tormentors. The next six hours witnessed one of the most ruthless battles ever to take place on English soil. Thousands fell to sword, lance, and spear. Finally, late in the day, the Yorkist Duke of Norfolk (John Mowbray VI) came up with fresh troops to smash into the Lancastrians' exposed flank. Henry's men broke and fled. Hundreds of heavily armored knights drowned trying to ford the waters of the Cock. To be taken prisoner meant certain beheading. Queen Margaret and her young son Edward and the helpless king set out for the safety of the Scottish border.

Edward marched triumphantly into York, removed the heads of his father, Richard, and the other Yorkist nobles slain at Wakefield, and impaled the fresh skulls of Devonshire, Exeter, and other Lancastrian lords. On June 28 the new king was crowned at Westminster. The Yorkist victory seemed complete, but Margaret's will and thirst for vengeance remained unquenched. *See* Saint Albans II; Ferrybridge; Hedgeley Moor; Roses, Wars of the.

Toyotomi Castle (Conquest by Tokugawa Shogunate), 1614–1615. After his decisive victory at Sekigahara, Gen. Iyeyasu stood supreme over all of Japan except the Toyotomi Castle in Osaka. Here Hideyori, the sole surviving son of Toyotomi Hideyoshi, with his mother and some loyal followers, formed an island of resistance to the new shogun. In 1614 Iyeyasu laid siege to the castle. The defenders held out until the next year, when they surrendered. Iyeyasu put the prisoners to death, completing the establishment of his military dictatorship. *See* Sekigahara; Hara Castle.

Trafalgar Cape (Napoleonic Empire Wars), 1805. Although Napoleon I, emperor of France, had abandoned his position along the Channel Coast to march deep into Germany in 1805, both the French and British fleets remained alert and active off the western European coast. On October 19 Adm. Pierre de Villeneuve with 18 French and 15 Spanish ships slipped out of Cadiz, Spain, and headed for the Strait of Gibraltar. Two days later a British fleet of 27 warships under Adm. Lord Nelson sighted the allied vessels ten miles off Cape Trafalgar. At the approach of the British, Villeneuve turned north in a single line. Nelson promptly attacked in two columns, at right angles from the west. He struck at the enemy van and center with his flagship, *Victory,* and 11 other ships, while Adm. Cuthbert Collingwood (afterward Lord Collingwood) in the *Royal Sovereign* led the other division against the rear (south) of Villeneuve's line. The British assault, under Nelson's signal "England expects every man will do his duty," shattered the French-Spanish column. In a hard-fought melee, dominated by the more accurate British gunnery, 18 allied ships surrendered, 4 others were later taken off La Coruña, and the remainder escaped into Cadiz. One of the captured was Villeneuve's flagship, the *Bucentaure.* No British ship was lost, but Nelson was mortally wounded. He died at 4:30 P.M., certain of his com-

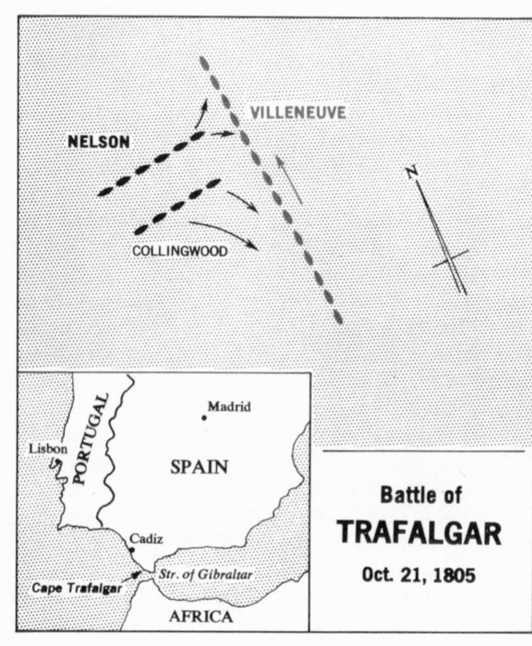

plete victory. Some 1,500 British seamen were killed or wounded; allied losses were 14,000, of whom about half were prisoners of war. Among the dead was the Spanish admiral Duque Federico de Gravina.

The battle of Trafalgar, the last great action fought by sailing ships, ended the naval power of France. It also established the supremacy of Great Britain on the seas for a hundred years. Thus it ranks as one of the decisive battles of history. *See* Finisterre Cape III; Ulm; Napoleonic Empire Wars.

Trasimeno Lake (Second Punic War), 217 B.C. After his major victory over Rome on the Trebbia River, Hannibal rested his Carthaginian army for two months at winter headquarters near modern Bologna. In the early spring he began marching south toward the Italian capital city. Crossing the Apennines to the western side of the peninsula, he was soon cutting a swath of destruction through central Italy.

To stop Hannibal, Rome sent two armies to the north—that of Gaius Flaminius, veteran of the Gallic wars, to Arretium (Arezzo) and the other, under Servilius Geminus, to Ariminum (Rimini), east of the Apennines. From the heights of Arretium, Flaminius let Hannibal pass by and then, ordering Servilius to join him, started in pursuit. The plan was to trap the Carthaginians between the two Roman armies. Upon reaching Lake Trasimeno, Hannibal took most of his 35,000-man army off the road and concealed them in wooded hills overlooking the water. On the mist-shrouded morning of June 21, Flaminius' 40,000 legionaries began moving along the lake road. The hidden Africans, Iberians, and Gauls suddenly assaulted the Roman column, which was strung out in marching formation. It was one of the bloodiest ambushes of history. The entire Roman army was either killed or taken captive. Among the dead was Flaminius. Carthaginian losses were about 2,500, mostly Gauls. Hannibal immediately turned east to recross the Apennines. Along the way he met and destroyed the 4,000 troops of Servilius, who had been hurrying forward to join the now nonexistent army at Lake Trasimeno.

The thoroughly frightened Roman Senate appointed a dictator, Quintus Fabius Maximus Verrucosus (Cunctator), to defend the city. For more than a year the new dictator avoided open combat with Hannibal, limiting the Roman army to harassing attacks as the Carthaginians marched southward on the Adriatic side of the peninsula. Although unpopular in the capital, the delaying tactics of Fabius (which gave rise to the adjective "fabian") gave Rome time to organize a new army for a major battle east of the Apennines. *See* Trebbia River I; Cannae; Punic Wars.

Trebbia River I (Second Punic War), 218 B.C. In his arduous six-month march from New Carthage in Spain, the redoubtable Hannibal probably lost 10,000 to 15,000 men through death, desertion, and military action, most of the casualties coming from his astonishing November crossing of the Alps. Yet he debouched into the Po Valley with a formidable army of 20,000 infantry, 6,000 cavalry, and the one or two elephants that had survived the extreme cold of the mountains.

Publius Cornelius Scipio, who had hurried back from his failure to intercept Hannibal in Gaul, now commanded the Roman outposts in the Po Valley. In December 218 B.C. on the Tincino River, a northern tributary of the Po, the Roman legions encountered the Carthaginians for the first time in the war. A brisk cavalry skirmish resulted. The swift, experienced African and Spanish horsemen soon routed the mounted Romans. Scipio, wounded in the fighting and deprived of his cavalry escort, pulled his legions back south of the Po.

The inconclusive action chafed Rome's second consul, Tiberius Sempronius Longus. Against the advice of Scipio, Sempronius crossed the Trebbia (a southern tributary of the Po) with 40,000 troops to attack the invaders in a snowstorm. Hannibal organized a defense that more than made up for his inferiority in numbers. His cavalry struck hard at the advancing flanks, bending back both Roman wings. Then, from a concealed gully, Mago, younger brother of the Carthaginian commander, led a fierce charge against the enemy rear. The encircled Romans battled desperately, but by the end of the day less than half of them had fought their way back to the camp at Placentia (Piacenza). The rest were fugitive, captured, or dead in the drifting snow.

The Carthaginian victory at the Trebbia delighted the Cisalpine Gauls, who had long warred against Rome. Some 10,000 Gallic warriors now attached themselves to Hannibal's army for the southward march toward Rome. *See* Saguntum; Trasimeno Lake; Punic Wars.

Trebbia River II (Wars of the French Revolution), 1799. As the French army in northern Italy under Gen. Jean Moreau continued to withdraw westward before the advance of the Russian-Austrian force, the Directory called up from Naples a second French army under Gen. Jacques Macdonald. Moreau had 25,000 men, Macdonald about 35,000. Between these two forces stood the 25,000 allied troops under the Russian field marshal Count Aleksandr Suvorov, assisted by the Austrian commander, Gen. Baron Michael von Melas. Determined to prevent the enemy armies from uniting against him, Suvorov turned to meet Macdonald on the Trebbia River, a southern tributary of the Po. Here, on June 17, 1799, the hostile forces clashed in a wild scramble along the banks and islands of the shallow river. The armies battled far into the night and throughout the next day. Finally, during the night of June 18–19, Macdonald pulled back, having lost 4,000 killed and 12,000 wounded, missing, and captured. Suvorov's total casualties were 6,000. France would make one more attempt to keep its foothold in Italy while its greatest commander, Napoleon Bonaparte, remained in the Middle East. *See* Cassano d'Adda II; Abukir; Novi Ligure; French Revolution Wars.

Trenton (War of the American Revolution), 1776. With the loss of forts Washington and Lee, which guarded the Hudson River, Gen. George Washington abandoned New York in November 1776 and retreated southwestward across New Jersey. He crossed the Delaware River into Pennsylvania on December 11, concentrating the American army behind the river line to cover the U.S. capital at Philadelphia. Congress fled to Baltimore. The British commander, Gen. Sir William Howe, had sent Gen. Lord Charles Cornwallis to harry the Continental retreat across New Jersey. But when Washington slipped across the Delaware, Howe ordered his troops into winter quarters.

The American commander in chief seized this opportunity to counterattack. On the night of December 25 he led 2,400 men across the ice-choked Delaware nine miles north of Trenton. The following morning he fell on the surprised garrison of 1,400 Hessian troops in Trenton. In a sharp street fight the German commander, Col. Johann Rall, was mortally wounded, 29 others were killed, and 918 captured. The Americans suffered only 5 casualties. After taking his prisoners back into Pennsylvania, Washington recrossed the river to occupy Trenton on December 30 and 31. Howe immediately sent out an army to try to retake the city. *See* Fort Washington; Princeton; American Revolution.

Treves (Gallic Revolt against Rome), A.D. 70. The violent upheavals that produced four different Roman emperors in A.D. 69 brought on a serious insurrection among several Gallic and Germanic tribes. Led by Julius Civilis, chief of the Batavi, who lived near the mouth of the Rhine, the civil conflict soon turned into a nationalist movement aimed at separation from the Roman Empire. The Treveri under Julius Classicus and Julius Tutor and the Lingones under Julius Sabinus joined the swelling revolt. To re-establish order, Petillius Cerealis marched into Gaul at the head of six loyal legions. Fortunately for Rome, disagreements among the rebels permitted Cerealis to subdue his opponents piecemeal. He crushed resistance in modern France and then moved east to Treves (Trier) on the Moselle. Here he attacked and routed Civilis and the Batavi. This defeat took the heart out of the rebellion. Before the year was over Cerealis dispersed the Treveri encampment at Bingen, 60 miles farther east. Emperor Vespasian then instituted administrative reforms that obviated all other separatist movements in the early empire. *See* Cremona I; Roman Empire.

Trevilian Station (American Civil War), 1864. While the Federal commander in chief, Gen. U. S. Grant, moved the Army of the Potomac across the James River against Petersburg, he ordered Gen. Philip Sheridan's cavalry to raid westward. Sheridan rode about 60 miles northwest to a point north of Louisa Courthouse on June 10. The Confederate general Wade Hampton, with his own and Gen. Fitzhugh Lee's cavalry divisions, pursued to Trevilian Station. Hampton had started northward against Sheridan on June 11 when suddenly Gen. George Custer's Federal cavalry brigade rode between the two Confederate divisions to Trevilian Station. In a confused fight Custer was contained. Hampton then dismounted to dig in against Sheridan's expected attack, which came the next day. The Federal assault was repulsed, Sheridan then turning back to rejoin Grant on June 28. He had suffered 735 casualties in the two-day battle. Hampton lost 612 men, Fitzhugh Lee about half that many. *See* Cold Harbor; Petersburg; American Civil War.

Tricameron (Wars of the Byzantine Empire). A village 18 miles southwest of Carthage, which was the site of a Vandal encampment stormed by the Byzantine army of Belisarius early in 534. *See* Carthage II.

Trifanum (Latin War), 338 B.C. During the inconclusive First Samnite War 343–41 B.C.), Roman and allied troops occupied the Campanian city of Capua. When Rome claimed sole honors for the achievement, the Latium cities revolted against the domineering rule of their former ally. For three years Latin and Roman troops clashed in the so-called Latin War. Finally, in 338 B.C., at the Latium town of Trifanum (near the mouth of the Liri River) the Roman general T. Manilus Torquatus won a decisive victory. Rome then annexed all of Latium to its growing string of conquests. *See* Caudine Forks; Roman Republic.

Trincomalee I (War of the American Revolution), 1782. Two months after the first British-French naval battle in the Bay of Bengal, the two hostile fleets clashed a second time. Again the opposing commanders were Adm. Sir Edward Hughes, with 11 British warships and Adm. Pierre André de Suffren with 12 French ships of the line. Hughes was sailing for the Ceylonese port of Trincomalee when the aggressive Suffren sought to intercept him, on April 12, 1782. (The same day another French fleet suffered a disastrous defeat at the hands of the British in Les Saintes Passage, in the West Indies.) In the hardest fight of the five engagements between these two commanders, the British suffered the greater personnel and ship casualties. Two of their vessels were so crippled as to be out of action for six weeks. But the French victory was so slight that Suffren could not alter the even balance of maritime power in the East. *See* Madras III; Saintes, Les; Cuddalore I; American Revolution.

Trincomalee II (War of the American Revolution), 1782. Following the indecisive naval battle off Cuddalore on the east coast of India, Adm. Pierre André de Suffren took his French fleet south to Ceylon. With 14 warships and carrying a detachment of soldiers, Suffren anchored off the British-held port of Trincomalee on August 25. The troops were landed the next night. Unable to resist the aggressive attack, the understrength British garrison surrendered on August 30–31. Three days later a British squadron of 12 ships under Adm. Sir Edward Hughes appeared over the horizon. Suffren, who loved to fight, sailed out to meet the enemy. In this fourth engagement in seven months between the same two commanders, the French fleet lost 82 killed and 252 wounded. But Hughes was driven off without regaining Trincomalee. *See* Cuddalore I; Cuddalore II; American Revolution.

Tripoli I (Moslem Conquest of Africa), 643. Following their rapid conquest of Egypt, the Moslems sent a column westward along the African coast of the Mediterranean. Under Abdullah ibn-Sa'd, the Arabian cavalry overran the Pentapolis cities of Cyrenaica—Apollonia, Arsinoë, Berenice, Cyrene, and Ptolemaïs—during 642–643. Pushing on to Tripoli, Abdullah found the city defended by a large force of Byzantine troops and African levies commanded by the prefect Gregory. Although the defenders had great numerical superiority, they were demoralized and uncertain in the face of the usual aggressive Arabian attack. During Abdullah's siege of Tripoli, the residents' will to resist declined even further. The Arabs finally stormed the city and captured it, inflicting heavy casualties on the defenders. Among the slain was Gregory.

Before the end of the century all North Africa would fall under Moslem rule. *See* Alexandria II; Carthage III; Moslem Conquests.

Tripoli II (U.S. War with Tripoli), 1804. When the pirates of the Barbary States—Algiers, Morocco, Tripoli, Tunis—declared open warfare on United States shipping in 1801, President Thomas Jefferson sent warships into the Mediterranean Sea to protect American vessels. On October 31, 1803, the 36-gun frigate USS *Philadelphia* (Capt. William Bainbridge) ran aground in the harbor of Tripoli and was captured. The pirates then turned the ship's guns against the American blockading fleet of Capt. Edward Preble. To eliminate this added enemy firepower, Lt. Stephen Decatur slipped into the harbor with 74 men on the night of February 16, 1804. Boarding the *Philadelphia,* Decatur's party set fire to the ship. Assured of its destruction, the Americans escaped under the fire of shore batteries, suffering only one casualty. The continuing blockade forced Tripoli to sue for peace the following year. *See* Tippecanoe Creek.

Tripoli, in Lebanon (Crusader-Turkish Wars), 1289. The death of the powerful Mameluke sultan of Egypt and Syria, Baybars I (Bibars), in 1277 gave the Frankish outposts in the Near East a respite from Moslem attacks. But in March 1289 the successors to Baybars settled their internal quarrels long enough to send a large army to besiege Tripoli. The northernmost of the remaining Christian fortresses, Tripoli came under the bombardment of heavy Egyptian war engines. When the walls began to crumble, first the Venetians and then the Genoese sailed away. On April 26 the Mameluke army launched a general assault against the fortress. Lucy, countess of Tripoli, who was the nominal ruler of the city, and many other notables fled to ships in the harbor and reached Cyprus in safety. Tripoli, which had been in Frankish hands since 1109, fell the same day. All male Christians in the town either died fighting or were killed later; the women and children were sold into slavery. The settlement suffered almost total destruction. To the other Frankish forts in Syria the fall of Tripoli signaled an ominous warning. *See* Antioch III; Tunis II; Acre II; Crusades.

Trnovo (Civil Wars of Bulgaria), 1218. The defeat suffered at Philippopolis (Plovdiv) at the hands of the Latin emperor of Constantinople weakened the rule of the Bulgarian king Boril, nephew of the great Kaloyan. Taking advantage of the discontent, John Asen, another nephew of Kaloyan, led a revolt in northern Bulgaria. Aided by some Russian troops, he laid siege to the capital of Trnovo (Tirnovo). In 1218 the rebels stormed into the city, captured Boril, and put out his eyes. John Asen II assumed the crown of Bulgaria, ruling wisely for the next 23 years. *See* Philippopolis II; Klokotnitsa.

Trojan War (1204–1194 B.C.). In a war in which legend seems irrevocably welded over historical fact, a Greek army, known as Achaeans, laid siege to the city of Troy in Asia Minor, just south of the Dardanelles. According to Greek mythology, the Greeks were commanded by King Agamemnon of Mycenae, brother of the king of Sparta, Menelaus. Supposedly, the war had begun when Helen, the wife of Menelaus, was enticed to Troy by Paris, son of the Trojan king, Priam. For nine years the Greeks failed to penetrate the sturdy walls of the city. In the tenth year Hector, another son of King Priam, was killed in individual combat with the temperamental Greek hero Achilles. Achilles in turn was slain by Paris.

The Greeks then sought to win the battle by trickery. They built a huge wooden horse in which a hundred warriors concealed themselves. The rest of the Greek army pretended to withdraw to the island of Bozcaada (Tenedos). The Trojans innocently brought the wooden horse inside their walls. That night the Greeks climbed out of their hiding place and opened the gates of the city to the main army, which had returned under cover of darkness. Troy was subdued and Helen returned to her husband.

The story of the Trojan War is told in the *Iliad, Odyssey,* and *Aeneid.* There seems to be considerable historical evidence that such a war did take place, although much of the legend has never been confirmed by scholars.

Truk (World War II), 1944. Early in World War II Japan developed a major naval and air base at the Caroline island of Truk, 1,500 miles west of Tarawa and 800 miles north of Rabaul. During the U.S. admiral Chester Nimitz' drive across the Central Pacific, the Truk base was neutralized in two devastating naval and air strikes. On February 17–18, 1944, Adm. Raymond Spruance's Fifth Fleet steamed into the Caroline group with the battleships *New Jersey* and *Iowa,* the cruisers *Minneapolis* and *New Orleans,* and four destroyers. While heavy naval guns blasted Japanese ships outside the Truk lagoon, Adm. Marc Mitscher's Task Force 58 sent 72 Hellcat fighters from his five fast carriers to attack inside the protected anchorage. The U.S. onslaught sank 2 light cruisers, 4 destroyers, 9 smaller naval vessels, and 24 merchantmen. Most of the 365 Japanese planes at Truk were destroyed or damaged. The attackers lost 25 aircraft; the carrier *Intrepid* was damaged.

Less than two months later, on April 28 and 29, Task Force 58 returned to make the second major strike aimed at completing the obliteration of Japan's "Gibraltar of the Pacific." Waves of carrier fighters and bombers pounded Truk for two days, sinking every Japanese vessel in sight and destroying 93 planes—59 in the air and 34 on the ground. Rescue operations saved more than half the 46 American pilots shot down.

With Truk effectively reduced, the next U.S. offensive swept northwest from the Marshalls, beyond the Carolines to the Marianas. *See* Tarawa-Makin; Kwajalein-Eniwetok; Mariana Islands; World War II.

Tsinan (Chinese Civil War), 1948. The Communist victory at Kaifeng in June and the impending greater triumph at Mukden began sounding the death knell for Generalissimo Chiang Kai-shek's regime. A new disaster started taking shape on September 14, when a People's Liberation Army of Mao Tse-tung attacked the northeastern city of Tsinan. After ten days of fighting, the Nationalist garrison of 80,000 men disintegrated. Many were neither casualties nor fugitives; they simply defected to the Communists. An even larger Nationalist defeat now loomed to the south. *See* Kaifeng; Mukden II; Hwai-Hai; Chinese Civil War.

Tsingtao (World War I), 1914. The Japanese Empire joined the Allied side early in the war, chiefly to pick off German holdings in the Far East. Japan's major objective was the port city of Tsingtao on the Shantung Peninsula of China, which had been under German control since 1898. On September 18, 23,000 Japanese troops landed above the city and were joined five days later by 1,500 British. The Allies then began a steady investment of Tsingtao, which was held by 4,000 German marines. While artillery pounded the fortress from the land side, Japanese and British warships added to the bombardment from the sea. By the night of November 6–7 Allied siege parallels had been constructed close enough to Tsingtao to permit a general assault. The German garrison surrendered the following morning, having suffered 700 casualties. Allied losses in this single battle of the war in the Far East were 1,800 Japanese and 70 British. *See* World War I.

Tsushima Strait (Russian-Japanese War), 1905. The unbroken succession of Japanese victories in Manchuria and Adm. Heihachiro Togo's domination of the seas prompted the Russian czar Nicholas II to send his Baltic fleet to the Far East late in 1904. Commanded by Adm. Zinovi Rozhde-

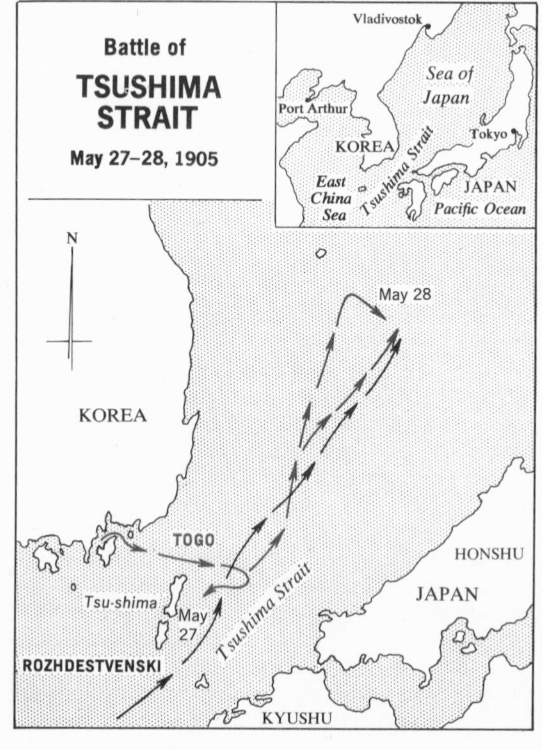

stvenski, 45 Russian ships, including 7 battleships and 6 cruisers, sailed through the East China Sea to enter the waters between Korea and Japan on May 27, 1905. Here, in the 63-mile-wide Tsushima Strait leading to the Sea of Japan, Togo intercepted the Russian vessels with a fleet of comparable size. The Japanese admiral held a marked advantage in the speed and firepower of his ships and in the training of his men. With a speed of 16 knots, Togo angled across the bows of the slower-moving (10 knots) Russian battleships in the van. In a fierce half-hour duel early in the afternoon, the Japanese sank one battleship, crippled another, and scattered the demoralized Russian line. Pressing his advantage, Togo blasted three more battleships to the bottom by nightfall.

Under cover of darkness Rozhdestvenski took his crippled fleet northward toward the shelter of Vladivostok. The alert Japanese pursued with destroyers and torpedo boats. Three more Russian ships were sunk during the night. With daylight on May 28 the pursuit continued, until all but 12 vessels of the harassed Russian fleet were sunk, captured, or driven ashore. Rozhdestvenski was wounded and captured. In the greatest sea battle since Trafalgar 100 years earlier, Togo lost only three ships—all torpedo boats. The stunning Japanese victory opened the way for both sides to accept the peace terms negotiated by U.S. President Theodore Roosevelt later that year. *See* Mukden I; Port Arthur II; Russian-Japanese War.

Tunis I (First Punic War), 255 B.C. The Roman naval victory at Ecnomus opened the way for an attack on Carthage itself. The following year Marcus Atilius Regulus landed on the North African coast at Tunis (Tunes), a few miles from the enemy capital, with four Roman legions composed of 17,000 infantry and a weak force of cavalry. Prior to this time Carthage had relied upon its fleet for protection and as a result had not built defensive walls around the city. Regulus demanded the surrender of the city. But Carthage refused and prepared to attack the invaders. The Carthaginian army, newly reorganized by the Spartan general Xanthippus and now commanded by him, had 12,000 infantry, 4,000 expert cavalry, and 100 elephants.

To defend against the elephants, Regulus abandoned the checkerboard arrangement of his legions and arranged both the second and third lines of maniples directly behind the first. This tactic worked successfully against the charge by the elephants—the huge beasts were simply driven to the rear through the open spaces in the Roman lines. But the arrangement proved fatal when the Carthaginian cavalry also charged through the undefended lanes and assaulted the Roman foot soldiers from the flank and rear. The legionaries were completely overwhelmed. Only 2,500 Romans escaped back to their ships (and many of these were lost when a storm devastated the fleet on the way home). Regulus was captured. He was later paroled to negotiate peace terms, but when that mission failed, he returned voluntarily to certain torture and death. *See* Ecnomus; Panormus; Punic Wars.

Tunis II (Eighth Crusade), 1270. Twenty years after the collapse of his crusade (the Seventh) against Egypt at El Mansûra, King Louis IX of France tried again. The future Saint Louis aimed his new attack on Tunis, where a victory would give the Christians the line Sicily-Malta-Tunisia across the central Mediterranean, thus isolating Islamic Spain and Morocco to the west (Sicily and Malta were then held by Louis's brother, Charles of Anjou). Another incentive for the expedition was the rumor that the Moslem emir of Tunis stood ready to embrace Christianity if he were supported by a crusading army.

In July 1270, Louis landed near Carthage with a strong force of French knights, supplemented by some Norman Sicilians under Charles. To the dismay of the crusaders, the emir of Tunis fought back fiercely from his capital. Louis had to besiege the city. A plague soon broke out in the Christian camp. By the end of August, Louis and many of his followers were dead. (Louis was canonized in 1297.) Charles promptly negotiated an indemnity from the emir and then led the survivors, who included the new French king, Philip III, back to Europe. So ended the last crusade. Although other Christian leaders tried to organize later attempts to win back the Holy Land, this was the final military offensive. *See* El Mansûra; Antioch III; Tripoli, in Lebanon; Crusades.

Tunis III (Invasion by Charles V), 1535. After the repulse of the Turks at Vienna in 1529, the chief threat to Europe came on the seas. The Ottoman sultan, Suleiman I, the Magnificent, made the Barbary pirate Barbarossa II (Khaireddin) supreme commander of the Turkish fleet. With a largely pirate force, Barbarossa began ravaging the Mediterranean coastline and in 1534 captured Tunis. Alarmed at the growing Turkish maritime power, Charles V, Holy Roman Emperor, organized a fleet of 600 ships under Andrea Doria of Genoa. This expedition crossed the Mediterranean in June 1535 and drove off the ships of Barbarossa. Veteran troops were landed in Tripoli. In July they attacked and captured Tunis, which was sacked in a three-day orgy. The victory crippled the sea power of the Turks only temporarily, however. Tunis was recaptured by Moslem forces in 1569, lost in 1573, and regained in 1575, and pirate raids would plague the Mediterranean for another 250 years. *See* Vienna I; Baghdad III; Preveza.

Tunisia (World War II), 1942–1943. The Anglo-American invasion of French Northwest Africa on

November 11 provoked a quick Axis reaction in Tunisia. By air and sea, German and Italian forces poured in to seize French military and naval installations. German bombers and fighters flew into Tunisian airfields. The German general Jürgen von Arnim concentrated most of the Axis strength in the northern cities of Tunis and Bizerte, which were also vital naval bases. By the end of November Arnim had 15,000 well-equipped troops, including the 10th Panzer Division. This rapid build-up thwarted the Allied aim of moving east from Algeria to take Tunisia ahead of the Axis and thus cut off the rear of Field Marshal Erwin Rommel's *Panzerarmee Afrika,* which was retreating from Libya.

In the race for Tunisia Gen. Dwight Eisenhower's Allied forces made deep penetrations before they were thrown back. On the north Gen. Kenneth Anderson's understrength British First Army reached Jefna, 32 miles southwest of Bizerte, and Tébourba, 12 miles short of Tunis, by November 28. But fierce Axis counterattacks pushed the British back 20 miles in seven days. On the south the American II Corps under Gen. Lloyd Fredendall was stopped in the Sbeitla-Gafsa sector of central Tunisia. Linking the two blocked wings of the Allied force was a French corps commanded by Gen. Georges Barré.

On December 24 Eisenhower ordered the Allies to assume defensive positions in front of the Axis bridgehead that extended from the coast south through Medjez-el-Bab, Ousseltia, and Faïd to the Mareth Line in the southeast. To speed the organization of the Allied line, Anderson assumed command of the entire front on January 24. Two weeks later Eisenhower became supreme commander of all Allied forces in Africa, with Gen. Sir Harold Alexander, head of the British forces advancing from Libya, his deputy and commander of ground forces (newly named the 18th Army Group).

There was little fighting throughout the winter, but in February the Axis launched a sudden attack. Early in the month Rommel, in flight from the British Eighth Army in Libya, had retreated behind the Mareth Line. Here the German Panzers were re-equipped with the 56-ton Mark VI Tiger tanks (four inches of armor, 88-mm. cannon, two heavy machine guns). On February 14 Rommel's 10th and 21st Panzer divisions of the veteran *Afrika Korps* lunged out of Faïd toward Kasserine Pass, the gateway to the communications hub of Tebessa. Holding this vital point were elements of Fredendall's 1st Armored Division and 168th Regimental Combat Team. The inexperienced Americans were driven back 21 miles in nine days, losing 192 killed, 2,624 wounded, and 2,459 prisoners and missing. Just when the Axis thrust promised to be a major success, it was blunted by stiffened American resistance, aided by strong air support and a counterattack from the north by the British 6th Armoured. Rommel's force suffered equivalent casualties and on February 22 began pulling back to its original positions. Two weeks later Gen. George Patton took over command of II Corps, which was built up to include the 1st Armored, and the 1st, 9th, and 34th Infantry divisions.

The German attack at Kasserine proved to be the last successful Axis offensive in Africa. On March 26 the British Eighth Army (Bernard Montgomery) breached the Mareth Line and on April 6 drove through enemy defenses at Gabès. The following day a patrol from Montgomery's 4th Indian Division met a patrol from the 9th American, linking all Alexander's ground forces for the final assault in Tunisia.

Continuing their drive up the eastern coast, the Eighth Army took Sfax on April 10, Sousse on April 12, and attacked the Axis positions at Enfidaville a day later. The Eighth Army now fought a containing action while the main Allied thrust shifted to the north. Here the II Corps, moved up from the south and now led by Gen. Omar Bradley, formed the left (northern) flank. (Patton was organizing the Seventh Army for the forthcoming invasion of Sicily.) The 1st Armored of Bradley's corps fought its way into Mateur on May 3; the 9th Infantry took Bizerte four days later. To the south, armored units of the British First Army, augmented by three veteran divisions from Montgomery's army, smashed toward Tunis on May 6. The 7th Armoured covered 30 miles in 36 hours to capture the city on May 7.

Three Axis divisions, trapped between Allied forces in Bizerte and Tunis, surrendered on May 9. On May 10 the British 6th Armoured raced southward across the base of the Cape Bon Peninsula. Two days later this force joined hands with the Eighth Army and the XIX French Corps in the south. The hopelessly pocketed Axis forces surrendered in droves. Throughout the battle of Tunisia, the British air chief marshal Sir Arthur Tedder's Mediterranean air force savagely attacked Axis aircraft and troops. The American general Carl Spaatz's tactical planes flew as many as 2,500 sorties in a day.

The last of some 250,000 Axis forces surrendered on May 13, including the desert-famed *Afrika Korps,* the Fifth Panzer Army (Von Arnim), and the First Italian Army (Giovanni Messe, who was in nominal charge of the Tunisian theater). Axis dead and wounded numbered about 40,000. The British First Army suffered 23,000 casualties, the Eighth Army about 10,000. American losses were 18,500, including 2,184 killed. The six-month battle of Tunisia ended the North African campaign. The Allied victory helped open the Mediterranean shipping line to the East and paved the way for an invasion of Sicily two months later. *See* Northwest Africa; Mareth Line; Sicily; World War II.

Tupelo (American Civil War), 1864. The severe Federal defeat at Brices Cross Roads prompted Federal leaders to launch another expedition against the Confederate cavalry leader Gen. Nathan Forrest. General Andrew Smith marched on Tupelo, in northeastern Mississippi, with 11,000 infantry, 3,000 cavalry, and 20 guns. To counter this Federal force, Gen. Stephen Lee assembled 6,600 Confederates, chiefly Forrest's troopers, at Columbus, Miss. Smith's army reached Tupelo on July 13 and began taking up a strong position. At 7 A.M. on the following morning the Confederates began a series of attacks that were all repulsed by heavy and accurate Federal fire. Lee pulled his men back, but that night Forrest made a new attack, seeking to envelop Smith's rear. Again the assault was beaten off. After checking still another attack on July 15, Smith began a careful withdrawal to Memphis. He had lost 77 killed, 559 wounded, and 38 missing. But he had dealt Forrest's men their most severe defeat to date—210 killed, 1,116 wounded (including Forrest himself). *See* Brices Cross Roads; Atlanta; American Civil War.

Turckheim (Second, or Dutch, War of Louis XIV), 1675. The aggressive campaigning of Louis XIV of France had brought the Holy Roman Empire of Leopold I into the war against him in 1674. Most of this fighting took place along the upper Rhine between two generals who had opposed each other a generation earlier in the Thirty Years' War—the marshal the Vicomte de Turenne of France and Count Montecuccoli of Austria. Late in the year both armies prepared to go into winter quarters in Alsace. But in a brilliant, cold-weather march, Turenne circled south of the Vosges Mountains and fell on the unsuspecting Imperial force at Turckheim, near Colmar, on January 5, 1675. The French army routed its enemy, pursuing them eastward as far as the Rhine. Turenne, the idol of Napoleon more than a century later, had won back all Alsace by a single stroke. *See* Enzheim; Sasbach; Louis XIV, Wars of.

Turin (War of the Spanish Succession), 1706. The last year of the war in Italy opened with the French under Marshal the Duc de Vendôme scattering the Imperial forces of the Holy Roman Empire in the spring (the so-called battle of Calcinato). Vendôme, however, was then recalled by Louis XIV to take command in Flanders, where the French had suffered a disastrous defeat at Ramillies. His successors in Italy, the Duc d'Orleans and Marshal Comte Ferdinand de Marsin, concentrated on a siege of Turin, in the northwest. Meanwhile, Prince Eugene of Savoy returned to the peninsula. Collecting the fragments of the Imperial army from the mountains of Lombardy, Eugene marched across the top of the Italian boot toward Turin. As he approached the besieged city, his cousin Victor Amadeus II, duke of Savoy, slipped through the French lines to join the Imperial army. On September 7 Eugene struck the besiegers with his augmented force. The French commanders failed to coordinate their defenses and were beaten in detail. Marsin died on the field, while D'Orleans fell back to Pinerolo with some 2,000 survivors of the 10,000-man army. Almost 6,000 French were lost through capture alone. The Savoy-Imperial battle casualties numbered only about 1,500, but almost 5,000 of the Turin garrison had perished from combat and disease during the siege. The defeat at Turin ended French attempts to conquer northern Italy. Archduke Charles (later Charles VI), brother of Holy Roman Emperor Joseph I, was proclaimed Charles III of Spain at Milan. *See* Cassano d'Adda I; Ramillies; Almansa; Spanish Succession, War of the.

Turkey. The major battles and wars of what is now the nation of Turkey are listed below.

Nishapur	1038
Manzikert	1071
See Crusades	
Philomelion	1116
Myriocephalon	1176
Erzincan	1230
Bursa	1317–1326
Adrianople VI	1365
Maritsa River	1371
Kossovo I	1389
Nicopolis	1396
Angora	1402
Salonika I	1430
Varna I	1444
Kossovo II	1448
Constantinople VII	1453
Belgrade I	1456
Negroponte	1470
Shkodër I	1478
Lepanto I	1499
Chaldiran	1514
Marj-Dabik	1516
Cairo	1517
Belgrade II	1521
Rhodes	1522
Mohács	1526
Vienna I	1529
Baghdad III	1534
Tunis II	1535
Preveza	1538
Malta I	1565
Szigetvár	1566
Astrakhan II	1569
Cyprus	1570–1571
Lepanto II	1571

Keresztes 1576
Khotin I 1621
Candia II 1646–1669
Szentgotthárd 1664
Khotin II 1673
Vienna II 1683
Harkány 1687
Slankamen 1691
Azov 1696
Senta 1697
Peterwardein 1716
Cesme 1770
Focsani 1789
Rimnik 1789
See Greek War of Independence
Varna II 1828
Kulevcha 1829
See Egyptian Revolt against Turkey
See Crimean War
See Russian-Turkish War, 1877–1878
Tyrnavos 1897
See Italian-Turkish War
See World War I
Sakarya River 1921

Turnhout (Netherlands War of Independence), 1597. The defeat of the Spanish Armada in 1588 by the English fleet (aided by severe storms) gave a new impetus to the Dutch War for Independence against Spain. Maurice of Nassau, leader of the northern provinces, with an army of 10,000 men liberated Breda in 1590; Zutphen, after a 7-day siege; Deventer, following an 11-day siege; and Nijmegen in 6 days, all in 1591; and the province of Groningen in 1594. Three years later the able Maurice made a forced march of 24 miles in nine hours to surprise a Spanish army at Turnhout, 26 miles northeast of Antwerp. On August 22, 1597, the Dutch overtook the troops of Albert, archduke of Austria, and cut them to pieces. Maurice inflicted 3,000 casualties on the Spaniards at small cost to himself. The resurgent Netherlanders continued to press their adversaries, building up to the largest pitched battle of the war. *See* Zutphen; Nieuwpoort; Netherlands War of Independence.

Tuttlingen (Thirty Years' War), 1643. The war in Germany, which had quieted down after the second battle of Breitenfeld in 1642, erupted again the following autumn. Marshal the Comte de Guébriant led a French army out of Alsace across the Black Forest into Württemberg. He seized Rottweil, on the upper Neckar, but was mortally wounded in the action. The French, under Gen. Josias von Rantzau, then moved across the watershed to Tuttlingen on the upper Danube. Here on November 24 they were attacked by a Bavarian army of the Holy Roman Empire (Ferdinand III) under Field Marshal Baron Franz von Mercy (and Gen. Johann von Werth, who led the cavalry in his first battle since Rheinfelden, where he had been taken prisoner). The Imperial assault caught the French by surprise and drove them back with heavy losses in men, artillery, and baggage. Rottweil was liberated.

Rantzau, who had been taken prisoner by the Bavarians, was succeeded by the marshal the Vicomte de Turenne, who was to become one of the greatest generals of his era. The following year Turenne and the French would be sorely tested by Mercy's resurgent Imperial army. *See* Breitenfeld II; Freiburg; Thirty Years' War.

Tyre I (Babylonian-Phoenician War), 585–573 B.C. Phoenicia's great commercial city of Tyre, on the eastern Mediterranean, was attacked by Nebuchadnezzar II of Babylonia's Chaldean dynasty in 585 B.C. Failing to capture the city, Nebuchadnezzar laid siege to it. For 13 years Tyre, under Ittobaal II, resisted the siege, which was finally raised in 573 B.C. The failure to take Tyre was the only major setback in Nebuchadnezzar's 57-year reign. *See* Jerusalem I; Sardis.

Tyre II (Macedonian Conquests), 332 B.C. Following Macedonia's decisive victory at Issus and the seizure of Damascus, all of Phoenicia submitted to Alexander the Great except for the strongly fortified seaport of Tyre. This city, which 250 years earlier had withstood a 13-year siege, stood on an island half a mile offshore. To reach this stronghold, Alexander began to build a mole across the channel. But this work was seriously hampered by Tyrian galleys from the city's two harbors, which attacked the workers and destroyed much of their equipment. Alexander then assembled his own fleet from captured Phoenician cities. These vessels provided protection for the Macedonian assault forces as well as for the floating batteries, built on barges to catapult stones, spears, and incendiaries into the besieged city. Finally, in August 332 B.C., the determined invaders breached Tyre's walls and stormed into the city. The stubborn seven-month resistance cost the defenders some 8,000 lives; another 30,000 were captured and sold into slavery. Alexander was now free to continue his southward march along the Mediterranean coast. *See* Issus; Gaza I; Macedonian Conquests.

Tyrnavos (Greek-Turkish War), 1897. Believing that the Greek government of George I had fomented the anti-Turkish uprisings in Crete in February 1897, Sultan Abdul Hamid II declared war on April 17. The major action took place in Thessaly, where the Ottoman general in chief, Edhem Pasha, had concentrated some 58,000 men. Here about 45,000 Greek soldiers under the overall command of the crown prince (future Constantine I) defended the frontier. On April 18 the Turks launched an advance all along the front. Pressed back, the Greeks resisted stubbornly in front of Tyrnavos, ten miles northwest of Larissa, on April 21 and 22. But when threatened on both flanks, the defenders began a retreat the next day that quickly became a rout. The demoralized army fled southward through Larissa to Pharsala. When the Turks moved on that town on May 5, the Greeks fled again after offering only brief resistance. At Domokos another Turkish attack, on May 17, brought but feeble opposition. Only the intervention of the Russian czar, Nicholas II, prevented a complete Greek collapse, for on the Epirus front Constantine's troops suffered a similar debacle in their efforts to drive back the Turks.

The fighting halted at this point while the European powers arranged a peace treaty. This was signed on September 20. Turkey received a large indemnity and a rectification of the frontier in Thessaly. Crete was placed under international control. *See* Plovdiv.

U

Ukraine (World War II), 1943–1944. The powerful German invasion of the Soviet Union in 1941 had swept through the Ukraine without serious hindrance. The following year found the Nazi armies still in the Ukraine and beyond. But by the spring of 1943 the Soviet Union had won a crucial victory at Stalingrad and had routed the German forces from the Caucasus. The stage was now set for a major Russian offensive that would drive southwest into the Ukraine on a 500-mile front between the Pripet Marshes on the north and the Black Sea on the south.

From Orel southward the Red armies were commanded by the generals Markian Popov, Konstantin Rokossovski, Nikolai Vatutin, Ivan Konev, Rodion Malinovski, Fedor Tolbukhin, and Ivan Petrov. Beginning on July 23, the Russian attacks, featuring tanks, aircraft, and the expert use of massed artillery, ground relentlessly forward. Only occasionally, and then for but a brief time, could the crumbling German defenses hold off the Soviet steam roller. Popov captured Orel on August 5. Vatutin took Belgorod, almost 200 miles to the south, the same day and then pressed southwest to aid Konev's attack on Kharkov. This battered communications hub and former capital of the Ukrainian S.S.R. had been lost a second time to the Germans earlier in the year. But now it was enveloped on three sides and won for the last time on August 23, despite Hitler's order that the city be held at all costs. Vatutin then turned back to the northwest to join with Rokossovski in a September breakthrough to Konotop, well inside the Ukraine.

Meanwhile, 200 miles south of Kharkov, Tolbukhin opened an attack on August 22 between Stalino and the Sea of Azov. Here Russian armor routed German militia troops and pushed into Taganrog on August 30. The back-up army of Malinovski took Stalino on September 7. Still farther south, Petrov struck at the last German bridgehead in the Caucasus, which extended from the Taman Peninsula southward to the city of Novorossisk. On September 15 the Red Army ended a year-long siege by breaking into Novorossisk. The remnants of eight German and six Rumanian divisions withdrew across the Kerch Strait into the Crimea on September 28. Here the German Seventeenth Army held out until the following spring.

As the Soviet onslaught continued across both central and southern fronts the Germans realized that their forced withdrawal to the vast, impassable Pripet Marshes would divide their forces. German generals then fought costly rear-guard actions to extricate major units northward into White Russia (Byelorussia) and southward into the Ukraine. In an effort to stabilize a winter position the German high command ordered Field Marshals Gunther von Kluge in the center and Erich von Manstein on the south to hold the line of the Dnieper. But the Red armies soon obliterated this position with advances on four numbered Ukrainian fronts.

In the north on the First Ukrainian Front, the next major Russian objective was the capital city of Kiev. On September 23 Rokossovski crossed the Desna River to take Chernigov, 75 miles northeast of Kiev. On his left, Vatutin bridged the Dnieper early in October north and south of Kiev and then took this famous old city from the rear on November 6. Vatutin pressed westward 100 miles in a week to Korosten and Zhitomir before Manstein threw back the advance with a desperate counterstroke, delivered by *Panzer* expert Gen. Hasso von Manteuffel.

On the Second Ukrainian Front, downstream on the Dnieper, Konev established a bridgehead across from Kremenchug early in October and then raced southwest halfway across the bulge formed by the river's eastward bend. This advance opened the Third Ukrainian Front, where Malinovski crossed the river to take Dnepropetrovsk on October 25 from Field Marshal Paul von Kleist's Army Group "A." With most of the German reserves pulled northward, the Fourth Ukrainian Front provided relatively easy going from Zaporozhe south. Tolbukhin thrust across the top of the Perekop Isthmus to reach the mouth of the Dnieper on the Black Sea early in November. The strong German force in the Crimea was now isolated.

In 1944, with no coherent German line in front

of them, the Red armies pushed across the western half of the Ukraine. Bursting out of the Kiev salient, Vatutin launched the winter offensive on December 24, 1943. By the end of that year he had recaptured Korosten and Zhitomir, and on January 4 he crossed the 1939 Polish frontier. A northern force then raced forward 100 miles to take Lutsk (Luck) on February 5. A southern thrust merged with Konev's right wing to encircle (on February 3) ten German divisions, which Hitler had ordered to cling to the southern face of the Kiev salient, on the Dnieper near Cherkassy. The futile German effort to relieve this hopelessly trapped group (18,000 surrendered on February 17) cost Manstein an additional 20,000 casualties and most of his reserves. As a result, Nikopol, in the eastern bend of the Dnieper, fell to Tolbukhin on February 8. Tolbukhin then halted to mop up south of the Dnieper bend and to attack through the Perekop Isthmus into the Crimea. Meanwhile, Malinovski pushed the Third Ukrainian Front forward to Krivoi Rog on February 22.

Early in March the able Vatutin suffered a fatal wound. Gen. Georgi Zhukov took over command of the First Ukrainian Army in time to launch the Russian spring offensive. On March 4 Zhukov lunged past the upper Bug to reach the outskirts of Tarnopol five days later. To the south Konev attacked on March 6, routed a *Panzer* force near Uman, and pushed on to the Bug. Crossing the river on March 15, he raced 70 miles westward to seize the German pontoon bridge over the Dniester at Mogilev. Behind this spearhead, Vinnitsa, Hitler's former headquarters in the Ukraine, fell on March 20. In the far south Malinovski kept pace by driving across the mouths of the Dnieper and the Bug, taking Kherson on March 13 and Nikolayev on March 28.

Before the end of March, Zhukov had crossed the upper reaches of both the Dniester and the Prut to enter prewar Rumania. Konev penetrated to the Prut near Jassy (Iasi) on March 28. This combined advance brought the Russians to the foothills of the Carpathians. A drive through Jablonica Pass, which Zhukov reached on April 1, would now bring the Red armies onto the Hungarian Plain. Hitler reacted swiftly by occupying Hungary. Further, a German counterattack from Lvov (formerly Lemberg) threw back Zhukov's spearhead. This was the first major German action directed by Gen. Walther Model, who had replaced the skillful but now discredited Manstein. At about the same time Gen. Ferdinand Schoerner replaced Kleist.

Konev, who also had been blocked along the northern Rumanian frontier, wheeled his left wing south down the Dniester. This movement threatened the rear of the Germans opposing Malinovski's drive along the north shore of the Black Sea. As a result the Germans were squeezed out of the port of Odessa on April 10.

The battle of the Ukraine was virtually over. When the Red armies resumed their offensive in July, the last important city still in German hands, Lvov, fell in two weeks (July 27). By then Russian troops were surging through the Balkans and Poland. *See* Stalingrad; Caucasus; White Russia; Crimea; Soviet Union (World War II); Balkans; Poland–East Prussia; World War II.

Ulm (Napoleonic Empire Wars), 1805. The two-year-old war of inaction between Great Britain (George III) and France (Napoleon I) burst into flame in 1805 when Austria, Russia, Sweden, and Naples formed the Third Coalition against France. Spain sided with the French. When Austrian troops, under the overall command of Holy Roman Emperor Francis II, began massing in the Tyrol and northern Italy, Napoleon resolved to strike at them through southern Germany. Turning his back on the Channel Coast and his threatened invasion of England, the French emperor sent his Grande Armée on the march on August 27. Four weeks later the French crossed the Rhine and headed southeast toward the Danube.

Meanwhile, an Austrian offensive, under the archduke Ferdinand (brother of Emperor Francis II) but directed by Gen. Baron Karl Mack von Leiberich, had pushed into Bavaria. Expecting Napoleon to debouch from the Black Forest, Mack concentrated at Ulm, on the upper Danube. Here he awaited the arrival of a Russian army coming up the Danube Valley. But on October 7 Mack learned that Napoleon was crossing the river in his rear (downstream), thus cutting his communications with Vienna. With the Russian army of Gen. Mikhail Kutuzov too far away to help, Mack tried to cut his way out. But Napoleon swung the biggest part of his 200,000 troops westward after crossing the Danube and began converging his columns on Ulm. North of the river Marshal Michel Ney's VI Corps fought its way into Elchingen on October 14 to hold the Danube bridge there open for Napoleon to shift more troops north of the river (Ney was later created Duc d'Elchingen).

The Austrians fell back into Ulm. Some divisions, including the archduke himself, escaped to the north or to the south. Mack, however, was penned up. On October 20 he formally surrendered his remaining 20,000 troops. In all, the campaign had cost the Austrians more than 50,000 men, largely prisoners, from their original army of 72,000. Napoleon now turned eastward to face Kutuzov, who had advanced as far westward as the Inn River. At sea, however, the French navy was suffering a disastrous defeat off the coast of Spain. *See* Oberhollabrunn; Trafalgar Cape; Caldiero II; Napoleonic Empire Wars.

Ulundi (Zulu-British War), 1879. Six months

after the initially successful Zulu uprising, the British in Natal launched a counteroffensive. Led by Gen. Lord Chelmsford and Sir Garnet Wolseley, a force of 5,000 men pressed forward to Ulundi, 115 miles northeast of Durban. Here stood the headquarters kraal of the Zulu chief, Cetewayo, guarded by some 20,000 warriors organized in impis (regiments). In a fierce fight on July 4, some 1,500 Zulus were killed, breaking the power of the tribe. British casualties were 15 killed and 78 wounded. Cetewayo was pursued and captured on August 28, ending the war. Zululand was gerrymandered among South African provinces and later incorporated into South Africa. *See* Rorke's Drift; Zulu-British War.

United States. The major battles and wars fought by the United States since colonial times are listed below.

Fort Caroline	1565
See Indian Wars in the United States	
See King William's War	
See Queen Anne's War	
See King George's War	
See French and Indian War	
Alamance Creek	1771
See American Revolution, War of the	
Tripoli II	1804
See War of 1812	
See Texan War of Independence	
See United States-Mexican War	
See American Civil War	
See Spanish-American War	
Philippine Insurrection	1899–1902
Columbus, N.M.	1916
Carrizal	1916
See World War I	
See World War II	
See Korean War	
See Vietnam War	

United States–Mexican War (1846–1849). A dispute over the territory between the Nueces and Rio Grande rivers led to open conflict between the United States and Mexico in April 1846. On May 13 the United States declared war. The fighting lasted 17 months, ending with American troops in possession of California, the Southwest, northern Mexico, and central Mexico from Veracruz to Mexico City. By the Treaty of Guadalupe Hidalgo, Mexico ceded the territories of California and New Mexico and all the land up to the Rio Grande. It also officially relinquished its claim to Texas. In return the United States paid $15 million and assumed its citizens' claims against Mexico, amounting to more than $3 million.

Fort Texas	1846
Palo Alto	1846
Resaca de la Palma	1846
Monterrey	1846
San Pasqual	1846
Buena Vista	1847
Chihuahua	1847
Veracruz	1847
Cerro Gordo	1847
Contreras-Churubusco	1847
Molino del Rey	1847
Chapultepec	1847
Puebla I	1847

Uruguay. *See* Latin America.

Ushant I (War of the American Revolution), 1778. The American victory at Saratoga brought France into the war against Great Britain on February 6, 1778. Six months later the fleets of the two long-time enemies met off Ushant (Île d'Ouessant), an island west of the tip of the Brittany Peninsula. The British fleet, sent out by King George III from Portsmouth, was under the command of Adm. Augustus Keppel. On July 27 Keppel with 30 ships of the line fought the first major naval battle of the war, against a French (Louis XVI) fleet of equal size under the admiral the Comte d'Orvilliers. The two fleets opened fire while moving in opposite, parallel directions. Despite the equality of the forces, neither admiral sought to do more than make this single pass. No ship was sunk or taken. Keppel returned to Portsmouth (he was later court-martialed but acquitted), while d'Orvilliers withdrew to Brest. Meanwhile another French fleet, under the admiral the Comte d'Estaing, sailed to North America in aid of the new United States. *See* Saratoga; Newport; American Revolution.

Ushant II (Wars of the French Revolution), 1794. The first naval battle of the war between the fleets of Great Britain and France took place 400 miles west of Ushant (Île d'Ouessant), off the Brittany peninsula. The French admiral Louis Villaret de Joyeuse, with the Brest fleet of 26 warships, was escorting a convoy of grain ships across the Atlantic when he was intercepted by a British squadron of equal size under Adm. Lord Richard Howe. After four days of skirmishing, the two hostile fleets clashed in a decisive action on June 1, 1794. Six French ships were captured and one was sunk, but the merchantmen slipped away safely to harbor at Brest. Howe's squadron was too battered to pursue. This battle is known in Great Britain as the "Glorious First of June." *See* Saint Vincent Cape II; French Revolution Wars.

Ustí nad Labem (Hussite Wars), 1426. When Andrew Procop, the Great, replaced Jan Zizka in 1424 as head of the Taborites, the Hussite military arm remained as strong as ever. The terrified German soldiers refused to take the field against the fierce Hussites despite the urging of the papacy and of Sigismund, king of Hungary and Bohemia and Holy Roman Emperor. Finally, in 1426, a force of some 50,000 Germans did make a stand at Ústí nad Labem (Aussig on the Labe [Elbe]

River) in northern Bohemia. But the battle was as disastrous for Sigismund's army as all previous engagements with the Bohemians had been. Procop's warriors, making maximum use of their mobile artillery, handguns, and brilliant tactics, killed more than a third of the enemy before the Germans fled in total rout.

The Hussites then took the offensive, burning and pillaging into Hungary, Austria, and Germany itself. No army could halt the invaders. The terror of eastern Europe came to an end only when a new civil war broke out among the Hussites. *See* Německý Brod; Český-Brod; Hussite Wars.

Utica I (Second Punic War), 203 B.C. Despite Publius Cornelius Scipio's dramatic conquest of Spain, the Roman senate was reluctant to let the young commander invade Carthage itself. Scipio (later Scipio Africanus) then went to Sicily where he recruited his own army of Roman volunteers, Syracusans, and two legions which had been exiled there after the humiliation at Cannae. In 204 B.C. Rome finally permitted this force to go to Africa. Scipio landed in midsummer at Utica, less than 20 miles west of Carthage. His expeditionary force was almost immediately hemmed in near the coast by Hasdrubal, son of Gisco, with a force of Carthaginians, and Syphax, the elderly king of the Numidians. But Scipio organized a strong defensive position, which included siege lines around the city of Utica, and made an alliance with another Numidian tribal chieftain, Masinissa.

In the spring of 203 Scipio launched a sudden attack against the forces containing his beachhead. The Africans withdrew inland to an area called the Great Plains, where they settled down to a leisurely reorganization. But the aggressive Roman commander took 16,000 men on a five-day forced march into the interior. He fell upon the surprised enemy camp in a fierce onslaught that routed 20,000 African troops. Syphax, the longtime friend of Hannibal, was wounded, captured, and sent to Rome in chains. Masinissa pressed on to capture the Numidian capital of Cirta and with it the beautiful young wife of Syphax, Sophonisba, whom he promptly claimed for his own. Meanwhile Scipio turned to the east and seized a position on the Bay of Tunis, threatening Carthage itself. The conclusive battle of the Second Punic War lay just ahead. *See* Ilipa; Metaurus River: Zama; Punic Wars.

Utica II (Wars of the First Triumvirate), 49 B.C. When Julius Caesar went to Spain to conquer Pompey's province there, he sent G. Scribonius Curio to take over North Africa. Curio landed at Utica with two legions. P. Attius Varro, in command of the Pompeian forces in modern Tunisia, left his entrenched position to attack the Caesarian legions. In a sharp struggle Curio's men turned back the enemy assault and then put them to rout. The victorious Curio moved inland to the Bagradas (Medjerda) River. *See* Ilerda; Bagradas River; First Triumvirate, Wars of the.

V

Vaal Krantz (South African War II), 1900. The town of Ladysmith, besieged by the Boers for more than three months, was the object of Gen. Sir Redvers Buller's third relief attempt, on February 5. With a British army of 20,000 men Buller forced a crossing of the Tugela River. On the following day he seized Vaal Krantz, just southwest of Ladysmith. The British held the village for two days against counterattacks by Gen. Louis Botha's Transvaal-Orange forces. But then Buller called off the offensive and again fell back beyond the Tugela. He had suffered 374 casualties. Boer losses were less.

This was the last major victory for the Boers, however. General Lord Frederick Roberts with Lord Kitchener as chief of staff had arrived the month before to take supreme command of the heretofore beleaguered British forces in South Africa. *See* Ladysmith; Spion Kop; Paardeberg; South African Wars.

Vadimonian Lake (Rise of Rome), 283 B.C. Despite their defeat at Sentinum, the Gauls and Etruscans continued to harass Rome's efforts to extend its northern borders. Finally, in 283 B.C., a Roman legion under Publius Cornelius Dolabella encountered a combined force of Gauls and Etruscans near Vadimonian Lake on the Tiber River 45 miles north of Rome. Dolabella caught the Etruscans as they were crossing the river and annihilated their last army. He then fell upon the Gauls and put them to flight with heavy losses. This battle ended the last resistance to Roman supremacy in central Italy. *See* Sentinum; Heraclea; Roman Republic.

Valcour Island (War of the American Revolution), 1776. While one British army under Gen. Sir William Howe tried to destroy Gen. George Washington's Continentals north of New York City in the fall of 1776, a second British force pushed up the Richelieu River from Canada toward Lake Champlain. Early in October Gen. Sir Guy Carleton arrived at the northern end of the lake with the advance guard of his 13,000-man army. The key to his thrust was a lake fleet of 29 vessels mounting 87 guns. Meanwhile Col. Benedict Arnold had been hurriedly building an American fleet of 16 vessels, carrying 83 guns, and manned by 800 soldiers.

On October 11 Carleton's ships encountered Arnold's fleet, which was moored between Valcour Island and the western shore. In a seven-hour battle the American flotilla was severely crippled and 60 crewmen were killed or wounded. That night Arnold led his surviving ships past the British line to the south. But Carleton pursued the next day, and at Split Rock the Americans were forced to abandon their ships and to set off overland for Crown Point, N.Y. Finding the latter post indefensible, Arnold's men retreated southward to Ticonderoga. Carleton occupied Crown Point but postponed an attack on Ticonderoga until the following year. Thus, although completely defeated at Valcour Island, Arnold's weak little fleet delayed the British advance on Albany until the fateful thrust of 1777. *See* Quebec III; Fort Ticonderoga III; American Revolution.

Valenciennes (Spanish-French Wars), 1656. The long war between Spain, now ruled by Philip IV, and France, under Louis XIV, entered its 22nd year in 1656. Neither side had been able to dominate the Spanish Netherlands and northern France, chief scene of the fighting. Much of the stalemate was due to the equal abilities of the two opposing commanders—Louis II, the Great Condé, the renegade French nobleman in the service of Spain, and the Vicomte de Turenne, marshal of France.

Early in the summer Turenne laid siege to the Spanish-held town of Valenciennes, in the northwest of modern France. On July 16, with the garrison on the point of surrender, Condé suddenly stormed the siege lines on both sides of the Schelde River. The French were routed with casualties of several thousand and forced to abandon the siege. Two years later near Dunkirk, however, the decisive battle of the so-called Spanish Fronde shaped up. It would serve as the basis for peace, after almost a quarter century of intermittent warfare. *See* Arras I; Dunes, The; Thirty Years' War.

Val-'es-Dunes (Rise of Normandy), 1047. William (the future Conqueror) of Normandy inherited the rule of northwestern France in 1035 from his father, Robert the Devil, duke of Normandy. But his claim was clouded by an illegitimate birth. Twelve years later a group of Norman nobles revolted against William. The 20-year-old duke appealed to King Henry I of France, who sent a cavalry force to Val-'es-Dunes, southwest of Caen. Here the rebel horsemen were attacked and thoroughly beaten. This battle secured William's position as duke of Normandy. He soon began building a military power that would rival the French and eventually conquer the English. *See* Hastings.

Valmy (Wars of the French Revolution), 1792. During the early stages of the French Revolution, Austria (Leopold II) and Prussia (Frederick William II) declared war on France in the spring of 1792. The ensuing conflict was called the War of the First Coalition. Along the border of the Austrian Netherlands (modern Belgium) the disorganized French army offered little resistance. On the northeast as well, the French fell back before the advance of an allied, chiefly Prussian, army commanded by Karl Wilhelm Ferdinand, duke of Brunswick. Longwy was lost on August 27, Verdun on September 2. The ponderous Prussian column of 34,000 men circled behind the French, who were guarding the passes through the Argonne Forest, to reach Valmy, near the Marne River, about 100 miles east of Paris. Here on September 20 the French generals Charles Dumouriez and François C. Kellermann turned their 36,000 troops to the west to make a stand north of the Châlons road. In a heavy fog the French artillery dueled the heavy enemy guns for several hours at a range of 1,300 yards. The Prussian infantry then advanced but halted before coming into musket range and turned back. This ended the fighting, with each side suffering only a few hundred casualties. Ten days later Brunswick retreated across the Rhine. Kellermann, whose men had borne the heaviest Prussian cannonade, was later made Duc de Valmy.

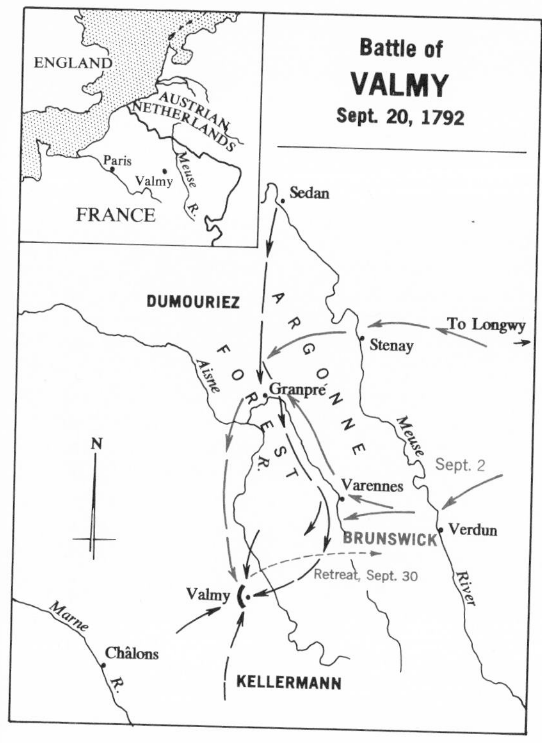

As a military action the battle of Valmy accomplished little. But the repulse of the Prussian invasion safeguarded the Revolutionary government and inspired the French to take the offensive. This set off a chain reaction that would continue for 23 years, until the battle of Waterloo. Thus Valmy ranks as one of the decisive battles of history. *See* Jemappes; French Revolution Wars.

Van Tuong Peninsula (Vietnam War), 1965. Increased United States military aid to South Vietnam led to the first large-scale combat for American troops since the Korean War, more than ten years earlier. During the summer of 1965 some 2,000 Viet Cong troops infiltrated the Van Tuong Peninsula just south of the major American air base of Chu Lai. To choke off this threat, Gen. Lewis Walt's Third Marine Division launched Operation Starlight. One company blocked the northern exit of Van Tuong, while two companies took a similar position to the south. Three companies then landed by helicopter west of the peninsula, trapping the Viet Cong against the sea, which American warships dominated completely. On August 30, 5,000 marines moved in to destroy the encircled enemy. The battle raged throughout the day and all that night. By midafternoon of the second day the attacking marines reached the beaches at the eastern end of Van Tuong, ending the last resistance. A total of almost 700 Viet Cong dead were counted, plus many more buried by aerial bombardment. United States losses were 50 killed and 150 wounded. *See* South Vietnam; Nam Dong; Plei Me; Vietnam War.

Varna I (Crusade against Ottoman Turks), 1444. The resurgent power of the Ottoman Empire in southeastern Europe prompted Pope Eugene IV to proclaim a new crusade. In 1443 János Hunyadi, a Transylvanian knight, marched into the Balkans at the head of a Christian army of Hungarians, Poles, Bosnians, Wallachians, and Serbians. The Turkish sultan Murad II thereupon agreed to a ten-year truce. But encouraged by the pope, the crusaders broke the peace in September 1444.

Commanded by Hunyadi, King Ladislas (Vladislav) III of Poland and V of Hungary, and Cardinal Guiliano Cesarini, the Christians advanced through Bulgaria to the Black Sea port of

Varna. Here they were to meet the ships of Venice. But the Venetians remained at Gallipoli and did not even prevent Murad from hurrying back to Europe from Asia Minor. On November 10 the sultan's Turkish army reached Varna. Hunyadi led an ill-advised frontal assault, which Murad repulsed. The Turks then attacked and quickly routed the poorly organized crusaders. Both Ladislas and Cesarini were killed, and Hunyadi barely escaped the ensuing massacre. Thus the Second Crusade ended as disastrously as had the first, 48 years earlier at Nicopolis. *See* Nicopolis; Salonika I; Kossovo II.

Varna II (Russian-Turkish War), 1828. To capitalize on the weaknesses of the Ottoman Empire, demonstrated in the Greek War of Independence, Czar Nicholas I of Russia declared war in the spring of 1828. Russian armies forced crossings of the Danube at several points but were stopped in their drive toward Constantinople by a series of strongly held fortresses in what is now northeastern Bulgaria. Prince Aleksandr Menshikov, in charge of the Russian advance, sent a force under Gen. Count Hans von Diebitsch to besiege Varna on the Black Sea. The Turkish soldiers of Sultan Mahmud II defended the town vigorously for three months until finally forced to yield Varna on October 12. However, the long resistance made it necessary for Russia to call off the campaign that year and go into winter quarters. *See* Navarino; Kulevcha.

Veii (Rise of Rome), 405–396 B.C. The long struggle for supremacy in Italy reached a turning point at the beginning of the fourth century B.C. for the contending settlements of Etruria, Rome, Latium, Samnium, Campania, and the Greek colonies of Magna Graecia. In 405 the Romans laid siege to the southern Etruscan stronghold of Veii, 12 miles north of Rome. After ten years of stalemate, the Roman general Marcus Furius Camillus took charge of the siege and in a determined assault conquered the city in 396 B.C. The Roman victory ended Etruscan power in central Italy. It also greatly enhanced Rome's prestige, for the battle had been won without the aid of its southern ally, the Latin League. From this time on Rome would cast an increasingly longer shadow. *See* Cumae; Allia; Roman Republic.

Vella Gulf (World War II). Site of a Japanese-American naval battle on August 6 and 7, 1943, during the fight for the Solomon Islands. *See* Solomon Islands.

Vella Lavella (World War II). A land and naval battle ending on October 7, 1943, between Japan and the United States in the fight for the Solomon Islands. *See* Solomon Islands.

Velletri (War of the Austrian Succession), 1744. The first serious fighting of the war in Italy shaped up when the Austrian general Johann Lobkowitz brushed past a Spanish force and headed southwest for the Neapolitan frontier during the summer of 1744. King Charles IV (son of Philip V of Spain) of the Two Sicilies hurriedly came to the assistance of the Spaniards. He formed a combined army at Velletri, 20 miles southeast of Rome. Here on August 11 the reluctant allies checked and then drove back the Austrian army of the Holy Roman Empire (Maria Theresa). Charles IV then again withdrew from the war, while Lobkowitz marched north to aid King Charles Emmanuel I of Sardinia (Savoy). *See* Toulon II; Cuneo; Austrian Succession, War of the.

Venezuela. *See* Latin America.

Venice (Italian Wars of Independence), 1849. During the Italian uprisings against Austrian rule in 1848, Venice proclaimed itself a republic (of Saint Mark) under the presidency of Daniele Manin on March 22. In little more than a year, however, the Italian rebels were put down in Lombardy, Rome, and Sicily. Venice, standing alone, then received the full force of Austrian might in Italy. Field Marshal Joseph Radetzky, who had crushed the Piedmontese in Lombardy, laid siege to the city on July 20, 1849. Blasted by bombardment, ravaged by cholera, and near starvation, Venice surrendered to the Austrians on August 28. Manin fled to exile in Paris. This defeat completed the suppression of the 1848–49 revolutionary movement. *See* Novara II; Rome VII; Magenta; Italian Wars of Independence.

Veracruz (U.S.-Mexican War), 1847. Convinced that Gen. Zachary Taylor could not win a final victory in northern Mexico, President James Polk ordered a new United States offensive early in 1847. Its aim was Mexico City, by way of a landing on the east coast at Veracruz, then the strongest fortress in the Western Hemisphere. On March 9 a fleet under Com. Matthew Perry (later succeeded by Com. David Conner) carried Gen. Winfield Scott and 13,000 troops to Veracruz. The army landed almost unopposed on the beaches south of the fortress in the first large-scale amphibious operation in American history. After building up their beachhead for two weeks, Scott's troops laid siege to Veracruz, defended by some 5,000 Mexicans under Gen. Morales. A six-day bombardment by artillery and naval guns brought a capitulation of the city and its castle of San Juan de Ulúa on March 27. The siege cost the defenders 80 military and 100 civilian casualties. American losses were 82, including 19 killed. Scott occupied Veracruz two days later and then began preparing for the march inland to Mexico City, 264 miles away. *See* Buena Vista; Cerro Gordo; U.S.-Mexican War.

Vercellae (Gauls' Attack on Rome), 101 B.C. The decision of the Gauls to divide their forces for separate invasions of Italy proved to be disastrous.

Concentrating his Roman army against the invasion from France, Gaius Marius had crushed the Teutones on the Rhone in 102 B.C. He then turned back to deal with the Cimbri, who had crossed the Alps through the Brenner Pass. Marius joined forces with Quintus Lutatius Catulus, who had been battling the invaders in northwestern Italy. At Vercellae, 39 miles southwest of Milan, the veteran Roman legions massacred the fierce but poorly organized Cimbri. This battle ended the last Gallic invasion of Italy and made Marius a national hero. *See* Aquae Sextiae; Roman Republic.

Verdun (World War I), 1916. To break the prolonged deadlock on the Western Front, the German chief of staff, Gen. Erich von Falkenhayn, organized a massive assault on the Verdun salient held by the French Second Army. Believing that for sentimental reasons the French would fight to hold this ground, he embarked upon a deliberate campaign of attrition. Crown Prince Friedrich Wilhelm's Fifth Army of a million men became the German instrument to bleed white the French army. The attack opened on February 21, behind a 12-hour bombardment by 1,400 artillery pieces, on an eight-mile front east of the Meuse River. The German infantry then stormed southward to capture the partially dismantled Fort Douaumont on February 25. On that day the French field marshal Joseph Joffre, preoccupied with planning his own offensive on the Somme River, sent Gen. Henri Pétain to take over the Verdun defenses.

South of Fort Douaumont, increased French resistance, particularly accurate artillery fire, slowed the German advance by the end of February. The Crown Prince then shifted his heaviest attacks to the west bank of the Meuse, on March 6. Here the French on Hill 295 (Le Mort Homme), six miles northwest of Verdun, and Hill 304, two miles farther west, held on so grimly that the Germans transferred their main efforts back to the right bank. (Hill 295 did not fall until May 29, Hill 304 was still partially held at the limit of the German penetration on this flank on August 8.) Pressing forward on the left flank, the attackers seized the village of Vaux, three miles from Verdun, on March 29 and finally overran Fort de Vaux on June 6. Although the German offensive had now been slowed to a crawl, the crown prince persisted. On June 23 he drove for the heights, east of the river, that commanded Verdun and the Meuse bridges. The assault was only narrowly repulsed. The last German attack, also beaten off by the slimmest of margins, came on July 11. The French had fulfilled their pledge *Ils ne passeront pas!* ("They shall not pass!") at a cost of 315,000 casualties. German losses were 280,000.

During the six-month attack the French made good use of their only line of communications. This was the secondary road to Bar-le-Duc, 40 miles to the south, which came to be known as la Voie Sacrée (the Sacred Road). An endless stream of trucks carried vital reinforcements and supplies along this road despite interdicting enemy artillery fire.

For the next three months the battleground remained relatively quiet. Then Gen. Robert Nivelle, who had replaced Pétain on May 1, launched a counterattack on October 24. The German Fifth Army, exhausted and decimated by casualties, gave up part of their hard-won gains,

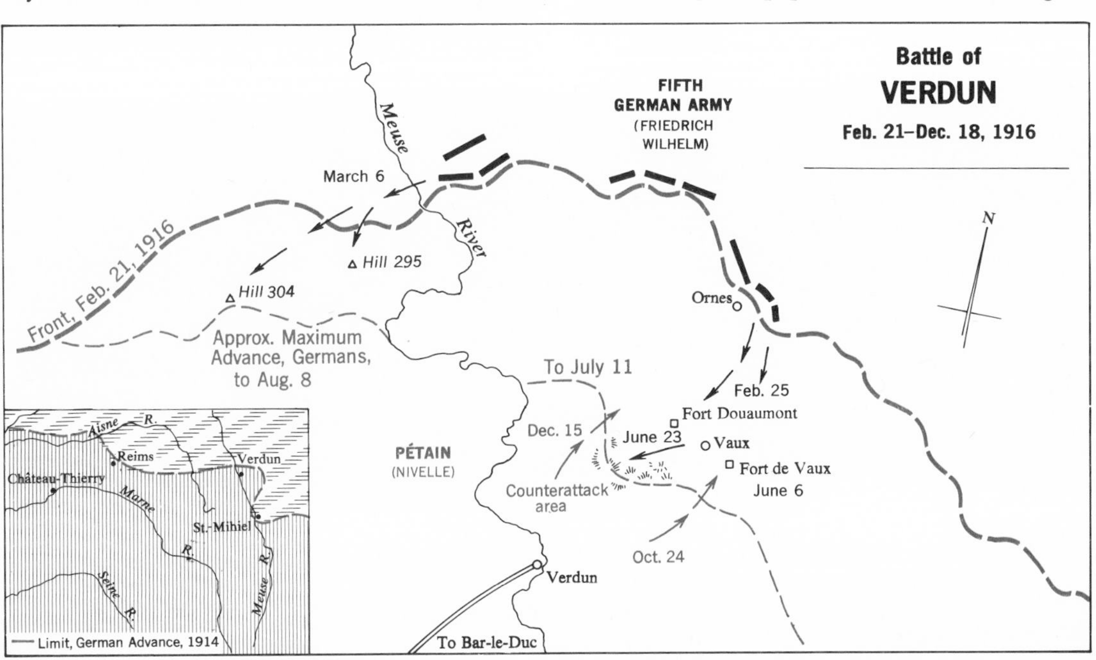

including forts de Vaux and Douaumont, on November 2. Another French counterthrust, on December 15, won back additional ground. In both of these attacks the leadership of the French general Charles Mangin stood out, first as a division, and later as a corps, commander. By December 18 fighting had ended, in one of the bloodiest battles in history. French losses totaled 542,000; German casualties, 434,000, in the longest engagement of World War I.

Meanwhile the other murderous battle of 1916, the Somme River, had opened and closed with equal lack of success and with even heavier casualties. Also, Falkenhayn had been replaced on the Western Front (August 29) by Field Marshal Paul von Hindenburg and his operational chief, Gen. Erich Ludendorff. *See* Artois-Loos; Somme River I; World War I.

Verneuil (Hundred Years' War), 1424. By mid-1424 the English army of the Duke of Bedford, regent for his youthful nephew Henry VI, had overrun most of northern France. In this campaign the English received help from the Duke of Burgundy. The Orleanist French, nominally ruled by the dauphin Charles (future Charles VII), resolved to make one more stand north of the Loire River. Much of the French determination came from a contingent of 5,000 Scots led by Archibald, 4th earl of Douglas.

The Scots and some 10,000 Orleanists commanded by the constable of France, the Earl of Buchan (John Stewart, son-in-law of Douglas), attacked the English at Verneuil, 50 miles west of Paris, on August 17. Although Bedford could deploy less than 9,000 men, most of them carried the deadly longbow. The long range (250 yards) and high velocity of their arrows repulsed a fierce and prolonged charge by the dismounted Scottish and French men-at-arms. After losing more than 7,000 men, including the great majority of the Scots, the shattered survivors retreated across the Loire. Both Douglas and Buchan lay dead on the field. Jean II, duc d'Alençon, who had led a futile flanking attack against the English rear, was a prisoner.

The battle of Verneuil ranks second only to Agincourt as the most decisive victory won by the English in the fifteenth-century phase of the Hundred Years' War. It also destroyed the last attempt by Scotland to provide major aid to its French ally. *See* Cravant; Orleans; Hundred Years' War.

Verona (Civil Wars of the Roman Empire), 312. Seven years after the abdication of Emperor Diocletian, Rome was torn by the claims of four major pretenders to the throne, all military commanders: Constantine I in Gaul, Valerius Maxentius in Italy, Licinianus Licinius in Illyria, and Valerius Maximinus in the East. The inevitable civil war erupted early in 312 when Constantine crossed the Alps into northwest Italy with 50,000 troops. Maxentius sent an army northward to block the advance, but Constantine pushed past resistance at Turin and marched down the Po Valley. Turning north at Verona, he laid siege to that city, defended by Pompeianus, a lieutenant of Maxentius. Pompeianus escaped and organized a force to relieve the siege. But Constantine's army wheeled about to crush these troops in a sharp struggle that resulted in the death of Pompeianus. Verona promptly surrendered.

Constantine, now master of the Po Valley, prepared to march on Maxentius' army at Rome. *See* Carrhae II; Saxa Rubra; Roman Empire.

Verulamium I (Caesar's Invasion of Britain), 54 B.C. Julius Caesar's first invasion of Britain was only a reconnaissance in Kent made with two legions in August 55 B.C. The following summer, however, Caesar landed five legions northeast of Dover. Brushing aside the weak resistance of the Britons, the Romans pushed inland and crossed the Thames near Brentford. The Briton chief Cassivellaunus wisely avoided a pitched battle, being content to harass Caesar's troops with war chariots and horsemen. Finally, at Verulamium (Saint Albans), 20 miles northwest of modern London, Cassivellaunus agreed to peace terms. He surrendered some hostages and promised to pay a tribute to Rome, whereupon Caesar retraced his route to the coast and re-embarked for Gaul. The invasion achieved no permanent gain (the tribute was never paid) except to open Britain to later Roman trade and influence. *See* Coblenz; Tongres; Medway River; Gallic Wars.

Verulamium II (Roman Conquest of Britain), A.D. 61. Under Emperor Nero, as under Claudius I before him, Roman rule over Britain was benevolent and constructive. The major exception was in East Anglia (modern Norfolk, Suffolk) where the death of the Iceni king in 61 opened the way to plunder and cruelties on the part of the occupying forces. The Iceni flew to arms under the leadership of the widow queen Boudicca (Boadicea). Descending on the undefended town of Camulodunum (Colchester), the frenzied tribesmen slaughtered the Roman settlers and the Britons who were collaborating with the conqueror.

Hurrying from Lindum (Lincoln) to put down the revolt, the Ninth Legion was overcome by sheer numbers and virtually annihilated. At Gloucester the Second Legion commander, Poenius Postumus, refused to leave the protection of his encampment. The other two legions in Britain, the Fourteenth and Twentieth, under Gov. Suetonius Paulinus, stood in Wales. Before they could intervene, Boudicca's rebels swept down on Londinium (London). The embryonic city was burned to the ground, its inhabitants massacred. The tide of terror then turned to the northwest where Verulamium (Saint Albans) suffered the same bloody obliteration. Some 70,000 people are reported to have been killed in the three onslaughts. But now Paulinus' two legions (10,000 men) had arrived on the scene following their forced march from Wales. Choosing his ground carefully to give maximum advantage to his vastly outnumbered soldiers, Paulinus directed a coordinated attack on the Briton horde. The battle was fought without mercy, even for the women and children in Boudicca's wagon train. At the end of the day Roman discipline and tactical skill had triumphed. Almost 80,000 Britons were reported killed at a loss of 400 dead legionaries and a somewhat larger number of wounded. The Iceni queen took poison, while at Gloucester the news of the battle induced Postumus to stab himself to death. The victory of Paulinus gave him rank with Domitius Corbulo, in the East, as the best Roman general of the first century A.D. *See* Mons Graupius.

Vesontio (Gallic Wars), 58 B.C. Moving 100 miles northeast from their victory at Bibracte, Julius Caesar's six Roman legions occupied the chief fortress of the Sequani Gauls at Vesontio (Besançon). A few days' march to the north brought the legionaries up against a Gallic force of seven tribes, commanded by the fierce Germanic chief Ariovistus. The Gauls attacked the Roman camp near Mulhouse. But again superior numbers proved to be unequal to the well-organized, hard-fighting Romans, and the Gauls suffered enormous losses. Caesar now went into winter quarters in Burgundy to rebuild his legions in preparation for the next year's campaign against the Belgic tribes in the northwest. *See* Bibracte; Sambre River; Gallic Wars.

Viborg (Wars of Scandinavia), 1157. For ten years after the death of Eric III, the Lamb, Denmark was torn by civil war between the houses ruled by Sweyn III and Canute V. When Canute was assassinated in 1157, a relative, Waldemar, whose father had also been murdered, claimed the crown. His forces met those of Sweyn at Viborg on the Jutland Peninsula later that year. Sweyn's army was routed. In fleeing the field, the king was overtaken and killed. The victor assumed the throne as Waldemar I. He was to earn the title "the Great" for his 25 years of strong and popular rule. *See* Stiklestad; Reval.

Vicksburg (American Civil War), 1863. In the West the chief objective of the Federal commander, Gen. U. S. Grant, was Vicksburg, Miss., a Confederate strong point blocking Union control of the Mississippi River. The first attack on the city, by way of Chickasaw Bluffs, had been repulsed at the end of 1862. During the first three months of 1863, Grant made four other unsuccessful attempts to capture or isolate Vicksburg—the Lake Providence route, a canal to bypass the city, Steele's Bayou route, and the Yazoo Pass route. Grant then planned a wide envelopment from the south and east. To camouflage his intent, he sent Col. Benjamin Grierson on a cavalry raid from La Grange, Tenn., on April 17. Riding hard, Grierson's 1,200 troopers swept 600 miles southward through Mississippi and northern Louisiana to reach Baton Rouge on May 2.

Under cover of the confusion caused by Grierson, Grant moved his army down the west side of the Mississippi below Vicksburg to Hard Times, La., during April 5–28. Two days later, protected by the gunboats of Adm. David Porter, Grant sent the corps of Gens. John McClernand (XIII) and James McPherson (XVII) across the river by transport ferry to Bruinsburg. No Confederate opposition was encountered. Distracted by Grant's diversions, the Confederate commander at Vicksburg, Gen. John Pemberton, had posted only 9,000 troops in this area—at Grand Gulf and Port Gibson, both to the north of Bruinsburg. When McClernand began marching inland, Gen. John Bowen tried to block the Federal advance at Port Gibson. McClernand, later supported by McPherson, attacked on May 1. The much larger Federal army turned Bowen's right (north) flank and forced his withdrawal. The Confederates evacuated Grand Gulf the following day. Learning that a Confederate army stood at Jackson, 45 miles east of Vicksburg, Grant marched boldly northeast to put his army between the separated wings of the enemy forces. On May 7 Gen. William Sherman's XV Corps crossed the Mississippi, bringing Grant's strength up to 41,000.

Moving three corps abreast, the Federal army pressed steadily forward. At Raymond the right flank corps of McPherson brushed past the Confederate brigade of Gen. John Gregg on May 12. Leaving McClernand to hold the Raymond–Clinton line against Pemberton's army, which was advancing toward him from Vicksburg, Grant turned McPherson and Sherman eastward to Jackson. Here Gen. Joseph Johnston, nominally the Confederate commander in the West, stood with the brigades of Gregg and Gen. William Walker, a total of 6,000 men. Grant's Napoleonic penetration had clearly divided the two Confederate armies.

On May 14 Grant attacked Jackson. Sherman, advancing from the southwest, overwhelmed Gregg's brigade, while McPherson, approaching from the west, routed Walker's men after a sharp struggle. The Federals entered the Mississippi capital at 4 P.M. Johnston's defeated army fled to the north.

Leaving Sherman to destroy war supplies in Jackson, Grant promptly turned westward with his other two corps on May 15. Meanwhile Pem-

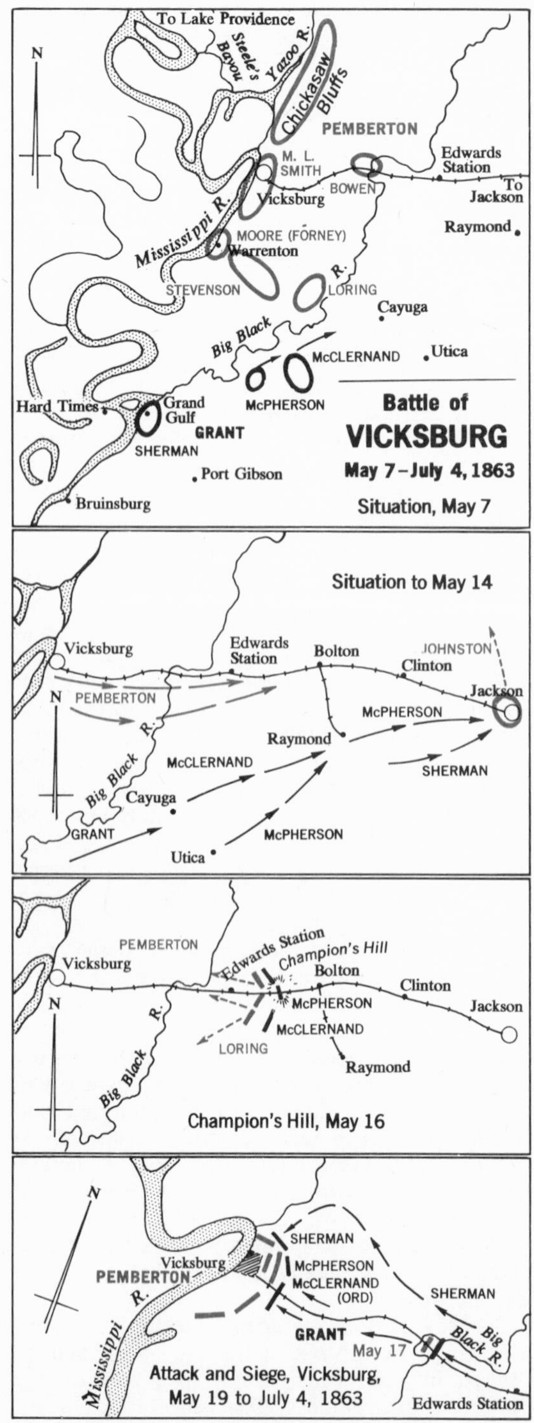

berton had been marching cautiously toward Jackson and now stood squarely in the path of the Federal army. The two hostile forces met at Champion's Hill, 20 miles east of Vicksburg, on May 16. McPherson attacked vigorously on the right (north) flank, but McClernand on the other flank moved so slowly as to neutralize Grant's numerical superiority, 29,000 to 22,000. In the hardest fight of the campaign so far, Champion's Hill changed hands several times before Pemberton ordered a withdrawal. General William Loring's division, charged with covering the retreat, was cut off from the main Confederate army and compelled to escape to the southeast. This force was thus lost to Pemberton for later defense of Vicksburg. In all, the Confederate army suffered 3,851 casualties, including 381 killed. Grant's losses were 410 killed out of a total of 2,441 casualties. Sherman did not arrive from Jackson until after the battle.

Pemberton fell back toward Vicksburg, leaving 5,000 men to hold a small bridgehead east of the Big Black River. But Sherman outflanked this position on the north, and on May 17 the rest of Grant's army overwhelmed the Confederate rear guard in an hour's fight, capturing 1,700 men and 18 guns. Grant pushed on to Vicksburg, where Pemberton had withdrawn with 20,000 men (ignoring Johnston's order to avoid being trapped inside the city). On May 19 the Federals attacked the city but the surprisingly strong defenses resisted capture. On this day Grant was able to reopen communications along the Mississippi, after his 18-day march of 200 miles into enemy territory.

On May 22 Grant launched a larger, better-coordinated assault against Vicksburg. Again the Confederates resisted stubbornly, repulsing the day-long attack and inflicting 3,200 casualties. Grant then methodically laid siege to the city, completely investing it, digging approaches, and employing mines and countermines. He built up his strength to 71,000 men, half of whom were deployed north and east to guard against a relief column that was being organized by Johnston at Jackson. The besieging force had Sherman's corps on the north, McPherson's on the east, and McClernand's (who was relieved by Gen. Edward Ord on June 18) on the southeast. Inside Vicksburg the 30,000-man garrison held on grimly despite increasing deprivations. The nine miles of Pemberton's well-organized defenses were manned by the divisions of Gens. Martin Smith, John Forney, and Carter Stevenson, from north to south. Gen. John Bowen's division constituted the reserve.

After May 22 Grant made no more direct assaults on Vicksburg. But constant shelling, disease, and the growing shortage of rations took a steady toll of the defenders. By July 4 one-half of Pemberton's command was dead, wounded, or sick. On that day the Confederates surrendered unconditionally.

As the Federal ring was closing tighter on Vicksburg, Johnston had begun marching to the city's relief with 31,000 men. He had reached the Big Black River on July 4 when he learned of

Vicksburg's capitulation. He promptly countermarched to Jackson.

At a cost of 9,362 casualties Grant had achieved one of the great victories in military history. The Mississippi was now a Federal highway (Port Hudson, downstream, fell five days later), and the Confederacy was split in two. The large Union army assembled by Grant was free to move against other objectives in the South. The capitulation of Vicksburg, coupled with the simultaneous defeat at Gettysburg, ended all hopes for a Confederate victory, although the war dragged on for almost two more years. *See* Chickasaw Bluffs; Gettysburg; Port Hudson; Chattanooga; American Civil War.

Vienna I (Siege by Turks), 1529. Suleiman I, the Magnificent, moved his Ottoman Turk army back into Hungary in 1528 to re-establish the rule of his puppet, John Zápolya. After routing the outpost forces of Ferdinand I (king of Hungary, archduke of Austria, and future Holy Roman Emperor) from Budapest, some 100,000 Turks marched 135 miles northwest up the Danube to Vienna. Holy Roman Emperor Charles V rushed veteran Spanish and German regiments to strengthen the defenses of the city, which were entrusted to Graf Nicolas zu Salm-Reifferscheidt.

On September 26, 1529, Suleiman laid siege to the great Christian outpost of eastern Europe. Here, too, was the seat of the Hapsburgs. The 20,000-man garrison beat off several assaults against the city's walls and in turn hurt the attackers with vigorous sorties through the three gates. In this valiant defense Vienna was aided by foul weather, which prevented the Turks from bringing up their artillery. Finally, after three weeks of failure, Suleiman abandoned the siege on

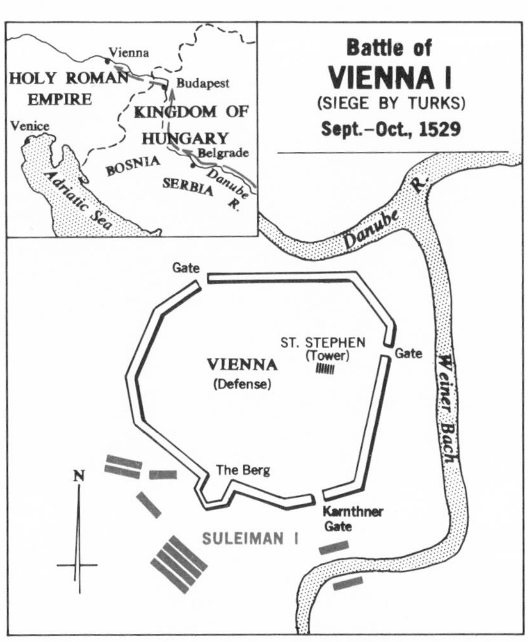

October 16. Hampered by deep snow and harassing cavalry attacks, the Turks lost heavily on the long road back to Adrianople. The repulse at Vienna is often considered the turning point in the Moslem advance against Christian Europe. The Turks, however, refused all offers of a peaceful settlement of the war until 1533. Then Suleiman agreed to terms on Hungary with Ferdinand; but the naval war with Charles V continued. *See* Mohács; Tunis III.

Vienna II (Austrian-Turkish Wars), 1683. Despite reverses in Poland and Russia, the Ottoman Turkish sultan Mohammed IV sent an army north to take Vienna. Under Grand Vizier Kara Mustafa, the Turks reached the city on July 17, 1683. Emperor Leopold I and his court fled, leaving the defense to Count Ernst Rüdiger von Starhemberg. When assaults against the city's walls failed, the Turks began mining operations, which seemed certain to succeed. But on September 12 John III Sobieski of Poland and Charles V, titular duke of Lorraine, arrived with a relieving army of 20,000 men. An attack on the Turkish siege lines routed the Mohammedans, ending the threat to Vienna. The defeated vizier was beheaded for his failure. This second battle of Vienna clearly confirmed the declining strength of the Ottoman Empire. *See* Khotin II; Harkány.

Vietnam War (1945–1954; 1961—). When French troops returned to Indo-China after World War II, they met ever greater resistance from Vietnam nationalists. The Communist victory of the Vietminh at Dienbienphu in 1954 overthrew French rule and led to the establishment of two Vietnams—North and South—divided at the 17th parallel according to the terms of an international conference at Geneva. When Communist guerrilla forces, called the Viet Cong (VC), began subverting the government of South Vietnam, the United States in 1961 sent increasing amounts of military aid and a growing number of military advisors to the South Vietnam government. Communist North Vietnam (ruled by Ho Chi-Minh) supported the VC, leading to a slow but steady development of open warfare between South Vietnamese forces, supported by American troops, on the one hand, and Communist guerrillas and, later, regular troops from North Vietnam, on the other.

Dienbienphu	1954
South Vietnam	1961—
Nam Dong	1964
Van Tuong Peninsula	1965
Plei Me	1965
Chu Pong–Ia Drang River	1965
An Lao Valley	1966
A Shau	1966
Tou Morong	1966

Vigo Bay (War of the Spanish Succession), 1702. In the first naval action of the war, Adm. Sir George Rooke and the 2nd Duke of Ormonde

(James Butler) led an Anglo-Dutch naval expedition against Cadiz in August 1702. The Spanish defenders, fighting for the new Bourbon king, Philip V, drove off the 50-ship fleet of the invaders. On the way back to England Rooke and Ormonde learned of a Spanish treasure fleet in Vigo Bay, on the northwest coast. With markedly more aggressiveness than they had displayed at Cadiz, the English commanders forced their way into the harbor on October 12. Every Spanish and French ship was sunk, burned, or captured, and a huge treasure of silver seized. This battle is sometimes called the affair of the Spanish Galleons. *See* Landau; Gibraltar I; Spanish Succession, War of the.

Vimeiro (Napoleonic Empire Wars), 1808. When Napoleon I occupied Portugal in 1807 and installed his brother Joseph as king of Spain the following year, most of the people of the peninsula rose in revolt. To take advantage of this unrest, the British government of George III sent an expeditionary force to Portugal. Under the command of Gen. Sir Arthur Wellesley (later Duke of Wellington), veteran of warfare in India, 30,000 troops began landing in July 1808 between Oporto and Lisbon. Wellesley took the road southward toward Lisbon, while Marshal Andoche Junot marched out from the Portuguese capital with 14,000 men to block the invaders.

Wellesley with 17,000 men pushed through Rolica on August 15 after a hard fight. At Vimeiro, 32 miles northwest of Lisbon, the two armies slammed together on August 21. The French reeled back with a loss of 1,800 men and 13 guns. British casualties totaled only 720. But Wellesley's senior commanders (Sir Harry Burrard and Sir Hew Dalrymple) arrived at the moment of victory. Instead of pursuing Junot's army, the British signed the Convention of Cintra (Sintra) on August 30, by which the French army agreed to evacuate Portugal in return for transportation back to France in English ships. Thus 26,000 of Napoleon's best troops were carried to Rochefort-sur-Mer, free to fight again. *See* Bailén; La Coruña; Napoleonic Empire Wars.

Viminacium (Wars of the Byzantine Empire), 601. The barbarian Avars, a Tatar tribe from Asia that had settled northwest of the Black Sea, pushed down to the Danube in 583 and ten years later raided southward to the gates of Constantinople. The Byzantine emperor Mauricius, busy rebuilding his armed forces and watching the Persian situation in the East, sent out an Imperial army to throw back the Avars. Led by Priscus, the Byzantine cavalry thrust northward to the Danube, killing barbarians on the way. At Viminacium, on the right bank of the river (in southeast modern Yugoslavia), Priscus met and defeated a large body of Avars. The Byzantines pushed on northwest to the Theiss (Tisza), a left bank tributary of the Danube, before turning back. In all, Priscus' expedition killed some 20,000 barbarians. It won only 18 years of peace, however. The Avars resumed raiding when the Persians advanced to within sight of Constantinople in 619. But the Avars were never able to storm the city's high walls. *See* Constantinople II; Jerusalem V.

Vimy Ridge (World War I). A dominant ridge ten miles north of Arras, taken briefly by the French on May 9, 1915; captured by the Canadian Corps of the British First Army on April 9, 1917. *See* Artois II; Arras II.

Vinaroz (Spanish Civil War), 1938. With the repulse of the Republican attack on Teruel, the Nationalist generalissimo Francisco Franco ordered a broad offensive eastward into Aragon and the Levante. On March 9, preceded by a heavy artillery and aerial bombardment, Gen. Fidel Dávila sent five columns plunging at the Republican lines. Overpowered by superior armament, government troops yielded as much as 60 miles of ground in eight days. One of the attacking columns (Juan de Yagüe) penetrated into Catalonia on March 25. Lérida was captured on April 3. A hundred miles to the south, Gen. Camilo Alonso Vega led a Navarrese division into Vinaroz, a fishing village on the Mediterranean about halfway between Barcelona and Valencia, on April 15. Franco's armies had cut Republican Spain in two. Alonso Vega's force turned southward but found increasing Republican resistance. Castellón de la Plana, 40 miles above Valencia, finally fell on June 14. To bolster the attack, Gen. José Varela set out from Teruel, attacking southeast. But Gen. Leopoldo Menéndez threw up such a stout defense that almost 20,000 Nationalists were killed, wounded, or captured during July 18–23. The attack then stalled, with Valencia still in government hands. *See* Teruel; Ebro River; Spanish Civil War.

Vincennes (War of the American Revolution), 1779. During the early years of the war American settlers in the Old Northwest (now Midwest) suffered from frequent raids by British, Loyalists, and Indians. The hated symbol of these outrages was the British lieutenant governor at Detroit, Lt. Col. Henry Hamilton (called the Hair Buyer). To put down the raiders and to win the support of local French settlers, George Rogers Clark of Harrodsburg (in what is now Kentucky), received a colonel's commission from Virginia. In May 1778 Clark sailed down the Ohio River with 175 rugged frontiersmen. Landing near the mouth of the river, he marched 120 miles overland to occupy Kaskaskia, Ill., without opposition on July 4. Other French towns in Illinois, and Vincennes, in Indiana, quickly submitted. But from Detroit, Hamilton marched southward to reoccupy Vincennes and its stronghold Fort Sackville on the Wabash River on December 17.

Clark reacted promptly. On February 6, 1779, at the head of 127 men, he began the 180-mile overland march to Vincennes. Despite incredible hardships, Clark's army reached the Wabash on February 20 and crossed it. Three days later the half-frozen, starving army entered the town at sunset. The Indians friendly to the British fled. Hamilton, with less than 100 men, holed up in Fort Sackville. After two days of fighting, the 80 surviving troops in the fort surrendered. Hamilton was sent back to Virginia under heavy guard. Clark now had complete control of the Illinois country, which he successfully held until the end of the war, although Detroit remained in British hands. *See* American Revolution.

Vinegar Hill (Irish Rebellion), 1798. To unite the Catholics and Protestants of Ireland in an effort to win political reforms from Great Britain, Theobald Wolfe Tone formed the Society of United Irishmen in 1791. When the group failed to obtain reforms, and later separation, by parliamentary means, it turned to revolution. The rebels asked France and then the Netherlands for aid but received no help. The British government of King George III sent Gen. Gerard Lake into Ireland to put down the insurrection. Lake disarmed Ulster in 1797 and captured the rebel leaders the following spring. He then marched into Wexford County where Father John Murphy had collected a strong rebel force. On June 21 Lake's troops attacked the Irish camp at Vinegar Hill, Enniscorthy. The British regulars were too much for the insurgents, routing them completely. This battle virtually ended the rebellion. Three years later Ireland became a part of the United Kingdom by act of Parliament. *See* Camperdown.

Vis (Italian Wars of Independence), 1866. Although the Austrian government of Franz Josef I agreed to cede Venice to Italy (via France) on July 3, 1866, the war with the new kingdom of Victor Emmanuel II continued. The fighting now shifted to the Adriatic where an Italian squadron of ten ironclads under Adm. Count Carlo di Persano was challenged by an Austrian fleet of seven ironclads and some wooden vessels commanded by Adm. Wilhelm von Tegetthoff. On July 20 off the island of Vis (Lissa), along the central coast of modern Yugoslavia, the Austrian ships virtually destroyed the embryonic Italian navy. But weakened by the loss of the Seven Weeks' War to Prussia, Austria could not pursue the conflict with Italy. A treaty of peace, which confirmed the cession of Venice, was signed at Vienna on October 19. *See* Custoza II; Sadowa; Mentana; Italian Wars of Independence.

Vistula River–Warsaw (World War I), 1914. To aid the crumbling Austrian army in Galicia, the German commander in chief on the Eastern Front, Field Marshal Paul von Hindenburg, moved the newly organized Ninth Army by rail from East Prussia into southern Poland. Taking up a position on the left of the Austrians, Gen. August von Mackensen sent his Ninth Army attacking eastward toward the upper Vistula River on September 28. To the south the Austrian First, Fourth, Third, and Second armies (all under Field Marshal Count Conrad von Hötzendorf) also advanced against the Russian armies of Gen. Nikolai Ivanov.

Outspeeding their Austrian allies, the Germans pressed forward to reach the Vistula on October 9. Three days later they were within 12 miles of Warsaw. However, the slow pace of the Austrians to the south and a Russian concentration by Gen. Nikolai Russki against the northern flank checked the German advance. On October 17 Hindenburg ordered a general retreat. By the end of the month the Central Powers were back on their starting line, closely pursued by the Russians. German losses were about 40,000.

The collapse of the German offensive against Warsaw again left Silesia vulnerable to Russian attack. To forestall the expected thrust, Hindenburg resolved to launch a new attack from the Posen-Thorn (Poznań-Toruń) area. *See* Galicia; Lódź; World War I.

Vitoria (Napoleonic Empire Wars), 1813. The disastrous French losses in Russia and subsequent enemy rebuilding of their forces along the Elbe forced Napoleon I to withdraw many troops from the Peninsular Campaign. Taking advantage of the reduced forces opposing him, Gen. Lord Wellington (Arthur Wellesley) marched from the Portuguese frontier into the north of Spain. King Joseph Bonaparte, older brother of Napoleon, evacuated Madrid and fled northward across the Ebro River. Here he relied on the 66,000-man army of Marshal Jean Jourdan to protect his ersatz Spanish government. But Wellington, with 79,000 British, Portuguese, and rebel Spanish troops, crossed the upper Ebro to outflank the French position. At Vitoria, 175 miles northeast of Madrid, Wellington attacked Jourdan on June 21, 1813. In a three-column assault the British general routed the French, inflicting 8,000 casualties and capturing most of the enemy artillery, transport, and booty. Allied losses totaled 5,000.

The battle of Vitoria ended Napoleon's domination of Spain. Joseph, now an ex-king, escaped across the Pyrenees into France. Wellington thrust northwest toward the western passes of the mountains while detachments of his command besieged San Sebastián (which fell on September 9), on the Bay of Biscay, and Pamplona (which fell on October 31), 40 miles to the south. Marshal Nicolas Soult hurried south from Bayonne, France, in a belated effort to check the enemy advance. But he was driven back across the Nive River in December. Wellington's army stood firmly on French soil. *See* Berezina River; Lützen II; Salamanca; Toulouse II; Napoleonic Empire Wars.

Vittorio Veneto (World War I), 1918. With the military strength of the Central Powers steadily diminishing in the autumn of 1918, the Italian supreme commander, Gen. Armando Diaz, prepared a final offensive against the Austrians stationed north of the Piave River. On the left (west) his First and Sixth armies were to fix the attention of the Austrian forces of Archduke Joseph in the Trentino. On the right five other Italian armies, which included British, French, and American units, stood ready to assault the enemy line held by the Austrian troops of Gen. Svetozar Borojević von Bojna. In all, Diaz had 57 divisions and 7,700 guns to oppose 58 divisions and 6,000 guns.

The Italian offensive began on October 24. On the left of the attack sector, the Fourth Army (Gaetano Giardino) struck at the hinge between the two Austrian army groups in the Monte Grappa area. For three days the Austrians fiercely held their ground, but the fighting drew in reserves from the lower Piave, where Diaz had scheduled his primary assault. Here three Italian armies established small bridgeheads north of the river during the first three days of the attack—on the left the Twelfth Army of French general Jean Graziani, in the center the Eighth Army of Gen. Enrico Caviglia, and on the right the Tenth Army of the British general Lord Cavan (Frederic Lambart). What had been a slow advance suddenly opened up on the afternoon of October 28. The bridgeheads were joined and a forward thrust was begun all along the line. The Eighth Army pressed forward to take Vittorio Veneto on October 30, while to its right the Tenth and Third armies lunged for the Livenza River, which was reached the same day. Checked for two days here, the troops of Diaz forced a crossing at Sacile on November 1. Austrian resistance now collapsed from the Trentino to the Adriatic Sea. Many units deserted en masse. Italian cavalry and armored cars rounded up the fleeing enemy in droves. Finally, late on November 3, the Austrians signed a truce at Villa Giusti, near Padua, which ended the fighting the following day. By this time about 500,000 prisoners had been taken. The Austrian armies ceased to exist. Italian casualties numbered 38,000. So ended the war on the Italian front—a struggle that had cost the Italians a total of 650,000 killed and almost 1,000,000 wounded. *See* Piave River; World War I.

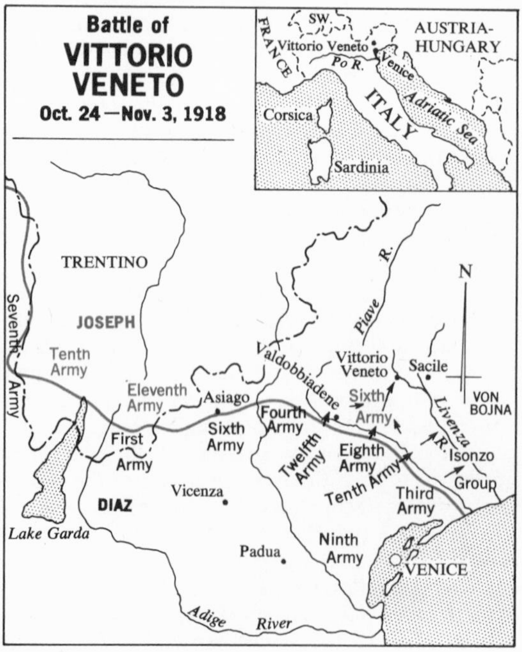

Battle of VITTORIO VENETO Oct. 24—Nov. 3, 1918

Vouillé (Rise of France), 507. After safeguarding his northern frontier against the Alamanni, the energetic Frankish king Clovis I turned on the Visigoths in the south. He crossed the Loire, intent on conquest. At Vouillé, a few miles northwest of Poitiers, Clovis encountered the army of Alaric II, who may have been trying to link up with the Ostrogoths in Italy under Theodoric the Great. The Frankish infantry with its deadly short-handled axes (the francisca) overpowered the Visigoths. Alaric was killed. The Goths abandoned their capital at Toulouse and retreated across the Pyrenees to Toledo, in modern Spain. Clovis, warmly supported by the Roman Catholic Church, now stood supreme as far south as Bordeaux and Toulouse. *See* Tolbiacum; Tertry.

Vyazma (World War II). The last German lunge toward Moscow trapped about 600,000 Russian troops in a pocket 125 miles southwest of Moscow; the pocket was reduced between October 2 and 13, 1941. *See* Moscow.

Vyborg (Finnish-Russian War), 1918. While Russia was torn by the Communist revolution, the grand duchy of Finland proclaimed its freedom, on July 20, 1917. But the ensuing Russian civil war between the Reds and counterrevolutionary Whites spread to Finland, where Bolsheviks and local Communists overran much of the southern part of the country early in 1918. General Baron Carl Gustav von Mannerheim then organized a Finnish White Army, which was supported by a German force under Gen. Baron Colmar von der Goltz. On April 13 Mannerheim's troops liberated Helsinki. Two weeks later they had marched on Vyborg (Viborg), 70 miles northwest of Leningrad. Here on April 29 the Whites defeated the Reds and drove them out of the country. Finland became an independent republic the following year. *See* Finland (World War II).

W

Wagram (Napoleonic Empire Wars), 1809. For six weeks after his withdrawal from Aspern-Essling, Napoleon I built up his French forces at Vienna and southward along the right bank of the Danube. In June 1809 he was reinforced by the army of his stepson, Eugène de Beauharnais, who had driven the Austrians out of Italy. Then, on the night of July 3–4, the emperor packed the bulk of his 189,000 troops onto Löbau Island, near the far shore. The following night his leading elements began landing on the east side of the Danube, pushing back weak Austrian opposition to expand their bridgehead. At 1 P.M. on July 5 Napoleon was across in force and pressing north and east against the 136,000-man army of Archduke Charles Louis, brother of the Austrian emperor Francis I. Charles yielded the Marchfeld (plain), but when the French attacked his main line along the Wagram plateau in the evening, the Austrians beat back the advance.

On the following day heavy fighting took place all along the five-mile front. Charles mounted an assault from his right wing along the river, aimed at cutting the French off at their crossing points. But the attack faltered against the resistance of Marshal André Masséna's IV Corps. Meanwhile Charles's own left was being relentlessly pushed in by Marshal Louis Davout's II Corps. Then at noon Gen. Jacques Macdonald, in a hollow oblong of three divisions (8,000 men), struck the Austrian right center and, despite cruel casualties, shattered the enemy line west of Wagram. Charles' army began falling back to the north. Later in the afternoon Charles's brother, Archduke John, made a tardy appearance from Pressburg (Bratislava) in the French rear. But he was quickly driven off. Too weary to pursue Charles until the next day, the French slept on the field that night. They had suffered almost 34,000 casualties, the Austrians between 40,000 and 43,000. Most of the killed and wounded fell from the heaviest concentration of artillery fire employed thus far in any war. Napoleon had used 488 guns, Charles 446.

After four days of retreat, Charles, slightly wounded at Wagram, asked for an armistice on July 10. (Napoleon's staunchest opponent for many years, the archduke never fought again.) Although Emperor Francis I planned to resume the war, he could not field another army and on October 14 signed the Treaty of Schönbrunn, which ceded 32,000 square miles of Austrian territory. Now only two obstacles stood in the way of Napoleon's complete mastery of continental Europe: the British-supported revolt in Spain and the hostility of Alexander I of Russia. *See* Aspern-Essling; Raab; Bussaco; Mogilev; Napoleonic Empire Wars.

Wakde Island (World War II). Part of the battle for New Guinea; the island was captured from the Japanese by Allied troops during May 18–21, 1944. *See* New Guinea.

Wakefield (Wars of the Roses), 1460. The compromise settlement after the Yorkist (white rose) victory of Northampton named Richard of York the successor to Henry VI. But it brought no peace to England. Queen Margaret assembled a Lancastrian (red rose) army from Wales and northern England and marched into Yorkshire, determined to assert the royal succession right of her (and Henry's) son Edward. Richard recklessly left the security of Sandal Castle and moved out to intercept the Lancastrians. At Wakefield on December 30, 1460, his army was surprised by Margaret's forces. In the bloodiest battle of the war to date the Yorkists suffered a crushing defeat. Richard, his son Edmund (the earl of Rutland), and the old Earl of Salisbury (Richard Neville) were all slain. The heads of the three nobles were impaled over the walls of York.

The battle of Wakefield completed the extinction of the older generation of nobles. Ascending to Yorkist leadership were Richard's sons Edward, George (Duke of Clarence), and Richard and Warwick, son of Salisbury. On the Lancastrian side the new lords Somerset, Clifford, and Exeter took command. With leaders on both sides mourning their slain fathers, the hatred and savagery of the struggle deepened significantly. *See* Northampton II; Mortimer's Cross; Roses, Wars of the.

Wake Island (World War II), 1941. One of the first targets of Japan's early offensive in the Pacific was the tiny U.S. atoll of Wake, 2,000 miles west of Hawaii. The island was defended by 449 combat marines under Maj. James Devereux, 69 navy men, and 6 army signalmen. Also present were 1,216 civilians, almost all construction workers from Guam. On December 8, 34 carrier-based Japanese bombers raided the island and knocked out 8 of Maj. Paul Putnam's 12 Wildcat fighter planes. Three days later an attempted Japanese landing was beaten off. But on December 23 a second amphibious assault by 2,000 specially trained seamen overwhelmed the Wake defenders. The island commander, Com. Winfield Cunningham, surrendered that same day to the Japanese admiral Sadamichi Kajioka. The invaders lost 820 killed and 335 wounded. Fifty marines and 70 civilians were killed, the others taken prisoner. The Japanese onslaught had now reached the Central Pacific. *See* Pearl Harbor; Guam I; Philippine Islands; World War II.

Walcheren (Netherlands War of Independence), 1574. The privateering Dutch fleet, called the Sea Beggars, was the strongest military arm of the Netherlands in that country's savage rebellion against the Spain of Philip II. Early in 1574 Don Luis de Requesens, second Spanish commander during the revolt in the Netherlands, sent out a naval force under Julian Romero to hunt down the Sea Beggars. Off Walcheren Island in the Schelde estuary, Romero found the Dutch ships, commanded by Louis de Boisot (Sieur de Ruart), on January 29. But the Spaniards were no match for the expert Dutch sailors and suffered a smashing defeat. Romero escaped only by crawling through a porthole of his burning flagship. On land, however, the Spanish infantry remained supreme. *See* Alkmaar I; Mookerheide; Leyden; Netherlands War of Independence.

Wallingford (The English Anarchy), 1153. The contest for the English throne between Stephen of Blois and Maud (Matilda) had dragged on for six years when Maud's chief supporter, her half brother Robert of Gloucester, died in 1147. Her son Henry Plantagenet, duke of Normandy, then assumed the leadership of her party. In January 1153 Henry landed in England and marched to Wallingford, where Stephen's men held the north bank of the Thames. Hampered by snow and cold, both sides readily accepted peace terms: Stephen would reign without dispute until his death; his successor would be Henry, the second of that name to wear the English crown. Signed later that year at Winchester and formally ratified at Westminster, the truce negotiated at Wallingford ended the Anarchy. *See* Winchester, England; Alnwick II.

Wandiwash (Seven Years' War), 1760. The British defense of Madras during 1758–59 proved to be a turning point in the war with the French in India. Under Lt. Col. (later Sir) Eyre Coote the British now went over to the offensive. With several thousand English and sepoy troops, Coote moved out from Madras early in 1760. At Wandiwash, 60 miles to the southwest, he encountered a mixed force of French and native soldiers under Louis XV's eastern commander, the Comte de Lally. Allied with the French was a strong Maratha cavalry force. But when the battle opened on January 22, the Marathas remained aloof. This made the two hostile armies about equal in size. In a severe struggle the English gained the upper hand and drove De Lally's beaten troops back to their Pondicherry base. *See* Madras II; Pondicherry; Seven Years' War.

Warburg (Seven Years' War), 1760. In contrast to the troubles Frederick II, the Great, had against the Russians and Austrians, his subordinate in the west steadfastly held off French advances against Prussia. Ferdinand, duke of Brunswick, with strong troop support from Great Britain (George II), stood in Westphalia in 1760 when 30,000 French under the Chevalier du Muy made a new thrust toward Hannover. Ferdinand, in slightly superior strength, met the attackers at Warburg on July 31. His British cavalry commander, the Marquis of Granby (John Manners), threatened the French flanks in a brilliant maneuver, which redeemed the British cavalry disgrace at Minden the previous year. The army of Louis XV then retreated with a loss of 3,000 in killed, wounded, and captured. Ferdinand pressed the French back to the Rhine at Wesel. But in October he withdrew to Lippstadt and Warburg. This campaign concluded the major fighting in the west. *See* Minden II; Liegnitz II; Seven Years' War.

War of 1812 (1812–1815). The second, and last, war between the United States and Great Britain took place 29 years after the former colonies had successfully revolted against the mother country. Most of the hostility between the two nations grew out of Great Britain's heavy involvement in the Napoleonic Empire Wars. President James Madison secured a declaration of war from the U.S. Congress on June 18, 1812, listing four major causes: (1) impressment of American seamen: (2) violation of the three-mile territorial limit; (3) blockade of American ports; and (4) the British Orders in Council. During the war the United States fought three battles with the Creek Indians in the Southeast. Peace terms were signed at Ghent, Belgium, on December 24, 1814. The treaty settled none of the issues that had provoked the conflict. The battle of New Orleans, the largest of the war, occurred two weeks after peace had been signed.

Fort Dearborn	1812
Detroit	1812
Queenston Heights	1812
Frenchtown	1813
Sackets Harbor	1813

Warsaw I (First Northern War), 1656. To extend Swedish control of the southern Baltic coast, King Charles X Gustavas prepared to invade Poland. First, however, he allied Sweden with Frederick William, elector of Brandenburg, in 1656. Later that year the army of Sweden marched into Poland, where King John II Casimir also claimed the Swedish throne. Charles' army reached Warsaw on July 28. The Poles battled furiously but were compelled to surrender two days later. Further Swedish conquests became blocked by a coalition of Russia, Denmark, and the Holy Roman Empire. When Brandenburg changed sides the following year, the Swedish army was driven out of Poland. But Charles' continued hostility toward his neighbors resulted in a series of treaties during 1660–61 that granted him Poland's last Baltic territories, while John II relinquished his claim to the Swedish throne. Denmark surrendered much of the southern part of the Scandinavian Peninsula. *See* Fehrbellin; Northern Wars.

Warsaw II (Polish Revolt against Russia), 1831. The Polish revolution against the rule of the Russian czar Nicholas I faltered largely because of strife between moderate and liberal factions. After the Polish defeat at Ostroleka on May 26, the remaining center of resistance was Warsaw. Here a garrison of about 30,000 troops under Gen. Henryk Dembiński entrenched themselves behind barricades and in redoubts. A Russian army twice as large, commanded by Field Marshal Ivan Paskevich (later Prince of Warsaw), attacked the city on September 6. For two days the Russians assaulted Warsaw's defenses, which the Poles defended bravely but unsuccessfully. On September 8 Paskevich's troops entered the center of the city and took its surrender. Many of the rebel leaders escaped to the west, particularly to Paris. Some 9,000 Poles died in the defense of Warsaw. Russia lost about 3,000 killed and twice as many wounded. The revolution ended with Russia in firm control. Paskevich became governor of Poland. *See* Grochów; Ostroleka; Polish Revolt against Russia.

Warsaw III (World War I). The Russian-held capital of Poland was within 12 miles of German capture on October 12, 1914, in the Vistula River–Warsaw offensive; it finally fell to Germany during August 4–5, 1915, in the Gorlice-Tarnów breakthrough. *See* Vistula River–Warsaw; Gorlice-Tarnów.

Warsaw IV (Polish-Russian War), 1920. Taking advantage of the confusion during the last days of World War I, Polish patriots under Marshal Józef Pilsudski proclaimed a republic of Poland on November 9, 1918. While the civil war in Russia raged to the east, Pilsudski formed an alliance with Simon Petlyura, who was directing the Ukrainian independence movement. Polish troops helped seize Kiev on May 7, 1920, and continued to advance eastward against the Red armies of the revolution. The Russians, however, rallied under the military leadership of Leon Trotsky and Gen. Mikhail Tukhachevski and on May 18, 1920, launched a counteroffensive both north and south of the Pripet Marshes. The Poles and Ukrainians, trying to hold a front of 800 miles, were soon overwhelmed. On the southern front the Russian cavalry leader Semën Budënny led a drive of 200 miles that reached Lvov (Lwów or Lemberg) by the end of July. Meanwhile, north of the marshes, a second thrust gained 300 miles to the Bug River and then pressed forward to the outskirts of Warsaw.

With the Russians threatening to take Warsaw, Polish forces rallied behind Pilsudski, who was advised by the French general Maxime Weygand. On August 15 Pilsudski, who had taken personal command of the five-division Fourth Army, launched a counterattack against the southern flank of the Russian forces in front of Brest Litovsk. In three days the Poles had broken through the enemy lines. With the southern Russian army blocked off by lack of initiative and the Pripet Marshes, the whole Red front crumbled. By August 25 the Polish attack had gained 200 miles. The Russian defeat was similar to the disaster suffered at Tannenberg in 1914. Some 70,000 troops were captured, with half that number fleeing into East Prussia to be interned by Germany. An armistice was signed at Riga on October 12, setting the boundary between Poland and the Soviet Union that would last until the outbreak of World War II in September 1939. *See* Russian Civil War; Poland (World War II).

Warsaw V (World War II). Caught between the pincers of two German armies, Warsaw surrendered on September 27, 1939, virtually ending the battle of Poland. *See* Poland (World War II).

Warsaw VI (World War II), 1944. During the crunching Russian offensive against Germany in the summer of 1944, the Russian general Konstantin Rokossovski thrust an armored column far ahead of the main front. This spearhead reached the Vistula River at Warsaw's eastern suburb of Praga on July 31. The Polish underground army of 40,000 inside the city then revolted under the command of Gen. Tadeusz Bor-Komorowski. Hitler ordered the uprising crushed by SS (*Schutzstaffel,* or Protective Corps) and police formations rather than by the military. Governor-General Hans Frank and SS Group Leader von dem Back-Zelewski directed the German force, which included the Kaminski Brigade of Russian prisoners and the Dirlewanger Brigade of German convicts. These units imparted their own brand of brutality to the desperate street fighting that spared neither women nor children. Food, medical supplies, and finally water gave out. Disease spread. Almost no babies survived.

The superior weapons of the German force gradually prevailed over the poorly armed Polish rebels. Much of the city was deliberately razed and thousands of Poles were shot in cold blood. Although the advancing Russian army won two bridgeheads over the Vistula during the revolt, no effort was made to aid the paramilitary Polish Home Guards fighting inside the city. Finally, on October 2, the last of the surviving rebels, including Bor-Komorowski, surrendered. Some 15,000 of the Polish troops were killed. German losses (testifying to the savagery of the fighting) totaled 10,000 killed, 7,000 missing, and 9,000 wounded. More than 200,000 civilians perished during the terrible 63-day ordeal. (Kaminski was executed by the Germans for atrocities committed during the fighting.)

Military action on this front remained dormant until the Red armies launched their last great offensive in January 1945. Warsaw was bypassed in this attack and fell on January 17. *See* Poland–East Prussia; World War II.

Wars of Liberation. *See* Napoleonic Empire Wars.

Washita River (Cheyenne and Arapahoe Wars), 1868. To quell the Indian uprisings in the Southwest, the U.S. Army launched a winter campaign on November 23, 1868. From Camp Supply in Indian Territory (now Oklahoma), Lt. Col. George Custer took the 7th Cavalry southward toward the Washita River. On November 27 the troopers surprised an encampment of Cheyennes and Arapahoes (plus some Kiowas, Comanches, and Apaches) along the river. In a sudden attack Custer's men killed more than 100 Indians, including the chief Black Kettle. When a large number of Indians rallied for a counterattack, the cavalrymen fell back to Camp Supply. They had lost 2 officers and 14 men killed, including the second-in-command, Maj. Joel Elliott. *See* Beecher Island; Salt River; Indian Wars in the United States.

Waterloo (Napoleon's Hundred Days), 1815. The battles of Ligny and Quatre Bras fought by Napoleon Bonaparte on June 16, 1815, drove a wedge between the allied armies in southern Belgium. To deepen the wedge and, if possible, destroy the Prussian army of Field Marshal Gen. Gebhard von Blücher, Napoleon put Marshal Marquis Emmanuel de Grouchy with 33,000 men in command of his right wing. He then concentrated his main army of 72,000 men at La Belle Alliance against the Anglo-Dutch army of the Duke of Wellington (Arthur Wellesley), which had fallen back to a low, narrow ridge at Mont-Saint-Jean, just south of Waterloo. Deploying his troops for an attack at 11 A.M. on June 18, Napoleon promised his lieutenants that they would sleep that night in Brussels, 12 miles away. Across the ridge Wellington placed his 68,000 men (24,000 British, 44,000 Dutch, Belgians, and Germans) and 156 guns astride the Brussels road.

Under cover of the fire of 246 guns, the French left, west of the road, moved forward at 11:20 A.M. They struck hard at the massive Château de Goumont, called Hougoumont, but soon became entangled in a bloody, fruitless struggle to take this gateway to the English right wing. Meanwhile, 80 French guns opened fire along the Brussels road, where Marshal Michel Ney launched the main attack just before 2 P.M. In a fierce assault, resisted with equal ferocity, the French drove at the key point of La Haye-Sainte. Infantry, cavalry, and artillery at point-blank range took a terrible toll on both sides. Ney was forced back, but in a second assault led by the marshal himself, La Haye-Sainte fell, about 6 P.M. The allied line, based on stubborn squares of English infantry, cracked but did not break.

As the battle raged in this sector, a dangerous threat developed on the French right. At Wavre, ten miles to the east, Blücher had eluded Grouchy. Holding off the French at the village, he sent the two Prussian corps of Field Marshal Gen. Count Hans von Zieten and Gen. Count Bülow von Dennewitz marching to Wellington's aid. Bülow with 31,000 men reached the village of Plancenoit late in the afternoon, perilously close to cutting the Brussels road in Napoleon's rear. With the entire battle hanging in the balance, the Count of Lobau yielded Plancenoit to the Prussians. Napoleon threw in reserves. The village was retaken by a bayonet attack. At 7 P.M. the French commander turned back to the main battle, ordering nine Old Guard infantry battalions forward against Wellington's center. Again Ney personally led the assault. In a savage collision the allied line held fast and the survivors staggered back down the ridge. The battle was lost to France by 8 P.M. Wellington then counterattacked while the Prussians thrust into Plancenoit once more. The French began falling back on the long, bitter retreat to-

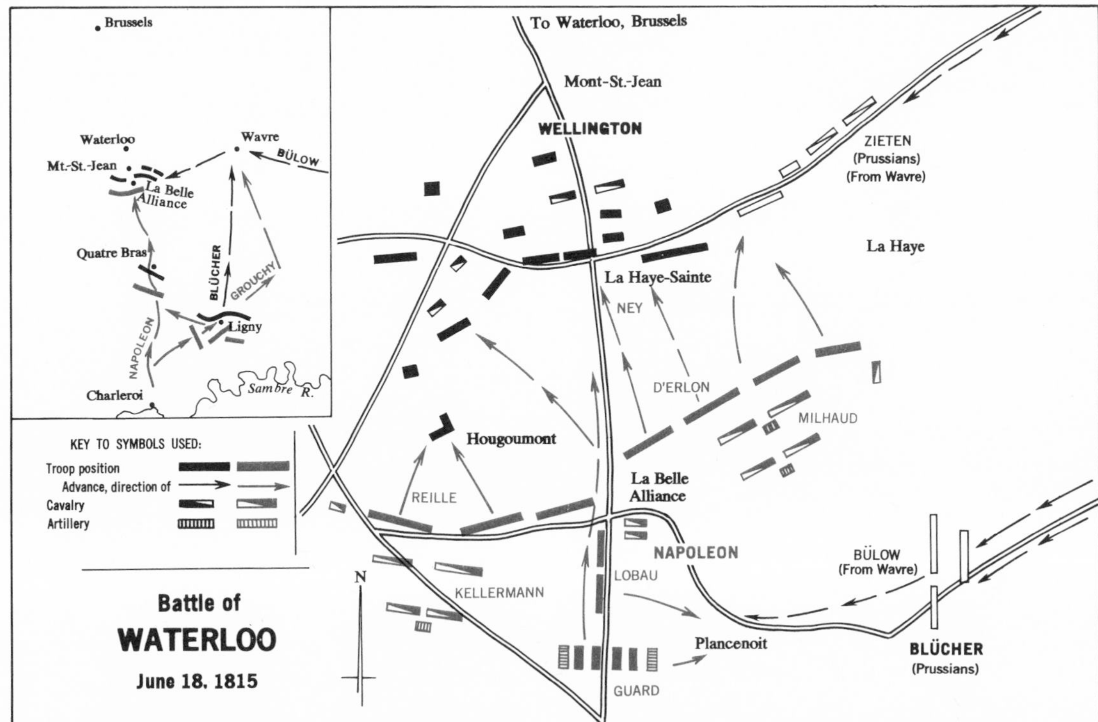

ward Paris. Blücher's troops took up the pursuit, but the retreating French fought off all attempts to crush them in flight. Waterloo cost Napoleon 26,000 killed and wounded, 9,000 captured, and 9,000 missing. On the allied side the Anglo-Dutch casualties totaled 15,000, plus several thousand temporarily missing; Prussian losses were 7,000.

Napoleon relinquished his command at Philippeville the following morning and returned to Paris. On June 22 he abdicated a second time. The allies entered Paris on July 7 and restored Louis XVIII to the throne. (Napoleon was exiled to the island of Saint Helena in the South Atlantic.) So ended not only the Hundred Days but 23 years of almost constant warfare between France and the other major powers of Europe. Thus Waterloo takes its place as one of the most decisive battles in history. *See* Ligny; Quatre Bras; Wavre; Napoleon's Hundred Days.

Wattignies (Wars of the French Revolution), 1793. The French forces of the National Convention, revitalized by Lazare Carnot to relieve Dunkirk in September 1793, next turned toward Maubeuge. Here the allied commander in chief, the Prince of Saxe-Coburg, was besieging the last remaining fortress that barred the way to Paris. Carnot sent Gen. Jean Jourdan with 50,000 men to attack the 26,000 allied troops, chiefly Austrians, stationed on the plateau of Wattignies. On October 15 the poorly organized Revolutionary army was beaten back. But that night the French leaders shifted 8,000 men from their stalled left wing to the right flank, near Wattignies village. This maneuver overlapped the Austrian left, and when the French renewed the assault the following day, Saxe-Coburg's line was rolled up. He fell back, abandoning the siege of Maubeuge, to go into winter quarters. The allied drive on Paris had been thwarted again. *See* Hondschoote; Tourcoing; French Revolution Wars.

Wavre (Napoleon's Hundred Days), 1815. When Napoleon Bonaparte's French army defeated the Prussians at Ligny on June 16, 1815, Field Marshal Gen. Gebhard von Blücher fell back northward to Wavre, also in Belgium. This withdrawal seemed to take the Prussians far enough to the east so that Napoleon could concentrate his offensive against the Duke of Wellington (Arthur Wellesley) at Waterloo, on the road to Brussels. To guard against any attack on his right flank, the French commander assigned Marshal Marquis Emmanuel de Grouchy to pursue the Prussians.

Uncertain of Blücher's position, Grouchy moved hesitatingly northward. As he approached Wavre on June 18, he found the village held in force. With his 33,000 troops, Grouchy attacked the larger Prussian army. But Blücher was not to be deflected from his primary mission of assisting Wellington. Leaving Gen. Baron Johann von Thielmann to hold Wavre and the line of the Dyle River, the aged field marshal and general pressed westward. Thielmann, with only 15,000 men, held on grimly, tying up Grouchy, who was desperately needed by Napoleon at Waterloo (especially now that he had let Blücher escape him). Oblivious to the crushing French defeat less than ten miles to the southwest, Grouchy kept hammering at Wavre. On the following morning he routed Thielmann completely in one of the most useless victories in history. Napoleon's army was beaten beyond hope of revival and the Hundred Days' regime had run its course. *See* Ligny; Waterloo; Napoleon's Hundred Days.

Waxhaw Creek (War of the American Revolution), 1780. When Charleston, S.C., surrendered to the British on May 12, 1780, Col. Abraham Buford with 350 Continentals and a small cavalry detachment stood 40 miles north of the city. Buford immediately turned about and began withdrawing toward North Carolina. From Charleston Col. Banastre Tarleton set out in pursuit at the head of several hundred mounted men. Riding 154 miles in 54 hours, Tarleton overtook the retreating Americans at Waxhaw Creek, S.C., near the border of North Carolina. The British swept down on the foot soldiers on May 29, enveloping both flanks. Buford raised a white flag, but the redcoats charged on with saber and bayonet. In a slaughter called "Tarleton's quarter," 113 Americans were killed, 150 wounded so severely they could not be moved, and 53 captured, some of whom were also wounded. American resistance in the South seemed hopelessly broken. *See* Charleston II; Camden; American Revolution.

Weihaiwei (Chinese-Japanese War I), 1895. The all-victorious Japanese land and sea forces carried the war to the Chinese mainland early in 1895. On February 4 the Japanese cut the boom protecting the harbor of Weihaiwei on the Shantung Peninsula. Torpedo boat attacks then began taking a steady toll of Chinese warships over the next several days and nights. Land batteries were set up to add to the onslaught. Finally, on February 12, the Chinese admiral Ting surrendered the rest of his fleet and the port to Gen. Count Iwao Oyama and then committed suicide. The Japanese seized Weihaiwei, forcing China to accept the Treaty of Shimonoseki two months later. *See* Port Arthur I; Chinese-Japanese War I.

Werben (Thirty Years' War), 1631. The devastation of Magdeburg in May 1631 made it necessary for Field Marshal the Count of Tilly to abandon the city as a base. He marched northward along the Elbe with his 22,000-man army of the Holy Roman Empire (Ferdinand II). At the junction of the Havel and Elbe rivers stood the invading army of Gustavus II of Sweden, some 16,000 strong. The Swedes made up for their inferiority of numbers by entrenching strongly at Werben (Havelberg). When Tilly attacked on July 22, his Bavarians were repulsed by concentrated musket and artillery fire. Regrouping the Imperial troops, Tilly launched a second assault six days later. Again he was beaten back. With total casualties of 6,000 men Tilly turned away southward and on September 4 marched into neutral Saxony. Here he received 14,000 fresh troops from the south and west. But now the wavering elector of Saxony, John George I, made an alliance with Gustavus. The combined Protestant armies hurried in pursuit of Tilly, who headed for Leipzig. *See* Magdeburg; Breitenfeld I; Thirty Years' War.

Wexford (English Civil War), 1649. Following his massacre of the Drogheda garrison, Lord Lieutenant Oliver Cromwell led his 10,000 veterans of the New Model army into southeast Ireland. At Wexford a garrison of Irish and English Royalists sought to defend that seaport. But the city could not hold out against the Roundhead attack, which carried inside the walls on October 11, 1649. Again the defenders were massacred, and Wexford was sacked. With this victory, Cromwell returned to England to rule the Commonwealth government. Ireland was given over to his lieutenants to subdue. This was accomplished by May 1652, but the ruthlessness, "the curse of Cromwell," left Ireland permanently embittered. The war site now shifted back to Scotland. *See* Drogheda; Carbiesdale; English Civil War.

White Mountain (Thirty Years' War), 1620. The embryonic Thirty Years' War flared into a continental struggle when Frederick V, elector palatine, left Heidelberg late in 1619 to assume the crown of Bohemia. In the following summer Maximilian I of Bavaria sent the army of the Catholic League, 25,000 men under the Bavarian field marshal the Count of Tilly, into Bohemia. The Bohemian forces, commanded by Christian I of Anhalt, fell back to defend their capital of Prague. West of Prague this Protestant army was joined by the troops of Bethlen Gabor (Gabriel Bethlen), Hungarian nobleman and adventurer. The combined force encamped on the chalk hill of White Mountain, west of the walls of Prague. On the morning of November 8, protected by a heavy mist and covered by an artillery bombardment, Tilly sent his Imperial army charging up the slope of the hill. The defenders, taken by surprise, reeled back with heavy losses and then broke and fled. One third of Anhalt's 15,000-man force was killed or captured.

Frederick, with his queen, Elizabeth, daughter of James I of England, fled Prague, thereby earning the title "Winter King" for his short reign. Tilly's men entered the city without opposition, sacked it, and re-established Catholic domination. All Bohemia again fell under the rule of the Holy Roman Empire of Ferdinand II. *See* Sablat; Wiesloch; Thirty Years' War.

White Plains (War of the American Revolution),

1776. When the British general Sir William Howe landed on Manhattan Island on September 15, 1776, he found Gen. George Washington's American army entrenching at Harlem Heights to the north. A British probing action the following day resulted in a sharp skirmish, which cost each side about a hundred casualties. Howe then decided against a frontal assault on the colonial position. On October 12 the bulk of the 20,000-man British army sailed up the East River, entered Long Island Sound, and landed behind Washington's lines at Pell's Point. The Americans hurriedly fell back northward to make a stand at White Plains. Howe, moving only 17 miles in ten days, did not attack until October 28. Then, in a turning assault on the left, the British captured Chatterton's Hill, which dominated the village of White Plains. The attackers suffered 300 casualties; American losses were 200. While Howe awaited reinforcements, Washington retreated five miles on November 1 to a new position at North Castle. But now the British turned back to clear their communication lines by attacking Fort Washington on upper Manhattan Island. *See* Long Island; Fort Washington; American Revolution.

White Russia (World War II), 1943–1944. In July 1943 Marshal Semën Timoshenko launched a great Russian offensive on the central (Moscow) front that soon routed Gen. Gunther von Kluge's German army group. The fall of German-held Smolensk on September 25 opened the way for four powerful Red armies to roar westward into White Russia (Byelorussia): Gens. Andrei Yeremenko to Polotsk, Vassili Sokolovski to Vitebsk, Markian Popov to the Orsha-Mogilev sector, and Konstantin Rokossovski to Gomel (north to south). Like a gigantic steam roller all four Russian armies smashed toward their objectives that autumn. The Germans fought desperately to hold a winter line on the upper Dnieper, but Popov bridged the waterway above and below Mogilev. On his left, Rokossovski took Gomel on November 25 and then drove along the northeastern edge of the Pripet Marshes. Earlier, Rokossovski's left wing had turned southwest to aid in conquering the Ukrainian capital of Kiev.

During the winter the Russian armies reorganized in preparation for a 1944 assault on the German Central Army Group, which was now commanded by Field Marshal Ernst Busch. The Russian attack resumed on June 22, with 146 infantry and 43 armored divisions divided into four armies. Within a week German defenses crumbled along a 350-mile front. On the north (right flank) Gen. Ivan Bagramian's First Baltic Army and Gen. Ivan Chernyakhovski's Third White Russian Army struck north and south of Vitebsk. The city was pinched out and fell on June 27, with a loss of five German divisions. The same day Chernyakhovski's left wing took Orsha. General Zakharov's Second White Russian Army captured Mogilev on June 28 and Rokossovski's First White Russian Army annihilated a force of 33,000 Germans at Bobruisk the following day.

The four-pronged attack soon thrust through White Russia. The Moscow–Smolensk highway was cut in two places west of Minsk, and converging Red armies took this communications center on July 3, trapping some 50,000 Germans in the city. It was a small-scale repetition of the German encirclement of Minsk three years before. In the center, the offensive pressed on through Baranowicze (July 8) to Grodno (July 16) on the postwar border of Poland. On the south, Rokossovski cleared the Pripet Marshes by taking Pinsk and Kowel on July 5. On the north, Bagramian turned west into the Baltic States to take both Vilnius (Wilno) in Lithuania and Daugavpils (Dvinsk) in Latvia on July 13. This thrust caved in the right wing of German Army Group North and split the front into two theaters of action—the upper Baltic States, occupied by the Germans who had besieged Leningrad, and the East Prussia–Poland sector, where the Russians now stood on the eastern border following their reconquest of White Russia. The 24-day Russian offensive eliminated 25 German divisions. Field Marshal Walther von Model now replaced Busch in command of the shattered German Army Group Center. *See* Leningrad; Ukraine; Soviet Union (World War II); Poland–East Prussia; World War II.

Wiesloch (Thirty Years' War), 1622. After the collapse of the Bohemian Protestant forces of Frederick V, elector palatine and, briefly, king of Bohemia, the site of the war shifted to The Palatinate. Here Gen. Ambrogio di Spinola had sent a 20,000-man army from the Spanish Netherlands under the command of Gonzales de Córdoba to occupy Mainz, Kreuznach, Oppenheim, and other Rhine strong points in the fall of 1621. (Sir Horace Vere's 2,000 English volunteers, shut up in Frankenthal and Mannheim, were unable to impede the relentless march of the Spanish.) During the winter Gen. Count Ernst von Mansfeld, at the head of a mercenary army employed by Frederick, encamped in Alsace. In the spring he crossed the Rhine to link up with an allied force under George Frederick, margrave of Baden-Durlach.

The combined armies then sought to prevent a junction between Cordoba and the Bavarian field marshal the Count of Tilly, who had marched into The Palatinate at the head of the army of the Catholic League (directed by Maximilian I of Bavaria). On April 22 Tilly came upon the Protestant rear guard at Wiesloch, 15 miles south of Heidelberg. He drove it in but upon encountering the main body was sharply rebuffed. Tilly pulled back. However, when Mansfeld stayed put, the Catholic commander marched around him to link up with Cordoba later that month. This put the Protestant forces at a distinct disadvantage until they could be reinforced by young Christian of Brunswick who was moving down from the north. *See* White Mountain; Wimpfen; Thirty Years' War.

Wilderness (American Civil War), 1864. The fourth year of the Civil War opened with Gen. U. S. Grant in charge of all Federal armies. The new commander took his place with the Army of the Potomac (George Meade) against the Confederate Army of Northern Virginia (Robert E. Lee), which stood south of the Rapidan River. The other major Federal army in the field, that of Gen. William Sherman, was ordered to attack the large Confederate army in northern Georgia, then under the command of Gen. Joseph Johnston.

The Federal offensive in Virginia got under way with a crossing of the lower Rapidan before dawn on May 4 in an attempt to turn Lee's right (east) flank. This move placed Meade's army deep in a wooded, tangled terrain aptly called the Wilderness. Lee shifted eastward to attack even though he could muster only 64,000 men and 274 guns against a total Federal strength of 119,000 men (of which Meade's army made up 99,000) and 316 guns. He sent the II Corps of Gen. Richard Ewell along the Orange–Fredericksburg Turnpike, the III Corps of Gen. Ambrose Hill along the Orange Plank Road. (Gen. James Longstreet's I Corps was closing up from the south.)

On the morning of May 5 Ewell collided with the V Corps of the Federal general Gouverneur Warren. The Federals turned right (westward) to meet this challenge. To the south, Hill also bumped into a Federal force along his road—Gen. George Getty's division of the VI Corps (John Sedgwick). General Winfield Hancock's II Corps, which had advanced farthest into the Wilderness, countermarched to support Getty. A desperate action took place on this front late in the day, but neither side gained an advantage before darkness halted the confused fighting.

On the following morning (May 6) Meade's army attacked early. Its right flank, composed of Sedgwick's and Warren's corps, was checked with heavy losses by Ewell. On the south, Hancock broke through Hill's corps, but as the Federals pursued the routed Confederates, they ran headlong into Longstreet's troops pushing forward along the Orange Plank Road. The fight now raged back and forth until about 11 A.M., when the whole front quieted down because of sheer exhaustion on both sides. During this lull, Longstreet sent four brigades under Gens. William Mahone and Gilbert Sorrel against Hancock's open (southern flank). The circling attack succeeded, but when Longstreet tried to supplement it with a renewed frontal assault, he was accidentally wounded by his own men. Hancock's main line held firm. To the north, also, both sides had renewed the battle, only to fight themselves out with no advantage by sundown.

There was no action the following day (May 7) as the two hostile forces worked to improve their defensive positions. That night Grant began moving southeast toward the important road junction of New Spotsylvania Court House. This ended the blind, blundering battle of the Wilderness. The Army of the Potomac suffered 17,666 casualties (of which 2,246 were killed and 12,073 wounded), including two generals killed, two wounded, and two captured. Lee's losses are estimated at 7,750. Here too the general officer casualties were high: 3 killed, 4 wounded. *See* Bristoe Station; Spotsylvania; American Civil War.

Williamsburg (American Civil War), 1862. When the Confederates began withdrawing up the peninsula from Yorktown on the night of May 3–4, Gen. Edwin Sumner's Federal II Corps pursued. Moving slowly over muddy roads, the Federals found the enemy holding a strong line two miles east of Williamsburg, on May 5. Here the Confederate generals James Longstreet and Daniel Hill had deployed 31,800 men to delay the Union advance. A Federal division under Gen. Joseph Hooker, supported by another division under Gen. Philip Kearny, attacked the center of the Confederate line without success. Late in the afternoon Gen. Winfield Hancock's brigade turned the Confederate left (northeast). With his escape route endangered Longstreet (and Hill) withdrew farther up the peninsula that night. The successful delaying action cost 1,603 Southern casualties. Sumner, who had committed less than half his available forces, lost 2,239 men out of the 40,700 engaged. The Federal commander in chief, Gen. George McClellan resumed his overcautious advance toward the Confederate capital of Richmond. *See* Yorktown II; Fair Oaks; American Civil War.

Wilson's Creek (American Civil War), 1861. Both the North and South struggled hard for control of the important border state of Missouri during the early months of the war. A fiery little regular army captain, Nathaniel Lyon, assumed charge of Federal military operations designed to keep Missouri in the Union. During the summer Lyon (now promoted to brigadier general) took up a position at Springfield, in the southwest, with some 5,400 troops. He then resolved to move against a Confederate force advancing from Arkansas under Gen. Ben McCulloch. On August 9 Lyon marched southwest to the Confederate encampment of 11,600 men at Wilson's Creek. The following morning Lyon attacked along the west side of the creek toward Oak Hill, held by the Missouri State

Guard, commanded by Gen. Sterling Price. Lyon's force successfully stormed the hill, but east of the creek his supporting force was routed. Worse news came from the south where Gen. Franz Sigel's encircling column was checked and then routed.

McCulloch was now free to mass his troops for a counterattack on Oak Hill. Three times the Confederates charged the height, but each time they were driven back. In this fight the capable Lyon, already twice wounded, was killed. His successor, Maj. (later Brig. Gen.) Samuel Sturgis, made the controversial decision to withdraw northeast to Rolla. The Confederates promptly occupied Springfield. Continuing northward, Price took the surrender of a Federal brigade at Lexington during September 18–20. He then moved eastward; many of his men participated in the battle of Belmont two months later. At Wilson's Creek the Federals lost 223 killed, 721 wounded, and 291 missing. Confederate casualties were 257 killed, 900 wounded, and 27 missing. *See* Belmont; American Civil War.

Wilton (Danish Invasions of Britain), 871. In the year 871 the Danes and West Saxons fought several fierce but inconclusive battles for supremacy in the kingdom of Wessex. Although the invaders usually won the field, they were unable to conquer the stubborn Saxons. During this time Ethelred I died and Alfred assumed the rule of Wessex. Late in the summer the Danes struck deep into Alfred's domain at Wilton in southern Wiltshire. When the Wessex army held its ground, the Vikings feigned retreat. The Saxons leaped forward to pursue, became disorganized, and suffered a severe loss when the wily invaders suddenly turned and counterattacked.

With his army now weakened by casualties and desertion, Alfred made peace with the Danes. Upon payment of a large tribute—the Danegeld—the invaders withdrew to London. During the five-year armistice that followed, Alfred rebulit his army, while the Vikings consolidated their conquest of the Midlands. *See* Reading; Chippenham; Danish Invasions of Britain.

Wimpfen (Thirty Years' War), 1622. Early in May 1622 the Protestant forces of the elector Frederick V in The Palatinate found themselves opposed by two Catholic armies—a Spanish contingent under Gonzales de Córdoba and the Catholic League army commanded by Field Marshal the Count of Tilly. To the north beyond the Neckar River an army led by Christian of Brunswick stood ready to help the Protestants. The Protestant plan was to combine their forces before risking a battle. To gain time, and hopefully to split the Catholic armies, Gen. Count Ernst von Mansfeld with his army of veteran mercenaries was to cross the Neckar near Heidelberg, while George Frederick, margrave of Baden-Durlach, moved upstream (eastward) with his German army to cross at Wimpfen.

The plan failed. Both Córdoba and Tilly marched against George Frederick and cut him off from the river near Wimpfen. The margrave deployed his outnumbered 14,000-man force on a low hill. Here on May 6 the Protestants fought bravely behind a strong artillery bombardment. But when a random Spanish artillery shell exploded the defenders' magazine, the Badener position was lost. The Catholics drove up the hill and shattered the Protestant army. George Frederick escaped to Stuttgart with only a few companions. Meanwhile Mansfeld crossed the Neckar and hurried to meet Christian of Brunswick at the Main. Córdoba and Tilly raced northward to prevent these Protestant forces from linking up. *See* Wiesloch; Höchst; Thirty Years' War.

Winchelsea (Hundred Years' War), 1350. During one of the many truces between England and France in the Hundred Years' War, Spain attempted to intervene on behalf of its continental neighbor. A Spanish fleet commanded by Carlos de la Carda put in at Sluys (Sluis). When it sailed out into the Channel, the English navy of Edward III attacked the intruder off Winchelsea, one of the Cinque Ports of southeastern England. Using the grappling and boarding tactics common to early sea battles, the English destroyed most of the Spanish vessels on August 29, 1350. Edward's mastery of the English Channel, which protected his communications with Calais, remained unimpaired. *See* Calais I; Poitiers; La Rochelle I; Hundred Years' War.

Winchester I (American Civil War), 1862. The Federal commander, Gen. Nathaniel Banks, was at Strasburg with about 8,500 men when he learned that Front Royal, on his east flank, had been attacked on May 23. Banks began withdrawing down the Shenandoah Valley to Winchester the following night. General Thomas (Stonewall) Jackson with 17,000 Confederate troops, including Gen. Richard Ewell's division, hurried to intercept the Federal retreat. Banks reached Winchester first but had no time to fortify the heights southwest of the city before Jackson arrived, at 1 A.M. on May 25. The Confederate general rested his tired "foot cavalry" until dawn and then attacked Winchester on three sides—west, south, and east. The coordinated assault crumpled the Federal lines. Banks retreated farther north, crossing the Potomac to safety the following day. He had lost an estimated 2,000 men at Winchester. Confederate casualties were about 350.

Jackson had pursued to within three miles of Harpers Ferry on May 29 when he heard of a combined Federal offensive designed to cut him off from the upper Shenandoah Valley. General John Frémont with 10,000 men was marching on

Strasburg from West Virginia, while Gen. James Shields's division, the advance guard of Gen. Irvin McDowell's corps, moved into the valley from Front Royal. Retreating quickly southward, Jackson cleared Strasburg on June 1, just before the Federal trap snapped shut. The wily Confederate had not only escaped; he had also persuaded the Federal government to withhold McDowell's 40,000 troops from the crucial Peninsula Campaign southeast of Richmond. *See* Front Royal; Cross Keys–Port Republic; American Civil War.

Winchester II (American Civil War), 1863. In June Gen. Robert E. Lee began shifting his Army of Northern Virginia toward the Shenandoah Valley preparatory to making his second invasion of the North. As an advance guard, Gen. Robert Rodes took his division into the lower valley, routing a Federal brigade at Berryville on June 13. The Federal commander in this area, Gen. Robert Milroy, had been ordered to withdraw from Winchester. But now it was too late, as Gen. Richard Ewell closed in with a full corps of Confederates on June 14. Working around to attack from the west, Ewell made Milroy's position untenable. The Federal commander began retreating toward Harpers Ferry on the night of June 14–15. He was cut off and defeated by pursuing Confederates. Milroy lost 4,443 men (of whom 3,358 were captured), a third of his command, and all his guns and supplies. Ewell suffered only 269 casualties. The main Confederate army pushed on northward through the Shenandoah and Cumberland valleys for a showdown battle at Gettysburg. *See* Brandy Station; Gettysburg; American Civil War.

Winchester III (American Civil War), 1864. To eliminate the Shenandoah Valley as a strategic route and supply source for the Confederacy, Gen. Philip Sheridan was given command of the Federal forces in the area. The 33-year-old general took charge on August 7 but did not receive permission to launch an offensive until mid-September. Then, with almost 38,000 troops, Sheridan attacked up the valley against the 12,000 Confederates of Gen. Jubal Early stationed at Winchester, Va., on September 19. In a hard, all-day fight Sheridan's three corps on the east pushed Early's men back into the town, while the Federal cavalry pressed down from the north. By evening the Confederates had given up Winchester, falling back southward through Strasburg to nearby Fisher's Hill. Sheridan pursued. The Federal losses at Winchester were 697 killed, 3,983 wounded, 330 missing. Confederate casualties were 276 killed (including a division commander, Robert Rodes), 1,827 wounded, 1,818 missing. *See* Kernstown II; Fisher's Hill; American Civil War.

Winchester, England (The English Anarchy), 1141. After the capture and imprisonment of Stephen of Blois, her rival for the English crown, Maud (Matilda) seemed to have the upper hand in 1141. Enthroned, she ordered the reduction of Wolvesey Castle in Winchester, still held by forces loyal to Stephen. While her troops were besieging the castle, they were attacked by another force of Stephen's supporters and routed. In the flight from Winchester on September 14, Maud's ablest commander, her half brother Robert of Gloucester, was captured at Stockbridge. To secure his release, Maud exchanged Stephen. The confused war dragged on, but now Maud's advantage dwindled away. *See* Lincoln I; Wallingford.

Windhoek (World War I), 1915. At the outbreak of war in 1914 the Germans, from their colony of Southwest Africa, occupied the British exclave of Walvis (Walfish) Bay on the Atlantic coast, 710 miles north of Cape Town. Until the end of the year South Africa was paralyzed by anti-British activity. Finally Gen. Louis Botha halted the rebellion and reoccupied the settlement at Walvis, on December 25, 1914. Marching inland 170 miles, Botha with 20,000 men stormed and captured Windhoek, capital of the German colony, on May 12, 1915. The German survivors fled to Grootfontein, 220 miles to the northeast. At Otavi, to the west, 3,500 surrendered on July 9, ending resistance in this area. German Southwest Africa became a protectorate of the Union (later Republic) of South Africa. *See* Rufiji River; World War I.

Winnington Bridge (Royalist Uprising in England), 1659. Eight months after the death of Oliver Cromwell, his son and successor, Richard, resigned as Lord Protector of England on May 25, 1659. While Parliament and the army struggled for control, royalist sentiment crystallized rapidly, particularly in the northwest. Here in Cheshire Sir George Booth (later Lord Delamere) collected a small cavalry force dedicated to the exiled Charles. But John Lambert, a veteran general of the Civil War, marched into the county at the head of 5,000 loyal troops. On August 19, 1659, at Winnington Bridge, Lambert's horsemen attacked and irrevocably scattered Booth's army. The uprising failed only because it was premature—on May 8 of the following year Parliament proclaimed Charles II king of England.

"Winter Battle of Masuria." *See* Masurian Lakes II.

Winwaed (Teutonic Conquest of Britain), 655. King Penda of Mercia (the Midlands) had assumed hegemony over the other six Anglo-Saxon kingdoms (together called the Heptarchy) following his successive defeats of the Northumbrian rulers Edwin and Oswald. However, Oswald's brother Oswy (Oswiu) rallied his Bernicians and at an unknown river near Leeds challenged the overlordship of Penda. Despite support by some East Angles and Britons, the Mercians were soundly defeated. Penda and the East Angle king were killed. The battle of Winwaed re-established the power of the kingdom of Northumbria, which included Bernicia and Deira in the north of Britain. Oswy ruled for another 15 years. During this time he presided over the Synod of Whitby in 664, which aligned Britain with the Roman Catholic Church. In the south, however, Mercia stood supreme for another century and a half. *See* Heavenfield; Maserfield; Nechtansmere; Ellandun.

Wissembourg (Franco-Prussian War), 1870. A blown-up dispute over a German candidate for the throne of Spain led to a French (Napoleon III) declaration of war against Prussia (Wilhelm I) on July 15, 1870. It was the precise opportunity Prussia's Iron Chancellor, Otto von Bismarck, had sought to weld the German states into a unified nation. His chief of the general staff, Gen. (later Count) Helmuth von Moltke, promptly launched three armies across the borders of France. The first battle developed on August 4 at Wissembourg (Weissenburg), 40 miles north of Strasbourg. Here the Prussian Third Army (25,000 men) under Crown Prince Frederick William (future Frederick III) attacked the town, held by 4,000 troops of the Comte de MacMahon's French army. The Prussians stormed Wissembourg in six hours with a loss of 1,500 men. The French suffered 2,300 casualties, including the immediate commander, Gen. Charles Abel Douay, who was killed. MacMahon pulled his army southwest for a stand at Wörth. *See* Wörth; Spicheren; Franco-Prussian War.

Wittstock (Thirty Years' War), 1636. After the shattering defeat at Nördlingen in 1634, the French-Swedish cause lay in eclipse for almost two years. The forced retreat of Bernhard, duke of Saxe-Weimar, across the Rhine left southern and central Germany exposed to attack by the Hapsburg army of the Holy Roman Empire (Ferdinand II). Augsburg, Hanau, Heidelberg, and other cities fell to the forces under Ferdinand of Austria (future Holy Roman Emperor). Along the Rhine, Spanish Hapsburg troops took Philippsburg and Treves. For a time even Paris was threatened by a joint attack from the Spanish Netherlands and Alsace. Meanwhile the Swedish army of Field Marshal Johan Banér was virtually isolated in Brandenburg.

In the fall of 1636 John George I, elector of Saxony with 30,000 Saxon and Imperial troops sought to cut off Banér from the Baltic. At Wittstock, 58 miles northwest of Berlin, the allied German army took up a strong position on a hill on October 4. Banér, with only 22,000 men (largely Swedes and Scots), could not attack the dug-in enemy. With only part of his force, including the Swedish general Lennart Torstenson, Banér advanced to the foot of the slope. Meanwhile he sent the Scottish general James King (later Lord Eythin) and field marshal Alexander Leslie (later Lord Leven) in a wide encircling maneuver. At the approach of the small enemy force to their front, the Germans left their positions to attack. Thus they were caught in the open when King and Leslie struck their flank and rear. Assailed on three sides, the Saxon-Imperial army caved in, losing 11,000 in killed and wounded and 8,000 captured. Swedish losses were 5,000. The victory gave new hope to the Protestant princes of North Germany who were still resisting Hapsburg domination. *See* Nördlingen I; Rheinfelden; Thirty Years' War.

Wolf Mountain (Sioux War II), 1877. After their overwhelming victory over U.S. soldiers at the Little Bighorn River in June, the huge (10,000) encampment of Sioux and Cheyennes broke up into small parties. Relentlessly pursued by the troops of Gens. Alfred Terry and George Crook, the Indians were defeated piecemeal—at Slim Buttes in northwestern South Dakota, on September 9, and at Crazy Woman Creek of the Powder River in Montana, on November 25. Sitting Bull escaped to Canada. Finally 1,000 Sioux warriors under Crazy Horse were trapped on Wolf Mountain along the Tongue River in Montana by Gen. Nelson Miles with 436 troops. On January 7, 1777, aided by two field guns, the American soldiers routed the last major group that had participated in the massacre of Lt. Col. George Custer's men. Crazy Horse himself surrendered later that year and was killed on September 5 trying to escape. *See* Little Bighorn River; Wounded Knee Creek; Indian Wars in the United States.

Wolgast (Thirty Years' War), 1628. While the Hapsburg army of Gen. Albrecht von Wallenstein was besieging Stralsund, King Christian IV of Denmark and Norway was organizing a new army to invade the Holy Roman Empire of Ferdinand II. Christian landed in Pomerania during the summer of 1628 and seized Wolgast on the coast. He then began to move to the south, planning to enter Mecklenburg. But his timing was wrong. Wallenstein, who had abandoned the siege of Stralsund early in August, intercepted Christian's march outside Wolgast on September 2. The Bohemian army fell on the Danes and shattered them. Christian, with only a handful of survivors, fled to his ships in the Baltic and then back to Denmark. This was the final defeat of the Danish king, who asked the emperor for peace, terms of which were signed at Lübeck the following June. Christian received back his lands on the promise of not interfering in German affairs. *See* Stralsund I; Frankfort on the Oder; Thirty Years' War.

Worcester (English Civil War), 1651. Despite their overwhelming defeat at Dunbar, the Scots proceeded to crown as their king Charles II, at Scone on January 1, 1651. Meanwhile Oliver Cromwell led his English army into Edinburgh.

The Roundhead general then continued his advance deeper into Scotland, marching for Perth. This presented Charles II and his veteran Scottish commander, Gen. David Leslie, with the opportunity to counterinvade England. At the head of a new army of 16,000 Scots, who were now more Royalist than Presbyterian, the young king marched southward. Cromwell wisely allowed the Scots to maneuver past him. He captured Perth on August 2, 1651, then took up the pursuit, cutting the Royalists off from their base. Unfortunately for Charles, few English flocked to his banner, and at Worcester, in west-central England, he was forced to make a stand. On September 3 Cromwell attacked with 20,000 veterans of the New Model army, supplemented by English militia to give him a 2-to-1 superiority. Although the Royalist Scots and English fought bravely, they were no match for the Cromwellians, who pressed forward along both sides of the Severn River. The larger, better-equipped, and well-trained army of the Commonwealth destroyed its enemies. Only a few Scots survived and Charles himself fled for his life. The future king of England had six weeks of narrow escapes before he found safety again on the Continent.

With the last Scottish army crushed, Cromwell sent Gen. George Monck (later duke of Albemarle) northward to subdue whatever resistance remained in the north country. This was accomplished by May of the following year. The nine-year Civil War, or Great Rebellion, thus ended with Cromwell the complete master of Ireland and Scotland as well as of England. *See* Dunbar II; English Civil War.

World War I (1914–1918). The long-building arms race and hostile alliances among the major powers of Europe finally erupted into war in 1914. Fusing the conflict was the assassination of Austria's Archduke Francis Ferdinand at Sarajevo (in present-day Yugoslavia), on June 28. Although an investigation failed to establish the complicity of the Serbian government (Peter I), Emperor Franz Josef of Austria-Hungary sent an ultimatum to Belgrade on July 23. Judging the Serbian reply unsatisfactory, the Austrian-Hungarian Empire declared war five days later. Russia (Nicholas II), committed to the support of Serbia, ordered a general mobilization on July 30. Two days later Germany (Wilhelm II), allied with Austria and Italy in the Triple Alliance, declared war on Russia, then, on August 3, on France (President Raymond Poincaré), which was leagued with Russia and Great Britain in the Triple Entente. On August 4 Germany declared war on Belgium (Albert I) and invaded that country. Great Britain (George V) came to Belgium's aid the same day. (Italy refused to support Germany and Austria-Hungary, finally entering the war against them the following May.)

Germany and Austria, soon to be called the Central Powers, were joined by Turkey on November 2 and by Bulgaria on October 14, 1915. Serbia, Russia, France, Belgium, and Great Britain came to be known as the Allies. Later active participants in the war on the Allied side were Montenegro (August 5, 1914), Japan (August 23, 1914), Italy (May 23, 1915), Portugal (March 9, 1916), Rumania (August 27, 1915), United States (April 6, 1917), and Greece (June 27, 1917). Another dozen nations declared war on the Central Powers but did not contribute to the fighting.

The fighting ranged around the world, with most of the battles taking place on the Western Front in northern France and Belgium; the Eastern Front along the Russian borders; the Italian Front facing Austria-Hungary; the Balkan Front in Serbia, Turkey, and Romania; the Turkish Front in Egypt, Palestine, and Mesopotamia; Africa; China; and at sea. These battles saw the origins of most of the more powerful military weaponry of World War II, particularly the tank, submarine, airplane, machine gun, and fast-firing artillery pieces.

Russia was the first major power to leave the war, on March 3, 1918. Bulgaria surrendered on September 29, Turkey on October 31, and Austria-Hungary on November 3. On the Western Front, after more than four years of stalemate, two huge Allied offensives, launched on September 26 and 27, 1918, crumbled the German armies. Kaiser Wilhelm II abdicated on November 9. Two days later an armistice ended the fighting. A series of treaties, signed in 1919, brought peace to Europe. In all, World War I cost almost 10,000,000 dead and about 20,000,000 wounded. The major power losses were:

ALLIES	*Dead*	*Wounded*
Great Britain	947,000	2,122,000
France	1,385,000	3,044,000
Russia	1,700,000	4,950,000
Italy	460,000	947,000
United States	115,000	206,000
CENTRAL POWERS		
Germany	1,808,000	4,247,000
Austria-Hungary	1,200,000	3,620,000
Turkey	325,000	400,000

Western Front

Liége I	1914
Mulhouse	1914
Haelen	1914
Namur II	1914

Frontiers of France 1914
Lorraine 1914
Ardennes I 1914
Charleroi 1914
Mons II 1914
Guise 1914
Le Cateau 1914
Marne River I 1914
Ourcq River 1914
Moselle River 1914
Aisne River I 1914
Artois I 1914
Antwerp II 1914
Ypres I 1914
Champagne I 1914–1915
Neuve-Chapelle 1915
Ypres II 1915
Artois II 1915
Champagne II 1915
Artois-Loos 1915
Verdun 1916
Fort Douaumont 1916
Fort de Vaux 1916
Somme River I 1916
Arras II 1917
Vimy Ridge 1917
Aisne River II 1917
Messines 1917
Ypres III 1917
Passchendaele 1917
Cambrai 1917
Somme River II 1918
Lys River 1918
Aisne River III 1918
Château-Thierry 1918
Cantigny 1918
Belleau Wood 1918
Noyon-Montdidier 1918
Marne River II 1918
Champagne–Marne River 1918
Aisne-Marne rivers 1918
Amiens 1918
Saint-Mihiel 1918
Meuse River–Argonne Forest 1918
Cambrai–Saint-Quentin 1918

Eastern Front

Gumbinnen 1914
Stallupönen 1914
Galicia 1914
Kraśnik 1914
Gnila Lipa River 1914
Lemberg I 1914–1915
Rava Russkaya 1914
Przemyśl 1914–1915
Tannenberg II 1914
Masurian Lakes I 1914
Vistula River–Warsaw 1914
Lódź 1914
Masurian Lakes II 1915
Gorlice-Tarnów 1915
Warsaw III 1915
Naroch Lake 1916
Kovel-Stanislav 1916
Lemberg II 1917
Riga II 1917

Italian Front

Isonzo River I–XI 1915–1917
Asiago 1916
Caporetto 1917
Piave River 1918
Vittorio Veneto 1918

Balkan Front

Jadar River 1914
Rudnik Ridges 1914
Gallipoli 1915–1916
Serbia 1915
Salonika II 1915–1918
Rumania 1916–1917

Turkish Front

Sarikamis 1914–1915
Kut-al-Imara I 1915
Ctesiphon III 1915
Kut-al-Imara II 1915–1916
Erzurum-Erzincan 1916
Rumani 1916
Baghdad IV 1917
Gaza II 1917
Ramadi 1917
Gaza III 1917
Megiddo III 1918
Sharqat 1918

Africa

Windhoek 1915
Rufiji River 1917

China

Tsingtao 1914

War at Sea

Heligoland Bight 1914
Coronel 1914
Falkland Islands 1914
Dogger Bank II 1915
Atlantic Ocean I 1915–1917
Dardanelles 1915
Jutland 1916

World War II (1939–1945). Many historians believe that the seeds of World War II were planted in the Treaty of Versailles that concluded World War I. A less controversial date of origin is January 30, 1933, when Adolph Hitler became chancellor of Germany. During the next six years Hitler rearmed Germany, reoccupied the Rhineland (1936), accomplished the *Anschluss* of Austria (March 1938), and dismembered Czechoslovakia (October 1938, March 1939). When Hitler invaded Poland on September 1, 1939, Great Britain and France, renouncing their previous policy of appeasement, declared war on Germany two days later. Poland was overrun in a month. In 1940, Denmark, Norway, Holland, Belgium, and France fell under the heel of Nazi Germany. Great Britain resisted heroically and alone until June 1941 when Hitler, after conquering Yugoslavia and Greece, invaded the Soviet Union, opening a new front in the war. A former German ally, the Soviet Union had defeated Finland the previous year. Another German ally, Italy, had already weakened the Berlin-Rome axis by bungling operations in North Africa and Greece. Other German allies—Bulgaria, Hungary, and Rumania—proved to be of little help.

On December 7, 1941, Japan entered the conflict by an attack on the United States and on British possessions in the Pacific. Germany and Italy declared war on the United States three days later. China, which had been resisting Japanese aggression since 1937, automatically became an Allied power. Allied victories in North Africa and Sicily drove Italy out of the war on September 8, 1943. The Allied second front (really the third after Russia and Italy), which opened in France on June 6, 1944, sealed the doom of Hitler's Germany. Squeezed from the east, west, and in Italy, the Nazis surrendered unconditionally on May 8, 1945.

Meanwhile, in the Pacific the Japanese string of early victories had been broken at Midway in June 1942 and in the Solomon Islands that autumn. Two largely American offensives, across the Central and Southwest Pacific, brought the Allies to the doorstep of Japan. The dropping of atomic bombs on August 6 and 9, 1945, forced the surrender of the third member of the Berlin-Rome-Tokyo axis on August 14. The entrance of the Soviet Union into the Pacific war six days earlier had no effect on the outcome.

Peace treaties were signed and put into effect in 1947 for Bulgaria, Finland, Hungary, Italy, and Rumania. During the Korean War of 1950–53 a treaty with Japan was signed (1952). An Austrian treaty was not effected until 1955. Meanwhile, the Cold War between the Soviet Union and the Western Allies blocked all attempts to complete a treaty with Germany. This delay helped harden the division of Germany into two distinct nations, East and West. More than 20 years after the end of the war a formal settlement seemed as remote as in 1945.

The casualty figures for World War II are far higher than for any other conflict in history. Battle deaths came to more than 9 million for the Allies, more than 5 million for the Axis. Civilian deaths from air bombing, starvation, epidemics, and deliberate massacres can only be broadly estimated but probably totaled more than the combined military losses.

ALLIES	*Dead*	*Wounded*
British Empire	354,000	475,000
China (1937–1945)	1,310,000	1,753,000
France	166,000	409,000
Greece	77,000	unknown
Italy (1943–1945)	17,000	unknown
Poland	125,000	141,000
U.S.S.R.	6,750,000	unknown
United States	294,000	671,000
Yugoslavia	75,000	unknown
AXIS		
Bulgaria	10,000	unknown
Finland	53,000	125,000
Germany	3,250,000	4,000,000
Hungary	75,000	unknown
Italy (1940–1943)	60,000	unknown
Japan	1,862,000	4,616,000
Rumania	80,000	unknown

The war may be divided into the following theaters: Europe, Africa and Middle East, Atlantic and Mediterranean, and Pacific.

EUROPE

German Offensive—West and South

Poland	1939
Warsaw V	1939
Finland	1939–1940
Suomussalmi	1939–1940
Mannerheim Line	1940, 1944
Norway	1940
Netherlands	1940
Flanders	1940
Dunkirk	1940
France	1940
Britain	1940–1941
Yugoslavia	1941
Greece	1940–1941
Crete	1941
Dieppe	1942

Eastern Front

Soviet Union	1941–1944
Minsk	1941
Smolensk II	1941
Kiev II	1941
Kursk	1943
Leningrad	1941–1944
Moscow	1941–1942
Vyazma	1941
Crimea	1941–1944
Sevastopol II	1941–1944
Caucasus	1942–1943
Stalingrad	1942–1943
Ukraine	1943–1944
White Russia	1943–1944
Poland–East Prussia	1944–1945
Warsaw VI	1944
Balkans	1944–1945

Hungary	1944–1945
Austria	1945
Czechoslovakia	1945
Germany, East	1945
Berlin	1945
Italian Front	
Sicily	1943
Italy, Southern	1943
Salerno	1943
Gustav-Cassino Line	1943–1944
Cassino	1944
Anzio	1944
Gothic Line	1944–1945
Po Valley	1945
Western Front	
Germany—Air Bombardment	1942–1945
Normandy	1944
Cherbourg	1944
German Vengeance-Weapon Bombardment	1944–1945
Saint-Lô Breakthrough	1944
Falaise-Argentan Pocket	1944
France, Northern	1944
Paris IV	1944
France, Southern	1944
Siegfried Line	1944
Arnhem	1944
Aachen	1944
Hürtgen Forest	1944
Ardennes II	1944–1945
Saint-Vith	1944
Bastogne	1944
Celles	1944
Rhineland	1945
Remagen	1945
Germany, West	1945
Ruhr Pocket	1945

AFRICA AND MIDDLE EAST

Dakar	1940
East Africa	1941
Habbaniya	1941
Malta III	1941–1942
First British Offensive	
Sidi Barrâni	1940
Bardia	1941
Tobruk I	1941
Beda Fomm	1941
First Axis Offensive	
Tobruk II	1941
Salûm–Halfaya Pass	1941
Second British Offensive	
Sidi-Rezegh	1941
Second Axis Offensive	
Gazala	1942
Tobruk III	1942
Mersa Matrûh	1942
El Alamein I	1942
Alam Halfa	1942
Third British Offensive	
El Alamein II	1942
Mareth Line	1943
Médenine	1943
Anglo-American Offensive	
Northwest Africa	1942
Tunisia	1942–1943
Kasserine Pass	1943

ATLANTIC AND MEDITERRANEAN

"Graf Spee"	1939
Atlantic Ocean II	1940–1944
Oran II	1940
Taranto	1940
Matapan	1941
"Bismarck"	1941
Dodecanese Island	1943

PACIFIC

Japanese Offensive	
Pearl Harbor	1941
Hong Kong	1941
Malaya	1941–1942
Wake Island	1941
Philippine Islands	1941–1942
China II	1941–1945
"Prince of Wales"–"Repulse"	1941
Guam I	1941
East Indies	1941–1942
Bataan-Corregidor	1942
Burma I	1942
Singapore	1942
Darwin	1942
Java Sea	1942
Ceylon	1942
Shangri-La	1942
Madagascar	1942
Coral Sea	1942
Turning Point	
Midway	1942
Allied Offensive—South and Southwest Pacific	
Solomon Islands	1942–1944
New Georgia	1943
Kula Gulf	1943
Vella Gulf	1943
Vella Lavella	1943
Bougainville	1943–1944
Guadalcanal	1942–1943
Guadalcanal—Naval Action	1942
Savo Island	1942
Eastern Solomons	1942
Esperance Cape	1942
Santa Cruz Islands	1942
Tassafaronga	1942
New Guinea	1942–1944
Wakde Island	1944
Biak Island	1944
Morotai	1944
Bismarck Sea	1943
Rabaul	1943–1944

Gloucester Cape	1943
Admiralty Islands	1944
Leyte	1944
Leyte Gulf	1944
Surigao Strait	1944
Engaño Cape	1944
Samar	1944
Luzon	1945
Southern Philippines–Borneo	1945
Allied Offensive—Central Pacific	
Tarawa-Makin	1943
Truk	1944
Kwajalein-Eniwetok	1944
Mariana Islands	1944
Saipan	1944
Guam II	1944
Tinian	1944
Philippine Sea	1944
Peleliu-Angaur	1944
Iwo Jima	1945
Okinawa	1945
Allied Offensive—Northern Pacific	
Aleutian Islands	1943
Attu	1943
Allied Offensive—Asia	
Burma II	1943–1945
Myitkyina	1944
Imphal	1944
Japan—Bombardment	1944–1945

Wörth (Franco-Prussian War), 1870. After driving the French army out of Wissembourg on August 4, the Prussian Third Army under Crown Prince Frederick William marched southwest to Wörth with 77,000 men. Here, in northeast France, the Comte de MacMahon concentrated 37,000 French troops to block the invasion. The Prussians attacked at dawn on August 6 under cover of an artillery barrage laid down by most of their 234 rifled, breech-loaded guns. This weapon stood markedly superior to the old muzzle-loaded French piece, of which MacMahon had only 101. However, the center-fire French rifle, called the chassepot, proved to have double the range of the Prussian needle rifle, and for eight hours the defenders held off the attacks. Augmenting the French firepower was the mitrailleuse, the first crude machine gun used in Europe. Finally, late in the afternoon, MacMahon had to retreat from Wörth (Fröschwiller) after suffering the loss of almost one-third of his force. He fell back behind the Vosges Mountains. The crown prince, who had lost 11,000 casualties, pursued slowly. Meanwhile, another French army suffered defeat at Spicheren, 40 miles to the northwest. *See* Wissembourg; Spicheren; Colombey; Franco-Prussian War.

Wounded Knee Creek (Ghost Dance War), 1890. Thirteen years after the last major battle between United States troops and the Indians at Bear Paw Mountains, the Sioux in South Dakota became aroused by a messianic religion (which included a ritualistic Ghost Dance) that was sweeping the western tribes. On December 15, 1890, Sitting Bull, who had returned from Canada in 1881, was killed by Indian police while being arrested. In panic, a Sioux tribe under Big Foot fled into the Badlands of South Dakota. Colonel James Forsythe with 470 men surrounded the Indians on December 28. When the troops of the 7th Cavalry started to disarm the Indians the following day, the 120 warriors in the tribe opened fire. In the six-hour massacre that followed, the Indians were overpowered, 145 men, women, and children being killed, including Big Foot. Some of the 33 wounded froze to death. The army lost 30 killed and 34 wounded. This was the last major Indian uprising in the West. *See* Wolf Mountain; Indian Wars in the United States.

Würzburg (Wars of the French Revolution), 1796. After turning back the French invasion at Amberg in August 1796, Archduke Charles Louis pursued the defeated army of the Sambre-and-Meuse, commanded by Gen. Jean Jourdan. The French Revolutionary force fell back northwestward to Würzburg. Here, on September 3, Jourdan made a stand. But he suffered a second defeat, from a sharp attack by the 45,000-man Austrian army of the Holy Roman Empire (Francis II, older brother of Charles). The French lost 2,000 men (out of about 40,000) and 7 cannon. Jourdan retreated across the Rhine.

Charles then turned south to challenge the second invading force, the Army of the Rhine-and-Moselle. This body of troops had lost its commander, Gen. Charles Pichegru, who had defected to the enemy. Without the support of Jourdan's army, Gen. Jean Moreau, now in command, retreated through the Black Forest before the Austrian advance. When Moreau too fell back west of the Rhine, the entire French offensive came to an end. In Italy, however, Napoleon Bonaparte was reversing the tide of French defeats at the hands of Austria. *See* Amberg; Caliano; French Revolution Wars.

Y

Yalu River I (Chinese-Japanese War I), 1894. At sea the Japanese held the same superiority in armament, training, and organization that they did on land. Aggressively seeking out the Chinese fleet, Adm. Yugo Ito sailed to the mouth of the Yalu River with ten cruisers and two gunboats. Here on September 17 he attacked the Chinese navy of two battleships and eight cruisers, under the command of Adm. Ting. Circling the line of Chinese ships, Ito's guns caused two enemy vessels to drop out and set two others afire. But Ting's other six ships fought back until sundown, when Ito called off the attack. The surviving Chinese vessels retired to Port Arthur on the Liaotung Peninsula. *See* Pyongyang; Port Arthur I; Chinese-Japanese War I.

Yalu River II (Russian-Japanese War), 1904. While Adm. Heihachiro Togo blockaded the Russian fleet at Port Arthur, the Japanese prepared a land offensive in Korea. Some 40,000 Japanese troops under Gen. Count Tamemoto Kuroki landed at Jinsen (Chemulpo) on the west coast and pushed northward. Russia's supreme commander in the Far East, Gen. Aleksei Kuropatkin, concentrated his forces at Liaoyang in southern Manchuria. He sent forward only 7,000 troops under Gen. Zasulich to hold the line of the Yalu River. Kuroki's First Army reached the river on May 1 and forced a crossing at Gishu (Wiju) in the face of weak Russian opposition, which cost the defenders a third of their force. This initial land battle of the war won widespread attention: it was the first time in modern history that European troops had been beaten by an Asiatic army employing Western arms and tactics. Kuroki pressed aggressively into Manchuria. *See* Port Arthur II; Liaoyang; Russian-Japanese War.

Yarmuk River (Moslem Conquest of Syria), 636. To throw back the Arabian invasion of Syria, the Byzantine emperor Heraclius sent two armies into the field—one from the north, the other from the Palestinian coast. The Arabian general Khālid ibn-al-Walīd pulled back his Moslem cavalry to the valley of the Yarmuk, an eastern tributary of the Jordan. Here he received reinforcements from Medina and from some tribes of Syrian Arabs, to bring the Moslem strength to about 25,000 warriors. The combined Byzantine force, under Theodorus Trithurius, was twice as large, but much of it was composed of Asiatic auxiliaries. On August 20, 636, the Moslems opened the battle with their usual slashing cavalry attacks. Although the first forays were beaten off, the Islamic horsemen continued to strike until the Byzantine lines collapsed, at the end of the day. In the rout that followed, the Imperial forces suffered enormous losses; some 4,000 Moslems were killed.

The defeat broke the Byzantine power in southern Syria and in Palestine. The Moslem wave swept on to Damascus without opposition. Here the capital of Islam was established for the next hundred years. Before pushing on to northern Syria, the Moslems turned to attack Jerusalem. *See* Damascus I; Jerusalem VI; Aleppo; Moslem Conquests.

Yellow Sea (Russian-Japanese War). Harassed by Japanese artillery ringing Port Arthur, the Russian fleet sought to evade destruction by escaping into the Yellow Sea; on August 10, 1904, the Japanese fleet under Adm. Heihachiro Togo turned back the fugitive ships to their eventual doom in the harbor of Port Arthur. *See* Port Arthur II.

Yellow Tavern (American Civil War), 1864. As Gen. U. S. Grant moved his large Federal army from the Wilderness to Spotsylvania, he sent the cavalry corps of Gen. Philip Sheridan on a raid against Richmond. With 10,000 troopers Sheridan rode out on May 9, circling west and south of the Confederate army of Gen. Robert E. Lee. Gen. J. E. B. Stuart, the Confederate cavalry leader, divided his smaller force of 4,500 men into two groups, one of which, under Gen. James Gordon, followed Sheridan, while Stuart, with the other, detoured eastward to intercept the Federals at Yellow Tavern, six miles north of Richmond. On May 11 Sheridan struck the blocking force and drove it off. Stuart was mortally wounded by a pistol shot from Pvt. John Huff. At the same time Sheridan's rear guard routed the Confederate force in its rear, killing Gordon.

Sheridan pressed on, passing north of Richmond and then south to the James River, where he obtained supplies from Gen. Benjamin Butler's Federal army at Haxall's Landing on May 14. Riding northward three days later, Sheridan rejoined Grant along the North Anna River on May 24. The raid cost the Federals 625 men. Its chief result was the killing of the spectacular but restless Stuart. *See* Wilderness; Spotsylvania; American Civil War.

Yenan (Chinese Communists' Long March), 1934–1935. Beginning late in 1930, Gen. Chiang Kai-shek's Nanking government waged an all-out campaign to eliminate the Communist hold on southern Kiangsi Province. The harried Communists finally resolved to leave the area and join up with their fellow rebels in northern Shensi, 6,000 miles away. On the night of October 16, 1934, some 90,000 Communist troops, led by commander in chief Chu Teh with Mao Tse-tung serving as political commissar, set out on their Long March, or Chang Cheng. Living off the land and fighting their way past hostile Nationalist and provincial armies, the Communist force crossed 24 rivers and 18 mountain ranges. The combat march finally ended on October 20, 1935, when the lead elements linked up with 10,000 fellow Communist partisans near Yenan. Only 20,000 men survived, but the epic mass movement probably saved Chinese Communism from extinction. Two years later Chu Teh took command of the Eighth Route Army in a loose alliance with Chiang against the Japanese invasion. Yenan became the Communist capital. *See* China I.

York (Danish Invasions of Britain), 867. The Danish raiders, who had begun their incursions into Britain in the late 700's, grew more bold in the following century. From East Anglia, Ivan, the Boneless, led a group north along the old Roman road to York in 867. His intent was to avenge the earlier killing of his father, Ragnar Lodbrok, in Northumbria. When Ivan laid siege to York, the two rival kings of Northumbria united against the Vikings and drove them back against the walls of the city. The garrison then made a sortie against the besiegers. But in the melee that followed, the Danes overwhelmed the combined Saxon forces with terrible loss of life. Both the Northumbrian kings were killed. This battle ended Saxon power in the north of Britain. York became a Danish stronghold. *See* Aclea; Hoxne; Danish Invasions of Britain.

Yorktown I (War of the American Revolution), 1781. From North Carolina, the British general Lord Cornwallis marched into Virginia in the spring of 1781. Here he received reinforcements which brought his army up to a strength of 7,500, much superior to the small American army in Virginia under the command of the French Marquis de Lafayette. In June Gen. Anthony Wayne and the Baron von Steuben reinforced Lafayette, increasing his force to 4,500. Although Cornwallis still had the overwhelming advantage in numbers, he turned eastward to the coast to maintain sea communications with Gen. Sir Henry Clinton in New York City. Reaching Yorktown on August 1, Cornwallis fortified both this town and Gloucester, to the north across the York River.

Meanwhile, above New York City, Gen. George Washington was joined by a French army under the Comte de Rochambeau. The combined allied force crossed the Hudson River on August 21, marching against Cornwallis. Covering 200 miles in 15 days, the allies arrived at the head of Chesapeake Bay to obtain ship transportation to Virginia. By September 18 all the troops were embarked by the French fleet of the Comte de Grasse, who was maintaining a sea blockade of Cornwallis' army, after having driven off the British fleet in the battle of Chesapeake Capes on September 5. Washington's army finished debarking near Williamsburg on September 26. Here it was joined by Lafayette's force (already reinforced by 3,000 French troops landed by De Grasse) to begin the siege of the 6,000-man enemy force at Yorktown.

From Williamsburg, the allied army marched eastward against the British defenses. Washington, with 8,845 men, commanded the right wing; Rochambeau led 7,800 French troops on the left. By October 6 the allied siege lines, including the heavy guns, were in place, and the first parallel was begun. Three days later 52 siege guns opened

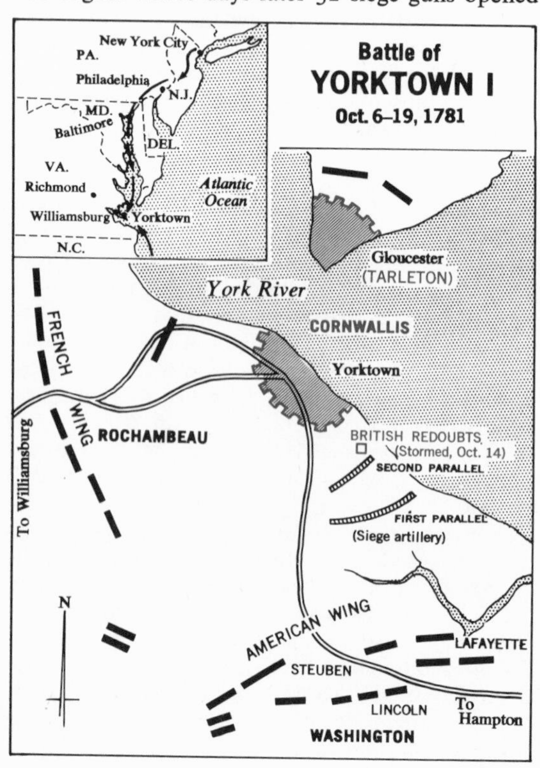

fire on the British in Yorktown. A second parallel, started on October 10, was blocked by two British redoubts near the river east of the town. These redoubts were stormed and carried four nights later. When a British sortie on October 16 failed to prevent the closer emplacement of the siege artillery, Cornwallis lost hope of holding out. The following morning all the allied guns began a cannonade of the doomed town. Cornwallis asked for an armistice and accepted terms of complete surrender. At two o'clock on the afternoon of October 19 the British army marched out of Yorktown and laid down its arms. Across the York River Col. Banastre Tarleton surrendered at Gloucester, bringing the total number of prisoners to 7,247 soldiers and 840 seamen. The siege had cost the British 156 killed, 326 wounded. American losses were 20 killed, 56 wounded; the French lost 52 killed, 134 wounded.

The British capitulation at Yorktown ended the fighting in America. Early the next year the House of Commons authorized King George III to make peace. The formal treaty acknowledging the independence of the United States was signed on September 3, 1783. Meanwhile the war between Great Britain and its European enemies continued in the West Indies, the Mediterranean, and in India. *See* Chesapeake Capes; Minorca II; American Revolution.

Yorktown II (American Civil War), 1862. After the Federal disaster at first Bull Run, President Abraham Lincoln put Gen. George McClellan in charge of what would become the Army of the Potomac. McClellan resolved to strike at the Confederate capital of Richmond from the southeast —up the peninsula between the York and James rivers. Arriving at Fort Monroe on April 2, the Union commander launched his offensive two days later. At Yorktown he found his route blocked by some 13,000 Confederates under Gen. John Magruder. Although McClellan had a superiority of 4 to 1, he was deceived into conducting a regular siege operation against Yorktown. Thus Magruder accomplished his mission of holding off the Federals until Gen. Joseph Johnston could move the main Confederate army southeast from Culpeper to protect Richmond.

By May 1 McClellan had the first of his heavy Parrott guns in position to open fire on Yorktown. Two nights later Magruder began a withdrawal toward Richmond, covered by the cavalry of Gen. James (Jeb) Stuart. General Edwin Sumner's II Federal Corps occupied Yorktown on May 4 and then took up the pursuit. *See* Ball's Bluff; Williamsburg; American Civil War.

Ypres I (World War I), 1914. At the close of the first battle of the Aisne River, Field Marshal Joseph Joffre began shifting the French armies and the British Expeditionary Force (BEF) northward against the open German flank at Noyon. The German commander, Gen. Erich von Falkenhayn, countered by trying to envelop the Allied left flank. This inaugurated a series of bloody but ineffective flanking maneuvers by both sides, until the Allies reached the North Sea at Nieuwpoort, Belgium, in the first half of October. As the so-called Race to the Sea ended, the Belgian army of King Albert I was driven out of Antwerp. The Belgians then occupied the extreme left of the Allied line from the coast southward to Ypres (Ieper). The BEF, under Field Marshal Sir John French, took over the line from Ypres south to La Bassée, while seven French armies dug in all the way eastward to the Swiss border. The Western Front had become stabilized.

To effect a penetration of the Allied line, Falkenhayn sent the Fourth and Sixth armies against Ypres on October 14. The German offensive pressed forward for nine days. It was finally halted by French reinforcements rushed to the area and by the Belgians on the left, who flooded their front by opening sluice gates from Diksmuide to the sea. During this attack King Albert lost 35 percent of his army. On October 20 Gen. Ferdinand Foch, who had assumed nominal command of the northern part of the Allied line, launched a counterattack. These assaults were no more productive than those of the Germans. When Foch called off his offensive on October 28, Falkenhayn renewed his attacks the following day. But again no gain could be made despite the frightful casualties suffered on both sides. Heavy rains and snow on November 11 finally brought the battle to a close. As both sides entrenched deeper for the winter, the British held a salient that jutted six miles eastward into the German lines. Ypres stood at the base of the salient. Despite this poor defensive position, the British grimly held their ground, for the small Belgian town had become a symbol of Allied resistance. Ypres, the last major battle on the Western Front in 1914, cost Sir John French 2,368 officers and 55,787 enlisted men—80 percent of the men in his original British Expeditionary Force of five and one-half divisions. France suffered about 50,000 casualties. German losses were at least 130,000 men. In the first three months of fighting on the Western Front, France lost 380,000 killed and 600,000 wounded, captured, and missing. Total German casualties were only slightly less. *See* Aisne River I; Champagne I; World War I.

Ypres II (World War I), 1915. The initial German offensive of 1915 came against the Allied salient at Ypres (Ieper), Belgium. It was preceded by the first employment of poison (chlorine) gas, early on April 22. The yellowish-green clouds created a four-mile gap in the Allied line, which the Germans of Gen. Erich von Falkenhayn began exploiting. The British Second Army commander, Gen. Sir Horace Smith-Dorrien, plugged the hole with Canadian troops. These units held during a second gas attack on April 24. Three days later Smith-Dorrien ordered a voluntary withdrawal to the outskirts of Ypres. Field Marshal Sir John French, in command of the British Expeditionary Force, promptly replaced Smith-Dorrien with Gen. Sir Herbert Plumer. The new Second Army chief did precisely what his predecessor planned, beginning on May 1. German attacks continued until May 25, when the battle ended. The poor tactical position around Ypres was demonstrated in the casualties of the battle. The defending Allies lost 60,000 men, or almost twice the 35,000 casualties suffered by the attacking Germans—a complete reversal of the defense-offense casualty ratio common to the Western Front. *See* Ypres I; Neuve-Chapelle; Artois II; World War I.

Ypres III (World War I), 1917. With the capture of Messines Ridge on June 7, the British field marshal Sir Douglas Haig stood ready to launch his major Flanders offensive. On July 31 the Fifth Army of Gen. Hubert Gough jumped off northeastward out of the three-year-old Ypres (Ieper) salient. The British drove forward two miles that day. Then heavy rains set in, flooding the thousands of shell holes created by the ten-day preliminary bombardment. When Gough bogged down, the main axis of attack was shifted southward to the Second Army of Gen. Sir Herbert Plumer. But the combination of waterlogged terrain and stubborn resistance by Gen. Friedrich Sixt von Armin's German Fourth Army reduced the British pace to a crawl. Langemarck, five miles north of Ypres, was taken on August 16, and Meenen Road Ridge and Polygon Wood to the east between September 20 and October 3. Even the German use of mustard gas failed to halt Plumer's methodical advance.

Finally, on November 6, two Canadian brigades stormed and held the village of Passchendaele, less than seven miles from Ypres. Here the battle ended. Haig received much criticism for the 240,000 British casualties suffered in the battle. However, he did succeed in taking the pressure off the French armies to the south, which were being reorganized after their mutiny in May. And his offensive had been weakened by the loss of five valuable divisions transferred during the battle to the Italian front following the Austrian victory at Caporetto. German losses were equally high, including 37,000 prisoners. *See* Messines; Cambrai; World War I.

Yugoslavia (World War II), 1941. The pro-German Yugoslav government of Prince Paul was overthrown on March 27, 1941, by Gen. Dušan Simovic, who installed young Peter II as ruler. Ten days later the German *Wehrmacht,* 27 divisions strong, plunged into Yugoslavia (and simultaneously into Greece) from four neighboring countries. From Austria and from Hungary, the German Second Army (Maximilian von Weichs) moved on Zagreb in the north and on Belgrade in the northeast; from Rumania and from Bulgaria, Field Marshal Siegmund List's Twelfth Army with 15 divisions smashed into central and southern Yugoslavia toward Belgrade and Bitolj (Monastir). Yugoslavia was unable to mobilize its planned 40 divisions. Fragmented by knifing German armored attacks, plus an Italian advance from the west and a Hungarian thrust from the north, the ill-equipped Yugoslav forces were destroyed in detail.

Belgrade, bombed with calculated ruthlessness for three days, on April 6–8, suffered 17,000 civilian deaths. It was occupied on April 12 by converging German columns, King Peter fleeing to London on a British plane. Sarajevo fell on April 14 and three days later Yugoslavia capitulated. Five of List's divisions, which had knifed through to Bitolj in the southwest and thus prevented a possible link-up of Yugoslav and Greek forces, now turned south toward Athens. In all, about 6,000 Yugoslavian officers and 335,000 enlisted men surrendered. German casualties totaled 558. *See* Greece (World War II); World War II.

Yungay (War of the Peruvian-Bolivian Confederation), 1839. Andrés Santa Cruz, who had helped in the Peruvian revolt against Spain during 1820–23, became president of Bolivia in 1829. Seven years later he organized the Peruvian-Bolivian Confederation, a virtual union of the two countries. Faced with the threat of domination by this confederation, Chile built up its army, commanded by Manuel Bulnes. The decisive battle was fought at Yungay in Chile, southeast of Concepción, on January 20, 1839. Bulnes' army won a clear-cut victory. Santa Cruz was overthrown, terminating the confederation. *See* Ingaví.

Z

Zab al Kabir (Moslem Civil Wars), 750. The rule of the Ommiad caliph Marwan II was torn by Moslem insurrections in all parts of the Arabian Empire. One of the strongest rebel forces was the Abbasids, who began carrying a black standard in Khurasan about 747. This aggressive group fought an 11-day battle with the Ommiad loyalists on the Great Zab River, an eastern tributary of the Tigris, in modern Turkey, in January 750. The Ommiads were routed. Marwan fled to Egypt where he was later killed. Abu-al-Abbas then became the first Abbasid caliph, a dynasty that would last 350 years. The center of Arab power now shifted from Damascus to Baghdad. *See* Kerbela; Heraclea Pontica; Moslem Conquests.

Zallaka (Spanish-Moslem Wars), 1086. When Alfonso VI, the Valiant, of Castile and León seized Toledo in 1085, the alarmed Moslems called for aid from Yusuf ibn-Tashfin, chief of the Almoravids, the Berber sect that had recently conquered northwestern Africa. Ibn-Tashfin landed at Algeciras, west of Gibraltar, in 1086 and marched north through Seville and Badajoz. At Zallaka (Zalaca) he met the army of Christian knights and infantry under Alfonso on October 23. The swift Berber horsemen utterly routed the Spanish, who had a marked superiority in numbers but lacked maneuverability and discipline. King Alfonso barely escaped with his life.

During the next 20 years ibn-Tashfin ruled with a firm hand all of Spain south of Toledo. The temporary exception was Valencia, which became an independent Moorish kingdom in 1094 under the Spanish soldier of fortune Rodrigo (Ruy) Díaz de Bivar, the Cid. The city reverted to Moslem control when the great folk hero was killed by the Almoravids five years later. *See* Toledo I; Huesca.

Zama (Second Punic War), 202 B.C. The Roman victory south of Utica in the spring of 203 B.C. terrified the council of Carthage. Hannibal, still in southern Italy, was called back to Africa to defend his home city. Despite the tight corner into which Rome had squeezed him, Hannibal slipped out of the port of Croton on the Gulf of Taranto with the bulk of his 12,000-man army in June. He landed on the east coast of modern Tunisia, about 80 miles below Carthage, in October of the same year. Hannibal immediately began forging a new army. His brother Mago, who had been in northwest Italy at the foot of the Alps, was also recalled to Carthage. Part of Mago's troops arrived safely, but the young Barca was lost at sea.

West of Carthage Publius Cornelius Scipio, in command of the Roman army near Utica, offered Carthage peace terms. When all efforts to reach a truce failed, Scipio abandoned the siege of Utica and marched up the Bagradas (Medjerda) River in the spring of 202 B.C., determined to draw Hannibal into combat. His 6,000 Numidian cavalrymen, under Masinissa, rode up just as the Romans came face to face with Hannibal's 37,000 troops near the village of Zama. Although Scipio's army was no larger, his men were better trained, especially his Numidian horsemen. As Hannibal unloosed his 80 elephants, the Romans stood their ground and soon scattered the great beasts. Then the Roman cavalry rode at the Carthaginian cavalry on the wings and, when the enemy riders fled, followed them across the plains. It now became a battle of infantry—the Roman legions attacking the three separate lines that Hannibal had organized. In a deadly test of strength the

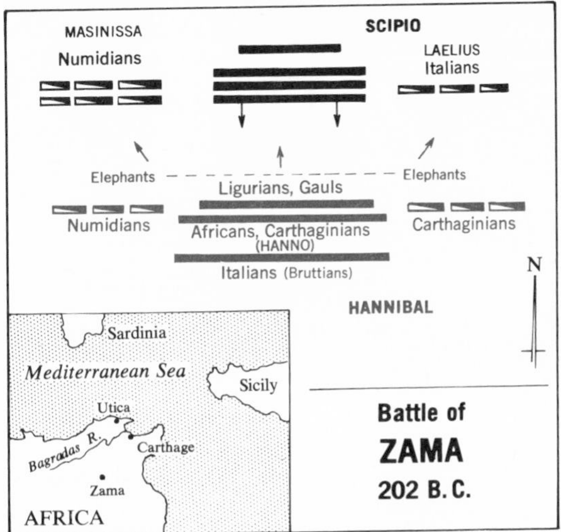

legionaries crushed the first line of Ligurians and Gauls from Mago's old army. Then they moved forward to take on the second line, composed of Africans under the command of Hannibal's long-time lieutenant Hanno. This line too was broken by the inexorable Roman advance. Scipio's near exhausted men regrouped to attack the still-fresh third line, made up of veterans from Italy directed by Hannibal himself. But at that moment the Roman cavalry arm returned from its successful chase and struck at the rear of the Carthaginian infantry. The combined attack smashed the last line of resistance. At the end of the day 20,000 Carthaginians lay dead on the battlefield and a similar number were captive. Some 1,500 Romans were killed. The Second Punic War was ended.

A prostrate Carthage ceded Spain and its Mediterranean islands to Rome. It surrendered all its warships except ten and began paying an indemnity of 200 talents a year for 50 years. Scipio received the surname Africanus, the first Roman leader to be distinguished with the name of the country he conquered. Hannibal, who had barely escaped the Zama disaster, returned to Carthage. He helped revitalize the city until forced into exile in 195. He allied himself with Antiochus III (the Great) of Syria. But the Roman victory over the Seleucid dynasty at Magnesia forced him to flee once again. In 183 he took poison to avoid capture by Rome. *See* Utica I; Magnesia; Carthage I; Punic Wars.

Zamora (Spanish-Moslem Wars), 939. The Moslems of Spain under the Ommiad caliph Abd-er-Rahman III reacted to the Christian counter-offensive by laying siege to Zamora, 130 miles northwest of Madrid. King Ramiro II of León marched to the aid of the city. His attack, supplemented by a sortie of the garrison, routed the large force of besiegers. Thousands of Moslems were killed and a large number drowned in the moat surrounding Zamora.

Through the next century the Christian counter-offensive in Spain made only slow progress. However, its path became easier when internal Moslem strife finally resulted in the collapse of the Ommiad caliphate at Córdova in 1031. Moorish rule then degenerated into a score of petty kingdoms. *See* Simancas; Toledo I; Moslem Conquests.

Zela (Wars of the First Triumvirate), 47 B.C. In the summer of 47 B.C. Julius Caesar left Egypt for the Roman province of Syria. Here a new threat to his rule was developing from the north. Pharnaces II, son of the resolute Mithridates VI, had established himself in Pontus on the southern shore of the Black Sea. Earlier in the year he had routed a Roman detachment at Nicopolis. Caesar now marched to meet him with seven legions. While the Romans were making camp on August 2 near Zela (Zile), in north-central Turkey, Pharnaces suddenly attacked. But the disciplined legionaries refused to panic. They quickly assembled in combat units and overwhelmed the ill-trained Pharnacians. Caesar, in a laconic message, reported back to Rome: *Veni, vidi, vici*. After re-establishing order in the East, Caesar sailed for Tarentum and Italy in September. *See* Alexandria I; Ruspina; First Triumvirate, Wars of the.

Zorndorf (Seven Years' War), 1758. While Frederick II, the Great, was campaigning against Austria in 1758, Czarina Elizabeth of Russia sent a ponderous army into East Prussia. Under the general Count William of Fermor, the Russians captured and plundered Posen, then moved westward into Brandenburg, besieging Cüstrin (Kostrzyn) on the Oder. Disengaging from the Austrian army of the Holy Roman Empire along the Silesian-Moravian border, the Prussian king hurried northwestward. He reached Frankfurt on the Oder on August 20 with 15,000 effectives. Uniting this force with the shaken army which had been trying to stem the Russian advance, Frederick marched to Cüstrin. Fermor raised the siege and retreated northward to take up a strong position at Zorndorf. The Russian commander had 42,000 men to Frederick's 36,000, but he dissipated much of his superiority by deploying into three large, irregular squares. Marshland between the squares prevented mutual support.

On August 25 Frederick marched across the Russian front to attack the square on their right. To the king's surprise the enemy fought back hard. His infantry was stopped cold until the cavalry of Gen. Friedrich von Seydlitz rode into the melee. In a savage, no-quarter struggle the Russian square was destroyed. Re-forming his troops, Frederick assaulted the center square. Again the Russians checked the infantry, only to be ridden down by the cavalry. Darkness ended the bloody battle, in which the Prussians lost 13,500 men (37.5 percent) and the Russians suffered 21,000 casualties (50 percent).

Both sides were too weakened to resume fighting the next day. Fermor began a slow withdrawal to the east, cautiously followed by a Prussian covering force. Frederick turned back to Saxony, where a new Austrian offensive was under way. *See* Olmütz; Crefeld; Hochkirch; Kay; Seven Years' War.

Zulu-British War (1879). When the British annexed the Transvaal in 1877, the Zululand boundary was adjusted to favor King Cetewayo on condition that he disband his army. To enforce this agreement, British troops invaded Zulu territory. Despite an initial defeat, the British destroyed Zulu military strength.

Isandhlwana	1879
Rorke's Drift	1879
Ulundi	1879

Zurich I (Wars of the French Revolution), 1799. After defeating the armies of the French Directory in Germany and Italy, the Second Coalition powers turned to Switzerland. This country, overrun by France and organized as the Helvetian Republic in April 1798, was held by 45,000 French troops under Gen. André Masséna. Archduke Charles Louis, the brother of Holy Roman Emperor Francis II and the liberator of Germany, moved from Baden into Switzerland in the spring of 1799. Masséna concentrated half of his force at Zurich. Here the archduke sent some 40,000 troops, chiefly Austrian. In a four-day battle during June 4–7, both sides suffered heavy casualties along a five-mile front. Masséna finally gave way and the Austrians took Zurich, the key to northern Switzerland. Soon after, however, illness forced the capable Charles Louis to turn his command over to the Russian general Alexander Korsakov. Masséna regrouped his forces for a counteroffensive. *See* Stokach I; Cassano d'Adda II; Zurich II; French Revolution Wars.

Zurich II (Wars of the French Revolution), 1799. After routing the French army in northern Italy, Field Marshal Count Aleksandr Suvorov took his Russian army through Saint Gothard Pass into Switzerland. To cover his march, he relied on the protection of the 30,000 Russian troops under Gen. Alexander Korsakov near Zurich. However, the veteran French mountain fighter Gen. André Masséna was alert to the danger of the Russian armies uniting against him. Sending a division to the pass to harass Suvorov's march, Masséna turned on Korsakov with the bulk of his forces on September 26. In the second battle of Zurich fought within three and a half months, the French routed the Russians, killing or wounding 8,000 and capturing many guns and prisoners. Masséna then concentrated against Suvorov, who fell back. The Russian retreat soon became a disaster. His troops weakened by starvation and French ambushes along the mountain roads, Suvorov lost half his 28,000-man army before he escaped eastward. It was the worst setback in the long career of the tough little Russian general. Back in Moscow, Czar Paul I, disgusted at the weak support received from his allies, withdrew from the Second Coalition on October 22. *See* Novi Ligure; Zurich I; Alkmaar II; French Revolution Wars.

Zusmarshausen (Thirty Years' War), 1648. After more than a quarter century of fighting that had brought no result except the despoliation of their lands, the German states allied to the Holy Roman Empire began to pull out of the war. Frederick William, elector of Brandenburg, sued for peace in 1644; John George I, Elector of Saxony, withdrew the following year. In March 1647 Maximilian I of Bavaria accepted peace terms, leaving only Austria in support of the Hapsburg position of Emperor Ferdinand III in Germany (the emperor's brother, Archduke Leopold William, commanded the Spanish Hapsburg forces in the Netherlands).

In the fall of 1647, however, Bavaria re-entered the war. This brought on a new invasion of this state by the combined forces of France (Vicomte de Turenne) and Sweden (Karl Wrangel, who had replaced Field Marshal Lennart Torstenson in 1646). The allied army outnumbered the defending 30,000 Austro-Bavarian troops, now under the command of Peter Melander, a Hessian general. On May 17 the invaders surprised the Imperials at Zusmarshausen, 14 miles west of Augsburg. Melander began falling back, leaving the Austrian general Count Raimund Montecuccoli to hold off the enemy with a rear-guard action. The withdrawal was severely handicapped by a train of 100,000 camp followers. When Melander fell fatally wounded, Montecuccoli abandoned the impedimenta and saved the combat troops by retreating to Landsberg. The French and Swedes overran Bavaria as far as the Inn River, but here they were checked by a second Imperial Army under Field Marshal Octavio Piccolomini. Meanwhile, another Swedish army had marched into Bohemia. *See* Nördlingen II; Prague II; Thirty Years' War.

Zutphen (Netherlands War of Independence), 1586. Following the successful Dutch defense of Leyden in 1574, the site of the Netherlands revolt against Philip II of Spain shifted to the southern provinces (modern Belgium). Thereupon the seven northern provinces formed the Union of Utrecht in 1579 and two years later declared their independence under William I (the Silent) of Orange. William, murdered in 1584, was succeeded by his son Maurice of Nassau. Queen Elizabeth I of England recognized the new nation and sent troops under the Earl of Leicester (Robert Sidney) to aid the Dutch. In 1586 the new allies laid siege to Zutphen in eastern Netherlands, defended by a Spanish garrison under the supreme command of the Duke of Parma. When the Spaniards sent a relief column to the town on September 22, Leicester tried to intercept it but was beaten off. His brother, Sir Philip Sidney, was mortally wounded in the battle. With Zutphen relieved, Leicester abandoned the siege. But five years later Maurice liberated the city in a renewed attack upon the Spanish forces in the Netherlands. *See* Antwerp I; Cadiz; Turnhout; Netherlands War of Independence.

SUGGESTIONS FOR FURTHER READING

The following is a selected bibliography of books that contain additional background and detail for the battles described in *A Dictionary of Battles*. The number of monographs dealing with single battles runs into the hundreds; this list includes only those books that deal with more than one battle. All titles are fairly recent and therefore are either still in print or readily available in most public libraries; many are in paperback.

General

Creasy, Sir Edward S., and Mitchell, Joseph B., *Twenty Decisive Battles of the World*. New York: Macmillan, 1964.

Esposito, Vincent J., ed., *The West Point Atlas of American Wars*. 2 vols. New York: Praeger, 1959.

Falls, Cyril, *The Art of War from the Age of Napoleon to the Present Day*. New York: Oxford University Press, 1961.

———, *Great Military Battles*. New York: Macmillan, 1964.

———, *A Hundred Years of War, 1850–1950*. New York: Macmillan, 1962.

Fuller, J. F. C., *The Conduct of War, 1789–1961*. New Brunswick, N.J.: Rutgers University Press, 1961.

———, *A Military History of the Western World*. 3 vols. New York: Funk and Wagnalls, 1954–1956.

Mahan, Alfred, *The Influence of Sea Power upon History, 1660–1783*. New York: Sagamore, 1957.

Potter, E. B., and Nimitz, Chester W., eds., *Sea Power: A Naval History*. Englewood Cliffs, N.J.: Prentice-Hall, 1960.

Pratt, Fletcher, *The Battles That Changed History*. New York: Doubleday, 1956.

Preston, Richard A., Wise, Sydney F., and Werner, Herman O., *Men in Arms: A History of Warfare and Its Interrelationships with Western Society*. New York: Praeger, 1962.

Ancient, Medieval, and Early Modern

Henderson, Bernard W., *Great War Between Sparta and Athens*. New York: Macmillan, 1927.

Herodotus, *History of the Persian Wars*. Vol. 6 of *Great Books of the Western World*. Chicago: Encyclopaedia Britannica, 1952.

Hignett, Charles, *Xerxes' Invasion of Greece*. New York: Oxford University Press, 1963.

McCartney, Eugene S., *Warfare by Land and Sea*. New York: Cooper Square, 1963.

Oman, C. W. C., *A History of the Art of War in the Middle Ages, A.D. 378–1485*. 2 vols. New York: Burt Franklin, 1959.

———, *A History of the Art of War in the Sixteenth Century*. New York: Dutton, 1937.

Perroy, Edouard M. J., *Hundred Years' War*. Tr. by W. B. Wells. New York: Oxford University Press, 1952.
Smail, R. C., *Crusading Warfare (1097–1193)*. New York: Cambridge University Press, 1956.
Thompson, James Westfall, *The Wars of Religion in France, 1559–1576*. New York: Ungar, 1958.
Warrington, John, ed., *Caesar's War Commentaries*. New York: Dutton, 1958.
Wedgwood, C. V., *The Thirty Years' War*. New Haven: Yale University Press, 1939.
Yadin, Yigael, *The Art of Warfare in Biblical Lands*. 2 vols. New York: McGraw-Hill, 1963.

Eighteenth Century

Boatner, Mark, III, *Encyclopedia of the American Revolution*. New York: McKay, 1966.
Esposito, Vincent J., and Elting, John R., eds., *A Military History and Atlas of the Napoleonic Wars*. New York: Praeger, 1964.
Hamilton, Edward P., *The French and Indian Wars*. New York: Doubleday, 1962.
Ketchum, Richard, ed., *American Heritage Book of the Revolution*. New York: Simon and Schuster, 1958.
Mitchell, Joseph B., *Decisive Battles of the American Revolution*. New York: Putnam, 1962.
Ward, Christopher L., *War of the Revolution*. Ed. by John Richard Alden. 2 vols. New York: Macmillan, 1952.

Nineteenth Century
(Except the U.S. Civil War)

Ardant du Picq, Charles J. J. J., *Battle Studies*. Tr. by John N. Greeley and Robert C. Cotton. Harrisburg, Pa.: Military Service, 1947.
Churchill, Winston, *The River War: An Account of the Reconquest of the Soudan*. New York: Scribner's, 1933.
Collier, Richard, *The Great Indian Mutiny*. New York: Dutton, 1963.
Delderfield, R. F., *Napoleon's Marshals*. Philadelphia: Chilton, 1966.
Downey, Fairfax, *Indian Wars of the U.S. Army, 1776–1865*. New York: Doubleday, 1963.
Esposito, Vincent J., and Elting, John R., eds., *A Military History and Atlas of the Napoleonic Wars*. New York: Praeger, 1964.
Freidel, Frank, *Splendid Little War*. Boston: Little, Brown, 1958.
Furneaux, Robert, *Zulu War*. Philadelphia: Lippincott, 1963.
Holt, Edgar, *Boer War*. Toronto: McClelland, 1958.
Horne, Alistair, *Fall of Paris: The Siege and the Commune*. New York: St. Martin's, 1966.
Howard, Michael, *The Franco-Prussian War*. New York: Macmillan, 1962.
Nichols, Edward J., *Zack Taylor's Little Army*. New York: Doubleday, 1963.
Pemberton, W. B., *Battles of the Crimean War*. New York: Macmillan, 1962.
Singletary, Otis A., *The Mexican War*. Chicago: University of Chicago Press, 1960.
Trevelyan, George M., *Garibaldi and the Thousand*. New Orleans: Pelican, 1965.

U.S. Civil War

Anderson, Bern, *By Sea and by River: The Naval History of the Civil War*. New York: Knopf, 1962.
Boatner, Mark, III, *The Civil War Dictionary*. New York: McKay, 1959.
Catton, Bruce, *The Army of the Potomac*. 3 vols. New York: Doubleday, 1962.
———, *Centennial History of the Civil War*. 3 vols. New York: Doubleday, 1961–1965.
Freeman, Douglas S., *Lee's Lieutenants: A Study in Command*. 3 vols. New York: Scribner's, 1942–1945.
Grant, Ulysses S., *Personal Memoirs*. Ed. by E. B. Long. New York: World, 1952.
Henry, Robert S., *Story of the Confederacy*. New York: Grosset & Dunlap, 1937.

Ketchum, Richard M., ed., *American Heritage Picture History of the Civil War*. New York: Doubleday, 1960.
Mandel, Paul, *Great Battles of the Civil War*. New York: Time, Inc., 1961.
Mitchell, Joseph B., *Decisive Battles of the Civil War*. New York: Putnam, 1955.
Williams, Kenneth P., *Lincoln Finds a General: A Military Study of the Civil War*. 5 vols. New York: Macmillan, 1949–1959.
Williams, T. Harry, *Lincoln and His Generals*. New York: Knopf, 1952.

Twentieth Century
(Except the two World Wars)

Fall, Bernard B., *Viet-Nam Witness: 1953–66*. New York: Praeger, 1966.
Fehrenbach, T. R., *This Kind of War*. New York: Macmillan, 1963.
Hailey, Foster, and Lancelot, Milton, *Clear for Action 1898–1964: A Photographic History of Modern Naval Combat*. New York: Duell, Sloan & Pearce, 1964.
Leckie, Robert, *Conflict: The History of the Korean War*. New York: Putnam, 1962.
MacArthur, Douglas, *Reminiscences*. New York: McGraw-Hill, 1964.
Stewart, George, *White Armies of Russia*. New York: Macmillan, 1933.
Thomas, Hugh, *The Spanish Civil War*. New York: Harper & Row, 1961.

World War I

Baldwin, Hanson W., *World War I*. New York: Grove, 1963.
Barnett, Correlli, *The Sword-Bearers: Supreme Command in the First World War*. New York: Morrow, 1964.
Esposito, Vincent J., *A Concise History of World War I*. New York: Praeger, 1964.
Falls, Cyril, *The Great War, 1914–1918*. New York: Putnam, 1959.
Hoehling, A. A., *The Great War at Sea*. New York: Thomas Y. Crowell, 1965.
Liddell Hart, B. H., *The Real War, 1914–1918*. Boston: Little, Brown, 1930.
Marshall, S. L. A., *The American Heritage History of World War I*. New York: Simon and Schuster, 1964.
Pitt, Barrie, *1918: The Last Act*. New York: Norton, 1963.
Stallings, Laurence, *The Doughboys: The Story of the AEF, 1917–1918*. New York: Harper & Row, 1963.
Tuchman, Barbara, *The Guns of August*. New York: Macmillan, 1962.

World War II

Alexander of Tunis, Earl, *The Alexander Memoirs 1940–1945*. Ed. by John North. New York: McGraw-Hill, 1963.
Baldwin, Hanson W., *Battles Lost and Won: Great Campaigns of World War II*. New York: Harper & Row, 1966.
Barnett, Correlli, *The Desert Generals*. New York: Viking, 1961.
Carell, Paul, *Hitler Moves East: 1941–1943*. Boston: Little, Brown, 1965.
Churchill, Winston, *The Second World War*. 6 vols. Boston: Houghton Mifflin, 1948–1953.
Clark, Alan, *Barbarossa: The Russian-German Conflict, 1941–45*. New York: Morrow, 1965.
Commager, Henry Steele, ed., *Story of the Second World War*. Boston: Little, Brown, 1945.
Eisenhower, Dwight D., *Crusade in Europe*. New York: Doubleday, 1948.
Esposito, Vincent J., *A Concise History of World War II*. New York: Praeger, 1964.
Freidin, Seymour, and Richardson, William, eds., *The Fatal Decisions: The Battles of Britain, Moscow, El Alamein, Stalingrad, France, 1944, and the Ardennes*. New York: Sloane, 1956.
Jacobsen, Hans A., and Rohwer, Jurgen, eds., *Decisive Battles of World War II: The German View*. Tr. by Edward Fitzgerald. New York: Putnam, 1965.
Leckie, Robert, *Strong Men Armed: The U.S. Marines Against Japan*. New York: Random House, 1962.

Suggestions for Further Reading

Liddell Hart, B. H., *German Generals Talk*. New York: Morrow, 1948.

Morison, Samuel Eliot, *The Two-Ocean War: A Short History of the United States Navy in the Second World War*. Boston: Little, Brown, 1963.

Potter, E. B., Nimitz, Chester W., and Adams, Henry, eds., *Triumph in the Atlantic: The Naval Struggle Against the Axis*. Englewood Cliffs, N.J.: Prentice-Hall, 1964.

Potter, E. B., and Nimitz, Chester W., eds., *Triumph in the Pacific: The Navy's Struggle Against Japan*. Englewood Cliffs, N. J.: Prentice-Hall, 1963.

Rothberg, Abraham, *Eyewitness History of World War II*. 4 vols. New York: Bantam, 1962.

Thompson, Laurence, *1940*. New York: Morrow, 1966.

Toland, John, *But Not in Shame: The Six Months After Pearl Harbor*. New York: Random House, 1961.

———, *The Last 100 Days*. New York: Random House, 1966.

Tourtellot, Arthur, ed., *Life's Picture History of World War II*. New York: Simon and Schuster, 1951.

U.S. Department of the Army, Office of the Chief of Military History, *Command Decisions*. Washington, D.C.: Government Printing Office, 1960.

Werth, Alexander, *Russia at War, 1941–1945*. New York: Dutton, 1964.

Wilmot, Chester, *The Struggle for Europe*. New York: Harper & Row, 1952.

Young, Peter, *World War 1939–1945*. New York: Thomas Y. Crowell, 1966.

INDEX

The Index contains the names of all persons and places mentioned significantly in the text. Names of wars and battles used as entry titles in the text are not repeated here, but alternative spellings not included as text cross references are indexed. The Index also contains titles of alliances and treaties, names of battleships that are not used as entry titles, and famous quotations, slogans, catch phrases, and battle cries.

"See" and "See also" references in SMALL CAPITALS direct the reader to entry titles in the body of the book; cross references to other Index entries are indicated by lightface roman type.

Index